Mark E. Noll

# abnormal psychology

## AN EXPERIMENTAL CLINICAL APPROACH

# abnormal psychology

Second Edition

## AN EXPERIMENTAL CLINICAL APPROACH

Gerald C. Davison
John M. Neale

John Wiley & Sons, Inc.
New York
Santa Barbara
London
Sydney
Toronto

Cover: Yzes Tanguy, "Five Strangers" Wadsworth Atheneum, Hartford. Ella Gallup Sumner and Mary Catlin Sumner Collection.



***Library of Congress Cataloging in Publication Data:***

Davison, Gerald C

Abnormal psychology.

1. Psychology, Pathological. I. Neale, John M., 1923– joint author. II. Title. [DNLM: 1. Psychopathology. WM100 D265a]

RC454.D3 1978 616.8'9 77-13940

ISBN 0-471-19923-0

Printed in the United States of America

10 9 8 7 6 5 4 3 2 1

To the memory of
Celia I. Davison (1910–1976)

GCD

---

To Sean

JMN

**Gerald C. Davison** received his B.A. from Harvard in 1961, studied the following year in Germany on a Fulbright scholarship, and obtained his Ph. D. from Stanford in 1965. After a postdoctoral clinical fellowship at the Veterans Administration Hospital in Palo Alto, California, he joined the faculty at the State University of New York at Stony Brook, where he is Professor of Psychology and Director of Clinical Training. He spent the 1975–76 academic year at Harvard as a National Institute of Mental Health Special Fellow. He has published widely in the general area of behavior therapy and personality, particularly on theoretical and philosophical issues, and is coauthor of *Clinical Behavior Therapy*. He is a Fellow of the American Psychological Association and has served on the Executive Committee of the Division of Clinical Psychology, on the Board of Scientific Affairs, on the Committee on Scientific Awards, and on the Council of Representatives. He is also a past-president of the Association for Advancement of Behavior Therapy. He is on the editorial board of several professional journals, including the *Journal of Consulting and Clinical Psychology, Cognitive Therapy and Research,* and *Journal of Homosexuality*. In addition to his teaching and research, he is a practicing clinical psychologist.

**John M. Neale**, a Canadian, received his B.A. from the University of Toronto in 1965 and his Ph.D. from Vanderbilt University in 1969. Thereafter he spent a year as Fellow in Medical Psychology at Langley Porter Neuropsychiatric Institute and since then has been at the State University of New York at Stony Brook, where he is Professor of Psychology. His major research interests are cognitive processes in schizophrenia, the study of children at high risk for the disorder, and research methodology. In 1974 he won the American Psychological Association's Early Career Award for his research in schizophrenia. He is a consulting editor for the *Journal of Consulting and Clinical Psychology* and for *Cognitive Therapy and Research*. In addition to being a reviewer and an active contributor to professional journals such as the *Journal of Abnormal Psychology,* he has coauthored three books, *Science and Behavior: An Introduction to Methods of Research, The Early Window: Effects of Television on Children and Youth,* and *Psychology*. And in addition to his research and teaching activities, he is involved in clinical supervision and training.

# Preface

Contemporary abnormal psychology is a field in which there are few hard and fast answers. Indeed, the very way the field should be conceptualized and the kinds of questions that should be asked are hotly debated issues. In this book we have tried to present what glimpses there are of answers to two primary questions: what causes deviant behavior and which treatments are most effective in reducing psychological suffering. But long after specific facts are forgotten, the student should retain a grasp of the basic problems in the field of psychopathology.

It has become commonplace in psychology to recognize the selective nature of perception. Certainly the writing of a textbook is guided by biases on the part of the authors, and our effort is no exception. We share a strong commitment to a scientific approach but at the same time appreciate the often uncontrollable nature of the subject matter and the importance of clinical findings. Rather than pretend that we are unbiased and objective, we have tried to alert readers to our prejudices. Forewarned in this manner, they may consider on their own the merits of our point of view. At the same time, we have tried as best we can to represent fairly and comprehensively the major alternative conceptualizations in contemporary psychopathology. A recurrent theme in the book is the importance of points of view or, to use Kuhn's (1962) phrase, paradigms. Our experience in teaching undergraduates has made us very much aware of the importance of making explicit the unspoken assumptions underlying any quest for knowledge. In our handling of the paradigms, we have tried to make the assumptions underlying them clear.

A related issue is the use of more than one model in studying abnormal psychology. Rather than force an entire field into, for example, a social-learning paradigm, we argue, from the available data, that different problems in psychopathology are amenable to analyses within different models. For instance, several of the organic disease models seem unavoidable when dealing with mental retardation, but in discussing therapy we prefer a learning conceptualization.

We also have had to choose among numerous topics for inclusion in the textbook. Some readers may be dismayed, for instance, to find that the names of Wilhelm Reich and Eric Berne appear nowhere in the text. At the same time, more recent and also lesser-known developments are included both for their intrinsic interest and for important questions raised at the paradigm level.

The book itself is divided into six major parts. Part I is introductory, providing information on history, paradigms of madness, issues in the diagnosis and assessment of abnormal behavior, and research methods. The next four sections each deal with a major category of abnormal behavior. At several points we have departed from the traditional diagnostic nomenclature. For example, we discuss depression in a single chapter even though the diagnostic manual breaks it down into several distinct categories. And several of the so-called personality disorders—for example, neurasthenic and cyclothymic personalities—are omitted because of lack of data and the diagnostic unreliability of these subcategories. Part II concentrates on anxiety and depression. Part III deals with social deviance—problems of addiction, antisocial behavior, and unconventional or inadequate human sexual behavior. Part IV discusses the problems of psychosis, adult and childhood schizophrenia, and infantile autism. Part V discusses brain dysfunctions and mental retardation. Part VI, on therapy, describes and evaluates a number of insight therapies, behavior therapy, and group, community, and somatic treatments. The discussion of therapy was reserved for a separate section of the book so that the various approaches to the modification of abnormal behavior could be discussed and criticized in depth.

Many people helped us in bringing our task to completion. We have been fortunate at Stony Brook to be surrounded by a talented and energetic group of students who read and criticized drafts of various chapters. Particularly helpful and extensive comments were offered by Crysta Casey, Emily Davison, Glenn Davidson, Marsha Linehan, Thomas Oltmanns, Kenneth Price, and Alan Rosenbaum. We are especially indebted and grateful to Nancy Fenrick, who lent her considerable expertise to Chapter 17, Mental Retardation. Thanks are also extended to a long list of colleagues who reviewed one or more of the chapters: Theodore X. Barber, Vernon T. Devine, Frederick Kanfer, Alan Marlatt, David Martindale, Richard McFall, David Pomeranz, Rita Poulos, Richard H. Price, Bernard Rimland, and John Stamm. We are grateful to Wiley Advisory Editor Brendan Maher, as well as to several other Wiley reviewers who remain anonymous. We hope that all reviewers will notice places where their suggestions improved the quality of the manuscript; the final decisions and the responsibility for the present form of the text, however, are ours. Mrs. Patricia Carl helped with the typing during the last stages of frenzied activity. Finally, gratitude that is difficult to put into words is extended to Mrs. Betty Hammer, who decoded and then retyped the many drafts of the manuscript. One aspect of the book—order of authorship—was unplanned, being decided by a toss of a coin.

December 1973

Gerald C. Davison
John M. Neale
Stony Brook, New York

## Preface to the second edition

Preparing this second edition has given us an opportunity to strengthen many parts of the book and to include significant new material that has appeared since completion of the first edition. Those familiar with our earlier effort will find that our basic orientation has not changed. We remain committed to an empirical approach to abnormal behavior and have tried to integrate scientific data with the clinical findings that are so important to the study of it. Our intent is to communicate to students our own excitement about our discipline, particularly the puzzles that challenge researchers in their search for the causes of psychopathology and for ways to prevent and ameliorate it. We try to encourage readers to participate with us in a process of discovery as we sift through the evidence on the origin of abnormal behavior and the effectiveness of specific treatments.

One of the major changes evident throughout the book is a stronger focus on modern psychodynamic theories and their relation to behavioral approaches. The sections on the physiology of abnormal behavior have also been extensively revised to reflect the most up-to-date information. We are fortunate to have had available draft versions of the forthcoming Diagnostic and Statistical Manual (DSM-III) and have referred to many of the proposed changes at appropriate points. The final chapter, almost entirely new, focuses on psychopathology and the law and on the ethical problems facing researchers and clinical practitioners.

The second edition has benefited greatly from the contributions of many consultants hired by Wiley to review the first edition and early versions of this one. Particularly helpful comments were received from Alan Evans, Robert Gatchel, Richard McFall, Advisory Editor Brendan Maher, Joseph Mendels, Norman Milgram, John Monahan, Oscar Parsons, Paul Wachtel, and David Wolitsky. As with the first edition, we were able to obtain assistance from talented students at Stony Brook: Joan Broderick, Patricia Chesleigh, Gail Glass, Gregory Mavrides, Mitchell Schare, and Wayne Regina. Letters from students using the first edition suggested several changes. We are grateful too for the editorial assistance of Carol M. Davison. And we wish to thank the staff at John Wiley for their expertise in the development and production of the book: Jack Burton, John Balbalis, F. A. Burke, Stella Kupferberg, Ron Nelson, and Debra Schwartz. Our deepest appreciation goes to Priscilla Todd, who lent her writing talents to what we hope is a lucid manuscript. Finally, we wish to acknowledge the secretarial work of Anne Thomas, Sharon Worksman, and Mary Rucklos.

September 1977

Gerald C. Davison
John M. Neale
Stony Brook, New York

# Contents

# abnormal psychology

## AN EXPERIMENTAL CLINICAL APPROACH

# part one
# introduction and basic issues

# chapter 1

## INTRODUCTION: HISTORICAL AND SCIENTIFIC CONSIDERATIONS

The Mental Health Professions
History of Psychopathology
Science: A Human Enterprise

Slumping in a comfortable leather chair, Ernest H., a thirty-five-year-old city policeman, looked skeptically at his therapist as he struggled to relate a series of problems. His recent inability to maintain an erection when making love to his wife was the immediate reason for his seeking therapy, but after gentle prodding from the therapist, Ernest recounted a host of other difficulties, some of them dating from his childhood but most of them originating during the previous several years.

Ernest's childhood had not been a happy one. His mother, whom he had loved dearly, died suddenly when he was only six, and for the next ten years he lived either with his father or with a maternal aunt. His father drank so heavily that he seldom managed to get through any day without some alcohol. Moreover, the man's moods were extremely variable; he had even spent several months in a state hospital with a diagnosis of "manic-depressive psychosis." The father's income was irregular and never enough to pay bills on time or to allow his son and himself to live in any but the most run-down neighborhoods. At times the father was totally incapable of caring for himself, let alone his son. Ernest would then spend weeks, sometimes months, with his aunt in a nearby suburb.

Despite these apparent handicaps, Ernest completed high school and entered the tuition-free city university. He earned his miscellaneous living expenses by waiting table at a small restaurant. During these college years his psychological problems began to concern him. He often became profoundly depressed, for no apparent reason, and these bouts of sadness were sometimes followed by periods of manic elation. His lack of control over these mood swings troubled him greatly, for he had observed this same pattern in his alcoholic father. He also felt an acute self-consciousness with people who he felt had authority over him—his boss, his professors, and even some of his classmates, with whom he compared himself unfavorably. He was especially sensitive about his dress—never quite in style and certainly much less elegant than that of his peers whose families had more money than his.

It was on the opening day of classes in his junior year that he first saw his future wife. When the tall, slender, "chic" young woman moved to her seat with grace and self-assurance, his were not the only eyes that followed her. He spent the rest of that semester watching her from afar, taking care to sit where he could glance over at her without being conspicuous. Then one day, as they and the other students were leaving class, they bumped into each other quite by accident, and her warmth and charm emboldened him to ask if she would join him for some coffee. When she said yes, he almost wished she had not.

Amazingly enough, as he saw it, they soon fell in love, and before the end of his senior year they were married. Ernest could never quite believe that his wife, as intelligent a woman as she was beautiful, really cared for him. As the years wore on, his doubts about himself, and about her feelings toward him, would continue to grow.

He had hoped to enter law school, and both his grades and law school boards made these plans a possibility, but he decided instead to enter the police academy. His reasons, as he related them to his therapist, had to do with doubts about his intellectual abilities, as well as his increasing uneasiness in situations where he felt himself being evaluated. Seminars had become unbearable for him in his last year in college, and he somehow felt that the badge and uniform of a police officer would give him the instant recognition and respect that he felt himself incapable of earning on his own.

To help him get through the academy, his wife quit college one year before graduation, against Ernest's pleas, and sought a secretarial job. He felt she was far brighter than he and saw no reason why she should sacrifice her potential to help him make his way in life. But at the same time he recognized the fiscal realities and grudgingly accepted her financial support.

The police academy proved to be even more stressful than college. His mood swings, although less frequent, still haunted him. And like his father, who was now confined to a state mental hospital, he drank to ease his psychological pain. He felt that his instructors considered him a fool when he had difficulty standing up in front of the class to give an answer that he himself knew was correct. But he made it through the physical, intellectual, and social rigors of the academy, and he was assigned to foot patrol in one of the wealthier sections of the city.

Several years later, when it seemed that life should be getting easier, he found himself in ever greater turmoil. Now thirty-two years of age, with a fairly secure job which paid reasonably well, he began to think of starting a family. His wife wanted this as well, and it was at this time that his problems with impotence began. He thought at first it was the alcohol—he was drinking at least six ounces of bourbon every night, except when on the swing shift. Soon, though, he began to wonder if he really was avoiding the responsibility of having a child, and later he began to doubt that his wife really found him attractive and desirable. The more understanding and patient she was in his sometimes frantic efforts to consummate sex with her, the less "manly" he felt himself to be. He was unable to accept help from his wife, for he did not believe that this was the "right" way to maintain a sexual relationship. The problems in bed spread to other areas of their lives. The less often they made love, the more suspicious he was of his wife, for she had become even more beautiful and vibrant as she entered her thirties. In addition, she had been promoted to the position of administrative assistant at the law firm where she worked. She would mention—perhaps to taunt him—long, martini-filled lunches with her boss at a posh uptown restaurant.

The impetus for his contacting the therapist was an ugly argument with his wife one evening when she came home from work after ten. Ernest had been elated and agitated for several days. To combat his fear that he was losing control, he had consumed almost a full bottle of scotch each night. By the time that his wife walked in the door on that final evening, Ernest was already very drunk, and he attacked her both verbally and physically about her alleged infidelity. In her own anger and fear, she questioned his masculinity in striking a woman and taunted him with the disappointments of their lovemaking. Ernest stormed out of the house, spent the night at a local bar, and the next day somehow got himself together enough to seek professional help.

Every day of our lives we have to deal with people and try to figure out why they conduct themselves as they do. Yet, how difficult it is to understand why another person does or feels something. Indeed, it is sometimes hard to understand why we ourselves feel and behave the way we do. Acquiring insight into what we consider the normal range of expected behavior is arduous enough, requiring much of our attention and thought, but how far more perplexing is human behavior beyond the normal range, such as that of the policeman just described.

Our conversational allusions to odd behavior are frequently couched in phrases such as "He's out of his mind," "He's all screwed up," "He's a maniac," "She's an hysteric," or "She's really paranoid." Such terms indicate that as observers we have found a person's behavior inexplicable and can attribute it only to an unbalanced mind. These minds are very often much sounder than such phrases and adjectives imply. Terrifying instances of unusual behavior, however, although not personally observed by most of us, are very much in the public eye. Hardly a week passes that a violent act, such as an ugly axe murder or multiple slayings, is not reported. The assailant is diagnosed by a police officer or mental health authority as a "mental case" and is found to have had a history of mental instability. Sometimes we learn that the person has previously been confined in a mental hospital.

This book is concerned with the whole range of abnormal behavior and with the various explanations for it, both past and present. There are, however, numerous pitfalls in seeking valid explanations that must be pointed out. To study abnormal psychology, we must have what might be called "great tolerance for ambiguity," an ability to be comfortable with very tentative, often conflicting pieces of information. Much less is known with certainty about the field than we might hope, presenting problems both for the professional and for the beginning student. Indeed, as already indicated, precious little is known of why human beings behave in a normal fashion, to say nothing of their abnormal behavior. In approaching the study of psychopathology, we do well to keep in mind that the subject offers few hard and fast answers. Although we shall report such findings as there are, many of the facts that will be introduced will undoubtedly be outdated in a matter of years. And yet, as will become evident when we discuss our orientation to scientific inquiry, the study of abnormal behavior is no less worthwhile because of its ambiguities. The kinds of questions asked rather than the specific answers available at any particular time constitute the very essence of the field.

Another problem that professionals share with laypeople is the closeness of any human being to the subject matter of behavior. Physicists, for example, would seem better able to detach themselves emotionally from their subject matter than psychologists, particularly those who specialize in the study of abnormal behavior. The pervasiveness and disturbing effects of abnormal behavior intrude on our lives. Who, for example, has not experienced irrational thoughts and feelings? Or who has not known someone, a friend or perhaps a relative, whose behavior was impossible to fathom? If you have, you realize how frustrating and frightening it is to try to understand and help a person suffering psychological difficulties.

Our closeness to the subject matter, of course, adds to its intrinsic fascination; no wonder that undergraduate courses in abnormal psychology are among the most popular in psychology departments and indeed in the entire college curriculum. Although familiarity with the subject matter encourages people to study abnormal psychology, it has one distinct disadvantage. All of us have already developed certain ways of thinking and talking about behavior, certain words and concepts that somehow seem to *fit*. For example, some may assert that the study of fear should concentrate on the immediate *experience* of fear; this is technically known as a *phenomenological* approach and is one formal way of setting about the study of human behavior. But it is not the approach of the authors of this book. We ourselves have had to grapple with the difference between what we may *feel* is the appropriate way to talk about human behavior and experience, and what as behavioral scientists we have learned to be more fruitful means of discussing behavior. Where most people might say "feeling of terror," we might be more inclined as behaviorally oriented psychopathologists to use a phrase such as "fear-response of great magnitude." In doing so we would not be merely playing verbal games. The word "games" does indeed apply in the sense that our procedures have rules, but it does not apply in the sense that we may be engaging in activities that do not mean very much or that might just as well be carried out in any other fashion. The crucial point is that the concepts and verbal labels we use in the serious study of abnormal behavior must be free of the subjective feelings of appropriateness that, as nonspecialists, we have come to attach to certain human phenomena. We may be asking you, then, to adopt frames of reference different from those that you are accustomed to, and indeed different from those we ourselves employ when we are not wearing our professional hats.

The case study with which this chapter began is open to a wide range of interpretations. No doubt you have some ideas about how Ernest's problems developed, what his primary difficulties are, and perhaps even how you might try to help him. We know of no greater intellectual or emotional challenge than deciding both how to conceptualize the life of a person with psychological problems and how best to treat him or her. In the next chapter we will refer back to the case of Ernest H. to illustrate how workers from different theoretical orientations might describe him and seek to help.

## The Mental Health Professions

The training of clinicians, the various professionals who are regarded as legitimate purveyors of psychological services, takes different forms. A *psychiatrist* is a physician who holds an M.D. degree and has taken postgraduate training, called a residency, wherein he or she has received supervision in psychotherapy. By virtue of the M.D. degree, the psychiatrist can also continue functioning as a physician—giving physical examinations, diagnosing medical problems, and the like. In actuality, however, the only aspect of medical practice that most psychiatrists engage in is prescribing *psychoactive drugs,* chemical compounds which are able to change how people feel and think.

The term *psychoanalyst* is reserved for those individuals who have received specialized training at a psychoanalytic institute; the program usually involves several years of clinical training as well as an in-depth psychoanalysis of the trainee. Although Sigmund Freud held that psychoanalysts do *not* require medical training (his daughter Anna, who does not have an M.D., is a so-called lay analyst), until recently most psychoanalytic institutes required of their graduates an M.D. and a psychiatric residency. After the B.A., then, it can take up to ten years to become a psychoanalyst. Psychoanalysts are usually in private practice, and their fees are extremely high.

To practice *clinical psychology* (the profession of the authors of this textbook) requires a Ph.D. degree, which usually entails four to five years of graduate study. Training is much like that for the other special fields of psychology—experimental, physiological, social, developmental, industrial—with a heavy emphasis on laboratory work, research design, statistics, and the empirically based study of human and animal behavior. As with these other fields of psychology, the degree is basically a research one, and candidates are required to write a lengthy dissertation on a specialized topic. In addition, however, clinical psychologists learn how to deal with patients (or, as many term them, clients) in therapy settings, much as a psychiatrist in training does. They receive this training both in courses in which they master specific techniques under close professional supervision, and, more intensively, in internship or postdoctoral training, during which the maturing clinician takes increasing responsibility for the care of clients.

Other professions are certified for psychotherapeutic practice. Some graduate schools have initiated Psy.D. (Doctor of Psychology) programs. The curriculum offered candidates for this new degree is generally the same as that available to Ph.D. students, but there is less emphasis on research and more on clinical training. The assumption is that clinical psychology has advanced to a level of knowledge that justifies—and even requires—intensive training in specific techniques of therapeutic intervention. A *psychiatric social worker* obtains a Master of Social Work degree. There are also master's and doctoral-level programs in *counseling psychology,* somewhat similar to graduate training in clinical psychology but usually with less emphasis on research. Recent years have seen a movement to "paraprofessional training," in which workers without advanced degrees learn to conduct various forms of therapy under the close supervision of professionals.

The actual therapy practiced by any of these individuals depends for the most part on the orientation of the school attended. By and large, except for the administration of drugs, specific therapies relate *very little* to the therapist's academic degree.

In addition to professionals who offer therapeutic services to the public, there is a highly diverse group who can be called *psychopathologists*. These people conduct research into the nature and development of the various disorders that their therapist colleagues try to treat. Psychopathologists can come from any number of disciplines; some are clinicians, but the educational backgrounds of others can range from biochemistry to developmental psychology, and their academic degrees can be at virtually any level. What unites them is their commitment to the study of how abnormal behavior develops. Since relatively little is known about psychopathology, the diversity of backgrounds and interests is an advantage, for it is too soon to be certain where major advances will be made. The work of psychopathologists is amply illustrated in Chapters 5 through 17 of this book, and the activities of clinicians are discussed at length in Chapters 18 through 21.

## History of Psychopathology

### Some General Remarks on Historical Analysis

Before we present a brief history of psychopathology in order to place contemporary developments in perspective, it may be useful to comment on the manner in which historians go about reconstructing the past. Let us consider what archaeologists conjecture about *trephining,* a crude surgical practice believed to have been prevalent in the Stone Age. They have assumed that people of very early periods chipped holes in the skulls of troubled comrades to allow the escape of evil spirits who were supposedly causing deviant behavior. But on what is this supposition based, since there are no known recorded interviews with people who practiced this primitive surgical art? First of all, skulls with holes in them have been found by archaeologists in certain parts of the world. The holes in these skulls seem to have been intentionally created by repeated impacts with sharp stones. But why do historians conclude that these holes were made for the purposes just mentioned rather than, for example, inflicted in the heat of combat?

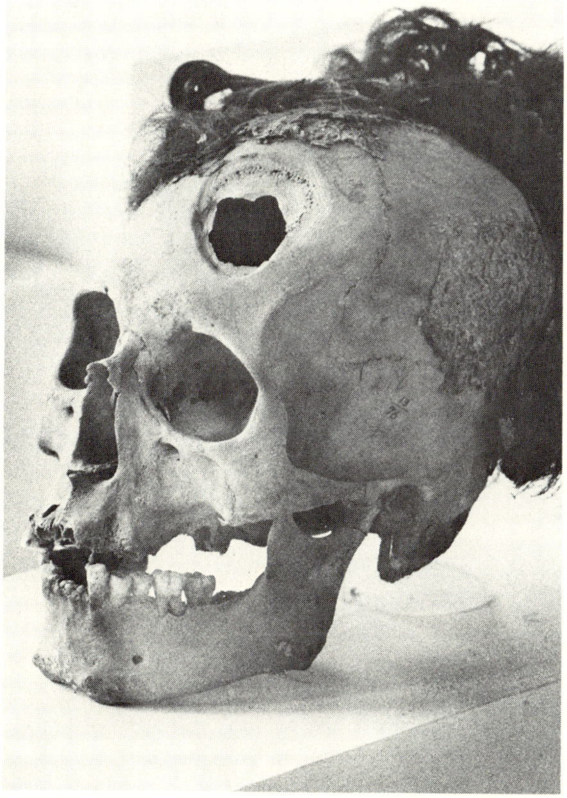

A trephined skull with some healing of the bone, indicating that the disturbed patient sometimes survived this crude Stone Age operation.

The currently popular interpretation of trephining as a practice to facilitate the exit of evil spirits from a person's mind and body is closely linked to what historians have been able to learn and conjecture about the nature of Stone Age man's social order and beliefs. Even before the trephined skulls were found, historians had anticipated that such practices were in vogue. Finding skulls with holes in them strengthened this supposition, although it is unclear how prehistoric man determined that the spirits were located in the head. Conjecture seems a reasonable means for trying to find out what happened in the preliterate past, but we must be mindful of the amount of inference resorted to.

Even when historians can rely on written records, they still have difficulty making generalizations. We often hear phrases such as "The Renaissance *began* with the . . ." What in fact does this mean? Consider a recent event that is likely to be discussed in future history books. When did the so-called drug culture begin? The onset of this important phenomenon might be traced to the visit of Dr. Timothy Leary to Mexico, where he was first exposed to the "magic mushrooms." We could look earlier to the publication of a fascinating little book by Aldous Huxley, entitled *Doors of Perception*. Or perhaps the drug culture "began" when Leary and his colleague Richard Alpert (who became known as Baba Ram Dass) left Harvard in 1962, for up until that time it seems reasonable to assert that only among graduate students at Harvard was psilocybin being used for the deliberate induction of "psychedelic" states. Not until

The migration of "flower children" to San Francisco's Haight-Ashbury district is sometimes thought of as one of the events heralding the "drug culture."

the two men went out into the world could their work have had a more general influence. Consider also the migration of the "flower people" to the Haight-Ashbury district of San Francisco in the 1960s. No doubt any adequate history of this period would have to include all these events and many more. But what brought about the phenomenon of taking psychedelic drugs? What are the dimensions of the phenomenon? How far back in time must we go to trace and *explain* the initial urge? These are formidable questions indeed, and perhaps in the course of this book some light may be shed on these issues; our point here is merely to indicate the difficulties inherent in making generalizations about the sweep of human events.

## Historical Overview

As psychopathologists, our interest is in the causes of deviant behavior. The search for these causes has gone on for a considerable period of time, long antedating what we generally regard as the age of scientific inquiry.[1] This search, moreover, has not been a mere scholastic exercise, for the manner in which people have explained deviant behavior has played a vitally important role in how they have attempted to deal with it. For example, if I believe that a man who hears voices from unseen sources is being visited by the devil and I consider the devil an evil force, I am likely to move against that force. If I want to help the man stop hallucinating, I must find some way of getting rid of or exorcising the devil within him. Moreover, my treatment will very likely be tailored to how I anticipate the devil will react to my efforts to cast him out from the person. If I think that the devil will respond to directions from God, I will probably choose prayer as a treatment. If my theology regards the devil as too strong or evil to respond even to God, I may consider it necessary to deal with him at his own level and resort to torture of the body that is possessed by the devil.

### Early demonology

The doctrine that a semiautonomous or completely autonomous evil being, such as the devil, may dwell within a person and control his or her mind and body is called demonology. We have already presented the current suppositions about trephining. Among the ancient Hebrews as well, many thousands of years later, behavior was considered to be controlled by good or bad spirits residing within the person. Christ is reported to have cured a man with an "unclean spirit" by casting out the devil from within him and hurling it onto a herd of swine. The animals were then said to have become possessed and to have run "violently down a steep place into the sea." Similar examples of demonological thinking can be found among the early Chinese, Egyptians, and Greeks. Treatment for such demons typically took the form of elaborate prayer rites, noise making, forcing the afflicted to drink terrible tasting brews, and on occasion more extreme measures such as flogging and

[1] Much of the following historical review is based on Zilboorg and Henry (1941).

starvation. As we have already suggested, the priests and medicine men practicing exorcism chose treatments they considered most likely to be effective against the particular demon to be removed. In the fifth century B.C. in Greece, Hippocrates received his early training in one of the Greek schools that specialized in treating deviant behavior with exorcism.

### Somatogenesis

Hippocrates (460–370 B.C.), often regarded as the father of modern medicine, operated outside the *Zeitgeist* or intellectual and emotional orientation of the times. He questioned the prevailing Greek belief that the gods arbitrarily ordained the mental dispositions of people, insisting instead that mental disorders had the same causes as other illnesses and hence should be treated like any other disease. Hippocrates regarded the brain as the organ of intellectual life, and it followed that if someone's thinking and behavior were deviant, there was some kind of brain pathology. He is often considered one of the very earliest proponents of a *somatogenic* hypothesis to explain disordered behavior—that something wrong with the *soma* or physical body disturbs thought and action. He also recognized that environmental and emotional stress can damage the body and mind. Hippocrates classified mental disorders into three categories, mania, melancholia, and phrenitis or brain fever. Through his teachings the phenomena of abnormal behavior became more the province of physicians than of priests.

The treatments suggested by Hippocrates were quite different from the earlier exorcistic tortures. For example, for melancholia he prescribed tranquility, sobriety, care in choosing food and drink, and abstinence from sexual activity. Such a regimen was presumed to have a healthful effect on the brain and the body. Because Hippocrates believed in natural causes rather than

The Greek physician Hippocrates held a somatogenic view of abnormal behavior, considering insanity a disease of the brain.

Medieval woodcuts of the four temperaments thought by Hippocrates to result from excesses of the four humors. From left to right: the man with changeable temperament, who has plenty of blood; the melancholy man, full of dark bile; the hot-tempered man, who has a surplus of choler or yellow bile; and the sluggish man with too much phlegm.

supernatural, he depended on his own keen observations. Remarkable clinical records describing many of the symptoms now recognized in epilepsy, alcoholic delusion, and paranoia have come down to us from him.

Hippocrates' physiology was rather crude, however, for he conceived of normal brain functioning, and therefore of mental health, as dependent on a delicate balance among four "humors" of the body, namely blood, black bile, yellow bile, and phlegm. An imbalance produced disorders. If a person was sluggish and dull, for example, the body supposedly contained a preponderance of phlegm. A preponderance of black bile was the explanation for melancholia, too much yellow bile explained irascibility, and too much blood changeable temperament. Hippocrates' humoral pathology has not withstood later scientific scrutiny. His basic premise, however, that human behavior is directly determined by bodily structures or substances, and that abnormal behavior is produced by some kind of imbalance or even damage, foreshadowed aspects of contemporary thought. In the few centuries before and after the birth of Christ, Hippocrates' somatogenic premise was generally accepted by other Greeks, such as Plato, Aristotle, and Galen, as well as by the Romans, who adopted the medicine of the Greeks.

## The Middle Ages

In a massive generalization, historians have often suggested that the death of Galen in the third century A.D. marked the beginning of the Dark Ages for the treatment and investigation of abnormal behavior. Galen, a Greek, had practiced in Rome and codified the medicine of antiquity. As Hippocrates before him, he had drawn attention to the role of the brain in mental disorders. But after Galen's death there were few medical advances, and many of the later Roman men of medicine again adopted popular superstitions. Galen's naturalistic approach to abnormal behavior yielded to ancient demonology, modified somewhat by the theology of the new religion. Toward the end of the fifth century A.D., Greek and Roman civilization collapsed. Medical pursuits and the scientific principles of systematic observation that had been established by the Greeks were almost completely abandoned in Europe. Furthermore, with the advent of the Christian world, possession could now be interpreted as an affront to the church and to God, doubling the jeopardy of the mentally afflicted.

An eighteenth-century engraving of a tarantula and two women thought to have been bitten by this large spider. Slow music and gentle dancing were regarded as a cure for those obsessed during periodic outbreaks of mass hysteria and madness.

The second part of the Middle Ages was marked by occasional outbreaks of mass madness. In the thirteenth century a phenomenon known as *tarantism,* a kind of possession by alien forces, originated in Italy and spread all through Europe. The bite of a tarantula during the height of the summer heat supposedly caused people to run out of their homes and to jump and dance around in a rather wild fashion. Others who had also been bitten by the spiders soon joined them, and so did those who had been bitten during earlier summers. Some of the reports of tarantism contain references to considerable imbibing of alcoholic beverages, which from our twentieth-century point of view might well account for the wild behavior. But tarantism and other outbursts of apparently manic behavior affecting whole groups of people might also have been a reaction to some of the terrible social oppression and famines, the uprisings and disintegration of institutions that plagued much of western Europe during the thirteenth through the sixteenth centuries.

Treatment of mental illness during the Middle Ages was generally in the hands of priests, who would pray and sprinkle the afflicted with holy water. In their zeal and well-intentioned attempts to strike a fatal blow to Satan's pride, however, they eventually came to curse him obscenely and at length. As time went on, terrible tortures took the place of prayers, for the devil within had to be punished and the body harboring him made uninhabitable.

Theology at first recognized two types of possession by the devil, neither of which stood the possessed person in very good social stead. In one form of supposed possession, the victim was unwillingly seized by the devil as God's punishment for sins. These were the mentally ill. Their possession was viewed as personal misfortune. In the second form a person became possessed by deliberately entering into a pact with the devil. These were the witches, and they were endowed with supernatural powers because they were doing the devil's work. They could injure their enemies, cause cattle to sicken, ruin crops, control the weather, make men impotent, and turn themselves into animals. Their possession was considered to place their communities in great physical and moral peril. By the end of the fifteenth century the distinction between the two forms of demoniacal possession had become blurred (Coleman, 1976). Numerous hapless individuals were labeled as witches or heretics on either of these bases, and their culpability grew. They were frequently accused of causing the pestilence and floods that were then rampant throughout western Europe and could not be explained or dealt with in naturalistic ways. Faced with vexing and inexplicable occurrences, people tend to seize on whatever explanation seems available, and in these times events conspired to heap enormous blame on witches. And it was not just evil or stupid people who held that those behaving peculiarly were possessed by or were in league with the devil. To quote from a respected authority of the sixteenth century, "The greatest punishment God can afflict on the wicked . . . is to deliver them over to Satan who with God's permission kills them or makes them to undergo great calamities. Many devils are in woods or in wildernesses, ready to hurt and prejudice people. . . . I conclude it is merely the work of the devil." The writer of these words was Martin Luther.

Earlier, in 1484, Pope Innocent VIII had issued a papal bull in which he exhorted the clergy of Europe to leave no stone unturned in the search for witches. The pope based his pronouncement on Exodus 22:18: "Thou shalt not suffer a witch to live." This papal decree ushered in one of the most tragic and brutal episodes in all Western history.

Two Dominican monks who had been appointed by the pope to act as inquisitors in northern Germany compiled a manual, *Malleus Maleficarum* ("the witches' hammer"), which provided some important justifications and procedures for hunting witches. First, it confirmed beyond doubt the existence of witches and asserted that those who did not believe in them were either stupid or heretical. Then it enun-

Pope Innocent VIII, whose 1484 decree launched a witch hunt that extended throughout Europe and lasted through three centuries.

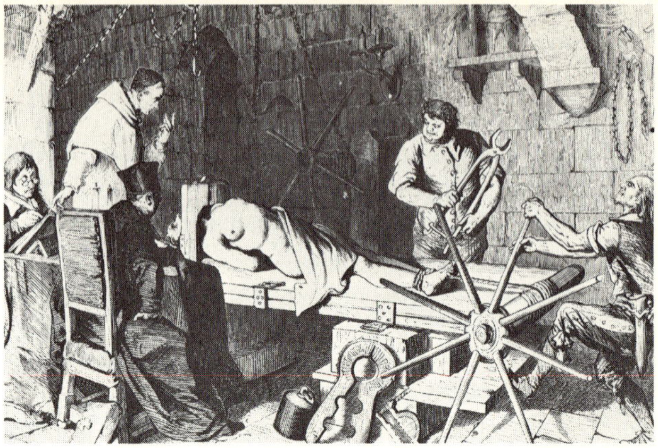

Tortures by which confessions were extracted from accused witches.

ciated various signs by which witches could be detected, for example, red spots or areas of insensitivity on the skin, supposedly made by the claw of the devil when touching the person to seal a pact. Various means of examining and sentencing witches were also detailed. Revered by Catholics and Protestants alike, the manual was eventually considered almost divinely inspired. Under its direction and for more than two hundred years, hundreds of thousands of mentally ill men, women, and even children were hunted, accused, and tortured to obtain confessions and, if found guilty, were publicly put to death.

During the seventeenth century witch hunting was also quite widespread in the colonies of the New World. Salem, Massachusetts, became the infamous center of the witch hunts of 1692. Within a few months hundreds were arrested, nineteen were hanged, and one was pressed to

Witch burning.

The dunking test. If the woman did not drown, she was thought to be in league with the devil.

death. It appears certain that at least some of those persecuted for being witches or for being otherwise in league with the devil were mentally disturbed. Deutsch (1949), for example, describes statements made by the servant of a Boston family in 1688, during her trial for having bewitched the children of her employers. "When asked by the judges whether she had any one standing by her, she replied that she had, but, looking very pertly into the air, she added, 'No, he's gone'" (p. 34). The woman was apparently hallucinating, that is, seeing someone who was, in fact, not there. Whereas today such behavior might be taken as a sign of schizophrenia, in the seventeenth century it was considered definitive proof of possession by the devil.

During a visit to the State House in Boston, Massachusetts, one of the authors of this textbook came upon a document of a proceeding of the 1957 Massachusetts State Legislature. A bill

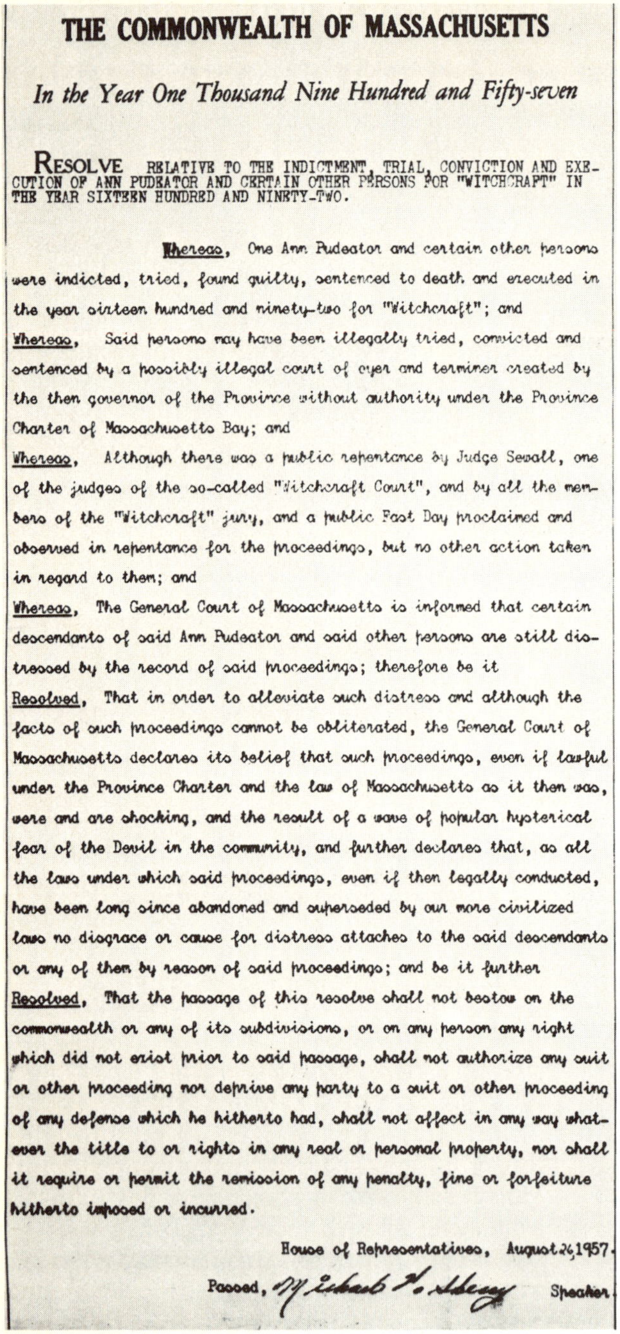

THE COMMONWEALTH OF MASSACHUSETTS

*In the Year One Thousand Nine Hundred and Fifty-seven*

RESOLVE RELATIVE TO THE INDICTMENT, TRIAL, CONVICTION AND EXECUTION OF ANN PUDEATOR AND CERTAIN OTHER PERSONS FOR "WITCHCRAFT" IN THE YEAR SIXTEEN HUNDRED AND NINETY-TWO.

Whereas, One Ann Pudeator and certain other persons were indicted, tried, found guilty, sentenced to death and executed in the year sixteen hundred and ninety-two for "Witchcraft"; and

Whereas, Said persons may have been illegally tried, convicted and sentenced by a possibly illegal court of oyer and terminer created by the then governor of the Province without authority under the Province Charter of Massachusetts Bay; and

Whereas, Although there was a public repentance by Judge Sewall, one of the judges of the so-called "Witchcraft Court", and by all the members of the "Witchcraft" jury, and a public Fast Day proclaimed and observed in repentance for the proceedings, but no other action taken in regard to them; and

Whereas, The General Court of Massachusetts is informed that certain descendants of said Ann Pudeator and said other persons are still distressed by the record of said proceedings; therefore be it

Resolved, That in order to alleviate such distress and although the facts of such proceedings cannot be obliterated, the General Court of Massachusetts declares its belief that such proceedings, even if lawful under the Province Charter and the law of Massachusetts as it then was, were and are shocking, and the result of a wave of popular hysterical fear of the Devil in the community, and further declares that, as all the laws under which said proceedings, even if then legally conducted, have been long since abandoned and superseded by our more civilized laws no disgrace or cause for distress attaches to the said descendants or any of them by reason of said proceedings; and be it further

Resolved, That the passage of this resolve shall not bestow on the commonwealth or any of its subdivisions, or on any person any right which did not exist prior to said passage, shall not authorize any suit or other proceeding nor deprive any party to a suit or other proceeding of any defense which he hitherto had, shall not affect in any way whatever the title to or rights in any real or personal property, nor shall it require or permit the remission of any penalty, fine or forfeiture hitherto imposed or incurred.

House of Representatives, August 26, 1957.

Passed, Michael F. Skerry Speaker

A bill passed in 1957 by the Massachusetts legislature exonorating a woman who had been executed for witchcraft in 1692.

was passed formally exonerating a woman who had been burned as a witch in seventeenth-century Salem. It is interesting to speculate on what led to the introduction of this bill and on how it was discussed by twentieth-century legislators. Apparently a family in Massachusetts still takes the charge of witchcraft seriously enough to have the stigma removed from a relative by formal state resolution.

### Early medical practices

Even during the period when throughout Europe persons suspected of witchcraft were being hunted by both clergy and laity, brought to trial, and often put to death, others expressed more rational views. One of these was a German physician, Johann Weyer. In the sixteenth century he published a book asserting that many if not all "witches" were really sick mentally or bodily and that the barbarous acts perpetrated against these people were terrible wrongs. Weyer was the first physician whose primary interest was mental disorders. His book also contained careful descriptions of mental illnesses, couched in kindly words that implored the reader's understanding. The recorded statement of a priest indicates the typical reaction to Weyer's work: "Recently Satan went to a sabbath [witches' gathering] attired as a great prince, and told the assembled witches that they need not worry since, thanks to Weyer and his followers, the affairs of the devil were brilliantly progressing." In spite of such unfavorable criticism, Weyer's book grew in importance, and he is frequently regarded as the founder of modern psychiatry.

In 1621 the *Anatomy of Melancholy* was first published. This book was to have five subsequent editions by 1651 and to be widely read. Robert Burton, an English scholar, writer, and clergyman, had set himself the task of preparing a medical treatise on melancholy, its causes, symptoms, and cures. This he accomplished with considerable style, common sense, and humanity. For example, he viewed various child-rearing practices as contributing to depression in adult life. "Parents, and such as have the tuition and

The sixteenth-century German physician Johann Weyer, who examined the problems of witchcraft and became convinced that some, if not all, "witches" were mentally ill rather than possessed.

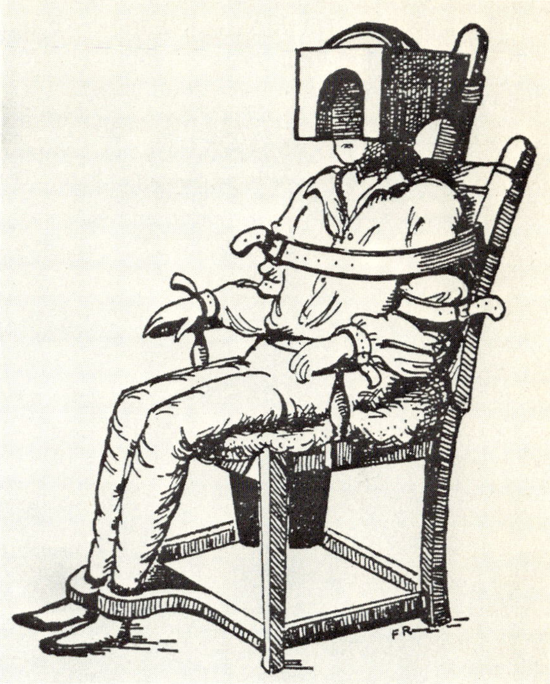

The "tranquilizing chair," used by Benjamin Rush as a means of treating mental disorders.

oversight of children, offend many times in that they are too stern, always threatening, chiding, brawling, whipping, or striking; by means of which, their poor children are so disheartened and cowed, that they never after have any courage, a merry hour in their lives, or take pleasure in any thing" (p. 215).

It should not be assumed, however, that the gradual inclusion of abnormal behavior within the domain of medicine led immediately to more humane and effective treatment. Benjamin Rush, who practiced medicine in the United States at the end of the eighteenth century and into the early nineteenth and is considered the father of American psychiatry, believed that mental disorder was caused by an excess of blood in the brain. Consequently, his favored treatment was to draw from "the insane" great quantities of blood, as much as six quarts over a period of a few months. Little wonder that patients so treated became less agitated (Farina, 1976)! Rush entertained another hypothesis, namely that many "lunatics" could be cured by frightening them. In one such recommended procedure the physician was to convince the patient of his impending death. A New England doctor of the nineteenth century implemented this prescription in an ingenious manner. "On his premises stood a tank of water, into which a patient, packed into a coffin-like box pierced with holes, was lowered. . . . He was kept under water until the bubbles of air ceased to rise, after which he was taken out, rubbed, and revived—if he had not already passed beyond reviving!" (Deutsch, 1949, p. 82).

## Development of asylums

Although many disturbed Europeans who had been considered too simple to be witches were tolerated in their local communities, large numbers were housed in dungeons and jails, which served simply to rid society at large of the necessity of having everyday commerce with the deranged. Then through the influence of Moorish physicians who still practiced medicine according to the precepts of Hippocrates, several asylums were established in Spain during the early fifteenth century. In northern Europe it took longer. Not until 1547 did Henry VIII hand over to the city of London the Hospital of St. Mary of Bethlehem, henceforth to be used solely for the confinement of the insane. The conditions in Bethlehem were deplorable. Over the years the word "bedlam," a contraction and popular name

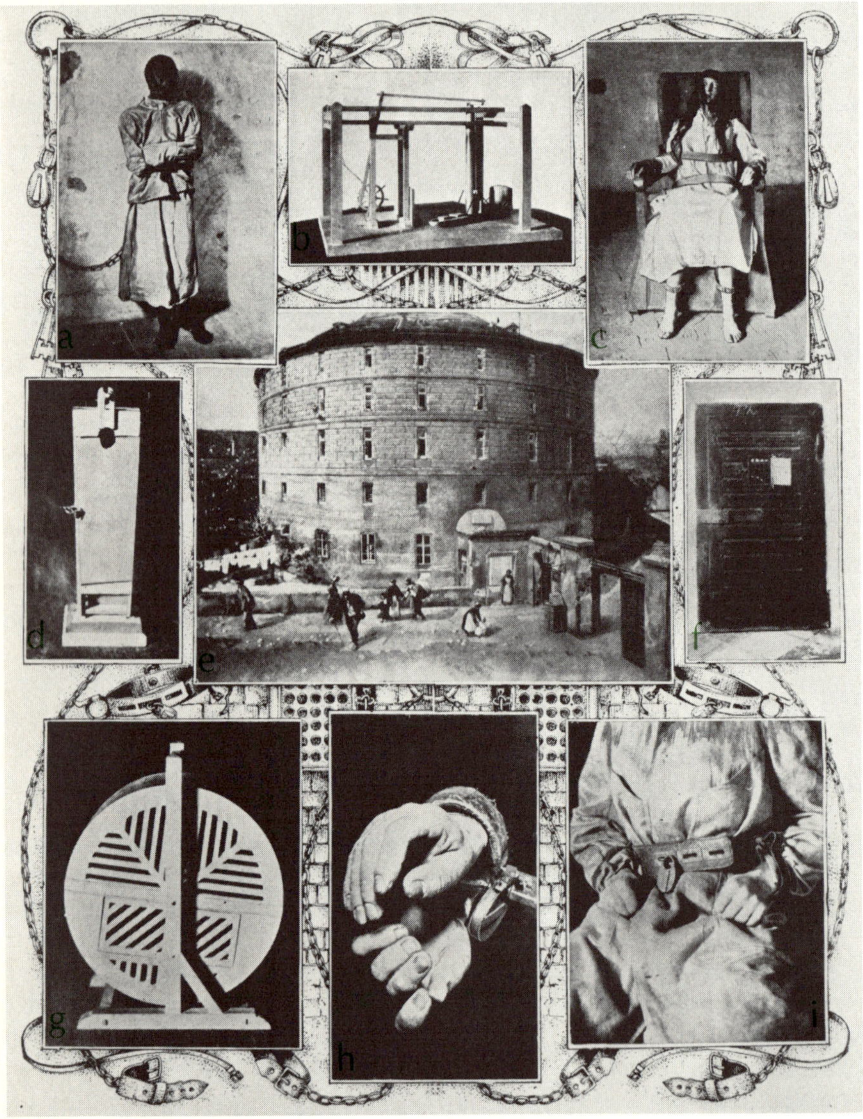


At the Lunatics' Tower (e, center) in Vienna, a remarkable collection of strange instruments and fetters were employed in the treatment of the insane. A lunatic in hood and straitjacket (a), padlocked to a cell wall. The machine (b) in which lunatics were swung until they were in a state of stupefaction and therefore remained quiet. A maniac strapped to a chair (c), in a position sometimes held for weeks. The "English coffin" (d) in which the lunatic was kept, his face at the hole, for discipline. The face and the box together resembled a standing clock. A cell door (f) with its iron "spy-hole." An enormous wheel (g), which turned each time the lunatic inside it moved. A maniac's hands in padlocked handcuffs (h). Another straitjacketed lunatic (i).

for this hospital, became a descriptive term for a place or scene of wild uproar and confusion. In the Lunatics' Tower, constructed in Vienna in 1784, patients were confined in the spaces between inner and outer walls. There they could be looked at from below by passersby. Even as late as the nineteenth century, viewing the violent patients and their antics was considered entertainment, and tickets of admission to Bedlam were sold. The first mental hospital in the United States was founded in Williamsburg, Virginia, in 1773.

A primary figure in the movement for humanitarian treatment of those in asylums was Philippe Pinel. In 1793, while the French Revolution raged, he was put in charge of a large asylum in Paris known as La Bicêtre. A historian has written of the conditions at this particular hospital.

A tour of St. Mary's of Bethlehem (Bedlam) provides amusement for these two upper-class ladies. Hogarth captures the poignancy of the scene in this eighteenth-century painting.

> [*The patients were*] *shackled to the walls of their cells, by iron collars which held them flat against the wall and permitted little movement. . . . They could not lie down at night, as a rule. . . . Oftentimes there was a hoop of iron around the waist of the patient and in addition . . . chains on both the hands and the feet. . . . These chains* [*were*] *sufficiently long so that the patient could feed himself out of a bowl, the food usually being a mushy gruel—bread soaked in a weak soup. Since little was known about dietetics,* [*no attention*] *was paid to the type of diet given the patients. They were presumed to be animals . . . and not to care whether the food was good or bad* (*Selling, 1940, p. 54*).

Pinel was reluctantly allowed to remove the chains of the people imprisoned in La Bicêtre and to treat them as sick human beings rather than as beasts. Many who had been excited and completely unmanageable became calm and much easier to handle. Formerly considered dangerous, they strolled through the hospital and grounds with no inclination to create disturbances or to harm anyone. Some who had been incarcerated for years were soon restored to health and were eventually discharged from the hospital.

Freeing the patients of their restraints was not the only humanitarian reform advocated by Pinel.[2] He believed that the mental patients in his care were essentially normal people who should be approached with compassion and understanding and treated as individual human beings with dignity. Their reason supposedly having left them because of severe personal and social problems, it might be restored to them through comforting counsel and purposeful activity. Of course not all asylums adopted these so-called moral practices, but the smaller ones that did achieved remarkable successes. Unfortunately, this personal attention to the patients was no longer possible when the large mental hospitals that are prevalent today began to be built (Bockhoven, 1963).

[2] Not all scholars agree that Pinel deserves as much adulation as he enjoys. Thomas Szasz (1974), whose influential writings on involuntary hospitalization are reviewed in Chapter 21, points to sections of Pinel's famous *A Treatise on Insanity* (1801). They indicate that he relied on terror and coercion in dealing with patients of the lower classes.

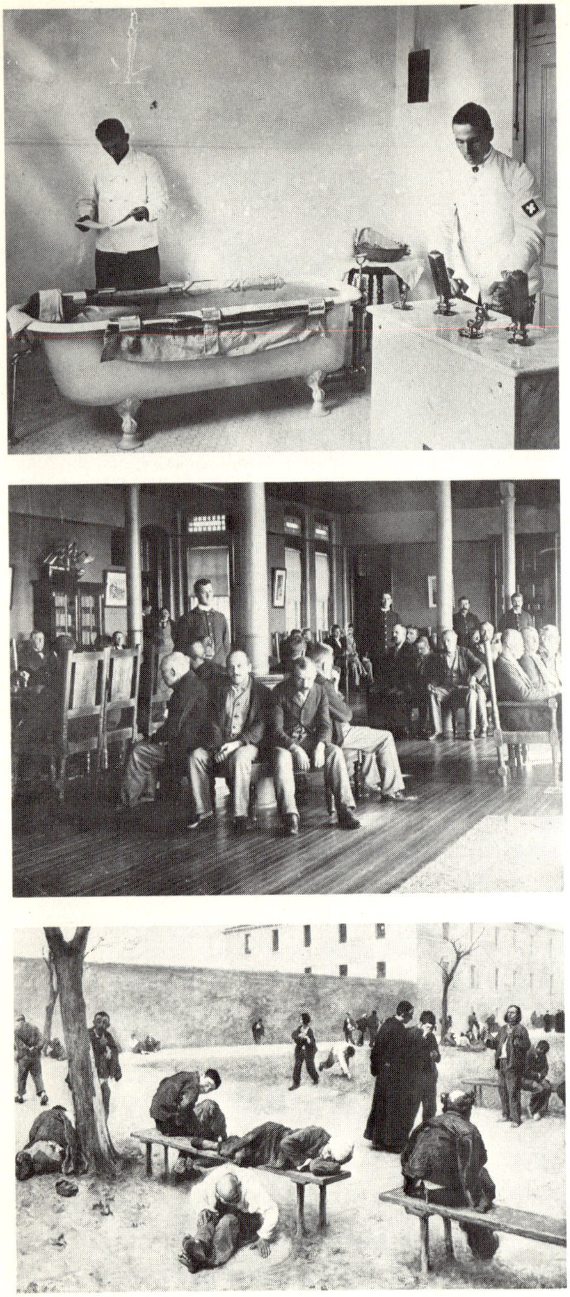

Scenes from some earlier asylums. A patient taking the "tepid bath cure"; inmates gathered in a day room at Mattewan Insane Hospital, New York, early in this century. The painting by Silvio surveys patients in the yard of an asylum near Rome.

### The beginning of contemporary thought

Earlier Hippocrates was described as the first to enunciate a somatogenic hypothesis of mental illness. His view was revived in Europe in the middle of the nineteenth century by a German physician, Wilhelm Griesinger. This clinician insisted that any diagnosis of mental disorder specify a physiological cause. A textbook of psychiatry, written by his well-known follower, Emil Kraepelin, and published in 1883, furnished a classification system to help establish the organic nature of mental illnesses. Kraepelin discerned among mental disorders a tendency for a certain group of symptoms, called a *syndrome,* to appear together regularly enough to be regarded as having an underlying bodily and physical cause, much as a particular medical disease and its syndrome may be attributed to a physiological dysfunction. He regarded each mental illness as distinct from all others, having its own genesis, symptoms, course, and outcome. Even though cures had not been worked out, at least the course of the disease could be predicted. Kraepelin was able to recognize two major groups of mental diseases: dementia praecox, an early term for schizophrenia, and manic-depressive psychosis. He postulated a chemical imbalance as the cause of schizophrenia and an irregularity in metabolism as the explanation of manic-depressive psychosis. Kraepelin's scheme for classifying these and other mental illnesses became the basis for the present psychiatric categories, which will be described more fully in Chapter 3.

Much was being learned about the nervous system in the second half of the nineteenth century but not enough yet to reveal the potential abnormalities in structure underlying mental disorders. Perhaps the most striking medical success was the discovery of the full nature and origin of syphilis. The venereal disease syphilis had been recognized for several centuries, and since 1798 it had been known that a number of mental patients manifested a similar and steady deterioration of both physical and mental abilities. These patients were observed to suffer multiple impairments, including delusions of grandeur and progressive paralysis. Soon after these symptoms were recognized, it was realized that these patients never recovered. In 1825 this deterioration in mental and physical health was designated a disease, general paresis. Although in 1857 it was established that some patients with paresis had earlier had syphilis, there were many competing theories of the origin of paresis. For example, in attempting to account for the high rate of the disorder among sailors, some supposed that sea water might be the cause. And Griesinger, in trying to account for the higher incidence among men, speculated about the importance of liquor, tobacco, and coffee. Then in the 1860s and 1870s Louis Pasteur established the germ theory of disease. It thus became possible to demonstrate the relation between syphilis and general paresis. In 1897 Richard von Krafft-Ebing inoculated paretic patients with matter from syphilitic sores. The patients did not develop syphilis, indicating that they had been infected earlier. Finally, in 1905, the specific microorganism causing syphilis was discovered. Fortunately, measures that can detect the presence of syphilis and prevent its spread were developed soon after the discovery of the spirochete that causes it.

Two portrayals of Franz Anton Mesmer's procedure for transmitting animal magnetism from the *baquet* to his patients. The caricature shows the process as a form of exorcism. Ordered to leave Austria, Mesmer took up practice in Paris. Benjamin Franklin was a member of the French commission that investigated his activities in 1784.

## Psychogenesis

The search for somatogenic causes dominated psychiatry until well into the twentieth century, no doubt partly because of the stunning discoveries made about general paresis. But in other parts of western Europe, in the late eighteenth century and throughout the nineteenth, mental illnesses were considered to have an entirely different genesis. Various *psychogenic* points of view, attributing mental disorders to psychic malfunctions, were fashionable in France and Austria. For reasons that are not clear to us even today, many people in western Europe were at that time subject to *hysterical states:* they suffered from physical incapacities that made absolutely no anatomical sense (see page 158). For example, in "glove anesthesia" the person had no feeling in his or her hand, but sensation was present just beyond the wrist and on up into the arm. Since the nerves run continuously from the shoulder down to the fingertips, there is no known physiological explanation for such an anesthesia.

Franz Anton Mesmer, an Austrian physician practicing in Vienna and Paris in the late eighteenth century, believed that hysterical disorders were caused by a particular distribution of a universal magnetic fluid in the body. Moreover, he felt that one person could influence the fluid of another to bring about a change in the person's behavior. He conducted meetings cloaked in mystery and mysticism, during which afflicted patients sat around a covered *baquet* or tub with iron rods protruding through the cover from the bottles of various chemicals which were beneath. Mesmer would enter a room, clothed in rather outlandish garments, and take various of the rods from the tub and touch afflicted parts of his patients' bodies. The rods were believed to transmit "animal magnetism" and adjust the distribution of the universal magnetic fluid, thereby removing the hysterical disorder. Whatever we may think of what seems today to be a questionable theoretical explanation and procedure, the fact remains that Mesmer seemingly helped quite a number of people overcome their hysterical problems. Our discussion of Mesmer's work under the rubric of psychogenic causes is rather arbitrary, since Mesmer regarded the hysterical disorders as strictly physical. Because of the setting in which Mesmer worked with his patients, however, he is generally considered one of the earlier practitioners of hypnosis (see Box 1.1). (The familiar word mesmerize is the older term for hypnotize.)

A great Parisian neurologist, Jean Martin Charcot, also studied hysterical states, not only anesthesia but blindness, deafness, paralysis, convulsive attacks, and gaps in memory brought about by hysteria. Practicing in the second half of the nineteenth century, Charcot initially espoused a somatogenic point of view. One day, however, some of his enterprising students hypnotized a

Jean Martin Charcot, a French neurologist and teacher of immense influence. He studied hysteria in relation to hypnosis and wrote on the cerebral localization of brain diseases.

normal woman and suggested to her certain hysterical symptoms. Charcot was deceived into believing that she was an actual hysterical patient. When the students showed him how readily they could remove the symptoms by waking the woman, Charcot changed his mind about hysteria and became interested in nonphysiological interpretations of these very puzzling phenomena. Further psychological theorizing and research was done by Pierre Janet, one of Charcot's pupils. He believed that in hysteria subconscious thoughts broke loose through a weakness of the nervous system.

In Vienna, toward the end of the century, a physician named Josef Breuer treated a woman who mumbled to herself when in a dreamlike state called a fugue. Perhaps not knowing what else to

## BOX **1.1** Hypnosis

A discussion of hypnosis could appear in several chapters of this book; inasmuch as it played a central role in the development of psychogenic theories of psychopathology, we include it here.

An initial question to be asked is what exactly is hypnosis. In view of how often psychologists and psychiatrists employ the term, it is sobering to realize how much heated controversy there is about its very nature. Hilgard (1965) suggests the following characteristics.

1. *Increased suggestibility.* Hypnotized subjects seem much more open to suggestions from the hypnotist than they would be in a waking state. Indeed, many hypnotized subjects show annoyance when the hypnotist directs them to do some planning of their own while they are hypnotized. Many theorists believe that hypnosis is nothing more than a state of heightened suggestibility.

2. *Redistribution of attention.* Hypnotized subjects appear extremely attentive to what the hypnotist is saying, thereby becoming less aware of other stimulation, such as noises in an adjacent room. Although the hypnotist often suggests that the subject pay attention only to him, there may be a tendency, even without direct suggestion, for hypnotic subjects to focus on the hypnotist rather than on other things.

3. *Heightened ability to fantasize.* Clinical evidence suggests that visual images are more vivid under hypnosis, although there is a notable lack of controlled experimental data on this point.

4. *Increased tolerance for persistent distortion of reality.* Many hypnotized subjects readily accept all kinds of perceptual distortions that they would not tolerate when awake. Thus hypnotized subjects may accept suggestions that an animal is talking to them or that someone is present in the room when no one is actually there. The logic that operates during a hypnotic trance, allowing a person to perceive the world in a way remarkably different from how he or she regards it when awake, has been called "trance logic" (Orne, 1959).

5. *Role behavior.* Subjects have a greater ability to assume a particular role when hypnotized than when awake. Indeed, Sarbin (1950) has constructed an entire theory about the nature of hypnosis in terms of role taking.

These, then, are what many workers regard as characteristics of hypnotized subjects. As in all aspects of human behavior, not all people manifest all these characteristics in the same way, and it is indeed possible for subjects who otherwise appear to be deeply hypnotized not to give all these noticeable indications at any one time.

Our historical review mentioned Mesmer's therapy for hysterical disabilities and subsequent work by Charcot, Janet, and Breuer. During the same period of time surgeons were "mesmerizing" patients to block pain. For example, in 1842 a British physician, W. S. Ward, amputated the leg of a patient after hypnotizing him. Apparently the patient felt nothing during what would otherwise have been an excruciatingly painful operation. And in 1849 a mesmeric infirmary was opened in London. Hundreds of apparently painless operations were performed while the patients were under hypnotic trances. In the same decade, however, ether was proved to produce insensibility to pain. The term anesthesia had heretofore been applied to the numbness felt in hysterical states and paralysis. Oliver Wendell Holmes is credited with suggesting that it be applied to the effects of this new agent and others like it, and that the agents be called anesthetics. The availability of these chemicals for surgical operations seems to have forestalled the continuing use of hypnosis as an alleviator of pain.

The person who coined the modern term hypnotism is usually considered to be James Braid (1795–1860), a British physician who was also hypnotizing people to reduce pain. Unlike Mesmer, however, Braid did not break with his profession, describing what happened in terms that were more consistent with the *Zeitgeist*. He characterized the trance as a "nervous sleep," from which came the name "neurohypnology," later shortened to hypnotism. Braid rejected the mystical orientation of Mesmer and yet continued to experiment with the phenomenon as he saw it. He sought a physiological cause and felt he had found one in his discovery that trances could be readily induced by having people stare at a bright object located somewhat above the line of vision. The object was placed in front of a person in such a way that the levator muscles of the eyelids had to be strained in order to keep it in view. Braid suggested that the muscles were markedly affected by having them remain fixed in this position for a given period of time and that somehow this led to nervous sleep or hypnosis. He therefore placed the cause of the sleep inside the subject rather than external to him, as Mesmer had suggested with his concept of animal magnetism. In this way he was able to perform many public demonstrations without incurring the disapproval of his medical colleagues.

As already indicated, the discovery of drugs for anesthesia discouraged the use of hypnosis in medicine, for drugs are clearly more reliable, although more dangerous as well, than hypnotic inductions. In clinical work many practitioners have employed hypnotic procedures for psychotherapeutic purposes, especially during World War II. To relieve shell shock the frightened soldier was hypnotized and encouraged to relive traumatic events in his imagination.

The scientific study of hypnosis had to await the development of relatively objective measures in the 1950s. Perhaps the principal device is that developed at Stanford University by Weitzenhoffer and Hilgard (1959), the Stanford Hypnotic Susceptibility Scale. In the application of this scale, or, more properly, scales, since there are a number of them, the subject is hypnotized and then asked to undertake a series of tasks. For example, the hypnotist may suggest to a subject that his right hand is so heavy that it is doubtful whether he can raise it. Then the hypnotist will ask the subject to try to lift the heavy hand even though he probably will not be able to do so. The hypnotist observes the degree to which the subject can or cannot raise the hand and gives a plus or minus score. After the subject has been observed at a number of tasks, he is given a score ranging from zero to twelve, and this score is regarded as a measure of how deeply hypnotized he is.

Most of these scales, however, do not measure the more subjective aspects of hypnosis. For example, many hypnotized subjects, even though they have not been specifically told that it may happen, experience sensations such as floating or spinning. Many hypnotists consider such subjective experiences at least as important as the more observable performances tapped by the various scales. As we might expect, this divergence of interests contributes to the controversy within the field, with the more clinically oriented hypnotists rejecting the validity of such scales as the Stanford. They instead content themselves with what subjects report of their subjective reactions.

do, Breuer hypnotized her and repeated some of her mumbled words. He succeeded in getting her to talk more freely and ultimately with considerable emotion about some very troubling past events. Upon awakening from these hypnotic sessions, she would frequently feel much better. With other hysterical patients Breuer found that the relief and cure of their symptoms seemed to last longer if, under hypnosis, they were able to recall the original precipitating event for the symptom and if, furthermore, their original emotion was expressed. This reliving of an earlier emotional catastrophe and the release of the emotional tension produced by previously forgotten thoughts about the event was called abreaction or catharsis. Breuer's method became known as the *cathartic method.* In 1895 one of his colleagues joined him in the publication of *Studies in Hysteria,* a book considered to be a milestone in abnormal psychology. Breuer's collaborator was Sigmund Freud, whose thinking we shall examine later.[3]

[3] Anna O., the young woman treated by Breuer with the cathartic method, or "talking cure," has become one of the best-known clinical cases in all psychotherapy literature, and, as stated above, the report of this case in 1895 formed the basis of Freud's important contributions later on. But historical investigations by Ellenberger (1972) cast serious doubt on how accurate Breuer's reporting was. Indeed, Anna O.—in reality Bertha Pappenheim, member of a well-to-do Viennese family—was apparently helped only temporarily by Breuer's talking cure! Carl Jung, Freud's renowned colleague, is quoted as saying that, during a conference in 1925, Freud told him that Anna O. had never been cured. Hospital records discovered by Ellenberger confirmed that she continued to rely on morphine to ease the "hysterical" problems that Breuer is reputed to have removed by catharsis. In fact, evidence suggests that some of her problems were organic, not psychological. It is fascinating and ironic to consider that psychoanalysis traces its roots back to an improperly reported clinical case.

## Science: A Human Enterprise

In the dramatic space explorations of recent years, highly sophisticated satellites are sent aloft to make observations. Astronauts have also been catapulted to the moon, where they use their human senses as well as man-made machines to make still more observations. It is possible, however, that certain phenomena are being missed because our instruments do not have sensing devices capable of recording the presence or absence of such phenomena, and because people are not trained to look for them. When the Viking 1 and Viking 2 Mars landers began to forage for life in July and September of 1976, space scientists repeatedly cautioned against concluding that there was no life on Mars just because instruments failed to detect any. Scientists are sophisticated enough by training to know that they are in a bind. Life on another planet can be looked for only with the instruments they themselves have developed, but these devices are limited by their own preconceptions. The tests run on Mars make *assumptions* about the nature of living matter that may not match what has evolved on this distant planet. Carl Sagan, renowned Cornell space scientist, has cautioned that we may simply be asking the wrong questions. The Viking experiments can determine only whether the Martian soil samples contain earthlike life, but life on Mars could be based on an entirely different chemistry (*Time,* August 2, 1976, p. 23).

This discursion on outer space exploration is by way of pointing out that scientific observation is a human endeavor, reflecting both the strengths of human ingenuity and scholarship as well as our intrinsic incapacity to be fully knowledgeable about the nature of our universe. Scientists are able to design instruments to make only the kinds of observations about which they have some initial idea. They realize that certain observations are not being made because our knowledge about the general nature of the universe is limited. Thomas Kuhn, a well-known philosopher of science, has put the problem this way: "The decision to employ a particular piece of apparatus and to use it in a particular way carries an assumption that only certain sorts of circumstances will arise" (1962, p. 59). Robert Pirsig, in *Zen and the Art of Motorcycle Maintenance* (1974), expressed the issue somewhat more poetically: "We take a handful of sand from the endless landscape of awareness around us and call that handful of sand the world" (p. 75).

## Subjectivity in Science: The Role of Paradigms

We believe that every effort should be made to study abnormal behavior according to scientific principles. It should be clear at this point, however, that science is *not* a completely objective and certain enterprise. Rather, as we can infer from the comment by Kuhn, subjective factors, as well as limitations in our perspective on the universe, enter into the conduct of scientific inquiry. Central to any application of scientific principles, in Kuhn's view, is the concept of *paradigm,* which may be defined as a conceptual framework within which a scientist works. A paradigm, according to Kuhn, is a set of basic assumptions that outline the *particular* universe of scientific inquiry, specifying both the kinds of concepts that will be regarded as legitimate as well as the methods that may be used to collect and interpret data. Indeed, every decision about what constitutes a datum, or scientific observation, is made within a paradigm. A paradigm has profound implications for how scientists operate at any given time, for "Men whose research is based on shared paradigms are committed to the same rules and standards for scientific practice" (Kuhn, 1962, p. 11). Paradigms specify what problems scientists will investigate and how they will go about the investigation.

Although made explicit only when scientists address themselves to philosophy, paradigms are nonetheless an intrinsic part of a science, serving the vital function of indicating how the game is to be played. In perceptual terms a paradigm may be likened to a general *set,* a tendency to see certain factors and not to see others.

Consider the following experiment (Davison, 1964a). Having volunteered for a study on perception, you find yourself sitting in front of a screen on which color slides are being projected. Your task is to identify, as best you can, what the slides depict. Each is initially projected so far out of focus that it is virtually impossible to make out the image. Over a period of two minutes, the slide is very gradually brought into focus; as this happens your ideas of it change. Figure 1.1 shows one of these slides at varying degrees of focus. We invite you to examine these pictures before reading further. If you are like the students who participated in the actual study, the slide may at first seem to show "a bunch of balls floating in water" or "children's tops." After a minute or so you suddenly realize that you are gazing at a fire hydrant. You experience the familiar "Aha!" of recognition which comes when the solution of a difficult problem finally occurs to us. The interesting question is what effect the original hypothesis has on the ultimate recognition of the content of the slide. In fact, subjects tended to get *stuck* within a particular interpretation for each of the slides because they had had to look at them when they were impossible to identify correctly. Even though the students appeared to be changing their minds, in most instances they kept looking at each in a particular way and were prevented from seeing the slides correctly until they became clearer. In the case of the fire hydrant portrayed in Figure 1.1, subjects assumed that they were viewing several separate objects. Any organization of the visual field into disconnected figures is quite different from the actual composition given on the slide, which is a view of a single object. Indeed, in another experiment, subjects recognized these same pictures more quickly if they were warned about the most common error of interpretation. Before viewing the slide of the fire hydrant, they were told, "Do not make the mistake of looking at this pic-

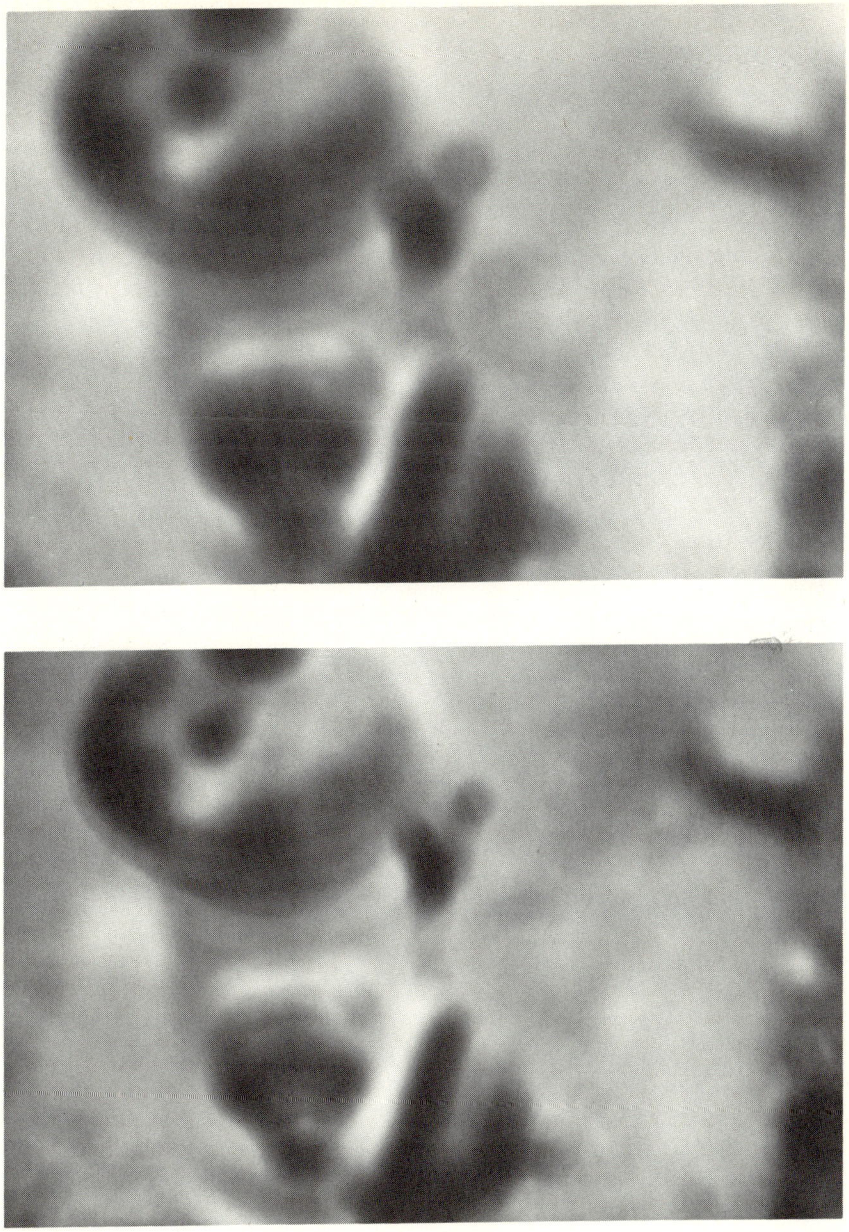

FIGURE **1.1**
Try to determine the subject matter of these photographs. Beginning with the first, decide what you think you see. Then look at the second, guess again, and so on through the third and fourth on the following page. Did your early hypotheses "blind" you from seeing the later photographs correctly?

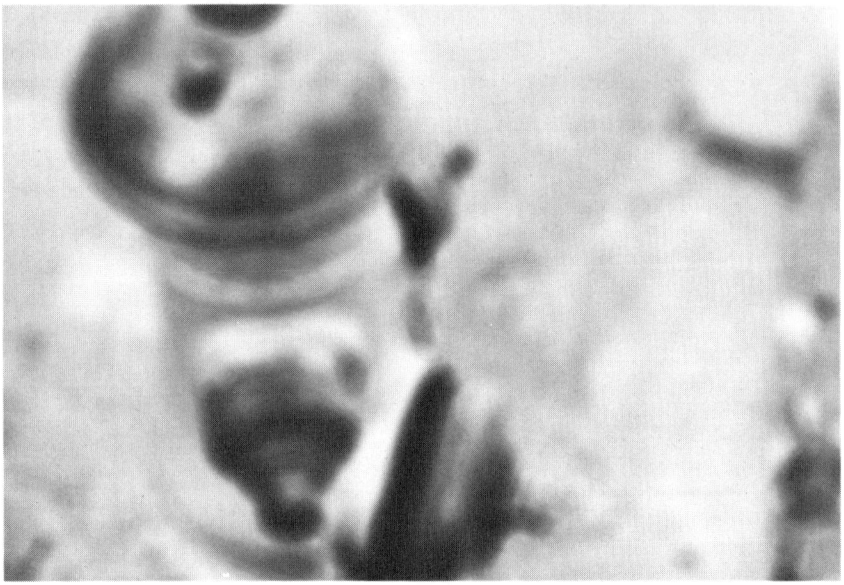

ture as though it were composed of several objects."

What does this study have to do with Kuhn's concept of paradigm? We believe that scientists investigating abnormal behavior are faced with a task similar to that of identifying out-of-focus slides. Psychopathology and its treatment are at a very poor stage of focus; knowledge is limited. Faced with this challenge, we adopt overall points of view—paradigms—that channel our thinking in certain directions. We may believe that we are remaining flexible as we alter our specific ideas, but we tend to get caught in a particular way of looking at the world, and our perceptions fall within that domain. Because input is not very good, we may often be wrong. The lesson to be drawn is that we must be aware of our biases—our most basic beliefs, our paradigms—so that we can shift points of view when they do not prove serviceable. None of us can afford to be smug about the paradigm we adopt. Within contemporary psychology behaviorism and psychoanalysis may be regarded as two separate paradigms. How difficult it is for people operating within different paradigms even to talk with one another will become evident when we later explore the specifics of these two schools of psychology.

In addition to injecting inevitable biases into the definition and collection of data, a paradigm may also affect the interpretation of facts. In other words, the meaning or import attributed to data may depend to a considerable extent on a paradigm. Let us look briefly at the classic example of how for nearly 1400 years a particular paradigm influenced the interpretation of data about the heavens. From the second until the sixteenth century A.D., astronomy was dominated by the Ptolemaic paradigm. The earth was viewed as the center of the universe and the various planets and stars were considered to revolve around it. Although such a point of view seems rather absurd when examined in the light of current scientific knowledge, it was in fact, with some embellishments, able to provide relatively good predictions of the positions of the planets, the sun, and the moon and of such phenomena as eclipses.

Fairly accurate observations and measurements of planetary positions and motions had been made by Hipparchus, 300 years earlier, and Ptolemy had extended this work. The astronomical data to be encompassed by any paradigm interpreting the heavens was therefore considerable. To explain the retrograde, or westward, motion of planets and other orbital eccentricities—changes of position actually reflecting the revolution of the earth about the sun—the Ptolemaic system postulated a number of complicated concepts. A planet was thought to move in a small circle, the epicycle, the center of which was at the same time traveling an orbit, the planet's deferent, around the earth. The earth was not located in the exact center of the diameter of the deferent but a little to the side, at the eccentric (Figure 1.2). The equant was yet another position on the diameter of the deferent, the same distance from the center as the eccen-

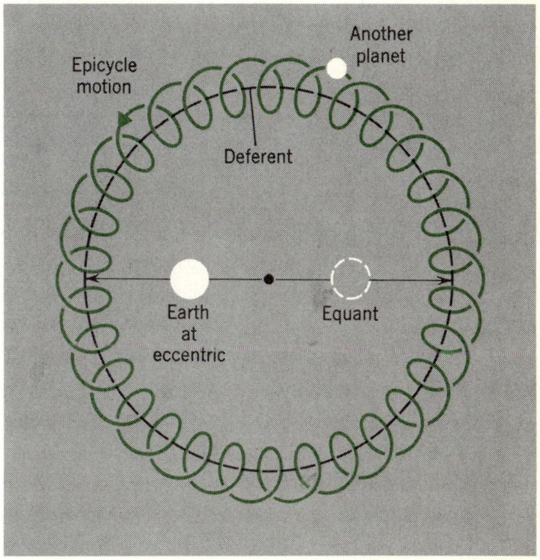


FIGURE **1.2**
Planetary movements in the Ptolemaic system, showing the epicycle, deferent, eccentric, and equant.

tric. Around this point the center of each planet's epicycle appeared to move with uniform speed. To the proponents of the Ptolemaic system, who were certainly no fools, such motions seemed eminently reasonable because they explained a universe of which the earth was the immovable center. Although some minor discrepancies between the predictions and the actual observations of planetary motions remained unexplained, these discrepancies did not lead people to doubt the basic assumption, that the earth was the center of the universe. The task of astronomy for fourteen centuries was the refinement of the Ptolemaic system to improve its predictions.

Kuhn (1959) has labeled such a period "normal science." Astronomers during these centuries shared a common view of the phenomena in which they were interested. Because this shared view, that the earth was the center of the universe, was so strongly held, it was never questioned when contradictory evidence was discovered. Instead, scientists attempted to readjust aspects of the paradigm. To bring the Ptolemaic system more in line with any new observations of the positions and movements of the planets, astronomers elaborated the arrangement of deferents and epicycles.

In 1543 Copernicus proposed a radically different paradigm as a theoretical basis for astronomy. Specifically, he suggested that the sun rather than the earth be considered the center of the universe. Moreover, orbits should be regarded as perfectly circular and uniform and not be subject to complexities such as the equant. *It is important to note that the Copernican revolution was not based on the acquisition of new data.* Rather, the data available to Copernicus were but little different from those available to Ptolemy over 1400 years earlier. What, then, led to the revolution in thought, the paradigm shift?

Two points seem to have been particularly important to Copernicus in his rejection of the Ptolemaic system. First, he recognized its great complexity and lack of elegance. The Ptolemaic view of the universe had become inordinately flexible and complex—encompassing additional and eccentric epicycles—in order to avoid being disproved. Second, based on religious-cosmological considerations, Copernicus believed that planetary orbits "ought to be" circular since the circle was the most perfect form in nature. Thus we see that the postulation of a paradigm to interpret observed data can depend heavily on *subjective,* nonscientific views held by the theorist. In fact, when the Copernican system was initially proposed, it provided no increment in predictive power over what could be obtained by adhering to the Ptolemaic system. At least initially, the adoption of the Copernican paradigm was based on factors other than the adequacy with which it could account for the available data.

Subjective factors such as those we have discussed in relation to the Copernican revolution have also greatly affected theorizing about psychopathology. We have already examined several instances of what might be called "paradigm clashes" in the history of thinking about the problems of abnormal behavior (see Box 1.2). Hippocrates' revolt against demonology, Weyer's denunciation of witch-hunting, and the treatment reforms of Pinel can all be considered attempts to change radically the way in which abnormal behavior was viewed. Moreover, at the time these men proposed what we consider more rational approaches to abnormal behavior, they had no definitive proof that their new visions would be better than the old.

## An Example of Paradigms in Abnormal Psychology

As implied earlier, there is perhaps no poorer communication within the field of psychology than that between the psychoanalysts and the behaviorists. The chasm that exists between these two camps is made apparent by examining a widely quoted and rather controversial report by three behaviorists, Ayllon, Haughton, and Hughes (1965). These investigators were interested in the etiology of psychiatric symptoms, that is, in what factors may account for their development. Being skeptical about prevailing

## BOX 1.2 Paradigm Clash in the Study of Hypnosis

Box 1.1 reviewed some of the history of hypnosis and its generally accepted characteristics. There is an interesting paradigm clash about hypnosis, for the very idea that we should talk *at all* about a state called hypnosis has been challenged. Probably the most outspoken critic of "state theories" of hypnosis—conceptions of hypnosis that assume a separate state underlying the phenomena—is an experimental psychologist, Theodore X. Barber. Barber's line of reasoning, presented in scores of theoretical papers and experiments (for example, Barber, 1969), is essentially as follows.

1. "Hypnosis," as a state, is inferred solely on the basis of the presence of behavioral phenomena that it is alleged to cause. A subject's inability to lift his or her hand when extreme heaviness is suggested is, at the same time, interpreted to be both a sign of hypnosis and a result of hypnosis. To say that the heaviness indicates that the person is hypnotized and then to conclude that the heaviness is caused by hypnosis is to engage in circular reasoning. Nothing has really been explained.

2. Behavior generally regarded as caused by hypnosis can be readily produced in subjects who are not given a hypnotic induction. Barber and Calverley (1964b) found that subjects will report a variety of vivid auditory and visual hallucinations, seeing or hearing something that is not really present, when they are simply urged to try very hard to hallucinate.

3. Therefore it is not scientifically useful nor is it necessary to employ a state concept of "hypnosis."

Not surprisingly, Barber's position has been attacked, sometimes vehemently, by investigators who operate under the assumption that we can talk meaningfully of a state of hypnosis. Spanos (1970), one of Barber's associates, has reviewed and replied to the principal criticisms. State theorists have suggested that the subjects in Barber's experiments, although not given a formal hypnotic induction, nonetheless slip into a hypnotic trance and *therefore* shows signs of hypnosis. Spanos points out that this is a purely *post hoc* argument, an "explanation" offered only after the data are in, and is therefore impossible to refute. If nonhypnotized subjects do something hypnotic, they can be said to have slipped into a trance; but if, like many subjects, they fail to "look hypnotized," they can always be said *afterward* not to have been in a trance.

Barber's critics (for example, Conn and Conn, 1967) have also proposed that independent evidence of hypnosis can be found in verbal reports of whether subjects are or are not hypnotized. Spanos replies that scientists do not always believe what subjects tell them and that the tendency to regard a self-report as valid or invalid is itself affected by the scientist's point of view. For example, suppose a subject tells a hypnotist that she cannot lift her arm because the devil is holding it down. How many present-day scientists would conclude that hypnosis is the devil's doing? Similarly, an investigator must initially believe that there is a separate state of hypnosis *before* attributing validity to the report of a subject that he or she has been hypnotized.

On the experimental level, some of Barber's research has questioned the very existence of behavioral phenomena that state theorists have accepted on the basis of self-support. For instance, some hypnotized subjects report deafness after it has been suggested to them that they may not be able to hear. Barber and Calverley (1964a) decided to assess deafness in a less obvious fashion, one that would not rely on self-report. Delayed auditory feedback is a procedure whereby subjects hear through headphones what they are saying, although it is delayed by a given period of time, for example, one second. Numerous studies have shown that such delayed feedback of speech invariably causes stuttering in otherwise fluent people. Barber and Calverley reasoned that if people could truly be rendered deaf by hypnotic suggestion, they would not stutter when their words were fed back to them. In a carefully controlled experiment, subjects who were, according to objective measures, deeply hypnotized, were given a suggestion of deafness. Afterward they reported that they could not hear, but they were nonetheless markedly affected by delayed auditory feedback of their own speech.

The authors of this book are sympathetic to the arguments of Barber and his colleagues. At the same time, it seems quite reasonable to study phenomena that have been labeled as hypnotic, as indeed Barber himself has done for many years. In our clinical work we occasionally make use of hypnotic inductions to achieve certain specific ends, for example, helping people to relax. It seems possible to do this without affirming allegiance to either state or nonstate theories of hypnosis. The expectations a person has about being hypnotized would seem to be the important factor. Whether a hypnotic induction *really* produces a *state* in which a person imagines more vividly than when awake seems to be secondary in importance to the possibility that a hypnotic induction may make a person *believe* that he or she can imagine more vividly.

psychoanalytic explanations of psychopathological phenomena, Ayllon and his colleagues set out to demonstrate that "The etiology of many so-called psychotic symptoms exhibited by hospitalized patients or those in need of hospitalization does not have to be sought in the obscure dynamics of a psychiatric disturbance" (p. 5). To prove their point, they chose a female patient hospitalized for chronic schizophrenia and proceeded to encourage her to hold a broom, without sweeping with it, by giving her cigarettes whenever she followed their instructions. They felt that the purposeless behavior they had devised for the woman could be regarded as abnormal. Then to determine how the broom holding would actually be judged, they arranged for unsuspecting psychiatrists to comment on the patient's behavior. One of the doctors described the broom-holding behavior as follows:

> *Her constant and compulsive pacing, holding a broom in the manner she does, could be seen as a ritualistic procedure, a magical action . . . her broom would be then: (1) a child that gives her love and she gives him in return her devotion, (2) a phallic symbol, (3) a sceptre of an impotent queen . . . (Ayllon et al., 1965, p. 3).*

As the investigators point out, the psychiatrist was not aware of the *contrived* origin of this behavior.

What did this demonstration really prove? Ayllon and his colleagues asserted that in persuading the woman to hold the broom by rewarding her, they had illustrated how psychotic behavior develops in the real world, under nonlaboratory conditions. The fact that the psychiatrists, who were ignorant of the experimental ruse, regarded the behavior as a symptom of the woman's psychosis helped to convince the investigators that they had actually shown how abnormal behavior originates.

If we assume that even bizarre-appearing behavior can be learned in the same way as behavior not designated as abnormal, we must postulate a world of psychopathology far different from that in which deviant phenomena are considered an expression of internal repressed impulses.[4] Although we do not know what the psychiatrists who commented on the broom-holding woman were actually thinking at the time of their observation, it is safe to assume that their psychoanalytic orientation did not allow them even to consider the possibility that she had been taught this behavior. On the other hand, it is significant that Ayllon and his colleagues, in their apparent eagerness to debunk the psychoanalytic approach, committed an error in logic. Because they had shown that under certain contrived circumstances a patient already diagnosed as schizophrenic could easily be encouraged to hold a broom by occasionally giving her cigarettes, they inferred that they had cast light on the manner in which psychotic behavior develops. They committed the error of "affirming the consequent." They assumed that simply because behavior is generated under one set of circumstances, a set of like controlling conditions accounts for its occurrence in nature (Davison, 1969; Maher, 1966).

Thus subjective factors pervade psychology and very much affect our conception of the nature of abnormal behavior. Scientists do not resign from the family of man when they formulate hypotheses and conduct controlled research. Perhaps it is especially appropriate for the psychologist-as-scientist to remain aware of this simple, although frequently overlooked, point.

## Summary

The study of abnormal behavior is a search for why people behave in unexpected, sometimes bizarre, and typically self-defeating ways. Much less is known than we would like; this book will focus on the ways in which psychopathologists have been trying to learn the causes of abnormal behavior and what they know about alleviating it.

A brief history of the field was provided, indicating its origins in ancient demonology and crude medical theorizing. Since the beginning of scientific inquiry into abnormal behavior, two major points of view have vied for attention: the somatogenic, which assumes that every mental aberration is caused by a physical malfunction; and the psychogenic, which assumes that the sufferer's body is intact and that difficulties are to be explained in psychological terms.

Scientific inquiry was presented as a special way in which human beings acquire knowledge about their world. In a very important sense people see only what they are prepared to see, and certain phenomena may go undetected because scientists can discover only those things about which they already have some general idea. There is subjectivity in science as there is in everyday perception and problem solving.

Hypnosis was reviewed in some detail, both because it occupies an important position in the historical development of the field and because the controversies about hypnosis provide a good example of how the paradigms of science—the sets of basic assumptions that determine the kinds of scientific questions to be asked and the procedures to be used in collecting data—can vary and thus affect the conclusions drawn.

[4] Additional details of psychoanalytic thinking are given in Chapters 2, 5, and 18.

# chapter 2

## CURRENT PARADIGMS IN ABNORMAL PSYCHOLOGY



This chapter is concerned with the principal paradigms or perspectives that have been used to conceptualize abnormal behavior. Some authors have applied the term model rather than paradigm to these points of view. The term model implies that concepts from one domain, for example, learning theory, are applied to another, such as abnormal psychology, with the expectation that understanding of the second will be increased. Or, as another example, the brain can be thought of as a computer. Adopting a computer model of the brain would not mean that we believe the brain to *be* a computer, constructed of electronic circuitry, tape decks, and typewriter terminals. Rather, we would be assuming that the *functioning* of the brain might be better understood by likening it to the operation of a computer (Maher, 1966; Price, 1972a).

The term model, however, implies a degree of precision that does not seem characteristic of the way people have thought about abnormal behavior. Instead of formulating models, different investigators have adopted various perspectives, loose sets of *general assumptions* about what should be studied, how to gather data, and how to think about such behavior. We shall discuss four major paradigms of contemporary abnormal psychology, the *statistical* paradigm, the *physiological,* the *psychoanalytic,* and the *learning*. The particular postulates of each paradigm cannot be listed item by item. Instead, we shall try to convey the flavor of the four general points of view. Many people go about the study of abnormal psychology without explicitly considering the nature of the paradigm that they have adopted. As we hope to show in this chapter, the choice of a paradigm has some very important consequences for the way abnormal behavior is defined and investigated. The assumptions made by the holders of the various paradigmatic positions must be examined.

## The Statistical Paradigm

Those who adopt the statistical approach measure specific characteristics of people, such as personality traits and ways of behaving, and the distribution of these characteristics in the population. One type of population distribution, the normal curve (Figure 2.1), depicts the majority of people as being in the middle as far as any particular characteristic is concerned: that is, very few people fall at either extreme. Within a statistical paradigm an assertion that a person is normal implies that he or she does not deviate from the average in a particular trait or behavior pattern. For example, if we consider anxiety as one dimension of abnormality, persons who are "average" in anxiety level will be considered normal. In contrast, people who are extremely anxious and people who suffer little or no anxiety will be considered abnormal. To use more traditional diagnostic labels (see Chapter 3), a person with considerable anxiety is regarded as neurotic and a person with very little anxiety as sociopathic. Similarly, a person very low in intelligence will be considered abnormal and so will a genius. To make a decision about a person's normality or abnormality, we merely assess the characteristic in question and determine the person's position on the bell-shaped curve.

As an example, let us consider how Eysenck (1960) diagnoses people. He bases his classification on what he believes are the three most pertinent dimensions of personality. The first, neuroticism, refers primarily to emotionality, or the ease with which people can become aroused. The second, introversion-extroversion, refers for the most part to conditionability: extroverts are said to acquire conditioned responses slowly and to lose them rapidly, whereas the reverse is true of introverts. The third, psychoticism, relates to the person's contact with reality. Each of the three dimensions is assumed to be measurable through various techniques, such as personality questionnaires, laboratory tests, and the like. By determining people's scores on each of the three dimensions, we can fit them into the more traditional diagnostic scheme. Figure 2.2 indicates how this can be done for two of the dimensions, neuroticism and introversion-extroversion.

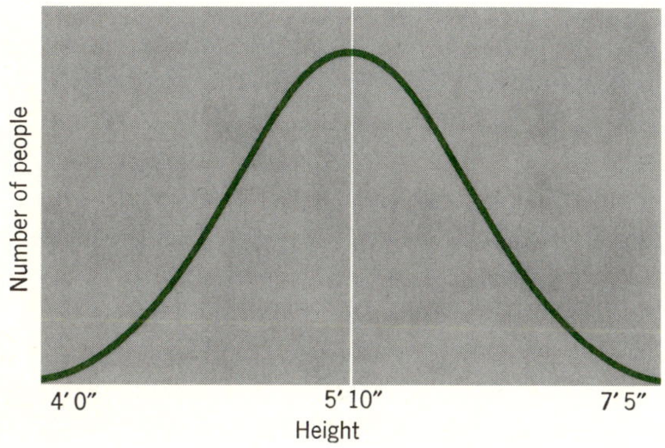


FIGURE **2.1**
The distribution of height among adults, illustrating a normal or bell-shaped curve.

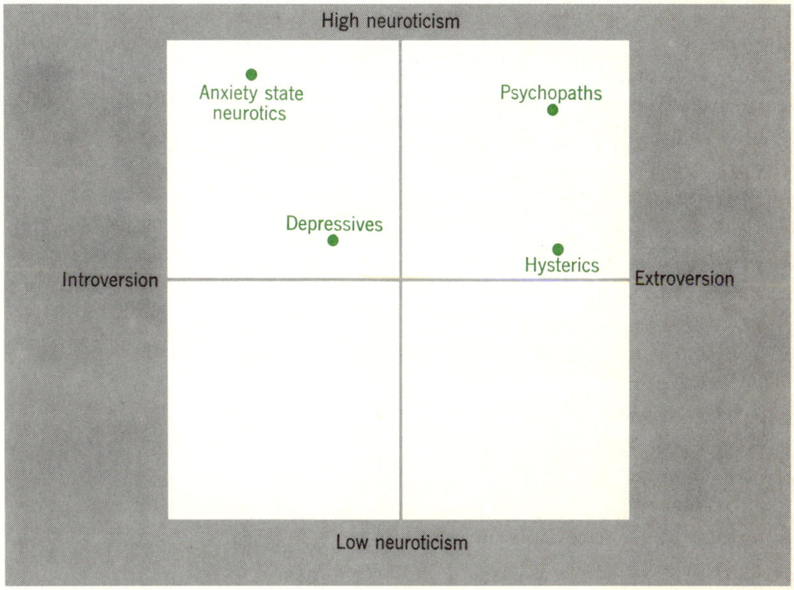


FIGURE **2.2**
Eysenck's statistical paradigm, indicating how various clinical groups can be described according to their positions on the dimensions of neuroticism and introversion-extroversion.

Those persons who are deviant, that is, those who are rated either high or low on a particular dimension, are judged abnormal; for example, someone rated high in both neuroticism and extroversion is regarded by Eysenck as psychopathic.[1]

How may the statistical approach to abnormal behavior be evaluated? First, the investigator relies on the fact that a low frequency of occurrence is defined as deviant. Low-frequency behavior is indeed often regarded as abnormal, but there are also instances in which this relationship breaks down. Low IQs may be a proper subject for study by abnormal psychologists, but can the opposite, high IQs, be considered within their province? And just how low does the frequency of occurrence have to be to judge the behavior abnormal? Moreover, the paradigm fails to specify what phenomena we should measure and gives us no hints about what variables may be related to the development of abnormal behavior. Few of us would seriously make decisions about psychological normality or abnormality on the basis of characteristics such as height, weight, and hair color; rather, a person's tendency to be anxious or to hallucinate would generally be viewed as more appropriate criteria. Any decision, then, about *which* variables or dimensions to measure must be made on some other basis. Therefore, although providing a partial description of abnormality, the statistical paradigm must be considered inadequate.

[1] Eysenck's view of psychopaths as having a high level of neuroticism conflicts with most other theoretical accounts, as will be discussed in Chapter 9.

## The Physiological Paradigm

What we designate as the physiological paradigm of abnormal behavior is often referred to as the medical or disease model. We prefer our term for two reasons. First, it has proved difficult to define exactly what is meant by medical model. Second, and more important, arguments about the so-called medical model most often reduce to whether or not behavior is abnormal because of physiological defects.

Let us first examine the prevalent definition of the medical model. As indicated in Chapter 1, the study of abnormal behavior is historically linked to medicine. Many early workers and many contemporaries as well have used the model of physical illness as the basis for defining deviant behavior. Clearly, within the field of abnormal behavior the terminology of medicine is pervasive. As Maher (1966) has noted, "[deviant] behavior is termed *pathological* and is classified on the basis of *symptoms,* classification being called *diagnosis*. Processes designed to change behavior are called *therapies* and are applied to patients in mental *hospitals*. If the deviant behavior ceases, the patient is described as *cured*" (p. 22).

The critical assumption of the medical model is that abnormal behavior may be likened to a disease. To determine how a disease model can be applied to abnormal behavior, we must first examine the concept of disease as it is employed in medicine. During the Dark Ages a disease was thought to consist simply of observable signs and symptoms, such as a rash and high temperature. As medical science, particularly autopsy studies, increased in sophistication, the observable symptoms were attributed to internal malfunctions. Then, when Louis Pasteur discovered the relation between bacteria and disease, and soon thereafter postulated viruses, the *germ theory of disease* provided a new explanation of pathology. External symptoms were assumed to be produced through infection of the body by minute organisms and viruses. For a time this germ

## BOX **2.1** Criticisms of the Medical or Disease Model of Abnormal Behavior

Although we have argued that the term medical model is not very valuable, it is so widely discussed by psychopathologists and clinicians that an overview of some of its problems may be useful. A common criticism is that in examining the abnormal behavior of an individual, there are no independent means of verifying the existence of a disease. In medicine both the symptoms and the factors producing them, that is, the disease process, can often be assessed. It is possible, for example, to determine that an individual has a temperature of 104 degrees. Moreover, the particular germ or microorganism that has initiated the processes producing the heightened temperature can also be independently determined, say by taking a throat culture and analyzing what foreign organisms are present. When a disease model is applied to abnormal behavior, however, it is often not possible to assess independently both the symptoms and the supposed cause of the symptoms. Certain behavior or symptoms are categorized as mental illnesses and given names, but then the name of the illness itself is often cited as an explanation for or cause of these same symptoms. For example, a patient who is withdrawn and hallucinating is diagnosed as schizophrenic: however, when we ask why the patient is withdrawn and hallucinating, we are often told that it is *because* the patient is schizophrenic. Thus the label schizophrenia is applied to certain behavior and then in addition is specified as a cause of this same behavior, a clear example of *circular reasoning.*

This criticism of the way mental illnesses are assessed is reasonable, but it is not always entirely applicable. Someone holding a medical or disease model point of view could take a somewhat more sophisticated position. He or she could assert that we may make a diagnosis of schizophrenia on the basis of symptoms without claiming that these symptoms are produced by the presence of schizophrenia. This diagnostician would propose that although we do not know the cause of the symptoms, such knowledge will eventually be forthcoming. Some deviant chemical may eventually be located within schizophrenics and be identified as the cause of the disorder. In sum, the more sophisticated disease modeler may acknowledge that we currently have little information about causes, but that when such information becomes available, it will, in principle, be possible to assess independently both the symptoms and the etiology as is the case in medicine.

A second common criticism of applying medical models to abnormal behavior involves an alleged difference between the symptoms of physical illness and the symptoms of mental illness. This argument, most often associated with Thomas Szasz (1960), holds that so-called mental symptoms are a patient's communications about himself and others. When we call such statements symptoms, Szasz asserts, we are making a judgment within a particular social and cultural context. For example, a patient's belief that he is Christ might be enough for an observer to make a diagnosis of paranoid schizophrenia. Even in this extreme case, however, the diagnosis depends on the observer's disbelieving the patient's assertion. If the observer gives credence to the patient's assertion, the behavior will clearly not be judged a symptom of mental illness.

In evaluating this criticism, we should consider the allegation by Szasz and his followers that the symptoms of mental illness are *subjective,* whereas those of physical illness are *objective.* This assertion has some merit, but the distinction is not as clear-cut as Szasz would have it (Ausubel, 1961b). For example, a patient who has entered a physician's office may complain that he is suffering pain. But because tolerance of pain differs widely among individuals, how can the physician determine the actual amount of pain the patient is experiencing? Although the importance of subjective factors as they enter into the definition of so-called mental illness should not be minimized, distinguishing between mental and physical illnesses on this basis alone is a questionable procedure. Subjective factors appear to be implicated in determining the presence of physical diseases as well, although the exact nature of a medical disorder is likely to be assessed further by objective laboratory tests.

Finally, many people have alleged that so-called mental illnesses have neither a specific etiology nor a specific set of symptoms and thus do not qualify as diseases (for example, Milton and Wahler, 1969). Our knowledge of the etiologies of psychopathologies is indeed extremely limited. The fact that these etiologies have not been uncovered as yet, however, does not necessarily mean that we should stop looking for them.

Our failure to define specific sets of symptoms for many categories of deviant behavior may be a more damning criticism. Evidence has accumulated that specific syndromes have simply not been discerned for all psychopathologies. Again, however, a person wishing to maintain a medical model for mental illness may counter this criticism with the following line of reasoning. Many medical diseases do *not* have a set of specific symptoms. Paresis is a good example. Before it was discovered to be infectious, there was considerable debate whether the symptoms had a physical cause or whether paresis should be considered a psychological disturbance. Proponents of the psychological view argued that the symptoms were not entirely consistent from one person to another, for some patients suffer depression rather than delusions of grandeur. Therefore they did not consider paresis a medical disease. Although paresis was indeed found to have a *single* causal agent, the manifestations of its *later* stage may *differ markedly from patient to patient*. Thus even an infectious disease may not necessarily have a homogeneous set of symptoms.

Any judgment about whether to view abnormal behavior as a medical disease made on the basis of the information just presented is a good illustration of how subjective factors may have to be resorted to in science. The medical model is subject to many potential criticisms. For each of these, however, there is a possible rejoinder.

theory was the paradigm of medicine. But it soon became apparent that not all diseases could be explained by the germ theory. Diabetes, for example, a malfunction of the cells of the pancreas that secrete insulin, is not produced by infection. Nor does it even have a single cause. As another example, consider heart disease. A multitude of factors—genetic makeup, stress produced by smoking and obesity, a person's degree of physical fitness—are all related to the frequency of heart disease. Is there a single paradigm here?

We think not. Because medical diseases themselves vary in their causes and symptoms, asserting that abnormal behavior can be considered a disease clarifies little (see Box 2.1). But all diseases *are* disturbances of the body's physiological processes. This is why we have chosen the term physiological paradigm. It is meaningful to say that a behavioral abnormality may be attributed, at least in part, to a disruption in one or more physiological processes.

There is now a considerable literature, both research and theory, dealing with physiological factors relevant to psychopathology. Some, for example, believe that heredity predisposes a person, through physiological malfunction, to develop schizophrenia (see Chapter 14). Depression may result from a failure of the usual processes of neural transmission (Chapter 8). Neurotic behavior has been considered to stem from a defect within the autonomic nervous system that causes a person to be too easily aroused (Chapter 6). Other so-called organic brain syndromes can be traced to impairments in structures of the brain (Chapter 16). In each case a type of psychopathology is viewed as caused by the disturbance of some physiological process. Those working with this paradigm assume that answers to the puzzles of psychopathology will be found by concentrating on somatic, that is, bodily, causes.

## The Psychoanalytic Paradigm

Probably the most widespread paradigm in psychopathology is the psychodynamic or psychoanalytic, originally developed by Sigmund Freud.

### Structure of the Mind

Freud came to divide the mind or the psyche into three principal parts, the id, ego, and superego; each of these are metaphors for specific functions or energies. The id is present at birth and is the part of the personality that accounts for all the energy to run the psyche. Freud, trained as a neurologist, regarded the source of all energy of the id as physiological; it is later converted by some means into psychic energy, all of it unconscious, below the level of awareness.

Within the id Freud postulated two basic instincts, Eros and Thanatos. The more important is Eros, which Freud saw as a life-integrating force, principally sexual. The energy of the instinct Eros is called libido. Eros, libido, and sexual energy are sometimes indiscriminately equated, but libido and Eros are also occasionally expanded to include all integrative, life-furthering forces, some of which may not be strictly sexual. Thanatos, the death instinct, plays a relatively small role in Freudian thinking, and indeed its energy never received a name.

The id seeks immediate gratification and operates on what Freud called *the pleasure principle*. When the id is not satisfied, tension is produced, and the id strives to eliminate this tension as quickly as possible. For example, the infant feels hunger, an aversive drive, and is impelled to move about, sucking, in order to reduce the tension arising from the unsatisfied drive. This behavior, called reflex activity, is one means by which the id obtains gratification; it represents the organism's first commerce with the environment. The other means is *primary process,* generating images of what is desired. The infant who wants its mother's milk imagines the mother's breast and thereby obtains some short-term satisfaction of the hunger drive through its wish-fulfilling fantasy. Even in adult life id impulses remain relatively dissociated from the reality-oriented, adaptational processes of the ego. The id, with its need to reduce and eliminate tension, seeks a state of quiescence, which, perhaps ironically, can be achieved only in death.

The second part of the personality, primarily conscious and called the ego, begins to develop out of the id in the second six months of life. The ego is the part of the id that is modified by the direct influence of the environment. It must deal with reality and hence often attempts to delay the immediate gratification desired by the id. The ego frowns upon primary process, for fantasy will not keep the organism alive. Through its planning and decision-making functions, called *secondary process,* the ego realizes that operating on the pleasure principle at all times, as the id would like to do, may not be the most effective way of maintaining life. The ego then operates on the *reality principle* as it mediates between the demands of reality and those of the id.

The ego, however, derives all its energy from the id and may be likened to a horseback rider who receives energy for riding from the horse. But a real horseback rider directs the horse with his or her own energy, not depending on that of the horse for thinking, planning, and moving. The ego, on the other hand, derives *all* its energies from the id and yet must direct what it is entirely dependent on for energy.

The superego is the third part of the personality, being essentially the carrier of society's moral standards as interpreted by the child's parents. The superego develops through the resolution of the oedipal conflict, to be discussed shortly, and is generally equivalent to what we call conscience. When the id pressures the ego to satisfy its needs, the ego must cope not only with reality constraints but also with the "right-wrong" moral judgments of the superego. The behavior of the human being, as conceptualized by Freud, is thus a complex interplay of three psychic systems, all vying for the achievement of goals that cannot always be reconciled. This interplay of active forces is referred to as the psychodynamics of the personality.

Freud was drawn into studying the mind by his work with Breuer on hypnosis and hysteria (see page 23). The apparently powerful role played by factors of which patients seemed unaware led Freud to postulate that much of our behavior is determined by forces that are inaccessible to awareness. Both the id instincts and many of the superego's activities are not known to the conscious mind. The ego is primarily conscious, for it is the metaphor for the psychic systems that have to do with thinking and planning. But the ego too has important unconscious aspects, the *defense mechanisms* which protect it from anxiety; these will be discussed in Chapter 5. Basically, Freud considered most of the important aspects of behavior to be unconscious.

Freud saw the human personality as a closed energy system; at any one time there is a fixed amount of energy in the id to run the psychic apparatus. The three parts of the personality therefore battle for a share in a specific amount of energy. Moreover, Freud regarded the mind as totally deterministic. Natural scientist that he was, Freud saw every bit of behavior, even seemingly trivial slips of the tongue, as having specific unconscious causes.

## Stages of Psychosexual Development

Freud conceived of the personality apparatus as developing through a series of four separate psychosexual stages. At each stage a different part of the body is the most sensitive to sexual excitation and therefore the most capable of providing libidinal satisfaction to the id. The first is the *oral* stage, during which the infant derives maximum gratification of id impulses from excitation of the sensory endings around the mouth. Sucking and feeding are the principal pleasures. In the second year of life the child enters the *anal* stage as enjoyment shifts to the anus and the elimination and retention of feces. In the *phallic* stage, which extends from age three to age five or six, maximum gratification comes from stimulation of the genitalia. Between ages six to twelve the child is in a *latency* period, during which the id impulses presumably do not play a direct role in motivating behavior. The child behaves asexually, although according to Freud's theoretical schema all behavior is *basically* driven by id impulses. The final and adult stage is the *genital*, during which heterosexual interests predominate.

The manner in which the growing person at each stage resolves the conflicts between what the id wants and what the environment will provide determines basic personality traits that will last throughout the person's life. A person who in the anal stage experiences either excessive or deficient amounts of gratification, depending on his or her toilet training regimen, and thus does not progress beyond this stage, is called an *anal per-*

*sonality*. One type, the anal retentive, is considered stingy and sometimes obsessively clean. These traits, appearing throughout life but receiving the greatest attention in adulthood, when people typically consult psychoanalysts, are traced back to early events and to the manner in which gratification was provided or denied the child. Freud referred to this "freezing" of development at an earlier psychosexual stage as *fixation*.

Perhaps the most important crisis of development occurs during the phallic stage, around age four, for then, Freud asserted, the child is overcome with sexual desire for the parent of the opposite sex. Through the threat of dire punishment from the parent of the same sex, he or she may repress the entire conflict, unconsciously pushing it into the unconscious. This desire and repression is referred to as the Oedipus complex for the male and the Electra complex for the female. The dilemma is usually resolved through increased identification with the parent of the same sex and through the adoption of society's mores, which forbid the child to desire its parent. Through this learning of moral values the superego is developed.

Freud's theorizing, presented here in bare outline, changed almost continuously over his lifetime. His students and colleagues have also made important changes in psychoanalytic theory. The ego analysts in particular dispute the relatively weak role that Freud assigned to the ego. They have concentrated their attention on the independent decision-making and planning functions of this predominantly conscious part of the personality, and many talk of ego energy that is independent of the id. Ego analysis will be discussed in greater detail in Chapter 18.

The analytic view of abnormal behavior focuses on the way the conflicts that occur in various psychosexual stages are resolved. Most neuroses, for example, are traced back to difficulties in resolving the oedipal conflict. Neurosis takes different forms, depending on the defense mechanisms resorted to for handling the anxiety that this unresolved conflict has created.

## Methodological and Conceptual Problems in Freud

Perhaps no investigator of the vagaries of human life has been honored and criticized as much as Freud. During the late nineteenth century, when he was first espousing his views of infantile sexuality, he was personally vilified. At that time sexuality was little discussed among adults. How scandalous, then, to assert that infants and children were also motivated by sexual drives! In the history of science few have shown greater intellectual integrity and personal bravery than Freud.

Because of his very great importance in the field, some current criticisms of his methodology and concepts will be reviewed. There are several weaknesses in Freud's methodology that are to be found to some extent in *all* case study work. Although we attach considerable importance to case reports compiled by clinicians who are "on the front line," clinical reporting by its very nature presents problems that are extremely difficult to avoid. Freud's theorizing, and to a lesser extent the thinking of the "neo-Freudians," those who have adapted and changed his basic framework, rest primarily on case studies. Like many clinicians, Freud did not take careful notes during his sessions and had to rely very heavily on his recollections. The reliability of his perceptions and recollections is impossible to evaluate. Furthermore, the behavior of a listener has been demonstrated to change what the speaker says. For example, Truax (1966) has shown that during supposedly *nondirective* therapy sessions, Carl Rogers (see Chapter 18) selectively attended to certain kinds of verbal statements from clients and ignored others; the frequency of the statements that were attended to increased. It is possible that Freud's patients were similarly influenced, at least to some degree, to talk about the childhood events that he was most interested in.

The inferential leaps that are made by Freud and other psychoanalysts may be difficult to accept unless one has a prior commitment to the point of view. The distinction between observation and interpretation is sometimes blurred.

Consider an example from the analyst Main (1958). "The little boy who babbles tenderly to himself as he soaps himself in his bath does so because he has taken into himself his tender soaping mother." What, in fact, is readily observed by the average onlooker is the child bathing himself. To *see* his mother incorporated in the soapy bath play is to operate at a very high level of inference. The paradigm problem is once again evident. What we perceive is strongly colored by the paradigm we adopt.

There is considerable disagreement whether Freud's theorizing should be considered scientific, for it is difficult to disprove or prove. Few of the statements are very explicit. If our view of science requires concepts to be measurable, and theories testable, psychoanalytic thinking cannot be regarded as scientific.

Freud's findings do not have general applicability because his sample of patients was very selective and small. Nearly all his patients were from the upper middle class of early twentieth-century Vienna, hardly a representative sampling of human beings. Nonetheless, Freud was prepared to apply his findings to all mankind. In a related vein, after making limited observations, Freud held that a repressed homosexual inclination was the basis for all paranoid disorders. But he never considered, nor for that matter have others who have accepted his point of view, how many paranoids have not had homosexual desires in the past and, indeed, how many people with repressed homosexuality do not develop into paranoids.

Although Freud insisted that he used concepts like id, ego, superego, and the unconscious as metaphors to describe psychic functions, they seem reified, that is, they are made into independent, behavior-determining agents whose own actions must still be explained. For example, Freud speaks of ". . . immediate and unheeding satisfaction of the instincts, such as the id demands. . . . The id knows no solicitude about ensuring survival . . ." (1937, p. 56). Thus the id "demands" immediate satisfaction and "knows" certain things. In spite of occasional reminders in psychoanalytic writings that these concepts are meant as metaphors, or as summary statements of functions, they are typically written about as if they had an existence of their own and had a power to push things around, to think, and to act.

It should be obvious by now that the authors of this book view the validity and usefulness of Freud's work with skepticism. On the other hand, it would be a serious mistake to minimize his importance in psychopathology or, for that matter, in the intellectual history of Western civilization. Freud was an astute observer of human nature. Moreover, his work has elicited the kind of critical reaction that helps to advance knowledge. He was instrumental in getting people to consider nonphysiological explanations for disordered behavior. It is impossible to acquire a good grasp of the field of abnormal psychology without some familiarity with his writings.

## Behaviorism and Learning Paradigms

### The Rise of Behaviorism

Before we discuss learning paradigms, it will be helpful to trace briefly the rise of behaviorism within psychology. Early twentieth-century psychology was dominated by structuralism, which held that the proper subject of study was conscious experience. The goal of psychology was to learn more about what goes on in people's minds. To do this, psychologists used what is called the *introspective method.* Trained subjects were asked to report on their conscious experience. What, for example, is the experience "red" like? During this same period a controversy raged whether thought did or did not always involve images. Understandably, such a controversy was extremely difficult to resolve and, even with the advances that have been made, is still unsolved today. But because introspection provided no means of settling this question at that time, psychologists became discouraged with it as a method and began to question the definition of psychology as the study of conscious experience. This dissatisfaction was brought to a head by John B. Watson, who in 1913 revolutionized psychology with statements such as the following:

> *Psychology as the behaviorist views it is a purely objective branch of natural science. Its theoretical goal is the prediction and control of behavior. Introspection forms no essential part of its methods, nor is the scientific value of its data dependent upon the readiness with which they lend themselves to interpretation in terms of consciousness (p. 158).*

To replace introspection, Watson looked to the work of contemporary psychologists who were concerned with learning. In this way learning rather than thinking became the dominant focus of psychology in the post-Watsonian period. The task of psychology was now viewed as an attempt to obtain information about which stimuli would elicit which directly observable responses. With such information it was hoped that human behavior could be both predicted and controlled.

John B. Watson (1878–1958), American psychologist, who was influential in making psychology the study of observable behavior rather than an investigation of subjective experience.

Ivan P. Pavlov (1849–1936), Russian physiologist and Nobel Laureate, responsible for extensive research and theory in classical conditioning. His influence is still very strong in Soviet psychology.

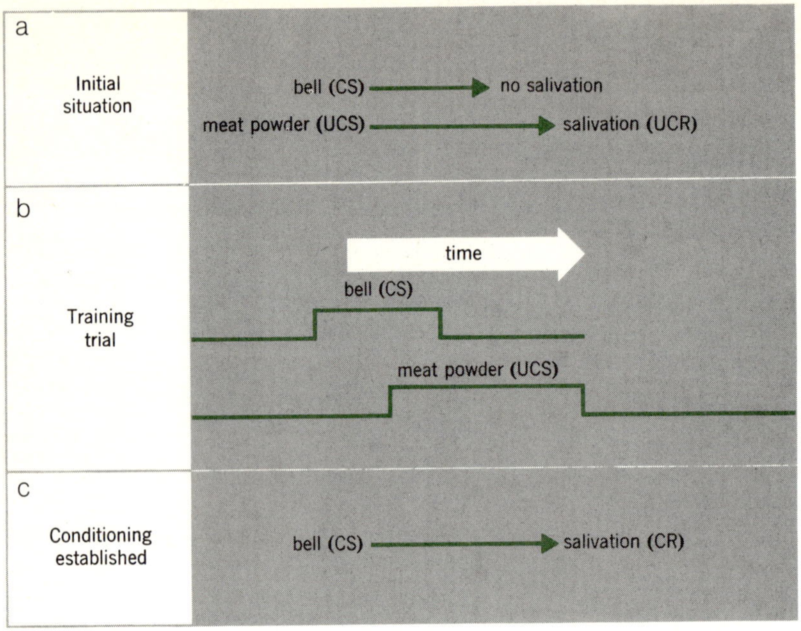


FIGURE **2.3**
The process of classical conditioning: (a) before learning the meat powder (UCS) elicits salivation (UCR), but the bell (CS) does not; (b) a training or learning trial consists of presentations of the CS, followed closely by the UCS; (c) classical conditioning has been accomplished when the previously neutral bell elicits salivation (CR).

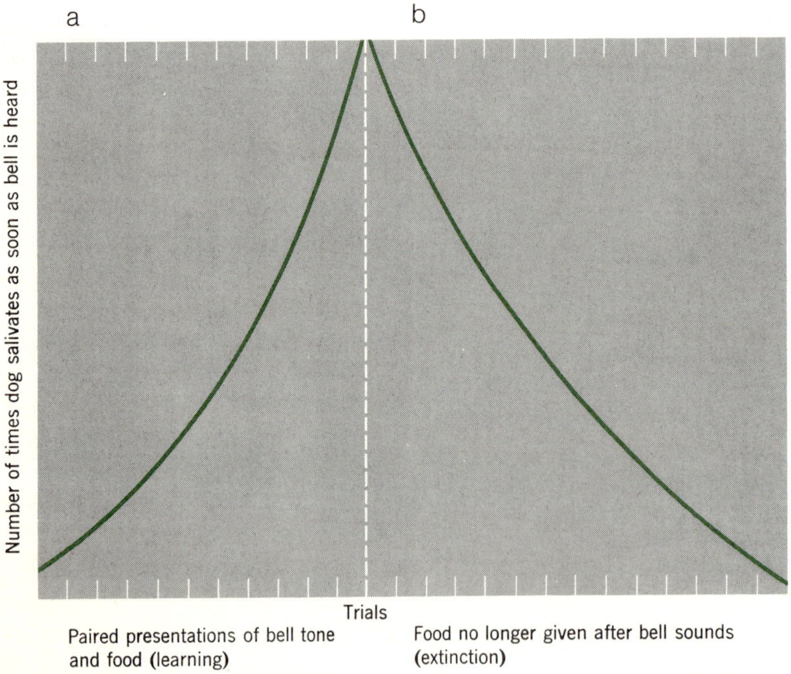


FIGURE **2.4**
Classical conditioning: typical learning curve (a); typical extinction curve (b).

With the focus of psychology now on learning, a vast amount of research and theorizing was generated. Two types of learning soon began to attract the research efforts of psychologists. The first type, *classical conditioning,* had originally been discovered quite by accident by the Russian physiologist Ivan Pavlov at the turn of the century. In his studies of the digestive system, a dog was given meat powder to make it salivate, the amount of saliva then being measured with the help of a complicated apparatus in which the dog was restrained. Before long Pavlov's laboratory assistants became aware that the dog began salivating when it saw the person who fed it and then even earlier, when it heard the footsteps of its feeder. Pavlov was intrigued and excited by what his laboratory had happened upon and decided to study the dog's reactions systematically. In the first of many experiments, the dog was positioned facing a window, a bell was rung behind the animal, and then the meat powder was placed in its mouth. After this procedure had been repeated a number of times, the dog began salivating as soon as it heard the bell ring.

When the dog is first given meat powder, it salivates instinctively without prior learning. Since the meat powder automatically elicits salivation, the powder is termed an *unconditioned stimulus* (UCS) and the response of salivation an *unconditioned response* (UCR). Then when the offering of meat powder is preceded several times by a neutral stimulus, the ringing of a bell (Figure 2.3), the sound of the bell itself (the *conditioned stimulus,* CS) is able to elicit the salivary response (the *conditioned response,*[2] CR). Figure 2.4a is a typical learning curve. As the number of paired presentations of the bell tone and the meat powder increases, the number of salivations elicited by the bell increases. The extinction curve in Figure 2.4b indicates what happens to the established CR when the repeated soundings of the bell tone are later not followed up by the administrations of meat powder. Fewer and fewer salivations are elicited, and the CR is extinguished rather rapidly.

Another famous experiment, one which made an eleven-month-old boy fear a white rat (Watson and Rayner, 1920), indicates the possible relation between classical conditioning and the development of certain emotional disorders, in this instance a phobia. When the infant, Little Albert, was first shown the white rat, he indicated no fear of the animal and appeared to want to play with it. But whenever he reached for the rat, the experimenter made a loud noise (the UCS) by striking a steel bar behind Albert's head, causing him great fright (the UCR). After five such experiences Albert became very disturbed (the CR) by the sight of the white rat, even when the steel bar was not struck. The fear initially associated with the loud noise had come to be elicited by the previously neutral stimulus, the white rat (now the CS).

The second principal type of learning, *instrumental learning,* draws primarily on the work of Edward Thorndike. Rather than investigating the association between stimuli as Pavlov was to do, Thorndike was interested in the effect that consequences have on behavior. He had observed that alley cats, angered by being caged and making furious efforts to escape, would eventually and accidentally hit the latch that freed them. Recaged again and again, they would soon immediately and purposely touch the latch. Thorndike formulated what was to become an extremely important principle, the law of effect: behavior that is followed by consequences satisfying to the organism will be repeated, and behavior that is followed by noxious or unpleasant consequences will be discouraged. Thus the behavior or response that has consequences serves as an instrument, encouraging or discouraging its own repetition. This basic principle has been applied by B. F. Skinner in studying many different aspects of human behavior. The goal of Skinner (1953) and the Skinnerians, like

[2] Some research (for example, Kimble, 1961) has suggested that the CR is sometimes different from the UCR. Moreover, a number of writers believe that the terms "unconditional" and "conditional" are preferable to "unconditioned" and "conditioned." Such subtleties, although important for the learning theorist, are relatively unimportant for our purposes and are beyond the scope of this book.

B. F. Skinner (1904– ), perhaps the most influential living psychologist, responsible for the in-depth study of operant behavior and for the extension of experimental findings to American education and society as a whole.

that of Watson, is the prediction and control of behavior. These experimenters hope that by analyzing behavior in terms of stimuli, responses, and consequences, they will be able to determine when certain responses will occur. The information gathered should then help to indicate how behavior develops and how it can be changed. In the Skinnerian approach, often called the operant approach because it studies behavior that operates on the environment, abstract terms and concepts are avoided. For example, references to needs, motivation, and wants are conspicuously absent in Skinnerian writings. To provide an entirely satisfactory account of human behavior, Skinner believes that psychology must restrict its attention to directly observable stimuli, responses, and consequences or reinforcements. Psychologists who hold this view do *not,* as human beings, deny the existence of inner states of mind and emotion. Rather, they urge that investigators not employ such *mediators* in trying to develop a science of behavior.

In a prototypical operant conditioning experiment a hungry rat might be placed in a box that has a bar located at one end (the well-known "Skinner box"). Initially the rat will explore its new environment and, by chance, will come close to the bar. At this time the experimenter may drop a food pellet into the receptacle located near the bar. After a few such rewards the animal will come to spend more and more time in the area around the bar. But now the experimenter drops a pellet into the receptacle only when the rat happens to touch the bar. After capitalizing on a few chance touches, the rat begins to touch the bar frequently. With bar touching well established, the experimenter can make the criterion for reward more stringent. The animal must actually press the bar. Thus the desired behavior, bar pressing, is gradually *shaped* by rewarding a series of responses that are *successive approximations.* The number of bar presses increases as soon as they become the criterion for the release of pellets and decreases as soon as the pellet is no longer dropped into the receptacle after a bar press (Figure 2.5).

In recent years there has been an increased interest in yet a third type of learning, *modeling.* We all realize that we learn by watching and imitating others. Experimental work has proved that witnessing someone perform certain activities can increase or decrease diverse kinds of behavior, such as sharing, aggression, and fear. For example, Bandura and Menlove (1968) used a modeling treatment to reduce fear of dogs in children. After witnessing a fearless model engage in various interactions with a dog, initially fearful children showed a marked increase

FIGURE **2.5**
Operant conditioning (a), or instrumental learning, is concerned with the development and maintenance of behavior as a function of its consequences; a typical learning curve (b), showing increases in responding when the operant behavior is reinforced; a typical extinction curve (c), showing decreases in responding when the accustomed reward is withheld.

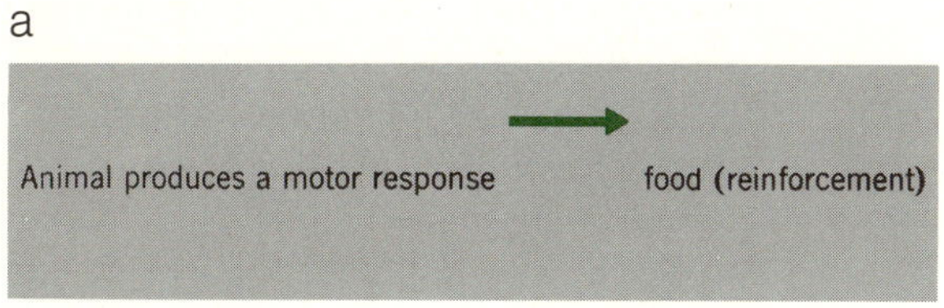


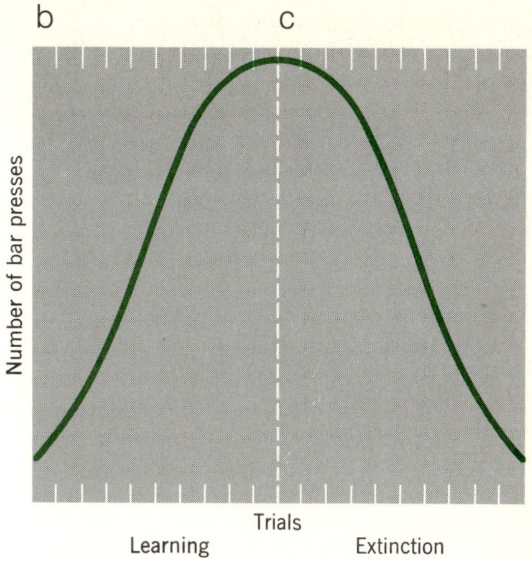


in their willingness to approach and interact with a dog.

By now it should be apparent that there is no single learning paradigm. Although some investigators (Ullmann and Krasner, 1969; Bijou and Baer, 1961) study learning in terms of the observable stimuli, responses, and reinforcements of strict Skinnerian behaviorism, by no means do all learning theorists avoid the use of *mediating constructs,* such as drives and beliefs, or limit themselves to the operant approach. These theorists also consider themselves behaviorists and have contributed importantly to the study of internal states and overt behavior within what is often referred to as a mediational framework. In *mediation theory* a stimulus does not initiate a direct response but instead activates an intervening process which in turn initiates the response. The mediating construct is a thought or other internal process, an entity inferred as actually existing, although it cannot be observed. These learning theorists work within a paradigm holding that, under certain conditions, it is legitimate to go beyond the observables. In physics and chemistry scientists similarly make ample and effective use of variables that are not directly observable but whose existence is guessed at or inferred.

Albert Bandura, pioneer in the study of modeling and in the alleviation of neurotic fears through imitation.

Theorists like Bruner (Bruner, Olver, and Greenfeld, 1966), Piaget (for example, 1955), Bower (1970), and Levine (1975) have dealt with *cognition,* a very important extension of mediation theory. They offer several hypotheses about how people think, reason, and judge, how they process information, how they conceive of their world. The following example illustrates how a *cognitive set* may alter the way information is processed and remembered.

> *The man stood before the mirror and combed his hair. He checked his face carefully for any places he might have missed shaving and then put on the conservative tie he had decided to wear. At breakfast, he studied the newspaper carefully and, over coffee, discussed the possibility of buying a new washing machine with his wife. Then he made several phone calls. As he was leaving the house he thought about the fact that his children would probably want to go to that private camp again this summer. When the car didn't start, he got out, slammed the door and walked down to the bus stop in a very angry mood. Now he would be late (Bransford and Johnson, 1973, p. 415).*

Now read the excerpt again, but add the word "unemployed" before the word "man." Now read it a third time, substituting "stockbroker" for "man." Notice how differently you understand the passage. Ask yourself what parts of the newspaper these men read. If this query had been posed on a questionnaire, you might have answered "the want ads" for the unemployed man, "the financial pages" for the stockbroker. In actual fact, the passage does not specify which part of the paper was read. Your answers would have been erroneous, but in each instance the error would have been a meaningful, predictable one.

Most cognitive psychologists have themselves paid little systematic attention to how their research findings bear on psychopathology or how they might help generate effective therapies. But cognitive explanations now come up more and more often in the search for the causes of abnormality. To take an example that will be examined in greater length in Chapter 8, a widely held view of depression holds a person's sense of helplessness to blame. Those who are depressed supposedly believe themselves to have no important effect on the environment, regardless of what they do. The thought "Nothing I do makes any difference" may be important in developing the condition that clinicians term depression.

## Applying the Learning Point of View to Deviant Behavior

We are now ready to examine the general application of behavioral principles to the study of deviant behavior. The crucial assumption of learning approaches is that abnormal behavior is learned in the same manner as most other human behavior. This view minimizes the importance of physiological factors. It focuses instead on elucidating the learning processes that supposedly produced the maladaptive behavior. The gap between normal and abnormal behavior is reduced, since both are viewed within the same general framework; thus a bridge is forged between general experimental psychology and the field of abnormal psychology. Moreover, according to many who have adopted a learning paradigm, abnormality is a *relativistic* concept. Labeling someone or some behavior as abnormal is inextricably linked to a particular social or cultural context. For example, in the United States hallucinating may be one of the grounds for commitment to a mental institution. In some African tribes, however, witch doctors and shamans rely on their trances and visions to help them cure the sick and predict events affecting the welfare of their people.

One very important advantage of applying a learning view in psychopathology is the increased precision of observation. Stimuli must be accurately measured, responses reliably recorded, and relationships among stimuli, responses, and outcomes carefully noted. Although we judge this and other features of learning approaches to deviant behavior to be extremely advantageous, it is difficult to persuade those not already committed to the paradigm that it is adequate. The learning paradigm of abnormal behavior is in much the same position as the physiological. Just as pertinent physiological malfunctions have not been uncovered, abnormality has not yet been convincingly shown to result from particular learning experiences, as will be documented in later chapters. Although adopting a learning explanation of abnormal behavior has clearly led to many treatment innovations (see Chapter 19 on behavior therapy), the effectiveness of these treatments does not bear on the adequacy of the learning account of the particular deviant behavior in question. The fact that a treatment based on learning principles is effective in changing behavior does *not* show that the behavior was itself learned in a similar way. For example, if the mood of depressed persons is elevated by providing them with rewards for increased activity, this fact cannot be considered evidence that the depression was initially produced by an absence of rewards (Rimland, 1964). The problem in logic may perhaps be made clearer by another example. Because electroconvulsive shock treatment temporarily relieves depression, it does not follow that depression is produced by not receiving electroshock during the formative years.

## Consequences of Adopting a Paradigm

The student of abnormal behavior who adopts a particular paradigm necessarily makes a prior decision concerning what kinds of data will be collected and how they will be interpreted. Thus he or she may very well ignore possibilities and overlook other data in advancing what seems to be the most probable explanation (see Box 2.2). A behaviorist is prone to attribute the prevalence of schizophrenia in lower-class groups to the paucity of social rewards that these people have received, the assumption being that normal development requires a certain amount and patterning of reinforcement. A physiologically oriented theorist will be quick to remind the behaviorist of the many deprived people who do *not* become schizophrenic. The behaviorist will undoubtedly counter with the argument that those who do not become schizophrenic had different reinforcement histories. The physiologically oriented theorist will reply that such *post hoc* or after-the-fact statements can always be made.

Our physiological theorist may suggest that certain biochemical factors that predispose both to schizophrenia and to deficiencies in the intellectual skills necessary to maintain occupational status account for the observed correlation between social class and schizophrenia. The behaviorist will be entirely justified in reminding the physiological theorist that these alleged factors have yet to be found, to which the physiological theorist might rightfully answer, "Yes, but I'm placing my bets that they are there, and if I adopt *your* behavioral paradigm, I may not look for them." To which the learning theorist may with justification reply, "Yes, but *your* assumption regarding biochemical factors makes it less likely that you will look for and uncover the subtle reinforcement factors that in all likelihood account for both the presence and the absence of what you call schizophrenia."

The fact that our two colleagues are in a sense

"THERE ARE SEVERAL REASONS FOR YOUR PROBLEM: ENVIRONMENTAL STRESS, EARLY CHILDHOOD EXPERIENCE, CHEMICAL IMBALANCE, AND, PRIMARILY, THE FACT THAT BOTH OF YOUR PARENTS ARE AS CUCKOO AS A BAVARIAN CLOCK."

correct and in another sense incorrect is at the same time both exasperating and exciting. They are both correct in asserting that certain data are more likely to be found through work done within a particular paradigm. But they are incorrect to become unduly agitated because each and every social scientist is not assuming that one and the same factor will ultimately be found crucial in the development of mental disorders. The field of abnormal behavior is too diverse to be explained adequately by any of the current paradigms. As we subsequently examine various categories of psychopathology, we will find substantial differences in the extent to which physiological and learning paradigms are applicable. And we will often see that a plausible way of looking at the data is to assume multiple causation. A particular disorder may very well develop through an interaction of physiological defects and learning factors.

### Diathesis-stress: A proposed paradigm

A general point of view, one that meaningfully links both physiological and learning factors, does in fact guide our own search for answers. Termed the *diathesis-stress* approach, it considers the often subtle interactions between a predisposition toward disease—the diathesis—and environmental, or life, events affecting people—the stress. Diathesis refers most precisely to a constitutional predisposition toward illness, but the term may be extended to any tendency or inclination a person may have to respond in a particular way to an environmental stress. The cognitive set already mentioned, the chronic feeling of helplessness sometimes found in the depressed, may be considered a diathesis for depression.

It is a fact that some people break down in certain ways when exposed to certain stressors, whereas others come through even more terrible trauma apparently unscathed. Certain people have, for example, inherited a physiological predisposition that places them at high risk for schizophrenia (see Chapter 14). Given a certain amount of stress, they are so physiologically constituted that they stand a good chance of becoming schizophrenic. Other people, those at low risk, are not likely to develop schizophrenia, regardless of how difficult their lives are.

As for future discoveries, it is well that psychologists do *not* agree on which paradigm is the *best.* We know far too little to make hard-and-fast decisions on the exclusive superiority of any one paradigm, and there is enough important work to go around.

It will be useful to recall now the case of the policeman with which the first chapter of this book began. The material provided is open to a number of interpretations, depending on the paradigm adopted. For instance, if you hold a physiological point of view, you might be attentive to the similarity between the man's tendencies to be alternately manic and depressed and the cyclical swings of mood his father suffered. You would be mindful of the research (to be reviewed in Chapter 8) that suggests a genetic factor in manic-depression. You would not, how-

## BOX **2.2** Psychopathology Can Be in the Eye of the Beholder

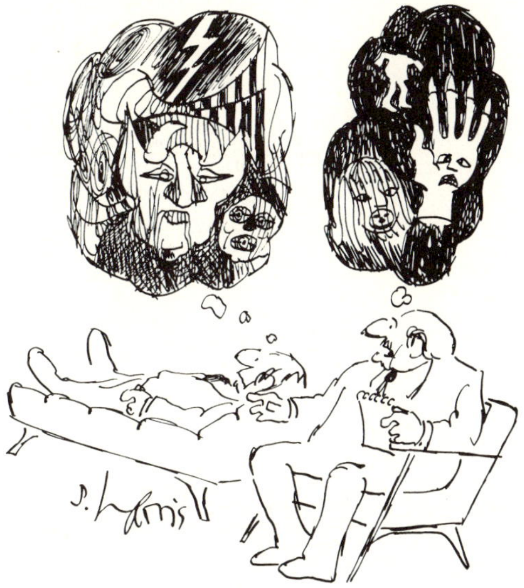

"FORGET IT—HALLUCINATIONS ARE NOTHING."

We have been examining Kuhn's concept of paradigm—a set of assumptions which are shared by investigators and determine not only what they will consider "legitimately" scientific but also how they will perceive data. A striking demonstration of this "I'll see it when I believe it" feature of science is provided in an experiment by Langer and Abelson (1974). They were interested in how different theoretical orientations might affect the ways in which trained clinicians view the "adjustment" of a person. They reasoned that behavior therapists, operating within a learning paradigm of psychopathology, might be swayed less by an illness label applied to a given client than would clinicians trained in a more traditional orientation. To test this supposition, they conceived the following experiment. A group of behavior therapists and another of therapists trained in psychoanalysis were shown a videotape of an interview in progress between two men. Before viewing this videotape, half the subjects in each group were told that the interviewee was a job applicant, the other half that he was a patient. It was predicted that the traditional clinicians who were told that the interviewee was a patient would generally rate him as more disturbed than would those who considered him a job applicant. It was also predicted that ratings of behavior therapists would be affected less by illness labeling than those of traditional therapists.

The videotape shown to all subjects depicted a bearded professor interviewing a young man in his mid-twenties. The interviewee had been recruited through a newspaper advertisement that offered ten dollars to someone who had recently applied for a new job and was willing to be interviewed and videotaped. The fifteen-minute segment chosen from the original interview contained a rambling, autobiographical monologue by the young man in which he described a number of his past jobs and dwelt on his conflicts with bureaucrats. His manner was considered by Langer and Abelson to be intense but uncertain; they felt that he could be regarded either as sincere and struggling or as confused and troubled.

A questionnaire measured the clinicians' impressions about the mental health of the interviewee. When the young interviewee was identified as a job applicant, there were no significant differences in the adjustment ratings given by the traditional clinicians and the behavior therapists. But the patient label, as expected, produced sharp differences (Figure 2.6). When the interviewee was identified as a patient, the traditional clinicians rated him relatively disturbed—significantly more so than did the traditional clinicians who viewed the man as a job applicant. In contrast, the behavior therapists rated the interviewee as relatively well adjusted, in fact, no less adjusted than the other behavior therapists rated the man they considered a job applicant.

Qualitative evaluations obtained from the clinicians supported their ratings. Whereas the behavior therapists described the man as "realistic," "sincere," and "responsible," regardless of label, the traditional clinicians who viewed him as a patient used phrases such as "tight, defensive person," "conflict over homosexuality," and "impulsitivity shows through his rigidity."

Why, in this particular experiment, did the behavior therapists appear to be unbiased? Langer and Abelson explain it this way. The behavioral approach encourages clinicians to concentrate on overt or manifest behavior and to be skeptical about illness that is not readily apparent. Those with such an orientation had the advantage in this particular study because, however the interviewee rambled, his behavior on balance was not overtly disturbed. The traditional therapists, on the other hand, had presumably been trained to look beyond what is most obvious in a client. Therefore, when the traditional therapists heard the negative ramblings about bureaucrats, they probably paid too much attention to them.

Langer and Abelson properly alert readers to the limitations of the experiment, reminding them that a different study—perhaps using an interviewee who is obviously disturbed—might put behavior therapists at a disadvantage. The purpose of the experiment, and this discussion of it, is not to pit one orientation against another, but rather to illustrate how a theoretical orientation can affect perception. Indeed, psychopathology can be in the eye of the beholder.

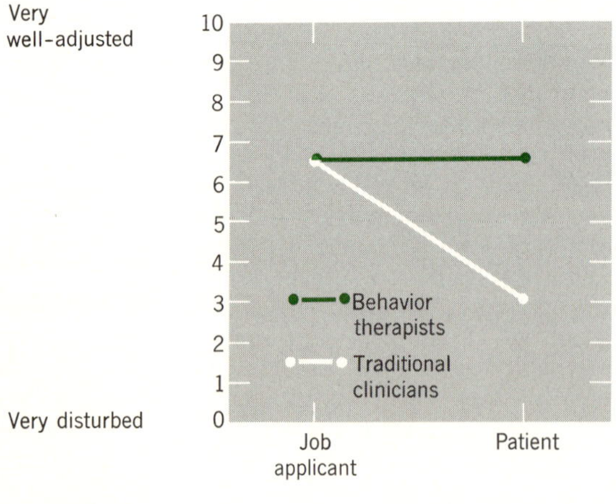


FIGURE **2.6**
The mean adjustment ratings given the interviewee, by the investigators' description of him and by the diagnosticians' training. Adapted from Langer and Abelson, 1974.

ever, discount the importance of environmental factors in contributing to his problems, but you would hypothesize that he was *predisposed* by some inherited, probably biochemical, defect to break down under stress. After all, not everyone who experiences a difficult childhood and adolescence develops the kinds of problems Ernest H. had.

Now suppose that you are committed to a learning perspective, which encourages you to analyze human behavior in terms of reinforcement patterns as well as cognitive variables. You might focus on his self-consciousness at college, which seemed related to the fact that he had grown up with few advantages, compared to his fellow students. Economic insecurity and hardship may have made him unduly sensitive to criticism and rejection. Moreover, he perceived his wife as "chic," more elegant than he, pointing up his own lack of social skills. Alcohol was his escape from such tensions. But heavy drinking, coupled with persistent doubt about his own worthiness as a human being, interfered with sexual functioning, worsening an already deteriorating marital relationship.

A psychoanalytic point of view would cast Ernest H. in yet another light. Believing that events in early childhood are of great importance in later patterns of adjustment, you might hypothesize that Ernest had blamed his father for his mother's early death. Such strong anger at the father would be repressed, but Ernest would be unable to regard him as a competent, worthwhile adult and to identify with him. Fixation at the oedipal stage of psychosexual development could have produced Ernest's anxieties about authority and hampered his functioning as an adult male.

## Summary

This chapter has reviewed the major paradigms, or points of view, that are current in the study of psychopathology. In the *statistical* paradigm a characteristic, such as anxiety, is measured in a group of people, and a distribution of scores is derived. Individuals whose levels of anxiety are at either extreme are designated as abnormal. Which particular behavior or trait is to be measured is decided outside the purview of this paradigm, however. The *physiological* paradigm assumes that psychopathology is caused by an organic defect. Previous discussions of this point of view have taken the form of arguments, pro and con, about a "medical" or "disease" model. But an examination of the meaning of the term medical model reveals that it is actually too vague about etiology to enjoy the status of a formal model of psychopathology. The medical model does have one implication—that psychopathology may be attributed to physiological malfunctions and defects. Therefore we have proposed instead the physiological paradigm. The third paradigm derives from the work of Sigmund Freud. This *psychoanalytic* point of view directs our attention to repressions and other unconscious processes that are traced to early childhood conflicts. Whereas present-day ego analysts who are part of this tradition place greater emphasis on conscious ego functions, the psychoanalytic paradigm has generally focused on searching the unconscious and early life of the patient for the causes of abnormality. *Behavioral,* or *learning,* paradigms suggest that aberrant behavior has developed through classical conditioning, operant conditioning, modeling, and particular cognitive sets. Investigators who believe that abnormal behavior may have been learned share a commitment to examine carefully all situations affecting behavior, as well as to define concepts carefully. The *diathesis-stress* paradigm is one that may integrate the best features of several points of view. People are assumed disposed to react differently to particular environment stresses. The diathesis may be constitutional, as appears to be the case in schizophrenia, or it may be extended to the psychological, for example, the chronic sense of helplessness considered a factor contributing to depression.

The most important implication of paradigms is that they determine where and how investigators look for answers. Paradigms necessarily limit their perceptions of the world, for they will interpret data differently according to their points of view. To our minds it is fortunate that workers are not all operating within the same paradigm, for too little is known about psychopathology and its treatment to settle on any one of them as superior at this point.

# chapter 3

## CLASSIFICATION AND ASSESSMENT



By the end of the nineteenth century, medicine had progressed far beyond the stage it had been in during the Middle Ages, when virtually all physical problems were treated by a common technique, bloodletting. It was gradually recognized that different illnesses required different treatments. Diagnostic procedures were improved, diseases subclassified, and applicable treatments administered. Impressed by the successes that new diagnostic procedures had effected in the field of medicine, investigators of abnormal behavior also sought to develop classification schemes that grouped disorders according to symptoms. Moreover, advances in other sciences such as botany and chemistry had followed the development of classification systems, reinforcing hope that similar efforts in the field of abnormal behavior might bring progress.

In this chapter we first review the diagnostic system of the American Psychiatric Association, which relies much on Kraepelin's groupings of mental disorders and also incorporates many psychoanalytic concepts. Recently, the nomenclature committee of the American Psychiatric Association has been circulating several drafts of a third version of the *Diagnostic and Statistical Manual of Mental Disorders* (DSM-III), which is slated to appear in 1979 or 1980. Some new disorders are listed, and some familiar ones have been dropped. In addition, more specific criteria define each disorder (Spitzer, Endicott, and Robins, 1975; Spitzer, 1976, personal communication). The changes in DSM-III will be discussed at appropriate points throughout this textbook, but our own organization of the field is not markedly affected by its forthcoming publication.[1] We also examine here some criticisms, both of the general concept of classification and of the DSM itself, and describe several assessment procedures that provide the data on which diagnostic decisions are based. Finally, we direct our attention to recent advances in behavioral assessment that rely little on the DSM.

[1] The development of DSM-III is surrounded by some political controversy. Many psychologists believe that the American Psychiatric Association is trying to appropriate all psychopathology and its treatment by defining mental disorders as medical in nature. As this book goes to press, with DSM-III still in draft form, it would be premature to pass judgment.

## The Diagnostic System of the American Psychiatric Association

The current diagnostic system (DSM-II) has six major categories and numerous subcategories of abnormal behavior. Table 3.1 outlines only the major classes and subcategories. Subsequent chapters will treat the subcategories in greater detail.

1. **Mental retardation.** In the diagnostic manual mental retardation is defined as subnormal intellectual functioning associated with impairments in learning, social adjustment, and maturation. The manual specifies that the impairment may be attributed to one of several factors such as infection, gross brain disease, chromosomal abnormality, and environmental deprivation. Within the general category of retardation, various degrees are specified, ranging from mild to profound.

2. **Organic brain syndromes.** Organic brain disorders are caused by impaired brain functioning that is attributed to tissue or structural lesions. Many human capacities such as intelligence, memory, and the emotions may of course be affected by brain dysfunction. A psychotic organic brain syndrome is defined in the following way. "Patients are described as psychotic when their mental functioning is sufficiently impaired to interfere grossly with their capacity to meet the ordinary demands of life. . . . Deficits in perception, language and memory may be so severe that the patient's capacity for mental grasp of the situation is effectively lost" (American Psychiatric Association, 1968, p. 23). Brain dysfunctions that are not severe enough to produce behavior categorized as psychotic according to the preceding definition constitute nonpsychotic brain syndromes.

3. **Psychoses not attributed to physical conditions.** The definition of this large and important category of deviant behavior is identical to that of psychoses attributable to brain dysfunctions. The important difference is that they are *not* considered to be caused by the physical conditions that produce organic brain syndromes. There are three major

TABLE **3.1**
List of DSM-II Diagnoses

1. Mental Retardation
2. Organic Brain Syndromes
   A. Psychoses
   B. Nonpsychotic disorders
3. Psychoses Not Attributed to Physical Conditions Listed Previously
   A. Schizophrenia
   B. Major affective disorders
   C. Paranoid states
4. Neuroses
5. Personality Disorders and Certain Other Nonpsychotic Mental Disorders
   A. Personality disorders
   B. Sexual deviation
   C. Alcoholism
   D. Drug dependence
6. Psychophysiological Disorders

distinctions within the general category of psychosis.

*Schizophrenia.* A group of disorders characterized by a breakdown of integrated emotion, thought, and behavior and by withdrawal from human contact and reality.
*The major affective disorders.* Severely disabling disturbances of mood and feeling, such as psychotic depression and manic-depressive illness.
*Paranoid states.* Disorders in which patients either have delusions or mistaken beliefs that they are being persecuted or hold grandiose ideas about themselves.

4. **Neuroses.** According to DSM-II the principal characteristic of a neurosis is conscious or unconscious anxiety. There are no gross distortions of reality, nor is the personality significantly disorganized. As with other major categories, several distinctions are made.

   *Anxiety neurosis.* Pervasive or free-floating anxiety, without apparent object or cause.
   *Hysterical neurosis.* An involuntary loss of the function of a part of the body or alterations in consciousness, such as amnesia and sleepwalking.
   *Phobic neurosis.* An intense fear of an object or situation that the patient recognizes as presenting no real danger to himself.
   *Obsessive-compulsive neurosis.* Preoccupation with persistent, unwanted thoughts, or the compulsion to repeat a certain act again and again.
   *Depressive neurosis.* A deep, prolonged, and excessive sadness caused by some external circumstance such as the loss of a loved one.

5. **Personality disorders and certain other nonpsychotic disorders.** Personality disorders are defined as "deeply ingrained" maladaptive patterns of behavior that are different from those observed in psychoses and neuroses.[2] Included in this category are motivational and social maladjustments such as sexual deviations, drug dependencies, and alcoholism. In addition, many disorders previously noted in the psychotic and neurotic categories are found within this category in what appear to be somewhat less debilitating forms. For example, within this general category are subcategories such as paranoid personality, obsessive-compulsive personality, and hysterical personality.

6. **Psychophysiological disorders.** These disorders are characterized by physical symptoms produced in part by emotional factors. Various organ systems may be implicated. For example, the respiratory system may be debilitated by asthma, the cardiovascular system by high blood pressure, the gastrointestinal system by ulcers, the genitourinary system by impotency, and the skin by hives.

[2] The DSM-II does not explain very well how personality disorders are different from neuroses and psychoses. For example, obsessive-compulsive personality is defined as ". . . excessive concern with conformity and adherence to standards of conscience. Consequently, individuals in this group may be rigid, over-inhibited, over-conscientious, over-dutiful, and unable to relax easily. This disorder may lead to an *obsessive compulsive neurosis* from which it must be distinguished" (p. 43). Exactly *how* to distinguish an obsessive-compulsive personality from an obsessive-compulsive neurosis is not spelled out.

## Issues in the Classification of Abnormal Behavior

The preceding review of the major categories of abnormal behavior has been brief, for they will be examined in more detail throughout this volume. On the basis of this overview, however, we may scrutinize the usefulness of the system as it exists today. In recent years the diagnosis of mental disorders has been frequently attacked. Two major lines of criticism can be distinguished. One group of critics argue that classification per se is irrelevant to the field of abnormal behavior. These critics hold that there is a *continuum* ranging from adjustment to maladjustment and consider discrete judgments inappropriate. The second group of critics find specific deficiencies in the current diagnostic system.

### Classification Views: Pro and Con

Those opposed to classifying argue that whenever we do so we lose information and hence overlook some of the uniqueness of the subject being studied. To understand this argument better, let us take the simple example of casting dice. Any of the numbers one through six may come up on a given toss of a single die. Let us suppose, however, that we classify each outcome as odd or even. Whenever a one, three, or five comes up on a roll, we call out "odd," and whenever a two, four, or six appears, we say "even." A person who is listening to our calls will not know whether the call "odd" refers to a one, three, or five, or whether a two, four, or six has turned up when he or she hears "even." In classification some information must inevitably be lost.

What matters, however, is whether the information lost is relevant, which in turn depends on the *purposes* of the classification system. Any classification system is designed to group together objects having a common property and to ignore differences among the objects that are not relevant to the purposes at hand. If our intention is merely to count odd and even rolls, it is irrelevant whether a die comes up one, three, or five or two, four, or six. In judging abnormal behavior, however, we cannot so easily decide what is wheat and what chaff, for the relevant and irrelevant dimensions of abnormal behavior are uncertain. Thus when we do classify, we may indeed be grouping people together on rather trivial bases while ignoring extremely important differences among them.

It may also be argued that classification, because it often postulates discrete entities, does not allow the continuity between normal and abnormal behavior to be taken into consideration. Those who advance this argument, for example psychopathologists operating within a learning paradigm, hold that abnormal behavior and normal behavior differ only in intensity or degree and not in kind. Therefore the discrete diagnostic categories of DSM-II foster a false impression of discontinuity. Rimland (1969) has summarized this position and, in our opinion, effectively criticized it.

> . . . *The idea is that if it is difficult to make a distinction between two neighboring points on a hypothetical continuum, no valid distinctions can thereafter be made even at the extremes of the continuum. There are thus persons who would argue that the existence of several variations of gray precludes a distinction between black and white. Hokum. While I will agree that some patients in mental hospitals are saner than nonpatients, and that it is sometimes hard to distinguish between deep unhappiness and psychotic depression, I do not agree that the difficulty sometimes encountered in making the distinction between normal and abnormal necessarily invalidates all such distinctions* (pp. 716–717).

In other words, the fact that some distinctions are difficult to make, such as deciding whether sundown is night or day, does not mean it is impossible to distinguish between noon and midnight.

## BOX **3.1** On Being Sane in Insane Places

A controversial study by Rosenhan (1973) illustrated in dramatic fashion the kinds of errors that can be committed in working with the *Diagnostic and Statistical Manual.* Over a period of three years Rosenhan arranged for a number of sane people to be admitted to various psychiatric hospitals across the country. Care was taken to ensure that none of the participants had had psychiatric problems or was otherwise malfunctioning. Each pseudopatient complained at the admissions desk of hearing voices that said "empty," "hollow," and "thud."

But this one symptom, chosen by Rosenhan because it is nowhere reported in the clinical literature, was the only one they feigned. Rosenhan wanted to limit the symptoms because a diagnosis of schizophrenia is properly made on the basis of disturbances in thinking and affect, as well as for withdrawn or bizarre behavior, but not solely for having had an hallucination. Furthermore, each pseudopatient accurately reported family history and the circumstances of his present life, except for the psychologists in the research group. Being identified as a fellow mental health professional might have unduly affected the behavior of the staff.

All pseudopatients were diagnosed as psychotic; on eleven occasions the diagnosis was schizophrenia, and on one occasion manic-depressive psychosis. And all were admitted to the hospital, where they stayed an average of nineteen days. *In no instance did any of the staff detect that the pseudopatient was actually quite sane,* even though, immediately after admission was secured, *the pseudopatient stopped talking about the alleged hallucinations and behaved in his usual fashion.* The anxiety of the initial period after admission, which was felt by all the participants, quickly disappeared; if anything, the pseudopatients tended to be somewhat bored. The only instances of detection were those made by the actual hospitalized patients.

Rosenhan found that the circumstances of the patients' past history were sometimes distorted to "explain" the disordered behavior seen on admission. He provides the example of one pseudopatient who had reported accurately a close relationship with his mother and a remote one with his father. As he grew up, however, the pseudopatient had become closer to his father and somewhat alienated from his mother. The discharge summary concluded that "This white thirty-nine-year-old male . . . manifests a long history of considerable ambivalence in close relationships, which begins in early childhood. . . . Affective stability is absent. His attempts to control emotionality with his wife and children are punctuated by angry outbursts and, in the case of the children, spankings. And while he says that he has several good friends, one senses considerable ambivalence embedded in those relationships also . . . " (1973, p. 253).

Rosenhan comments on the tendency of those who think within an illness model to interpret almost any behavior as a *presumed* illness. But since the behavior of the pseudopatients was completely unremarkable, the only basis for construing their behavior as abnormal was the fact that they were encountered as patients on a psychiatric ward and bore a diagnostic label describing them as psychotic. Thus, Rosenhan argues, the psychiatric diagnosis had little or no relationship to the patients' actual behavior. If this is true, then current psychiatric diagnosis is surely a worthless enterprise.

As we might expect, Rosenhan's article elicited a rash of comments from many mental health professionals. Indeed, some even alleged that the study is so flawed that it was irresponsible of *Science* magazine to have published it or for textbooks to discuss it favorably. Let us examine what appear to be the crucial issues.

Each patient was diagnosed twice, on admission and then again on discharge. So we must examine these diagnoses and their relation (or lack of it) to behavior. On admission the patients reported a single symptom, auditory hallucinations. There is no psychiatric diagnosis that can be made on such a basis. But the presence of auditory hallucinations is *consistent with* a diagnosis of psychosis. So at this point we can say that the diagnosis did have some relation to behavior, but that it was based on rather flimsy evidence. In such a case a diagnostician has the option of deferring diagnosis until more information is collected. Yet this tack was not taken by any of the clinicians observed in Rosenhan's study.

From Rosenhan's point of view the discharge diagnoses are even more telling. Upon release from the hospital, nearly all the patients were given a diagnosis of schizophrenia, in remission. Thus psychiatric labels are "sticky," Rosenhan argues, taking on an independent existence of their own. Since the patients behaved normally after admission, how can it be said that they were schizophrenic, even with the qualifier "in remission," on discharge? The discrepancy between the diagnoses and the patients' behavior is obvious. Robert Spitzer (1975), however, has challenged Rosenhan's interpretation by carefully analyzing the meaning of the term "in remission." By examining the records of several hospitals, he determined that it is rarely used as a discharge diagnosis for schizophrenics. Instead, schizophrenics are usually discharged with diagnoses of schizophrenia, somewhat improved, or schizophrenia, much improved. Therefore, Spitzer argues, the diagnosticians in Rosenhan's study had indeed recognized that the patients were normal on discharge and chose the "in remission" phrase to make this point.

Spitzer's arguments are not totally acceptable. His data may indicate that discharge diagnoses did have some relation to behavior, but another DSM-II diagnostic category, "no mental disorder," could and should have been used by the diagnosticians. This diagnostic term "is used when, following psychiatric examination, none of the previous disorders [the whole range of psychiatric diagnoses] is found. It is not to be used for patients whose disorders are in remission" (APA, 1968, p. 52). If the psychiatrists had been truly attentive to the behavior of the patients, we should have expected the "no mental disorder" diagnosis to be used. But it was not.

Another criticism asks whether the pseudopatients really acted as though they were normal once they were admitted. This is a key point, for Rosenhan's conclusions rest on the assumption that the pseudopatients behaved normally. The pseudopatient did not immediately ask to be released. Would not the normal person wrongfully hospitalized seek to get out? This question raises the issue of what behavior is normal in a mental hospital. In our view, the pseudopatients had committed themselves to a project that required them not only to be admitted to a mental hospital but to remain there in order to make the kinds of observations that form part of the published report. Hence they would have been remiss in their responsibilities if they had sought release right after admission. Research protocol demanded that they stay. Many patients who are properly admitted to hospitals immediately ask to be released. Indeed, such requests are sometimes viewed as an indication of severe disturbance. Therefore the relationship between seeking release and being normal is unclear.

In sum, Rosenhan has documented the fact that diagnoses are not as closely related to behavior as would be desirable. He has also alerted us to the kinds of errors that even skilled professionals can make. But, as we have tried to show, the diagnoses were not totally *un*related to behavior either. Thus we cannot conclude that psychiatric diagnosis is worthless. Indeed, in later chapters we will show that diagnoses have helped psychopathologists gather important information on how human conduct can go awry.

Another problem of classification lies in its application. Clinicians working within an illness model may tend to see pathology even where it does not exist (see Box 3.1). An incident witnessed in part by one of the authors illustrates how preconceptions can destroy perspective and in this instance even common sense.

A patient hospitalized for anxiety and depression was observed by both the ward psychiatrist and the patient's own therapist. The ward psychiatrist eventually came to feel that the man was hallucinating and reported to the therapist what he considered the significant incident. The previous day, in talking about how depressed he had been feeling, the patient had looked behind him, up toward the ceiling, and declared "It's that little black cloud following me around." On the basis of this single comment, the ward psychiatrist had suggested changing the diagnosis of the patient's condition from a neurosis to a psychosis.

The therapist, however, had observed no signs of psychosis and decided to investigate further. The next time the therapist visited the patient, he queried him: "Can you tell me a little bit about the black cloud that you mentioned to Dr. X the other day?" The patient looked at him quizzically for a long moment and then asked, "You mean that black thing hovering over my left shoulder and my head? Well, what would you like to know about it?" As a more precise description of the cloud was requested, the patient grinned broadly and asked rhetorically, "Haven't you ever heard of a metaphor?"

Assuming that various types of abnormal behavior do differ one from the other, however, it is essential to classify them, for these differences may constitute keys to the causes and treatments of the various deviant behaviors. For example, one form of mental retardation, phenylketonuria, is attributable to a deficiency in the metabolism of the protein phenylalanine, resulting in the release of incomplete metabolites which injure the brain (see page 453). One means of treatment is to provide a diet drastically reduced in phenylalanine. As Mendels (1970) has noted, however,

> . . . *had we taken 100, or even 1000, people with mental deficiency and placed them all on the phenylalanine-free diet, the response would have been insignificant and the diet would have been discarded as a treatment. It was first necessary to recognize a subtype of mental deficiency, phenylketonuria, and then subject the value of a phenylalanine-free diet to investigation in this specific population, for whom it has been shown to have value in preventing the development of mental deficiency* (p. 35).

Forming classes may thus further knowledge, for once a class is formed, additional information may be ascertained about it. Even though the class is only an asserted and not a proven entity, it may still be heuristically useful in that it facilitates the acquisition of new information. Only after a diagnostic class has been formed can people who fit its definition be studied in hopes of uncovering factors that were responsible for the development of their problems and of devising treatments that may help them.

## Criticisms of the Current Diagnostic System, DSM-II

More specific criticisms are commonly made of the current psychiatric classification scheme. Although the studies to be discussed were done on the previous classification system of the American Psychiatric Association, DSM-I, the two editions are so similar that there is no reason to expect that the findings are not applicable to DSM-II. The principal complaints are that the diagnostic classes are heterogeneous and that they are neither reliable nor valid.

### Heterogeneity within diagnostic classes

In a classification scheme each grouping that categorizes a person and his or her particular pattern of behavior must convey specific and discriminating information about that person. If we know that a given patient is classified as "obsessive-compulsive neurotic," the system is useful only if membership in that category reveals something specific about the patient that differentiates him or her from nonmembers of the class. One of the defining characteristics of an obsessive-compulsive are intrusive thoughts which the patient seems unable to control, for example, worrying continually about the presence of germs. In order for the relation between this symptom and its category to be truly meaningful, people *not* diagnosed as obsessive-compulsive should *not* display this particular kind of behavior. By the same token, intrusive thoughts should be found in any and all persons diagnosed as obsessive-compulsive. To state this point another way, whenever a class is formed, the behavior of all its members should be similar along the dimensions distinguishing the classification. Thus, pursuing the example, if we were to examine a group of people who had been labeled obsessive neurotics, we would expect all of them to have intrusive thoughts. Others not classified as obsessive neurotics should *not* have intrusive thoughts.

Science, alas, is a difficult taskmaster, for research indicates that this important criterion of homogeneity is frequently not met. For example, in a well-known study Zigler and Phillips (1961) found that knowing what diagnostic category a patient falls into does not allow us to predict with great accuracy the actual behavior of the person. Similarly, they found that certain symptoms appeared in a number of diagnostic categories, thus making it difficult to move reliably from a specific symptom to a specific diagnostic category.

Table 3.2 summarizes the principal findings of the study Zigler and Phillips conducted on 793 patients. After reviewing the hospital records, these investigators categorized the patients into four relatively broad diagnostic groups. Next, they examined the frequency of particular symptoms in each of these groups. As indicated in the second line of the table, for example, each diagnostic category contained a substantial number of patients who were rated as tense: 32 percent of the manic-depressives, 46 percent of the neurotics, 33 percent of those with character disorders, and 36 percent of the schizophrenics. Thus knowing only that a patient was tense tells us very little about the category to which he or she was assigned. Similarly, knowing that a person was schizophrenic allows us to make only a rather poor guess whether or not the individual was regarded as tense, for the table shows that only 36 percent of the schizophrenics were considered to have this symptom. Moreover, all the percentages for tenseness are within fourteen points of one another, although many of the other characteristics do show a wider range from category to category.

Although these data raise an important question about DSM-II, they do not totally negate its usefulness. The symptom tenseness, for instance, may not be useful in differential diagnosis, but others may prove more valuable in this regard. We would suppose the symptom of depression to characterize many manic-depressives and neurotics, and indeed the figures of 64 percent and 58 percent respectively bear out our expectations. Again, since one of the subcategories of schizophrenia is paranoid schizophrenia, characterized by suspiciousness, it is not surprising that 65 percent of the schizophrenics in this study were regarded as suspicious. This figure is substantially and significantly greater than the percentage figures for suspiciousness in the other three categories.

Furthermore, we must keep in mind that the four diagnostic categories used by Zigler and Phillips were indeed *very broad,* and thus their study cannot be considered a definitive test of the point that they were trying to make regarding homogeneity. For example, the general category of schizophrenia is itself made up of several smaller categories; the percentage figures for suspiciousness might be considerably higher for a subcategory such as paranoid schizophrenia.

The Zigler and Phillips study was necessarily limited because it looked only at the presence or

TABLE **3.2**
Percentage of Individuals in Each Diagnostic Category Showing Particular Symptoms
(from Zigler and Phillips, 1961)

| Symptom | All patients ($N$ = 793) | Manic-depressive ($N$ = 75) | Neurotic ($N$ = 152) | Character disorder ($N$ = 279) | Schizo-phrenic ($N$ = 287) |
|---|---|---|---|---|---|
| Depressed | 38 | 64 | 58 | 31 | 28 |
| Tense | 37 | 32 | 46 | 33 | 36 |
| Suspiciousness | 35 | 25 | 16 | 17 | 65 |
| Drinking | 19 | 17 | 14 | 32 | 8 |
| Hallucinations | 19 | 11 | 4 | 12 | 35 |
| Suicidal attempt | 16 | 24 | 19 | 15 | 12 |
| Suicidal ideas | 15 | 29 | 23 | 15 | 8 |
| Bodily compaints | 15 | 21 | 21 | 5 | 19 |
| Emotional outburst | 14 | 17 | 12 | 18 | 9 |
| Withdrawn | 14 | 4 | 12 | 7 | 25 |
| Perplexed | 14 | 9 | 9 | 8 | 24 |
| Assaultive | 12 | 5 | 6 | 18 | 5 |
| Self-depreciatory | 12 | 16 | 16 | 8 | 13 |
| Threatens assault | 10 | 4 | 11 | 14 | 7 |
| Sexual preoccupation | 10 | 9 | 9 | 6 | 14 |
| Maniacal outburst | 9 | 11 | 6 | 7 | 12 |
| Bizarre ideas | 9 | 11 | 1 | 2 | 20 |
| Robbery | 8 | 0 | 3 | 18 | 3 |
| Apathetic | 8 | 8 | 8 | 4 | 11 |
| Irresponsible behavior | 7 | 3 | 7 | 9 | 7 |
| Headaches | 6 | 7 | 10 | 4 | 5 |
| Perversions (except homosexuality) | 5 | 0 | 5 | 10 | 2 |
| Euphoria | 5 | 17 | 2 | 2 | 5 |
| Fears own hostile impulses | 5 | 4 | 9 | 5 | 2 |
| Mood swings | 5 | 9 | 5 | 4 | 4 |
| Insomnia | 5 | 11 | 7 | 3 | 5 |
| Psychosomatic disorders | 4 | 7 | 6 | 3 | 5 |
| Does not eat | 4 | 9 | 4 | 2 | 4 |
| Lying | 3 | 0 | 1 | 7 | 0 |
| Homosexuality | 3 | 3 | 3 | 8 | 2 |
| Rape | 3 | 0 | 3 | 8 | 1 |
| Obsessions | 3 | 8 | 3 | 1 | 4 |
| Depersonalization | 3 | 4 | 1 | 0 | 6 |
| Feels perverted | 3 | 0 | 3 | 1 | 5 |
| Phobias | 2 | 4 | 5 | 0 | 2 |

absence of specific isolated symptoms. Most psychiatric diagnostic categories are defined by the *joint presence* of a *number* of particular symptoms, rather than simply by the presence or absence of a single one. Psychiatrists and psychologists who find DSM-II useful emphasize the importance of syndromes or clusters of symptoms. For example, schizophrenia is generally defined by a number of symptoms such as delusions, hallucinations, and bizarre motor behavior. The problem is that the current diagnostic system does not adequately describe these symptoms, nor does it specify how *many* of these various symptoms must be present in order to make a diagnosis, or the degree to which they must be manifest. If psychologists decide to continue working within the current diagnostic scheme, or a revised one, they will need to address themselves to these more quantitative questions. Indeed, the new DSM-III will attempt to handle some of these important issues.

### Lack of reliability

Whether or not different diagnosticians will agree that a given diagnostic label should be applied to a particular person is the test of its *reliability*. Clearly, for a classification system to be useful, those applying it must be able to agree on what is and what is not an instance of a particular class. Thus reliability becomes the primary requisite for judging any classification system.

Before the evidence is discussed, (a problem assessing the reliability of the present diagnostic system should be reviewed (see page 35).) In medicine a diagnosis made by a physician can usually be checked by some sort of laboratory test. That is, an objective measurement is available by which the reliability of a physician's diagnosis can be determined. For diagnosing abnormal behavior no such infallible measurement exists; the only means of assessing reliability is whether or not diagnosticians agree.

The reliability of psychiatric diagnosis has been well researched. One exemplary investigation has been reported by Beck and his colleagues (1962). Four highly experienced psychiatrists diagnosed 153 patients within one week of their admission to a psychiatric facility. Each patient was interviewed twice in succession by two different psychiatrists. Before beginning their study, the four psychiatrists had met to discuss the current diagnostic manual so that they could agree on its application. No attempt was made to ensure that the four interviewers would employ the same techniques in gathering the information necessary to make their diagnoses, however.

The overall agreement among the psychiatrists, calculated as the number of diagnoses on which they agreed divided by the total number of diagnoses made, was a disappointingly low 54 percent. The amount of diagnostic agreement within the six most frequently applied categories is presented in Table 3.3. The percentage of agree-

TABLE **3.3**
Percentage of Diagnostic Agreement Within Various Diagnostic Categories
(from Beck et al., 1962)

| Category | Number of diagnoses | Agreement, percent |
|---|---|---|
| Neurotic depression | 92 | 63 |
| Anxiety reaction | 58 | 55 |
| Sociopath | 11 | 54 |
| Schizophrenic reaction | 60 | 53 |
| Involutional melancholia | 10 | 40 |
| Personality trait disturbance | 26 | 38 |

ment varied considerably from one category to another, ranging from a low of 38 percent in personality trait disturbance to a high of 63 percent for neurotic depression. Later, the same data were reanalyzed using only three larger categories, psychosis, neurosis, and character disorder. Diagnostic agreement then reached 70 percent, approaching levels that satisfy most clinical researchers.

The percentage of agreement in the Beck study may be atypically low, for studies by Kreitman and others in 1961 and by Sandifer and his colleagues in 1964 had percentages of agreement in the range of 73 to 74 percent for individual, specific diagnostic categories. Other features make the Beck study a noteworthy piece of work, however. In addition to diagnosing the patients, the psychiatrists in this study were also asked to rate the certainty of their diagnosis on a three-point scale. There are always "gray areas" in making diagnostic judgments. Some individuals may be easily classified, whereas others fall into larger indeterminate groups for which diagnosis becomes uncertain. In the Beck study, when both psychiatrists felt sure of their choice, agreement was 81 percent, even in applying the full range of categories. This evidence supports the view that some individuals, the so-called clear-cut cases, can be reliably classified. Moreover, in one-third of the cases that were seen, the psychiatrists were asked to make a second choice in addition to their primary diagnosis. Presumably, if the diagnostician is presented with a case that is somewhat ambiguous, he or she will probably be able to narrow the diagnosis down to two categories. According to this line of reasoning, the proportion of cases in which neither the primary nor the alternative diagnoses of the two psychiatrists are in agreement should be very small. This is precisely what the Beck study found, for in only 16 percent of these fifty-one cases was there a total absence of agreement on diagnosis. Thus a substantial number of individuals *can* be reliably classified with the current psychiatric classification scheme.

As for the patients about whose diagnosis the psychiatrists are less likely to agree, there are several reasons why the diagnostic system is inadequate. First, as others (for example, Maher, 1966) have pointed out, the scheme for categorizing patients is not a taxonomy in the strictest sense of the word, for it is not based on a single, uniform principle. Organic brain syndromes, for instance, are classified according to the causes of the damage to the patient's brain. Disorders such as neuroses are defined largely on the basis of psychoanalytic theory, to wit, that neuroses are characterized by unconscious anxiety. The presence of physiological brain damage and of unconscious anxiety must be determined by vastly different means. Moreover, the usefulness of a psychoanalytic term such as "unconscious anxiety" can and has been questioned, for psychoanalytic theory itself is rather uncertain ground on which to build any part of a classification scheme (see Chapter 2).

The data of the Beck study were later reexamined in an attempt to determine why diagnosticians might disagree (Ward et al., 1962). Meeting again after they had completed the interviews and made their diagnoses, the psychiatrists found three major reasons why they had not always reached the same determination. First, accounting for 5 percent of the disagreements, were *inconsistencies on the part of the patient.*

> *A young woman was referred for evaluation of a somatic complaint which neither diagnostician could be sure was psychogenic in nature. One of the diagnosticians could therefore make only the diagnosis of "no psychiatric disease." However, to the other examiner, the patient volunteered the history of a previous gastric ulcer . . . information she had previously directly denied to the first examiner. The second physician therefore diagnosed psychophysiological gastrointestinal reaction* (*p. 200*).

The second major group of diagnostic disagreements, 32.5 percent of them, were attributed to *inconsistencies on the part of the diagnostician.* Differences in interview techniques, in judging the importance of particular symptoms, and in interpreting the same pathology constituted most of these inconsistencies.

> *Weighing symptoms differently was a sizable factor . . . especially in cases where the diagnostic choice fell between two neuroses. . . . Often what was initially advanced as a chief complaint did not develop to be the predominant area of distress. . . . For example, a patient whose chief complaints were of tension and palpitation was considered by the second examiner to be actually more disturbed by . . . mood impairment, fatigue, self-depreciative thought, and loss of interest. When directly asked in the second examination, the patient gave his opinion that the low spirits were more troublesome than the tension. Diagnostic conflict: anxiety reaction with depressive features vs. neurotic depressive reaction with anxiety features* (p. 200).

The third and largest group of disagreements, comprising 62.5 percent of them, were considered to stem from *inadequacies of the diagnostic system.* The diagnosticians found the criteria unclear. Either too fine distinctions were required, or the classification system seemingly forced the diagnostician to choose a major category that was not specific enough.

> . . . A twenty-one-year-old single white female . . . was seen whose chief complaints were nervous tension and self-consciousness since she was three years old. In recent years, she had been unable to hold down a job, although she had some secretarial training. . . . She had received various forms of psychiatric treatment over the past four years and had seen twelve psychiatrists in all, remaining with only one for a period as long as seven months and leaving all of them with open hostility. . . . It was open knowledge in the family that the patient was supposed to have been a boy; and her parents, especially the somewhat alcoholic father, had told her that she was no good because she was a girl and had approved of her only when she was successfully competitive with boys. The patient finished high school with difficulty, having to leave one school because of her marked discomfort in efforts to make speeches before mixed groups, and also because of much daydreaming, which still continued. She now felt frustrated, bitter, and had long felt that life was not worthwhile. She had never had a serious interpersonal involvement of a positive nature, and to the extent that she let herself react with others, the pattern was that of hostile anticipation, poorly modulated aggression, and suspiciousness. She often wished she were dead and had frequent thoughts of turning on the gas or jumping in front of a car, but at the same time she was aware of an excessively strong fear of death. She was compelled to wash her hands after touching certain articles of furniture; she had phobias of eating with other people. She had many physical symptoms of . . . anxiety and autonomic tension. . . . She had a sleep pattern which was a mixture of anxiety and depression, was not rarely awakened by nightmares in which she saw herself dead or bad things happening to her family. She had on several occasions [experienced] . . . visual images upon awakening from these dreams and had remained anxious and unable to sleep long afterwards. However, she definitely had had no auditory or visual hallucinations in the waking state and had had no clear delusions. There was a peculiar quality to her affect which suggested flatness or a manifestation of depression, though it was hard to distinguish between the two, and neither observer felt that she was making any substantial attempt to be melodramatic or impressive.

Both observers were impressed with the borderline nature of her problem. One was reminded of a previous patient who became "overtly psychotic"; the resemblance was less in specific, recognizable details and more in terms of a vague general feeling of the examiner's. He was also impressed with the chronicity, quantity, and multiplicity of her symptoms. The other examiner volunteered that on another day he might well agree, but as the patient struck him now, after an hour's interview, he felt she had a certain integration and inner consistency; he had seen similar patients who consolidated themselves and improved their adjustment without any clearly psychotic episode. In view of the absence of any clear break with reality; because of the reactive elements in the picture; because the patient was intelligent and did well on routine tests of similarities, differences, and proverb interpretation; because of the potential damage to the patient of being labeled with a psychotic diagnosis; and because of personal antipathy to the poorly conceived phrase "chronic undifferentiated schizophrenic," he gave the patient the benefit of a very sizable doubt as to where schizoid personality left off and schizophrenia began. Diagnostic conflict: chronic undifferentiated schizophrenic reaction vs. chronic anxiety reaction in a severely schizoid personality[3] (pp. 203–204).

Although the reliability of DSM-II diagnosis is not as great as we would like, we should not conclude that considerable diagnostic reliability is unattainable. A somewhat different system, for example, is used in Great Britain. The British diagnostic manual contains much more detailed descriptions of various categories, and reliabilities are indeed higher (for example, Wing et al., 1967). Similarly, new research diagnostic systems being used in the United States are also producing reliabilities higher than those previously reported (for example, Spitzer et al., 1976). These systems also specify much more precisely the criteria for diagnosis. The DSM-II description of mania is contrasted with that from the Research Diagnostic Criteria (Spitzer, Endicott, and Robins, 1975) in Table 3.4. Hopefully, greater clarity of definitions will increase the reliability of the forthcoming DSM-III.

### Lack of validity

Whether or not valid statements and predictions can be made about a class once it has been formed is the test of its validity. We should state at the outset that validity bears a particular relation to reliability; the less reliable a category is, the more difficult it is to make valid statements about the category. Since the reliability of the current diagnostic system is not entirely adequate, we can expect that its validity will not be either.

A psychiatric diagnosis can have three kinds of validity: etiological, concurrent, and predictive. It has etiological validity if the same historical antecedents have caused the disorder in the patients diagnosed. In other words, for a diagnosis to be considered etiologically valid, the same factors must be found to have caused the disorder in the people who comprise the diagnostic group. Consider, for example, the supposition that manic-depressive illness is, in part, genetically determined. According to this theory, manic-depressives must have a "family tree" that contains other manic-depressives. As we shall see in Chapter 8, evidence that supports this theory has been collected, giving this diagnostic category some etiological validity.

A psychiatric diagnosis has concurrent validity if symptoms or disordered processes not previously distinguished are discovered to be characteristic of those diagnosed. Finding that most

[3] Schizoid personality is a personality disorder characterized by seclusiveness, oversensitivity, and eccentricity.

TABLE **3.4**
Criteria for Diagnosing Manic Disorder in DSM-II Versus the Research Diagnostic Criteria

**DSM-II** (APA, 1968, p. 36)
*Manic-depressive illness, manic type.* This disorder consists exclusively of manic episodes. These episodes are characterized by excessive elation, irritability, talkativeness, flight of ideas, and accelerated speech and motor activity. Brief periods of depression sometimes occur, but they are never true depressive episodes.

**Research Diagnostic Criteria** (Spitzer, Endicott, and Robins, 1975, pp. 13–14).
*Manic disorder.* This category is for an episode of illness characterized by predominantly elevated or irritable mood accompanied by the manic syndrome. It should also be used for mixed states in which manic and depressive features occur together, or when a subject cycles from a period of depression to a period of mania, or the reverse, in which case the duration should refer to the manic symptoms only (the depressive symptoms would be recorded elsewhere).

A through E are required for the episode of illness being considered.

A. One or more distinct periods with a predominantly elevated or irritable mood. The elevated or irritable mood must be a prominent part of the illness and relatively persistent although it may alternate with depressive mood. Do not include if apparently due to alcohol or drug intoxication.

B. If mood is elevated, at least three of the following symptom categories must be definitely present to a significant degree (four if mood is only irritable). (For past episodes, because of memory difficulty, one less symptom is required.) Do not include if apparently due to alcohol or drug intoxication.

1. More active than usual—either socially, at work, sexually, or physically restless.
2. More talkative than usual or felt a pressure to keep talking.
3. Flight of ideas . . . or subjective experience that thoughts are racing.
4. Inflated self-esteem (. . . which may be delusional).
5. Decreased need for sleep.
6. Distractibility, i.e., attention is too easily drawn to unimportant or irrelevant external stimuli.
7. Excessive involvement in activities without recognizing the high potential for painful consequences, e.g., buying sprees, sexual indiscretions, foolish business investments, reckless driving.

C. Overall disturbance is so severe that at least one of the following is present:

1. Meaningful conversation is impossible.
2. Serious impairment socially, with family, at home, at school, or at work.
3. In the absence of 1 or 2, hospitalization.

D. Duration of manic features at least one week (or any duration if hospitalized).

E. None of the following which suggests schizophrenia is present. [Five symptoms of schizophrenia are listed. If any one is present, the diagnosis of mania is ruled out.]

people with paranoid delusions also hallucinate is an example. Predictive validity refers to similar future behavior on the part of the disorder or patient. The disorder may have a particular "natural history," that is, take a certain course. Or members of a diagnostic group may be expected to respond in a similar way to a particular treatment. Manic-depressive patients, for example, tend to respond well to a relatively new drug, lithium carbonate. The fact that this drug does not work well for people in other diagnostic classes supports the predictive validity of the manic-depressive diagnosis. Clearly, because we have organized this book around the major diagnostic categories, we believe that they indeed possess some validity. Certain categories have greater validity than others, however; these differences will become apparent as we discuss each diagnostic classification.

## The Assessment of Abnormal Behavior

The account with which this book began, that of the policeman with drinking and marital problems, allowed no opportunity to find out why he was behaving as he was. We had no possibility of learning more about him by any of the means commonly available to clinicians—interviews, tests, and a variety of other procedures for assessing behavior. These modes of assessment may occasionally be given different, perhaps more impressive-sounding names. An interview may be called "the psychiatric interview," "the diagnostic interview," or "a depth interview"; tests "psychologicals" or "projectives." All assessment procedures are more or less formal ways of finding out what is wrong with a person, what may have caused a problem or problems in the past, and what steps may be taken to improve the individual's condition.

### Clinical Interviews

Most of us have probably been interviewed at one time or another, although the conversation may have been so informal that it was not regarded as an interview. To the layperson the word interview connotes a formal, highly structured conversation, but we find it useful to construe the term as any interpersonal encounter, conversational in style, in which one person, the interviewer, uses language as the principal means of finding out about another, the interviewee. Thus a Gallup pollster who asks a housewife whom she will vote for in an upcoming presidential election is interviewing with the restricted goal of learning which candidate she prefers. And a clinical psychologist who asks a patient about the circumstances of his most recent hospitalization is similarly conducting an interview.

One way in which a clinical interview is perhaps different from a casual conversation and from a poll is the attention the interviewer pays to *how* the respondent answers—or does not answer—questions. For example, if a client is recounting her marital conflicts with her husband, the clinician will generally be attentive to any emotion accompanying her comments. If the woman does not seem upset about a difficult situation, her answers will probably be interpreted differently than if she cries while relating her story.

The paradigm within which an interviewer operates determines the type of information sought and obtained. A psychoanalytically trained clinician can be expected to inquire about the person's childhood history. He or she is also likely to remain skeptical of the verbal reports because the analytic paradigm holds that the most significant aspects of a disturbed or normal person's developmental history are repressed into the unconscious. By the same token, the behaviorally oriented clinician is likely to focus on current environmental conditions that can be related to changes in the person's behavior, trying to determine, for example, the circumstances under which the person may become anxious. Thus the clinical interview does not follow a prescribed course, varying rather with the paradigm adopted by the interviewer. Clinical interviewers in some measure find only the information they look for.

Great skill is necessary to carry out good interviews, particularly clinical interviews, for they are conducted with people who are often under considerable personal stress. Vast amounts of information can be obtained by means of the interview; its importance in abnormal psychology is unquestioned. Whether the information gleaned can always be depended on is not so clear, however. In one study, for example (Ward et al., 1962), it was established that patients sometimes gave different interviewers different information in response to the same questions. Often clinicians tend to overlook *situational* factors of the interview that may exert strong influences on what the patient says or does. Consider, for a moment, how a teen-ager is likely to respond to the question "How often have you used illegal drugs?" when it is asked by a young, long-haired psychologist in jeans and again when it is asked by a sixty-year-old, bald-headed psychologist in a three-piece suit.

Interviews may also vary in the degree to which they are structured. In practice, most clinicians operate from only the vaguest outlines. The authors of this textbook, in their behaviorally oriented clinical work, conduct an intake (initial) interview in order to answer the questions shown in Table 3.5. Exactly *how* such information is collected is left largely up to the particular interviewer. Through years of clinical experience and of both teaching and learning from students and colleagues, each of us has developed ways of asking questions with which we are comfortable and which seem to extract the information that will be of maximum benefit to the client. Thus, to the extent that an interview is unstructured, the interviewer must rely on intuition and general experience, which may be either good or bad, for obvious reasons.

One system of imposing more structure in interviewing is the Current and Past Psychopathology Scales, developed by Spitzer and Endicott (1969). This instrument consists of an interview guide geared to elicit specific information. During the interview itself the patient's responses to various questions are scored on scales, as indicated in the two examples of Table 3.6. Again, these questions can be understood only within the context of the investigators' views of human behavior. Spitzer and Endicott, and anyone else who uses their scales and asks similar questions, assume that the information collected in their interview bears importantly on a patient's current status and perhaps also on how he or she will respond to treatment, or, indeed, on whether treatment is even needed.

## Psychological Tests

Psychological tests structure still further the process of assessment. The same test is administered to many people at different times, and the responses collected are analyzed to indicate how certain kinds of people tend to respond.

TABLE **3.5**
Example of a Form Used To Report the Information Collected During an Interview

INTAKE REPORT

*Name:* *Age:* *Sex:* *M* *F*

*Class:* *Fr* *So* *Jr* *Sr* *Grad* *Date of Interview:*

I. *Behavior During Interview and Physical Description:*

II. *Presenting Problem:*
   A. Nature of problem:
   B. Historical determinants:
   C. Current determinants:
   D. Dimensions of problem (duration, pervasiveness, frequency, magnitude, etc.):
   E. Consequences of problem (mood, efficiency, satisfaction, productiveness, interpersonal functioning, etc.):

III. *Other Problems:*

IV. *Personal Assets (physical, aptitudes, abilities, interests, etc.):*

V. *Target(s) for Modification:*

VI. *Recommended Treatment(s):*

VII. *Motivation for Treatment:* low medium high does not apply

VIII. *Prognosis:* 1. very poor 2. poor 3. fair 4. good 5. very good does not apply

IX. *Priority for Treatment:* none low medium high

Statistical norms for the test can thereby be established as soon as the data collected are extensive enough. This process is called standardization. The responses of a particular patient can then be compared to the statistical norms. Psychological tests may be easier to administer and interpret than an interview. Several classes of psychological tests have been developed: projective personality tests, personality inventories, tests of organic damage and tests of intelligence.

TABLE **3.6**

## Two Questions and Scales from a Structured Diagnostic Interview, the Current and Past Psychopathology Scales

(from Spitzer and Endicott, 1969)

| | | | | | | |
|---|---|---|---|---|---|---|
| **Agitation—Excitement** Have there been any times recently when you weren't able to sit still . . . or you fidgeted a lot . . . or anything else like that? | 1 None | 2 Minimal | 3 Mild | 4 Moderate | 5 Severe | 6 Extreme |

| | | | | | | |
|---|---|---|---|---|---|---|
| **Grandiosity** Do you feel that you are a particularly important person or that you have certain special powers or abilities? | 1 None | 2 Minimal | 3 Mild | 4 Moderate | 5 Severe | 6 Extreme |

### Projective personality tests

The Rorschach inkblot test and the Thematic Apperception Test are perhaps the best-known projective techniques. In both of these tests a set of standard stimuli, vague enough to allow variation in responses, is presented to an individual. In an inkblot test the subject is shown a series of blots, one at a time, and asked to tell what figures or objects he or she sees in each of them. Similarly, in the Thematic Apperception Test the examinee is shown a series of pictures one by one and asked to tell a story related to each. In both these tests it is assumed that because the stimulus materials are unstructured, the patient's responses will be determined primarily by unconscious processes and will reveal his or her own attitudes, motivations, and modes of behavior. This is referred to as the *projective* hypothesis. For example, reporting eyes on the Rorschach has been said to indicate paranoia. Those of the psychoanalytic bent tend to favor such tests, since they presumably afford an opportunity for the unconscious to express itself. By the same token, those who use these tests tend to think in psychoanalytic terms. This preference for ambiguous stimuli is entirely consistent with the psychoanalytic assumption that people defend against unpleasant thoughts and feelings by repressing them into the unconscious. In order to bypass the defense mechanism of repression (see page 120) and get to the basic causes of distress, the real purposes of a test are best left unclear.[4]

As might be imagined, the interpretation of the responses to projective tests poses a severe problem, for the examinee is not merely answering yes or no to a series of questions or indicating which of a series of statements are true and which false. Rather, the person is providing a complex response to a complex stimulus,

[4] A behaviorist might also make use of projective tests, although for different purposes. The Rorschach and the TAT, being unstructured, may be viewed as making ambiguous demands on the person taking them. Determining the degree of tension evidenced by the respondent when asked to operate in these highly unstructured situations may then be considered a sample of his or her typical reactions to life stresses.

Picture from the Thematic Apperception Test, devised in 1935 by Henry Murray and his associates at the Harvard Psychological Clinical. Like the Rorschach, this projective test is designed to reveal unconscious conflicts and concerns.

which is, by design, open to a fantastic range of interpretations. In many instances the reliability of the scoring of the Rorschach and Thematic Apperception tests is quite low. With extensive training in a particular scoring system, however, examiners can achieve satisfactory levels of agreement (Goldfried, Stricker, and Weiner, 1971). A more serious problem is the often woefully low validities of responses in projective tests. We assume that these responses tell us something important and useful about the person. Generally, the information gathered through a projective technique concerns unconscious conflicts and repressed anxieties. Behavioral psychologists find it difficult to assess the validity of such data, for how can it be known whether the test is in fact measuring unconscious conflicts and repressed anxieties if they are by definition hidden from direct observation?

On the other hand, the inferences drawn from projective test data do sometimes permit attempts at validation. For example, if a patient is asserted to be homosexual on the basis of his Rorschach responses, the validity of this assertion can be determined. But the inferences made about aspects of personality through projective testing do not generally prove accurate. After conducting an extensive survey of the literature, Nunnally (1967) has written that

> *. . . Most projective techniques do a rather poor job of measuring personality traits. . . . In applied settings, the evidence is clear that projective techniques have, at most, only a low level of validity. . . . They do a poor job of differentiating normal people from people who are diagnosed as neurotic and they do a poor job of differentiating various types of mentally ill persons* (p. 497).

Certain responses to projective tests continue to be viewed as diagnostic signs, even though an association between the response and a particular diagnosis does not exist. Many clinicians rely to a considerable extent on such signs in making their diagnoses. Moreover, as noted by Chapman and Chapman (1969), clinicians often show considerable consensus in assigning meanings to various signs, even though there is little evidence to back up their interpretations. Let us examine this issue of consensus.

Chapman and Chapman conducted a study that you may participate in right now. Imagine yourself part of a psychological experiment in which you are asked to rate the amount of association between homosexuality and particular Rorschach responses. Specifically, you are to rate the degree to which each of the responses signifies homosexuality, using the following six-

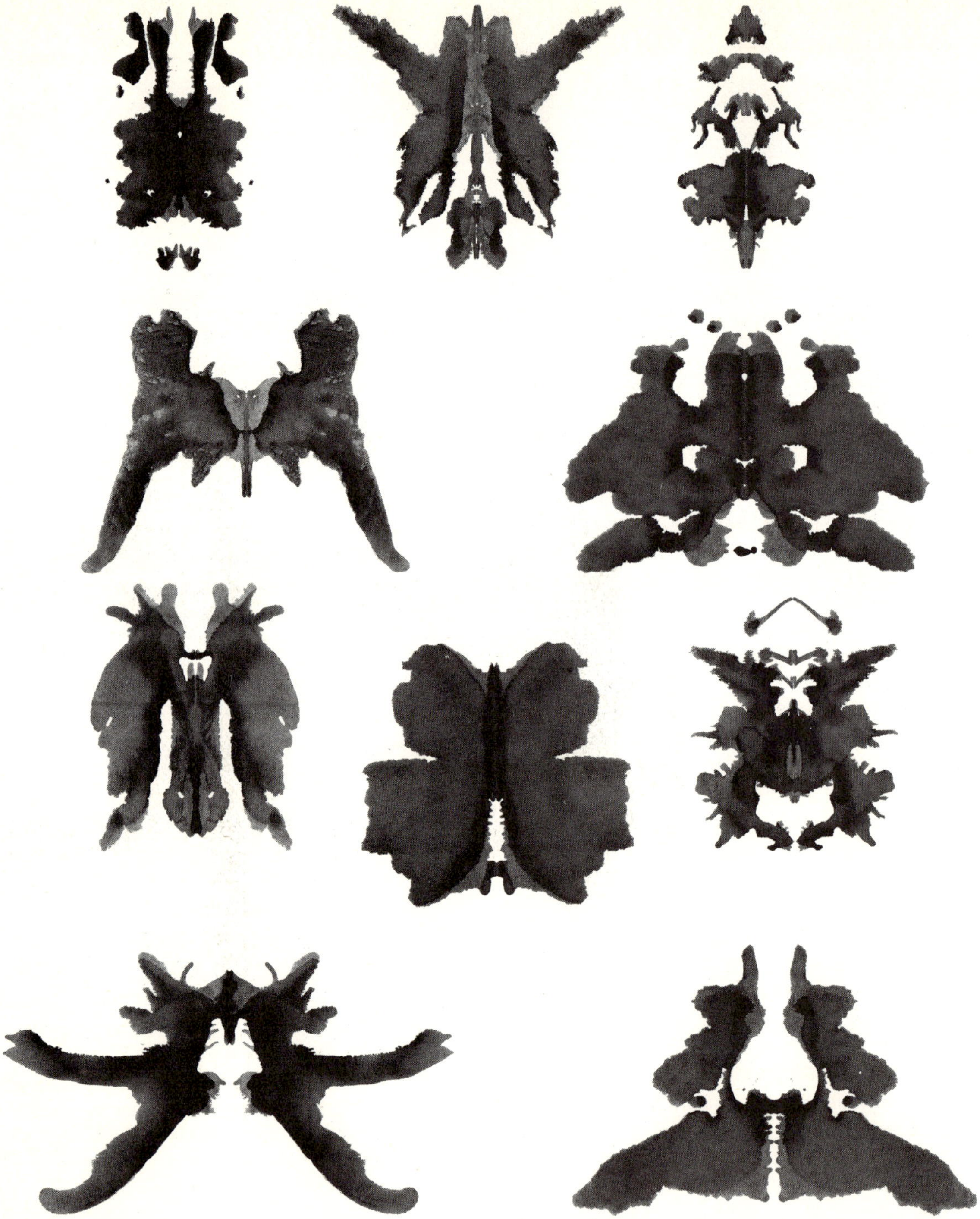

Inkblots resembling those used by Rorschach.

Hermann Rorschach (1884–1922), Swiss psychiatrist who introduced the famous inkblot test. It was designed to uncover motivations and conflicts that are said to be unavailable to consciousness.

point scale; 6, very strong; 5, strong; 4, moderate, 3, slight; 2, very slight; and 1, no tendency at all. The eight Rorschach responses to be rated are presented in Table 3.7.

Now you may compare your ratings to those actually obtained from a sample of undergraduate students. In Table 3.8 the responses are divided into three different classes. The popular invalid signs are those that clinicians tend to *believe* reflect homosexuality, although they have *not* been validated by research evidence. The unpopular but valid signs are infrequently listed by clinicians, but they do have some modest research support as being indicators. The filler items are unrelated to homosexuality and to how clinicians assess it. The students in the Chapmans' study gave much higher ratings to the *popular but invalid signs* than to the other responses.

Professional clinicians may rely on particular signs in making a diagnosis because they *assume* such responses are valid indicators of homosexuality. But as Chapman and Chapman themselves noted, "The popular meanings of many test signs. as reported by clinicians, are *illusory correlations* [italics added] based on verbal associative connection of the test sign to the symptom" (p. 272). No research has established such connections through observation. Chapman and Chapman are saying that, in our culture, we all seem to have developed similar ideas of what homosexuals say, think, or do. In this study of how students rated Rorschach responses, the students *assumed,* as clinicians have, that homosexuals would be inclined to see such things as buttocks in the inkblots and accepted such

## TABLE **3.7**
## Rorschach Responses To Be Rated as Signs of Homosexuality

| Response | Rating |
|---:|---|
| Feminine clothing | |
| Food | |
| Rectum and buttocks | |
| Maps | |
| Figure, part man–part woman | |
| Sexual organs | |
| Monsters | |
| Figure, part animal–part human | |

TABLE **3.8**

Mean Rated Strength of Association Between Particular Rorschach Responses and Homosexuality

(from Chapman and Chapman, 1969)

| Response | Rated strength |
|---|---|
| **Popular invalid signs** | |
| Rectum and buttocks | 4.38 |
| Figure, part man–part woman | 3.53 |
| Feminine clothing | 3.12 |
| Sexual organs | 4.47 |
| **Unpopular valid signs** | |
| Figure, part animal–part human | 1.93 |
| Monsters | 1.68 |
| **Filler items** | |
| Food | 1.09 |
| Maps | 1.09 |

responses as indicators. But these accepted popular signs are *not* valid. There is no evidence to indicate that such responses differentiate between homosexuals and heterosexuals, yet they continue to be taken as signs and to be applied in diagnoses.

### Personality inventories

In personality inventories a large number of statements are typically presented to the examinee, who is asked to indicate whether they do or do not apply. The investigators who have been involved in the construction of such instruments have usually been well schooled in the general principles of test construction and standardization. It is therefore rare for a personality inventory to lack reliability. Validity, however, still presents a problem, especially if the personality inventory has been designed to reveal unconscious conflicts and the like. Some personality inventories have been constructed with more specific purposes in mind. Perhaps the best-known of these is the Minnesota Multiphasic Personality Inventory (MMPI), which was developed in the early 1940s as an inexpensive device to simplify the differential diagnosis of mental patients.

In developing the test, the investigators relied on factual information. First, many clinicians provided large numbers of statements that they considered indicative of various mental problems. Second, these items were rated as self-descriptive or not by people already diagnosed as abnormal according to the DSM. Items that served to discriminate among the patients were retained: that is, items were selected if one clinical group responded to them more often in the same way than did other groups. With additional refinements, sets of these items were established as scales for determining whether or not a respondent should be diagnosed in a particular way. If the individual answered a large number of the items in a scale in the same way as had a certain diagnostic group, the more likely was his or her behavior to resemble that of the particular diagnostic group. The scales of the instrument do, in fact, relate well to psychiatric diagnoses (see Box 3.2). Thus the MMPI has been widely used to screen large groups of people for whom clinical interviews are not feasible. Items similar to those on the various scales are presented in Table 3.9.[5]

We may well wonder whether answers that would designate the subject as normal might not be easy to fake. A superficial knowledge of contemporary abnormal psychology would alert even a seriously disturbed person to the fact that, if he wants to be regarded as normal, he must not admit to worrying a great deal about germs on doorknobs. In fact, there is evidence that

[5] The manner in which the MMPI was constructed is referred to as *empirical,* that is, relying on data or experience rather than speculation. It is also worth noting that the MMPI's diagnostic scheme is based on symptoms listed in DSM. Not surprisingly, clinicians who dislike DSM are unenthusiastic about the MMPI.

TABLE **3.9**
## Typical Clinical Interpretations of Items Similar to Those on the MMPI

(adapted from Kleinmuntz, 1967)

| Scale | Sample Item | Interpretation |
|---|---|---|
| Cannot say | This is merely the number of items marked in the "cannot say" category. | A high score indicates evasiveness. |
| Lie | I have never had a bad night's sleep (false).* | Persons trying to look good (i.e., wholesome, honest) obtain high scores. |
| Frequency | Everything tastes salty (true). | High scores on this scale suggest disinterest or a wish to appear abnormal. |
| Correction | I am more satisfied with my life than most of my friends (true). | High scores on this scale suggest a guarded test-taking attitude. |
| Hypochondriasis | I wake up tired most mornings (true). | High scorers have been described as cynical and dissatisfied. |
| Depression | I rarely see the bright side of things (true). | High scorers are usually withdrawn, sad, and troubled. |
| Hysteria | My fingers sometimes feel numb (true). | High scorers have multiple bodily complaints. |
| Psychopathic deviate | I did not like school (true). | High scorers tend to be adventurous and antisocial. |
| Masculinity-femininity | I do not like sports (true). | Men with high scores tend to be artistic and sensitive. High-scoring women have been described as rebellious and assertive. |
| Paranoia | I am envied by many people (true). | High scorers on this scale tend to be suspicious and jealous. |
| Psychasthenia | I have a great deal of self-confidence (false). | High scorers are described as anxious, self-doubting, and rigid. |
| Schizophrenia | I sometimes smell strange odors (true). | Adjectives such as seclusive and bizarre describe high scorers. |
| Hypomania | I never have any difficulty making decisions (true). | High scorers tend to be outgoing and impulsive. |
| Social introversion–extroversion | I avoid getting together with people (true). | High scorers are modest and shy; low scorers are sociable and exhibitionistic. |

* The true or false responses in parentheses indicate the answer expected if the respondent is to accumulate a high score on this scale.

these tests *can* be "psyched out." In many testing circumstances, however, people do not *want* to falsify their responses, for they want to be helped. Moreover, the test designers have included as part of the MMPI several scales designed to detect deliberately faked responses (see Table 3.9). In one of these, the lie scale, a series of statements sets a trap for the person who is trying to "look too good." One such item from the lie scale declares "I read the newspaper editorials every night." The assumption is that few people would be able to endorse such a statement honestly. Thus persons who do endorse a large number of the statements in the lie scale might well be attempting to present themselves in a particularly good light. Their scores on other scales are usually viewed with more than the usual skepticism.

Tests such as the MMPI are subject to certain other difficulties. It has been found that many people tend to answer test questions on bases other than the specific content of the question. For example, suppose the statement is "I attend a party at least once a week." If the individual answers "Yes," or "True," can we conclude without reservation that he or she really attends social gatherings frequently? Research suggests that such answers cannot be accepted as necessarily true, for a certain test-taking or questionnaire "set" may have determined the response.

Several types of *response sets,* as these orientations are called, have been identified. *Response acquiescence,* or "yea saying," is the tendency to agree with statements regardless of their content. *Response deviation* is the tendency to answer items in an uncommon way regardless of their content. People with a *social desirability* response set will give what they judge to be the most socially acceptable answer, whether or not the response accurately describes them. For instance, in the example just given, individuals who abhor and avoid parties may say that they attend them at least once a week because they wish to be viewed as typical and believe that such a response is likely to be considered "right" or appropriate.

One obvious means of avoiding this problem is to structure the test-taking situation in such a way that the respondent is motivated to answer honestly. If we are working with an individual in a clinical setting, this is not too difficult to accomplish. But what can be done if the test is administered to a group or as part of a research project, where it is difficult to motivate all respondents to answer frankly? The pioneering work of Edwards (1957) illustrates one way of handling the response set of social desirability. He began with an investigation designed to assess the relation between the social desirability of an item and the likelihood that it would be endorsed. First, a large number of undergraduates were asked to judge 140 different self-descriptions on a nine-point scale in terms of ". . . the degree of desirability or undesirability of these traits in people. . . ." Among the items were the following.

1. *To like to punish your enemies.*
2. *To like to read psychological novels.*
3. *To like to make excuses for friends.*
4. *To like to go out with your friends.*

In the next phase of the study Edwards presented the same 140 items to a different sample of undergraduates who were asked to respond yes if the particular item was characteristic of their own behavior and no if it was not. The percentage of subjects responding yes to each of the items was computed and then correlated with the judged social desirability of the response. An impressively high correlation was obtained, leading Edwards to conclude that if we know where a statement lies on the social desirability-undesirability dimension, ". . . we can then predict, with a high degree of accuracy, the proportion of individuals who will say, in self-description, that the statement does describe them" (p. 3). Moreover, even when respondents are led to believe that they will remain anonymous, they still ascribe to themselves socially

## BOX 3.2 Predictive Validity in Clinical Assessment Procedures

Strictly speaking, our discussion of the validity of the MMPI and other assessment devices has been restricted to concurrent validity, the extent to which one measure correlates with other currently available data. Thus the depression scale of the MMPI has concurrent validity if an individual who has been diagnosed as depressed on the basis of other information receives a high score on this scale.

Predictive validity, or the degree to which a measure can predict a characteristic or behavior that will develop at a later time, is also important. For example, we might wish to predict, on the basis of an MMPI profile, how well a person will do in psychotherapy, or, indeed, how well he or she will do without it. The assessment devices we have reviewed possess little validity for this purpose. Is it because the tests are poor? Perhaps. The authors of this textbook suggest, however, that the tests cannot predict the usefulness of psychotherapy because we know so little about therapy. When we examine theory and research in various forms of therapy (Part Six), it will become painfully clear how little is known about whether psychotherapy works, and if it seems to, under what conditions and why. It is therefore premature to expect an assessment procedure to be able to predict a future outcome that is itself not well understood. To draw an analogy, suppose that a personality test is examined for its validity in predicting how well examinees will get along with Martians. How can we expect good prediction without knowing what is required to get along with such extraterrestrial beings? Personality tests have been expected to predict a great many ill-defined outcomes. For this reason their disappointing predictive validity is not surprising and, indeed, should probably have been anticipated (Mischel, 1968).

desirable attitudes and activities.[6]

Several methods have been devised for controlling the social desirability response set. In one of these methods, the *forced-choice inventory,* items that describe different attitudes and activities, which have been independently determined equal in terms of the social desirability of the behavior, are given in pairs to the respondent. Thus the person is forced to choose between two statements describing equally desirable or undesirable alternatives. Edwards himself used this technique in constructing his Personal Preferences Schedule. The manner in which this method forces respondents to make a content-related response is indicated by the following two examples.

*Choose A or B for each of the following items:*

*Item I*
- *A: I like to tell amusing stories and jokes at parties.*
- *B: I would like to write a great novel or play.*

[6] There is more than one possible interpretation of these data. For example, if behavior that is judged the most desirable in a particular culture is also the most common, the probability of endorsing statements describing such behavior would be high, even when subjects were not misrepresenting themselves. But the evidence does not favor this interpretation.

| | | |
|---|---|---|
| | *A:* | *I feel like blaming others when things go wrong for me.* |
| *Item II* | | |
| | *B:* | *I feel that I am inferior to others in most respects.* |

Like others who have judged these statements before them, respondents will probably consider the alternatives of each pair equivalent in social desirability. Thus they are more likely to choose the statement that actually describes themselves.

The forced-choice inventory is a widely used technique for reducing the likelihood that questionnaire responses will reflect only the degree to which the respondent wishes to appear conventional or likable. By excluding or at least minimizing the role of social desirability factors, those who rely on data from personality inventories can with greater confidence regard responses as valid indicators of the personality characteristics the particular test purports to measure.

### Tests for organic brain dysfunction

As indicated at the beginning of this chapter, one major section of the DSM-II refers to behavioral problems brought on by brain abnormalities. Neurological tests such as checking the patellar reflex, examining the retina for any indication of blood vessel damage, and evaluating motor coordination and perception are useful procedures in diagnosing brain dysfunction. The X-ray can sometimes detect tumors, and the electroencephalograph (EEG) abnormalities in the brain's electrical activity. We might reasonably assume that neurologists and physicians, with the help of such procedures and technological devices, can observe the brain and its functions more or less directly and thus assess brain abnormalities. Many brain abnormalities, however, involve alterations in structure so subtle that they have thus far eluded direct physical measurement. Moreover, we still know very little about how the brain works.

Since the way the person functions is the problem—what he or she does, says, thinks, or feels—a number of tests assessing behavioral disturbances that are caused by organic brain dysfunctions have been developed by psychologists. The literature on these tests is extensive and, as with most areas of psychology, so too is disagreement about them. The weight of the evidence, however, does seem to indicate that psychological tests have some validity in the assessment of brain damage. The best psychological test of brain damage is Reitan's modification of a battery or group of tests previously developed by Halstead. The concept of using a battery of tests, each tapping different functions, is critical, for only by studying a person's pattern of performance can an investigator judge accurately whether the person is indeed brain-damaged. But the Reitan-Halstead battery can do even more than this, locating the area of the brain that has been affected. Some of the tests in the battery are the following.

1. **Tactual Performance Test.** The subject tries to fit blocks into spaces while blindfolded, using each hand in turn. After finishing the test the subject tries to draw the board showing the blocks in their proper spaces.
2. **Trail-Making Test**—see Figure 3.1.

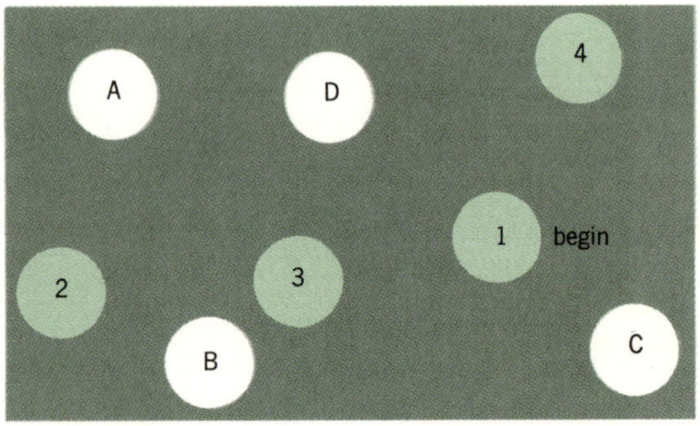


FIGURE **3.1**
Sample item from the Trail-Making Test. The subject is instructed to alternate numbers and letters, for example, by drawing a line from 1 to A, A to 2, 2 to B, and so on.

3. **Finger Oscillation.** In this procedure the subjects taps the index finger as fast as he or she can for five trials of ten seconds each. The index finger of each hand is tested.

4. **Aphasia Screening Test.** A number of language abilities are studied by asking the subject to name digits, spell, read, write, and so on.

Performance on the tests is interpreted by drawing on knowledge of the relation between certain brain structures and behavior. Finger tapping, for example, is thought to be controlled by a brain area just in front of the central sulcus (see Box 16.1, page 412). And control of speech and language tends to be localized in the left cerebral hemisphere. Thus particular deficits suggest that a problem exists in a specific brain area and in one or the other hemisphere. In examining sixty-four brain-damaged patients, Reitan (1964) was able to locate the affected brain area specifically and accurately about 70 percent of the time. That is, his predictions based on test performance were highly related to results of neurological procedures, such as brain scans and surgery.

### Intelligence tests

Psychological measures of intelligence enter into diagnoses of mental retardation. Alfred Binet, a French psychologist, originally constructed mental tests to help the Parisian school board predict which children would profit most from schooling. Intelligence testing has since developed into one of the largest psychological industries. The word aptitude is frequently applied to these widely used standardized procedures. The Scholastic Aptitude Test and the individually administered tests, such as the Wechsler Adult Intelligence Scale and the Stanford-Binet, are all based on the assumption that one sample from an individual's current intellectual functioning can predict how well he or she will perform in school.

When such tests are evaluated, it is important to keep in mind two points that are only infrequently made explicit by those who have a heavy professional commitment to intelligence testing. First, strictly speaking, the tests measure only what a psychologist considers intelligence to be. The tasks and items on an IQ test are, after all, invented by psychologists—they did not come down to us inscribed on stone tablets. Second, the tests are widely used because they do indeed accomplish what they were designed for, that is, predict who will succeed in our educational system. If and when there are major changes in our school systems, we can expect analogous changes in our definition and assessment of intelligence.

## Behavioral Assessment

Except for the IQ tests just described, many of the assessment devices in use today are intimately related to the DSM as well as to variations of psychoanalytic theory. As already mentioned, within a psychodynamic framework it makes sense to use a projective test because truly important material is assumed repressed in the unconscious, and ambiguous stimuli rather than direct questions are viewed as the best means to bypass defense mechanisms. Although the MMPI is a more direct, self-report measurement, it too is intimately related to psychodynamic theory because the test itself was standardized on the basis of categories from the DSM.

In recent years, as part of the continuing development of behavioral approaches to the study of psychopathology and treatment, interest has been growing in assessment procedures that are different from those examined so far. The various learning perspectives described in Chapter 2 indicate that behaviorists are interested in *situational determinants* of behavior, that is, in environmental conditions that precede and follow certain responses.[7] In addition, with the growing

[7] Principal sources for the following discussion are Goldfried and Sprafkin (1974) and Mischel (1968).

interest in cognitive explanations, we can expect behavioral assessment to be oriented toward self-report as well; but, as we shall see, interpretations of self-reports within a behavioral framework differ from those in more traditional assessment.

Traditional assessment concentrates on measuring underlying traits or personality structures, such as "anal personality," "obsessive personality," and "paranoid personality"; behavioral assessment focuses on specifying conditions under which behavior does or does not occur. But, as the social-learning theorist Mischel (1968) has pointed out, most laypeople, including clients, are personality trait theorists in the way they explain their own behavior and that of others. "A chief aim of the trait approach is to infer the underlying personality structure of individuals and to compare persons and groups on trait dimensions" (1968, pp. 5–6). Clients typically consult a therapist with vague generalized complaints such as "I'm all messed up," or "I'm depressed all the time." It is a considerable challenge to the behavior therapist to obtain from clients who begin interviews in this way information that can prove useful in analyzing the problem in learning terms and, more importantly, for planning various therapy programs.

Several methods of behavioral assessment are currently available. These include direct observation of the behavior in real life as well as contrived settings, self-report, role playing in the consulting room, and physiological measurement.

### Direct observation of behavior

It is not surprising that behavior therapists have paid considerable attention to careful observation of behavior in a variety of settings. But it should not be assumed that they simply go out and observe behavior. Like other scientists, they fit actual physical events into categories that have been set up beforehand. This excerpt from a case report by Patterson and his colleagues (1969), describing an interaction between a boy named Kevin and his mother, father, and sister Freida, serves as the first part of an example.

> *Kevin goes up to father's chair and stands alongside it. Father puts his arms around Kevin's shoulders. Kevin says to mother as Freida looks at Kevin, "Can I go out and play after supper?" Mother does not reply. Kevin raises his voice and repeats the question. Mother says "You don't have to yell; I can hear you." Father says "How many times have I told you not to yell at your mother?" Kevin scratches a bruise on his arm while mother tells Freida to get started on the dishes, which Freida does. Kevin continues to rub and scratch his arm while mother and daughter are working at the kitchen sink* (p. 21).

This informal description could probably be provided by any observer. But a behavioral observer would divide the uninterrupted sequence of behavior into various parts and apply terms that make sense within a learning framework. "Kevin begins the exchange by asking a routine question in a normal tone of voice. This ordinary behavior, however, is not reinforced by the mother's attention, for she does not reply. Because she does not reply, the normal behavior of Kevin ceases and he yells his question. The mother expresses disapproval—punishing her son—by telling him that he does not have to yell. And this punishment is supported by the father's reminding Kevin that he should not yell at his mother." This behavioral rendition acknowledges the consequences of ignoring a child's question. At some point the behavior therapist will undoubtedly advise the parents to attend to Kevin's requests when expressed in an ordinary tone of voice, lest he begin yelling.

It is difficult to observe most behavior as it actually takes place, and little control can be exercised over where and when it may occur. For this reason many therapists contrive artificial situations in their consulting rooms or in a laboratory so that they can observe how a client or a family acts under certain conditions. The sequence just described might well have happened in such a contrived setting.

The foregoing illustration in the operant vein employs no inferential concepts; the observations are interpreted in a fairly straightforward way. Behavioral assessment techniques can also be applied within a framework that does make use of mediators (to be discussed in greater detail in Chapter 4). For instance, Gordon Paul (1966) was interested in assessing the "anxiety" of public speakers. He decided that a good way to measure the anxiety of the speaker was to count the frequency of behavior that is deemed indicative of this emotional state. One of his principal measures, the Timed Behavioral Checklist for Performance Anxiety, is shown in Table 3.10. Subjects were asked to deliver a speech in front of a group, some members of which were raters trained to consider each subject's behavior every thirty seconds and to record the presence or absence of twenty specific behaviors. By summing the scores, Paul arrived at a behavioral index of anxiety.[8] This study is one example of how observations of overt behavior have been used to measure an internal state.

Like all means of assessment, direct behavioral observation is not without its problems. The most obvious is that of *reactivity,* namely the *phenomenon of behavior changing because it is being observed.* The very fact that people know that they are being observed can change their behavior. Investigators have been sensitive to this source of bias and have taken such tacks as not informing the person initially which behavior is being observed at a given time. Ethical considerations would preclude making observations that are kept completely secret and never revealed to a subject.

Another difficulty has come to be called the "Rosenthal effect." In a series of ingenious experiments, Rosenthal (1967) demonstrated that experimenters can often influence the outcome of a study, without being dishonest, by virtue of having certain expectations about the results. But in an interesting demonstration by Kent, O'Leary, and their colleagues (1974), experimenter bias was shown to affect overall conclusions rather than specific behavioral observations. In this study observers used a behavioral coding system as they watched videotapes of children who were being treated for disruptive behavior. One group of observers was told that the treatment would decrease disruptive behavior, whereas the others were told that no change was expected. As Rosenthal's data would suggest, observers afterward reported an increase in disruptive behavior if they had been told it was expected. More importantly, however, their *specific behavioral recordings* did not show bias. These results indicate the usefulness of relatively objective coding schemes in observing behavior.

Daniel O'Leary observing and recording the behavior of children in a classroom. He is coding their behavior at regular intervals according to a predetermined set of dimensions.

[8] Additional details of this important experiment are discussed in Chapter 19. Paul used the behavioral index of anxiety in determining the relative efficacy of several forms of therapy devised to reduce anxiety about public speaking.

TABLE **3.10**
Timed Behavioral Checklist for Performance Anxiety

(from Paul, 1966)

| Behavior observed | Time period 1 | 2 | 3 | 4 | 5 | 6 | 7 | 8 | Σ |
|---|---|---|---|---|---|---|---|---|---|
| 1. Paces | | | | | | | | | |
| 2. Sways | | | | | | | | | |
| 3. Shuffles feet | | | | | | | | | |
| 4. Knees tremble | | | | | | | | | |
| 5. Extraneous arm and hand movement (swings, scratches, toys, etc.) | | | | | | | | | |
| 6. Arms rigid | | | | | | | | | |
| 7. Hands restrained (in pockets, behind back, clasped) | | | | | | | | | |
| 8. Hand tremors | | | | | | | | | |
| 9. No eye contact | | | | | | | | | |
| 10. Face muscles tense (drawn, tics, grimaces) | | | | | | | | | |
| 11. Face "deadpan" | | | | | | | | | |
| 12. Face pale | | | | | | | | | |
| 13. Face flushed (blushes) | | | | | | | | | |
| 14. Moistens lips | | | | | | | | | |
| 15. Swallows | | | | | | | | | |
| 16. Clears throat | | | | | | | | | |
| 17. Breathes heavily | | | | | | | | | |
| 18. Perspires (face, hands, armpits) | | | | | | | | | |
| 19. Voice quivers | | | | | | | | | |
| 20. Speech blocks or stammers | | | | | | | | | |

### Self-report measures

As we have already seen, traditional assessment relies very heavily on self-report, both in interviews and in personality inventories. It has sometimes been thought that a learning paradigm of behavior precludes paying attention to what clients can tell a clinician about their problems, their needs, and so forth. This is not the case, particularly as behavior therapy takes more and more the cognitive direction already alluded to in Chapter 2 and discussed at great length in Chapter 19. As psychoanalytically oriented clinicians have insisted for many years, an important part of a person's world is not just his overt behavior but what he thinks about what he is doing. In an example taken from Goldfried and Sprafkin (1974), a little boy is playing with a worm. He suddenly pulls out a knife and cuts the worm in half. Is this an example of destructive, aggressive behavior? An observer might find out, through questioning the child, that he believed he was giving the worm a playmate, saying to himself as he cut the worm, "There, now you have someone to play with." As with other self-report measures, questioning and interviews are of course open to various response biases. But if a clinician takes care to create an atmosphere encouraging honesty and frankness, there is every reason to give considerable credence to the words of the person being examined.

The self-report inventories that behavior therapists develop are a great deal more specific and detailed than those that are typically used by nonbehavioral clinicians. For example, McFall and Lillesand (1971) employed a Conflict Resolution Inventory, containing thirty-five items which focus on the ability of the respondent to refuse unreasonable requests. Each item describes a specific situation in which a person is asked something unreasonable, for example, "You are in the thick of studying for exams when a person you know slightly comes into your room and says 'I'm tired of studying, mind if I come in and take a break for a while?' " Subjects are asked to indicate the likelihood that they would refuse such a request and how comfortable they would be in doing so. This and similar inventories have helped behavioral researchers measure the outcome of clinical interventions and can be used by the practicing clinician as well.

### Role playing

Because some clinical problems cannot be observed directly in the real-life situation, many behavior therapists enact little plays, if you will, in the consulting room. The therapist assumes the role of a particular individual in the client's life and creates an opportunity for observing responses. Not infrequently clients object that the created scene is "just make believe, too artificial, could not possibly show anything." But in many instances the client becomes quite involved in the role playing assessment, enabling the therapist to obtain useful information about how the client responds in real life.

### Physiological measurement

In recent years experimentally minded psychopathologists and therapy researchers have employed sophisticated procedures to measure behavior that is not detectable by those already described in this chapter. The discipline of *psychophysiology* is concerned with the bodily changes that accompany psychological events. For example, we know that the heart rate of most people will increase markedly under conditions of psychological, as well as physical, stress. Experimenters have studied such changes, as well as alterations in the conductivity of the skin (see page 115), tension in the muscles, blood flow in various parts of the body, and even brain waves (see page 233) while subjects are afraid, depressed, asleep, imagining, solving problems, and so on. Special attention has also been paid to the *patterning* of such responses, as when heart rate increases while skin conductivity remains constant.

As the technology has improved, psychopathologists have come to realize that a more complete picture of the human being is obtained by assessing physiological functioning as well as overt behavior and cognitive activity. If experimenters wonder whether showing schizophrenic patients pictures of their mothers is stressful, they can, in addition to asking the patients how they feel about looking at the pictures, measure their heart rate and electrical skin activity. Psychophysiological measuring procedures are relatively unobtrusive. Once the person has adapted to having electrodes pasted on his or her arm, for example, measurement of heart rate does not interfere with the assigned experimental task, such as listening to a story or solving a mathematical problem.

Inasmuch as psychophysiology employs highly sophisticated electronic machinery, and inasmuch as many psychologists aspire to be as scientific as possible (see Box 3.3), it sometimes happens that they rely on these apparently objective assessment devices without appreciating their real limitations and complications. Many of the measurements do not differentiate clearly among different emotional states. Heart rate, for example, increases with a variety of emotions, not only with anxiety. Special care must be taken to ensure a proper setting for taking measurements so that the data collected are meaningful. And experimenters can still introduce bias by the way in which they treat their willing subjects.

### Behavioral assessment for behavioral change

We have seen that people operating within a learning paradigm of psychopathology and treat-

## BOX 3.3 Psychophysiological Assessment of Sexual Arousal

Let us examine closely some important innovations in psychophysiological measurement. In 1966 Masters and Johnson startled researchers and lay people alike by their direct physiological assessments of men and women during states of great sexual arousal. The measures they used primarily were two already mentioned, muscle tension and measurement of blood volume in various parts of the cardiovascular system. In addition, they employed ingenious photographic devices to record changes in the color of various tissues of the vagina during the sexual arousal of women. More recently behavioral researchers have been using two genital devices for measuring sexual arousal in men and in women, and each of them enjoys considerable validation in giving rather specific measurements of sexual excitement. Both are sensitive indicators of vasocongestion of the genitalia, that is, the flooding of their veins with blood, a key process in sexual arousal.

The penile plethysmograph (Freund, 1963; Bancroft, Jones, and Pullan, 1966) has been used successfully to measure the sexual arousal of men in a variety of experiments. A plethysmograph is a device that measures blood flow. The most widely used penile plethysmograph is a strain gauge, consisting of a very thin rubber tube filled with mercury or a circular piece of light surgical steel, either of which can be placed around the penis (Barlow et al., 1970) with ease and in privacy. As the penis fills with blood during sexual excitement, the tube or steel stretches, changing the electrical resistance of the mercury or steel; through appropriate wiring the increase in resistance is transformed into tracings on a complex apparatus called the polygraph. Increase in the length of the penis correlates highly with increase in circumference, and both of them are a function of engorgement of the penis with blood during sexual excitement. The strain gauge, then, provides a very useful measure of sexual responding in men.

Until recently, similarly direct and specific measurement of female sexual arousal was not possible. Only indirect measures such as those used by Masters and Johnson were available, and these are unsatisfactory for both aesthetic and practical reasons. Fortunately, a vaginal plethysmograph was recently invented by Sintchak and Geer (1975). This device is shaped like a small menstrual tampon and has a light at the tip. The light reflected from the vaginal walls is recorded and provides a measure of the amount of blood in the walls of the vagina. Like the penile strain gauge, the vaginal probe is a reliable instrument and is easily put in place by subjects in total privacy. An important validational study of this device was reported by Geer, Morokoff, and Greenwood (1974). They showed female undergraduates erotic and nonerotic films and measured engorgement of their vaginal walls during the viewings. In the erotic film a young man and a young woman have an explicit sexual encounter, including foreplay, oral-genital sex, and intercourse. The nonerotic film, entitled *The Crusades,* depicts battle scenes and court life during the time of the Crusades. Since each film was readily identified as erotic or nonerotic, any differences between the measurements of the two groups of subjects obtained with the vaginal probes could be taken as evidence that the instruments do provide a valid measure of sexual excitement. The women watching the sexual film showed much greater blood flow than did the subjects watching the control film. It is of interest that heart rate measurements taken concurrently did not differentiate the two groups of subjects, confirming the desirability of specific genital measures.

In addition to the obvious advantages of genital plethysmographs in providing specific measures of sexual arousal, subjects soon become relatively unaware of their presence on their bodies and of the wiring to the polygraph. This degree of unobtrusiveness, desirable in any assessment procedure, is particularly important in studying sexual behavior, about which many people are self-conscious. The technical innovations and availability of these devices have spurred a remarkable volume of research on human sexual behavior. Of course, it would be naive to assert that these genital devices have no effect on how subjects respond in a laboratory. And as valuable as these new devices appear to be in assessing sexual arousal, it would be unwise to view them as able to gauge all sexual interest. A value that a particular image or idea holds for a man or a woman may not always be translated directly into an increase in penile size or vaginal blood flow. Not all sexuality can be measured in terms of genital responding.

The data being collected by sex researchers around the world do indicate that, at least with those volunteering for such experiments, meaningful and important studies can be done. The accumulating literature is beginning to shed light on an area of human conduct previously shrouded in mystery, embarrassment, and an often harmful mythology.

ment do not ignore the inner life of the individual, but it is accurate to say that they pay considerably more attention to overt behavior than do other theoreticians and practitioners. A principal difference between behavioral assessment and the traditional personality assessment reviewed earlier in this chapter is its closer tie to procedures for changing behavior. Behavior therapists search thoroughly for the situational determinants of behavior because they believe it can be altered by manipulating the environment. One behavior therapy procedure, systematic desensitization, seems to be effective in reducing a variety of fears. Without going into the specifics of the technique at this point (see Chapter 19), suffice it to say that the therapist must know the particular situations that make the patient fearful. Rather than making a general diagnosis, such as phobic reaction, and then beginning to search for underlying personality dynamics, behavior therapists believe that quicker and greater progress can be made by ascertaining the specific situations in which people are phobic and lessening their fears of them.

## The Consistency and Variability of Behavior

Mischel (1968) has argued that the environment is a more important determinant of behavior than are personality traits. Trait theorists, as suggested earlier, believe that human beings can be described as having a certain "amount" of a characteristic, such as "stinginess," or "obsessiveness," and that their behavior in a variety of situations can be predicted by the degree to which they possess this characteristic. This position implies that people will behave consistently across a variety of situations—for example, an aggressive person will be aggressive at home, at work, and at play. Mischel's careful analysis of the evidence bearing on this question, however, indicates that the behavior of people is not very consistent from situation to situation.

In an attempt to shed light on this controversy, Bem and Allen (1974) administered to a large undergraduate class a questionnaire which presented the students with a number of situations and asked them to indicate whether they would be consistently or variably friendly and conscientious in these circumstances. Bem and Allen then obtained permission from a small number of these men and women to have their behavior observed and rated by people familiar to them, including their parents and roommates. In addition, Bem and Allen arranged for several unobtrusive measures to be taken of these subjects. For example, "spontaneous friendliness" was measured by having each subject observed as he or she waited in a room with a confederate of the experimenter; the observer recorded how long it took the subject to initiate a conversation with the confederate.

Bem and Allen divided their subjects into those with great or little variability in friendliness and conscientiousness, based on the subjects' own ratings of themselves via the questionnaire. They next compared this self-rated consistency or variability with how consistently friendly and conscientious subjects had appeared in the observed real-life situations. The results showed that people can be predicted to behave in a friendly fashion in a number of circumstances *if* they view themselves as consistently friendly. But the behavior of subjects who believe themselves to vary considerably in friendliness from situation to situation could *not* be predicted. Basicially, Bem and Allen conclude that certain people—those who believe that they are consistent—will generally be so in all situations. In contrast, the behavior of others depends on the specific situation.

A different critique of the situational approach comes from a psychodynamic theorist, Paul Wachtel (1977). Wachtel argues that social-learning theorists like Mischel ignore current psychoanalytic thinking, which is sensitive to the way behavior varies across different situations. But, Wachtel argues, the behavior of individuals whom clinicians tend to encounter may indeed by predictable on the basis of some underlying trait or disposition. Clinical problems may, in fact, be associated with a rigidity or inflexibility to changing conditions.

Wachtel also suggests that people tend to perceive certain kinds of situations in a particular fashion; the perception in effect renders situations that look different to an experimenter equivalent in their own eyes. For example, a person who might be described as paranoid sees threats in seemingly innocuous situations. Insensitivity to circumstances is not his or her problem; rather this person perceives a great many situations as threatening events. In addition, people can *elicit* certain kinds of reactions from their environment. The paranoid individual may not only perceive people as threatening but make them so by attacking them first. In effect, he transforms different situations into similar and dangerous ones. As a result his own behavior varies little.

Wachtel goes on to argue that the experiments Mischel attends to are generally done with normal college undergraduates, whose behavior is probably more flexible than that of patients. As just mentioned, one of the hallmarks of mental disorder may be rigidity and inflexibility, which is another way of saying that behavior is consistent in a variety of situations. Therefore, by studying basically normal people, social-learning theorists have concluded that people are more variable than they might had they studied patients.

Thus, contrary to what some behavioral critics contend, contemporary psychodynamic thinkers do not dispute the important role that environmental events play in determining behavior. They argue instead that people perceive events in certain ways, even transforming their environment, and then respond in a rather consistent manner.

Mischel, in an important paper published in 1973, replies to some of his critics by suggesting that social-learning theory can indeed incorporate certain personality variables in a more systematic fashion than was made clear in his original pronouncements in 1968. He suggests a set of primarily cognitive "person variables." The expectancy of affecting or not affecting the environment may, for example, be a major factor determining behavior and allowing its prediction. This and other person variables should be derived, argues Mischel, from experimental research and not from speculation, as tends to be the case in psychodynamic theorizing.

A synthesis may be emerging whereby social-learning theorists pay considerable attention to personality variables, but only those validated by experimental personality research.

## Summary

The six major categories of abnormal behavior—mental retardation, organic brain syndromes, psychoses, neuroses, personality disorders, and psychophysiological disorders—comprising the current diagnostic and statistical manual, DMS-II, were briefly described. Three major criticisms of DSM-II were discussed: heterogeneity of symptoms within diagnostic classes, insufficient reliability, and lack of validity. Although these criticisms are indeed partially deserved, they are not serious enough to justify abandoning all attempts at classification. Some sort of classification or measurement seems essential whenever we wish to learn something new. The recent trends to present more detailed criteria for reaching a diagnosis were discussed. Greater clarity may reduce some of the problems of current psychiatric classification.

The remainder of the chapter dealt with techniques for assessing abnormal behavior. The clinical interview was seen to vary widely in format, for the paradigm of the interviewer inevitably determines the direction of questioning. Psychological tests—projective techniques, personality inventories, tests for brain damage, and intelligence tests—were also reviewed. Projective tests such as the Rorschach were judged to have little value, but the other classes of psychological tests may be useful in some situations. A number of assessment procedures based on the learning paradigm, which emphasizes situational determinants of behavior, were also described. Finally, we examined whether personality trait or the situation is more important in predicting how people will behave in a variety of circumstances. Recent developments in psychoanalytic theory and new data from personality researchers suggest ways of settling this controversy, which has divided trait and learning theorists.

# chapter 4

## RESEARCH METHODS IN THE STUDY OF ABNORMAL BEHAVIOR



From our discussion of different ways of conceptualizing abnormal behavior and of problems in its classification and assessment, it should be clear that there is less than total agreement on how abnormal behavior ought to be studied. Our approach to the field is based on the belief that more progress will be made through scientific research than armchair speculation. Abnormal behavior as we have already noted, has been the subject of theorizing for centuries. We are studying a field that has a high ratio of speculation to data. Because facts are hard to come by, it is important to discuss in some detail the contemporary research methods that are applied in psychopathology.

### Science and Scientific Methods

In Chapter I we emphasized the important role of subjective factors in the collection and interpretation of data, indeed, in the very definition of what constitutes an observation. Thus there is actually no one science or scientific method, although we often read in college textbooks of "*the* scientific method." The phrase "as currently practiced" should really be added.

Let us consider science from the point of view of Baruch Spinoza, a famous Dutch philosopher of the seventeenth century. He believed that the scientist's role was to discover God's law. Today we say that Spinoza did not hold a "constructive" view of science. We do not necessarily imply that Spinoza's views were not useful, rather that they can be differentiated from perspectives that emphasize man's role in constructing laws and principles. Contemporary scientists tend to view the laws and theories in existence as constructions or inventions made by scientists. And the rules to be followed in formulating and evaluating these hypotheses and laws are also constructed by people and might very well be changed at any time. Science, as currently practiced, is the pursuit of systematized knowledge through observation. Thus the term refers to a method, the systematic acquisition and evaluation of information. It also refers to a goal, the development of principles that explain the information. Contemporary science strives for explanations that are an outgrowth of, and can be modified by, publicly observed evidence. Both observations and explanations must meet certain criteria.

Testability A scientific approach requires that all claims be exposed to systematic probes and tests, any one of which could negate the scientist's expectations about what will be found. Statements, theories, and assertions, regardless of how plausible they may seem, must be testable in the public arena. The attitude of science is an extremely doubting one. It is not enough to assert that particular traumatic experiences during childhood may produce psychological maladjustment in adulthood, or that various stresses in adult life may create problems. These are no more than possibilities or propositions. According to a scientific point of view, such propositions must be amenable to testing.

Reliability Closely related to testability is the demand that the observations forming a scientific body of knowledge be reliable. Whatever is observed must occur under prescribed circumstances not once but repeatedly. The event cannot be seen or detected only by a single individual or individuals in a given laboratory, community, or country. Instead, it must be reproducible under the circumstances stated, anywhere, anytime, and anyplace. If the event cannot be reproduced, scientists become wary of the legitimacy of the original observation.

The Inferences of Unobservables Even with its emphasis on observables, science often resorts to nonobservable or theoretical concepts in explaining phenomena. Although theoretical concepts are inferred from observable data, they go beyond what can actually be seen or measured. Several advantages may thus be gained. First, theoretical concepts often bridge spatiotemporal relations. For example, in early physics it was noted that a magnet placed close to some iron filings would cause some of the filings to move toward it. How does one piece of metal influence another over the spatial distance? The inferred concept of magnetic fields proved to be very useful in accounting for this phenomenon. Similarly, in abnormal psychology we may often want to bridge temporal gaps with theoretical concepts. If a child has had a particularly frightening experience and his or her behavior is changed for a lengthy period of time, we need to explain how the earlier event is able to exert an influence over subsequent behavior. The unobservable and inferred concept of *acquired fear* has been very helpful in this regard.

Theoretical concepts may also be used to account for already observed relationships. Let us take a classic example proposed by a philosopher of science, Carl Hempel (1958). An early observer of nature has been studying what happens to various objects as they are placed in water. He formulates some lawlike generalizations, such as "Wood floats in water, iron sinks." In addition to the fact that a large number of such generalizations would be needed to describe exhaustively the behavior of all objects placed in liquids, exceptions to the generalizations are likely. Iron in a particular shape (boatlike) will float on water. A waterlogged piece of wood will sink. The solution is to propose a theoretical term, in this case specific gravity, which can both simplify descriptions of what will and will not float and allow errorless statements to be made. Specific gravity is the ratio of the weight of an object to its volume. And with this theoretical term we can now easily and without error specify what will happen to *any* body placed in *any* liquid. If the specific gravity of the object is less than that of the liquid, the object will float.

Let us now examine a similar instance, closer to the field of abnormal behavior. We may observe that people who are taking an examination, who expect a momentary electric shock, or who are fighting with a companion all have sweaty palms, trembling hands, and a fast heartbeat. If we ask them how they feel, they all report that they are agitated. The relationships can be depicted as shown in Figure 4.1a. Or we could say that all the situations have made these individuals anxious, and that anxiety has in turn caused the reported agitation, the sweaty palms, the faster heartbeat, and the trembling hands. Figure 4.1b shows anxiety as a theoretical concept explaining what has been observed. The first part of the figure is much more complex than the second, where the term anxiety becomes a mediator of the relationships.

With these advantages in mind, we must consider the criteria to be applied in judging the legitimacy of a theoretical concept. One earlier school of thought, the *operationist,* proposed that each such concept take as its meaning a single observable and measurable operation. In this way each theoretical concept would be nothing

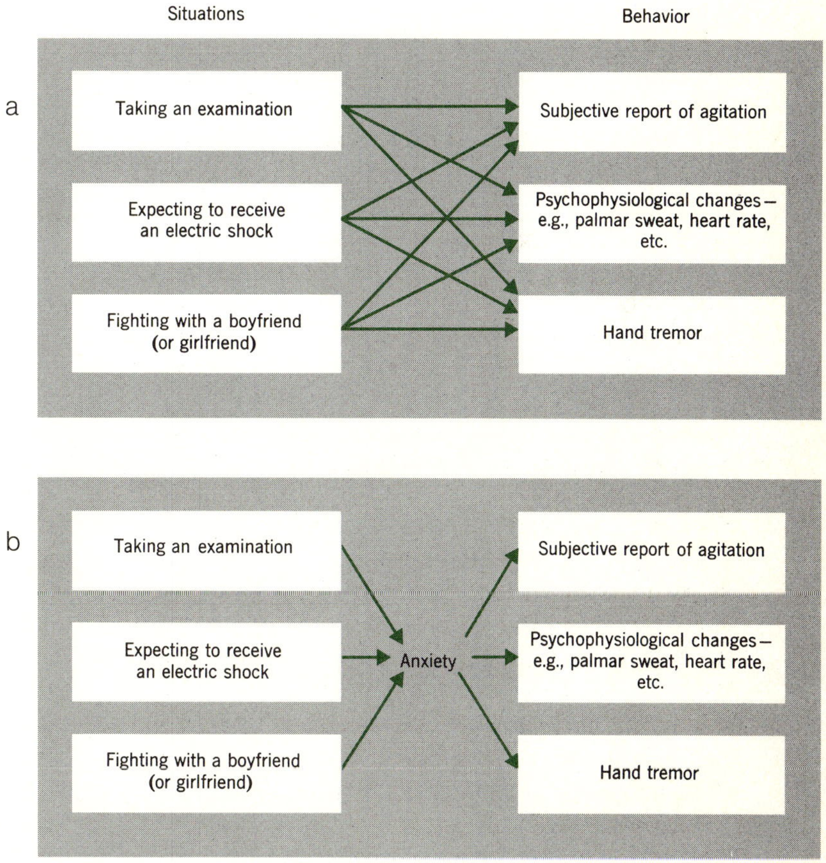


FIGURE **4.1**
An illustration of the advantages of using anxiety as a theoretical concept. The arrows in part b are fewer and more readily understood. After Miller, 1959.

more than one particular measurable effect. For example, anxiety might be identified as *nothing more* than scoring 50 on an anxiety questionnaire. It was soon realized, however, that this approach would take away from theoretical concepts their greatest advantage. If each theoretical concept is *operationalized* in only one way, its generality is lost. If the theoretical concept of learning, for instance, is identified as a *single* operation or effect that can be measured, such as how often a rat presses a bar, other behavior such as a child performing arithmetic problems or a college student studying this book cannot also be called learning, and attempts to relate the different phenomena to one another might be discouraged. The early operationist point of view quickly gave way to the more flexible position that a theoretical concept can be defined by *sets* of operations or effects. In this way the concept may be linked to several different measurements, each of which taps a different facet of the concept (see Figure 4.1b).[1] Research in different laboratories, carried out with different subjects and experimental arrangements, can then be integrated.

[1] There are also risks when we permit an unobservable concept to be operationalized, or measured, in more than one way. We shall examine some of these when we consider the topic of anxiety in the next chapter.

## The Research Methods of Abnormal Psychology

We turn now to a consideration of various research procedures that are currently applied in the study of abnormal behavior. The four most common—the experiment, the correlation, the mixed design, and single-subject research—vary in the degree to which they allow scientific propositions to be probed and reliable data collected.

### The Experiment

The experiment is generally considered to be the most powerful tool for determining causal relationships between events. As an introduction to the basic components of experimental research, let us consider a study of how violence seen on television influences the aggressive behavior of children (Liebert and Baron, 1972). A group of 136 children participated in the research. Each child was first taken to a room containing a television monitor and was told he could watch it for a few minutes until the experimenter was ready for him. For all the children the first two minutes of film consisted of two commercials. After that, *half* the children viewed a sequence from "The Untouchables" which contained a chase, two fistfights, two shootings, and a knifing. The remaining children saw an exciting sports sequence. For all subjects the last minute of the film was another commercial.

Each child was then escorted to a nearby room and seated in front of a large box which had wires leading to another room. On the box was a white light, below which were a green button labeled HELP and a red button labeled HURT. The experimenter explained that the wires were connected to a game a child in the other room was going to play. The game involved turning a handle, and each time the other child did this the white light would come on. The experimenter explained that by pushing the buttons the subject could either help the other child by making the handle easier to turn or hurt him by making the handle hot. Each time that the white light came on, the subject was to push one of the buttons, and the longer he pushed it, the more he would help or hurt the other child. After making certain that the instructions were understood, the experimenter left the room. Each subject was given twenty trials; that is, the white light came on twenty times.

Table 4.1 shows the average length of time that a subject in each of the two groups—the children who had seen the violent episodes on television and those who had seen the sports sequence—pushed the HURT button. Children who had viewed the violent television sequences were more aggressive than those who had not.

TABLE **4.1**
Effect of Television Viewing on the Aggressiveness of Children
(from Liebert and Baron, 1972)

| Television program viewed | Average duration of each aggressive response, seconds |
|---|---|
| Aggressive—"The Untouchables" | 9.92 |
| Nonaggressive—sports sequence | 7.03 |

### Basic features of experimental design

The foregoing example illustrates many of the basic features of an experiment. The researcher typically begins with an *experimental hypothesis*. Liebert and Baron hypothesized that viewing violence would stimulate aggressive behavior. Second, the investigator chooses an *independent variable* that can be manipulated, that is, some factor that will be under the control of the experimenter. Liebert and Baron exposed some children to an aggressive sequence on television and others to a nonaggressive sequence. Finally, the researcher arranges for the measurement of a *dependent variable,* which is expected to depend on or vary with manipulations of the independent variable. The dependent variable in this study was the duration of the HURT response, an operational definition of aggression. When in such an investigation differences between groups are indeed found to be a function of variations in the independent variable, the researcher is said to have produced an *experimental effect.*

### Internal validity

An additional feature of any experimental design is the inclusion of at least one *control group.* A control group is necessary if the effects in any experiment are to be attributed to the manipulation of the independent variable. In the Liebert and Baron study the control group saw the nonviolent sports sequence.

To illustrate this point with another example, consider a study of the effectiveness of a particular therapy in modifying some form of abnormal behavior. Let us assume that persons with initially poor self-concepts have asked for treatment and that they undergo therapy designed to remedy their condition. At the end of six months the patients are reassessed, and it is found that their self-concepts have improved compared to what they were at the beginning of the study. Unfortunately, such an investigation would not produce valid data. The improvement in self-concept from the beginning of the treatment to the end could have been brought about by several factors in addition to or instead of the particular treatment employed. For example, it may be that certain environmental events occurred within the six months and produced the improvement. Or it may be that people with a poor self-concept acquire better feelings about themselves with the mere passage of time. Variables such as these are often called *confounds;* they make the results impossible to interpret. Studies in which the effect obtained cannot be attributed with confidence to the independent variable are called *internally invalid* studies. The design of *internally valid* research, that is, research in which the effect obtained can be confidently attributed to the manipulation of the independent variable, is a primary goal in the social sciences.

In the example just outlined, internal validity could have been secured by the inclusion of a *control group*. Such a group might have consisted of individuals with poor self-concepts who did *not* receive the therapeutic treatment. Changes in the self-concepts of these control subjects would constitute a *base line* or standard against which the effects of the independent variable can be assessed. If a change in self-concept is brought about by particular environmental events, quite beyond any therapeutic intervention, the experimental group receiving the treatment and the control group receiving no treatment are equally likely to be affected. On the other hand, if a difference is shown between the self-concepts of the treated group and those of the untreated control group, we can be relatively confident that this difference is, in fact, attributable to the treatment.

The mere inclusion of a control group, however, does not always ensure internal validity. To illustrate, let us consider another study of therapy, this time the treatment of two hospital wards of psychiatric patients. An investigator may decide to select one ward to receive an experimental treatment and then select another ward as a control. When the researcher later compares the frequencies of deviant behavior in these two groups, he or she will want to attribute any differences between them to the fact that one received treatment and the other did not. But the researcher cannot legitimately draw this inference, for a competing hypothesis cannot be disproved—that even before treatment the ward patients who happened to receive therapy might have had a lower level of deviant behavior than the ward patients who became the control group. The principle of experimental design disregarded in this defective study is that of *random assignment*.

Random assignment is achieved by ensuring that every subject in the research has an equal chance of being assigned to any of the groups. For example, in a two-group experiment a coin can be tossed for each subject. If the coin turns up heads, the subject is assigned to one group; if tails, he or she is assigned to another. This procedure minimizes the likelihood that differences between or among the groups after treatment will reflect pretreatment differences in the samples rather than true experimental effects.

Even with both a control group and random assignment, the results of the research may still be invalid. An additional source of error is the potential biasing influence of the experimenter or observers. This is the "Rosenthal effect" already mentioned in Chapter 3. As Rosenthal (1966) has suggested, the expectancies of an investigator about the outcome of a study may conspire to produce results favorable to the initial hypothesis. He or she may subtly manipulate the subject to give expected and desired responses. Although the pervasiveness of these effects has been questioned (Barber and Silver, 1968; Kent et al., 1974), investigators must remain on guard lest their results be tainted by their own expectations. To avoid biases of this type, many studies apply the so-called *double-blind* procedure. For example, in an investigation comparing the psychological effects of two drugs, the person dispensing the pills is kept ignorant (that is, blind) about their actual content, and the subject is also not informed about the treatment he or she is receiving. With such controls the behavior observed during the course of the treatment is probably not influenced by biasing.

Earlier, we briefly defined the term experimental effect, but we have yet to learn how it can be decided that an effect is important. To evaluate importance researchers employ the concept of *statistical significance*. Essentially, statistical significance has to do with the likelihood or probability that the results of an experiment were produced by chance. A *significant difference* between groups is one that has little probability of occurring by chance alone. Thus this difference can be expected to be found again whenever the same experiment is repeated. Traditionally, in psychological research, a difference is considered statistically significant and therefore admissible as evidence if the likelihood is five or less in one hundred that it is a chance finding. This level of significance is called the .05 level, commonly written as $p < .05$ and read as "probability less than 5 percent." Statistical significance should not be confused with the social or real-life significance of research results. An experiment can yield findings that are statistically significant yet devoid of practical importance. Moreover, the level of statistical significance considered acceptable is determined by *social convention,* that is, the rules by which contemporary scientists agree to play the game. Thus if the results of an experiment have a probability of .10 or less that they occurred by chance rather than a probability of .05 or less, it is nowhere mandated that these are chance events and therefore totally worthless. Investigators may decide that, given the kind of experiment run, these results are quite encouraging and should not be disregarded. Then they must convince their colleagues that these findings are indeed valid. In a sense, science is a game of *persuasion.*

### External validity

The extent to which the results of any particular piece of research can be generalized beyond the immediate experiment is the measure of their *external validity.* For example, if investigators have demonstrated that a particular treatment helps a group of patients they have tried it on, they will undoubtedly want to determine whether this treatment will also be effective in ministering to other patients, at other times, and in other places. Liebert and Baron would hope that the findings of their television experiment apply to violence of many kinds, shown on home television sets to children other than those who served as experimental subjects.

The external validity of the results of a psychological experiment is extremely difficult to determine. For example, merely knowing that one is a subject in a psychological experiment often alters behavior, and thus results are produced in the laboratory that may not automatically be produced in the natural environment. In many instances results obtained from investigations with laboratory animals such as rats have been generalized to human beings. Such generalizations are hazardous, since there are enormous differences between *Homo sapiens* and *Rattus norvegicus.* Researchers must be continually alert to the extent to which they claim generalization for findings, for there are, in fact, no entirely adequate ways of dealing with the question of external validity. The best that can be done is to perform similar studies in new settings with new participants so that the limitations, or the generality, of a finding can be determined.

### Analogue experiments

*Although the experimental method is judged to be the most telling way to determine cause-effect relationships, the method has in fact been little used by those seeking the causes of abnormal behavior.* Suppose that a researcher has hypothesized that a child's emotionally charged, overdependent relationship with his or her mother causes schizophrenia. An experimental test of this hypothesis would require assigning infants randomly to either of two groups of mothers! The mothers in one group will have undergone an extensive training program to ensure that they are able to create a highly emotional atmosphere and foster overdependence in children. The mothers in the second group will have been trained not to create such a relationship with the children they care for. The researcher then waits until the subjects in each group reach adulthood and determines how many of them become schizophrenic. Obviously, such an experimental design contains insurmountable practical problems. But practical issues are hardly the only ones that must concern us. Consider also the ethics of such an experiment. Would the potential scientific gain outweigh the suffering that would surely be imposed on some of the participants? In almost any person's view it would not.

Experiments are used, though, in some areas of abnormal psychology. The effectiveness of treatments for psychopathology is usually evaluated by the experimental method, for it has proved a powerful tool for determining whether a therapy reduces suffering. Experimental research on the causes of abnormal behavior, however, has taken the *analogue* approach. Investigators have attempted to bring a *related* phenomenon, that is, an analogue, into the laboratory for more intensive study. In this way internally valid results may be obtained, although the problem of external validity may be accentuated. In one type of analogue study, behavior is rendered temporarily abnormal through experimental manipulations such as the administration of drugs, hypnotic suggestions, sensory deprivation, and operant shaping. If "pathology" can be experimentally induced by any one of these manipulations, the same variable, existing in the natural environment, might well be a cause of the disorder. We have already noted the problems involved in this reasoning (see Chapter 1), in the discussion of the broom-holding demonstration of Ayllon and his colleagues (1965). Results of such experiments must be interpreted with great caution, although they provide valuable hypotheses about the origins of psychopathology.

Whether the animal experiments mentioned earlier are regarded as analogues depends not on the experiment itself but rather on the use to which it is put. We can very readily study avoidance behavior in a white rat by running experiments with rats. The data collected from such studies are not analogue data if we limit our discussion to the behavior of rats. They become analogue data only when we draw implications from them and apply them to other domains, such as anxiety in man.

In the next chapter we shall have occasion to review experimental work on anxiety. This work often has been done with white rats, although the results have been generalized to human beings. It will be important to keep in mind, therefore, that we are arguing by analogy when we attempt to relate reactions to stress of white rats to anxiety in human beings. At the same time, however, we do not agree with some who regard such analogue data as totally and intrinsically worthless as far as the study of human behavior is concerned. In particular, the discussion of behavior therapy in Chapter 19 will indicate that some important treatments for abnormal human behavior were originally developed through research with animals. Although man and other mammals differ on many important dimensions, it does not follow that principles of behavior derived from animal research are necessarily irrelevant to human behavior.

## The Correlational Method

Correlational techniques address questions of the form "Are variable *X* and variable *Y* associated in some way so that they vary together (correlate)?" In other words, questions are asked concerning relationships; for example, "Is schizophrenia related to social class?" or "Is anxiety related to scores obtained on college examinations?" Thus the correlational method establishes whether there is a relationship between or among two or more variables. Numerous examples can be drawn from everyday life. Income correlates positively with the number of luxuries purchased: the higher the income, the more luxuries purchased. Height tends to be positively correlated with weight: taller people are usually heavier. This second relationship, that between height and weight, is by no means perfect, for many individuals are "overweight" or too fat for their height and "underweight" or too thin for their height. The relationship, however, is a strong one.

The correlational method involves obtaining pairs of observations, such as height and weight, on each member in a group of subjects (Table 4.2). Once such pairs of observations are obtained, we can determine how strong the relationship is between the two sets of observations.

TABLE **4.2**
Data for Determining a Correlation*

| Individuals | Height | Weight, pounds |
|---|---|---|
| John | 5′10″ | 170 |
| Asher | 43″ | 40 |
| Eve | 52″ | 56 |
| Carol | 5′6″ | 120 |
| Gail | 5′3″ | 105 |
| Jerry | 5′10″ | 172 |
| Bob | 6′1″ | 175 |
| Marv | 5′8″ | 168 |
| Jim | 6′2″ | 200 |
| Harry | 5′9″ | 175 |
| Alan | 5′7″ | 150 |
| Sean | 28″ | 28 |

* For these figures $r = +.87$.

The most prevalent means of measuring such a relationship was devised by Karl Pearson and is referred to as the *Pearson product moment correlation coefficient,* denoted by the symbol *r*. This statistic may take any value between −1.00 and +1.00 and measures both the *magnitude* and the *direction* of a relationship. The higher the *absolute value* of *r*, the larger or stronger the relationship between the two variables. An *r* of either +1.00 or −1.00 indicates a perfect relationship, whereas an *r* of .00 indicates that the variables are unrelated. If the sign of *r* is positive, the two variables are said to be *positively related.* As the values for variable *X* increase, those for variable *Y* also tend to increase. Conversely, when the sign of *r* is negative, variables are said to be *negatively related;* in this instance as values for one variable increase, those for the other tend to decrease. The correlation between height and weight, based on the data in Table 4.2, is +.87, indicating a strong positive relationship; as height increases so does weight.

Plotting a relationship graphically will often impart a better feel for it. Figure 4.2 presents diagrams of several of the correlations just discussed. In the diagrams each entry point corresponds to two values determined for the given subject, the value of variable *X* and that for variable *Y*. In perfect relationships all the points fall on a single straight line: if we know the value of only one of the variables for an individual, we can state with certainty the value of the other variable. Similarly, when the correlation is relatively large, there is only a small degree of scatter about the line of perfect correlation. The values tend to scatter increasingly and become dispersed as the correlations become lower. When the correlation reaches .00, knowledge of a person's score on one variable tells us nothing about his or her score on the other.

The results of any correlational investigation, like those of the experiment, can be evaluated for their statistical significance. Correlations that could be expected to occur by chance alone fewer than five times in one hundred are conventionally spoken of as being statistically significant. In general, as the size of the correlation coefficient increases, the result is more and more likely to be statistically significant.[2]

Although it is much more widely used in the field of abnormal psychology than the experiment, the correlational method has a serious

[2] Whether a correlation attains statistical significance also depends on the number of observations that were made. The greater the number of observations, the smaller *r* needs to be in order to reach statistical significance. Thus a correlation of $r = .30$ is statistically significant when the number of observations is large, for example, 300, although it would not be significant if only 30 observations have been made.

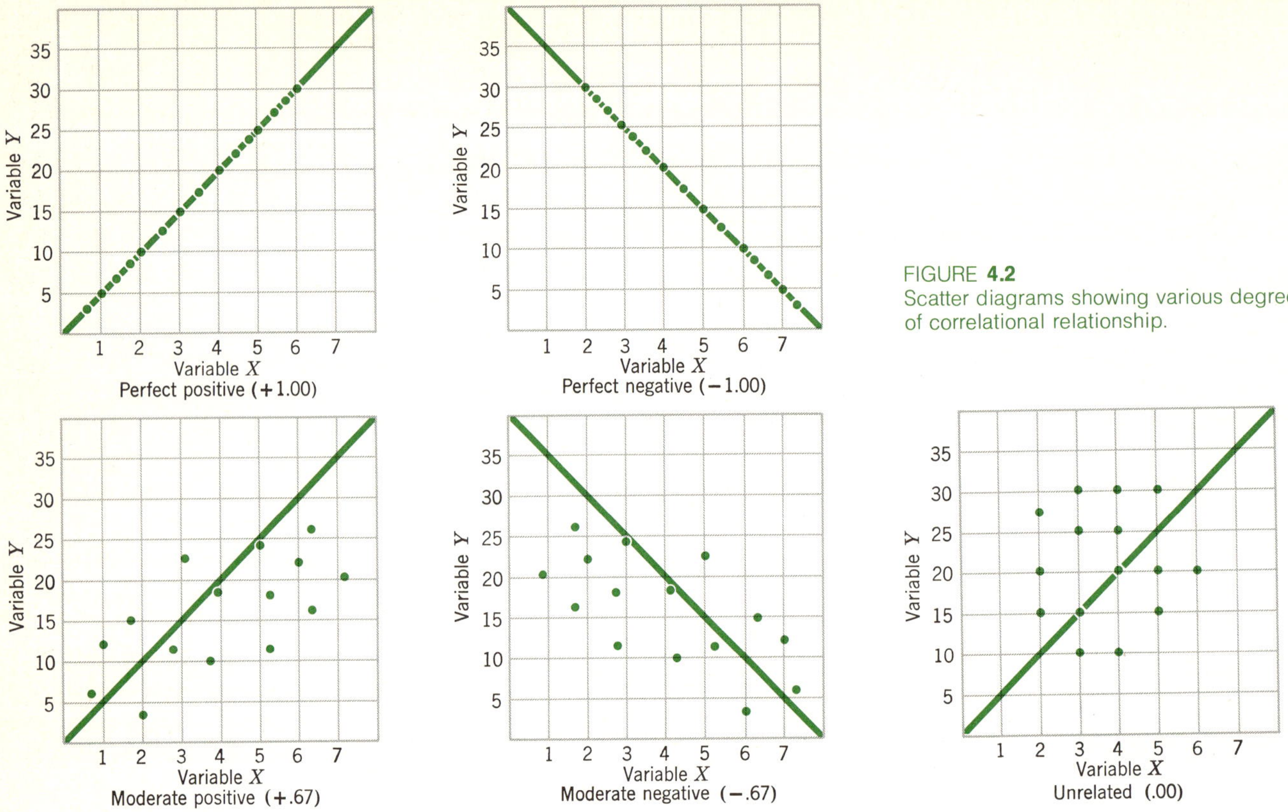


FIGURE **4.2**
Scatter diagrams showing various degrees of correlational relationship.

flaw—it does not allow us to determine cause-effect relationships. But so-called "organismic variables" such as sex, age, social class, and body build are exceedingly difficult or impossible to manipulate in an experiment, for both practical and moral reasons. Moreover, the direct manipulation of certain variables might be acceptable at some levels but not at those found in the natural environment. For example, inflicting mild pain or discomfort might (or might not) be an ethically legitimate experimental procedure, but it would clearly be unethical to induce extremely painful but psychologically significant experiences of the kind people are only too often subjected to. Finally, as we have already indicated, the experimental production of any kind of serious psychopathology would clearly be indefensible. Thus the correlational technique is the major strategy used in research studying the vagaries of psychopathology. By this technique the psychopathologist can determine whether the responses and characteristics of a person correlate with his or her abnormality as compared with those of control group members who are considered normal.

Many investigators have compared the performances of schizophrenics and normal people on laboratory tasks such as proverb interpretation and size estimation (for example, Kopfstein and Neale, 1972). Often these investigations are not recognized as correlational, perhaps because the subjects come to a laboratory for testing. Yet a comparison of a diagnostic group with some control group is not an experiment: no variable has been manipulated, since the schizophrenics had already been classified as abnormal before they took the tests.

### Directionality and third-variable problems

A correlation cannot be interpreted in causal terms because of two major problems of interpretation, the *directionality problem* and the *third-variable problem*. With respect to directionality, a sizable correlation between two variables tells us only that they are related or tend to covary with one another, but we do not really know whether one is caused by the other, or even if they are at all causally related. For example, correlations have been found between the diagnosis of schizophrenia and social class; lower-class people with emotional problems are more frequently diagnosed as schizophrenic than are middle- and upper-class people. One possible explanation is that the stresses of living in the lower social classes produce the behavior that is subsequently labeled schizophrenic. But a second and perhaps equally plausible hypothesis has been advanced. It may be that the disorganized behavior patterns of schizophrenic individuals cause them to lose their jobs and thus to become impoverished. The problem of directionality is present in many correlational research designs; hence the often-cited dictum "Correlation does not imply causation."[3]

As for the third-variable problem, it may be that neither of the two variables studied in the correlation produces the other. Rather, some as yet unspecified variable or process may be responsible for the correlation. Consider the following example, which points out an obvious third variable.

> *. . . One regularly finds a high positive correlation between the number of churches in a city and the number of crimes committed in that city. That is, the more churches a city has, the more crimes are committed in it. Does this mean that religion fosters crime or does it mean that crime fosters religion? It means neither. The relationship is due to a particular third variable–population. The higher the population of a particular community the greater . . . the number of churches and . . . the frequency of criminal activity (Neale and Liebert, 1973, p. 86).*

Are there any solutions to the directionality and third-variable problems? In general, the answer is yes, although the solutions are only partially satisfactory and do not permit unambiguous causal inferences to be made from correlational data (Neale and Liebert, 1973). In the field of abnormal psychology, there are in fact fewer problems with directionality than with third variables. If, for example, we find that schizophrenia is correlated with slowness to react, few people would argue that slow reactions cause schizophrenia. The possibility that the relationship is produced by a third variable, such as drugs, remains very real, however (see Box 4.1). For this reason we shall discuss ex post facto analysis, the technique which is most often used in attempting to control third variables.

### Ex post facto analysis

In ex post facto analysis subjects are matched on a third variable in an effort to simulate experimental procedures. For example, the investigator may be comparing the performance of schizophrenics and hospital aides on a test of cognitive ability. Let us assume that the schizophrenics are found to perform much more poorly than the aides. Clearly, the investigator is interested in attributing the difference between the two groups to the fact that one group is schizophrenic and the other not. Because the variable of interest,

[3] Although correlation does not imply causation, the determination of whether or not two variables correlate may allow for the *disconfirmation* of certain causal hypotheses. That is, *causation does imply correlation*. For example, if an investigator has asserted that cigarette smoking causes lung cancer, he or she implies that lung cancer and cigarette smoking will be positively correlated. Studies of the two variables must show this positive correlation, or the theory will be disproved.

## BOX 4.1 The Problem of Controlling for Drug Effects in Correlational Research with Institutionalized Patients

Schizophrenics are very likely to be on a heavy regimen of tranquilizing medicine. Comparing them with normal people is complicated by the fact that drugs might well introduce differences between the two groups that have nothing to do with schizophrenia. This problem has been approached in several ways. First, if hospital authorities will cooperate, the schizophrenic patients may be withdrawn from their drug regimen for several weeks, the period of time that is required for the drug to leave the body completely. Chapman (1963), however, has noted that the hospital staff may object to the increased pathology manifested by certain patients when medication is withdrawn. Because the greater number of disturbing symptoms of these patients upsets or threatens members of the staff responsible for them, pressure is brought to bear on the investigator to put these patients back on their medicine. The sample of patients remaining off the drug at the end of the "drying out" period is thus a biased one, comprised of individuals with a schizophrenic diagnosis who did not react adversely to the termination of medication.

A second strategy of investigators is to withhold medication from newly admitted patients until a given study has been completed. But in addition to the possible ethical considerations raised by such a procedure, a large percentage of newly admitted patients are already taking medication. Moreover, many new patients are in such a disorganized state that they cannot participate in psychological research. This second strategy has been applied rather infrequently.

Finally, some investigators have tried to assess the potential effects of drugs by correlating level of dosage with the ability of the schizophrenic to perform an experimental task. Since only the schizophrenic and not the control group is likely to be medicated, the correlation is calculated only within the schizophrenic group. If a significant relationship emerges—for instance, the higher the dosage, the poorer the performance—it might be argued that schizophrenics perform more poorly than controls because of their medication. Such an argument is flawed, however. The relationship between dosage level and performance may be produced by a third variable, such as severity of pathology, for patients showing the most severe symptoms may also be those who are given the most medication. Thus the practical problem of controlling for the effects of drugs remains unsolved in most investigations of psychiatric patients.

schizophrenia, has not been manipulated, however, the presence of a third variable may affect the results. By ex post facto analysis the investigator attempts to match subjects on what seem particularly plausible third variables. In the example we are considering, variables such as social class, intelligence, and years of education are likely candidates as factors for such a matching process. If the effects of these variables can be eliminated, the investigator can with more confidence attribute any differences between the two groups to the presence of schizophrenia in one of them.

The ex post facto technique, however, cannot entirely eliminate the problem of the third variable. First, regardless of the number of variables on which matching occurs, there can be no guarantee that some other unknown variable is not the important controlling factor determining the differences between the two groups. In other words, the term "third variable" is really a misnomer, for *any* number of variables might account for the observed effects in a way that is masked by the correlational research design.[4]

The ex post facto technique is also subject to other difficulties. For example, matching may drastically reduce the generality or external validity of any conclusions that may be drawn from a study. Let us assume that schizophrenics generally complete less schooling than do hospital aides. Noticing this fact, the investigator decides to match subjects on amount of education in order to eliminate the effects of this variable as a potential confound. He or she may then be forced to select for study only the schizophrenics who have educational levels close to those of the hospital aides. Thus the researcher ends up studying an *unrepresentative subpopulation* of schizophrenics. The results of such an investigation cannot be generalized to the entire population of schizophrenics, for the subjects who were studied have, on the average, completed more education than most schizophrenics.

With no viable alternative method available, investigators who study clinical groups must rely on correlational techniques. But they must always keep in mind that certain differences between clinical groups and control groups may make the correlations very difficult to interpret.

[4] This is but one illustration of why scientists seldom make absolute statements. There always seems to be a qualification that must be added in any scientific generalization or conclusion.

## Mixed Designs

The experimental and correlational research techniques that we have just discussed can be combined in what is called a *mixed design*. In a mixed design subjects who can be divided into two or more discrete and typically nonoverlapping populations are assigned as groups to different experimental conditions. The two different types of populations, for example, schizophrenics and neurotics, constitute correlational variables. That is, the variables schizophrenia and neuroticism were not manipulated, nor were they created by the experimenter, and they can only be correlated with the manipulated conditions, which are true experimental variables.

To illustrate how a mixed design is applied, we shall consider an investigation of the effectiveness of three types of therapy (the experimental variable) on psychiatric patients who have been divided into two groups on the basis of the severity of their illnesses (the correlational, nonmanipulated variable). The question was whether the effectiveness of the treatments varies with the severity of illness. The hypothetical results from such a study are presented in Figure 4.3. The b part of the figure shows the results obtained. The a part illustrates the misleading conclusions that could have been drawn from this research if the patients had not been divided into those with severe and less severe illnesses. Thus Figure 4.3a indicates that treatment 3 produced the greatest amount of improvement when the patients were not separated into groups on the basis of the severity of their illness. When no

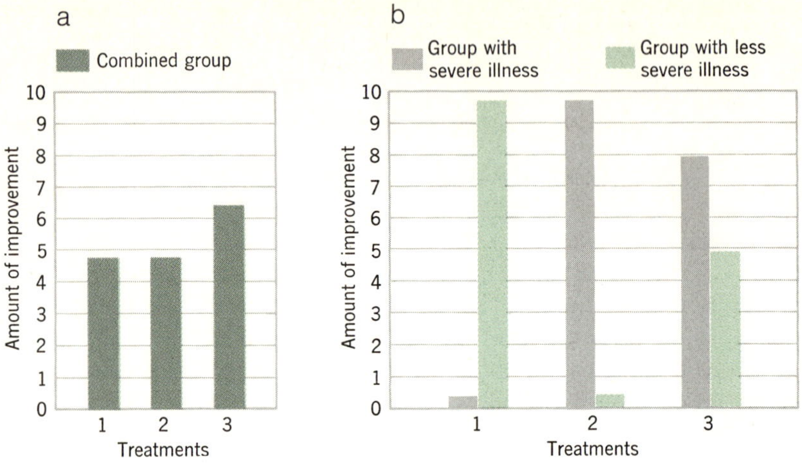


FIGURE **4.3**
Effects of three treatments on patients whose symptoms are severe and less severe. The amount of improvement brought about by each treatment varies, depending on how it is administered. When the severity of the illness is not known, the patients are treated together (a). When the severity is known, they are divided into two groups and treated separately (b).

information about differential characteristics of the patients is available, treatment 3 would be preferred. When the severity of the patients' difficulties is considered, however, treatment 3 would no longer be the therapy of choice for *any* of the patients. Rather, as seen in Figure 4.3b, for those with less severe illness treatment 1 would be selected and for patients with more severe illness treatment 2 would be preferred. Thus a mixed design can identify which particular treatment applies best to which group of subjects.

The results of mixed designs are analyzed by the same statistical procedures that are employed with pure experimental designs, tempting us to interpret the results as if all the variables were, in fact, manipulated. As we have previously noted, however, one of the variables in a mixed design (severity of illness in our example) is not manipulated. Therefore the problems we have previously noted in interpreting correlations are to be found in interpreting the results of mixed designs as well.

## Single-Subject Research

Research does not always have to be conducted on *groups* of people. In this section we shall consider research designs for studying a single subject. Two major procedures have been developed, the *case study* and *single-subject experiment.*

The strategy of relying on a single subject appears to violate many of the principles of research designs that we have discussed. No control group can act as a check on a single subject, and the individual who does serve as our research participant cannot, of course, have been randomly assigned to a particular experimental situation. Moreover, generalizations will be difficult because the findings may relate to a particular or unique aspect of the one individual whose behavior we have explored. Hence the study of a single individual would appear unlikely to yield any findings that could possess the slightest degree of internal or external validity. But, as we shall see, the study of a single subject *can* be an effective research technique for certain purposes.

### The case study

In making a case study, the clinician collects historical and biographical information on a single individual. Although case reports from practicing clinicians usually lack the degree of control and objectivity of research done by other methods, these descriptive accounts have played some important roles in the study of abnormal behavior. Specifically, the case history has been used in each of the following ways: (1) to demonstrate important, often novel, methods or procedures of interviewing, diagnosis, and treatment; (2) to provide a detailed account of a rare or unusual phenomenon; (3) to disconfirm allegedly universal aspects of a particular theoretical proposition; and (4) to generate hypotheses that can be tested through controlled research.

A famous case history of *multiple personality* reported by Thigpen and Cleckley in 1954 serves several of the foregoing purposes. The investigators described a patient, "Eve White," who displayed at various times three very distinct personalities.

Eve White had been seen in psychotherapy for several months because she was experiencing severe headaches accompanied by blackouts. Her therapist described her as a retiring and gently conventional figure. One day during the course of an interview, however, she changed abruptly and in a surprising way.

> *As if seized by sudden pain, she put both hands to her head. After a tense moment of silence, both hands dropped. There was a quick, reckless smile, and, in a bright voice that sparkled, she said, "Hi there, Doc!" The demure and constrained posture of Eve White had melted into buoyant re-*

*pose. . . . This new and apparently carefree girl spoke casually of Eve White and her problems, always using she or her in every reference, always respecting the strict bounds of a separate identity. . . . When asked her name, she immediately replied, "Oh, I'm Eve Black" (p. 137).*

After this rather startling revelation, Eve was observed over a period of fourteen months in a series of interviews that ran to almost a hundred hours. During this time still a third personality, Jane, emerged. At first Jane appeared to be only a composite of the two Eves, but later she became a well-integrated person in her own right.

The case of Eve White, Eve Black, and Jane constitutes a valuable classic in the literature because it is one of only a few detailed accounts of a rare phenomenon, multiple personality. Moreover, in addition to illustrating the phenomenon itself, the original report of Thigpen and Cleckley provides valuable details about the interview procedures that they followed; and it sheds light on the way in which the woman's behavior may have developed and how the treatment progressed in this one case of multiple personality.[5]

As an example of how the case history can be used effectively to demonstrate various methods of treatment, we include an excerpt from the case study of a mute psychotic woman. Through a combination of reinforcement and imitative learning procedures, she was successfully coaxed to speak clearly and loudly enough to be understood (Neale and Liebert, 1969). The excerpt provides reasonably detailed information about a novel aspect of the procedure that was developed and thus serves as the basis for its further application by others.

During these sessions a device was introduced to facilitate the patient's acquisition of more audible responses. From the beginning of treatment Martha's low volume has posed a constant problem. . . . This puts a heavy load on the discriminative capacity of T (the therapist), [making it difficult to know when the responses were correct and should be rewarded]. The device consisted of a microphone, amplifier, and neon light. T controlled the volume necessary to turn on the light by a rheostat. If one of Martha's responses was insufficient in volume, she was asked to repeat the response. Food was withheld until Martha's volume increased sufficiently to turn on the light.

The effect of this device was dramatic. Martha's volume increased markedly and this change was maintained throughout subsequent sessions. On session 13, when the light was first introduced, Martha produced 47 responses which did not turn on the light. On session 17, however, only 3 responses were produced which were not of sufficient volume (pp. 831–832).

[5] Chris Sizemore, in a book recently published (Sizemore and Pittillo, 1977), has cast serious doubt on the accuracy of Thigpen and Checkley's original account. This woman—the real Eve White—claims that, following her period of therapy with these two men, her personality continued to fragment. In all, twenty separate and distinct "strangers" came to inhabit her body at one time or another. One set of personalities would weaken and fade, to be replaced by others. During a single day and night she might become a number of these persons in split-second, midsentence switches that resembled flipping television channels. The debilitating round robin of changes and the fierce battle for dominance among her selves filled her entire life.

Case histories can provide especially telling instances that negate an assumed universal relationship or law. Freud, for example, initially believed that his female patients' reports of sexual assaults by their fathers or uncles were accurate descriptions of events, and moreover that these events had a bearing on the problems being treated. Later, on the basis of a chance finding that the supposed sexual assailant of one of his patients could not have been physically present at the time indicated, he came to recognize that some of these sexual assaults were fantasies. This single case provided a negative instance and led Freud to reject his previously held belief that his patients' recollections of early sexual assaults were necessarily true.

Finally, the case study plays a unique and important role because it is very often exploratory in nature. Circumstances are permitted to "vary as they will," with the often desirable revelation of new and perhaps important hypotheses that could not have been uncovered in a more controlled investigation.

> . . . *It is a serious mistake to discount the importance of clinical experience per se. There is nothing mysterious about the fact that repeated exposure to any given set of conditions makes the recipient aware of subtle cues and contingencies in that setting which elude the scrutiny of those less familiar with the situation. Clinical experience enables a therapist to recognize problems and identify trends that are usually beyond the perception of novices, regardless of their general expertise. It is at this level that new ideas will come to the practitioner and often constitute breakthroughs that could not be derived from animal analogues or tightly controlled investigations. Different kinds of data and different levels of information are obtained in the laboratory and the clinic. Each is necessary, useful, and desirable (Lazarus and Davison, 1971, p. 197).*

Thus case studies often provide important hypotheses which experimenters can later subject to more controlled investigation. In the presentation of a case history, however, the controls for confirming one hypothesis and ruling out alternative hypotheses are usually absent. To illustrate this lack of validity, let us consider another case that received a great deal of public attention, in the 1950s, the case of "Bridey Murphy."

When hypnotized, a sedate New England woman "regressed," apparently beyond her early childhood and back into an earlier life in which she claimed to be Bridey Murphy, an Irish lass. Under hypnosis the woman was able to report, in a distinct Gaelic brogue, many remarkable details of a town in Ireland which she had never visited. Her case history supposedly demonstrated a true instance of reincarnation. Later, however, it was learned that the woman had been reared, in part, by an Irish maid who had described to her most of the long-ago happenings later reported under hypnosis. The maid had also provided an excellent model for the brogue that the hypnotized subject used so convincingly. In this instance the reincarnation hypothesis presented by the case history was discounted.

### Single-subject experimental designs

The experimental method, which we have previously discussed in connection with groups of subjects, may also be applied with a single subject, improving on the internal validity of the case report. A method developed by Tate and Baroff (1966) for reducing the self-injurious behavior of a nine-year-old boy, Sam, serves as an example. The lad, who had been diagnosed as psychotic, engaged in a wide range of self-injurious behavior, such as banging his head against the floors and walls, slapping his face with his hands, punching his face and head with his fists, hitting his shoulder with his chin, and kicking himself. Despite his self-injurious behavior, Sam was not entirely antisocial. In fact, he obviously enjoyed contact with other people and

A teaching box used to increase a child's attention span. When the boy is attending and working well, the therapist rewards him with a small piece of food.

would cling to them, wrap his arms around them, and sit in their laps. This affectionate behavior gave the investigators the idea for an experimental treatment.[6]

The study ran for twenty days. For a period of time on each of the first five days, the frequency of Sam's self-injurious actions was observed and recorded. Then on each of the next five days the two adult experimenters accompanied Sam on a short walk around the campus, during which they talked to him and held his hands continuously. The adults responded to each of Sam's self-injurious actions by immediately jerking their hands away from him and not touching him again until three seconds after such activity had ceased. The frequency of the self-injurious acts was again recorded. As part of the experiment, the schedule was then systematically reversed. For the next five days there were no walks, and Sam's self-afflicting behavior was again merely observed. Then for the last five days the experimenters reinstated their experimental procedure. The dramatic reduction in undesirable behavior induced by the treatment is shown in Figure 4.4. Such designs, usually referred to as *reversal* (or ABAB) *designs,* involve the careful measurement of some aspect of the subject's behavior during a

[6] The use of the adjective experimental in this context prompts us to distinguish between two different meanings of the word. As applied to the methods that have been discussed, the adjective refers to the manipulation of a variable that allows conclusions of a cause-effect relationship to be drawn. But here the word refers to a treatment whose effects are unknown or only poorly understood. Thus an "experimental drug" is one about which we know relatively little; however, such a drug might well be used in a correlational design.

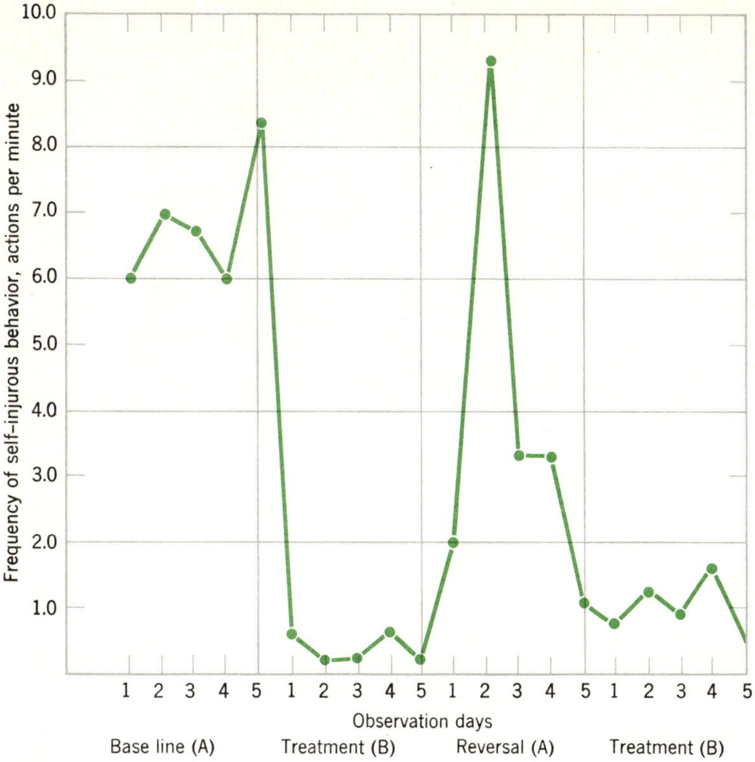


FIGURE **4.4**
Effects of a treatment for injurious behavior, in an experiment with an ABAB single-subject design. Adapted from Tate and Baroff, 1966.

given time period, the base line (A), during a period when a treatment is introduced (B), during a reinstatement of the conditions that prevailed in the base line period (A), and finally during a reintroduction of the experimental manipulation (B). If behavior in the experimental period is different from that in the base line period, reverses when the experimentally manipulated conditions are reversed, and "re-reverses" when the treatment is again introduced, there is little doubt that the manipulation, rather than chance or uncontrolled factors, has produced the change.

The reversal technique cannot always be employed, however, for the initial state of a subject may not be recoverable, as when treatment produces an irreversible change. Moreover, in studies of therapeutic procedures, reinstating the original condition of the subject or patient would generally be considered an unethical practice. Most therapists would be extremely unwilling to act in any way that might bring back the very behavior for which a client has sought help, merely to prove that a particular treatment was indeed the effective agent in changing the behavior.

When the reversal technique does not apply, the *multiple-base-line* procedure, wherein two or more behaviors are chosen for study, is the method of choice. For example, if a child has "learning problems," both mathematical and reading performances might be selected as the two areas for treatment. When observing the child, the investigator may notice that he or she is inattentive during lessons and proceed to collect base line data on the degree of attentiveness during *both* mathematics *and* reading sessions. Rewards are then given the child for attention paid to the mathematics lessons but not for attention paid during reading sessions. Again, the attentiveness of the child during both kinds of lessons is measured. Finally, in a third phase of the experiment, the child is rewarded for attention paid during reading as well as mathematics lessons.

A hypothetical pattern of the attentiveness of the child during the course of the experiment is shown in Figure 4.5. If such a pattern were indeed obtained, it would provide convincing evidence that the introduction of reward, and not other factors, was responsible for modifying the child's behavior. Had some uncontrolled environmental influence improved the child's attention, it presumably would have worked equally well during both mathematics and reading classes. Moreover, if reward were not the agent responsible for change, attentiveness during mathematics lessons would not have markedly improved as compared to attentiveness during reading sessions. Thus, by choosing two base lines of behavior to be modified (hence the term multiple base lines), the investigator was able to eliminate certain possible sources of invalidity.

As indicated earlier, even though an experiment with a single subject demonstrates an experimental effect, no generalization may be possible. The fact that a particular treatment works for a single subject does not necessarily imply that the treatment will be universally effective. If the search for more widely applicable treatment is the major focus of an investigation, the single-subject design has a serious drawback. It may well help investigators to decide whether large-scale research with groups is warranted, however.

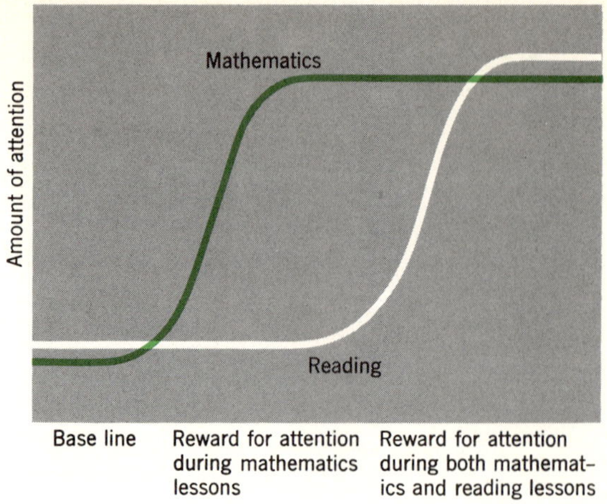


FIGURE **4.5**
Outcome of a multiple-base-line, single-subject experiment that rewarded attention, initially during lessons in mathematics, ultimately during both mathematics and reading instruction.

## Summary

Science represents an agreed-upon problem-solving enterprise, with specific procedures for gathering and interpreting data in order to build a systematic body of knowledge. Scientific statements must have the following characteristics: they must be testable in the public arena, they must entail reliable observations, and although they may infer unobservable processes, the concepts inferred must be linked to observable and measurable events or outcomes.

It is important to consider the various methods that scientists employ to collect data and arrive at conclusions. The experimental method entails the manipulation of independent variables and the careful measurement of their effects on dependent variables. An experiment usually begins with a hypothesis to be tested. Subjects are generally assigned to at least two groups: an experimental group, which experiences the manipulation of the independent variable, and a control group, which does not. If differences between the experimental and control groups are observed on the dependent variables, we can conclude that the independent variable had an effect. Furthermore, it is important to ensure that experimental and control subjects do not differ from one another before the introduction of the independent variable; thus they are usually assigned randomly to groups. Experimenters must guard against bias by keeping themselves unaware of what group a given subject is in, experimental or control. If these conditions are met, the experiment has internal validity. The external validity of the findings, whether they can be generalized to situations and people not studied within the experiment, can be assessed only by performing similar experiments in the external domain with new subjects.

Since most variables in abnormal psychology cannot be experimentally manipulated, correlational methods are the important means of conducting research. Statistical procedures allow us to determine the extent to which two or more variables correlate or co-vary. Unlike experimental findings, however, conclusions from nearly all correlational studies cannot legitimately be interpreted in cause-effect terms, although there is great temptation to do so.

Mixed designs are combinations of experimental and correlational methods. For example, two different kinds of patients (the correlational variable) may be exposed to various treatments (the experimental variable).

Finally, a single individual can be studied in several ways. Clinical case studies serve unique and important functions in psychopathology, such as allowing rare phenomena to be studied intensively in all their complexity. Certain single-subject experimental designs that expose one subject to different treatments over a period of time provide scientifically acceptable information.

A science is only as good as its methodology. Thus students of abnormal psychology must appreciate the rules that social scientists currently abide by if they are to be able to evaluate the research and theories that form the subject matter of the remainder of this book.

# part two

# anxiety and depression

# chapter 5

## VIEWS ON ANXIETY



*How would you like to be a tame, somewhat shy and unaggressive little boy of nine, somewhat shorter and thinner than average, and find yourself put three times a week, every Monday, Wednesday, and Friday, as regularly and inexorably as the sun sets and the sky darkens and the globe turns black and dead and spooky with no warm promise that anyone anywhere ever will awaken again, into the somber, iron custody of someone named Forgione, older, broader, and much larger than yourself, a dreadful, powerful, broad-shouldered man who is hairy, hard-muscled, and barrel-chested and wears immaculate tight white or navy-blue T-shirts that seem as firm and unpitying as the figure of flesh and bone they encase like a mold, whose ferocious, dark eyes you never had courage enough to meet and whose assistant's name you did not ask or were not able to remember, and who did not seem to like you or approve of you? He could do whatever he wanted to you. He could do whatever he wanted to me (Heller, 1966, p. 236).*

This excerpt from Joseph Heller's second novel, *Something Happened,* portrays the terrified helplessness of a nine-year-old boy who has to interact every other school day with a burly gym teacher. As described by his equally fearful father, the youngster has an overwhelming anxiety about his gym class, a situation into which he is forced and from which he cannot escape, a situation which makes demands on him that he feels utterly unable to meet. Once again a gifted novelist captures the phenomenology—the direct experience—of an important human emotion in a way that speaks vividly to each of us.

There is, perhaps, no other single topic in abnormal psychology that is as important and controversial as anxiety. This emotional state is considered a symptom of almost all psychopathologies and in particular of the neurotic disorders. Furthermore, anxiety plays an important role in the study of the psychology of normal people as well, for very few of us go through even a week of our lives without experiencing in at least some measure what we would all agree is the emotion anxiety or fear. But the briefer periods of anxiety that beset the normal individual are hardly comparable in intensity or duration, nor are they as debilitating, as those suffered by the neurotic.

In the theoretical and research literature the terms anxiety, fear, nervousness, and tension seem to be employed interchangeably. Those of a psychoanalytic persuasion prefer to reserve the term anxiety for fear that is experienced in the absence of external danger; most learning theorists, on the other hand, apply the term anxiety to fear learned in the presence of specific harmless stimuli (for example, Maher, 1966). There is much inconsistency. For our purposes we shall employ all these terms interchangeably, specifying only the conditions that seem to elicit a given response. Thus we shall have occasion to speak of unrealistic anxiety or fear and neurotic anxiety or fear, in contrast with realistic anxiety or fear and objective anxiety.

## The Assessment of Anxiety

### Methods of Measurement

Besides their overriding concern about how to apply the term anxiety, psychopathologists have needed to measure the emotion. They rely on three methods: self-report questionnaires, observation of overt behavior, and physiological measurements.

Allowing subjects to describe the phenomena of their emotions in their own terms makes it difficult to compare their experience with those of others and, even more important, to quantify what they say. Researchers have therefore devised various *self-report questionnaires* which attempt to direct the individual's impressions into standardized terms. The following are some sample items from the Taylor Manifest Anxiety Scale (Taylor, 1953), which consists of fifty items drawn from the MMPI.

| | |
|---|---|
| *I work under a great deal of strain.* | <u>True</u> False |
| *I am usually calm and not easily upset.* | True <u>False</u> |
| *I sweat very easily even on cool days.* | <u>True</u> False |
| *I always have enough energy when faced with difficulty.* | True <u>False</u> |
| *My sleep is restless and disturbed.* | <u>True</u> False |

An anxious person would underline the true and false responses as indicated. The test is scored by simply summing the number of "anxious" responses made by the subject. This score is then assumed to represent the person's general level of anxiety.

The second means of assessing anxiety is to *observe overt behavior* for reactions and movements that are believed to reflect the internal emotional state. A person would be judged anxious when he or she can be observed to tremble, perspire, bite his or her nails, or flee from a situation—in short, when behaving in ways assumed to reflect anxiety. We have already described in Chapter 3 how anxiety can be measured by watching and recording overt behavior. The observers trained to administer Paul's (1966) Timed Behavioral Checklist for Performance Anxiety (see page 82) time-sampled the overt behavior of subjects in a stressful situation, recording instances of twenty indices of anxiety whenever they were observed.

*Physiological measurements* of activities of the autonomic nervous system and the output of certain endocrine glands also indicate level of anxiety. Some physiological changes that supposedly indicate anxiety can be seen by even a casual observer, for example, rapid breathing and sweating, but they may also be monitored with sophisticated instruments for more precise determinations (see Box 5.1). The availability of sensitive electronic as well as chemical instrumentation has encouraged researchers to define anxiety in physiological terms.

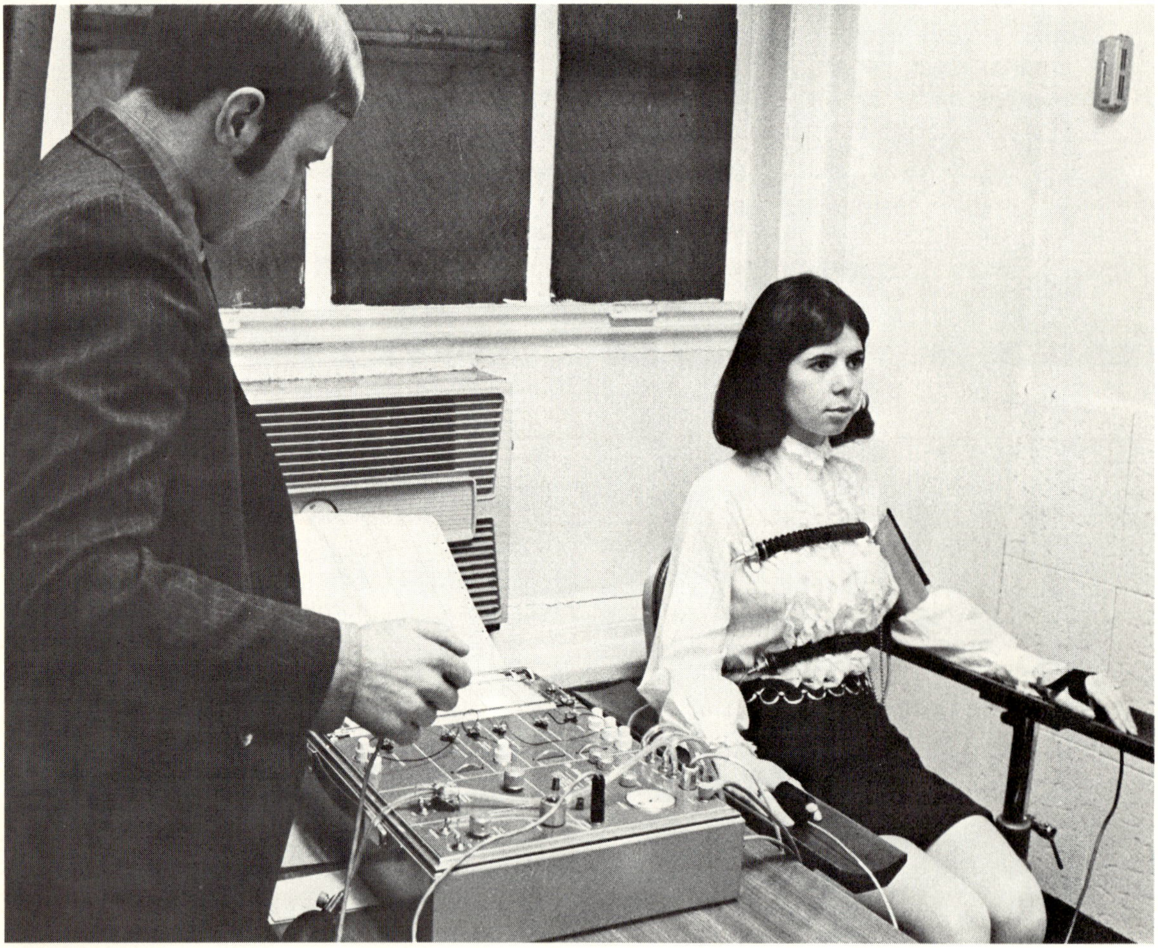

The autonomic nervous system activity of this young woman—heart rate, respiration,and electrodermal responses—are being recorded by the polygraph.

## BOX **5.1** Measurement of Autonomic Nervous System Activity

The mammalian nervous system can be considered to have two relatively separate functional divisions: the somatic or voluntary, and the autonomic or involuntary. Because the autonomic nervous system is especially important in the study of emotional behavior, it will be useful to review its principal characteristics and the ways in which its activity can be monitored.

Skeletal muscles, such as those that move our limbs, are innervated by the voluntary nervous system. Much of our behavior, however, is dependent on a nervous system that operates generally without our awareness and has traditionally been viewed as beyond voluntary control. Hence the term autonomic. The autonomic nervous system (ANS) innervates the endocrine glands, the heart, and the smooth muscles which are found in the walls of the blood vessels, stomach, intestines, kidneys, and other organs. This nervous system is itself divided into two parts, the sympathetic and parasympathetic nervous systems (Figure 5.1), which sometimes work against each other, sometimes in unison. The sympathetic portion of the ANS, when energized, accelerates the heartbeat, dilates the pupils, inhibits intestinal activity, and initiates other smooth muscle and glandular responses that prepare the organism for sudden activity and stress. Indeed, some physiologists view the sympathetic nervous system as primarily excitatory, whereas the other division, the parasympathetic, is viewed as responsible for maintenance functions and more quiescent behavior, such as deceleration of the heartbeat, constriction of the pupils, and speeding up contractions of the intestines. Division of activities is not quite so clear-cut, however, for the parasympathetic system may be active during situations of stress. Animals, and humans to their consternation, may urinate and defecate involuntarily when extremely frightened.

The activities of the ANS are frequently assessed by electronic and chemical measurements and analyses in attempts to understand the nature of emotion. One important measure is heart rate. Each heartbeat generates spreading changes in electric potential which can be recorded by an electrocardiograph or on a suitably tuned polygraph. Electrodes are usually placed on both arms and lead to a galvanometer, an instrument for measuring electric currents. The deflections of this instrument may be seen as waves on an oscilloscope, or a pen recorder may register the waves on a continuously moving roll of graph paper. Both types of recordings are called electrocardiograms. More recently available is the cardiotachometer, a device that measures the precise elapsed time between two heartbeats and then instantaneously provides heart rate on a beat-to-beat basis. This technological advance is especially important for experimental psychologists, who are typically interested in bodily changes that occur over short periods of time in response to rapidly shifting circumstances. Generally a fast heart rate is taken to indicate increased arousal.

A second measure is electrodermal responding, sometimes referred to as the galvanic skin response (GSR). Anxiety, fear, anger, and other emotions elicit greater sweat gland activity. The electrophysiological processes in the cells of these glands change the electric conductance of the skin as well as producing sweat. There are two methods of measuring the electrodermal response. Skin potential may be measured by recording with surface electrodes the very small differences in electric potential that always exist between any two points on the skin. This voltage shows a pronounced rise after the sweat glands have been stimulated to activity. Or we may determine the current that flows through the skin when a known small voltage derived from an external source is passed between two electrodes pasted to the palm and back of the hand. This current also shows a pronounced increase after activation of the sweat glands. The percentage of change from the normal or base line reading is for either method the measure of reactivity. High conductance, or alternatively low resistance, is thought to reflect increased autonomic activity. Since the sweat glands are innervated only by the sympathetic nervous system, increased sweat gland activity indicates sympathetic autonomic excitation and is often taken as a measure of anxiety.

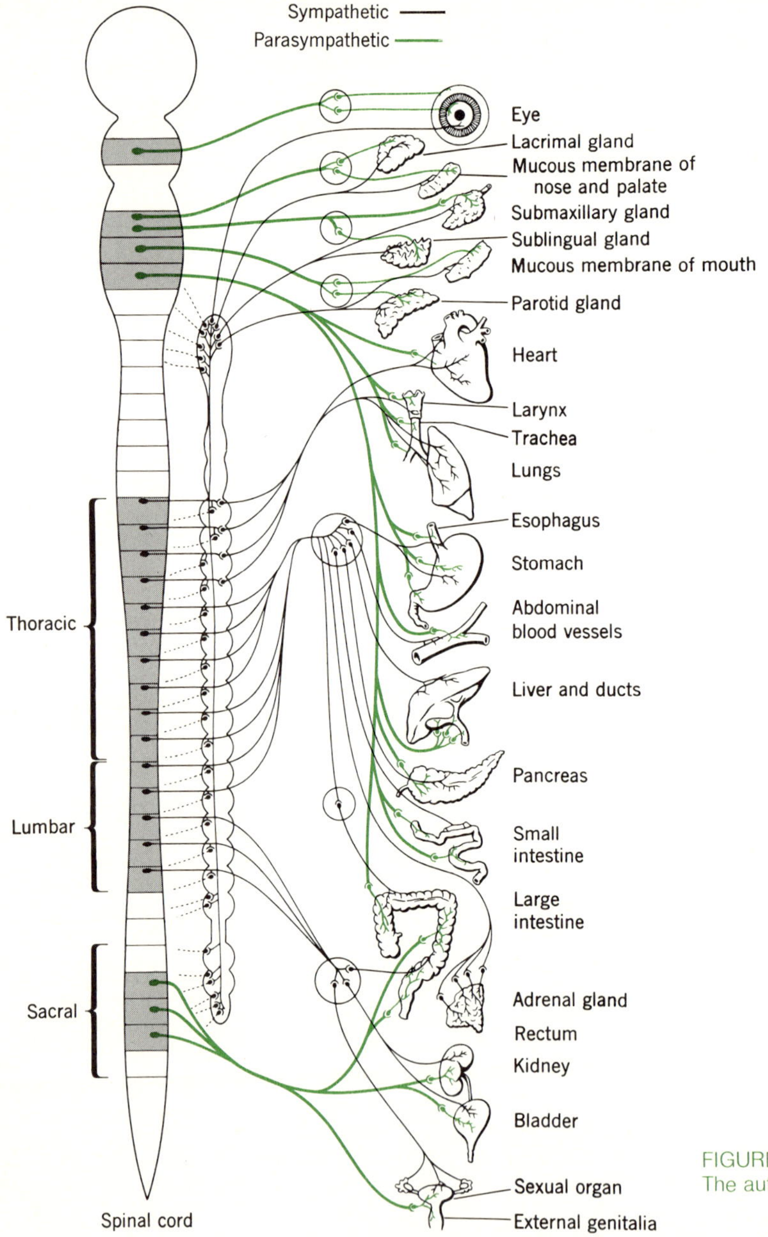


FIGURE **5.1**
The autonomic nervous system.

## Anxiety as a Construct

In the foregoing description of how anxiety is assessed, something important is left out, namely the situation in which measures are being taken. What would be revealed, for example, if recording electrodes were attached to a woman who is about to have sexual relations? Both before and during sexual activity the heartbeat is very likely to be faster, blood pressure higher, perspiration greater, and breathing more rapid, all physiological responses that are generally regarded as indicators of sexual excitement as well as of anxiety. But why would we not conclude that our female subject is, indeed, anxious as she contemplates sexual intercourse? As we shall see in Chapter 11, many people are debilitated by fear in sexual situations. How can an investigator distinguish rapid breathing that reflects sexual excitement from rapid breathing that reflects anxiety? Part of the answer necessarily lies in other observations being made concurrently. If at the time physiological measures are being taken the female subject convincingly reports that she is looking forward to what is to come, and if she ultimately derives great enjoyment from her sexual partner, we would almost certainly choose to interpret her rapid breathing and other physiological responses as indicating sexual arousal. The situation and her self-report of it must be taken into consideration.

Would that things were so simple, that a distinction between two emotional states could always be made on the basis of situational cues and verbal reports. The many measures of anxiety, besides being indicators of other emotional states, have been found time and again *not* to correlate well with one another (see Martin, 1961; Lang, 1969). In a stressful situation such as being threatened with painful electric shock, many people report being very nervous, but their heart rates may be lower rather than elevated. An individual taking an important examination for which he or she is ill-prepared may deny feeling anxious and yet be observed trembling. In spite of these *low* intercorrelations, many workers continue to regard the concept of anxiety as a useful one for organizing and interrelating data from numerous sources. Maher (1966) and Lang (1969), for example, consider anxiety to be a hypothetical *construct,* a convenient fiction or inferred state that mediates between a threatening situation and the observed behavior of an organism. They also assume that the construct is multifaceted or multidimensional, and that each facet is not necessarily evoked by a given stressful situation or always expressed to the same degree, thus explaining the low intercorrelations of the measures of anxiety.[1]

As a scientific construct, anxiety must be tied to observables, the conditions that produce it and the effects that follow its induction. For this reason Skinner (1953), as we indicated earlier (see page 44), argues that mediators are *not* essential in accounting for behavior. Since the construct of anxiety is linked to stimuli and responses, why not dispense with it and talk only of observables? Furthermore, might not the inference of an internal state lead us to believe that an adequate explanation has been found and thereby discourage the continuing search for ways to predict and control behavior?

These are cogent objections, and they have forced workers to exercise great care in their use of the anxiety construct. As noted in Chapter 4, investigators who employ mediators such as anxiety do so in hopes of better organizing their data and of generating hypotheses. We seldom find experimental psychologists speaking about anxiety without being able at any time to explain how and why they infer that the emotional state

[1] It is worth mentioning that similar problems of low intercorrelations plague other areas of psychology. For instance, one construct in conditioning is "strength of learning," often operationalized as the number of times a response continues to be evoked after reward has been withdrawn (extinction). Strength of learning, however, is not reflected in a single measurement; rather, the concept is measured in a number of different ways by different investigators. For example, they may set up their experiments to measure the force with which a response is made as it is being extinguished, the latency of responses while they are being extinguished, and so forth. Simultaneous measurements of numbers, force, and latency of the responses during extinction do not correlate highly. Once again, we can appreciate the need to specify what operations are to be identified as the measures of a particular construct.

exists. Furthermore, certain experiments would not be undertaken or could not be explained without inferring a mediating state.

To illustrate, let us consider an experiment reviewed by Rescorla and Solomon (1967). Dogs were taught to avoid a stimulus (CS) by pairing it repeatedly with a painful shock (UCS). Then they were totally paralyzed with injections of curare, a drug which prevents movement of the skeletal muscles. One group of animals, while paralyzed, were repeatedly presented with the CS, but shock did not accompany it. In Pavlovian, classical conditioning terms, these would be considered attempts to extinguish the conditioned response. Did these animals learn, while paralyzed and unable to move, that the CS was in fact no longer followed by shock? Phrased another way, did the previously learned fear of the CS undergo any extinction? The answer was obtained on a subsequent day when the dogs in this group had completely recovered from the curare and were confronted with the CS. The unshocked presentations of the CS a day or two earlier had indeed reduced avoidance behavior, even though no overt response could have occurred during the curare paralysis. The control animals, who had been confronted with no stimuli while paralyzed, did not show a reduction in avoidance behavior.

How do we account for such remarkable findings? Rescorla and Solomon deem it necessary, and legitimate, to infer a mediating fear which was lessened when the dogs were presented with the CS while paralyzed with curare. Clearly, something was being unlearned during the time that the dogs could not respond by avoiding the CS. By positing a mediating fear, we can make sense of these findings and relate them to a wealth of other theory and research. The experiment just described does indicate that anxiety, or fear, can be useful as an explanatory device. We turn now to major theories of how neurotic or unrealistic anxiety develops.

## Theories of Anxiety

### Psychoanalytic Theory

Freud proposed two different theories of anxiety. In the first formulation, published in 1895, neurotic anxiety was regarded as stemming from the blockage of unconscious impulses. Such impulses are blocked, for example, under conditions of extreme sexual deprivation. When repressed they become susceptible, according to Freud's first theory of anxiety, to transformation into neurotic anxiety. The first theory did not pay much attention to the circumstances surrounding the repression of an unconscious impulse. In his second theory, proposed in 1926, Freud made more explicit the situations that may cause the individual to repress an unconscious impulse, and he reversed the relationship between neurotic anxiety and repression. According to the first theory, neurotic anxiety develops through repression of impulses. In the second, anxiety about impulses signals the need for their repression. In a sense, according to the first theory we become anxious because we want things that we do not get; according to the second we are anxious because we fear our wants (Wachtel, 1977).

The second theory viewed birth as the prototypic anxiety situation, for the infant is flooded with excitation over which it can exert no control. After the development of the ego in the first year of life (see Chapter 2), anxiety becomes a signal of impending overstimulation. The person is warned that he or she is in danger of being reduced to an infantile state of helplessness through overstimulation by id impulses and other forces. Anxiety thus plays a functional role, signaling the ego to take action before being overwhelmed.

Three kinds of anxiety were differentiated by Freud, depending on their source. *Objective anxiety* refers to the ego's reaction to danger in the external world, as for example the anxiety felt when life is in real jeopardy. This kind of anxiety is the same as realistic fear. *Moral anxiety*, experienced by the ego as guilt or shame, is really fear of the punishment that the superego imposes for failure to adhere to standards of moral conduct.

The form of anxiety that has bearing on this chapter is *neurotic anxiety,* the fear of the disastrous consequences that are expected to follow if a previously punished id impulse is allowed expression. Neurotic anxiety has its roots in reality anxiety. As Hall (1954) has noted,

> *Neurotic anxiety is based upon reality anxiety in the sense that a person has to associate an instinctual demand with an external danger before he learns to fear his instincts. As long as instinctual discharge does not result in punishment, one has nothing to fear from [the instincts]. . . . However, when impulsive behavior gets the person into trouble, as it usually does, he learns how dangerous the instincts are. Slaps and spankings and other forms of punishment show the child that impulsive instinctual gratification leads to a state of discomfort. The child acquires neurotic anxiety when he is punished for being impulsive* (p. 67).

What must be added is that this conflict between desiring something and fearing that desire *has to be repressed,* or driven out of conscious awareness, before we can properly speak of neurotic anxiety.

Perhaps because Freud's early views on anxiety held that repression of id impulses would create neurotic anxiety, we often hear that Freudians preach as much gratification of impulses as possible, lest a person become neurotic. But this is not the case. For Freudians the essence of neurotic anxiety is *repression,* a tenet accepted nowadays even by the ego analysts, who attach less importance than did Freud to the id. Being unaware of conflicts lies at the core of neurotic anxiety, rather than simply being reluctant, unwilling, or unable to reduce the demands of the id. A celibate Catholic priest and a nun, for example, are not considered candidates for neurosis provided they consciously acknowledge their sexual or aggressive tendencies. Such individuals do not have to act on these felt needs in order to avoid neurotic anxiety. They must only remain aware of these needs whenever they vie for expression.

Initially, Freud postulated that traumatic childhood sexual experiences lay behind the neurotic problems of his patients. But by 1897 he came to realize that perverted acts against children would have to be far more prevalent than he was willing or able to assume. He then coupled his patients' reports of such trauma with his own supposition that the unconscious does not distinguish between fact and fantasy. Performing what one commentator has termed a stunning intellectual tour de force (Wachtel, 1977), he proposed that his patients were reporting to him not actual events of their childhood but rather their fantasies. Young children, he assumed, have to deal with intense feelings and longings. Ill-equipped to do so, they are prone to *invent* gratifications. Scientists, wishing to retain certain tenets of their theorizing, can be remarkably creative in adjusting particular aspects of their thinking in order to accommodate newly emerging evidence. By switching from actual events to fantasies, Freud was able to retain the importance of early childhood trauma in the etiology of neurotic anxiety.

### Forms of neurotic anxiety

Neurotic anxiety can be expressed in several ways: as free-floating anxiety, as phobia, and as panic reaction. The stimuli triggering all these expressions of neurotic anxiety are actually internal, stemming from previously punished id impulses. In free-floating anxiety the person appears to be apprehensive nearly all the time, in the absence of reasonable danger. The theory assumes that the person is actually afraid of his own id—which, of course, is with him all the time. Phobias are characterized by an intense irrational fear and avoidance of specific objects and situations, such as kittens, open spaces,

closed spaces, and nonpoisonous snakes. The feared objects and situations are hypothesized to be symbolic representations of the object or situation chosen earlier for gratification of the id impulse. That choice and thus the impulse were subsequently punished, and then the whole conflict was repressed. "Behind every neurotic fear there is a primitive wish of the id for the object of which one is afraid" (Hall, 1954, p. 65). Finally, neurotic anxiety may become manifest as a panic reaction, a sudden and inexplicable outburst of severe and prolonged fear.

### Defense mechanisms

According to Freud, the discomfort experienced by the anxious ego can be reduced by several maneuvers. Objective anxiety, rooted in reality, can often be dealt with by removing or avoiding in a rational way the danger in the external world. Neurotic anxiety, and sometimes moral anxiety, may be handled through an unconscious distortion of reality by means of one of the *defense mechanisms.* A defense mechanism is a strategy, unconsciously utilized, which serves to protect the ego from anxiety. Perhaps the most important is *repression,* whereby impulses and thoughts unacceptable to the ego are pushed into the unconscious. Repression not only prevents awareness but also keeps buried desires from growing up (Wachtel, 1977). By remaining repressed, these infantile memories cannot be corrected by adult experience and therefore retain their original intensity. Another defense mechanism, important in paranoid disorders (see Chapter 14), is *projection,* or the attribution to external agents of characteristics or desires that are possessed by an individual and yet are unacceptable to conscious awareness. For example, a hostile person may *unconsciously* find it aversive to regard herself as angry at others and may project her angry feelings onto them. Other defense mechanisms are *displacement,* redirecting emotional responses from a perhaps dangerous object to a substitute, for instance, kicking the cat instead of the boss; *reaction formation,* converting one feeling such as hate into its opposite, love; and *regression,* retreating to the behavioral patterns of an earlier age. All these defense mechanisms allow the ego to discharge some id energy while at the same time not facing frankly the true nature of the motivation. Because defense mechanisms are more readily observed than other symptoms of a disordered personality, they very often make people aware of their troubled natures and persuade them to consult a therapist.

### Evaluation

Since Freud's theorizing on anxiety is inseparable from other aspects of his system, as described in Chapter 2, the criticisms voiced in that chapter also relate to his first and second theories of neurotic anxiety. How, for example, can the theory be adequately tested? How can we determine whether the id and ego are actually in conflict? It is difficult to make predictions based on Freud's theory of anxiety, since it is stated in such general terms. When direct tests have been attempted, results have been discouraging (for example, Sears, Maccoby, and Levin, 1957). Similarly, attempts to find differences in the childhood experiences of normal and neurotic adults have not been successful (Frank, 1965). Finally, efforts to alleviate anxiety using methods suggested by psychoanalytic theory have only occasionally been proved successful by controlled evaluations (see Chapter 18).

## A Stimulus-Response Analysis of Anxiety: Mowrer and Miller

Until the 1930s American learning theorists, working mostly with rats, were little concerned with behavior commonly thought to reflect anxiety. The study of anxiety was at the time more actively pursued by clinicians, particularly Freudians. Mowrer (1939) is credited with bringing the study of anxiety into the mainstream of experimental psychology. Instead of construing anxiety in psychoanalytic terms, as the threat of or the flooding of the ego by excessive and worrisome stimulation from impulses, he suggested that we conceptualize anxiety as an internal response which can be learned by means of classical conditioning.

In a typical experiment rats were shocked repeatedly in the presence of a neutral stimulus such as the sound of a buzzer. The shock (UCS) produced a UCR of pain, fear, and flight. After several pairings the fear that was naturally produced by the shock came to be produced by the buzzer, fear being assumed the learnable component of the pain-fear response. It was observed that shock could eventually be omitted, and yet the animal would continue to react fearfully to the previously neutral stimulus (CS). In addition, it was shown (for example, Miller, 1948) that the rat could learn new responses to avoid the CS. The question became how to conceptualize the finding that animals would learn to *avoid* a harmless event. Mowrer (1947) and others suggested that in this, a typical *avoidance learning* experiment, two bits of learning were taking place (Figure 5.2): (1) the animal, by means of *classical* conditioning, learned to fear the CS, that is, acquired a fear-drive; and (2) the animal, by means of *instrumental* conditioning, learned an overt behavior to remove itself from the CS and thus to reduce the fear-drive.

### Fear as response, stimulus, and drive

The foregoing makes sense only in the context of an unfortunately complicated conceptual scheme. We have called fear a drive, but at the same time it is viewed as an internal response that can be classically conditioned. How can fear be both a response and a drive?

Additional assumptions are necessary. First, according to Mowrer and Miller, every response, whether overt or covert, produces its own stimulus. One way to understand this is to close your eyes and bend a finger; in spite of the absence of visual cues, you can *feel* that the finger is bent. In Mowrer-Miller terms, the response of finger bending generates its own perceptible stimuli. The sensations of bending the finger act as stimuli to the brain, telling it what has happened. Conceived in this way, a response such as fear can also be said to function as a stimulus.

Second, drives are said to be strong stimuli. Strong responses, like fear, generate their own stimuli which are strong and thus can be considered as drives. In this fashion fear as a strong internal response is said to function as a drive. Thus fear can be spoken of in three ways, as a response, as a stimulus, and as a drive.

Finally, as a drive, fear functions in the Mowrer-Miller learning model to impel the rat to run away from the sound of the buzzer. As the rat increases its distance from the CS, the fear-drive is reduced, which reinforces the avoidance behavior.

The essential features of this admittedly complicated theorizing are that fear or anxiety can be conceived of both as an internal response, which can be learned as observable responses are learned, and as a drive, which can mediate avoidance behavior. The study of anxiety, then, becomes amenable to the same kind of experi-

FIGURE **5.2**
Schematic representation of Mowrer's account of avoidance learning. The dotted line indicates that the subject is learning to fear the buzzer tone, the solid line that the subject is learning to avoid the shock.

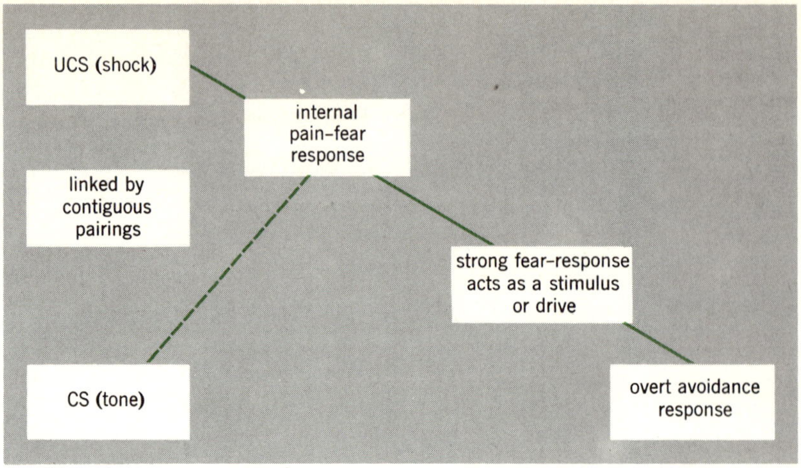

Neal Miller (above) and O. Hobart Mowrer (below), learning theorists who pioneered in studying anxiety experimentally.

mental analysis employed in the investigation of observable behavior. Mowrer and Miller have *assumed* that a useful way to talk about the internal life of organisms is to liken it to overt behavior. They speak of "mediating fear-responses" to point up this assumption that such responses, although inferred, are much the same as overt responses. Hopefully, the knowledge that has been gleaned about overt behavior can be transferred to the study of mental and emotional life (see Box 5.2). For instance, if we know that repetition of an overt response without reinforcement leads to the extinction of the response, we can predict, as Rescorla and Solomon have indeed shown, that repeated evocation of a fear-response while withholding the expected pain or punishment will reduce the fear. This is no trivial possibility, and indeed, as will be indicated in Chapter 19 when behavior therapy is discussed, treatments based on such reasoning have helped people become less fearful of animals and of objects and situations that do not merit such reactions.

Building on his own earlier work and that of Mowrer, Miller together with Dollard (1950) translated Freud's theorizing into mediational stimulus-response terms. In this fashion the anxi-

## BOX 5.2 A Study of the "Thinking-Response"

An early experiment by Miller (1935) was designed to assess the usefulness of construing mental life in mediational stimulus-response terms. Imagine that as a subject in his experiment you have shock electrodes attached to your left hand. The experimenter then repeatedly presents to you the letter T and the number 4; you are shocked every time the T is presented but never when the number 4 is presented. Careful electrophysiological recordings are made of your sweat gland activity when the letter T and the number 4 appear. Results show that you perspire more when T is presented than when 4 is presented. The most interesting part of the experiment then follows: you are instructed on a particular signal to *think* of either the letter T or the number 4. What happens?

Thinking about the letter T, which had previously been paired with shock, elicits more sweat gland activity than thinking about the number 4. This outcome is consistent with the assumption that the image or thought of the letter T functions in the same way as the actual physical presentation of the letter. Thought, like fear, is thus construed as a response, which in turn, functioning as a stimulus, can elicit the sweat gland activity.

ety that according to psychoanalytic theory is generated by excessive stimulation of the ego was conceptualized as an intense response which is learned as are other responses and which functions as a drive. Moreover, Dollard and Miller proposed that thinking could be similarly construed in mediational terms and spoken of as a "thinking-response" or "planning-response." The various defense mechanisms were similarly transformed into covert or unobservable avoidance responses, acquired and maintained because they manage to reduce anxiety or fear.

Many scientifically oriented workers in psychopathology have regarded Dollard and Miller's book as virtually useless, for what are the advantages of translating the problematical theory of Freud into other terms? Our own assessment is much more positive, for the work of Dollard and Miller offered the possibility of studying internal mental life by means that had proved useful in the study of overt behavior. Thus it is their *mode of analysis* that has been of enduring value, contributing to the intensive study of anxiety and its relationships to learning. Moreover, Dollard and Miller's book was an early application of the methods and principles of general psychology to a domain of human behavior historically considered the province of medicine.

### Evaluation

As useful as this learning model of the development of anxiety appears, it cannot be accepted uncritically. Mowrer and Miller assume that an association, or pairing, between a previously neutral stimulus and some sort of strong anxiety-provoking event will endow that stimulus with aversive properties. There are several problems with this classical conditioning formulation. In the first place, there is very little experimental evidence to support the contention that human beings can be classically conditioned to fear neutral stimuli even when such stimuli are paired repeatedly with primary aversive stimuli, such as electric shock (for example, Davison, 1968b). Ethical considerations have of course restrained most researchers from employing highly aversive stimuli with human beings, but considerable evidence indicates that fear is extinguished rather quickly when the CS is presented a few times without the reinforcement of moderate levels of shock (Bridger and Mandel, 1965; Wickens, Allen, and Hill, 1963). Moreover, only a few isolated studies have, in fact, shown that a human being can be conditioned to fear something that does not warrant being feared (for example, Watson and Rayner, 1920; Campbell, Sanderson, and Laverty, 1964), and there have been unsuccessful attempts to replicate the Watson and Rayner experiment in which Little Albert was made fearful of a rat (English, 1929). In the face of such weak and even contradictory evidence, it is surprising that the Mowrer-Miller theory continues to be viewed by some behaviorists as the sole explanation of neurotic fear and avoidance.[2]

Another criticism of the Mowrer-Miller view comes from Skinnerian learning theorists and behavior therapists. They have argued that avoidance behavior in humans can be eliminated simply by reinforcing people for approaching nearer and nearer the things they fear, without attending to any anxiety that is presumably motivating the avoidance (for example, Leitenberg et al., 1969). On the more theoretical level, Herrnstein (1969) has attempted to explain in nonmediational, Skinnerian terms the avoidance phenomena that mediational theorists have pointed to in justifying their inferences of anxiety or fear. In our view the argument between the Skinnerians and the mediationalists—yet another example of paradigm clash, although on a scale considerably more modest than that between behaviorism and psychoanalytic theory—is not likely to be settled on the basis of the data now available.

[2] When we discuss learning views of phobias in Chapter 6, a physiologically based hypothesis that may allow investigators to retain a classical conditioning hypothesis of neurotic anxiety (see Box 6.1) will be mentioned.

As a final criticism of the Mowrer-Miller theory, we should mention that although the past histories of many anxious people contain what appear to be classical conditioning experiences —for example, a woman may fear to leave her home after being terrified in the street—such experiences are just as often, perhaps more often, *not* found in the histories of those who are unrealistically or neurotically fearful. Grinker and Spiegel (1945) documented many examples of soldiers who suffered shell shock from the strains of modern warfare, but in the same war many men experienced the same horrors *without* developing neurotic symptoms. *Why?*

One answer lies in postulating a diathesis that could make some people more likely to develop anxiety when they encounter stress.

It has often been suggested that different experiences with stress in childhood account for different reactions to stress in adulthood. Soldiers who were not incapacitated in combat by extreme fear may have had a childhood that somehow prepared them well for emotional turmoil in adulthood. Unfortunately, the same data cited earlier in criticizing Freud's views on anxiety (Frank, 1965) are relevant here as well: it has not yet been shown that the development of neurotic anxiety in adulthood relates to particular childhood experiences.

Physiologically oriented researchers have sought predisposing factors or diatheses in the autonomic nervous system. Inasmuch as anxiety is generally assumed to involve this system, it is reasonable to propose that the learning of neurotic anxiety may depend importantly on its arousability, that is, the ease with which a given amount of stimulation triggers it. Soldiers who cannot cope with the ordeal of combat may have an autonomic nervous system that is especially sensitive to stress. This line of reasoning is plausible, but as yet little direct supporting evidence has been collected.

In sum, satisfactory answers to why only some people become chronically anxious remain to be found, and learning points of view, although adequate in accounting for much animal behavior, are as inadequate as the psychoanalytic paradigm in explaining why human beings sometimes fear what is harmless.

## Control and Helplessness: A Cognitive View

Mandler (1966) suggests that the feeling of not being in control is a central characteristic of all views of neurotic anxiety. According to psychoanalytic theory, the ego is anxious because it is threatened with overstimulation that it cannot control. Learning theory sees people as confronted with painful stimuli over which they have no control until they learn to avoid them. This concept of helplessness had earlier been examined by workers in several disciplines.

Richter (1957), in an article entitled "On the Phenomenon of Sudden Death in Animals and Man," quoted the following anthropological observation from an earlier source.

> *A Brazilian Indian condemned and sentenced by a so-called medicine man is helpless against his own emotional response to this pronouncement—and dies within hours. In Africa a young Negro knowingly eats the inviolably banned wild hen. On discovery of his "crime" he trembles, is overcome by fear and dies in twenty-four hours. In New Zealand a Maori woman eats fruit that she only later learns has come from a taboo place. Her chief has been profaned. By noon of the next day she is dead. In Australia a witch doctor points a bone at a man. Believing that nothing can save him, the man rapidly sinks in spirits and prepares to die. He is saved only at the last moment when the witch doctor is forced to remove the charm* (Basedow, 1925, cited in Richter, 1957, p. 191).

That such seemingly supernatural events actually occur in primitive societies may be difficult for us to believe. Walter Cannon, a well-known American physiologist of the earlier part of this century, studied reports of such "voodoo" deaths and concluded that they do take place and are worthy of serious scientific study (Cannon, 1942). He drew on his own experimental work involving the emotions of rage and fear in cats to propose that a person whose autonomic nervous system is maintained in a highly aroused state, with little opportunity for effective action to reduce the tension, may indeed die. The doomed individual has no means of controlling his fear of what he regards as all-powerful forces ordaining his death. Under such tension, Cannon suggested, certain vital bodily organs can be irreparably harmed, and death is actually brought about by severe fright.

Bettelheim's (1960) descriptions of the reactions of certain prisoners to conditions in the Nazi concentration camps indicate another instance in which a feeling of having lost control overcame people.

> *Prisoners who came to believe the repeated statements of the guards—that there was no hope for them, and that they would never leave the camp except as a corpse—*who came to feel that their environment was one over which they could exercise no influence whatever [*emphasis added*], *these prisoners were in a literal sense, walking corpses. . . . They were people who were so deprived of affect, self esteem, and every form of stimulation, so totally exhausted, physically and emotionally, that they had given the environment total power over them* (pp. 151–152).

These people, typically well educated, reacted in a helpless and self-defeating manner because they believed that they had no control over their lives.

Experimental psychologists have also been interested in related phenomena. Maier (1949) conducted a series of studies in which he presented unsolvable problems to laboratory rats. The behavior of the rats usually became rigid

A medicine man attempting to cure a paralyzed patient with a live chicken. He rubs the patient with the chicken to draw the paralysis or tension into it. Then the bird is killed and with it the evil that caused the paralysis. The medicine man can also instill life-taking tension and terror.

and stereotyped. They would jump in only one direction, even though this movement solved the problem only part of the time. Indeed, after the problem was made solvable, the animals frequently did not recognize the solution and continued instead to jump in only one direction.

The studies just mentioned have an important drawback, however; another group of animals was not allowed control over the same aversive situation. The earliest experiment designed to allow one group of animals control and another group none was performed by Mowrer and Viek (1948). Rats were trained to obtain food by making a particular instrumental response. Then they were all shocked at the feeding place. One group was able to terminate the shock by jumping. Each member of the second group was yoked to, that is, paired with, a member of the first so that the amount and duration of shock received by the pair were identical. But the members of the second group were unable to jump in a way that would give them control. The group of rats who had control over shock exhibited less fear than did those animals who were yoked helplessly to a partner.

Thus far we have examined anecdotal accounts of human helplessness and reports of animals rendered helpless by experiments. But rats are not people, and uncontrolled variables make it impossible to know what may really cause voodoo deaths and extreme apathy in prisoners. Fortunately, some experimental work has been done with human beings. Haggard (1943) showed that human subjects who administered electric shocks to themselves were less anxious about the situation than those who received the same amount and intensity of shock but who had no control over its administration. Further-

## BOX 5.3 Trait versus Situation Anxiety: Two Methods of Assessment

In Chapter 3 we contrasted assessing traits and assessing reactions to situations as means of gaining insight into psychopathology. A comparison of different self-report anxiety questionnaires provides an opportunity to examine further these two contrasting methods. The aim of the Taylor Manifest Anxiety Scale, mentioned earlier, is to place a person somewhere on a continuum with respect to anxiety. People scoring as highly anxious on the MAS are assumed to carry this personality trait around with them at all times. This ongoing level of tension helps to determine how they will behave as compared, for example, with individuals with a low MAS score.

Contrasting with this scale to measure the trait of anxiety is one developed by Mandler and Sarason (1952). Their scale assesses individual differences in anxiety during examinations. Like the MAS, the Test Anxiety Scale has contributed to our understanding of the relationship between anxiety and behavior. Individuals with high test anxiety scores typically perform more poorly on exams than do those who have low scores on this scale.

What are the relative contributions of trait and situation to individual differences in anxiousness? One questionnaire directed toward this issue, the S-R Inventory of Anxiousness, asks subjects to indicate how they respond to a number of situations (Endler, Hunt, and Rosenstein, 1962). The questionnaire presents situations such as "You are going to meet a new date," and "You are entering a competitive contest before spectators." Subjects indicate their degree of reaction to each of these situations on variables such as "Heart beats faster," "Perspire," and "Experience nausea." A complete sample item appears in Table 5.1.

### TABLE 5.1 Sample Item from the S-R Inventory of Anxiousness

"You are just starting off on a long automobile trip."

| | | | |
|---|---|---|---|
| 1. Heart beats faster | Not at all | 1 2 3 4 5 | Much faster |
| 2. Get an uneasy feeling | None | 1 2 3 4 5 | Very strongly |
| 3. Emotions disrupt action | Not at all | 1 2 3 4 5 | Very disruptive |
| 4. Feel exhilarated and thrilled | Not at all | 1 2 3 4 5 | Very strongly |

| | | | | |
|---|---|---|---|---|
| 5. Want to avoid situation | Not at all | 1 2 3 4 5 | Very strongly |
| 6. Perspire | Not at all | 1 2 3 4 5 | Perspire much |
| 7. Need to urinate frequently | No | 1 2 3 4 5 | Very frequently |
| 8. Enjoy the challenge | Not at all | 1 2 3 4 5 | Very much |
| 9. Mouth gets dry | Not at all | 1 2 3 4 5 | Very dry |
| 10. Become immobilized | Not at all | 1 2 3 4 5 | Very immobilized |
| 11. Stomach feels full | Not at all | 1 2 3 4 5 | Very full |
| 12. Seek such experiences | Not at all | 1 2 3 4 5 | Very much |
| 13. Have loose bowels | Not at all | 1 2 3 4 5 | Very loose |
| 14. Experience nausea | Not at all | 1 2 3 4 5 | Very nauseous |

This inventory therefore provides separate scores on how anxious people rate themselves in a variety of settings. They may, for example, consider themselves highly anxious about taking a test but not very anxious about situations involving interpersonal relations. The inventory is important because it allows us to examine how much variability in anxiety is attributable to situations and how much to the trait of anxiousness. Research with the questionnaire has indicated that neither situation nor trait alone can best account for anxiety. Instead, both the person's general anxiety level and the situations he or she fears must be determined. Such information allows us to consider the interaction of trait and situation and provides the most telling account of anxiety. Bowers (1973), after a comprehensive review of similar studies, came to a similar conclusion, that both general anxiety level and situations feared must be known, and then their interaction charted.

more, Pervin (1963) found that electric shocks that could be controlled were preferred to those that could not be controlled. Another study has indicated that intellectual performance is superior when the subjects believe that they have control over the order in which they take a series of tests (Neale and Katahn, 1968). And in yet another study, in which human beings received aversive stimulation, Staub, Tursky, and Schwartz (1971) indicated that "The ability to predict and control events in the environment is important for the comfort and safety of organisms. Consequently . . . lack of control . . . may become intrinsically aversive" (p. 157). In all this experimental work with human beings, stressful events that the subjects could exert some control over were less anxiety-provoking than those over which no control could be exercised.

The work done with both animals and human beings led Geer, Davison, and Gatchel (1970) to ask whether a relevant variable might be the subject's *perception* of his control in a situation rather than the actual amount of control exercised by him. The possibility existed that stress might be reduced if the experimental arrangements induced in the subject a *belief* that he can control the amount of stress to which he is subjected. This hypothesis seemed testable, at least for human beings, if a situation could be devised that would make people believe they have control over aversive stimulation, although in actuality they have none. If such subjects are less upset by aversive stimulation than are subjects who share the same actual lack of control, but not the false belief that they have control, it may be assumed that an important variable for human beings is their *perception* of the situation rather than its objective reality.

In a base line test to establish the amount of arousal produced by uncontrolled aversive stimulation, subjects were presented with a series of ten painful electric shocks. The subjects were instructed to press a switch as each shock was administered so that the amount of time it took them to react could be determined. Each shock lasted six seconds and was always preceded by a ready signal. The amount of arousal, as measured by the electrodermal response, was recorded for each shock (Figure 5.3). In the next part of the study, half of the subjects, those who were to perceive themselves in control, were told that the duration of each of the next ten shocks would be cut in half if their reaction time achieved a certain speed. Thus these subjects were led to believe that they could exert control over the next ten shocks. The remaining subjects were simply told that the next ten shocks would be of shorter duration. In actuality, the experimenter arranged for *all* subjects to receive three-second shocks in the second part of the experiment rather than six-second shocks, thus holding constant the actual amount of aversive stimulation.

As expected, during the second part of the experiment, the subjects who assumed that they could control the duration of shocks evidenced significantly less arousal, as measured by the GSR. Believing that they could control the amount of shock—even though they really were not able to do so—made the shocks easier to tolerate. These findings are all the more striking when we consider that the subjects who considered themselves in control might well have been *more* on edge because they were performing work—trying to reduce their reaction time—in order to achieve a goal. Other research indicates that such situations typically lead to an *increase* in the kind of arousal that was measured in this experiment. As Geer and his colleagues state at the end of their report, "Man creates his own gods to fill in gaps in his knowledge about a sometimes terrifying environment, creating at least an illusion of control which is presumably comforting. Perhaps the next best thing to being master of one's fate is being deluded into thinking that he is" (pp. 737–738).

The helplessness theory of anxiety suggests a novel explanation of how anxiety develops. Most theories propose that anxiety is a learned response to certain situations. But perhaps anxiety is instead an *unlearned* response to a situation in which people are helpless or believe they have

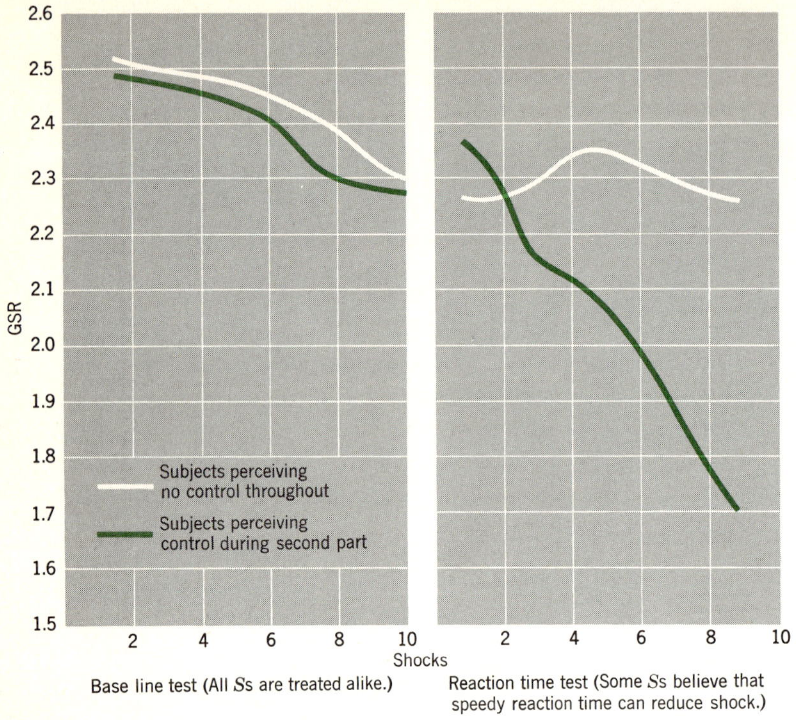


FIGURE **5.3**
Anxiety as a function of whether subjects perceive themselves as capable of shortening the duration of shock. Adapted from Geer, Davison, and Gatchel, 1970.

no control. Later, they may develop a certain amount of control by adopting behavioral repertoires that allow them to deal with challenging environmental situations. By this process they may *learn* both control and *how not to be anxious*.

The research and theory on control and helplessness offer a promising way to view anxiety. Not only does this theory have direct support from adequately controlled experiments, but it can also be applied to the views of Freud and the learning theorists. Moreover, contemporary ego analysts, whose therapies will be scrutinized in Chapter 18, seem also to emphasize the importance of control by the ego in reducing unwarranted fears. We will find the helplessness hypothesis very useful when examining neuroses, psychophysiological disorders, and depression.

## Summary

Anxiety is regarded as a construct, an unobservable state, which is considered useful in explaining and integrating data and in generating hypotheses regarding the way people deal with stress. An inferred state must be tied to observables; anxiety has been measured in terms of self-report, overt behavior, and physiological changes. Three major views of anxiety were examined. Freud considered anxiety to be a signal of the ego's incapacity to deal with stimulation from id impulses, external danger, and the prohibitions of the superego. Many learning theorists construe anxiety as an internal response that initiates behavior which will remove the individual from the situation that distresses him. We discussed also trait versus reaction to situation as they relate to anxiety and concluded that both should be considered in accounting for the anxiousness of people in a variety of life situations. Finally, the inability to minimize the feeling of helplessness in the face of threat is regarded as an important factor in determining the extent of anxiety. In fact, it may be the most important variable in explaining the high levels of anxiety found in neurotic disorders.

# chapter 6

## NEUROTIC DISORDERS

Phobias
Anxiety Neurosis
Obsessive-Compulsive Neurosis
Hysterical Neuroses
Existential Neurosis

By the late nineteenth century the fascination with hysteria and hypnosis was nearly a century old and had fostered considerable psychogenic theorizing on the etiology of certain emotional disorders. The prevailing belief was that the paralysis and anesthesia of hysteria had no organic cause and could be removed and even induced by hypnosis. Thus hysteria came to be regarded as some form of self-hypnosis. If one mental disorder had a psychological cause, so might others. Our historical review in Chapter 1 ended with Freud's collaboration with Breuer on *Studies in Hysteria,* a book important for the impetus it gave to the systematic study of psychological factors in mental disorders, particularly in the neuroses.

The prevailing conceptualizations of the neuroses, as elaborated in DSM-II and accepted by the greater part of the professional community, did indeed develop out of Freud's work with hysterics and other neurotics and are thus inextricably bound up with psychoanalytic theory. According to DSM-II,

> *Anxiety is the chief characteristic of the neuroses. It may be felt and expressed directly, or it may be controlled unconsciously and automatically by conversion, displacement and various other psychological mechanisms. Generally, these mechanisms produce symptoms experienced as subjective distress from which the patient desires relief* (p. 39).

The major neurotic syndromes are summarized in Table 6.1. As we review the more important types of neuroses, it will become clear how thoroughly Freudian theory permeates our conceptions of them. Indeed, the very existence of the category neurosis depends on Freudian theory. The problems evident in people with different "types of neurosis" are quite varied—the avoidance of phobics, the unwanted and uncontrollable thoughts of obsessives, the paralyses of conversion hysterics. How can such diverse problems be grouped into a single category? Although the observed symptoms differ,

TABLE **6.1**
Neurotic Disorders, According to DSM-II

| Type | Major symptom patterns |
|---|---|
| Phobic neurosis | Extreme fear and avoidance of an object or situation which the person is able to recognize as harmless |
| Anxiety neurosis | Anxiety felt in so many situations that it appears to be "free-floating," without specific cause |
| Obsessive-compulsive neurosis | Flooding of the mind with persistent and uncontrollable thoughts, or the compulsion to repeat a certain act again and again |
| Hysterical neurosis, dissociative type | Alterations in consciousness, manifested as amnesia, fugue, somnambulism, and multiple personality |
| Hysterical neurosis, conversion type | Paralysis, lack of sensation, and sensory disturbances without organic pathology |
| Neurasthenic neurosis | Chronic fatigue and weakness |
| Depersonalization neurosis | Feelings of unreality and estrangement from the self and the environment |
| Depressive neurosis | Extreme sadness in reaction to a specific event |
| Hypochondriacal neurosis | Preoccupation with bodily functions and with imagined illnesses |

all neurotic conditions are *assumed,* according to the psychoanalytic theory of neuroses, to reflect an underlying problem with repressed anxiety. Many psychopathologists have begun to question this assumption, however, and their doubts are reflected in the draft version of DSM-III, in which *the class neurosis no longer exists.* Instead, there are three new categories. The "Anxiety Problems" category includes several classes of disorders, such as phobias and obsessions-compulsions, in which a subjective feeling of anxiety is indeed present. In the remaining two categories—termed *hysterical disorders* in DSM-II—anxiety is not a key debility. The "Somatoform Disorders" category covers those in which physical problems, without an organic basis, are the primary symptoms. Included in the "Dissociative Disorders" category are multiple personality and amnesia, which are characterized by alterations in consciousness.

According to DSM-II, neurotic individuals commonly have problems in several areas of their lives. They feel inadequate and inferior and tend to avoid challenge rather than face it. They also lack insight into the motives for their behavior and are rigid rather than flexible in handling different problems. In varying circumstances they fail to adopt alternative, more appropriate courses of action. Neurotics have difficulty maintaining satisfying interpersonal relationships and suffer considerable guilt and unhappiness about the way they conduct themselves and their lives. This self-consciousness causes them to color their world in the light of their own distress. Minor obstacles and minor transgressions, their own and those of others toward them, loom very large indeed. And though neurotics see no way out of their own difficulties, they have enough self-knowledge to recognize that in some way their perceptions of the world are distorted and their reactions to it maladaptive.

Both learning theorists and psychoanalysts regard the symptoms just described as *derivatives* of neurotic anxiety. For example, Wolpe (1969), influenced heavily by the animal research on anxiety reviewed in the preceding chapter, considers the most important aspect of neurotic behavior to be fear of previously harmless stimuli, acquired through classical conditioning. The object of the fear must then be avoided. From this core of fear and avoidance, Wolpe would *derive* the remaining clinical symptoms of neurosis. Thus the agoraphobic, someone who is neurotically fearful of leaving the home, may well feel inferior, avoid challenge, respond in the same stereotyped way when confronted with different problems, have few friends, suffer great unhappiness and guilt, be anxious a great deal of the time, and remain unaware of the reasons for his or her behavior. Psychoanalytic theory would hold that these same symptoms are derived from what they consider to be the core of neurosis, the repression of childhood conflicts.[1]

[1] Omitted from the following discussion are neurasthenic neurosis, depersonalization neurosis, and hypochondriacal neurosis. Very few data exist concerning these categories. Depressive neurosis will be treated in Chapter 8.

## Phobias

Psychopathologists define a phobia as a fear-mediated avoidance, out of proportion to the danger posed by a particular object or situation. For example, when people are extremely fearful of heights, closed spaces, snakes, or spiders, provided there is no objective danger, the label phobia is likely to be applied to their avoidance and fear.

Over the years complex terms have been formulated as names for such unwarranted avoidance patterns. In each instance the suffix -phobia is preceded by a Greek word for the feared object or situation. Some of the more familiar terms are claustrophobia, fear of closed spaces; agoraphobia, fear of open spaces and of leaving the house; and acrophobia, fear of heights. More exotic fears have also been given Greek-derived names, for example, ergasiophobia, fear of writing; pnigophobia, fear of choking; and taphephobia, fear of being buried alive. All too often the impression is conveyed that we understand how a particular problem originated or even how to treat it merely because we have an authoritative-sounding name for it. Nothing could be further from the truth, however. As with so much else in the field of abnormal psychology, there are more theories and jargon pertaining to phobias than there are firm findings.

In comparison to other diagnostic categories, phobias are relatively common in the general population. For example, Agras, Sylvester, and Oliveau (1969) found a rate of 77 per 1000 in a population study done in New England. This same investigation, however, revealed that most of the phobias were relatively mild, only 2.2 per 1000 being rated as severely disabling. Indeed, many specific fears do not cause enough hardship to compel an individual to seek treatment. If a person with an intense fear or phobia of nonpoisonous snakes lives in a metropolitan area, he or she will probably have little direct contact with the feared object and may therefore not believe that anything is seriously wrong.

206 . ADVERTISEMENTS.

**WOMEN AND MICE**

The reason why a woman is afraid of a mouse is a profound mystery—indeed, it has never been very closely proved that she is. But some women are constantly in such a nervous irritable condition, that the slightest thing annoys and startles them. The cause of this unfortunate state of affairs is usually some functional derangement, some distressing or painful irregularity, some derangement or peculiar weakness incident to her sex; or it may be due to inflammation, ulceration, or displacement of some of the pelvic viscera or to other organic lesions peculiar to her sex. From whichever cause it may arise, Dr. Pierce's Favorite Prescription is a *positive remedy*, so certain in its curative results that its manufacturers sell it, through druggists, under a *guarantee* of its giving satisfaction in every case, or money paid for it will be *promptly refunded*. As a soothing and strengthening nervine, "Favorite Prescription" is unequaled, and is invaluable in allaying and subduing nervous excitability, irritability, exhaustion, prostration, hysteria, spasms, and other distressing nervous symptoms commonly attendant upon functional and organic disease of the womb. It induces refreshing sleep and relieves mental anxiety and despondency.

Copyright, 1888, by World's Dispensary Medical Association, Proprietors.

**Dr. Pierce's Pellets,** Anti-Bilious Granules, are Laxative or Cathartic, according to size of dose. By Druggists.

## The Psychoanalytic Theory of Phobias

As is true of many of the neuroses, Freud was the first to attempt to account systematically for the development of phobic behavior. According to Freud, phobias result from anxiety that is produced by repressed id impulses. The anxiety is displaced from the id impulse that is feared to an object or situation that has some symbolic connection to this threat. These objects or situations then become the phobic stimuli. A classic case, reported by Freud in 1909, was that of a five-year-old boy, Little Hans, who was afraid of horses and thus would not venture out of his home. The importance of this case is attested to by many psychoanalytic scholars. Ernest Jones, Freud's famous biographer, calls it "the brilliant success of child analysis" (1955, p. 289); and Glover, a respected scholar, terms it "a remarkable achievement . . . [constituting] one of the most valued records in psychoanalytic archives" (1956, p. 76).

Freud's analysis of Little Hans was based on information reported in letters written to Freud by the boy's father; Freud actually saw the child only once. Before the development of his phobia, when he was three, Hans was reported to have "a quite peculiarly lively interest in the part of his body which he used to describe as his widdler." When he was three and a half his mother caught him with his hand on his penis and threatened to arrange for his penis to be cut off if he continued "doing that." At age four and a half, while on summer vacation, Hans is described as having tried to "seduce" his mother. As his mother was powdering around his penis one day, taking care not to touch it, Hans said, "Why don't you put your finger there?" His mother answered "Because that would be piggish." Hans replied "What's that? Piggish? Why?" Mother: "Because it's not proper." Hans, laughing: "But it's great fun." These events were taken by Freud as proof that Hans had strong sexual urges, that they were directed toward his mother, and that they were repressed for fear of castration. According to the first theory of anxiety (see page 118), this sexual privation would ultimately be transformed into neurotic anxiety.

The first signs of the phobia appeared about six months later while Hans was out for a walk with his nursemaid. After a horse-drawn van had tipped over, he began crying, saying that he wanted to return home to "coax" (caress) with his mother. Later he indicated that he was afraid to go out because a horse might bite him, and he soon elaborated on his fears by referring to "black things around horses' mouths and the things in front of their eyes."

Freud considered this series of events to reflect Hans's oedipal desires to have his father out of the way so that he could possess his mother. His sexual excitement for his mother was converted into anxiety because he feared that he would be punished. Hans's father was considered the initial source of his son's fear, but the fear was then transposed to a symbol for his father—horses. The black muzzles and blinders on horses were viewed as symbolic representations of the father's eyeglasses and moustache. Thus, by fearing horses, Hans was said to have succeeded unconsciously in avoiding the fear of castration by his father—even though it was the *mother* who had threatened this punishment—while at the same time arranging to spend more time at home with his principal love-object, his mother.

There are many other details in the case study, which occupies 140 pages in Freud's *Collected Papers*. In our brief account we have attempted to convey the flavor of the theorizing. We agree with Wolpe and Rachman (1960) that Freud made large inferential leaps from the data of the case. First, the evidence for Hans's wanting sexual contact with his mother is minimal, making it debatable that Hans wanted to possess his mother sexually and replace his father. Second, there is little evidence that Hans hated or feared his father, and in the original case report it is stated that Hans directly denied any symbolic connection between horses and his father. This denial was interpreted as evidence *for* the connection, however. Third, there is no evidence, or any reason to believe, that intense

*"Why can't you be more like Oedipus?"*



sexual excitement was somehow translated into anxiety. Indeed, the fact that Hans became afraid of horses after being frightened by an accident involving a horse may be more parsimoniously explained by the classical conditioning model, which we shall now discuss.

## Behavioral Theories of Phobias

As in psychoanalytic theory, the primary assumption of all behavioral accounts of phobias is that such reactions are learned. But the exact learning mechanisms and what is actually learned in the development of a phobia are specified differently in the various behavioral theories.

### The classical conditioning model

Historically, Watson and Rayner's (1920) demonstration of the apparent conditioning of a fear or phobia in Little Albert (see page 124) is considered the model of how a phobia may be acquired. A major problem exists in the application of this model, however. The fact that fear was acquired by Little Albert in this particular study can *not* be taken as evidence that *all* fears and phobias are acquired through conditioning. Rather, the study demonstrates only the *possibility* that some fears *may* be acquired in this particular way.

As mentioned in Chapter 5, other attempts to demonstrate the acquisition of fear via classical conditioning have *not* been successful. For example, English (1929) attempted to condition fear in a fourteen-month-old girl by pairing the presentation of a duck with a loud noise. Despite fifty trials, no conditioned response to the duck was established. In a more extensive investigation, Bregman (see Thorndike, 1935) tried to condition fear in fifteen infants of about the same age as Little Albert, using various CSs and a loud bell as the UCS. Again, relatively few fears were acquired by the subjects. From an ethical point of view, it is fortunate that these workers failed to produce phobias in their young subjects.

In spite of these failures to replicate the Watson and Rayner demonstration, many learning theorists still construe phobias as acquired through classical conditioning. They have elaborated on the case of Little Albert by asserting that the classically conditioned fear of an objectively harmless stimulus forms the basis of an instrumental avoidance response. This formulation, based on the two-factor theory originally proposed by Mowrer (1947) and described in Chapter 5 (see page 121), holds that phobias develop from two related sets of learning. (1) Via classical conditioning, a person can learn to fear a neutral stimulus (the CS) if it is paired with an intrinsically painful or frightening event (the UCS). (2) Then, like the rat in the Miller experiment, the person can learn to reduce this conditioned fear by escaping from or avoiding the CS. It is assumed that this second kind of learning is instrumental conditioning; the response is acquired and maintained by its reinforcing consequences.

Certain clinically reported phobias seem to fit such a model rather well. For example, a phobia of a specific object has sometimes been reported to have developed after a particularly noxious experience with that object. Some people become intensely afraid of driving an automobile after a serious accident, or of descending stairs after a bad fall. Other phobias apparently originate in similar fashion.

> A young boy would often pass a grocery store on errands and when passing would steal a handful of peanuts from the stand in front. One day the owner saw him coming and hid behind a barrel. Just as the boy put his hand in the pile of peanuts the owner jumped out and grabbed him from behind. The boy screamed and fell fainting on the sidewalk.
>
> The boy developed a phobia of being grasped from behind. In social gatherings he arranged to have his chair against the wall. It was impossible for him to enter crowded places or to attend the theater. When walking on the street he would have to look back over his shoulder at intervals to see if he was closely followed (Bagby, 1922).

But other clinical reports suggest that phobias may also develop *without* prior frightening experience. Many individuals with severe fears of snakes, germs, airplanes, and heights report to clinicians that they have had no particularly unpleasant experiences with any of these objects or situations.[2] Similarly, many people who have had an unpleasant automobile accident or bad fall do *not* become phobic to these situations. Thus the classical conditioning model cannot account for the acquisition of all phobias.

Questions have also been raised whether laboratory avoidance behavior and phobic reactions are really analogous. It has been proposed that conditioned avoidance responses do resemble phobic reactions in that both appear to be particularly resistant to extinction. Once an avoidance response has been established in an animal, these responses tend to be repeated for long periods of time, even though the animal is never again shocked or directly encounters whatever else served as the UCS. The avoidance behavior is maintained in the absence of any direct traumatic experience. Similarly, clinical phobias also appear to persist for long periods of time, even though nothing bad ever happens to the person when he or she encounters the feared situation. Most of the work on which the accounts of avoidance learning are based, however, was done with dogs and rats. The resistance to extinction of avoidance responses appears to be somewhat species-specific. Other animals show wide differences in both the facility with which they acquire specific avoidance responses and their resistance to extinction of these responses (Bolles, 1970). Human beings, in particular, extinguish their laboratory fears very quickly once the UCS is omitted (see Chapter 5). Thus it may be hazardous to generalize about human behavior on the basis of that of infrahuman species, especially when the relevant behavior varies widely in these animals.

Another point of dissimilarity was noted by Costello (1970).

[2] Such accounts are called *retrospective* reports, that is, reports made by people looking back into their past, sometimes for many, many years. Since memory of long-ago events is often distorted, such reports must be viewed with some skepticism. The fact that many phobics cannot recall traumatic experiences with their now-feared objects may indeed be distortions of memory. Accounts of traumatic episodes may be questioned on the same grounds. Retrospective reports are discussed again on page 229.

> *Responses learned in the usual avoidance procedure are* adaptive [*emphasis added*] *because they enable the animal simply to avoid a noxious stimulus. If this were true also . . . of phobic behaviors, they could not be considered maladaptive and would not come to the attention of clinicians. But phobias are maladaptive because they prevent the occurrence of behaviors desired by the individual (e.g., the claustrophobic person cannot sit in a lecture theater or a cinema) and/or desired by society* (*as in the case of the child with school phobia*) (*p. 250*).

In sum, the data we have reviewed suggest that not all phobias are learned through classical conditioning. Such a process *may* be involved in the etiology of some phobias, but other processes must also be implicated in their development (see Box 6.1).

### Modeling

Phobic responses may also be learned through imitating the reactions of others. As we have previously noted (see page 44), a wide range of behavior, including emotional responses, may be learned by witnessing a model. The learning of phobic reactions by modeling behavior after that of another person is generally referred to as vicarious conditioning. In one study Bandura and Rosenthal (1966) arranged for subjects to watch another person, the model, in an aversive conditioning situation. The model was hooked up to an impressive-looking array of electrical apparatus. Upon hearing a buzzer, the model withdrew his hand rapidly from the arm of the chair and feigned pain. The physiological responses of the subjects witnessing this behavior were recorded. After the subjects had watched the model "suffer" a number of times, they showed an increased frequency of emotional responses when the buzzer sounded. The subjects began to react emotionally to a harmless stimulus even though they had had no direct contact with a noxious event.

Vicarious conditioning may also be extended to include the direct verbal instruction of phobic behavior. That is, phobic reactions can be learned through another's description of what might happen as well as by observing another's fear. As an example from everyday life, a mother may repeatedly warn her child not to engage in some activity lest dire consequences ensue. Vicarious examples can apparently be provided through words.

As with the classical conditioning formulation, however, vicarious learning experiments fail to provide an adequate model for all phobias. In the first place, the vicarious fear extinguishes quickly. Second, phobics who seek treatment do not often report that they became frightened after witnessing someone else's distress. And third, many people have been exposed to the bad experiences of others but have not themselves developed phobias.

### Operant conditioning

Finally, we may consider the possibility that phobic reactions are learned by virtue of the consequences they produce. Avoidance responses may be directly rewarded and thereby learned. For example, a child who wants to stay close to her mother may invent excuses so that she does not have to attend school. If the mother gives in to these excuses, the child is directly rewarded by the positive consequence of being allowed to stay home with her mother. In this instance fear is not mentioned as a mediator. The child avoids school simply because it produces favorable results.

Although some phobias may develop because of the payoff provided by the environment, the fact that many phobics suffer because they are compelled to avoid harmless situations strains the plausibility of the theory.

## Physiological Factors Predisposing to the Development of Phobias

Both psychoanalytic and learning theories look to the environment for the cause and mainte-

## BOX 6.1 Classical Conditioning and Preparedness

Perhaps the classical conditioning view of phobias would be more valid if modified slightly to take into account the fact that certain neutral stimuli may be more likely to become conditioned stimuli than others. Pavlov (1928) did not address this question, stating that ". . . every imaginable phenomenon of the outer world affecting a specific receptive surface of the body may be converted into a CS" (p. 88).

Seligman (1971) has suggested that phobias may well reflect classical conditioning to stimuli that an organism is physiologically predisposed to be sensitive to. Accordingly, classical conditioning experiments that show quick extinction of fear may have employed CSs that the organism is not well "prepared" to learn to associate with UCSs.

An example from the research that has given rise to this preparedness notion may make this hypothesis clearer. Garcia and his associates (Garcia, McGowan, and Green, 1972) found that rats could learn to avoid the *taste* of a given food if nauseated following its ingestion—even if the nausea did not begin for many hours. In contrast, they could not be negatively conditioned to the *sight* of food if they were nauseated in its presence but had not actually tasted it. Similarly, rats could readily learn to avoid a light paired with shock (a common experimental finding), but they could not learn to avoid taste paired with shock. Thus, as seen in Figure 6.1, gustatory sensations and illness (taste-nausea) are read-

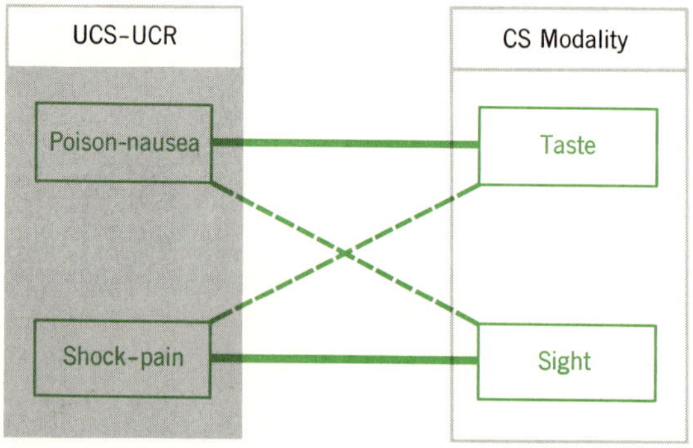


FIGURE **6.1**
The organism may be prepared through innate sensitivity to learn certain associations but not be prepared to learn others. Solid lines indicate easily made associations; dotted lines connect classes of stimuli that are difficult to associate.

ily associated, as are visual and tactile modalities (light-shock). But visual stimuli and illness (sight of food-nausea) and gustatory and tactile sensations (taste-shock) are not.

Seligman has provided a personal illustration of the operation of this process.

*Sauce Béarnaise is an egg-thickened, tarragon-flavored concoction, and it used to be my favorite sauce. It now tastes awful to me. This happened several years ago. . . . After eating filet mignon with Sauce Béarnaise, I became violently ill and spent most of the night vomiting. The next time I had Sauce Béarnaise, I couldn't bear the taste of it. At the time I had no ready way to account for the change, although it seemed to fit a classical conditioning paradigm: CS (sauce) paired with US (illness) and UR (vomiting) yields CR (nauseating taste). [Although I learned that flu had caused the nausea and others with me did not get sick . . .], I could not later inhibit my aversion (Seligman and Hager, 1972, p. 8).*

This and related research prompted Seligman to hypothesize that some associations, and thereby phobias, are easily learned by human beings and thus are not readily extinguished. Marks (1969), in a related observation, points to the *nonarbitrary* objects and events that human beings tend to be afraid of. People may have phobias of dogs, cats, and snakes—but few lamb phobics have been encountered. It is even more striking to consider how few people phobically avoid electrical outlets, even though they present certain dangers under specified circumstances.

Some more direct evidence for this position comes from a conditioning study in which different types of stimuli were used as the CS (Öhman, Erixon, and Löfberg, 1975). All subjects viewed three sets of pictures varying in content—snakes, houses, and faces. Half the participants received a shock (UCS) immediately after viewing each slide of snakes. The remainder received shocks after viewing slides either of houses or of faces. The GSR served as the CR and was analyzed for both the conditioning trials and for a subsequent extinction series. During the conditioning part of the study, the GSRs of the groups of participants receiving shocks after viewing slides of any of the three classes of stimuli were about the same. During extinction, however, the CR to the slides of houses or faces quickly diminished, whereas the CR to slides of snakes remained strong. Thus the CR was more durably associated with the sight of snakes, which is a fairly common elicitor of clinical phobias. The study suggests that people are "prepared" to acquire fears of snakes, given an unpleasant experience with them.

Seligman has also linked his preparedness theory to psychoanalytic concepts. He proposed that the kind of symbolism mentioned in psychoanalytic theory may one day be found to have a basis in the sensitivities of people and what they are prepared to associate and to learn. Hans, after all, came to fear horses after he saw one of them fall down in the street in a rather memorable incident. But he did not become afraid of the van which tipped over, and he must have observed other incidents involving other intriguing stimuli during his walks with the nursemaid. Although the symbolic connection with the father is still unclear unless Freud's hypothesis is accepted, it does seem significant that the particular incident mentioned in the case report loomed larger than others, and that in its aftermath Hans came to be afraid of horses. Even though not all investigators are convinced that people are prepared to acquire some conditioned responses to certain stimuli (see Bitterman, 1975; Evans, 1976), the preparedness hypothesis nevertheless appears worth exploring.

nance of phobias. Indeed, as already indicated, the primary assumption of both theories is that phobias—and in fact all neurotic disorders—are learned. But what is the best way to conceptualize this learning and, most importantly, why do some people acquire unrealistic fears whereas others do not, given similar opportunities for learning? Perhaps those who are adversely affected by stress have a physiological malfunction (the diathesis) that somehow predisposes them to develop a phobia following a particular stressful event.

### Autonomic nervous system

What characteristics may be important in determining the susceptibility of individuals to particular environment experiences? One way people may react differently to certain environmental situations is the degree to which their autonomic nervous systems become aroused. Lacey (1967) has referred to a dimension of autonomic activity which he calls stability-lability. Labile or "jumpy" individuals are those whose autonomic systems are easily aroused by a wide range of stimuli. Clearly, because of the extent to which the autonomic nervous system is involved in fear and hence in phobic behavior, a dimension such as autonomic lability would assume considerable importance. Since there is reason to believe that autonomic lability is to some degree genetically determined (Eysenck, 1957; Lacey, 1967), the heredity (see Box 6.2) of individuals may very well have a significant role in the development of phobias.

## BOX 6.2 Behavior Genetics

Life begins at the moment of conception when the *ovum,* the female reproductive cell, joins with the male's *spermatozoan,* producing the zygote or fertilized egg with its forty-six *chromosomes,* the number characteristic of the human being. Each chromosome is made up of thousands of *genes.* The genes are the carriers of the genetic information that is passed on from parents to child. Each cell of the human body will contain a full complement of chromosomes and genes in its nucleus.

Behavior genetics is the study of individual differences in behavior that are attributable in part to differences in genetic makeup. The total genetic makeup of an individual, consisting of genes, is referred to as the *genotype.* An individual's genotype is the unobservable, physiological genetic constitution, in contrast to the totality of observable characteristics which is referred to as the *phenotype.* The genotype is fixed at birth, whereas the phenotype changes and is generally viewed as the product of an interaction between the genotype and experience. For example, an individual may be born with the capacity for high intellectual achievement. Whether he or she develops this genetically given potential depends on such environmental factors as rearing and education. Any measure of intelligence (IQ) is therefore best viewed as an index of the phenotype.

On the basis of the distinction made between phenotype and genotype, we realize that various clinical syndromes are disorders of the phenotype. Thus it is not proper to speak of the direct inheritance of schizophrenia or neuroses. At most, only the genotypes of these

In family studies the investigator capitalizes on the degree of genetic similarity in family members. Shown here is a marked similarity in physical appearance.

disorders can be inherited. Whether these genotypes will eventually engender the phenotypic behavioral disorder will depend on environment and experience; a predisposition (diathesis) may be inherited but not the disorder itself.

The two major methods of study in behavior genetics are to compare members of a family and pairs of twins. Members of a family are compared because we can determine, on the average, how many genes are shared by two blood relatives. For example, children receive half their genes from one parent and half from the other. Siblings will, on the average, be identical in 50 percent of their genetic background. In contrast, relatives not as closely related share fewer genes. For example, an uncle shares 25 percent of the genetic makeup of his nephews or nieces. If a predisposition for a mental disorder can be inherited, a study of the family should reveal a correlation between the number of shared genes and the incidence of the disorder in relatives. The starting point in such investigations is to collect a sample of individuals who bear the diagnosis in question; these are referred to as *index cases* or *probands.* Then relatives are studied to determine the frequency with which the same diagnosis might be applied to them.

In the twin method dizygotic (DZ) and monozygotic (MZ) pairs of twins are compared. MZ twins develop from a single fertilized egg and are genetically identical. DZ pairs develop from separate eggs and on the average are only 50 percent alike genetically, actually no more alike than two siblings. MZ twins are always the same sex, but DZs or fraternal twins can be either the same sex or opposite in sex. Again, such studies begin with diagnosed cases and then search for the presence of the disorder in the other twin. When the pair of twins are similar diagnostically, they are said to be *concordant*. To the extent that a predisposition for a mental disorder can be inherited, concordance for the disorder should be greater in MZ pairs than in DZ pairs.

Although the methodology of the family and twin studies is clear, the data they yield are not always easy to interpret. Let us assume that neurotic parents have been found to produce more than the average number of neurotic offspring. Does this mean that neurosis is genetically transmitted? Not necessarily. The increased frequency of neurosis could as well reflect child-rearing practices and exposure of the children to neurotic adult models. Consider also a finding of greater concordance for schizophrenia among MZ than among DZ twins. Again, such data do not necessarily implicate heredity, since MZ twins, perhaps because they look so much alike, may be raised in a more similar fashion than are DZs, thus accounting for the greater concordance for schizophrenia among them. There are, however, special but infrequent cases that are not subject to the aforementioned problems: children reared completely apart from their abnormal parents and MZ twins reared separately from very early infancy. A high frequency of neurosis in children reared apart from their neurotic parents would offer convincing support for the theory that genetic factors figure in neurosis. Similarly, greater concordance among separately reared MZ twins than among DZ twins would offer compelling evidence that a predisposition for a disorder can be inherited.

### Genetic studies of neurosis

Several studies have questioned whether a genetic or innate factor is involved in neurosis or anxiety, although none has been directly concerned with whether such a factor is implicated in the formation of phobias per se. Brown (1942) investigated the incidence of neuroses in relatives of people who had already been diagnosed as neurotic. Consistent with the view that a predisposition for a disorder can be genetically transmitted, he found the incidence of neurosis in first-degree relatives—siblings, mothers, and fathers—to be 16.8 percent. In contrast, for a control group made up of nonneurotic individuals, the incidence of neurosis in first-degree relatives was only 1.1 percent. Rosenthal (1970) has summarized the available studies of the incidence of neurosis in the co-twins of neurotic probands. Again, consistent with the theory of genetic transmission, among monozygotic or identical pairs of twins there was a 53 percent concordance or similarity in diagnosis. Among dizygotic or fraternal pairs of twins there was only a 40 percent concordance.

These data do not unequivocally implicate innate factors, however. Although close relatives share genes, they also have considerable opportunity to observe one another. The fact that a son and his father are both afraid of heights may indicate not a genetic component but rather direct modeling of the son's behavior after that of his father. In sum, although there is some reason to believe that genetic factors are involved in the etiology of phobias, there has as yet been no clear-cut demonstration of the extent to which they may be important.

Identical or monozygotic twins are genetically identical. Fraternal or dizygotic twins are no more alike genetically than siblings and can be either the same or opposite in sex.

## Subclassification of Phobias

Up to now we have been discussing phobias as though they are alike in every respect except the object or situation that is fearfully avoided. Behaviorists have been remiss in not considering whether the differences between fearing a small animal and fearing the prospect of leaving the house are important. This neglect of the content of the phobia seems consistent with the fact that behaviorists take a *functional* stance rather than a topographical one (Wilson and Davison, 1969). Topography here means specification of the actual physical behavior. Thus avoidance of a snake is topographically different from avoidance of heights, for the simple reason that a snake is not a height. According to the functional approach adopted by most behaviorists, however, the two responses may be treated as equivalent because both perform the same function, removing the individual from a fear-eliciting situation. Within a functional framework fear of snakes and fear of heights are viewed as equivalent in the means by which they are acquired, in how they might be changed, and so on.

If behaviorists underplay the content of phobias, analysts go to the other extreme, seeing great significance in the phobic object as a symbol of an important unconscious fear. Little Hans, it will be recalled, was afraid of encountering horses if he went outside. Freud paid particular attention to Hans's reference to the "black things around horses' mouths and the things in front of their eyes." The horse was regarded as "standing for the father," who wore eyeglasses and had a moustache. Freud theorized that fear of the father had become transformed into fear of horses, which were then avoided by Hans. Countless other such examples might be cited; the principal point is that psychoanalysts believe that the content of phobias has important symbolic value.

Marks (1969) has an extensive scheme for classifying various phobias. He has noted many potentially important differences, which behaviorists have paid little if any attention to, and which analytically oriented workers have also ignored, but for other reasons. The variables examined by Marks are frequency, sex distribution, age of onset, whether or not additional symptoms are present, the course of the problem, and psychophysiological responses.

### Agoraphobia

A complicated syndrome, agoraphobia is a cluster of fears centering around open spaces. Fears of other situations such as shopping, encountering crowds, and traveling are often a part of agoraphobia. From a patient's point of view, agoraphobia is surely very distressing. Consider how limiting it must be to be afraid of leaving the house. Perhaps for this reason agoraphobia is the most common phobia seen in the clinic, constituting roughly 60 percent of all phobias examined. The restrictive nature of the syndrome forces the agoraphobic to seek help. Most agoraphobics are women, and the majority develop their problems in adolescence and early adulthood. Numerous other neurotic symptoms are also evident, including panic attacks, tension, dizziness, depression, depersonalization, and obsessions. Psychophysiological responses confirm the clinical impression that agoraphobics are subject to a rather diffuse, nonspecific anxiety. Recordings taken of their autonomic activity typically show high levels of arousal, even when they are supposedly relaxing (Marks, 1969).

### Social phobias

A social phobia is a collection of fears generally linked to the presence of other people. Eating, speaking, or virtually any other activity that might be carried out in the presence of others can elicit extreme anxiety. Although this phobia is not uncommon, social phobics seek help much less frequently than do agoraphobics. Women are seen in therapy for these difficulties slightly more often than are men. As might be expected, onset is generally during adolescence, when social awareness and interaction with others are assuming much more importance in the person's life. Few additional symptoms are generally present, although recordings of psychophysiological responses indicate rather high levels of arousal.

### Animal phobias

Although easy to define, phobias of animals are the rarest seen in clinical practice. Only 3 percent of all phobics have them. The majority of animal phobias occur in women, and they begin very often in early childhood (Marks and Gelder, 1966). It is likely that among boys and girls animal phobias are quite common, but that boys extinguish their phobias because of social pressures. Thus in adulthood the problems are much more common in women. Recordings of autonomic activity while the subject is at rest indicate that arousal levels are within the normal range. Presenting the phobic stimulus, however, does increase arousal.

### Miscellaneous specific phobias

Included in this catch-all category are phobias of heights, thunder, darkness, travel, closed spaces, driving, infections, running water, and the like. Few other symptoms are generally present. Further evaluation of this category is not possible because few data have been collected.

### Phobias of childhood

Most children have many fears that are apparently "outgrown" in the normal course of development. For example, Jersild, Markey, and Jersild (1933) interviewed 398 children of ages five to twelve. Fears of the following were expressed by substantial numbers: supernatural events, for example, ghosts and witches, 19.2 percent; being alone, in the dark, or in a strange place, being lost, 14.6 percent; attack or danger of attack by animals, 13.7 percent; bodily injury, falling, illness, operations, hurt and pains, 12.8 percent. The results of a similar study of generally younger children appear in Figure 6.2.

Should these fears be regarded as phobias? For the most part, the answer would appear to be no. The childhood fears reported in various studies are transitory, and little information is given to indicate that the feared situation is actively avoided. It is generally agreed that to be classified as a phobia, a fear should be of substantial duration and should entail definite avoidance. One situation, however, attending school, does appear to generate a fear in children that warrants the name phobia. Waldfogel (1959) offers the following definition of school phobia.

> *School phobia refers to a reluctance to go to school because of acute fear associated with it. Usually this dread is accompanied by somatic symptoms with the gastrointestinal tract the most commonly affected. . . . The somatic complaints come to be used as an auxiliary device to justify staying at home and often disappear when the child is reassured that he will not have to attend school. The characteristic picture is of a child nauseated or complaining of abdominal pain at breakfast and desperately resisting all attempts at reassurance, reasoning, or coercion to get him to school. In its milder forms, school phobia may be only a transient symptom; but when it becomes established, it can be one of the most disabling disorders of childhood, lasting even for years (pp. 35–36).*

The frequency of school phobias has been estimated at 17 per 1000 children per year (Kennedy, 1965), and they are more common in girls than in boys. The most prevalent view of the etiology of school phobia may be termed a *separation anxiety* theory. From one investigation, which consisted of an intensive study of several cases, the following account emerged (Johnson et al., 1941).

First, some environmental event, which may be related to the school setting itself, elicits increased anxiety in the child. At the same time the mother becomes increasingly anxious about some problem of her own. A dependent relationship between mother and child may then conspire to increase further the anxiety that occurs naturally when mother and child are separated

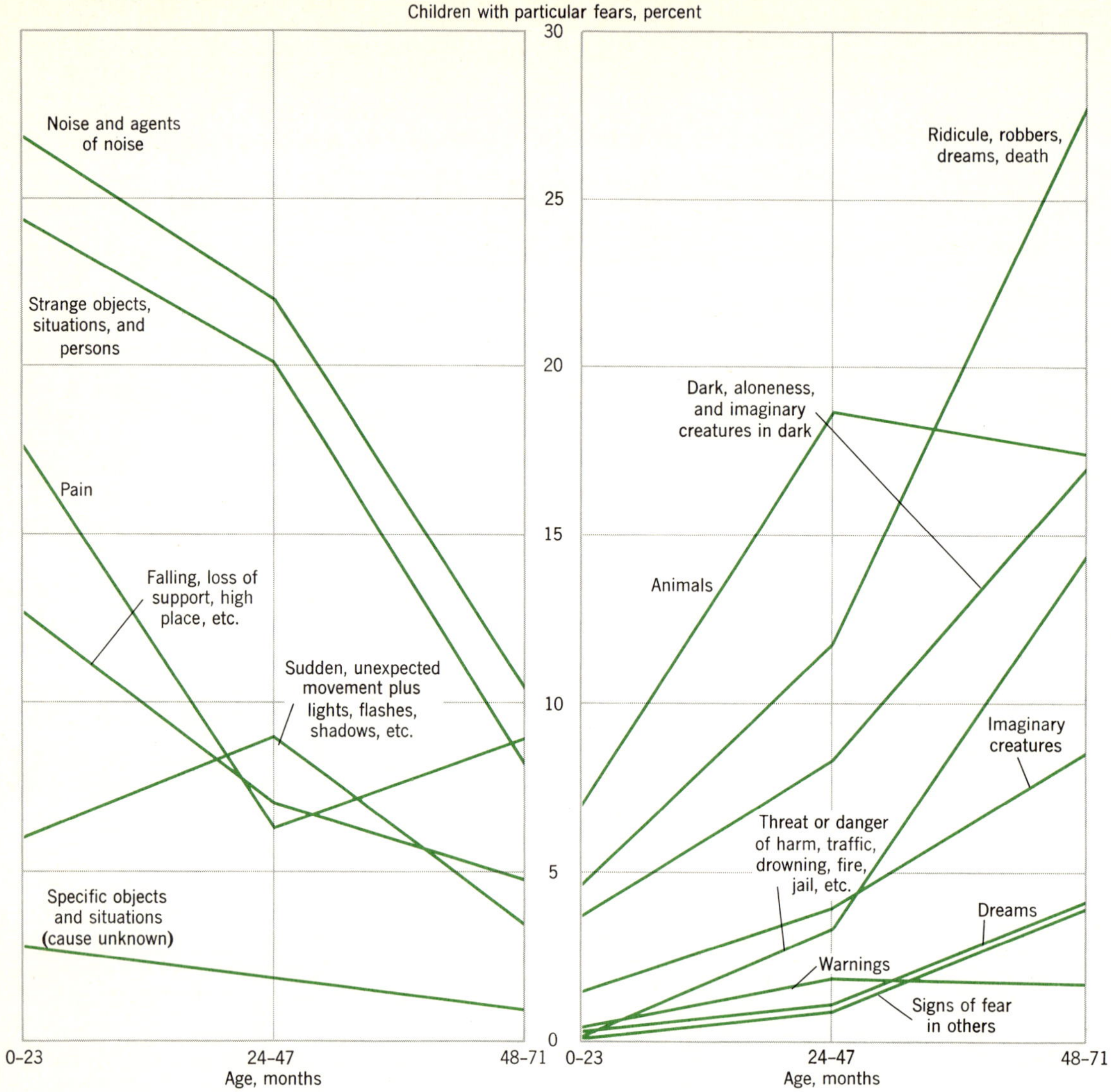


FIGURE **6.2**
Relative frequency of fears of various kinds shown by children of different ages who were observed by parents and teachers in the Jersild and Holmes (1935) study. After Gray, 1971.

by the child's going to school. Thus the child starts to avoid school, and the mother does not protest too strongly. She may even unwittingly reward the child's nonattendance for her own purposes. Given that the dependent relationship works both ways, the child being dependent on the mother and the mother being dependent on the child, the mother may not wish to lose her child to the school each day. A similar view has also been suggested by behaviorally oriented

TABLE **6.2**
## Summary of Classification of Phobias
(adapted from Marks, 1969)

| Variables | Animal phobias | Agoraphobia | Social phobias | Miscellaneous | School phobia |
|---|---|---|---|---|---|
| Frequency | Rare | Common | Not uncommon | Not uncommon | Not uncommon |
| Sex incidence | 95% women | 75% women | 60% women | 50% women | More common in girls |
| Onset age | Childhood | After puberty | After puberty | Anytime | Childhood |
| Associated symptoms | Few | Multiple—general anxiety, depression, panic | Few | Not determined | Nausea, vomiting, diarrhea |
| Psychophysiology | Normal | High arousal | High arousal | Not determined | Not determined |

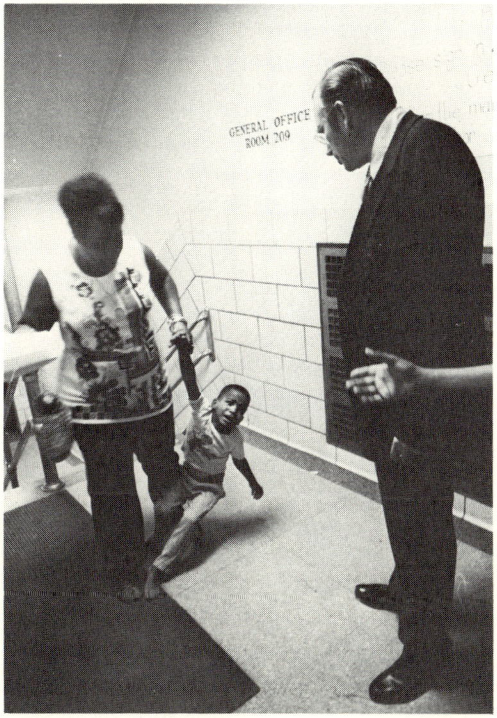

School phobia is common and worrisome, upsetting thousands of American children and their parents.

psychologists Lazarus, Davison, and Polefka (1965), who regard the avoidance of school as comprising two separable although interrelated elements: intense fear of going to school and reinforcement of avoidance by the mother.

A summary of the important differences among various clinical phobias appears in Table 6.2. Some, like agoraphobia and social phobias, are associated with high arousal levels, indicating that the autonomic nervous system may be especially important in their etiology. Therapy procedures aimed at reducing such fears may have to take this high level of autonomic arousal into account. Similarly, any attempt to deal with school phobia should probably include changing the mother's behavior. Therefore the topographical features of a phobia have important implications for both etiology and treatment.

## Anxiety Neurosis

Anxiety neurosis is characterized by anxious overconcern which may amplify to become panic. Somatic symptoms are frequently associated with this anxiety, which may occur in any circumstance and is not restricted to specific situations or objects. This syndrome is sometimes referred to as "free-floating anxiety." The person is anxious in so many different situations and so much of the time that many psychopathologists have regarded as fruitless any systematic search for specific eliciting causes. Individuals diagnosed as having anxiety reactions are likely to be tense, irritable, and subject to episodes of acute panic. They are also overly sensitive to criticism and easily discouraged. Patients report apprehension, feelings of being out of control, premonitions of impending disaster, and the like. Danger preoccupies their thoughts and fantasies (Beck, Laude, and Bohnert, 1974). Generally there are many physiological concomitants such as rapid heart rate, irregular breathing, excessive sweating, and dizziness. Insomnia, restlessness, fatigue, muscular tension, and difficulty in concentrating and making decisions are other symptoms often reported.

The patient, a thirty-one-year-old mechanic, had been referred for psychotherapy by his physician, whom he had consulted because of dizziness and difficulties in falling asleep. He was quite visibly distressed during the entire initial interview, gulping before he spoke, sweating, and continually fidgeting in his chair. His repeated requests for water to slake a seemingly unquenchable thirst were another indication of this extreme nervousness. Although he first related his physical concerns, a more general picture of pervasive anxiety soon emerged. He reported that he nearly always felt tense and that "If anything can go wrong, it will." He was apprehensive of possible disasters that could befall him as he worked and interacted with others. He reported a long history of difficulties in interpersonal relationships which had led to his being fired from several jobs. As he put it, "I really like people and try to get along with them, but it seems like I fly off the handle too easily. Little things they do upset me too much. I just can't cope unless everything is going exactly right."[3]

**Psychoanalytic theory** regards the source of anxiety neurosis as an unconscious conflict between the ego and id impulses. The impulses are usually sexual or aggressive in nature and are struggling for expression, but the ego cannot allow this because it fears that punishment will follow. Since the source of the anxiety is unconscious, the person experiences apprehension and distress without knowing why. For the individual suffering from anxiety neurosis, the true source of anxiety, namely previously punished id impulses which are striving for expression, is ever present. In a sense there is no way to evade anxiety; if the person escapes the id, he is no longer alive. Anxiety is felt nearly all the time.

**Learning theorists** (for example, Wolpe, 1958) attempting to account for anxiety neurosis would, by the very nature of their paradigm, reject a concept of "free-floating anxiety." Instead, they look with greater persistence for external causes. For example, a person anxious most of his waking hours might well be fearful of social contacts. If that individual spends a good deal of time with other people, it may be more useful to regard the anxiety as tied to these circumstances rather than to any internal factors. This behavioral model of anxiety neurosis, then, is identical to the learning view of phobias. Anxiety is

[3] Case reports such as this one, when not referenced, have been drawn from our own clinical files. Identifying features are changed to protect the confidentiality of the individual.

viewed as having been classically conditioned to external stimuli, although the range of conditioned stimuli is considerably broader.

A **cognitive** model might focus on control and helplessness. Consider an individual who has not learned effective responses for coping with a variety of challenges. Since we have already indicated that a lack of control engenders anxiety (Chapter 5), we would expect such a person to exhibit pervasive anxiety.

Another cognitive theory is worth considering. Albert Ellis has proposed that anxiety neurotics learn ways of thinking about their world that create anxiety. Consider, for example, how much anxiety you might create for yourself if you believed that to be a worthwhile person you had to be perfectly competent in everything you do. Or how socially anxious might you be if you considered it essential to be loved or approved of by everyone whom you meet? Ellis believes that these thought patterns are learned by neurotics and that it is these *irrational beliefs* that create anxiety. Some support for Ellis's theory comes from a study in which a questionnaire, designed to assess a person's degree of endorsement of various beliefs, was administered to neurotics, normal controls, and patients with personality disorders (Newmark et al., 1973). As expected, many more neurotic subjects than others endorsed the irrational beliefs that Ellis has proposed as causing anxiety (Table 6.3). In Chapter 19 we shall examine a type of behavior therapy that uses Ellis's theory as the basis for treating anxiety.

TABLE **6.3**
Responses to Ellis's Set of Irrational Beliefs by Neurotics, Normal Controls, and Patients with Personality Disorders
(from Newmark et al., 1973)

| Irrational belief | Neurotic, percent | Normal, percent | Personality disorder, percent |
|---|---|---|---|
| It is essential that one be loved or approved by virtually everyone in his community. | 65* | 2 | 5 |
| One must be perfectly competent, adequate, and achieving to consider oneself worthwhile. | 80 | 25 | 30 |
| It is easier to avoid than to face certain life difficulties and responsibilities. | 75 | 29 | 34 |
| Past experiences and events are the determinants of present behavior; the influence of the past cannot be eradicated. | 89 | 38 | 45 |
| Some people are bad, wicked, or villainous and therefore should be blamed or punished. | 70 | 40 | 48 |

* Entries are percentages of subjects in each group who endorsed the statement. The table shows only the items on which the groups differed substantially.

**Genetic researchers** have also examined anxiety neurosis. In one study (Slater and Shields, 1969) comparisons were made of seventeen identical pairs of twins and twenty-eight fraternal pairs of twins; one twin of each pair had been diagnosed as having anxiety neurosis. Of the identical co-twins, 49 percent were also diagnosed as having anxiety neurosis. In contrast, only 4 percent of the fraternal co-twins were so diagnosed. Although this pattern of incidence is consistent with genetic transmission, the more crucial adoptee studies, and those of identical twins reared apart, have not been done. Thus we can draw no firm conclusion.

## Obsessive-Compulsive Neurosis

Obsessive-compulsive neurosis, the least common of any of the neurotic disorders (Ingram, 1961), generally has its onset in early adulthood. Obsessions are intrusive and recurring thoughts which appear irrational and uncontrollable to the individual experiencing them. Whereas many of us may have similar fleeting thoughts, the obsessive experiences them with such force and frequency that functioning is interfered with. Cameron (1963) gives an example illustrating the onset of an obsessive thought in a forty-two-year-old mother.

> She was serving the family dinner one evening when she dropped a dish on the table and smashed it. The accident appalled her. While clearing up the fragments she was seized with an unreasonable fear that bits of glass might get into her husband's food and kill him. She would not allow the meal to proceed until she had removed everything and reset the table with fresh linen and clean dishes. After this her fears, instead of subsiding, reached out to include intense anxiety over the possibility that she herself and the children might be killed by bits of glass (p. 384).

A compulsion is an irresistible impulse to repeat some ritualistic act over and over again. Lady Macbeth washed her hands continually after the murder of King Duncan. Virtually any behavior can be viewed as a compulsion if the individual reports an irresistible urge to perform it and experiences considerable distress if prevented from doing so. Often an individual who continually repeats some action fears dire consequences if the act is not performed. The sheer frequency with which an act is repeated may often be staggering. One woman treated by the authors of this book washed her hands over 500 times per day, despite the painful sores that resulted. She reported that she had a very strong fear of contamination by germs and could temporarily alleviate this concern only by washing her hands.

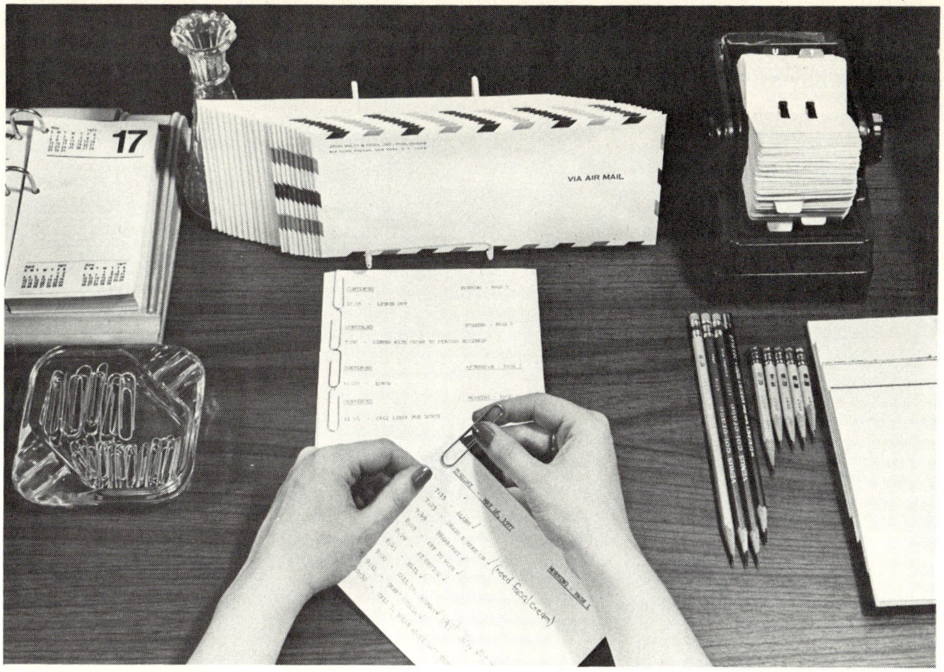


The orderly world of the obsessive-compulsive.

The content of obsessions and compulsions have been investigated by Akhter and his colleagues (1975). After interviews with eighty-two obsessive-compulsive patients, five distinguishable forms of obsession and two of compulsion were identified.

## Obsessions

1. **Obsessive doubts.** Persistent thoughts that a completed task had not been adequately accomplished were found in 75 percent of the patients. "Each time he left his room a twenty-eight-year-old student began asking himself 'Did I lock the door? Am I sure?' in spite of a clear and accurate remembrance of having done so" (p. 343).
2. **Obsessive thinking.** Seemingly endless chains of thoughts, usually focusing on future events, were reported by 34 percent of those interviewed. A pregnant woman tormented herself with these thoughts: "If my baby is a boy he might aspire to a career that would necessitate his going away from me, but he might want to return to me and what would I do then, because if I . . ." (p. 343).
3. **Obsessive impulses.** Seventeen percent had powerful urges to perform certain actions, ranging from rather trivial whims to grave and assaultive acts. "A forty-one-year-old lawyer was obsessed by what he understood to be the nonsensical notion of drinking from his inkpot but also the serious urge to strangle an apparently beloved only son" (p. 343).

4. **Obsessive fears.** Twenty-six percent were anxious about losing control and doing something that would be socially embarrassing. "A thirty-two-year-old teacher was afraid that in the classroom he would refer to his unsatisfactory sexual relations with his wife, although he had no wish to do so" (p. 344).

5. **Obsessive images.** Persisting images of some recently seen or imagined event plagued 7 percent of the sample. A patient "'saw' her baby being flushed away in the toilet whenever she entered the bathroom" (p. 344).

## Compulsions

1. **Yielding compulsions.** Obsessive urges seemingly forced actions on 61 percent of the patients. "A twenty-nine-year-old clerk had an obsessive [notion] that he had an important document in one of his pockets. He knew that this was not true, but found himself impelled to check his pocket, again and again" (p. 344).

2. **Controlling compulsions.** Diverting actions apparently allowed 6 percent of the patients to control an obsessive urge without giving in to it. "A sixteen-year-old boy with incestuous impulses controlled the anxiety these aroused by repeatedly and loudly counting to ten" (p. 344).

In **psychoanalytic theory** obsessions and compulsions are viewed as similar, resulting from instinctual forces, primarily aggressive, which are not under control because of overly harsh toilet training. The person is thus fixated at the anal stage. The symptoms observed represent the outcome of the struggle between the id and the defense mechanisms; sometimes the id predominates, sometimes the defense mechanisms. For example, when obsessive thoughts of killing intrude, the forces of the id are dominant. More often, however, the observed symptoms reflect the partially successful operation of one of the defense mechanisms. An individual fixated at the anal stage may by *reaction formation* resist his urge to soil and become compulsively neat, clean, and orderly. Similarly, in *undoing,* the individual engages in a ritualistic behavior which represents a magical attempt to cancel out the forbidden impulse. Or the ritual may serve as penance for misdeeds in order to erase guilt.

**Behavioral accounts** of obsessions and compulsions (Meyer and Chesser, 1970) consider them learned behavior reinforced by their consequences. One set of consequences is the reduction of fear. For example, compulsive hand washing is viewed as an instrumental escape-response which reduces an obsessional preoccupation with contamination by dirt or germs. Anxiety as measured by self-report (Hodgson and Rachman, 1972) and psychophysiological responses (Carr, 1971) can indeed be reduced by such compulsive behavior.

Or the consequences may be a more direct but chance reward, as in Skinner's famous demonstration of the acquisition of so-called superstitious behavior in pigeons. The birds were reduced to 75 percent of their normal body weight and then presented with food at regular intervals, whatever their behavior happened to be. In this way and quite by chance, as Skinner described it,

> *One bird was conditioned to turn counter-clockwise about the cage. . . . Another repeatedly thrust its head into one of the upper corners of the cage. A third developed a "tossing" response, as if placing its head beneath an invisible bar and lifting it repeatedly (1948, p. 168).*

The implication is that obsessive behavior in human beings is similarly learned through chance reward. As plausible as these formulations appear, we still have much more to learn about the etiology of obsessive-compulsive neurosis.

## Hysterical Neuroses

The last major category of neurotic disorders is hysteria, or to use its more contemporary name, hysterical neurosis. According to DSM-II, hysterical neuroses are divided into two major types, dissociative and conversion reactions. Dissociative reactions are defined as departures from normal states of consciousness. Partial paralysis, anesthesias, disturbances of vision, and the like, all of them occurring in the absence of physical damage of any kind, are examples of conversion reactions. In DSM-III conversion reactions will be considered somatoform disorders.

There are also two related disorders. The *hysterical personality,* usually female, is prone to histrionics and exaggeration and tends to be seductive and overdemanding in interpersonal relationships. As Chodoff (1974) notes, however, hysterical personality is "one of the most loosely used phrases in the lexicon of [psychopathologists]. . . . Hysterical personality can be used as a pejorative label to denigrate someone whom the psychiatrist believes to be insufficiently serious. I have had the impression that susceptible young male residents [physicians training to become psychiatrists] may classify as a hysterical personality any reasonably attractive woman with whom they come into therapeutic contact" (p. 1076). A second disorder related to hysteria is *Briquet's syndrome.* People with this disorder have many physical complaints. Hospitalizations are frequent, and unnecessary surgery may even be performed. True conversion reactions and histrionics are other symptoms (Woodruff, Clayton, and Guze, 1971). Briquet's syndrome, which has some similarity to hypochondriacal neurosis, is slated to appear in DSM-III as a somatoform disorder.

### Dissociative Reaction

It is believed that there are four types of dissociative neuroses. *Amnesia* involves loss of memory for a period of time, during which the amnesiac cannot remember his name, where he lives, or anything about his previous life. He will not recognize his relatives or friends but he retains his ability to talk, read, and reason, and perhaps his talents and the knowledge that he has acquired of the world and how to function in it. The duration of an amnesic state varies from several hours to several years. *Fugue* also involves loss of memory, but in addition the person flees from his usual surroundings, frequently moving to a new geographic location and starting an entirely new life. *Somnambulism,* commonly referred to as sleepwalking, is also considered a dissociative reaction. It is as though an unknowing part of the person controls bodily movements while the knowing mind sleeps. *Multiple personality,* the presence of separate and different personalities within the same individual, is perhaps the most dramatic type of dissociative reaction.[4]

According to the **psychoanalytic view** of each of the four types of dissociative reaction, one part of the mind or consciousness splits off or becomes dissociated from another part. The individual engages in activities of which he or she later claims to be unaware. The types of dissociative reaction are tied together etiologically in psychoanalytic theory, being viewed as instances of a massive repression, usually relating back to the unacceptable infantile sexual wishes of the oedipal stage. In adulthood these oedipal yearnings increase in strength until they are finally expressed, usually as an impulsive sexual act. The ordinary form of repression is obviously no longer sufficient; the whole event must be obliterated from consciousness. The person succeeds in this by splitting off an entire part of the personality from awareness (Buss, 1966) and by acquiring a new identity for the dissociated portion of the self (see Box 6.3).

[4] Cases of multiple personality are frequently mislabeled in the popular press as schizophrenic reactions. This diagnostic category, discussed in greater detail in Chapters 13 and 14, derives part of its name from the Greek root *schizo,* which means "splitting away from." Hence the confusion. A split in the personality, wherein two or more fairly separate and coherent systems of being exist alternately in the same person, is different from the split between cognition and affect that is said to produce the schizophrenic's inappropriate behavior.

## BOX 6.3 The Three Faces of Evelyn

Consider what it would be like to have a multiple personality. People have told you about things you have done that seem out of character, events that you have no memory of. You yourself have been waking up each morning with the remains of a cup of tea by your bedside—and you do not like to drink tea. How can you explain these happenings? If you were to seek treatment, might you not worry whether the psychiatrist or psychologist will believe you? Perhaps the clinician will think you psychotic.

Each of us has days when we are not "quite ourselves." This is assumed to be quite normal and is not what is meant by multiple personality. According to DSM-II, a proper diagnosis of multiple personality requires that a person have at least two separate "ego states," two different modes of being and feeling and acting that exist independently of each other, coming forth at different times. Each ego state has no contact with the other, that is, the person in ego state A has no memory for what state B is like, or even any knowledge of having an alternate state of being. The existence of different states must furthermore be chronic and severe, not attributable to the ingestion of some drug, for example.

Until recently the case of Eve White, alluded to in Chapter 4, was the most carefully documented report of multiple personality in the clinical literature. But then in 1976 another case was detailed in the *Journal of Abnormal Psychology*. "The Three Faces of Evelyn" is a detailed history by Robert F. Jeans, the psychiatrist who treated the woman. The case history is accompanied by exchanges between him and a team of psychologists at a distant university. The investigators had been asked whether they would be interested in describing the patient and advancing some hypotheses about her past history on the basis of her scores on a particular psychological test, taken while she was in each of her different "ego states." Thigpen and Cleckley had adopted a similar procedure in 1954 in their work with Eve White. Osgood, Luria, and Smith's intriguing bit of psychological detective work both sheds light on the fascinating phenomenon of multiple personality and offers some concurrent validation of a psychological test, the Semantic Differential, which is meant to reveal how a person feels about a number of people, situations, and ideas (Table 6.4).

### TABLE 6.4
### Sample Item from the Semantic Differential

(from Osgood, Suci, and Tannenbaum, 1957)

| My mother | | |
|---|---|---|
| valuable | *___ ___ ___ ___ ___ ___ ___ | worthless |
| clean | ___ ___ ___ ___ ___ ___ ___ | dirty |
| tasty | ___ ___ ___ ___ ___ ___ ___ | tasteless |
| large | ___ ___ ___ ___ ___ ___ ___ | small |
| strong | ___ ___ ___ ___ ___ ___ ___ | weak |
| deep | ___ ___ ___ ___ ___ ___ ___ | shallow |
| fast | ___ ___ ___ ___ ___ ___ ___ | slow |
| active | ___ ___ ___ ___ ___ ___ ___ | passive |
| hot | ___ ___ ___ ___ ___ ___ ___ | cold |
| relaxed | ___ ___ ___ ___ ___ ___ ___ | tense |

* Subjects mark any one of the lines between each pair of adjectives.

Jeans provides the following background on his patient. He was consulted in December 1965 by a Gina Rinaldi, referred to him by her friends. Gina, single and thirty-one-years old, lived with another single woman and was at the time working successfully as a writer at a large educational publishing firm. She was considered an efficient, businesslike, and productive person, but her friends had observed that she was becoming forgetful and sometimes acted out of character. The youngest of nine siblings, Gina reported that she had been sleepwalking since her early teens; her present roommate had told her that now she would sometimes scream in her sleep.

Gina described her mother, then age seventy-four, as the most domineering woman she had ever known. She reported that as a child she had been quite a fearful and obedient daughter. At age twenty-six Gina got braces for her teeth, and at age twenty-eight she had had an "affair," her first, with a former Jesuit priest, although it was apparently not sexual in nature. Then she became involved with "T.C.," a married man who assured her he would get a divorce and marry her. She indicated that she had been faithful to him since the start of their relationship. Partly on the basis of Jeans's analysis of one of Gina's dreams, the psychiatrist concluded that she was quite uncomfortable about being a woman, particularly when a close, sexual relationship with a man might be expected of her. But T.C. did not come through with his promised divorce, stopped seeing Gina regularly, and generally fell out of her favor.

After several sessions with Gina, Jeans began to notice a second personality emerging. "Mary Sunshine," as she came to be referred to by Jeans and by Gina, was quite different from Gina. She seemed to be more childlike, more traditionally feminine, ebullient, and seductive. Gina felt that she herself walked like a coal miner, but Mary certainly did not. Some quite concrete incidents indicated Mary's existence. Sometimes Gina found in the sink cups that had had hot chocolate in them—neither Gina not her roommate liked this beverage. There were large withdrawals from Gina's bank account that she could not remember making. One evening while watching television, Gina realized that she was crying and remarked to herself that it was stupid to feel sad about the particular program she was viewing. She even discovered herself ordering a sewing machine on the telephone, although she disliked sewing; some weeks later she showed up for her therapy session wearing a new dress that Mary had sewn. At work, Gina reported, people were finding her more pleasant to be with, and her colleagues took to consulting her on how to encourage people to work better with one another. All these phenomena were entirely alien to Gina. Jeans and Gina came to realize that sometimes Gina was transformed into Mary.

Then one day T.C. showed up again. Gina was filled with scorn and derision for him, yet she heard herself greeting him warmly with the words "Gee, I missed you so much! It's good to see you!" (Apparently the psychoanalytically oriented therapy was softening the hitherto impermeable boundaries between the separate ego states of Gina and Mary.) Gina was also surprised to hear T.C. reply on this occasion, "All you ever wanted was to please me. You've done nothing but cater to my every whim, nothing but make me happy." Mary must have been active in the earlier relationship that Gina had had with this man.

Now more and more often Jeans witnessed Gina turning into Mary right before his eyes in the consulting room. T.C. accompanied Gina to a session during which her posture and demeanor became more relaxed, her tone of voice warmer. When T.C. explained that he really cared for her, Gina, or rather Mary, said warmly, "Of course, T., I know you do."

At another session Mary was upset and, as Jeans puts it, chewed off Gina's fingernails. Then the two of them started having conversations with each other in front of Jeans.

A year after the start of therapy, an apparent synthesis of Gina and Mary began to emerge. At first it seemed that Gina had taken over entirely, but then Jeans noticed that Gina was not as serious as before, particularly about "getting the job done," that is, working extremely hard on the therapy. Jeans, probably believing that Mary wanted to converse with him, encouraged Gina to have a conversation with Mary. The following is what was said by the patient: "I was lying in bed trying to go to sleep. Someone started to cry about T.C. I was sure that it was Mary. I started to talk to her. The person told me that she didn't have a name. Later she said that Mary called her Evelyn. . . . I was suspicious at first that it was Mary pretending to be Evelyn. I changed my mind, however, because the person I talked to had too much sense to be Mary. She said that she realized that T.C. was unreliable but she still loved him and was very lonely. She agreed that it would be best to find a reliable man. She told me that she comes out once a day for a very short time to get used to the world. She promised that she will come out to see you [Jeans] sometime when she is stronger" (Jeans, 1976, pp. 254–255).

Throughout January Evelyn appeared more and more often, and Jeans felt that the patient was improving rapidly. During this stage of therapy he administered the Semantic Differential to each of the three personalities, for now he had access to all three ego states. Within a few months the patient seemed to be Evelyn all the time, and this woman soon married a physician. Now, years later, she still has had no recurrence of the other personalities.

On the basis of the Semantic Differential responses of Gina, Mary, and Evelyn, Osgood, Luria, and Smith (1976) were able to describe the patient in ways that concurred impressively with Jeans's clinical data. Not only do their conclusions have concurrent validity—each personality is described in a manner consistent with Jeans's clinical reports; but their work has etiological validity as well—Osgood and his colleagues were able to suggest accurately various features of the patient's earlier history, for example, that her father was less dominant than her mother. The similarity of their conclusions and Jeans's observations, although not total, is impressive.

**Learning theorists** have generally construed these rare phenomena as avoidance responses that serve to protect the individual from highly stressful events. Although not employing the concept of repression and not emphasizing the overriding importance of infantile sexual conflicts, the behavioral view of dissociative reactions is not dissimilar to psychoanalytic speculations about these disorders.

We are unfortunately able to go little beyond these rather vague accounts, since there are so few concrete data available on this type of problem. Information is scant, principally because of the rarity of the disorder. Abse (1966), for example, reviewed the literature and was able to find only 200 documented cases of various dissociative reactions, most of them descriptive clinical accounts. Dissociative reactions remain among the most poorly understood clinical syndromes.

## Conversion Reaction

In conversion reactions the operations of the musculature or sensory functions are impaired, although the bodily organs themselves are sound. We find reports of partial or complete paralyses of arms or legs; anesthesias (Figure 6.3), the loss or impairment of sensations; and analgesias, insensitivity to pain, all occurring in physiologically normal people. Vision may be seriously disturbed: the person may become partially or completely blind or have "tunnel vision," wherein the visual field is constricted as it would be were the observer peering through a tunnel.

Hysteria, the earlier term for such disorders, has of course a long history dating back to the earliest writings on abnormal behavior. Hippocrates considered it an affliction limited solely to women and brought on by the wandering of the uterus through the body. The Greek word *hystera* means womb. Presumably the wandering uterus symbolized the longing of the body for the production of a child. The consensus among writers is that conversion reactions are found primarily

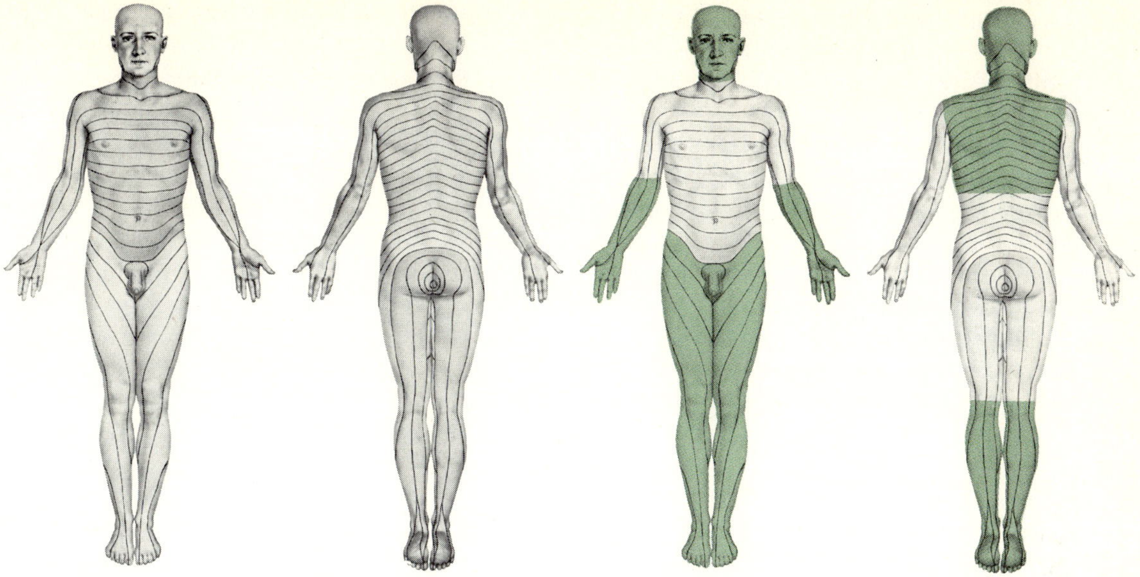

FIGURE **6.3**
Hysterical anesthesias can be distinguished from neurological dysfunctions. On the left are shown the patterns of neural innervation of the skin. On the right are superimposed typical areas of anesthesias in hysterical patients. The hysterical anesthesias do not make anatomical sense. (Left, copyright © 1963, 1972 CIBA Pharmaceutical Company, Division of CIBA-GEIGY Corporation. Reproduced with permission from The CIBA Collection of Medical Illustrations, by Frank H. Netter, M.D. All rights reserved.)

in females. During both world wars, however, a large number of males also developed conversionlike difficulties in combat (Ziegler, Imboden, and Meyer, 1960).

Diagnostically, it is important to distinguish a hysterical paralysis or sensory dysfunction from similar problems that have a true neurological basis. Sometimes this is an easy task, as when the paralysis does not make anatomical sense. But in other cases the diagnostic decision is more difficult and may require special procedures. A case in point was described by Theodor and Mandelcorn (1973). The patient, a sixteen-year-old girl, had experienced a sudden loss of peripheral vision, reporting that her visual field had become tubular and constricted. Although a number of neurological tests proved negative, the authors wanted to be even more certain that they were not dealing with a neurological problem. So they arranged a special visual test in which a bright, oval target was presented either in the center or in the periphery of the girl's visual field. On each trial there were two time intervals which were bounded by the sounding of a buzzer. The target was illuminated during one of the intervals, and the girl's task was to report which one.

When the target was presented in the center of the visual field, the girl always correctly identified the time interval during which it was illuminated. This had been expected since she had not reported any loss of central vision. What happened when the oval was presented peripherally? The girl could be expected to be correct 50 percent of the time by chance alone; the authors reasoned that this would be the outcome if she were truly "blind" in peripheral vision. For the peripheral showings of the target, however, the girl was correct only 30 percent of the time. She had performed significantly more poorly than would a person who was indeed blind! The clinicians reasoned that the girl must have been in some sense aware of the illuminated stimulus, and that she wanted, either consciously or unconsciously, to preserve her "blindness" by performing poorly on the test.

A second diagnostic problem with conversion disorders is differentiating them from *malingering,* which is faking an incapacity in order to avoid a responsibility. In trying to discriminate conversion reactions from malingering, clinicians may try to decide whether the symptoms have been consciously or unconsciously adopted. This means of resolving the issue is at best a dubious one, for it is difficult if not impossible to know with any degree of certainty whether behavior is consciously or unconsciously motivated. One aspect of behavior is sometimes revealing, however, *la belle indifférence* of hysterics. Some hysterics do not seem upset by their problems, adopting a blasé attitude toward their symptoms. But they also appear willing and eager to talk endlessly and dramatically about them. In contrast, the malingerer is likely to be more guarded and cautious, perhaps because he or she considers interviews a challenge or threat to the success of the lie. But this distinction is not foolproof, for only about one-third of hysterics show *la belle indifférence* (Stephens and Kamp, 1962).

### Misdiagnosis of conversion reaction

Since the majority of paralyses, analgesias, and sensory failures do have organic causes, are true neurological problems sometimes misdiagnosed as conversion reactions? Slater and Glithero (1965) have investigated this possibility. Their study was a follow-up of patients who nine years earlier had been diagnosed as suffering from conversion reaction. An unexpected number, in fact 60 percent, of these individuals had either died in the meantime or developed symptoms of physical disease! A high proportion had diseases of the central nervous system. Similarly, Whitlock (1957) compared the incidence of organic disorders in patients earlier diagnosed as having conversion reactions and in patients earlier diagnosed as having depressive reactions, anxiety reactions, or both. Organic disorders were found in 62.5 percent of the patients earlier diagnosed as having conversion reactions and in only 5.3 percent of the other groups. The most common organic problem was head injury, generally found to have occurred about six months before the onset of the conversion symptoms. Other common organic problems were stroke, encephalitis, and brain tumor. From these data we can see that some symptoms labeled as conversion reactions and thought to have psychological causes may, in fact, be physical disorders. We have already learned that the assessment of organic problems is still rather crude. Therefore it is not always possible to distinguish between psychologically and organically produced symptoms. The diagnosis of conversion reaction may be applied too frequently; some individuals diagnosed in this way may have an organic problem that has gone undetected. The damage that such inappropriate diagnoses can do is sobering to contemplate.

### Theories of conversion reaction

According to classical **psychoanalytic theory,** conversion reactions, like dissociative reactions, are rooted in an early unresolved Electra complex. The young female child becomes incestuously attached to her father, but these early impulses are repressed, producing both a preoccupation with sex and, at the same time, an avoidance of it. At a later period of her life, sexual excitement or some happenstance reawakens these repressed impulses, at which time they are expressed or *converted* into physical symptoms that represent in distorted form the repressed libidinal urges. Modern psychoanalytic theorists, however, do not all agree that conversion hysteria stems from the Electra complex. Some (for example, Sperling, 1973) see the problem originating much earlier, during the oral period.

**Sociocultural theories** are based on the supposed decrease in conversion reactions over the last century. Although Charcot and Freud seemed to have had an abundance of female patients with this sort of difficulty, contemporary clinicians rarely see anyone with such problems. A number of hypotheses have been proposed to explain this apparent decrease. For example, those of a psychoanalytic bent point out that in the second half of the nineteenth century, when the incidence of conversion reactions was apparently high in France and Austria, sexual attitudes were quite repressive and may have contributed to the increased incidence of the disorder. The decline of the conversion reaction, then, is attributed to the greater sophistication of twentieth-century culture and a general relaxing of sexual mores.

A study by Proctor (1958) is often cited as providing evidence for this theory. The incidence of conversion reaction was found to be particularly high among children who were patients at the University of North Carolina Medical School Psychiatric Clinic. In interpreting this very high incidence, the author noted that most of the children came from rural areas where the socioeconomic status of the inhabitants was low and little education was provided for them. Moreover, the religious background of these people was generally strong and fundamentalist. The conditions in this area of North Carolina may have approximated in some respects those prevailing in nineteenth-century France and Austria.

Ironically, *there is in fact little evidence that the incidence of conversion reactions is decreasing.* For example, Stephens and Kamp (1962) compared the outpatient diagnoses of two periods, the first from 1913 to 1919 and the second from 1945 to 1960. In both they found the incidence of conversion reaction to be 2 percent. We can also find reasons that explain away the seemingly high incidence of conversion disorders found in the nineteenth century. The large numbers seen by clinicians such as Charcot and Freud may have reflected a selective process. Patients with these particular difficulties may have come to these clinicians because they were known to be successful in treating hysterias. Similarly, the high incidence of conversion reactions reported by Proctor may reflect not a "true" high incidence but rather differences in diagnostic practices. In view of the difficulties in assessing incidence at different periods of time, it would seem ill-advised to use alleged changes in frequency of occurrence as validation for an etiological theory of a disorder.

A **behavioral account** of the development of conversion reactions has been proposed by Ullmann and Krasner (1969). In their opinion the person with a conversion reaction attempts to behave according to his or her own conception of how a person with a disease affecting the motor or sensory abilities would act. This theory raises two questions. Are people capable of such behavior? Under what conditions might such behavior be most likely to occur?

Considerable evidence supports an affirmative answer to the first question, that people can adopt patterns of behavior that match many of the classic conversion reaction symptoms. For example, paralyses and analgesias can be induced in people under hypnosis. Similarly, chemically inert drugs called placeboes have reduced the pain of patients who had been considered truly ill. As a partial answer to the second question, Ullmann and Krasner specify two conditions that increase the likelihood that motor and sensory disabilities will be imitated. First, the individual must have some experience with the role to be adopted. He or she may have had similar physical problems or may have observed them in others. Second, Ullmann and Krasner note that the enactment of a role must be rewarded. An individual will feign a disability only if it can be expected either to reduce stress or to reap other positive consequences.

Ullmann and Krasner describe the case of a veteran originally reported by Brady and Lind (1961). Two of the patient's aunts had been totally blind during their last years. While in the army the patient had developed a problem in one of his eyes, which had greatly reduced visual acuity. Thereafter he was given a medical discharge from the army and a small pension. During the twelve years following his discharge, he held a series of semiskilled jobs, remaining at none more than a year and often returning to the hospital with recurrences of his visual problem. Each time after returning to the hospital he applied for a larger pension, but he was refused because there had been no additional loss of vision.

Twelve years after his discharge, while shopping with his wife and mother-in-law, he suddenly "became blind" in both eyes. At this time, the authors state, "His wife and mother-in-law were being more demanding than usual, requiring him to work nights and weekends at various chores under their foremanship. One immediate consequence of his blindness was, then, partial escape from this situation." During the next two years the patient received various treatments and was enrolled in a course of training for the blind. In addition, he was awarded a special pension for his total disability and received financial assistance from the community for his children and some money from his relatives. Ullmann and Krasner's contention that conversion reactions may develop when the role that is to be adopted is known and rewards are to be expected is plausible; yet, except for case studies like this one reported by Brady and Lind, their theory has not been substantiated.

**Genetic and physiological factors** have been suggested as playing some role in the development of conversion reactions. Slater (1961) investigated concordance rates in twelve identical and twelve fraternal pairs of twins. Probands of each pair had been diagnosed as having the disorder, but none of the co-twins in either of the two groups manifested a conversion reaction. Similarly, Gottesman (1962) found the reactions of identical twins to statements on the hysteria scale of the MMPI to be no more similar than those of fraternal twins. Genetic factors, then, from the studies done so far, seem to be of no importance.

An intriguing case study of a conversion hysteric suggests the possible neurophysiological mechanisms by which a conversion reaction involving a sensory system is produced (Hernández-Peón, Chávez-Ibarra, and Aguilar-Figueroa, 1963). The patient was a fifteen-year-old girl with an analgesia in the left arm. To determine the basis of her affliction, these investigators recorded electrical activity of the brain while her arms were pricked by a pin. The usual pattern of cortical responses was found for the right arm, but no brain response was detected when the left analgesic arm was pricked. These data, consistent with clinical reports, suggest that sensory input to the left arm was being inhibited. Other research has demonstrated that neural pathways descending from the cortex can exert an inhibitory influence on incoming sensory pathways. That is, certain messages from the brain can block out or inhibit the impulses traveling along incoming sensory nerves. An increase in the activity of these descending inhibitory pathways, then, may be a mechanism by which sensations are altered in conversion reactions. But the possibility that neural pathways are implicated in conversion reactions need not mean that the explanation for these disorders is somatogenic rather than psychogenic, for the increased activity of these descending pathways would still have to be accounted for in some manner.

## Existential Neurosis

At least implicit in Freud's theorizing is the idea that normal personality development entails a balance or compromise between the physiologically based urges of the id and the reality (ego) and moral (superego) considerations imposed upon the individual by the external world and society. From a behavioral point of view, to grow up without experiencing an appreciable amount of unrealistic anxiety, the individual must not be subjected to too many stressful traumatic situations, and must acquire the social skills that effectively permit a life in society. These two views of personality development have a great deal in common—if for no other reason than that both neglect one aspect of human nature, freedom, which is given particular emphasis in the writings of existential philosophers and psychologists.

In recent years clinicians have noticed the emergence of what seems to be a completely different kind of neurotic disorder, *existential neurosis*. Although not recognized as a syndrome by DSM-II, it is somewhat similar to depersonalization neurosis. Even though little research has been done on this disorder, our account of neuroses would be incomplete without at least a description.

> *The cognitive component of the existential neurosis is meaninglessness or chronic inability to believe in the truth, importance, usefulness, or interest value of any of the things one is engaged in or can imagine doing. The most characteristic* [emotional] *features . . . are blandness and boredom, punctuated by periods of depression which become less frequent as the disorder is prolonged. As to the realm of action, activity level may be low to moderate, but more important than the amount of activity is the introspective and objectively observable fact that activities are not chosen. There is little selectivity, it being immaterial to the person what if any activities he pursues. If there is any selectivity shown, it is in the direction of ensuring minimal expenditures of effort and decision making* (*Maddi, 1967, p. 313*).

Basing his views on the philosophical and often extremely subjective writings of existentialists, Maddi suggests that even before the individual suffers from existential neurosis, he or she has developed a *premorbid personality*. Such a person plays social roles, perhaps very well indeed, and satisfies physiological needs quite adequately. These talents are indeed important, as Maddi hastens to point out. People whose lives consists *only* of these acquired skills, however, are candidates for existential neurosis, for they have merely "gone along with" society instead of creating a personal destiny. Such people will feel a great sense of emptiness and lack of fulfillment, *in spite of the fact that they may be extremely effective in satisfying society's demands in every possible way*. Conditions of stress—for example, the imminence of death; a gross disruption in the social order, such as war or an economic depression; or the repeated failure to experience other people and their own feelings at what Maddi regards as a "deep and comprehensive level"—can easily trigger the onset of the neurosis itself.

Central to any existential theory is the idea that people are capable of making free and independent choices among alternatives. According to this view, individuals are initiators in their world, rather than the passive and purely reactive organisms implied by both psychoanalytic and behavioral theories. Maddi does not feel, however, that it is impossible to study existential neurosis scientifically, for any person's moment-by-moment ability to make the choices among alternatives is a link in the causal chain of all phenomena. Maddi is indeed very serious in suggesting that children can be taught to become premorbid existential neurotics if they are valued and rewarded only for their increasing ability to satisfy their physiological needs and for their performance of society's social roles. For a more healthy development they should be encouraged to make independent decisions based on some system of values, which may be shared by other people, and to have an active internal life, which they can maintain whatever happens in the external world.

## Summary

According to DSM-II, anxiety is central to all neurotic disorders. But only in some of the disorders considered to be neurotic is anxiety observed. Hysterical disorders, for example, do not involve anxiety that can be readily detected. Phobias are fear-mediated escape or avoidance reactions that are out of proportion to the dangers presented by objects or situations. Anxiety neurosis is a more pervasive fear, not clearly elicited by particular objects or situations. A person with an obsessive-compulsive neurosis has intrusive thoughts, or performs the same act again and again, or is troubled in both ways. In a hysterical dissociative neurosis consciousness is altered. Paralyses, loss of sensation, and sensory disturbances that occur without known organic damage are called hysterical conversion reactions. Existential neurosis, a recently suggested type of neurotic disorder, is the feeling that life is meaningless.

According to psychoanalytic views, neuroses develop when the expression of id impulses is blocked and the conflict is repressed. The maladaptive behavior of any neurotic is an attempt to reduce the overstimulation of the ego by impulses. For example, in phobias the fear of an actual object is displaced to an object symbolically related to the actual source of fear. Little Hans's fear of his father was displaced onto horses, which could then be avoided.

Learning theorists view neurotic behavior as responses reinforced either because they reduce fear or because the consequences that they produce are positive. The development of the original fear has been viewed in both classical conditioning and modeling terms. In addition, there are cognitive views which attribute anxiety to aberrant thought patterns the person has learned.

All theories rest on little direct evidence. None can account well for the fact that among individuals who have experienced stress only *some* become neurotically anxious. It may be that a few people are more predisposed than others to develop neurotic anxiety, and that lability of the autonomic nervous system is the important diathesis or predisposing factor.

# chapter 7

## PSYCHOPHYSIOLOGICAL DISORDERS



In Chapter 5 we discussed voodoo death, a seemingly supernatural phenomenon whereby a curse from a witch doctor dooms his victim to extreme physical suffering and death. To explain such events, Cannon (1942) proposed that vital bodily organs are irreparably harmed if the autonomic nervous system is maintained in a highly aroused state through prolonged psychological stress without the opportunity for effective action. Inasmuch as the arousal of the autonomic nervous system is also regarded as one of the bodily indications of emotion, it is not surprising that psychopathologists have concerned themselves with physical diseases involving this system, in the belief that psychological factors may be implicated. In the expression of emotion, the bodily changes of autonomic arousal are viewed as transient; in psychophysiological disorders the usually reversible autonomic and hormonal responses to stress cause irreversible tissue damage (Meyer and Chesser, 1970).

Psychophysiological disorders ". . . are characterized by physical symptoms that are caused by emotional factors and involve a single organ system, usually under the control of the autonomic nervous system" (DSM-II, 1968, p. 46). At the outset, two important points must be firmly established. First, a psychophysiological disorder is a real disease involving damage to the body. The fact that such disorders are viewed as being caused by emotional factors does not make the affliction imaginary. People can just as readily die from "psychologically produced" asthma or ulcers as from similar diseases produced by infection or physical injury. Second, psychophysiological disorders should be distinguished from the hysterical reactions that were discussed in Chapter 6. Hysterical disorders do not involve actual organic damage to the body, and they are generally considered to affect function of the voluntary musculature. In contrast, in psychophysiological disorders bodily tissues *are* damaged.

Nine different types of psychophysiological disorders are listed in DSM-II. All are attributed in part to the emotional state of the patient; the most obvious difference among them is the part of the body affected.

1. Psychophysiological skin disorders. Skin reactions such as neurodermatitis (inflammation), pruritis (itching), and hyperhydrosis (dry skin).
2. Psychophysiological respiratory disorders. Bronchial asthma, hyperventilation (breathing very rapidly), sighing, and hiccups.
3. Psychophysiological cardiovascular disorders. Tachycardia (heart racing), hypertension (high blood pressure), and migrain headache.
4. Psychophysiological hemic and lymphatic disorders. Disturbances of the blood and lymphatic systems.
5. Psychophysiological gastrointestinal disorders. Peptic ulcers, chronic gastritis, ulcerative or mucous colitis, constipation, hyperacidity, and heartburn.
6. Psychophysiological genital-urinary disorders. Disturbances in menstruation and urination, dyspareunia (painful sexual intercourse), and impotence (difficulty obtaining or maintaining an erection, or both).
7. Psychophysiological endocrine disorders. Malfunctions of the various endocrine glands.
8. Psychophysiological disorders of a sense organ. Any disturbance in one of the sensory organs in which emotional factors play a causative role.
9. Psychophysiological musculoskeletal disorders. Backache, muscle cramps, and tension headaches.

The present term, psychophysiological disorders, is now preferred to one that is perhaps better known, psychosomatic disorders. Psychosomatic connotes quite well the principal aspect of these disorders, that the psyche or mind is having an untoward effect on the soma or body. The structure of both these terms, in fact, implies that mind and body are separate and independent, although they may, at times, influence each other (see Box 7.1). Dualism is a deeply ingrained paradigm of human thought. And yet the hope was that these terms would foster a monistic rather than dualistic view of the human being, since ". . . all functioning and all diseases are both mental and physical, because both mental and physiological processes are going on continuously" (Sternbach, 1966, p. 139). Instead of speaking of the emotions as causing body dysfunctions, we could instead, as Graham (1967) has noted, regard the psyche and soma as one and the same. Psychological and physical explanations of disease are then simply two different ways of describing the same events. Here we shall accept the modern concept of a unitary organism, but at the same time allow that psychological and physical aspects can be distinguished one from the other for purposes of separate study.

Psychophysiological disorders do *not* appear in the draft of DSM-III. Because virtually all diseases are now viewed as potentially related to psychological stress, a psychophysiological disorders category would become a complete listing of all diseases. Instead of such a cumbersome, overlapping system, DSM-III recommends that the physician make a medical diagnosis and then specify the extent to which the illness is related to stress.

A number of instruments have been developed to measure life stress. One such test, whose items appear in Table 7.1, is the Social Readjustment Rating Scale (SRRS). In using the SRRS, the respondent simply checks off the life events that have been experienced during the time period in question. But merely summing the *number* of events would not work, for different *amounts* of stressfulness are inherent in different events. To solve this problem, Holmes and Rahe (1967) obtained data from a large group of subjects who were asked to rate each item according to the ". . . intensity and length of time

# BOX **7.1** Descartes and the Mind-Body Problem

One of the most influential statements about the "mind-body" problem is found in the writings of the brilliant French philosopher of the seventeenth century, René Descartes. Being a deeply religious Catholic, he assumed that human beings differed from other animals by virtue of having a soul and thus being partly divine. But like the other animals, human beings had a body as well. Although the body was said to work on mechanical principles—Descartes was fascinated by the mechanical models of the body's workings that were prevalent at the time—these mechanics were seen to be under the control of the soul, or mind. But how could the body, operating like a machine, be affected by the soul, which is spiritual and nonphysical? How could two such basically different substances, in fact, "touch" each other? If the mind was to affect the body, there must be some point of *contact*. The pineal gland, located in the midbrain, was postulated by Descartes as the locus of this critical interaction, the point at which the mind could direct the mechanics of the body. By dualizing human beings in this way, with this vital connection between the mind and the body, Descartes felt that he could retain his religious view of people as being partly divine and yet an integral part of the rest of the animal world.

René Descartes (1596–1650), the French philosopher who proposed a dualistic view of mind and body.

TABLE **7.1**
## Social Readjustment Rating Scale

(from Holmes and Rahe, 1967)

| Rank | Life event | Mean value |
|---|---|---|
| 1 | Death of spouse | 100 |
| 2 | Divorce | 73 |
| 3 | Marital separation | 65 |
| 4 | Jail term | 63 |
| 5 | Death of close family member | 63 |
| 6 | Personal injury or illness | 53 |
| 7 | Marriage | 50* |
| 8 | Fired at work | 47 |
| 9 | Marital reconciliation | 45 |
| 10 | Retirement | 45 |
| 11 | Change in health of family member | 44 |
| 12 | Pregnancy | 40 |
| 13 | Sex difficulties | 39 |
| 14 | Gain of new family member | 39 |
| 15 | Business readjustment | 39 |
| 16 | Change in financial state | 38 |
| 17 | Death of close friend | 37 |
| 18 | Change to different line of work | 36 |
| 19 | Change in number of arguments with spouse | 35 |
| 20 | Mortgage over $10,000 | 31 |
| 21 | Foreclosure of mortgage or loan | 30 |
| 22 | Change in responsibilities at work | 29 |
| 23 | Son or daughter leaving home | 29 |
| 24 | Trouble with in-laws | 29 |
| 25 | Outstanding personal achievement | 28 |
| 26 | Wife begins or stops work | 26 |
| 27 | Begin or end school | 26 |
| 28 | Change in living conditions | 25 |
| 29 | Revision of personal habits | 24 |
| 30 | Trouble with boss | 23 |
| 31 | Change in work hours or conditions | 20 |
| 32 | Change in residence | 20 |
| 33 | Change in schools | 20 |
| 34 | Change in recreation | 19 |
| 35 | Change in church activities | 19 |
| 36 | Change in social activities | 18 |
| 37 | Mortgage or loan less than $10,000 | 17 |
| 38 | Change in sleeping habits | 16 |
| 39 | Change in number of family get-togethers | 15 |
| 40 | Change in eating habits | 15 |
| 41 | Vacation | 13 |
| 42 | Christmas | 12 |
| 43 | Minor violations of the law | 11 |

* Marriage was arbitrarily assigned a stress value of 500; no event was found to be any more than twice as stressful. Here the values are reduced proportionally and range up to 100.

necessary to accommodate . . . *regardless of the desirability of the event.*"[1] Marriage was assigned a stress value of 500; all other items were then evaluated using this reference point. For example, an event twice as stressful as marriage would be assigned a value of 1000, and an event one-fifth as stressful as marriage would be assigned a value of 100. The average ratings assigned to the events by the respondents in Holmes and Rahe's study are also shown in Table 7.1

The ratings that indicate differential stressfulness of events are totaled for all the events actually experienced to produce a Life Change Unit (LCU) score, a weighted sum of events. The LCU score is then related to illness. Rahe and Holmes (unpublished), for example, studied a sample of 200 physicians. Health problems (infectious diseases, allergies, musculoskeletal problems, and psychophysiological disorders) were strongly related to LCU scores. With an LCU score of less than 200, 37 percent of the life crises were associated with deterioration of health. But with an LCU score greater than 300, 79 percent of the life crises were accompanied by health problems. Other studies have shown that LCU scores are related to heart attacks (Rahe and Lind, 1971), fractures (Tollefson, 1972), leukemia onset (Wold, 1968), and colds and fevers (Holmes and Holmes, 1970).

We have, then, some promising information on the relationship between psychological stress and physical illness. But caution is in order before we assert that the relationship is a causal one. Many of the studies have used a retrospective method; participants were asked, for example, to recall both the illnesses and the stressful life events that they had experienced over the previous two years. In this type of study causal inferences are hazardous indeed. Recall is less than perfect, and it is difficult to unravel

[1] Note that Holmes and Rahe's rating procedure makes *change* the crucial variable, not whether an event is pleasant or unpleasant. There is considerable controversy whether change per se or pleasantness-unpleasantness is the best way to assess life stress.

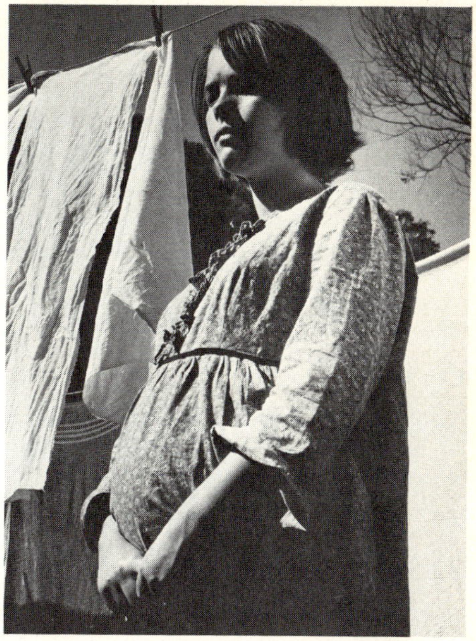

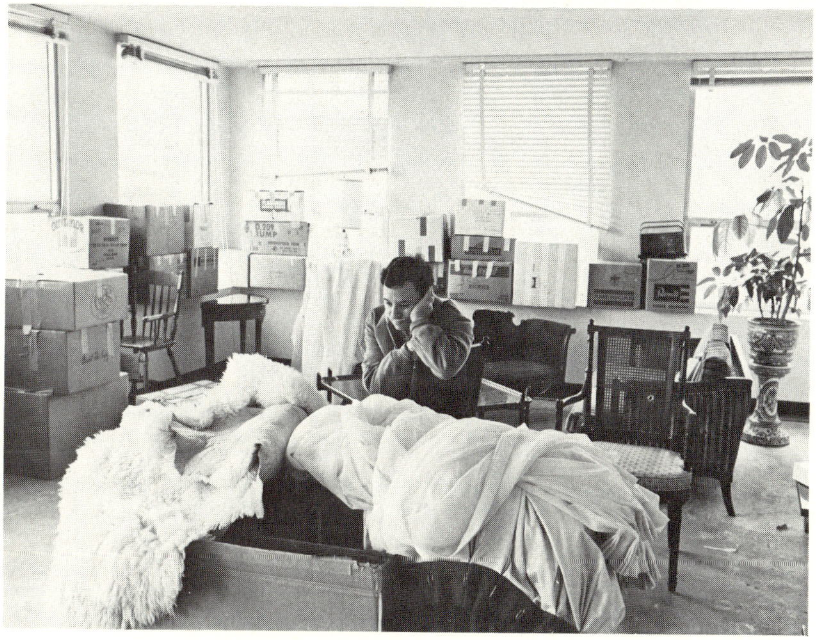

Major life events bring stress which can in turn cause medical and psychological problems.

cause and effect. Illness, for example, could cause a high life change score, as when chronic absenteeism brings dismissal from a job. And the reports of stressful events in such studies could also be contaminated by knowledge of subsequently occurring illnesses.

A few studies have used a prospective methodology wherein individuals are followed over time, and life changes and illness are repeatedly assessed (for example, Holmes and Holmes, 1970). Even these investigations, however, are subject to the possible influence of third variables; a factor could cause both the life events preceding the illness and the illness itself. Definite conclusions about the effects of life stresses await further studies that use prospective methodologies and also try to assess the potential role of third variables.

## Theories of Psychophysiological Disorders

We have known for some time that various *physical* stresses can produce physiological damage (Selye, 1956). In studying psychophysiological disorders we are concerned with *psychological* stressors such as emotional tension, conflict, and bereavement. Can they also elicit physiological changes and thus cause a psychophysiological disorder? In considering this issue we are confronted with three questions: (1) Why does stress produce difficulties in only *some* people who are exposed to it? (2) Why does stress sometimes cause a psychophysiological disorder and not another disorder such as a neurosis? (3) Given that stress produces a psychophysiological disorder, what determines which one of the many possible disorders it will be? Indeed, we have already discussed the concept of stress as it is related to various neurotic syndromes, and we shall discuss it further in the chapters on schizophrenia. How is it that this general concept can be used to "account for" such a wide range of disorders?

Answers to these questions have been sought by both physiologically and psychologically oriented theorists. A number of the theories concern the specificity of psychological disorders. Physiological approaches attribute particular psychophysiological disorders to specific weaknesses or overactivity of an individual's organ systems in responding to stress. Psychological theories account for specificity by positing particular stresses for particular disorders.

### Physiological Theories of Psychophysiological Disorders

#### Somatic-weakness theory

Genetic factors, earlier illnesses, diet, and the like may selectively disrupt a particular organ system, which may then become weak and vulnerable to stress. According to the somatic-weakness theory, the connection between stress and a particular psychophysiological disorder is the weakness in a specific bodily organ. By way of analogy, a tire blows out at its weakest or thinnest portion. And in the human body a congenitally weak respiratory system might predispose the individual to asthma.

### Specific-reaction theory

Some investigators argue that there are differences, probably genetically determined, in the ways individuals respond to stress. People have been found to have their own particular patterns of autonomic response to stress. The heart rate of one individual may increase, whereas another may react with increased respiration rate but no change in frequency of heartbeats (Lacey, 1967). Thus individuals respond to stress in their own idiosyncratic way, and the body system that is the most affected may be a likely candidate for the locus of a subsequent psychophysiological disorder. Someone reacting to stress with secretion of stomach acid may be more vulnerable to ulcers, and someone reacting to stress with blood pressure elevation may be more susceptible to essential hypertension. Later in this chapter, when we consider particular psychophysiological disorders, substantial evidence in support of both the somatic-weakness and specific-reaction theories will be given.

### Evolution theory

What are now considered psychophysiological disorders may have become so through evolutionary advances. Simeons (1961) and Wolf and Goodell (1968) have emphasized the initially adaptive function of psychophysiological disorders and consider them to be formerly useful protective reactions. For example, the increased pressure of arterial blood flow now known as hypertension may have once been the body's protection against threatened loss of blood. The increased secretion of digestive juices that now produces duodenal ulcer may have originally prepared the body to devour food under trying circumstances. Simeons has speculated that the diencephalon in the lower forebrain, the region of the brain most closely associated with visceral functions (see Box 16.1, page 412), primarily prepared primitive man to flee or fight in an emergency. Modern man does not for the most part find such measures necessary or indeed even possible.

> *The diencephalon knows nothing of the cortical artifacts which have rendered physical escape unnecessary, and so it keeps on trying to make the body run. . . . Modern man's behavior is like that of an inexperienced driver who does not realize that the engine is running by itself. He keeps his finger pressed down on the self-starter and then wonders what is producing all the unpleasant noise* (p. 150).

## Psychological Theories of Psychophysiological Disorders

### Psychoanalytic theory

Franz Alexander (1950) has perhaps been the most prominent of the psychoanalytic theorists who have concerned themselves with psychophysiological reactions. In his view the various psychophysiological disorders are products of unconscious emotional conflicts specific to each disorder. For example, ". . . it would appear that the crucial factor in the pathogenesis of ulcer is the frustration of the dependent, help-seeking and love-demanding desires. When these desires cannot find gratification in human relationships, a chronic emotional stimulus is created which has a specific effect on the functions of the stomach" (p. 103). Alexander assumed that ulcer patients have repressed their longing for parental love in childhood, and that this repressed impulse causes the overactivity of the parasympathetic nervous system and of the stomach, leading to ulcers. Physiologically, the stomach is continuously preparing to receive food, which the person has symbolically equated with parental love.

Undischarged hostile impulses are viewed as

creating the chronic emotional state responsible for essential hypertension.

> *The damming up of his hostile impulses will continue and will consequently increase in intensity. This will induce the development of stronger defensive measures in order to keep pent-up aggressions in check. . . . Because of the marked degree of their inhibitions, these patients are less effective in their occupational activities and for that reason tend to fail in competition with others, . . . envy is stimulated and . . . hostile feelings toward more successful, less inhibited competitors are further intensified* (p. 150).

Alexander formulated his theory on the basis of his observations of patients undergoing psychoanalysis. Attempts to provide corroborative evidence, however, have not been successful. Cochrane (1973), for example, studied volunteers in a heart attack prevention clinic, before the onset of any clinical disorder. Participants were given the Maudsley Personality Inventory as a measure of neuroticism and the Direction of Hostility Questionnaire to assess how they customarily handle their angry impulses. After the initial assessment some of the participants did develop hypertension. But, contrary to Alexander's theory, these individuals had not differed from the other subjects on the personality measures.

### Specific-attitudes theories

Graham has proposed another psychological theory to account for the specificity of psychophysiological disorders. According to him, particular attitudes, rather than chronic emotional states, are associated with particular patterns of physiological changes and hence specific psychophysiological disorders (Grace and Graham, 1952). A number of patients having psychophysiological disorders were interviewed to determine their characteristic attitudes. A partial list of psychophysiological disturbances and the attitudes that were found to be related to them follows.

1. Urticaria (hives). Patients see themselves as being mistreated and are preoccupied with what is happening to them, not with retaliation.
2. Eczema. Individuals feel that they are being interfered with or prevented from doing something and cannot overcome the frustration. They are more concerned with the interference or the obstacle than with remedying the situation.
3. Raynaud's disease (cold hands). The individual wants to undertake hostile physical action but may not have any idea what the actual activity should be.
4. Asthma. Patients are facing a situation that they would rather avoid or escape. The most important part of their attitude is their desire to have nothing to do with the situation at all and to deal with it by simply ignoring it.
5. Hypertension. Individuals feel that they must be constantly on guard and prepared to ward off the ever-present threat of danger.
6. Duodenal ulcer. Individuals are seeking revenge and wish to injure the person or thing that has injured them.

The seeming remoteness of connection between such attitudes and these psychophysiological disorders makes Graham's findings quite striking. But the connections are, of course, correlational in nature and hence subject to the problems of interpretation discussed in Chapter 4. An experimental analogue study was undertaken to test these suggested correlations. After hypnotizing normal subjects, Graham, Stern, and Winokur (1958) gave them suggestions designed to produce the attitudes specific either to hives or to Raynaud's disease. These two disorders were selected for comparison because skin temperature changes with both but in different directions. The skin temperature of someone suffering from hives is higher than normal, that of the person with Raynaud's disease lower than normal. After the particular attitude had been induced in the subject, the temperature of his or her skin was measured. The actual instructions given to the subjects were as follows.

> Hives. *Dr. X is now going to burn your hand with a match. When he does so you will feel very much mistreated, but you will be unable to do anything about it. You can't even think of anything you want to do about it. You are thinking only of what happened to you.*
> Raynaud's disease. *Dr. X is now going to burn your hand with a match. You feel mistreated and you want to hit Dr. X. You want to hit him as hard as you can, you want to hit him and choke him and strangle him. That's all you are thinking about, how much you want to hit him.*

Each subject was tested twice, receiving first one set of instructions and then the other. The results, presented in Figure 7.1, show that the "hives attitude" produced a small rise in skin temperature of a finger and that the "Raynaud's disease attitude" produced a decrease. In another study the hypertension attitude was induced and produced an increase in blood pressure (Graham, Kabler, and Graham, 1962). These demonstrations support Graham's theory to some extent, although it must be remembered that hives, Raynaud's disease, and hypertension were not actually produced.

A more recent study, however, provided data much less supportive of Graham's theory. Peters and Stern (1971) studied a group of subjects who tested high in hypnotic susceptibility. Each subject participated in several sessions during which the Raynaud's disease or hives attitude was induced, either through or without hypnosis. Temperature of the skin of a finger was recorded continuously during each session. When hypnotized the subjects showed a *de-*

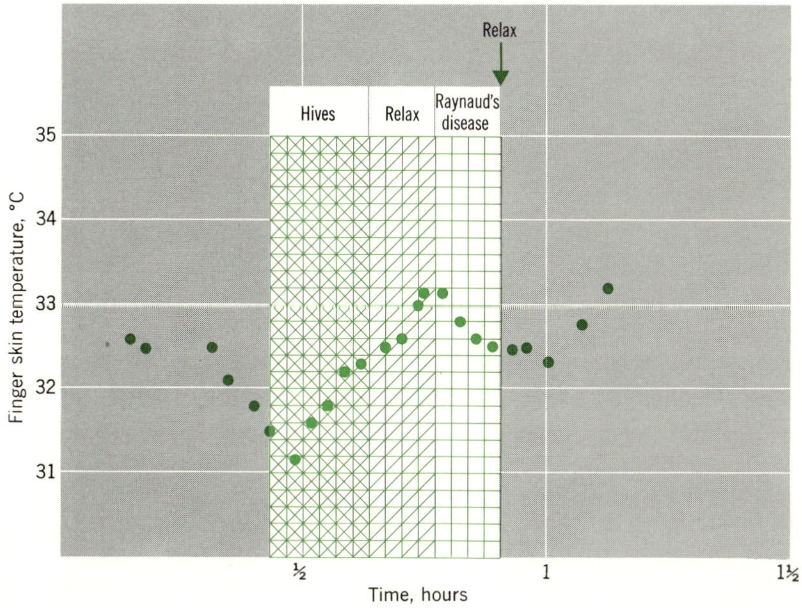


FIGURE **7.1**
Changes in skin temperature of a finger during the course of an experimental session. When the hives attitude was induced, there was a sustained rise after a small initial drop. With the induction of the Raynaud's disease attitude, skin temperature of the finger dropped steadily. After Graham, Stern, and Winokur, 1958.

*cline* in skin temperature of the finger, whichever disease attitude was suggested. When not hypnotized the subjects showed temperature *increases* as either attitude was induced. Given these contradictory findings, Graham's theory should be viewed with skepticism.

An interesting variation on the specific-attitudes theory of psychophysiological disorders, one which concerns hypertension, has recently been offered by David McClelland (1975), who for many years has worked on schemes to standardize scoring of the Thematic Apperception Test. It will be recalled from Chapter 3 that the TAT is composed of a set of pictures about which subjects or clients are instructed to tell stories. The assumption is that people will project into these stories needs or fears that they may not be willing or able to verbalize directly. One of the needs that McClelland assumes can be measured in the stories told is the need for power (n Power), more specifically, the desire to have an impact on others. A person receives a high score on n Power if his or her stories contain many elements reflecting argumentation, attempts to persuade others or to control them, and efforts to help people who have not themselves requested aid. Interscorer reliabilities of 90 percent and higher have been achieved by scorers trained by McClelland.

How might n Power relate to essential hypertension? First, McClelland saw in the hypertension literature that sufferers are frequently described as extremely competitive, aggressive, and impatient; they feel constantly pressed for time (Jenkins, 1971). These characteristics suggest chronically high levels of sympathetic nervous system activity. Furthermore, people who score high in n Power on the TAT may be described in a similar way, indicating a possible connection between n Power and essential hypertension. The question then becomes how to test the strength of this relationship.

McClelland has followed several lines of inquiry. Laboratory studies have indicated, for example, that n Power scores can be raised if TAT stories are told after viewing an inspirational film (Steele, 1973). Furthermore, these "power-aroused" subjects had higher levels of epinephrine in their urine after seeing the film, one which showed President John F. Kennedy giving his inaugural address. That this elevation in n Power scores and epinephrine level could not be attributed to an overall arousal of needs is suggested by the fact that scores on the need for achievement (n Ach), another need revealed in TAT stores and studied by McClelland, were not similarly increased. Therefore sympathetic nervous system activity may be associated with the desire to exercise power over others.

The next question is whether these short-term analogue findings are supported by data with more clinical relevance. What evidence is there that the power motive might be the kind of chronic, long-term activation that is related to hypertension and cardiovascular disease? To

David McClelland, Harvard psychologist, who uses the TAT to assess motivation. One of his theories links hypertension and cardiovascular disease to a strong need for power.

examine this problem, McClelland turned to longitudinal TAT data collected over many years on college students from a selective Eastern private college. In the fall of 1960, 235 male college freshmen took a TAT test and also had their blood pressure measured as part of their physical examination as incoming students. Those who scored high in n Power on the TAT had significantly higher blood pressure than those who scored low. Moreover, McClelland obtained access to data on men who had graduated from this college between 1939 and 1944 and who had been followed up regularly since their college years. Available in the files were n Power TAT data as well as blood pressure measurements. McClelland found that blood pressure at about age fifty-one could be predicted from n Power scores obtained when the men were thirty years of age. In addition, there was a clear link between n Power scores and cardiovascular disease: of twenty-five men who had cardiovascular disease in their early fifties, fourteen had scored high in n Power years earlier.

In evaluating this web of evidence, we should be mindful, as McClelland is, of the host of uncontrolled factors in all this research, especially in the longitudinal work. Many things happen to people after they leave college that could bear on the development of hypertension and heart disease as well—financial reverses, marital difficulties, legal entanglements, and the like. In addition, McClelland does not rule out a role for physiological factors in the development of hypertension. Given the additional factors that might have a role, the possible relationships revealed between the disorder and n Power by laboratory and historical investigations are all the more remarkable.

### Conditioning theories

Both classical and instrumental conditioning have been suggested as having a role in psychophysiological disorders, although conditioning is probably best viewed as a factor that can exacerbate an already existing illness rather than cause it. Consider a person who is allergic to pollen and thus subject to asthma attacks. It has been theorized that through classical conditioning, neutral stimuli paired with pollen could also come to elicit asthma, thus broadening the range of stimuli that can bring on an attack (Bandura, 1969). The asthmatic attacks might also be viewed as instrumental responses producing rewards. For example, a child could "use" asthma as an excuse for not participating in unpleasant activities. *Neither of these accounts excludes the importance of physiological factors in psychophysiological disorders, for the original occurrence of the illness must still be accounted for.* Both classical and instrumental conditioning hypotheses assume that the physical symptoms already exist. Thus any learning model of a psychophysiological disorder requires a physiological predisposition, a diathesis of some kind.

Our overview of theories concerning the etiology of psychophysiological disorders is complete. We turn now to a detailed review of the disorders that have attracted the most attention from researchers—ulcer, hypertension, and asthma. We will see that a combination of a physiological predisposition and stress—the diathesis-stress paradigm introduced in Chapter 2—seems to fit and explain most of the clinical and experimental evidence.

## Ulcer

A peptic ulcer is a lesion or hole in the lining of the stomach or duodenum that is produced by excessive secretion of hydrochloric acid (HCl). In the digestive process HCl and various enzymes act on ingested food to break it down into components that the body can use. The inner wall of the stomach is protected from the destructive effects of HCl by a layer of mucus. Production of excess amounts of acid for long periods of time erodes the mucous layer, and the acid may digest the stomach wall. Ulcer patients suffer periodic attacks of pain and have to alter their diets to include only bland foods. The following case history illustrates the development of an ulcer.

> *Background.* As a child, Mr. A was quiet and obedient, whereas his brother who was three years older was aggressive and independent. Socially, Mr. A was very close to his brother and his brother's companions and was always under the protection of his brother. Mr. A also spent much time with his parents, who provided him with much attention.
> *Emotion-Arousing Situations.* When Mr. A was thirteen his brother died; about two years later his father also died. Both of those events were of major significance in Mr. A's young life. Following the death of his father, his mother became psychologically dependent on him, consulting him about important problems and requiring him generally to substitute for both his older brother and his father, a situation for which Mr. A was completely unprepared intellectually and otherwise. While maintaining a secure outer appearance, Mr. A was aroused emotionally, and his emotional reactions were repeatedly intensified by the excessive expectations of his mother. . . . At age eighteen, Mr. A experienced a short period of stomach discomfort that was followed by the initial hemorrhaging of a duodenal ulcer. When psychotherapy began about five years later, X-ray findings and general symptoms indicated an active ulcer.
> *Follow-up.* Follow-up study during a three-year period after conclusion of this initial psychotherapy disclosed the following facts. Mr. A had a mild relapse shortly after his marriage when he accepted a very strenuous assignment abroad and had an unsuitable diet; a second mild relapse occurred immediately prior to the birth of his first child, which corresponded in time with his mother's considering remarriage. A few psychotherapeutic consultations at that time involved examination of the existing emotion-provoking problems and apparently resulted in the resumption of more stable functioning. At the end of the three-year period (following conclusion of initial psychotherapy), Mr. A was on a normal diet with minimal daily medication (Lachman, 1972, pp. 1–2).

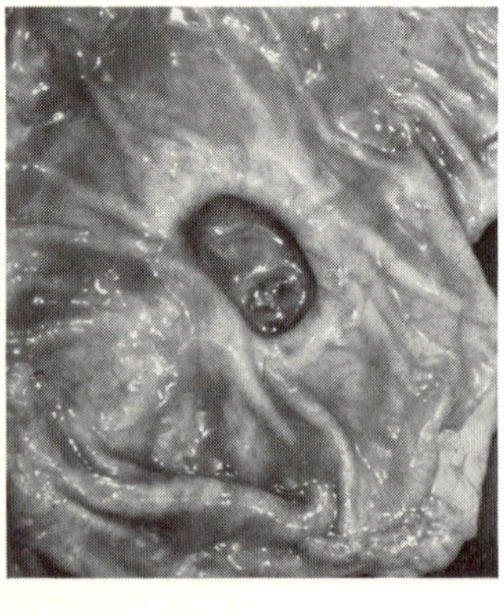

A stomach ulcer.

### Psychological stress

Although many stressors bring about an increase in the secretion of HCl, the approach-avoidance conflict is the one that has been the most extensively researched. Sawrey devised several illustrative experiments with rats to investigate whether prolonged approach-avoidance conflicts produce ulcers. The animals lived in an environment in which shock was administered whenever they approached food or water. Thus they were in conflict over whether to approach the food or avoid the shock. At the end of approximately two weeks many had developed ulcers,

"THE FUNNY THING IS, I GOT MY ULCER AFTER I BECAME A BUM."

and some had even died from hemorrhages (Sawrey and Weisz, 1956; Conger, Sawrey, and Turrell, 1958).

### Physiological predisposition

In Sawrey's animal research only *some* of the rats exposed to the approach-avoidance conflict developed ulcers. Thus stress can be only part of the story in the development of ulcers. We need also to locate a factor that can interact with stress and greatly increase the probability that an individual having this particular characteristic will develop an ulcer.

A prime candidate for a physiological predisposition is the amount of pepsinogen secreted by the peptic cells of the gastric glands in the stomach. Pepsinogen is converted into pepsin, the stomach enzyme which digests proteins and which in combination with HCl is the principal active agent in gastric juice. Pepsinogen levels are therefore measures of gastric activity, and hence we might expect them to be implicated in the formation of ulcers. By taking measurements through the umbilical cord, Mirsky (1958) was able to detect marked individual differences in pepsinogen levels in newborns. Furthermore, young infants with high levels of pepsinogen were found to be members of families with a high incidence of excessive pepsinogen levels. That only some people secrete large amounts of pepsinogen, depending on their genetic inheritance, does demonstrate that this variable has a possible causal role in the development of ulcers. Much stronger evidence would come from a demonstration that individuals who do not yet have ulcers but do have high levels of pepsinogen secretion are more likely to develop ulcers than another group, also without ulcers but with lower pepsinogen levels.

Such an investigation has in fact been conducted (Weiner et al., 1957). These researchers measured the level of pepsinogen in 2073 newly inducted draftees. From this large number two smaller groups were selected, the 63 with the highest levels of pepsinogen and the 57 with the lowest levels. A complete gastrointestinal examination, given before basic training, showed that none had ulcers at that time. The majority of these men were then reexamined during the eighth and sixteenth weeks of their basic training. Nine cases of ulcers had developed, all of them in the group with high pepsinogen levels. Another study (Mirsky, 1958) of a population of children and civilian adults who had earlier been classified as high and low pepsinogen secreters revealed a similar tendency for ulcers to develop among those with high levels of pepsinogen.

In sum, the data available on peptic ulcers are clearly consistent with a diathesis-stress theory implicating in their development both stress and the physiological predisposition to secrete excessive amounts of pepsinogen. Consistent with the specific-reaction theory, individuals who develop ulcers appear to be predisposed to react to stress with excessive gastric secretions, which then produce lesions.

## Essential Hypertension

Without question, the most serious psychophysiological disorder is hypertension, commonly called high blood pressure. This disease disposes people to atherosclerosis (clogging of the arteries), heart attacks, and strokes (see Chapter 16). It is estimated that more than half the deaths each year in the United States are caused by these diseases of the heart and brain. Were this statistic not alarming enough, in recent years the incidence of high blood pressure and related illnesses has increased markedly in younger age groups; heart attacks in men in their thirties are no longer as uncommon as they once were (Benson, 1975).

The pressure produced in the arteries as the heart pumps blood through them is referred to as blood pressure. Blood pressure may be elevated by increased cardiac output (the amount of blood leaving the left ventricle of the heart per minute), by increased resistance to the passage of blood through the arteries, that is, by vasoconstriction, and by an increase in fluid volume. Essential hypertension is a disorder characterized by chronic high blood pressure that cannot be traced to an organic cause; recent estimates are that varying degrees of hypertension are found in 15 to 33 percent of the adult population of the United States, and that no more than 10 percent of these cases are attributable to physical causes (Benson, 1975).

Constriction in the walls of the arteries seems to be the most important factor. Cochrane (1971) has speculated that increased sympathetic nervous system activity produced by stress causes greater secretions of norepinephrine; ultimately sodium is retained in the muscles of the arteries. This higher level of sodium sensitizes the arterial walls so that they overrespond to normal neural firings, producing greater vasoconstriction and hence hypertension. Lyght (1966) has offered the following description of the course of hypertension and the symptoms associated with the disorder.

> *. . . Hypertension frequently is present for many years without symptoms or signs other than an elevated blood pressure. In the majority of cases, increased blood pressure first appears during early adult life (mean age of onset, the early thirties). These patients may complain of fatigue, nervousness, dizziness, palpitation, insomnia, weakness and headaches at the same time in the course of the disorder. . . . The mean age of death for untreated patients is in the fifties, and their average life expectancy probably is close to twenty years from the onset, with extremes of from several years to many decades* (pp. 218 ff).

## Control over Stress and Blood Pressure Increase

### Short-term effects

Various stressful conditions have been examined to determine their role in the etiology of essential hypertension. Stressful interviews, natural disasters, anger, and anxiety have been found to produce elevations in blood pressure (Innes, Millar, and Valentine, 1959; Ruskin, Board, and Schaffer, 1948; Ax, 1953). More recently, Kasl and Cobb (1970) have examined the effects of the loss of employment on blood pressure. They studied a group of workers beginning two months before their jobs were to be terminated and for two years subsequent to loss of employment. A control group, consisting of men in similar occupations who did not lose their jobs, was examined for the same twenty-six-month period. Each participant in the study was visited at home by a nurse about every two weeks so that blood pressure could be measured. For the control subjects there were no overall changes in blood pressure. In the experimental subjects, however, elevated blood pressure was found both in anticipation of job loss and after termination of employment.

In another group of studies (Hokanson and

Burgess, 1962; Hokanson, Burgess, and Cohen, 1963; Hokanson, Willers, and Koropsak, 1968; Stone and Hokanson, 1969), based in part on psychoanalytic theory, researchers have attempted to determine whether blood pressure elevation is associated with the inhibition of aggression. The subjects are placed in two experimental situations in the course of these investigations. In the first the subject is given a task to perform, counting backward from 99 by two's, and is then harassed by a confederate of the experimenter. The subject, however, believes that this confederate is a fellow subject in the investigation. During the harassment it is found that blood pressure tends to rise. Later, half the subjects are given the opportunity to aggress against the confederate and half are not, and blood pressure is then remeasured. In the second situation the subject and the experimenter's confederate are together in a chamber. In front of each is a panel with three buttons labeled SHOCK, REWARD, and NO RESPONSE. On a signal from the experimenter, the confederate is allowed to press whichever button he "wishes," depending on how he feels at the moment. The confederate consistently shocks the subject, which produces an increase in his blood pressure. The dependent variable is the time it takes for the subject's blood pressure to return to normal as a function of which of the buttons he in turn chooses to press. In the control group the subjects are never given the opportunity to shock the confederate because the experimenter always signals that it is the confederate's turn to respond.

The results of this extensive series of investigations indicate that, for males, aggressing against a source of frustration helps blood pressure to decrease. With no opportunity to aggress against the frustrator, blood pressure is significantly slower to decrease after frustration. Only aggression directed at a low-status frustrator (college student) proved helpful in decreasing blood pressure, however, not that directed toward a high-status frustrator (visiting professor). These findings did not hold for female subjects. Rather, for them making a *positive response*—pressing the REWARD button—decreased their blood pressure.

Alexander has postulated that individuals who develop hypertension handle their aggression poorly and tend to repress aggressive impulses. Because of this repression, they are supposedly unable to find outlets for their aggression; their hostile impulses accumulate and grow in intensity to produce hypertension. The results of Hokanson's investigation offer some corroborative evidence for Alexander's theory concerning the etiology of hypertension. Alexander's theory, however, deals with repressed hostility, and in Hokanson's work there is no demonstration of a repression process operating unconsciously. Moreover, other studies performed by Hokanson and his colleagues demonstrate that aggression against a frustrator in itself may not be the key factor in increasing and decreasing blood pressure. Hokanson himself favors the following interpretation of his data: ". . . *Any* social response can be viewed as having arousal-reducing concomitants, if that response has been previously instrumental in terminating or avoiding aggression in others" (Stone and Hokanson, 1969, p. 72).

Hokanson's interpretation explains why aggression directed toward a high-status frustrator was not effective. Presumably, subjects have learned that it does not pay to retaliate against a high-status aggressor. Thus an aggressive response will *not* help to reduce arousal since such responses have not previously been rewarding. Similarly, Hokanson's position accounts for the fact that aggressive responses do not seem to reduce arousal for females. Social and cultural conditions prevailing for them when these studies were conducted dictated that the response to frustration not be aggression. This sex difference may disappear with growing social support for greater assertiveness in women.

The results of these studies seem to indicate that any response which gives *control* to the subject can decrease blood pressure. This possibility was directly examined in a study (Hokanson et al., 1971) in which subjects performed a symbol-matching task, with shocks being delivered for poor performance. The task was set up so that subjects would receive, on the average, one shock every forty-five seconds. Subjects were to spend twenty minutes working at the task but were allowed to take one-minute rest breaks so they would not "become overly fatigued." Subjects who had "control" could take as many breaks as they wanted whenever they wanted. "No control" subjects were matched to the "control" subjects in the amount of time spent working and resting, but the number and timing of their rest periods were determined for them. The results (Figure 7.2) indicated clearly that control, not actual amount of rest, produced lower levels of blood pressure. Not having control, then, is an elicitor of increased blood pressure and perhaps of essential hypertension.

A recent study (Harburg et al., 1973) extends Hokanson's ideas to the natural environment and to the high incidence of hypertension among black Americans. Harburg and his colleagues chose two areas of Detroit in which to conduct their investigation. In one area, the high-stress location, the crime rate was substantial, population density, mortality rates, and frequency of marital breakups were all high, and the socioeconomic status of residents was generally low. Conditions in the low-stress area were more favorable.

In each area groups of married black and white men were selected for study. During a visit to the participants' homes, a nurse collected blood pressure readings, the respondents were interviewed, and a specially designed test was administered. The test presented hypothetical situations and asked the participants how they would respond. An example follows.

> *Now imagine that you were searching to find another place to live in, and finally found one for sale or rent which you liked, but the owner told you he would not sell or rent to you because of your religion, national origin or race. How would you feel about that? The response categories . . . were as follows:* (1) *"I'd get angry or mad and show it,* (2) *I'd get annoyed and show it,* (3) *I'd get annoyed, but would keep it in,* (4) *I'd get angry or mad but would keep it in,* (5) *I wouldn't feel angry or annoyed"* (*p. 280*).

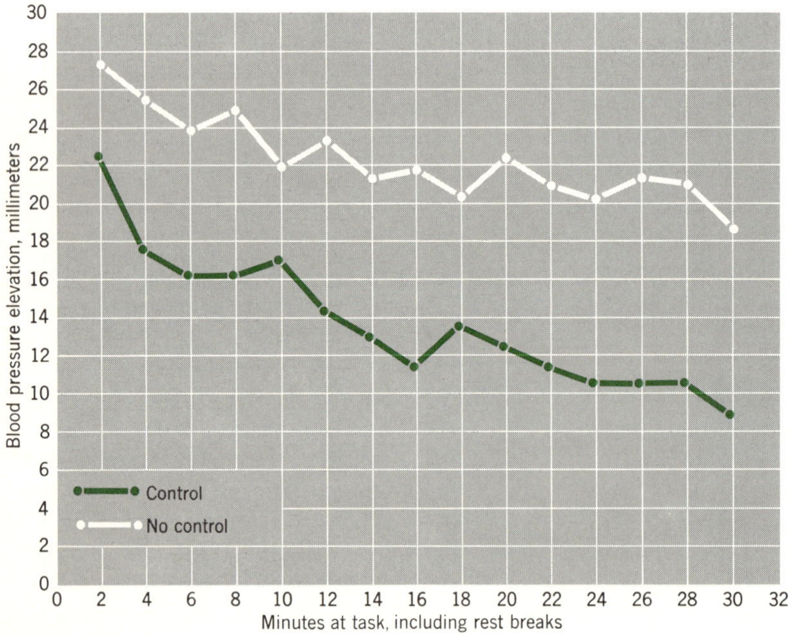


FIGURE **7.2**
Differences in blood pressure of subjects who controlled their rest breaks while performing a task and of subjects who did not, although they rested as much. After Hokanson et al., 1971.

Participants were also asked how they would feel if they had become angry and showed it. The dimension assessed here was guilt, and the possible responses ranged from very guilty to no feelings of guilt at all.

Blood pressure was higher among the black males than among the whites; and blacks living in the high-stress area had higher blood pressure than blacks living in the middle-class neighborhoods. Thus previous statistics revealing racial differences in blood pressure were substantiated, but with the important reservation that environmental stress is also a major factor. When responses on the test were related to blood pressure, the following pattern emerged. For all subjects except blacks in the low-stress area, holding anger in and guilt were related to higher blood pressure levels. The connection to Hokanson's work seems clear: not expressing anger or feeling guilty if anger is expressed would both be correlates of a sense of having no control. So again we see that lack of control may be a crucial variable in determining blood pressure.

### Long-term effects

Thus far we have discussed stressors that can produce a temporary increase in blood pressure in normal individuals. But can such short-term increases develop into sustained, long-term hypertension? The mechanism inducing long-term hypertension would necessarily involve some structural changes in the organism. No direct work has been done with human beings to determine whether short-term increases in blood pressure will develop into prolonged hypertension, but some research has been done on animals. Maher (1966) cites a study by Schunk in which cats were exposed to the barking of dogs for a number of months, presumably a stress for them. About half of these cats developed hypertension. Similarly, crowded living conditions and extended exposure to experimental avoidance conditioning procedures have been shown to elicit long-lasting elevations in blood pressure (Henry et al., 1971; Forsyth, 1969).

## Predisposing Factors

The research reviewed thus far suggests that lack of control over stress may be an important factor in producing hypertension. But we must also attempt to account for the fact that only some individuals exposed to particular stresses develop hypertension. Unfortunately, the data on physiological predispositions for hypertension are not as extensive or clear as those on the physiological predispositions for ulcers. Several studies have, however, demonstrated that hypertensives show greater blood pressure reactivity, reacting to stress with blood pressure increases that are higher than those of normal people (Engel and Bickford, 1961; Shapiro, 1961). In the Engel and Bickford study twenty female hypertensive patients and twenty control subjects were exposed to various stressors. Fifteen of the twenty hypertensives showed an increase in blood pressure, but only five of the controls did. In a similar vein Hodapp, Weyer, and Becker (1975) studied the blood pressure of hypertensive patients and normal controls while they rested, while they attended to colored slides of landscapes, and while they performed a demanding cognitive task (the stressor). The blood pressure of all subjects increased during the stress task. But in the hypertensives blood pressure was elevated, in relation to that recorded during the rest period, even when they were simply viewing the slides.

The research on blood pressure reactivity as a possible physiological predisposition cannot be regarded as conclusive, however, for the individuals being studied were *already* hypertensive. Their reactivity might have been a *result* rather than a *cause* of their hypertension. To be conclusive, studies must begin with individuals who have the predisposition but have not yet developed essential hypertension. In any event, the diathesis-stress theory of hypertension, the most promising of the etiological speculations, clearly implicates a predisposition toward a malfunction of some portion of the circulatory system.

# Asthma

## A Characterization of the Disease

Purcell and Weiss (1970) have described asthma in the following way.

> *Asthma is a symptom complex characterized by an increased responsiveness of the trachea, major bronchi, and peripheral bronchioles to various stimuli, and is manifested by extensive narrowing of the airways which causes impairment of air exchange, primarily in expiration,* [*thus inducing*] *wheezing.* [*The airways may be narrowed*] *because of edema* [an accumulation of excess watery fluid in the tissues] *of the walls, increased mucus secretion, spasm of the bronchial muscles, or the collapse of the posterior walls of the trachea and bronchi during certain types of forced expiration* (*p. 597*).

The major structures of the respiratory system are shown in Figure 7.3.

Most often, asthmatic attacks begin suddenly. The patient has a sense of tightness in the chest, wheezes, coughs, and expectorates sputum. Subjective reactions include panic-fear, irritability, and fatigue (Kinsman et al., 1974). A physician will notice that the asthma sufferer takes a longer time than normal to expire air and that whistling sounds can be detected throughout the chest. These sounds are referred to as rales. Symptoms may last an hour or less or may continue for several hours or sometimes even days. Between attacks no abnormal signs may be detected when the individual is breathing normally, but forced, heavy expiration will often allow the doctor to hear the rales.

One patient, to be described, had his first attack at age nine. His condition worsened until he was thirteen, after which he was symptom-free for ten years. From that time on, however, his condition deteriorated to an unusual degree, and the patient eventually died of respiratory complications—an outcome which fortunately is rare.

> Abundant data from this patient's life suggest the importance of emotional factors in precipitating exacerbations of his asthma. He gives a graphic description of developing wheezing and shortness of breath upon separation from his mother. Once, while away on a trip with either her or his grandmother (it is not clear which), in a strange hotel, separated from his companion by a wall, he suffered through the night, having the feeling that his wheezes might be loud enough to be heard and bring her in to rescue him.
>
> He described clearly the relationship of his symptoms to odors. His response to the scent of flowers may have had an allergic basis. That seems less likely in the case of the scent of "lovely ladies," which he stated also gave him asthma. So did certain "bad" smells, of asparagus and cigar smoke. . . . He had many conflicts around weeping, frequently described being dissolved in tears, but always with the implication that he never really was exhausting the reservoir of "sobbing." . . .
>
> At the time of his brother's marriage, the patient was jealous; he managed to forget to mail the 150 invitations to the ceremony that had been entrusted to him. In the church he was almost more prominent than the bride, walking down the aisle just before the ceremony, gasping for breath, and wearing a fur coat, although the month was July (Knapp, 1969, p. 135).

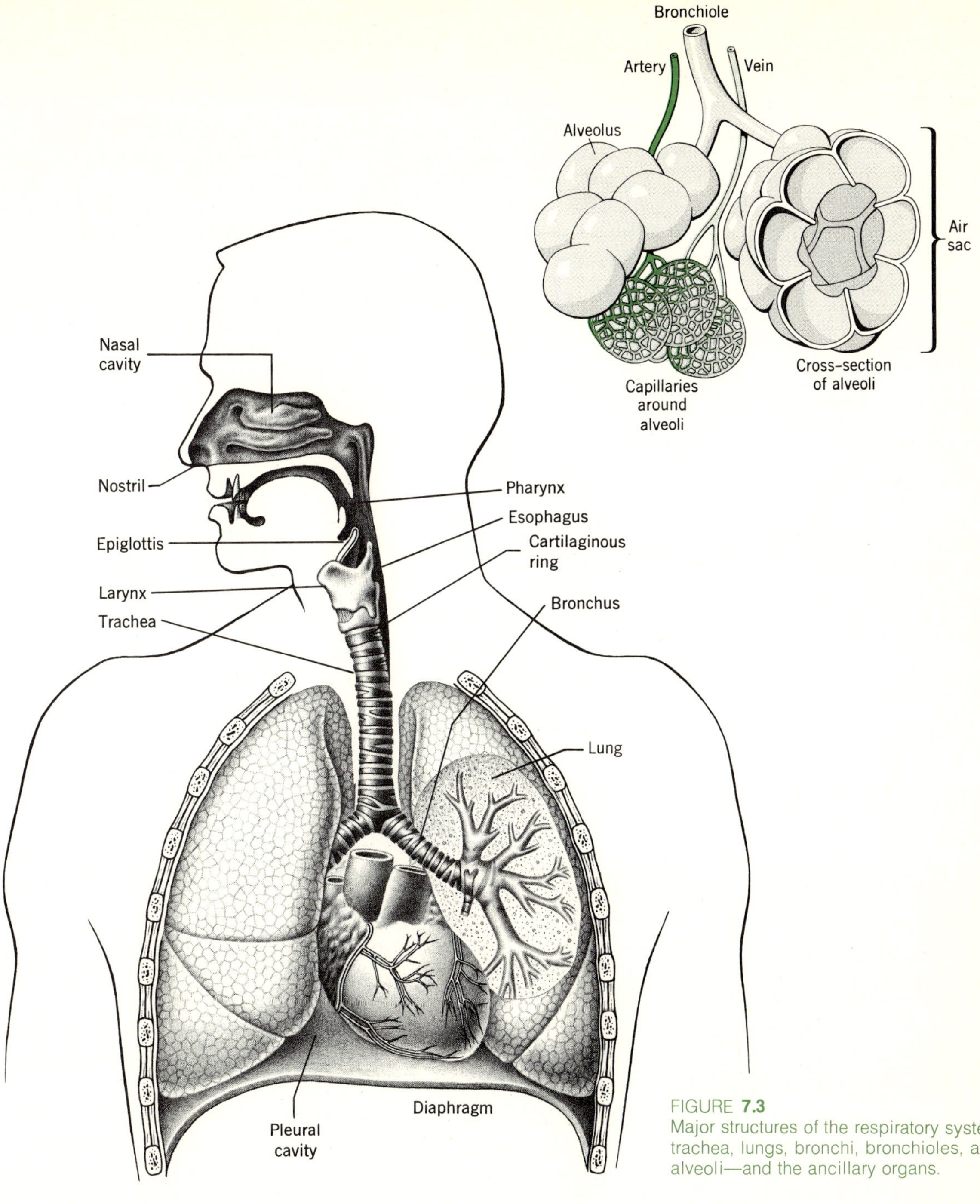


FIGURE **7.3**
Major structures of the respiratory system—trachea, lungs, bronchi, bronchioles, and alveoli—and the ancillary organs.

Somewhere between 2 and 5 percent of the population is estimated to have asthma, and it is more common in males than females (Graham et al., 1967). Williams and McNicol (1969) studied 30,000 seven-year-old Australian school children. They found a high correlation between the age of onset of the symptoms and the length of time the disorder lasted. If the age of onset was less than one, 80 percent were found to be still wheezing five years later. With ages of onset from three to four, 40 percent were still wheezing five years later, and with an onset age of five or six, only 20 percent were still wheezing five years later. Thus the earlier the disorder begins, the longer it is likely to last.

TABLE **7.2**
Relative Importance of Allergic, Infective, and Psychological Factors in the Etiology of Asthma
(from Rees, 1964)

| Factors | Relative importance, percent | | |
|---|---|---|---|
| | Dominant | Subsidiary | Unimportant |
| Allergic | 23 | 13 | 64 |
| Infective | 38 | 30 | 32 |
| Psychological | 37 | 33 | 30 |

## The Etiology of Asthma

Much of the debate concerning the importance of psychological factors in the development of asthma relates to whether or not emotionality is always implicated. To investigate the etiology of asthma, Rees (1964) divided the various possible causes into three categories, allergic, infective, and psychological. The cells in the respiratory tract may be especially sensitive to one or more substances or allergens such as pollen or dust, bringing on asthma. Respiratory infections, most often acute bronchitis, can also make the respiratory system vulnerable to asthma. Anxiety, tension produced by frustration, anger, depression, and anticipated pleasurable excitement are all examples of psychological factors that may, through induced emotionality, disturb the functioning of the respiratory system and thus cause asthma.

The part played by allergic factors was assessed through the case histories that were taken and by making cutaneous and inhalation reaction tests with suspected allergens. Patients were also exposed to suspected allergens and inert substances without their knowing which was which. The importance of infective factors was determined through the case histories and X-rays, by examining sputum, and by searching for pus or other evidence of infection in the nose, sinuses, and chest. The potential importance of psychological factors was assessed through the case histories and by direct behavioral observations. The principal results of Rees's study demonstrate the importance of conceptualizing asthma as a disease with multiple causes. As can be seen from Table 7.2, psychological factors were considered a dominant cause in only 37 percent of the cases. And in 30 percent of the cases psychological variables were regarded as totally unimportant—a conclusion at odds with the popular notion that asthma is always psychosomatic.

Rees's data showed also that the different causes of asthma varied in importance depending on the age of the individual. For those asthmatic individuals less than five years of age, the infective factors predominated. From ages six to sixteen the infective factors still predominated, but psychological variables increased in importance. In the range from ages sixteen to sixty-five, psychological factors decreased in importance until about the thirty-fifth year, thereafter becoming more consequential again.

### Psychological factors producing asthma

Rees's studies have demonstrated that some, but by no means all, cases of asthma have psychological factors as a primary cause. Yet even when asthma is originally induced by an infection or allergy, psychological stress can precipitate attacks. Eysenck (1965), for example, has related a case study originally described by Katsch, who had

> *. . . arrived at the hypothesis that the patient's mother-in-law, with whom he had many conflicts, constituted the source of the emotional trouble producing the asthmatic attacks and that a very large picture of her which hung in the bedroom of the patient was a . . . stimulus for these attacks. . . . [This hypothesis was tested as follows.] Katsch turned the mother-in-law's face to the wall, as it were, and immediately the asthmatic attacks ceased. They could be brought back at will, by turning the picture round again, and they could again be terminated by turning it to the wall once more; in other words, Katsch had achieved complete control over the asthmatic attacks of his patient (p. 207).*

In another study exploring somewhat the same ground, Kleeman (1967) interviewed twenty-six patients over an eighteen-month period. According to the reports of these patients, 69 percent of their attacks began with an emotional disturbance.

Dekker and Groen (1956) were able to produce asthma attacks in the laboratory using the following procedure. Before the actual investigation twelve asthmatic patients had described environmental situations that precipitated attacks. When these situations were reproduced in actual or pictorial form in the laboratory, three of the twelve patients developed full-blown asthma attacks, and three others showed less severe respiratory symptoms. The stimuli to which the subjects ascribed their asthma included the national anthem, perfume, the sight of dust, horses, and waterfalls.

Finally, another study indicates the "power of suggestion" in inducing asthma attacks, even among individuals whose allergic reactions are regarded as the primary cause of their disorder (Luparello et al., 1971). Forty asthmatics and a control group of another forty persons were told that they were participating in a study of air pollution. The investigator explained to each subject that he wanted to determine what concentrations of various substances would induce wheezing. The asthmatics were told that they would inhale five different concentrations of an irritant or allergen that had previously been established as a contributing cause of their asthma attacks. They were led to believe that each successive sample would have a higher concentration of the allergen, but in fact they were given only five nonallergenic saline solutions to inhale. The control subjects were told that they were inhaling pollutants which could irritate the bronchial tubes and make it difficult for them to breathe. Fourteen out of the forty asthmatic patients reacted with significant airway obstruction, and twelve went on to develop full-fledged attacks. None of the controls exhibited pathological respiratory reactions. Later the twelve subjects who had developed asthma attacks were given the same saline solution to inhale but were told that the solution was a bronchodilator. The condition of all twelve improved, confirming the role of suggestion in some asthmatics.

### Classical conditioning

The two investigations just described suggest the possibility that asthma may be induced in a variety of situations as a result of conditioning. One conditioning experiment done with human beings as subjects had almost completely negative results, however. Dekker, Pelse, and Groen (1957) paired a known allergen with a neutral solvent. The classical conditioning hypothesis would argue that through repeated pairings of the CS and UCS, the CS should acquire the ability to elicit the asthmatic reaction. In this study, after repeated pairings, only two of a hundred subjects were found to have been successfully conditioned. Moreover, "In a personal communication dated October, 1961, Dekker reported that he was unable to replicate even these results" (Purcell and Weiss, 1970, p. 607). At this time there is no support for a classical conditioning account of asthma.

### The role of the family

Several researchers have considered parent-child interactions to be important in the etiology of asthma. The investigators at the Children's Asthma Research Institute and Hospital in Denver routinely categorize their patients into those for whom psychological factors are considered the primary cause and those whose respiratory tracts are more greatly disturbed by other factors. In one investigation Purcell and his colleagues (1969) chose a group of twenty-two children. For thirteen children psychological factors were considered the principal precipitants of their asthma. For the other nine, allergic or infective factors were considered more significant. These twenty-two children were studied over a considerable length of time which was subdivided into four periods. The first was an initial base line period. In the second period the children lived with their families, in the third they lived in their own homes but with substitute parents, and in the fourth they were reunited with their parents. If the psychological factor disturbing one subgroup was the parent-child relationship, these children should improve when their parents lived apart from them. The children whose asthma was considered induced principally by allergic or infective factors would show no such improvement. The data supported the predictions remarkably well. Daily measurements and observations were made of the following variables: peak expiratory air flow, amount of medication required, wheezing, and frequency of asthma attacks. Seventy percent of the group who were predicted to do well without their parents improved during the separation phase (Figure 7.4). Of the nine children who were not predicted to do well without their parents, only one benefited from being separated.

Another study by Rees (1963) supports the theory that disturbed parent-child relationships may be a cause of asthma. He classified the attitudes of the parents of hospitalized asthmatic children as either satisfactory—the parents promote feelings of security and are affectionate and accepting; or unsatisfactory—parents are rejecting, perfectionistic, and overprotective. Only 44 percent of the parents of asthmatics were rated as having satisfactory attitudes, whereas 82 percent of the parents of control children (accident cases in the same hospital) were rated in this way.

The research that we have discussed reveals the importance of the home life of asthmatics. It should be noted, however, that we cannot always tell whether various familial variables are causal agents or maintaining agents. Although certain emotional factors in the home may be important in eliciting early asthmatic attacks in some children, in others the illness may originally develop for nonfamilial reasons, and then the children's parents may unwittingly reward various symptoms of the syndrome. For example, the parents may cater to the child and treat him specially because of his asthma. Current recommendations for the treatment of asthmatic children supply indirect support for this thesis. Doctors prescribe no special treatment and no overprotection. Instead, asthmatic children are urged to lead as normal a life as possible, even to the extent of participating in athletic events. An attempt is made, then, to keep the children from considering their sickness as the dominating factors in their lives. This attitude is well illustrated in the following interaction presented by Kluger (1969).

*Patient:* I can't go to school today because my asthma is worse.

*Doctor:* I know, but since it's not contagious why can't you be in school?

*Patient* (irritated): Because I'm having trouble breathing!

*Doctor:* I can see that, but you'll have trouble breathing whether you go to school or not. Remaining in bed won't help your breathing.

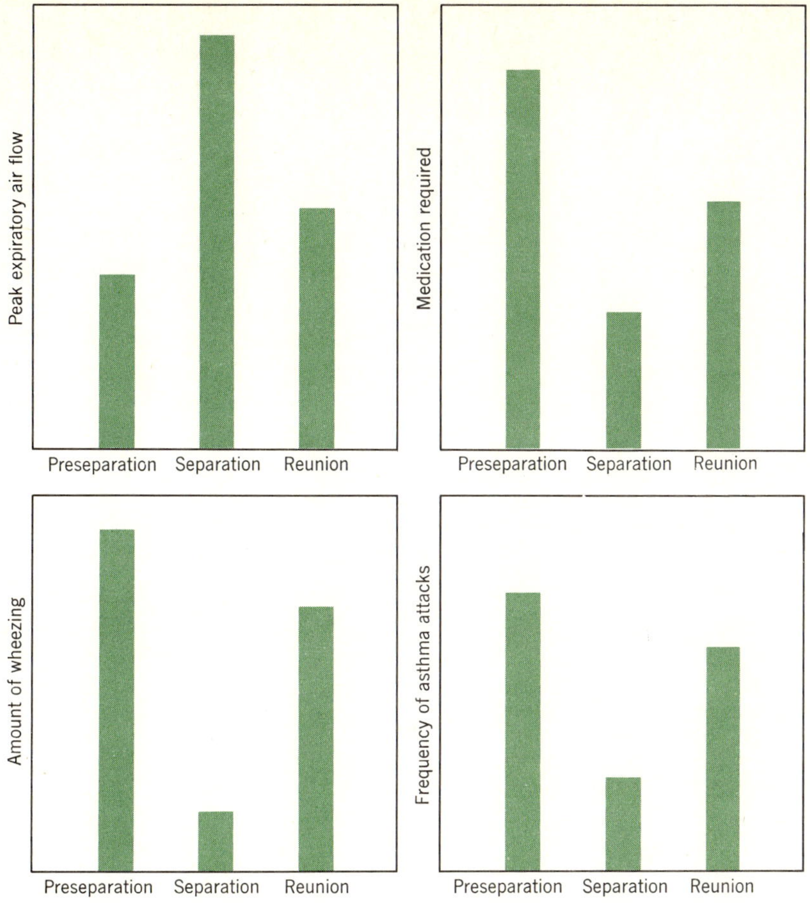


FIGURE **7.4**
Improvement on several measures of asthma among children who were predicted to do well after being separated from their parents. After Purcell et al., 1969.

*Patient* (Disgustedly): Boy, they don't even let you be sick in this hospital! (p. 361).

### Personality and asthma

It has often been suggested that asthmatic individuals display particular constellations of personality traits. Several investigators have found that asthmatic individuals have a great many so-called neurotic symptoms: dependency and maladjustment (Herbert, 1965), meekness, sensitivity, anxiety, meticulousness, perfectionism, and obsessions (Rees, 1964). But most of this work consisted of comparing asthmatics to a normal control population. Neuhaus (1958) compared the personality test scores of asthmatic children to those of both a normal group of children and a group of children with cardiac conditions. As in other studies, the asthmatics were found to be more neurotic than those who were normal. But, and this is the important point, *the cardiac children were also more neurotic than normal children*. Thus the increased neuroticism of asthmatic children may reflect only reactions to a chronic illness; neuroticism scores on personality tests are always higher the longer the patient has been sick (Kelly and Zeller, 1969).

### Physiological predisposition

Now that the importance of various stresses in eliciting asthmatic attacks has been documented, we must attempt to account for the fact that not all individuals exposed to such stressors develop asthma. Rees (1964) found that 86 percent of the asthmatics examined had a respiratory infection before asthma developed. Only 30 percent of his control subjects had been so afflicted. This study can be regarded as evidence that inheriting a weak organ, establishing a reaction pattern, or both may figure in the etiology of asthma. Individuals whose asthma is primarily allergic may have an inherited hypersensitivity of the respiratory mucosa which then overresponds to usually harmless substances such as dust or pollen. There is evidence that the incidence of asthma has a familial pattern consistent with genetic transmission (Konig and Godfrey, 1973). Finally, there is some indication that asthmatics have a less than normally responsive sympathetic nervous system (Miklich et al., 1973; Mathe and Knapp, 1971). Activation of the sympathetic nervous system is already known to reduce the intensity of an asthmatic attack.

In conclusion, a diathesis-stress explanation once again seems to fit the data on a psychophysiological disorder. Once the respiratory system is predisposed to asthma, any number of psychological stressors can interact with the diathesis to produce the disease.

## Summary

Psychophysiological disorders are physical diseases produced by psychological factors, primarily stress. Such disorders usually affect organs innervated by the autonomic nervous system, such as those of the respiratory, cardiovascular, gastrointestinal, and endocrine systems. Research has focused on the question of how psychological stress produces a particular psychophysiological disorder. Some workers have proposed that the answer lies in the specifics of the stressor. They say, for example, that aggressive impulses may create conflicts for an individual and give him an ulcer. The evidence does not generally favor this view. A more viable hypothesis is that stress interacts with a physiological diathesis. Ulcer may be induced by stress and a tendency of the stomach to secrete too much acid, hypertension by stress and a labile circulatory system, and asthma by stress affecting a respiratory system that overresponds to an allergen or one that has been weakened by prior infection. Although we have spoken of psychological stress affecting the body, it must be remembered that the *mind* and the *body* are best viewed as two different ways of talking about the same organism.

# chapter 8

## AFFECTIVE DISORDERS



Melancholia, a term derived from the Greek words *melan* meaning black and *choler* meaning bile, was one of the three types of madness recognized by Hippocrates in the fourth century B.C. By the second century A.D. the Cappadocian physician Artaeus had suggested a relationship between melancholia and an apparently opposite emotional state, which is now called mania. In the late nineteenth century, as we have seen, the famous German psychiatrist Emil Kraepelin divided psychoses into two types. One, schizophrenia, will be discussed in Chapters 13 and 14. The other, manic-depressive illness, which was considered to be the disturbance of all patients showing "affective excess," is the subject of this chapter.

## General Characteristics of Depression and Mania

### Depression

"Depression is the common cold of psychopathology, at once familiar and mysterious" (Seligman, 1973). Just as most people experience at least moments of anxiety every week of their existence, so will each of us probably have more than an ample amount of sadness during the course of our lives, although perhaps not to the degree or with the frequency that the label depression is warranted. It has been estimated that 5 percent of men and 10 percent of women are depressed at least once during their lives (Woodruff, Goodwin, and Guze, 1974). Often depression is associated with other psychological problems and with medical conditions. The man who has trouble maintaining his erection during intercourse is usually depressed about his sex life. The woman who has had a hysterectomy often suffers depression over what she incorrectly believes to be a loss of her femininity. Agoraphobics may become despondent because of their inability to venture out of their homes. In these and countless other instances depression is best viewed as secondary to another condition. Our discussion of depression in this chapter will focus on people for whom this affective disorder is the primary problem.

The following eloquent account is from a person who would be regarded as suffering from profound depression. Clearly, anxiety also plays a part in deepening the despair.

> *I was seized with an unspeakable physical weariness. There was a tired feeling in the muscles unlike anything I had ever experienced. A peculiar sensation appeared to travel up my spine to my brain. I had an indescribable nervous feeling. My nerves seemed like live wires charged with electricity. My nights were sleepless. I lay with dry, staring eyes gazing into space. I had a fear that some terrible calamity was about to happen. I grew afraid to be left alone. The most trivial duty became a formidable task. Finally mental and physical exercises became impossible; the tired muscles refused to respond, my "thinking apparatus" refused to work, ambition was gone. My general feeling might be summed up in the familiar saying "What's the use." I had tried so hard to make something of myself, but the struggle seemed useless. Life seemed utterly futile (Reid, 1910, pp. 612–613).*

Depression has been studied from several perspectives in addition to such phenomenological reports. Psychoanalytic views emphasize the unconscious conflicts associated with grief and loss; cognitive theories focus on the depressed person's self-defeating thought processes; learning theorists contend with the curtailment of activity associated with depression; and physiological theorists concentrate on what the central nervous system is doing at the neural-chemical level.

### The clinical picture

There is general agreement on the most common signs and symptoms of depression (Robins and Guze, 1970).

1. Sad, apathetic mood (dysphoria).
2. Negative self-concept (self-reproach, self-blame).
3. Desire to hide, to stay away from others.
4. Loss of sleep, appetite, and sexual desire, but sometimes a tendency to sleep an abnormally great amount.
5. Shift in activity level, becoming either lethargic or agitated.
6. Recurrent thoughts of death or suicide.
7. Difficulty in concentrating.

Depressed people may also neglect personal hygiene and appearance and make numerous hypochondriacal complaints of aches and pains that apparently have no physical basis. They feel generally dejected and completely worthless and may be apprehensive, anxious, and despondent much of the time.

A single individual seldom shows all the aspects of depression; the diagnosis is typically made if at least a few signs are evident, particularly a mood of profound sadness that is out of proportion to the person's life situation. Fortunately, most depression, although recurrent, tends to dissipate with time. The following case description conveys the course of depression.

Mr. J. was a fifty-one-year-old industrial engineer who, since the death of his wife five years earlier, had been suffering from continuing episodes of depression marked by extreme social withdrawal and occasional thoughts of suicide. His wife had died in an automobile accident during a shopping trip which he himself was to have made but had canceled because of professional responsibilities. His self-blame for her death, which became evident immediately after the funeral and was regarded by his friends and relatives as transitory, deepened as the months, and then years, passed by. He began to drink, sometimes heavily, and when thoroughly intoxicated would plead to his deceased wife for forgiveness. He lost all capacity for joy—his friends could not recall when they had last seen him smile. His gait was typically slow and labored, his voice usually tearful, his posture stooped. Once a gourmet, he had lost all interest in food and good wine, and on those increasingly rare occasions when friends invited him for dinner, this previously witty, urbane man could barely manage to engage in small talk. As might be expected, his work record deteriorated markedly, along with his psychological condition. Appointments were missed and projects haphazardly started and then left unfinished. He was referred by his physician for psychotherapy after he had spent a week closeted in his home. Not long afterward, he seemed to emerge from his despair and began to feel his old self again.

### Laboratory findings on depression

Thus far, we have considered the clinical description of depression. A few controlled studies should also be reviewed in order to give a more complete picture. Then we will have a better idea of the various aspects of depression that any given theory must seek to explain.

The clinical lore tells us that depressed patients complain of decreased ability to think and to solve problems. Most controlled studies do suggest that some depressives suffer from intellectual deficits. Miller (1974), for example, found that depressed college students were significantly slower in solving anagrams than were nondepressed controls. Other laboratory research concerns the perception of time. Depressed people frequently complain that time drags by, almost interminably, and this was confirmed by Mézey and Cohen (1961), who also found that the distortion tended to diminish as the patients improved clinically. A study done with TAT cards provides evidence that normal people are more future-oriented than either depressed or schizophrenic patients (Dilling and Rabin, 1967).

Motor retardation, or slowness in moving, is a generally accepted hallmark of most types of depression. Laboratory data confirm that depressives do in fact perform more poorly than normal controls on a range of tasks requiring quick responses. But on most tasks their performance is similar to that of schizophrenics, suggesting that slowness is not specific to depression (Miller, 1975).

Taken together, studies do indicate that as a group depressed people suffer from a host of sometimes severe psychological deficits (Miller, 1975). What is not clear is whether all people who are depressed suffer in the same way. Nor is it certain whether the observed deficits uniquely characterize depressives or whether they are found also in people who fit into other diagnostic categories.

## Mania

The symptoms of mania include disturbances in

1. **Mood.** The patient may be elated and overconfident yet easily angered and irritable.
2. **Thought.** The patient will generally speak rapidly, often talking about grandiose, sometimes

delusional, plans for the future. He or she may change topics frequently—the so-called flight of ideas.

3. **Motor activity.** There is a marked increase in motor activity, sometimes to the point that some of it is apparently purposeless.
4. **Sleep.** The patient sleeps fitfully and infrequently.
5. **Attention.** The patient is easily distracted and accomplishes little that he or she sets out to do.

The following description of a manic episode comes from our files. The irritability that is often part of this state was not found in this patient.

*Therapist:* Well, you seem pretty happy today.

*Client:* Happy! Happy! You certainly are a master of understatement, you rogue! (Shouting, literally jumping out of seat.) Why I'm ecstatic. I'm leaving for the West coast today, on my daughter's bicycle. Only 3100 miles. That's nothing, you know. I could probably walk, but I want to get there by next week. And along the way I plan to follow up on my inventions of the past month, you know, stopping at the big plants along the way having lunch with the executives, maybe getting to know them a bit—you know, Doc, "know" in the biblical sense (leering at therapist seductively). Oh, God, how good it feels. It's almost like a non-stop orgasm.

## Formal Diagnostic Categories

### DSM-II Listings

The DSM-II lists depression in three major diagnostic categories—*major affective disorders, depressive neurosis,* and *psychotic depressive reaction.* Listed under the major affective disorders heading are the manic-depressive illnesses and involuntional melancholia. The concept of *manic-depressive illness,* as developed by Kraepelin to cover all cases of "affective excess," is *not* meant to identify only those individuals who show the alternations between mania and depression, the circular type. It is also applied both to people who are exclusively depressed (depressed type) and to those who are exclusively manic (manic type).

The other major affective disorder, *involutional melancholia,* is said to occur at the "change of life," when both men and women go through physiological changes that make it less likely that they will be able to reproduce. It used to be thought that these changes were the physical cause of this kind of depression. But no evidence substantiates this belief. We know that, in addition to somatic changes, individuals in their forties and fifties face considerable other difficulties: doubts about sexual attractiveness, realization that certain life goals may never be achieved, and loss of contact with children. All are likely contributors to depression in people of this age.

The two remaining DSM-II categories, neurotic and psychotic depressions, are distinguished, in part, from manic-depression, depressed type, by the fact that an environmental event is assumed to have elicited the reactions. But deciding whether depression was indeed caused by an environmental stress proves troublesome. Mendels (1970) has pointed out some of the problems.

> *. . . The fact that a patient reports an association between a stressful life experience and the onset of an illness, and that he believes the two to be associated, does not in itself constitute proof that the reported stress caused the illness. Several*

*explanations must be considered:*

*1. The stress is a temporal coincidence. We all experience difficulties and strains in the course of everyday living, and only a minority of us develop symptoms sufficiently severe after such experiences to bring them to a psychologist or a psychiatrist. It is therefore possible that the stress events that the patient associates with the onset of his illness are unrelated to the illness.*

*2. The so-called stress event may arise as a consequence of the illness. This is exemplified in a man who explains his depression as a result of having recently lost an important position. Careful [investigation] might reveal that he had lost his position because of increasing inefficiency associated with the earlier onset of the depression.*

*3. The stress experience may interact with an underlying predisposing factor or in some way activate a latent problem in a vulnerable personality.*

*4. The stress event may, in fact, have been the major cause of the depression, either because of the nature or the intensity of the stress. An example would be a woman who is depressed because her husband and children were all killed in a motor accident.*

*Thus while there is often no definite causal relationship between adverse environmental events and the onset of a reactive depression, there is no doubt that for many individuals the onset is related in some way to adverse circumstances. We are far from understanding the exact nature of this relationship (p. 28).*

It is difficult then to distinguish between neurotic and psychotic depressions on the one hand and manic-depression, depressed type, on the other. What of the distinction between neurotic and psychotic depressions? Most research (for example, Beck, 1967) indicates the major difference to be severity (Table 8.1). The

TABLE **8.1**
Frequency of Clinical Symptoms in Neurotic Depressive Reaction (NDR) and Psychotic Depressive Reaction (PDR)
(from Beck, 1967, p. 85)

| | Symptom present | | Symptom present to severe degree | |
|---|---|---|---|---|
| **Clinical symptom** | **NDR, % (*N* = 50)** | **PDR, % (*N* = 50)** | **NDR, % (*N* = 50)** | **PDR, % (*N* = 50)** |
| Sad faces | 86 | 94 | 4 | 24 |
| Stooped posture | 58 | 76 | 4 | 20 |
| Speech: slow, etc. | 66 | 70 | 8 | 22 |
| Low mood | 84 | 80 | 8 | 44 |
| Diurnal variation of mood | 22 | 48 | 2 | 10 |
| Hopelessness | 78 | 68 | 6 | 34 |
| Conscious guilt | 64 | 44 | 6 | 12 |
| Feelings of inadequacy | 68 | 70 | 10 | 42 |
| Somatic preoccupation | 58 | 66 | 6 | 24 |
| Suicidal wishes | 58 | 76 | 14 | 40 |
| Indecisiveness | 56 | 70 | 6 | 28 |
| Loss of motivation | 70 | 82 | 8 | 48 |
| Loss of interest | 64 | 78 | 10 | 44 |
| Fatigability | 80 | 74 | 8 | 48 |
| Loss of appetite | 48 | 76 | 2 | 40 |
| Sleep disturbance | 66 | 80 | 12 | 52 |
| Constipation | 28 | 56 | 2 | 16 |

## BOX 8.1 Endogenous-Exogenous Depression

A widely applied system of classification distinguishes between endogenous and exogenous depression. Endogenous means "originating within the body" and is an adjective applied to a disorder assumed to have an *internal physical cause.* In other words, a physiological malfunctioning is believed to bring on endogenous depression. Exogenous, "originating outside the body," is applied to sadness with an *environmental cause;* sometimes the word reactive identifies this type of depression.

How valid are the exogenous and endogenous diagnoses? Surely depressives diagnosed as exogenous should have suffered more environmental stress just prior to their depression than patients diagnosed as endogenous. But this has not been demonstrated. Leff, Roatch, and Bunney (1970), for example, obtained careful histories from patients diagnosed as having either exogenous or endogenous depression. They failed to find any significant differences in the frequency and types of stresses preceding the two kinds of depression. Other studies (Akiskal and McKinney, 1975) have similarly failed to isolate undue psychosocial stresses on depressives who are supposed to have become ill because of them. Such evidence argues against trying to distinguish between depressions that have environmental and organic sources.

The difficulties involved in determining whether the depression is directly attributable to an environmental event has changed the way in which the endogenous-exogenous distinction is made. The labels no longer indicate whether a precipitating event can or cannot be found. Rather they are applied to different patterns of behavior. In several different studies the following symptoms were found more often among patients labeled as endogenous depressives than among those with exogenous depression (Mendels and Cochrane, 1968): motoric retardation, deep depression, lack of reactivity to the environment, loss of interest in life, bodily symptoms, insomnia in the middle of the night, and no self-pity.

But even this reliance on behavior patterns has not led the exogenous-endogenous distinction out of the realm of controversy. Some believe that the endogenous-exogenous distinction, like the psychotic-neurotic, primarily reflects severity rather than any real difference in kind (for example, Klerman and Paykel, 1970).

patient diagnosed as psychotic depressive generally has the common indications of depression to a significantly greater degree. It may not, however, be very useful to have two distinct categories, neurotic and psychotic depressions, if we are talking only about severity (see Box 8.1).

To sum up the numerous problems with the DSM-II classification of depression,

1. Reliance on the presence or absence of stress to distinguish between categories is problematic.
2. The involutional melancholia category is based on the unsupported theory that its cause is physiological.
3. Neurotic and psychotic depressions are differentiated only by severity; it appears more straightforward to speak of people who are either profoundly or moderately depressed.

### DSM-III on Affective Disorders

The draft version of the DSM-III classification of affective disorders is simplicity itself compared to the cumbersome system just examined. Three categories are proposed—*manic disorder; depressive disorder;* and *bipolar affective disorder,* which covers alternating episodes of mania and depression. Stress is no longer a differentiating factor; the problematic neurotic-psychotic distinction has been discarded; and the outmoded involutional melancholia category is gone. The DSM-III system is based solely on current behavior and the patient's history. As we shall see later, particularly when examining whether genetic factors figure in depression, solid evidence supports making a distinction between bipolar-mood disorder and depressive disorder. ■

## Psychological Theories of Depression

As is true of theorizing about other abnormal syndromes, that concerning depression points to both psychological and physiological factors. It will be seen that each theoretical position emphasizes one or another aspect of depression at the expense of others. In this section we discuss several theories that are couched in psychological terms.

### Psychoanalytic Theory

It is not always easy to distinguish between sadness, which is normal, and depression, which is not. The contrast between normal grief and abnormal depression is the focal point of Abraham's (1911) original attempt to interpret depression through psychoanalytic theorizing and of Freud's (1917) celebrated paper, "Mourning and Melancholia." Abraham was Freud's student. They both saw self-centeredness as differentiating depression from normal grief. There are several variations on this thesis, well summarized by Mendels (1970); our own expository purposes are served by restricting critical attention to Freud's original work, which was an elaboration of Abraham's theorizing.

Predictably, Freud saw the potential for depression being created early in childhood. He theorized that during the oral period the child's needs may be insufficiently or oversufficiently gratified. The person therefore remains "stuck" in this stage and dependent on the instinctual gratifications particular to it. With this arrest in psychosexual maturation, this fixation at the oral stage, he or she may develop a tendency to be excessively dependent on other people for the maintenance of self-esteem.

From this happenstance of childhood, how can the adult come to suffer from depression? The reasoning is complex, assuming as it does that several unconscious processes are a part of mourning. Freud hypothesized that after the loss of a loved one the mourner first *introjects* or incorporates the lost person: he or she identifies with the lost one, perhaps in a fruitless attempt to undo the loss. Because, as Freud asserted, we unconsciously harbor negative feelings against those we love, the mourner now becomes the object or his or her own hate and anger. In addition, the mourner also resents being deserted and feels guilt for real or imagined sins against the lost person. The period of introjection is followed by the period of *mourning work,* during which the mourner recalls memories of the lost one and thereby separates himself from the person who has died and loosens the bonds that introjection has imposed.

The grief work can go astray in overly dependent individuals and develop into an ongoing process of self-abuse, self-blame, and depression. Such individuals do not loosen their emotional bonds with the person who has died, continuing to castigate themselves for the faults and shortcomings perceived in the loved one who has been introjected. The mourner's anger toward the lost one continues to be directed inward. This theorizing is the basis for the widespread psychodynamic view of depression as anger turned against oneself.

One further point must be made. Since many people can become depressed and remain so *without* having recently suffered the loss of a loved one, it became necessary to invoke the concept of "symbolic loss" in order to keep the theoretical formulation intact. For example, a person may unconsciously interpret a rejection as a total withdrawal of love.

We see numerous problems in this formulation. First, since the person presumably both hates and loves the individual he or she has lost, why is it that only the hate and anger are turned inward and not the love that is also there? Since the depressed person is said to have introjected the loved one, thus directing inwardly the feelings previously directed to the loved one, why do anger and resentment predominate? If the mourner directed positive feelings about the lost one inwardly, he or she would be a happy person rather than a depressed one. Psychoanalytic theorists have tried to resolve this inconsistency by postulating that the loss of a loved one is viewed as a rejection or withdrawal of affection. Interpreted in this way, a negative emotional state is more likely to predominate. The crucial point, though, is the absence of direct evidence that depressives do interpret death as rejection by the deceased.

A second difficulty is common to all Freud's hypotheses that involve the concept of fixation at an earlier psychosexual stage of development. Freud states that fixation at the oral stage can come about *through either too little or too much gratification.* How much, it could be asked, is *enough* to prevent fixation? Freud's theory, being nonquantitative, does not deal adequately with this question.

The concept of "symbolic loss" presents a third problem. From our critical perspective, this concept is introduced only after the fact to account for depression when no actual object loss can be specified. The concept would not be invoked for people who are not depressed. If it is inferred only *after* a diagnosis of depression and only *after* no actual object loss can be discerned, the diagnostician is engaging in the kind of confused reasoning referred to as *post hoc, ergo propter hoc,* after this, therefore because of this.

Little research has been generated by psychoanalytic points of view, neither Freud's nor those of others that are not discussed here. Our assessment is in agreement with that of Mendels (1970), who finds little to support these views other than the often-repeated assertions by adherents that things are as they conceive them to be. The conceptual system itself is elastic enough to explain any finding, *after the fact.*

At the same time, however, these views have found their way into more recent theorizing. For instance, irrational self-statements such as "It is a dire necessity that I be universally loved and approved of," to which Ellis attributes neurotic suffering, might plague Freud's "oral personality" in the deepening depression following the loss of a loved one. Although Freud cloaked his clinical impressions in theoretical terms that have been rejected by many contemporary writers, we must appreciate that some of his basic suppositions have a continuing influence.

## Cognitive Theories

Discussions of the feeling of helplessness in Chapter 5 and of Ellis's concept of irrational beliefs in Chapter 6 indicate that cognitive processes play a decisive role in emotional behavior. In some theories of depression as in some concerning anxiety, thoughts and beliefs are regarded as causing the emotional state. In a way Freud is a cognitive theorist too, for he viewed depression as resulting from a person's *belief* that loss is a withdrawal of affection.

Perhaps the most important contemporary theory of depression to regard thought processes as causative factors is Beck's (1967). His central thesis is that depressed individuals feel as they do because they commit characteristic logical errors. From an examination of his therapy notes, he found that his depressed patients tended to distort whatever happened to them in the direction of self-blame, catastrophes, and the like. Thus an event interpreted by a normal person as irritating and inconvenient, for example, the malfunctioning of an automobile, would be interpreted by the depressed patient as yet another example of the utter hopelessness of life. Beck's position is not that depressives think poorly or illogically in general. Rather, depressives draw illogical conclusions in evaluations of themselves.

Beck calls these errors in thinking "schemata" or characteristic sets which color how the person actually perceives the world. The depressed person is seen as operating within a schema of *self-deprecation* and *self-blame.* This set disposes the individual to interpret or label events in a way that justifies saying "What a jerk I am," or "How hopeless this is."

Beck describes several logical errors committed by depressed people in interpreting reality.

1. **Arbitrary inference.** A conclusion drawn in the absence of sufficient evidence or of any evidence at all. For example, a man concludes that he is worthless because it is raining the day that he is hosting an outdoor cocktail party.

2. **Selective abstraction.** A conclusion drawn on the basis of but one of many elements in a situation. A worker blames herself entirely for the failure of a product to function, even though she is only one of many people who have produced it.

3. **Overgeneralization.** An overall sweeping conclusion drawn on the basis of a single, perhaps trivial, event. A student regards his poor performance in a single class on one particular day as final proof of his worthlessness and stupidity.

4. **Magnification and minimization.** Gross errors in evaluating performance. A woman believes that she has completely ruined her car (magni-

Aaron T. Beck, psychiatrist at the University of Pennsylvania. His cognitive theory of depression suggests that it is caused by excessive self-blame.

fication) when she sees that there is a slight scratch on the rear fender; or a man still believes himself worthless (minimization) in spite of a succession of praiseworthy achievements.

It is important to appreciate the thrust of Beck's position. Whereas many theorists have seen people as victims of their passions, creatures whose intellectual capacities can exert little if any control over feelings—this is Freud's basic position—in the theory just outlined the cause-effect relationship operates in the opposite direction. Our emotional reactions are considered to be a function of how we construe our world, and indeed the interpretations of depressives are found not to mesh very well with objective reality. Beck sees depressives as the victims of their own illogical self-judgments.

At least two points need to be demonstrated when evaluating Beck's theory. First, depressed patients, in contrast to nondepressed individuals, must actually judge themselves in the illogical ways that Beck has enumerated. This first point has been tentatively confirmed by Beck's clinical observations, which suggest that depressed patients do, in fact, manifest at least some of the errors in logic listed by him (Beck, 1967).

Second, it should be demonstrated that this cognitive distortion is not a function of a primary emotional disturbance, that it does in fact *cause* the depressed mood. Many studies in experimental psychology have in a general way shown that a person's feelings can be influenced by how he or she construes events. The Geer, Davison, and Gatchel study (1970), for example, indicated that people are less aroused when they believe that they have control over painful stimulation, even when that belief is false. No study that we know of, however, directly demonstrates that the various noncognitive aspects of depression are truly secondary to or a function of the distorted cognitive schemata that Beck believes operate in this disorder. Beck has found that depression and cognitive distortions are *correlated,* but a specific causal relationship cannot be determined from such data; depression could cause illogical thoughts or illogical thoughts could cause depression. Or the relationship could reflect some third variable, such as a biochemical disturbance.

In spite of these difficulties, an important advantage of Beck's theory is that it is testable and has encouraged considerable research on depression. Even more important, it has encouraged therapists to work directly on depressed patients' thinking in order to change and alleviate their feelings (Beck, 1976).

## Learning Theories

**Depression through reduction in reinforcement**

One current learning conceptualization of depression bears some resemblance to Freud's theory, although, of course, the metaphors differ. Freud proposed as a causative factor the loss of a loved one by people whose oral dependencies retained from childhood make them particularly vulnerable to a lessening of external supports. It seems but a short step to connect depression to the reduction in activity that occurs when accustomed reinforcement is withdrawn. When a loved one dies, an important source of positive reinforcement is certainly lost.

For some learning theorists the concept of reduction in reinforcement is central (Eastman, 1976); unconscious mourning processes and introjection of the lost loved one play no part in their explanation of depression. Once people stop behaving as they used to do before the loss, when reinforcement was plentiful (Ferster, 1965; Lazarus, 1968b), the new lower level of activity may itself be reinforced (Ullmann and Krasner, 1975). For example, depressed people may receive sympathy or special dispensations from others, who expect less of them than they did before the loss of the loved one. The outlook for improvement is all the more bleak for those who lack social skills for acquiring in new or different ways the rewards that used to be available. In fact, this learning theory explains more directly than did Freud the depression that is not preceded by the loss of a loved one; accustomed reinforcements may be cut off for a number of reasons, for example, changes in occupational status or of locale.

The learning conceptualization attributing depression to a reduction in activity when reinforcement is lacking has been elaborated on and researched by Lewinsohn and his colleagues (for example, Lewinsohn, 1974). Figure 8.1 is a schematic representation of Lewinsohn's model of depression. The following assumptions are made.

1. The feeling of depression and other symptoms of the clinical syndrome, such as fatigue, are elicited when behavior receives little reinforcement.
2. This "thin" schedule of positive reinforcement, in turn, tends to reduce activity even more, and then reinforcements are even fewer.
3. The amount of positive reinforcement is a function of three sets of variables: (*a*) the number of potential reinforcers available to an individual as a function of personal characteristics, such as age, sex, and attractiveness to others; (*b*) the number of potential reinforcers available as a function of the environment that the person is in, such as being at home rather than in prison; and (*c*) the person's repertoire of behavior that can gain reinforcement, for example, vocational and social skills.

As Figure 8.1 indicates, a low rate of positive reinforcement reduces still further the activities and expression of qualities that might be rewarded. Both activities and rewards decrease in a vicious circle. A little reflection will reveal how difficult it would be to collect data that confirm this model. Careful, yet unobtrusive trained raters, such as those in the Paul study (page 81), would have to count the number of reinforcements individuals receive in their everyday lives. Only after such a study could we state that depressed people receive fewer reinforcements than nondepressed individuals. We would also have to demonstrate that the activity of the individual is indeed less because of the reduced rates of positive reinforcement rather than other factors. Many studies from Lewinsohn's group confirm to some degree the central hypothesis,

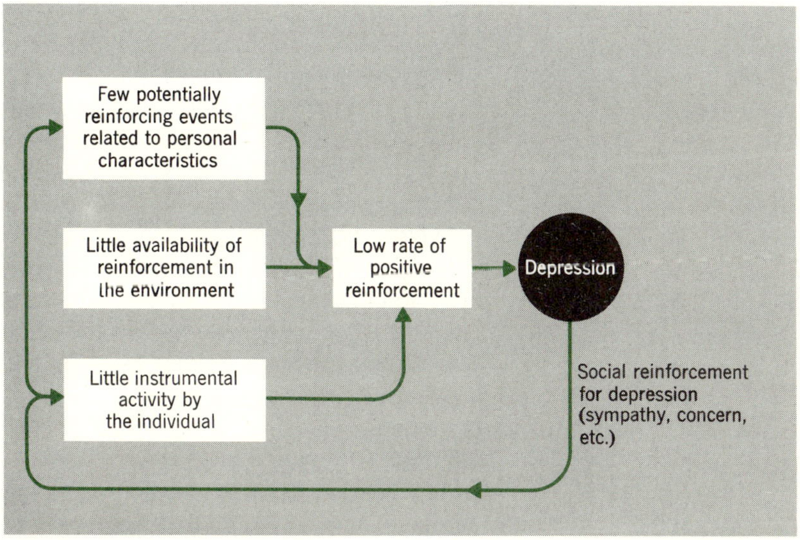


FIGURE **8.1**
Schematic of Lewinsohn's model of depression, which takes into account the inactivity and dejection of the depressive. After Lewinsohn, 1975.

that depression is associated with low rates of positively reinforced activity (Libet and Lewinsohn, 1973; Lewinsohn and Libet, 1972), but considerable research is still needed to establish specific causal relationships between reinforcement and mood.

### A cognitive–learning view

A cognitive model of depression as *learned helplessness* has been proposed by Seligman (1974). He suggests that although anxiety is the initial response to a stressful situation, anxiety is replaced by depression if the person comes to believe that control is unattainable. In some ways this model is similar to the ego analytical view of Bibring (1953), who proposed that depression follows ". . . the ego's shocking awareness of its helplessness in regard to its aspirations" (p. 39).

Both Lewinsohn's reduced-activity–low-reinforcement view of depression and Seligman's learned-helplessness model are learning-based theories of depression. There are, however, important differences between them. The first view is a noncognitive one, assuming that inactivity and depressed mood are a direct function of environmental consequences. If a person's reinforcement becomes "thin," activity will be reduced in frequency, positive reinforcement will become even scarcer, and the person will feel depressed. Seligman's cognitive formulation emphasizes the way in which the individual learns to *construe* the relationship between activity and outcome, which is that he or she is helpless and all efforts will be in vain.

To examine Seligman's theory we will first describe a typical learned-helplessness experiment with animals. Dogs receive painful electric shock in two different situations. In the first part of the experiment some dogs are subjected to numerous painful electric shocks from which they cannot escape. In the second part these animals, as well as dogs who did not have this prior experience with inescapable shock, are placed in an avoidance apparatus. Painful shock can be avoided if the dogs learn to run to another compartment of the box as soon as they hear a warning buzzer or see a light come on. The behavior of the dogs is markedly affected by whether they were earlier exposed to inescapable shock. Animals who have not had the earlier experience become quite upset when they receive the first few electric shocks, but fairly soon thereafter they learn to run when they hear or see the conditioned stimulus and thereby avoid further painful shock. The animals who have had the earlier experience with inescapable shock behave quite differently. Soon after receiving the first shocks they stop running around in a distressed manner; instead they seem to give up and passively accept the painful stimulation. Not surprisingly, they do not acquire the avoidance response as efficiently and effectively as the control animals do. Such experiments imply that animals can acquire what might be called a "sense of helplessness" when confronted with uncontrollable aversive stimulation. This helplessness later tends seriously and deleteriously to affect their performance in stressful situations that *can* be controlled. They appear to lose the ability and motivation to learn to respond in an effective way to painful stimulation.

On the basis of this and other work on the effects of uncontrollable stress, Seligman felt that learned helplessness in animals can provide a model for at least certain forms of human depression. He documented remarkable similarities between the manifestations of helplessness observed in animal laboratory studies and at least some of the symptoms of depression (Table 8.2). Like many depressed people, the animals appear passive in the face of stress, failing to initiate action that might allow them to cope. They develop anorexia, having difficulty in eating or retaining what is eaten, and lose weight. On the physiological level, one of the neurotransmitter chemicals, norepinephrine, was found to be depleted in Seligman's animals (see Box. 8.5, page 210). Drugs that increase levels of norepinephrine have been shown to alleviate depression in human beings. Although effectiveness of treatment does not, as we have often indicated, prove etiology, the fact that depression is re-

TABLE **8.2**
## Seligman's Learned-Helplessness Model of Depression

| | Learned helplessness in animals | Depression in humans |
|---|---|---|
| **Manifestations** | Passivity in face of stress | Passivity, "paralysis of the will" |
| | Retardation in learning to deal with stress | Negative expectations in dealing with stress or challenge, even when performance is adequate; feelings of hopelessness |
| | Dissipation of effect with time | Dissipation with time, although the length of time is very indefinite, ranging from days to years |
| | Anorexia | Anorexia |
| | Weight loss | Weight loss |
| | Brain norepinephrine depletion | Improvement when norepinephrine increases |
| **Etiology** | Uncontrollable stress—not stress per se but learning that no response reliably reduces aversive stimulation | Inability to control events in life, such as loss of a loved one and physical disease, and failure to act either to relieve suffering or to gain gratification |

duced by a drug that increases the level of norepinephrine is consistent with the finding that learned helplessness in animals is associated with lower levels of the chemical.

Building on these behavioral and physiological parallels, Seligman then examined possible commonalities in the causes of helplessness and depression. What makes the dog behave in a helpless, apparently depressed manner is known, for the carefully controlled experiments *create* the condition. The causes of human depression are much less clear, for the information available consists primarily of clinical observations. It is striking, however, how often clinicians of diverse theoretical persuasions remark on events over which the depressed person has had little or no control, such as the loss of loved ones, physical disease, aging, and failure.

Now experiments with human beings have yielded results similar to those of experiments done with animals. People who have been subjected to inescapable noise and inescapable shock and confronted with unsolvable problems fail later to escape noise and shock and solve simple problems (for examples Hiroto and Seligman, 1975; Roth and Kubal, 1975). Moreover, the performance of college students who rate as depressed on the Beck Depression Inventory (Beck, 1967) has been found similar to that of nondepressed students who have earlier been subjected to these same helplessness-inducing experiences (Miller, Seligman, and Kurlander, 1975; Klein and Seligman, 1976). This is very important, for it suggests that we can, in a laboratory setting, elicit from nondepressed subjects behavior similar to that observed in depressed individuals. Figure 8.2 illustrates this phenomenon. The mean escape latency, their slowness to move away from an unpleasant noise, constituted the dependent measure of how poorly or well subjects coped with a solvable problem. Klein and Seligman found that these latencies were the same for depressed students who had not earlier been subjected to noise (D-NN in Figure 8.2) and for nondepressed students who in an earlier phase of the experiment *had* been

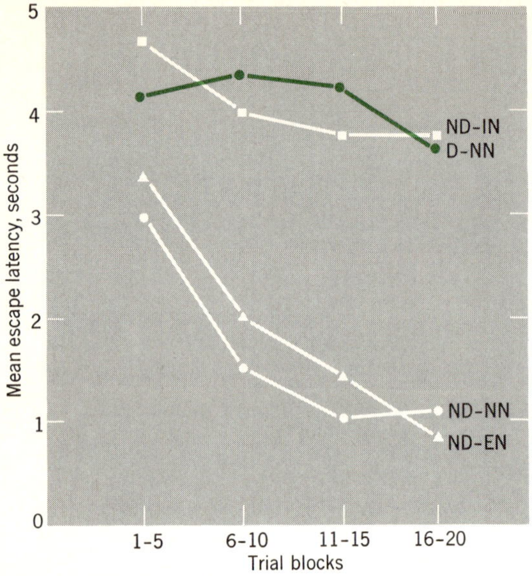


FIGURE **8.2**
Subjects who were depressed and those who were not depressed but had experienced inescapable noise acted more slowly to escape noise than did those in the other groups. After Klein and Seligman, 1976.

D-NN: *S*s rated as depressed on Beck Depression Inventory; were not previously subjected to noise.
ND-NN: *S*s rated as nondepressed; were not previously subjected to noise.
ND-IN: *S*s rated as nondepressed; were previously subjected to inescapable noise (the "helpless" group).
ND-EN: *S*s rated as nondepressed; were previously subjected to escapable noise.

exposed to inescapable noise (ND-IN). This pattern of results indicates that a helplessness-inducing experience (1) interferes with the handling of a subsequent problem that is solvable; and more importantly, (2) renders the nondepressed subjects as unable to cope as the depressed subjects. A precursor to at least certain kinds of human depression may well be the belief that one cannot act to solve problems, to reduce suffering, and to gain gratifications (see Box 8.2).

An ingenious experiment by Miller and Seligman (1973) offers additional corroborative evidence. This effort focused on a related cognitive distortion of depressed people, namely their disinclination to be encouraged by successes, ostensibly because they do not believe their behavior to have any effect on what happens to them. College students were classified as either depressed or nondepressed on the basis of the Beck Depression Inventory. Then they were given several trials on each of two kinds of problems. One task consisted of guessing which of two slides would appear on a given occasion, the order being randomized. Success was a purely chance event. The second task required them to move a platform upward in such a way that a steel ball was kept from rolling off it; success apparently required skill. After each trial the subjects were asked whether they expected to be successful on the next. How was each subject's expectation of success on the next trial affected by success or failure on a given trial? If depressed people do not readily perceive that any activity they engage in will bring them rewards, their expectancy for success when performing a task requiring skill should be less affected by previous success than would be the case for a nondepressed person. In carrying out a task for which success depends on chance, both depressed and nondepressed subjects should have similar expectations about success. Seligman does not consider depressives to have a distorted view of situations whose outcomes do not depend on their behavior.

As can be seen in Figure 8.3, the results of the experiment strongly confirmed the hypothesis. Keeping the steel ball on the platform during one trial made the nondepressed subjects feel rather confident of success on the next trial, the depressed subjects less so. No differences were found in the expectancies of the two groups of subjects as they made guesses about the order of the slides.

What is noteworthy—and what points up the role played by the subject's thinking—is that success on *both* tasks was controlled by the experimenter in order to make reinforcements of all subjects the same. A hidden electric switch enabled the experimenter to decide whether, on a given trial, a subject would perform the skilled

## BOX **8.2** Depression in Women: A Consequence of Learned Helplessness?

As indicated at the beginning of this chapter, depression appears to occur more often in women than in men. But why? A recent large-scale survey carried out by the National Institute of Mental Health Center for Epidemiologic Studies (Radloff, 1975) suggests some reasons.

More than 2500 men and women of all ages and from a broad range of educational and socioeconomic backgrounds were interviewed in two American cities. Among the questions asked were twenty that comprised a self-report measure of depression, such as how often had the person slept restlessly during the previous week, and how often had he or she felt sad.

Several of the numerous findings are important for our present purposes.

1. Consistent with work done previsouly, married men were found to be significantly less depressed than married women.

2. Contrary to earlier thinking (for example, Gove and Tudor, 1973; Bernard, 1973) however, it was concluded that the role of housewife per se does not account for the higher levels of depression in married women, for working wives were also more depressed than married men. Having a job outside the home, then, does not appear to insulate married women from depression. Indeed, working wives were no less depressed than those who did not have outside employment.

3. Contrary to the findings of previous studies, the working wives were not more depressed than working men because they felt overworked by having two jobs, one as homemaker and one outside the house. Although the working wives did more housework than working husbands, this was not associated with their higher levels of depression.

Radloff speculates that the higher levels of depression among women are best explained as a consequence of learned helplessness. The feminist literature would agree (for example, Bernard, 1973; Chesler, 1972), for it blames the greater incidence of mental problems among women on their lack of personal and political power. Feminists take the position that more women than men become depressed because their social roles do not encourage them to feel competent. What women do does not seem to count compared to the greater power that men have in society. In fact, it may be that little girls are *trained* to be helpless (Broverman, Broverman, and Clarkson, 1970). And the more helpless woman, unable to tolerate the single life (Bernard, 1973), is probably more likely to marry.

These are interesting hypotheses, even plausible ones. But we need to know, for example, whether a woman's depression is preceded by a series of events that force her to recognize a feeling of helplessness already instilled in her. This and other questions have to be dealt with before lending too much credence to a helplessness explanation of depression in women. Learned helplessness may, however, prove a fruitful framework within which to conduct research on the depression of women.

task successfully or not. The efforts of the subjects were not really effective or for that matter ineffective; they were simply irrelevant. The experimenter created the mistaken *belief* of success or failure on a given trial. The fact that the task was a ruse, and that depressed and non-depressed subjects had the same number of "successes" and "failures," demonstrates the overriding importance of the subjects' beliefs about themselves in relation to the environment. The depressed subject was sometimes successful in performing the skilled task, but this favorable outcome did not increase the expectancy of succeeding on the next trial. A person may be profoundly depressed in the midst of environmental gratification that he or she has earned. If the person does not believe that the rewards have been earned, Seligman's model predicts no lifting of depression.

One final note on this experiment. None of the items on the Beck Depression Inventory, Seligman's measure of depression, seems to predict in any precise way the results of the Miller-Seligman experiment. One item, for instance, asks whether the person has suicidal thoughts. We would suppose, of course, that highly de-

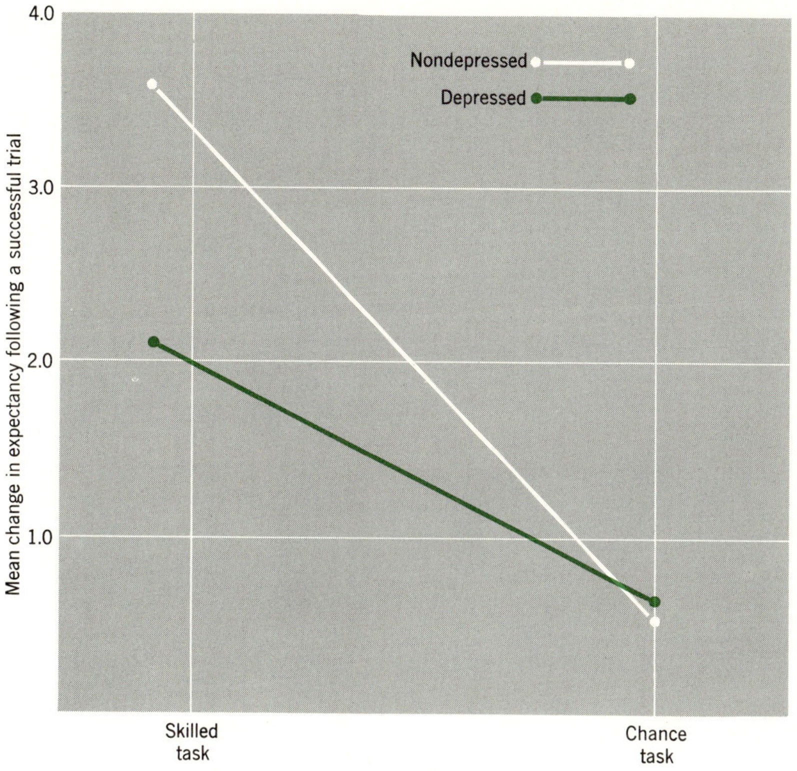


FIGURE **8.3**
Average changes in expectancy of success of depressed and nondepressed subjects after success on a task requiring skill and on one depending on chance. Adapted from Miller and Seligman, 1973.

pressed subjects are *generally* more pessimistic about their ability to solve problems. But the learned-helplessness model makes a more specific prediction, namely that only on tasks that require skill will the expectations of depressed and nondepressed subjects differ. The fact that this hypothesis, derived from the helplessness model, was so strongly confirmed is impressive evidence of the usefulness of Seligman's theory.

It is worth bearing in mind, as Seligman himself has cautioned, that the research from his lab has thus far yielded only *analogue* findings. The "depressed" college students participating in these experiments, although they attained scores on the Beck Depression Inventory that are similar to those of patients considered mildly depressed (Metcalfe and Goldman, 1965), nonetheless functioned in a highly demanding academic environment (University of Pennsylvania) and were available for study because they responded to a newspaper advertisement asking for subjects for a psychological experiment, not because they were hurting enough to seek professional help. Moreover, the activities engaged in by the subjects—pressing buttons when lights come on and moving handles to escape an unpleasant noise—are remote from the ordinary concerns of human beings. But we can expect studies to go forward and to examine in more naturalistic settings people who are truly incapacitated by depression.

Seligman (1975) has recently done more work on the cognitive part of his theory. He was impressed by the fact that human subjects in helplessness experiments quickly improve their performance when informed by the experimenter that the task they could not accomplish had been rigged to assure failure. Why should the typical performance deficits caused by helplessness-inducing experiences (fortunately) vanish as soon as subjects are told that their assumption of helplessness was contrived by the experimenter? The rats and dogs used in the earlier studies required repeated "therapy" trials before overcoming learned helplessness. But people, after all, *think* about why they behave as they do! Seligman proposes that a crucial factor in helplessness and depression is to what subjects *attribute* their failures to perform. His subjects rid themselves of their inability to perform because they could attribute it to a temporary circumstance.

Table 8.3 gives Seligman's schema of attribution, which is similar to an earlier proposal by Weiner and his colleagues (1971). A college student who has failed the mathematics portion of the Graduate Record Examination is taken as an example. Three questions are asked. Are the reasons for failure believed to be internal or environmentally caused? Is the problem believed to be stable or short-term? How all-inclusive or specific is the inability to succeed perceived to be? We would expect a person to feel more helpless and depressed if failure on a skill task like the GRE is regarded as internal (I have some personal problem that caused me to fail); if the problem is believed to be relatively persistent (I am incompetent and am *unlikely to change*); and if the defect is perceived to be all-inclusive and far-reaching (I have a *general* sort of incompetence that will prevent me from carrying out a wide variety of assignments). And we would predict that a person making the depressing internal, stable, and all-inclusive attributions would expect to do poorly on the verbal portion of the exam.

Not all evidence supports Seligman's learned-helplessness model (see Greer, 1976; Rizley, 1976), but the majority of studies testing it indicate that further exploration is warranted (Box 8.3). Moreover, Seligman's laboratory research has hopeful implications for treating depressed people. Teaching them that they *can* control their behavior and its consequences to some degree should prove effective therapy against one of the most widespread and crippling of human psychological disablements (for example, Klein and Seligman, 1976).

TABLE **8.3**
Seligman's Attributional Schema of Depression: Why I Failed My GRE Math Exam

| | **Internal** | | **External** | |
|---|---|---|---|---|
| **Degree** | **Stable** | **Unstable** | **Stable** | **Unstable** |
| All-inclusive | I lack intelligence. | I am exhausted. | These tests are all unfair. | It's an unlucky day, Friday the thirteenth |
| Specific | I lack mathematical ability. | I am fed up with math. | The math tests are unfair. | My math test was numbered "13." |

## BOX **8.3** Self-Blame and Learned Helplessness: A Paradox in Depression?

Although the views of Beck and Seligman are generally regarded as similar (for example, Akiskal and McKinney, 1975), they actually have an interesting incompatibility, which has recently been examined by Abramson and Sackeim (1977). Beck views the depressive as approaching life with a cognitive set that interprets unfortunate events as instances of personal failure. Depressed people blame themselves excessively for what goes wrong around them. But according to Seligman's learned-helplessness model, individuals become depressed because they believe that their behavior does not matter, that reinforcement is not contingent on what they do or do not do. "The discrepancy between these two views resides in the question of whether individuals assume responsibility for events that they believe they neither cause nor control" (Abramson and Sackeim, 1977, p. 839).

Does this conceptual paradox, this inconsistency between two theories, point to a paradox to be found in the actual thinking of depressives? The answer appears to be yes. In the study by Hiroto and Seligman (1975), for instance, subjects who were confronted with inescapable noise and unsolvable problems, and who thereafter acted helpless on a subsequent task, tended to attribute their failure both to the unsolvable nature of the tasks and to their own lack of ability. Basically, they were saying that the problems were unsolvable but that they also had failed. Other studies reviewed by Abramson and Sackeim similarly confirm that it is possible for depressed people, and for college students rendered "temporarily helpless," to hold two seemingly inconsistent beliefs, namely that they are both helpless to control what happens to them and are themselves to blame for failures.

Is there a reasonable way to resolve this paradox, assuming that research continues to support the view that depressed people blame themselves for events they also feel they cannot influence? One possibility is that depressed individuals blame themselves for failure but do not take credit or "blame themselves" for success. If an action has a good outcome, depressives may regard it as happenstance or attribute it to the effectiveness of others; but failures they take unto themselves. Abramson and Sackeim suggest that holding two contradictory beliefs is a paradox only in the view of people who are not clinically depressed. To a profoundly depressed individual it may not be paradoxical to consider the self simultaneously impotent and omnipotent, capable of nothing and yet responsible for many things. Appreciation of this phenomenon may help us better understand what depression is all about.

## Physiological Theories of Depression

Since physiological processes are known to have considerable effects on moods, it is not surprising that investigators have sought physiological causes for depression. At the outset we should indicate that disturbed physiological processes must be part of the causal chain if a predisposition for depression can be genetically transmitted. Evidence indicating that depression is, in part, inherited would, then, provide some support for the theory that depression has a physiological basis.

### The Genetic Data

Research on genetic factors in depression has very often used the twin and family methods and has typically focused on bipolar or unipolar depressives. Bipolars have suffered episodes of depression and mania, unipolars only depression. Unipolar depression is identical to depressive disorder as it is defined in the draft version of DSM-III. Estimates of the frequency of bipolar depression in first-degree relatives of bipolars range from about 10 to 20 percent (Slater, 1938; Perris, 1969; Brodie and Leff, 1971; Hays, 1976). These figures are substantially higher than the 1 to 2 percent figure usually taken as the morbidity risk for the general population. And the relatives of bipolar depressives are also found *not* at high risk for unipolar depression, thus supporting the bipolar-unipolar distinction. Zerbin-Rüdin (1968) compiled concordance data for depression of identical twins. The probands had bipolar depression. Overall, the concordance rate for depression was 70 percent, and the vast majority of the disturbed co-twins were bipolar depressives. In contrast, Price (1968) estimates the concordance rate for bipolar depression in fraternal twins at only 23 percent. The evidence clearly supports the notion that bipolar depression has a heritable component, although we must of course caution that the more conclusive adoption studies have not been performed (see Box 8.4).

Less research has been done on unipolar depression, but the information available indicates that genetic factors, although important, do not figure to the same extent that they do in bipolar depression. Perris (1969), for example, found that 7.4 percent of the first-degree relatives of unipolar index cases also had experienced a depressive episode. Cadoret, Winokur and Clayton (1971), in addition to uncovering the same amount of depression among the first-degree relatives of unipolar depressives, found that these relatives, especially the ones who themselves become depressed at an early age, appear to be at risk for other disorders, notably alcoholism and sociopathy.

### Biochemistry and Depression

Two major theories that have been proposed relate depression to neurotransmitters (see Box 8.5). One theory suggests that depression results from low levels of norepinephrine; the other points to low levels of serotonin. The norepinephrine theory also postulates that an excess of this neurotransmitter causes mania (Schildkraut, 1965).

The actions of drugs provided the clues on which both theories are based. In the 1950s two particular groups of drugs (see Chapter 20) were found to be effective in relieving depression. Studies revealed that they also increase the levels of both serotonin and norepinephrine in the brains of animals. This information only suggested that depression is caused by low levels of these substances, but it encouraged further explorations. Another piece of evidence favoring both theories was provided by reserpine, a drug now used primarily in the treatment of hypertension. Early in the same decade reserpine had been isolated by a research team working in Switzerland. It is an alkaloid[1] of the root of

[1] Alkaloids are organic substances that are found for the most part in seed plants, usually not singly but in mixtures of similar alkaloids. They all contain nitrogen and are the active agents that give a number of natural drugs their medicinal and also their toxic properties.

## BOX **8.4** A Testable Theory of the Genetic Transmission of Bipolar Depression

Throughout this book we have often been faced with theories couched in sufficiently vague terms to be untestable. A notable exception is the proposal of Winokur and his colleagues at the University of Iowa, that bipolar depression is caused by a dominant gene on the X chromosome, one of two which together determine the sex of the fetus. The theory is easily tested. According to Mendelian genetics, the forty-six chromosomes in the body cells of human beings, and the genes they carry, act together in pairs. A dominant gene is one that will find expression, regardless of the other gene it is paired with. Women have a pair of similar sex chromosomes, XX, men a dissimilar pair, XY. The fetus gets one of its pair from the ovum of the mother and one from the spermatozoan of the father; each of these sex cells contains only twenty-three chromosomes, for the pairs have divided. The mother, then, always contributes an X chromosome; if the father also contributes an X chromosome, the child will be female. If the father contributes a Y chromosome, the child will be male.

Winokur's theorizing grew out of an early study of the family histories of patients with affective disorder (Winokur and Clayton, 1967). The patients were separated into two groups, those whose families had incidences of affective disorder and those whose families did not. In the first group 96 percent of 112 probands were bipolars. In the second only 3 percent of 129 probands were bipolars. The relatives of bipolar probands were obviously at high risk. To investigate bipolar patients further, Winokur, Clayton, and Reich (1969) collected a new sample of 89 index cases. The data from this investigation are shown in Table 8.4. The A part of the table indicates that female relatives were at much higher risk than

### TABLE **8.4**
### A Study of the First-Degree Relatives of Manic Probands

(from Winokur, Clayton, and Reich, 1969)

| | | |
|---|---|---|
| **A.** | Morbidity risk of relative of a proband | |
| | *Relationship to proband* | *Risk, percent* |
| | mother | 55 |
| | father | 17 |
| | sister | 52 |
| | brother | 29 |
| **B.** | Relationships of depressive pairs | Number of pairs |
| | father–son | 0 |
| | father–daughter | 13 |
| | mother–son | 17 |
| | mother–daughter | 17 |

males, which would bear out the prediction that manic-depression is controlled by a dominant gene on the X chromosome. Part B of the table shows no instances of father-son pairs of manic-depressives. Again, this is precisely what Winokur's theory predicts. The reasoning is as follows. The gene causing manic-depression in a father is on his X chromosome. Since the father gives only his Y chromosome to a male child, his son cannot be affected.

Winokur's data supported his theory, but before long disconfirmations appeared. Both Goetzl and his colleagues (1974) and Hays (1976) have reported father-son pairs of manic-depressives. Although it is unlikely that Winokur's theory will survive, he has contributed valuable information increasing our knowledge of the genetics of bipolar-mood disorder. The early demise of his theory is, in a sense, a positive state of affairs. We have far too many long-lived theories in psychopathology, long-lived not because they are true but because they cannot be disproved.

*Rauwolfia serpentina,* a shrub which grows in India. Hindu physicians have for centuries administered powdered rauwolfia as a treatment for mental illness. Reserpine became one of the compounds to initiate the modern era of psychopharmacology and to revolutionize the care and treatment of mental patients. This drug and chlorpromazine (see page 555) were given to schizophrenics to calm their agitation. Reserpine did indeed relax and sedate them but was soon contraindicated, for a serious side effect in about 15 percent of the patients taking it was depression (for example, Lemieux, Davignon, and Genest, 1956). Reserpine was discovered to reduce levels of both serotonin and norepinephrine and of all the brain amines. It impairs the process by which these substances are stored within the synaptic vesicles and allows them instead to become degraded by monoamine oxidase.

So far we have examined *indirect* evidence for each theory. It would be ideal if the levels of norepinephrine, serotonin, or both could be measured within the brains of depressed people. This is not possible with existing technology, so we must take another tack. Two approaches have been used. The first measures metabolites of these neurotransmitters, the by-products of the breakdown of serotonin and norepinephrine, as they are found in urine, blood serum, and the cerebrospinal fluid. The problem with such measurements is that they may not be direct reflections of *brain* levels of either serotonin or norepinephrine, since serotonin is involved in other bodily processes and norepinephrine acts in the peripheral nervous system. 3-Methoxy-4-hydroxyphenylethylene glycol (MHPG), for example, is considered to be a major metabolite of norepinephrine. Although several studies have found low levels of MHPG in the urine of depressives (for example, Greenspan et al., 1970), the inactivity of individuals can also decrease MHPG levels (Post et al., 1973). Since depressives are typically less active than is normal, their urine may contain lesser amounts of MHPG after the onset of depression rather than before.

A second strategy would be to choose drugs other than the antidepressants and reserpine that are known either to increase or to decrease the brain levels of serotonin and norepinephrine. A drug raising the level of a neurotransmitter

# BOX **8.5** Communication in the Nervous System

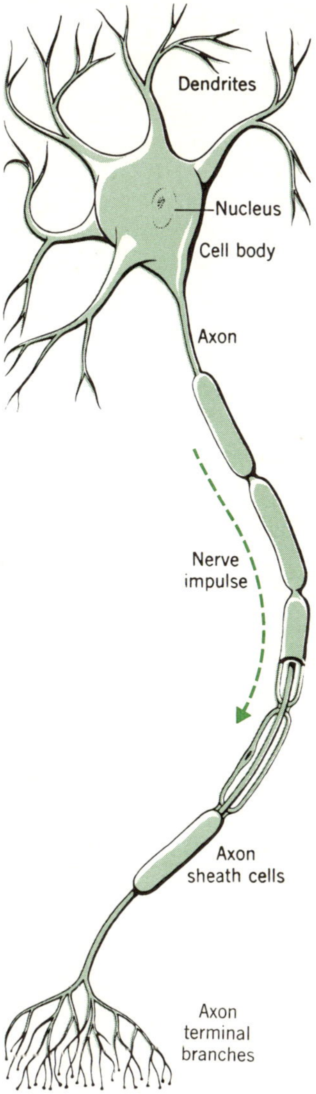


FIGURE **8.4**
The neuron, the basic unit of the nervous system.

The nervous system is composed of billions of neurons. Although differing in some respects, each neuron has four major parts (Figure 8.4): (1) the cell body; (2) several dendrites, its short and thick extensions; (3) one or more axons, but usually only one, long and thin, extending a considerable distance from the cell body; and (4) terminal buttons on the many end branches of the axon. When a neuron is appropriately stimulated at its cell body or through its dendrites, a nerve impulse, which is a change in the electric potential of the cell, travels down the axon to the terminal endings. Between the terminal endings of an axon and other neurons there is a small gap, the synapse (Figure 8.5). For a nerve impulse to pass from one neuron to another, it must have a way of bridging the synaptic cleft.

The terminal buttons of each axon contain synaptic vesicles, small structures that are filled with chemicals called neurotransmitters. Each neuron synthesizes and stores only one particular neurotransmitter. The nerve impulse causes the synaptic vesicles to release their transmitter substance, which floods the synaptic cleft and can then stimulate an adjacent neuron. The molecules of the transmitter fit into receptor sites in the postsynaptic neuron and thereby transmit the impulse.

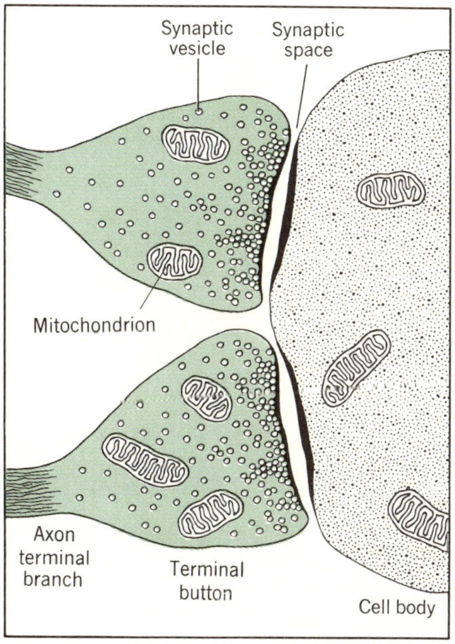


FIGURE **8.5**
A synapse, showing the terminal buttons of two axon branches in close contact with a single cell body.

Several neurotransmitters have been identified; those belonging to two major compound groups, the catecholamines and the indoleamines, have been implicated in mood and emotion and therefore in psychopathology. Substances in both groups are monoamines, which means that their molecules contain a single amino group ($NH_2$). The catecholamines, each with a catechol portion ($C_6H_6O_2$), are norepinephrine, epinephrine, and dopamine. The two indoleamines, each with an indole portion ($C_8H_7N$), are serotonin and tryptamine. Histamine, another related monoamine, is also present in the brain. Serotonin, tryptamine, and histamine are found in greater quantities in other bodily tissues than in the central nervous system. Serotonin, for example, occurs in large amounts in cells of the mucous membranes of the intestines. Its release from these cells helps to regulate peristalsis. Norepinephrine is a neurotransmitter of the peripheral sympathetic nervous system. Of these monoamines, norepinephrine, dopamine, and serotonin appear for certain to be neurotransmitters of the central nervous system. At least some of the particular pathways in the brain served by these transmitters have been identified.

To understand the theory and research relating neurotransmitters to psychopathology, we need to know how these substances are synthesized within the neuron from the amino acids tryosine and tryptophan. Table 8.5 presents this information. Finally, we need to consider the mechanisms by which the neurotransmitters are inactivated following their release. The catecholamines norepinephrine and dopamine are for the most part reabsorbed into the presynaptic neuron. The remàinder of these substances is deactivated in the synapse by the enzyme catechol-*O*-methyltransferase (COMT). Catecholamines within the presynaptic neuron can be deactivated by the enzyme monoamine oxidase (MAO), which is present in the mitochondria, the powerhouses supplying the energy for the activities of all cells. Serotonin is deactivated within the presynaptic neuron and in the synapse by MAO.

## TABLE **8.5**
## Biosynthesis of the Catecholamines and Indoleamines

| **Catecholamines** | **Indoleamines** |
|---|---|
| Tyrosine | Tryptophan |
| ↓ tyrosine hydroxylase* | ↓ tryptophan hydroxylase; → tryptophan decarboxylase → Tryptamine |
| Dopa | 5-Hydroxytryptophan |
| ↓ dopa decarboxylase | ↓ dopa decarboxylase |
| Dopamine | Serotonin |
| ↓ dopamine-β-hydroxylase | |
| Norepinephrine | |
| ↓ norepinephrine-*N*-methyltransferase | |
| Epinephrine | |

* The substances on the arrows are the enzymes that catalyze the reactions.

should alleviate depression; one reducing it should deepen depression or induce it in normal subjects. This strategy also has its problems. Most drugs have multiple effects, making it difficult to choose one that accomplishes a specific purpose without complicating side effects. The drug L-Dopa, for example, *should* enter the brain and allow a greater amount of catecholamines, including norepinephrine, to be produced. If the norepinephrine theory were true, L-Dopa should be therapeutically effective in depression. But it is not (Mendels et al., 1975). This evidence, though, is not regarded as a conclusive refutation of the norepinephrine hypothesis. L-Dopa may not really increase levels of norepinephrine in the brain, and it has other potential effects, including a reduction in serotonin levels.

Significant evidence has been collected by these strategies, however.

1. **Low levels of serotonin.** 5-Hydroxyindoleacetic acid (5-HIAA), the major metabolite of serotonin that is present in cerebrospinal fluid, can be measured to determine the level of the transmitter in the brain and spinal cord. A fairly consistent body of data indicates that 5-HIAA levels are low in the cerebrospinal fluid of depressives (Ashcroft, Crawford, and Eccleston, 1966; Mendels et al., 1972; Van Praag, Korf, and Schut, 1973). Studies also show that ingestion of L-tryptophan, which acts as a serotonin precursor, relieves depression, especially when used in combination with other drugs (Coppen et al., 1972; Mendels et al., 1975). Furthermore, *p*-cholorophenylalanine (PCPA), which suppresses serotonin synthesis by blocking tryptophan hydroxylase, reduces the therapeutic effect of drugs that usually lessen depression (Shopsin, Friedman, and Gershon, 1976).

2. **Catecholamines as determiners of mania or depression.** A series of studies on bipolar depressives was performed by Bunney and Murphy and their colleagues at the National Institute of Mental Health. The norepinephrine levels of a group of bipolar patients were watched over a period of time as patients cycled through stages of depression, mania, and normalcy. Urinary levels of norepinephrine increased as patients became manic (Bunney, Goodwin, and Murphy, 1972) and decreased when patients became depressed (Bunney et al., 1970). This study was able to relate the low and high levels of norepinephrine more closely to the onset, rather than the aftermath, of depression and mania.

A promising synthesis of the theories on levels of serotonin and norepinephrine has been proposed by Prange and his associates (1974): a low level of serotonin may be a predisposing factor for affective disorders in general; and an imbalance of norepinephrine determines the direction of bipolar-mood disorder, a low amount producing depression and a high level producing mania.

These biochemical data lend some support to theories that depression has physiological causes. Does this mean that psychological theories are irrelevant or useless? Not in the least. To assert that behavioral disorders have a basis in somatic processes is to state the obvious. No psychogenic theorist would deny that behavior is mediated by some kinds of bodily changes. The question rather is how psychological and physiological factors interact. We have already grappled with this philosophical issue in Chapter 7. It may well be, for example, that depletion of norepinephrine does cause certain kinds of depression, but that an earlier link in the causal chain is "the sense of helplessness" or "paralysis of will" that psychological theorists have proposed as the disabler.

## Suicide

In some religions suicide is considered a mortal sin. As late as 1823 a citizen of London who took his own life was buried with a stake pounded through his heart (Shneidman, 1973). Moreover, until 1961, suicide in England was a criminal offense. Sanctions, then, have been quite strong in many societies. And yet it is fair to say that the idea of killing oneself comes to many people at one time or another. To "explain" the thought, or the deed, by asserting that it is caused by depression or insanity is more likely to hinder the search for answers than to facilitate it. The fact that many depressives have suicidal thoughts and sometimes make genuine attempts to take their own lives is the rationale for including a discussion of suicide in this chapter. A significant number of people who are not depressed, however, make suicidal attempts and commit the act. An adequate understanding of suicide cannot come by concentrating only on the tendency of many depressed people to think about suicide.

### Facts about Suicide

No single theory is likely to take into account all the available information about suicide. The diversity of facts that are known about the act may help us appreciate how complex and multifaceted self-intentioned death is (Resnik, 1968; Gibbs, 1968; Douglas, 1967; Shneidman, 1973; Seiden, 1974).

1. Every thirty minutes someone in the United States kills himself, and this rate is probably a gross underestimate. It is likely that up to ten times as many attempt suicide.
2. Three times as many men kill themselves as women.
3. Three times as many women as men attempt to kill themselves but do not die.
4. Suicide is found in both the very old and the very young—even in those older than ninety years and younger than ten years.
5. Suicide is found at all social and economic levels.
6. No other kind of death leaves in friends and relatives such long-lasting feelings of distress, shame, guilt, puzzlement, and general disturbance.
7. Guns are the most common means of suicide in the United States. Men in particular usually choose to shoot themselves. Women are more likely to use sleeping pills. Elsewhere in the world methods vary by country; for example, coal gas is chosen most often in England, gas and hanging in Austria, pills and poisons in the Scandinavian countries.
8. Suicide ranks tenth as a leading cause of death among adults and third among college students.
9. Most of the people who kill themselves in the United States are native-born Caucasian males between forty-five and sixty years of age.
10. The rates for suicide among black and native American youths are more than twice those for whites.
11. There are close to 500 self-inflicted deaths of adolescents and children each year in the United States.
12. Suicide rates go up during depression years, remain stable during years of prosperity, and decrease during war years.

### Theories of Suicide

Mintz (1968) has summarized the numerous motivations for suicide mentioned in the literature: aggression turned inward; retaliation by inducing guilt in others; efforts to force love from others; efforts to make amends for "perceived" past wrongs; efforts to rid oneself of unacceptable feelings, such as sexual attraction to members of one's own sex; the desire for reincarnation; the desire to rejoin a dead loved one; and the desire or need to escape from stress, deformity, pain, or emotional vacuum. Two principal theoretical positions are currently espoused by suicidologists, the psychoanalytic and Durkheim's sociological theory.

### Psychoanalytic theories of suicide

Freud proposed two major hypotheses to account for suicide. One is an extension of his theory of depression. When a person loses someone whom he or she has ambivalently loved and hated, and introjects that person, aggression is directed inward. If these feelings are strong and murderous enough, the person will commit suicide. The second theory postulates that the death instinct, Thanatos, can turn inward and make the person take his or her life.

Freud's views on suicide are subject to many of the problems raised earlier in this text about psychoanalytic theorizing. Moreover, a careful analysis of suicide notes by Tuckman, Kleiner, and Lavell (1959) has provided information that is in marked disagreement with the psychoanalytic position. They found that only a very small minority of the notes expressed hostility. In fact, about half expressed gratitude and affection for others. A possible rebuttal—which we find unsatisfactory—might be that a suicide note, written at the conscious level, could not be expected to reflect repressed hostility.

### Durkheim's sociological theory of suicide

Durkheim (1897), after analyzing the records of suicide for various countries and during different historical periods, distinguished three different kinds of self-annihilative behavior. *Egoistic suicide* is committed, according to Durkheim, when a person has too few ties to the society and community. These people feel alienated from others, cut off from the social supports that are important to keep them functioning adaptively as social beings. *Altruistic suicides,* in contrast, are viewed by Durkheim as responses to societal demands. Some people who commit suicide feel very much a part of a group and sacrifice themselves for what they take to be the good of society. The self-immolations of Buddhist monks during the Vietnam war would fit into this category. Finally, *anomic suicide* may be triggered by a sudden change in a person's relations to society. A successful businessman who suffers severe financial reverses may experience *anomie,* a sense of disorientation, because what he believed to be his normal way of living is no longer possible for him.

As with all sociological theorizing, Durkheim's hypotheses have trouble accounting for the different reactions of individuals in a given society to the same demands and conditions. Not all those who unexpectedly lose their money commit suicide. It appears that Durkheim was aware of this problem, for he suggested that individual temperament would interact with any of the social pressures that he found causative. Perhaps at the most general level a person's suicide may be regarded as what he or she considered the best means for withdrawing from a particular and apparently unsolvable problem in living. Even this suggestion, however, is inadequate, for it does not explain why person A chooses suicide whereas person B withdraws from stress by "going crazy." All explanations remain strictly *post hoc* until and unless a theory better predicts why individuals differ in their reactions to the same set of social conditions.

## Prediction of Suicide from Personality Tests

Psychologists have recently attempted to predict suicide on the basis of personality. It would of course be of great theoretical and practical advantage to be able to predict the act from the results of personality tests. Theoretically, knowing what characteristics a potential suicide has would help us understand what makes people consider killing themselves. On practical, social-action grounds, being able to detect who is likely to make an attempt would obviously help those who wish to intervene and save lives.

Many investigators have studied the personality characteristics of those who have attempted suicide and of those who have been successful, but the overall results are quite discouraging (Lester, 1970). One principal difficulty stems from the fact that personality tests can seldom be given to numbers of people who may *later* kill themselves. Furthermore, in addition to this problem of obtaining data before a suicide attempt has been made, it is impossible to obtain information, other than biographical accounts from relatives and a few other sources, after the deed has been done. The literature, then, consists mostly of reports of psychological tests given to people *after* they have made an aborted attempt at suicide. Clearly, the information obtained from such tests will reflect the fact that those tested have recently tried and failed to kill themselves. Their state of mind is likely to be quite different from what it had been before the attempt. For example, many who have tried unsuccessfully to take their lives feel extremely guilty and embarrassed. It is impossible to know with any exactness how test scores and interview behavior are affected by such postattempt factors.

What do we discover when we compare questionnaires answered by those who have only thought of suicide and by others who have made an attempt? A few studies have collected such important information. Rosen, Hales, and Simon (1954) compared the MMPI scores of fifty patients who had attempted suicide, a hundred who had thought about suicide, and, as a control, several who had never attempted or thought about suicide. Generally, the results showed that members of the group who had only thought about suicide but had not attempted it were more deviant than those who had made an attempt, as well as being more deviant than those in the control group. In a later study Simon and Gilberstadt (1958) compiled MMPI data on successful suicides, the tests obviously having been administered prior to the act. They then compared these data with the MMPI scores of Rosen's subjects, those who had thought of or attempted suicide. In general, the scores of the groups were *not* different. Data from other studies on suicide are either similarly inconclusive or utterly uninterpretable because experimental blunders were made, such as not testing a nonsuicidal control group for comparison purposes.

A more recent investigation by Leonard (1974) casts serious doubt on the relation often assumed to exist between depression and suicide attempts or completed suicide. Leonard gave the MMPI and the Self-Rating Depression Scale (Zung, 1965) to ninety patients voluntarily admitted to a psychiatric hospital. About one-third of them were rated as seriously suicidal by these tests. The most astonishing finding was that suicidal inclination did not correlate strongly with depression, rather with a feeling of being out of control and a sense of physical disequilibrium. Perhaps the person felt extremely restless or believed that his or her heart beat faster than usual, that it was not as easy to do things as it once had been. Problems in channeling energy emerged rather than the hopelessness and despondency that characterize depression.

## Prediction of Suicide from Demographic Variables

Rather than employing psychological tests devised for other purposes, many workers advocate the development of assessment procedures specifically designed to predict suicide. Attention is paid to demographic factors such as age, sex, marital status, and living arrangements, which turn out to be very useful predictors—more helpful than the personality variables just considered.

Suicide prevention centers, such as those in Los Angeles and in Buffalo, rely on demographic factors (Shneidman, Farberow, and Litman, 1970). In the Buffalo Suicide Prevention and Crisis Service, for example, workers receiving phone calls from people in suicidal crises have before them a checklist to guide their questioning of each caller, for they must immediately assess how great the risk of suicide may be. For

## BOX **8.6** Some Myths about Suicide

There are many prevalent misconceptions about suicide (Pokorny, 1968; Shneidman, 1973).

1. *People who discuss suicide will not commit the act.* The fact is that up to three-quarters of those who take their lives have communicated the intent beforehand, perhaps to ask for help, perhaps to taunt.

2. *Suicide may be committed without warning.* The falseness of this belief is readily indicated by the preceding statement. There seem to be many warnings, such as the person's saying that the world would be better off without him, or making unexpected and inexplicable gifts to others.

3. *Only people of a certain class commit suicide.* Suicide is actually neither the curse of the poor nor the disease of the rich. People in all classes commit suicide.

4. *Membership in a particular religious group is a good predictor that a person will not consider suicide.* It is mistakenly thought that the strong Catholic prohibition against suicide makes the risk that Catholics will take their lives much lower. This is not supported by the evidence, perhaps because an individual's formal religious identification is not an accurate index of true beliefs.

5. *The motives for suicide are easily established.* The truth is that we have only the poorest understanding of why certain people commit suicide. For example, the fact that a severe reverse in finances precedes a suicide does not mean that the reversal adequately explains the suicide.

6. *Most of the people who commit suicide are depressed.* This fallacy may account for the tragic fact that signs of impending suicide are overlooked because the person is not depressed. Although reliable data are difficult to collect, some experts believe that many of the people who take their lives are *not* depressed.

7. *A person with a terminal physical illness is unlikely to commit suicide.* A person's awareness of impending death does not preclude suicide. Perhaps the wish to end their own suffering or that of their loved ones impels many to choose the time of their death.

8. *To commit suicide is insane.* Although most suicidal persons are very unhappy, most do appear to be completely rational and in touch with reality.

9. *A tendency to commit suicide is inherited.* Since suicides often run in families, the assumption is made that the tendency to think in terms of self-annihilation is inherited. There is no evidence for this.

10. *Suicide is influenced by seasons, latitude, weather fronts, barometric pressure, humidity, precipitation, cloudiness, wind speed, temperature, and days of the week.* There are no good data to substantiate any of these myths.

11. *Suicide is influenced by cosmic factors such as sunspots and phases of the moon.* No evidence confirms this.

12. *Improvement in emotional state means lessened risk of suicide.* The fact is that people often commit the act after their spirits begin to rise; this appears to be especially true of depressed patients.

13. *Suicidal people clearly want to die.* Most people who commit suicide appear to be ambivalent about their own deaths.

example, a caller would be regarded as a lethal risk if he were male, middle-aged, divorced, and living alone and had a history of previous suicide attempts. And usually the more detailed and concrete the suicide plan, the higher the risk.

Another procedure is the "psychological autopsy," pioneered at the Los Angeles Suicide Prevention Center (Shneidman et al., 1970). In effect, these workers analyze information obtained from crisis phone calls, from interviews with relatives and friends of those who are thinking about suicide or have committed the act, and from notes left behind by those who have ultimately killed themselves. This type of clinical case study has yielded a wealth of provocative and often useful information.

Of particular interest is a study (Shneidman and Farberow, 1970) of notes left by people who subsequently committed suicide. At least in the Los Angeles area, about 15 percent of suicides do leave notes, and the contents of these notes were analyzed by judges trained to rate them on the presence or absence of instructions and specific themes, such as self-blame, discomfort, death as relief, and the like. Having determined that such ratings could indeed be made reliably by independent judges, Shneidman and Farberow compared these actual suicide notes with simulated notes prepared for them by individuals who were *not* oriented toward killing themselves but who were matched to those who had on such demographic variables as age, sex, and social class. These control subjects had been instructed to write *as if* they were about to commit suicide. The genuine notes contained a greater number of instructions, such as explicit orders about how to dispose of the body; there was also evidence of significantly more anguish.

As is the case in nearly all areas of abnormal psychology, not as much is known about suicide as we would like. In this instance the lack of information is all the more worrisome, since the very existence of many people is at stake. Fortunately, those who have devoted their professional lives to preventing suicide are not waiting for all the data to come in before attempting to intervene. The absence of a good theory does not preclude action. Working principles can be derived from available statistical studies, which already identify at least some of the individuals who are likely to make lethal attempts.

## Summary

In DSM-II depression is found in a number of categories, principally manic-depressive illness, depressive neurosis, and psychotic depression. The distinctions made among these categories have been based on severity and on whether precipitating events can be found. More recently, workers have distinguished between exogenous and endogenous depression on the basis of different patterns of affect and behavior. All these distinctions create serious problems; the draft version of DSM-III simplifies matters by distinguishing among manic, depressive, and bipolar affective disorders.

Psychological theories of depression have been couched in psychoanalytic, cognitive, and learning terms. Psychoanalytic formulations stress unconscious identification with a loved one whose desertion of the individual has made him or her turn anger inward. Beck's cognitive theory ascribes causal significance to illogical self-judgment. Operant learning theorists attribute depression to an inactive, unrewarding existence. And according to Seligman's cognitive–learning appraisal, early experiences in inescapable, hurtful situations instill a sense of helplessness which can evolve into depression. Physiological theories suggest an inherited predisposition for bipolar-mood disorder and relate the phenomena of depression and mania to abnormally depleted and copious amounts of the neurotransmitters that pass on neural impulses in particular nerve tracts of the brain.

Finally, the topic of suicide was explored, although self-annihilative tendencies are not restricted to those who are depressed. A review of the facts and myths about suicide suggest that any single theory is unlikely to account for its great diversity, but that the information already gathered can be applied to prevent it.

# part three
# social problems

# chapter 9

## PERSONALITY DISORDERS: SOCIOPATHY



In this chapter and the three that follow we turn our attention to disorders that are classified together in DSM-II as "Personality Disorders and Certain Other Non-Psychotic Mental Disorders." This broad category has four subunits—*personality disorders, sexual deviations, alcoholism,* and *drug dependence*—clearly a very broad range of human problems. Indeed, the draft version of DSM-III no longer contains the general category and instead has three separate ones—"Personality Disorders," Psychosexual Disorders," and "Drug Use Disorders."

The focus of this chapter is on personality disorders, defined by DSM-II as

> . . . *deeply ingrained maladaptive patterns of behavior that are perceptively different in quality from psychotic and neurotic symptoms. Generally, these are life-long patterns, often recognizable by the time of adolescence or earlier (p. 41).*

A number of specific subcategories are listed.

**Paranoid Personality** The paranoid personality is unduly sensitive and rigid, holds unjustified suspicions, and is overly envious or jealous of others. Such individuals, possessed with an excessive amount of self-importance, tend to blame others for their own mistakes and to mistrust the motives and intentions of other people.

**Cyclothymic Personality** The cyclothymic personality undergoes recurrent, alternating periods of elation and depression that are not easily linked to changes in life circumstance. The elation is a healthy state of energetic activity, ambition, liveliness, enthusiasm, and warmth. Depression takes the form of gloom, worry, and a sense of futility.

**Schizoid Personality** The schizoid diagnosis is applied to overly sensitive, shy, and seclusive people who avoid interpersonal relationships, particularly close ones. They daydream but without losing their grip on reality. They have great difficulty expressing ordinary aggression and hostility and become detached when faced with stress or calamity.

**Explosive Personality** The explosive personality is subject to outbursts of extreme rage and of physical and verbal aggression. During these intense outbursts the person's behavior is quite different from normal; he or she usually expresses profound regret afterward and tries to make amends. But any form and degree of stress is likely to trigger another explosion beyond the control of this excitable person.

**Obsessive-Compulsive Personality** People with the obsessive-compulsive behavior pattern are excessively concerned with rules and standards and with conforming to them. Overly conscientious, inhibited, dutiful, meticulous, and rigid, they have great difficulty relaxing.

**Hysterical Personality** The diagnosis of hysterical personality (also mentioned in Chapter 6) covers emotional lability and overly dramatic behavior. Excitable, immature, vain, self-centered, and seductive, these people seek to be the center of attention.

**Asthenic Personality** The defining characteristics of the asthenic personality are a low energy level, fatigability, oversensitivity to physical and emotional stress, and a seeming incapacity to enjoy or become enthusiastic about anything in life.

**Passive-Aggressive Personality** The passive-aggressive personality apparently feels considerable hostility and aggression yet cannot express these feelings directly. Instead the aggression is revealed in a passive way, such as by being intentionally late or inefficient, by not returning phone calls, and by general and thoroughgoing stubbornness, procrastination, and inactivity.

**Inadequate Personality** The diagnosis of inadequate personality is applied to someone who, although neither mentally or physically deficient, behaves in a generally inept and incompetent manner, especially in any situation that places emotional, social, intellectual, and physical demands on the person. Such individuals lack emotional and physical stamina to judge and adjust to any circumstance out of the ordinary.

Obviously, these subcategories encompass a great diversity of behavior. In some instances they are similar to other diagnostic categories. For example, the asthenic personality is similar to neurasthenic neurosis, and the cyclothymic personality to manic-depressive psychosis. Although DSM-II states that personality disorders "are perceptibly different in quality from psychotic and neurotic symptoms" (p. 41), it does not really provide much information to help the diagnostician make the necessary distinctions. Small wonder then that the subcategories of personality disorder as given in DSM-II have very little diagnostic reliability and that empirical data are few.

One personality disorder, the antisocial personality, not yet described, is the single exception to the preceding statement. DSM-III will retain this subcategory essentially unchanged. The rest of this chapter will be devoted to what is known about the disruptive and essentially self-destructive individuals whose deep-seated ethical and moral maladjustments frequently bring them into serious conflict with society.

## Antisocial Personality (Sociopathy)

In DSM-II antisocial personalities are described as

> . . . *individuals who are basically unsocialized and whose behavior pattern brings them repeatedly into conflict with society. They are incapable of significant loyalty to individuals, groups, or social values. They are grossly selfish, callous, irresponsible, impulsive, and unable to feel guilt or to learn from experience and punishment. Frustration tolerance is low. They tend to blame others or offer plausible rationalizations for their behavior. A mere history of repeated legal or social offenses is not sufficient to justify this diagnosis* (p. 43).

In current usage the term sociopath is employed interchangeably with antisocial personality and psychopath. The concept has an interesting history. In the eighteenth century Philippe Pinel conceived of *manie sans délire,* mania without delirium, and in the nineteenth Pritchard described the disorder moral insanity in an attempt to account for behavior so far outside the usual ethical and legal codes that it seemed a form of lunacy. Pinel's term was first applied to an easily angered aristocrat who had whipped a horse, kicked a dog to death, and thrown a peasant woman into a well. Since the early concept was used to explain a wide range of strange behavior, it is not surprising that it came to function somewhat as a wastebasket diagnosis, encompassing those inclined not only to violence but to unconventional practices as well.

Before considering current views of these problems, we shall examine excerpts from two case histories that reveal the scope of sociopathic reactions. The first case illustrates many of the classic characteristics of the sociopath but is unusual in that the person described was neither a criminal nor in psychiatric treatment at the time that the data for the case study were collected. This is an important point, for the majority of sociopaths who are the subjects of research studies have broken the law and been caught for doing so. Only rarely do we have the opportunity to examine in detail the behavior of an individual who fits the diagnostic definition but yet has managed not to break the law. The second case history presents the more usual picture of the criminal sociopath.

### The Case of Dan

This case history was compiled by a psychologist (McNeil, 1967) who happened to be a personal friend of Dan's.

Dan was a wealthy actor and disc jockey who lived in an expensive house in an exclusive suburb and generally played his role as a "personality" to the hilt. One evening, when the two men were out for dinner, Dan made a great fuss over the condition of the *Shrimp de Johnge* that he had ordered. McNeil thought that the whole scene had been deliberately contrived by Dan for the effect it might produce, and he said to his companion,

> *"I have a sneaking suspicion this whole scene came about just because you weren't really hungry." Dan laughed loudly in agreement and said, "What the hell, they'll be on their toes next time." "Was that the only reason for this display?" . . . "No," he replied, "I wanted to show you how gutless the rest of the world is. If you shove a little they all jump. Next time I come in, they'll be all over me to make sure everything is exactly as I want it. That's the only way*

*they can tell the difference between class and plain ordinary. When I travel I go first class."*

*"Yes, . . . but how do you feel about you as a person—as a fellow human being?"*

*"Who cares?" he laughed. "If they were on top they would do the same to me. The more you walk on them, the more they like it. It's like royalty in the old days. It makes them nervous if everyone is equal to everyone else. Watch. When we leave I'll put my arm around that waitress, ask her if she still loves me, pat her on the fanny, and she'll be ready to roll over any time I wiggle my little finger"* (p. 85).

Another incident occurred when a friend of Dan's committed suicide. Most of the other friends whom Dan and McNeil had in common were concerned and called the psychologist to see whether he could provide any information about why the man had taken his life. Dan did not. Later, when McNeil mentioned the suicide to Dan, all he could say was "That's the way the ball bounces." In his public behavior, however, Dan's attitude toward the incident appeared quite different. He was the one who collected money and presented it personally to the new widow. In keeping with his character, however, Dan remarked that the widow had a sexy body that really interested him.

These two incidents convey the flavor of Dan's behavior. McNeil had witnessed a long succession of similar events which led him to conclude that

*[The incidents] painted a grisly picture of life-long abuse of people for Dan's amusement and profit. He was adept at office politics and told me casually of an unbelievable set of deceptive ways to deal with the opposition. Character assassination, rumor mongering, modest blackmail, seduction, and barefaced lying were the least of his talents. He was a jackal in the entertainment jungle, a jackal who feasted on the bodies of those he had slaughtered professionally* (p. 91).

In his conversations with Dan, McNeil was also able to inquire into Dan's life history. One early and potentially important event was uncovered.

*I can remember the first time in my life when I began to suspect I was a little different from most people. When I was in high school my best friend got leukemia and died and I went to his funeral. Everybody else was crying and feeling sorry for themselves and as they were praying to get him into heaven I suddenly realized that I wasn't feeling anything at all. He was a nice guy but what the hell. That night I thought about it some more and found that I wouldn't miss my mother and father if they died and that I wasn't too nuts about my brothers and sisters for that matter. I figured there wasn't anybody I really cared for but, then, I didn't need any of them anyway so I rolled over and went to sleep* (p. 87).

The moral depravity described long ago by Pinel and Pritchard clearly marks Dan's behavior. A person may be otherwise quite rational and show no loss of contact with reality and yet behave in a habitually and exceedingly unethical manner. The final excerpt illustrates Dan's complete lack of feeling for others, a characteristic that will later be seen to have considerable relevance in explaining the behavior of the sociopath.

## The Case of Jim

Jim, the fourth child in a family of five, grew up in the lower social class of a small Midwestern town. During his childhood the member of his family who made the greatest impression on him was his older brother, whom he described as follows.

> *He was always a bully, promiscuous, and adventurous. He was always involved with some local girl, before I was even old enough to realize what was going on. He started drinking early, and had several scrapes with the law. He had rough companions, whom I later inherited, who helped me on my way.*
>
> *He married a tramp, ended up in a stolen car, and was given the choice of jail or the army, as this was the Korean war time. I cannot directly link him to my life of crime, although he introduced me to those who later helped me along. Also, he condoned some of my early petty thievery (Bintz and Wilson, as reprinted in Milton and Wahler, 1969, p. 92).*

During early adolescence Jim engaged in many petty antisocial acts. For example, on one occasion he stole some change from his mother's pocketbook. His father reacted by whipping both brothers until Jim confessed. Once Jim had admitted taking the money, however, the punishment ended. This became standard practice for the family, with Jim being able to avoid punishment by confessing as soon as he was accused of misbehavior, regardless of whether or not he was guilty. Moreover, the petty thievery that Jim committed in the community was generally successful, and even when he was caught consequences were minimal.

Jim's first serious trouble with the law occurred when he was charged with raping a girl whom he had picked up at the local skating rink. He was sentenced to five years at a reform school but received an immediate parole on the condition that his sentence would be activated if he violated it. After several parole violations such as petty theft, and being detained for speeding, he was sentenced to one year at the reform school. By the time he returned to his hometown a year later, he had become a young hoodlum. Jim himself stated that the principal consequence of the year in reform school had been the opportunity afforded him to fraternize with more experienced thieves. Shortly thereafter Jim and a friend committed their first major theft, stealing $1700 from a tavern safe. Then the same pair attempted to burglarize a lumberyard but were unable to open the safe. The next day they were arrested, and the burglary tools were found in Jim's car. He served a ninety-day sentence for attempted burglary. Three months after being released, Jim was incarcerated again, this time for statutory rape. As soon as he was free again, he and a friend planned another robbery. They reasoned that a bootlegger would be a good target for a holdup for, being outside the law himself, he would be reluctant to report the incident to the police.

They bungled the job badly, however, and both were sentenced to five-year terms. Jim served three of the five years and upon his release met the girl he was soon to marry. He described her as follows.

> *Diane was a tramp, I could tell from the start. She forced the introduction and the first date. I had sexual relations with her on the first date, she was my third sexual partner on that particular day. She was neat, but not really attractive. The next four and a half months we were intimate almost every night. She wanted to marry, I did not. I could not see myself married to this plain-looking tramp. In fact, toward the last, I was trying to think of a scheme to get rid of her . . . (p. 100).*

During this period Jim held a job, but he soon began to get deeper and deeper into debt. Eventually, an opportunity for another theft presented itself. Again the job was spectacularly unsuccessful and Jim was sentenced to ten years in the state penitentiary. While in the county jail, before the trial, he was visited often by Diane and finally married her just before going to prison. As a substitute for a wedding ring, Jim had the words "Love me, Diane" tattooed on his penis.

## Cleckley's Concept of Sociopathy

Both of these case histories illustrate many of the symptoms of the sociopathic syndrome as it has been defined by Cleckley (1964). On the basis of his vast clinical experience, he has formulated a set of criteria by which to recognize the disorder.

1. Superficial charm and average or superior intelligence.
2. Absence of irrationality and other commonly accepted symptoms of psychosis. No neurotic anxiety; at ease in situations that would unsettle the average individual.
3. No sense of responsibility, in matters of little and great import.
4. No sense of shame.
5. A cavalier attitude about telling the truth; unperturbed whether lies will be detected.
6. Antisocial behavior with no apparent regret.
7. Poor judgment; regularly fails to learn from experience.
8. Lack of genuine insight.
9. Callousness, insincerity, and incapacity for love and attachment.
10. Little response to special considerations and kindness.
11. No history of genuine suicide attempts.
12. Unrestrained and unconventional sex life.
13. Failure to have a life plan and to live in in any ordered way except to follow a persistent pattern of self-defeat.
14. Onset of sociopathic characteristics no later than early twenties.

These fourteen characteristics are quite similar to the description of antisocial personality found in DSM-II. But some appear to be more central than others. Perhaps the most critical aspect to be considered in making a diagnosis of sociopathy are the reactions of the individual to his or her antisocial behavior. Thus Cleckley's criteria *no sense of responsibility* and *no sense of shame* are particularly important. The sociopath is viewed as not responding emotionally after committing an act that generally elicits shame and guilt in most people. Moreover, the lack of these affective reactions is presumably linked to the sociopath's inability to learn from experience, particularly to avoid punishment. The sociopath continues to engage in the same antisocial activities, even though they prove unsuccessful. Learning to avoid actions that continually fail may be mediated by emotional arousal; because sociopaths do not become emotionally aroused, they are less likely to suffer from and to change their unproductive and antisocial ways.

Before examining the existing research on the sociopathic syndrome, we should emphasize that most of it has been conducted on sociopaths who have already been convicted as criminals. Individuals such as Dan have rarely been studied

## BOX 9.1 A Methodology for Studying Noninstitutionalized Sociopaths

Until recently the problem of collecting for study a sample of "successful" psychopaths who have avoided incarceration seemed unsolvable. Now Widom (1977) has proposed a method that may allow them to be contacted in sufficient numbers.

In order to recruit subjects, Widom placed an advertisement in a "counterculture" newspaper in the Boston area. The ad attempted to attract the attention of sociopaths by referring to key aspects of their behavior in a nondemeaning way.

*Wanted charming, aggressive, carefree people who are impulsively irresponsible but good at handling people and at looking after number one. Send name, address, phone, and short biography proving how interesting you are . . . .*

The ad ran for eight months, and in this period of time forty-five males and twenty-three females responded. Its message was apparently deciphered by one respondent, who wrote "Are you looking for hookers or are you trying to make a listing of all the sociopaths in Boston?" On the basis of the biographies, and in some instances telephone conversations, twenty-three males and five females were selected as likely sociopaths. These subjects were then contacted, and appointments were arranged for rather extensive testing.

The critical question that these tests were meant to answer was whether these subjects, upon closer examination, would actually prove to have the rather clear-cut characteristics of sociopaths. Seventy-eight percent of the sample fit Robins's (1966) description of sociopathy: they had poor work and marital histories, used drugs excessively, drank heavily, and were physically aggressive and sexually promiscuous. True to the MMPI sociopathic profile, they peaked on the mania and psychopathic deviate scales of this questionnaire. Other results, for example, low scores on empathy and socialization tests, corroborated the conclusion that the members of this sample were truly sociopathic. Thus it now seems possible to collect subjects who can be studied to determine etiology of sociopathy in noncriminal populations.

in research settings. We must therefore keep in mind that the available literature may not allow us to generalize about the behavior of sociopaths who elude arrest and the subsequent label of criminal.[1] A recently described method that may allow these noncriminal sociopaths to be studied is presented in Box 9.1.

[1] Nor indeed are all criminals sociopaths. In fact, the majority of criminals cannot be described as sociopathic.

# Theory and Research on the Etiology of Sociopathy

## The Role of the Family

Since much sociopathic behavior violates social norms, it is not surprising that many investigators have focused on the primary agent of socialization, the family, in their search for the explanation of such behavior. Many sociopaths have apparently experienced the trauma of losing a parent. Greer (1964) found that 60 percent of his sample of sociopaths had lost at least one parent during childhood, whereas only 28 percent of the control sample of neurotics and 27 percent of a control sample of normal subjects had. In a similar vein, McCord and McCord (1964) concluded, on the basis of a review of the literature, that lack of affection and severe parental rejection were the primary causes of sociopathic behavior. Several other studies have related sociopathic behavior to the parents' inconsistencies in disciplining their children and in teaching them their responsibilities to others (Bennet, 1960). Furthermore, the fathers of sociopaths are likely to be antisocial in their behavior.

But such data on early rearing must be interpreted with extreme caution. They were gathered by means of *retrospective reports.* Information about early family experiences and about how the child was taught to behave socially was obtained either from an adult sociopath or from parents, relatives, and friends at a time very much later than events actually occurred. Recent studies of the reliability of the information obtained in this way indicate that such data may be of little use. As Garmezy has noted,

*Studies of normal families have revealed the unreliability of the case history, with its exclusive reliance on retrospective reconstruction of an earlier time period. . . . Investigations conducted with normal mothers of primary school age (and younger) children provide evidence that not*

*only do mothers suffer deficits in recalling events in the early years of their children's lives but that the deficiency is particularly acute [in remembering] emotions and affectively-tinged attitudes . . . (1971, p. 105).*

When people are asked to recollect the early events in the life of someone who is now known to be a sociopath, their knowledge of adult status may have some effect on what they remember or report about childhood events. Potentially deviant incidents are more likely to be recalled, whereas those that do not dovetail with the person's current behavior may be overlooked.

One way of avoiding the problems of retrospective data is to follow up in adulthood a large group of individuals who as children were seen at a child guidance clinic. In one such study very detailed records had been kept on the children, including the type of problem that had brought them to the clinic and information on numerous variables related to the family (Robins, 1966). Ninety percent of an initial sample of 584 cases were located thirty years after their referral to the clinic.[2] In addition to the clinic cases, 100 control subjects who had lived in the same geographic area served by the clinic but who had *not* been referred to it were also followed up in adulthood.

By interviewing the now-adult individuals chosen for both the experimental and control samples, the investigators were able to diagnose and describe any maladjustments of these individuals. Then adult problems were related back to the characteristics that these people had had as children to find out which of them predicted sociopathic behavior in adulthood. Robins summarized these as follows.

*If one wishes to choose the most likely candidate for a later diagnosis of sociopathic personality from among children appearing in a child guidance clinic, the best choice appears to be a boy referred for theft or aggression who has shown a diversity of antisocial behavior in many episodes, at least one of which could be grounds for Juvenile Court appearance, and whose antisocial behavior involves him with strangers and organizations as well as with teachers and parents . . . . more than half of the boys appearing at the clinic [with these characteristics were later] diagnosed sociopathic personality. Such boys had a history of truancy, theft, staying out late, and refusing to obey parents. They lied gratuitously, and showed little guilt over their behavior. They were generally irresponsible about being where they were supposed to be or taking care of money. They were interested in sexual activities and had experimented with homosexual relationships . . . (p. 157).*

In addition to these characteristics, variables related to family life that were mentioned earlier were again found to be important. Both inconsistent discipline and no discipline at all predicted sociopathic behavior in adulthood, as did antisocial behavior of the father.

In sum, the data we have reviewed emphasize the importance of child-rearing practices. The fathers of sociopaths appear to provide a model for antisocial behavior. We must caution, however, that poor training in socialization has been implicated in the etiology of a number of clinical syndromes including delinquent, neurotic, and even psychotic behavior (Wiggins, 1968), and that many individuals who come from what appear to be similarly disturbed social backgrounds do *not* become sociopaths or develop any other behavior disorders. This point is important: adults may have no problems whatsoever in spite of the inconsistent and otherwise undesirable manner of their rearing. Thus family experience may be important in the development of sociopathic behavior, but it can *not* be the whole story.

[2] It should be appreciated that being able to track down this large a percentage of individuals thirty years after their contact with the clinic is an incredible feat.

## Genetic Correlates of Sociopathic Behavior

### Twin and adoptee studies

Most of the studies concerned with the possible genetic basis for sociopathic behavior have focused on criminality rather than on sociopathy per se. The data collected are therefore difficult to interpret since, as already emphasized, not all sociopaths are criminals nor are all criminals sociopaths. Lange's research (1929) comparing concordance rates for criminality in identical and fraternal twins showed them to be a great deal higher for identical twins, supporting the theory that genetic factors may be involved. Kranz (1936), in a study that used better sampling procedures, found the following patterns of concordance: identical twins, 66 percent; fraternal twins of the same sex, 54 percent; fraternal twins of the opposite sex, 14 percent. Although at first glance these data also seem to support the notion that genetic factors are important, they in fact give only slight support to this hypothesis. The critical piece of information is the marked *difference* in concordance rates of fraternal twins of the same sex and those of fraternal twins of the opposite sex. Both of these pairs of twins are equally alike genetically, but we can expect the parental rearing practices to which they are exposed to be markedly different. Fraternal twins of the same sex are probably treated more alike than are fraternal twins of the opposite sex. This evidence, in point of fact, implicates environmental factors.

But recent adoptee studies conducted in Denmark suggest that heredity may indeed play a role in both criminality and sociopathy. Hutchings and Mednick (1974) examined rates of criminality in the adoptive and biological relatives of adoptees who had acquired criminal records, and Schulsinger (1972) performed a similar study with sociopathy as the variable of interest. Hutchings and Mednick found a higher rate of criminality in the biological relatives of criminals than in the general population, and Schulsinger found more sociopathy in the biological relatives of sociopaths. Thus the evidence on hand suggests that a disposition to become sociopathic may be inherited.

### XYY

One genetic aberration that has recently received considerable publicity is the presence of an extra male sex chromosome in men who have committed particularly violent crimes.[3] As indicated in Box 8.4, the normal male cells have one X and one Y chromosome, the normal female cells two X chromosomes. The cells of some men have recently been reported to have one Y chromosome too many, XYY, and thus they may be considered "supermales." But Rosenthal (1970) has noted that of the large number of criminals and delinquents tested to date, only about 1.5 percent have shown this pattern. And these studies, because only criminals have been tested, cannot provide definitive information on the relation between the XYY syndrome and violence.

A more adequate study has recently been performed in Denmark by Witkin and a large group of investigators. All men born in Copenhagen between 1944 and 1947 ($N = 31{,}436$) formed the population, and from this group the investigators culled for study those who were over six feet tall ($N = 4591$). Height was used as a selection criterion to ensure that an adequate number of XYY males would be found; previous research had shown that XYY males tend to be taller than average. Over 90 percent of the selected group participated in the research, which involved taking blood and a buccal smear—one from the mucous membranes of the cheek—so that the sex chromosomes could be studied. Existing records of criminal offenses were the measure of aggression-criminality; school reports and army screening tests provided estimates of intelligence.

Twelve XYY men were found, a prevalence rate of 2.9 per thousand. Five of these (41.7 percent) had been convicted of one or more criminal

[3] Again we must caution that such data may be of only limited relevance to sociopathy.

offenses; the nature of their crimes is indicated in Table 9.1. Of the 4579 normal XY men, 9.3 percent had been convicted of a crime. Thus with superior methodology it has now been shown that XYY men are more likely to be convicted of crimes. But do the convictions reflect a greater tendency of these men to be aggressive and violent? Inspection of Table 9.1 reveals that only one man committed an act of aggression against another person. Thus the XYY male, at least in his criminal offenses, does not appear to be highly violent. Why, then, are XYY men more likely to be convicted of crimes? Their lower intelligence is a possible explanation. The XYY

TABLE **9.1**
Nature of Offenses of XYYs Convicted on One or More Criminal Charges
(adapted from Witkin et al., 1976).

**Case 2.** This man is a chronic criminal who, since early adolescence, has spent 9 of 15 years in youth prisons and regular prisons. By far his most frequent criminal offense, especially in his youth, has been theft or attempted theft of a motor vehicle. Other charges included burglary, embezzlement, and procuring for prostitution. On a single occasion he committed a mild act of violence against an unoffending person; for this together with one case of burglary he received a sentence of around three-quarters of a year. This aggressive act was an isolated incident in a long period of chronic criminality. Except for this act, and the charge of procuring, all his nearly 50 offenses were against property, predominantly larceny and burglary. His single most severe penalty was somewhat less than a year in prison. Most of his crimes were committed in the company of other persons.

**Case 3.** This man committed two thefts, one in late adolescence, the second when he was in his early twenties. The penalties for both were mild—a small fine for the first and less than 3 months in prison for the second. His last offense was committed 7 years ago.

**Case 5.** Ten years ago as a young adult this man committed two petty offenses, the second within a short time of the first. One was the theft of a motorcycle, the other a petty civil offense; the penalties were detentions of approximately 2 weeks and less than 2 weeks, respectively.

**Case 7.** Five years ago when in his twenties this man committed his only criminal offenses within a short period of time: falsely reporting a traffic accident to the police and starting a small fire. On both occasions he was intoxicated. The penalty was probation.

**Case 12.** This man was under welfare care as a child and has spent only 3 to 4 of the last 20 years outside of institutions for the retarded. He is an episodic criminal. When very young he committed arson. Later his crimes included theft of motor vehicles, burglary, larceny, and embezzlement. His more than 90 registered offenses were all against property, mostly theft and burglary. For crimes committed while he was free, the penalty imposed was placement in an institution for the mentally retarded. For crimes committed while he was in such an institution—once theft of a bicycle, another time theft of a quantity of beverage—the penalty was continued institutionalization.

men were significantly lower than the XYs on both measures of intelligence. And the data revealed that low intelligence was related to higher rates of criminality. It may be, then, that low intelligence is causally related to criminality. It is equally possible, though, that people of low intelligence are less able to escape detection once they have committed a criminal act. The XYY men may have a higher rate of being *apprehended* for crimes, rather than a higher rate of committing them.

## Central Nervous System Activity and Sociopathy

Many studies have examined patterns of brain wave activity (see Box 9.2) in sociopaths and various groups of control subjects. Ellingson (1954) reviewed these studies and reported that in thirteen out of fourteen of them, investigating a total of about 1500 sociopaths, between 31 and 58 percent showed some form of electroencephalogram (EEG) abnormality. The most frequent form of abnormality was slow-wave activity, which was generally widespread throughout the brain. There is, however, some evidence that among extremely impulsive and aggressive sociopathic individuals the EEG abnormalities are localized in the temporal lobes of the cerebral hemispheres (Hill, 1952). Finally, some individuals who respond with impulsive, aggressive, and destructive acts to seemingly trivial stimuli show what are referred to as *positive spikes*. These occur in the temporal area of the brain and consist of bursts of activity with frequencies of 6 to 8 cycles per second (cps) and 14 to 16 cps. Hare

### BOX **9.2** The Electroencephalogram

The electroencephalogram or EEG is a graphic recording of the electrical activity of the brain. The brain is known to be continuously active, chemically and electrically, throughout life, even in sleep. Individual neurons of the central nervous system fire spontaneously at regular or irregular intervals, creating differences in electric potentials, that is, fluctuations in voltage. The fluctuations in voltage in the cortex, the portion of the brain immediately below the skull, can be picked up by two or more sensitive electrodes pasted to the scalp. The recording machine, the electroencephalograph, amplifies the pulsations one to two million times and connects them to a pen recorder (or recorders) which registers them on a continuously moving role of graph paper as a pattern of oscillations. The spontaneous activity of the brain, known as its waves, varies in different cortical areas and in the other less accessible portions of the brain. Perhaps most importantly, the dominant brain waves reflect the degree to which the brain has been aroused.

In a normal adult subject, awake but resting quietly with eyes closed, the dominant rhythm has a frequency of between 8 and 13 pulsations or cycles per second (cps) and an amplitude of from 40 to 50 microvolts. This low-frequency, high-voltage wave is called the *alpha* rhythm. When a stimulus is presented, the alpha rhythm is replaced by a high-frequency (14 to 25 cps), low-voltage rhythm, the *beta* rhythm. If very low frequency waves are found dominant in the awake adult, they are considered abnormal. These slow waves, which are sometimes found in sociopaths while they are awake, are referred to as the *theta* (4 to 7 cps) and the *delta* (less than 4 cps) rhythms. Delta rhythms occur during deep sleep; theta waves are commonly recorded from subcortical parts of the brain. Examples of these various rhythms as well as the positive spikes referred to in the text may be seen in Figure 9.1.

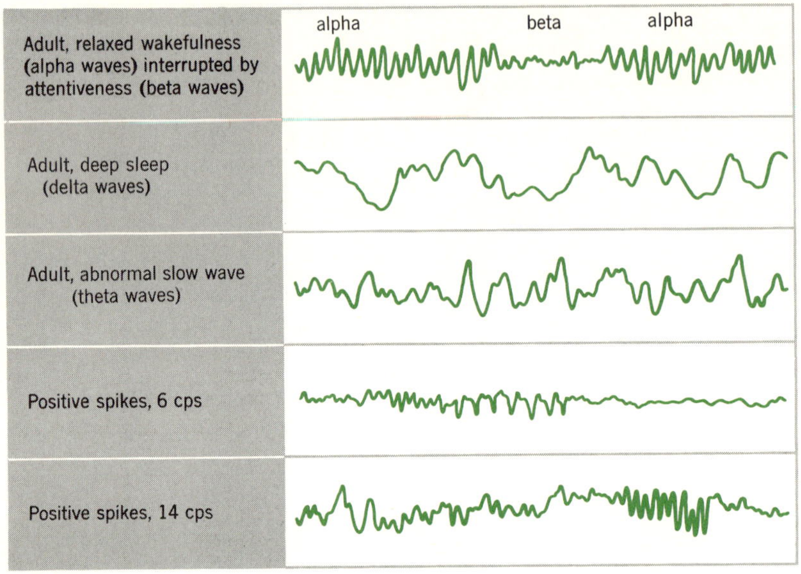


FIGURE **9.1**
Patterns of electrical activity in the brain recorded by the electroencephalograph. After Hare, 1970.

(1970) has interpreted these EEG data as follows.

> *It is quite possible . . . that these EEG abnormalities reflect some sort of dysfunction in the underlying temporal and limbic mechanisms [which] are involved in sensory and memory processes and in the central regulation of emotional and motivational behavior. . . . The limbic mechanisms appear to play a particularly important role in the regulation of fear-motivated behavior, including learning to inhibit a response in order to avoid punishment. . . . The temporal slow-wave activity frequently observed in the EEG records of psychopaths reflects a malfunction of some limbic inhibitory mechanism and this malfunction makes it difficult to learn to inhibit behavior that is likely to lead to punishment* (pp. 33–34).

Thus Hare links the various EEG abnormalities of sociopaths, some of which can be regarded as immaturities of the brain, to poor inhibition and thereby to their inability to avoid punishment. It is this subject of punishment and the failure to learn to avoid it that we shall now discuss as a fourth correlate of sociopathy.

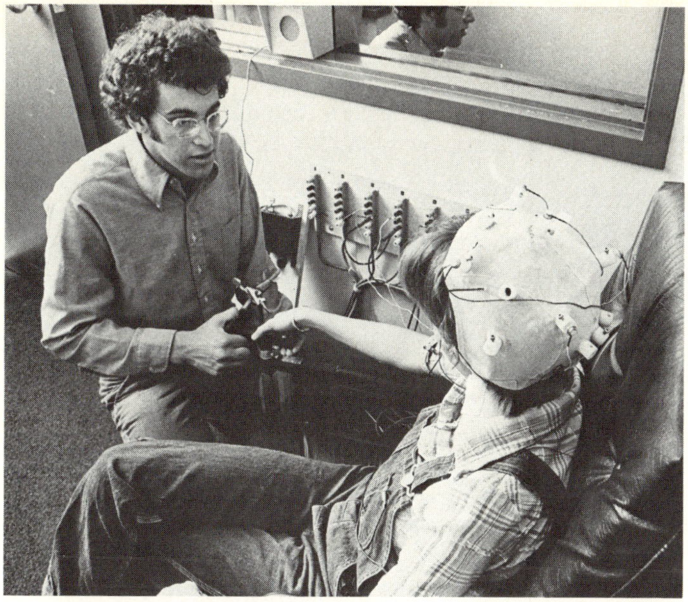

At top, a subject being prepared for an electroencephalogram. The cap ensures that the recording electrodes will contact the proper locations on the skull. Below, a room containing the equipment for amplifying the brain's electrical activity and recording it.

## Avoidance Learning and Sociopathy

As we have previously noted, in defining the sociopathic syndrome, Cleckley pointed out the inability of these persons to learn from experience. In particular, they seemingly feel no need to avoid the negative consequences of social misbehavior. Cleckley also remarked that they were not neurotic and seldom anxious. Lykken (1957) deduced that sociopaths may have few inhibitions about committing antisocial acts because they experience so little anxiety. He performed several tests to determine whether sociopaths do indeed have low levels of anxiety. One of these tests involved avoidance learning.

A group of male sociopaths, judged to be so on the basis of Cleckley's criteria for recognizing the syndrome, was selected from a penitentiary population. Their performance on an avoidance learning task was compared to that of nonsociopathic penitentiary inmates[4] and of college students. It was of course critical that only avoidance learning and not learning mediated by other possible rewards be tested. If a subject perceives that his task is to learn to avoid pain, he may be motivated not only by the desire to avoid the pain but also by a desire to demonstrate his cleverness to the investigator. To ensure that no other motives would become manifest, Lykken made the avoidance learning task *incidental*. He used the following apparatus. On a panel in front of the subject there were four red lights in a horizontal array, four green lights below each of the red ones, and a lever below each column, as illustrated in Figure 9.2. The subject's task was to learn a sequence of twenty correct lever presses, but for each he first had to determine by trial and error which of the four alternatives was correct. The correct lever turned on a green light. Two of the remaining three incorrect levers turned on red lights, indicating an error. The third incorrect lever delivered an

[4] In the literature such people are sometimes referred to as neurotic sociopaths. We have avoided using this confusing term since, by definition, a sociopath is not neurotic.

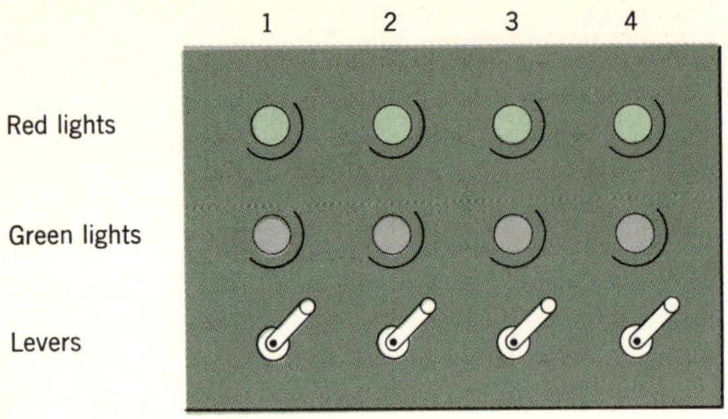


FIGURE **9.2**
The apparatus devised by Lykken (1957) for his study of avoidance learning in sociopaths.

For the first lever press assume that lever 3 is correct, that is, that pressing it lights the green bulb; that levers 1 and 4 are incorrect, lighting red bulbs; and that pressing lever 2 lights a red bulb and gives the subject a shock. For the second lever press the meaning of the levers may change entirely; for example, lever 2 may be correct, levers 3 and 4 incorrect, and lever 1 may give the shock. The subjects had to learn a sequence of twenty correct lever presses.

electric shock to the subject. The location of the correct lever was of course not always the same. The subject was told simply to figure out and to learn the series of twenty correct lever presses. He was not informed that avoiding shock was desirable or possible, only that shock was randomly administered as a stimulant to make him do well. Thus the task yielded two measures of learning: the total number of errors made before the subject learned the correct sequence of twenty presses and the number of errors made that produced shock. Avoidance learning is measured by this second index.

In terms of the overall number of errors made, there were no significant differences among any of the groups in Lykken's study. The college students, however, were apparently best able to remember the sequence of presses that produced shock and thus sharply decreased their proportion of shocked errors. The sociopaths made the most shocked errors, but the differences between their shocked errors and those of the other penitentiary inmates only approached statistical significance. The results of Lykken's investigation therefore tentatively support the hypothesis that sociopaths operate under lower levels of anxiety than do normal individuals.

Lykken also tried to verify his reduced-anxiety hypothesis by giving his subjects standard psychological tests for measuring anxiety, such as the Taylor Manifest Anxiety Scale. On these tests the sociopaths did indeed show lower levels of anxiety. In addition, Lykken devised his own instrument, the Activity Preference Questionnaire, which presents subjects with a series of items, each forcing a choice between two unpleasant events. One is unpleasant in a social way, such as having an accident in a borrowed car or spilling a glass of water in a restaurant. The other is merely distasteful or tedious, such as cleaning up a bottle of syrup or draining and cleaning a cesspool. It was thought that, by virtue of their minimal anxiety in social situations, sociopaths would choose relatively more of the socially unpleasant incidents. Control subjects, on the other hand, were expected to choose more of those that were unpleasant but not socially so. Lykken's hypothesis again received clear support: sociopaths chose more of the socially unpleasant incidents than did the controls, indicating less sensitivity to social mores.

Lykken's pioneering work was subsequently followed up by Schachter and Latané (1964). These investigators reasoned that if sociopaths do not learn to avoid unpleasant stimuli because they have little anxiety, a procedure that increases their anxiety should make them learn to shun punishment. Inasmuch as anxiety is viewed as being related to activity of the sympathetic nervous system, they injected Adrenalin, an agent whose effects mimic sympathetic activity, in order to increase anxiety.

Sociopathic and nonsociopathic prisoners from a penitentiary were studied with the same task and apparatus that had been devised by Lykken. This time each subject was tested twice. The subjects were led to believe that the effects of a hormone on learning were being investigated. Half received a placebo injection on the first day of testing and half an injection of Adrenalin. On

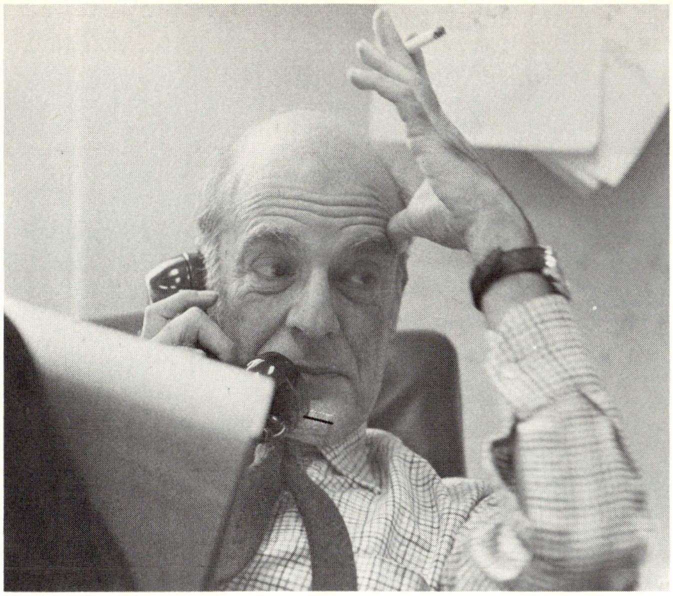

Stanley Schachter, social psychologist at Columbia University, known for his theory that emotion has both cognitive and physiological aspects. He has investigated the relation between arousal in the nervous system, emotion, and sociopathy.

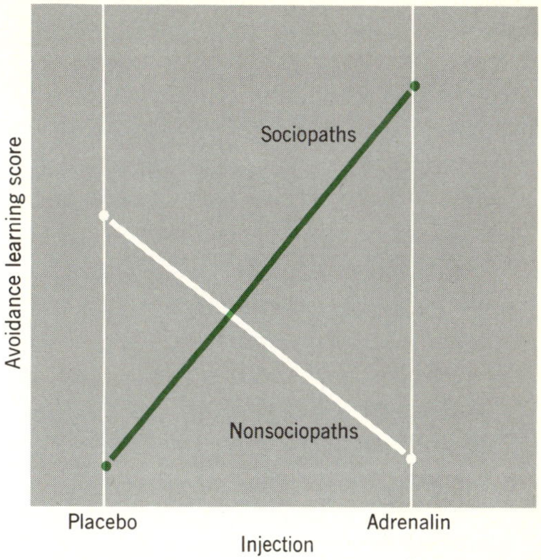


FIGURE **9.3**
Results of Schachter and Latané's study (1964) of the effects of Adrenalin on avoidance learning in sociopathic and nonsociopathic prisoners. Higher scores reflect better avoidance learning; arousal through Adrenalin helped the sociopaths to learn to avoid shock by activating their otherwise underaroused autonomic nervous system.

the second day of testing the injections received by the subjects were reversed.

The results of Schachter and Latané's experiment were important in several ways. First, the overall number of errors provided confirmation for Lykken's results: no difference was found between the sociopathic and nonsociopathic prisoners in the total number of errors committed in learning the sequence, whether they had been injected with Adrenalin or the placebo. Second, the nonsociopathic prisoners injected with the placebo markedly reduced their proportion of shocked errors after a number of runs, but the sociopaths injected with the placebo showed no such improvement. In this part of the study the difference between the performances of the two groups of prisoners was greater than that revealed in Lykken's experiment and considerably larger than the amount necessary for statistical significance. Third, and most important, when injected with Adrenalin, the sociopaths showed a great reduction in the number of shocked errors, but the prisoners who were not sociopaths were adversely affected by the Adrenalin and did not learn to avoid the shock in their state of high arousal (Figure 9.3). Thus the hypothesis of the anxiety-free and underaroused sociopath received considerable support from the work of Schachter and Latané.[5]

Chesno and Kilmann (1975) have provided further confirmation of Schachter and Latané's work. Sociopaths, as well as several other groups of subjects, participated in a shock avoidance learning test. While they performed the task the subjects were exposed to bursts of noise

[5] The finding that the Adrenalin injection apparently worsened the avoidance learning performance of the nonsociopathic prisoners is difficult to interpret. A follow-up test by Schachter and Latané did not reproduce this effect.

which varied in intensity. One-third of the subjects in each group were exposed to noise of 35 decibels, one-third to 65 decibels, and the remainder to 95. The varying levels of noise were expected to produce different levels of arousal, as had the Adrenalin injections in Schachter and Latané's work. And the sociopaths were expected to learn to avoid shock more readily as noise became more intense, which is exactly what happened.

An avoidance learning study by Schmauk (1970) qualifies the findings of Lykken as well as those of the other studies we have discussed. He showed that a particular kind of punishment, losing money, *can* have an effect on sociopaths. His study involved three groups, sociopathic prisoners, nonsociopathic prisoners, and a control group consisting of farmworkers and hospital attendants. As in the previous studies, an avoidance learning task was devised, but this time three different aversive stimuli could be avoided: a physical punishment—electric shock; a tangible punishment—losing a quarter from an initial pile of forty; and a social punishment—the experimenter's saying "wrong" to the subject. There were again no differences among the groups in the total number of errors made before the task has been mastered. The major finding of this study (Figure 9.4) indicated that the sociopath's avoidance performance varies with the nature of punishment. When the punishments confronting them were physical and social, the members of the control group were vastly superior to the sociopaths in learning to avoid punishment. But the sociopaths outdid them in learning to avoid the tangible punishment of losing a quarter. The nonsociopathic prisoners did better than the sociopaths in learning to avoid physical punishment but less well in avoiding social punishment.

It appears then that sociopaths *can* learn to avoid punishment. The differences found between sociopaths and nonsociopaths in previous investigations may reflect *not* a general deficit in avoidance learning ability but rather the fact that some punishments have no meaning for the sociopath. Evidently, sociopaths will learn to avoid punishment that is relevant to their system of values, and money may very well be particularly important to them. According to this hypothesis, then, sociopaths differ from nonsociopaths in that they do not view *certain* consequences as negatively as others do.

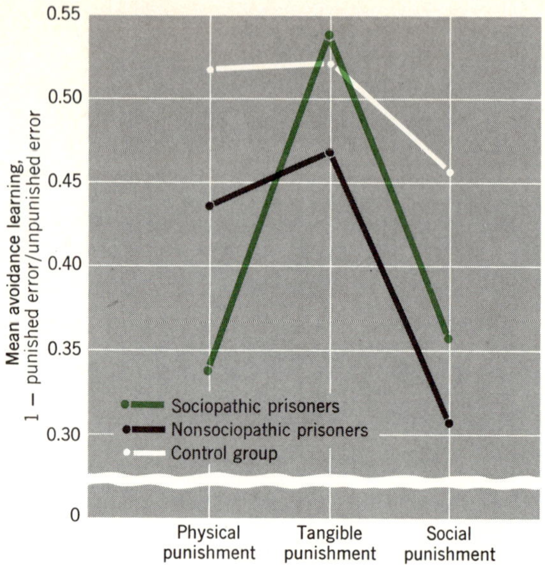


FIGURE **9.4**
Mean avoidance learning scores plotted for three subject groups confronted by three different punishments, physical, tangible, and social. The sociopaths readily learned to avoid punishment when it cost them money. After Schmauk, 1970.

## Underarousal and Sociopathic Behavior

Sociopaths have often been described as not responding emotionally when confronted by both familiar and new situations that most people would find either stressful or unpleasant. Cleckley (1964) has written about this aspect of their behavior.

> *Regularly, we find in* [*the sociopath*] *extraordinary poise rather than jitteriness or*

*worry, a smooth sense of physical well-being instead of uneasy preoccupations with bodily functions. Even under concrete circumstances that would for the ordinary person cause embarrassment, confusion, acute insecurity, or visible agitation, his relative serenity is likely to be noteworthy* (p. 267).

This description is remarkably consistent with the Schachter and Latané finding that sociopaths do not ordinarily avoid electric shock but that they do so when their autonomic arousal is increased by injections of Adrenalin. Because of the assumed central role of the autonomic nervous system in states of emotion, several investigators have examined sociopaths both for their resting levels of autonomic activity and for their patterns of autonomic reactivity to various classes of stimuli. Hare (1970) has summarized the results of many of these investigations.

> *During periods of relative quiescence* [sociopathic] *subjects tend to be hypoactive* [less active than normal] *on several indices of skin conductance and autonomic variability* [spontaneous fluctuations in GSR and cardiac activity]. *Although these findings must be interpreted with caution, they are at least consistent with most clinical statements about the psychopath's general lack of anxiety, guilt, and emotional "tension." The situation with respect to autonomic responsivity is more complex. Nevertheless, it appears that psychopaths may give relatively small electrodermal responses to "lie detection"* [tests] *and to situations that would ordinarily be considered stressful* (p. 57).

The data showing such underarousal in the sociopath have additional implications. Quay (1965) has suggested that the sociopath's impulsiveness, thirst for excitement, and inability to tolerate routine and boredom are fostered by a state of lowered arousal. This reasoning is based on the hypothesis that there is an optimal level of arousal for human beings. When arousal is too high an individual will take steps to reduce it, and when it is too low the individual will take steps to increase it. Much of the sociopath's "thrill seeking" behavior could then be viewed as an attempt to increase his or her arousal enough to approach this optimal state.

If it is true that sociopaths seek excitement to raise their arousal levels, we might expect their performance on a tedious and monotonous task to be especially poor. Orris (1967) has tested prisoners on such a task. The findings bore out the prediction. Sociopathic prisoners performed less well than did the others. We might also predict that given a choice, sociopaths will prefer novel and complex stimuli. Such stimuli are generally viewed as having high-arousal properties, and thus the sociopath might be expected to show a preference for them. Skrzypek (1969) tested this hypothesis on a sample of sociopathic and other prisoners and found that sociopaths indeed showed a somewhat greater preference for novelty and complexity than did the other prisoners.

The case histories, studies, and theories that we have reviewed show the sociopath to be an individual who does not experience the same emotions that most of us do. Thus anxiety can have no deterrent effect. Moreover, because the sympathetic nervous system of the sociopath is less active than that of normal human beings, arousal is actually sought. These are possible reasons for the sociopath's misconduct without regret and thrill seeking without regard for society's rules.

## Summary

The category of personality disorders is an extremely broad and heterogeneous one. There is little information on most of them. The notable exception is sociopathy, the dominant pattern of which is repeated antisocial behavior without regret or shame. In addition, sociopaths are thought to be unable to learn from experience, to have no sense of responsibility, and to establish no genuine emotional relationships with other people. Research on their families indicates that sociopaths had fathers who themselves were antisocial. Genetic studies, particularly those using the adoptee method, suggest that a predisposition to sociopathy is inherited. The core problem of the sociopath may be that impending punishment creates no inhibitions about committing antisocial acts. A good deal of overlapping evidence supports this view: (1) sociopaths have abnormal amounts of slow-wave EEG activity, which may reflect a failure of the usual inhibitory processes; (2) sociopaths are slow at learning to avoid shock, a deficit which can be reduced by heightening the sociopath's level of physiological arousal; and (3) sociopaths are hypoactive in measures of autonomic nervous system functioning.

# chapter 10

## DRUG USE DISORDERS



From prehistoric times man has used various substances in the hope of reducing physical pain or altering states of consciousness. Almost all peoples have discovered some intoxicant that affects the central nervous system, relieving physical and mental anguish or producing euphoria. Whatever the aftermath of taking such substances into the body, their effects are usually pleasing, at least initially.

Alcoholic beverages from the fermentation of many fruits and grains, of milk, honey, and molasses, and even of tree sap; opium, the dried milky juice obtained from the immature fruit of the opium poppy; hashish and marihuana from *Cannabis,* the hemp plant; and cocaine, an alkaloid extracted from coca leaves—these are the major natural drugs that have a long history of both use and abuse, and that continue today to present problems for society. In the United States and other Western countries, morphine, an alkaloid extracted from opium, and heroin, derived from morphine, are more prevalent than the raw opium, and dried marihuana is used more often than hashish. Also available are a number of newer synthetic and synthesized drugs, most importantly the barbiturates, the amphetamines, and LSD. Of all the potentially dangerous drugs, the one craved by the greatest number of people is nicotine, the principal alkaloid of tobacco.

The current diagnostic system, DSM-II, has classified drug dependence and addiction with personality disorders and designated them more generally as nonpsychotic mental disorders. This categorization assumes excessive use of alcohol and other drugs to be a manifestation of underlying personality disturbances. But as we have indicated, in the draft version of DSM-III this assumption is no longer made, and the disorders discussed in this chapter are termed simply "Drug Use Disorders."

Drug dependence is defined as the habitual use of a drug, frequently out of a perceived sense of need. The term dependence is sometimes used interchangeably with addiction, but there are important distinctions between the two. *Addiction* is a physiological process by which the body responds to certain drugs. When addicting drugs are ingested for prolonged periods of time, greater and greater amounts of them are *tolerated.* The bodily systems habituate to the particular chemical so that larger and larger doses are necessary to maintain similar intoxicating effects. Then when the frequency of ingestion or the amount of the drug is suddenly decreased, the person suffers *withdrawal reactions.* The prolonged use of the drug has so altered the physiological conditions of the body that it is disturbed when the drug is not administered. For example, an addict who suddenly ceases to take morphine usually suffers from hypertension and cramps, is restless, and sweats profusely.

The physiological mechanisms responsible for tolerance and withdrawal reactions are as yet unknown. In the case of alcohol, it is evident that tolerance can *not* be attributed to the drug's entering the bloodstream at a slower rate and being more rapidly metabolized by the liver (see page 243). Most current hypotheses focus on alterations in the process of neural transmission, but none has unequivocal support.

But not all drugs, even if they are taken regularly, bring on either tolerance or the later withdrawal reactions when their use is terminated. For this reason the concept of *psychological dependency* was proposed to describe reliance on drugs that are *not* addicting. A drug may be taken because its effects make stressful or anxiety-provoking situations more bearable. But the dosage of the drug does not have to be continually increased to produce these effects, nor is there a withdrawal reaction if the drug is not taken. This is not to say that the individual with a psychological dependence on a drug feels no unpleasant effects when the drug is not available. If people are deprived of *anything* that they have come to rely on, they are likely to react negatively to its absence by becoming restless, nervous, or otherwise upset. These reactions sometimes resemble the withdrawal symptoms obtained with addictive drugs, but they should not be regarded as such *unless* there is also evidence of tolerance.

## Alcoholism

Written reports of the use of wines, beers, and other alcoholic beverages date back to 3000 B.C., but not until about 800 B.C. was the distillation process applied to fermented beverages, making possible the preparation of the highly potent liquors that are available today. It has been estimated that in the United States about 100 million people consume alcohol and about 12 million are judged alcoholic according to some definitions. There are about 200,000 new cases of alcoholism each year, and in the 1970s teenage alcoholism has greatly increased. Male alcoholics outnumber females by about four to one. Although most of the people who have a drinking problem do not seek professional help, alcoholics do constitute a large proportion of new admissions to mental and general hospitals. Moreover, some estimate that they account for 25,000 highway deaths each year. Alcohol also presents law enforcement problems, for 31 percent of all arrests in the United States are for public drunkenness. Homicide is an alcohol-related crime; and parental child abuse and suicide are also frequently associated with excessive drinking (Brecher, 1972). The World Health Organization has defined alcoholics as

> . . . *excessive drinkers whose dependence on alcohol has attained such a degree that they show noticeable mental disturbance or an interference with their mental and bodily health, their interpersonal relations and their smooth social and economic functioning; or who show the prodromal* [*beginning*] *signs of such developments* (Kessel and Walton, 1965, p. 18).

The essential points made by this definition are that *control over the consumption of the beverage is lost* and that *consumption disrupts the individual's life.*

The definition established by the World Health Organization applies only to those people who would by DSM-II be diagnosed as *addicted* to alcohol. In the following discussion we will not consider in any depth individuals who are excessive habitual drinkers, and for whom DSM-II also has a subcategory. Rather, our study will concentrate on alcohol addiction.

## Short-Term Effects of Alcohol

After being swallowed, alcohol does not undergo any of the processes of digestion. A small part of the alcohol ingested passes immediately into the bloodstream through the stomach walls, but most of it goes into the small intestines and from there is absorbed into the blood. It must then be metabolized by a process referred to as oxidation. In this process alcohol fuses with oxygen and is broken down so that its basic elements leave the body as carbon dioxide and water.[1] The primary site of oxidation is the liver, which can break down about one ounce of 100 proof (that is, 50 percent alcohol) whiskey per hour. Quantities in excess of this amount remain in the bloodstream. Whereas absorption of alcohol can be very rapid, removal is always slow. Many of the effects of alcohol vary directly with the level of concentration of the drug in the bloodstream, which in turn depends on the amount ingested in a particular period of time, the presence or absence in the stomach of food to retain the alcohol and reduce its absorption rate, the size of the individual's body, and the efficiency of the liver.

Because the drinking of alcoholic beverages is accepted in most societies, alcohol is rarely regarded as a drug, especially by those who drink. But it is indeed a drug, affecting the central nervous system. Alcohol, acting as a depressant, first numbs the higher brain centers, those that are primarily inhibiting. Thus the initial effect of alcohol is stimulating. Tensions and inhibitions are reduced, and the individual may experience an expansive feeling of sociability and well-being. Larger amounts interfere with complex thought processes; then motor coordination, balance, speech, and vision are impaired. Alcohol is capable of blunting pain and in larger doses of inducing sedation and sleep. Before modern techniques of anesthesia were discovered, liquors were often administered to a patient about to undergo surgery.

Studies have determined that short-term effects of alcohol on social drinkers are complex (see Box. 10.1). Jones and Parsons (1975) have reviewed a number of experiments that suggest, among other things, that effects vary depending on whether the person is becoming drunk or sobering up. In one such experiment Jones and Parsons (1971) assessed the abstract problem-solving ability of drinkers. Those on the downward part of the curve, that is, drinkers becoming sober, performed significantly better with a particular level of alcohol in their blood than did those who were getting high and had the same level. A person apparently thinks better, at a given stage of intoxication, if he or she is becoming less drunk than if becoming more so. The short-term memories of those becoming sober appear to be similarly good and those becoming intoxicated to be similarly poor (Jones, 1973).

Other studies have addressed a problem experienced by many social drinkers, namely remembering clearly what happened while they were drinking. It seems indeed that the state of consciousness entered through intoxication is somewhat separate from the normal, sober state. Overton (1966) demonstrated what he termed "state-dependent learning" in a series of experiments with rats. A rat taught something while drugged remembers that behavior better when tested later in a drugged state than when tested in an undrugged state. The same phenomenon has been demonstrated with alcohol intoxication and the learning and retention of human beings (Goodwin et al., 1969).

[1] Various types of alcohol differ in the rate at which they can be oxidized. Ethyl alcohol, the type found in alcoholic beverages, oxidizes the most rapidly, whereas methyl or wood alcohol oxidizes much more slowly. Because of slow oxidation, large amounts of methyl alcohol may accumulate in the blood, causing death or blindness. Another type of alcohol, denatured alcohol, is a deadly poison because of the toxic substances added to it.

## BOX **10.1** Expectancy and the Short-Term Effects of Alcohol

Are the host of short-term effects attributed to alcohol invariably caused by the drug itself? Could some of the effects reflect peoples' expectations? Let us consider aggression. Folklore and some scientific data as well suggest that alcohol stimulates aggressiveness, but perhaps those who drink become aggressive simply because of the cultural beliefs people have about alcohol. To address this question, Lang, Marlatt, and their associates (1975) set up an experimental situation in which the direct effects of alcohol and those caused by expectancy could be teased apart.

College students who had been designated heavy social drinkers were recruited for a study of the effects of alcohol on motor performance. After arriving at the laboratory, half the subjects were told that they would be receiving alcohol and the remaining undergraduates were told that they would not. Thereafter half the participants in each of the two groups were given a rather strong dose of vodka mixed with tonic (enough for their blood concentration levels to reach 0.1 percent—6 ounces of vodka will do it for a 150-pound man) and the remaining half were given only tonic.* Thus four groups of subjects were formed: expect alcohol–receive alcohol, expect alcohol–receive tonic, expect tonic–receive alcohol, expect tonic–receive tonic. Another variable was also manipulated. After drinking, participants were introduced to "another subject"—these individuals were actually confederates of the experimenters—who would perform the motor task with them. For half the subjects the task was rigged so that their confederates did especially well and then belittled the intelligence of the subjects. The confederates of the remaining participants performed at about the same level as they did and made no critical remarks.

Aggression was measured by having the confederate perform a second task and the subject administer shocks to the confederate each time he made an error. The subject freely determined both the intensity and duration of the shocks. As expected, the subjects who had been insulted tended to deliver more intense and longer shocks to their confederates. More important, however, were the relative effects of alcohol and the expectancy manipulations. Subjects who thought that they had drunk alcohol gave more intense and longer shocks than those who thought that they had drunk tonic, *regardless of whether they had actually received alcohol*. The *belief* that alcohol had been drunk, rather than the drinking of it, made the imbibers more aggressive. Thus the "effects" of alcohol must be cautiously interpreted, for it is possible that behavior in addition to aggression is determined by expectations rather than by actually drinking the beverage.

Relatively high levels of alcohol in the blood are known to inhibit sexual arousal in men (Briddell and Wilson, 1976; Farkas and Rosen, 1976). Women are similarly affected (Wilson and Lawson, 1976). But alcohol in small to moderate amounts is widely believed to "promote sexual activity by lowering inhibitions, causing euphoria and greasing the wheels of social interactions" (Gebhard, 1965, p. 485). Perhaps in sexual behavior, as in aggression, expectations are more determinative than the consumption of alcohol. Wilson, a researcher at the Rutgers Alcohol Behavior Research Laboratories, set up the same four expectancy-manipulating groups of male undergraduates that Lang had: expect alcohol–receive alcohol, expect alcohol–receive tonic, expect tonic–receive alcohol, expect tonic–receive tonic. The students were shown erotic films; the penile plethysmograph measured arousal. The young men who believed that they had drunk vodka were more aroused than the others, whether or not they had actually consumed alcohol. The vodka itself had no effect on sexual arousal.

* The two beverages were carefully pretested so they could not be discriminated by taste.

## Long-Term Effects of Prolonged Alcohol Use

The possible long-term effects of prolonged drinking are vividly illustrated in the following case history.

> At the time of his first admission to a state hospital at the age of twenty-four, the patient, an unmarried and unemployed laborer, already had a long history of antisocial behavior, promiscuity and addiction to alcohol and other drugs. . . . There had been eight brief admissions to private sanatoria for alcoholics, a number of arrests for public intoxication and drunken driving, and two jail terms for assault.
>
> The patient had been born into a wealthy and respected family in a small town. The patient's father, a successful and popular businessman, drank excessively and his death at the age of fifty-seven was partly due to alcoholism. The mother also drank to excess. The parents exercised little control over the patient as a child, and he was cared for by nursemaids. His father taught him to pour drinks for guests of the family when he was very young and he reported that he began to drain the glasses at parties in his home before he was six; by the time he was twelve he drank almost a pint of liquor every weekend and by seventeen was drinking up to three bottles every day. His father provided him with money to buy liquor and shielded him from punishment for drunken driving and other consequences of his drinking.
>
> The patient was expelled from high school in his freshman year for striking a teacher. He then attended a private school until the eleventh grade, when he changed the data on his birth certificate and joined the Army paratroops. After discharge, he was unemployed for six months; he drank heavily and needed repeated care at a sanatorium. When a job was obtained for him he quit within a month. On his third arrest for drunken driving he was jailed. His father bailed him out with the warning that no more money would be forthcoming. The patient left town and worked as an unskilled laborer—he had never acquired any useful skills—but returned home when his father died. During the next few years he was jailed for intoxication, for blackening his mother's eyes when he found a male friend visiting her, and for violating probation by getting drunk. He assaulted and badly hurt a prison guard in an escape attempt and was sentenced to two additional years in prison. When released, he began to use a variety of stimulant, sedative and narcotic drugs as well as alcohol (Rosen, Fox, and Gregory, 1972, pp. 312–313).

The life histories of alcoholics are considered to share a common progression. On the basis of an extensive survey of 2000 alcoholics, Jellinek (1952) described the male alcoholic as passing through four stages on the way to his addiction. The first *prealcoholic* phase lasts from several months up to two years. In this stage the individual drinks socially and also on occasion rather heavily to relieve tension and to forget about his problems. At first the heavy drinking is infrequent, but in time the crises and the occasions for seeking the bolstering effects of alcohol recur with greater regularity. In the second *prodromal stage* drinking may become furtive and may also be marked by blackouts. The drinker remains conscious, talks coherently, and carries on other activities, without even appearing to be greatly intoxicated, but later he has no recall of the occasion. Alcohol begins to be used more as a drug and less as a beverage. The individual becomes preoccupied with drinking, feeling guilty about it but at the same time worrying where and when he will have his next drink.

Jellinek terms the third phase *crucial,* choosing this adjective because he sees the alcoholic in this stage as being in severe danger

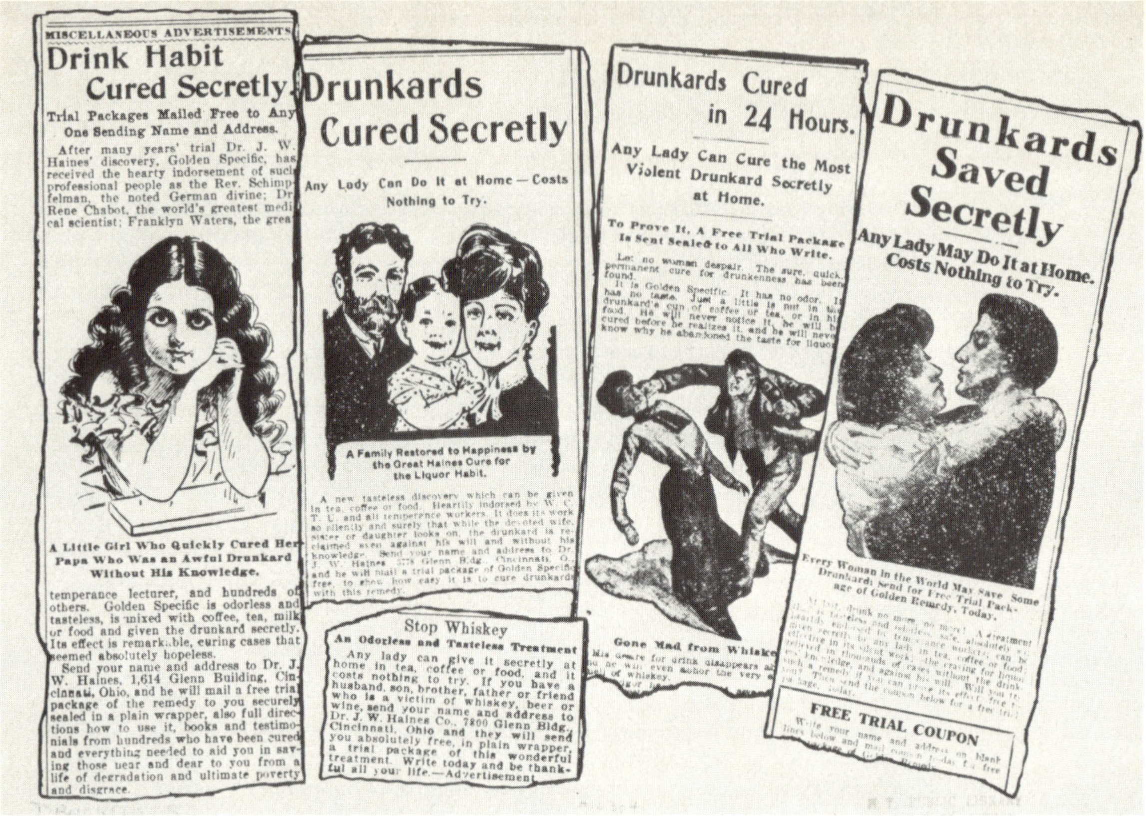


of losing everything that he values. He has already lost control of his drinking. Once he takes a single drink, he continues to consume alcohol until he is too sick or in too much of a stupor to drink anymore. The individual's social adjustment also begins to deteriorate. He starts to drink during the day, and this becomes evident to his employer, family, and friends. The alcoholic neglects his diet, has his first bender, a several-day period of excessive drinking, and may experience hallucinations and delirium when he stops drinking. At this stage the individual still has the ability to abstain. He can give up alcohol for several weeks or even months at a time, but if he has just one drink the whole pattern will begin again. The alcoholic even comes to feel that he needs a drink to steady himself for the day, and he starts to drink in the morning.

In the final *chronic stage* drinking is continual, and benders are frequent. The individual lives only to drink. His bodily systems have become so accustomed to alcohol that they must be supplied with it or he suffers withdrawal reactions. If liquor is not available to him, he will consume any liquid he can find that contains alcohol—shaving lotion, hair tonic, various medicinal preparations, whatever. He suffers from malnutrition and other physiological changes. He neglects his personal appearance and, having lost his self-esteem, feels little remorse about any aspect of his behavior. Finally, he ceases to care at all about family and home, about

Nineteenth- and early-twentieth-century advertisements and campaigns to cure and discourage drinking.

friends, occupation, and social status.

Jellinek's description has been widely cited, but the available evidence is not always corroborative. One study found that blackouts do *not* occur in conjunction with modest drinking and that many alcoholics have never experienced a blackout (Goodwin, Crane, and Guze, 1969). More recent evidence questions the commonly accepted notion that a single drink stimulates an irresistible impulse to continue drinking (Marlatt, Demming, and Reid, 1973). Alcoholics "primed" with an initial drink, one they believed to be nonalcoholic, later consumed no more alcohol than did social drinkers.

In addition to the psychological deterioration brought on by alcoholism, severe physiological

Alcoholism cuts across age groups and all strata of society.

damage is also a serious consequence of chronic drinking. Almost every tissue and organ of the body is affected by the prolonged consumption of alcohol. The malnutrition suffered may be severe. Because alcohol provides calories, the alcoholic greatly reduces food intake. But alcohol, although it furnishes energy, does *not* supply any of the nutrients essential for health. In the older chronic alcoholic a deficiency of B-complex vitamins is believed to cause severe memory loss (Korsakoff's psychosis, page 420). A drastic reduction in the intake of protein causes cirrhosis of the liver, a disease in which an excessive amount of fibrous connective tissue is formed, replacing active liver cells and thus impeding blood circulation. Other common physiological changes include damage to the endocrine glands, heart failure, hypertension, and capillary hemorrhages, which are responsible for the swelling and the redness in the face, and especially of the nose, of chronic alcoholics. Prolonged use of alcohol also appears to produce brain damage, especially in the frontal lobes (Parsons, 1975; see Box 16.1, page 412).

The effects of the abrupt withdrawal of alcohol from an alcoholic may be rather dramatic, for the body has become profoundly accustomed to the drug. Subjectively, the patient is often frightened, depressed, weak, restless, and unable to sleep. Tremors of the muscles, especially of the small musculature of the fingers, face, lips, and tongue, may be marked, and there is an elevation of pulse and blood pressure. An alcoholic who has been drinking for a number of years may also suffer from *delirium tremens* (DTs) when the level of alcohol in the blood drops suddenly. He sweats profusely, and the pupils of his eyes react slowly to changes in light. He becomes delirious as well as tremulous. His hallucinations are primarily visual but they may be tactile as well. Unpleasant and very active creatures—snakes, cockroaches, spiders, and the like—may appear to be crawling up the wall or all over the alcoholic's body, or they may fill the room. Feverish, disoriented, and terrified, the alcoholic may claw frantically at his skin to rid himself of the vermin, or he may cower in the corner to escape an advancing army of fantastic animals.

Delirium tremens would certainly seem to constitute a physiological withdrawal reaction, one of the criteria for considering a drug addictive. Increased tolerance is also evident. Mello and Mendelson (1970) found that alcoholics could drink a quart of bourbon a day without showing signs of drunkenness. Moreover, levels of alcohol in the blood were unexpectedly low after what would usually be viewed as excessive drinking.

In short, *the psychological, physiological, and social effects of prolonged consumption of alcohol are extremely serious.* Because the alcoholic's own functioning is so severely disrupted, the people he interacts with are also deeply affected and hurt by his conduct. Society too suffers, for the alcoholic is unlikely to be able to hold a job. The accumulated costs—the money spent in maintaining the necessary supply of liquor, the time lost in work efficiency, the damage of traffic accidents caused by impaired coordination, the expense of physicians and psychologists—run to millions of dollars each year. The human tragedy, much more devastating, is virtually incalculable.

Scene from a nineteenth-century play depicting the hallucinations often experienced during delirium tremens.

## Theories of Alcoholism

In trying to understand alcoholism, we must draw a distinction between conditions that induce a person to *start* drinking and those that play the central role in *maintaining* the behavior. Chronic drinking becomes an addiction; an alcoholic eventually continues drinking because his or her body demands alcohol. But the later physical need does not explain why an individual initially develops a drinking habit. Those who attempt to explain the origins of habitual drinking refer to either psychological or physiological factors. Within each of these two broad categories there are several theories.

### Psychological Theories

#### Psychoanalytic views

Most analytic accounts of alcoholism point to fixation at the oral stage of development as the precipitating cause. Early mother-child interactions supposedly either frustrate dependency needs during this stage of maturation or satisfy them to too great an extent. The various psychoanalytic theories therefore differ in the function attributed to excessive drinking. For example, Knight (1937) proposed that the male alcoholic's experience with an overprotective mother has developed a strong need to remain dependent. When this need is frustrated, he becomes angry and aggressive and feels guilty about his impulses. He drinks heavily to reduce these impulses and also to punish those who withhold affection from him. Fenichel (1945), in contrast, stated that being neglected by the mother turns the young male child toward his father, which in turn produces unconscious homosexual impulses. These repressed impulses compel him to drink in bars with other men, an activity that supposedly allows the alcoholic to obtain some of the emotional satisfaction he has not received from women. (It is not clear what the psychodynamic significance of solitary drinking would be.) Bergler (1946), emphasizing the self-destructive nature of alcoholism, hypothesized that alcohol addiction is a means of attempting to destroy a bad mother with whom the individual has identified. Little evidence is available to support these notions.

Other analytic accounts of alcoholism describe excessive drinking as a defense mechanism adopted to reduce emotional conflicts or eliminate guilt (see Box 10.2). A common analytic quip defines the superego as the part of the personality that is soluble in alcohol. The notion that the consumption of alcohol can reduce distress is also advanced in learning-based accounts of alcoholism.

#### Learning views

An early experiment by Conger (1951) demonstrated that alcohol can relieve fear. First, animals were trained in a classic approach-avoidance situation: after having been trained to feed in a particular place, the animals were subjected to shock when they approached their food. Half of the animals were then injected with alcohol. These animals were found to approach the food more readily than did the controls. The fear that had become associated with the goal was apparently decreased by the alcohol in the bloodstream of the animals. Some recent investigations have replicated this work and also shown that conflict increases alcohol consumption (Freed, 1971; Von Wright, Pekanmaki, and Malin, 1971).

Generalizing from these studies, we might argue that drinking alcohol is a learned response that is acquired and maintained because it reduces distress. Alcohol, however, has other effects besides the immediate allaying of tension, as our review of the long-term deleterious effects of continual drinking has revealed. Should not these extremely serious long-term negative effects outweigh the transient relief from stress felt when alcohol is first consumed? Dollard and Miller (1950) offered as a solution to this seeming paradox the concept of a *delay of reward gradient.* According to this formulation, the effectiveness of both rewards and punishments,

## BOX 10.2 Alcoholism and the Need for Power

David McClelland has advanced a rather novel psychodynamic theory of the origins of both social and excessive drinking, linking them to a personality trait, the need for power (McClelland et al., 1972). He proposes that men drink to increase their sense of power. Ingesting alcohol in small doses supposedly brings to mind a greater number of thoughts about social power—being able to affect others for their own good—and larger doses increase thoughts of personal power, and in particular of sexual and aggressive conquests.

In one experiment lending support to the theory, men were recruited to participate in a study of the effects of social atmosphere on imaginativeness. On arriving at the laboratory, each member of the group responded to a series of four TAT-like pictures. Twenty-five minutes of social interaction followed, during which the experimental manipulation took place. Half the men were allowed to drink alcohol, but the others consumed only soft drinks. Then the subjects responded to four more TAT cards. In support of the theory, only those who drank alcohol told in the second testing a greater number of power-related TAT stories—stories that involved prestige, dramatic settings, and positive feelings aroused in others—than they had related in the first testing.

According to McClelland's theory, the need for personal power that makes the alcoholic drink heavily is intense and excessive. Moreover, instead of fostering instrumental behavior that might indeed earn increased power, this excessive need impels the alcoholic to choose drinking as an alternate path to his goal. Two studies did indeed show that the experimental induction of concerns about power led to increased drinking. What remains unclear is how an excessive need for power develops, and why some individuals with this need attempt to fulfill it by drink rather than action.

in terms of their impact on any particular behavior, tends to decrease as they become farther and farther removed in time from the response. Thus a small but immediate reward can often exert a more powerful effect than can a larger one that does not immediately follow the response. Similarly, an immediate punishment is a much more effective agent of change than a punishment imposed several days, weeks, or even months later. In this sense the short-term reduction of distress offered by alcohol is seen as a rather large and immediately reinforcing benefit. Conversely, the longer-term effects of alcohol are relatively ineffective in discouraging its consumption because they are suffered so long after the actual drinking.

The theory that the alcoholic drinks because alcohol reduces tension must be viewed as an incomplete explanation, however. First, studies of the effect of alcohol on other behavior related to tension, such as avoidance, have not always provided data supporting the theory (Cappell, 1975). Furthermore, the theory may explain why many people *begin* drinking, but it does not appear to account for the continuation of drinking over long periods of time. For example, Nathan and his colleagues have reported a study in which alcoholics residing in a specially designed hospital ward were carefully observed (Nathan et al., 1970). The patients were allowed to work to obtain points which could later be exchanged for alcohol. Although the patients themselves reported that they drank to relieve anxiety and depression, an assessment of their moods by means of a self-report adjective checklist indicated that they were actually *more* anxious and depressed after drinking. Similar results were reported by Mendelson (1964).

We might well ask why it has so long been assumed that drinking is initially maintained because it reduces anxiety. Perhaps the theorists have failed to distinguish between chronic consumption of alcohol and social drinking. Those who have theorized about alcoholism are, after all, unlikely to be chronic or addicted alcoholics. They are more likely to be social drinkers who enjoy an occasional cocktail in the company of others, especially after a trying day. It may be, then, that closeness to the subject matter has prevented until recently a critical examination of the view that prolonged drinking reduces tension.

### Personality and alcoholism

Many investigations have attempted to measure the personalities of alcoholics. Two points must be made about this research. First, no profile of a single "alcoholic personality" has been obtained. More typically a number of personality patterns are found among alcoholics (for example, Skinner, Jackson, and Hoffman, 1974). Second, the research design of such studies suffers from the problems of interpretation that are inherent in correlational work. For example, if a given personality pattern is highly correlated with alcoholism, did the former cause the latter, or vice versa? Some studies, though, have employed the more appropriate longitudinal design.

In the 1930s a long-term research project was begun in Oakland, California. Called the Oakland Growth Study, it examined a large sample of children in great detail and followed them up at periodic intervals. In the mid-1960s many of these middle-aged individuals were contacted again and interviewed concerning their current alcohol consumption patterns, their reasons for drinking, their attitudes toward drinking, and the like (Jones, 1968, 1971). On the basis of their answers to these questions, the individuals were classified into five categories: (1) problem drinkers, (2) heavy drinkers (two or three drinks every day), (3) moderate drinkers, (4) light drinkers, and (5) nondrinkers and abstainers. The information that had been collected on the members of the population sample during their junior and senior high school years was extensive. Parents had contributed details about background and homelife, teachers had reported on classroom behavior, classroom peers had rated one another, and the individuals in the sample had rated themselves on personality tests and in interviews. All these data collected during their adolescence were correlated with the subjects' adult drinking patterns.

Jones found that the adult male problem drinkers still had some of the same traits that had characterized them in adolescence: impulsiveness which was never controlled, extroverted behavior, and a tendency to overemphasize their masculinity. Moreover, as compared to high school contemporaries who did not later become excessive drinkers, adult male problem drinkers had been described in adolescence as less aware of impressions made on others, less productive, less calm, more sensitive to criticism, and less socially perceptive. The traits of the future problem drinker had apparently caused him social difficulties even in high school. Later these difficulties may have served as the source of stress that induced him to begin drinking.

Among the women, the picture was much less clear, for Jones found marked similarities in adolescence between those who later became problem drinkers and those who abstained altogether from alcohol in adulthood. Both groups had been characterized in high school as vulnerable, withdrawn, dependent, irritable, and sensitive to criticism. The pattern of apparently poor social adaptation—which correlated with heavy drinking in men—was in women associated with *either* problem drinking *or* total abstinence.

### The sociocultural view

It has been argued that ethnic groups such as the Jews, Italians, and Chinese, who specify appropriate ceremonial, nutritional, or festive uses of alcohol, have lower rates of alcoholism. Although these people condone the drinking of alcohol under specified circumstances, they frown on overindulgence. For other national groups, such as the Irish and the English, the circumstances in which the consumption of alcohol is deemed appropriate are less clear.

A study carried out by McCord, McCord, and Gudeman (1959, 1960) reveals the importance of ethnic and cultural backgrounds in the etiology of alcoholism of males in the United States. Young men who had been intensively studied several years earlier as adolescents were followed up. In examining the earlier histories of those who had become alcoholics, the investigators found no support for theories relating the habit to oral fixation, parental pampering, or self-destructive tendencies, but they did find the relation of alcoholism and ethnic background to be significant. More young men with American Indian, western and eastern European, and Irish backgrounds were alcoholic than were those of Italian and other Latin extractions. The investigators also found a relation between alcoholism and social class: more of the alcoholics were from the middle class than from the lower class.

Although social and cultural factors are clearly important, they obviously cannot be the only ones. The relationship between ethnic background and alcoholism is not one to one; some Jews are alcoholics, and not every Irishman is addicted to the beverage. Furthermore, comparisons among various countries reveal a pattern of alcoholism not entirely consistent with this view. The rate of alcoholism in Ireland, for example, is in the bottom third of the list given in Table 10.1. Italians have the second highest rate.

## Physiological Theories

The psychosocial theories just reviewed attempt to account for the origins of heavy drinking. None of the views enjoys great support from the available data. Inasmuch as chronic alcoholism becomes a physiological addiction, other theorists point to physiological factors in attempting to explain why some people begin a drinking pattern that eventuates in addiction.

Williams (1959) has proposed that alcoholism develops from a metabolic deficiency. He suggests that alcoholics have an inherited inability to produce certain enzymes and thus cannot digest certain nutrients. The excessive consumption of alcohol somehow assuages the physiological need for the substances their digestive systems cannot assimilate. In formulating his theory, Williams relied heavily on an early study in which vitamin-deprived rats were found to prefer alcohol to water. It appeared that their consumption of liquor might be a response to the dietary deficiency.

Other research, however, has offered little support for Williams's theory. Lester and Greenberg (1952) studied the effects of dietary deficiencies on alcohol consumption in a situation somewhat similar to that set up by Williams for his study. In addition to allowing rats to choose between alcohol and water, however, they also provided a sucrose solution. In their study sucrose was greatly preferred to alcohol. Thus a vitamin deficiency may give the animal a nonspecific hunger for *any* nutrient. When water is the only alternative, alcohol is preferred, but it will not be if another nutrient is available.

Other data, though, do suggest that physiological variables may be of importance. Among animals a preference for alcohol or indifference to it varies with the species. By selective mating within a species showing a preference, animals that greatly prefer alcohol to other beverages can be bred (Segovia-Riquelme, Varela, and Mardones, 1971). And there is evidence that alcoholism in human beings is, in part, heritable. A number of studies indicate that relatives and children of alcoholics have higher than expected rates of alcoholism. Such findings might of course suggest that these individuals become alcoholics through exposure to drinking.

TABLE **10.1**
Annual Drinker Consumption, Estimated Rates of Alcoholism, and Rates of Death from Cirrhosis of the Liver

(from de Lint and Schmidt, 1971)

| Country | Liters of absolute alcohol consumed by each drinker, 1966 or 1967* | Estimated rates of alcoholism per 100,000 population aged 15 and older† | Rate of death from cirrhosis of the liver per 100,000 population aged 15 and older, 1963, 1964, or 1965‡ |
|---|---|---|---|
| France | 25.9 | 9405 | 45.3 |
| Italy | 20.0 | 5877 | 27.3 |
| Portugal | 19.5 | 5652 | 42.7 |
| Spain | 17.1 | 4635 | 24.3 |
| Austria | 16.0 | 4212 | 35.0 |
| West Germany and West Berlin | 16.0 | 3978 | 26.7 |
| Switzerland | 15.8 | 3901 | 19.7 |
| Luxembourg | 12.5 | 2988 | 34.2 |
| Hungary | 12.4 | 2952 | 12.9 |
| United States | 12.0 | 2198 | 18.4 |
| Czechoslovakia | 11.4 | 2655 | 13.1 |
| Canada | 11.1 | 2272 | 10.0 |
| England and Wales | 10.9 | 1946 | 3.7 |
| Republic of Ireland | 10.9 | 1946 | 4.5 |
| Denmark | 9.4 | 1848 | 10.2 |
| Belgium | 9.3 | 2052 | 12.9 |
| Poland | 9.0 | 1752 | 8.6 |
| Sweden | 8.4 | 1515 | 7.9 |
| Netherlands | 7.7 | 1456 | 4.9 |
| Finland | 5.9 | 945 | 4.6 |
| Norway | 5.9 | 945 | 4.7 |

* Alcohol consumption data were taken from the 1968 Annual Report of the Dutch Distillers' Association.

† Alcoholics are defined as drinkers of daily averages in excess of 150 milliliters of absolute alcohol. Their numbers were tabulated on the basis of data provided in J. Hyland and S. Scott, Alcohol consumption tables: An application of the Ledermann equation to a wide range of consumption averages, 1969.

‡ Figures were taken from United Nations, *Demographic Yearbook, 1966*, New York: 1967.

A more recent study, however, examined alcoholism in the adopted offspring of alcoholics, thus allowing the role of heredity to be more precisely specified (Goodwin et al., 1973). One hundred seventy-four subjects were chosen from an initial pool of 5483 male babies (males are more prone to alcoholism than females) who were adopted in Copenhagen between 1924 and 1947. Subjects were divided into the three following experimental and control groups.

1. $N = 67$: One and sometimes both biological parents of each subject (proband) in the experimental group had been hospitalized for alcoholism. The probands had been adopted within six weeks of birth by nonrelatives and

had had no subsequent contact with biological relatives.

2. $N = 70$: Each subject in this control group was matched for age and time of adoption with a subject in group 1. None of the biological parents of these control subjects had a record of psychiatric hospitalization.

3. $N = 37$: The subjects in this control group were matched for age and time of adoption with subjects in group 1. At least one biological parent of each of these control subjects had been hospitalized for a psychiatric condition other than alcoholism or schizophrenia.

When this original sample was followed up, 133 subjects were located and interviewed. (Those who could not be located or who refused to be questioned were proportionately distributed across groups.) The subjects, who had a mean age of thirty at the time of the follow-up, were interviewed by a psychiatrist blind to their group assignment. Questions covered their drinking practices, psychopathology, and demographic variables. Since the subjects in the two control groups did not differ on any of the variables, they were combined into one comparison group for purposes of analysis. Variables that significantly discriminated between the experimental group and the comparison group are given in Table 10.2.

As can be seen, the two groups are easily distinguished one from the other on the basis of alcohol-related measures. Thus the results suggest that a predisposition toward alcoholism can be inherited. Such a predisposition could help explain why only some of the people who drink eventually become addicted.

TABLE **10.2**
The Alcohol-Related Problems of Offspring of Alcoholics, Adopted and Raised by Others, Compared with Those of Controls
(from Goodwin et al., 1973)

| Problems | Probands, percent ($N = 55$) | Controls, percent ($N = 78$) |
|---|---|---|
| Ever divorced | 27 | 9 |
| Any psychiatric treatment | 40 | 24 |
| Psychiatric hospitalization | 15 | 3 |
| *Drinking problems* | | |
| Hallucinations (as withdrawal symptoms) | 6 | 0 |
| Loss of control | 35 | 17 |
| Repeated morning drinking | 29 | 11 |
| Treated for drinking | 9 | 1 |
| Alcoholic diagnosis | 18 | 5 |

## Hard Drugs

Until 1914 addiction to drugs was disapproved in the United States, but it was tolerated. The 1914 Harrison Narcotics Act changed this, making the unauthorized use of various drugs illegal and those addicted to them criminals. The drugs to be discussed, not all of which are illegal, may be divided into two general categories. The major *sedatives,* called "downers," slow the activities of the body and reduce its responsiveness. In this group of drugs are the organic narcotics—opium and its derivatives morphine, heroin, and codeine—and the synthetic barbiturates. The second group, *the stimulants* or "uppers," act on the brain and the sympathetic nervous system to increase alertness and motor activity. The amphetamines are synthetic stimulants; cocaine is a natural stimulant extracted from the coca leaf.

### Sedatives

#### Narcotics

Opium, the principal drug of illegal international traffic, was known to the people of the Sumerian civilization dating back to 7000 B.C. They gave the poppy that supplied this narcotic the name by which it is still known and which means "the plant of joy." Opium is a mixture of about eighteen alkaloids, but until 1806 people had no knowledge of these substances to which so many natural drugs owe their potency. In that year the alkaloid morphine, a bitter-tasting powder, was separated out from raw opium. It proved to be a powerful sedative and pain reliever. Before its addictive properties were noted, it was commonly used in patent medicines. In the middle of the century, when the hypodermic needle was introduced in the United States, morphine began to be injected directly into the veins to relieve pain. Many soldiers wounded in battle and suffering from dysentery during the Civil War were treated with morphine and returned home addicted to the drug. Concerned about administering a drug that could disturb the later lives of patients, scientists began studying morphine.

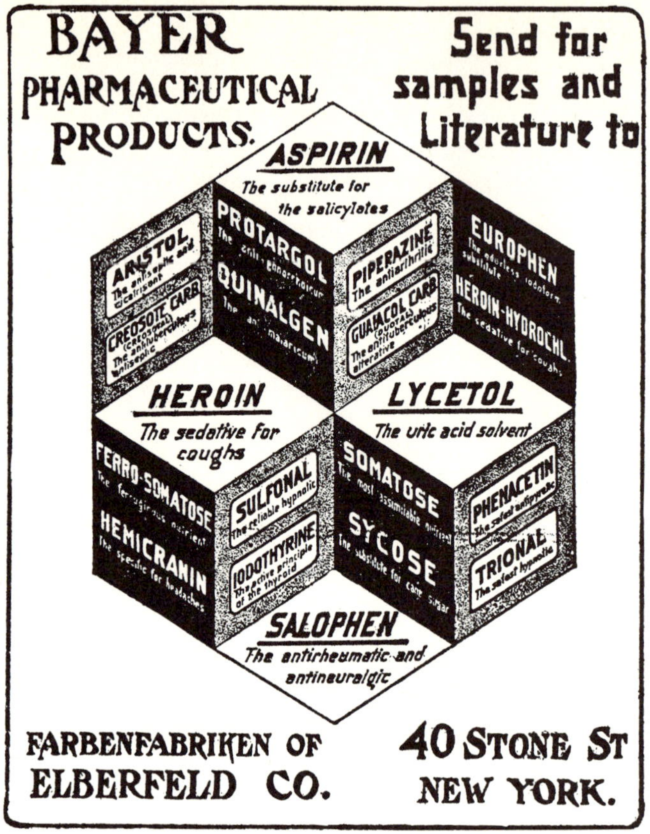


Early advertisement from the Bayer Company illustrating the legal sale of heroin as a medicant for coughing.

They thought that part of its molecule might be responsible for relieving pain and another part for its addictiveness. In 1874 they found that morphine could be converted into another powerful pain-relieving drug which they named heroin. It was used initially as a cure for the withdrawal symptoms of morphine and was substituted for morphine in cough syrups and other patent medicines. So many maladies were treated with heroin that it came to be known as G.O.M. or "God's own medicine" (Brecher, 1972). Heroin proved to be even more potent than morphine, however, acting more quickly and with greater intensity, and it is more addictive. By 1909 President Theodore Roosevelt was calling for an international investigation of opium and the opiates.

Opium and its derivatives morphine and heroin produce euphoria, drowsiness, reverie, and sometimes a lack of coordination. Heroin has an additional initial effect, the "rush," a feeling of ecstasy immediately following an injection. Because these drugs are central nervous system depressants, they relieve pain. All three are clearly addicting in the physiological sense, for users show both increased tolerance of the drugs and withdrawal reactions when they are unable to obtain another dose.

A recent breakthrough may greatly increase our understanding of the process of addiction to opiates. In the early 1970s several laboratories reported the presence in vertebrate brains of what appeared to be specific opiate receptors, that is, cell components to which opiates bind to produce euphoria and analgesia. Because it seemed unlikely that such receptors had been developed to interact with opiate alkaloids in the environment, a search began for internally produced (endogenous) opiates. By 1975 such compounds, called endorphins, had been discovered in several species, including man (Goldstein, 1976). Apparently we all can produce our own opiates. Endorphins may play a crucial role in addiction. Ingesting an exogenous opiate, such as heroin, may halt the normal production of endorphins. If later the exogenous substance is no longer supplied, an individual could be left with no opiates in the body, either exogenous or endogenous, precipitating withdrawal reactions.

It has been estimated that the frequency of narcotics addiction in the general population is about one person per 3000 (Richard and Carroll, 1970). Among certain groups, however, the rate is much higher. One in every hundred physicians is reported to be addicted, for example, and there are a greater number of addicts in large cities. Moreover, there is also a sex difference: male addicts outnumber female addicts by about eight to one.

Deaths, often attributed to overdoses, are also frequent, but the actual cause remains in doubt (see Box 10.3). Among the possible effects of prolonged narcotic addiction are malnutrition from poor eating habits, loss of sexual interest, and respiratory difficulties. In addition, there is an ever-present danger of abscesses and of contracting bloodstream infections, tetanus, and hepatitis from the use of unsterile needles.

Reactions to the abrupt withdrawal of narcotics can be severe, at least after high tolerance has built up. Within the first twelve hours the individual will typically have muscle pain, will sneeze, sweat, become tearful, and yawn a great deal. Within about thirty-six hours the withdrawal symptoms become more severe. There may be uncontrollable muscle twitching, cramps, chills alternating with excessive flushing and sweating, and a rise in heart rate and blood pressure. The addict is unable to sleep, vomits, and has diarrhea. These symptoms typically persist for about seventy-two hours and then diminish gradually over a five- to ten-day period.

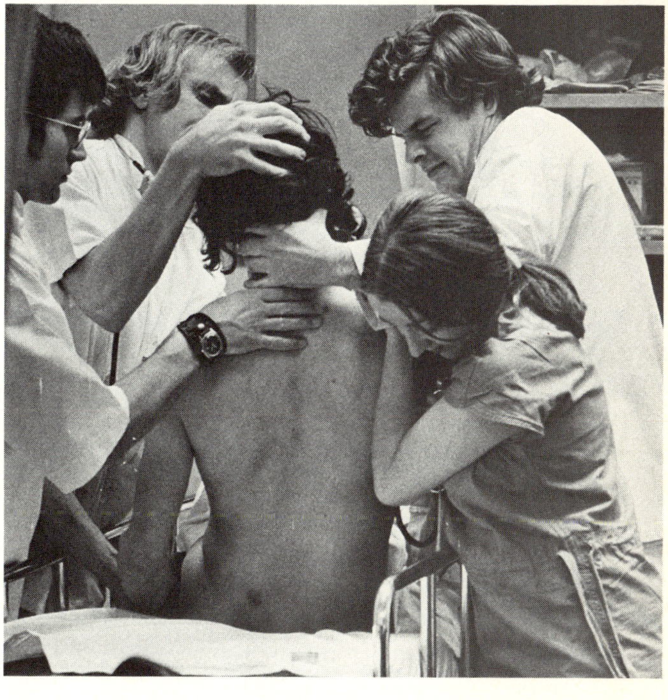

Medical team trying to revive a heroin OD case.

## BOX **10.3** The Heroin Overdose Mystery

The rate of deaths attributed to heroin overdose has risen dramatically—by 50 percent in the 1950s, by 70 percent by 1969, and by 80 percent in 1970. But the deaths do *not* appear to be a result of injecting a particularly powerful dose. The estimates of what constitutes a lethal dose range from 120 to 350 milligrams, but the average dose contained in a New York City "bag" is only 10 mg. Furthermore, when packets of heroin are found near the bodies of dead addicts, they do not differ from the usual dose. After the coroner has ruled out death by suicide, violence, or "natural causes," the evidence that he or she relies on to substantiate the verdict of heroin overdose is, in fact, nothing more than the knowledge that the deceased had been an addict. Contrary to widespread belief, there is no real evidence that these deaths are caused by heroin (Brecher, 1972).

But if not heroin, what? The fact that the frequency of such deaths has recently increased must be regarded as significant. Is there another factor or variable that has increased during this same period? One hypothesis proposes that the quinine used to "cut" heroin is the culprit. Quinine was introduced in 1939 when New York City addicts were hit by an epidemic of malaria spread by contaminated needles. Since then the use of quinine as a cutting agent has gradually become widespread. Quinine can cause a rapid flooding of the lungs with fluid, a condition found in many of the so-called overdose deaths.

Another hypothesis suggests an interaction between alcohol and heroin. Evidence does indicate that alcohol can dramatically reduce the amount of narcotic that need be taken for it to be a lethal dose. Many early studies found that heroin addicts disliked alcohol, using it only as a substitute during withdrawal. Recently, however, addicts seem to alternate between alcohol and heroin because the price of heroin is so high. Thus deaths such as the following may be caused by an interaction between alcohol and heroin.

> *The quart bottle of Southern Comfort that she held aloft onstage was at once a symbol of her load and a way of lightening it. . . . Last week, Janis Joplin died on the lowest and saddest of notes. Returning to her Hollywood motel room after a late-night recording session and* some hard drinking [*emphasis added*] *with friends at a nearby bar, she apparently filled a hypodermic needle with heroin and shot it into her left arm* (Time, *October 19, 1970*).

Even more serious than the physical effects are the social consequences of narcotic addiction. Since narcotics are illegal, addicts must deal with the underworld in order to maintain their habits. The high cost of the drugs—addicts must often spend $100 per day for their narcotics—means that they must either have great wealth or acquire money through illegal activities. Thus the correlation between addiction and criminal activities is rather high, undoubtedly contributing to the popular notion that drug addiction per se causes violence. A comparison of the ways in which addicts are treated in America and in Great Britain belies this conclusion, however, and indicates that the correlation need not exist.

The first United States laws against opium were racist, directed principally against Chinese

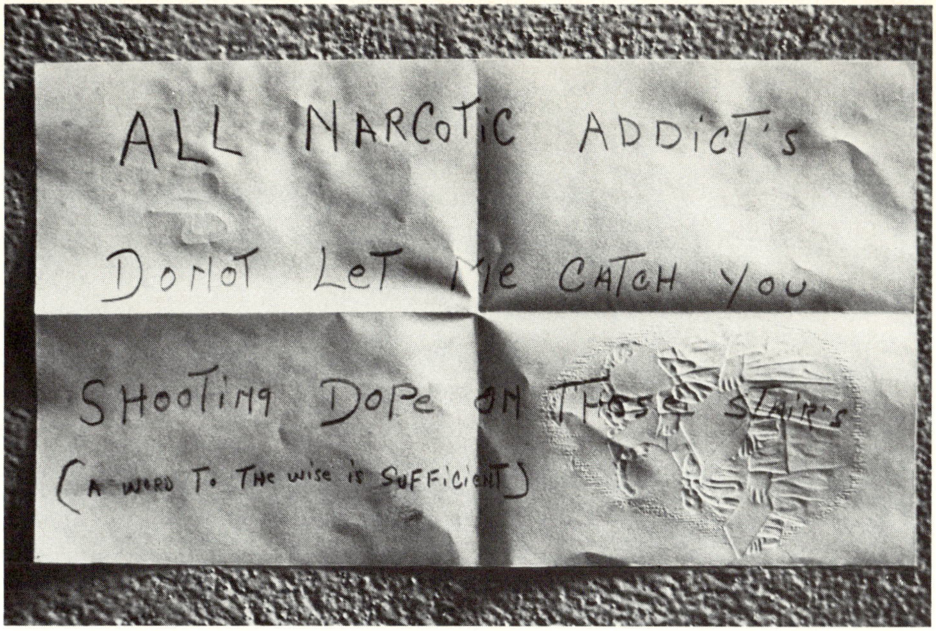


opium smokers. By 1914 there were twenty-seven such laws, but the amount of imported opium had risen steadily. So in this year the Harrison Narcotics Act was passed, regulating the processing and use of opium and of cocaine as well. The law, however, was interpreted to mean that a physician could no longer prescribe heroin for an addict. Underground drug trafficking and use immediately increased. Then in 1924 a new law was passed banning heroin altogether. Again failure. And so it went—new laws, stiffer penalties, and an ever-increasing problem.

In England drugs have been administered to addicted individuals under the care of a physician since 1924, and there is no compulsory treatment for addicts. An earlier report by Schur (1965) compared the American and British systems and concluded

> *This entire approach* [*the British one*] *has worked remarkably well. . . . All the evidence indicated that there are very few addicts other than those receiving their supplies through legal channels. No sizable underworld drug traffic exists. The addict furnishes no economic incentive for contraband peddling and needn't become a thief or prostitute to pay for drugs. . . . It would seem that by refusing to treat the addict as a criminal, Britain has kept him from becoming one (p. 153).*

Since this assessment was offered, there has been an increase of drug use in England. As of 1969, there were 1530 addicts, and the number of teen-age addicts had increased from none in 1959 to 764 in 1968. Although these figures are small indeed compared to those for the United States, the British have moved toward tighter controls, limiting the number of sources of legally prescribed heroin. Overall, though, the British system must be viewed as highly successful in restraining illegal drug trafficking.

## Barbiturates

Barbiturates were synthesized as aids for sleeping and relaxation. The first was produced in 1903 and since then over fifty derivatives of barbituric acid have been made. Two types are usually distinguished—long-acting barbiturates for prolonged sedation and short-acting barbiturates for prompt sedation and sleep. The short-acting drugs are usually viewed as addicting. Initially, the drugs were considered highly desirable and were prescribed very frequently. In the 1940s, however, a campaign was mounted against them because they were discovered to be addicting, and physicians prescribed barbiturates less frequently. Today in the United States they are manufactured in vast quantities, enough, it is estimated, to supply each man, woman, and child with thirty pills per year. Many are shipped legally to Mexico and then brought back into the country and trafficked illegally (*U.S. News and World Report,* December 27, 1971, p. 44).

"ACTUALLY I TAKE ONE PILL FOR MY HITTING, ONE FOR MY FIELDING, AND ONE FOR A GENERAL EUPHORIA."

Barbiturates are depressants,[2] relaxing the muscles and in small doses producing a mildly euphoric state. Excessive doses, however, may cause irritability and loss of weight. The impairments of cognitive functioning may be extreme. Very large doses can be fatal because the diaphragm muscles relax to such an extent that the individual suffocates. As we have indicated in Chapter 8, barbiturates are frequently chosen as a means of suicide.

Barbiturates are the second most common class of drugs to which people become addicted. Increased tolerance follows prolonged use, and the withdrawal reactions after abrupt termination are particularly severe and long lasting. The following is a description of one stage of the withdrawal reaction of a middle-aged woman who had been taking barbiturates for many years.

> She has a marked tremor and was unsteady on her feet. She had hallucinated, thought she heard the voice of her husband telling her that he was coming to get her in a taxi and she cried out to him. Soon she began seeing people climbing trees and looking through the window at her. She became violent and abusive to the staff. Even after receiving sedative medication she remained restless, muttering to herself incoherently. Her tremor increased, her face became flushed and she began to perspire excessively. At times she twitched convulsively. A little later she began picking up imaginary objects and muttering "thank you" as if someone were handing them to her. Later she was observed reaching for an imaginary glass and drinking from it. She ate imaginary food and picked imaginary cigarettes out of the air; she heard nonexistent doorbells and an ambulance siren (Rosen, Fox, and Gregory, 1972, pp. 317–318).

[2] Methaqualone, a sedative sold under the trade names Quaalude and Sopor, is similar in effect to barbiturates and has more recently become a popular "street" drug. Besides being addictive, its other dangers are internal bleeding, coma, and even death from overdose.

## Stimulants

### Amphetamines

In seeking a treatment for asthma, the Chinese-American pharmacologist Chen studied ancient Chinese descriptions of drugs. He found a desert shrub mahuang commended again and again as an effective remedy. After systematic effort Chen was able to isolate an alkaloid from this plant, which belongs to the genus *Ephedra;* ephedrine did indeed prove highly successful in treating asthma. But relying on the shrub for the drug was not viewed as efficient, and so a search began for a synthetic substitute. The amphetamines were the result of this search (Snyder, 1974).

The first amphetamine, Benzedrine, was synthesized in 1927. Almost as soon as it became commercially available in the early 1930s as an inhalant to relieve stuffy noses, the public discovered its stimulating effects. Physicians thereafter prescribed it and the other amphetamines soon synthesized to control mild depression and appetite. During World War II soldiers on both sides were supplied with the drugs to ward off fatigue; today amphetamines are used to treat hyperactive children (see page 557).

Amphetamines such as Benzedrine, Dexedrine, and Methedrine produce effects similar to those of norepinephrine in the sympathetic nervous system. Wakefulness is heightened, intestinal functions are inhibited, and appetite is reduced—hence their use in dieting. The heart rate is increased, and blood vessels in the skin and mucous membranes dilate. The individual becomes euphoric and more outgoing and is possessed with seemingly boundless energy. Larger doses can make the person nervous, agitated, and confused, subjecting him or her to palpitations, headaches, dizziness, and sleeplessness. There are some reports of extremely large doses inducing a state quite similar to paranoid schizophrenia.

Although amphetamines are not considered to be physiologically addictive, increased tolerance does develop rapidly so that mouthfuls of pills are required to produce the stimulating effect. As tolerance increases, the user may stop taking pills and inject Methedrine, the strongest of the amphetamines, directly into the veins. The so-called speed freaks give themselves repeated injections of the drug and maintain intense and euphoric activity for a few days, without eating or sleeping, after which they are exhausted and sleep or "crash" for several days. Then the cycle starts again. After several repetitions of this pattern, the physical and social functioning of the individual will have deteriorated considerably. Behavior will be quite erratic, and the speed freak may become a danger to himself and to others.

### Cocaine

The Spanish conquistadors introduced *coca* leaves to Europe. The Indians of the Andean uplands, to which the coca shrubs are native, chew the leaves, but the Europeans chose to brew them instead in beverages. The alkaloid co-

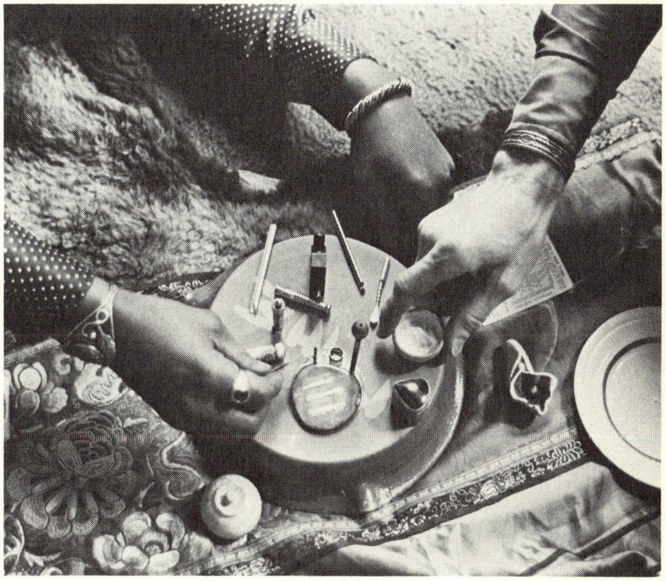

Cocaine, which is expensive and provides a notable euphoria, has become a fashionable drug of the rich.

caine was extracted from the leaves of the coca plant in 1844 and has been used since then as a local anesthetic. In 1884, while still a young neurologist in Vienna, Sigmund Freud began using cocaine to combat his depression. Convinced of its wondrous effects, he prescribed it to a friend with a painful disease and published one of the first papers on the drug, "Song of Praise," which was an enthusiastic endorsement of the exhilarating effects he had experienced. One of the early products using coca leaves in its manufacture was Coca-Cola, first marketed in the United States in 1896. For the next ten years Coke was the real thing, but by 1906 the manufacturer had switched to coca leaves from which the cocaine had been removed.

In addition to its pain-reducing effects, cocaine acts on the cortex of the brain, increasing mental powers and inducing a state of euphoria. Sexual desire is accentuated, and feelings of self-confidence and well-being suffuse the user's consciousness. An overdose may produce psychotic symptoms and hallucinations, which tend to be terrifying. The use of cocaine seems to have increased significantly in the 1970s.

# Theories of the Origins of Addiction to Hard Drugs

## Physiological Theories

Many have regarded the physiological changes in the body effected by drugs as the most important factor in drug addiction. Because the physiology of the body has been changed by the drug, it reacts when the substance to which it has become accustomed is no longer administered. To avoid withdrawal reactions, the addict continues taking the drug. Physiological alterations are, in turn, viewed as having been established through accident or curiosity. A person may take the drug by chance or because he or she wants to experience its effects. The person is then ensnared by changes in bodily chemistry and the concomitant severity of withdrawal reactions. The addict is regarded as an unwitting victim of physiological reactions, continuing to use the drug to ward off the distress of withdrawal.

Ausubel (1961a) has challenged this interpretation by alleging that the effects of withdrawal are in reality no more severe than a bad case of influenza. Anecdotal evidence exists to support Ausubel's claim that the effects of withdrawal are not as severe as is often imagined. Synanon (Yablonsky, 1967), a self-governing corporation which offers a community-living treatment for drug addiction, does not "allow" a severe withdrawal reaction among the participants in its program. Rather, the addict is told that the effects of withdrawal will not be severe and that he or she will be able to continue ordinary daily life. In fact, strong social pressures are applied to make the addict meet responsibilities during withdrawal. Apparently the method has some success, and severe withdrawal reactions are not often reported among people who live at the various Synanon centers.

Even though the real effects of withdrawal may not be severe, we must consider what the average addict, one who is not being helped by organizations such as Synanon, *believes* withdrawal to be. If the addict believes that severe cramps, retching, sweating, chills, and loss of control are inevitable consequences of abstaining, it may matter little what the actual withdrawal reaction is like. As we learned in Chapter 5, even a belief based on illusion can strongly affect behavior. This is not to say that drug addiction is entirely unrelated to physiological processes, rather that psychological variables may play an important role in the maintenance of the habit as well as in the initial taking of the drug.

## Psychological Theories

Psychological theories of the origin of drug addiction usually emphasize reduction of distress and the pleasant feeling and euphoric state that the drugs produce. These theories also attempt to explain why particular kinds of people seem to "need" these effects. An association has often been noted between criminality, drug abuse, and the sociopathic personality. In this context drug abuse may be considered as part of the thrill-seeking behavior of the sociopath discussed in Chapter 9. We might also expect narcotics to be used by anxious individuals in order to reduce the distress that they often experience. Drug addicts have also been found to be deviant on various personality questionnaire measures. But we must question whether these personality characteristics antedated the addiction and caused it. For example, we might find that drug addicts tend to be more suspicious than nonusers. To conclude that suspiciousness contributes to the use of drugs would not be justified, for it might well be the addict's *reaction to* his illegal status as a drug user. Longitudinal data on personality variables such as those that were collected by Jones on alcoholism (page 252) are not available on narcotics addiction.

Some similarities in family background have been identified in the life histories of drug addicts (Chein et al., 1964). In many cases the father is absent from the home of the future addict. If the father is present, he tends to be a shadowy figure or to be overtly hostile and distant. If present he may also serve as a model for criminal behavior, and the relations between the mother and father are likely to be stormy. Chein and his colleagues therefore proposed that the personality defects of the drug addict, whatever they are, were developed through family background. Initial experiences with addicting drugs were also shown to be nonaccidental. Most addicts were found to have been introduced knowingly to the drugs, not by an adult but rather by a member of their peer group, suggesting the importance of peer pressure and curiosity. Boredom and aggravation are probably contributing factors. In ghettoes where narcotics are readily available, and the culture of the streets prevails, the incidence of drug use is especially high.

In sum, there is little evidence available concerning the origins of drug addiction. Personality characteristics, peer pressure, family background, the ease with which the drug can be acquired, and the frequency with which it is used in a particular culture are all possible factors, but as yet the role of any of them has been only vaguely specified.

## Nicotine and Smoking

The history of tobacco smoking bears much similarity to the use of other addictive drugs (Brecher, 1972). The use of tobacco spread through the world from Columbus's commerce with the native American Indians. It did not take long for sailors and merchants to imitate the Indians' smoking of rolled leaves of tobacco—and to experience, as the Indians did, the increasing craving for the stuff. When not smoked, tobacco was chewed or else ground into small pieces and inhaled as snuff.

Some idea of the addictive qualities of tobacco can be appreciated by considering how much people would sacrifice to maintain their supplies. In sixteenth-century England, for example, tobacco was exchanged for silver *ounce for ounce*. Poor people squandered their meager resources for their several daily pipefuls. Even the public tortures and executions engineered by the Sultan Murad IV of Turkey during the seventeenth century could not dissuade those of his subjects who were addicted to the weed. Today the threat of ill health, documented convincingly by the United States Surgeon General, is similarly failing to force smokers to reduce their tobacco consumption, even though the overwhelming majority of them believe the dire predictions. Nor do the compulsory warnings on cigarette packages and advertisements—"Warning: The Surgeon General Has Determined That Cigarette Smoking Is Dangerous to Your Health"—appear to deter them.

Probably a majority of smokers have tried at least once to check the habit. Perhaps one of the most tortured addicts was Sigmund Freud, who continued smoking up to twenty cigars a day in the full knowledge that the nicotine was taxing his heart and causing cancerous growths in his mouth. With his jaw later almost entirely removed, Freud suffered great difficulty swallowing and endured excruciating pain, but he was still unable to bear the anguish of abstaining. Although many heavy smokers do succeed in stopping, Freud's tragic case was certainly not the exception.

In recent years various local governments have passed, or tried to pass, ordinances regulating

"FIRST WE HAVE TO CONVINCE THE PEOPLE THAT GOOD HEALTH ISN'T EVERYTHING."

where cigarettes may or may not be smoked in public places. In New York City it is against the law to smoke in supermarkets and on elevators. The City Council of Cambridge, Massachusetts, debated in 1975 whether to require restaurants to set aside no-smoking areas to protect nonsmokers from being irritated and even harmed by the smoking of other patrons. Many nonsmokers expressed enthusiastic approval of the proposed measures, but pressure from smokers forced the council to abandon its plans. The objections of smokers to what they view as undue infringement of their rights often find virulent expression. Otherwise amiable, law-abiding people become defensive and even combative when threatened with restrictions on their freedom to use this drug, which appears consistent with the view that heavy cigarette smoking is an addiction.

In the literature on smoking there is, however, considerable controversy whether nicotine is an addictive drug. It would be a serious mistake to overlook social and psychological factors. For some, lighting up a cigarette definitely reduces tension (see Box 10.4), whereas others seem to consider smoking a necessary accompaniment of their relaxing activities. One authority speculates that cigarette smoking is part and parcel of the achievement and coping ethic of our society, and that therefore is benefits may outweigh the accepted physical dangers.

> . . . *Cigarette smoking, for many people, is an important source of ego strength. It not only yields a variety of pleasurable sensations but, more important, helps the smoker cope with the demands of life, eases and promotes his or her social interactions, and is a valuable aid to the establishment of a sense of identity. As such, the activity of smoking is congruent with the dominant problem-solving, achievement-oriented values of high Western society. There is little wonder that people find it so hard to give it up or that social response to the dangers of smoking has been so weak. The search for effective means of changing social values associated with smoking may be the main order of business in the years ahead for those who seek to accomplish any large-scale change in smoking behavior* (*Mausner, 1973, pp. 125–126*).

Part of the confusion may stem from a failure to distinguish among different kinds of smokers. Those smoking more than two packs a day may well be addicted to nicotine, whereas those who limit their smoking, for example, to social situations and consume less than a pack a day do indeed smoke from habit, but they may not be addicted. The evidence, at any rate, is somewhat equivocal; workers interpret the same results in different ways. Consider a well-controlled experiment that attempted to determine whether nicotine is the "culprit."

On the assumption that "nicotine hunger" plays an important role in maintaining smoking, Lucchesi, Schuster, and Emley (1967) recruited cigarette smokers and required them to sit in a laboratory and smoke as much as they wanted while various chemical solutions were steadily dripped into a vein via a catheter. Periods during which a saline (salt) solution was injected were alternated with periods during which varying amounts of nicotine solution were injected directly into the vein. The subjects were expected to smoke significantly fewer cigarettes when the injected solution contained nicotine if, in fact, the body does crave the substance. While 4 mg of nicotine per hour was being injected—an amount equivalent to the nicotine obtained by smoking two average cigarettes per hour—smoking was 60 percent less than during the period in which subjects were receiving the saline solution. Thus injecting nicotine directly into the blood did reduce the number of cigarettes smoked. The findings can be interpreted in several ways, however. The authors themselves concluded that "The results obtained suggest that nicotine plays a small but significant role in the smoking habit and that part of the craving for a cigarette can be satisfied by the intravenous administration of the alkaloid. . . . [But] if the

## BOX **10.4** Smoking—Arousing, Relaxing, or Both?

Most cigarette smokers report that their habit is relaxing (Ikard, Green, and Horn, 1968), yet smoking a cigarette typically increases the heart rate from fifteen to twenty-five beats per minute, as well as elevating blood pressure (United States Department of Health, Education and Welfare, 1964). An experiment was designed to investigate these two paradoxical effects.

Nesbitt (1973) arranged for both smokers and nonsmokers to undergo a series of increasingly uncomfortable electric shocks under three conditions: when not smoking, when smoking a high-nicotine cigarette, and when smoking a low-nicotine cigarette. He reasoned that if smoking is at the same time physiologically arousing yet psychologically relaxing to *regular smokers,* they would endure greater levels of painful shock when smoking and would also endure even more shock when smoking a high-nicotine cigarette than smoking one low in nicotine. Inasmuch as nonsmokers were not expected to experience a cigarette as relaxing, he did not believe that he would find this improvement in ability to endure shock among the subjects of the nonsmoker control group.

First, by monitoring the heartbeats of his subjects with the electrocardiograph, he was able to demonstrate that smoking a cigarette does indeed increase heart rate, especially when the cigarette contains a high concentration of nicotine. More interesting was the ability of a regular smoker to endure increasingly higher-voltage electric shock as a function of whether he was smoking. As Figure 10.1 indicates, regular smokers took more shock when smoking, especially when smoking a high-nicotine cigarette. Smoking did not alter the shock-taking behavior of the nonsmokers.

Assuming that increased endurance of shock is a valid measure of the reducing of anxiety, Nesbitt concluded that smoking is relaxing to those who are accustomed to smoking, even while physiological arousal is increasing. Nonsmokers, unfamiliar with the effects of smoking—indeed, feeling even somewhat queasy—do not relax psychologically while physiologically aroused by cigarettes. The paradox was thus confirmed: smoking psychologically relaxes those accustomed to it while it arouses them physiologically. Why this happens is by no means clear.

pleasure of smoking or craving for tobacco were due to the general effects of the alkaloid we should have observed a much greater reduction in the smoking frequency" (p. 795). In his well-known review of the role of nicotine in cigarette smoking, Jarvik (1970) seems to vacillate between regarding this study as strong evidence that smoking is a hunger for nicotine and accepting it as evidence that nonnicotine factors, such as habit, are the culprits that keep people lighting cigarettes.

Recent evidence collected in Stanley Schachter's laboratory more clearly supports the notion that smoking is an addiction. He has shown that smokers adjust their habit to maintain a relatively constant level of nicotine in their systems (Schachter, 1977) and has suggested further that their rate of smoking is controlled by the pH (a measure of acidity-alkalinity) of the urine. Said another way, "The smoker's mind is in his bladder" (Schachter, Silverstein and Perlik, 1977). Urinary pH is related to smoking in

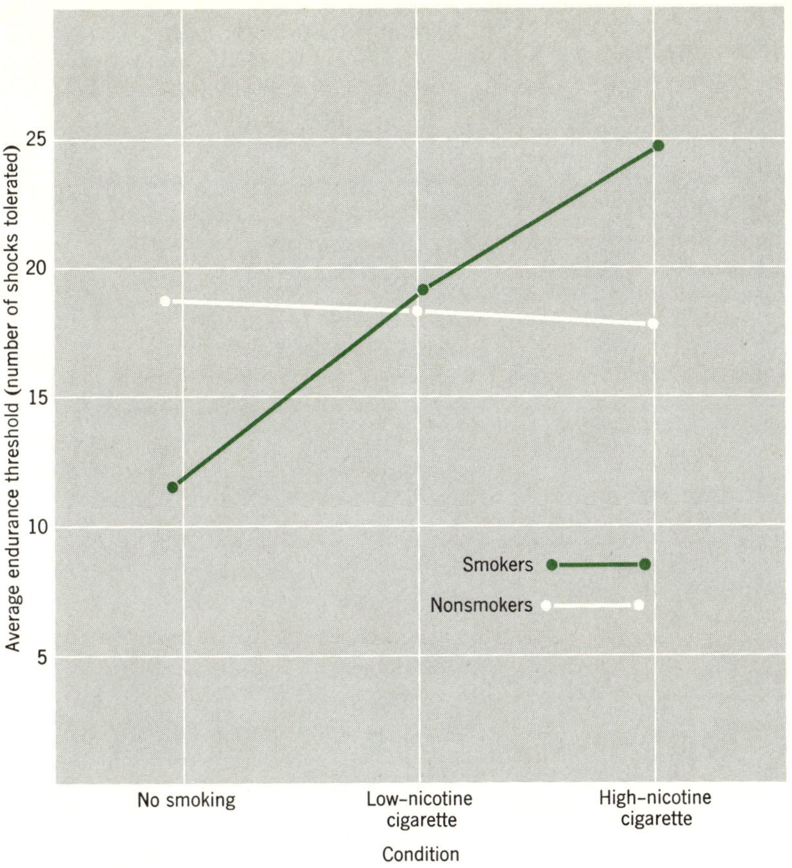


FIGURE **10.1**
Average numbers of shocks endured by smokers relaxed by their habit compared to those endured by nonsmokers taking in the same amounts of nicotine. After Nesbitt, 1973.

the following way. When urine is acidic, nicotine is excreted at a greater rate than when urine is nonacidic. Therefore when urine is acidic, there should be more smoking to replace the nicotine being excreted. This prediction was confirmed in a study in which smokers ingested vitamin C; their urine was acidified and their rate of smoking increased (Schachter, Kozlowski, and Silverstein, 1977). Furthermore, if Schachter's thesis is correct, smoking should also increase in other environmental situations that acidify the urine. Stress appears to operate in this fashion, increasing both the acidity of the urine and smoking (Silverstein, Kozlowski, and Schachter, 1977; Schachter et al., 1977). The usual effects of stress can even be short-circuited via a manipulation that prevents urine from becoming too acidic. After drinking sodium bicarbonate, which makes urine more alkaline, subjects under stress did not increase their smoking (Schachter, Silverstein, and Perlik, 1977).

Although it is unrealistic to expect total agreement among investigators—Bernstein (1969), for example, disagrees with the addiction view—it is probably fair to say that *some* smokers are addicted. Indeed even members of organizations that engage in antismoking campaigns are sometimes unable to overcome their habit. Brecher (1972) makes the case for addiction rather convincingly. First, cessation of smoking does seem to produce fairly consistent withdrawal symptoms—nervousness, drowsiness, and headaches. Second, people do seem to develop a tolerance to nicotine, although there is of course an upper limit on how much nicotine can be taken into the body, for people can smoke just so much during their waking hours.

## Marihuana

Marihuana consists of the dried and ground leaves and stems of the hemp plant, *Cannabis sativa*. It is most often smoked, but it may be chewed, prepared as a tea, or eaten in baked goods. Hashish, much stronger than marihuana, is produced by drying the resin of the marihuana plant. Both marihuana and hashish have been known to mankind for thousands of years, and their poor reputation among the general public dates back many centuries. For example, the English word assassin comes from the Arabic word *hashshāshīn,* which means those addicted to hashish, and which was the name given an order of Muslims who took hashish and murdered Christians at the time of the Crusades. In early American history the plant was extensively cultivated, not for smoking but for its fibers, which were used in the manufacture of cloth and rope. By the nineteenth century the medicinal properties of *Cannabis* resin were noted, and it was a recommended treatment for rheumatism, gout, depression, cholera, and neuralgia, as well as being smoked for pleasure. Until 1920 marihuana was little seen in the United States, but with the passage of the Eighteenth Amendment, which prohibited the sale of alcohol, marihuana began to be brought across the border from Mexico and smoked for intoxication by members of the lower classes. Unfavorable reports in the press attributing crimes to marihuana use led to the enactment of a federal law against the sale of the drug in 1937.

### Patterns of Marihuana Use

According to surveys discussed in the 1975 *Marihuana and Health,* an annual report to the United States Congress required of the Secretary of Health, Education and Welfare, marihuana use has increased significantly in recent years. Table 10.3 summarizes trends for people eighteen years and older, and Table 10.4 shows use among young people. These figures reveal several important points.

Early recreational use of hashish in a fasionable apartment in New York City. An 1876 issue of the Illustrated Police News carried this picture with the title "Secret Dissipation of New York Belles: Interior of a Hasheesh Hell on Fifth Avenue."

1. From 1971 to 1974, the percentage of adults ages eighteen to twenty-five who had tried marihuana at least once jumped from 39 to 53 percent.
2. In this same age group one in four reported having used the drug in the month preceding the 1974 survey (and some may be assumed to have used the drug several times that year).
3. Among adults twenty-six through thirty-four—hardly the "youth culture"—29 percent reported having used marihuana at least once, a 50 percent increase over the 19 percent who so reported in 1971.
4. Among those younger than eighteen, 12 percent are current users, whereas 6 percent were in 1971.

The report also stated that one-third of those who had used the drug indicated that they planned to do so again, and another third that they might. And as the younger people in the sample grow older, it is possible that the percentages of marihuana smokers in the over-eighteen groups will continue to increase. Two Gallup polls taken of college students in 1967 and again in 1974 suggest such a possibility. Whereas only 5 percent of those questioned in 1967 reported having used the substance, 55 percent had done so seven years later. And these percentages seem to hold for high school drop-outs as well; the use of the drug, at least among all young adults, appears to be growing.

Surveys of a large sample of both private and public high schools across the country in 1975 indicate that almost half the 16,000 seniors questioned had used marihuana at least once. Twenty-nine percent had used it during the month preceding the survey, which is somewhat higher than the 25 percent of adults ages eighteen to twenty-five reported in Table 10.3 as current users in 1974, and almost 10 percent higher than the 20 percent of young people ages sixteen and seventeen reported in Table 10.4 as current users only one year earlier.

Survey data show also that about 2 percent of youth between the ages of twelve and seventeen use marihuana *daily;* for seventeen-year-olds the figure rises to 5 percent. Further, of males between the ages of twenty and thirty—whose overall use of marihuana is highest—as many as 9 percent (almost two million men) are estimated to be daily users.

In sum, although there are regional differences (use being greater in the West than in the South, for example), overall trends indicate that in this country more and more people, ranging considerably in age but from the high school ranks in particular, are smoking marihuana.

## Short-Term Effects of Marihuana

As with the intoxicating effects of most drugs, those of marihuana depend in part on potency and size of the dose. Users report that smoking marihuana makes them feel relaxed and sociable. The effects of the dried leaves contained in the typical American marihuana cigarettes are mild. In fact, it is often said that the smoker has to *learn* to get a "high" from a marihuana cigarette, which he or she often shares with others (Becker, 1963). Nonetheless, like any intoxicant, marihuana can impair visual and motor functions; activities such as driving a car are dangerous after using marihuana.

The major active chemical in marihuana has been isolated and named tetrahydrocannabinol (THC). Although there are wide ranges in potency,[3] the marihuana available in the States typically contains less than 1 percent THC. Hashish is much stronger and often contains between 5 percent and 12 percent THC. Large doses of marihuana have been reported to produce rapid emotional changes, a dulling of attention, fragmented thought, impaired memory, and in some cases a feeling of enhanced insight. Extremely heavy doses have sometimes been found to induce hallucinations and other effects similar to those of LSD. Occasionally, marihuana elicits intense anxiety, but usually only among novices who may fear that the changes taking place are not produced by the drug or that they are irreversible.

In one of the studies reported by the National Commission on Marihuana and Drug Abuse (1972), the following description of the short-term effects of marihuana was offered.

> *. . . No harmful effects were observed on general bodily functions, motor functions, mental functions, personal or social behavior, or work performance. Total sleep time and periods of sleep were increased. Weight gain was uniformly noted.*
>
> *No evidence of physical dependence [i.e., addiction] or signs of withdrawal were noted. In the heaviest smokers, moderate psychological dependence was suggested by an increased negative mood after cessation of smoking. . . . Neither immediate or short-term (twenty-one-day) high-dose marihuana intoxication decreased motivation to engage in a variety of social and goal-directed behavior. . . . Marihuana smoking appeared to affect patterns of social interaction. Although use of the drug was found to be a group . . . social activity around which conversation and other types of social behavior were centered, it was not uncommon for some or all of the smokers to withdraw from social interaction and concentrate on the subjective drug experience. During the first part of the smoking period, both intermittent and daily users demonstrated a marked decrement in total interaction. Total interaction continued to diminish among intermittent users but increased . . . among the daily users during the later part of the smoking period. The quality of the interaction was more*

[3] The potency of the leaves is thought to vary with the region in which the hemp plant is cultivated. The leaves of plants grown in hot, relatively dry climates contain larger amounts of THC.

TABLE **10.3**
Marihuana Use Among Adults, 1971–1974

| Adult groups | Ever used, percent | | | Current use,* percent | | |
|---|---|---|---|---|---|---|
| | 1971 | 1972 | 1974 | 1971 | 1972 | 1974 |
| All adults | 15 | 16 | 19 | 5 | 8 | 7 |
| *By age* | | | | | | |
| 18–25 | 39 | 48 | 53 | 17 | 28 | 25 |
| 26–34 | 19 | 20 | 29 | 5 | ? | ? |
| 35–49 | 9 | 6 | 7 | 1 | 1 | 1 |
| 50+ | 6 | 2 | 2 | – | – | – |
| *By sex* | | | | | | |
| Male | 21 | 22 | 24 | 7 | 11 | 9 |
| Female | 10 | 10 | 14 | 3 | 5 | 5 |

* Used during last month.

TABLE **10.4**
Marihuana Use Among Youth, 1971–1974

| Youth groups | Ever used, percent | | | Current use,* percent | | |
|---|---|---|---|---|---|---|
| | 1971 | 1972 | 1974 | 1971 | 1972 | 1974 |
| All youth | 14 | 14 | 23 | 6 | 7 | 12 |
| *By age* | | | | | | |
| 12–13 | 6 | 4 | 6 | 2 | 1 | 2 |
| 14–15 | 10 | 10 | 22 | 7 | 6 | 12 |
| 16–17 | 27 | 29 | 39 | 10 | 16 | 20 |
| *By sex* | | | | | | |
| Male | 14 | 15 | 24 | 7 | 9 | 12 |
| Female | 14 | 13 | 21 | 5 | 6 | 11 |

* Used during last month.

*convivial and less task-oriented when marihuana was available to the group. Additionally, an assessment of the effect of marihuana on risk-taking behavior revealed that daily users tended to become more conservative when engaging in decision-making under conditions of risk (p. 74).*

## Long-Term Effects of Marihuana

Much of the current public attention given marihuana stems from concern about the alleged consequences of long-term use of the drug. *The Official Report of the National Commission on Marihuana and Drug Use* (1972) has refuted some of these allegations. First, it has been claimed that marihuana smoking leads to antisocial and criminal behavior. It is true that early studies had demonstrated heavier use of marihuana among criminals. But that association was more pronounced before the rapid upswing in marihuana smoking in the 1960s. The National Commission noted on the basis of their studies that "if anything, marihuana generally seems to inhibit [violent and aggressive] behavior" (p. 91). Second, it has been claimed that smoking marihuana is a steppingstone to addiction to heroin and other more harmful drugs, for it is known that among heroin addicts there are a large number of former marihuana users. The National Commission undertook research to determine the association between marihuana smoking and the use of other drugs. As can be seen in Table 10.5, only 2 percent of all who habitually use marihuana now also take heroin, and then only several times a year. Nineteen percent of marihuana smokers have tried mescaline and cocaine, but few are daily users. Thus, although most heroin addicts have used marihuana, it is also true that most marihuana users do not go on to heroin. The widely known "steppingstone" theory has little support. Third, it has often been claimed that marihuana smoking can cause psychosis. Evidence to support this assertion is not convincing. In cases in which marihuana apparently did precipitate some sort of disturbed behavior, the individual had an earlier history of psychiatric problems. Fourth, marihuana has been thought to produce genetic damage. Again, there is no definitive evidence to support this assertion. Finally, even though marihuana is not physiologically addictive, it has been asserted that heavy long-term use may lead to an undesirable psychological dependence on the drug, the so-called *amotivational syndrome;* the individual is said to lose interest in virtually all activities, become lethargic, and show moral, social, and personal deterioration.

Two elaborate studies relating to the amotivational syndrome have been reported (*APA Monitor,* 1976). They have been the center of much controversy, for social scientists and lawmakers are eager for research findings that support their particular positions on decriminalizing or even entirely deregulating marihuana use. The so-called "Jamaica study," funded by the National Institute of Mental Health and conducted by two

TABLE **10.5**
### Frequency with Which Marihuana Users Try Other Drugs
(from National Commission on Marihuana and Drug Abuse, 1972)

| | Percent who take | | | |
|---|---|---|---|---|
| **Substance** | **Once to several times a year** | **Several times a month** | **Several times a week** | **Daily** |
| Hashish | 31 | 21 | 5 | 0 |
| LSD | 4 | 0 | 0 | 0 |
| Mescaline | 19 | 0 | 0 | 2 |
| Psilocybin | 4 | 0 | 0 | 0 |
| Heroin | 2 | 0 | 0 | 0 |
| Codeine | 11 | 0 | 0 | 2 |
| Amphetamines | 7 | 0 | 4 | 0 |
| Barbiturates | 10 | 4 | 0 | 0 |
| Cocaine | 19 | 2 | 4 | 0 |
| Glue | 0 | 0 | 0 | 0 |

anthropologists (Rubin and Comitas, 1975), studied 2000 regular users in Jamaica over a period of two years. Ganja, the Indian term for marihuana, has been widely smoked in Jamaica for more than 200 years, and its daily use is widespread and very heavy, at least by North American standards. Most working-class men smoke an average of seven cigarettes a day. The THC content of the cigarettes is 10.2 percent, making them far stronger than those generally available in the United States. Even women and children use the drug.

What appears crucial about the reaction of the Jamaicans to ganja is that they believe it to be a beneficial drug: it is said to help them solve problems and get to sleep and even to make food more tasty. Young children are given ganja to drink in tea to help them do better in school. Apparently these favorable attitudes about ganja correlate with its observed effects! Not only do workers assert that the drug helps them concentrate and work better, but careful behavioral observations confirm that their output increases after ingestion of marihuana. Thus, rather than taking the drug to "drop out," Jamaicans seem to take it to "stay in." In addition, ganja use is not related to taking hard drugs or to crime.

A sample of thirty smokers and thirty nonsmokers were examined more closely in the laboratory for chromosome damage, thinking deficits, and brain damage. The two groups did not differ; according to this examination, chronic ganja use is not physically harmful. This study thus lends no support to the widespread belief that long-term, heavy use of marihuana is a direct cause of an amotivational syndrome. It

Ganja smoking is widespread in Jamaica, even among children.

serves furthermore to allay growing fears that smoking marihuana does serious bodily harm.

A second study was conducted in Costa Rica (Coggins, in press). This inquiry did reveal fewer red blood cells in the ganja users as compared to matched nonsmoker controls, but all counts were within the normal range. Of particular interest, since earlier workers had claimed such damage, was the finding that levels of serum testosterone were not lower among male users.

Taken together, the findings suggest that marihuana is not psychologically or physiologically dangerous. Why then are societal reactions against its use so strong? Marihuana smoking increased dramatically during the period of the hippie movement and the development of the radical youth counterculture. In the minds of many people, unconventional life styles, diminished interest in vocational achievement, and dropping out of society probably became associated with the dramatic increase in the smoking of marihuana. Thus marihuana has perhaps been viewed as abetting the destruction of the current social order. There are few threats a society reacts more strongly against than that of its own destruction.

## Reasons for Use

Both the National Commission and the Secretary of HEW in his report *Marihuana and Health* found that the motivations for smoking marihuana varied, depending on how often it was smoked. Those who smoked the drug less than once a month reported that they did so primarily out of curiosity and the desire to share a social experience with their peers. Intermittent users, those smoking the drug from two to ten times per month, started for the same reason but continued because they enjoyed the socializing and recreational aspects of the drug and found that it contributed to the formation of close social relationships. Moderate and heavy users, those smoking marihuana from eleven times per month up to several times per day, mentioned the "kicks" of the drug more often than did other groups. They also reported relying on the drug to relieve anxiety and boredom. There is some indication of an association between personality traits and the use of marihuana. In a study reported by the National Commission, 148 undergraduates filled out the California Psychological Inventory anonymously. Marihuana users were found to have greater social presence, flexibility, empathy, and inclinations for independent achievement. In contrast, adamant nonusers were found to have greater responsibility and self-control and to be conformists in their outlook.

Why is marihuana the favorite drug of so many? There are several plausible explanations. It has been suggested (Marin and Cohen, 1971) that a strong desire for new and interesting phenomenological experiences plays a central role in the use of drugs such as marihuana. It is perhaps no accident that many of those who enjoy marihuana also show an interest in meditation. We must also remember that the United States, even before the upswing in the use of marihuana, was already a drug-taking culture. Sleeping preparations, tranquilizers, diet pills, pep pills, and alcohol were all widely ingested by a great many Americans. Therefore it is hardly surprising that our society has adopted yet another drug.

Given the conflicting claims of earlier studies, and given the clear outcomes of the superior Jamaican and Costa Rican efforts, it is difficult to conclude that marihuana poses psychological and health hazards to justify the continuation of harsh legal penalties. And, indeed, in the past few years a number of states have markedly reduced the penalties for possession and use (Alaska, California, Colorado, Maine, Minnesota, New York, Ohio, Oregon, South Dakota). Advancing arguments why people should not be punished for using a drug that is apparently less harmful than tobacco and alcohol is not the same as advocating its use. As medical researchers have known for years, drugs are never entirely harmless; and there is always the possibility that later research will reveal unsuspected dangers.

"RECENT EVENTS DICTATE THAT WE START CONVERTING SOONER THAN PLANNED. MARIJUANA WILL SOON BE LEGAL. TOBACCO WILL NOT."

Nonetheless, whether people *should* ingest one or another chemical, particularly for recreational purposes, seems a *moral* problem, not a scientific or legal one. The trend does appear to favor giving adults the freedom and therefore the responsibility of deciding for themselves whether to alter mood by using marihuana.

## LSD and Related Drugs

In 1943 a Swiss chemist, Albert Hofmann, recorded a description of an illness he had seemingly contracted.

> *Last Friday . . . I had to interrupt my laboratory work . . . I was seized with a feeling of great restlessness and mild dizziness. At home, I lay down and sank into a not unpleasant delirium, which was characterized by extremely exciting fantasies. In a semiconscious state with my eyes closed . . . fantastic visions of extraordinary realness and with an intense kaleidoscopic play of colors assaulted me (cited by Cashman, 1966, p. 31).*

Earlier in the day Dr. Hofmann had manufactured a few milligrams of *d*-lysergic acid diethylamide, a drug which he had first synthesized in 1938. Reasoning that he might have unknowingly ingested some and that this was the cause of his unusual experience, he deliberately took a small dose and confirmed his hypothesis.

After Hofmann's experiences with LSD in 1943, the drug was referred to as psychotomimetic because it was thought to produce effects similar to the symptoms of a psychosis. More recently, the term psychedelic has been applied to emphasize the subjectively experienced expansion of consciousness reported by users of LSD and two other drugs, *mescaline* and *psilocybin*. In 1896 mescaline, an alkaloid and the active ingredient of peyote, was isolated. Peyote is obtained from small, disklike growths of the top of the peyote cactus, most of which extends below ground. The drug has been used for centuries in the religious rites of Indian peoples living in the Southwest and northern Mexico. Psilocybin is a crystalline powder which was isolated from the mushroom *Psilocybe mexicana*.

During the 1950s these drugs were dispensed by physicians and scientists in research settings and used to produce what were thought to be psychotic experiences. In 1960 Timothy Leary and Richard Alpert of Harvard University began an investigation of the effects of psilocybin on institutionalized prisoners. The early results, although subject to several confounds, were encouraging: released prisoners who had had a psilocybin trip proved less likely to be rearrested. At the same time the investigators started taking trips themselves and soon had gathered around them a group of people interested in experimenting with psychedelic drugs. By 1962 their activities had attracted the attention of law enforcement agencies. As the investigation continued, it became a scandal, culminating in Leary and Alpert's departure from Harvard. The scandal seemed to give tremendous impetus to the use of the psychedelic drugs, particularly since the manufacture of LSD and the extraction of mescaline and psilocybin were found to be relatively easy and inexpensive. After leaving Harvard, Leary and Alpert founded the International Foundation for Internal Freedom, an organization which emphatically espoused the desirability of properly guided psychedelic trips. It can probably be said that the proselytizing efforts of Leary and Alpert shifted attention from the supposedly psychotic experiences induced by the drugs to their mind-expanding effects. The user's state of consciousness and intensification of sensory perceptions were considered extremely positive and beautiful.[4]

The typical dose of LSD is from about 100 to 350 micrograms, administered as a liquid absorbed in sugar cubes or as capsules or tablets; for psilocybin the usual dose is about 30,000 micrograms; and for mescaline the usual dose is between 350,000 and 500,000 micrograms. The effects of LSD and mescaline usually last about twelve hours, those of psilocybin about six.

[4] Like many of the "old-timers" in the psychedelic drug revolution, Alpert has for the past several years espoused an Eastern meditation philosophy that urges people to forsake drugs and work instead on creating their own meaningful internal "trips" without the aid of chemical agents. Known as Baba Ram Dass, he has lectured and written eloquently about the possibility of cultivating expanded states of consciousness; those who would devote the necessary time and energy to meditation techniques will be open to such experiences, according to Ram Dass.

The effects of varying doses of LSD were studied by Klee and his associates (1961). Neither the subjects nor the observers knew the amounts of drug that had been administered. Nonetheless, experienced observers could readily judge the dose levels ingested by a particular subject from his reports of visual effects and from his somatic or bodily reactions, particularly of the sympathetic nervous system; intellectual impairment and also confusion increased with higher doses.

The effects of the psychedelics, like those of other kinds of drugs, depend on a number of psychological variables in addition to the dose itself (see Box 10.5). A subject's set, that is, attitudes, expectancies, and motivations about taking drugs, are widely held to be important determinants of reactions to psychedelics. In an excellent review of the literature, Barber (1970) specified the effects of psychedelic drugs and related them to variables such as dose, personality, set, and situation (Table 10.6).

Some of the individual studies on psychological variables have been relatively simple, others complex. Expectancies were examined by Metzner, Litwin, and Weil (1965). Before receiving 25,000 to 30,000 micrograms of psilocybin, subjects were asked, "How apprehensive are you about taking the drug?" and "How good do you feel about taking the drug today?" Reports of greater apprehension about taking the drug correlated significantly with increased anxiety, headache, and nausea during the drug experience itself. Similarly, Linton and Langs (1964) administered a battery of personality tests before giving the subjects a dose of 100 micrograms of LSD. Those who were judged to be guarded and overdependent on the basis of the personality tests had the greatest number of bodily reactions, particularly of the sympathetic nervous system, and experienced the greatest anxiety during the LSD session. Persons who had shown themselves to be mistrustful, complaining, and fearful had paranoiac reactions from taking LSD (Klee and Weintraub, 1959; Von Felsinger, Lasagna, and Beecher, 1956).

## BOX **10.5** A Psychological Explanation of Flashbacks

One of the principal concerns about ingesting LSD is the possibility of flashbacks—"the transient recurrence of psychedelic drug symptoms after the pharmacologic effects of such drugs have worn off and [there has been] a period of relative normalcy" (Heaton and Victor, 1976, p. 83). Little is known about these flashback "trips" except that they cannot be predicted or controlled. The available evidence does not support the hypothesis that they are caused by drug-produced physical changes in the nervous system. For one thing, only 15 to 30 percent of users of psychedelic drugs are estimated ever to have flashbacks (for example, Stanton and Bardoni, 1972). Moreover, there is no independent evidence of measurable neurological changes in these drug users.

Heaton and Victor (1976) determined to explore a possible psychological explanation of flashbacks. Heaton had been mindful of previous evidence indicating that extreme relaxation and sensory deprivation can produce in some people sensations and experiences that are closely similar to those reported during flashbacks. In an earlier study (1975) he had demonstrated that *expectancy* of a flashback increased the chances that former LSD users, after swallowing a placebo capsule and then undergoing mild sensory deprivation, would report such experiences, whether or not they had previously had flashbacks. The belief that they had taken a drug that would produce a flashback proved more important than a past history of such phenomena.

Heaton and Victor therefore speculated that some drug users, believing that flashbacks are likely, may *attend selectively* to naturally occurring altered states of consciousness and then *label* them flashbacks of a previous drug trip. But why would they allow their thinking to take such a course? Employing various scales from the MMPI, the two researchers developed measures of thinking in a logical, reality-oriented fashion and in a looser, inner-fantasizing mode. They then recruited thirty male volunteer drug users from clinics and counseling agencies serving young people, including "street people," in a Western metropolitan area. Half claimed no previous history of flashbacks; the others reported such experiences. The two groups, satisfactorily matched on variables such as age and numbers of previous psychedelic experiences, were tested on the selected MMPI scales. Then all subjects swallowed a capsule, which they were told would probably produce a flashback in experienced drug users like themselves, and underwent brief sensory deprivation. On a second occasion all subjects were given a different capsule, this time with the expectation that it would *not* produce a flashback. Both capsules were placeboes.

The group of LSD users reporting earlier flashbacks did show significantly more loose fantasizing, as measured by the MMPI scales. They were also found to have poorer social and sexual adjustment, an uneven school and work history, and often a history of bizarre thinking. And the subjects who scored especially high in loose thinking did indeed report many flashback experiences during the sensory deprivation, even when they had been told that the capsule ingested would *not* produce such effects.

Although it is impossible to know whether the personality described predated the tendency to have flashbacks, the results are useful. They suggest that

> *Under environmental conditions which pull for altered states of consciousness anyway,* [*loose-thinking*] *subjects have less ability* (*and possibly less desire*) *to maintain reality-oriented mental activity. . . .* [*Furthermore,*] *if the subject labels his initial sensations as the beginning of a flashback, expectations. . . are self-fulfilling to the extent that they selectively direct attention to psychedelic sensations* (*Heaton and Victor, 1976, p. 89*).

TABLE **10.6**
Reactions and Aftereffects of Psychedelic Drugs, with the Variables Most Strongly Related to the Effects
(adapted from Barber, 1970)

| Variables | Reactions | Aftereffects |
|---|---|---|
| A. Drug: chemical structure and dose<br><br>B. Situation: where the drug is administered, the way subject is treated by experimenter and by others, the emotional atmosphere, whether subject is alone or in a group<br><br>C. Set: subject's attitudes, expectancies, and motivation<br><br>D. Subject's personality characteristics | 1. Somatic-sympathetic effects: pupillary dilation; increased blood pressure; increased body temperature; occasional nausea; subjective reports of weakness and giddiness (variable A)<br><br>2. Changes in body image: strange and distorted feelings about body or limbs (variable A)<br><br>3. Dreamy, detached feelings: light-headedness and detachment from reality; unusually rapid flow of ideas (variable A)<br><br>4. Reduced intellectual proficiency: impaired performance on tests measuring memory, mathematical skills, and ability to accomplish other tasks requiring focused attention (variable A)<br><br>5. Changes in time perception: marked slowing of the passage of time (variable A)<br><br>6. Changes in sensory experience: increased richness of colors; heightened sensitivity to touch and smell; changes in depth and size perception; occasional synesthesias, for example, "smelling a sound" or "feeling a color" (variable A)<br><br>7. Changes in moods and emotions: highly variable, ranging from ecstasy and transcendental experience to great anxiety, depression, and despair (variables A, B, C, D) | 1. Chromosomal damage: reported in some early studies, but not replicated and currently believed not to be a danger<br><br>2. Positive psychological effects: self-reports of improved functioning, but little adequately controlled documentation (variables A, B, C, D)<br><br>3. Negative psychological effects: rare instances of psychoticlike reactions, most often in people with a past history of psychopathology; occasional "flashbacks," vivid reexperiencing of some portion of an earlier drug experience (variables A, B, C, D) |

Pahnke (1963) performed a considerably more remarkable and original piece of research. He attempted to maximize all the situational variables that might contribute to a religious or mystical experience. Subjects in his investigation were theological students who first attended a meeting at which they were told of the possibilities of having religious experiences after taking psilocybin. Twenty students were given psilocybin and twenty an active placebo by a double-blind procedure. Nicotinic acid was given as the placebo because it does produce some effects, such as a tingling sensation in the skin. After receiving the drug or the placebo, each subject participated in a two-and-a-half-hour-long religious service which included meditation, prayers, and the like. To heighten the significance of the occasion, Pahnke had chosen to conduct the experiment on Good Friday. After the service each subject wrote a description of his experience and answered an extensive questionnaire. The mystical and transcendental experiences of the group who took psilocybin were found to be significantly greater than those of the group who took the placebo.

## Summary

The habitual use of drugs is regarded by DSM-II as a symptom of an underlying personality disorder. The assumption seems to be that only a mentally disordered person would continue using a drug that is not only harmful but sometimes illegal as well. Little evidence was found to support this view. Therefore attention was focused on the variables that appear to play a role both in the individual's initial taking of a drug and in the continuing use of it, even though he or she may want to stop.

A number of psychological and social factors figure in the initial use of many legal and illegal drugs; these variables include peer pressure, a need to relieve tension, irritation, curiosity, boredom, cultural approval of drug use, and perhaps even a desire of most people to alter their states of consciousness.

Once people are using a drug with some regularity, their bodies may become addicted to it, thereby making it extraordinarily difficult to abstain. Taking drugs such as alcohol, nicotine, heroin, and the barbiturates for prolonged periods appears to develop true physiological addictions: increasing dosages are required to achieve the same effect, and the withdrawal symptoms when the particular drug is no longer taken are fairly predictable.

In recent years dispassionate observers have questioned both the sense and morality of the harsh punishments legislated for the use of nonaddicting drugs like marihuana, when at the same time the promotion and sale of harmful drugs such as alcohol and nicotine are allowed. Many prohibitions against marihuana have already been relaxed.

# chapter 11

## UNCONVENTIONAL SEXUAL BEHAVIOR AND HUMAN SEXUAL INADEQUACY



Of all the aspects of human functioning that receive the attention of psychopathologists, perhaps none has been the object of as much bad counsel as sexual activity. Most people recall from their own development some concerns about sexuality. All too often their worries originated with, or were at least exacerbated by, some piece of explicit misinformation from authorities. The *Boy Scout Manual* used to counsel maturing young men against masturbation, falsely inculcating in them the fear that self-stimulation might weaken their minds. Some psychiatrists and psychologists have been known to admonish an individual who is sexually attracted to members of his or her own sex that giving in to homosexual ways will lead to psychical ruination. Simultaneous orgasms have been held up as the pinnacle and goal of lovemaking. A substantial proportion of the average psychotherapist's time is, or should be, devoted to undoing the harm caused by such misinformation. It has indeed been estimated (Masters and Johnson, 1970) that more than half of all marriages in the United States are marked at some time by sexual difficulties, sometimes of such severity that tenderness itself is lost, let alone the more intense pleasure of sexual activity.

## Categories of Unconventional Sexual Behavior

We have already commented several times on the relativistic, often subjective nature of psychiatric labeling. The clinician's judgment of the appropriateness and intensity of sadness, for example, plays a role in determining whether or not it will be considered depression. In decisions about what sexual behavior is unconventional, psychiatric diagnosis becomes extremely arbitrary. Let us examine first how problems are listed in DSM-II. Two disorders typically regarded as sexual in nature and already alluded to in Chapter 7, namely impotence in the male and dyspareunia or painful intercourse in both sexes, are not considered sexual deviations but rather psychophysiological disorders. These and other relatively widespread sexual inadequacies are discussed in the second part of this chapter. Our attention in this first section is directed to the so-called sexual deviations which, like addiction, are classified with personality disorders, all of them being given in DSM-II the more general designation nonpsychotic mental disorders. The subcategory *sexual deviation* is applied to

> . . . *individuals whose sexual interests are directed primarily toward objects other than people of the opposite sex, toward sexual acts not usually associated with coitus, or toward coitus performed under bizarre circumstances as in necrophilia* [sexual relations with dead bodies], *pedophilia* [sexual contacts with children], *sexual sadism and fetishism. Even though many find their practices distasteful, they remain unable to substitute normal sexual behavior for them. This diagnosis is not appropriate for individuals who perform deviant sexual acts because normal sexual objects are not available to them* (*DSM-II, p.44*).

This definition is problematic for several reasons.

1. It is assumed, from the general definition of personality disorders, that sexual deviations are "deeply ingrained . . . lifelong patterns," as contrasted with behavior that might originate in adulthood and not be a "core" part of the individual.
2. To feel sexually toward a member of the same sex is regarded *ipso facto* as abnormal.
3. It is asserted that sexual activity is abnormal unless it is "associated with coitus." According to this definition, someone who prefers an orgasm produced by manual stimulation to one produced by intercourse may be considered abnormal.
4. To decide whether intercourse is performed "under bizarre circumstances" clearly demands a definition of what is bizarre.

In Freud's (1905) scheme sexual deviations, or unconventional sexual behavior as we choose to speak of them here, are examined in terms of *object chosen* and *activity engaged in*. Thus, when the individual chooses someone of the same sex, the behavior is homosexuality; an inanimate object or part of the body, fetishism; a close relative, incest; a child, pedophilia. The second category, unconventional activity, may have some connection with the first, choice of an unconventional object. In addition to or instead of engaging in sexual intercourse, the individual may prefer to watch others undress or engage in sexual behavior, which is voyeurism; expose his or her genitals to some audience, which is exhibitionism; obtain sexual gratification forcibly, which is rape; inflict pain, which is sadism; or endure pain, which is masochism. Two other forms of unconventional behavior are more difficult to fit into these two major categories: transvestism, dressing in the clothing of the opposite sex; and transsexualism, believing that one is actually a member of the opposite sex and has been "trapped" from birth in the wrong body. Transvestism does, however, somewhat resemble fetishism, except that the person carries the behavior one step further and dons the inanimate object.

A number of other sexual activities would fall into the DSM-II open categories of "other unspecified" sexual deviations. Some are defined briefly in the following list (McCary, 1967).

Troilism. Having sexual relations with or in the presence of more than one person.
Sexual oralism. Exclusive reliance on oral-genital contact for sexual gratification.
Sexual analism. Exclusive reliance on the anus instead of the vagina for penile insertion.
Zoophilia (bestiality). Sexual contact with animals, either intercourse or masturbation.
Frottage. Obtaining sexual satisfaction by rubbing or pressing against another person, typically without engaging in sexual intercourse.
Saliromania. Obtaining sexual gratification from soiling or mutilating female bodies or clothing.
Gerontosexuality. Preference for older people as sexual partners.
Mate swapping. Exchange of marital partners.
Coprophilia. Obtaining sexual gratification from handling feces.

In DSM-III sexual deviations will probably become "Psychosexual Disorders" and be divided into the following three new subcategories.

1. *Gender identity or role disorders:* covering primarily transsexualism and transvestism.
2. *Paraphilias:* sexual attractions to unusual objects—fetishisms, incest, and pedophilia; and sexual activities unusual in nature, such as sadism and rape.
3. *Psychosexual dysfunctions:* sexual inadequacies, such as impotence and dyspareunia; formerly classified as psychophysiological disorders, which in DSM-III will no longer constitute a category.

Little is known about how patterns of sexual behavior, whether conventional or not, develop and are maintained. In psychoanalytic theories each of the sexual deviations is viewed as some kind of defensive maneuver against intolerable levels of anxiety aroused by the threat of engaging in "normal" sexual activity, that is, having intercourse with a person of the opposite sex. Thus the male exhibitionist who shows his genitalia to others under inappropriate social circumstances is considered to be fearful of coitus because he connects it with castration. Male homosexuality is viewed as having a similar etiology. Learning accounts of the different problems are more varied, but neither they nor the psychodynamic theories are supported by reliable data.

Homosexuality, a significant social and personal problem, will not be discussed in this chapter but will receive separate and extended consideration in Chapter 12.

## Unconventional Choices of Sexual Object

### Fetishism

Many men take particular pleasure in observing and fondling certain parts of women's bodies. In our society a woman's breasts and legs hold the attention of a majority of males. A woman may place great importance on the size of a man's penis or be sexually excited by the shape and texture of his hands. Through cultural and personal preferences, certain physical attributes come to be regarded as sexually arousing. But interest in a particular part of the body is not considered a fetishism unless it is so strong that the rest of the person is disregarded. For a fetishist a particular inanimate object or a part of the body is the center of all or nearly all sexual interest. Subjectively, the attraction felt by the person toward the object or part of the body is involuntary and irresistible. In other words, the attraction has a strong compulsive quality and may be a dominant force in the person's life. For example, a man may be so enthralled with women's ankles that he takes a job as a shoe salesman, even though he could qualify for a better-paying position. He prefers instead to titillate himself with frequent and close contacts with female ankles.

The inanimate objects that are common sources of arousal for fetishists, who are usually men, are underwear, shoes, stockings, gloves, toilet articles, and the like. Or a man may be uncontrollably aroused by the sight of and contact with furs or even a baby carriage, a fetish which seems to be far more prevalent in Great Britain than in the United States. Often fetishistic objects are used in masturbation, although they may also serve as the arousing factor for conventional heterosexual intercourse—as when a husband demands that his wife wear black net stockings and leather gloves during lovemaking.

As already indicated, psychoanalyic theorists generally consider fetishisms, like other deviations, to serve some sort of defensive function, warding off anxiety about normal sexual contacts. Learning theorists usually invoke some kind of classical conditioning in the person's social-sexual history. For example, a young boy may, early in his sexual experiences, masturbate to pictures of women dressed in black leather. Indeed, one experiment (Rachman, 1966) lends some mild support to learning propositions. Male subjects were repeatedly shown slides of nude and alluring females interspersed with slides of women's boots. The subjects were eventually aroused by the slides of the boots alone. The "fetishistic attraction" induced, however, was weak and transient.

Box 6.1 (page 140) discussed the possibility that people are "prepared" to learn to become phobic to certain objects. It is also possible that human beings are prepared to learn to be sexually stimulated by certain classes of stimuli. If mere association with sexual stimulation were all there is to acquiring a fetish through classical conditioning, would not objects such as ceilings and pillows be found high on the list (Baron and Byrne, 1977)? At this point it would be premature to conclude that fetishisms are established through classical conditioning.

### Transvestism and transsexualism

When a person is sexually aroused by dressing in the clothing of the opposite sex while still regarding himself as a member of his own sex, the term *transvestism* is applied to his behavior. Transvestites, male and female, may also enjoy appearing socially as a member of the opposite sex. When arousal is the primary motivation of transvestites, they often masturbate when cross-dressed. Transvestism should not be confused with homosexuality; many transvestites are heterosexual and not all homosexuals "go in drag." In most jurisdictions it is illegal to appear cross-dressed in public.

If a man dresses as a woman because he truly believes that he is of that sex and that nature has played an unfair trick on him by giving him the wrong body, he is called a *transsexual*. These individuals, usually men, maintain their belief despite firm evidence that their bodies are, in fact, physiologically male in every respect (Benjamin, 1953).[1] Case histories suggest that this belief originates in early childhood and is reinforced by parents' allowing the child to dress up repeatedly and frequently in clothing of the opposite sex (Green, 1974). When transsexuals are cross-dressed, *they* regard themselves as properly clothed. Indeed, more and more often transsexuals are taking the drastic step of undergoing sex-change surgery. In men, for example, the genitalia are almost entirely removed, with some of the tissue retained to form an artificial vagina. Appropriate female hormones are given before the operation to produce bodily changes such as development of the breasts and softening of the skin (Green and Money, 1969).

The first sex-change operation took place in Europe in 1930, but the surgery that attracted

A transvestite imitating Marilyn Monroe in a Parisian nightclub act.

[1] Hermaphrodites actually have both male and female sexual organs, but this physical disorder is rare.

world-wide attention was performed on an ex-soldier, Christine (originally George) Jorgenson in Copenhagen in 1952. More recently, Jan (originally James) Morris, a well-known journalist, published *Conundrum* (1974), a sensitive and highly personal account of her life as a man and her subsequent alteration to a female. Perhaps the most widely known American facility for these operations—and for the psychological support that must precede and follow them—is the Gender Identity Clinic at Johns Hopkins School of Medicine, directed by John Money, a leading figure in sex research. It has been estimated that over 2500 Americans have had their sex altered by surgery (Gagnon, 1977).

Both psychoanalysts and learning theorists seem to agree that transvestism and transsexualism develop under circumstances in which the person is confused about which sex he or she belongs to—*gender identity* is not well established or is even reversed. The literature on transvestism, as well as that on transsexualism, contains case histories in which the male child is praised for dressing up in his mother's clothing. But nonsexual factors have been implicated in transvestism. Some clinicians have treated transvestites who regard cross-dressing as a refuge from the responsibilities that they have to bear as men in our society. The clothing, then, has a particular *meaning* for them that is more complex than sheer sexual arousal and role playing. In other words, conceptualizing transvestism solely in sexual terms may be an oversimplification.

To most people it would seem that only a psychotic could possibly believe that he or she is trapped in the body of the opposite sex. How can a physiologically normal man believe that he is a woman unless he is psychotic? This commonsense view has been challenged in recent years by research examining whether transsexuals are, in fact, neurotically or psychotically impaired. In a correlational study, Roback, McKee, and Webb (in press) gave the MMPI to

The left-hand pair of pictures shows young Judy Patton and Jude Patton as he is today. The right-hand pair shows Renée Richards before and after a sex-change operation.

three groups of patients: ten women who had been seeking sex reassignment surgery and who had been living as men for at least six months; ten morbidly obese women who were candidates for a radical operation in which a portion of the small intestine would be bypassed to help them lose weight; and ten women who had applied for outpatient psychotherapy at the same university hospital. Subjects in these three groups were matched for age and IQ to rule out differences in these variables as possible explanations of the results of the questionnaire.

The study did not confirm the hypothesis that female transsexuals are mentally ill, a finding consistent with the verdict of research done on biological males who believe that they are women. To be sure, the transsexual women did deviate from the MMPI norms on two scales—psychopathy and masculinity-femininity—but these deviations were neither large enough nor of such a nature to indicate neurotic or psychotic disorder. Considering the immense social pressures that transsexuals are under to conform, their MMPI scores were unremarkable. Although some sex-change candidates are flagrantly psychotic (Finney et al., 1975), in the main transsexuals cannot be said to suffer a mental disorder that in any way explains their unconventional desire to have their bodies radically altered to conform to a strongly held belief that they are of the opposite sex.

### Incest

The taboo against incest seems virtually universal in human societies. A notable exception were the marriages of Egyptian pharoahs to their sisters or other females of their immediate families. In Egypt it was believed that the royal blood should not be contaminated by that of outsiders. Some anthropologists consider the prohibition against incest to have served the important function of forcing larger and wider social ties than would have been likely had family members chosen their mates only from among their own.

Incest, which includes all varieties of sexual relations that culminate in at least one orgasm, seems most common between brother and sister—especially in lower-income homes where siblings tend to share the same beds. The next most common form, which is considered more pathological, is between father and daughter. Gebhard and his associates (1965) found, in their well-known study on sex offenders, that most fathers who had relations with physically mature daughters tended to be very devout, moralistic, and fundamentalistic in their religious beliefs.

Statistics on the incidence of incest are notoriously difficult to collect; since this behavior occurs within the family, other members are very reluctant to report the offenders to the authorities. Explanations of incest run the gamut from sexual deprivation to the Freudian notion that human beings have basic human desires for such relationships. Gagnon (1977) speculates that an incestuous relationship between father and daughter begins when the father is under considerable stress outside the home and yet receives insufficient emotional and sexual support from his wife. He turns to an available, sometimes prepubescent daughter, who takes on the role of substitute wife. Whether the incest continues depends in large measure on the response of the man's wife, who may choose to ignore what is going on in the interest of keeping the family together. The reactions of the daughter are, of course, highly variable and can be expected to change over time. Perhaps initially flattered that she can take good care of daddy, the growing young woman may later feel trapped by the whole affair and run away from home. Or she may become pregnant, thus *forcing* other family members to deal with the father's behavior. There is little firm evidence bearing on the long-term effects of incest on either children or parents.

### Pedophilia

Pedophiles are adults, usually men at least as far as police records indicate, who derive sexual gratification through physical and often sexual contact with children. Although violence is seldom a part of the molestation, society's reaction to pedophiles is far more punitive than it is toward rapists, who employ physical force. Often the pedophile is content to stroke the child's hair, but he may also manipulate the child's genitalia, encourage the child to manipulate his, and less often, attempt intromission. The molestations may be repeated over a period of weeks, months, or years if they are not discovered by other adults or protested by the child. There are both heterosexual and homosexual pedophiles, but it is of interest that most homosexuals restrict their sexual attentions to other adults and regard with disdain those who do not.

Pedophiles tend to be rigidly religious and moralistic. As with most of the aberrant sexual behavior that has been described, there is a strong subjective feeling of compulsion in the attraction that draws the pedophile to the child. According to Gebhard and his colleagues (1965), pedophiles typically know the children they molest, being a next-door-neighbor, friend of the family, or relative. Most older heterosexual pedophiles are or have been married at some time in their lives.

A group of pedophiles were investigated by Mohr, Turner, and Jerry (1964). The pedophiles in their sample were found to cluster into three age groups, adolescent, mid-to-late thirties, and mid-to-late fifties, with the mid-thirties group the largest. Adolescent pedophiles were found to be sexually inexperienced with people of their own age. Those in their mid-thirties had developed serious mental and social maladjustments, including alcoholism, which was frequently associated with the act. The older pedophiles were better adjusted but usually suffered from loneliness and isolation. These differences indicate that etiological factors vary with the age of the offender.

It has been suggested that the drive to approach a child sexually can reflect a sense of having failed in the adult world, socially and professionally as well as sexually. Occasionally, though, an adult predisposed toward pedophilia may be aroused by a child's innocent, uninhibited show of affection. Unbeknown to the child, the pedophile perceives sexual overtones in demonstrativeness. If we accept the Gebhard (1965) finding that the pedophile approaches children as old as twelve, some of the youngsters may well be physically mature, and given recent similar styles of clothing for both children and adults, may appear older than their chronological age. In defining pedophilia, state laws prescribe an upper age limit for those who are to be considered children, making it a crime to approach sexually any younger person. The age varies in different states.

When a child tells a parent that an adult has fondled him or her, the parents face the dilemma of how to react. Many experts feel that the child tends not to interpret the interaction in the same sexual terms that adults do (Gagnon, 1977). Even if the molester has an orgasm, it is not always clear to the child what has happened, and to react with adult alarm can lend needless negative meaning to an unfortunate incident. But at the same time the young child must be protected from a prolonged and harmful sexual relationship with an adult.

## Unconventional Choices of Sexual Activity

Unconventional sexual acts with adult members of the opposite sex are generally considered abnormal if they are preferred to conventional, heterosexual relations between consenting adults. When the acts are performed *in addition to* conventional activities or under conditions of involuntary deprivation of these activities, the diagnostic label is not usually applied.

### Voyeurism ("Peeping")

Now and then a man may by chance happen to observe a nude woman without her knowing he is watching her. If his sex life is primarily conventional, his act is voyeuristic, but he would not generally be considered a voyeur.

> *Strictly speaking, voyeurism is viewed as a deviation when it is preferred to coitus or indulged in at serious risk. . . . The typical voyeur is not interested in ogling his own wife or girl friend. In 95 percent of incidents he observes strangers. What draws him to peep through windows is in large measure the danger and excitement entailed. . . .* [*He typically masturbates*] *while watching or immediately thereafter* (Katchadourian and Lunde, 1972, pp. 288–289).

A true voyeur, who is almost always a man, will not find it particularly exciting to watch a woman who is undressing for his special benefit. The element of risk seems important, for he is excited by his anticipation of how the woman will react if she finds out he is watching. Some voyeurs derive special pleasure from secretly observing couples having sexual relations. As with all categories of behavior that are against the law, frequencies of occurrence are difficult to assess, since the majority of *all* illegal activities go unnoticed by the police.

From what we know, voyeurs tend to be fearful of more direct sexual encounters with others, their peeping serving as substitute gratification and possibly giving them a sense of power over those watched. They do not seem to be otherwise disturbed, however. After all restrictions against the sale of pornographic materials to adults had been lifted in Denmark, one of the few observed effects of this liberalization was a significant reduction in peeping, at least as reported to the police (Kutchinsky, 1970). It may be that the increased availability of completely frank pictorial and written material, which is typically used in masturbation, satisfies the needs that had earlier made some men without other outlets voyeurs.

### Exhibitionism

Voyeurism and exhibitionism together account for close to a majority of all sexual offenses that come to the attention of police. Again, the frequency of exhibitionism is much greater among men. A quip holds that a man surreptitiously looking at a nude woman is a voyeur, but that a woman looking at a naked man is watching an exhibitionist. Like many statements about human sexuality, this one implies that women are less sexual than men.

> *Exhibitionism is a deviation when an adult male obtains sexual gratification from exposing his genitals to women or children who are involuntary observers, usually complete strangers. In a typical sequence the exhibitionist drives or walks in front of a passing woman with his genitals exposed. He usually, but not always, has an erection. Usually, as soon as she has seen him, he flees. Sometimes he wears a coat and exposes himself periodically while riding on a subway or bus. . . .*
>
> *The exhibitionist, in common with the voyeur, does not usually attack or molest his "victim." His gratification comes from observing her reaction, which is predictably*

These photographers, delighted with their pastime of viewing a partially nude woman, would not be considered voyeurs. A voyeur must obtain most of his sexual enjoyment from peeping and do so in a socially disapproved fashion. Could the woman be regarded as an exhibitionist?

> *surprise, fear, disgust, and so on. . . . Some men ejaculate at the scene of exposure; others merely enjoy the psychic release. Others become highly aroused and masturbate right afterward* (Katchadourian and Lunde, 1972, pp. 289–290).

The urge to expose seems overwhelming and virtually uncontrollable to the exhibitionist and is apparently triggered by anxiety and restlessness as well as by sexual arousal. Because of the compulsive nature of the urge, the exposures may be repeated rather frequently and even in the same place and at the same time of day. Generally the exhibitionist is immature in his approaches to the opposite sex and otherwise unsuccessful in all interpersonal relationships, although these failures cannot be said to cause exhibitionism, at least by themselves. Over half of all exhibitionists are married, but their sexual relationships with their wives are unsatisfactory (Mohr, Turner, and Jerry, 1964).

Younger exhibitionists may not manifest other kinds of psychopathology, but some of those who expose themselves come from the ranks of the mentally retarded and the senile. Some who exhibit do so while having a temporal lobe epileptic seizure (see page 431). Because the behavior of these men may be without deliberation and intent, it is problematic whether they should be considered exhibitionists. When the label of exhibitionism is applied, not only overt behavior but also intent should be established, which may be difficult.

The fact that the exhibited penis is sometimes flaccid raises interesting questions about the *sexual* aspects of the act. How sexually arousing can it be for a man to expose himself if his penis is not erect when doing so? It may be that his arousal is diminished by guilt over what he is doing or fear that he will be apprehended by the police. Or the exhibitionist, deficient as he seems to be in more conventional social skills, may regard his act of exposure as the best social interaction that he can manage. The fact that a nonchalant reaction on the part of the observer is not satisfying to the exhibitionist confirms that he is seeking to startle those to whom he exposes himself. These are only a few of the aspects of exhibitionism about which we have no certain knowledge at present.

The search to determine how exhibitionism develops has turned up very little. An intriguing learning hypothesis emphasizes the reinforcing aspects of masturbation. McGuire, Carlisle, and Young (1965) reported on the development of exhibitionism in two young men who were surprised during urination by an attractive woman. When the embarrassment had passed and they were in private, the thought of being discovered in this way aroused them and they masturbated while fantasizing the earlier experience. After repeated masturbating to such fantasies, they began to exhibit. The report suggests that repeated association of sexual arousal with images of being seen by a woman classically conditioned the men to become aroused through exhibiting. There is no experimental evidence, however, that clearly supports a learning explanation of exhibitionism.

### Rape

Few other antisocial acts are viewed with more disgust and anger than the obtaining of sexual gratification forcibly and often violently through rape. A special category, statutory rape, refers to sexual intercourse between a male and any female who is a minor. The typical age of consent, as decided by state statutes, is eighteen years. It is assumed that a younger person should not be held responsible for her sexual activity. A charge of statutory rape can be made even if it can be proved that the girl entered into the situation knowingly and willingly. Thus statutory rape need not involve force, being simply a consummated intercourse with a minor that was reported to the police. The focus here is on rape other than statutory.

In the past rape was considered an offense not against the victim but against the property rights of the woman's husband, father, or brothers. Even now a forcible sexual assault by a husband on his wife is not legally recognized as rape. Definitions of rape vary greatly in different police jurisdictions, making it extremely difficult to draw meaningful comparisons between the incidences in various cities and locales. For example, in Los Angeles the police classify as forcible rape any encounter between a man and a woman in which the man seeks sexual gratification from her against her will. This broad definition includes instances in which no sexual intercourse takes place. In Boston the fondling of immature girls by physically immature boys has been considered rape; not only may no intercourse take place, but the offenders may not be adults (Chappell et al., 1971). In other jurisdictions such episodes would be categorized as delinquent behavior, not rape.

Certain women have "bad" reputations with the police of their communities. Under these circumstances a truly forceful and even violent rape may not be categorized as such in the stationhouse, especially when the status in the community of the boy or man involved is higher than that of the victim. In this way a biased incidence of rape, as well as of other unconventional sexual behavior, may be obtained if attention is restricted to police records. Overriding these considerations, however, is the unfortunate fact that the woman may feel great shame is attached to her involuntary role in rape. Many times as many rapes are estimated to occur as are reported to the police.

Rape victims are often traumatized by the experience, both mentally and physically. Masters and Johnson (1970) have provided several case histories indicating how the experience of rape can leave a psychological mark on a woman for many years afterward, giving her a negative attitude toward her sexual relationship with her husband. Rapists usually inflict at least a degree of bodily injury in forcing themselves sexually upon their victims. And if a woman struggles against her attacker, ligaments in the pelvic area can be torn. Some rapists may, after the sex act, murder and mutilate the women they have attacked. The vast majority of rapes are almost surely planned—it is a myth to say that rape is the spontaneous act of a man whose sexual impulses have gone out of control (Harrington and Sutton-Simon, 1977). The rapist may have a sadistic streak, but unlike the sadist he often does not know the victim beforehand and attacks someone who is unwilling. Moreover, the sadist usually has an established, ongoing relationship with a masochist. In many cases a pattern of repeated rape is part of a sociopathic life style (see page 226). Because rape is a mixture of both sex and aggression, the motivation is difficult to determine.

Sexism and the subjugation of women through rape have been explored in depth by Susan Brownmiller (1975) in her best-selling book *Against Our Will*. Her thesis holds rape to be "nothing more or less than a conscious process of intimidation by which all men keep all women in a state of fear" (p. 5). She garners evidence from history, both ancient and modern. In the Babylonian civilization (3000 B.C.), for example, a married woman was the property of her husband. If she was raped, both she and the rapist were bound and tossed into a river. The husband could choose to save her, or he could let her drown, just punishment for her *adultery*. The views of the ancient Hebrews were no more enlightened: a married woman who had been raped was commonly stoned to death along with her attacker. When an unbetrothed virgin was raped within the walls of the city, she was similarly stoned, for it was assumed that she could have prevented the attack simply by crying out.

These penalties that different societies have imposed on raped women, together with the fact that men with their generally superior strength can usually overpower women, buttress Brownmiller's argument that rape has served in the past and still serves to intimidate women. The Crusaders raped their way across Europe in the eleventh through thirteenth centuries on their holy pilgrimages to free Jerusalem from the Muslims, the Germans in World War I raped as they rampaged through Belgium, and American forces raped in Vietnam as they "searched and destroyed." Brownmiller contends that rape is actually *expected* in war. In her view membership in the most exclusive males-only clubs in the world—the fighting forces of most nations—encourages a perverse sense of masculine superiority and creates a climate in which rape is acceptable.

Emerging from the study of rape, and of other patterns of unconventional sexual behavior, is the fact that sexuality can serve many purposes. Indeed, an act we label as sexual because it involves the genitalia may sometimes be better understood in nonsexual terms. Rapists, in the opinion of many (for example, Brownmiller, 1975; Gagnon, 1977), aggress against others for reasons having only remotely to do with sex per se (see Box 11.1). The classic study of sex offenders (Gebhard et al., 1965) concluded that up to 33 percent of rapists carried out the act to express aggression rather than for sexual satisfaction. Many feminist groups object to the classification of rape as a *sexual* crime at all, for it can mask the basically assaultive and typically brutal nature of the act, and creates an atmosphere in which the sexual motives of the *victim* are questioned. Although a person who is beaten and

## BOX **11.1** A Psychophysiological Analysis of Rape

Discussions of rape are based almost entirely on the work of historians, sociologists, political analysts, and journalists. Recently, experimental psychologists have been trying to bring something of the phenomenon into the laboratory. The work of Abel and his colleagues (in press) is a good example of this kind of research.

In their initial study, these workers developed a methodology that relied on the penile plethysmograph to help them distinguish between rapists and nonrapists. Rapist subjects were recruited from referrals by psychiatrists, psychologists, attorneys, and the courts. Most of the rapists had long histories of forcible sexual assaults on women, and some on men as well. Control subjects, who came from the same referral sources, had histories of other types of unconventional sexual behavior, such as exhibitionism, pedophilia, and homosexuality.

The independent variable in the experiment consisted of two kinds of erotic audiotapes. The story recorded on one tape was of mutually enjoyable intercourse with a suitable partner; the other audiotape was of a rape of that same partner. The enjoyable scene of intercourse portrayed the partner as willing, loving, and utterly involved with the subject. In the rape scene the victim resisted and was in physical as well as emotional pain. According to the plethysmograph, rapists were significantly more aroused by the rape tape than were the nonrapist subjects, the expected pattern. But interestingly, the rapists were highly aroused by the mutually enjoyable intercourse tape as well! In fact, this tape aroused them no less than the rape scene. And the nonrapists, although much more aroused by the lovemaking than by the rape, nonetheless showed some mild arousal when listening to the rape story.

The finding that the rapists were responsive to the enjoyable sex scene as well as to the rape scene does not support the usual image of the rapist as a man who is *incapable* of finding stimulation in conventional, loving intercourse. It is possible, however, that had Abel and his colleagues queried the subjects afterward, they would have found that the rapists were adding violence and hurtful elements to the loving encounter in an attempt to enjoy it more.

Abel then went on to use the same method to investigate the rapist's response to aggression. Are rapists aroused by aggression if the incident does not conclude with sexual assault? How does arousal from aggression relate to arousal from rape? Some of the rapists already studied listened to three additional tapes. One of them depicted a rapist slapping, hitting, and holding a woman down against her will, but without ensuing intercourse. On the second the man had forcible intercourse with the same victim. The rapists also listened to a tape of nonviolent sexual intercourse with a willing partner. Results revealed that the aggression scene generated some sexual arousal, but only 40 percent of that generated by the rape scene and an even smaller percentage of that generated by the tape of mutually satisfying, nonaggressive intercourse.

Abel and his colleagues went on to compare the polygraph records of individual rapists with their case histories. Some case histories indicated a preference for conventional intercourse, with rape resorted to if the victim was unwilling. These men had relatively small erections to the aggression story, greater response to the rape, and the greatest response to the conventional intercourse. For other rapists, whose histories showed repeated, often sadistic assaults on women, erections to mutually enjoyable intercourse were minimal, but arousal was markedly augmented when aggression was added to sex to equal rape. Moreover, high levels of arousal were elicited by the aggression tape. Hence the picture is not a simple one. Some men apparently resort to rape only when loving intercourse is unavailable, whereas others seem to *require* violence-with-sex forced on an unwilling and frightened victim.

How does this sort of research relate to the discussions in the text? Consider, for example, Brownmiller's thesis that rape is man's way of intimidating, even denigrating, women. Her historical-political analysis might at first appear a world apart from the laboratory research of Abel. But this is not really the case, even though investigators like Brownmiller and experimentalists seldom converse. Abel and his colleagues have shown that some rapists do, indeed, become sexually aroused by scenes depicting aggression, and that this arousal can be greater than that they experience when scenes of conventional intercourse are presented. The question this kind of laboratory research does not address—and can probably *never* address—is *why*. Why are certain men sexually stimulated when pain is inflicted on an unwilling victim? What is there about the one-down relationship between a rapist and his victim that excites him? Brownmiller and others find the causes in the broad sweep of history and more particularly in the power relationships between men and women. Their independent variables, if you will, are male machismo, the deliberate degradation of women, and the desire to intimidate by aggression. Abel and others in their laboratory work examine men at the end of a long behavior-shaping process. The rapists they have studied are products of their social-learning history. To figure out *why* they aggress is the larger, more important question. The search should take investigators into the domain of sociologists, political scientists, and historians.

robbed (without being sexually abused) is hardly suspected of secretly wanting to be attacked, by cruel irony the victims of rape must often prove their moral "purity" to husbands, friends, police—and even to themselves. What, after all, did *they* do that might have contributed to the incident, especially if the rapist was not a complete stranger? But there are indications that the stigma of rape is being removed by more enlightened views, coming in large measure from women's liberation groups and from books such as Brownmiller's.

### Sadism and masochism

The majority of sadists, as indicated earlier, establish relationships with masochists to derive mutual sexual gratification. The sadist may derive full orgastic pleasure by inflicting pain on his or her partner, and the masochist may be completely gratified by being subjected to pain. For other partners the sadistic and masochistic practices are a prelude to sexual intercourse. A married couple seen for behavior therapy had practiced the following ritual.

> *As a prelude to sexual intercourse, the young man would draw blood by cutting a small incision on the palm of his wife's right hand. She would then stimulate his penis, using the blood of her right palm as a lubricant. Normal intercourse would then ensue, and the moment the wife felt her*

Marquee of a New York City movie theater catering to sadists and masochists.

*husband ejaculating, she was required to dig her nails deep into the small of his back or buttocks* (*Lazarus and Davison, 1971, pp. 202–203*).

Some sadists murder and mutilate; fortunately, however, most of the time sadism and masochism are restricted to fantasies. The increasing number of "sex shops" in large cities do a lucrative business in providing pictorial and written materials to those who need at least the vicarious experience of pain in order to satisfy themselves sexually. One young man who sought help found it sexually stimulating to imagine an attractive woman tied to stakes on the ground and tearfully trying to extricate herself. His sexual life was restricted to masturbation and thinking of this and similar images of women in pain or extreme discomfort (Davison, 1968a).

How can it happen that a person, often quite normal in other respects, must inflict or experience suffering, directly or vicariously, in order to become sexually aroused? If it is assumed, as some psychoanalysts do, that pain provides sexual pleasure, the answer is readily available; unfortunately, this "explanation" really explains nothing. Another psychoanalytic theory, restricted to men, holds that the sadist has a castration complex and inflicts pain to assure himself of his power and masculinity. It may also be that in childhood or adolescence sadomasochistic elements were present while orgasms were experienced. Although it is plausible to suggest that classical conditioning may have occurred, there are as yet no data to support this theory. A related hypothesis suggests that the physiological arousal from inflicting and experiencing pain is not, in fact, dissimilar to sexual excitement. In the early stages of being sexualized, discriminations may be more difficult to make, especially if the pain-inducing act also includes sexual elements. In this way the individual may learn to label pain-produced arousal as sexual. Interesting as it may be, this hypothesis is also purely speculative at this point.

## Human Sexual Inadequacy: The Work of Masters and Johnson

Thus far in this chapter the unconventional patterns of sexual behavior of a small minority of the population have been described. But many "ordinary" people are likely to have problems that interfere with conventional sexual enjoyment at least to some extent during the course of their lives. In examining these problems, we shall be drawing extensively on the clinical and research data on dysfunctional human sexual behavior collected by Masters and Johnson (1966, 1970) in the context of their extensive research and therapy programs in St. Louis, Missouri.

### Background of the Masters and Johnson Work

Inquiry into human sexual behavior has not always been a common and acceptable field of scientific activity as it is today. While still a medical student at the University of Rochester, William H. Masters decided to undertake a scientific and clinical investigation of human sexual response for the principal reason that very little was known about the physiology of human sexual functioning. Like other sex researchers before him, Masters chose obstetrics and gynecology as his speciality; during his residency he worked on hormone problems of the aging. The medical profession has seldom been known as particularly innovative in a social and political sense; Masters was repeatedly rebuffed and discouraged by his older colleagues before he was able to begin his pioneering research on sexual response. Fortunately, his earlier very reputable and conservative work in hormone replacement therapy encouraged Washington University to sponsor him. He obtained permission to set up a laboratory in 1953 and started the actual work in July 1954.[2]

Masters realized that he was risking his professional reputation by working in this area.

> *If you do cancer research for ten years and don't come up with anything noteworthy, nobody is going to question you professionally. I went into sex research with full knowledge that I had to win. I had to come up with something or I would have been destroyed professionally. Even with results sex research invites criticism* (Belliveau and Richter, 1970, pp. 19–20).

For about ten years Masters's work was supported by Washington University, some private grant money, and some funding from the National Institutes of Health. These sources of funds were eventually exhausted, however, and in 1963 and 1964 he moved to private quarters, setting up his own clinic, the Reproductive Biology Research Foundation, entirely separate from the University. He had been joined in 1957 by Virginia Johnson, in what has become an extremely fruitful collaboration.

The initial work was not directed toward developing therapy techniques but proposed to measure in the laboratory the physiological responses of normal human subjects to sexual stimulation. One of the first problems was to set up the instruments necessary for observation and measurements. For example, an artificial penis was constructed out of clear plastic through which the vagina could be filmed during sexual excitement. Finding suitable volunteer subjects was another challenge. For over a year only female prostitutes were studied, but because prostitutes frequently do not have orgasms, other subjects were eventually sought. Masters and Johnson let it be known in the university com-

[2] The studies carried out by Alfred Kinsey and others in the 1940s and 1950s will be reviewed in detail in Chapter 12. Although it is generally assumed that the Kinsey data were based almost entirely on interviews, John Gagnon, formerly associated with Kinsey's Institute for Sex Research in Bloomington, Indiana, has called attention to the extent to which Masters and Johnson built on work done earlier at the Institute. Many findings of the Kinsey group, published later in the Kinsey reports, were obtained through the direct observation and filming of sexual activity. The social climate of the day, however, discouraged Kinsey from acknowledging that his group had, in fact, gathered information on human sexuality through direct behavioral observation (Gagnon, 1977).

The noted sex researchers and therapists, William H. Masters and Virginia Johnson. Their pioneering work helped launch a more candid and scientific appraisal of human sexuality.

munity that volunteer subjects were needed; in this liberal setting they came forth without too much hesitation. Extensive interviewing and history taking established that the subjects included in the study were not emotionally disturbed and were capable of normal sexual functioning, that is, able to have an orgasm with sufficient physical and psychological stimulation. The persons tested were in no sense a random sample of the population, nor did Masters and Johnson ever claim that they were. All potential subjects knew that they would be observed during acts of intercourse or masturbation, and that their physiological responses would be recorded. Of course, confidentiality was absolutely assured.

## Sexual Response in Men and Women

After eleven years of study the principal findings of the laboratory research on normal volunteers were reported in the first Masters and Johnson book, *Human Sexual Response* (1966). The responses of men and women had unexpectedly been found to be quite similar; Masters and Johnson were able to delineate a four-stage cycle of sexual arousal for both sexes (Figure 11.1).

*The* excitement phase *is initiated by whatever is sexually stimulating to a particular individual. If stimulation is strong enough,*

FIGURE **11.1**
Graphs of male (a) and female (b) sexual response cycles. The green lines indicate the most common patterns of response, the white lines variations. The female cycle does not always climb to orgasm, but when it does there is not the inevitable refractory period found in the male cycle. After Masters and Johnson, 1966, p. 5.

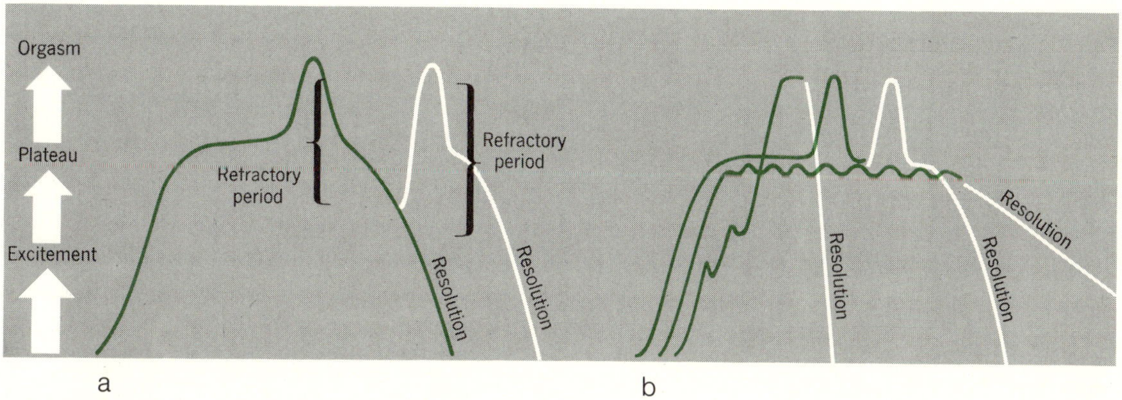

*excitement builds quickly, but if it is interrupted or if it becomes objectionable, this phase becomes extended or the cycle may be stopped. If effective sexual stimulation is continued, it produces increased levels of sexual tension. . . . This increased tension is called the* plateau phase. *If the individual's drive for sexual release in this phase is not strong enough, or if stimulation ceases to be effective or is withdrawn, the man or woman will not experience orgasm, but will enter a long period of gradually decreased sexual tension. The climactic or* orgasmic phase, *a totally involuntary response, consists of those few seconds when the body changes resulting from stimulation reach their maximum intensity. During the* resolution phase, *after orgasm, there is a lessening of sexual tensions as the person returns to the unstimulated state. Women are capable of having another orgasm if there is effective stimulation during this phase. The resolution period in the male includes a time, which varies among individuals, when restimulation is impossible. This is called the refractory period. In both sexes, the basic responses of the body to sexual stimulation are myotonia (increased muscle tension) and vasocongestion (filling of the blood vessels with fluid), especially in the genital organs, causing swelling. Of course these basic physiologic responses take on a different appearance in a man than they do in a woman. Interestingly enough, the basic physiologic sexual responses remain the same regardless of the stimulation—coital, manipulative, mechanical, or fantasy. However, intensity and duration of responses vary with the method of stimulation used. Masturbation produced the most intense experiences observed in the laboratory, partner manipulation the next, and intercourse the least (Belliveau and Richter, 1970, pp. 33–34).*

It is important to note that the sexual response cycle does not represent, nor was it ever intended to, actual quantitative changes in any particular physiological or psychological dimension. Heart rate, or vaginal lubrication, or engorgement of the penis does not steadily increase during excitement, remain constant during plateau, shift markedly upward during orgasm, and slowly diminish during resolution. Nor did Masters and Johnson claim to have shown the sexual interest of their subjects to wax and wane in the manner portrayed in Figure 11.1. These tracings represent a useful overall scheme for talking about all the facets of human sexuality during high levels of sexual arousal. The scheme is an *invention* of the scientist, a device for organizing and discussing a body of information (Gagnon, 1977).

The impact of the first book by Masters and Johnson has been very great, contributing immensely to our knowledge of the physiology of human sexuality. Even before the book was published, the information obtained through research was put to use in the treatment phase of the project. By knowing how the body works to achieve maximum sexual response, Masters and Johnson were able to elaborate methods of treating sexual dysfunction. Some of the treatments that they developed are discussed in Chapter 19.

The fact that the circumstances of these findings were artificial limits their generality somewhat, however. And we should be mindful how little physiological research can tell us about the *psychological* components of human sexuality. They were nonetheless able to provide firm data on certain controversial points and to dispel a few myths.

1. Although the clitoris (Figure 11.2) is quite important in transmitting sexual stimulation in the female, it has been a mistake to advise men to try to stimulate it continually during intercourse. During the plateau phase the clitoris retracts, making access to it extremely difficult and even painful for some women. In point of fact, it is very difficult to have inter-

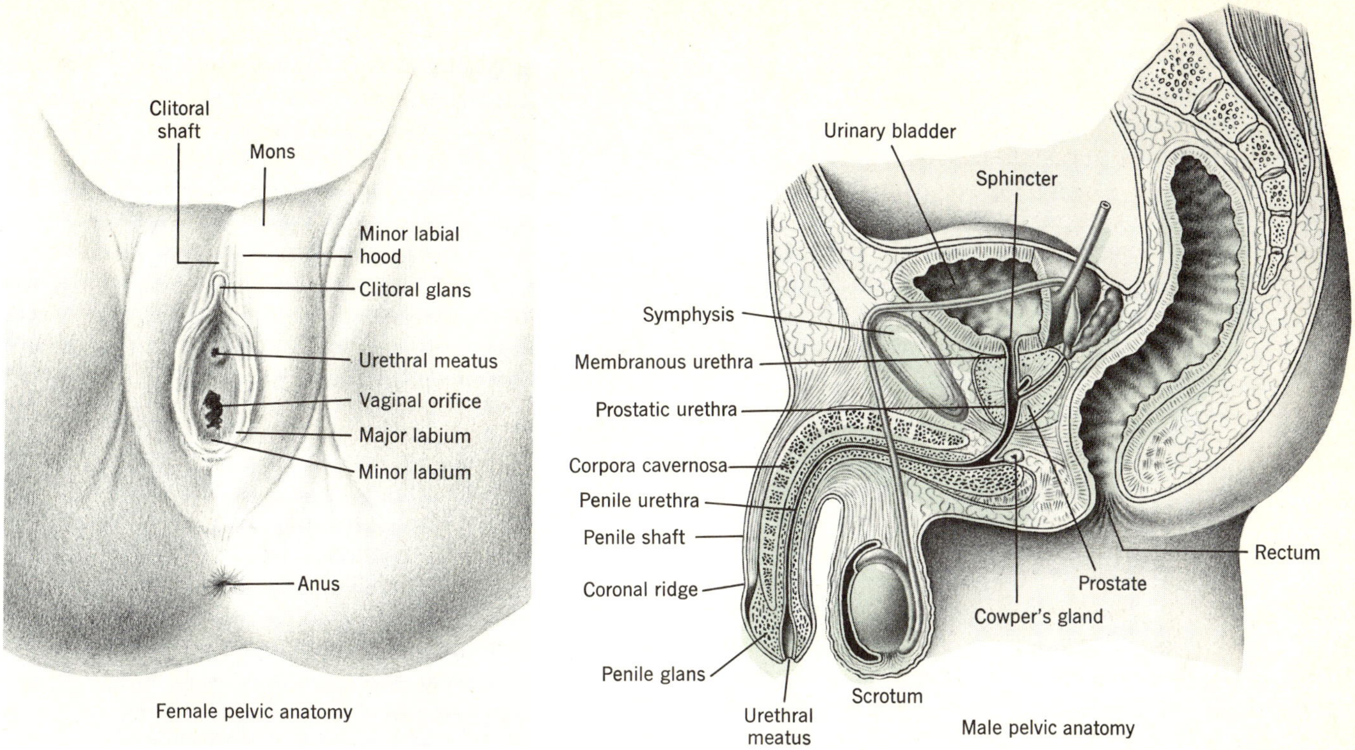


FIGURE **11.2**
Exterior view of female genitalia, cross section of male. (From Alvin Nason and Robert DeHaan, *The Biological World*, New York: Wiley, 1973.)

course without stimulating the clitoris *indirectly,* which is the type of stimulation that some women seem to prefer.

2. Masters and Johnson were able to prove with hard data that orgasms in women obtained from stimulation of the clitoris, without entrance into the vagina, are as intense as and indeed objectively indistinguishable from orgasms obtained by having an erect penis in the vagina.

Probably few pieces of misinformation have caused more consternation than Freud's insistence that the vaginal orgasm is superior to the clitoral orgasm. He asserted, and practitioners have parroted to hundreds of thousands of people for years since, that a woman who can have an orgasm only by stimulation of her clitoris is settling for second best; further, that failure to have an orgasm via stimulation of the vagina by the man's penis is a sign of psychosexual fixation and immaturity. The Freudian theory has been explained rather precisely by John Gagnon.

*Everyone goes through certain psychosexual stages, one of which involves masturbation as the important overt sexual activity. This stage occurs early in life as part of the parade of changes toward heterosexual genital maturity, that is, intercourse with a person of the opposite sex. Masturbation is infantile; intercourse is mature; being mature is better than being infantile. When women masturbate, they touch the clitoris; when women have inter-*

*course, they have a penis in the vagina. Since masturbation is infantile, pleasures achieved by touching the clitoris are infantile. Sexual maturity* [*therefore*] *requires that women move from having orgasms produced by touching the clitoris to having orgasms produced by the penis in the vagina. The site of sensation* [*is*] *supposed to move from clitoris to vagina (From* Human Sexualities, *p. 138. Copyright © 1977, by Scott, Foresman and Company. Reprinted by permission.*)

Even before the work of Masters and Johnson, some sexologists had been trying to disabuse people of this notion (for example, Ellis, 1961), pointing out that the walls of the vaginal barrel are poorly supplied with sensory nerve endings, whereas the clitoris, like the glans of the penis, is amply supplied. The fact that orgasms achieved by masturbation and manual manipulation by the partner, both of which typically concentrate on the clitoris and surrounding areas, were found to create at least as much excitation as intercourse pretty much puts to rest the bugaboo about clitoral orgasms. Of course, these findings about the clitoris in no way imply that conventional intercourse (penile-vaginal containment) is not extremely enjoyable! Once again, the Masters-Johnson data do not address the *psychological* aspects of sex. What is the most effective stimulation for one person may prove less so for another.

3. The goal of having simultaneous orgasms, held up in numerous marriage manuals as a sign of true love and compatibility, was shown to be hardly a mark of superior sexual achievement. Instead, it can often distract each of the partners from his or her own sexual pleasure.
4. It was also found that not only do most women *not* object to intercourse during menstruation, but they even tend to enjoy it more, particularly during the second half of the period.
5. During the second three months of pregnancy, women seem to desire intercourse at least as much as when not pregnant. Although there is some danger of spontaneous abortion in the early stages, particularly for women who have a history of spontaneous miscarriage, most women continue to desire sexual stimulation, sometimes until they go into labor. At any rate, little harm seems to come to the woman and to the fetus in the uterus through intercourse, at least during the first six months of the pregnancy.
6. Various facts about the male's penis were also confirmed. The size of a man's erect penis was not found to be a factor in the enjoyment he can derive himself and impart to his sexual partner. The vagina is a potential not an actual space; that is, it distends just enough to accommodate the penis. Hence a very large penis will not create more friction for the man or the woman than a smaller one. Furthermore, penises that are small when flaccid may double in size when erect, whereas penises that are large in the limp state increase less proportionately. In other words, there does not seem to be as much variation in the size of the *erect* penis as had been assumed. The idea that the size of a man's penis is an index of his virility was completely dispelled.[3]

## Types of Human Sexual Inadequacy

Masters and Johnson separate the sexual response system into two interfacing subsystems, the *biophysical* and the *psychosocial*. Severe physiological damage or deficit, such as low levels of hormones, may hinder sexual responses, but such impairments are very rare. Most human beings will respond sexually to appropriate sensory stimulation if their acquired

[3] Some women have voiced disagreement with Masters and Johnson's conclusion about the merits of a large penis. No doubt psychological variables, as well as the purely physiological ones that Masters and Johnson have dealt with, play a part in determining how an individual woman reacts.

psychosocial system does not interfere. In other words, assuming adequate biological endowment and given sensory stimulation such as stroking of the genitalia, it is inevitable that a person will respond sexually when their reactions are unhindered by fear or disgust.

The following types of sexual inadequacy are discussed by Masters and Johnson as being largely psychosocial in origin.

1. **Primary impotence.** The man has never been able to achieve an erection sufficient for successful intercourse, either heterosexual or homosexual.
2. **Secondary impotence.** The man is at present unable to achieve an erection sufficient for successful intercourse, either heterosexual or homosexual, but he has been able to do so at least once in the past.
3. **Premature ejaculation.** The man is unable to inhibit ejaculation long enough for his female partner to have orgasm in 50 percent of their contacts. Masters and Johnson were keenly aware that this definition is highly arbitrary, for women vary widely in the amount of stimulation required for orgasm.[4] In some cases ejaculation occurs without an erection.
4. **Ejaculatory incompetence.** A man with this rare disability cannot ejaculate intravaginally, although erections and intromissions are not problematic.
5. **Dyspareunia.** Intercourse is painful in some way for the man or woman.
6. **Primary orgasmic dysfunction.** The woman has never had an orgasm from either masturbation or intercourse.
7. **Situational orgasmic dysfunction.** The woman is unable to have orgasms in particular situations. She may, for example, climax easily when on vacations but never at home.
8. **Vaginismus.** The outer third of the vaginal barrel is subject to involuntary spastic contractions, often making the insertion of the penis or even a finger impossible.

[4] The draft version of DSM-III tries to eliminate this arbitrariness by defining the disorder as that of a man who wishes ejaculation to occur less quickly but is often unable to maintain control.

## Etiology of Human Sexual Inadequacy

Masters and Johnson found in the backgrounds of the individuals they examined a number of untoward attitudes and events that they consider responsible for the development of sexual problems. The two researchers distinguish *historically* relevant factors and two *currently* relevant variables that they believe underlie the *maintenance* of all human sexual inadequacies (Figure 11.3). Sexual disorders are maintained because during intercourse one or both of the participants either adopt a *spectator role* or have crippling *fears about performance*. These two attitudes focus undue attention on performance rather than allowing a relatively passive and uncritical acceptance of sexual stimulation, which if unimpeded leads naturally to sexual enjoyment, including orgasm. As Masters and Johnson have stated, "fear of inadequacy is the greatest known deterrent to effective sexual functioning, simply because it so completely distracts the fearful individual from his or her natural responsivity by blocking reception of sexual stimuli . . ." (1970, pp. 12–13). People adopt the spectator role and are fearful about performance because of the unfortunate attitudes instilled by their upbringing and the difficult experiences of earlier years. It should be noted, however, that a great many individuals have unfortunate attitudes and experiences *without* developing sexual dysfunctions. Other factors must also be important in determining whether a given individual develops a sexual problem.

### Historical factors

Religious Orthodoxy One or both partners may have negative attitudes toward sex because they have been brought up with strict religious beliefs that denigrate sexual enjoyment. For example,

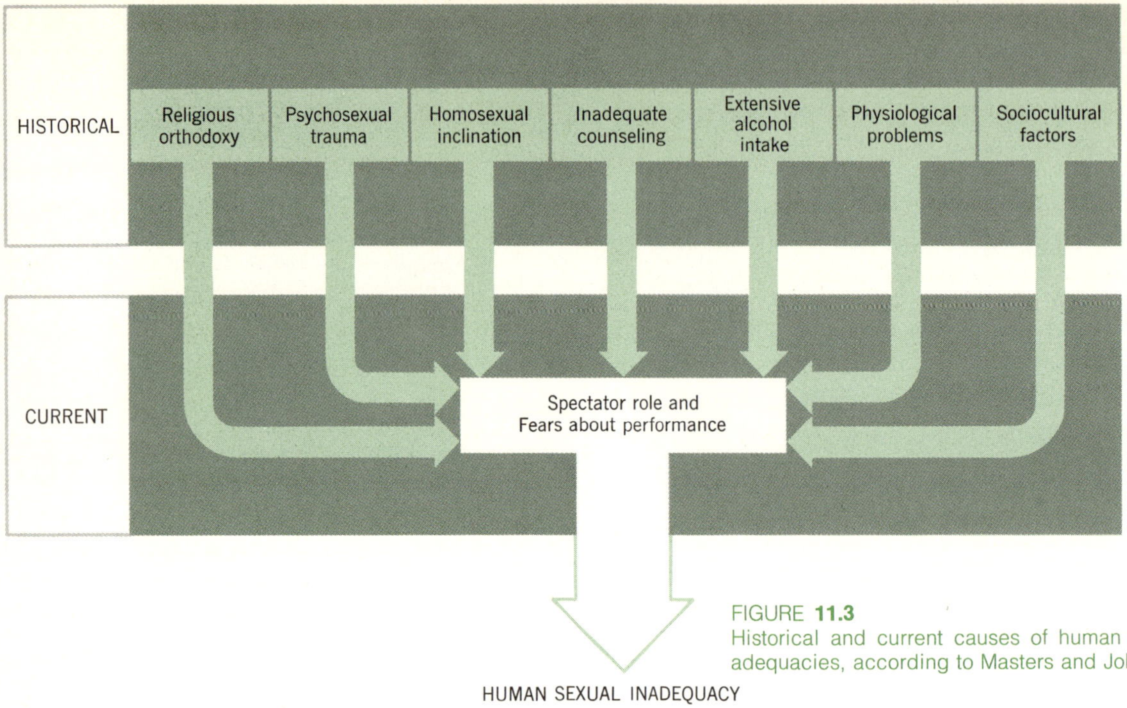


FIGURE **11.3**
Historical and current causes of human sexual inadequacies, according to Masters and Johnson.

a woman with vaginismus who was interviewed by Masters and Johnson had been

> *. . . taught that almost any form of physical expression might be suspect of objectionable sexual connotations. . . . She was prohibited when bathing from looking at her own breasts either directly or from reflection in the mirror for fear that unhealthy sexual thoughts might be stimulated by visual examination of her own body. Discussion with a sibling of such subjects as menstruation, conception, contraception, or sexual functioning were taboo. . . . Mrs. A. entered marriage without a single word of advice, warning, or even good cheer from her family relative to marital sexual expression. The only direction offered by her religious advisor relative to sexual behavior was that coital connection was only to be endured if conception was desired (p 254).*

Psychosexual Trauma Some patients trace their fears of sexual contact to particularly frightening or degrading experiences during initial sexual exposures. One young man had been assured by a prostitute that "He would never be able to get the job done for any woman—if he couldn't get it done here and now with a pro." One woman could date her vaginismus to a gang rape from which she suffered severe physical and psychological damage.

Homosexual Inclinations Impotent men and inorgasmic women may be unable to enjoy heterosexual relations because they have homosexual inclinations.

Inadequate Counseling Bad advice from professional workers may create or exacerbate sexual inadequacies. Some men were told by physicians that secondary impotence is incurable, others that it is a natural part of the aging process. A few had been warned by clergymen that their impotence was God's punishment for sins.

Excessive Intake of Alcohol Secondary impotence sometimes begins with undue concern about a normal reduction in sexual responsiveness brought on by excessive drinking. In the typical pattern suggested by Masters and Johnson, a man who works very hard may develop a habit of drinking a good deal. Large amounts of alcohol are known to interfere with erections, while at the same time, ironically, lowering inhibitions. Having drunk too much, the man may find that no erection develops. Instead of attributing his lack of sexual arousal to his drinking, however, he begins to ruminate. Fear accumulates, and after a number of failures he may become secondarily impotent. The wife often attempts to be understanding and supportive of the husband. He, for any number of reasons, interprets this solicitude as further questioning of his masculinity. Or the wife, concerned that she may no longer be sexually attractive to her husband, pushes for sexual encounters, aggravating the situation. Soon she may refrain from any physical contact whatsoever, even affectionate hugs and kisses, for fear that the husband will interpret this as a demand for intercourse. The communication of the couple worsens, aggravating the man's anxiety and setting a pattern difficult to reverse without professional assistance.

Vaginismus As yet another example of the intimate relation between the sexual reactions of the two partners, Masters and Johnson found that some men develop secondary impotence because of the partner's vaginismus.

Physiological Causes Some of the disorders are attributable to physical damage. Clitoral or vaginal infections, torn ligaments in the pelvic region, scarred tissue at the vaginal opening from incisions made during childbirth (episiotomies), and—especially in older, postmenopausal women—insufficient lubrication of the vagina may make intercourse painful for women. Infection of the glans of the penis, which can develop when it is not kept clean, may make intercourse painful for men. A minority of men with secondary impotence are found to suffer from metabolic problems of diabetes, and in some cases sexual arousal is dulled by the use of certain tranquilizers.[5]

Sociocultural Factors Especially in female dysfunctions, cultural biases play a role. "Sociocultural influence more often than not places woman in a position in which she must adapt, sublimate, inhibit, or even distort her natural capacity to function sexually in order to fulfill her genetically assigned role. Herein lies a major source of woman's sexual dysfunction" (p. 218). The man has the blessing of society to develop sexual expressiveness, but the woman, at least until recently, has not had this freedom, and her needs have often been ignored. Compounding her difficulties is the fact that she does not require sexual arousal in order to function adequately as a partner during sexual intercourse.

According to laboratory studies reported in *Human Sexual Response,* women seem capable of more sustained and more frequent sexual arousal than men, which makes the neglect of their sexuality particularly ironic.

### Evaluation

As Masters and Johnson caution, these factors are *hypothesized* to be the reasons why, during intercourse, individuals assume a spectator role and have crippling fears about performance. The data are based entirely on the retrospective reporting of the couples who were treated at the foundation between 1959 and 1969. As already indicated, such data are notoriously open to bias and distortion. At the same time there are at present no better sources of information.

But the Masters and Johnson data, and the interpretation of them, do present other problems. First, their 1966 book, *Human Sexual Response,* contains very few actual measurements. Although many ingenious physiological measures

[5] Spinal cord lesions, depending on how complete they are and where they are located, may cause paralysis and loss of sensation either in the legs (paraplegia) or in both arms and legs (quadraplegia). A person who cannot move his or her arms and legs is sometimes considered incapable of sexual excitement. This is not so. A recent review by Higgins (in press) documents erections and ejaculations in a number of paralyzed men.

were taken, no polygraph tracings and few actual numbers are provided. Second, Masters and Johnson assert that sexual arousal will develop naturally if the "biophysical system" is adequate and if the "psychosocial system" is not clouded by negative attitudes and fears. But it can be argued that human beings must *learn* to be sexual, that is, must learn to respond sexually to some of the infinite variety of events around them. This view of human sexuality has been elaborated on by Gagnon and Simon (1973; Gagnon, 1977). Their basic thesis is that people must be *taught* to be sexually aroused by breasts, penises, various odors, and even the sensations that are felt when the genitals are handled. To put it more graphically, "There is no automatic connection between touching a woman's breasts and blood flow into the genitals" (Gagnon, 1977, p. 118). In fact, in many societies the breast is considered sexually neutral. Much as the scientist sees what he or she has learned to see (see Chapter 1), we may come to endow portions of our world with sexual meanings. Gagnon and Simon, then, would say that learned and stored in the "psychosocial system" discussed by Masters and Johnson are not only the fears and misconceptions that people acquire with experience but also the more positive aspects of sexuality.

## Summary

This chapter has dealt with unconventional sexual behavior and human sexual inadequacy. The first category includes "sexual deviations" characterized either by unusual choice of object—fetishism, transvestism, transsexualism, incest, and pedophilia; or by unconventional activities—voyeurism, exhibitionism, rape, sadism, and masochism. Psychoanalytic theories tend to explain virtually all this behavior as a defense against anxiety aroused by the idea of engaging in conventional heterosexual intercourse. Learning theorists have considered sexual arousal to be conditioned to stimuli that happen to be present during early erotic experiences. Few data support either of these hypotheses. Moreover, the fact that what is considered unacceptable or unconventional behavior often depends on cultural definitions raises the question whether some of these activities should be categorized as abnormal.

The clinical research of Masters and Johnson has dealt with problems that interfere with the full enjoyment of conventional sexual relations. Their basic hypothesis holds that virtually all disorders such as impotence and frigidity are maintained because the individual assumes a spectator role and has fears about performance. The etiology of these inadequacies was sought in excessively puritanical religious beliefs, earlier unpleasant sexual experiences, misinformation, and other factors in the individual's background.

# chapter 12

## HOMOSEXUALITY



In the first edition of this textbook, we began this chapter by observing that the decision to include homosexuality was difficult, for we do not believe such behavior should be regarded as psychopathological. Whether to retain the chapter in this second edition was even more troubling. We again have opted to include the topic because we believe that students of abnormal psychology should be provided the opportunity to reflect on the history and nature of an aspect of human sexuality that has generally been viewed as a sign of emotional disturbance.

Imagine for a moment that you are an anxious person and that being anxious is against the law. You must try to hide your fears from others. Your own home may be a safe place to feel anxious, but a public display of apprehension can lead to arrest or at least to social ostracism. At work one day an associate looks at you suspiciously and says, "That's funny. For a crazy moment there I thought you were anxious." "Heck no," you exclaim a bit too loudly, "*not me*!" You begin to wonder if your fellow worker will report his suspicions to your boss. If he does, your boss may inform the police, or will at least change your job to one that requires less contact with customers, especially with those who have children.

There are many parallels between the way an anxious person is treated in this seemingly improbable fantasy and the current plight of homosexuals. In the United States alone it is estimated that at least four million people are predominantly homosexual. If each such individual makes an average of two contacts per week, nearly a quarter of a billion homosexual acts are engaged in each year in this country. Millions of other people who are bisexual are involved in homosexual activity from time to time (Gebhard,

1972). In this chapter we shall examine the extent and nature of homosexual behavior, its legal status, and some of the consequences of the attitudes that most citizens harbor toward homosexuality.

Sexual attraction among members of the same sex has been amply documented throughout recorded history as well as in many different cultures. In many societies homosexual practices have been suppressed by harsh laws, and indeed in most states of contemporary America laws exist by which homosexuals can be arrested and imprisoned, although not all these statutes are rigidly enforced. Never have societal sanctions eliminated homosexuality, nor does it seem likely that they ever will. The widespread prevalence of homosexuality, even though such practices are often threatened by punishment, has led some workers to believe that this aspect of sexuality is, in some important way, part of human nature.

Ford and Beach's (1951) survey of the anthropological literature suggests that forty-nine out of seventy-six primitive societies on which fairly reliable data were available considered some form of homosexual activity quite normal and acceptable, although seldom sanctioning such sexual behavior as desirable for large numbers of the community. One North African tribe considered it odd for a man not to have sexual affairs with both women and other men. Other tribes have believed that sodomy, so named for its prevalence in the "sinful" biblical city of Sodom, makes young men strong. Some North American Indians recognized and tolerated groups of exclusively homosexual men and women within their predominantly heterosexual cultures.

Homosexual love flourished and was celebrated in ancient Greece. It is believed that the Greeks regarded such love as especially noble and beautiful. The bodies of young male athletes were particularly admired. An older man was often a mentor to a younger one, providing advice, tutelage, and a substantial measure of sexual gratification. Those who have read Plato's *Symposium* will remember that it contains an endorsement of homosexual love by Greece's leading philosophers.

But homosexuality, like heterosexuality, has not always been associated with the noblest impulses. In early imperial Rome it was common and fashionable but was not held in esteem. In fact, homosexual acts took their place among the debaucheries and tortures that were practiced.

> *Nero's disgusting and cruel orgies, in which men and women suffered equally, reached the depths of squalor. He had Sporus, his favourite, castrated, after which he went through all the ceremonies of marriage and made the unfortunate youth his "wife"* (*West, 1967, p. 25*).

Thus the widespread desire of some human beings to be sexually intimate with members of their own sex has been vilified or dignified depending on the particular cultural mores. Other historical figures are understood to have loved members of their own sex. The erotic poetry of Virgil and Horace was often about men. Michelangelo addressed love sonnets to a young man, as did Shakespeare. Julius Caesar was regarded as "every man's woman." And serious commitments to homosexuality are to be found as well in the lives of Marlowe, Tchaikovsky, Whitman, Proust, and Wilde (Magee, 1966). All and all, there is nothing new or rare about homosexuality (see Box 12.1).

## BOX 12.1 Homophobia and Exclusive Homosexuality

Those who argue that heterosexuality is normal and homosexuality abnormal often make the statement that exclusive homosexuality is unknown in the animal kingdom when members of the opposite sex are available. It is also proposed that heterosexual contacts are maximized in all species so that adequate reproduction can take place. Moreover, it is apparently the case that in no human culture has exclusive homosexuality been encouraged for sizable numbers of people.

These arguments are cogent, but they overlook one essential characteristic of human sexuality, namely that *bisexuality is more prevalent than exclusive homosexuality*. Churchill (1967) has made the provocative suggestion that exclusive homosexuality may well be encouraged by antihomosexual societies such as our own. Because sexual contacts between members of the same sex are so severely condemned, some bisexuals may be forced into making a choice and *thereby* become committed to contacts with members of their own sex rather than continuing to find sexual relationships with members of both sexes meaningful. What some call "homophobia" (Weinberg, 1972) may actually help create exclusive homosexuality.

# Survey Data on Homosexuality

## The Kinsey Surveys

The fact that homosexuality can be mentioned in most social settings without anyone's becoming apoplectic reflects a considerable and fairly recent liberalization of attitude toward at least the discussion of this aspect of sexuality. Without question the pioneering, brave work of Alfred Kinsey and his co-workers in the 1940s and 1950s under the auspices of the Institute of Sex Research contributed importantly to lifting the

Alfred C. Kinsey, renowned Indiana University biologist. His courageous explorations of sexual practices in the United States helped establish the respectability of scientific sex research in this country.

taboos on sex research and increased considerably our knowledge of human sexuality.

A biologist by training, Kinsey was appalled at the lack of even minimally reliable information on American sexual practices. He was interested in removing the taboos about the scientific study of sexuality and in instigating dispassionate research into its bases and very nature. He rightly pointed out that it is difficult to understand the nature or significance of any aspect of human behavior until we have some firm idea of its prevalence and patterning.

Kinsey trained sensitive people to elicit self-reports on present and past sexual practices by means of a comprehensive interview and then sent them out to see as many members of a given social group as would agree to talk to them. The groups were chosen to achieve a wide geographic, economic, and socioreligious distribution. For example, a Kinsey interview team would arrange to speak to an Elk Lodge, explaining the scientific purposes of the project and the careful safeguards that would be taken to ensure confidentiality. Interviews were then scheduled with those present who agreed to donate their time and reveal intimate information about themselves to total strangers. Indeed, it seems likely, since the interviews were conducted in the 1940s, that many who participated had never openly discussed with another human being such topics as masturbation, premarital intercourse, and homosexual acts.

Self-reporting is of course open to many sources of bias, such as a desire to appear normal and to avoid disapproval. And all self-reports are subject to the distortions that time may impose on memory. But the Kinsey data have remained the most comprehensive information on American sexual customs. The skills of the interviewers, who were reassuringly matter-of-fact when asking about intimate details of the participants' lives, argue in favor of taking the information seriously until better data are collected. The findings of other more limited surveys of sexual behavior, both here and abroad, have not been dissimilar to Kinsey's (Gebhard, 1972; Gagnon, 1977).

### The Kinsey study on men

Until Kinsey's first survey (Kinsey, Pomeroy, and Martin, 1948) very little was known about the incidence of homosexuality. The evidence collected very much surprised America, for many of the men in the sample were found to be neither exclusively heterosexual nor exclusively homosexual. Indeed, Kinsey concluded that it was fruitless to speak in terms of "the homosexual" and "the heterosexual." He came to think of sexuality as a continuum between them, where many of us fall, and reported instead relative frequencies of each kind of sexual response. Figure 12.1 shows graphically the heterosexual-homosexual rating scale devised by the Kinsey group (see also Box. 12.2).

The report on men emphasizes objective descriptions. The meaning that various sexual activities had for the respondents was completely ignored. As a biologist Kinsey was not used to concerning himself with how the objects of a study *felt* about what they were doing. Thus the information collected is restricted to whether the male had performed a particular sexual act. He

FIGURE **12.1**
Kinsey rating scale for heterosexuality-homosexuality: O, entirely heterosexual; 1, largely heterosexual, but with incidental homosexual history; 2, largely heterosexual, but with a distinct homosexual history; 3, equally heterosexual and homosexual; 4, largely homosexual, but with distinct heterosexual history; 5, largely homosexual, but with incidental heterosexual history; 6, entirely homosexual.

## Box **12.2** Sexual Preference and Our Understanding of Human Behavior

The Kinsey reports documented for the first time that a great many men and women have homosexual feelings at various times in their lives. So it became less and less defensible to divide people up into two mutually exclusive categories based on the gender of their sexual partners. A continuum, like that pictured in Figure 12.1, seemed more appropriate. But, as Gagnon has pointed out, the very fact that homosexuality and heterosexuality appear at opposite ends of Kinsey's continuum reveals an *assumption* that human behavior will be better understood if individuals are placed somewhere on a continuum of sexual preference. An infinite array of characteristics might have anchored Kinsey's scale:

*In United States culture the gender of one's sexual partner is crucial, and therefore leads to a key label; however, let us think of a society where gender does not matter, but where it is very important what emotions one feels during sex. People would then divide up by the kind of* feeler *that they are . . . love-feelers or lust-feelers* (*the former would obviously be "better" people*)*. In our studies we would find that there are many love-feelers in the society and only just a few lust-feelers; in the middle we would find bi-feelers. Soon we would have theories about why people felt lust* (*and not love*)*; their childhoods would be studied; the fact that they were not able to feel correctly would tell us that they were immature, neurotic, perhaps even criminal.* (*From* Human Sexualities, *p. 236. Copyright © 1977, by Scott, Foresman and Company. Reprinted by permission.*)

Gagnon questions whether Western society's long-held concern with sexual orientation is a useful one. Is our understanding of Michelangelo's genius furthered by our knowing that he had strong homosexual interests? Many have remarked that his sensitive sculpture "David" is a manifestation of his homosexuality, that his brilliant representation of a young man came from his sexual love for men and for the person who was the model for the sculpture. Are we then to "explain" the beauty of the Sistine Chapel in a similar fashion?

was not asked whether he enjoyed it or was ashamed of it, and what it really meant to him.

Kinsey's findings on homosexuality in men, based on interviews with 5300 white males, can be summarized as follows.

1. Thirty-seven percent of men have experienced homosexual orgasm at some time since the onset of adolescence.[1]
2. An additional 13 percent have felt homosexual urges without acting upon them.
3. Of the males who remain bachelors until thirty-five, 50 percent have had homosexual experience to the point of orgasm since the onset of adolescence.
4. Twenty-five percent of men have more than incidental homosexual experiences between the ages of sixteen and fifty-five (these men would rate between 2 and 6 on the Kinsey scale).
5. Eighteen percent of men have at least as much of the homosexual as the heterosexual in their histories (ratings, 3, 4, 5, and 6) for at least three years between the ages of sixteen and fifty-five.
6. Ten percent are almost exclusively homosexual (ratings 5 and 6) for at least three years between the ages of sixteen and fifty-five.
7. Four percent are exclusively homosexual throughout their lives, after the onset of adolescence.
8. Homosexuality is found among all social and occupational groups.

### The Kinsey study on women

While collecting and writing up the data on male sexual behavior, Kinsey, Pomeroy, Martin, and Gebhard (1953) were also working on a similar report on female sexuality. Some improvements were made, one being to add to the interview questions about the emotions aroused by overt sexual acts and the woman's attitudes toward her behavior.

The interviews of 5940 white women indicated a much lower incidence of homosexuality than that found among the men surveyed in the 1948 report. Whereas 37 percent of men had experienced homosexual orgasm after the onset of adolescence, the figure for women was 13 percent. Furthermore, only about 3 percent of the women had been primarily or exclusively homosexual at any given age period, compared with a figure of 10 percent for men. The pattern was also different; whereas men were often highly promiscuous, 71 percent of the women who made homosexual contacts restricted them to a single partner or two.

[1] This widely cited figure may have been inflated by the inclusion of a disproportionately large number of men who had been imprisoned. Homosexual encounters are higher among prisoners than in the general population. A more accurate estimate might be several percentage points less (Gagnon, 1977). But this sampling problem does not undermine the import of this and other findings: homosexual feelings and behavior are not confined to a small and deviant segment of the population.

*"Well, I'm sure Dr. Kinsey never spoke to anyone in Upper Montclair."*

### Methodological problems in the Kinsey data

Because of their controversial nature, the Kinsey reports received searching and critical evaluations. It should be stated at the outset, however, that Kinsey himself was very much surprised by the high incidence of homosexuality, especially by that among men. It seems unlikely that the investigators found the amount of sexual contact among members of the same sex that they did because they were looking for it.

Problems in the Interview Terman (1948) pointed out that the exact wording of each question of the standard interview was not published, and we know that each interviewer was free to rephrase and probe at his own discretion, depending on what he perceived the requirements at the moment to be. We know from numerous other sources that interviewers may not produce comparable data when such innovation is allowed. Moreover, all interviewers for both studies were male. We know from other studies that the sex of the interviewer is an important variable in what the respondent reports, especially if the interview pertains to sex. More sexual experiences are reported when interviewer and respondent are of the same gender (Walters, Shurley, and Parsons, 1962).

Some subjects may have been gently coerced into falsely admitting to certain activities. Terman points out, for instance, that the interviewer was instructed to convey the assumption that a given practice had been engaged in unless the respondent strongly denied it. In one method employed, "proving the answer" (Kinsey et al., 1948, p. 55), the interviewer pretends that he has misunderstood a negative reply and asks additional questions as though the original answer had been in the affirmative, for example, "Yes, I know you have never done that, but how old were you the *first time* you did it?"

Another possibility is that some respondents might have simply lied. Kinsey was clearly aware of this problem and believed that he had overcome it through the anonymity of the interview and the generally trusting atmosphere that the highly skilled and sensitive interviewers are said to have created. But a lower-class male respondent might find it easier to admit to premarital coitus than to frequent masturbation. Sociological studies reveal that classes differ in their opinion of what is acceptable sexual behavior. The fact that lower-class males reported less masturbation than college-educated men may therefore not be a completely reliable indication of the actual frequencies.

Sampling Problems Through lectures and other public relations efforts, various organizations throughout the country were asked to participate, and efforts were made to persuade everyone at a given meeting to sign up. Not every member of a given group was in attendance at that recruitment meeting, however. The purpose of the meeting had been announced in advance, and we cannot know anything about people who did not attend even this session. We do know that in the male sample, for instance, sixty-two groups yielded 100 percent samples, and that the members of forty-two of these groups had generally attended college. This statistic strongly suggests greater willingness among men who have attended college to participate in a study involving potential embarrassment. But the manner in which the data were reported precludes an assessment of the effects of this greater willingness of better-educated groups to participate. Perhaps the most glaring sampling deficiency was the intentional exclusion of nonwhites. Properly speaking, then, both reports refer to white Americans.

The Generality of the Data Terman (1948) also examined several of Kinsey's tables very carefully to determine the numbers of respondents on which some of the sweeping conclusions about men were based. Thus the generalization already mentioned, that among men who remained unmarried until age thirty-five, 50 percent have had homosexual orgasm, is in fact based on the responses of fewer than 200 individuals.

### Scientific and social implications

In view of the past and continuing intolerance of

homosexuality in a considerable portion of American society, Kinsey's findings on the social realities of this form of sexual expression are of special interest. Unless we wish to regard half of American men as abnormal, it is difficult to entertain the notion that homosexuality is, by itself, evidence of psychopathology. Some homosexuals may be disturbed, but in view of the pressures society imposes on them, it seems possible that their emotional problems stem from society's reactions rather than that emotional disturbance preceded or caused their homosexuality.

Kinsey believed that the prevalence of homosexuality in ancient Greek civilization, coupled with the wide diversity of Americans who his investigation determined have homosexual experiences, argues in favor of a conception of the human being as eminently conditionable to respond to erotic stimulation from the same sex, the opposite sex, or both. According to this theory, human beings are neither inherently homosexual nor inherently heterosexual. Rather they are inherently sexual, with the direction of attraction being determined importantly or entirely by circumstance. If there is one aspect to being human that psychologists have established without doubt, it is our fantastic capacity to change as a function of experience. Whatever else we may be, we are certainly organisms who can learn a wide variety of things. Different people may, through learning, find a tremendous variety of human characteristics sexually arousing.

> *Exclusive preferences and patterns of behavior, heterosexual or homosexual, come only with experience or as a result of social pressures which tend to force an individual into an exclusive pattern of one or the other sort. Psychologists and psychiatrists, reflecting the mores of the culture in which they have been raised, have spent a good deal of time trying to explain the origins of homosexual activity; but considering the physiology of sexual responses and the mammalian background of human behavior, it is not so difficult to explain why a human animal does a particular thing sexually. It is more difficult to explain why each and every individual is not involved in every type of sexual activity (Kinsey et al., 1953, p. 451).*

## A Survey of Gay Groups

Since publication of the two Kinsey volumes, homosexual behavior has been the subject of several other investigations. Saghir and his colleagues (Saghir and Robins, 1969; Saghir, Robins, and Walbran, 1969) conducted interviews with male and female members of gay groups. To be included in the samples, people had to be experienced homosexually and could never have been hospitalized in a psychiatric setting or arrested for sexual offense. Both samples, then, were admittedly not truly representative of homosexuals in general—for all the men and women had "come out of the closet," at least to the extent of joining a homosexual organization. They tended also to be of relatively high socioeconomic class.

Information was gathered on a number of variables, including frequency of masturbation, degree of sexual arousal, extent and nature of sexual behavior, and nature of personal relationships. The major findings can be summarized as follows.

1. The male homosexuals began masturbating much earlier than the females and continued to do so much more often, even when involved in an active homosexual relationship.
2. Both groups reported definite sexual arousal to people of the same gender at a very early age, usually before adolescence.
3. The male homosexuals, by the end of adolescence (defined as age nineteen), were engaging in overt homosexual behavior to a significantly greater extent than the females.
4. A given male or female tended to alternate

between "active" and "passive" roles in homosexual relationships.

5. The frequency of homosexual contacts in adulthood was much higher for the men.
6. The men were much more "promiscuous" than the women, having fewer long-term relationships with a single lover and, even when involved in an ongoing relationship, caring little about fidelity.
7. The males engaged in much more oral-genital contact (fellatio) than the females, who tended to favor manual stimulation of the clitoris.
8. Both groups engaged in periodic sexual activity with members of the opposite sex during adolescence, but in adulthood they lost interest in heterosexual encounters.

These findings are revealing in a number of ways. First, a very early onset of homosexual interests, typically before physical maturity, was reported. Second, the men seemed much more "genital" and explicitly sexual in their homosexuality. Third, the men enjoyed many "one-night stands," whereas the women tended to opt for long-term relationships, which, moreover, were not as explicitly sexual as the men's.

Perhaps the most significant conclusion to be drawn by Saghir and his colleagues was that ". . . when it comes to sexual behavior homosexual men are more like heterosexual men (or the stereotype) and homosexual women are more like heterosexual women (or the stereotype)" (Saghir, Robins, and Walbran, 1969, p. 228). A study of factors underlying the choice of a same-sexed person as a sexual partner will, by implication, tell us less about male and female homosexuality than will a consideration of how people of both sexes are sexualized and socialized in our society.

With these survey data as background, we turn now to an examination of several theories on homosexuality—psychoanalytic, learning, physiological, and sociological.

## Theories of Homosexuality and Related Research

The theorizing about and search for factors that contribute to a person's becoming homosexual have been more extensive and active than any probing into the sources of heterosexuality. We know as little about how people become heterosexual as we do about why they come to prefer same-sexed partners. There is a usually unspoken belief that human beings will become heterosexual if only nothing "bad" interferes.

> *Both folklore and psychoanalytic theory assert that heterosexuality is the necessary outcome of undamaged socialization. Alternative sexual outcomes are read as fixations, phobias, perversions, errors in learning. . . .* [*The therapies adopted to eliminate homosexual behavior imply*] *that if we only reduce the frequency of the unconventional behaviors or preferences, the natural heterosexual pattern will flower like a plant newly moved from the shade to the sun* (Gagnon and Davison, 1974).

As for the research on homosexuality, most of it is flawed by serious methodological problems. Even more damaging are logical errors that make it impossible to learn anything of interest from the research (see Box 12.3, page 315). All human beings are subject to lapses in the clarity of their thinking; this section confirms the simple truth that scientists are only human.

### Psychoanalytic Theory

A review of psychoanalytic theories explaining any form of behavior reveals divergent points of view. The psychoanalytic theories of homosexuality are no exception. Klein and her colleagues (1952) and Bergler (1957) suggest that another man's penis is desirable because it represents the breast to the orally fixated male homosexual. The basic premise of most psychoanalytic interpretations of homosexuality, however, can be summed up in one word, *heterophobia,* which means fear of sexual contact with the opposite sex (Bieber et al., 1962; Rado, 1949). This fear is traced back to events in early life. Although Freud suggested that human beings have genetically determined predispositions toward activity, or masculinity, and passivity, or femininity, he did not clarify the formative role of these predispositions. Most of his theorizing on homosexuality treats it as learned behavior.

We have already indicated the importance that Freud and most of his followers attached to the oedipal conflict; how this dilemma of each person's life is resolved is regarded as crucial in determining the direction of sexual preference. In the early years the child is bisexual, responding libidinally to any human contact regardless of that person's gender. Around the age of four, however, the male child begins to note differences between his mother and father. Incestuous wishes come to the fore, the boy child wishing to replace the father in the mother's affections. The gratification of these sexual desires is thwarted, however, by the threat of punishment from the father-rival, the paramount threat being that of castration. The conflict is sometimes increased by seductive behavior on the part of the mother, especially when the marriage is not a happy one. Moreover, the father sometimes withdraws from the mother and child and fails thereby to provide a good model for the son to identify with. If the boy cannot resolve the conflict by repressing his desire for his mother and identifying with his father, he may try to escape from his oedipal conflict by avoiding all sexual contact with women. They come to represent to the maturing young man's unconscious his unresolved incestuous feelings toward his mother. The mother may also contribute to the heterophobia by discouraging masculine assertiveness and heterosexual approaches to girls his own age, thereby keeping her son close to her. As he reaches adulthood, the unresolved conflict may make the young man fantasize that his penis will be injured by insertion into a woman's vagina. The sight of a woman's genitalia, because she is without a penis, can trigger castration anxieties, making his thoughts dwell on the possibility of losing his own penis. The young man can then have sexual relations only with another male, who will not remind him of the threat of castration. Presumably in less severe cases heterophobia renders the man impotent only when he is with women who in some way remind him of his mother. But intercourse may be possible with prostitutes, whom the man sharply differentiates from his mother.

### The Bieber study

This psychoanalytic theory was examined in a well-known study by Bieber and his associates (1962). The case records of 106 homosexual patients and 100 heterosexual control patients who were being seen by 77 New York psychoanalysts in their private practices were made available for the study. In addition to their qualitative, clinical observations, all the analysts were asked to collect certain specific bits of information in the course of their interviews with their patients. Some of the questions asked were the following.

Was the patient the mother's favorite?

Did the mother express affection for the patient? In physical acts such as hugging and kissing?

Does the analyst consider that the mother was seductive in her activities with the patient? Did the patient sleep with the mother? Was there dressing or undressing with the patient?

Did the mother encourage masculine attitudes and activities?

Did the patient consider the father sexually potent?

Did the father encourage masculine attitudes and activities?

Did the patient feel "babied" by the mother?

Did the mother give the patient frequent enemas?

On the basis of the information gathered from these and other questions, Bieber concluded that his study had provided strong support for the psychoanalytic interpretation of homosexuality.

> *A considerable amount of data . . . has been presented as evidence that fear of heterosexuality underlies homosexuality, for example, the frequent fear of disease or injury to the genitals, significantly associated with fear and aversion to female genitalia. . . . The capacity to adapt homosexually is, in a sense, a tribute to man's biosocial resources in the face of thwarted heterosexual goal achievement. Sexual gratification is not renounced; instead, fears and inhibitions associated with heterosexuality are circumvented and sexual responsivity with pleasure and excitement to a member of the same sex develops as a pathologic alternative (1962, p. 303).*

Particular importance was placed on the "close-binding intimate" mother, who "exerted an unhealthy influence on her son through preferential treatment and seductiveness on the one hand and inhibiting, over-controlling attitudes on the other. In many instances, the son was the most significant individual in her life and the husband was usually replaced by the son as her love object" (p. 47). The most common behavioral pattern among the fathers of homosexual patients was detachment and hostility. Although not all the homosexual patients had such parents, "We are led to believe that . . . maternal close-binding intimacy and paternal detachment-hostility is the 'classic' pattern and most conducive to promoting homosexuality . . . in the son" (p. 144)." . . . the chances appear to be high that any son exposed to this parental combination will become homosexual or develop severe homosexual problems" (p. 172).

Bieber's study is widely cited as proof of the validity of psychoanalytic theory in explaining male homosexuality. (As is typical in Freud's writing, short shrift is given to female sexuality.) But the way in which the investigation was conducted presents a few problems.

1. Those who collected the data were psychoanalysts, already biased in favor of the psychoanalytic theory. "We assumed that the dominant sexual pattern of the adult is the adaptive consequence of life experiences interpenetrating with a basic biological tendency toward heterosexuality" (p. 28). That is, the basic outlines of the theory had been accepted before any of the data were collected.
2. To obtain answers to the questions, a high degree of inference was necessary on the part of the analyst.
3. Many of the questions required the patient to think back over a number of years for answers.
4. All the homosexuals had sought psychoanalytic treatment. They are therefore representative neither of homosexuals who undergo other forms of psychotherapy nor of homosexuals en masse, most of whom are not in therapy of any kind.

Perhaps because of these obvious difficulties, workers who already find psychoanalytic theorizing problematic question whether the family backgrounds of homosexuals are as Bieber found them. But a replication of the Bieber study on homosexuals not undergoing therapy might obtain important information on the etiology of male homosexuality. Such a study has been reported.

### A replication of Bieber's study

Evans (1969) adapted the questions used by the psychoanalysts in the Bieber study to construct a twenty-seven-item questionnaire. Instead of having therapists rate their patients, he recruited male subjects from a nonpatient population of homosexuals and heterosexuals. In the context of a study on cardiovascular disease, he had 43 homosexuals (all members of a Los Angeles homosexual organization) and 142 heterosexuals report on their recollections of childhood. In addition to answering the twenty-seven questions, the homosexual subjects rated themselves on the Kinsey scale and completed a short "sexual identification" questionnaire designed to determine the extent to which they regarded themselves as masculine or feminine.

Of the twenty-seven items on the questionnaire, twenty-four discriminated very strongly between the male homosexuals and heterosexuals. And in every instance Bieber's findings were confirmed.

> *Specifically in retrospect, the homosexuals more often described themselves as frail or clumsy as children and less often as athletic. More of them were fearful of physical injury, avoided physical fights, played with girls and were loners who seldom played baseball and other competitive games. Their mothers more often were considered puritanical, cold toward men, insisted on being the center of the son's attention, made him her confidant, were "seductive" toward him, allied with him against the father, openly preferred him to the father, interfered with his heterosexual activities during adolescence, discouraged masculine attitudes, and encouraged feminine ones. The fathers of the homosexuals were retrospectively considered as less likely to encourage masculine attitudes and activities. . . . [The subjects] spent little time with their fathers, were often aware of hating him and afraid he might physically harm them, less often were the father's favorite, felt less accepted by him, and in turn less frequently accepted or respected the father. Unlike Bieber's patients, these homosexuals were no different from the heterosexuals in amount of time they estimated their parents spent together or in the interests shared by their parents (Evans, 1969, pp. 130, 133).*

Another outcome is of interest: 95 percent of the subjects considered themselves as moderately or strongly masculine, consistent with the opinions of the Bieber analysts, who rated only 2 percent of their homosexual patients markedly effeminate.

Evans cautions against assigning the various child-rearing factors etiological significance, for the research methodology of the study does not allow definite cause-effect inferences to be drawn. The study was also a retrospective one, with the usual problems of recalling past happenings and attitudes.[2] Evans calls attention to this point and urges that prospective studies be done.

And yet the differences between heterosexuals and homosexuals are remarkably similar to those revealed by the Bieber study, done several years earlier in an entirely different part of the country and with men who were in psychoanalytic therapy. The serious scientist cannot dismiss the findings of the Bieber and the Evans studies, but questions can be raised about what such data mean (see Box 12.3).

## Learning Theory

Interestingly enough, one of the most widely known learning accounts of homosexual behavior comes not from experimental psychologists but from the Kinsey group, whose speculations on the role of conditioning in the development of sexual preferences have already been mentioned. They see the human organism as neither intrinsically heterosexual nor intrinsically homosexual, but responsive to stimuli from both sexes. Sexual preference is considered to be entirely a

[2] The reports of homosexuals might also have been biased by their reading of the popular and scientific literature on the topic. Homosexuals tend to be more thoughtful and more knowledgeable about their sexuality than are people of conventional orientation. "Unlike the young heterosexual, who can drift into adulthood, sex, marriage, and children with scarcely a thought, a homosexual preference requires a fairly high level of personal and emotional self-consciousness about sexuality" (Gagnon, 1977, p. 245).

## BOX **12.3** Do Differences Imply Pathology?

The theories and studies reviewed in this section have to do with differences in the rearing, heredity, and hormones of homosexuals and heterosexuals. The implication is that differences between the two groups constitute evidence that homosexuality is disordered and abnormal. But such differences cannot be considered pathological unless the assumption is made beforehand that homosexuality is pathological. Nor can they be considered to cause pathology unless pathology has been assumed!

Let us take an analogous situation. Suppose we found that women who are now good golfers had as children attended public schools more often than did women who are poor golfers. Suppose also that the difference in their golfing ability is the only consistent one between the two groups. Under what circumstances would we conclude that childhood experiences in private schools are pathogenic, causing pathology or illness? The answer is simple: going to a private school is pathogenic if its outcome, being a poor golfer, has already been judged pathological. If we do not make this a priori judgment, we cannot talk of a difference between two groups as indicative of pathology in one of the groups, and we cannot regard the presumed cause a pathogenic one. The most we can say is that the two groups are *different* from each other.

This logic can be applied to Bieber's widely cited study.

> . . . *Does the finding that male homosexuals have similar child-rearing experiences different from [those of] male heterosexuals demonstrate pathology? My answer is no. One cannot attach a pathogenic label to a pattern of child rearing unless one a priori labels the adult behavior pattern as pathological. For example, Bieber et al. found that what they called a "close-binding intimate mother" was present much more often in the life histories of the male homosexual patients than [in those of] the heterosexual controls. . . . What is wrong with such a mother unless you happen to find her in the background of people whose current behavior you judge beforehand to be pathological?* (Davison, 1976, p. 159).

function of conditioning experiences, with neither kind of behavior regarded as normal or abnormal.

More recently, Feldman and MacCulloch (1971) have proposed a theory that incorporates both physiological and learning elements. They distinguish between primary and secondary homosexuals, the first group having no history of heterosexual arousal or behavior. On the basis of information indicating that sexual behavior in rats can be altered dramatically by injecting hormones into the pregnant mother's uterus,

Feldman and MacCulloch suggest that "there are 'male' and 'female' areas in the human foetal brain which are critically susceptible to circulating levels of male and female hormones" (pp. 168–169). In other words, the brain of the human fetus may be "preset" before birth to foster the development of "masculine" (for example, aggressive) or "feminine" (for example, preference for playing with dolls) behavior in early childhood. If the actual biological gender of the child is male, and if his brain has been affected by female hormones while in the womb, he will in childhood tend to behave in a feminine way, especially if his parents encourage feminine behavior. Although the predisposition supplied by the female hormones will not inevitably make him a homosexual, it is hypothesized that they lean him that way. He may later be readily conditioned into forming homosexual attachments, in which case he is called a primary homosexual.

In contrast, secondary homosexuals are assumed by Feldman and MacCulloch to show conventional development of heterosexual interests into puberty. At some point, however, they have an unpleasant experience with a woman and begin to be afraid of approaching females. They justify their growing fear and avoidance of women by changing their attitudes toward them. Women were previously considered sexually desirable but are now derogated as sexual objects and emotional companions. And sexual attachments to men, which were previously viewed negatively, now become more appealing. The young man experiments. If his experiences are pleasurable, men become even more attractive to him. Having ruled out the possibility of heterosexual outlets, the adolescent or young man, whose sex drive is strong, is eager for sexual encounters of *some* kind. Obviously, the particular subculture in which he finds himself will markedly affect the extent to which homosexual attractions develop.

The Feldman-MacCulloch theory is of interest for several reasons. First, the hypothesis explaining the development of secondary homosexuality closely resembles Bieber's heterophobic theory, although there is no reference to early parent-child relationships or to repression. Perhaps of greater interest is the unsupported assumption about primary homosexuality—that a man who loves another man is more feminine than one who loves women, and that lesbians are more masculine than women who prefer men. Primary homosexuals are in their nonsexual behavior assumed to be prone to act more like a member of the opposite sex. A primary homosexual is likely as a child to have played with dolls and to have been less aggressive than the boy whose brain was not affected in utero by female hormones. As he grows up, he continues to behave in a way that is alien to his own gender, namely by loving members of his own sex, and he becomes a primary homosexual. This view, then, assumes that homosexual behavior develops out of an error in *gender identity,* that is, the sense that each one of us has of being either a man or a woman (see Box 12.4).

Our evaluation of Kinsey's thinking and of that of Feldman and MacCulloch is that the data are far from in. Neither position enjoys the direct support of experimental research. Moreover, any theory that speaks in terms of heterophobia will have to account in some way for the impressive amount of heterosexual interest and activity among both male and female homosexuals, especially during their adolescence (Saghir, Robins, and Walbran, 1969; Saghir and Robins, 1969).

## Physiological Bases of Homosexuality

Not all workers attach as much importance to learning as Kinsey and Bieber did. We have just summarized the views of Feldman and MacCulloch on a possible physiological predisposition for homosexuality. Other work on genetic factors and hormones has been done.

### Genetics of homosexuality

Rosenthal's (1970) review of what little data are available indicates that homosexual tendencies

## BOX 12.4 Gender Identity and Homosexual Preference

Gender identity is the deeply held belief that one is either a man or a woman. Transsexuals, by definition, have a gender identity opposite to their anatomical endowment; to have a penis and at the same time to believe that one is female is to have a gender identity at variance with one's body.

Psychoanalytic theory, and to a degree Feldman and MacCulloch's learning theory, regard male homosexuality as a problem in gender identity: a man can become homosexual because he has not adopted his society's definition of manhood. Making love to a man rather than to a woman is assumed to be possible only for men who do not share a given society's conception of masculinity.

Many theorists and writers dispute whether homosexuals have an inappropriate gender identity. Churchill (1967), for example, refers to the comradeship and homosexual love that existed among many Greek warriors; Plato commented on the military advantages of homosexual relationships, for they seemed to foster great ferocity in battle on the part of men driven to protect their lovers. Is it reasonable to regard a brave soldier as lacking a masculine gender identity?

Moreover, in the Bieber study (1962) only 2 percent of the homosexuals were rated by their analysts as "effeminate"; this finding of masculinity among male homosexuals was replicated in the Evans (1969) study, in which 95 percent of the homosexuals rated themselves as "moderately or strongly masculine." Indeed, in his renowned "Three Contributions to the Theory of Sex" (1905), Freud asserted, "In men, the most perfect psychic manliness may be united with . . . homosexuality."

Many male homosexuals have a firm identification of themselves as men (Silverstein, 1972); the same holds true for lesbians, who usually identify themselves as women (Martin and Lyon, 1972). To be sure, the stereotype of the limp-wristed, lisping "fag" probably contributes to the misconception, or at least overgeneralization, of male homosexuality as feminine behavior. And the stereotype of the "butch" or "dyke" who wears her hair clipped and dresses in tailored clothing similarly fosters the misconception that the lesbian is somehow less of a woman, more of a man. But we must bear in mind that homosexuals grow up in the same cultures as everyone else! They learn that preferring a same-sexed partner implies being less of a man or less of a woman and they may consciously adopt traits of the opposite gender. To explain homosexuality itself as simply an error in gender identity is probably wrong. "Gender roles are not a mold in which we pour our sexuality" (Gagnon, 1977 p. 242).

are probably not inherited. Although a few studies (for example, Kallmann, 1952a,b) report 100 percent concordance rates for homosexuality in identical twins and less than 15 percent concordance for fraternal twins, Kallmann himself was very cautious in the conclusions he drew. Moreover, others have failed to replicate his unusually high concordance rates (for example, Parker, 1964), finding numerous identical twin pairs in which only one member is homosexual. The necessary adoptee studies to determine the concordance rates of homosexuality for identical twins who have been separated from their natural parents at an early age and raised by others have yet to be done.

### Hormonal bases of homosexuality

Probably because homosexual feelings and behavior appear to be so resistant to change—either through therapy or through threat of legal prosecution—many have suggested that homosexuality is caused by some kind of imbalance of sex-related hormones. Testosterone is regarded as crucial to the proper development of all secondary sex characteristics typical of mature men, such as growth of facial hair, deepening of the voice, and, in particular, the enlargement of the testes for production of sperm. Estrogen serves the important function of making a woman what she is physically. The physiologically oriented researchers who first investigated levels of the sex hormones in homosexuals expected them to be lower or imbalanced. Loraine and his colleagues (1971) did in fact find that the urine of homosexual men contained less testosterone than that of heterosexual men. In lesbians urinary levels of testosterone were higher, those of estrogen lower, than in heterosexual women.

Findings consistent with those of Loraine and his colleagues were reported by another group led by Kolodny (1971). They determined the levels of testosterone in the blood and the nature and quantity of sperm in young, physically healthy male homosexuals, comparing them with those of male heterosexuals. Exclusive and near-exclusive homosexuals had lower levels of plasma testosterone as well as markedly lower sperm counts and more misshaped sperm than did the controls.

Recent attempts to replicate the findings of Kolodny and his associates have not been successful, however, and have even produced directly contradictory evidence. For example, Barlow and his co-workers (1974) found that plasma testosterone levels in a group of fifteen homosexual men seeking therapy for their homosexuality to be *as high* as those of Kolodny's heterosexual controls. Another study (Birk et al., 1973) produced similar results. Brodie and his associates (1974) compared levels of plasma testosterone in nineteen male homosexuals, drawn from a gay community at a West coast university, with those found in twenty heterosexual men. In both sample groups contact with sexual partners had been exclusively homosexual or heterosexual for at least the preceding year. Levels of plasma testosterone were significantly *higher* in the homosexual group.

Therefore it cannot now be said that homosexuality in human beings has a hormonal basis. With improvements in technology, future research on hormones and sperm of homosexuals and heterosexuals might conceivably uncover differences. Even so, such findings would still be open to the interpretation offered by Kolodny and his co-workers (1971) in discussing their pioneering work: hormonal differences found in people already functioning as homosexuals and as heterosexuals may be the result of, rather than the cause of, respective patterns of sexual behavior.

## Sociological Views on Homosexuality

Most of the theoretical accounts considered thus far, although different in major respects, have emphasized what happens early in life. The guiding assumption has been that an understanding of homosexuality will come from an examination of prenatal events and of the experiences of childhood and adolescence. Sociologists have instead tried to concentrate on the adult lives of homosexuals. Gagnon and Simon (1973), two sociologists who were formerly affiliated with the Kinsey group, suggest that we have allowed

> *. . . the homosexual's sexual object choice to dominate and control our imagery of him* (or her). *We have let this single aspect of his* (or her) *total life experi-*

*ence appear to determine all his products, concerns and activities. This prepossessing concern on the part of nonhomosexuals with a purely sexual aspect of the homosexual's life is something we would not allow to occur if we were interested in the heterosexual. . . . the mere presence of unconventional sexuality seems to give the sexual content of life an overwhelming significance.* [But] *homosexuals . . . vary profoundly in the degree to which their homosexual commitment and its facilitation become the organizing principle of their lives* (p. 137).

A full understanding of homosexuality, then, requires an appreciation of how homosexuals handle the kinds of problems that all people face in society and with themselves. In addition to preferring members of the same sex as sexual partners, homosexuals also hold jobs, have their likes and dislikes, own things, live somewhere—in short, engage in the common activities of adulthood. Furthermore, homosexuals can be men *or* women; until recently the psychological literature has been barren of discussion of female homosexuality and its similarities to and differences from male homosexuality. Some ideas and observations from the sociological literature, hypotheses as well as data, should provide a much broader perspective on the subject.

Most sociologists rely heavily on the Kinsey evidence. They integrate his findings with other information collected in recent years both through interviews and through participant observations. Sociologists have entered into homosexual settings as unobtrusively as possible in order to observe, as well as an outsider is able, the various homosexual life styles.

## Male homosexuality

Life Styles How do homosexuals find partners? Where do they live and work? Are some homosexuals married? As in the heterosexual world, those desiring homosexual contacts have many options for meeting partners socially and sexually. With the growing acceptance of homosexuality as an alternative life style, like-minded men may meet through gay counseling organizations, gay student organizations, and even groups within large professional organizations, for example, the Association of Gay Psychologists, a formal subgroup of the American Psychological Association.

Homosexual men can also meet in certain bars, gyms, and movie houses, at beaches, at particular highway rest areas, behind or inside trucks, and in public toilets, referred to as "tearooms." These are the locations where men look for "impersonal sex" (Humphreys, 1970). After appropriate signaling, an arrangement is made for a contact that is purely sexual in nature—words are often never spoken.

Performing fellatio in a men's toilet can be quick and easy, but it can also bring arrest by a plainsclothesman. If the homosexual is older, or unattractive, he may have to pay a male prostitute for gratification (see Box 12.5). Men may enter into homosexual marriages, complete with household. The sexual activities engaged in by male homosexuals are similar to those of heterosexuals. There may be kissing and general fondling, especially when the partners know and love each other. The practices leading to orgasm include fellatio, manipulation of the penis, and insertion of the penis or fingers in the anus.

Many, perhaps most, male homosexuals can be said not to "look" it. The "swishy" effeminate man who avoids "masculine" pursuits is the stereotype. Male hairdressers are often considered to be homosexual, even though many are not, and football players may be regarded as surely not, even though some are. Some homosexuals dress in female attire, called "going in drag," perhaps even passing themselves off to heterosexual men as female prostitutes; this may account for the frequent confusion of homosexuality with transvestism (see Chapter 11).

Deciding how far "out of the closet" to move can become a central question. Although sexuality typically plays a minor role in a heterosex-

## BOX 12.5 Male Homosexual Prostitution

The appeal of youth and the general search for desirable partners make homosexual prostitution an established and flourishing sexual institution, but one that varies in some respects from heterosexual prostitution. A female prostitute is paid by a male heterosexual so that the male can have an orgasm, but in homosexual prostitution the male prostitute or "hustler" is usually paid for *his* having an orgasm. In the heterosexual world the female prostitute is regarded as degraded, but in the male prostitute world the homosexual who pays for sex is degraded (Gagnon and Simon, 1973).

In addition to the older confirmed homosexuals who seek new and youthful partners, clients include married men who are especially vulnerable to disclosure of their homosexuality. By going to the homosexual prostitute and paying for sex, they face less risk of discovery. But fee-paying customers are sometimes beaten up and robbed by delinquent adolescents who act as prostitutes but may then also prey on their customers. Or an inexperienced prostitute may panic when he feels pleasure, fearing that he too may be "queer," and resort to violence to reassert his sense of masculinity (Reiss, 1961).

With male prostitutes who are predominantly or entirely heterosexual, a rather regimented set of procedures minimizes the homosexual nature of the contact. The male prostitute maintains his erection and has an orgasm without apparently compromising his conception of himself as heterosexual. The hustler's ability to do so is an example of how human beings are able to "script" their behavior (Gagnon and Simon, 1973), giving it a meaning they create in their heads.

> *[First,] the act may occur only a few times, with different men for money—the activity is "playing the queers," not homosexuality. . . . Commonly such young men refuse to allow hugging or kissing or anything sexual to occur above the waist. As long as the head is below the belly button and contact is on the penis, it is the other person who is homosexual. Without affection . . . and reciprocity . . . there is no reason to define the self as homosexual. . . . Further, it is possible for the young man to think about his girl friend or other women while the act is going on—some do, in fact, report that they cannot become aroused unless they have another scenario in their heads. (From John H. Gagnon,* Human Sexualities, *p. 264. Copyright © 1977, by Scott, Foresman and Company. Reprinted by permission.)*

Some of these young men are, however, homosexually inclined themselves or may become so through repeated orgastic pleasure with men. They may then engage reciprocally in these paid encounters, which makes them less attractive to the homosexual who wants to reduce his own sense of deviancy by fellating a heterosexual male and confirming his belief that all men have a streak of homosexuality.

Hustlers are not the only male homosexual prostitutes. Pittman (1971) describes a range of activities available to men who are willing to pay for sexual gratification with other men, many of them similar to special services provided by female prostitutes. Sadism and masochism, discussed in Chapter 11 in the context of heterosexuality, are practiced in certain male houses of prostitution. Fellatio is available for, rather than by, the customer, as is anal intercourse in both directions. A "watch queen" or voyeur pays to watch a nude male prostitute walk around the room, masturbate, or have sex with another male prostitute. Unconventional sexual practices are not restricted to the world of the heterosexual.

ual's choice of occupation, leisure activities, and place of residence, sexual orientation will matter when the homosexual who chooses to live openly makes these decisions. For example, a gay wanting to be entirely open about himself may feel more comfortable living in a certain part of town, or of the country, and working in settings where knowledge about his orientation is not a disadvantage, for example, tending a gay bar. Or the gay male may remain within the general heterosexual culture and be open about his homosexuality if he enters certain stereotyped jobs, such as being a hairdresser or interior decorator (Gagnon, 1977). At the same time, many gays are announcing themselves, regardless of their occupation, and facing the consequences that their openness may bring.

Male Homosexuals in Heterosexual Marriages
Kinsey (1948) determined that 10 percent of married American men between the ages of sixteen and twenty-five have had homosexual experiences. Since married men would probably wish to hide such activity, even from a professional interviewer, this figure is likely to be a gross underestimate of homosexual inclinations and behavior among married men. Moreover, as Humphreys (1970) has shown in his study of homosexual behavior in toilets, substantial numbers of married males have impersonal sexual encounters with men, in circumstances that magnify their fear and guilt. Indeed, such men, especially if they are well-off, are prime targets for extortion and blackmail.

The fact that a man can be homosexual to some degree and have a conventional heterosexual marriage may seem contradictory, but it is not. Heterosexual and homosexual men alike marry for all sorts of reasons, perhaps particularly to obtain what in our society constitutes the heterosexual package—a home, long-term companionship, and children. Moreover, as the survey data examined earlier revealed, a substantial proportion of men are bisexual.

The Aging Homosexual It is widely assumed by both homosexuals and heterosexuals that growing old occasions for homosexuals more distress and loneliness than experienced by heterosexuals. The pun "Nobody loves you when you are old and gay . . ." (Stearns, 1961, p. 202) is believed to be a sad statement of fact.

To examine whether this generalization is really valid, Weinberg (1970) enlisted the help of the Mattachine Society of New York. An extensive questionnaire, to be filled out anonymously, was mailed to over 3000 male homosexual members. Weinberg was also able to obtain data from a sample of homosexuals in Chicago who were not members of any homosexual society. Unfortunately, only 30 percent of the questionnaires were returned. Weinberg himself was aware of problems in generalizing from such a restricted sample. Nonetheless, the findings are of considerable interest.

The data confirmed the widely held belief that male homosexuals who are forty-five or older have relatively few sociosexual contacts with other homosexuals. Whereas homosexual bars and clubs were visited at least once a month by more than half the homosexuals under age twenty-six, only a quarter of those who were forty-six or older visited bars and clubs that often. Older homosexuals were also more likely to be living alone and to be having far less homosexual sex than they had had as younger men.

The loneliness and psychological distress of older gays, however, appeared to be no greater than that of younger homosexuals. Indeed, the older gays appeared to be less worried about their homosexuality and more accepting of themselves. Weinberg reasoned that both homosexuals and heterosexuals lower their aspirations as they age, settling for less in many areas of life. By the time the homosexual is middle-aged, he has probably come to terms with himself, including his sexuality. Younger homosexuals are more likely to be torn by conflict and guilt.

## Female homosexuality

Our review of the Kinsey data has indicated that the incidence of lesbianism is apparently much,

much lower in America than the incidence of male homosexuality. Moreover, the amount of research and writing done on female homosexuality has been much less than that on male homosexuality.

**The Nature of the Lesbian Relationship** It has been proposed that female homosexuals follow the same developmental patterns as female heterosexuals, and that their attitudes are in ways similar to those of female heterosexuals (Gagnon and Simon, 1973; Martin and Lyon, 1972). Gagnon and Simon speculate that during puberty sexual development for boys is primarily genital, with nearly all young males experiencing orgasm, usually from masturbation, within two years of the onset of biological maturation. In contrast, girls are introduced to sexuality through social learning organized around romance and marriage, not through orgastic arousal. Not until they have reached their late twenties do women generally experience the number of orgasms that seventeen-year-old males do. Masturbation is for teen-age boys "detached sex activity—activity whose only sustaining motive is sexual" (Simon and Gagnon, 1970, p. 32). During it they generally fantasize a great deal, seeing

> . . . *large parts of the environment in an erotic light.* [*They have*] *the ability to respond, sexually and perhaps poetically, to many visual and auditory stimuli. . . .* [*On the other hand*] *girls appear to be well-trained precisely in that area in which boys are poorly trained—that is, a belief in and a capacity for intense, emotionally-charged relationships and the language of romantic love. When girls during this* [adolescent] *period describe themselves as having been aroused sexually, they more often report it as a response to romantic, rather than erotic, words and actions* (pp. 33–36).

In maturity, according to Gagnon and Simon, the separation of sexual gratification from emotional and romantic involvement is not appealing to most women, whether heterosexual or homosexual. The Kinsey data, for example, showed that only 29 percent of those interviewed who were exclusively lesbians had had sexual relations with three or more partners. This figure is very similar to the number of male partners female heterosexuals have and is much, much lower than that for men. Furthermore, sexual arousal tends to be restricted to "legitimizing emotional circumstances"; it is not detachable from some kind of meaningful relationship with another person. A female homosexual relationship, then, is said to be built more on caring than on sexual need. And lesbian relationships tend to last longer than those of male homosexuals. The image of the lesbian as a counterfeit man does not appear accurate.

What we have stated so far are massive generalizations, which, even if generally accurate, may well change as sexual mores in the society at large change. The women's liberation movement may have a decided impact. As female heterosexual relationships become freer and more orgastic, it is possible that lesbian relationships will follow suit.

**Life Styles and Adjustment** Gagnon and Simon (1973) conducted extensive interviews with about two dozen lesbians. Although some did fit the "butch" or "dyke" stereotype, Gagnon and Simon did not view this occasional "masculine" behavior pattern as confirming the psychoanalytic notion that homosexuality is some failure in appropriate gender identification. Rather, they relate this behavior to the fact that lesbians must be more aggressive than female heterosexuals in making sexual contacts. Furthermore, a lesbian is more likely than a heterosexual woman to assume responsibilities largely defined as masculine—for example, repairing household appliances. The masculinity of some "butch" lesbians may reflect the necessary assumption of certain aspects of the male role.

Like the gay males discussed earlier, lesbians have to make decisions on how to deal with family, how to earn a living, what kind of friends to seek, how to find a partner, and how to achieve some degree of self-acceptance. Obviously these problems in living are made all the more difficult by societal sanctions, but more and more gay women are living openly and accepting the risks of social disapproval.

Regardless of the obstacles they face, the general mental well-being of lesbians has been attested to. From interviews that were conducted with sixty-five females who were exclusively homosexual, Hedblom (1972) found little support for the contention that homosexuality is a sign of psychopathology. More than three-fourths of the respondents felt strongly that homosexuality was as normal as heterosexuality. The lesbians also felt that homosexuals are highly creative and sensitive individuals. In this nonpsychiatric sample, 91 percent said that they had never sought help for their homosexuality, although 26 percent had sought professional advice on nonsexual problems.

Finally, Hedblom and others have reported that the initial sexual encounters between women already inclined sexually toward each other are overwhelmingly positive, apparently because of the greater understanding one woman has of another's physiological and psychological needs. Kinsey and his workers (1953) commented in a similar vein that arousal techniques used by two women with each other are virtually identical to those used in heterosexual petting or foreplay and at least as effective. Percentages of female orgasm reported in heterosexual intercourse during the first five years of marriage were significantly lower than those reported for women with five years of homosexual experience.

It would be rash and inaccurate to state, however, that a greater degree of familiarity can by itself account for female, or male, homosexuality. Intimate physical contact, as physicians and their patients are well aware, is readily desexualized if the setting is not construed as sexual. Even the most sensitive bodily stimulation by another person will be reacted to with sexual arousal only if that person is accepted as a legitimate partner beforehand.

## Conclusion

Theories about the development and maintenance of homosexual behavior are as diverse as those explaining other behavioral phenomena. What they attempt to account for, homosexuality, also has considerable range. It seems unlikely that any single theory could ever encompass it. Moreover, at least as much remains to be learned about heterosexuality as homosexuality. Therefore our present body of knowledge does not allow any determination of the causes of a presumed deviance from normal development.

People appear to become involved in same-sexed erotic pursuits for a multitude of reasons, and perhaps also for different reasons at different times. It is also possible that some homosexuals are preset by the hormonal balance in the uterus of the mother to acquire later same-sexed preferences. Attempts to demonstrate that homosexuality is genetically or hormonally determined have so far failed, however, which may be another indication that it is heterogeneous in origin and maintenance. In any given sample of homosexuals, at least some individuals probably differ from one another with respect to the cause of their sexual behavior. By lumping them all together in one group—homosexuals—we may be assuming homogeneity where there is none.

## Legal and Social Implications of Homosexuality

Earlier in this chapter the reader was invited to reflect on how he or she might react if anxiety were against the law, even if the emotion were felt in private. In this section we shall examine more closely the legal status of homosexual behavior, its consequences for homosexuals and other citizens, and the ways in which the laws affecting homosexuality are being changed.

The legal restrictions that Western society has imposed on homosexuals through the centuries have been extremely punitive. The Jews of the Old Testament were very intolerant of homosexual behavior, and this attitude was clearly reflected in the laws under which they lived. In Leviticus 20:13, it is stated, "If a man also lies with mankind, as he lieth with a woman, both of them have committed an abomination; they shall surely be put to death; their blood shall be upon them." The story of Lot reveals the attitude of Judaism toward homosexuality. Lot, who lived near the gate of Sodom, gave lodging for the night to two men, actually the Lord's angels. Male citizens of Sodom who wanted to have homosexual relations with the guests came to Lot's house and asked to be given the travelers. So abhorrent was this request, and so degraded were women in those days, that Lot offered the Sodomites his virgin daughters rather than hand over the two male visitors. When the Sodomites tried to break down Lot's door, the angels smote them with blindness. The next day the angels led Lot and his family from the city. "Then the Lord rained upon Sodom and upon Gomorrah brimstone and fire from the Lord out of heaven; and He overthrew those cities, and all the plain, and all the inhabitants of the cities, and that which grew upon the ground" (Genesis 19:24, 25).

### The Laws Affecting Homosexuality

The Jewish prohibition against homosexuality was introduced into Christianity by St. Paul and has come down to us through both Roman law and English church and civil law. In medieval England sodomists were tried in the ecclesiastical courts and could, according to the church laws, be buried alive, burned alive, or put to death by other means. In 1533, during the reign of Henry VIII, an act was passed that absorbed the church laws into English civil law, making it a felony punishable by death to "commit the detestable and abominable vice of buggery with mankind or beast" (quoted in Crompton, 1976, pp. 277–278). The death penalty for anal intercourse was not reduced to a maximum of life imprisonment until 1861. Laws generally reflect the values of *people* in a given society at a given point in time. The following remarks by the judge sentencing Oscar Wilde in 1895 at the Old Bailey voice the passions behind the English laws against homosexuality.

> *Oscar Wilde . . . the crime of which you have been convicted is so bad that one has to put stern restraint upon one's self to protect one's self from describing, in language which I would rather not use, the sentiments which arise to the breast of every man of honour who has heard of the details of these two terrible trials. . . .*
>
> *It is of no use for me to address you. People who can do these things must be dead to all sense of shame, and one cannot hope to produce any effect upon them.*
>
> *I shall, under the circumstances, be expected to pass the severest sentence that the law allows. In my judgment it is totally inadequate for such a case as this* (Regina v. Wilde).

The Puritans of Massachusetts Bay Colony brought both English law and biblical precepts to America. They incorporated in their famous "Body of Liberties" (1641) the words of Leviticus 20:13, thus declaring homosexuality a capital offense. In 1655 the New Haven colony enacted a code similar in tone. The extreme of mandating execution began only very slowly to disappear from colony laws over the next hundred years.

But Virginia, like most of the other states, did not remove the death penalty until the end of the eighteenth century, although even then retaining it for slaves who committed sodomy. In South Carolina sodomy was punishable by death up until 1873 (Crompton, 1976).

The so-called sodomy laws now on the books of thirty-one of the United States do not outlaw homosexuality per se, rather certain sexual *acts*—anal intercourse and oral-genital contacts—which are practiced by heterosexuals as well as homosexuals (Hoffman, 1968). The Constitution, in its guarantee of the right of privacy—"The right of the people to be secure in their persons, houses, papers, and effects, against unreasonable searches and seizures . . . and no warrant shall issue but upon probable cause"—makes arrests on the basis of these laws difficult. Most arrests of homosexuals are for violations of vaguely worded misdemeanor statutes prohibiting disorderly conduct, soliciting in public places, loitering, and exposure. Police sometimes act as decoys to attract homosexuals. Officers, usually young and handsome, are accompanied by a fellow policeman who keeps out of sight and witnesses what happens. The law distinguishes between "entrapment," which is not proper, and "enticement," the distinction being "whether the intent to commit the crime originated in the mind of the defendant or in the mind of the officer." In practice it is the word of the arresting officer against the word of the defendant that must be judged in drawing this very fine line. Civil libertarians have for some time recommended that police manpower not be used for this kind of enforcement of law.

As already stated, the acts for which homosexuals are arrested are the very same ones performed frequently by heterosexuals, who only rarely are arrested for them. Indeed, numerous sex manuals available in the soberest of bookstores advise heterosexuals to engage in such practices on occasion. If these heterosexual practices are also taken into account, it is likely that 96 percent of American men could be arrested for violation of sodomy laws (Churchill, 1967).

Hoffman (1968) believes that society views the male homosexual as a violent threat to heterosexuals, especially boys. But most sex that involves violence is in fact heterosexual in nature; moreover, the adult homosexual who does have relations with a boy usually masturbates or fellates him but does not have anal intercourse, which might be more injurious. The men who molest children, however, are not generally homosexuals (see page 286).

The Roman Catholic Church's stand against homosexuality rests not only on the presumed unnaturalness of the act but also on its being separated from procreation. Sex without the possibility of conception is viewed askance by the Catholic hierarchy, a position which was reaffirmed by the Vatican in January 1976, when the Church insisted that "homosexual acts are intrinsically disordered and can in no case be approved of."

The Catholic Church is not a monolith, however, and it is common knowledge that the laiety do not always go along with the Vatican's views on issues such as contraception and extramarital relations. The same diversity of opinion prevails concerning homosexuality. A book called *The Church and the Homosexual* (McNeill,1976), published by a Catholic priest who is a celibate homosexual, argues against the Church's long-standing abhorrence of homosexuality. Younger priests are likely to take a far more liberal view of human sexuality than does the pope. Formal marriage ceremonies for homosexual couples have been conducted by ministers of many denominations.

## Gay Liberation

### The beginnings of the movement

In reaction against the downtrodden legal and social status of homosexuals and the view of many mental health professionals that homosexuality is pathological, there has developed a militant and radical sociopolitical movement to achieve recognition of the normality of homosex-

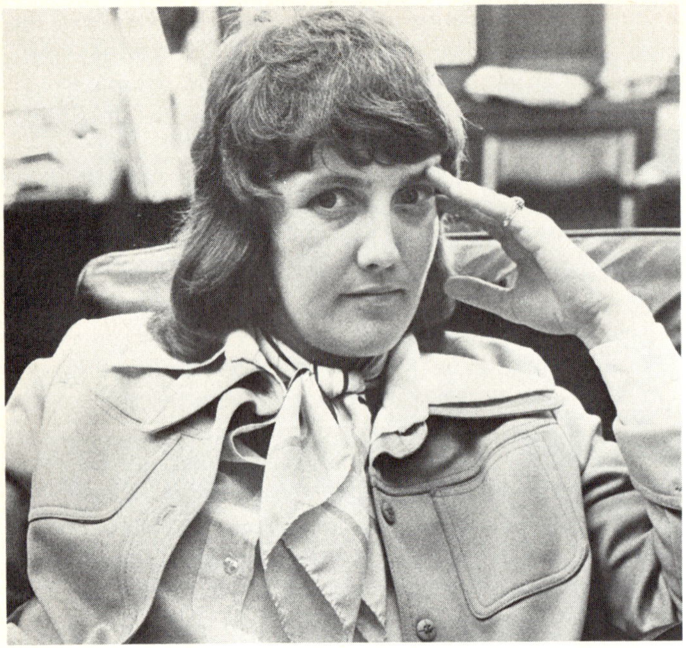

Changing attitudes toward homosexuality are reflected in open declarations of sexual preference. Above, Elaine Noble, a Massachusetts legislator, and Merle Miller, a well-known author. At left, the late Dr. Howard Brown, former New York City official. (Above right, Israel Shenker/NYT Pictures; bottom, Gene Maggio/ NYT Pictures.)

uality. The slogan of this group proclaims that "Gay is good."

In June of 1969, outside a gay bar called the Stonewall in Greenwich Village, New York City, homosexuals rioted openly in the streets, objecting to what they regarded as police harassment. Many view this as the explosive beginning of gay liberation, although forces had already been developing to make such a public revolt inevitable. The originally social Mattachine societies in various large cities had during the early 1960s become outspoken in their efforts to establish rights for homosexuals. One of the most articulate and militant of the gay liberation people, Franklin Kameny, soon proclaimed on behalf of their movement,

> *We have been shoved around for some 3,000 years. We're fed up with it and we're starting to shove back. If we don't get our rights and decent treatment as full human beings which we deserve, and get them now, there is going to be a lot more shoving back* (*1971, p. 19*).

In "Refugees from Amerika: A Gay Manifesto," Wittman (1970) offers indirect criticisms of Bieber, as well as support for the Kinsey position.

> *Nature leaves undefined the object of sexual desire. The gender of that object has been imposed socially . . .* [*Homosexuality*] *is not a makeshift in the absence of the opposite sex; it is not hatred or rejection of the opposite sex; it is not genetic; it is not the result of broken homes. . . . Homosexuality is the capacity to love someone of the same sex.*

The gay liberation movement has formed alliances with other oppressed groups and supports humanitarian and political causes. The principal concern is with the rights of individuals to conduct their lives as they see fit, provided they not infringe on the rights of others.

### Homosexuality and the mental health establishment

The gay liberation movement lent impetus to the drive to have homosexuality dropped from DSM-II and thereby be formally recognized by the mental health professions as a "normal variant" of sexual behavior rather than as a disorder or illness. A hearing was held before the Nomenclature Committee of the American Psychiatric Association, on February 8, 1973. Statements were made by several gay activists in an effort to persuade the psychiatrists. Charles Silverstein, a gay psychologist, reminded the committee that earlier psychiatric manuals had contained such obsolete and now-humorous categories as "vagabondage," "pathologic mendacity," and "cruel." He argued that no evidence indicates greater emotional disturbance among male and female homosexuals than among heterosexuals. Letters from recognized authorities—including Wardell Pomeroy, one of the original Kinsey researchers, and the American Psychological Association—strongly supported the stand taken by the coalition of gay groups.

By 1974 "homosexuality" had been formally dropped from DSM-II, but not without vehement protests from a number of renowned psychiatrists who have long held a pathological view of homosexuality. A new subcategory was invented, "sexual orientation disturbance," to refer to those who are sexually oriented to people of the same sex and are disturbed by their orientation, perhaps wishing to change it. The American Psychiatric Association *voted* on the issue, a comment on the conduct of science in the twentieth century.[3]

Other professional groups have moved in similar directions. In September 1976, for example, the American Psychological Association voted to oppose discrimination on the sole basis of sexual orientation in cases involving the custody of children. "The sex, gender identity, or sexual orientation of natural, or prospective adoptive or foster parents should not be the sole or primary variable considered in custody or placement cases." Two years earlier, the Association for Advancement of Behavior Therapy, a 3000-member organization of professionals advocating

[3]DSM-III is slated to call this new category "dyshomophilia"; homosexuality will, as now, be omitted from the listing of recognized mental disorders. The draft available as this book goes to press defines dyshomophilia as the disorder of people who not only are sexually aroused by same-sexed stimuli but "are distressed by such arousal, because homosexual stimuli are incompatible with the individual's conscience. The distress must be consciously perceived. An individual with homosexual arousal may be distressed because he or she is not accepted by society. However, unless the distress is a result of an internal conflict . . . the essential features of Dyshomophilia are not met." It is unclear at this point how the diagnosing clinician is to determine that the distress is internal rather than caused by social pressures.

behavioral approaches to treatment, had issued the following statement.

> *The AABT believes that homosexuality is in itself not a sign of behavioral pathology. The Association urges all mental health professionals to take the lead in removing the stigma of mental illness that has long been attributed to these patterns of emotion and behavior. While we recognize that this long-standing prejudice will not be easily changed, there is no justification for a delay in formally according these people the basic civil and human rights that other citizens enjoy.*

## Reform of Our Sex Laws

The legal status of homosexuals was altered somewhat even before the gay liberation movement gained its momentum and the psychiatric community acknowledged their normality. In this century civil libertarians had become convinced that the state has no right to legislate concerning the private sexual activities of consenting adults. In 1954 the House of Lords in England commissioned a study of homosexuality, chaired by Sir John Wolfenden. The well-known Wolfenden report of 1957 came out strongly in favor of repealing England's prohibitions against homosexual acts, arguing that sexual behavior in private between consenting adults is not the law's business. But not until ten years later, in 1967, were the recommendations implemented by parliamentary repeal of the centuries-old statutes. In 1955 the American Law Institute made recommendations similar to those of the Wolfenden report. And in 1961 Illinois became the first state to drop the laws against sodomy. Eighteen other states have followed suit. In a large number of major and smaller cities, civil rights bills have been passed protecting homosexuals from discrimination when they seek housing and employment.

What have been the consequences of decriminalizing homosexual relations among consenting adults? Has it encouraged child molesting, as some opponents have warned? Do homosexuals now force themselves sexually on others? One thing we do know is that decriminalization may not necessarily reduce police harassment. In Chicago the laws governing public conduct have not been changed; making contacts and arrangements for later private relations is still illegal. Ironically, the police in Chicago *increased* their arrests of homosexuals in the five years following repeal of the sodomy laws of Illinois (Hoffman, 1968).

In an effort to gain more comprehensive information on the effects of changes in the law, Geis and his associates (1976) mailed questionnaires to police departments and prosecuting attorneys in cities in each of the seven states that had decriminalized private homosexual behavior at the time of the survey. Questionnaires were sent also to a number of homosexual organizations in the same localities. As is generally the case with mail surveys, the response rates were disappointingly low for each group—24 percent of the police departments, 33 percent of the prosecuting attorneys, and only 13 percent of the homosexual organizations. These findings must be interpreted with considerable caution, but they clearly suggest that no dire predictions have come to pass. More specifically, these are some of the findings.

1. An overwhelming majority of all three groups of respondents felt that there had been no increase in the use of force by homosexuals.
2. All three groups tended to believe that involvement of homosexuals with minors had not increased (80 percent of the attorneys, 96 percent of the homosexual groups, and 69 percent of the police officers).
3. To the question whether homosexual activity had increased, 63 percent of the homosexuals, 71 percent of the attorneys, and 54 percent of the police answered no.
4. About half of each group of respondents believed there were more gay bars. Only

3 percent of the homosexual groups felt that public solicitation had increased, but 59 percent of the police officers believed that it had.

5. A sizable portion of each group (44 percent of homosexuals, 52 percent of police, and 45 percent of attorneys) believed that the social condemnation of homosexuals had decreased.
6. Half the police officers felt that discriminalization had given them more time to pursue serious crimes.

This preliminary survey suggests that few if any negative consequences to society at large ensue from decriminalizing private homosexual behavior. As for its easing the lot of the homosexual, the argument advanced by civil rights groups in the 1950s applies. Although prejudice cannot be directly legislated against, it may be weakened by removing laws that justify the derogation of particular groups. And it cannot but help those who feel they must be secretive about their emotional and sexual attachments to have the government affirm their right to a particular mode of self-expression. Cory noted in his classic book *The Homosexual in America,* "A person cannot live in . . . a society that outlaws and banishes his activities and desires . . . without a fundamental influence on his personality" (1951, p. 21).

## Summary

This chapter has reviewed data and speculation on the nature, origins, and extent of homosexuality. The most extensive sources of data are the two Kinsey reports, which indicate a considerable amount of homosexual behavior and interests among American men and women. Kinsey regarded the choice of a sexual partner of the opposite or of the same sex as being dependent on early sexual experiences. Psychoanalysts have tended to favor a heterophobic conception, according to which the male homosexual, having mishandled his oedipal dilemma, develops a neurotic fear of castration which often turns into a fear of the vagina. Some learning theorists also propose a heterophobic interpretation of homosexuality. There is no evidence for a genetic factor, and correlational data fail to demonstrate that homosexuals and lesbians have lower levels of appropriate sex hormones. Sociological studies have tended to concentrate on how a homosexual organizes his or her life and how sociosexual contacts are made. Of considerable interest is the finding that the socialization and sexualization of female homosexuals are apparently more nearly like those of female heterosexuals than of male homosexuals. Thus trying to understand a homosexual's life by concentrating on its sexual aspects may impede scientific understanding. The legal problems of homosexuals were also reviewed, as well as the significant movements for the recognition of their rights. Many experts agree that a serious reexamination of our attitudes is in order.

# part four
# the schizophrenias

# chapter 13

## SCHIZOPHRENIA: DESCRIPTION



Schizophrenia must be considered as one of the most serious of the behavioral disorders. About 50 percent of hospitalized mental patients are diagnosed schizophrenic. And even though the typical length of the period of hospitalization for these patients has shortened markedly over the past decade, rehospitalization is frequent. Within two years following initial discharge, about 50 percent of schizophrenics have reentered mental hospitals (Gunderson et al., 1974). Thus, understandably, schizophrenia has been one of the most thoroughly investigated disorders in the field of abnormal psychology. In this chapter and the following we shall review the literature on schizophrenia. In this first chapter we examine the various forms of the disorder, its symptoms, and other descriptive aspects. In Chapter 14 we shall consider the different theories of the etiology of schizophrenia and the data that support them.

In various editions of his famous nineteenth-century textbook of psychiatry, Emil Kraepelin applied the term dementia praecox to a syndrome that consisted of such symptoms as hallucinations, delusions, inappropriate emotional responses, stereotyped motor behavior, and deficient attention. He viewed dementia praecox as one of the two major groups of endogenous or organically caused psychoses, differentiating it from manic-depressive illness. Kraepelin supposed that the sex glands malfunctioned, producing a chemical imbalance which in turn affected the nervous system. The Latin adjective *praecox,* meaning premature, was applied to the disorder because it was believed to begin in adolescence, the noun *dementia* because a mental deterioration from which there could be no recovery was considered the inevitable progression.

In 1911 Eugen Bleuler wrote a monograph on what he termed "the group of schizophrenias";

in it he modified some of Kraepelin's early notions. Bleuler suggested the term *schizophrenia* because he viewed the essential feature of these disorders as a *schizein* or splitting of various functions of the *phren,* the mind. He proposed that in schizophrenia normally integrated processes such as thoughts and emotions are fragmented through a "loosening of associative threads." Although Bleuler agreed with Kraepelin that the cause of the disorder was probably organic, he differed with him on other important points. He did not believe that the disorder always began in adolescence or that deterioration was inevitable. He felt that schizophrenia could be arrested at any stage and that the condition of some who suffer from it may improve. The pioneering efforts of these two workers, Kraepelin and Bleuler, continue to have an impact on contemporary conceptions of schizophrenia.

Emil Kraepelin (1856–1926), the German psychiatrist whose descriptions of dementia praecox have proved remarkably durable in the light of contemporary research.

Eugen Bleuler (1857–1939), the Swiss psychiatrist who contributed importantly to our conceptions of schizophrenia and coined the term.

## The Diagnosis of Schizophrenia

We must present not one but two approaches to diagnosis, for American and European practices differ. Two principal formalized diagnostic statements about schizophrenia are those of DSM-II and the British Glossary (1968). Their criteria for schizophrenia are presented in Table 13.1. Both systems place schizophrenia within the more general category of functional psychoses, that is, psychoses not considered to have an organic cause.

Let us examine these two definitions of schizophrenia more closely. The brief DSM-II definition merely points out several aspects of the disorder: (1) thought disorder, including delusions and hallucinations; (2) mood disorders, such as ambivalence and constricted or inappropriate emotional responsiveness; and (3) disturbed behavior, such as regression and withdrawal. In contrast, the definition in the British Glossary is much more elaborate; hallucinations and other symptoms are much more fully described. Importantly, the British Glossary also provides a criterion to *exclude*

TABLE **13.1**
Formal Definitions of Schizophrenia

**American Psychiatric Association Diagnostic and Statistical Manual** (1968). This large category includes a group of disorders manifested by characteristic disturbances of thinking, mood and behavior. Disturbances in thinking are marked by alterations of concept formation which may lead to misinterpretation of reality and sometimes to delusions and hallucinations, which frequently appear psychologically self-protective. Corollary mood changes include ambivalent, constricted and inappropriate emotional responsiveness and loss of empathy with others. Behavior may be withdrawn, regressive and bizarre.

**British Glossary** (1968). Under this heading are included . . . illnesses . . . characterized from the outset by a fundamental disturbance of the personality involving its most basic functions, [those that] give the normal person his feeling of individuality, uniqueness and self-direction. . . . [Although the state of consciousness evidently remains clear, the person bares to others his] inmost life, thoughts, feelings and acts. . . . [The patient has] explanatory delusions that [his] thoughts etc. are influenced by outside forces which may be natural or supernatural. . . . Hallucinations are common, predominately auditory, in the form of "voices" which may comment on the patient's thoughts and actions, and somatic or tactile. [There are] unpleasant sensations which the patient may be unable to describe in ordinary language and which again usually [have] delusional interpretation. An important symptom of schizophrenia, not however evident in all cases, is a curious disturbance of thinking. . . . Peripheral, marginal and irrelevant features of a total concept, [normally] inhibited . . . are brought to the forefront and utilized in place of the elements relevant and appropriate to a given situation. Thus thinking becomes vague, elliptical and obscure and its expression in speech [is] often incomprehensible. Sudden breaks in the flow of thought ("blocking") are frequent, and there is difficulty in retaining thoughts, which is often interpreted delusionally as "thought withdrawal" by outside agencies. Hearing one's thoughts spoken aloud is common and is believed to be diagnostically significant. Perception is also disturbed so that irrelevant features of a percept become all-important. . . . The patient [may] believe that every-day objects and situations, e.g. statements in the press, possess a special, usually sinister, meaning especially intended for him. The affective state becomes capricious and often inappropriate to a given situation. It should . . . be borne in mind that a minority of cases . . . clear up apparently without residual defect.

some patients from the schizophrenia category. If consciousness is not clear, that is, if the person is disoriented for time or place, he or she is not considered schizophrenic. (As we shall see in Chapter 16, disorientation is a primary symptom of organic brain disorders.)

Have these different definitions had consequences in their applications? Apparently, the answer is yes. In America the concept of schizophrenia has over the years been extended considerably. At the New York State Psychiatric Institute, for example, about 20 percent of patients were diagnosed schizophrenic in the 1930s. This figure increased through the 1940s and in 1952 peaked at a remarkable 80 percent. In contrast, the European concept of schizophrenia is narrower and has remained so. The percentage of patients diagnosed schizophrenic at the Maudsley Hospital in London remained relatively constant over a forty-year period (Kuriansky, Deming, and Gurland, 1974).

The United States–United Kingdom Cross National Project (Cooper et al., 1972) has intensively studied the differences between American and British diagnoses. In one part of the overall investigation a number of patients admitted consecutively to several hospitals in London and New York were interviewed by members of the project staff, who later reached diagnoses. These diagnoses were then compared with those made on the same patients by the staffs of the respective institutions.

The numbers of patients diagnosed schizophrenic by the special project staff were about the same, in New York hospitals 59, in London hospitals 61. The numbers of schizophrenic diagnoses made by the staffs of each institution, in New York 118 and in London 59, were not the same. The difference between New York staff and project staff diagnoses can be pinpointed by examining how the project staff diagnosed the patients considered schizophrenic by the New York staff but not by them. Table 13.2 indicates that a substantial proportion of New York-diagnosed schizophrenics were considered to have an affective illness by the project staff. In fact, many patients considered by the project staff to fit in all categories other than schizophrenia were regarded as schizophrenic by New York diagnosticians. "Sixty-three percent of those with a project diagnosis of depressive psychosis, 91 percent of those with a project diagnosis of mania, 69 percent of those with a project diagnosis of neurosis, and 63 percent of those with a project diagnosis of personality disorder all have hospital diagnoses of schizophrenia" (Cooper et al., 1972, p. 104). Thus the American concept of schizophrenia (or at least the New York concept) was shown to be considerably broader than that used either by project staff or by hospital staff in London (Figure 13.1).

TABLE **13.2**
Project Diagnosis of Patients Considered Schizophrenic by New York Staff

| Project diagnoses | Of New York schizophrenics |
|---|---|
| Schizophrenic | 50 |
| Affective illness | 42 |
| Neuroses | 3 |
| Personality disorder | 5 |
| Other | 18 |

Having established that there are clear differences between American and British diagnostic practices, we must now ask whether one system is in some ways better than the other. Since there is no absolute criterion by which to judge, we can only examine the reliability and validity of each approach. The British system seems superior on both counts. Using British diagnosis, Wing and his associates (1967), for example, found an interjudge reliability of 92 percent for schizophrenia. Contrast this with the 53 percent figure found in America by the Beck (1962) study discussed in Chapter 3! Validity can be assessed by relating diagnosis to other meas-

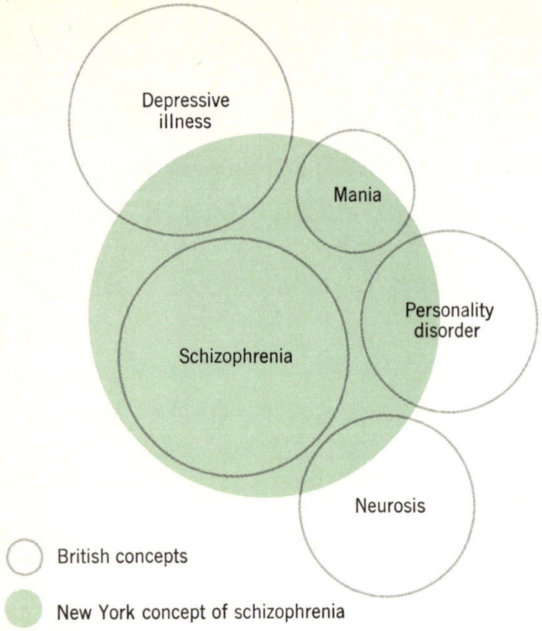


FIGURE **13.1**
A Venn diagram indicating the difference between the New York and British concepts ot schizophrenia. The British concept is narrower than the New York one and does not overlap with other diagnostic categories. After Cooper et al., 1972.

ures such as performance on laboratory tasks and evidence of predisposition in the family. Although few studies have compared the validity of different diagnostic systems, those that have suggest that a narrower definition of schizophrenia is preferable.[1] We will discuss two such studies, one later in this chapter (Oltmanns, O'Hayon, and Neale, in press) and one in the next (Gottesman and Shields, 1972).

With the foregoing as background, the behavior of schizophrenics can be examined in greater detail. This discussion, drawing on many sources of information, leans toward a European conceptualization of schizophrenia. It also draws heavily on the results of a large-scale investigation of the definition of schizophrenia, the International Pilot Study of Schizophrenia (IPSS), conducted by the World Health Organization (Sartorius, Shapiro, and Jablonsky, 1974).

[1] In fact, there is now a strong move to bring the American concept of schizophrenia more in line with the British one. Experimental diagnostic systems already in use in America (for example, Spitzer, Endicott, and Robins, 1975) are quite close to the British definition, and the current draft of DSM-III defines schizophrenia in a more European way.

## Schizophrenic Behavior

The disordered behavior of schizophrenic patients can be organized into disturbances in several major areas—thought, perception and attention, motor behavior, affect or emotion, and contact with reality. The range of problems of people diagnosed as schizophrenic is very extensive, although patients who are so diagnosed will typically have only *some* of them. The diagnostician has to decide how many problems must be present, and in what degree, to justify the diagnosis. The heterogeneity of the behavior suggests that it would be appropriate to try to subdivide schizophrenics into types who manifest particular constellations of problems. After reviewing the major symptoms, we shall examine the subcategorizing of schizophrenic behavior.

### Disorders of thought

One disturbance observed in most schizophrenics is thought disorder. The term refers to problems both in the *form* of thought—the organization of ideas, speaking so that a listener can understand; and in its *content*—the actual ideas that are expressed. We shall first examine the form of thought in schizophrenia.

**Disorders of Thought Form** In response to an initial, seemingly simple question to a schizophrenic patient, this conversation ensued.

> *"How old are you?"*
> *"Why I am centuries old, sir."*
> *"How long have you been here?"*
> *"I've been now on this property on and off for a long time. I cannot say the exact time because we are absorbed by the air at night, and they bring back people. They kill up everything; they can make you lie; they can talk through your throat."*
> *"Who is this?"*
> *"Why, the air."*
> *"What is the name of this place?"*
> *"This place is called a star."*
> *"Who is the doctor in charge of your ward?"*
> *"A body just like yours, sir. They can make you black and white. I say good morning, but he just comes through there. At first it was a colony. They said it was heaven. These buildings were not solid at the time, and I am positive that this is the same place. They have others just like it. People die, and all the microbes talk over there, and prestigitis you know is sending you from here to another world. . . . I was sent by the government to the United States to Washington to some star, and they had a pretty nice country there. Now you have a body like a young man who says he is of the prestigitis."*
> *"Who was this prestigitis?"*
> *"Why, you are yourself. You can be prestigitis. They make you say bad things; they can read you; they bring back Negroes from the dead"* (White, 1932, p. 228).

This excerpt illustrates the *incoherence* sometimes found in the conversation of schizophrenics. Although the patient may make repeated references to central ideas or a theme, the images and fragments of thought are not connected. It is difficult to understand exactly what the patient is trying to tell the interviewer. In addition, the patient uses the word "prestigitis" several times, a *neologism* or new word which he has made up himself and which is probably meaningless to the listener.

Thought may also be disordered by *loose associations,* in which case the patient may be more successful in communicating with a listener but has difficulty sticking to one topic. He or she seems to drift off on a train of associations evoked by some idea from the past. Schizophrenic patients have themselves provided descriptions of this state.

> *My thoughts get all jumbled up. I start thinking or talking about something but I never get there. Instead, I wander off in the wrong direction and get caught up with all sorts of different things that may be con-*

*nected with things I want to say but in a way I can't explain. People listening to me get more lost than I do. . . .*

*My trouble is that I've got too many thoughts. You might think about something, let's say that ashtray and just think, oh! yes, that's for putting my cigarette in, but I would think of it and then I would think of a dozen different things connected with it at the same time (McGhie and Chapman, 1961, p. 108).*

Another aspect of the schizophrenic's associative problems is termed *clang associations*. The patient's speech contains many rhyming words, for example, "How are you today by the bay as a gay, Doctor?" The words follow one another because they rhyme, not because they make grammatical or logical sense.

**Disorders of Thought Content** The thoughts of 97 percent of schizophrenics in the IPSS were found disordered in another, more fundamental way, through "lack of insight." When asked what they thought was wrong or why they had been hospitalized, schizophrenics seemed to have no appreciation of their condition and little realization that their behavior was unusual. In addition, many schizophrenics are subject to delusions, holding beliefs that the rest of society would generally disagree with or view as a misinterpretation of reality.

No doubt each of us is, at one time or another, rather concerned because we believe that others think badly of us. Perhaps much of the time this belief is well justified. Who, after all, can be universally loved? Fortunately, we either learn to live with this belief, or, if it is false, are readily able to dispel it. Consider for a moment, however, what life would be like if you were firmly convinced that numbers of people did not like you, indeed that they disliked you so much that they were plotting against you. Some of these persecutors have sophisticated listening devices which allow them to tune in on your most private conversations and gather evidence in a plot to discredit you. None of those around you, including your loved ones, is able to reassure you that these people are not spying on you. In fact, even your closest friends and confidants are gradually joining your tormenters and becoming members of the persecuting community. You are naturally quite anxious or angry about your situation, and you begin your own counteractions against the imagined persecutors. Any new room you enter must be carefully checked for listening devices. When you meet a person for the first time, you question him or her at great length to determine whether he or she is part of the plot against you.

Besides the *persecutory* pattern just described, which was found in 64 percent of the IPSS sample, schizophrenics may have delusions of *grandeur* or *control*. With delusions of grandeur they believe that they are especially important or powerful individuals, such as a great explorer or Napoleon reincarnate. With delusions of control they fear that they are being controlled by some alien force or perhaps by radar, television, or other wavelike emanations.

Delusions that appear fleetingly in the verbal reports of newly admitted mental patients may be distinguished from those that become *systematized*. For example, in our own clinical experience we saw a young woman who had been admitted to a mental hospital in a severe psychotic state. During an initial interview she attributed her current difficulty to a treatment she had received for her skin problem. She had come to believe that the physician was surreptitiously administering a hormone that would increase her sexual desire for him. She had decided that the physician planned to increase the dose gradually and then sexually assault her. After a brief period of drug therapy, the patient no longer mentioned these beliefs. When queried about them, she merely said that she must have been mixed up to say such things.

In contrast, schizophrenics may sometimes have delusions that become the dominant focus in their lives. Such systematized delusions are well illustrated in an extensive report by Rokeach, called *The Three Christs of Ypsilanti*

(1964). Interested in the processes that underlie changes in attitudes and beliefs, Rokeach canvassed a number of mental hospitals to find men who believed that they were Christ. After locating three, he managed to have them all transferred to a single state mental hospital at Ypsilanti, Michigan. Furthermore, he arranged for these three Christs to meet with one another on a regular basis. Each man believed strongly that he was Christ, and this conviction dominated most of his daily activities. How would each man react to meeting two others who also alleged that they were Christ? The Christian belief that there was only one Son of God had little impact on the delusions of the three men. In the face of seemingly conflicting evidence, each steadfastly maintained his own belief that he was the Christ.

The German psychiatrist Kurt Schneider's (1959) description of an additional group of delusional beliefs plays an important role in how schizophrenia is more specifically diagnosed in Britain. The following catalogue of these delusions is drawn from Mellor (1970).

Kurt Schneider, a German psychiatrist, proposed that particular forms of hallucinations and delusions, which he calls first-rank symptoms, are central to defining schizophrenia.

1. **Delusional percept.** A normal perception, for some reason, takes on a special significance for the patient and an often elaborate delusional system quickly develops. To give an example of such a transformed percept.

   *A young Irishman was at breakfast with two fellow-lodgers. He felt a sense of unease, that something frightening was going to happen. One of the lodgers pushed the salt cellar towards him (he appreciated at the time that this was an ordinary salt cellar and his friend's intention was innocent). Almost before the salt cellar reached him he knew that he must return home, "to greet the Pope, who is visiting Ireland to see his family and to reward them . . . because Our Lord is going to be born again to one of the women. . . . And because of this they [all the women] are all born different with their private parts back to front"* (p. 18).

2. **Somatic passivity.** The patient is a passive, unwilling recipient of bodily sensations imposed by an external agency.

   *A twenty-nine-year-old teacher described "X-rays entering the back of my neck, where the skin tingles and feels warm, they pass down the back in a hot tingling strip about six inches wide to the waist. There they disappear into the pelvis which feels numb and cold and solid like a block of ice. They stop me from getting an erection"* (p. 16).

3. **Thought insertion.** Thoughts, which are not the patient's own, have been placed in his or her mind by an external source.

*A twenty-nine-year-old housewife said "I look out of the window and I think the garden looks nice and the grass looks cool, but the thoughts of Eamonn Andrews come into my mind. There are no other thoughts there, only his. . . . He treats my mind like a screen and flashes his thoughts on to it like you flash a picture"* (p. 17).

4. **Thought broadcast.** The patient's thoughts are transmitted so that others know them.

   *A twenty-one-year-old student [found that] "As I think, my thoughts leave my head on a type of mental ticker-tape. Everyone around has only to pass the tape through their mind and they know my thoughts"* (p. 17).

5. **Thought withdrawal.** The patient's thoughts are "stolen" from his or her mind by an external force—suddenly, unexpectedly, and without arousing anxiety.

   *A twenty-two-year-old woman [described such an experience]. "I am thinking about my mother, and suddenly my thoughts are sucked out of my mind by a phrenological vacuum extractor, and there is nothing in my mind, it is empty . . ."* (p. 16–17).

The next three delusions pertain to the experiencing of feelings and the carrying out of actions and impulses that have been imposed on the patient by some external agent.

6. **"Made" feelings.** *A twenty-three-year-old female patient reported, "I cry, tears roll down my cheeks and I look unhappy, but inside I have a cold anger because they are using me in this way, and it is not me who is unhappy, but they are projecting unhappiness onto my brain. They project upon me laughter, for no reason, and you have no idea how terrible it is to laugh and look happy and know it is not you, but their emotions"* (p. 17).

7. **"Made" volitional acts.** *A twenty-nine-year-old shorthand typist described her [simplest] actions as follows: "When I reach my hand for the comb it is my hand and arm which move, and my fingers pick up the pen, but I don't control them. . . . I sit there watching them move, and they are quite independent, what they do is nothing to do with me. . . . I am just a puppet who is manipulated by cosmic strings. When the strings are pulled my body moves and I cannot prevent it"* (p. 17).

8. **"Made" impulses.** *A twenty-nine-year-old engineer [who had] emptied the contents of a urine bottle over the ward dinner trolley [tried to explain the incident]. "The sudden impulse came over me that I must do it. It was not my feeling, it came into me from the X-ray department, that was why I was sent there for implants yesterday. It was nothing to do with me, they wanted it done. So I picked up the bottle and poured it in. It seemed all I could do"* (p. 18).

### Disorders of perception and attention

Schizophrenic patients frequently report that the world seems somehow different to them. Some mention changes in the way their bodies feel. Parts of their bodies may seem too large or too small, objects around them too close or too far away. Or there may be numbness or tingling; or the body may become so depersonalized that it feels as though it is a machine. Others remark that the world is not as it used to be, that it appears flat and colorless. Some schizophrenics report difficulties in attending to what is happening around them.

*I can't concentrate on television because I can't watch the screen and listen to what is being said at the same time. I can't seem to take in two things like this at the same time especially when one of them means watching and the other means listening. On the other hand I seem to be always taking in too much at the one time, and then I can't handle it and can't make sense of it. . . . [Or, as another patient stated] When people are talking, I just get scraps of it. If it is just one person who is speaking, that's not so bad, but if others join in then I can't pick it up at all. I just can't get in tune with the conversation. It makes me feel all open—as if things are closing in on me and I have lost control* (McGhie and Chapman, *1961, p. 106*).

The most dramatic distortions of perception are called *hallucinations,* sensory experiences in the *absence* of any stimulation from the environment. They occur most often in the auditory modality and less often in the visual. Seventy-four percent of the IPSS sample reported having auditory hallucinations.

As with delusions, some hallucinations are thought to be particularly important diagnostically. Schneider (1959) has described these, and we again rely on Mellor (1970) for examples.

1. **Audible thoughts.** *A thirty-two-year-old housewife complained of a man's voice speaking in an intense whisper from a point about two feet above her head. The voice would repeat almost all the patient's goal-directed thinking—even the most banal thoughts. The patient would think "I must put the kettle on" and after a pause of not more than one second the voice would say "I must put the kettle on." It would often say the opposite "Don't put the kettle on"* (*p. 16*).
2. **Voices arguing.** *A twenty-four-year-old male patient reported hearing voices coming from the nurse's office. One voice, deep in pitch and roughly spoken, repeatedly said "G. T. is a bloody paradox," and another higher in pitch said "He is that, he should be locked up." A female voice occasionally interrupted, saying "He is not, he is a lovely man"* (*p. 16*).
3. **Voices commenting.** *A forty-one-year-old housewife heard a voice coming from a house across the road. The voice went on incessantly in a flat monotone describing everything she was doing with an admixture of critical comments. "She is peeling potatoes, got hold of the peeler, she does not want that potato, she is putting it back, because she thinks it has a knobble like a penis, she has a dirty mind, she is peeling potatoes, now she is washing them. . . ."* (16).

### Motor symptoms

Disturbances in motor activity are obvious and bizarre. The schizophrenic may grimace or adopt strange facial expressions. He or she may gesture repeatedly, using peculiar and sometimes complex sequences of finger, hand, and arm movements—which often seem to be purposeful, odd as they may be. Some schizophrenics manifest an unusual increase in the overall level of activity. There may be much excitement, wild flailing of the limbs, and great expenditure of energy similar to that seen in mania. At the other end of the spectrum is *catatonic immobility:* unusual postures are adopted and maintained for very long periods of time. A patient may stand on one leg, with the other tucked up toward the buttocks, and remain in this position virtually all day. The limbs of catatonic patients may have what is referred to as *waxy flexibility.* Another person can move them about and put them into strange positions that will then be maintained.

### Affective symptoms

Three affective abnormalities are often found in schizophrenic patients. In some affect is said to be *flat;* virtually no stimulus can elicit an emotional response. This shallowness or complete blunting of emotions renders the schizophrenic apathetic. The patient may stare vacantly, the muscles of his face flaccid, his eyes lifeless. When spoken to he answers in a flat and toneless voice. Flat affect was found in 66 percent of the IPSS schizophrenics. Other patients display *inappropriate affect.* The emotional responses of these individuals are out of context—the patient may laugh on hearing that her mother has just died or become enraged when asked a simple question about how a new

This patient, diagnosed as a catatonic schizophrenic, spends nearly all his waking hours in a crouching position.

garment fits. These schizophrenics are likely to shift rapidly from one emotional state to another for no discernible reason. Finally, the affective responses of some schizophrenic patients can be *ambivalent*. A single person or object may simultaneously arouse both positive and negative emotions. A patient may express strong hatred and strong love toward another person at about the same time.

**Withdrawal and autism**

Autism is a withdrawal from contact with the world and a consequent overemphasis on one's own thoughts and fantasies. Schizophrenics become unable to distinguish between reality and the products of their own imaginations and are often spoken of as "being out of contact." Because schizophrenics are often buried in their own private and inner world, they lack interest in what is happening around them, being particularly withdrawn from any sort of social interaction. They frequently have few friends, little interest in the opposite sex, and a history of actively avoiding close social contacts with others.

## Subcategories of Schizophrenia

### The Kraepelinian Subtypes

Three of the subtypes of schizophrenic reaction that are now included in the current diagnostic and statistical manual—hebephrenic, catatonic, and paranoid—were initially proposed by Kraepelin many years ago. Later, after Bleuler had written about the disorders, Kraepelin added a fourth, the simple type. The present descriptions of Kraepelin's original subtypes provide further information on what schizophrenia is like and on the great diversity of behavior that relates to the diagnosis.

#### Simple schizophrenia

The British Glossary contains the following definition of simple schizophrenia.

> *This form is characterized by insidious development, perhaps over some years, of oddities of conduct, difficulties in social contact, unreasonableness, extreme intolerance of relations and friends who seek to induce the patient to conform in his own interests to the demands of society, and by decline in total performance. As a result social derailment occurs and the patient sinks into vagrancy. . . ."*

The simple schizophrenic chooses to live in the least demanding manner possible. Minimal motivation, apathy and languor, slowness of thought and wit, inattention, orneriness, meager conversation, continual daydreaming, reclusiveness, and a slovenly appearance are all implied by this definition. Because it is conspicuous for the absence of several of the accepted symptoms of schizophrenia, we shall not consider further this questionable subcategory.

#### Catatonic schizophrenia

The most obvious symptoms of the *catatonic* type of schizophrenia are the motor disturbances discussed earlier. Such individuals typically alternate between catatonic immobility and wild excitement, but one or the other type of motor symptoms may predominate. The onset of catatonic reactions may be more sudden than other forms of schizophrenia, although the person has probably already shown some apathy and withdrawal from reality. The limbs of the immobile catatonic may become stiff and swollen; in spite of apparent obliviousness, he or she may later relate all that has happened during the stupor. In the excited state the catatonic may shout and talk continuously and incoherently, all the while pacing with great agitation. There are some indications that this form of schizophrenia is becoming relatively rare, perhaps because drug therapy is now so frequently administered (Arieti, 1955). The following description is taken from our files.

> Bob, a twenty-two-year-old, was admitted to the hospital after a brief period of bizarre behavior at home. His parents reported that for several days he had stayed in his room, coming out only for meals. Then, at dinner one evening, he suddenly "became rigid." Alarmed, the parents called the family physician, but by the time he arrived Bob had entered a period of intense activity. He ran through the house, rolled on the floor, and strenuously resisted efforts to restrain him. Finally, he was sedated and taken to the hospital.
>
> In the hospital Bob continued to alternate between periods of catatonic immobility and wild excitement. He refused to speak or eat and often did the exact opposite of what was requested of him, remaining in bed when asked to get up and remaining up when asked to go to bed.
>
> Initially, Bob was placed on a drug therapy regimen which lasted for several months. He showed little improvement. Then a course of electroconvulsive therapy was begun, but again there was little improvement. The periods of excitement abated, but Bob remained mute and withdrawn and frequently adopted catatonic postures.

### Paranoid schizophrenia

A more common subdiagnosis is *paranoid* schizophrenia. The key to this diagnosis is the presence of numerous and systematized delusions. Usually they are of persecution, grandeur, and being controlled by an alien force, as well as others similar in nature, as already described. Vivid auditory and visual hallucinations may also accompany the delusions. These patients often develop what are referred to as *ideas of reference:* they incorporate unimportant events within a delusional framework, reading personal significance into the seemingly trivial activities of others. They think that phrases of overheard conversations apply to them, and the continual appearance of a person on a street where they customarily walk means that they are being watched. What they see on television or read in magazine also somehow refers to them. Paranoid schizophrenics are confused, agitated, and afraid. But they are more alert and verbal than other schizophrenics, and their thought processes, although deluded, have not fragmented.

Another case from our records illustrates these symptoms.

> Roger was initially seen as an outpatient. He had come for treatment because he had been rejected by the army for psychiatric reasons and "wanted to do whatever was necessary to get into the army and go to Vietnam." He thought that he was a "born soldier" and related several incidents to support this assertion. In one of them he had been registering at a hotel desk, and the clerk had asked him how long his "leave" was going to be. Roger was unable to see that his short hair, marching gait, and the fact that he wore an army jacket were the likely cues the clerk was responding to.
>
> Over the course of several weeks of outpatient therapy little happened. Roger remained very guarded and maintained that there really wasn't anything wrong. He showed almost no affective responses and claimed that his ideal was Mr. Spock, the intellectual, unemotional Vulcan of "Star Trek." One week, as he was leaving, he announced that he had "figured out what was going on and knew what to do."
>
> Three days later he was hospitalized. He had threatened to blow up an army recruiting post, claiming that aliens from another planet had taken over. He now believed that he was one of the last "true" earthmen. The aliens had already infiltrated the bodies of most human beings, beginning first with those of army men and then moving into the bodies of the rest of the human race as well.

### Hebephrenic schizophrenia

The *hebephrenic* form of schizophrenia is characterized by a variety of rather diffuse and regressive symptoms. Hallucinations and delusions—sexual, hypochondriacal, religious, and persecutory—are profuse and less organized than those of the paranoid schizophrenic. The patient may be subject to bizarre ideas, often involving deterioration of the body. Much of the patient's behavior is marked by a pattern of silliness and absurdity. He may grimace or have a meaningless smile on his face. He giggles childishly and speaks incoherently, stringing together similar-sounding words and inventing neologisms. All in all, his life is often a tangled nightmare of distortion and delusion. He frequently deteriorates to the point that he becomes incontinent, voiding anywhere and at anytime. And he completely neglects his appearance, never bathing, brushing his teeth, or combing his hair.

> The patient was a twenty-four-year-old single woman. After graduation from college she worked for two years with an advertising agency. During both her college days and later she was very seclusive and had few friends. She had never had any sexual experience, either homosexual or heterosexual. In the few weeks before hospitalization she had

stopped going to work, remaining in her apartment and becoming inattentive to personal hygiene and grooming.

When she was admitted to the hospital, she was unkempt, disheveled, and dirty. Meaningful conversation with her seemed impossible. She maintained a silly grin and occasionally would burst into spontaneous and wild fits of laughter, even though she might be describing how her bones were melting. Her verbal behavior was nonsensical. Asked whether she wanted to go on a ward outing, she replied, "Outing, inning, being out is in and in is out" (*laughter*).

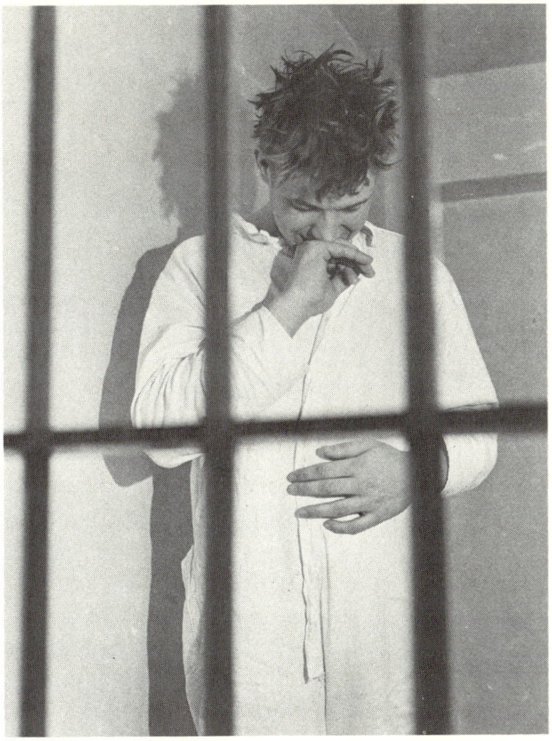

A man diagnosed as a hebephrenic schizophrenic, largely because of his inappropriate mirth.

## Evaluation

The Kraepelinian subtypes still form the basis of current diagnostic systems, yet many have questioned their usefulness. Making subtype diagnoses such as these is extremely difficult, which often means that diagnostic reliability is dramatically reduced. Furthermore, the subtypes have little validity: knowing that a patient has been diagnosed as having one or another form of schizophrenia does not give us information that will be helpful in treatment or in predicting the course of the problems. Finally, there is considerable overlap among the subtypes. For example, patients with all forms of schizophrenia may have delusions. Thus the Kraepelinian system of subtyping has not proved to be an optimal way of trying to deal with the variability in schizophrenic behavior.

Supplemental subtypes that have been added in both the British Glossary and the DSM are also flawed, as definitions of two of them, the *latent* and *residual* types, will indicate. "[Latent schizophrenia] is used to designate those abnormal states in which, in the absence of obvious schizophrenic symptoms, the suspicion is strong that the condition is in fact a schizophrenia" (British Glossary, 1968). The category schizophrenia, residual type, "is for patients showing signs of schizophrenia but who, following a psychotic schizophrenic episode, are no longer psychotic" (DSM-II, 1968). Little wonder that the diagnostic reliability of these subtypes is low. For the many patients who do not fit neatly into one of the subtypes, having instead a "mixed" pattern of disturbances, *chronic undifferentiated,* now the most frequently used subtype from the DSM, was created. These are the "patients who show mixed schizophrenic symptoms and who present definite thought, affect, and behavior not classifiable under the other types of schizophrenia." It might be supposed that this diagnosis is applied only to patients who have been hospitalized for long periods of time. This is not the case, for the label chronic undifferentiated is often applied on a patient's first admission. It has become something of a wastebasket category.

## Dimensions of Schizophrenia

Some differentiations among schizophrenics may be useful, however, in view of the great diversity of symptoms. Researchers have found several variables or dimensions that appear to be helpful to them in the study of adult schizophrenics—paranoid-nonparanoid, acute-chronic, and good-poor premorbid adjustment. The paranoid-nonparanoid distinction is based primarily on the Kraepelinian subtype and is the only one of his categories that has proved helpful in contemporary research. Schizophrenics distinguished according to this dimension are classified in two groups, those who do and those who do not have delusions.

### Acute-chronic

The acute-chronic dimension has been defined in two ways. In DSM-II we find diagnostic types referred to as acute and chronic schizophrenics. The difference between them lies in the symptomatology being exhibited and in the suddenness with which the symptoms begin. Acute patients show a rapid onset and more obvious and florid symptomatology. Very often the disorder appears to have developed just after an emotionally painful experience. The chronic patient has more gradually withdrawn from others. The onset of symptoms has been insidious and apparently related to no particular incident.

In actual research practice, however, this distinction has referred primarily to length of hospitalization. Patients who have been hospitalized for only a short period are designated acutes, and those who have lived longer terms in an institution are called chronics. Although the exact cutoff points have varied, many workers have accepted two years after first admission as the upper limit of time for continuing to regard patients as acute (Neale and Cromwell, 1970). This cutoff point was chosen because after patients have remained in a hospital two years, it is unlikely that they will be subsequently discharged (Brown, 1960).

The research definitions of the acute-chronic dimension very likely relate to two aspects of schizophrenia. First, schizophrenics with shorter periods of hospitalization will be more likely to show the clear-cut, often bizarre and intense symptomatology of the acute patient. Schizophrenics with longer periods of hospitalization are likely to be apathetic and withdrawn. Second, the research definition is also relevant in attempting to determine the effects of prolonged institutionalization. There is reason to believe that institutionalization itself can profoundly and adversely influence behavior (Goffman, 1961). Thus the research definition divides patients according to the extent that they may have been affected by hospitalization.

### Premorbid adjustment

A person's social and sexual adjustment before the onset of symptoms is referred to as premorbid adjustment. Several means of assessing premorbid adjustment have been devised, the most prominent being the Phillips Scale (1953), which was initially developed as a method of predicting the success of electroconvulsive therapy (Chapter 20). Although it was somewhat useful in determining whether this therapy should be tried, the Phillips Scale proved better at predicting prognosis among schizophrenics, regardless of the treatment chosen, on the basis of what it revealed about their earlier adjustment. The scale is filled out by the researcher from case history material that has been collected on the patient's social and sexual functioning during adolescence and early adulthood. On the basis of earlier behavior as rated by the scale, patients can be divided into those who showed good premorbid adjustment and those who showed poor premorbid adjustment. Patients with good premorbid adjustment had adequate interpersonal and sexual relations before the onset of their problems, but those with poor premorbid adjustment were socially and sexually incompetent.

Actually, the total amount of information collected on the Phillips Scale reveals no more about the premorbid adjustment of a male schizophrenic than asking a single question. Has he ever been married (Held and Cromwell, 1968)? The behavior that designates a male schizophrenic as having good premorbid adjustment—having friends, dating, and the like—may also have eventuated in his marriage. In contrast, such traits as having few interests, not dating, and avoiding others are likely to lead to a solitary life, at least for men. In women similar behavior may be interpreted as shyness or demureness, attributes that have not generally been considered socially undesirable for them. Therefore a relatively "schizoid" adolescent female may be more likely to become married than her male counterpart would. The traditional social role of women conspires to make marriage a poorer measure of the premorbid adjustment of a female schizophrenic. Perhaps the growing equality between the sexes will eventually make marriage as valid a measure of the premorbid adjustment of female schizophrenics as it is now for males.

Later in this chapter we shall examine how premorbid adjustment is reflected in the laboratory performances of schizophrenic patients. Here its connections with nonlaboratory aspects of schizophrenia will be explored. Most important perhaps are onset, symptomatology, and prognosis. A patient who has had a good premorbid adjustment has a more rapid onset of more severe symptoms and improves more rapidly than do those who have had a poor premorbid adjustment (Phillips, 1953). Until the rapid onset of his difficulties, most people considered the good premorbid to be a relatively normal individual. Then in response to some stress, such as a divorce or the loss of a loved one, his behavior suddenly becomes bizarre and psychotic. Almost overnight the patient has found the world changed, and he is perplexed and depressed. Other people believe that he has lost his mind. His thinking and speech are disorganized, and he may have delusions and be in a great panic because he does not understand what is happening to him. He is confused and terrified by the loss of control over his thoughts and feelings, but he is also likely to be quite verbal and intensely excited.

In contrast, the patient with poor premorbid adjustment appears to have been a relatively deviant individual for a long period of time. He probably had difficulties at school and did not date much or have many friends. Gradually, he has become more seclusive and more withdrawn, until finally his deterioration cannot be ignored and he is hospitalized. Rather than manifesting particularly severe and bizarre symptomatology, however, he is uncommunicative, apathetic, and inactive, and he seems to accept the way he is. Having suffered insidious yet massive depletion of thought, emotions, interests, and activity, and having functioned marginally for so long, the schizophrenic with poor premorbid adjustment is unresponsive to treatment and has a poor prognosis. Thus he is more likely to remain in the hospital and to become chronic according to the research definition of that term. Therefore, even though we know that one group of schizophrenic patients had good earlier adjustment and the other poor, we cannot be certain that the differences observed at present between the two groups stem from the varying earlier adjustments or from the longer hospitalizations of the members of one of the groups.

Although the premorbid-adjustment distinction has been widely used in American studies of schizophrenia, some questions can be raised about it. In Europe, for example, some patients who would be considered to have had good premorbid adjustments are not viewed as "true" schizophrenics at all. Instead, they are assigned a separate category such as schizophreniform (schizophreniclike) psychosis. Furthermore, schizophrenics with good and poor premorbid adjustments differ in so many ways—the pace of onset, prognosis, cognitive processes, response to drug therapy—that applying a single term schizophrenia to both groups may be inappropriate. Indeed, the notion that a schizophrenic might have had a good premorbid adjustment may contribute in a major way to the excessive use of the diagnosis in the United States.

## Laboratory Research with Adult Schizophrenics

In their quest for a better understanding of schizophrenia, researchers have examined a number of psychological processes, among them motivation, learning, perception, and cognition. The primary goal of this research has been to obtain a detailed and precise knowledge of processes that may become deviant and are thus relevant to certain important types of schizophrenic behavior. Researchers attempt to answer questions such as "Why do schizophrenics make deviant associations?" "What produces hallucinations?" "How is schizophrenic attention deviant?"

We have already noted, for example, that clinicians view disorders of thought and language as crucial signs of schizophrenia. But what exactly is disordered in thought disorder? Chapman and Chapman (1973) report the following answer that a schizophrenic patient gave to the question "Why do you think people believe in God?"

> *Uh, late, I don't know why, let's see balloon travel. He holds it up for you, the balloon. He don't let you fall out, your little legs sticking out down through the clouds. He's down to the smoke stack, looking through the smoke trying to get the balloon gassed up you know. Way they're flying on top that way, legs sticking out, I don't know, looking down on the ground, heck, that'd make you go dizzy you just stay and sleep you know, hold down and sleep there. The balloon's His home you know up there. I used to sleep outdoors, you know, sleep outdoors instead of going home. He's had a home but His not tell where it's at you know* (p. 3).

The patient's response is clearly disordered, but can we specify the nature of the disorder more precisely? It would seem that the patient wanders off the topic, bringing in details, such as sleeping outdoors, that seem irrelevant to the question asked. Chapman and Chapman note that different observers might account for irrelevancy in varying ways.

1. The patient is unable to organize his thoughts coherently. A disordered associative process leads the patient from thinking of God's home, which he believes to be in the sky, to thinking of balloons because they are also in the sky.

2. The patient can deal with only one idea at a time.

3. The question was too abstract for the patient.

4. The patient's own personal feelings of being weak and alone intrude into his answer. He mentions the possibility of "falling out," "little legs," and so on.

These several descriptions of a single bit of schizophrenic dialogue illustrate how clinical data can be explained in a variety of ways. Laboratory research tries to determine which account is best by arranging special tests that pit the competing explanations against one another and allow incorrect ones to be discarded.

In any research on pertinent psychological processes, the performance of a group of adult schizophrenics is compared to that of a nonschizophrenic control group. Generally, schizophrenics are found to do more poorly than the control group, and the poor performance of the patients is termed a *psychological deficit.* The major difficulty of this research, discussed previously in Chapter 4, is that it is correlational in nature. The variable of primary interest is schizophrenic-nonschizophrenic, which has *not* been manipulated by an experimenter. Thus differences between schizophrenic and control groups in addition to the diagnosis may be regarded as plausible rival hypotheses to account for the varying performances. And there are many such differences and rival hypotheses. The schizophrenic and control groups are likely to vary in intelligence and social class, as indicated earlier; moreover, the schizophrenics are likely to be taking a tranquilizing medication and to be institutionalized. We must keep in mind that because this research is correlational, the conclusions drawn can be only tentatively accepted.[2]

We turn now to a selective review of three areas that have attracted much attention from researchers—effects of punishment, perception, and cognition.

## The Effects of Punishment on Schizophrenics

Why does the schizophrenic lose contact with reality? One answer to this question, proposed by Rodnick and Garmezy (1957), is that schizophrenics are especially sensitive to failure or censure. In many life situations a person may experience a sense of not measuring up or of having incurred the disapproval of others. He or she may say the wrong thing to a group of friends or perform poorly in school or at work. If schizophrenics are particularly sensitive to the pain of failure, they might be expected to take steps to reduce this source of distress. One means would be to withdraw into a private world.

Comparing the reactions of schizophrenics and normal people to criticism is one way of testing the theory that schizophrenics are sensitive to failure. Garmezy (1952) compared the performance of schizophrenic and control subjects on a perceptual task after each had been censured or praised. In support of the theory, the schizophrenics were found to make more errors after censure than after praise, in contrast to the members of a control group, who improved their performances after being censured. Similar results were found by Webb (1955) on a conceptual task, by Bleke (1953) on a memory task, and by Alvarez (1957) on a size judgment task. These studies had also subdivided their schizophrenics

[2] Much of the research on the etiology of schizophrenia, which is discussed in the next chapter, is also correlational in design and thus subject to the same problems mentioned here.

Norman Garmezy, a psychologist at the University of Minnesota, theorizes that a key component of schizophrenia is extreme sensitivity to censure.

into these who had had good premorbid adjustment and those who had had poor. Schizophrenics with poor premorbid adjustment were found to suffer more from censure.

Not all investigators, however, have found that punishment or censure makes schizophrenic patients perform more poorly. In fact, the results of a number of these investigations have indicated the opposite. As Buss and Lang (1965) noted, "in all studies employing physical punishment there has been a definite reduction, and in a few instances a temporary elimination, of psychological deficit. . . . both a negative evaluation and specific verbal or physical punishment for errors can lead to a significant improvement in performance rather than further deficit" (pp. 10-11).

Garmezy (1966) has attempted to reconcile these two seemingly conflicting sets of data. He still assumes that schizophrenics are particularly sensitive to censure, but he proposes that the effects of censure depend on the situation in which it occurs. Censure, Garmezy surmises, makes schizophrenics perform more poorly when it is not directly connected to the task and cannot be avoided. In contrast, when censure follows an incorrect response, it helps them eliminate that response on future occasions. In reanalyzing the data from several earlier studies. Garmezy demonstrated that schizophrenics, especially those with poor premorbid adjustment, avoided censured responses more often than did members of various control groups. Whether this avoidance of the censured response facilitated or hindered performance depended on the nature of the task at hand. In one study, performance on a reaction time task (see next page) was *facilitated* by censuring slow responses. In this instance, being sensitive to censure, schizophrenics reacted more quickly in order to avoid censure (Cavanaugh, Cohen, and Lang, 1960). But another task might, for example, require the subject to learn a sequence of lever presses A and B, with incorrect responses being censured. The correct order might be A, B, A, A, A, B. Suppose that a schizophrenic presses A twice; his second press would then be censured because B is the correct response. Since he is sensitive to censure, after an A response proves incorrect, he is likely to avoid the A lever and press B on the third trial. But A is the correct third response. In this task censure would produce *poor* performance. In an experiment similar to this, Bleke (1953) did find that censure interfered with performance.

This finding that schizophrenics are especially sensitive to censure fits well with certain aspects of their behavior. Their social withdrawal and their reluctance to seek work may indicate that they wish to avoid the possible failure and censure that might ensue if they did try to find friends and a job. Garmezy (1977) points out that the theory has also received support from Brown's investigations of the relation between the homelife of patients and the course of schizophrenic disorders (for example, Brown et al., 1962; Brown, Birley, and Wing, 1972).

In Brown's 1972 study the families of a large sample of schizophrenics were interviewed at the time of the patient's admission to the hospital. The clinicians noted not only what had been happening in the home but also the feelings that family members expressed toward the patient during the course of the interview. If family members have negative emotions about the patient, we would expect these to have a bad effect on the schizophrenic, perhaps even sending him or her back to the hospital once released. This is exactly what was found when an overall index of negative emotion expressed by family members was related to data on relapse collected over a subsequent nine-month period. Among families expressing few negative emotions, patients' relapse rates were 16 percent; among families expressing many, the figure was 58 percent. In this more naturalistic study a punishing family environment apparently played upon the schizophrenics' heightened sensitivity to censure, with a very unfavorable outcome for the patients.

## Perceptual Research

### Attention

Disordered attention has long been viewed as an important aspect of schizophrenia. And schizophrenics themselves report difficulty in attending to the world around them (see page 340). But what does it mean to say that attention is disordered in schizophrenics? Recent research has construed the concept of attention in two different ways, as alertness or readiness to respond and as a selective process. The first interpretation of attention, namely alertness and readiness to respond, has been the focus of numerous studies performed by David Shakow and his colleagues.

Reaction time is the amount of time it takes to make a response to a particular stimulus. A frequently used reaction time task requires a subject to lift his or her finger from a telegraph key as soon as a light comes on or a buzzer is sounded. Schizophrenics have consistently been shown to have slower reactions on such tests than various other control subjects. This slowness is more marked in chronic and nonparanoid patients than in acute and paranoid patients (Shakow, 1963). The finding that the schizophrenic's reaction time is slow does not, of course, point directly to a deficit in attention, for difficulty in making voluntary motor responses could also be responsible. Other studies on reaction time make lack of attention a plausible interpretation, however.

The preparatory interval in a reaction time task is a highly significant determinant of reaction time performance; this interval is the time between the onset of the warning signal and the showing of the actual stimulus. Chronic patients take much longer to react to the actual stimulus when the preparatory interval is long, eight or more seconds. They do not appear to be able to maintain a readiness to respond to the upcoming stimulus.

A comparison of the effects of regular preparatory intervals versus irregular backs up this conclusion. Normal controls respond more quickly when the preparatory intervals are regular—for example, a series of trials with a three-second preparatory interval, then a series with six-second intervals, and so on—than when the length of the preparatory interval is irregular and varies randomly from trial to trial. Schizophrenics, on the other hand, make only limited use of the information provided by regularity in length of preparatory interval and may be slower when preparatory intervals are regular than when they are irregular (Shakow, 1962; Bellissimo and Steffy, 1972).

The second interpretation of attention, that it is a selective process, points up the fact that there is simply too much information present in our world for us to process, making some selection necessary. The cognitive disorganization shown by many schizophrenic patients may very well reflect a failure to resist the impact of distracting information. In fact, some research has found schizophrenics to be particularly distractible. Rappaport (1967) investigated the performance of schizophrenic and normal subjects on a competing-message task. Several auditory messages were presented simultaneously. The subjects were required to attend to only one of them and then to repeat it back. The number of simultaneously presented messages varied from one to seven. The performance of the schizophrenics was always deficient whenever more than one message was offered. But not all research has found that schizophrenics are especially distractible (for example, Taylor and Hirt, 1975). Perhaps the conflicting results can be attributed in part to differences in the way the schizophrenic populations of the various studies had been diagnosed. This question, as well as several others, was studied by Oltmanns, O'Hayon, and Neale (in press).

Testing distractibility in relation to diagnosis required a complicated procedure. The role of diagnosis in distractibility was pursued by diagnosing the patients according to two different systems. First, patients who had been diagnosed schizophrenic by hospital personnel were chosen as subjects. Distractibility was tested by a digit span task. In the no-distractor version of the task selected, subjects heard a voice presenting a sequence of numbers at a rate of one every two seconds. After listening to the string, the participant tried to recall as many digits as possible. In the distractor version another voice presented several *irrelevant* digits between each relevant one. The difference in performance of these two tasks was the measure of distractibility. Hospital-diagnosed schizophrenics were no more distractible than controls, at least to no statistically significant degree. But then the schizophrenic subjects were rediagnosed using more stringent, Europeanlike diagnostic rules developed by Spitzer, Endicott, and Robins (1975). The schizophrenics separated out by the second diagnosis were found to be quite distractible, significantly more so than both the normal controls and the remaining patients who had now been judged not schizophrenic.

Additional evidence collected by Oltmanns and his colleagues also attests to the potential importance of distractibility in schizophrenia. The symptoms of each patient as recorded in their case histories were graded and then related to distractibility. Since distractibility is hypothesized to be a determinant of thought disorder, the correlation between these two variables was expected to be high. This is exactly what was found. Finally, a new sampling of patients, some still receiving medication, others not, was tested. Since certain drugs are known to improve schizophrenic behavior (see page 555), they should affect distractibility, if indeed it is an important component of schizophrenia. The schizophrenics who had been withdrawn from medication were found more distractible than those who were not.

The findings on the attention of schizophrenics can be summed up by two statements.

1. Schizophrenics have difficulty maintaining a readiness to respond.
2. Schizophrenics are especially distractible.

The two points may be related. Perhaps the schizophrenic fails to maintain a readiness to respond because of the "pull" of distracting, irrelevant information. Both points may help to explain the schizophrenic's thought and speech disorders. Because he or she does not discriminate between relevant and irrelevant information, "cognitive clutter" is the result. There is simply too much information for schizophrenics to process; when they try to order their thoughts, they become incoherent and confused. This confusion plus an inability to maintain attention then becomes evident in the irrelevancies and loose associations of schizophrenic speech.

### Hallucinations

Another kind of schizophrenic perceptual disturbance that has been researched is the hallucination. Mintz and Alpert (1972) hypothesized that having a predisposition for vivid imagining and an impaired perception of reality may explain why schizophrenics hallucinate. They administered two tests to three groups of hospitalized mental patients—hallucinating schizophrenics, nonhallucinating schizophrenics, and nonschizophrenic patients. In the first test the subject was asked to close his eyes and imagine hearing a phonograph record playing "White Christmas" with both words and music. After thirty seconds the subject rated the vividness of the image he was able to produce on a scale ranging from "I heard a phonograph record of 'White Christmas' clearly and believed that the record was actually playing" to "I did not hear the record." For a second test earphones were placed on the subject through which he was to hear a set of twenty-four sentences, each with an intelligibility level of about 50 percent. Each time a sentence was presented, the subject tried to repeat exactly what he had heard and rated his confidence in the accuracy of his rendition on a scale ranging from "positive correct" to "positive incorrect."

On the imagination task 85 percent of the hallucinating schizophrenics reported either that they had heard "White Christmas" and believed that the record was actually playing or that they had heard the song clearly but knew that a record was not really playing. One of the hallucinating schizophrenics who had not heard "White Christmas" said that his voices were talking too loudly for him to listen to the record. In contrast, only 5 percent of the nonhallucinating schizophrenics reported having heard the record with any vividness. The accuracy scores on the sentence detection task and the ratings by which the subject had indicated his confidence in his own renditions were compared. The correlation was +.54 for the hallucinating schizophrenics and +.84 for the nonhallucinating schizophrenics. Hallucinating schizophrenics were poorer at judging the accuracy of their performance.

What do these results reveal about hallucinations? How well the subject imagined hearing "White Christmas" was assumed to reflect his vividness of imagery. His capacity to perceive reality was supposedly measured by the correlation between the actual accuracy of his sentence renditions and his confidence in their accuracy—for anyone in contact with reality is assumed able to assess accurately his performance of a task. Hallucinating schizophrenics showed *both* vivid imagery *and* a defective capacity for perceiving reality. Hallucinations may therefore reflect a failure to discriminate between self-produced images and stimulation in the external world. A greater capacity for vivid imagery and loss of contact with reality should increase the likelihood of hallucinations.[3]

In a corroborative study McGuigan (1966) instructed patients to press a key whenever they experienced an auditory hallucination. At the same time recordings were made of electrical activity in the subject's larynx. In this fashion McGuigan could compare the outputs of the larynx when the patient was experiencing auditory hallucinations and when he was not. The patient's report that he was hallucinating correlated remarkably with an increase in electrical activity in the larynx. Patients reporting auditory hallucinations may merely be talking to themselves but interpreting the internal speech as coming from the external world.

## Cognitive Research

Researchers have also tried to elucidate the deviant cognitive processes that may contribute to the incoherent speech of schizophrenics. Many investigators have attempted to demonstrate qualitative differences between the associative responses of schizophrenic and those of normal subjects. Structured word association tests, for example, have been used to determine whether the patient's associations to common words are particularly deviant. In these tests a standard list of words is read to patients after they have been instructed to respond to each with the first word that comes to mind. Schizophrenics, especially chronics, have frequently been found to make

[3] The correlation between vivid imagery and hallucinations may also indicate that the experience of hallucinating facilitates vivid imaginings.

more unusual associations than various control groups (Dokecki, Polidoro, and Cromwell, 1965). For example, instead of responding "dog" to the word "bark," the schizophrenic might say "moon."

Most theoretical explanations of deviant schizophrenic associations involve the notion of a response hierarchy. Any stimulus can evoke a number of responses, which vary in the likelihood of occurrence. For example, the stimulus word "table" may evoke several responses varying from the very probable "chair" to a less probable "tennis," down to rare responses such as "night." Broen and Storms (1966) have proposed that the response hierarchies of schizophrenics have partially collapsed, and that the probabilities of the dominating and competing responses have become more nearly equal (Table 13.3). The result, of course, would be both more deviant and idiosyncratic responses. But not all evidence favors the view of an idiosyncratic associative repertoire.

Cohen and Camhi (1967) tested schizophrenic and control subjects in a word association task somewhat similar to the television game "Password." One subject, the speaker, is shown a series of word pairs, one pair at a time. For each word pair, for example, "car-automobile," the experimenter designates one of the words as the target. The speaker is then told to provide a one-word clue that will help another person distinguish the target word from the other one. Effective clues to the word "car," in the car-automobile pair, might be "sports," "hop," or "railroad." The words "crash," "vehicle," and "wheels" would be less effective clues. A second subject, the listener, is given each word pair and the speaker's clue. The listener's task is to guess which member of each word pair is the target.

Four groups of subjects were studied—schizophrenic speakers with schizophrenic listeners, schizophrenic speakers with normal listeners, normal speakers with schizophrenic listeners, and normal speakers with normal listeners. The results (Table 13.4) reveal that schizophrenic speakers were inferior to normal speakers. That is, the clue words chosen by schizophrenics made the listeners perform significantly more poorly whether they were schizophrenic or normal. In contrast, with a normal speaker, schizophrenic listeners were about as accurate as their normal counterparts in choosing the correct target word.

These results are difficult to explain if it is simply assumed that schizophrenics have deviant associative hierarchies. Such a deficit should make them perform as poorly as listeners as they do as speakers. The listener must decide which word

TABLE **13.3**
Hypothetical Probabilities of Associative Responses to a Stimulus

| Stimulus word | Associative responses | Probability that normal subjects will give response | Probability that schizophrenic will give response |
|---|---|---|---|
| table | chair | .60 | .23 |
| | top | .25 | .18 |
| | tennis | .11 | .16 |
| | car | .02 | .13 |
| | run | .01 | .14 |
| | shoe | .01 | .16 |

is the target on the basis of what associations best link the clue word to one of the paired words. To the extent that the listener's associative hierarchies are idiosyncratic, linking of clue words to the target would supposedly be less accurate. The finding that the schizophrenic's accuracy as listener matches that of the normal control indicates that, at least with regard to word association hierarchies, there may not be a *qualitative* difference between the two populations.

With the help of Nachmani and Rosenberg, Cohen (1974) has now followed up his earlier work on schizophrenics' associations deficits. Colors were presented on disks in displays that varied in two ways, the number of disks and the "hue steps" between disks. Twenty-four first-admission schizophrenics and twenty-four medical center employees were tested individually in the speaker role. Each participant was shown a series of disk displays; for each display he was asked to describe the color of the disk designated by the experimenter "so that another person with the same colors in front of him will know which color you are talking about." The subject's descriptions were tape-recorded and his reaction times—the number of seconds between presentation of the display and the beginning of his response—were noted. Later, to measure the associative accuracy of these tape-recorded descriptions, they were played for a panel of people who were asked to pick out the colored disk that had been described. Finally, a week after the subjects were initially tested in the speaker role, they were tested as listeners to their own descriptions.

As expected, schizophrenics were significantly poorer at devising useful descriptions than were the controls. When depending on their descriptions of the colors, the listener panel made substantially more errors in choosing the correct disk, except when the disks in the display were not very similar in color. For example, with quite dissimilar colors, a purple-blue and a red, and with the purple-blue as the referent, the following descriptions were given.

*Normal S1:* "Purple."

*Normal S3:* "This is purple-blue."

*Schizophrenic S1:* "Blue."

*Schizophrenic S3:* "The bluer."

But with similar colors, a red and a slightly more yellowish red, and with the red as the referent, the following descriptions were typical.

*Normal S1:* "Both are salmon-colored. This one, however, has more pink."

*Normal S3:* "My God this is hard. They are both the same except that this one might be a little redder."

*Schizophrenic S2:* "This is the stupid color of a shit ass bowl of salmon. Mix it with mayonnaise. Then it gets tasty. Leave it alone and puke all over the fuckin' place. Puke fish."

*Schizophrenic S3:* "Make-up. Pancake make-up. You put it on your face and they think guys run after you. Wait a second! I don't put it on my face and guys don't run after me. Girls put it on them."

Schizophrenics were also less accurate than the controls when choosing disks on the basis of

TABLE **13.4**
Schizophrenics as Speakers and Listeners
(from Cohen and Camhi, 1967)

| | Communication accuracy, percent of correct choices made by each speaker-listener group | |
|---|---|---|
| | Listeners | |
| Speakers | Schizophrenic | Normal |
| Schizophrenic | 66 | 67 |
| Normal | 72 | 74 |

their own recorded descriptions. Finally, the reaction times of the schizophrenics were usually longer than those of the controls. When the displays contained more disks or disks of similar color, the reaction times of members of both groups were longer than when disks were few and dissimilar, reflecting the greater difficulty of the task. But the reaction times of the schizophrenics were more than proportionately longer.

In discussing their results, Cohen, Nachmani, and Rosenberg evaluated several models that might explain the schizophrenics' associative inadequacy. In all the models they evaluated, the associative process was conceptualized as consisting of two stages, sampling and comparison. In the sampling stage the person thinks of a number of ways of describing the referent. In the comparison stage he or she determines the degree of association between each of the tentative descriptive phrases and the referent, decides whether they distinguish it from the nonreferent colors, and then picks the best phrase.

One model, called the *Tower of Babel,* asserts that schizophrenics sample from a repertoire of idiosyncratic phrases. Thus they would be poor describers but, and this is the important point, they should be able to respond accurately to their own descriptions. Since the outcome belied this second prediction, the model was abandoned. The *impulsive-speaker* model asserts that schizophrenics sample normally from a nondeviant repertoire of phrases but then fail to go through the comparison stage, that is, they fail to self-edit. Failure to self-edit should lessen the effectiveness of the schizophrenic's description for both the listener panel and self. These two predictions of the impulsive-speaker model were supported by the data. If schizophrenics spend no time comparing phrases, however, their reaction time should *not* change when the number of disks in a display is increased or when their colors are more similar. The findings indicated otherwise. Finally, the authors consider and tentatively accept a *perseveration-chaining* model. This position asserts that schizophrenics are unable to ignore a phrase that occurs to them, even though they recognize that it constitutes a poor description. Most phrases would rather inadequately distinguish among many and similar disks. The schizophrenic therefore perseverates or samples and resamples the same inappropriate phrase until it is emitted as a response. Then the schizophrenic begins the chaining process, uttering a new response evoked by the one already given, and then another and another one to each immediately preceding response. This model predicts the inadequacy of the descriptions, both for the listener panel and self and also the observed increases in reaction time. Finally, this model implies that the utterances of schizophrenics should be longer than normal, which they were.

Adopting a somewhat different approach, other investigators have sought *quantitative* abnormalities in schizophrenic associations. On the basis of the results of several investigations, Loren Chapman and his colleagues have proposed that the types of errors characterizing schizophrenic performance are also committed, although less frequently, by normal subjects. In many instances schizophrenics do not make errors that are *qualitatively different* from those made by normal individuals. Rather they make *more* of the *same* kinds of errors (Chapman, Chapman, and Miller, 1964).

In an early study Chapman (1958) employed a card-sorting task in which single words were printed on cards. The subject was shown an array of three different cards, then handed a fourth card and asked to place it with the card that belonged to the same category. For example, on one trial the subject was given the word "gold." The alternatives with which it could be sorted were "fish," an incorrect response which is related associatively to "gold"; "steel," the correct response, also a metal; and "typewriter," an irrelevant, incorrect response. The inclination to respond to "gold" by selecting "fish" is a normal error. Chapman hypothesized that schizophrenics would produce significantly more errors of this type than normal subjects, but that they would not produce more irrelevant errors ("typewriter"). This was in fact found to be the case, lending support to the assertion that the thought processes of schizophrenics are quantitatively but not qualitatively different from those of normal individuals.

In a related series of studies, Chapman, Chapman, and Miller (1964) demonstrated that schizophrenics frequently interpret double-meaning words on the basis of the stronger of their two meanings, even when the context indicates that the weaker one is appropriate. They constructed a test composed of items such as the following.

> *When the farmer bought a herd of cattle, he needed a new pen. This means*
> *A. He needed a new writing implement. (Incorrect response in this context, but the usual definition of the word.)*
> *B. He needed a new fenced enclosure. (Correct response in this context, but a less usual definition of the word.)*
> *C. He needed a new pick-up truck. (Irrelevant response.)*

The schizophrenics chose the A alternative more often that did the normal subjects. Neither group made the error of choosing C with any great frequency. On the basis of these and other findings, the investigators concluded that an exaggeration of normal errors explains the frequent misinterpretation of words by schizophrenics.

Although Chapman has thus far tested his quantitative theory only in studies of the schizophrenic's misuse of words, it has potentially much greater implications. In particular, there is a strong similarity between the results of these studies and those, discussed in an earlier section, that revealed the distractibility of the schizophrenic. The cognitive distortions of schizophrenics may reflect their susceptibility to irrelevant cues when they are processing information. ■

## Summary

The diagnosis of schizophrenia is complicated by differences between American and European practices. The American concept of schizophrenia is considerably broader than the European one; the available evidence indicates that the European definition is preferable because of its increased reliability and validity. The basic symptoms of schizophrenia are autism and withdrawal as well as disturbances in cognition and thought—thought disorder, loose associations, and delusions; in perception and attention—hallucinations and difficulties in maintaining attention; in motor behavior—grimacing, gesturing, and flailing of the limbs or catatonia and waxy flexibility; and in affect—flat, inappropriate, and ambivalent. A review of the schizophrenic subtypes proposed by Kraepelin and in DSM-II indicated the great variability in the behavior of schizophrenic patients. Although the Kraepelinian system has not proved useful in research, except for the paranoid-nonparanoid dimension, distinguishing schizophrenics by premorbid adjustment and chronicity has facilitated research. The performance of schizophrenics on laboratory tasks has indeed furthered our understanding of some schizophrenic behavior. For example, schizophrenics may withdraw from social relationships because of a heightened sensitivity to censure. Perceptual research has shown that schizophrenics have difficulty in maintaining attention and that they are especially distractible. Cognitive research has tried to pinpoint crucial processes that may explain thought disorder; much work has been done on associative looseness. Cohen's research has shown that schizophrenics' association problems may result from perseveration and chaining. In selecting descriptive words, schizophrenics are unable to ignore a poor choice and then give further associations to that choice. Any theory of the etiology of schizophrenia will have to account for the descriptive and laboratory data presented in this chapter. ■ ■

# chapter 14

## SCHIZOPHRENIA: THEORY AND RESEARCH ON ETIOLOGY



The preceding chapter summarized research undertaken to determine how schizophrenics differ from normal people in the ways they think, feel, and behave. What can explain their delusions and bewildering hallucinations, their wanting or inappropriate emotions, the scattering and disconnections of their thoughts? To borrow from the words of a poet, we might ask "What could frame their fearful dissymmetries?" Several major theoretical views—psychoanalytic, social-learning, and the experiential theory of R. D. Laing—will be reviewed first. Then the research on etiological factors such as social class, the family, genetic background, biochemical abnormalities, and the developmental histories of individuals who have later in life become schizophrenic will be examined.

## Major Theoretical Positions

### Psychoanalytic Theory

Because Freud himself dealt primarily with neuroses, he had relatively little to say about schizophrenia. He did occasionally speculate on its origins, though, using some of the psychoanalytic concepts that he applied to all disordered personalities. His basic notion was that schizophrenics have regressed to a state of "primary narcissism," a phase early in the oral stage before the ego has differentiated from the id. There is thus no separate ego to engage in reality testing—a crucial function whereby the ego takes actions that test the nature of its social and physical environment. By regressing to narcissism, schizophrenics have effectively lost contact with the world; they have withdrawn the libido from attachment to any objects external to themselves. Freud thought that the cause of the regression was an increase, during adulthood, in the intensity of id impulses, especially sexual ones. Contemporary psychoanalytic theorists give primacy to aggressive impulses. Whether the threats of the intense id impulses provoke schizophrenia or a neurosis depends on the strength of the ego. Neurotics, having developed a more stable ego, will not regress to the first psychosexual stage, as schizophrenics do, and will not lose contact with reality.

Some of the major symptoms of schizophrenia—lack of interpersonal relationships and passivity—are considered reflections of this regression. Other symptoms such as hallucinations and bizarre speech are regarded as the outcomes of attempts to deal with the id impulses and with reality—attempts to cope with the flood of id impulses demanding discharge and at the same time to reestablish contact with something other than the self. The patient, having withdrawn from reality, creates an inner world of hallucinations.

Few data bear on the psychoanalytic position. The theory has generated speculative analysis of case history material (see Box 14.1) but little research. The material on cognitive deficits presented in Chapter 13 as well as similar data collected by analytically oriented researchers (for example, Bellak, Hurvich, and Gediman, 1973) could be said to demonstrate that the egos of schizophrenics have been impaired. But even so, ego impairment need not be precipitated by an increase in id impulses, nor need it end in a regression to a childhood state. Finally, no one has presented evidence that ego impairments cause schizophrenia.

## Social-Learning Theory

*"The crucial behavior, from which other indications of schizophrenia may be deduced, lies in the extinction of attention to social stimuli to which 'normal' people respond"* (p. 357). In these few italicized words Ullmann and Krasner (1975) have summarized their position on the development of schizophrenia. They view faulty attention as causing much of the classic schizophrenic behavior discussed in the previous chapter. They argue that a dysfunction in attention whereby other than usual cues are heeded can account for the loose associations and irrelevancies of the schizophrenic's speech. At the same time, inattention to the cues that are part of the culture, and that consist very importantly of other people, makes the individual appear aloof and socially isolated.

In addition, Ullmann and Krasner see schizophrenia as a social role, one which the mental health professionals and the psychiatric hospital to a great extent determine. In short, they see the mental health professional as selectively rewarding schizophrenic behavior. This is an important and sensitive issue in the study of schizophrenia and has both scientific and social significance. Many of the descriptions of schizophrenia refer to behavior observed within a mental hospital, making it difficult to know how much of the peculiar behavior is caused by the presumed illness and how much is caused, in part, by the social setting of the mental institution. Ullmann and Krasner hold that the behavior we term schizophrenic must be regarded for the most part as a reaction to the reinforcement it receives within the mental hospital. According to this theory, patients "talk crazy" because hospital staff members attend more to them when their verbalizations are bizarre than when they are quiet and rational.

A series of studies performed by Braginsky and his colleagues is regarded as support for the view that schizophrenia is a learned social role. One investigation (Braginsky, Grosse, and Ring, 1966) was designed to examine whether hospitalized patients can manipulate the impressions they create on others. Acute and chronic patients completed a short form of the MMPI. Some pa-

## BOX 14.1 Paranoia and Repressed Homosexuality

According to DSM-II paranoid delusions may occur in both paranoid schizophrenia and in the so-called paranoid state. The paranoid state is a more transitory psychosis characterized principally by delusions. The patient's contact with reality is impaired, but his or her behavior is not as disordered as that of a schizophrenic. Freud's theory of paranoia, commonly accepted even today, is that delusions result from repressed homosexual impulses which are striving for expression. The anxiety stemming from their threatened expression is handled primarily by the defense mechanism of projection, attributing to others feelings that are unacceptable to one's own ego (Freud, 1915). The basic unconscious thought is "I, a man, love him" (or "I, a woman, love her"). Freud considered the common paranoid delusions of persecution and grandiosity to derive from distortions, and then projection, of this basic homosexual urge.

In *delusions of persecution* the homosexual thought "I, a man, love him," being unacceptable to the ego, is converted into the less threatening statement "I, a man, hate him." Since the emotion expressed by this premise is also less than satisfactory, it is further transformed by projection into "He hates me, so I am justified in hating him." The final formulation may be "I hate him because he persecutes me." Freud asserted that the persecutor of a paranoid is always a person of the same sex who is unconsciously a love object for the individual.

*Delusions of grandiosity* (*megalomania*) begin with a contradiciton of the homosexual impulse. The sentence "I, a man, love him" is changed into "I do not love anyone." But since libido must be invested in or attached to something or someone, the psychic reality becomes "I love only myself."

One of Freud's lesser-known cases of a patient with paranoid delusions is of special interest, for it seems initially to challenge Freud's basic tenet that the persecutor must be a person of the same sex. The kinds of inferences that constitute the argument of this case study are typical of those made by Freud in his attempts to understand his clinical data and to test his hypotheses.

Freud was consulted by a lawyer in Vienna who had been hired by a woman to sue a male business associate for making indecent allegations about her. She stated that the man had had photographs taken of them while they were making love and was now threatening to bring disgrace upon her. Because of the unusual nature of her allegation, the lawyer had persuaded her to see Freud so that he could offer an opinion.

The woman, about thirty years of age, was an attractive single person who lived quietly with her mother, whom she supported. A handsome man in her firm had recently begun to court her. After much coaxing he had persuaded her to come to his apartment for an afternoon together. They became intimate, at which point she was frightened by a clicking noise coming from the direction of a desk in front of the window. The lover told her that it was probably from a small clock on the desk. As she left the house that afternoon, she encountered two men, one of them carrying a small package. They appeared to whisper something to each other secretively as she passed. By the time she reached home that evening, she had put together the following story. The box was a camera, the men were photographers, and her lover was an untrustworthy person who had arranged for photographs to be taken of them while they were undressed. The following day she began to berate the lover for his untrustworthiness, and he tried equally hard to change her mind about her unfounded suspicions. Freud read one of the letters that the man had written to the woman. It struck him that the lover was indeed sincere and honest in denying involvement in such plot.

At this point Freud faced a dilemma common in scientific inquiry. What should the investigator do when confronted by an instance that negates his hypothesis? The persecutor of the young woman appeared to be a member of the opposite sex. Freud could, of course, have completely abandoned his theory that paranoia originates in homosexual impulses. Instead, he looked more closely into the case to see whether there were subtle factors that would allow him, in the end, to preserve the integrity of his theory.

During a second meeting with Freud, the woman changed the story somewhat. She admitted that she had visited the man twice in his apartment, not once, and that only on the second occasion had she heard the suspicious noise. After the first and uneventful visit—as far as her paranoia was concerned—she had been disturbed by an incident that she had witnessed at the office. The next day she had seen her new lover speaking in low tones to an older woman who was in charge of the firm. This older person liked the younger woman a great deal, and the younger woman in turn found that her employer reminded her of her own mother. She was therefore very concerned about their conversation and became convinced that her suitor was telling the woman about their lovemaking the previous afternoon.

Then it occurred to her that her lover and her employer had been having a love affair for some time. At the first opportunity she berated her lover for telling their employer of their lovemaking. He naturally protested and after a while succeeded in undoing her suspicions. Then she made her second visit to his apartment and heard the reputed clicking.

Let us examine Freud's comments on this portion of the case history.

*These new details remove first of all any doubts as to the pathological nature of her suspicion. It is easy to see that the white haired elderly manageress is a mother-substitute, that in spite of his youth the lover had been put in the place of the father, and that the strength of the mother-complex has driven the patient to suspect a love-relationship between these ill-matched partners, however unlikely such a relation might be. Moreover, this fresh information resolves the apparent contradiction with the view maintained by psychoanalysis, that the development of a delusion of persecution is conditioned by an over-powerful homosexual bond. The original persecutor—the agency whose influence the patient wishes to escape—is here again not a man but a woman. The manageress knows about the girl's love-affairs, disapproves of them, and shows her disapproval by mysterious allusions. The woman's attachment to her own sex hinders her attempts to adopt a person of the other sex as a love object (1915, p. 155).*

To protect herself from her own homosexual impulses, the young woman is presumed to have developed a paranoid delusion about the man and her employer. A crucial aspect of the case, according to Freud, was the click that the woman had heard and interpreted as the sound of a camera shutter. Freud assumed that this click was actually a sensation or beat in her clitoris. Her sexual arousal, then, provided the basis for her paranoid delusion of being photographed.

Freud allowed himself a remarkable amount of unverified inference in this particular case. Because he wanted to hold to a homosexuality-based theory of paranoia, he inferred that the woman regarded her female superior as a substitute for her mother, that she had an undue homosexual attachment to her own mother and by generalization to this older woman, and that the click which she had heard was sexual excitation, construed in a paranoid fashion to be the sound of a camera shutter.

tients were told that the more items answered true, the more severely ill they were, and the more likely they were to remain in the hospital for a long time. Others were told that the more items answered true, the more they knew about themselves, the less severely ill they were, and the more likely they were to remain in the hospital for only a short period.

It was hypothesized that the chronic patients, who had been in the hospital for a long period of time, actually wished to remain there since they had adjusted to the hospital milieu. In contrast, acute patients were thought to be eager to leave. Assuming that patients can indeed manage the impression that they create on others, the following outcomes were expected. Acute patients would give more true responses when they thought these answers reflected self-insight, fewer when they believed them to reflect mental illness. Chronic patients would give more true responses when they believed them to prove mental illness, fewer when they considered them to prove self-insight. The results (Table 14.1) clearly supported the hypotheses. It indeed appeared that patients would try to manipulate the impression that they created on others in order to enhance their chances of either staying in the hospital or leaving it.

TABLE **14.1**
Average Number of "True" Responses Made by Chronic and Acute Patients
(from Braginsky et al., 1966)

| Groups | True means mental illness | True means self-insight |
|---|---|---|
| Chronic patients | 18.80 | 9.70 |
| Acute patients | 13.00 | 18.80 |

There have been problems in replicating this study (Price, 1972b; Ryan and Neale, 1973). Moreover, what does the fact that a hospitalized mental patient might try to create a particular impression in an interview or testing situation imply? That a person diagnosed as schizophrenic will attempt to look "less sick" if told how to do so does not in itself justify the conclusion that schizophrenia is nothing more than adoption of a social role. If a person with a stomachache that is caused by a viral infection is told his admission of discomfort will bring negative consequences, he may lie to a physician and not report the pain in his stomach. But this does not mean that he does not have a stomachache or a viral infection. Similarly, the fact that the schizophrenics in the Braginsky study answered true on the MMPI so as to create a particular impression does not demonstrate that schizophrenia is merely a social role. It indicates that schizophrenics can, under certain circumstances, be sensitive to social cues. The patients in the Braginsky study, it must be borne in mind, were not discharged on the basis of their faked MMPI responses! It must also be noted that although Ullmann and Krasner use Braginsky's data as support for their position, Braginsky's demonstration is inconsistent with the hypothesis that schizophrenics have withdrawn their attention from social stimuli.

Ullmann and Krasner's theory has little direct support. Indeed, the genetic studies reviewed later in this chapter contradict the theory that schizophrenia is learned entirely through the person's social interaction or the lack of it.

## An Experiential Theory

Ronald Laing has offered a view of schizophrenia that is similar in some respects to Ullmann and Krasner's. For him schizophrenia is not an illness but a label for a certain kind of problematic experience and behavior.

> . . . *The experience and behavior that gets labelled schizophrenic is a special sort*

*of strategy that a person invents in order to live in an unlivable situation . . . the person has come to be placed in an untenable position. He cannot make a move or make no move without being beset by contradictory pressures both internally, from himself, and externally, from those around him. He is, as it were, in a position of checkmate (1964, p. 186).*

Laing considers the family to be the primary culprit producing the behavior that is labeled schizophrenia. Rather than trying to remove the patient's symptoms, Laing argues that we should accept his or her experience as valid, understandable, and potentially meaningful and beneficial. The schizophrenic is on a psychedelic trip, necessitated by untenable environmental demands, and is in need of guidance—not control—if the destination of that trip is to be a state of enlightenment.

Ronald D. Laing, the British existential psychiatrist who believes that schizophrenia is a behavioral strategy adopted as a means of escaping the reality of an unlivable world.

Laing's ideas are popular among those who object to what they consider to be hypocrisies of society and of the mental health establishment. Those who experience the suffering associated with schizophrenia may also take comfort in the belief that they are going through a positive growth process. At this point, however, there is little evidence that experiencing schizophrenia can make a "better person" of the patient. When released from the hospital, most schizophrenics who had a poor premorbid adjustment live a marginal existence, isolated from social relationships. Nor, as we shall see later in this chapter, is there much evidence to support Laing's assertion that schizophrenia is caused by familial experiences.

## Conclusion

In sum, none of the major theoretical positions discussed has much support. Freud's views on regression to the oral stage, social-learning theories that emphasize role taking reinforced by the attitudes of family and mental hospital staff, and Laing's hypothesis that schizophrenia is a trip to improved functioning—all are without substantiating evidence.

Rather than construct elaborate theories, it may prove more fruitful to determine the etiological significance of particular discrete variables. A review of these variables will indicate how very complicated a theory will have to be to account for the problems called schizophrenia.

# Research on the Etiology of Schizophrenia

## Social Class and Schizophrenia

Numerous studies have shown a relation between social class and the diagnosis of schizophrenia. The highest rates of schizophrenia are found in central city areas inhabited by the lowest socioeconomic classes (for example, Hollingshead and Redlich, 1958; Srole et al., 1962). The relationship between social class and schizophrenia does not show a continuous progression of higher rates of schizophrenia as the social class becomes lower. Rather, there is a sharp *discontinuity* between the number of schizophrenics in the lowest social class and those in others. In the ten-year Hollingshead and Redlich study of social class and mental illness in New Haven, Connecticut, the rate of schizophrenia was found to be twice as high in the lowest social class as in the next to lowest. In addition, the correlation between schizophrenia and class appeared to be particularly strong among women. The findings of Hollingshead and Redlich have been confirmed cross-culturally by similar community studies carried out in countries such as Denmark, Norway, and England (Kohn, 1968).[1]

The correlations between social class and schizophrenia are consistent, but still difficult to interpret in causal terms. Some people believe that being in a low social class may in itself cause schizophrenia. The degrading treatment a person receives from others, the low level of education, and the unavailability of rewards and opportunity, taken together, may make membership in the lowest social class such a stressful experience that the individual develops schizophrenia.

But another explanation of the correlation between schizophrenia and low social class has also been suggested. During the course of their developing psychosis, schizophrenics may "drift" into the poverty-ridden areas of the city. The growing cognitive and motivational problems besetting these individuals may so impair their earning abilities that they cannot afford to live elsewhere. Or they may by choice move to areas where little social pressure will be brought to bear on them and where they can escape intense social relationships.

One way of resolving the conflict is to study the social mobility of schizophrenics. Three studies (Schwartz, 1946; Lystad, 1957; Turner and Wagonfeld, 1967) have found that schizophrenics are downwardly mobile in occupational status. But an equal number of studies has shown schizophrenics *not* to be downwardly mobile (Hollingshead and Redlich, 1958; Clausen and Kohn, 1959; Dunham, 1965). Kohn (1968) has suggested another way of examining this question. Are the fathers of schizophrenics also from the lowest social class? If they are, this could be considered evidence in favor of the hypothesis that lower-class status is conducive to schizophrenia, for class would be shown to *precede* schizophrenia. If the fathers are from a higher social class, the drift hypothesis would be the better explanation.

Goldberg and Morrison (1963) conducted such a study in England and Wales. The occupations of male schizophrenic patients were found to be less remunerative and prestigious than those of their fathers. Similarly, Turner and Wagonfeld (1967) found that schizophrenics failed to achieve as high an occupational level as would have been expected of them, judging from their family's social class. These data contradict the hypothesis that being brought up as a member of a lower social class may somehow induce schizophrenia.

Perhaps, though, social class has different effects that depend on premorbid adjustment. From the description of the schizophrenic with poor premorbid adjustment offered in Chapter

[1] There is perhaps one exception to this finding: the relationship may disappear in nonurban areas (Clausen and Kohn, 1959).

13, it seems reasonable to predict that such a person would fail to achieve the expected level of social status. In contrast, the patient with good premorbid adjustment functions adequately but then becomes schizophrenic in response to stress, perhaps the stress associated with the disheartening and disruptive experiences of lower-class existence. A final resolution of the role of social class in schizophrenia awaits data relevant to these questions, but it *can* be asserted that available data do not support the view that being in a low social class causes schizophrenia in any simple fashion (see Box 14.2).

## The Role of the Family

Many theorists have regarded family relationships, especially those between a mother and her son, as crucial in the development of schizophrenia. This view has been so prevalent that the term "schizophrenogenic mother" has been coined for the supposedly cold and dominant,

### BOX 14.2 The Adequacy of Indices of Schizophrenia

Perhaps the most important decision facing a researcher interested in the relationship between social class and schizophrenia is determining how schizophrenia will be indexed. Many studies use hospital admission rates, especially those of state hospitals. But lower-class individuals are more likely to come to a public hospital than to a private one. Furthermore, many studies have shown that some people who suffer serious mental disorders never enter a mental hospital at all.

Researchers have attempted to make their sampling more complete by picking individuals from all treatment facilities in a given area. But the same kind of problem holds. For example, there are social class differences between people who have been treated for mental illness and severely impaired people who have never had any kind of treatment (Srole et al., 1962). Thus using treatment as an index of schizophrenia is suspect.

An alternative approach is to go into the community and examine everyone, or a representative sample of everyone. The problem of relying exclusively on treatment is solved, but other difficulties are raised. Operating in the community makes diagnostic reliability and even the definition of abnormal behvior a difficult proposition. The raters employed in the community studies have usually received much less training than those who conduct studies in psychiatric facilities. In addition, community studies settle for what is termed *prevalence* rather than *incidence* data. Incidence refers to the number of new cases found in various population groups during a particular period of time and thus is theoretically the most relevant measure in an investigation of this sort. In community studies, however, a simple count of the number of abnormal people is made. This prevalence measure is somewhat inappropriate, for it reflects both incidence and duration of illness. Since there is a correlation between duration of illness and social class (Hollingshead and Redlich, 1958), we cannot determine from prevalence data whether a correlation between social class and schizophrenia reflects incidence or duration of the disorder.

All in all, however, workers have continued to find a relation between social class and schizophrenia, whatever the methodologies employed, indicating that their data can be accepted.

conflict-inducing parent who is said to produce schizophrenia in her offspring. These mothers have also been characterized as rejecting, overprotective, self-sacrificing, impervious to the feelings of others, rigid and moralistic about sex, and fearful of intimacy.[2]

### Methods of study

Three methods have been employed to assess the potential role of the family. First, when patients are in treatment, their families can be studied by the *clinical observational method.* Although such studies may provide hypotheses, the data collected cannot serve as scientific proof (see Chapter 4). Second, in *restrospective studies of child rearing,* parents and other relatives and friends of the patient being treated are questioned about historical events related to family life. The information collected by this method is also subject to a severe problem, the fallibility of recall over time. Third, in the *family interaction method* structured situations are devised to reveal how family members interact with one another. One of these procedures is the *revealed-differences technique.* Members of a family are given several questions to respond to, such as "What is the appropriate time for teen-agers to begin dating?" Then they are asked to resolve any differences in the answers given by the individual members of the family. As they attempt to resolve their differences, their interaction is video-recorded so that the information can be reliably coded. The family interaction method has a clear advantage over the other two in the quality of the evidence that it can provide. It also has limitations, however, for knowledge that the family conversation is being studied may alter communication patterns. Moreover, since one member of the family is already psychotic, the validity of the information collected rests on the assumption that the currently observed family interaction patterns are the same as those existing *before* one member of the family became schizophrenic. The parents, however, may be *reacting* to the fact that an offspring is schizophrenic rather than acting as they did earlier when they may have been instrumental in causing the development of the disorder. If problems are noticeable in the family of a schizophrenic, the directionality of the correlation is therefore difficult to ascertain. The family problems may have caused schizophrenia in one of its members, or the schizophrenia may be causing family problems that did not exist earlier.

Fontana (1966) has found that the great majority of family studies are inadequate in various ways and has recommended some basic rules about methodology that should be followed in setting up these studies. Only families of schizophrenics should constitute the experimental group, the families of male and female patients should be analyzed separately, and all the diagnoses of schizophrenia should be reliable. Moreover, families of patients hospitalized for a physical illness must constitute the control group, for *all* families with a member hospitalized for any reason have been found to have problems.

Of the hundreds of family studies of schizophrenia, Fontana was able to find only five that met these criteria. And on the basis of these five he was able to draw only two conclusions.

1. There is more conflict between the parents of schizophrenics than between the parents of control patients.
2. Communication between the parents of schizophrenics is more inadequate than that between control parents.

When the most stringent controls are applied, conflict and poor communication between parents assume more significance than any qualities of the supposed schizophrenogenic mother. But whether the difficulties between the parents antedate the development of schizophrenia in an offspring remains to be settled. Two noteworthy attempts to resolve this issue are described in Box 14.3.

[2] It is noteworthy that most theories implicating family processes in the etiology of abnormal behavior focus almost exclusively on the mother. Sexism?

## BOX 14.3 Trying To Unravel the Direction of Causality in Family Studies of Schizophrenia

In a detailed and careful study, Mishler and Waxler (1968) attempted to determine what family interaction patterns correlated with schizophrenia. They used the revealed-differences technique with two sessions for each family. In one session the parents participated with their schizophrenic child, and in the other with a nonpsychotic offspring of the same sex and approximately the same age as the patient. The design included in the experimental group both male and female patients and patients with good and poor premorbid adjustment. The control families had pairs of normal siblings of the same sex and nearly the same age. An attempt was made to balance the two groups so that family incomes, father's occupation, parents' education and religion, and parents' and grandparents' birthplaces were not too different.

By having two revealed-differences sessions, the researchers hoped to determine whether the patient's presence or absence affected the parents' behavior. If, for example, the parents expressed less emotion and were uncommunicative only in the session with the patient, their behavior might be interpreted as a *response* to the disturbed child. But if the parents of a schizophrenic child were unexpressive and uncommunicative toward both the disturbed child *and* the normal sibling, their behavior was less likely to be a specific reaction to a schizophrenic child.

Strategies of control were one of the variables studied in the two sessions. In normal families there was a coalition between mother and father and a clear status hierarchy. In contrast, in families with a schizophrenic son the father was excluded and a coalition between mother and son was formed. In families with a schizophrenic daughter, she was the excluded one. These patterns were evident only when the patient was present, not during the session that the parents had with their normal offspring, suggesting that control strategies were a reaction to the schizophrenic child's behavior.

Speech disruptions—fragments of thought, repetitions, and incomplete sentences—were also observed. Contrary to expectation, the greatest frequency of speech disruptions occurred in the sessions with families of normal children. They were less noticeable in the conversations of families whose schizophrenic child was a poor premorbid and even less frequent in the conversations of families whose schizophrenic child had had a good premorbid adjustment. Thus disrupted verbal communications could not be implicated as causative factors.

Overall, Mishler and Waxler were unable to establish a definite causal relationship between any aspect of parental behavior and the development of schizophrenia in an offspring, but their study did go well beyond a simple and general comparison of the behavior of normal families and that of families with a schizophrenic child.

In another study, one which focused on communication, Liem (1974) had a number of families with a schizophrenic son and control families with a normal son participate in an object identification task. The "communicator" was given the task of describing common objects, such as a lamp or match, and concepts, such as teacher or child, so that a listener could identify them. During a session five "communications" about each of three objects or concepts were tape-recorded. Each schizophrenic son and each normal son had a turn in the role of communicator. Each set of parents took the role together as a communicating pair. Later parents and sons responded to different tapes, giving an answer after each description. The parents responded to tapes made by their own son, by an unknown nonschizophrenic son, and by an unknown schizophrenic son. The sons responded to tapes made by their own parents, unknown parents of a normal son, and unknown parents of a schizophrenic son.

How does this study relate to the possible role of the family in the etiology of schizophrenia? If unclear communication by the parents of a schizophrenic is assigned a *causal* role, we might expect their descriptions to be indeed inadequate and confusing to anyone who listens to them. In contrast, if the parents of a schizophrenic are *reacting* to their child's disorder, we would not expect their descriptions to be inadequate, but we would expect *all* parents to have difficulty interpreting the tape-recorded communications of a schizophrenic son. This second pattern is the one borne out by Liem's study.

On several measures of adequacy of communication, there were no important differences between the parents of normal and schizophrenic sons. The schizophrenic sons were inferior to normal sons, however, as would be expected from Cohen's work described in Chapter 13. *All* parents were confused by the descriptions formulated by schizophrenic sons, making more misidentifications when they listened to their own schizophrenic son's tape or that of an unknown schizophrenic son. In the author's own words,

> *The communication disorder of schizophrenic sons had an immediate, observable, negative effect not only on the parents of schizophrenic sons but on all parents who heard and attempted to respond to them. Disorder was not observed in the communications of parents of schizophrenic sons nor were their communications found to adversely affect sons who heard and responded to them (p. 445).*

## The double bind

Thus far we have examined the role of the family in a rather general way and found the amount of conflict and accuracy of communication to be problems. More specific hypotheses have also been advanced, the most prominent being the *double bind* proposed by Bateson and his colleagues (1956). These writers believe that an important factor in the development of schizophrenic thought disorder is the constant subjection of an individual to a so-called double-bind situation. A double bind has the following aspects.

1. The individual has an intense relationship to another, so intense that it is especially important to be able to understand communications from the other person accurately so that the individual can respond appropriately.
2. The other person expresses two messages when making a statement, one of which denies the other.
3. The individual cannot comment on the mutually contradictory messages and cannot withdraw from the situation or ignore the messages.

The parent rarely communicates with the child in a simple and direct way. What a mother says to her son may be contradicted by how she says it, by what she does, or by emotion conveyed in other ways. And the child cannot complain that he does not understand, nor can he ask for clarification. It becomes impossible for him to order his thinking; his responses may eventually become even more confused than the communications he receives. In their original paper Bateson and his colleagues gave the following example.

> *A young man who had fairly well recovered from an acute schizophrenic episode was visited in the hospital by his mother. He was glad to see her and impulsively put his arm around her shoulders whereupon she stiffened. He withdrew his arm and she asked, "Don't you love me anymore?" He then blushed and she said, "Dear, you must not be so easily embarrassed and afraid of your feelings." The patient was able to stay with her only a few minutes more and following her departure he assaulted an aide. . . .*
>
> *Obviously, this result could have been avoided if the young man had been able to say, "Mother, it is obvious that you become uncomfortable when I put my arm around you, and you have difficulty accepting a gesture of affection from me." However, the schizophrenic patient doesn't have this possibility open to him. An intense dependency in training prevents him from commenting upon his mother's communicative behavior, though she comments on his and forces him to accept and to attempt to deal with the complicated sequence. . . .*
>
> *The impossible dilemma thus becomes: "If I am to keep my tie to my mother, I must not show her that I love her, but if I do not show her that I love her then I will lose her"* (pp. 258–259).

Although the double bind has been a popular and widely known explanation of how schizophrenia develops, it is not supported as a factor of great etiological significance by any available data. Most of the literature on the double-bind hypothesis is uncontrolled and descriptive, consisting of case histories and transcripts of therapy sessions. In one controlled study Ringuette and Kennedy (1966) had different groups of judges try to identify double binds communicated in letters.[3] Two sets of letters were used, those written by parents to their hospitalized schizophrenic and nonschizophrenic offspring, and letters that had been written by volunteers instructed to compose them as though they were writing to hospitalized offspring. The groups of judges included three of the people closely involved in originally formulating the double-bind hypothesis, psychiatric residents who had been taught earlier how to recognize a double-bind communication, and experienced clinicians who also knew the double-bind interpretation.

The judges did not agree on which letters did and did not contain a double-bind communication. *The correlation among the judgments of the experts was only +.19.* Furthermore, the experienced judges were unable to discriminate between the letters written by the parents of a schizophrenic and those written by the other parents and by volunteers. This investigation, then, provided little support indeed for the viability of the double-bind hypothesis.

At this point we can clearly put to rest the two theories proposing the schizophrenogenic mother and the double bind as causes of schizophrenia. Although both theories have been around for over twenty years, no evidence lending them any definite support has been collected. Information on hand does indicate that communication is often unclear, however, and that there is much conflict in families with a schizophrenic son or daughter. But whether these family processes should be viewed as playing a causal role in the development of schizophrenia is questionable. It is equally plausible that the conflict and unclear communication are a response to having a

[3] Although the use of letters in this study may seem strange, many of those who have studied the double bind have paid particular attention to the contents of letters written by parents of schizophrenics, for they believe that written communications are likely to resemble spoken ones.

young schizophrenic in the family. Indeed, some evidence favors this interpretation (for example, Liem, 1974). A final resolution of the issue is not possible given the research on hand. The family interaction patterns of children at risk for schizophrenia should be carefully studied before any of the children have developed the disorder.

## The Genetic Data

Suppose that an individual who will one day be diagnosed as schizophrenic must be selected and that no behavior patterns or other symptoms can be considered. This problem, suggested by Paul Meehl (1962), has one solution with at least an even chance of picking a potential schizophrenic. *Find an individual who has a schizophrenic identical twin.* There now exists a convincing body of literature indicating that a predisposition for schizophrenia is transmitted genetically. The major methods employed in this research, as in other behavior genetics research projects, are the family and twin studies (see Box 6.2 page 142). The findings obtained from them will be discussed first and thereafter studies of adopted children.

David Rosenthal, a psychologist who has made a major contribution to understanding the genetics of schizophrenia and of other mental disorders.

### The family studies

A summary of the available studies using the family method is presented in Table 14.2. The data vary markedly. The morbidity risk for the parents of a schizophrenic index case ranges from 0.2 to 12.0 percent. Fourteen of the sixteen studies, however, show a risk estimate higher than the incidence expected in the general population, which is about 1.0 percent. The risk that siblings of schizophrenic probands will develop the disorder ranges from 2.6 to 14.3 percent, according to the studies examined. These risk estimates are uniformly higher than would be expected for members of the general population.

When a parent of the schizophrenic proband

TABLE **14.2**
Morbidity Risk Estimates for Parents and Siblings of Schizophrenic Index Cases

| Study | Morbidity risk, percent | |
|---|---|---|
| | Parents | Siblings |
| Brugger, 1928 | 4.3 | 10.3 |
| Bleuler, 1930 | 2.0 | 4.9 |
| Schulz, 1932 | 2.6 | 6.7 |
| Luxenburger, 1936 | 11.7 | 7.6 |
| Smith, 1936 | 1.2 | 3.3 |
| Galatschjan, 1937 | 4.9 | 14.0 |
| Strömgren, 1938 | 0.7 | 6.7 |
| Kallmann, 1938 | 2.7 | 7.5 |
| Bleuler, 1941 | 5.6 | 10.4 |
| Kallmann, 1946 | 9.2 | 14.3 |
| Böök, 1953 | 12.0 | 9.7 |
| Slater, 1953 | 4.1 | 5.4 |
| Hallgren-Sjögren, 1959 | 0.2 | 5.7 |
| Garrone, 1962 | 7.0 | 8.6 |
| Winokur et al., 1972 | 1.8 | 2.6 |
| Reed et al., 1973 | 11.0 | 8.3 |

also has the disorder, the morbidity risk for all siblings increases dramatically. Garrone (1962) found a morbidity risk of 33.7 percent among the siblings of schizophrenics if there was also one schizophrenic parent. The offspring of two schizophrenic parents has a likelihood of about 35 percent of becoming schizophrenic (Rosenthal, 1970).

In sum, the data gathered by the family method support the notion that a predisposition for schizophrenia can be transmitted genetically. And yet relatives of a schizophrenic proband share not only genes but also common experiences. A schizophrenic parent's behavior could be very disturbing to a developing child.

### The twin studies

A summary of the available twin studies appears in Table 14.3. The concordance rates reported in the several studies of identical twins range with great variability from 0 to 86 percent. The rates of concordance for the fraternal twins range from 2 to 14 percent. Concordance for the identical twins is generally greater than that for the fraternal, but it is always less than 100 percent. This is important, for if genetic transmission were the whole story of schizophrenia and one twin was schizophrenic, the other twin would be guaranteed a similar fate because MZ twins are genetically identical.

Gottesman and Shields (1972) have studied

TABLE **14.3**
Concordance Rates in the Major Twin Studies of Schizophrenia
(adapted from Rosenthal, 1970)

| Study | Country | MZ twins | | DZ twins | |
|---|---|---|---|---|---|
| | | Number of pairs | Concordance, percent | Number of pairs | Concordance, percent |
| Luxenburger, 1928, 1934 | Germany | 17–27 | 33–76.5* | 48 | 2.1 |
| Rosanoff et al., 1934–35 | United States | 41 | 61.0 | 101 | 10.0 |
| | and Canada | 7–11 | 14–71 | 24 | 8.3–17 |
| Essen-Möller, 1941 | Sweden | 174 | 69–86.2 | 517 | 10–14.5 |
| Kallman, 1946 | New York | 37 | 65–74.7 | 115 | 11.3–14.4 |
| Slater, 1953 | England | 55 | 36–60 | 17 | 6–12 |
| Inouye, 1961 | Japan | 16 | 0–6 | 21 | 4.8 |
| Tienari, 1963, 1968 | Finland | | | | |
| Gottesman and Shields, 1966 | England | 24 | 41.7 | 33 | 9.1 |
| Kringlen, 1967 | Norway | 55 | 25–38 | 172 | 8–10 |
| Fischer, 1968 | Denmark | 16 | 19–56 | 34 | 6–15 |
| Hoffer and Pollin, 1970 | United States | 80 | 13.8 | 145 | 4.1 |

* The ranges in the concordance figures reflect different definitions of what would constitute a concordant pair.

all twins treated at the Maudsley and Bethlem hospitals in London, England, between the years 1948 and 1964. One of the problems of any twin study of schizophrenia is how to judge concordance. Recognizing the potential problems and biases involved in making psychiatric diagnoses, often of people who were not hospitalized, Gottesman and Shields devised a three-grade system of concordance. All probands were, of course, hospitalized schizophrenics. The co-twins with the first grade of concordance were also hospitalized and diagnosed schizophrenic. Co-twins with the second grade of concordance were hospitalized but not diagnosed as schizophrenic; those with the third grade were abnormal but not hospitalized. Concordance rates for the MZ and DZ twins in the sample, figured cumulatively for the three grades, are shown in Table 14.4. As the definition of concordance is broadened, its rate increases in both MZ and DZ pairs, but concordance of the MZs is always significantly higher than that of the DZs.

The data in Table 14.4 are of cases in which British hospital diagnoses were the basis for deciding concordance and discordance of pairs. But Gottesman and Shields went beyond this, having each case rediagnosed from case history material by a group of eminent psychopathologists from several countries. Concordance rates obtained by pooling their diagnoses were for MZs 50 percent and for DZs 9 percent. More interesting, though, are the differences the judgments of individual American diagnosticians bring to concordance rates. These data were alluded to in Chapter 13 as evidence of the low validity of the broad American concept of schizophrenia. The greatest number of schizophrenia diagnoses were made by an American psychopathologist; when his diagnoses were used, the concordance rates for MZ and DZ pairs were 54 and 21 percent respectively. When those of some conservative diagnosticians who found fewer cases of schizophrenia were applied, the concordance rate for MZs was four times as large as for DZs.

Gottesman and Shields have also examined the relationship between severity of schizophrenia in the proband and the rate of concordance. Severity was defined in terms of the total length of hospitalization and the outcome, that is, whether the patient recovered enough to leave the hospital and then engage in gainful employment. When one of a MZ pair was judged severely ill, concordance rates went up dramatically. For example, pairs of MZ twins were divided into two groups; in one group the probands had had less than two years of hospitalization, in the other more than two years of hospitalization. The concordance rate for the first group was 27 percent, for the second 77 percent.

Questions have been raised about the interpretation of data collected on twins. Some have argued that the experience of being an identical twin may itself predispose toward schizophrenia. If schizophrenia is considered an "identity problem," it might be argued that being a member of an identical pair of twins could be

TABLE **14.4**
Concordance in MZ and DZ Twins as Defined in Three Ways
(from Gottesman and Shields, 1972)

| Definition of concordance | Concordance, percent MZ | Concordance, percent DZ |
|---|---|---|
| 1. Hospitalized and diagnosed schizophrenic | 42 | 9 |
| 2. Hospitalized but not schizophrenic, plus those with first-grade concordance | 54 | 18 |
| 3. Not hospitalized but abnormal, plus those with first- and second-grade concordance | 79 | 45 |

particularly stressful. But schizophrenia occurs about as frequently in single births as in twin births. If the hypothesis were correct, simply being twins would have to increase the likelihood of becoming schizophrenic—which it does not (Rosenthal, 1970).

But the most critical problem of interpretation remains. Since the twins have been reared together, a common environment rather than common genetic factors could account for the concordance rates. A few pairs of identical twins, at least one of whom developed schizophrenia, have been reared apart from very early childhood, enabling the relative contributions of heredity and environment to be separately determined. Of the sixteen cases in the literature, ten were concordant and six discordant (Rosenthal, 1970). The concordance rate of this limited sample was therefore 62.5 percent, a finding that certainly supports the view that a predisposition for schizophrenia is genetically transmitted. Because of the small sample size, however, the data cannot be regarded as conclusive.

### Adoptee studies

Fortunately, recent studies of children of schizophrenic mothers reared from early infancy by adoptive parents provide more definitive data. These studies eliminate the possible effects of a deviant environment. Heston (1966) was able to follow up forty-seven people who had been born to schizophrenic mothers while they were in a state mental hospital. The infants were taken away from the mothers shortly after birth and given either to relatives or to foundling homes. Fifty control subjects were selected from among the residents of the same foundling homes that the children of the schizophrenic mothers had been sent to. The follow-up assessment consisted of an interview, MMPI, IQ test, social class ratings, and the like. A dossier on each of these subjects was then rated independently by two psychiatrists, and a third evaluation was made by Heston. Ratings were made on a 0 to 100 scale of overall disability and, whenever possible, psychiatric diagnosis was offered. Ratings of disability proved to be quite reliable, and when the number of diagnostic categories was reduced to four—schizophrenia, mental deficiency, sociopathy, and neurosis—diagnostic agreement was also acceptable.

The control subjects were rated as less disabled than were the children of schizophrenic mothers. Similarly, thirty-one of the forty-seven children of schizophrenic mothers (66 percent) were given a psychiatric diagnosis, but only nine out of fifty control subjects (18 percent) were. None of the control subjects was diagnosed schizophrenic, but 16.6 percent of the offspring of schizophrenic mothers were so diagnosed.[4] In addition to this greater likelihood of being diagnosed schizophrenic, the children of schizophrenic mothers were more likely to be diagnosed mentally defective, sociopathic, and neurotic (Table 14.5). They had spent more time in penal institutions, had been involved more frequently in criminal activity, and had more often been discharged from the armed services for psychiatric reasons. Heston's study clearly supports the importance of genetic factors in the development of schizophrenia. Children reared without contact with their so-called "pathogenic mothers" were still more likely to become schizophrenic than were the controls.

A study similar in intent to Heston's has been carried out in Denmark under Kety's direction (1968). The starting point for the investigation was a culling of the records of all children who had been adopted at an early age between the years 1924 and 1947. All adoptees who had later been admitted to a psychiatric facility and diagnosed schizophrenic were selected as the index cases. From the remaining cases the investigators chose a control group who had no psychiatric history and who were matched to the index group on variables such as sex and age.

[4] The 16.6 percent figure was *age-corrected*. By this process raw data are corrected to take into account the age of the subjects involved. If a subject in Heston's sample was only twenty-four at the time of the assessment, he might still have become schizophrenic at some later point in his life. The age correction procedure attempts to account for this possibility.

TABLE **14.5**
Subjects Separated from Their Schizophrenic Mothers in Early Infancy
(from Heston, 1966)

| Assessment | Offspring of schizophrenic mother | Control offspring, mothers not schizophrenic |
|---|---|---|
| Number of subjects | 47 | 50 |
| Mean age at follow-up | 35.8 | 36.3 |
| Overall ratings of disability (low score indicates more pathology) | 65.2 | 80.1 |
| Number diagnosed schizophrenic | 5 | 0 |
| Number diagnosed mentally defective | 4 | 0 |
| Number diagnosed sociopathic | 9 | 2 |
| Number diagnosed neurotic | 13 | 7 |

Both the adoptive and the biological parents and the siblings and half-siblings of the two groups were then identified, and a search was made to determine who of them had a psychiatric history. As might be expected if genetic factors figure in schizophrenia, the biological relatives of the index cases were more often diagnosed schizophrenic than members of the general population. The adoptive relatives were not.

Although only preliminary data are as yet available, we turn finally to what may prove a remarkable study, clinching the case for the importance of genetic makeup in the etiology of schizophrenia. Using the adoptee method, Wender and his associates (1974) have examined several groups, including one not encountered before in the literature—children born to nonschizophrenic parents who were adopted and reared by families in which one parent was schizophrenic or borderline schizophrenic. The importance of such a group should be obvious, for it discloses the impact of being reared by a deviant adoptive parent. These adoptees were contacted as grown-ups and interviewed in depth. Two other groups served as controls and were also interviewed: people with normal biological parents who were adopted at an early age and reared by parents not related to them; and people with a schizophrenic biological parent who were adopted at an early age and reared by parents not related to them. On the basis of the interview, subjects were assigned to categories, one of which is of particular interest. It consisted of people who were described by the interviewer as having a disorder ranging from possible acute schizophrenia to chronic schizophrenia. The percentages of subjects in each group who fell into this category are shown in Table 14.6.

More of the subjects with schizophrenic biological parents fall into the deviant category than do subjects from either of the two other groups. The role of a schizophrenic adoptive parent in the etiology of schizophrenia seems negligible, for only slightly more adoptees reared by a schizophrenic parent (10.7 percent) are deviant than those reared by normal parents (10.1 percent).

TABLE **14.6**

Deviancy in Adoptees in Relation to Parentage, Normal and Schizophrenic, Biological and Adoptive

(from Wender et al., 1974)

| Adoptee groups by parentage | Adoptees judged schizophrenic or "near schizophrenic" based on interview, percent |
|---|---|
| Normal biological–normal adoptive parents | 10.1 |
| Schizophrenic biological–normal adoptive parents | 18.8 |
| Normal biological–schizophrenic adoptive parents | 10.7 |

### Evaluation

All the data collected so far indicate that genetic factors play an important role in the development of schizophrenia. Earlier twin and family studies deserved the criticism of environmentalists, who found that investigators had not acknowledged upbringing as a possible contributing factor. But later studies of children of schizophrenic mothers and fathers, who were reared in foster and adoptive homes, plus the follow-up of relatives of adopted schizophrenics, indicate the importance of genetic transmission, for the potential biasing influence of the environment had been virtually removed. As Seymour Kety, the highly regarded schizophrenia researcher, has quipped, "If schizophrenia is a myth, it is a myth with a heavy genetic component" (1974).

We cannot conclude, however, that schizophrenia is a disorder completely determined by genetic transmission. The less than 100 percent concordance rate of identical twins would argue against this conclusion, and we must always keep in mind the distinction made between phenotype and genotype (see page 142). The diathesis-stress model, introduced in Chapter 2, seems appropriate for explaining schizophrenia. Genetic factors can only be predisposers for a disorder. Stress is required to render this predisposition an observable pathology.

## Biochemical Factors

Speculation concerning possible biochemical[5] causes of schizophrenia began almost as soon as the syndrome was identified. Kraepelin, as already indicated, thought that poisons secreted from the sex glands affected the brain to produce the symptoms, and Carl Jung suggested the presence of "toxin X," which he thought would eventually be identified. The demonstrated role of genetic factors in schizophrenia also suggests that biochemicals should be investigated, for it is through the body chemistry that heredity may have an effect.

The extensive and continuing search for possible biochemical causes has a principal diffi-

[5] This section is necessarily technical, and it may be unusually difficult to follow for readers who have not studied biochemistry. We want to provide the details, however, for those who have this background. For those who lack it, we hope at least to convey the logic and general trends in the research on biochemical factors.

Seymour Kety, a prominent figure in research into both the genetics and the biochemistry of schizophrenia.

culty to overcome. If an aberrant biochemical is found in schizophrenics and not in control subjects, the difference in biochemical functioning may have been produced by a third variable rather than by the disorder. Most schizophrenic patients take tranquilizing medication. Although the effects of such drugs on behavior diminish quite rapidly once they are discontinued, traces of them may remain in the bloodstream for very long periods of time, making it difficult to attribute a biochemical difference between schizophrenic and control subjects to schizophrenia per se. Institutionalized patients may smoke more, drink more coffee, and have a less nutritionally adequate diet than various control groups. They may also be relatively inactive. All these variables can conspire to produce biochemical differences in schizophrenic and control patients that confound attempts to seek deviant biochemicals in the schizophrenics. Nonetheless, the search for biochemical causes of schizophrenia proceeds at a rapid rate. Tremendous advances now allow a much greater understanding of the relation between biochemistry and behavior. At present no biochemical theory has unequivocal support. But because of the great amount of effort that continues to be spent in the search for biochemical causes of schizophrenia, we shall review several of the best-researched factors.

### Early theories

Over the past two decades, two major classes of biochemical theories of schizophrenia have been advanced. One type has proposed deviant blood proteins as a factor. Heath, for example, theorizes that schizophrenics produce a gamma globulin, a deviant antibody called taraxein, which interferes with neural functioning (Heath and Krupp, 1967). Frohman has proposed that an alpha globulin (a lipoprotein), one with a deviant molecular structure, may disrupt normal neural transmission (Frohman et al., 1971). The other type of theory has suggested that the bodily systems of schizophrenics add methyl ($CH_3$) portions to the neurotransmitters dopamine, serotonin, and tryptamine, making the molecules of these substances structurally more similar to those of hallucinogens such as mescaline and psilocybin (for example, Friedhoff and Van Winkle, 1962). The methylated transmitters are supposedly capable of bringing on the psychosis. These theories have not been supported by all investigations, however. Another theory having to do with dopamine appears more promising at this time.

### Excess dopamine activity

The theory that schizophrenia is brought on by excess activity of the neurotransmitter dopamine is based principally on information concerning the mode of action of drugs that are effective in treating schizophrenia. If the biochemical activity of a therapeutically effective drug is understood, or at least hypothesized, the process responsible for the disorder may be guessed at too. The phenothiazines (see page 555), in addition to alleviating schizophrenia, produce side effects resembling Parkinson's disease. Parkinsonism is known to be caused, in part, by low levels of dopamine in a particular nerve tract of the brain (see page 426). It is therefore supposed that phenothiazines interfere with dopamine activity. Phenothiazine molecules are assumed, because of their structural similarities to the dopamine molecule (Figure 14.1), to fit into and thereby block postsynaptic receptors in dopamine tracts. From this speculation about the action of the drugs that help schizophrenics, it is but a short inductive leap to view schizophrenia as resulting from excess activity in dopamine nerve tracts, although the specific dopaminergic tracts malfunctioning in schizophrenia have not been identified.

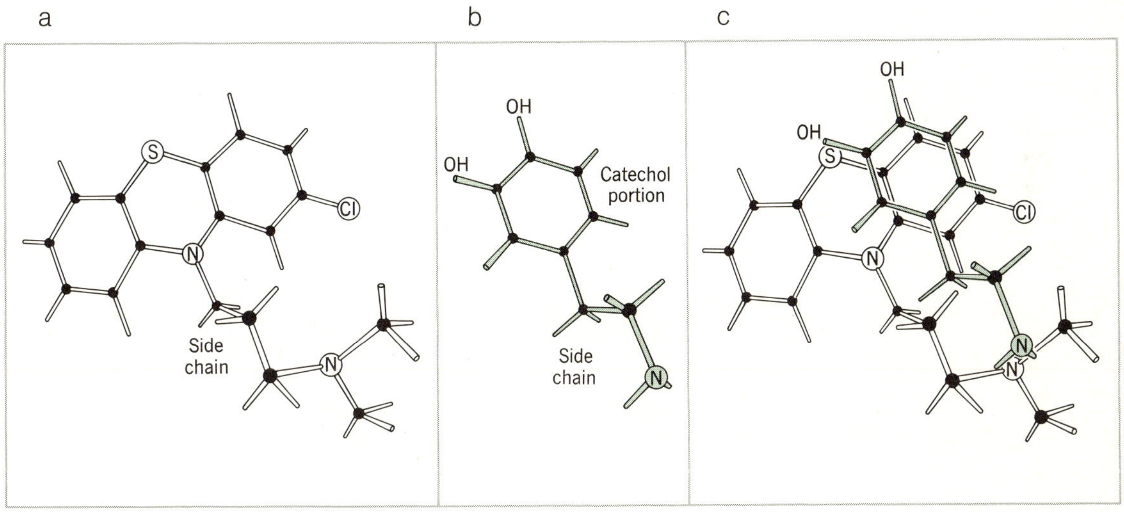


FIGURE **14.1**
Conformations of chloropromazine (a), a phenothiazine, and dopamine (b) and their superimposition (c), determined by X-ray crystallographic analysis. Chlorpromazine blocks impulse transition by dopamine by fitting into its receptor sites. Adapted from Horn and Synder, 1971.

Further indirect support for the theory of excess dopamine activity comes from the literature on amphetamine psychosis. There is general agreement that amphetamines can produce a state that closely resembles paranoid schizophrenia and that they can exacerbate the symptomatology of a schizophrenic (Angrist, Lee, and Gershon, 1974). The amphetamines are thought to act either by directly releasing catecholamines into the synaptic cleft or by preventing their inactivation (Snyder et al., 1974). We can be relatively confident that amphetamines act by way of dopamine, rather than norepinephrine, for phenothiazines are antidotes to amphetamine psychosis.

Work has been done on monoamine oxidase, for a deficiency of this enzyme, which can inactivate dopamine within the presynaptic neuron, might explain excess dopamine activity. Murphy and Wyatt (1972) studied blood platelet MAO in thirty-three chronic schizophrenics and twenty-two normal controls matched for age and sex. The blood platelets of schizophrenics were much lower in MAO than those of the controls; a subsequent investigation with drug-free patients confirmed this result. But acute schizophrenics were not found to differ from controls in platelet MAO levels (Carpenter, Murphy, and Wyatt, 1975). Moreover, Friedman and his colleagues (1974) studied platelet MAO of schizophrenics, depressives, and normal controls and found no significant differences. Postmortem studies of levels of MAO in the brain of eight schizophrenics and nine controls by Schwartz and his colleagues (1974) found no differences, nor did similar work done by Domino, Krause, and Bowers (1973).

The major metabolite of dopamine, homovanillic acid, has also been examined, with the expectation that it would be present in greater amounts in schizophrenics. Homovanillic acid can be measured in cerebrospinal fluid by treating patients with probenecid, a drug which prevents the transfer of homovanillic acid from cerebrospinal fluid to blood. But Bowers (1974) found that before drug treatment schizophrenics had lower levels of homovanillic acid than patients with affective illness, and that levels of homovanillic acid in schizophrenics increased when they were reassessed during treatment. Post and his colleagues (1975) found no differences in levels of homovanillic acid in schizophrenics and several control groups.

Meltzer, Sachar, and Frantz (1974) have also indirectly evaluated the excess-dopamine-activity hypothesis, by examining levels of the hormone prolactin. The dopaminergic system controls to some extent the release of prolactin inhibiting factor and thus prolactin levels in blood serum. If schizophrenics have excessive dopamine transmission, more inhibiting factor should be released and blood serum should contain less prolactin. Serum prolactin of thirty newly admitted drug-free patients was compared to that of a sample of normal controls, and no differences were found.

The theory of excess dopamine transmission is not strongly refuted by the evidence collected in the studies of MAO, homovanillic acid, and prolactin. Dopaminergic overactivity has not, perhaps, been specified precisely enough. The predictions of depleted MAO and increased levels of homovanillic acid assume that the dopamine-releasing neurons are overactive. But it may be that in schizophrenia dopamine *receptors* are overactive or oversensitive. In fact, the work on the phenothiazines' mode of action would suggest that the dopaminergic receptors are a more likely locus of disorder. If increased activity of the dopaminergic receptors is the key to schizophrenia, the data concerning levels of MAO and homovanillic acid are not crucially relevant. As for serum prolactin, its levels are affected by a host of variables, including stress, and thus it is hazardous to conclude that they provide an accurate reflection of the activity of dopaminergic neurons.

In sum, we concur with Snyder's (1976) position regarding the excess-dopamine-transmission theory. It indeed has two powerful, but indirect, pieces of evidence in its favor: the effectiveness of phenothiazines in treating schizophrenia, through the supposed blocking of dopamine receptors; and the inducement of a paranoidlike psychosis by amphetamines, through the release of dopamine into the synaptic cleft or a forestalling of its inactivation. But the theory has not been supported by all investigations and cannot therefore be enthusiastically endorsed until more evidence is available.

### Evaluation

The history of research on whether biochemicals figure in schizophrenia has been one of discovery followed by failures to replicate. Many methodological problems plague this research, and many confounds, unrelated to whether or not a subject is schizophrenic, can produce biochemical differences. Thus we must maintain a cautious attitude toward the excess-dopamine theory. Furthermore, studies on biochemicals can indicate only that a particular substance and its physiological processes are associated with schizophrenia. Excess dopamine activity could be induced *after* rather than *before* the onset of the disorder.

## High-Risk Studies of Schizophrenia

Many studies are primarily concerned with fashioning a picture of how an individual develops schizophrenia. The earlier method of constructing developmental histories was to examine the childhood records of those who later became schizophrenics. This research has indeed shown that those who were to become schizophrenics were different from their contemporaries even before any serious problems were noted in their behavior. Albee and Lane and their colleagues have repeatedly found preschizophrenics to have a lower IQ than members of various control groups, which usually consist of siblings and neighborhood peers (Albee, Lane, and Reuter, 1964; Lane and Albee 1965). Investigations of the social behavior of preschizophrenics have yielded some interesting findings; schizophrenics have been described in childhood, for example, as disagreeable by their teachers (Watt et al., 1970) and as delinquent and withdrawn (Berry, 1967).

But these findings are gross and nonspecific; certainly the traits mentioned would also be found in children and adolescents who are not destined to become schizophrenic. The major limitation of this type of developmental research is that the data on which it relies were not originally collected with the intention of describing preschizophrenics or of predicting the development of schizophrenia from childhood behavior. More specific information is required if developmental histories are to be a source of new hypotheses.

Perhaps the most desirable way of collecting information about the development of schizophrenia would be to select a large sample of individuals and follow them for the twenty to forty-five years that are the period of risk for the onset of schizophrenia. But such a method would be prohibitively expensive, for only about one individual in a hundred eventually becomes schizophrenic. The yield of data from such a simple longitudinal study would be small indeed. The *high-risk method* overcomes this problem; only individuals whose risk of becoming schizophrenic in adulthood is greater than the average are selected for study. In most of the current research projects using this methodology, individuals who have a schizophrenic parent are selected as subjects for, as we saw earlier, having a schizophrenic parent increases a person's risk for developing schizophrenia.

This method has three major advantages.

1. Variables that have direct relevance to the development of schizophrenia can be chosen for study.
2. The data are collected before the individual becomes schizophrenic. Therefore, unlike studies of hospitalized adult schizophrenics, these investigations will not be confounded by variables such as drugs, diet, and inactivity.
3. Finding variables that predict the occurrence of schizophrenia in adulthood may allow early intervention and the prevention of this serious disturbance.

In the early 1960s one of the first and most extensive high-risk studies was begun in Denmark by Sarnoff Mednick and Fini Schulsinger. Denmark was chosen because individuals can be followed up much more easily than is possible in America. In Denmark a lifelong and up-to-date listing of the address of every resident is kept, and a National Psychiatric Register maintains records on every psychiatric hospitalization in the country.

Mednick and Schulsinger selected as their high-risk subjects young people whose mothers were chronic schizophrenics and had had poor premorbid adjustment. It was decided that the mother should be the parent suffering the disorder because paternity is not always easy to determine and because schizophrenic women have more children than do schizophrenic men. Low-risk subjects, individuals whose mothers were not schizophrenics, were matched to the high-risk subjects on variables such as sex, age, father's occupation, rural-urban residence, years of education, and institutional upbringing versus rearing by the family. A summary of the design and expected results may be seen in Figure 14.2.

Now a number of other high-risk projects are in progress, and descriptions of the characteristics of high-risk children based on several studies are available.

## Characteristics of high-risk children

**School Adjustment** Since the social problems of the adult schizophrenic are so obvious, we might expect to find some early indications of them in the school-aged child. Several studies have indeed found this to be so (Beisser, Glasser, and Grant, 1967; Rolf, 1972). In one conducted by Weintraub, Liebert, and Neale (1975) teachers rated the classroom behavior of three groups of children. Members of one group had schizophrenic mothers, those of the second depressed mothers, and those of the third normal mothers. The two groups whose mothers were patients disturbed the classroom with their impatience, disrespect, defiance, inattentiveness, and withdrawal. Their teachers also rated both groups as low in comprehension and creative initiative and remote in their relationships to their teachers.

Sarnoff Mednick and Fini Schulsinger, pioneers in applying the high-risk longitudinal method of studying schizophrenia.

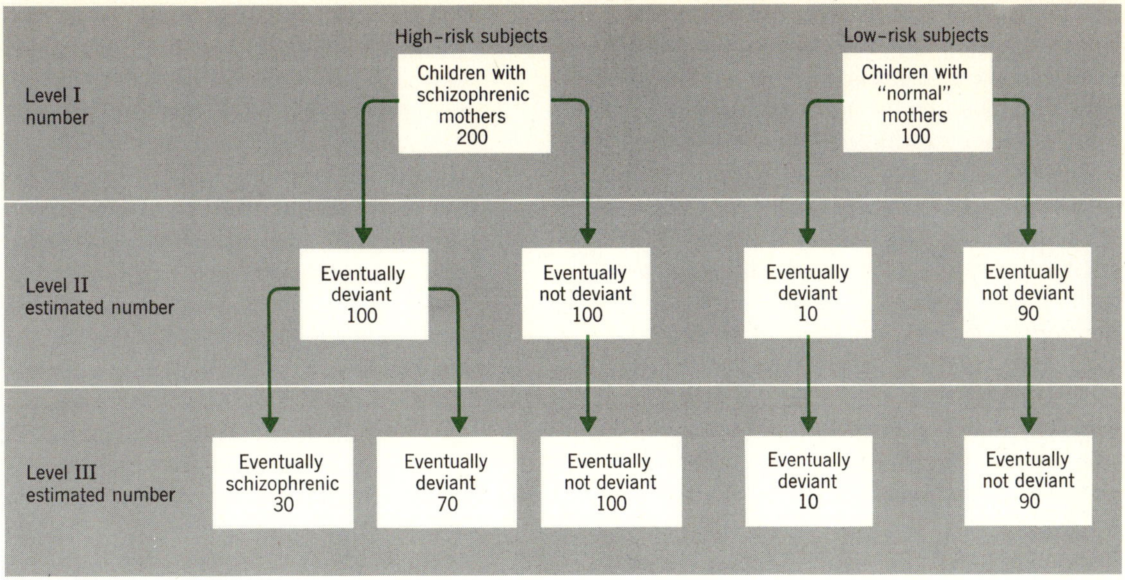


FIGURE **14.2**
Design and expected results of Mednick and Schulsinger's studying (1968) of young people with a high risk of developing schizophrenia.

Although the social and academic difficulties experienced by the children of schizophrenics seemed severe, these young people could *not* be differentiated from the offspring of depressive mothers. Thus the disruptive behavior described is unlikely to be specific predictor of schizophrenia.

Psychophysiology Many hypotheses link schizophrenia to alterations in levels of arousal and responsiveness. Perhaps the psychophysiological patterns in the high-risk children will resemble those seen in adult schizophrenics.

Itil (1972) has analyzed the EEG tracings from the cortexes of children with schizophrenic mothers, children with a parent who has another psychological problem, and children with normal parents. The offspring of schizophrenics had more delta and beta brain waves and fewer alpha than the controls. Furthermore, the tracings of the brain waves of high-risk children showed smaller amplitudes and less variability of amplitude. These are important findings, for the pattern reported for adult schizophrenics (for example, Goldstein et al., 1965) is quite similar.

The principal study of autonomic nervous system psychophysiology is Mednick and Schulsinger's (1966). Heart rate, muscle potential, and GSR were measured during a conditioning situation in which a neutral buzzer (CS) was paired with an irritating 96-decibel noise (UCS). After the children had been conditioned to react to the neutral buzzer, others similar in tone but of slightly different frequencies were sounded. The responses to them indicated the extent to which the conditioning of the children became generalized and carried over to similar stimuli.

The high-risk children differed from their controls on several measures, showing stronger GSR to the UCS as well as stronger conditioning. They also showed less of what is called habituation. If a person becomes habituated to stress, their GSRs occur only after lengthening periods of time. In contrast to the controls, the high-risk children showed no habituation. In fact, their GSRs occurred with increasing speed, suggesting greater responsiveness. Finally, the time it takes for the skin to return to base line conductance after the presentation of a stimulus, which is called GSR recovery, was determined. This measure discriminated between the groups better than any other, with the high-risk children showing particularly rapid recovery. Overall, then, the high-risk children showed a pattern of autonomic overreactivity. Other high-risk projects, however, have been unable to duplicate these findings (for example, Erlenmeyer-Kimling, 1975).

**Measurements of Thought Processes and Attention** Several teams have found in high-risk children deficits in thought processes and attention that closely resemble those of adult schizophrenics. Mednick and Schulsinger (1966), for example, found that on a continuous-association task high-risk children tended to drift away from the stimulus word. Instead of continuing to give associations to a single stimulus, as they had been instructed to do, the children gave them to words that they themselves were using as responses. Oltmanns, Weintraub, and Neale (1976) found that the conceptual patterns of high-risk children were quite similar to those of schizophrenics. Asarnow and his co-workers (1977) compared high-risk children, adopted away from their schizophrenic mothers, to other adoptees and nonadopted controls, using an entire battery of attention-measuring tasks. Among the best discriminators in this battery was a task assessing their ability to pick up briefly presented information. The adopted high-risk children, like adult schizophrenics (Neale, 1971), were notably deficient in apprehending within brief spans of time.

To sum up, the data on the characteristics of high-risk children appear significant. The high-risk children, although not in treatment or viewed as highly disturbed, differ from controls on a variety of measures. But will these differences predict what happens in adulthood? Only one high-risk study has been underway long enough to have collected data on this question, Mednick and Schulsinger's.

### Longitudinal data

During the initial phase of Mednick and Schulsinger's study, an alarm network was set up to ensure that children who began to show psychiatric difficulties would be detected. In a 1968 report the histories of twenty of the initial high-risk group who had by then required psychiatric care were reviewed. For comparison purposes each of these disturbed high-risk young people was matched with one high-risk subject who had not broken down and with one low-risk subject. The matching variables were age, sex, and social class. In addition, the disturbed high-risk subjects were matched with the well high-risk subjects in their 1962 level of adjustment rating, which had been determined by a psychiatrist's interview. The major findings of these comparisons were as follows.

1. Young people in the disturbed high-risk group tended to lose their mothers to a mental hospital early and permanently. Their mothers were also rated as being more severely ill. These facts can be interpreted in two ways. Losing one's mother is stressful; or the severity of the mother's illness may mean that a stronger genetic predisposition is passed on. In a later report B. Mednick (1973) presented data on the characteristics of the fathers of the disturbed and nondisturbed high-risk subjects. Eighteen fathers of the young people in the disturbed group could be traced. Seven of them had themselves had psychiatric treatment for disorders "that ranged from chronic paranoid schizophrenia to chronic alcoholism." None of the fathers of children in the nondisturbed high-risk group had a psychiatric history. This impressive finding raises into prominence the role of the father, either genetic or rearing, in potentiating schizophrenia in a predisposed person.

2. Teachers had reported that more members of the disturbed high-risk group, once they had become upset or excited, remained that way for a longer period of time than did members of the other two groups. More members of the disturbed high-risk group had also been rated by the teachers as being aggressive, domineering, and disturbing to the class.
3. During the continuous-association test, members of the disturbed high-risk group had tended to drift away from the original stimulus word, to an even greater extent than had the high-risk young people who were still well.
4. The disturbed high-risk group had shown to an even greater degree than the well high-risks the pattern of psychophysiological responding already described for high-risk children in general—greater responsiveness to the UCS, greater generalization of the conditioning, less habituation, and faster GSR recovery.

In interpreting all the information collected, Mednick focused on the psychophysiological responses. In an earlier paper (Mednick, 1958) he had postulated that schizophrenia is a learned thought disorder produced by autonomic hyperactivity. The tangential thinking of schizophrenics was suggested to be a set of instrumentally conditioned avoidance responses that help the individual control his or her autonomic responsiveness. These avoidance responses—the irrelevant thoughts—are learned on those occasions when the preschizophrenic escapes from arousal by switching to a thought that interrupts the arousal stimulus. Because the irrelevant associations enable the individual to avoid a stressful stimulus, they are reinforced by less arousal and the probability is great that the preschizophrenic will engage in similar behavior in the future. The data from his present study led Mednick to modify one aspect of his earlier theory, for he had thought at that time that the schizophrenic is slow to recover from the momentary autonomic imbalance registered as the GSR.

> *According to the earlier version of the theory the preschizophrenic is especially prone to learn this avoidant pattern [in his thought processes] because of his extreme hyperresponsivity, excessive generalization and slow recovery from autonomic imbalance. However, the hypothesis of slow recovery has always caused critics to point out that this would cause the preschizophrenic to be reinforced more slowly and meagerly for avoidance than even the normal. The finding of an abnormally fast rate of recovery has forced us to alter the theory. It is now our hypothesis that one of the determining features of the preschizophrenic is his abnormally fast recovery; because of this fast rate of recovery he is more easily, quickly and thoroughly reinforced for avoidance than the normal. This taken together with the tendency to chronic hyperarousal will, in a harsh environment, inexorably push him to learn conditioned avoidant thought mechanisms (Mednick and Schulsinger, 1968, p. 289).*

In a later report (Mednick, 1970) additional significant information was presented. Earlier Mednick and Schulsinger had examined the frequency of individual birth complications in the various groups in their study. The many complications that might have been reported by the midwife—prematurity, anoxia or oxygen deprivation, prolonged labor, placental difficulty, umbilical cord complications, illness of mother during pregnancy, multiple births, and breech presentations (baby emerging feet first instead of head first)—were analyzed separately, but no conclusions could be drawn. One of Mednick's students, after grouping all the pregnancy and birth complications into a single category, made a startling finding. Seventy percent of the mothers of disturbed high-risk children had suffered one or more pregnancy or birth complication (PBC) while carrying or delivering the child, as compared to 15 percent of the mothers of the nondisturbed but high-risk group and 33 percent of the mothers of the controls. Then in reexamining the psychophysiological differences previously discussed, Mednick determined that psychophysiological responses were deviant only in the subjects whose mothers had had one or more PBCs. Thus complications in the birth process may upset bodily control of responses to stress and thereby potentiate schizophrenia in a predisposed individual.[6]

The high-risk method holds great promise of furthering our understanding of schizophrenia. By using specially selected samples, the investigator is able to study the actual unfolding of the disorder. In the next few years the high-risk investigations that are already in progress may yield important information on the development of schizophrenia, pinpointing the environmental factors that potentiate a genetically transmitted diathesis.

[6] The mechanism by which PBCs may produce their effect is the subject of debate. Mednick (1970) proposed that they produce brain damage through anoxia, and that the hippocampal area is particularly vulnerable, but a good deal of other evidence (reviewed by Kessler and Neale, 1974) does not favor this view.

## Summary

Broad theoretical views such as those of Freud, Ullmann and Krasner, and Laing have not had great impact on research undertaken to determine the etiology of schizophrenia. Each of these workers placed undue and unsupported emphasis on particular causal factors. Freud thought that schizophrenia resulted from regression to the first psychosexual stage in which the ego is not differentiated from the id. Ullmann and Krasner postulate that schizophrenics do not attend to the social stimuli to which most people respond. They also regard schizophrenia as a social role maintained in large part by mental health professionals who reinforce "sick" behavior. For Laing schizophrenia is a label for the experience and behavior that constitute a person's attempts to cope with an impossible situation. Although popular and plausible, these theories lack empirical support. New information appears pertinent and suggests other explanations.

Most research has tried to determine the etiological role of more specific variables such as social class, the family, and genetic and biochemical factors. The diagnosis of schizophrenia is most frequently applied to members of the lowest social class. Although some view the stresses of lower-class existence as a cause of schizophrenia, the available data are more consistent with the hypothesis that schizophrenics fail to achieve higher social status because of the disorder. Vague communications and conflicts are evident in the family life of schizophrenics, but it is unclear whether such factors contribute to schizophrenia or whether the presence of a schizophrenic family member disrupts the home.

The data on genetic transmission are impressive. The adoptee studies, which are relatively free from most criticisms that can be leveled at family or twin studies, show a strong relation between having a schizophrenic parent and the likelihood of developing the disorder. Perhaps the genetic predisposition has biochemical correlates, although research in this area permits only tentative conclusions. At this time the excess-dopamine-activity theory appears the most promising. Much of the data we have reviewed are consistent with a diathesis-stress view of schizophrenia. Recently, investigators have turned to the high-risk method, studying children who are particularly vulnerable to schizophrenia by virtue of having a schizophrenic parent. They have found that these children are indeed different from controls in a variety of measurable ways—for example, in psychophysiology, thought processes, and attention—that have also been studied in adult schizophrenics. Mednick and Schulsinger have found that two characteristics of high-risk offspring—complications during the baby's term and birth and GSR responsiveness—predicted maladjustment in adulthood.

# chapter 15

## CHILD PSYCHOSES



We have concentrated thus far on abnormal behavior in adulthood. Many psychogenic theorists, both of a psychodynamic and behavioral bent, regard childhood as a stage in life during which the seeds of later disorders are sown. But disordered behavior does not become evident only with physical maturity. Children—even those of preschool age—can suffer from debilitating psychological problems. In Chapter 17 we shall discuss mental retardation, an intellectual impairment. This chapter is devoted to a study of serious childhood psychopathology.

Profound psychotic disorders may make their appearance very early in life. The two major categories of these childhood psychoses are *early infantile autism* and *childhood schizophrenia*. Early infantile autism, proposed by Leo Kanner in 1943, is a newcomer to the literature on psychiatric classification and is not included in DSM-II. It is likely to appear in DSM-III, however. The development of the concept of childhood schizophrenia and views about its etiology have been linked quite closely to descriptions of adult schizophrenia and theories advanced about its causes. Terms such as "dementia praecocissima" and childhood schizophrenia appeared shortly after Kraepelin coined his phrase dementia praecox and Bleuler his term schizophrenia. And as we shall see, theories of the etiology of adult and childhood schizophrenia do have many similarities. At the same time, however, because of the much earlier age of onset, there are clear-cut differences between the behavior manifested in adult schizophrenia and the disturbances that mark the behavior of children diagnosed as schizophrenic.

We will first describe the clinical syndromes of the two categories, autism and childhood schizophrenia, and then the theories that try to explain them.

# Infantile Autism

Some diagnosticians view autism as an early form of childhood schizophrenia and believe that the clinical pictures of the two disorders blend. Others consider autism to be a separate disorder. The autistic child when first observed may seem to be normal and attractive, moving well and quickly with good coordination and appearing bright, although perhaps pensive or preoccupied. But the child makes his or her inaccessibility evident by rejecting any social overture. For many diagnosticians this detachment and its apparent onset "from the moment of birth" make autism a very distinct and unique syndrome.

## Descriptive Characteristics

As described by Kanner (1943), Rimland (1964), and Rutter (1974), autism consists of a specific constellation of behaviors.

### Extreme autistic aloneness

An inability to relate to people or to any situation other than being alone in a crib is found from the very beginning of life. Autistic infants are often reported to be "good babies," apparently because they do not place many demands on their parents. They do not coo or fret or demand attention, nor do they reach out or smile or look at their mothers when being fed. When they are picked up or cuddled, they arch their bodies away from their caretakers rather than molding themselves against the adult as normal babies do. Autistic infants are content to sit quietly in their playpens for hours, never noticing the comings, goings, and doings of other people. After infancy they do not form attachments with people but instead may become extremely dependent on mechanical objects, such as refrigerators or vacuum cleaners. Because they avoid all social interaction, they fall rapidly behind their peers in development.

The autistic child's failure to relate to people has been studied in laboratory settings. Hutt and Ounsted (1966) observed autistic and control children in a room that had five masks mounted on the walls. There were two human faces, one happy and one sad, a blank oval mask, and two animal masks, a monkey and a dog. The children were allowed to explore the room and spend as much time as they wanted viewing the various masks. They were observed through one-way mirrors, and the time spent viewing each face was recorded. Corroborating clinical impressions, the autistic children spent significantly longer periods viewing the animal faces. In a similar manner, Black, Freeman, and Montgomery (1975) examined the behavior of autistic children as they played in several different environments. Again consistent with clinical lore, the autistic children related more often to objects than to peers and frequently engaged in solitary, repetitive behavior.

### Communication problems

Even before the period when language is usually acquired, autistic children show deficits in communication. Babbling, a term used to describe the utterances of children before they actually begin to use words, is less frequent in autistic children and conveys less information than does that of other children. Ricks (1972), for example, played tape recordings of the babbling of both autistic and mentally retarded children to their own mothers and to other mothers. Although all

The solitary play of autistic children.

mothers understood best the meaning of the noises of their own children, the babbling of the autistic children was less meaningful to other mothers than was the babbling of the mentally retarded children. Even on a nonvocal level, autistic children manifest a communication deficit. They do not, for example, use gesture as a substitute for speech, and it has proved difficult to try to train them to do so (Bartak, Rutter, and Cox, 1975).

The difficulties that older autistic children have with language are even more pronounced. *Mutism,* complete absence of speech, is prevalent; about 50 percent of all autistic children never learn to speak (Rutter, 1966). Even when they do, many peculiarities are found, among them *echolalia*. The child echos, usually with remarkable fidelity, what he or she has heard another person say. In "delayed" echolalia the child may not repeat the sentence or phrase until hours or weeks after hearing it. In one of our own cases, for example, speech was limited to the repetition of television commercials. In fact, the child's memory for these commercials seemed limitless. Mute children who later do obtain some functional speech through training must usually first pass through a stage of echolalia before they can learn to respond meaningfully to questions or to use labels.

Another abnormality common in the speech of autistic children is *pronoun reversal*. The children refer to themselves as "he," or "you," or by their own proper names; the pronouns "I" or "me" are seldom used and then only when referring to others. Pronoun reversal is closely linked to echolalia. Since autistic children often use echolalic speech, they will refer to themselves as they have heard others speak of them; pronouns are of course misapplied. For example,

*Parent:* "What are you doing, Johnny?"

*Child:* "He's here."

*Parent:* "Are you having a good time?"

*Child:* "He knows it."

As normal speech is built up, this pronoun reversal might be expected to disappear. It has been reported, however, to be highly resistant to change (Tramontana and Stimbert, 1970); some children have required very extensive training even after they have stopped parroting the phrases of other people.

Communication deficiencies are clearly one of the most serious problems of autistic children. The fact that about 75 percent of autistic children score in the mentally retarded range on IQ tests is undoubtedly a reflection of these deficiencies. They may also leave a lasting mark of social retardation on the child. The link between social skills and language is made evident by the often spontaneous appearance of affectional and dependent behavior in these children after they have been trained to speak (Churchill, 1969; Hewett, 1965).

An autistic child's ability or inability to speak is often an effective means of predicting later adjustment, an additional indication of the central role of language. Rutter (1967) found that of thirty-two autistic children without useful speech at five years of age, only seven had acquired speech when followed up about nine years later. Eisenberg and Kanner (1956) had earlier followed up a sample of eighty autistic children classified according to whether or not they had learned to speak by age five. Fifty percent of the children who had been able to speak at this age were later rated as showing fair or good adjustment, but only 3 percent of the nonspeaking children were so rated. More recent studies have also shown a close link between the acquisition of language and later adjustment (Lotter, 1974; Treffert, McAndrew, and Dreifuerst, 1973).

### Preservation of sameness

Autistic children become extremely upset over changes in daily routine and their surroundings. An offer of milk in a different drinking cup or a rearrangement of furniture may make them cry or bring on a temper tantrum. Even common greetings must not vary.

*. . . A beautiful girl of five, with autism, finally made contact with her teacher. Each morning she had to be greeted with the set phrase, "Good morning, Lily, I am very, very glad to see you." If even one of the very's was omitted or another added she would start to scream wildly (Diamond, Baldwin, and Diamond, 1963, p. 304).*

### Other signs

In addition to the three major signs just described, autistic children have problems in eating, often refusing food or eating only one or a few kinds of food. They may also have difficulty walking but be quite proficient at twirling and spinning objects and in performing ritualistic hand movements. Other rhythmic movements, such as endless body rocking, seem to please autistic children. They may also become preoccupied with manipulating a mechanical object and be very upset when interrupted. Often the children have sensory problems. Some autistic children are first diagnosed as being deaf because they never respond to any noise; some appear even to be insensitive to noise or to light. Bowel training is frequently delayed, and head banging and other self-injurious behavior are common (Rutter, 1974). Finally, autistic children have been shown to be negativistic, turning their backs on others and actively resisting whatever is expected of them (Cowan, Hoddinott, and Wright, 1965).

### Prognosis in infantile autism

What happens to such severely disturbed children when they reach adulthood? Kanner (1973) has reported on the adult status of nine of the eleven children whom he had described in his original paper on autism. Two developed epileptic seizures; by 1966 one of them had died, and the other was in a state mental hospital. Four others had spent most of their lives in institutions.

*Originally fighting for their aloneness and basking in the content that it gave them, originally alert to unwelcome changes and, in their own way, struggling for the status quo, originally astounding the observer with their phenomenal feats of memory, they yielded readily to the uninterrupted self-isolation and soon settled down to a life not too remote from a nirvanalike existence (p. 185).*

Of the remaining three, one had remained mute but was working on a farm and as an orderly in a nursing home. The last two have made at least somewhat satisfactory recoveries. Although both still live with their parents and have little social life, they are gainfully employed and have some recreational interests. Other follow-up studies corroborate this generally gloomy picture of adult autistics (for example, Rutter, 1967; Treffert, McAndrew, and Dreifuerst, 1973; Lotter, 1974).

## Case Example

Robbie was four years of age when his parents first sought behavior therapy for him. At that time he was virtually uncontrollable. He would do little that either of his parents told him to and, in fact, would often do the opposite of what they suggested. Although he "looked intelligent," he had never spoken. He seemed to be particularly fond of only one activity, unscrewing nuts and bolts. Whenever left to himself, Robbie would begin, working with just his fingers, to try to undo any nuts he could find. Often he puttered for hours with a single one until it would begin to move. After unscrewing the nut and bolt, he would typically swallow them. He also showed great upset over any change in daily routine, or indeed over any change at all in his environment. On one occasion, after his parents had bought new living room furniture, Robbie went into a rage that lasted until he fell asleep from exhaustion.

In interviews Robbie's parents described him as having been a "good baby," not crying very much and not placing very many demands on them. In thinking back to the time when they first noticed that something might be wrong, both parents agreed on one early phenomenon, which they had not considered particularly significant at the time. Robbie had actually seemed *not* to enjoy being held and cuddled by either of his parents. Often, when they tried to hold him and to look into his eyes, he would avoid their gaze and stiffen, seemingly becoming anxious and upset. As Robbie grew older, of course, the parents became worried about their lack of control over his behavior, his negativism, and his failure to talk. And as their concern deepened, they began to seek professional assistance. At various times Robbie had been diagnosed as retarded, as a childhood schizophrenic, as a symbiotic psychotic, as an anaclitic depressive,[1] and as autistic.

In the initial treatment sessions with Robbie, several other aspects of his behavior were clearly exhibited. He apparently had the capacity to understand at least some speech, even though he often appeared not to listen and did the opposite of what was requested. Four players, one of them being Robbie, gathered in a circle for a game of ball. Robbie was asked each time to throw the ball to a different person. In thirty trials not once did he throw the ball to the person whom he had been requested to throw it to. He always threw the ball to someone else. Even if he did not understand the requests, he would be expected to throw the ball to the correct person about one-third of the time simply by chance. The fact that he *never* made the correct response is evidence that he understood and chose deliberately not to comply with the request.

Robbie often gave the appearance of being tired, bored, and passive. When things became difficult during a language training session, for example, he might seem placid and calm and yawn a great deal. His outward appearance, however, was not an accurate reflection of Robbie's internal state. In one instance Robbie, barefoot, got up and walked across the room and left glistening footprints on the tile floor. His feet were literally dripping with sweat.

[1] Symbiotic psychosis, which is said to occur at about four years of age, is marked by an extreme reluctance to be separated from the mother (Mahler, 1952). Anaclitic depression is a term applied to the infant's profound sadness when separated from his mother for a prolonged period. Because there has been little systematic investigation of these syndromes, we mention them only in passing.

## Childhood Schizophrenia

### Descriptive Characteristics

The term childhood schizophrenia is generally applied to the psychotic behavior of a child over five years of age whose history indicates that he or she has regressed from an earlier higher level of adjustment, although some studies of child schizophrenics indicate that many have been profoundly backward in development from their earliest months. DSM-II defines childhood schizophrenia in the following way.

> *This category is for cases in which schizophrenic symptoms appear before puberty. The condition may be manifested by autistic, atypical and withdrawn behavior; failure to develop identity separate from the mother's; . . . gross immaturity* [and general unevenness] *and inadequacy of development (p. 35).*

In the United States Lauretta Bender has been the most prominent worker in this field. She has focused on several physiological and motoric signs that she believes to be particularly important in the diagnosis of childhood schizophrenia (Bender, 1955). She finds that these children show an upset in physiological rhythms so that eating and sleeping are disordered. She also notes vasomotor disturbances: either the walls of the blood vessels do not constrict or expand as they should in response to heat and cold, or they overrespond, as evidenced by excessive pallor and flushing. She proposed that schizophrenic children are poorly coordinated and show a particular motoric response called "whirling." To test for this an examiner has the child close his eyes and stretch out both arms while he rotates the child's head. A schizophrenic child turns his body (whirls) to keep it in line with his moving head. Normal children over six years of age respond this way very rarely, trying instead to maintain their bodies in the same position.

Childhood schizophrenia, as the name and its

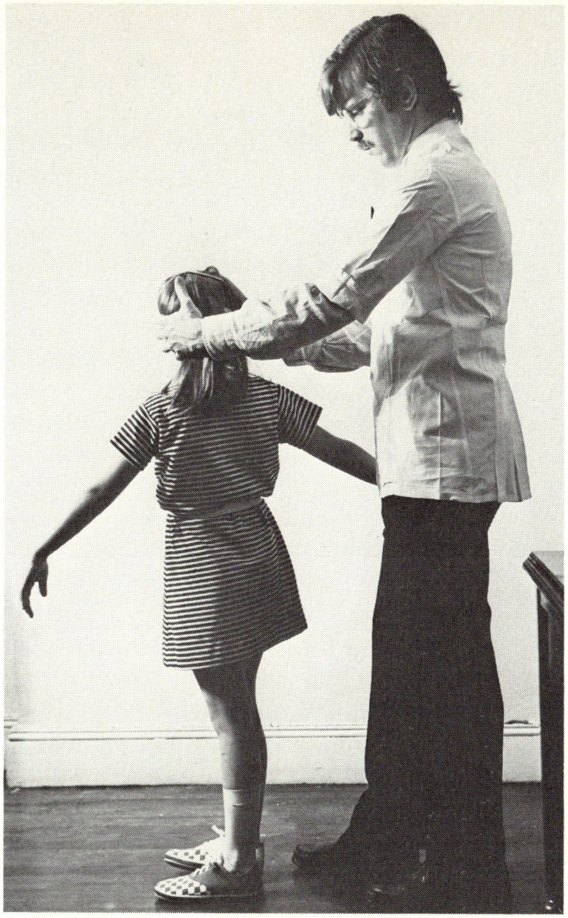

Pictured here is an examiner testing for the presence of the whirling response, behavior which Bender considers an important diagnostic sign of childhood schizophrenia When the schizophrenic child's head is turned, she swings the rest of her body in the same direction.

description in DSM-II suggest, is supposedly an early form of adult schizophrenia. There are indeed some similarities. In both there are problems with interpersonal relationships and distorted patterns of behavior and affect. The similarities are not pervasive, however. Although both groups, for example, have language disturbances, schizophrenic children's speech may be echolalic whereas that of adult schizophrenics is not. And there are several more significant differences between the two categories. For example, delusions and hallucinations do not seem to be prevalent among schizophrenic children. Although the sex ratio is about equal among adult schizophrenics, childhood schizophrenia is more common among males. Lotter (1966) has indicated the ratio as 2.5 to 1, but Rutter (1967) has placed it at 4.3 to 1. Moreover, unlike adult schizophrenia, there is no preponderance of childhood schizophrenia among the lower classes. Finally, schizophrenic children do not perform like adult schizophrenics on a variety of tasks (for example, Wortis et al., 1974; Caldwell, Brane, and Beckett, 1970).

Bender (1970, 1973) has been able to follow the life course of a hundred childhood schizophrenics who were seen in Bellevue Hospital in New York City. Two-thirds of these individuals were found in mental institutions, and ninety-four were thought to be schizophrenic. Thus, according to Bender's study, despite differences between adult and childhood schizophrenia, one link appeared strong: schizophrenic children may become schizophrenic adults. But others have questioned Bender's data on several grounds. First, she employs a diagnostic class broad enough to have included many brain-damaged individuals (Wortis et al., 1974). Second, in a well-executed ten-year follow-up study of psychotic children, many of whom could be regarded as childhood schizophrenics, Lockyer and Rutter (1969) did not find that they had become adult schizophrenics. We must therefore conclude that the evidence does not favor viewing child and adult schizophrenia as two closely related disorders. A more appropriate label for the first might be the simple term, childhood psychosis, and this change appears in the draft outline of DSM-III. Nonetheless, much of the research literature, as it now stands, is based on the childhood schizophrenia category; thus we are forced to use the term in the remainder of the chapter.

## Case Example

Kenny was five and a half when his parents sought professional help. His first five years had been uneventful. He developed language normally, played often with several close friends, and got along well with his siblings. He then began kindergarten and the teacher soon complained that Kenny did not seem mature enough to attend school. She said that he refused to talk or to participate in games with other children. Often, when she tried to encourage him to join in certain activities, he would throw a tantrum.

At this time the parents did not notice anything unusual about Kenny's behavior at home, but as the year progressed he became more aloof and uncommunicative. At times he would appear panic-stricken for no apparent reason, running through the house crying in abject terror.

When the child was seen professionally, his poor coordination and clumsiness were evident. In addition, he exhibited the classic whirling response of schizophrenic children.

## Childhood Schizophrenia and Infantile Autism: Different Syndromes?

Is there a basis for making the differentiation between the two categories infantile autism and childhood schizophrenia? Bernard Rimland (1964) answers with a very definite yes.

> *. . . [There is] sufficient information to demonstrate clearly that early infantile autism is* not *the same disease or cluster of diseases which has come to be called childhood schizophrenia [or childhood psychosis], and that autism can and should be differentiated from it at all levels of discourse. Indeed, on reading many of the papers which describe schizophrenic children as autistic the writer is reminded of the story of the two men who were indistinguishable in appearance except that the tall thin one had red hair and only one leg (p. 68).*

Rimland contends that the label autistic is applied far too frequently, and that only about 10 percent of psychotic children should actually be so diagnosed. He has proposed criteria by which autistic and schizophrenic children can be differentiated. Several of them have the support of experimental evidence.

1. **Onset and course.** Autism is said to begin shortly after birth and is detectable at least by the time the child is two or three. In contrast, childhood schizophrenia is viewed as beginning later in life, after a period of seeming normality. Furthermore, the prognosis of autistic children is worse than that of schizophrenic children (Rutter, 1968).
2. **Health and appearance.** Autistic children are usually described as especially healthy and good-looking (Kanner, 1949). Schizophrenic

children, on the other hand, have many health problems and are not distinguished by any particular level of physical attractiveness (Bender, 1955).

3. **Physical responsiveness.** Unlike autistic infants, those who are to become schizophrenic do mold to the bodies of their caretakers and are not reported as stiff and unresponsive (Bender, 1955).

4. **Autistic aloneness.** Rimland argues that the schizophrenic child, unlike the autistic, does not isolate himself.

5. **Need to preserve sameness.** Rimland says that the schizophrenic child does not have the autistic child's need for a set routine and unchanged surroundings.

6. **Motor performance.** Autistic children are often described as graceful and dexterous in finger movements. Schizophrenic children are usually described as awkward and poorly coordinated.

7. **Language.** The specific language difficulties of autistic children, echolalia and pronoun reversal, are not found as frequently in schizophrenic children.

8. **Parents.** The parents of autistic children are often found to be well educated and to have high IQs. Moreover, there is a low incidence of familial mental disorders. In contrast, the parents of schizophrenic children do not have high IQs, and the incidence of mental disorders in their families is greater than that in the general population.

9. **Idiot savant performance.** Rimland contends that many autistic children suffer from a particular kind of mental retardation which is characterized by extraordinary talents in isolated and limited areas (see Box 17.1, page 452). For example, he cites the case of an autistic child who, at seventeen months of age, could recite a complete aria from *Don Giovanni*. Such performances are not found in schizophrenic children.

Basing his work in part on the differences just listed, Rimland (1964) developed a checklist to help in differentiating autistic children from other children examined clinically. The instrument is filled out by the parents and covers aspects of behavior such as eating, cuddliness, and sensory responsiveness. In one report Rimland (1971) started with a sample of 2218 cases, about 10 percent of which were judged autistic on the basis of the rating scale. A comparison between autistic and nonautistic children on several of the key items appears in Table 15.1.

TABLE **15.1**
Comparison of Autistic and Psychotic Children on Several Items from Rimland's Diagnostic Checklist

| Item | Autistic, % | | Nonautistic, % |
|---|---|---|---|
| | Speaking (*N* = 65) | Mute (*N* = 53) | (*N* = 230) |
| **21.** Did you ever suspect the child was very nearly deaf? | | | |
| __1 Yes | 77 | 94 | 54 |
| __2 No | 23 | 6 | 46 |
| | 100 | 100 | 100 |

TABLE **15.1**
*(continued)*

| Item | Autistic, % | | Nonautistic, % |
|---|---|---|---|
| | Speaking (*N* = 65) | Mute (*N* = 53) | (*N* = 230) |
| **29.** (Ages 2–5) Is he cuddly? | | | |
| __1 Definitely, likes to cling to adults | 2 | 2 | 20 |
| __2 Above average (likes to be held) | 8 | 8 | 18 |
| __3 No, rather stiff and awkward to hold | 90 | 88 | 56 |
| __4 Don't know | 0 | 2 | 6 |
| | 100 | 100 | 100 |
| **33.** (Ages 3–5) How skillful is the child in doing fine work with his fingers or playing with small objects? | | | |
| __1 Exceptionally skillful | 71 | 75 | 33 |
| __2 Average for age | 6 | 9 | 23 |
| __3 A little awkward, or very awkward | 15 | 8 | 33 |
| __4 Don't know | 8 | 8 | 11 |
| | 100 | 100 | 100 |
| **40.** (Ages 3–5) How interested is the child in mechanical objects such as the stove or vacuum cleaner? | | | |
| __1 Little or no interest | 19 | 9 | 23 |
| __2 Average interest | 4 | 0 | 21 |
| __3 Fascinated by certain mechanical things | 77 | 91 | 56 |
| | 100 | 100 | 100 |
| **45.** (Ages 3–5) Does child get very upset if certain things he is used to are changed (like furniture or toy arrangement, or certain doors which must be left open or shut)? | | | |
| __1 No | 4 | 2 | 29 |
| __2 Yes, definitely | 87 | 86 | 41 |
| __3 Slightly true | 9 | 12 | 30 |
| | 100 | 100 | 100 |
| **71.** (Ages 3–5) Does the child typically say "Yes" by repeating the same question he has been asked? (Example: You ask "Shall we go for a walk, Honey?" and he indicates he does want to by saying "Shall we go for a walk, Honey?" or "Shall we go for a walk?") | | | |
| __1 Yes, definitely, does not say "yes" directly | 94 | 12* | 22 |
| __2 No, would say "Yes" or "OK" or similar answer | 0 | 3 | 8 |
| __3 Not sure | 4 | 6 | 8 |
| __4 Too little speech to say | 2 | 79 | 62 |
| | 100 | 100 | 100 |

* Speech item not applicable to the mute group.

Rimland's report, coupled with the descriptive differences he has listed, supports the notion that autistic children can be differentiated from the larger population of psychotic children. Nonetheless, diagnosing autism correctly may still present a serious problem. The usefulness of a test in diagnosis is affected by the base rate of the disorder in question, that is, the frequency of its occurrence in the general population. The base rate of childhood psychoses is reported to be about 4.5 cases per 10,000 in the general population (Lotter, 1966). According to Rimland, the base rate of autism among psychotic children is about one in ten. Thus the base rate for autism would be only 0.45 cases per 10,000 children in the general population, making its diagnosis extremely difficult.

To understand this point, consider what would happen if the diagnostician, wanting to make the maximum number of correct diagnoses of autism, decides to use no other information than the low base rate. By calling all the psychotic children seen nonautistic, the diagnostician would be correct 90 percent of the time! Of course in this extreme example all the autistic children would be misdiagnosed. The point is that with such a low base rate, there are few diagnoses of autism to make, and therefore the diagnostic validity of the checklist is difficult to demonstrate. This point was well illustrated in a study that found Rimland's checklist to improve only slightly on base rate diagnoses (Masters and Miller, 1970).

# Etiology of Autism and Childhood Schizophrenia

We turn now to an evaluation of the theory and research on autism and childhood schizophrenia. A note of caution is in order. Some theorists attempt to account specifically for autism, but others deal more generally with childhood psychosis. Moreover, the diagnoses of the children referred to in many of the research reports are often questionable, with the diagnosis of autism perhaps being made too frequently.

## Physiological Bases of Autism and Childhood Schizophrenia

Several considerations make organic accounts of autism and childhood schizophrenia plausible. First, the age of onset is very early; autism is supposedly detectable in the first two years of life, and childhood schizophrenia also develops in early childhood. Were a psychological stress to precipitate such disorders, it would indeed have to be a particularly noxious event. Yet the available evidence does not indicate that psychotic children are reared in especially unpleasant environments or that they have suffered some severe trauma. Second, a syndrome quite similar to the symptoms of autism and childhood schizophrenia may develop in the aftermath of brain diseases such as encephalitis. Third, mental subnormality is often associated with some kind of brain dysfunction (discussed in Chapter 17), and the majority of children with childhood psychoses have low levels of intelligence (see Box 15.1).

Within the general framework of physiological accounts of childhood psychoses, we can identify several topics of investigation: pregnancy and birth complications, abnormal EEGs and other neurological findings, and genetic factors. There has also been some interest in levels of brain amines, especially of serotonin, but thus far no conclusions can be drawn (Campbell et al., 1974; Yuwiler et al., 1975).

## BOX 15.1 Autism and Mental Retardation

The fact that autistic children perform very poorly on intelligence tests is not sufficient grounds to regard them as merely mentally retarded. Between one-quarter and one-third of autistic children have a normal IQ. Furthermore, performance may vary widely depending on the ability being tested. Children diagnosed as autistic perform more poorly on verbal tests and relatively better in matching designs in block design tests and in putting together disassembled objects (DeMyer, 1975; Rutter and Lockyer, 1967). Furthermore, prognosis is worse for autistic children than for retardates, and most retardates are not autistic. Thus autism cannot be viewed simply as a form of mental retardation.

Some controversy, though, surrounds the interpretation of the low IQ scores of autistic children. Kanner (1943) observed that autistic children "looked intelligent"; and their isolated areas of great talent have suggested to some that their IQ scores do not accurately reflect their mental ability. A variety of factors, other than poor cognitive ability, may account for poor performance on an IQ test. In one study, for example, autistic children were asked to choose red or square objects from a stimulus array; each correct response was rewarded. Over 80 percent of the children tested made *fewer* correct responses than would be expected on the basis of chance alone. In other words, they actively avoided making correct responses (Cowan, Hoddinott, and Wright, 1965). Such a negativitistic response set would, of course, make it difficult to obtain an accurate estimate of intelligence. But other evidence suggests that negativism is not the whole story of the low IQs of autistic children. If it were, the IQs of autistic children would be less reliable and valid than those obtained from testing other groups. But they are not. The IQs of autistic children prove to be stable on test-retest reliability (Lockyer and Rutter, 1969) and predict later adjustment and educational attainment as well as do those of normal children (Rutter, 1974).

**Pregnancy and Birth Complications** Given that the onset of psychotic behavior in children is at a relatively young age, a likely candidate for early damage to the central nervous system might be brain insult during the term of the fetus or at birth. Although pregnancy and birth complications (PBCs) are no more common in the gestation periods and deliveries of autistic children than in those of infants throughout the general population (Kanner, 1954; Kanner and Lesser, 1958), the majority of studies have indeed found a higher incidence of PBCs in the births of schizophrenic children (for example, Hinton, 1963; Gittelman and Birch, 1967). But even in the studies that have found *more* PBCs among schizophrenic children, the frequency has not been particularly high. For example, in the Gittelman and Birch study (1967) only 35 percent of the schizophrenic children's births were found to have been difficult. We must therefore look further for a physiological cause of autism and childhood schizophrenia.

**Neurological Findings** If autism or childhood schizophrenia is related to abnormal brain functioning, this should be detectable in their EEGs or through a neurological examination, although such correlational evidence would not be sufficient to prove causation. The majority of studies of the electrical activity in the brains of schizophrenic children have found abnormal brain rhythms. In fact, about 80 percent are reported to have an abnormal EEG, usually of an immature type (Taterks and Kety, 1955).

The picture is similar in autism. Although in an early study (Kanner and Eisenberg, 1955) only three of twenty-eight cases had abnormal EEGs, more recent studies have reported a higher incidence. Hutt and his colleagues (1964) reported low-amplitude, high-frequency waves and used them as evidence in proposing an overaroused cortex as the cause of autism. Others have failed to find this specific pattern, however, detecting instead slow-wave activity (Hermelin and O'Connor, 1968). Lotter (1974) reports that one-third of autistic children appear to have a neurological dysfunction, either seizures or an abnormal EEG. Similarly, Rutter and Lockyer (1967) reported that 14 to 20 percent of autistic children later develop seizures.

Neurological examinations have also revealed signs of neurological damage, such as difficulties in motor coordination and the vasomotor disturbances noted by Bender, in a large percentage of schizophrenic and autistic children. These percentages range from 41 to 84 percent in various studies (Bosch, 1970; DeMyer et al., 1973; Goldfarb, 1961; Gubbay, Lobascher, and Kingerlee, 1970). Thus a large proportion of both autistic and schizophrenic children appear to have a neurological dysfunction, as assessed by EEG and other neurological tests.

**Genetic Factors** In the major twin study of childhood schizophrenia, Kallmann and Roth (1956) reported concordance rates for identical and fraternal pairs. Twelve co-twins of seventeen monozygotic probands were diagnosed as schizophrenic before adolescence, and another three were so diagnosed after the age of fifteen. Six co-twins of thirty-five dizygotic probands were diagnosed as schizophrenic in preadolescence, and another two were so diagnosed after the age of fifteen. Thus the concordance rates were 88.2 percent of the identical twins and 22.9 percent for the fraternal. In a family study Bender (1955) found that 40 percent of a sample of schizophrenic children had one schizophrenic parent, and that *both* parents of 11 percent of them were schizophrenic. These findings support the importance of genetic factors in childhood schizophrenia, although the crucial studies of adoptees and of identical twins reared apart have not been done.

The role of genetic factors in autism is less clear. In examining parents, grandparents, uncles, and aunts of autistic children, Kanner (1954) found that only 1.3 percent of them could be diagnosed as psychotic. Those who have investigated the rate of autism in the siblings of autistic children have found it to be about 2 percent (Kanner and Lesser, 1958; Creak and Ini, 1960; and Rutter, 1965). Although this incidence rate is higher than that in the general population—the generally accepted rate of autism being, as stated earlier, about 0.45 per 10,000—this percentage does not approximate the high concordance rates found in family studies of schizophrenic children. Genetic factors cannot be dismissed in the etiology of autism, but they do not appear to be major contributors.

## Physiological Theories of Autism and Childhood Schizophrenia

Having reviewed some of the major data on physiological factors that may figure in childhood psychoses, we can now examine what use several theorists make of them.

### Lauretta Bender

It has been suggested by Bender that a genetically transmitted predisposition for childhood psychosis is precipitated by some kind of intrauterine difficulty or birth complication. The child is thereafter afflicted with a disorder in maturation, particularly in the development and functioning of the central nervous system. Not only does the child fail to develop normally, but he may also regress to earlier levels of functioning. Because the child does not mature, he is unable, according to Bender, to form an adequate body image or ego boundary; his psychotic symptoms manifest this failure.

Bender's theory integrates many of the data reviewed—genetic factors, PBCs, neurological impairments, and immature patterns of the EEGs. The last part of her theory, however, that concerning the failure to form an adequate body image, is highly speculative. The data reviewed have little relation to concepts such as body image and ego boundary. Furthermore, this last part of her theory rests on the psychoanalytic assumption that psychotic behavior represents a failure of ego processes, a view which, as indicated in Chapter 14, has few data to support it.

### Bernard Rimland

In an influential book Rimland (1964) proposed that the autistic child is genetically predisposed to superior development, but that this potential advantage also makes the child particularly vulnerable to damage in the reticular formation, a primitive netlike area of nerve tissue in the central core of the brainstem. Damage to a certain area of the reticular formation is known to cause slow-wave activity in the cortex, which means that the brain is maintained in a state of underarousal. The end result, as Rimland sees it, is a cognitive impairment, an inability to relate new stimuli to remembered experience. Thus, through a physiological route, Rimland derives a basic cognitive defect which he believes can account for the behavior of autistic children.

What evidence is available to support this theory? Data that might indicate that autistic children may be predisposed toward higher intelligence are equivocal. Their parents have typically been found to be higher than average in educational achievement (Treffert, 1970) but, contrary to Rimland's claim, they have not always been found to have high IQs (Levine and Olson, 1968).[2]

Rimland's supposition that the reticular formation in the brainstem is damaged is quite speculative. Furthermore, the notion that autistic children are characterized by a low level of arousal is supported only by the slow-wave activity found by Hermelin and O'Connor (1968) and is contradicted by other work.[3]

Finally, we should consider whether any evidence exists to support Rimland's claim that the primary defect leading to autism is an inability to relate new stimuli to remembered experience. Rimland believes that this inability to make new associations prevents the autistic child from deriving meaning from anything that happens to him. The child fails to develop an affectionate relationship with his family because he makes none of the normal associations between feeding and physical contact with the mother and derives none of the pleasure from this association that the normal child usually experiences. The autistic child's insistence that nothing in his surroundings or routine be altered is interpreted in a similar fashion. Environmental changes are considered by normal people to be minor or irrelevant because they are easily integrated with past experience. But because the autistic child can achieve no comprehensive ordering of the world, any slight change in surroundings causes him great emotional distress. In our opinion this part of the theory may be overstated, for autistic children *can* learn and thus are able to relate new stimuli to previous experience.

### Moore and Shiek

A theory similar to Rimland's has been proposed by Moore and Shiek (1971). They agree with Rimland that autistic children may be geniuses "gone awry," but they differ in the mechanism proposed for this arrested development. Their theory focuses on the possibility that the child may have been sensorially deprived while still in the womb. Moore and Shiek argue that because of accelerated development the autistic child is

[2] Actually, there are considerable data on the IQ, educational attainments, and social position of the parents of psychotic children. But most of the studies (for example, Florsheim and Peterfreund, 1974) did not sample just the parents of autistic children and thus are not completely relevant as evidence for or against Rimland's theory.

[3] It should be noted that Rimland does not commit himself to the reticular formation as the locus of damage. He focuses rather on the *psychological function* that is impaired and speculates that this malfunction *might* be explained by damage to the reticular formation.

"ready" to be born and to respond and to socialize before the end of the usual pregnancy term. By not being born until the full nine months have passed, the child suffers from restricted sensory stimulation and a lack of social experience.

> *Given a fetus with a brain in an advanced state of developmental readiness for stimulation but residing within a restricted uterine environment, what would be the probable results? What are the effects of sensory restriction and failure to experience primary socialization when these two circumstances occur simultaneously* (p. 454)?

Moore and Shiek note that the restriction of early environmental stimulation for animals dramatically affects their emotionality, learning ability, social behavior, and perception (Harlow and Harlow, 1966). And Rimland (1964) has remarked on the similarities between the behavior of autistic children and that of individuals who have experienced sensory deprivation. Subjects who are deprived of sensory stimuli for any length of time are "detached from the external environment" and "stare right at you but never see you" (p. 104).

Moore and Shiek also point out similarities between the behavior of autistic children and that of animals who have not been properly imprinted. Imprinting is a process whereby a neonate becomes attached to and learns from other members of its own species during a "critical period" of development. During this period the animal is inclined to follow a moving object in its vicinity, which is usually its mother. If by chance the object is other than a member of its own species and the animal follows and mimics it, the animal will thereafter lack interest in its own kind, much as the autistic child avoids human contact. Imprinting occurs only during one period of the neonate's development, usually just after birth. But if the autistic child were to reach the critical period while still in the womb, he or she might imprint on this intrauterine environment. Moore and Shiek have wondered,

> *Does the autistic child's insistence on sameness in the environment, his repetitive and stereotyped behaviors, his hand regarding, and his failure to develop speech suggest that he was imprinted by an atypical environment at a critical period in his primary socialization? In this essentially unchanging environment, the fetus has only the heartbeats of himself and his mother, and perhaps the other rhythms of their bodies, to affect him. Is it possible that the autistic child is so imprinted with this relatively featureless, secluded, and limited world during critical developmental periods, when he should be vividly stimulated and experiencing primary socialization, that he in fact seems to be living "in his own world" after birth? Does it explain his apparent need to maintain environmental sameness? . . . Are autistic children, by their frequent obsessions with inanimate objects, demonstrating . . . that an individual at the proper time in life can become attached to both living and nonliving things in the surrounding environment* (pp. 454–455)?

What kind of data could support this theory? First, like Rimland's theory, this account rests on the notion that autistic children are predisposed to precocious development and high intelligence. As we have just seen, the evidence on this point is equivocal. Second, the theory asserts that autistic children become accustomed to a low level of stimulation while in the womb. The autistic child should therefore be unable to accept "normal" levels of environmental stimulation and be overaroused by them. The data on EEG patterns are inconclusive on this point.

Moore and Shiek's hypothesis is fascinating and able to account for many facets of the behavior of autistic children. But it is, of course, a theory, and there are no direct research data to support it as yet. Indeed, it is interesting to reflect on what kind of research could produce data to support this highly speculative theory.

## Psychological Theories of Autism and Childhood Schizophrenia

As might be expected, theorists of a psychogenic bent attribute childhood psychoses to early experiences, especially those shared by the mother and child. An inadequate diet of mothering, the nutrient which, in dynamic theories, is so essential for development, is considered to bring on childhood psychoses.

### Bruno Bettelheim

Perhaps the best-known of the psychological theories was formulated by Bruno Bettelheim (1967). The basic supposition of Bettelheim's theory is that autism closely resembles the apathy and hopelessness found among inmates of German concentration camps during World War II (see page 125). Bettelheim hypothesizes that the young infant is able to perceive the negative feelings of his rejecting parents. He finds that his own actions have little impact on their unresponsiveness. The mother, on the one hand, may expect too much of the infant and be easily disappointed. Or the mother may expect too little, treating the child as a passive object. In either case the child comes to believe "that one's own efforts have no power to influence the world, because of the earlier conviction that the world is insensitive to one's reactions" (p. 46).

This experience of helplessness is viewed as extremely frustrating for the child. But he is unwilling to communicate his frustration because he feels that nothing good can come from it. He continues to withdraw from the world, his only activities—his ritualistic hand movements and echolalic speech—being more a means of shutting out the world than truly meeting it. An elaborate fantasy life is created, and insistence on sameness is the rule that brings permanence and order to the world. Autistic children remain safe only if everything about them stays put. Since the essential purpose of activity is to bring about change, autistic children avoid any sort of action; their universe centers on a static environment, beyond which they will not move.

Bettelheim's theory rests primarily on the hypothesis that at early critical periods, when the effect on the child is profound, the parents mistreat him by not loving him. In his early papers Kanner described the parents of autistic children as cold, insensitive, meticulous, introverted, distant, and highly intellectual (Kanner and Eisenberg, 1955). He summed up his theory of how such traits affect the children by saying that they are reared in "emotional refrigeration." Others (for example, Singer and Wynne, 1963; Rimland, 1964) have also noted the detachment of parents of autistic children, although Rimland has used less pejorative adjectives. Singer and Wynne have described several means by which these parents "disaffiliate" themselves from their children. Some are cynical about all interpersonal relations and are emotionally cold; others are passive and apathetic; and still others maintain an obsessive, intellectual distance from people. But a more recent investigation (Cox et al., 1975) has failed to confirm these earlier findings. When the parents of autistic children were compared to those of children with receptive aphasia (a disorder in understanding speech), the two groups did *not* differ in warmth, emotional demonstrativeness, responsiveness, and sociability.

Even if we were to ignore these recent findings, the direction of a possible correlation between parental characteristics and autism is not easily determined. The deviant parental behavior that has been reported could be a reaction to the child's abnormality rather than the other way around. And if parental behavior causes autism, why is the incidence of similar difficulties so low in siblings? Moreover, although autism is a severe disorder, the parental behavior that has been discussed does not appear likely to be more than mildly damaging. It would seem that only very gross mistreatment, such as keeping the child in a locked closet, could precipitate severe problems so early in life. There have been few reports of exceedingly harsh treatment of autistic children.

Recently, one aspect of Bettelheim's theory, admittedly one somewhat more limited in range, has been tested directly. According to Bettelheim, autistic children fail to use the pronoun "I" because they selectively reject a part of speech that would emphasize their own existence. But Bartak and Rutter (1974) thought that the typical pattern of autistic children's echolalia coupled with a common feature of English grammar could explain avoidance of the pronoun. The children tend to repeat the final part of a sentence, and "I" usually appears at the beginning; the use of "I" would therefore be infrequent. To pit the two theories against each other, Bartak and Rutter selected a group of autistic children who never spontaneously said "I" and who were echolalic. A number of three-word sentences were then constructed using various pronouns (he, she, me, I, and you) in each possible position in the sentence. These sentences were then presented to the children when they were paying attention, such as during play. As expected, the frequency of echoing was greatest for words in the last position, then the second, and finally the first. More important, and in direct contradiction to Bettelheim's theory, there was no difference in the frequency with which the various pronouns were echoed. The autistic children did not selectively avoid "I."

### Social-learning theory

Social-learning theorists, like those who are psychoanalytically oriented, have postulated that certain childhood learning experiences cause psychotic childhood disorders. Ferster (1961), in an extremely influential article, suggested that the inattention of the parents, especially of the mother, prevents establishment of the associations that make human beings reinforcers. And because the parents have not become reinforcers, they cannot control the child's behavior. Ferster's reasoning is as follows.

1. Behavior is controlled primarily by its consequences.
2. Initially, the young child responds only to primary reinforcers, such as food and milk.
3. As children grow older, their behavior comes more under the control of secondary and generalized reinforcers, such as praise and love, and these social rewards acquire their reinforcing properties through contiguous association with primary rewards.
4. The behavior of severly disturbed children is a consequence of inadequate secondary and generalized reinforcers.
5. The parents of disturbed children, especially those of autistic children, neglect the child, for example, by being involved in professional and other non-family-oriented activities.
6. Thus the child learns to function alone or autistically and never becomes responsive to human contact, having been deprived of it during the earlier stages of life.

An interesting consequence of Ferster's paper was a flurry of therapeutic work aimed at shaping the behavior of severely disturbed children (Davison, 1964b; Wolf, Risley, and Mees, 1964; Lovaas et al., 1965). The investigators' partial and short-term successes in modifying behavior by applying primary and secondary reinforcers did not of course demonstrate that Ferster's etiological hypotheses were correct. Indeed, Rimland may well insist that a physiological dysfunction causes autism and yet, with perfect consistency, agree with Ferster's proposals about how best to handle these children.

If the effectiveness of the treatment recommended by Ferster must be disregarded, what is left to support his theory? Very little. Many of the comments made about Bettelheim's position are again applicable. Lack of parental attention seems inadequate to explain severe behavioral disturbances among children (see Box 15.2).

### Developmental-disability theories

Rutter (1968, 1974) considers the basic defect that produces autism to be severe disruption of communication skills. The association of language

## BOX 15.2 A Special Note about Psychogenic Theories

Readers of this book have no doubt noticed that the authors are very critical of the various psychogenic theories, both psychoanalytic and learning. In addition to our aspirations to provide as scientifically accurate a textbook as possible, we are concerned about the impact that theories may have on people. Consider, for a moment, what your feelings might be if a psychiatrist or psychologist were to tell you that your unconscious hostility has caused your child to be mute at the age of six. Or how would you feel if you were told that your commitment to professional activities has brought about the autistic behavior patterns of your child? The fact is, of course, that the truth of these allegations has yet to be demonstrated, and some information even contradicts these views. But in the meantime a tremendous emotional burden is placed on parents who have, over the years, been told that they are at fault. But, you might say, have we not evidence that the families of disturbed children are "peculiar"? In Chapter 14 we have already shown how inconclusive such data are, and the strong possibility exists that any home problems are reactions to the behavior of the particular child rather than the cause of them, especially when there are normal siblings.

As Rimland has suggested, considering autism psychogenic in origin may be not only an inadequate hypothesis but also a pernicious one.

difficulties with the syndrome and the prognostic significance of the autistic child's acquiring speech are major pieces of evidence supporting his position.

Research has provided further insights. In intelligence testing autistic children do well on tasks involving immediate memory, for example, in digit span tests in which they must repeat a series of digits after hearing them. But they do very poorly on tests involving verbal concepts, abstraction, and symbolization (Rutter, 1968; Bartak, Rutter, and Cox, 1975). Hermelin (1966) tested autistic children for their recall of eight-word messages which consisted either of two nonsense phrases—such as "half egg a pick"; "might got dress up"; or two meaningful sentences—"watch these green lights"; "eat bread and jam." The normal children in the control group recalled the meaningful sentences better than the nonsense phrases. In contrast, the autistic children typically recalled only the last part of a message, regardless of whether it was meaningful or not. Acquiring knowledge of the structure of language facilitates storage of word sequences. Without knowing this structure, sentences can be stored no more efficiently than can a string of unrelated words. The outcomes of both intelligence testing and experimental studies suggest, then, a basic impairment in language.

But are the language problems *primary,* or could they result from social withdrawal? Although some emotional disturbances might stem from the inability to comprehend language, problems in social relationships are often noticeable even before verbal skills are acquired. Early in infancy autistic children have problems in communicating via babblings and gesture, however, as Ricks and Rutter have indicated. Therefore a communication deficit may precede the problems autistic children have in social relationships.

Another theory, proposed by Lovaas, attributes autism to a particular psychological deficit, stimulus overselectivity. In one study supporting this position, groups of autistic, retarded, and normal children were given a discrimination learning test (Lovaas, et al., 1971). In the training phase three different cues—a red floodlight, a noise, and the tactile sensations from the inflation of a blood pressure cuff—were all presented simultaneously. Each time subjects pressed a bar in response to this multidimensional cue, they were rewarded with candy. Once the response had been established, subjects moved to the testing phase; in addition to the complex combination of stimuli used in training, each stimulus was presented separately.

The most important part of the test was how the children responded when each of the three stimuli was presented by itself. Autistic children responded to only one of the three separately presented stimuli, retardates to two, and normal children to all three. Later work has extended and replicated this study (Koegel and Wilhelm, 1973). Lovaas makes a plausible case in explaining how such overselectivity might account for the autistic child's failure to learn socially appropriate behavior. Taking an associational view of learning, Lovaas notes that the stimuli that are to be associated in any situation are often complex and multidimensional. The child who attends to only one dimension at a time will have difficulty learning to associate complex stimuli and will remain socially inept.

In contrast to the single-process theories of Rutter and Lovaas, Wing (1970) has proposed that autism results from a multiplicity of impairments. In an earlier study (Wing, 1969) autistic children had been compared with groups of children with receptive aphasia—difficulties in comprehending speech—and with executive aphasia—difficulties in speaking; with children who were both partially blind and deaf; with retarded children who had been born with mongolism (Down's syndrome); and with normal children. All groups were given a number of tasks to perform and stimuli to respond to, and other aspects of behavior were observed. The results indicated that the pattern of impairments shown by autistic children was different from the pattern of any of the other groups. For example, both autistic and aphasic children had difficulty with the tasks requiring speech. The aphasic children, however, could use nonvocal communication to compensate whereas the autistic children did not. Moreover, the autistic children tended to use peripheral vision rather than central and could not copy skilled movements or tell left from right. Wing concluded that

> *At the present stage, the most reasonable way of formulating the problem which takes* [everything] *into account is to say that autistic children appear to suffer from multiple impairments (which can vary in severity) affecting comprehension and use of speech, comprehension and use of gesture, auditory perception, visual perception, control of skilled movements, posture, autonomic function, and certain aspects of physical development. Each of these impairments can occur independently of the others in various chronic childhood conditions. When they occur together, the affected child will show the behavior pattern typical of early childhood autism . . .*(1970, p. 263).

The primary difficulty with all these explanations is the lack of directly supporting evidence. The Wing (1969) study shows only a *correlation* between a considerable number of impairments and the diagnosis of autism. Similarly, Rutter and Lovaas have shown only that autistic children are deficient in communication skills and attention. Autistic behavior may plausibly follow from such developmental disabilities, but the studies that might prove them causative have not been done.

## A Diathesis-Stress Hypothesis

We have seen that both physiological and psychological theories about the causes of childhood psychoses have some credibility. Various neurological problems characterize *some* of these children and the parents of *some* may be rather aloof and detached. Yet none of the theories by itself accounts for the syndrome; an interaction of several factors may offer a better explanation. Kanner himself (Kanner and Eisenberg, 1955), although noting the lack of affection by the parents, concluded that psychotic children have some inborn defect. A diathesis-stress model that includes both a physiological predisposition and psychological stresses may prove more satisfactory. We shall examine such a theory, proposed by Zaslow and Breger (1969), to illustrate in more detail the aspects of this approach.

Zaslow and Breger view autism as a failure to establish social relationships because the interactions between mother and child are from the very beginning unsatisfactory.[4] The early sensorimotor interactions—when the mother feeds the child and holds him if he is distressed—are considered formative. Mother, and by generalization other people, take on positive valence as they reduce stresses such as hunger and discomfort. This is the basis on which social attachment is built.

> *In autism, a lack of satisfying sensorimotor interaction, in which the infant passes from a startle-like state of arousal and stress to a comfortable state of relaxation in human contact, may lead to a failure in adequate attachment. The autistic child then continues to show an aroused, startle-like reaction to people and holding* (pp. 251–252.)

Evidence indeed supports the notion that a child's response to being held may be inborn. Shaffer and Emerson (1964), for example, have indicated that infants may be classified as "cuddlers" and "noncuddlers," even before they have had much experience in being held. The noncuddlers resisted close physical contact with their mothers almost immediately and were found to be less intensely attached to them at the end of twelve months.

Zaslow and Breger point out that other factors may also decrease the amount of physical contact; the infant may be very active, or he may have physical ailments that make him cry and stiffen when held. Intellectual, aloof, and disaffiliating parents may be expected to pick up and play with their children less often. An inexperienced mother may find it difficult to cope with a child who seemingly rejects her attempts to comfort it, which may explain why the rate of autism is higher among firstborn children (Rimland, 1964).

How do Zaslow and Breger account for the other aspects of the syndrome?

> *The autistic child's need for sameness in the environment, his tremendous sensitivity to small changes in the arrangement of objects in the immediate world, and his propensity for intense rage and upset over such changes all attest to his great reliance on place security over person security. Lacking the positive affective bond to mother which forms the secure base from which exploration and eventual mastery of the environment normally proceeds, the autistic child has become attached to his immediate and familiar environment and relies on this for security.*[5]

[4] Although Zaslow and Breger consider their theory to be an explanation of autism, they hold a broader definition of the disorder than workers such as Rimland.

[5] Research with monkeys has indeed shown that they are more willing to explore a novel environment when their mothers are present.

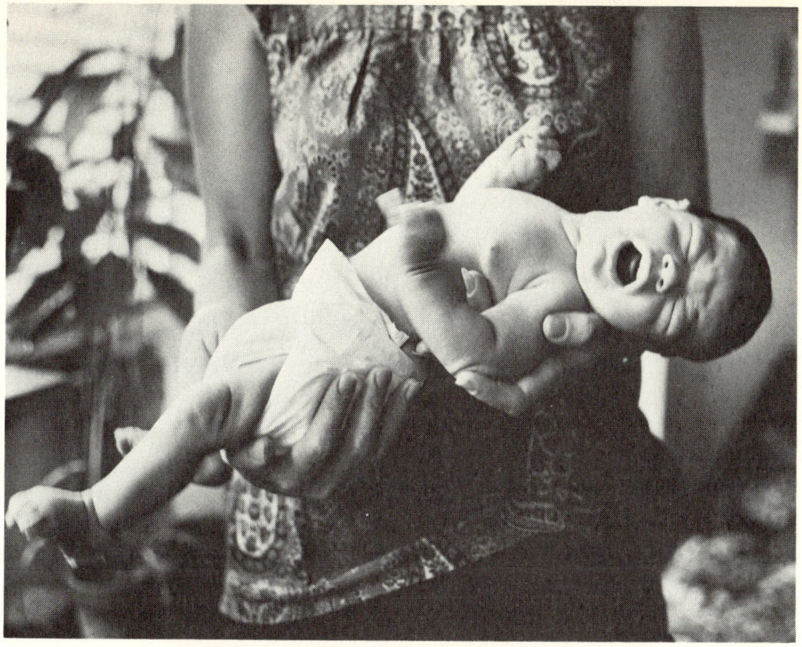

Most babies, like the one below, enjoy being held. The infant above is arching its back and resisting close physical contact. The parents of autistic children often remember this response pattern as the first indication of the disorder.

> *The autistic child's attachment to objects such as mechanical appliances is part of the same process. . . . Most normal infants and children become attached to certain physical objects such as a blanket, a special doll or toy. . . . In autism we see an intensification of this process due to the lack of a satisfying human attachment . . . the attachment to . . . objects increases . . . as the positive attachment to mother decreases* (pp. 263–264).

Zaslow and Breger's diathesis-stress model is indeed a plausible account of much of the extant data, focusing on the child's aversion to being held as the diathesis and on parental detachment as the stress. Other possible predisposing factors, such as neurological impairments, are not dealt with in their theory but will probably be part of a more adequate account that is put together someday.

## Summary

In this chapter we have reviewed research and theory related to the severe psychotic disturbances of children. The information available suggests that two syndromes, infantile autism and childhood schizophrenia, can be identified. Autism, a relatively new diagnostic category proposed by Kanner, is slated to appear in DSM-III. An inability to relate to people, communication problems, and a need to preserve sameness are indications of the disorder. Childhood schizophrenia, as the name implies, is supposedly an earlier version of adult schizophrenia. The evidence, though, suggests that the two are not related to any great extent.

Physiological factors may be important in etiology. For childhood schizophrenia significant concordance among identical twins suggests that genetic factors may be important. Both schizophrenic and autistic children frequently show signs of neurological impairment, such as abnormal EEGs and seizures. Psychological theories have focused on the characteristics of the children's parents. Some but not all autistic children appear to be born to highly intelligent parents who may not be physically comforting to them. Several researchers have pointed to the autistic child's language deficiencies, inability to attend to more than one stimulus, and failure to develop a number of perceptual and physical skills. The theoretical accounts of both autism and childhood schizophrenia must be regarded as highly speculative at this time.

# part five
# organic syndromes

# chapter 16

## BRAIN DYSFUNCTIONS AND HYPERACTIVITY



The focus of this chapter is on behavioral disturbances that are clearly linked to organic dysfunctions of the brain. Its tissues may be injured and destroyed through infection and accident and by chemicals; disease can cause biochemical imbalances and deterioration. The clinical syndromes that are attributable to brain pathologies bring to mind the so-called functional psychoses—those in which one or more of the normal activities of the individual are severely disturbed, but without known change in tissues or condition of the brain. The DSM, in effect, indicates the similarities of all psychoses by giving them the same definition, except that some are "not attributed to physical conditions." The symptoms of brain pathologies do in important respects resemble those of the major functional psychoses, manic-depression and schizophrenia. Some workers reason, therefore, that although no organic causes have been demonstrated with certainty for functional psychoses, eventually they will be established. The suspected damage to the central nervous system at birth of schizophrenics, the brain amine disturbances suspect in the same disorder and in the depressions, and the possible neurological damage of autistic and schizophrenic children might all prove to be such organic causes or at least diatheses.

Disordered behavior that can be traced to an organic impairment of the brain is not as circumscribed and predictable as might be surmised. It does not always depend simply on the brain area affected or the extent of the damage. In the first place, determining the exact area and extent of a brain lesion is difficult. Second, even when two persons have what appears to be the same lesion in a particular area of the brain, the impairments of behavior may vary widely. The preexisting personality of the individual may interact with the brain injury in determining the symptoms that are observed. Well-adjusted persons who do not succumb to psychological stress are also better able to withstand the physical stress of brain damage. Thus the manifestations of an organic brain disorder depend on other factors, even though the primary cause is an injury or a pathological change in the brain.

## Clinical Features of Brain Dysfunction

According to DSM-II any of the following impairments can occur in an organic brain syndrome.

1. **Impairments of orientation.** The individual may not know who he is or where he is and loses all track of time, forgetting not only the day of the week but also the year. These three impairments are usually called disorientation for person, place, and time.
2. **Impairment of memory.** Memory loss is especially great for recent events, less so for earlier life. The patient may resort to *confabulation,* making up stories to fill in the gaps in memory.
3. **Impairment of intellectual function.** The individual may have difficulties in comprehension, learning, and making judgments. He or she is unable to formulate plans or reason effectively. The progressive deterioration of these intellectual functions is referred to as *dementia.*
4. **Emotional impairments.** Emotions may be labile or all affect may be blunted.

The preceding list indicates that most symptoms of brain disorders are cognitive and intellectual malfunctions. The primacy of *cognitive* deficits helps distinguish the organic syndromes from the neuroses and depressions, in which emotional problems are paramount. Similarly, although schizophrenics have severe impairments in cognition and perception, they seldom show memory loss. The emotional impairments that a brain-damaged individual suffers may result directly from the brain injury, but they may also reflect the individual's *reaction to being cognitively impaired.* You may yourself have experienced the frustrations of trying in vain to remember another person's name. Life can become quite upsetting when this sort of problem is faced dozens of times a day. Kolb (1968) has described the distress and discouragement of such a patient.

> *Confronted with a problem he cannot solve, the brain-injured individual becomes suddenly anxious and agitated and may appear dazed. A change in his color may appear, he fumbles at the task, and he may present other evidence of autonomic disturbances, such as irregular pulse and changes in respiratory rate. If he was initially in good spirits, he now becomes evasive, sullen, irritable, and even aggressive* (pp. 215–216).

Organic brain dysfunctions are diagnosed on the basis of a detailed history of the onset of cognitive and behavioral difficulties; a neurological examination of sensory and motor responses, especially of the reflexes, to determine whether there are localized impairments of the nervous system; EEGs and brain X-rays; an analysis of cerebrospinal fluids to determine whether infections, poisons, or blood are present; and psychological tests such as the Rorschach and Reitan's modification of the Halstead Battery (see page 78), which assess the patient's perceptual, motor, and intellectual functions. When the brain pathology is serious, few diagnostic problems exist; injuries, alterations in structure, or other impairments are so severe that it does not take sophisticated procedures to determine that the patient has an organic dysfunction and to identify its nature. When the alterations are subtle, however, the sophisticated diagnostic tests developed for their detection are not always helpful. Nor is behavior a reliable key to the nature of the dysfunction. Patients who have *different* organic problems may show similar behavioral deficits and patients with the *same* organic impairment may behave quite differently. And, of course, the overriding difficulty in diagnosis is our woefully inadequate knowledge of the enormously complex brain (see Box 16.1 for a review of brain structure and function).

## BOX **16.1** Structure and Function of the Human Brain

The brain is located within the protective covering of the skull and is enveloped with three layers of nonneural tissue, membranes referred to as *meninges*. The three membranes are the outer, tough *dura mater,* the intermediate, weblike *arachnoid,* and the inner, soft *pia mater.* Viewed from the top, the brain is divided by a midline fissure into two mirror-image cerebral hemispheres; together they constitute most of the cerebrum. The major connection between the two hemispheres is a band of nerve fibers called the *corpus callosum.* Figure 16.1 shows the surface of one of the *cerebral hemispheres.* The upper, side, and some of the lower surfaces of the hemispheres constitute the *cerebral cortex.* The cortex consists of six layers of tightly packed neuron cell bodies with many short, unsheathed interconnecting processes. These neurons, estimated to be 10 to 15 billion in number, make up a thin outer covering, the so-called gray matter of the brain. The cortex is vastly convoluted; the ridges are called *gyri* and the depressions between them *sulci* or fissures. Deep fissures divide the cerebral hemispheres into several distinct areas, called lobes. The *frontal lobe* lies in front of the central sulcus; the *parietal lobe* is behind it and above the lateral sulcus; the *temporal lobe* is located below the lateral sulcus; and the *occipital lobe* lies behind the parietal and temporal lobes. Different functions tend to be localized in particular areas of the lobes—vision in the occipital; discrimination of sounds in the temporal; reasoning and other higher mental processes, plus the regulation of fine voluntary movements, in the frontal; initiation of movements of the skeletal musculature in a band in front of the central sulcus; in a band behind this sulcus, receipt of sensations of touch, pressure, pain, temperature, and body position from skin, muscles, tendons, and joints.

The two hemispheres of the brain have different functions. The left hemisphere, which generally controls the right half of the body by a crossing over of motor and sensory fibers, is usually dominant; it is responsible for speech and for analytical thinking in right-handed people and in a fair number of left-handed people as well. The right hemisphere controls the left side of the body and specializes in discerning spatial relations and patterns and in intuition.

If the brain is sliced in half, separating the two cerebral hemispheres (Figure 16.2), additional important features can be seen. The gray matter of the cerebral cortex does not extend throughout the interior of the brain. Much of the interior is *white matter* and is made up of large tracts or bundles of myelinated (sheathed) fibers which connect cell bodies in the cortex with those in the spinal cord and in other centers lower in the brain. These centers are additional pockets of gray matter, referred to as *nuclei.* Some cortical cells project their long fibers or axons to motor neurons in the spinal cord, but others project them only as far as these clusters of interconnecting neuron cell bodies. Four masses are deep within each hemisphere, called collectively the *basal ganglia,* and other important areas and structures of the brain also contain nuclei. The nuclei serve both as way stations, connecting tracts from the cortex with other ascending and descending tracts, and as integrating motor and sensory control centers. Deep within the brain too are cavities, called *ventricles,* which are continuous with the central canal of the spinal cord and which are filled with cerebrospinal fluid.

In Figure 16.2 are shown four important functional areas or structures.

1. The *diencephalon,* connected in front with the hemispheres and behind with the midbrain, contains the *thalamus* and the *hypothalamus,* which consist of groups of nuclei. The thalamus is a relay station for all sensory pathways except the olfactory. The nuclei making up the thalamus receive nearly all impulses arriving from the different sensory areas of the body before passing them on to the cerebrum, where they are interpreted as conscious sensations. The hypo-

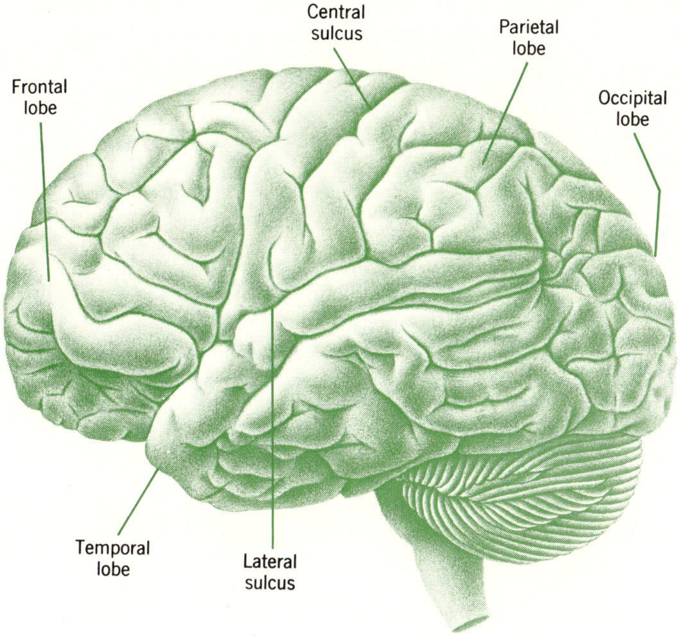


FIGURE **16.1**
Surface of the left cerebral hemisphere, indicating the lobes and the two principal fissures of the cortex.

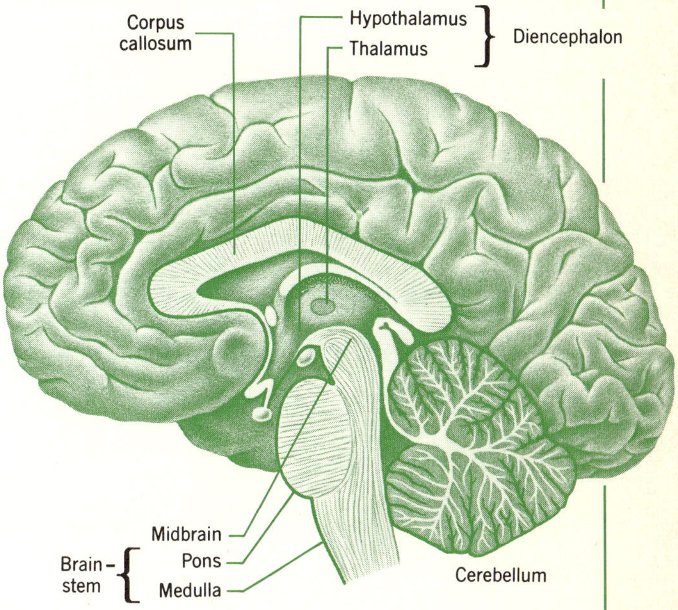


FIGURE **16.2**
Slice of brain through the medial plane, showing the internal structures.

thalamus is the highest center of integration for many visceral processes. Its nuclei regulate metabolism, temperature, water balance, sweating, blood pressure, sleeping, and appetite.

2. The *midbrain* is a mass of nerve fiber tracts connecting the cerebral cortex with the pons, the medulla oblongata, the cerebellum, and the spinal cord.

3. The *brainstem* is made up of the *pons* and *medulla oblongata* and functions primarily as a neural relay station. The pons contains tracts that connect the cerebellum with the spinal cord and the cerebellum with motor areas of the cerebrum. The medulla oblongata serves as the main line of traffic for the spinal cord tracts ascending to or descending from the higher centers of the brain. At the bottom of the medulla, many of the motor fibers cross to the opposite side. The medulla also contains nuclei that maintain the regular life rhythms of the heartbeat, of the rising and falling diaphragm, and of the constricting and dilating blood vessels. In the core of the brainstem is the *reticular formation,* sometimes called the reticular activating system be-

cause of the important role that it plays in arousal and in the maintenance of alertness. The tracts of the pons and medulla send in fibers to connect with the profusely interconnected cells of the reticular formation, which in turn send fibers to the cortex, the basal ganglia, the hypothalamus, the septal area, and the cerebellum.

4. The *cerebellum,* like the cerebrum, is made up for the most part of two deeply convoluted hemispheres with an exterior cortex of gray matter and an interior of white tracts. The cerebellum receives sensory nerves from the vestibular apparatus of the ear and from muscles, tendons, and joints. The information received and integrated relates to balance and posture and to the smooth coordination of the body when in motion.

A fifth important part of the brain, not shown in Figure 16.2, is the *limbic system,* structures which are continuous with one another in the cerebrum, and which developed earlier than did the mammalian cerebral cortex. This system is made up of cortex that is phylogenetically older than the so-called neocortex, which covers most of the hemispheres. The *juxallocortex,* which consists of four or five layers of neurons, surrounds the corpus callosum and the underlying thalamus. The cingulate gyrus stretching above the corpus callosum is an important structure made up of this juxallocortex. The *allocortex,* with only three layers of neurons, makes up the cortex of the septal area, which is anterior to the thalamus; the long, tubelike hippocampus, which stretches from the septal area into the temporal lobe; and the part of the lower temporal lobe that surrounds the under portions of the hippocampus and the amygdala (one of the basal ganglia), which is embedded in its tip. The amygdala and the septal area itself, which also consists of nuclei, are sometimes considered part of the limbic system because of their anatomical and functional connections to its other structures. The limbic system controls the visceral and physical expression of emotion—quickened heartbeat and respiration, trembling, sweating, and alterations in facial expressions—and the expression of appetitive and other primary drives—hunger, thirst, mating, defense, attack, and flight.

TABLE **16.1**
Summary of Brain Disorders Classified by Etiology

| **Infections** | **Traumas** | **Nutritional deficiencies** | **Cerebrovascular diseases** |
|---|---|---|---|
| Encephalitis<br>Meningitis<br>Neurosyphilis | Concussion<br>Contusion<br>Laceration<br>Skull fracture | Wernicke and Korsakoff syndromes<br>Beriberi<br>Pellagra | Atherosclerosis<br>Cerebral thrombosis<br>Cerebral hemorrhage |
| **Tumors** | **Degenerative diseases** | **Toxins** | **Endocrine dysfunctions** |
| Benign<br>Malignant | Alzheimer's disease<br>Pick's disease<br>Huntington's chorea<br>Parkinson's disease<br>Senile dementia | Lead<br>Mercury<br>Arsenic<br>Carbon dioxide<br>Etc. | Graves' disease<br>Myxedema<br>Addison's disease<br>Cushing's syndrome |

DSM-II classifies organic dysfunctions in two ways, by etiology and by particular clinical signs. When classification is by etiology, the agent that produced the dysfunction is specified. The most important of these are infection, brain trauma, nutritional deficiencies, cerebrovascular disease, tumors, degeneration, toxins, and metabolic and endocrine disturbances (Table 16.1). All the organic syndromes described by DSM-II are classified by etiology except for epilepsy, which is designated by type of seizure. Hyperactivity in children, although it is not included in the brain disorder section of DSM-II, will be discussed at the end of this chapter.

# Organic Brain Syndromes Classified by Etiology

## Brain Disorders Caused by Infection

### Encephalitis and meningitis

Encephalitis is a generic term that refers to inflammation of brain tissue. A large number of living and nonliving agents can enter the body by various routes and inflame the brain. Most are living, and the most important are several viruses, usually carried by insects such as mosquitoes and ticks. In other cases, though, infection may have spread from another part of the body, for example, the sinuses and ears. One form of encephalitis, now only of historical interest, was referred to as sleeping sickness because those infected were extremely lethargic and slept for prolonged periods, days and weeks at a time. The epidemics of sleeping sickness, widespread in the United States and Europe about the time of World War I, are suspected of having had an influenza virus as their cause. The virus apparently vanished from the face of the earth, for the epidemics stopped occurring around 1926.

The major symptoms of encephalitis are vomiting, headache, drowsiness and lethargy, a stiff neck and back, fever, tremors, and sometimes convulsive seizures and coma. In the acute phase of the disease patients are delirious and disoriented. Later they may remain depressed and irritable and experience difficulties in concentration and memory. Recovery is usually complete, but some patients may have permanent paralysis of an arm or leg, uncontrollable tremors, seizures, deafness, and speech and intellectual disturbances. If the disorder occurs in infants, they will often be mentally retarded; their developing brains are particularly susceptible to damage from infection (see page 455). Moreover, an older well-behaved child, after recovering from encephalitis, may become hyperactive and aggressive and generally offensive in behavior. He or she may cheat, lie, strike and torment others, vandalize property, and run away from home. The disruption of the child's personality may persist into adulthood, when hospitalization may be required.

The symptoms of meningitis, an inflammation of the meninges, are quite similar to those of encephalitis. The causes are varied but usually bacterial. The principal epidemic form, meningococcal meningitis, occurs all over the world, epidemics of major proportions happening every eight to twelve years.

### Neurosyphilis

In the past ten years the number of reported cases of syphilis has doubled in the United States. Because of the stigma associated with venereal disease, many more go undetected and untreated; in 1970, for example, it was estimated that there were one million untreated cases in the United States (Ford, 1970). Several decades from now a large number of individuals may be hospitalized with neurosyphilis or general paresis. The spirochete *Treponema pallidum* invades the body through mucous membranes after being contracted during either intercourse or oral-genital contact. The disorder may also be transmitted from an infected mother to her fetus. The first indication of the disorder is a small sore on the site of the infection—lips, genitals, or anus—which appears after ten to twenty days and then in a few weeks disappears. Before the sore disappears, a diffuse, copper-colored rash may cover the body. Fatigue, headache, and fever may accompany the rash, as well as sore throat, inflammation of the eyes, vague pains in bones and joints, and lesions in the mucous membranes of mouth and genitalia.[1] Thereafter no overt difficulties are evident for many years, but during this period spirochetes may be invading the lymph glands, the bone marrow, and other tissues and organs of the body. Damage usually becomes observable when the individual is in his or her forties or fifties and the spirochetes have either invaded the walls of the heart, causing a heart attack, or penetrated neural tissue. About 30 percent of those infected will ultimately have neurological impairment. The clinical picture depends on the area of the nervous system affected. In some cases the meninges of the brain are infected, in others the motor nerves of the spinal cord. The most severe damage is done when the cerebral cortex is invaded, producing the syndrome called general paresis.

The first symptoms of general paresis are irritability, fatigue, depression, and impairments in judgment and concentration. Later, deterioration becomes severe and diffuse; emotions are poorly controlled. Some patients have absurd and expansive delusions of grandeur.

Physical and neurological symptoms are variable. Headache, flashes of pain, usually in the legs, weight loss, and loss of tone in the facial muscles are frequent signs. Disturbances in the eyes are almost universal; in one such disturbance, the so-called Argyll-Robertson sign, the pupil responds normally to changes in distance, contracting properly for near vision, but does not contract for light. Loss of control of the voluntary musculature may be evidenced in tremors of the eyelids, lips, facial muscles, and fingers, mispronunciation and slurring of words, deterioration of handwriting, and a wobbly gait.

The two following cases illustrate the wide variety of symptoms.

[1] Unfortunately, these early signs do not always appear, making detection of the disease difficult. For this reason blood tests are recommended if there is any suspicion of venereal disease after sexual contact with a highly experienced person or with a relative stranger.

A woman of twenty-six was brought to the hospital because she had become lost when she attempted to return home from a neighboring grocery store. About seven months before the patient's admission, her husband noticed that she was becoming careless of her personal appearance and neglectful of her household duties. She often forgot to prepare the family meals, or, in an apparent preoccupation, would burn the food. She seemed to have little appreciation of time and would not realize when to get up or go to bed. The patient would sit idly about the house, staring uncomprehendingly into space.

At the hospital the patient entered the admission office with an unsteady gait. There, by way of greeting, the physician inquired, "How are you today?" to which she replied in a monotonous, tremulous tone, "N-yes-s, I was-s op-er-a-ted on for pen-pendici-ci-tis." She never made any spontaneous remarks and when, a few days after her admission, she was asked if she were sad or happy, she stared vacantly at the physician, and, with a fatuous smile, answered, "Yeah." The patient sat about the ward for hours, taking no interest in its activities. Sometimes she would hold a book in her lap, aimlessly turning the pages, never reading but often pointing out pictures like a small child and showing satisfaction when she found a new one to demonstrate. Neurological examination showed dilated pupils that reacted but slightly to light on convergence. There was a tremor of lips and facial muscles on attempting to speak. The protruded tongue showed a coarse tremor.

---

M., aged forty-one, a roofing salesman, was transferred to a state hospital from the jail to which he had been sentenced for violation of the motor vehicle laws. The [early] symptoms of the patient's oncoming disease were apparently slight. The informant, his sister, who had seen him but infrequently, stated that she had not noticed any change in him except that for a year he had seemed somewhat "worried." While driving his car, he disregarded the collector at a toll bridge and drove across the structure at high speed. When overtaken by a police officer, the patient was found to have no license to drive an automobile, the permit having been revoked several years previously. Three days later, while awaiting trial for this offense, he was again arrested for driving an automobile without a license. He was given a short sentence in jail, where a physician soon recognized the patient's disorder and had him committed to the hospital.

On arrival at the admission office of the hospital, he told the office attendant that he was going to give her a million dollars because she was "a nice lady." As he was being questioned for the usual admission data, he began to boast of his wealth, claiming that he had three automobiles, thousands of dollars in the bank, a "diamond watch," and much other valuable jewelry. His son, he said, was lieutenant governor of the state, was soon to be governor, and later would be president of the United States. After having expressed various absurdly grandiose plans, he added, "I have another plan, too. I'm going to the wardens of the prisons in this state and all the other states and I'm going to buy the prisoners. I'll have an agreement with the warden to take their prisoners and put them to work on farms, and I'll charge each prisoner $300 for doing it and for getting him out of jail. I made $105,000 with prisoners just last week, and when I get going, I'm going to make plenty of money" (Kolb, 1968, pp. 237–238).

In general paresis there is widespread atrophy of the cerebral cortex; the sulci are widened and the brain actually shrinks in size. Scar cells multiply and blood vessels are kept from functioning. Even to the naked eye such a brain appears "moth-eaten" (see color plate 1). In the final stages the individual is paralyzed, inarticulate, and subject to convulsions, for the mind and body have all but ceased functioning.

## Brain Disorders Caused by Trauma

Head injuries are now very common. The primary culprit is the automobile. These injuries may take one of four forms—concussions, contusions, lacerations, and skull fractures. There is some degree of hemorrhaging with almost any head injury, for the tiny blood vessels in the affected area rupture. In very severe injuries blood vessels may burst throughout the brain.

**Concussion** If the injury is a concussion, loss of consciousness is temporary, from several minutes to a few hours. A blow that forces the head to move abruptly, such as a knockout punch in boxing, jars the brain and disrupts circulatory and other functions momentarily. On regaining consciousness the individual is typically somewhat disoriented and may not remember events immediately preceding the insult. Some of the effects—nausea, dizziness, headache, confusion, and inability to concentrate—may persist for several weeks. There is, however, no permanent damage.

**Contusion** Contusions are bruises of the neural tissue. The blow to the head is so severe that the brain, normally held in a fixed position, shifts and is compressed against the opposite side of the skull. The surface of the brain is actually bruised by being pushed against bone. The resulting coma may last several hours or even days, followed sometimes by a period of delirium. After consciousness is regained, behavior is generally similar to that after a concussion except that the disorientation is more severe. The injured person may be unable to speak or may go into convulsions. Severe headaches are likely, and the person may become irritable, being especially sensitive to noise and light. A series of severe blows to the head can eventually lead to a brain syndrome called "punch-drunkenness." Areas of brain tissue become permanently damaged by the accumulation of injuries; the individual cannot pay attention or concentrate, and memory as well as motor functions are disturbed. The person speaks as though slightly drunk. Emotions are unstable and poorly controlled; intellectual impairment is sometimes profound.

**Laceration** When an object actually enters the skull and pierces, ruptures, or tears brain tissue, the injury is called a laceration. The effect of the injury of course varies with the site of the brain tissue destroyed and the extent of the damage. The injured person is likely to lose consciousness immediately; sometimes coma and death follow. If the individual does survive, intellect may be impaired and parts of the body may be paralyzed. The personality sometimes changes, and several years later the person may develop epilepsy. But if the damage, although extensive, is not in a strategic location and if the patient's personality is well integrated, chances for recovery with adequate function are good.

**Skull Fracture** Two particularly serious problems can result when the skull is fractured and pushed toward the brain. In an *extradural hematoma* the broken bone is pushed across a meningeal artery, causing it to rupture. The bleeding between the skull and the dura mater brings confusion, coma, and death, unless proper surgical steps are taken. In a *subdural hematoma* a head injury produces tears in the arachnoid membrane, causing blood to fill the subdural space between the dura mater and the arachnoid. The course is similar to that of an extradural hematoma. A case history of a patient with an extradural hematoma follows (see color plate 2).

[A] twenty-two-year-old airman, during a winter storm, was involved in an auto accident at 11:30 P.M. in which he struck his head against the windshield. He also sustained minor abrasions of the shoulder, hands, and chest.

The patient apparently was dazed, perhaps unconscious for a matter of seconds to minutes. He was taken by ambulance to the emergency room of the nearby army hospital where a brief evaluation indicated that the patient was alert, without definite neurological findings, and apparently without significant injuries. Skull X-rays did indicate a linear fracture over the right temporal area, not, however, definitely crossing the major groove of the middle meningeal artery. The patient was therefore admitted to the intensive care ward for head injury observation.

The patient was apparently alert upon his arrival on the ward. . . . the major attention of the physicians in the emergency room and of the nurses on the intensive care ward was given to four other patients from the same accident who had sustained very severe and obvious injuries. However, by 5 A.M. the patient was reported by the nurses to be agitated and confused.

NEUROLOGICAL EXAMINATION 8:00 A.M.

1. *Mental status:* The patient was agitated and unable to cooperate. He was sitting up in bed, holding his head, and moaning and hyperventilating to a marked degree. He answered only occasional questions and then with a yes or no answer.
2. *Cranial nerves:* . . .
   b. Pupils: There was a bilateral but sluggish response to light. A minimal asymmetry was present. The right pupil was perhaps slightly larger and slightly more sluggish than the left.
   c. The remainder of cranial nerves: Intact.
3. *Motor system:*
   a. All limbs were moved spontaneously.
   b. There was a variable increased resistance to passive motion, but this was apparently due to the patient's inability to cooperate.
4. *Reflexes:*
   a. Deep tendon reflexes were increased bilaterally.
   b. Plantar responses were equivocal but apparently flexor.
5. *Sensation:* Pain sensation appeared to be intact.
6. *Neck:* There was variable resistance to attempted flexion.
7. *Head:* The patient moaned when palpated over left or right temporal areas. . . .

[Deterioration of function was progressive. By 4 P.M. the airman's limbs were stiffly extended. Movement of them by the civilian neurosurgeon caused spasms. The patient, no longer breathing spontaneously, required the assistance of a respirator. The brainstem was clearly being compromised. The patient was operated on immediately.] An epidural hematoma over the right temporal-parietal area was evacuated and the bleeding middle meningeal artery branch was coagulated.

Follow-up examination approximately two months later indicated that the patient had returned to active duty but was experiencing some problems [with] recent memory and [with] changes in motivation and personality. [There were] no significant motor or sensory [impairments] (Curtis, Jacobson, and Marcus, 1972, pp. 576–577).

## Nutritional Deficiencies Producing Brain Dysfunction

At one time beriberi, a deficiency in vitamin $B_1$, and pellagra, a deficiency in niacin, were common causes of disturbed behavior. Improved nutrition has now made both conditions rare in the United States, leaving Wernicke-Korsakoff disorder as the major deficiency syndrome to consider.

*Wernicke's disease,* caused by a deficiency in the B-complex vitamins, is frequent among alcoholics, who often do not eat properly. Symptoms include confusion and drowsiness, partial paralysis of the muscles that control eye movements, and an unsteady gait. Autopsy reveals lesions in the pons and cerebellum and in the mammillary bodies, two small, rounded structures of the hypothalamus that contain nuclei. In addition, there is atrophy in the gray matter surrounding several of the ventricles.

A sizable number of patients with Wernicke's disease also develop *Korsakoff's psychosis.* The primary symptoms are *anterograde* amnesia, a loss of memory for events that have just occurred, and *confabulation,* a filling in of these memory gaps with obviously false material. Shortly after dinner a patient with Korsakoff's psychosis may be asked what he had for the evening meal. Unable to recall the details, he quickly provides a description of an imaginary meal. It often happens, however, that such descriptions are patently false. A patient in a mental institution may state that he has just finished a meal of Beef Wellington with a delightful sauce containing truffles, apparently not recognizing the extreme improbability of being served such a meal. A group of researchers have been studying patients with Korsakoff's psychosis in order to learn more about their inability to store new memories (Cermak and Butters, 1972). Consistent with clinical impressions, it has been shown that the recent memories of these patients are particularly vulnerable to interference from subsequent experiences and that the patients are deficient at storing material either by its meaning or by forming images of it (DeLuca, Cermak, and Butters, 1975).

Patients with Korsakoff's psychosis are usually lucid and friendly, yet they lack judgment, being unaware of the implausibility of the stories they tell and only poorly planning other aspects of their lives. They may become apathetic and sometimes grossly confused and severely disoriented. On autopsy, these patients reveal a pattern of brain damage similar to that of Wernicke's disease. But in addition they also have lesions in the thalamus.

## Cerebrovascular Diseases

The blood vessels supplying the brain are subject to several types of malfunction. In *atherosclerosis* deposits of fatty material narrow the lumen, or inner passageway, of the arteries of the body. When those in the brain are affected, some areas may not receive enough blood and hence insufficient oxygen and glucose. If the shortage is prolonged, the brain tissue, which is particularly dependent on receiving adequate supplies, softens, degenerates, and is even destroyed. The effects of cerebral atherosclerosis vary widely, depending on what area of the brain has clogged arteries and whether it is also supplied by nonaffected blood vessels. About three million Americans are incapacitated in some way by cerebral atherosclerosis (Terry and Wisniewski, 1974).

In *cerebral thrombosis* a blood clot forms at a site narrowed by atherosclerosis and blocks circulation. Carbon dioxide builds up and damages the neural tissues. The loss of consciousness and control is referred to as apoplexy or *stroke*. The patient may die, suffer paralysis of half the body or of an arm or leg, or lose other motor and sensory functions. The impairments of the patients who survive may disappear spontaneously, or they may be lessened through therapy and determined effort. Usually there is some residual damage. When only a small vessel is suddenly blocked, the patient suffers transient confusion and unsteadiness. A succession of these small strokes will bring cumulative damage, however.

A frequent impairment is *aphasia,* a disturbance of the ability to use words. The cause of this damage may be a clot in the middle cerebral artery supplying the parietotemporal region, usually of the dominant cerebral hemisphere. A right-handed person depends on the parietotemporal region in the left hemisphere for language skills; a left-handed person may depend on this region in the right hemisphere or in the left. Interestingly, damage to the right hemisphere in a right-handed person and to the left in a left-handed person does disturb the ability to use language, but to a lesser extent.

Aphasia is generally divided into two types, receptive or sensory and executive or motor. In sensory aphasias individuals have difficulty in understanding the meaning of words. They may have auditory aphasia and not understand the words spoken to them or visual aphasia and not understand the printed word. They will, however, be able to speak properly; and they may, for example, be able to read but not understand spoken speech, or they may understand spoken speech but not be able to read. With motor aphasia a person suffers no deficit in comprehension but has problems in speaking words and sentences. He or she may transpose syllables, utter words of a sentence out of order, or be unable to recall names of common objects.

In *cerebral hemorrhage* a blood vessel ruptures because of a weakness in its wall, damaging the brain tissue on which the blood spills. Cerebral hemorrhages are frequently associated with hypertension. The psychological disturbance produced depends on the size of the vessel that has ruptured and on the extent and the location of the damage. Often the person suffering a cerebral hemorrhage is overtaken suddenly and rapidly loses consciousness.

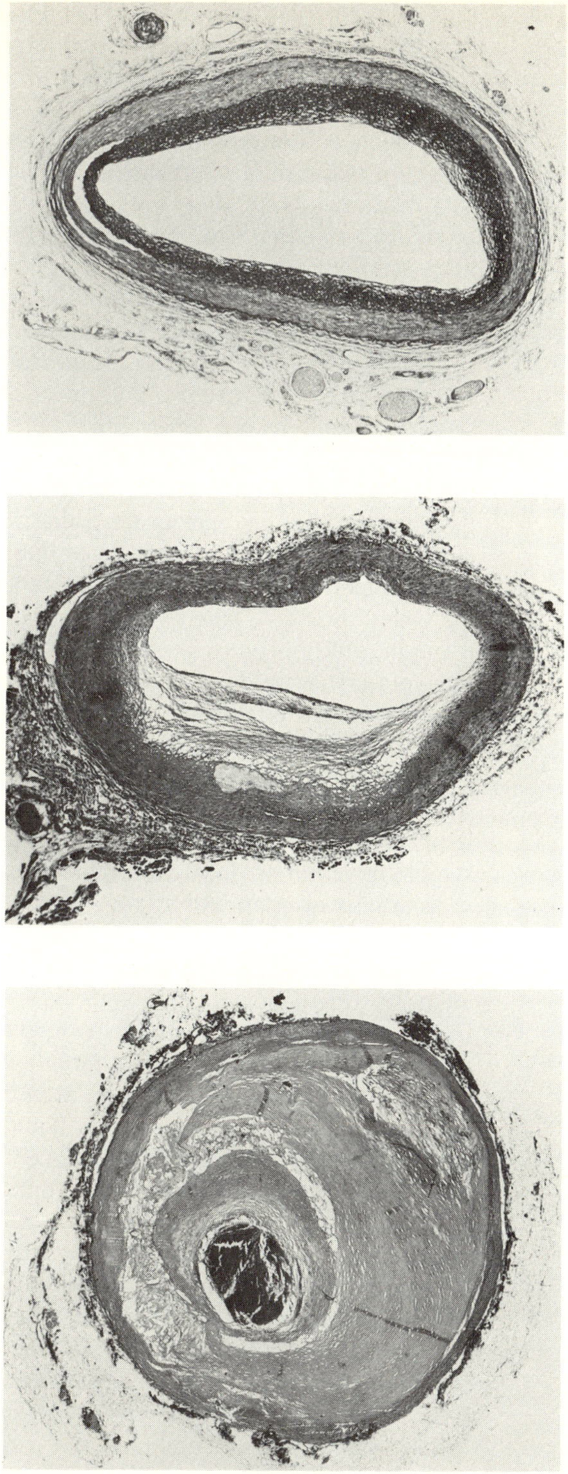

A normal artery (top); an artery whose inner space has been narrowed by a buildup of fatty deposits (center); and a narrowed artery blocked by a blood clot (bottom).

When a large vessel ruptures, the person suffers a major stroke. All functions of the brain are generally disturbed—speech, memory, reasoning, orientation, and balance. The person usually lapses into a coma, sometimes with convulsions, and may die within two to fourteen days. If the person survives, he or she will probably have some paralysis and difficulties with speech and memory, although in some cases appropriate rehabilitation restores nearly normal functioning. Cerebral thromboses and hemorrhages together kill about 200,000 Americans each year (Terry and Wisniewski, 1974).

A psychosis may be brought on by cerebral atherosclerosis. The onset may be gradual or follow suddenly after a stroke. When the illness begins gradually, the first symptoms are fatigue, headache, dizziness, periods of confusion, and an inability to concentrate. Efficiency and zest may be lost. Later memory deteriorates, affect becomes labile, and personal hygiene is neglected. With sudden onset an initial period of rather great confusion and incoherence is typical. The patient is disoriented for time, place, and person and may be subject to convulsions. Physiological signs identifying the psychosis as atherosclerotic are blackouts, cardiac insufficiency, kidney failure, and hypertension. This psychosis is also marked by extreme irritability and by alternating periods of lucidity and confusion. Recall of long-ago events similarly fluctuates; they are remembered in considerable detail one day and completely forgotten the next. This psychosis may appear in the young and middle years but usually not until the early seventies.

## Brain Tumor

A *brain tumor* or neoplasm is an abnormal growth which can produce a wide variety of psychological as well as physical symptoms. Tumors are either malignant or benign. Malignant growths interfere directly with neural functioning by destroying the original brain tissue from which they started to grow. Benign tumors do not destroy tissue but may, as they grow, increase intracranial pressure and thus disrupt the normal functioning of the brain. Brain tumors usually originate either in glial cells—which support and protect neurons, determine their supply of nutrients and enzymes, and remove dead cells—or in the dura. Metastatic tumors, though, can invade the brain after being carried by the blood from another area of the body such as the lung (see color plate 3).

The clinical picture is highly variable, reflecting the size and location of the tumor, how fast it is growing, whether there is pressure, and whether brain tissue has been destroyed. Early physical symptoms are persistent headaches, vomiting, and visual problems. By looking into the eye through the pupil, a physician can detect a "choked disk" at the back of the retina. Intracranial pressure forces cerebrospinal fluid into the optic nerve. The area at the back of the retina where the nerve enters the eyeball, called the optic disk, becomes swollen and protrudes. The very first symptoms of a tumor that is located beneath the brainstem are sudden outbursts of emotion, inappropriate spells of laughing or crying which last for thirty to ninety seconds. Listlessness, depression, and a vague sense of anxiety may precede the physical symptoms of tumors located in other areas.

As the tumor continues to grow and intracranial pressure increases, vision may become double, reflexes may be impaired, and memory, attention, orientation for time and place, and reasoning are likely to be poor. Consciousness may seem to keep slipping away; there are often convulsive seizures and eventually stupor. The damage from a tumor in particular motor and sensory areas of the brain may produce localized disturbances of these functions. Coordination may be impaired, or the patient may have visual, olfactory, and auditory hallucinations. Tumors in the frontal, temporal, and parietal lobes may disturb the personality. The individual may be preoccupied and confused, depressed and irritable, and careless about dress, appearance, and work. Very occasionally the person explodes in a sudden and destructive outburst, totally out of character and completely incomprehensible to family, friends, and society at large. After the event it is usually realized, however, that the individual has had earlier warning symptoms and has even communicated them.

If either a benign or a malignant tumor continues to grow, the patient usually dies. Even if the tumor is removed, the functions that have been lost through the destruction of neural tissue do not return.

## Degenerative Diseases

A large number of organic diseases appear to be correlated with advancing age. With the increased longevity of citizens in many modern societies, these problems of the later years are becoming much more prevalent than they once were.

### Presenile dementias

Rare forms of mental deterioration that begin when the individual is in the forties or fifties are referred to as presenile dementias. Alzheimer's disease, Huntington's chorea, and Parkinson's disease are such disorders.

Alzheimer's Disease  Many of the characteristics of the presenile disorder Alzheimer's disease are illustrated in the following case history.

> The first noticeable sign of difficulty was the fifty-one-year-old woman's jealousy toward her husband. Then a rapidly increasing loss of memory was observed. She could not find her way around her own apartment. Moreover, she sometimes thought that someone wanted to kill her and began shrieking loudly.
>
> Her behavior in the institution reflected total perplexity, and she was disoriented in time and place. Periodically she was delirious—she dragged her bedding around, called her husband and her daughter, and seemed to have auditory hallucinations. She often shrieked for many hours.
>
> Her ability to remember was severely disturbed. If one pointed to objects, she could name most of them correctly, but she forgot events immediately after they occurred. When reading she merged one line with another. When writing, she repeated some syllables and omitted others. When talking she used perplexing phrases and such . . . expressions as "milk-pourer" for "cup." She seemed no longer to understand the use of some objects. The generalized dementia continued. At the end, she was stuporous and laid in her bed with her legs drawn up under her.
>
> Four and one-half years after the onset of the disease, the patient died (Wilkins and Brody, 1969, p. 110).

The brain tissue deteriorates rather rapidly in Alzheimer's disease, death usually occurring four or five years after the onset of symptoms. The disorder is three times more prevalent among women than among men. The disease was first described by the German neurologist Alois Alzheimer in 1860. It commences with difficulties in concentration; the individual appears absent-minded and irritable, shortcomings which soon begin to interfere with the way she leads her life. She blames others for personal failings, and has delusions of being persecuted. Memory continues to deteriorate, with the individual becoming increasingly disoriented and agitated.

The primary physiological change in the brain, evident at autopsy, is a general atrophy of the cerebral cortex as neurons are lost. The fissures widen and the ridges become narrower and flatter (see color plate 4). Moreover, senile plaques are found scattered throughout the cortex—small round areas in which tissue has degenerated into granular material and filaments—and tangled threadlike structures replace normal nerve cells in the basal ganglia. Alzheimer's disease is probably *not* simply an early variant of senile dementia. It occurs much more abruptly and is distinguished by symptoms that are not notable in senile dementia, such as speech impairments, involuntary movements in the limbs, hyperactivity and agitation, and occasional convulsions, as well as by a much more rapid mental deterioration.

Pick's Disease Another presenile disorder was first described by Arnold Pick, a Prague physician, in 1892. Pick's disease is a degenerative disorder of the central nervous system in which the frontal and temporal lobes atrophy. As the disease progresses, the deterioration becomes more and more pervasive. The total weight of the brain may be reduced to less than 1000 grams from the usual weight of about 1300 grams. As in Alzheimer's disease, the age of onset is generally in the forties and fifties, and symptoms of the two disorders are also similar. The patient has difficulties with memory and in abstract thinking; he or she is confused and unable to concentrate and has transitory speech impairment. But in Pick's disease affect may be blunted, and the patient is likely to become apathetic and inactive. Life expectancy after onset is usually four to seven years.

Huntington's Chorea This degenerative disorder was first described by the American neurologist George Huntington in 1872, after his father and grandfather, both physicians, had observed the disease in several generations of a family. Symptoms usually begin when the individual is in the thirties, and thereafter deterioration is progressive. The early behavioral signs are slovenliness, disregard for social convention, violent outbursts, depression, irritability, poor memory, euphoria, poor judgment, delusions, suicidal ideas and attempts, and hallucinations. The term chorea was applied to the disorder because of the patient's choreiform movements—involuntary, spasmodic twitching and jerking of the limbs, trunk, and head. These signs of neurological disturbance do not appear until well after behavior has already started to deteriorate. Facial grimaces, a smacking of the lips and tongue, and explosive, often obscene speech are other symptoms. The afflicted individual is likely to have severe problems in speaking and walking. Eventually, there is a total loss of bodily control. Death is inevitable, but it may be delayed for ten to twenty years after the onset of illness. The incidence is about 5 cases per 100,000 persons (Boll, Heaton, and Reitan, 1974).

The following excerpts from the biography of the American folksinger Woody Guthrie illustrate the development of the disorder, some of the prominent clinical symptoms, and the personal tragedy of the illness.

> [Describing the first signs, Woody's wife, Marjorie, commented] "What confused me, and Woody himself, in the early stage of the illness was that by nature he was a rather moody person. As early as 1948, we began to notice that he was more reflective, and often depressed by trivial things. . . . [Shortly thereafter] the symptoms of the disease had become more obvious. Woody developed a peculiar lopsided walk and his speech became explosive. He would take a deep sigh before breathing out the words. The moods and depressions became more exaggerated and more frequent. . . ." [In 1952 the first serious attack occurred. As his wife described it,] "Woody had a violent outburst and foamed at the mouth." [He was hospitalized for three weeks and diagnosed as an alcoholic. After his release he had another violent seizure which, this time, led to a three-month hospitalization. Later] "the disease was making rapid progress. Woody found it increasingly difficult to control his movements, appearing to be drunk even when he wasn't drinking. Friends watched with apprehension as he dived into traffic, oblivious of danger, Chaplinlike, warding off each car as it sped toward him."

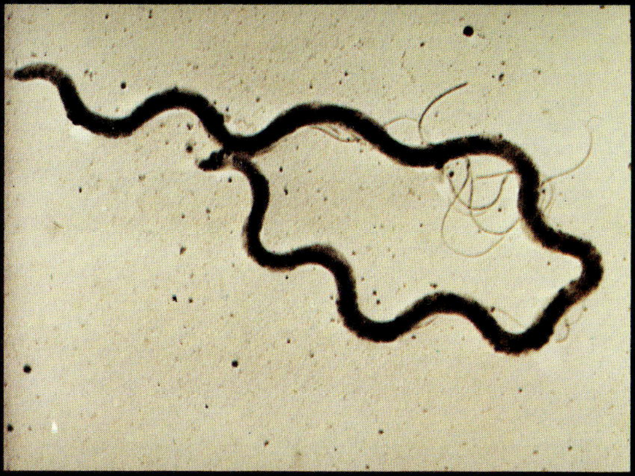

The syphilitic spirochete, *Treponema pallidum*, is transmitted from an already infected person by sexual intercourse or oral-genital contact.

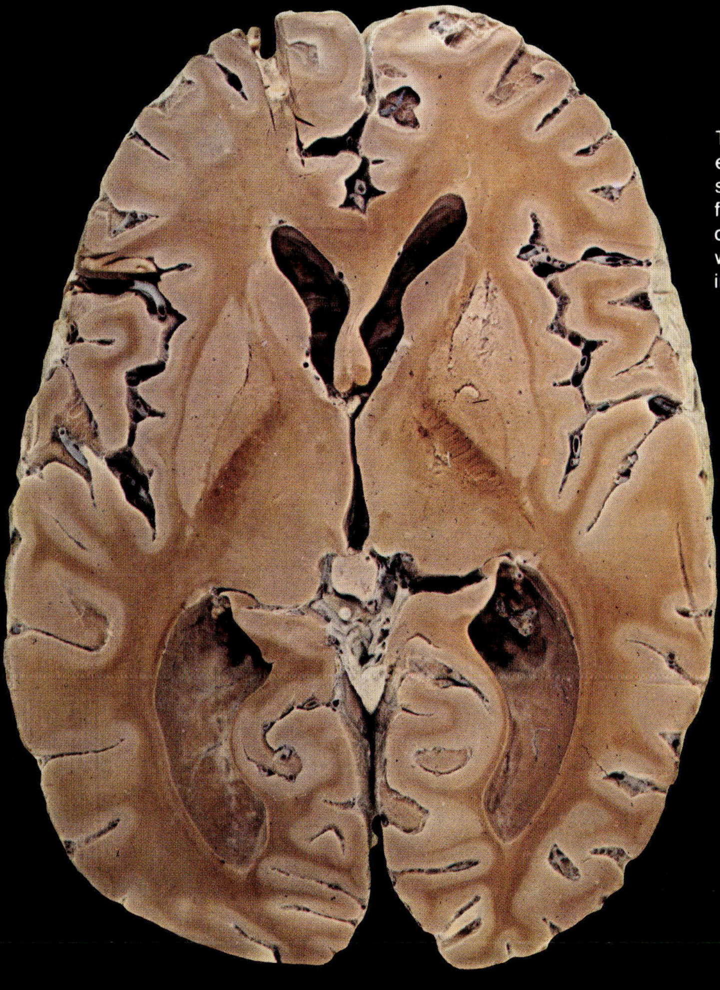

The effects of neurosyphilis (general paresis) shown in horizontal section of the cerebrum. The diffuse atrophy of the convolutions of the cortex and of the associated white matter is evident, especially in the frontal lobes.

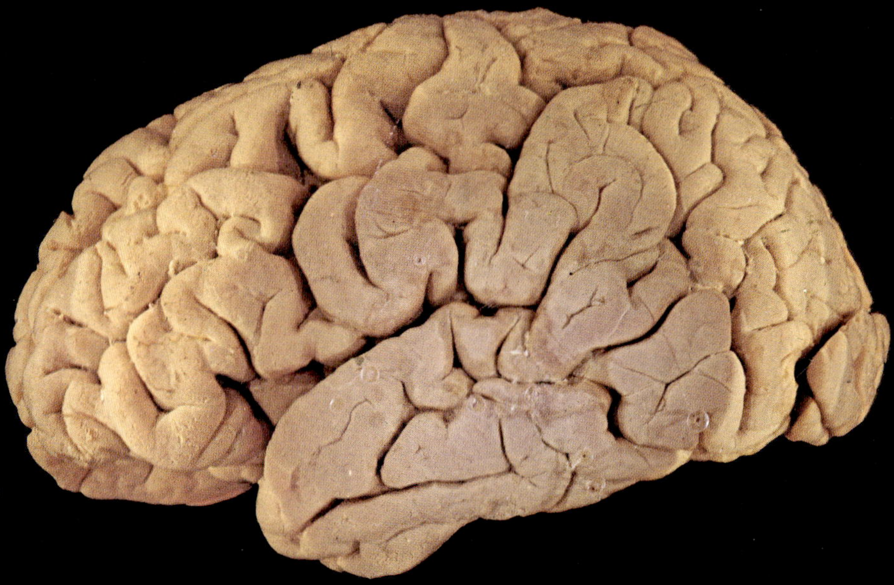

The surface of the right cerebral hemisphere of a normal brain. Below, a right hemisphere with multiple areas of hemorrhage after a skull fracture.

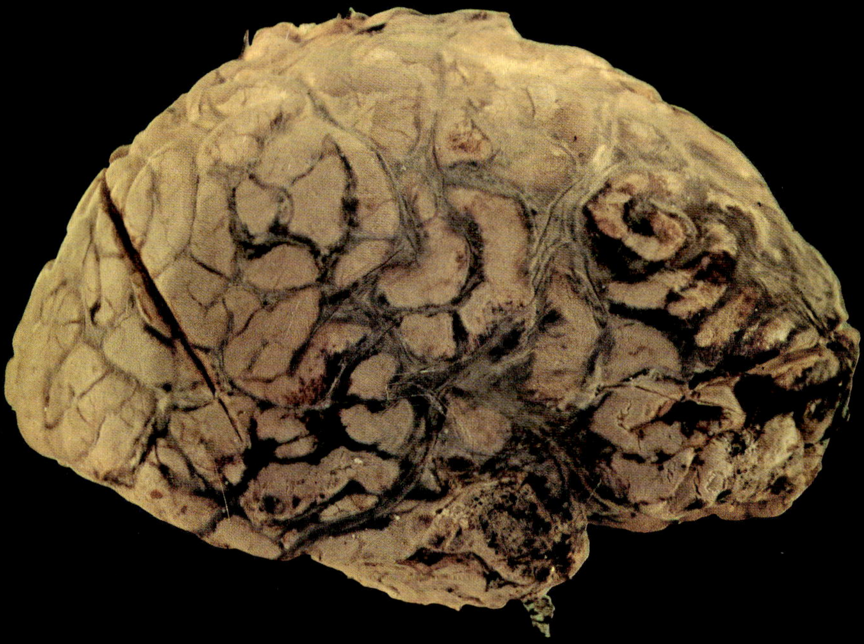

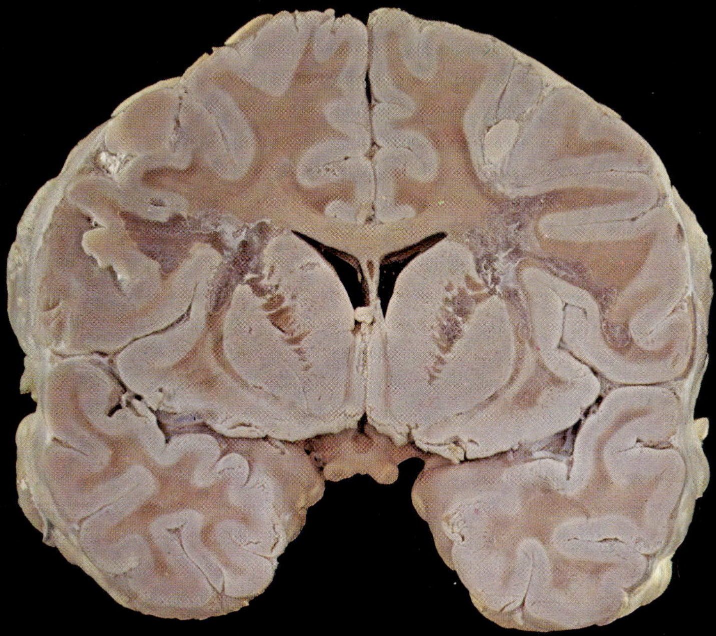

Cross section of the cerebrum of a normal brain.

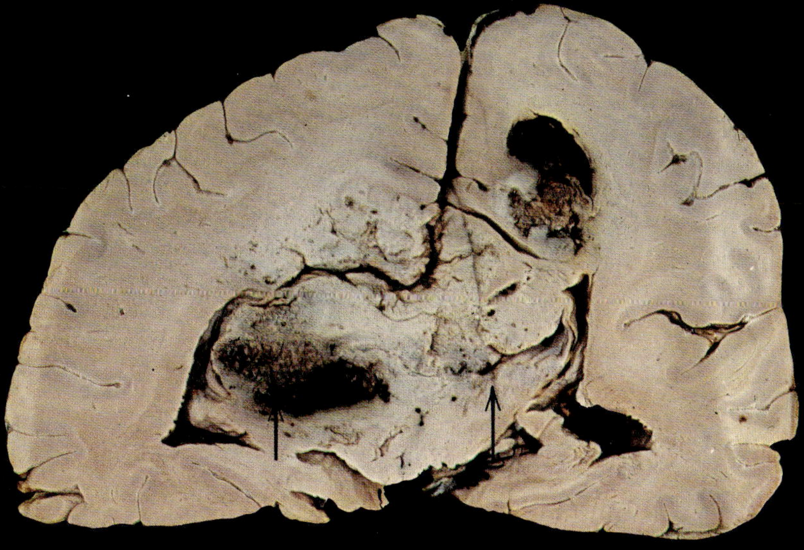

Cross section of the cerebrum showing a malignant tumor (arrows) extending from one hemisphere to the other through the corpus callosum. The gyri are noticeably flattened and the sulci narrowed.

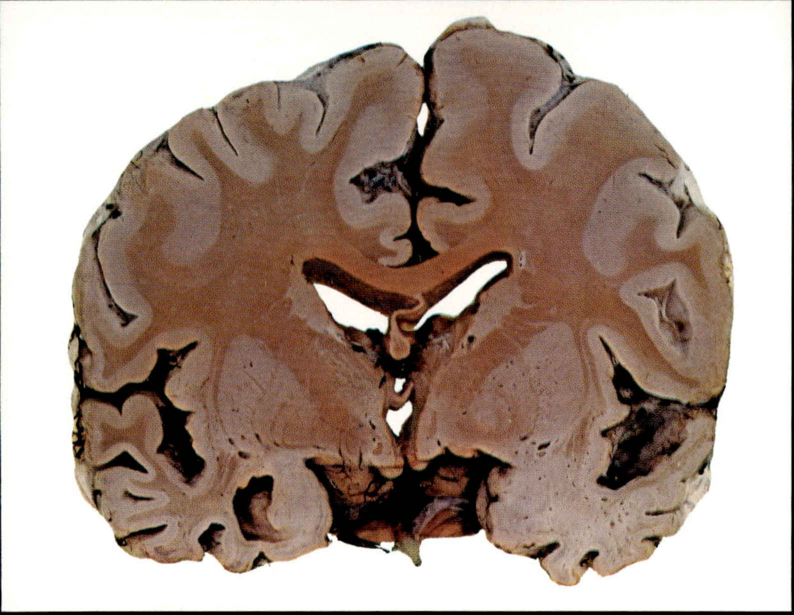

The diffuse cortical atrophy associated with Alzheimer's disease, one of the presenile dementias, is shown in this cross section of the cerebrum. The sulci have widened considerably.

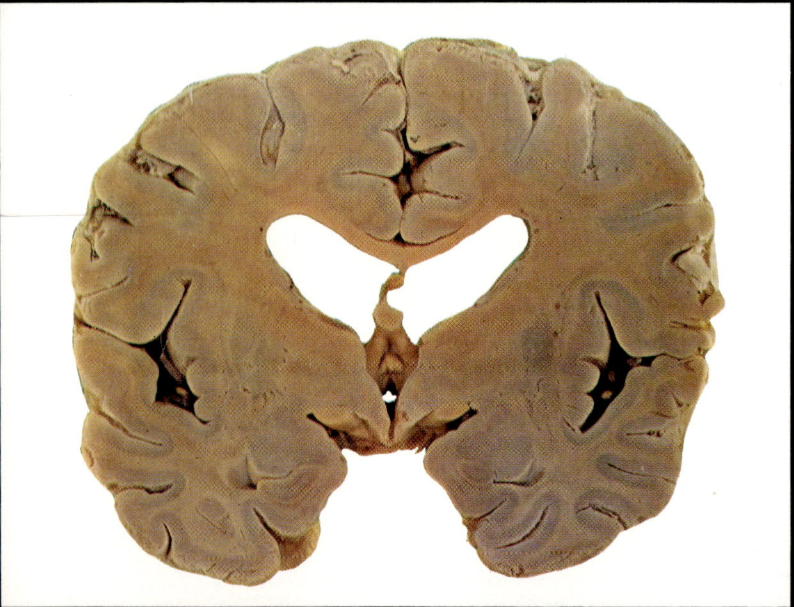

In Huntington's chorea, a presenile dementia, the interior cavities (ventricles) are enlarged through atrophy of the brain, especially of the caudate nucleus, a basal gang lion forming part of the floor of the lateral ventricle in each hemisphere

[Finally, in 1956, it was recognized that Guthrie had Huntington's chorea, and he spent his remaining years in hospitals. One incident related by his wife, which occurred shortly after his hospitalization, is especially poignant.] "In the early years of his stay in hospitals, Woody would leave every now and then on his own. One day he took the wrong bus and landed in some town in New Jersey. Noticing his disheveled appearance, his distraught air and halting gait, a policeman picked him up, took him to the local police station, and booked him on a vagrancy charge.

"Woody told the police that he was not a homeless bum but a sick man. He explained that he was staying at a New York hospital and begged them to get him home. 'Well,' they said, 'if you're sick you can stay in our hospital.' Finally, they let him call me and I went tearing out to New Jersey.

"When I arrived I was received by a staff doctor, a Viennese psychiatrist. 'Your husband is a very disturbed man,' he said imperiously, 'with many hallucinations. He says that he has written a thousand songs.'[2]

'It is true,' I said.

'He also says he has written a book.'

'That's also true.'

'He says that a record company has put out nine records of his songs!' The doctor's voice dripped disbelief.

'That is also the truth.' I said" (Yurchenco, 1970, pp. 139–148).

The disorder is a genetically determined one, passed on by a single dominant gene. The offspring of an individual with the disorder have a 50 percent chance of being afflicted. A postmortem examination of the brain of an individual with Huntington's chorea reveals widespread atrophy and scarring. The major pathological change is a loss of neurons in the caudate nucleus, one of the basal ganglia. The cerebral cortex also atropies, especially the frontal areas (see color plate 4). High levels of dopamine in the caudate nucleus appear to be primarily responsible for the choreiform movements.

**Parkinson's Disease** In 1817 James Parkinson described this disease which begins later in life, between the ages of fifty and seventy. The primary symptoms are severe and continual muscular tremors, usually occurring at a rate of four to eight movements per second, which rhythmically agitate the limbs, hands, neck, and face. The tremor may begin in one hand or arm, spread to the leg of that side, then to neck, jaw, and face, and finally to the two other limbs. Only muscles that are at rest are subject to tremors, however, not those that are engaged in a coordinated movement. But manual skills may eventually be lost, and speech, swallowing, and chewing are laborious. Other physiological effects include muscular rigidity, akinesia—an inability to initiate movements—and defects in balance. The face later becomes masklike and expressionless, the gait stiff and distinctive, with the upper part of the body moving forward ahead of the legs. The individual may have difficulty concentrating, become apathetic, and withdraw from social contact. About 90 percent of patients with Parkinson's disease are depressed, and in 30 percent intellectual deterioration is evident (DeJong and Sugar, 1971). About one and a half million Americans are afflicted with the disorder (Stang, 1970).

The etiology of Parkinson's disease varies. It is at times attributable to atherosclerosis; other cases are the aftereffects of encephalitis. The basic brain pathology is a loss of the deeply pigmented nerve cells in the substantia nigra, a nucleus within the midbrain which is an important

[2] In addition to misdiagnosing Mr. Guthrie, the physician had confused the concepts of delusion and hallucination.

motor relay station. The neurons in the substantia nigra that are destroyed are those that release dopamine. One by-product of dopamine metabolism is melanin, which gives the substantia nigra its characteristic color. A reduced number of these cells means not only that the substantia nigra loses color but that less dopamine is released in the corpus striatum, to which the axons of these neurons normally extend. The corpus striatum consists of the caudate and lenticular nuclei, two of the basal ganglia. Tracts of white matter between them give the mass a striped appearance. With reduced amounts of dopamine in the corpus striatum, the action of the neurotransmitter acetylcholine released by the cholinergic motor neurons in the caudate nucleus is insufficiently opposed. And because the neurotransmitter of the cholinergic tracts is not under the inhibitory control of dopamine, too many of the postsynaptic motor neurons fire, producing the uncontrollable muscular tremors and stiffness of Parkinson's disease. Parkinsonism can be treated either by administering anticholinergic drugs to reduce the action of the cholinergic neurons, or by giving the patient a precursor of dopamine, L-Dopa.

### Senile dementia

In senile dementia there is a gradual deterioration in functioning. The individual may first be somewhat careless in personal hygiene and grooming and may surprise friends with impulsive bursts of unexpected or unusual behavior. Gradually, memory impairment, especially for recent events, becomes evident. Alertness lessens, and incoherence, disorientation, and an intolerance for change cloud and agitate the mind. The patient may be easily irritated and weep readily. Some become incontinent and eventually grossly psychotic.

> The patient had been widowed at the age of fifty and thereafter lived with one or another of her five children. She had always been easy going, happy, and contented. Although she liked things to be neat and tidy, she was not exceptionally meticulous or compulsive. All her life she had been physically active and had an excellent memory. The first indication of difficulty came in her late sixties when she lost some money that had been given to her. Soon thereafter she set out to visit one of her children but lost her way and needed police assistance. After this incident she was observed to lose her former interest in reading, writing letters and knitting. During most of the year preceding hospitalization she was unable to recognize her children and frequently her conversation was unintelligible. She ate without assistance but had to be dressed, undressed, and taken to the toilet to avoid incontinence.
>
> Consistent with her life-long personality traits, her manner in the hospital was pleasant and cooperative. However, her comprehension and social behavior were grossly impaired. She walked down the corridor with her arm around a physician's waist and tickled his ribs. She misinterpreted everyday situations: when given her first bath in the hospital she said, "I don't want to get in the boat—the current is too swift." Her stream of talk rambled. The following is a verbatim sample: "While it is not so bad in the morning—that girl was over and she was saying that there was nothing better than the bottom ones, and the cows and the calves were off and she was making out that . . . [unintelligible] . . . but I made out I never heard her. When they go out—you see—they don't bother taking the boxes. They just take everything with them." Her memory for both recent and remote events was close to zero. She was able to give her name correctly but when asked her age said, "I am twenty-one to twenty-two anyway, every minute." She could not give her birthday, year of her birth, or any information about her previous life. Six months after admission, she died of pneumonia, a frequent cause of death in senile patients (Rosen, Fox, and Gregory, 1972, p. 330).

Postmortem examinations reveal generalized brain atrophy, especially in the frontal lobes. The brain itself is smaller, having fewer cells; the cortical convolutions are narrower and the fissures between them wider. Senile plaques are scattered throughout the cortex. These changes may be the simple process of aging, whereby cells decay, or they may be the cumulative effects of the toxic processes—carbon monoxide, alcohol, minor strokes—to which a person is exposed in his or her life-span.

Of course, not all individuals who enjoy a long life become psychotic in their last years. All brains are known to deteriorate to a certain extent in old age, but only some lose sanity. Social isolation may be important. Williams and Jaco (1958), for example, found that a married person of age sixty is only a third as likely to develop a disorder of aging as are those whose spouses have died. Furthermore, more women than men develop these disorders, perhaps because women typically outlive their husbands by about five years and are socially isolated during their widowhood. A genetic factor may also be involved. Kallmann (1950) examined concordance rates for senile psychosis in identical and fraternal twins. The age-corrected concordance rate was found to be 43 percent among the identical twins and only 7 percent among fraternal twins.

In 1970, 700,000 elderly people were in hospitals for mental disorders and it is estimated that this figure will pass the million mark by 1980 (Ford, 1970). Increasing longevity, coupled with institutional care, appears responsible for a greater incidence of senility. Estimates of the prevalence of senility in nursing home residents range from 21 to 80 percent; yet in the general population of elderly persons the incidence of brain deterioration severe enough to warrant institutionalization is estimated at only 1 to 2 percent (MacDonald, 1973).

MacDonald has eloquently summarized the plight of our institutionalized elderly.

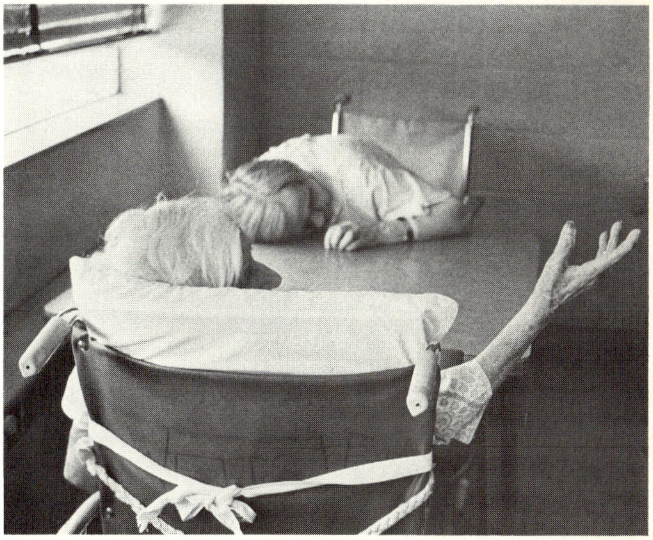

The impersonal surroundings and inactivity of the nursing home may contribute considerably to the deterioration of elderly residents.

> *There is a minority group in our country today that is growing stronger in numbers but weaker in voice. There is no legislated oppression explicitly imposed on this minority. . . . Yet these people have been victims of discrimination, both job . . . and housing. They are continually derided in the mass media . . . and they virtually have been sentenced to life incarceration without due process of law. The*

*members of this group cannot be identified by accent or skin pigmentation or religious preference. They are designated solely by being old and problematical enough to be placed in a nursing home (1973, p. 272).*

MacDonald argues that the nursing home itself is responsible for the apparent increase of senility in the aged. She reviews three possible causative factors.

1. The staffs of nursing homes expect the aged to become senile and treat them in a manner that fosters such behavior.
2. Various somatic illnesses may produce confusion and other signs often indicating senility. Although the illness would be reversible if properly treated, the symptoms are *assumed* to reflect senility and thus the illness is not attended to. The generally poor health care provided for nursing home residents would also be a contributing factor.
3. The sheer environmental deprivation that is experienced by some nursing home residents may bring on senility.

## Toxic Agents

Brain dysfunctions can be produced by the ingestion of a variety of toxic substances such as drugs, gases, and heavy metals. Difficulties in concentration, disorientation, emotional instability, hyperactivity, and psychotic delusions and hallucinations are common symptoms, seizures a less common one. In Chapter 10 the effects of alcohol and other drugs on behavior were discussed; here we need note only that the affective, behavioral, and cognitive difficulties associated with drugs can be considered brain syndromes.

Other toxic agents such as lead, mercury, manganese, carbon monoxide, copper, and arsenic can seriously impair brain functioning. With excessive intake of lead, fluid accumulates in the brain, increasing intracranial pressure. Employees of manufacturing plants in which lead is used may suffer severe lead poisoning. They may hallucinate, become delirious, especially at night, and be subject to tremors and convulsions. Children who suffer from lead poisoning may become mentally retarded, a pressing problem in ghetto areas where young children are likely to eat the crumbling plaster and old paint that have fallen from the walls (see page 457). Both are lead-based and can induce a toxic state. Children who chew on old toys and furniture painted with lead-based paints may also ingest too much of the poison. The exhaust from automobiles burning leaded gasoline is a danger of any continuously congested city street. Vomiting, facial pallor, and crying are early symptoms of lead-poisoned children.

Most mercury and manganese poisonings are the aftermath of accidents that occur in the industrial use of these metals. The first signs that too much mercury has been ingested are irritability, memory loss, and difficulties in concentration. Later the individual experiences impairments in hearing and speaking. Tunnel vision restricts the visual field to centrally located objects, and coordination becomes poor. In severe cases paralysis and death follow. Mercury was once used extensively in the manufacture of hats, and the effects suffered by some workers were the source of the phrase "mad as a hatter."

Manganese poisoning impairs the brain and spinal cord. The gait and speech are affected, and the patient is restless and emotionally upset.

## Endocrine Dysfunctions

Endocrine glands secrete their hormones directly into the bloodstream. Thus these powerful substances are delivered to nearly every cell in the body, including the neurons of the brain. Either oversecretions or undersecretions of the thyroid gland may bring on behavioral problems. In hyperthyroidism or *Graves' disease,* described by an Irish physician, Robert Graves, in the first part of the nineteenth century, an oversecretion of the hormone thyroxin speeds up metabolic processes, inducing a state of apprehension, restlessness, and irritability. Thinking proceeds at a rapid pace and may become confused in the process. About 20 percent of hyperthyroid patients may have transitory delusions and hallucinations. Hypothyroidism, which brings on a condition called *myxedema* in adults, is a deficiency in thyroid hormone. Metabolic processes are slowed down and so too are speech and thinking. The individual has poor emotional control and suffers from fatigue. He or she moves as little as possible and loses interest in activities and surroundings. As the disorder progresses, the skin becomes dry and brittle, and hair is lost from the eyebrows and the genital area. In severe cases depression may be deep enough to be considered psychotic. In children the disorder causes mental retardation (see page 456). Fortunately, hypothyroidism is a very rare condition today, for the iodine of iodized salt prevents it.

The *adrenal cortex* is centrally involved in the activation of emergency physiological responses and the energy needs of the human organism. Thus it is not surprising that a malfunction of the adrenals can cause an organic syndrome. A chronic insufficiency of cortisone secretion by the adrenal cortex produces *Addison's disease,* first described by the English physician Thomas Addison. The patient loses weight, suffers from low blood pressure, and is irritable and easily fatigued; skin and mucous membranes also darken. The person may be moderately depressed and become less sociable and ambitious. When abnormal growths on the cortices of the adrenal glands make them secrete too much cortisone, the condition produced is called *Cushing's syndrome*. Harvey Cushing, the American brain surgeon, described this rare disease, which usually affects young women. The afflicted individual has severe mood swings, none of them pleasant. She is most often depressed but may then become anxious, agitated, and irritable. Physical changes, some quite disfiguring ones—obesity, muscle wasting, changes in skin color and texture, and bone porosity which may bring spinal deformity—can also occur. ■

## Epilepsy

The incidence of epilepsy in the United States has been reported to be 29.8 cases per 100,000 people of the general population, with a slightly higher rate among males than females (Ervin, 1967). Epilepsy is not easily defined. One definition might state that epilepsy is a group of convulsive disorders brought on by pathology of the central nervous system. Certainly, the lay conception of epilepsy involves the notion of convulsion. In the neurology literature, however, forms of epilepsy in which no convulsion occurs are described. The definition must therefore refer to altered states of consciousness accompanied by sudden changes in the usual rhythmical electrical activity of the brain. In terms of neural functioning, epileptics are best regarded as representing one end of a continuum. They are individuals in whom a wide variety of circumstances can elicit a seizure. At the other end of the continuum are normal people in whom seizures or sudden discharging of neurons can be induced only by very unusual stimuli, such as the current used in electroconvulsive therapy.

For many years epileptics have carried the additional burden of being regarded as insane, mentally retarded, and, in general, emotionally unstable. These negative judgments are unsupported, except for some cases of psychomotor epilepsy (see page 431). The brains of epileptics do unquestionably function abnormally on occasion, and they do often discharge excessively even between seizures. Moreover, during a seizure the epileptic is obviously not behaving normally. But between seizures, and this fortunately accounts for most of the time, the psychological functioning of epileptics is usually fine.

A variety of conditions can precipitate an epileptic attack. First, a number of agents predispose a neuron to discharge, for example, strychnine poisoning and a low blood sugar level or hypoglycemia. Second, an attack may be triggered by external stimuli such as flashing lights or particular musical notes. Or brain infections such as multiple sclerosis, neurosyphilis, and encephalitis may predispose neurons to discharge more readily. Patients with brain trauma, hemorrhage, tumor, and toxicity are, as already indicated, also subject to convulsions. Finally, epileptic attacks can be brought on by stress and emotional difficulties (Smith, 1965).

Convulsions are generated by a massive discharge of groups of neurons. At first the discharge may be localized, but if it spreads the body is seized with the so-called grand mal convulsion. The areas involved in the spread of the discharge function as they would under normal conditions of stimulation: if the discharge spreads across visual areas, for example, the individual will have visual sensations during the seizure.

Epilepsy is usually classified into four types.

1. **Grand mal** (great illness). The grand mal attack, the most severe form of seizure, is usually described as consisting of four phases. The *aura* is considered a signal or warning of the impending convulsion. It may take the form of dizziness, fear, or an unusual sensory experience such as ringing in the ears or a peculiar odor. The aura, the Latin word for breeze, usually precedes the "storm" of neuron discharge by a few moments, which can give the epileptic just enough time to sit or lie down. In the *tonic phase,* the beginning of the actual seizure, the muscles of the body suddenly become rigid. The patient loses consciousness and falls heavily to the ground if he has not been able to prepare for the attack. The trunk and arms are flexed, the legs outstretched; the eyes are open and pupils dilated; corneal and light reflexes are absent. During this part of the convulsion breathing is suspended and the face darkens. The EEG tracing shows fast (8 to 20 cps) spike discharges. But then after about half a minute the muscular tension gives way to the spasms of the *clonic phase,* which lasts another one or several minutes. Now the muscles alternately contract and relax, producing violent contortions and jerking movements of the limbs. Breathing resumes. The jaws also open and close, and saliva collects on the lips. During this phase the individual can bite his tongue and lose sphincter control. Here the EEG tracing continues to show spiking but with decreasing frequency. Eventually, as the convulsive movements dissipate, the epileptic seizure passes from the clonic phase into *coma.* The individual remains unconscious and the muscles relax. Upon awakening, perhaps almost immediately or only after several hours, the individual has no memory of what happened after the beginning of the tonic phase.

2. **Petit mal.** In a milder and briefer form of epilepsy, the petit mal attack, there is neither an aura nor a convulsion. Petit mal, more frequent in children and rare after twenty years of age, is only a short (15 to 50 seconds) disturbance or alteration of consciousness. The person stops what he is doing and his eyes roll up. There may be a few twitches of the eye and face muscles, but in most instances such seizures are difficult to recognize. The person may be aware only that his mind has gone blank for a few moments. These absences usually happen many times a day. The EEG tracing reveals bursts of spike and slow-wave (3 to 5 cps) activity (Figure 16.3).

3. **Jacksonian or focal epilepsy.** The English neurologist J. Hughlings Jackson first described epilepsy in which muscle spasms are limited to particular areas of the body. There are several variants, depending on the area of the brain in which the neurons discharge. A motor seizure may begin with discharge near the lateral sulcus and be manifested as twitches of the thumb and index finger. A discharge beginning in the visual cortex may produce hallucinations. Sometimes these seizures remain localized and there is no loss of consciousness. But they may also spread, perhaps beginning with the thumb and index finger and then extending to the hand, arm, and shoulder, and sometimes ultimately throughout the entire body. The attack is then much like

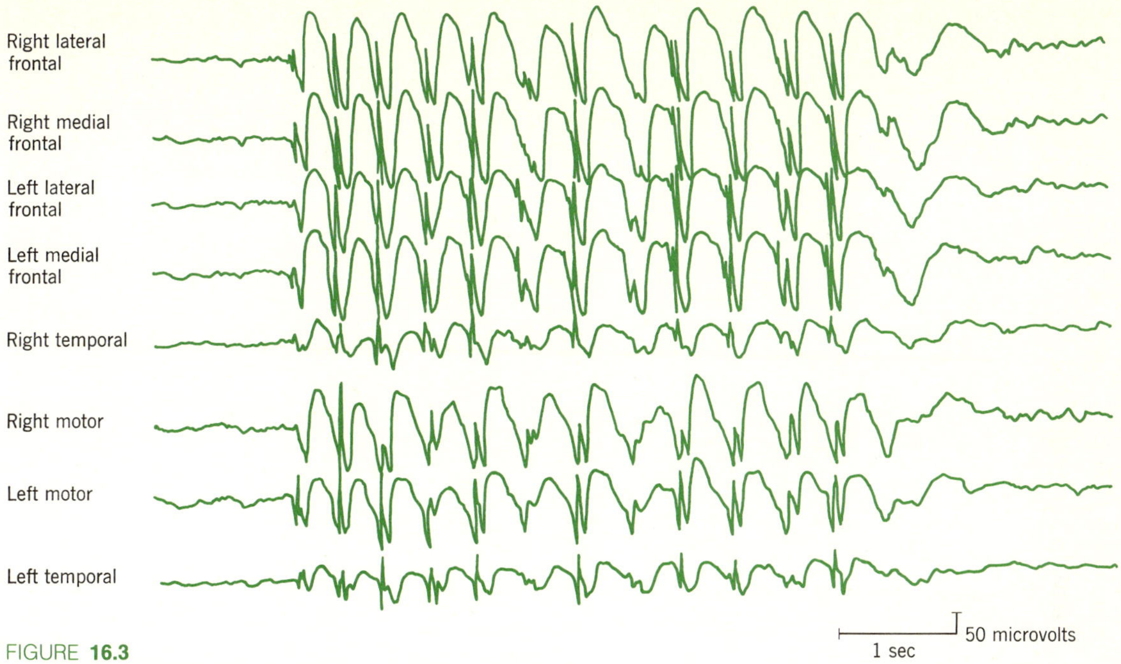


FIGURE **16.3**
Electroencephalogram taken during a short petit mal attack. Electrical activity increases at all the recording sites and in a pattern of spike and slow-wave discharges.

that of grand mal epilepsy (Smith, 1965).

4. **Psychomotor epilepsy.** A psychomotor seizure begins with an aura and is followed by a complete loss of contact with the environment. But during the attack the epileptic appears conscious and engages in some sort of routine or organized activity. The act may be simple and repetitive, such as chewing or moving the limbs in a particular way, or the epileptic may engage in a complex and prolonged series of activities. Psychomotor seizures may last only a few seconds or minutes but occasionally much longer. After the attack individuals have no memory for their actions. The behavior of these people is often otherwise psychotic, even between seizures (Glaser, Newman, and Schafer, 1963).

*F. F. Age 44. This woman has had a history of psychomotor seizures since the age of eighteen. During the seizure she would, in a stereotyped way, stroke or pat articles of furniture or curtains, salivate, groan, and clutch her mouth, as well as occasionally wander about in automatic fashion. She was frequently preoccupied with inadequate feelings concerning running her home, taking care of her family, and [her] social relationships. [She had] frequent episodes of paranoid psychosis . . . with delusions of reference and persecution, particularly concerning her neighbors* (*p. 351*).

Psychomotor epilepsy is associated for the most part with abnormal electrical discharge from the temporal lobes. Although some reports indicate that antisocial and violent acts are committed during such seizures, a survey by Gunn and Fenton (1971) found that of 434 epileptics who had engaged in so-called automatisms, violence was extremely unusual. They found that the automatic behavior typically lasted only minutes, and that no attempt was made to conceal the acts undertaken during the seizure. They also surveyed epileptics in prisons and found that only 10 out of 150 cases reported a seizure within twelve hours before or after their last offense. There was little evidence that their criminal acts had been automatisms.

Genetic factors appear to be of some importance in epilepsy, but that importance varies with the type. The evidence for a predisposition to develop petit mal epilepsy is strongest; one study found an 84 to 85 percent concordance rate in identical twins. For psychomotor epilepsy the concordance rate in identical twins was 75 percent (DeJong and Sugar, 1972). What may be inherited in epilepsy is an instability of nerve cells. As indicated earlier, seizures can be induced in anyone, but the kind of stimuli that can elicit them varies. Epilepsy can be treated with drugs such as Dilantin, but individuals vary in their response to it. When a tumor causes epilepsy, it is removed if at all possible.

## Hyperactivity and Minimal Brain Dysfunction

Jerry was a four-year-old child whose mother stated that she had never noticed anything unusual about him until he was almost two years old. At that point he had a severe case of mumps and this illness seemed to be the turning point from a calm infancy to a disruptive preschool period. The abruptness of the change suggests that his mumps *may* have been a mumps encephalitis with subsequent brain damage, but there was no mention of this possibility in his pediatric history. His activity [coupled] high speed . . . with an erratic quality. He rarely stood still: when he was not running, jumping, or climbing he jiggled up and down in place much as a boxer does while waiting for his opponent's next move. He lacked fine motor skill and some of his gross motor behavior was characterized by clumsiness and awkwardness. He spent a major part of each morning running, climbing, and swinging. If an adult offered to push him or help him with any project he sometimes accepted the help, but at other times he burst into screams of rage and often pounded the adult with his fists. When he went to the toy corner he would throw all the toys off the shelves until he found the one he wanted. If another child had the toy he wanted, he took it by force; then, when an adult intervened, he had a tantrum. He had a short attention span and was unable to sit in a group and listen to a short story.

His speech was somewhat delayed. Although his IQ on the Stanford-Binet was 120, he never seemed to learn from experience; he repeatedly tried to stand on the seat of his tricycle even though he had many nasty falls. He rarely cried on falling but he often sobbed disconsolately over minor frustrations and hurts. At times he seemed almost desperate for attention and would engage in what could best be described as daredevil and reckless behavior to get it. On one occasion he climbed a tall tree in the preschool yard and attracted a fascinated audience by his promises to "go down the chimney like Santa Claus." To reach the roof he had to make a difficult jump from the tree, which he did without any hesitation or overt evidence of fear, and was prevented from going down the chimney only because it was too small for him to enter. When he was brought down from the roof he exhibited only pleasure at his feat and at "having all the kids watch me like that." On another occasion he picked up some bottles of prescription pills that had been carelessly discarded in a trash can and set himself up as doctor outside the preschool, dispensing pills to children as they entered (many came by themselves from a nearby housing development). When he was severely reprimanded his only comment was that he liked having "every kid do what I tell them." His behavior in any one session had a Jekyll and Hyde quality, with periods of calm interspersed with frequent . . . intense upset. The other children generally feared him, so even his serene periods were never reinforced by positive peer attention. Although he appeared to enjoy the preschool he often tried to climb the fence and was successful on several occasions (Ross, 1961, as reprinted in Ross and Ross, 1976, pp. 34–35).

Hyperactivity or hyperkinesis in children is defined as a behavioral pattern of persistent restlessness and inattentiveness that begins in early childhood. Such children are not simply more active than their peers; rather they seem to have particular difficulty in controlling their activity in situations that call for sitting still, such as at school or at mealtime (Pope, 1970). *Minimally brain-damaged* is another term applied by some writers to hyperactive children. This label designates a *presumed* etiology for the behavior pattern of restlessness and inattentiveness. Hyperactive children do *not* give clear evidence of specific brain damage, although they often have what are termed "soft" neurological signs, such as clumsiness and confusion of right and left, as well as problems in learning and perceiving. On the basis of these signs, it has been inferred that these children have "minimal" brain damage. We prefer the term hyperactivity because it does not carry with it a presumption concerning etiology. Indeed, as we shall see later, hyperactivity may have multiple causes.

In addition to their core problems, hyperactive children have a number of difficulties. As evidenced by poor academic and test performance (Weiss et al., 1971), between 40 and 50 percent have the learning problems already mentioned. Misconduct at school is found in about 80 percent (Satterfield et al., 1972). And hyperactive children are commonly described by adults as immature. They may choose to play with children younger than themselves and with toys inappropriate to their age; they also persist in baby talk (Weiss et al., 1971).

The problems of hyperactive children begin in early infancy: they are more likely than their peers to develop colic (Stewart et al., 1966), and they fail to reach developmental milestones at the expected ages (Denhoff, 1973). Furthermore, even during infancy there are deviations in activity level; some are overactive but others, interestingly enough, are too passive (Werry, Weiss, and Douglas, 1964). By the preschool years their overactivity and inattentiveness are evident. At this stage in their lives, they are often considered temperamental and emotional children (Schain and Reynard, 1975). But their problems continue into the elementary school years; eventually most of them come to the attention of mental health professionals. One study (Stewart et al., 1966) compared teacher ratings of the behavior of hyperactive and control children (Table 16.2). The actions and attitudes rated make a good catalogue of hyperactivity.

It is estimated that 8 to 9 percent of elementary school boys and 2 to 3 percent of girls are hyperactive (Miller, Palkes, and Stewart, 1973). At one time it was thought that hyperactivity simply went away by adolescence. Problems

TABLE **16.2**
## Classroom Behavior of Hyperactive and Control Children
(from Stewart et al., 1966)

| Behavior | Control, percent (*N* = 33) | Hyperactive, percent (*N* = 37) |
|---|---|---|
| Overactive | 33 | 100 |
| Can't sit still | 8 | 81 |
| Fidgets | 30 | 84 |
| Leaves class without permission | 0 | 35 |
| Can't accept correction | 0 | 35 |
| Temper tantrums | 0 | 51 |
| Fights | 3 | 59 |
| Defiant | 0 | 49 |
| Doesn't complete project | 0 | 84 |
| Doesn't stay with games | 3 | 78 |
| Doesn't listen to whole story | 0 | 49 |
| Moves from one activity to another in class | 6 | 46 |
| Doesn't follow directions | 3 | 62 |
| Hard to get to bed | 3 | 49 |
| Unpopular with peers | 0 | 46 |
| Talks too much | 20 | 68 |
| Wears out toys, furniture, etc. | 8 | 68 |
| Gets into things | 11 | 54 |
| Unpredictable | 3 | 59 |
| Destructive | 0 | 41 |
| Unresponsive to discipline | 0 | 57 |
| Lies | 3 | 43 |

with activity level do diminish somewhat, but adolescent youngsters still have difficulty maintaining attention (Weiss et al., 1971). Moreover, deficits in learning and perception remain (Mendelson, Johnson, and Stewart, 1971), and social relationships at home and with peers are unsatisfactory (Huessy, Metoyer, and Townsend, 1974).

## Physiological Theories

A predisposition toward hyperactivity does appear to be inherited. Morrison and Stewart (1971), for example, found that 20 percent of hyperactive children had a parent who had been hyperactive. The corresponding figure for control children was 5 percent. Similar results have been reported by Gross and Wilson (1974), and the findings have held up in more methodologically sophisticated adoption studies (Morrison and Steward, 1973; Cantwell, 1975).

A biochemical theory of hyperactivity, proposed by Feingold (1973), has enjoyed much attention in the popular press. He had been treating a woman for allergies while she was concurrently being seen by a psychiatrist for uncontrollable, frenetic behavior. Feingold thought that the patient might be allergic to aspirin and other salicylate compounds, so he prescribed a diet free of them. Both her allergic symptoms and her overactivity rapidly and dramatically diminished. Feingold soon noted the prevalence of salicylates and other similar chemicals in food additives and embarked on a study in which hyperactive children were kept on a diet free of food additives. Many responded favorably, and his work was subsequently replicated (Hawley and Buckley, 1974). Thus it is possible that the central nervous systems of some hyperactive children, perhaps through a genetically transmitted predisposition, are upset in some way by food additives. It is unlikely, though, that all cases of hyperactivity are caused by sensitivity to food additives. Recent studies of the Feingold diet have found that only a minority of such children respond positively (Goyette and Conners, 1977).

The signs that hyperactive children show of possible brain damage are consistent with their histories. Their mothers typically have difficult pregnancies (Pasamanick, Rogers, and Lilienfeld, 1956) and in infancy hyperactive children are more likely to have had seizures, encephalitis, cerebral palsy, and head injury (Conners et al., 1972). Furthermore, hyperactivity can be brought on by lead poisoning (Wiener, 1970). And many hyperactive children show abnormal EEGs (Gross and Wilson, 1974) in addition to the soft neurological signs already mentioned. All this evidence points to some brain malfunction, but what parts of the brain might be impaired? Or is the problem biochemical, not structural? Unfortunately, no data currently available allow greater and more meaningful specification of the vague term brain damage (Sroufe, 1975).

## Psychological Theories

Bettelheim (1973) proposed a diathesis-stress theory, suggesting that hyperactivity develops when a predisposition to the disorder is coupled with unfortunate rearing by parents. A child with a disposition toward overactivity and moodiness is stressed further by a mother who easily becomes impatient and resentful. The child is unable to cope with the mother's demands for obedience, the mother becomes more and more negative and disapproving, and the mother-child relationship ends up a battleground. With a disruptive and disobedient pattern already established, the demands of school cannot be handled, and the behavior of the child is usually and often in conflict with the rules of the classroom.

The Fels Research Institute's longitudinal study of child development supplies some evidence that is consistent with Bettelheim's position (Battle and Lacey, 1972). Mothers of hyperactive children were found to be critical of them and relatively unaffectionate, even during the children's infancy. These mothers continued to be disapproving of their children and dispensed severe penalties for disobedience. The parent-child relationship, however, is bidirectional, the behavior of each being determined by the actions and reactions of the other. It is plausible, though, that a critical and unaffectionate mother might exacerbate the problems of a hyperactive child.

Finally, two ways in which learning might figure in hyperactivity should be mentioned. First, hyperactivity could be reinforced by the attention it elicits, even negative attention, as Jerry's was. Second, as Ross and Ross (1976) suggest, hyperactivity may be modeled on the behavior of parents and siblings.

## Summary

In this chapter we have reviewed the literature on organic brain syndromes, those classified by etiology and one, epilepsy, that is classified by type of seizure. The primary symptoms of these syndromes are cognitive dysfunctions—disorientation, memory loss, and dementia—although affective symptoms and psychotic delusions and hallucinations may also be evident. A wide variety of conditions can cause an organic syndrome. Among the most important are infection, brain trauma, nutritional deficiencies, cerebrovascular disease, tumors, degenerative diseases, toxic agents, and malfunctions of the thyroid and adrenal glands. The symptoms of a particular brain injury or degeneration are quite variable, suggesting that the behavior exhibited by a brain-injured person is *not* simply related to his or her neurological pathology. Other as yet poorly understood factors seem to *interact* with brain injury in producing the symptoms that are observed.

Epilepsy is a group of disorders characterized by abnormal brain activity and altered states of consciousness. The major types of epilepsy—grand mal, petit mal, Jacksonian, and psychomotor—can be precipitated by a variety of causes such as stress, particular sensory stimuli, and brain diseases. Available evidence also suggests the importance of genetic factors.

Hyperactivity in children, sometimes referred to as minimal brain damage, is defined as a pattern of persistent restlessness and inattentiveness beginning in early childhood. It appears, in part, to be inherited. Biochemical, neurological, and psychological theories of its cause have been proposed, though none enjoys clear support.

# chapter 17

## MENTAL RETARDATION



"What is retardation? It's hard to say. I guess it's having problems thinking." More technical descriptions of mental retardation will be presented, along with theories of some of the causes of this disorder, but we have not encountered a more straightforward definition than this one. It is particularly meaningful and poignant because it comes from a twenty-six-year-old man who, at the age of fifteen, was placed in a state institution for the retarded. An account of his life, in his own words, indicates his sensitivity and thoughtfulness.

> When I was born the doctors didn't give me six months to live. My mother told them she could keep me alive, but they didn't believe it. It took a hell of a lot of work, but she showed with love and determination that she could be the mother to a handicapped child. I don't know for a fact what I had, but they thought it was severe retardation and cerebral palsy. They thought I would never walk. I still have seizures. . . .
>
> When I was at school, concentrating was almost impossible. . . . That was my major problem all through school that I daydreamed. I think all people do that. It wasn't related to retardation. I think a lot of kids do that and are diagnosed as retarded, but it has nothing to do with retardation at all. It really has to do with how people deal with the people around them and their situations. . . . I kind of stood in the background—I kind of knew that I was different—I knew that I had a problem, but when you're young you don't think of it as a problem. . . . The problem is getting labeled as being something. After that you're not really as a person [sic]. . . . In the fifth grade—in the fifth grade my classmates thought I was different, and my teacher knew I was different. One day she looked at me

and she was on the phone to the office. Her conversation was like this, "When are you going to transfer him?". . . . She looked at me and knew I was knowledgeable about what she was saying.

My mother protected me. . . . I can remember trying to be like the other kids and having my mother right there pulling me away. . . . Sometimes I think the pain of being handicapped is that people give you so much love that it becomes a weight on you and a weight on them.

[When he was fifteen, the young man's parents died, and after brief stays with family friends and at an orphanage, he and his sister were sent to a state school.] Right before they sent me and my sister to the State School, they had six psychologists examine us to determine how intelligent we were. I think that was a waste of time. They asked me things like, "What comes to mind when I say 'Dawn'?"—so you say, "Light." Things like that. What was tough was putting the puzzles together and the mechanical stuff. They start out very simple and then they build it up and it gets harder and harder. . . . Another guy I talked to was a psychiatrist. That was rough. For one thing I was mentally off guard. . . . You don't figure what they're saying and how you're answering it and what it all means—not until the end. When the end came, I was a ward of the State. . . . When the psychiatrist interviewed me he had my records in front of him—so he already knew I was mentally retarded. It's the same with everyone. If you are considered mentally retarded there is no way you can win. . . .

I don't like the word vegetable, but in my own case I could see that if I had been placed on the low grade ward I might have slipped to that. I began feeling myself slip. . . . If I would have let that place get to me and depress me I would still have been there today. . . . They had me scheduled to go to P-8—a back ward. . . . There was this supervisor, a woman. She came on to the ward and looked right at me and said: "I have him scheduled for P-8." An older attendant was there. He looked over at me and said, "He's too bright for that ward. I think we'll keep him." . . . She made a remark under her breath that I looked pretty retarded to her. . . .

Of course I didn't know what P-8 was then, but I found out. I visited up there a few times on work detail. That man saved my life. . . . At that point I'm pretty positive that if I went there I would have fitted in and I would still be there. . . .

It's funny. You hear so many people talking about IQ. The first time I ever heard the expression was when I was at Empire State School. I didn't know what it was or anything, but some people were talking and they brought the subject up. It was on the ward, and I went and asked one of the staff what mine was. They told me forty-nine. Forty-nine isn't fifty, but I was pretty happy about it. I mean I figured that I wasn't a low grade. I really didn't know what it meant, but it sounded pretty high. Hell, I was born in 1948 and forty-nine didn't seem too bad. Forty-nine didn't sound hopeless. I didn't know anything about the highs or the lows, but I knew I was better than most of them. . . .

[Eight years later the young man was discharged. He has been working as a janitor and living in a boardinghouse with other former residents of state institutions. His thoughts go to a young woman named Joan, whom he had met at the institution.] Is there still any magnetism between that woman and me? I haven't seen her in three months, but there is still something, I can tell. . . . We got pretty close psychologically and physically—not that I did anything. They don't have programs at the Association for Retarded Children that say to adults you are an adult and you can make it. . . . The first time I noticed her was in the eating area; I was having lunch. I looked around and she was the only one there that attracted me. There was just something about her. . . .

Being at the State School and all you never have the chances romantically like you might living on the outside. I guess I was always shy with the opposite sex even at Empire.

> We did have dances and I felt that I was good looking, but I was bashful and mostly sat. I was bashful with Joan at the movie. In my mind I felt funny, awkward. I didn't know how to approach her. Should I hug her? You can't hug the hell out of her because you don't know how she would take it. You have all the feeling there, but you don't know what direction to go in. If you put your arm around her she might scream and you're finished. If she doesn't scream you're still finished. . . .
>
> As I got older I slowly began to find myself becoming mentally awake. I found myself concentrating. Like on the television. A lot of people wonder why I have good grammar. It was because of the television. I was like a tape recorder—what I heard I memorized. Even when I was ten to twelve I would listen to Huntley and Brinkley. They were my favorites. As the years went by I understood what they were talking about. People were amazed at what I knew. People would begin to ask me what I thought about this and that. Like my aunt would always ask me about the news—what my opinions were. I began to know that I was a little brighter than they thought I was. . . .
>
> I don't know. Maybe I used to be retarded. That's what they said anyway. I wish they could see me now. I wonder what they'd say if they could see me holding down a regular job and doing all kinds of things. I bet they wouldn't believe it (Bogdan and Taylor, 1976, pp. 47–52).

The foregoing comes from edited transcripts of conversations between this man and two psychologists who came to know him. Bogdan and Taylor hold the view that retardation is nothing more than a social construct, a label rather arbitrarily applied to other human beings. They object to the unfortunately widespread tendency to draw sharp distinctions between the "normal" and the "retarded," and their apparent purpose in publishing the article from which the foregoing excerpts were taken was to argue how faulty and damaging such generalizations are.

It is important to consider seriously this line of argument, for as the research and theorizing on retardation is reviewed, we must resist the tendency to dehumanize the people so labeled. A person may have "problems thinking," but he is still able to have his feelings hurt, to know justifiable anger, to love, and to reflect on his life and where it seems to be going. In other words, his commonalities with those of us who score well on the standard tests and who adapt relatively easily are to be appreciated as well as his differences.

But, as will become clear in this chapter, we ourselves cannot accept the thesis that mental retardation is nothing more than a social label. Although there is an important gray area between the intellectually normal and those of subnormal IQ, and yes, although to be labeled mentally retarded can be demeaning, consistent differences *do* exist between many retardates and normal individuals, and careful consideration of these differences by behavioral scientists will bring greater understanding, help, and tolerance.

There is an additional issue to raise at the outset, namely whether a chapter on mental retardation should be included in an abnormal psychology textbook. The central concern of those who work with the retarded is the *intellectual deficit* that defines mental retardation. In contrast, most of abnormal psychology is concerned with behavioral and emotional problems. But people who suffer extreme neurotic anxiety often do not think clearly, and, conversely, someone with an IQ of 60 is likely to have trouble adapting to our complex society and therefore have negative feelings about himself or others. So the lines of separation are fuzzy.

One easy way out is to say that students and teachers of abnormal psychology have come to expect a chapter on mental retardation in this kind of textbook. But there is a more substantive reason, namely that abnormal psychology is concerned with the whole range of problems in adaptation and creative living. A person who cannot acquire information as easily as others may have as much difficulty living as someone who thinks he is Napoleon, or as someone whose anxious concern that others think well of her interferes with her ability to concentrate.

According to the most recent manual of the American Association on Mental Deficiency, an organization to which many professionals in the field belong, mental retardation ". . . refers to significantly subaverage general intellectual functioning existing concurrently with deficits in adaptive behavior, and manifested during the developmental period" (Grossman, 1973, p. 11). In the view of these professionals, a low IQ score does not by itself designate an individual as a mental retardate; he or she must also be unable to adapt to the natural and social demands of the environment. Moreover, the problems of retardates manifest themselves early in life, well before the eighteenth year, distinguishing them from those whose intelligence is impaired later in life, through a severe contusion, for example. Thus three variables must be considered in deciding whether a person is mentally retarded: measured IQ, degree of social adaptation, and whether the difficulties were early in onset. The AAMD asserts also that a person can *cease* being retarded, as seems to have happened to the man whose thoughts on retardation began this chapter.

■

# Classification and Diagnosis of Mental Retardation

## Levels of Retardation

The current AAMD manual differs in an important respect from the earlier one (Heber, 1961). The category "borderline retardation" has been dropped; a person is now considered retarded only if his or her IQ score falls two standard deviations below the mean of the intelligence test being used.[1] Thus on the Stanford-Binet, which has a standard deviation of 16, an individual would be labeled mildly retarded if his or her score is between 52 and 67; on the Wechsler test the cutoff scores would be slightly higher, between 55 and 69, since that test was constructed to have a standard deviation of 15. These may seem obscure statistical niceties, but they have important consequences. In the 1960s professionals became concerned that people with IQs as high as 83 on the Stanford-Binet were stigmatized as borderline retarded. Intellectual deficits formerly regarded as major no longer seemed so, for even our highly technological society has less demanding situations into which those with IQs in the 70s fit without marked difficulty (Robinson and Robinson, 1976).

Four levels of mental deficiency are now recognized by the AAMD, each of them a specific subaverage range on the far left of the normal distribution curve of measured intelligence (see page 33). In order to be considered retarded, people who score in these ranges must also have significant problems in social adaptation. This criterion is discussed separately and more fully in a later section of this chapter. In the United States those considered retarded by these two measures number close to seven million. The fol-

[1] The standard deviation is a statistic used to describe the amount of variability in a set of scores. If we know that a person is two standard deviations below the mean, we also know that he or she is in the lower 3 percent of the population.

lowing is a summary of how individuals at each level of mental retardation are described by Robinson and Robinson (1976).[2]

**Mild Mental Retardation** (Stanford-Binet IQ 52 to 67). The mildly retarded comprise about 90 percent of all those who have IQs of less than 67. As children they are eligible for special classes for the educable mentally retarded. Adults are likely to be able to maintain themselves in unskilled jobs or in sheltered workshops, although they may need help with social and financial problems. Only about one percent are ever institutionalized, usually in adolescence for behavioral problems. Many of the mildly retarded show no signs of brain pathology and are members of families whose intelligence and socioeconomic levels are low.

**Moderate Mental Retardation** (Stanford-Binet IQ 36 to 51). About 6 percent of those with IQs of less than 67 are moderately retarded. Brain damage and other pathologies are frequent. During childhood these individuals are eligible for special classes for trainable retardates in which the development of self-care skills rather than academic achievement is emphasized. Many are institutionalized. Although most can do useful work, few hold jobs except in sheltered workshops or in family businesses. Most live dependently within the family. Few have friends of their own, but they may be left alone without supervision for several hours at a time. Their retardation is likely to be identified in infancy or early childhood, for their sensorimotor coordination remains poor, and they are slow to develop verbal and social skills. In contrast to mildly retarded children, moderate to profound retardates are found in all socioeconomic groups.

**Severe Mental Retardation** (Stanford-Binet IQ 20 to 35). About 3 percent of those with IQs of less than 67 are severely retarded. Most are institutionalized and require constant supervision. For children in this group to be able to speak and take care of their own basic needs requires prolonged training; the self-care training that is provided in the special classes within the school system is usually inadequate except for the upper portion of this group. As adults the severely retarded may be friendly but can usually communicate only briefly on a very concrete level. They engage in very little independent activity and are often lethargic, for their severe brain damage leaves them relatively passive and the circumstances of their lives allow them little stimulation. Genetic disorders and environmental insults, such as severe oxygen deprivation at birth, account for most of this degree of retardation.

**Profound Mental Retardation** (Stanford-Binet IQ below 20). Only about one percent of the retarded are profoundly so, requiring total supervision and often nursing care all their lives. Very little training is usually given them because it is assumed that they can learn little except possibly to walk, utter a few phrases, feed themselves, and use the toilet. Many have severe physical deformities as well as neurological damage and cannot get around on their own. There is a very high mortality rate during childhood.

These categories are difficult to apply, partly because of the assessment devices that are used to measure intelligence and adaptive behavior, and partly because human beings seldom lend themselves to precise categorization. Moreover, the social implications of labeling a child as mildly or moderately retarded must be considered. Ross (1974) points out that social agencies, such as schools, make inferences about the future development of children with low IQ scores, and that these expectations affect markedly the kind of educational settings in which such children are placed. A child labeled as moderately retarded, since he or she has an IQ score between 36 and 51, is generally judged to be "trainable." Those who are categorized as mildly retarded, with an IQ above 52 but below 67, are considered "educable." Educable children are

[2] The draft of DSM-III has levels of retardation consistent with the AAMD scheme.

expected to reach a sixth-grade level of academic achievement, but trainables are generally considered unable to learn any of the subject matter usually taught in schools. So-called trainable children tend not to be given adequate opportunity to surpass the levels that are expected of them, which means, as Ross points out, that the prophecy of low achievement is self-fulfilling.

Over the past two hundred years attitudes have swung like a pendulum from optimism and interest in educating the retarded to bleak pessimism. Édouard Seguin, a French physician and educator of the eighteenth century, was convinced that education was a universal right and that "idiots" were among the neediest. Considering mental retardation a weakness in the nervous system, he devised teaching methods to correct specific disabilities. After leaving Paris in 1848, he settled in Ohio and was instrumental in setting up special schools throughout the northeastern United States. But disillusionment set in later in the century when the goals that had been confidently worked toward earlier were not attained. The children did not become normal, and the institutions grew and grew. Perhaps the retarded were just "born that way" and little could be done for them, except to maintain them and protect them from the intellectual demands of society. More recently, in this century, there have been more serious and systematic attempts to educate the retarded to as full an extent as possible. These efforts were spurred on, no doubt, by the infusion of federal moneys initiated by President Kennedy, himself the brother of a retarded woman (Crissey, 1975). Through the application of operant teaching principles, for example, some retarded children have acquired skills that they were formerly thought incapable of learning. If such successes continue, the

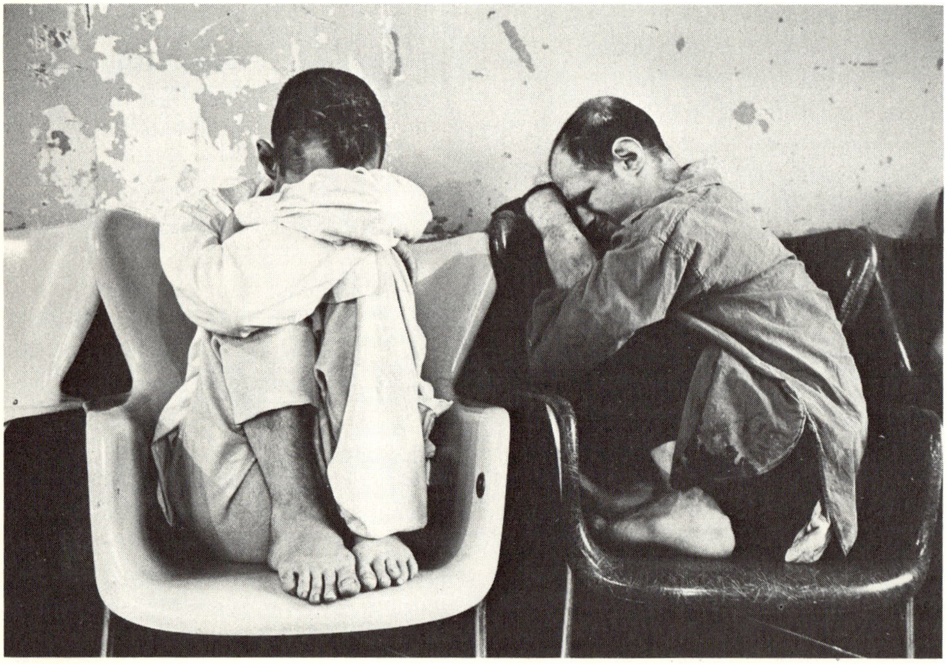

All too often the mentally retarded who are hospitalized as children spend the rest of their lives in the hopeless, inhospital environment of a state institution.

descriptions of each level of retardation will become inappropriate. In Chapter 19 this approach and its implications for teaching those previously thought to be unteachable will be described.

## Intelligence Test Scores as a Criterion

Because the principal means of diagnosing mental retardation are the IQ tests that are currently available, we should reexamine the nature of these tests (see page 79). An intelligence quotient[3] is actually nothing more than what an IQ test measures, even though the concept of intelligence has seemingly been reified by these tests, made into "a thing" that exists "out there."

When people take an IQ test, they demonstrate how many problems of those that are being presented to them—whether they be to generate definitions of words or to manipulate small colored blocks to form a design—they can solve at that particular time and place. Scores on IQ tests do allow useful predictions to be made; Binet, for example, succeeded in predicting school performance on the basis of his test. Current IQ tests are similarly good at predicting academic performance. And people can be categorized by IQ scores so that other aspects of their behavior are anticipated. But the predictive validity of the intelligence test should not blind us to the fact that intelligence itself is a construct, an entity which is inferred as actually existing and supposedly generating measurable phenomena, but which is not at present, and perhaps never will be, fully observable.

Traditional IQ tests pose special problems when they are used to diagnose mental retardation.

[3] Since the late 1930s the intelligence quotient has represented what is technically called a "deviation IQ." Although the mathematics need not concern us here [see Anastasi (1968), for example, for particulars], a person's raw score—the number of test items he or she passes—is transformed into a deviation IQ, which indicates how far the raw score falls away from the average raw score obtained by the age group on which a given test was standardized.

1. Most IQ tests have not been standardized on nonwhite populations or institutionalized populations, groups that are heavily represented in the prevalence figures for mental retardation. Items that sample intelligent behavior of a white noninstitutionalized population may be very different from those that ought to be used to measure the intelligent behavior of a nonwhite institutalized population of retardates.

2. Few of the intelligence tests have been validated for IQ scores of less than 70. Individuals of low intellectual functioning were not adequately represented in the groups taking the tests when the scales were being compiled and standardized.

3. Many diagnoses of retardation are made when the child is quite young, less than five years of age. Measurements of the intelligence of very young children do not necessarily correlate highly with those obtained when the child is older, although extremely low scores do predict subnormal intellectual functioning later in childhood.

4. The most reliable and frequently used tests for measuring the intelligence of children, the Stanford-Binet Intelligence Scale and the Wechsler Intelligence Scale for Children (WISC), were not devised to take into account other problems of the mentally retarded that may contribute to their poor performance on an IQ test. Children taking the Stanford-Binet test must repeat digits spoken to them by the tester, find objects in pictures, build simple structures with blocks to match those shown them, complete sentences, define simple words, detect fallacies in statements, supply rhyming words, and so on. The WISC consists of separate subtests, six of them verbal and testing the child's store of general information, comprehension and abstract thinking, vocabulary, and abilities to repeat series of numbers and to solve problems in arithmetic. The other subtests evaluate nonverbal per-

FIGURE 17.1
In the WISC block design test, blocks and a series of printed designs are presented to the examinee. He or she has to construct the design using the varicolored blocks. Each block has a white side, a colored side, and a side that is half and half, as well as sides with irrelevant colors.

formances such as completing pictures or arranging them to depict a meaningful story, reproducing designs with blocks (Figure 17.1), assembling objects, and substituting a set of unfamiliar symbols for digits. The intelligence of blind, deaf, and nonverbal individuals is extremely difficult to assess by either of these instruments, for children who are handicapped in these ways are physically unable to complete all parts of the tests. Those with poor motor coordination may work out an intellectual solution to a problem but have trouble translating it into the verbal or motor behavior required by the test. For these reasons special IQ tests have been developed for the blind, the Hayes-Binet; for the deaf, the Hiskey Nebraska; and for the nonverbal, for whom the second half of the WISC, the performance section of the test, is typically used.

5. Before the IQ test is given, the tester must establish a degree of rapport with the child in order to obtain maximum performance. A poor black child may not readily be put at ease by a white middle-class psychologist. But it is also unclear whether a black psychologist will "pull" maximum performance

from a black child, or a white psychologist maximum performance from a white child. The important point, however, is that establishing a relaxed atmosphere is especially necessary, for testing may present special problems for the retarded child.

6. Zigler, Butterfield, and Capobianco (1970) have shown that an institution can be a very socially depriving place for a child. When being tested the retarded child's atypical need for social reinforcement may make him attend too much to the adult and look to him for solutions to the test problems. The "outer-directedness" of the retarded child can keep him from concentrating on the tasks, resulting in a spuriously low IQ score.

The problems in testing the IQs of the retarded suggest that the scores obtained cannot be regarded as unerringly valid indicators of their intelligence. At the same time, however, such tests have proved useful in providing information about retardates and in predicting their later intellectual and social achievements.

## Adaptive Behavior as a Criterion

In addition to measured IQ, the American Association on Mental Deficiency's classification scheme emphasizes the importance of assessing adaptive behavior in determining the level of mental retardation. Two facets of adaptive behavior are described: "(1) the degree to which the individual is able to function and maintain himself independently, and (2) the degree to which he meets satisfactorily the culturally imposed demands of personal and social responsibility" (Heber, 1961, p. 61).

The standards of adaptive behavior vary with age. Individuals must always be evaluated in terms of how they meet the standards of personal independence and social responsibility set for their particular chronological age group. Unfortunately, there are few objective measures of adaptive behavior. The Vineland Social Maturity Scale (Doll, 1953) is perhaps the best measure currently available, although its norms are not as firmly established as those of the IQ tests. This scale is composed of 117 activities grouped into 8 categories of behavior. An interviewer asks a person well acquainted with the child, often a parent, to evaluate how well the child performs a variety of socially adaptive behaviors. Several sample items are shown in Table 17.1.

TABLE **17.1**
Sample Items from Vineland Social Maturity Scale with Age at Which Performance Is Expected
(from Doll, 1953)

| Age | Item |
|---|---|
| 0–1 | pulls self upright<br>does not drool |
| 1–2 | pulls off socks<br>eats with spoon |
| 2–3 | asks to go to toilet<br>dries own hands |
| 3–4 | plays cooperatively at kindergarten level<br>buttons coat or dress |
| 4–5 | uses pencil or crayon for drawing<br>washes face unassisted |
| 5–6 | prints simple words<br>is trusted with money |
| 6–7 | uses table knife for spreading<br>goes to bed unassisted |
| 7–8 | tells time to quarter hour<br>combs or brushes hair |
| 8–9 | uses tools or utensils<br>reads on own initiative |
| 9–10 | makes minor purchases<br>goes about town freely |

## Experimental Study of Specific Cognitive Processes

Intellectual functioning is for the most part judged on the basis of IQ scores, but a particular score provides only limited information on *how* a person thinks. The WISC may reveal that a child does very poorly on block design tasks (Figure 17.1), but why? What is there about the problem solving of this task that is particularly difficult and that psychologists might study? In the picture completion subtest of the WISC a series of pictures are presented to the child one at a time. He or she must identify the important part that is missing from each picture. This and other subtests have proved effective in picking out retardates. But what are the deficiencies in thinking that they reveal?

### Laboratory Testing of the Retardate

Experimental psychologists have for years divided intelligence into particular functions such as perception, motor skills, short-term memory, long-term memory, speech, discrimination learning, and other phenomena and have studied them in laboratories. But they have usually tested these functions in individuals whose IQ scores and social behavior are well within the normal range, if not above average. Since the early 1960s, many workers have been studying experimentally, in laboratory settings, the intellectual behavior of mental retardates, giving careful consideration to the specific intellectual functions that are poorly developed in them. Approaching mental retardation in this fashion would seem to have some advantages. Experimentalists may one day be able to isolate variables that underlie the development and maintenance of subnormal functioning. Through comparison studies they may find out how the learning of retardates differs from that of normal children, and through special studies of retardates they may determine what factors help them to achieve certain patterns and levels of performance. If laboratory work establishes means of manipulating specific subnormal functionings, this knowledge may help in formulating treatments.

### The Developmental versus Defect Controversy

Much of the experimental research in mental retardation has been devoted to determining whether the retarded person is *quantitatively* or *qualitatively* different from the normal person in thinking and learning processes. The essential question is whether the retardate's cognitive development is the same as that of a normal person but proceeding at a slower rate—the developmental position; or whether he or she suffers from some cognitive deficit that makes intellectual functioning different from that of normal persons—the defect position.

The major developmental theorist is Zigler (1969). He is concerned with the cultural-familial retarded, those who have no demonstrated brain pathology, are mildly retarded, and have at least one parent or sibling who is also retarded. He believes that the cultural-familial retardate "is characterized by a slower progression through the same sequence of cognitive stages . . . and a more limited upper stage of cognition . . . than is characteristic of the individual of average intellect" (p. 537).

Milgram (1973) is one of the major defect or difference theorists. His research attempts to isolate specific deficiencies of the retarded to which their low IQs can be attributed, with the hope that eventually deficiencies can be modified or retarded learning can at least be better understood.

The specific qualitative deficiency Milgram is concerned with is the failure of retardates to think of mediators to help them associate words. In a paired-associates learning task, for example, an individual is given several pairs of words to learn, cat-tree, spoon-table, knife-wall. Later he or she is given only the first item of each pair (cat, spoon, knife) and is required to recall the second item (tree, table, wall). Normal children commonly form verbal mediators to link the items of a pair—for example, the phrase "the CAT ran up the TREE." Milgram has argued that because retarded children do not usually form such mediators, they do poorly on this type of task. In support of his argument, he administered a paired-associates test to retarded and normal children under two conditions. First the children were given only the paired words, but in the second round the children were provided a mediator for each pair. The retarded children performed more poorly than the nonretarded *only when mediators were not provided,* confirming the hypothesis that retarded children have trouble producing verbal mediators.

The short-term memory, selective attention, distractibility, and physiological arousal of the mentally retarded have also been studied in the attempt to discover particular deficiencies. But in comparing normal children and retardates on laboratory cognitive tasks, investigators have great difficulty controlling the motivational, environmental, and educational variables other than intelligence that might contribute to poor cognitive performance. It is still unclear how best to account for the consistently poor performance of retarded children on these tasks. The developmental versus defect controversy remains a lively one.

## The Contributions of Piaget

A further attempt to study the mental processes that may underlie mental retardation comes from the tradition of work that originated with the famous Swiss researcher Jean Piaget (for example, 1952; Ginsburg and Opper,1969), and more particularly with his associate Bärbel Inhelder. Piaget has been studying the growth of intelligence and problem solving in normal children since the 1920s. His efforts to understand the development of adaptive behavior are probably more ambitious and more creative than the work of any other single theorist in this field. It is

Jean Piaget, the famous Swiss researcher whose theories of normal cognitive development are now being applied in the study of mental retardation.

not surprising that in recent years investigators have attempted to understand mental retardation in Piagetian terms. Before we review some of these efforts, it will be useful to outline briefly Piaget's view of the growth of intelligence.[4]

Piaget is a cognitive theorist, for he believes that human behavior must be understood in terms of how people construe their world, how they attempt to alter it to meet their needs, and how they change their own way of thinking and behaving in order to work within the constraints of the environment. Although identified professionally as a psychologist, Piaget was in fact trained as a zoologist. Perhaps this accounts for the notion central to his theory, that cognitive abilities develop in stages. At each stage the individual acquires not a simple quantitative advance in "brainpower" but a *qualitatively different* way of grappling with experience. Piaget's stages of intellectual growth are similar in concept to Freud's psychosexual stages of development. Neither theorist ignored the *interaction* between organism and environment, but both Piaget and Freud postulated a predetermined set of developmental stages through which every human being is thought to progress—unless, of course, there is some sort of aberration in development.

**Birth to Two Years: The Period of Sensorimotor Intelligence** At the beginning of the first period the innate reflexes of infancy, such as sucking, have already been acquired. By the end the ability to manipulate objects and even to anticipate the consequences of behavior has been developed. The very young child gradually learns to perceive, to recognize aspects of the environment, and to realize that he or she can have a predictable effect on it. The child knows that a rattle will move and make noise if grasped and shaken. Sensorimotor intelligence is essentially knowing by doing; presumably the young child does not have an internal, symbolic representation of the world. According to Piaget, the child is not interested in or capable of understanding *why* behavior affects things, only in the fact that it does. The child's thoughts are very much bound by concrete objects that are immediately in view, although the child eventually realizes that they continue to exist even when not seen. More reflective intelligence is assumed to develop in the next stage.

**Two to Seven Years: The Period of Preoperational Thought** The hallmark of this stage of development is the emergence of internal representations of the external world, in other words, images and thoughts about what may not be immediately present. Of course the acquisition of language is the most obvious and remarkable feature of these five years, and much of the child's language is conceptual—it reflects an increasing ability to transcend time and space, to think of the past, present, and future.

These are impressive gains, but preoperational intelligence is still limited. Piaget finds children in this period of development to be egocentric, unable to adopt differing points of view about problems. They tend not to reflect on their own thought processes, on how logical or illogical they are. Perhaps the best-known limitation of this stage of thinking is the difficulty children have in conserving volume. In one way of demonstrating this phenomenon, a child is first presented with identical tall, thin beakers containing equal amounts of water. After the child has agreed that both beakers contain exactly the same amount of liquid, the contents of one of the beakers are poured into a shorter but wider container. The child is then asked whether these two containers have the same amounts of water in them. A preoperational child usually answers no and states that the tall, thin beaker contains more. The child has focused on one salient characteristic of the beakers, namely their height, and has assumed that "taller" means "bigger in volume," which in this instance is not so. The child has not conserved volume when shape was changed.

[4] Much of the following discussion of Piaget is based on Robinson and Robinson (1976).

**Seven to Eleven Years: The Period of Concrete Operations** The principal advance at this stage is the acquisition of well-organized cognitive systems, such as notions of time, space, and number and the ability to add and subtract, to estimate and approximate. Piaget's theorizing becomes unusually intricate at this point, so suffice it to say that the child now thinks more and more like an adult—logically and in a complex fashion.

**Eleven Years Onward: The Period of Formal Operations** This final, highest stage of intellectual development frees the child and adult from the close dependence on concrete, external objects that characterizes the three preceding stages. During the period of formal operations the person can deal with the hypothetical, the possible. Readers can demonstrate this kind of thinking to themselves by formulating an experiment, such as one to test the effects of toilet training on adult attitudes toward parents. In designing such a study, they will be fully immersed in abstract, logical thinking.

Piaget's concepts and his research with normal children offer a way of *describing* the cognitive deficits of retarded children that takes the psychologist much farther than the mere reporting of an IQ score. In fact, Bärbel Inhelder (1968), one of Piaget's closest associates, has described different levels of retardation in terms of cognitive patterns à la Piaget, and her observations have been confirmed by others. She has found, for example, that severely and profoundly retarded adults (IQ from below 20 to 35) have not progressed beyond the sensorimotor stage; moderately retarded adults (IQ 36 to 51) have been described as limited to preoperational thought; and mildly retarded people (IQ 52 to 67) have been characterized as unable to pass beyond the concrete operations stage. And yet, as we have come to expect, people do not fit this neatly into categories. In general, although the overall findings in Piagetian research lend some support to Inhelder's observations, many retarded children and adults shift back and forth, showing at different times lesser or greater ability to solve problems that are believed to require one or another kind of thinking. As enthusiastic as they are about Piaget, Robinson and Robinson (1976), in their classic text on mental retardation, caution against falling into the trap of expecting all retarded children of a given IQ to function alike in Piagetian terms.

Robinson and Robinson (1976) have discussed other ways in which Piaget's theorizing has contributed to our understanding of mental retardation, and in particular how it has affected our general attitudes. As we have seen, the theory emphasizes *qualitative* changes in thinking as a person matures, and, as such, is consistent with Milgram's position. According to Piaget, knowledge does not simply get added on through experience; rather, individuals deal with their environments *differently* as they pass from stage to stage. Piaget's theory encourages (or should encourage) workers to appreciate the unique capabilities of retarded persons rather than emphasizing their obvious limitations.

Piaget has not been concerned with the possibility that children might be taught more effectively by developing to the fullest their cognitive competencies as they become evident. But his theory promises to guide other workers in planning curricula suited for children at particular levels of intellectual development (Ginsburg and Opper, 1969). And his work offers clues to the *content* of remedial programs that might challenge the retarded child just enough to maintain interest and curiosity, yet not be so difficult that they contribute to feelings of helplessness and incompetence.

■

## Organic Causes of Mental Retardation

The several forms of mental retardation are likely to be caused by any number of factors or combinations thereof. Through the years the issue of whether mental retardation should be attributed primarily to organic factors or to the environment has aroused great controversy. But this debate has really focused on only one level of the disorder, the first, mild retardation. Zigler (1968), Robinson and Robinson (1976), and others following their lead make a distinction between mild retardation on the one hand and moderate, severe, and profound on the other. Cultural-familial or environmental factors are considered likely to be formative in mild retardation; and a single pathological organic factor, such as a defective gene or a brain trauma, is considered determinative in the more severe forms of retardation.

Heber (1970) estimates that damage to the developing brain accounts for no more than 10 to 20 percent of the total population of the mentally retarded. These individuals generally have IQs of less than 51, falling into the moderate, severe, and profound retardation categories. They are fairly evenly distributed throughout all socioeconomic, ethnic, and racial groups. Unlike the so-called cultural-familial retardates, these children have parents with IQs across the entire range. The greatest proportion of the mentally retarded, the cultural-familial retardates, appear physically normal and give no indication of brain pathology that can at present be detected. Most are mildly retarded with IQs above 51, and the great majority of them are born and raised in deprived environments. Although the genes considered responsible for inheritance of intelligence have been implicated in their retardation, the effects of sociocultural impoverishment are now considered very important as well.

In Table 17.2 are listed a few of the many currently known diseases that are associated with

TABLE **17.2**
Illustrative Organic Diseases Associated with Mental Retardation

| When disease develops | Types of disease | | |
|---|---|---|---|
| | **Genetic** | **Infectious** | **Traumatic** |
| In utero (before birth)* | Down's syndrome<br>Klinefelter's syndrome<br>Phenylketonuria<br>Tay-Sachs disease<br>Niemann-Pick disease<br>Maple Syrup Urine disease<br>Hurler's syndrome<br>Lesch-Nyhan syndrome | Rubella<br>Syphilis<br>Toxoplasmosis<br>Encephalitis | Rh factor<br>Cretinism<br>Malnutrition<br>Poisoning (lead, carbon monoxide, X-ray)<br>Drugs |
| At or following birth | | Encephalitis<br>Meningitis | All the above (except Rh factor)<br>*plus*<br>Anoxia<br>Premature birth<br>Head Injury |

* Conditions in which the head size is grossly distorted are not listed because various factors may have impaired development. Examples are microcephaly or small head in which the development of the brain has been arrested; macrocephaly, large head with abnormal growth of supportive tissues; and hydrocephaly, large head with excessive cerebrospinal fluid.

mental retardation. They are grouped in two different ways, by when the problem develops, before or after birth, and by the nature of the disease, genetic, infectious, or traumatic. In some instances a problem will not show itself until some time after birth, but it is still categorized as prenatal if the physiological source of the difficulty was established while the child was still in its mother's uterus. Our knowledge is still so limited, however, that the distinctions made in the table should be viewed only as general guidelines. To take but one example, a chromosomal abnormality, which is categorized as a prenatal genetic disease, may itself be attributed to the mother's exposure to radiation (considered a traumatic disease) before the egg was even fertilized.

## Genetic Conditions Causing Mental Retardation

In genetic conditions the individual's abnormality is almost always determined at the moment of conception. Robinson and Robinson (1976) distinguish two important types, those caused by chromosomal aberrations and those attributable to the unfortunate pairing of two defective recessive genes. Mental retardation attributable to a dominant gene is very rare because the persons affected are generally not able to reproduce. Variations from the normal complement of forty-six chromosomes usually, but not always, cause very noticeable physical abnormalities in the developing child. When defective recessive genes are paired, production of an enzyme necessary for an important metabolic process is usually disturbed.

### Chromosomal aberrations

*Down's syndrome* or *mongolism,* first described by Langdon Down in 1886, is the most prevalent single-factor cause of mental retardation, accounting for at least 10 percent of moderately to severely retarded children. It has been estimated that one child in every 660 births is afflicted with this disorder (Robinson and Robinson, 1976). Mongoloid children seldom have an IQ over 50. Their many physical abnormalities are rather apparent: eyes slanted upward and outward, a vestigial third eyelid in the inner corner of the eye, flat face and nose, overly large and often deeply fissured tongue, misshapen teeth, small skull, stubby fingers, fingerprints with ℓ-shaped loops rather than whorls, protruding belly, underdeveloped genitalia, and arms and legs that are smaller than normal. Many children with Down's syndrome, perhaps 40 percent, have heart problems; a small minority may have blockages of the upper intestinal tract; and about 25 percent do not survive the first few years. As adults, mongoloids seldom exceed five feet in height. Menstruation in women tends to follow a normal course, but men are apparently sterile. Mortality after age forty is abnormally high; brain tissue generally shows signs of deterioration similar to that found in Alzheimer's disease (see page 423).

Down's syndrome is caused by a chromosomal abnormality. The vast majority of mongoloid children have forty-seven chromosomes instead of forty-six. During the earliest stage of an egg's development, the two chromosomes of pair 21 fail to separate, perhaps because they are so small. When the sperm and egg unite, chromosome pair 21 will thus have three chromosomes instead of the usual two. This is referred to as a trisomy of chromosome 21.

The risk of having a mongoloid child increases dramatically with the age of the mother. There is a one in 1500 chance of a mother in her twenties having such a child, and a one in 65 risk for a mother over forty-five. Fortunately, recently developed methods of testing the amniotic fluid in which the fetus is immersed within the uterus can reveal whether the child is mongoloid. In a much rarer and inherited form of mongolism the extra chromosome 21 becomes attached to another chromosome. The risk of bearing a child with this type of mongolism does not increase with maternal age.

Perhaps because children with Down's syndrome grow up in widely diverse situations, the

## BOX **17.1** Idiot Savant

One particularly interesting phenomenon, usually regarded as a special form of mental retardation, is the "idiot savant," a retardate with superior functioning in one narrow area of intellective activity. Perhaps the best-documented case history was kept by Scheerer, Rothman, and Goldstein (1945), who studied their subject intensively from his eleventh year through his sixteenth. During this period they gave the boy numerous problem-solving tasks and intelligence tests. L. was described as follows.

1. He had been failing at school, showing little interest in classroom activities and interacting minimally with classmates.

2. L. had developed the unusual talent of being able to provide, with little apparent thought, the day of the week for any date between 1880 and 1950. A favorite pastime was to ask people their birth dates and then immediately tell them on which day of the week they had been born and when their birthday would fall in any other given year, past or future. L. had been performing this feat since the age of seven. Scheerer and his colleagues point out, however, that he had no grasp of which of two people was the older, designating always the person whose birthday fell in an earlier part of the year. For example, he would regard anyone born on June 10 as being older than someone born on September 13, quite overlooking the year of birth or the physical appearance of the two people.

3. L. could quickly spell forward or backward practically any word pronounced to him, *but* without necessarily knowing its meaning or caring to.

4. The boy had a very well-developed but unusual musical ability. He could play many melodies on the piano by ear, that of Beethoven's "Moonlight Sonata," for example, but he seemed to have no grasp of what he was doing and took no enjoyment in it. He ignored any instructions or comments on his playing. Moreover, "He sings the accompaniment or the Italian words [to several operas] as they sound to him. Without knowing the language he reproduces it phonetically" (p. 2).

5. L.'s arithmetic ability was also unusual. He could, for example, add ten to twelve two-digit numbers as fast as they were recited to him, but he was unable to learn to add larger numbers. He could also count by 16 very rapidly—1, 17, 33, 49, and so on—but without any understanding of what the numbers meant; for instance, he could not state that 20 is larger than 8.

6. He easily learned the Gettysburg Address at age fourteen by rote memory, but without understanding its meaning.

Scheerer and his colleagues found L. to test at an IQ of 50 on the Binet scale, which classified him as moderately retarded. In their attempt to explain L.'s behavior, they rejected the idea that an idiot savant has a supernormal *ability* in one area. Rather they suggested that this kind of individual lacks the crucial ability to reason abstractly and that, given this serious handicap, he copes with the world by channeling his energy into rote memory feats. He develops rote skills to an unusually high degree because he can in essence do little else with his cortex. L.'s IQ rating was low because he could not perform tasks that children must handle in order to score in the normal range when they are eleven or older—namely tasks requiring abstract reasoning. For instance, shown an absurd picture of a man in the rain holding an umbrella upside down, the boy at age fifteen said "Yes, the man is holding an umbrella upside down. I don't know why, there is a lot of rain there" (p. 10). The overall problem was summarized by these workers as ". . . a general impairment of abstract capacity . . . , L. [even] succeeded in his own performance-specialities without having a genuine understanding of their meaning. . ." (p. 59).

rates at which they become toilet-trained and master walking vary more than might be expected from the description of the disorder. The interaction between diathesis, in this case the chromosomal anomaly, and stress, here the environment in which a person with a faulty brain is reared, is complex. The children do much better in a loving home than in an institution. With proper encouragement and instruction, adults with Down's syndrome can perform jobs such as simple carpentry and housework. Although it is unrealistic to expect even intensive remedial efforts to eradicate completely the adjustment problems of mongoloids, their potentials for intellectual and social growth have probably not been realized.

In *Klinefelter's syndrome* an extra X chromosome is usually at fault. This syndrome occurs only in males and accounts for about one percent of institutionalized male retardates. Only about 25 percent of males with this syndrome are retarded, and their retardation is likely to be mild or moderate rather than severe. The symptoms are usually noticed at puberty when the testes remain small and the boy develops feminine secondary sex characteristics such as enlarged hips.

### Recessive genes

When a pair of defective recessive genes misdirect the formation of an enzyme, metabolic processes are disturbed. The problem may affect development of the embryo in the uterus or may not become important until much later in life.

In *phenylketonuria* (PKU) the infant, born normal, soon suffers from a deficiency of liver enzyme, phenylalanine hydroxylase, which is needed to convert phenylalanine, an amino acid of protein foods, to tyrosine. Phenylalanine and its derivative phenylpyruvic acid build up in the body fluids, ultimately wreaking irreversible brain damage. The unmetabolized amino acid interferes with the process of myelination, the sheathing of neuron axons. This sheathing is essential for the rapid transmittal of impulses and thus of information in the nervous system. The neurons of the frontal lobes are particularly affected. Inasmuch as these areas of the cortex are known to be crucial for normal thinking—although *how* is not known—it is not surprising that

Children with Down's syndrome being taught in a special classroom.

A brother and sister, both of whom have PKU. The girl's diet was restricted early to reduce the serious consequences of the disease.

mental retardation is profound.

At about six months parents usually begin to notice a retardation in motor development and in general responsiveness. There may also be seizures and an unusual body odor from the presence of phenylpyruvic acid in the urine. Over 60 percent of children with PKU never learn to talk, about one-third cannot walk, and more than half have IQs of less than 20. In addition to their profound mental impairment, those with PKU have been described as unfriendly, restless, fearful, and occasionally destructive.

Although a very rare disorder, with an incidence of about one in 20,000 births, it is estimated that one person in seventy is a carrier of the recessive gene. Fortunately, prevention of extensive brain damage is facilitated by laboratory tests of an infant's blood for excessive phenylalanine. State laws require that this test be given four or five days after birth. If the test is positive, a diet low in phenylalanine is urged upon the parents as soon as possible. When the diet is restricted as early as the third month and until the age of six, when brain differentiation is relatively complete, cognitive development improves, sometimes to within the normal range (*Collaborative Study of Children Treated for Phenylketonuria,* 1975).

Hundreds of other recessive-gene disorders have been isolated, many of them causing mental retardation. Only a very minor percentage of the cases of mental retardation are accounted for by any single disorder, however. *Tay-Sachs disease,* a disorder of lipid metabolism transmitted by the pairing of single recessive genes, is found among Jews more often than any other ethnic group. In many metropolitan areas of the United States, large-scale screening programs provide Jewish couples with the blood tests that detect carriers. The child with Tay-Sachs disease suffers increasing muscular weakness, visual deterioration, and convulsions. He or she seldom lives beyond the third year (Kolb, 1968).

*Niemann-Pick disease,* also a fatal inherited dysfunction in lipid metabolism, causes gastrointestinal disturbances, malnutrition, and progressive paralysis. *Maple Syrup Urine disease* is an inherited defect in amino acid metabolism and receives its name from the odor of the infant's urine. Deterioration of the muscles accompanies cerebral deterioration, and the child seldom survives its first year. An infant afflicted with *Hurler's syndrome,* or gargoylism, soon develops an enlarged head with protruding forehead, bushy eyebrows, thick lips, and deformed limbs. Many of these children survive into their teens. Another metabolic disorder, the *Lesch-Nyhan syndrome,* is inherited through sex-linked recessive genes and seriously impairs the kidneys. It causes not only severe mental retardation but unusually aggressive and self-mutilating behavior. Although appearing normal at birth, these children, all of whom are boys, begin to manifest a delay in motor development at three to four months of age and then lose considerable motor control. Not surprisingly, institutionalization is the rule. These boys seem to be happiest when physically restrained. They appear terrified and are subject to loud, destructive outbursts when free to move about (Nyhan, 1973).

## Infectious Diseases Causing Mental Retardation

Even though the developing fetus has had a normal genetic beginning to its journey to life, it faces physical dangers that can bring on mental retardation. The speed and complexity of the development of the fetus's nervous system are unparalleled, especially during the first three months, or trimester. Later, by the time a baby is about six months old, cell division within the central nervous system ceases altogether and forever; the most serious consequence of this fact is that central nervous system cells can never be replaced if they are injured or destroyed. It sometimes appears miraculous that most human infants arrive on the scene unhurt and properly equipped and enter the first years of life unscathed by any degree of damage to the intricate brain. Fortunately, the overwhelming majority of births and subsequent early development are apparently quite normal and routine.

Both before birth—through contagion of the mother—and after birth, an inherently healthy fetus and infant can be subjected to an infection that causes mental retardation. If the mother is infected by *rubella* or German measles in the last six months of pregnancy, the fetus is usually not adversely affected. If, however, she contracts the disease during the first month of pregnancy, there is a 50 percent chance that her live-born child will suffer both mental abnormality and congenital physical defects, very often blindness. When the disease is contracted in the second month, the risk is reduced to 15 percent, in the third month to 10 percent (Kolb, 1968). Therapeutic abortions have been available for a number of years for pregnant mothers who have had German measles early in pregnancy; more importantly, vaccination to prevent rubella is now widely available.

*Syphilis* no longer causes as much mental retardation as it used to because in recent years pregnant women who are seen in prenatal clinics must have their blood tested. Many of the fetuses afflicted with congenital syphilis die before they are born. Others die during the first weeks of life. Congenital syphilis usually affects the child immediately if he or she lives, frequently causing mental retardation, blindness, and deafness. A rarer form is juvenile paresis. This disease begins to affect the central nervous system only after a number of symptom-free years, but thereafter intellectual deterioration is progressive (Robinson and Robinson, 1976).

Other very rare infectious diseases of the mother can affect the unborn child, among them *toxoplasmosis* (infection from a protozoanlike organism, *Toxoplasma*) and encephalitis. Heber (1970) concludes, however, that there are few "broad-based data upon which to assess the role of maternal infections (other than rubella and syphilis) in the production of mentally retarded offspring" (p. 46).

After birth, infectious diseases can also affect a child's developing brain. Encephalitis and meningococcal meningitis may cause irreversible brain damage and even death if contracted in infancy or early childhood. These infections in adulthood are usually far less serious, probably because the brain is largely developed by about the age of six. There are several forms of childhood meningitis, a disease in which the protective membranes of the brain are acutely inflamed and fever is very high. Even if the child survives and is not severely retarded, he or she is likely to be moderately or mildly so. Other disabling afteraffects are deafness, paralysis, and epilepsy.

## Traumas Causing Mental Retardation

Trauma of many kinds can cause mental retardation and other physical problems, either indirectly to the fetus through the mother or directly to the infant after birth. The specific forms and severity of disorders vary with the trauma; lead poisoning, Rh-factor incompatibility, carbon monoxide poisoning, too frequent exposure to X-rays, poor diet, birth injury, head injury, and certain drugs, including excessive alcohol intake by the mother, all have serious aftermaths.

*Rh factors* are substances that are present in the red blood cells of a large majority of human beings and other higher animals. When they are introduced into the blood of a person whose own does not contain them, they act as antigens or foreign substances and stimulate the production of antibodies. If the blood of a fetus contains Rh factors, through inheritance from the father, but that of the mother is Rh negative, lacking in Rh factors, these substances will be introduced into the mother's blood for the first time by the fetus. The mother produces antibodies which, when they in turn enter the bloodstream of the fetus, destroy red blood cells, and cause oxygen deprivation. Since it takes time for the mother to produce the antibodies, firstborn children are less likely to be affected by Rh incompatibility than are subsequent children. The brain damage from oxygen deprivation in Rh incompatibility can be extensive if not treated. In recent years newborn infants at risk have been given a complete blood transfusion, and most children recover. Heber's (1970) summary of various studies indicates that the IQs of children who have suffered from Rh incompatibility and been treated are lower than those of control group children, but they are still within the average range.

*Cretinism* is caused by a severe deficiency in the output of the thyroid gland and is characterized by profound intellectual deficit as well as physical defects. The untreated child who has suffered this deficiency since birth has a short, dwarflike body, coarse features, a swollen abdomen, and short, stubby limbs. Although several factors may diminish the activity of the thyroid, historically the major cause has been lack of iodine in the diet of the pregnant mother, iodine being the major ingredient needed for the production of the hormone thyroxin. The infant is born with defective thyroid glands which remain underdeveloped or atrophy. The symptoms of cretinism become apparent during the early months, for development is very slow, and the baby is not responsive or alert. The incidence of cretinism is now very low because of the widespread use of iodized salt. An infant born with a thyroid deficiency can be given thyroid extracts, making a relatively normal development possible in many instances.

It has been estimated that throughout the world 300 million preschool children suffer mild to moderate *malnutrition* (Behar, 1968). A poor diet, with protein deficiencies in particular, is believed to be especially harmful during the period of the brain's fastest growth. The consequences of moderate and chronic malnutrition are not as well known. The effects of malnutrition have been studied in several ways, by manipulating the diets of animals, by observing those of human beings, and by examining the brains of children who have died of malnutrition. Animal research has convincingly demonstrated the ill effects of poor diet on brain development (Davison and Dobbing, 1966). The total number of brain cells is permanently reduced if the animal suffers from malnutrition during periods when they are dividing. But we cannot easily generalize across species, and it would be unethical to try to replicate these studies with human infants. Some research, however, does reveal similar effects in human beings. In one study autopsies were performed on children who had died from malnutrition; all had a subnormal number of brain cells (Winick, Rosso, and Waterlow, 1970). In another study lower-class women were given multiple vitamins during pregnancy. They gave birth to children who, at age three, had higher IQs than those whose mothers had not had the special vitamin supplements (Harrell, Woodyard, and Gates, 1955). Thus there is some evidence that the pregnant woman's diet can influence the future IQ of the infant.

Recent years have seen heightened interest in and welcome action against the high levels of lead and mercury that have been allowed to poison the environment, causing brain damage and consequent mental retardation. Screening of children in some of our largest cities, both those who live in slums and those who do not, has often revealed toxic levels of lead in their blood. Slum children sometimes ingest lead by eating chips of paint. The paint applied indoors used to be lead-based. Now laws prohibit indoor household paint from containing lead, and landlords are instructed to remove old coatings that contain this poision. City children living in more fortunate circumstances may also have dangerously high blood levels of lead, apparently because they, as well as slum children, breathe in automobile emissions. For this reason, among others, newer cars are built to run on unleaded gasoline. Adults are not immune to the ravages of lead poisoning, but children, not surprisingly, are more susceptible to its effects (Robinson and Robinson, 1976).

Mercury has been similarly indicted as a cause of mental retardation; the accompanying neurological damage can bring on problems in kidney function and walking and can even cause cerebral palsy. Certain industrial wastes containing mercury, dumped carelessly into rivers and lakes, have led to tragic illnesses in Japan and in this country. Vigorous action has been brought against offending industries. Too often, however, economic considerations bring evasive maneuvers that delay control of both mercury and lead, and they continue to wreak irreversible brain damage.

If the cells of the brain are completely deprived of oxygen for even a few short seconds during any period of the life cycle, they will die. *Anoxia,* which is usually only partial but still

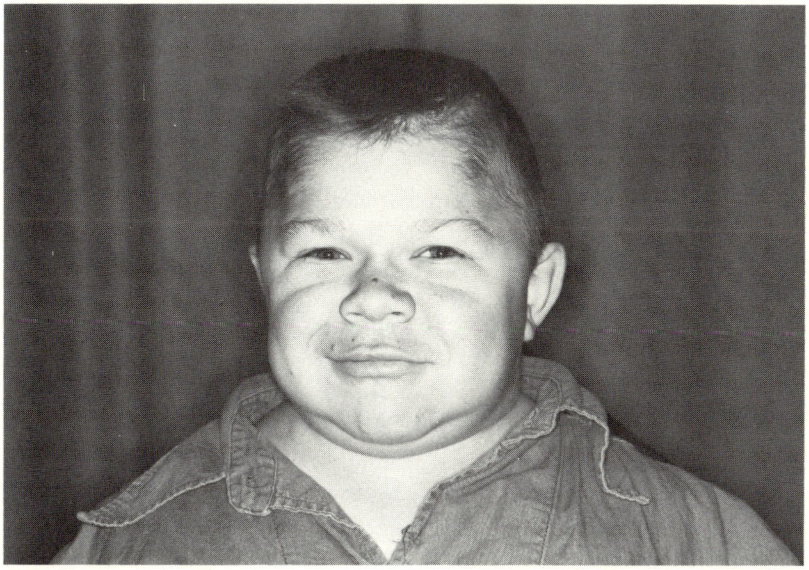

Cretinism, caused by a deficiency in the output of the thyroid gland, is one of the severe forms of mental retardation. The features of this afflicted child are characteristically coarse.

causes irreparable damage because the rate of metabolism in the brain is lowered, can occur before, during, or after birth. Research with animals has shown the harmful effects of oxygen deprivation, but generalization to human beings may be unwarranted. Summarizing the results of research with human beings, Heber (1970) concludes that children who suffered oxygen deprivation at birth do not differ greatly in intelligence from controls. He believes that studies stressing the role of neonatal anoxia as an important cause of retardation are usually based on retrospective analysis of the histories of retarded persons and have failed to include appropriate nonretarded control groups.

When *prematurity* of birth is separated from the other variables that commonly accompany it—poor socioeconomic status, maternal age, health, medical care—there seems to be little relationship between it and neurological deficit or mental retardation. Robinson and Robinson (1976) conclude that prematurity per se is not usually dangerous to mental development, although the risk of retardation in children who are very small at birth, whether or not they are premature, is quite high.[5]

[5] Of course, premature babies tend to be of below-average size at birth. Thus an infant premature enough to be very small has a higher risk of being mentally retarded.

## Cultural-Familial Causes of Mental Retardation

As serious as the retardations attributed to various known and suspected single-factor organic causes may be, the majority of people considered retarded are only mildly so and do not have any identifiable physiological damage. The diagnosis of cultural-familial retardation is made on the basis of three criteria: mild retardation, no indication of brain pathology, and evidence of retardation in at least one of the parents or in one or more of the siblings. Very often mild retardation does not become evident until the child has trouble in school.

### Family Backgrounds of the Cultural-Familial Retarded

Robinson and Robinson (1976) report that a sizable proportion of the cultural-familial retarded come from stable lower-class families. There is steady employment, and the child's physical needs are met fairly adequately. But the intellectual and educational level in the home is low; few of the parents have IQs that exceed the borderline range (Heber, 1970). A large number of families live at this low socioeconomic level, making the incidence of cultural-familial retardation very great.

Children classified as cultural-familial retarded may also come from unstable, poverty-stricken families. In such homes shelter, food, clothing, and medical care are inadequate. The intelligence and intellectual achievement of the parents is very low. The family is often disrupted and disintegrating, providing no social, emotional, or motivational support for the child.

Many research findings document the accuracy of these dismal characterizations of the homelife of the child with cultural-familial retardation. Benda and his colleagues (1963) studied the families of 205 institutionalized mentally retarded children. The children had no obvious neurological symptoms, were four to fifteen years old, and had IQs above 50. Only 13 of the 205 children came from homes in which there was no apparent mental retardation in the immediate family. Only one-fourth of the families were both intact and able to provide even minimum food, shelter, clothing, and protection from danger. In most of the families certain members had violated societal norms severely enough to have had legal action taken against them. This study was somewhat biased, however, for a mildly retarded child is usually institutionalized only when the family unit cannot provide for his or her needs. The backgrounds of these children were probably worse than those of retarded children in general.

Not all children who are reared in deprived environments are retarded, however. Heber (1970) correlated the IQ scores of eighty-eight mothers in a city slum with their children's test scores and found that a minority of the mothers had given birth to a majority of the children whose IQs were in the mildly retarded range. For example, 17 percent of mothers with IQs of less than 68 had reared 54.5 percent of the children in that range and 32.9 percent of the children with IQs of 68 to 83.

Offspring of mothers whose IQs were less than 80, approximately half the sample, showed a decrement in measured intelligence with increasing age; the older children of these mothers had lower IQ scores than their younger siblings. Only 20 percent of the children less than six years of age had IQs lower than 80, but 50 percent of the children between seven and twelve years of age tested below 80, as did over 90 percent of those thirteen years of age. This tendency for scores to decrease as children grow older in deprived socioeconomic environments is often interpreted as evidence of the serious effects of such environments on intellectual development. The children of mothers who scored closer to the normal range, however, showed no decrease in intelligence as they grew older. Fewer than 20 percent of these children, regardless of their age, had IQs of less than 80. The deleterious effects of living in an impoverished environment are less if the mother's IQ is near average.

## Problems of Interpretation

The effects of deprivation are very complex. Lower-class mothers tend to have poor diets, which can retard normal development of the fetus. As a growing child the ghetto youngster may eat chips of lead-based paint. The schools may not be as good, and the parents may never read books or even newspapers or intellectually stimulate their children. The family members may seldom venture from the few blocks of their neighborhood. But even knowing that a child is brought up in physical, cultural, and intellectual poverty does not always mean that environment is totally responsible for retardation. As Zigler (1968) has stated, "It is one thing to assert that the environment plays a role in determining the range of individual differences, and quite another to say that environmental events can cause the individual born with a normal intellect to be retarded or that they can prevent retardation" (p. 528).

Some, however, feel that the relationship between poverty and mental retardation should no longer be regarded as correlational. Hurley (1969) feels that the evidence is sufficient to demonstrate that *poverty causes mental retardation*. The child reared in poverty is affected by innumerable intellectually stunting factors—both organic and environmental—ranging from the poor nutrition and the lack of prenatal care of his mother to his own malnutrition, his emotionally and intellectually deprived home and neighborhood, and the failure of his school system. These factors, either singly or in combination, may cause the kind of retardation that has been termed cultural-familial. The implication drawn by Hurley is that by eradicating poverty the majority of cases of mental retardation would be eliminated.

## A Challenge to the Concept of Cultural-Familial Retardation

Family problems may lead to the inappropriate institutionalization of some children. In one part of a larger investigation, Braginsky and Braginsky

## BOX 17.2 Avoidable Mental Retardation

We were reminded earlier that despite the numerous dangers to the developing fetus in utero and to the growing child, the overwhelming majority of births yield intact babies. But it is also clear that parents must bear considerable responsibility to make certain that their babies are born healthy. Sensible care during pregnancy is not too difficult, given a minimum economic level. A woman who even suspects that she is pregnant can make sure that her diet is adequate, avoid unnecessary use of drugs, and decline medical X-rays, such as those that dentists take to detect cavities.

The controversial issue of eugenics must also be considered in any discussion of the control of childbearing and child rearing. It has been estimated that of the approximately 9000 mongoloid children born each year in the United States, two-thirds would not be conceived if women completed their childbearing by the age of forty (Sarason, 1972). We are now far afield of psychiatry and psychology per se, however, for what are the ethics of making a recommendation based on this estimate when the vast majority of pregnancies of mothers over forty do *not* yield mongoloid infants? And yet, as already noted, most states *require* testing an infant for PKU, and individual liberties do not appear thereby to have been infringed upon in any important way. But should society go so far as to advocate or require *sterilization* of those who have already given birth to deformed or severely retarded children? What about the mother who stands a one-in-ten chance of bearing a blind, retarded child because she has contracted rubella in her third month? Is our obligation to the unborn child better served by terminating a risky pregnancy or by taking the chance of allowing, or forcing, the birth of a child whose physical and mental handicaps may be devastating? Indeed, does the generally happy mongoloid child—especially if kept at home by courageous and loving parents—enjoy life any less than, for example, the harried suburban commuter who daily consumes 40 milligrams of Valium and 8 ounces of scotch, or the ghetto child whose opportunities may be significantly compromised by the color of his skin?

(1971) interviewed cultural-familial retarded children, asking them why they thought they had been institutionalized. Ninety-three percent did not believe that they were retarded and instead gave replies suggesting that difficulties within the family had prompted the decision to institutionalize them as retardates.

> *I hate to mention it. . . . I was living with my real mother and she died and so my father came home from the service and picked me up and my father found another woman so he married her and I'm his son and my brother's stepbrother. . . . My stepmother ain't so good to me. See my father wants me out, but my mother wants me here. My stepmother, she wants me here, my father wants me out. So I don't know which it's going to be (p. 140).*

Braginsky and Braginsky (1971) have argued that the concept of familial retardation should be abandoned altogether, for they feel that the label retarded simply does not apply. From a series of investigations they concluded that familial retardates could

> *. . . carry out successfully subtle manipulative strategies. They were capable of protecting their self-interests by using complex tactics of impression management such as ingratiating themselves with the staff. . . . Many of the retardates were able even to implement life styles that were counter to the values of the institutions (p. 175).*

In one of the studies that helped Braginsky and Braginsky to draw this conclusion, two groups of retarded children were told that they were going to be given an intelligence test. The experimenter instructed these two groups of retarded children separately as follows.

> I'm going to show you some pictures and say some words. When I say a word, show me which of the pictures best fits it. Some of the words are going to be rather hard. Just say you "don't know." (*Then after the subject completes the first test*) That was fine, but it was only a practice test. I'm going to throw this one away and give you another one very similar to the test you just took. (*Experimenter crumples test and tosses it in wastebasket.*) Before we start the real test I think I should tell you why we are testing you. The State is thinking about starting a new training program for mentally retarded youngsters. I can't tell you the details about the new program, but from what I've heard, I really don't think you would like it. To me it sounded really terrible. Well, they want us to test a group of kids to see if they should be put in this new training program. You see, they only want to take
>
> Condition I. kids who do well on this test—who get good IQ scores.
> Condition II. kids who do poorly on this test—who get really low IQ scores.
>
> Okay, now that you know why I'm testing you, let's begin the *real* IQ test. What's your name? (*Experimenter writes subject's name in obvious way.*) You have to do the same thing as before, only now there will be different words and different pictures (pp. 70–71).

A third group of retarded children, the control group, received the following instructions after the completion of the first test. "That was fine, but it was only a practice test. I'm going to throw this one away and give you another one very similar to the test you just took. Okay? What's your name?" (p. 71).

Figure 17.2 compares the results of the two tests taken by the three groups. The mental-age scores of those in the control group did not change, but those of subjects who took the second test under condition I decreased and those who took it under condition II increased. When a high mental-age score would have meant transfer to the presumably undesirable training situation, scores decreased from the first to the second session. Similarly, when a low score would have meant transfer, mental age increased. Clearly, the retardates in this study were sensitive and adaptive to the situation presented them. Should they be considered retarded?

We believe so. The Braginsky and Braginsky study does show that some retarded children can effectively manipulate what they consider to be their social environments. The children proved sensitive to certain social cues and were able to modify their test performance *within* certain limits. But such results do *not* necessarily indicate that the children are not retarded. Nor do they prove that these children cannot benefit from specially designed programs and do not sometimes need institutionalization. To abandon entirely the concept of familial retardation, one would have to demonstrate that these children are able to cope with normal school and social demands.

Yet the mildly retarded, who come primarily from culturally deprived backgrounds, are considered backward only within a cultural context that emphasizes the importance of the "three Rs"—reading, writing, and arithmetic. Only in modern societies such as our own have psychologists developed IQ tests to measure the intel-

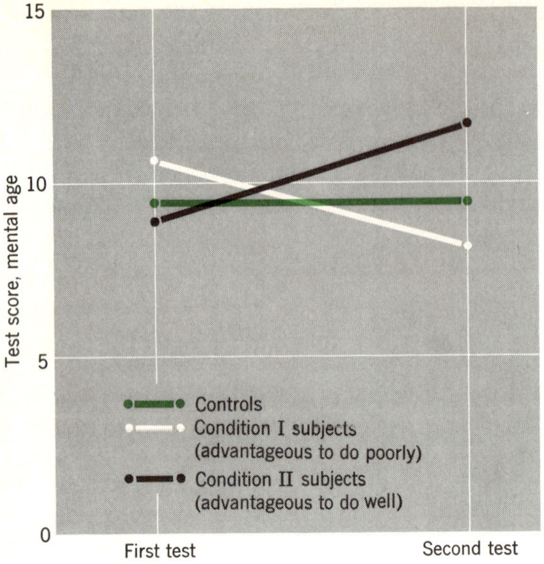


FIGURE **17.2**
Results of Braginsky and Braginsky's experiment (1971), indicating that cultural-familial retardates were able to alter their IQ scores when they thought it would help them avoid a new training program described as undesirable.

lectual functioning of children. Given the nature of our educational system and the society for which it is supposed to prepare people, IQ tests are very good at predicting how children will do in school. But it is only because of these tests that we have been able to talk about high IQs versus low and thereby designate children as bright or below normal. Nonindustrialized societies, which are without our kind of intelligence testing, would not conceive of cultural-familial retardation.

## Summary

A diagnosis of mental retardation is reserved for people who score below a certain level on IQ tests, adapt poorly to social demands and expectations, and show these problems before age eighteen. Several difficulties with determining intelligence and social adaptation were discussed. Much of the recent work in retardation has focused on an experimental analysis of what are believed to be the specific cognitive processes underlying intelligence and learning.

The search for causes, as has been true with all the other psychopathologies, encompasses both physiological and sociopsychological variables. Most of the severely retarded are known to suffer from prenatal and postnatal organic diseases. Serious physical abnormalities very often accompany the mental retardation caused by such diseases. Fortunately, some of these illnesses can be prevented or ameliorated by attention to diet and careful prenatal care.

Most mentally retarded, however, do not have physiological damage that has as yet been identified. This group, generally called the cultural-familial retarded, are assumed by many workers to have been exposed to environments that do not provide the intellectual stimulation and encouragement necessary for normal and superior mental growth. Unequivocal data, however, are not available, and it may be that many of these children actually suffer from traumatic organic disorders that are fostered by deprivation, and that have not yet been adequately distinguished. Whatever the original causes, the overwhelming majority of retarded children can achieve higher levels of intellectual and social functioning with appropriate training.

# part six
# treatment

# chapter 18

## INSIGHT THERAPY



Up to now we have reviewed the nature and development of abnormal behavior. Another important aspect of abnormal psychology is the work of clinicians, or therapists, who try to *relieve* the kinds of human suffering we have described. As we have seen, many myths prevail about the development of abnormal behavior; reliance on the unsubstantiated is at least as great in the field of psychotherapy. Once again, it will be important to maintain a skeptical, critical stance as we review what is known about therapy and how people are gathering new knowledge about it.

Shorn of its theoretical complexities, any psychotherapy is a set of procedures by which one person uses language to change the life of another—so-called "talking cures." The underlying assumption is that particular kinds of verbal interchanges in a trusting relationship can achieve certain specific goals, such as reduction of anxiety and elimination of self-defeating or dangerous behavior.

Simple as this definition may seem, there is little general agreement about what *really* constitutes psychotherapy. A person's next-door neighbor might utter the same words of comfort as would a clinical psychologist, but should we regard this as psychotherapy? In what way is psychotherapy different from such nonprofessional reassurance? Is the distinction made on the straightforward basis of whether the dispenser of reassurance has an academic degree or license? Does it relate to whether the giver of information has a theory that dictates or at least guides what he or she says? Does it depend on how sound the basic assumptions of the theory are? These are difficult questions, and, as in other areas of abnormal psychology, there is a lack of agreement about the answers to them.

Another problem in the study of psychotherapy is the great number and variety of therapeutic activities and theories. There are scores, perhaps hundreds, of schools of therapy, each with its band of enthusiastic adherents (both therapists and patients) proposing procedures ranging from screaming and writhing nude on the floor to forced inactivity and sleep for several weeks. One could almost say, "You name it, someone thinks it's therapeutic." Because it would be impossible and unenlightening to examine every school, we have opted for a focused review of the field, presenting sufficient detail about the more important approaches to allow a grasp of the basic issues and an overall perspective on the enterprise of changing behavior in a therapeutic context.

London (1964) categorizes psychotherapies into *insight* and *action* (behavioral) therapies. Behavior therapy is the subject of Chapter 19. Insight therapy, the topic in this chapter, assumes that behavior becomes disordered because people do not adequately understand what is motivating their actions, especially when different needs and drives conflict. Insight therapy tries to help them discover the true reasons they behave as they do. The assumption is that greater awareness of motivations will yield greater control over behavior and subsequent improvement in it. The emphasis is less on changing behavior directly than on uncovering its causes—both historical and current. To facilitate such insights, therapists of different theoretical persuasions have employed a variety of techniques, ranging from the free association of psychoanalysis to the reflective procedures of client-centered therapies.

The focus in this chapter and the next is on individual therapy, that is, therapy conducted by a clinician with one patient or client. But it should be noted that nearly everything said in these two chapters is relevant also for therapy in *groups,* a subject dealt with more completely as one of three principal topics in Chapter 20.

## The Placebo Effect

For reasons that will become clear, it is appropriate to begin our discussion of psychotherapy with what has become known as the *placebo effect.* The term refers to improvement in physical or psychological condition that is attributable to a patient's expectations of help rather than to any specific active ingredient in a treatment. Although the word placebo generally refers to a pill or capsule that has no pharmacologically active substance—the familiar "sugar pill"—the term placebo effect need not be restricted to therapy with an inert pill. It can also apply to therapeutic results, both psychological and physiological, brought about by any method that has no demonstrable specific action on the disorder being treated.

Shapiro (1960) concludes that until recently the history of medication has been largely a history of placebo effects, that drugs have benefited people only to the extent they were believed in. Frank (1973) relates placebo effects to faith healing in prescientific or nonscientific societies. For centuries, suffering human beings have derived benefit from making pilgrimages to sanctified places such as Lourdes and from ingesting sometimes foul-smelling concoctions.

Many people tend to dismiss placebo reactions as "not real" or second-best. After all, if a person has a tension headache, what possible benefit can he or she hope to get from a pill that is totally devoid of chemical action or direct physiological effect? The fact is, however, that such benefits are often significant and even long-lasting. For example, Lasagna and his colleagues (1965) reported impressive relief from pain in surgical patients receiving saline injections. And Frank (1973) furnishes extensive evidence attesting to improvement in a variety of physical and mental problems after the ingestion of pills and from exposure to other ministrations that, in themselves, could not possibly account for improvement.

A psychotherapist who places great stock in a particular theory may not like to think that his or her professional activities have no power other than to mobilize a person's expectancies for help. But research on psychotherapy offers scant reassurance to the contrary (Bergin, 1971). Many researchers agree that in psychotherapy, as in much of medicine, *the most reliable effect is the placebo effect.*

The phenomenon of the placebo effect has far-reaching implications concerning the controls that must be designed into experiments. If every therapy procedure—however rationalized by its proponents—has placebo elements, it is essential to include a placebo control group in any experiment examining the efficacy of a technique. A good example of this practice is Paul's (1966) experiment on systematic desensitization, discussed in the next chapter. The use of placebo controls in insight therapy research, in contrast, is quite rare.

## Psychoanalytic Therapy

Despite the numerous critical attacks made on psychoanalytic theory and the denials that psychoanalytic therapy is effective, psychoanalysis and its many offshoots remain the dominant force in American psychiatry and clinical psychology. In this section we will try to summarize the important features of both classical—that is, traditional—psychoanalysis and ego analysis.

### Basic Techniques of Psychoanalysis

Classical psychoanalysis relates to Freud's second theory of anxiety, according to which neurotic anxiety is the reaction of the ego when a previously punished and repressed id impulse presses for expression (Freud, 1949). Tension or anxiety is created when the unconscious part of the ego encounters a situation reminding it of a repressed conflict from childhood. The situation usually concerns sexual or aggressive impulses (see page 118). Psychoanalytic therapy attempts to remove this earlier repression and to help the patient face the childhood conflict and resolve it in the light of adult reality. The repression, occurring so long ago, has prevented the ego from growing in an adult fashion, and the lifting of the repression is supposed to enable this relearning to take place. Treatment typically extends over several years, with as many as five sessions a week.

The essence of classical psychoanalysis, and to a large extent that of ego analysis, has been captured by Paul Wachtel (1977) in the metaphor of the *woolly mammoth*. Some of these gigantic creatures, frozen alive eons ago, have been recovered so perfectly preserved that their meat can actually be eaten. Neurotic problems were considered by Freud to be the encapsulated residue of conflicts from long ago. Present adult problems are merely reflections or expressions of these "frozen" intrapsychic conflicts.

> *The patient's neurosis is seen as deriving most essentially from his continuing and*

The photograph at top left shows the room in which Freud saw many of the patients written about in his famous psychoanalytic cases. Below left, the ailing Freud sits working at his desk. Above is a portrait of Freud at twenty with his fiancée, Martha Bernays.

*unsuccessful efforts to deal with internalized residues of his past* [the "woolly mammoth"] *which, by virtue of being isolated from his adaptive and integrated ego, continue to make primitive demands wholly unresponsive to reality. It is therefore maintained that a fully successful treatment must create conditions whereby these anachronistic inclinations can be experienced consciously and integrated into the ego, so that they can be controlled and modified* (*Wachtel, 1977, p. 36*).

A number of techniques are used by psychoanalysts to facilitate the recovery of conflicts that have been repressed. Perhaps the best known and most important is *free association:* the patient, reclining on a *couch,* is encouraged to give free rein to thoughts and feelings, and to verbalize whatever comes into his mind. The assumption is that with enough practice free association will facilitate the uncovering of unconscious material. The analysand must follow the fundamental rule of reporting thoughts and feelings as accurately as possible, without screening out the elements he feels are unimportant or shameful. Freud assumed that thoughts and memories occurred in associative chains and that recent ones reported first would ultimately trace back to earlier crucial ones. In order to get to these earlier events, however, the therapist has to be very careful not to guide or direct the patient's thinking, and the patient must not monitor his thoughts. Ford and Urban (1963) have paraphrased the analyst's directions for free association.

> *In ordinary conversation, you usually try to keep a connecting thread running through your remarks, excluding any intrusive ideas or side issues so as not to wander too far from the point, and rightly so. But in this case you must talk differently. As you talk various thoughts will occur to you which you like to ignore because of certain criticisms and objections. You will be tempted to think, "That is irrelevant or unimportant, or nonsensical," and to avoid saying it. Do not give in to such criticism. Report such thoughts in spite of your wish not to do so. Later, the reason for this injunction, the only one you have to follow, will become clear. Report whatever goes through your mind. Pretend that you are a traveler, describing to someone beside you the changing views which you see outside the train window* (p. 168).

But blocks do arise, virtually thrusting themselves across the thoughts supposedly given free rein. Such obstacles to free association were noted by Freud and contributed to the development of the concept of repression. He asserted that interference with free association is traceable to unconscious control over sensitive areas; it is precisely these areas that psychoanalytic therapists must thoroughly probe.

Akin to free association is the *study of dreams*. Freud assumed that during sleep the ego defenses are lowered, allowing repressed material to come forth, usually in disguised form. The dreams take on a heavily symbolic content,

A moment in a psychoanalytic session.

which helps protect the conscious ego from the true significance of dream material. The substance of dreams, then, is distorted by unconscious defensive structures which continue to fight to protect the ego from repressed impulses.

As presumably unconscious material begins to appear, another technique comes into play, *interpretation*. According to Freud, this stage helps the person face the hitherto repressed and emotionally loaded conflict. At the "right time" the analyst begins to point out to the patient his defenses and the underlying meaning of his dreams. Interpretation is the analyst's principal weapon against the continued use of defense mechanisms. After noting that they are present, as revealed by obstacles in free association, the analyst makes the patient more aware of his defenses through interpretations. He points out how certain verbalizations of the patient relate to repressed unconscious material. He may also suggest what the manifest content of dreams *truly* means. If the interpretation is timed correctly, the patient can begin to examine the repressed impulse in the light of present-day reality. In other words, he can begin to realize that he no longer has to fear the expression of the impulse. This realization leads to further relaxation of defenses and to still greater accessibility of repressed material.

In order to achieve the goal of making the unconscious conscious through appropriately timed interpretation, the therapist has to create certain conditions within the therapy hour. He must attempt at all times to be neutral and objective, imposing no moral judgments on the person. He must at all costs not impose his own needs and desires on the patient's verbalizations and behavior, and it is for this reason that analysts, as part of their training, must go through psychoanalytic treatment, or a *Lehranalyse* (training analysis). Feeling safe under the undemanding conditions arranged by the analyst, the patient presumably uncovers more and more repressed material. Interpretations are held to be particularly helpful in establishing the meaning of *resistances* that disturb the patient's free association. The therapist points out how the patient avoids a topic, and it is common for the analysand to deny the interpretation. Interestingly, this denial is sometimes interpreted as a sign that the therapist's interpretation is correct rather than incorrect. In the slow process of "working through," the patient gradually faces up to the validity of the analyst's interpretations, often with great emotion. At the same time, however, the therapist must be careful not to force his interpretations on the patient.

The core of psychoanalytic therapy is the *transference neurosis*. Being a good observer, Freud noted that some of his patients acted toward him in an emotion-charged and unrealistic way. For example, a patient much older than Freud would behave in a childish manner during a therapy session. Although these reactions were often positive and loving, many times they were quite negative and hostile. Since these feelings seemed out of character with the ongoing therapy relationship, Freud assumed that they were relics of attitudes, *transferred* to him from those held in the past toward important people in the patient's history, primarily parents. That is, he felt that patients responded to him *as if* he were one of the important people in their past. Freud utilized this transference of attitudes, which he came to consider an inevitable aspect of psychoanalysis, as a means of explaining to patients the childhood origin of many of their concerns and fears. This revelation and explanation tended also to help lift repressions and allow the confrontation of hitherto buried impulses. In psychoanalysis transference is regarded as essential to a complete cure. Indeed, it is precisely when the analyst notices transference developing that he begins to believe that the important neurotic conflict from childhood is being approached. An analyst encourages the development of transference by intentionally remaining a shadowy figure, typically sitting behind the patient while the patient free-associates and serving as a relatively blank screen on which the important persons in the neurotic conflicts can be projected. Because the therapy setting is so different from the childhood

## BOX **18.1** Excerpt from a Psychoanalytic Session, an Illustration of Transference

*Patient* (a fifty-year-old male business executive): I really don't feel like talking today.

*Analyst:* (Remains silent for several minutes, then) Perhaps you'd like to talk about why you don't feel like talking.

*Patient:* There you go again, making demands on me, insisting I do what I just don't feel up to doing. (Pause) Do I always have to talk here, when I don't feel like it? (Voice becomes angry and petulant) Can't you just get off my back? You don't really give a damn how I feel, do you?

*Analyst:* I wonder why you feel I don't care.

*Patient:* Because you're always pressuring me to do what I feel I can't do.

**Comments.** This excerpt must be viewed in context. The patient had been in therapy for about a year, complaining of depression and anxiety. Although extremely successful in the eyes of his family and associates, he himself felt weak and incompetent. Through many sessions of free association and dream analysis, the analyst had begun to suspect that the patient's feelings of failure stemmed from his childhood experiences with an extremely punitive and critical father, a man even more successful than the client, and a person who seemed never to be satisfied with his son's efforts. The exchange quoted was later interpreted by the analyst as an expression of resentment by the patient of his *father's* pressures on him and had little to do with the analyst himself. The patient's tone of voice (petulant), as well as his overreaction to the analyst's gentle suggestion that he talk about his feelings of not wanting to talk, indicated that the patient was angry not at his analyst but at his father. The expression of such feelings to the analyst, that is, transferring them from the father to the analyst, was regarded as significant by the therapist and was used in subsequent sessions in helping the patient to reevaluate his childhood fears of expressing aggression toward his father.

situation, the therapist can readily point out to the patient the irrational nature of his fears and concerns (see Box 18.1).

An important implication of this review of classical psychoanalysis is the care the analyst must exercise *not* to become actively involved in helping the analysand deal with everyday problems. Such involvement, it is assumed, will detract from the development of the transference neurosis. The analyst assiduously avoids any intervention, such as a direct suggestion how to behave in a troublesome situation. Short-term relief might deflect the patient's efforts to uncover the repressed conflicts. This tactic is directly opposite to the thrust of behavior therapy. For now, suffice it to say that the behavior therapist, unconcerned with factors that are presumed by analysts to be buried in the unconscious, concentrates precisely on what the analyst ignores, namely helping patients change their attitudes, feelings, and overt behavior in concrete, current life situations. What the analyst, and to a large degree the ego analyst, terms "supportive therapy," the behavior therapist regards as the essence of therapy. By the same token, what the behavior therapist sees as unnecessary and even detrimental to the client—digging into the repressed past—is judged by the analyst to be essential to complete psychotherapeutic treatment.

We turn now to some of the recent modifications of psychoanalytic theory and therapy based on them.

## Ego Analysis

The most important modifications in psychoanalytic theory come from a group generally referred to as ego analysts. Their views are often seen as constituting contemporary Freudian psychoanalysis. The major figures in this loosely formed movement include Karen Horney (1942), Anna Freud (1946), Erik Erikson (1950), David Rapaport (1951), and Heinz Hartmann (1958). Basically, these writers regard Freud's model of man as too dependent on instinctual drives. Although Freud by no means ignored the interactions of the organism with the environment, his view was essentially a "push model" in which people are driven by intrapsychic urges. The ego analysts place greater emphasis on a person's ability to control the environment and to select the time and the means for satisfying certain instinctual drives. The concept of *control,* first introduced in Chapter 5, is quite important to ego analysts. They tend also to focus on current living conditions to a greater extent than Freud did, although they still advocate delving deeply into the historical causes of an individual's behavior.

*The ego analysts do not view man as an automaton pushed hither and yon by imperative innate energies on the one hand and by situational events on the other, constantly seeking some compromise among these conflicting influences. When behavior develops in a healthy fashion, man controls both it and the influence of situational events, selectively responding to consequences he has thoughtfully selected. . . . Man is not at the mercy of either [innate energies or situational events]. He can impose delay and thought between innate energies and action, thus postponing the reduction of such energies indefinitely. Learned responses, primarily thought, make this possible, and although originally they*

Karen Horney, one of the important ego analysts. They believe that the ego has substantial energy of its own, and that it can be helped to exert control over both the intrapsychic and the external environments.

> *may be learned as a consequence of their energy-reducing function, later they may become relatively independent of such influences (drives) and control them (Ford and Urban, 1963, pp. 187–188).*

We have, then, a set of important *ego functions* which are primarily conscious, capable of controlling both id instincts and the external environment, and which, more significantly, do not depend on the id for their energy. Ego analysts assume that these functions and capabilities are present at birth and then develop through experience. These ego functions, which Freud underemphasized, have energies and gratifications of their own, usually separate from the reduction of id impulses. And whereas society was, for Freud, essentially a negative inhibition against the unfettered gratification of libidinal impulses, the ego analysts hold that an individual's social interactions can provide their own special kind of gratification.

In spite of these changes, however, we cannot conclude that most ego analysts have entirely renounced Freud's repression ("woolly mammoth") theory. Consider this from Karen Horney.

> *The . . . task awaiting the patient is to change those factors within himself which interfere with his best development. This does not mean only a gross modification in action or behavior, such as gaining or regaining the capacity for public performance, for creative work . . . or losing phobias or tendencies toward depression. These changes will automatically take place in a successful analysis. They are not primary changes, however, but result from less visible changes within the personality . . . (1942, pp. 117–118).*

## The Interpersonal Views of Harry Stack Sullivan

The views on the development of normal and abnormal behavior held by the American psychiatrist Sullivan are generally considered to be a variation of ego psychology, although some writers label him "interpersonal," others neo-Freudian. His primary contributions derive from his emphasis on the interpersonal nature of emotional problems. The basic difficulty of patients, according to Sullivan, is so-called *parataxic distortions,* which are misperceptions of reality stemming from some disorganization in the interpersonal relationships of childhood. The disturbed attitudes toward people who were significant in the person's past are from that time forward projected unconsciously into all interpersonal relationships, including that between patient and therapist (Wolberg, 1954). The principal goal of therapy is to bring these distortions to the patient's consciousness so that he or she can evaluate present reality and separate it from past conditioning and learning.

So far Sullivan appears traditionally Freudian, with his strong emphasis on the childhood

Harry Stack Sullivan, the American ego analyst. He believed that psychological disturbance can be traced to anxiety about interpersonal relations learned in childhood, and that help lies in examining this anxiety in the context of the therapist-patient relationship.

sources of adult problems and the need to help the analysand achieve insight into the infantile origins of current difficulties. But he was also very directive and present-oriented, recommending that the therapist inform the patient of fairly predictable consequences of contemplated actions (Wachtel, 1977). Moreover, Sullivan is perhaps most noted for his conception of the analyst as a "participant observer" in the therapy process. In contrast to the classical or even ego-analytical view of the therapist as a blank screen for the transference neurosis, Sullivan argued that the therapist, like the scientist, is inevitably a part of the process he or she is studying. An analyst does not "see" patients without at the same time affecting them. What patients do and say—or do not do and say—is determined not only by what they bring to the therapy session but by how they interact with the therapist. Even a silent or "invisible" analyst will elicit a reaction from the patient (Sullivan, 1953).

Sullivan was relatively vague, however, about the means by which patients were actually to be changed. For example, it is not clear whether Sullivan assumed that realization on the part of the patient of the role a given interpersonal relationship has played in his discomfort will automatically lead to a reduction of anxiety. Like the other ego analysts, Sullivan provided relatively sparse descriptions of specific therapeutic techniques (Ford and Urban, 1963). He did, however, alert Freudians to the importance of using the interpersonal setting of therapy to help patients understand their maladaptive ways of dealing with the world.

## Evaluation of Analytic Therapy

There are few issues in clinical and experimental circles more controversial than the question whether psychoanalysis and related therapies work. Some clinicians are uneasy with the psychoanalytic concepts themselves, especially those that seem wedded to a notion of *an* unconscious. As Levy puts it, ". . . nothing can be said by the canons of modern philosophy of science, of the existence of the unconscious as a substantive entity: the assertion of its existence is in principle untestable and hence meaningless" (1963, p. 22).

This harsh judgment points up one of the underlying themes of this textbook, namely the problem of paradigms. Those who think in psychoanalytic terms might themselves take issue with "the canons of modern philosophy of science." This paradigmatic difference bears on any evaluation of the effectiveness of psychoanalysis (in all its various forms). What, for example, are the criteria for improvement? A principal criterion is the lifting of repressions, making the unconscious conscious. But how is that to be demonstrated? How do we determine whether a repression has been lifted? In practice, attempts to assess outcome have relied very heavily on projective tests like the Rorschach, which, in turn, rely heavily on the concept of the unconscious. Clearly, if that very concept is rejected a priori, there is little common ground for discussion.

Further controversies surround the central concept of insight. Rather than accept the view that insight entails the recognition by the client of some important, externally valid historical connection or relationship, several writers (for example, Bandura, 1969; London, 1964) propose that the development of insight is better understood as a *social conversion process,* whereby the patient comes to accept the belief system of his or her therapist. Marmor (1962) has suggested that insight means different things depending on the school of therapy; a patient treated by a proponent of any one of the various schools gets insights along the lines of its particular theoretical predilections. For example, Freudians tend to elicit insights regarding oedipal dilemmas, whereas Sullivanians produce insights regarding interpersonal relationships. Indeed, Levy (1963) goes so far as to say that the concept of the unconscious is actually nothing more than a disagreement between what a psychoanalytically oriented therapist and the analysand believe to be the explanation of the client's predicament.

Criticisms such as these are difficult to evaluate because the effectiveness of various therapies is difficult to judge. The insight therapists argue that the worth or validity of a particular insight is to be gauged by its efficacy in producing a desired and beneficial therapeutic change. But in the absence both of generally agreed upon criteria for assessing therapeutic change and of well-controlled outcome data, reliance on efficacy for evaluating insight is very tenuous.

With all these cautions in mind, let us consider what efforts people have made to evaluate the power of psychoanalytic and ego analytic therapy to effect desirable changes in behavior. Like all therapy research, psychoanalytic research can be divided into studies concentrating on *outcome* and on *process*. Outcome studies ask whether therapy works, and whether it works better under one set of conditions than another. Process studies focus on what happens *during* therapy that can be related to the outcome. For example, does transference have to occur for beneficial change to take place?

The following generalizations about Freudian psychoanalysis were made by Luborksy and Spence (1971), who relied on outcome research conducted with some measure of controlled observation.

1. Patients with severe psychopathology (for example, schizophrenia) do not do as well as neurotics. This is understandable in view of Freud's admitted emphasis on neurosis rather than psychosis and in view of the heavy reliance psychoanalysis places on verbal abilities—a factor that is important in some of the following conclusions as well.

2. The more education a patient has, the better he or she does in analysis, probably because of the heavy emphasis on verbal interactions.

3. The evidence whether the outcome of psychoanalysis is any better than what would be achieved through the mere passage of time or by engaging other professional help, such as a family doctor (Bergin, 1971; Eysenck, 1952), is conflicting. This is *not* to say that psychoanalysis does no good, only that clear evidence is as yet lacking. Given the great diversity in the characteristics of both patients and therapists, and in the severity of patients' problems, the question being asked is probably too complex to yield a single, scientifically acceptable answer.

Since the Luborsky and Spence review, an important comparative study of outcomes has been done at the Temple University Outpatient Clinic (Sloane et al., 1975). Three behavior therapists and three analysts—all of them highly experienced and recognized leaders in their respective fields—were to see a total of ninety adult patients from the university health service for a period of four months. In addition, to judge the effects of having taken steps to enter therapy, they included a wait-list control group, composed of people who were promised therapy but asked to wait while others were in treatment. These clients can best be described as neurotic; they were the individuals typically seen in outpatient clinics or in private consulting rooms. After being matched on age and sex, as well as severity of problem, the clients were randomly assigned to behavior therapy, to short-term analytic therapy (meaning ego analysis, presumably), or to the wait-list control group. Measures included various psychological tests, as well as reports from people who were very familiar with each client.

The most noteworthy finding is that both therapies were about equal in overall effectiveness; and both forms of therapy were clearly superior to waiting for therapy. Other comparative studies (such as Luborsky, Singer, and Luborsky, 1974) reveal few if any differences in the effectiveness of treatments given clients with "garden variety" neuroses.

It is difficult to draw general conclusions from process studies of analytic therapy, primarily because the variables are so complex and, as already stated, inextricably bound up with concepts referring to the unconscious. One of the variables, for example, is "associative freedom," or the extent to which the analysand can free-associate. If free association helps the analyst get to hitherto repressed material, great facility in free-associating should predict a good outcome. Unfortunately, the relationship is much more complex, for the patient's free association interacts with the analyst's interpretations, and the effectiveness of these, in turn, depends on their timing—not to mention their accuracy. Because of these difficulties, plus the problems of defining outcome criteria and of designing reliable measures, it is not surprising that there are no controlled data. The evidence on other process variables, such as accuracy of interpretations, is similarly inconclusive.

## Humanistic-Existential Therapies

Humanistic-existential therapies, like psychoanalytic therapies, are insight-oriented, being based on the assumption that disordered behavior can best be changed by increasing the individual's awareness of motivations and needs (see London, 1964). But there is a useful contrast between psychoanalysis and its offshoots on the one hand and existential approaches on the other: existential therapies place greater emphasis on the person's freedom of choice. Free will is regarded as the human being's most important characteristic. Free will is, however, a double-edged sword, for it not only offers fulfillment and pleasure but also threatens acute pain and suffering. It is an innately provided gift that *must* be used and that requires special courage to use. Not all of us can meet this challenge; those who cannot are regarded as candidates for any of several variations of humanistic-existential therapies, among which are client-centered therapy, existential analysis, and Gestalt therapy.

### Carl Rogers's Client-Centered Therapy

Carl Rogers is an American psychologist whose theorizing about psychotherapy grew slowly out of years of intensive clinical experience. After teaching at the university level for some time, he helped organize the Center for Studies of the Person in La Jolla, California. Rogers makes several basic assumptions about human nature and the means by which we can try to understand it (Ford and Urban, 1963; Rogers, 1951, 1961).

1. We must adopt a phenomenological point of view (see page 4). People can be understood only from the vantage point of their own perceptions and feelings. It is the way people construe events rather than the events themselves that the investigator must attend to.

Carl Rogers, the American humanistic psychologist. The aim of his client-centered individual and group psychotherapy is to provide a warm and sympathetic ambience in which the individual recognizes conflicts and goes on to broaden and extend the self.

2. Healthy people are aware of their behavior. In this sense Rogers's system is similar to psychoanalysis and ego analysis, for it emphasizes the desirability of awareness of motives.

3. People are innately good and effective; they become ineffective and disturbed only when faulty learning intervenes.

4. Behavior is purposive and goal-directed; people do not respond passively to the influence of their environment or to their inner drives. In this sense Rogers is closer to ego analysts than to orthodox Freudian psychoanalysts.

5. Therapists should not attempt to manipulate events for the individual; rather they should create conditions that will facilitate independent decision making by the client.

### Personality development

Rogers postulates an innate tendency to *actualize,* that is, to realize potentialities. This idea is basic to his conception of human beings and therefore crucial to understanding his approach to therapy. In common with Freud and most of the social-learning theorists discussed in the next chapter, Rogers holds that people try to reduce the physiological tensions of hunger, thirst, and pain. But Rogers proposes that people by nature seek also to learn new things and otherwise enhance their lives. In other words, people *seek out* pleasurable tension in addition to simply attempting to reduce unpleasurable tension. All behavior, for Rogers, originates in some way from this innate self-actualizing tendency. Furthermore, people evaluate behavior for its contribution to personal growth and tend to repeat activity that helps them approach this goal.

Rogers assumes that the most effective learning takes place when a person does not have to struggle for and concern himself with approval from others. The most important evaluations are to come from the person himself, for the self is oriented toward satisfying the innate self-actualizing tendency. When a person receives *unconditional positive regard* from others, he is not distracted and is better able to evaluate how his own behavior is contributing to the enhancement of self (self-actualization).

The natural sequence of healthy development can be interfered with by faulty learning. A person may accept evaluations by others instead of paying heed to the internal evaluations provided by his own psyche and body. For example, he may apply the denigrating evaluations of others to his own instrinsically good behavior and actually begin to accept their judgment, as when a student regards himself as a worthless human being after being criticized by a teacher. The result is a conflict between self and experience.

This conflict, or incongruence, creates anxiety. At some point the conflict begins to operate outside of the person's awareness. By the time he consults a therapist, an individual may not even know why he is unhappy.

### Therapeutic intervention

With this brief summary of Rogers's conception of people and the development of disordered behavior, we can now turn to an account of his client-centered psychotherapy. Consistent with the view that a mature and well-adjusted person makes his own judgments based on what is intrinsically satisfying and actualizing, Rogers prohibits the therapist from imposing goals upon the client. The therapist's job is to create suitable conditions so that during the therapy hour the client can return once again to his basic nature and judge for himself which course of life is intrinsically gratifying to him. Again, because of Rogers's very positive view of people, he assumes that their decisions will not only make them happy with themselves but also turn them into good civilized people.

As for the techniques of therapy, Rogers's thinking has evolved from a clear specification of techniques (Rogers, 1942) to an emphasis on the attitude and emotional style of the therapist and a de-emphasis of specific procedures (Rogers, 1951). The principal therapeutic task, as already indicated, is to create conditions that will allow the client to change by himself. By conveying complete acceptance and unconditional positive regard, the therapist enables the client gradually to attend to conflicts between his ideal self (the one whom he is capable of being) and the self he has become through accepting the conflicting evaluations of others.

The basic therapeutic tool—namely the acceptance, recognition, and clarification of feelings—is applied within the context of a warm therapeutic relationship. The therapist encourages the client to talk about his most deeply felt emotions and empathizes with him. He attempts to restate the emotional aspects, rather than the content, of what the client says (see Box 18.2). This mirroring of feelings back to the client is meant to

## BOX **18.2** Excerpt from a Client-Centered Therapy Session

*Client* (an eighteen-year-old female college student): My parents really bug me. First it was Arthur they didn't like, now it's Peter. I'm just fed up with all their meddling.

*Therapist:* You really are angry at your folks.

*Client:* Well, how do you expect me to feel? Here I am with a 3.5 GPA, and providing all sorts of other goodies, and they claim the right to pass on how appropriate my boyfriend is. (Begins to sob.)

*Therapist:* It strikes me that you're not just angry with them. (Pause) Maybe you're worried about disappointing them.

*Client:* (Crying even more) I've tried all my life to please them. Sure their approval is important to me. They're really pleased when I get the A's, but why do they have to pass judgment on my social life as well?

**Comments.** Although the emotion expressed initially was one of anger, the therapist felt that the client was really fearful of criticism from her parents. Previous sessions had suggested that the client worked hard academically primarily to please her parents and to avoid their censure. She had always been able to win their approval by getting good grades, but more recently the critical eyes of her mother and father were being directed at the boys she was dating. The client was beginning to realize that she was having to arrange her social life to please her parents. Her neurotic fear of disapproval from her parents became the focus in therapy.

remove gradually the emotional conflicts that are blocking self-actualization. The therapist, it should be noted, is not being truly nondirective (a term often applied to Rogers), for he selectively attends to evaluative statements and feelings expressed by the client, the assumption being that these are the matters the client should be helped to examine (see Truax, 1966).

If these therapeutic conditions are established, the client begins to talk in a more honest and emotional way about himself. Rogers assumes that such talk in itself is primarily responsible for changing behavior.

### Evaluation

Largely because of Rogers's own insistence that the outcome and process of therapy be carefully scrutinized and experimentally validated, numerous studies have attempted to evaluate client-centered therapy. Indeed, Rogers can be credited with stimulating the whole field of psychotherapy research. He and his students deserve the credit for removing the mystique and excessive privacy of the consulting room; for example, they pioneered the tape recording of therapy sessions for subsequent analysis by researchers.

Research on Rogerian therapy has focused principally on relating outcome to the personal qualities of therapists. As Truax and Mitchell (1971) explain,

> *Three characteristics of an effective therapist emerge . . . (1) an effective therapist is nonphony, nondefensive and authentic* or genuine *in his therapeutic encounter; (2) an effective therapist is able to provide a nonthreatening, safe, trusting, or secure atmosphere through his own acceptance, positive regard, love, valuing, or* nonpossessive warmth, *for the client; and (3) an effective therapist is able to understand, "be with," "grasp the meaning of," or have a high degree of* accurate empathic understanding *of the client on a moment-by-moment basis (p. 302).*

A study of four years of client-centered therapy with sixteen hospitalized schizophrenics illustrates the research done within the Rogerian school (Rogers et al., 1967). The control group of schizophrenics received the standard hospital regimen, principally drug therapy. At the end of treatment there were *no* overall differences between the two groups. But *within* the group that had received Rogerian therapy, there were outcome differences that were related to the personal qualities of the therapist. Patients seen by therapists who were exceptionally genuine and truly empathic had improved, whereas some patients seen by therapists who did not have these personal qualities to an appreciable degree actually did less well than patients in the control group.

In keeping with Rogers's phenomenological approach, self-reports by clients are the usual measures of the effectiveness of therapy. Research on Rogerian therapy pays practically no attention to how patients actually *behave* following therapy. Rogers's basic datum is the individual's own phenomenological evaluation and reaction to himself and events in his world; the overt behavior, it is held, follows from these perceptions and is not the proper object of study by the client-centered therapy researcher.

The paradigmatic neglect of behavior outside the therapy session can create problems for clients who have never learned to behave in particular ways. Even though feelings of inferiority are overcome during sessions, the client may very well be at a loss how to behave differently after leaving the consulting room. He may, for example, never have acquired an adequate repertoire of social skills. If he is truly to change his concept of himself, it would seem necessary to do more than help the client understand himself better—in this case he needs training in interpersonal skills.

Rogers's emphasis on subjective experience also raises important epistemological problems, for the therapist must be able to make accurate and incisive inferences about what the client is feeling or thinking. Although the method seems to rely entirely on what the client says, Rogers asserts that clients can be unaware of their true feelings; indeed, it is this lack of awareness that brings most of them into therapy in the first place. As with psychoanalysis, we must ask how a therapist is to make an inference about internal processes of which a client is seemingly unaware, and then by what procedures is the usefulness or validity of that inference to be evaluated.

Rogers may also be criticized for his assumption that there is a master motive of self-actualization. Postulating any innately given drive or motive raises difficulties. Rogers infers a self-actualization motive from his observation that people seek out situations that will offer fulfillment. But then the self-actualization tendency is offered as an *explanation* of the behavior that initially suggested the concept. Circular reasoning again!

Then, of course, there is the question of the therapist's own influence on what happens in the therapy session. Rogers no longer refers to his therapy as nondirective, evidently an admission of the influence inherent in the therapeutic situation. That a client's verbal statements are shaped by Rogerians was shown by an analysis of one of Rogers's own therapy transcripts (see Truax, 1966).

Another point to consider is how faulty ideas are learned from the evaluation of others. Why does the master motive not always predominate over the individual's learning? If the master motive is indeed always directing the person toward self-actualization, under what circumstances does faulty learning take place, and what motives and needs are satisfied by such faulty learning?

Recall also that Rogers assumes both that the psychologically healthy person makes choices to satisfy self-actualizing tendencies and that man by his very nature is good. But other social philosophers have taken a less optimistic view of human nature. Thomas Hobbes, for example, stated that life is "nasty, brutish, and short." How do we explain a person who is behaving in a brutish fashion and yet asserts that this behavior is intrinsically gratifying and, indeed, self-actualizing?

It may be that the problem of extreme unreasonableness was not adequately handled by Rogers because he and his colleagues have concentrated on people who are only mildly disturbed rather than on those with a psychotic disturbance. Rogerian therapy may not, in fact, be appropriate for a severe psychological disorder, as Rogers himself has warned. As a way to help unhappy people understand themselves better (and *perhaps* even to help them behave differently), client-centered therapy may very well be appropriate and effective. As with most forms of therapy, however, the effectiveness of Rogerian procedures has not been well demonstrated. This humanistic approach remains popular, however, especially in the encounter group movement (see page 527).

## Existential Analysis

Those most commonly associated with existential analysis are the Danish philosopher Kierkegaard, the German philosophers Husserl and Heidegger, and the Swiss psychiatrists Binswanger and Boss. In this country the principal proponents have been Rollo May and the late Abraham Maslow. The following presentation of existential analysis is a distillation of the points of view of these men. According to the existential position,

> *Man has the capacity for being aware of himself, of what he is doing, and what is happening to him. As a consequence, he is capable of making decisions about these things and of taking responsibility for himself. He can also become aware of a possibility of becoming completely isolated and alone, that is, nothing, symbolized by the ultimate nothingness of death. This is innately feared. He is not a static entity but in a constant state of transition. He does not exist; he is not a being; rather he is coming into being, emerging, becoming, evolving*

*toward something. His ways of behaving toward himself and other events are changing constantly. His significance lies not in what he has been in the past, but in what he is now and the direction of his development, which is toward the fulfillment of his innate potentiality* (Ford and Urban, 1963, p. 448).

### Basic concepts of existential analysis

This point of view is similar to Carl Rogers's emphasis on personal growth. A further similarity between the two approaches is the phenomenological means Rogerians and the existentialists propose for understanding people. The existential therapist attempts to understand people's problems through their own subjective points of view. In other words, the therapist tries to deal with reality not as he or she perceives it but rather as it appears to the client. This approach, of course, requires one human being to view the world through the perspective of another. This is no easy task! Existentialists are aware of the difficulty, and they recommend that therapists understand their own feelings and biases so that they can hold them in abeyance while they attempt to place themselves within the phenomenological world of a client.

Another key feature of existential therapy is helping people to relate *authentically* to others. The assumption is that people define their identity and existence in terms of their interpersonal relationships. A person is threatened with nonbeing—or alienation—if isolated from others. Even though he may be effective in dealing with people and his world (see the discussion of Maddi's views in Chapter 6), he can become anxious if deprived of open and frank relationships. Hence, although the existential view is a highly subjective one, it strongly emphasizes *relating to others* in an open, honest, and loving fashion. The encounter group movement owes much to existential analysis.

Like Rogers, the existentialists hold that behavior becomes disordered when man's natural tendency to fulfill his potential is interfered with. Events eliciting such anxiety that the person must expend his energies avoiding them are the usual happenstances by which the urge for self-fulfillment is blocked. Since in the existentialist view man creates his existence anew at each moment, the potential for disorder is ever-present. Everyone is confronted with anxiety-provoking situations; moreover, we are all limited in our ability to handle the inevitable stresses of life. Yet not everyone becomes neurotic or psychotic. Why, then, do some people break down and others do not? The response of the existentialists is that some people have developed a strong sense of their own identities and their worth as human beings. They are therefore less susceptible to existential breakdowns.

The goal of existential therapy is to make the patient more aware of his own potential for choice and growth. The person must be encouraged to accept the responsibility for his own existence and to realize that, within certain limits, he can redefine himself at any moment and behave and feel differently within his own social environment. Anxiety about relating authentically to others is assumed to interfere with becoming. Presumably therapy somehow reduces this anxiety so that the person's natural tendency to lead a meaningful existence is able to assert itself. The existential writers, however, are very vague about how such relearning takes place and about what therapeutic techniques will help the client achieve this goal. But clearly the therapeutic relationship should be an authentic encounter between two human beings so that the patient has some practice in relating to another individual in a straightforward fashion.[1]

[1] It is interesting to note that this approach, which places so much emphasis on a person's perceptions, understanding, feelings, and other internal processes, is in a way very behavioristic in the overt sense of the word. The person must at some point during therapy begin to behave differently, both toward the therapist and toward the outside world, in order for his own existential condition to be changed.

### Evaluation

Although existential therapists have published numerous case reports relating striking successes with a variety of clinical problems, no data approach scientific rigor. What may be of more interest is a critical examination of their phenomenological approach to knowledge. Existentialism is entirely different from the paradigm emphasized in this book. Existentialists believe that efforts to approach human beings in scientific ways deny the unique humanness of people. But the alternative that they propose, although interesting and compelling, has its own problems. Since by definition a person's subjective experience is unique to himself, how can the therapist know that he is truly understanding a patient's world as it appears to him? The evidence available to a therapist consists of the verbal and motor behavior of the client; everything else necessarily remains an *inference* on the part of the therapist. To be sure, such inferences may seem very convincing to the therapist and even to the individual whose phenomenological world is being inferred; nonetheless, we must ask whether the patient *really* is perceiving things the way a therapist reports that he is at any given time. And yet the attention that existentialists pay to subjective impressions is not necessarily bad, and the emphasis that they place on a person's freedom to choose and ability to change at any time may, in fact, be an important means of changing behavior. Without good outcome data, however, we cannot know how helpful such attention truly is to the patient.

## Gestalt Therapy

Another humanistic-existential therapy that has developed over the past twenty years is Gestalt therapy; its most important proponent was the late Frederick S. Perls (see Box 18.3). After receiving a medical degree in Germany in 1921,

### BOX **18.3** A Glimpse of Fritz Perls

Frederick (Fritz) Perls, colorful founder of Gestalt therapy.

As Joe got on the elevator, he hardly noticed the short, gray-bearded man standing against the wall. Then recognition hit him. "Uh, Dr. Perls, I'm, uh, honored to meet you. I've read your work, and it's such—such an honor to meet—to be in your presence. . . ." Joe's stammering speech trailed away with no effect. The old man did not move.

The elevator slowed and Joe, realizing that an opportunity was slipping away, heard himself say, hopelessly, "I'm really nervous." Perls turned and smiled at him. As the doors opened, he took Joe's arm and said, "Now let us talk" (Gaines, 1974).

Perls became a psychoanalyst. He was rejected by European analysts because he challenged some of the basic precepts of psychoanalytic theory, particularly the important place accorded to the libido and its various transformations in the development of neurosis. He emigrated to South Africa to escape the Nazi persecutions in Germany and ultimately took up residence in the United States, where his ideas and techniques of therapy have undergone impressive growth (Perls, Hefferline, and Goodman, 1951; Perls, 1970).

### Basic concepts of Gestalt therapy

Like Rogers, Perls holds that people have an innate goodness and that it is desirable to allow this basic nature to express itself. Psychological problems originate in frustrations and denials of this innate goodness. Like other humanistic approaches, Gestalt therapy tends to emphasize the creative and expressive aspects of people, rather than the negative and distorted features that most psychoanalytically oriented conceptualizations concentrate on.

A basic assumption of Gestalt therapy is that all of us bring our needs and wants to any situation. We do not merely perceive situations "as they are" but engage our social environment by projecting our needs, or fears, or desires onto what is "out there." Thus if I am talking to a stranger, I do not merely react to the person as that person exists; I react to the stranger in the context of my needs. Gestalt therapists working with groups sometimes have people pair off, close their eyes, and imagine the face of an individual to whom they have a strong emotional attachment. They are encouraged to concentrate on the feelings they have about that person. Then all open their eyes and look at their partner. After a few moments they are instructed to close their eyes again and think now of something neutral, such as an arithmetic problem. Then they open their eyes again and look a second time at their partner. Finally, they are asked whether there was an important difference in the ways they felt about their partner in the two situations. This exercise is designed to exaggerate what is assumed to happen inevitably in all our social interactions, namely the intrusion of our feelings into whatever is happening at any particular moment.

Perls and his followers concentrate on the here and now, placing considerable importance on the individual as an actor, as a being who is responsible for his or her own behavior and who is capable of playing a central role in bringing about beneficial changes.

> *The patient who comes for help, seeking to relate more adequately with other people and to be able to express his feelings more directly, is instructed to express what he is feeling at that moment to another person. The ways in which he stops, blocks, and frustrates himself quickly become apparent, and he can then be assisted in exploring and experiencing the blockings and encouraged to attempt other ways of expressing himself and of relating.*
>
> *Thus, the general approach of Gestalt theory and therapy requires the patient to specify the changes in himself that he desires, assists him in increasing his awareness of how he defeats himself, and aids him in experimenting and changing. Blocks in awareness and behavior emerge in the same way that they manifest themselves in a person's life; his increased awareness of his avoidances and his relief as he becomes able to expand his experience and behavior are felt immediately in increases in capacity for living* (Fagan and Shepherd, 1970, p. 2).

The foregoing description of the theorizing behind Gestalt therapy makes it difficult to distinguish this approach from what Rogers prescribes. Gestalt therapy is also supposedly related to Gestalt psychology, a branch of psychology concerned primarily with perception. Their closest similarity may be in their attention to *wholes*. Perls emphasized making a person *whole* once again, in touch with his or her feelings and thoughts, and able to behave in manner consonant with this unity.

The manner in which Gestalt therapy applies Gestalt psychology to personality development, and especially abnormal development, has been described by Wallen (1970). In the terminology of Gestalt psychology, the central aspects that we attend to as we view the world are referred to as *figure*. The remaining information is considered *ground*. The Gestalt therapist also believes that a human being must fulfill certain needs, and that failure to do so causes psychological suffering. As an example of how the two concepts of need and figure are brought together, consider a person reading alone in a room. As he concentrates on the book, the book is the figure and everything else in the room is the ground. Suppose, however, that the person becomes thirsty and notices that his mouth is dry. The mouth now becomes the figure and the book becomes part of the ground. Awareness of the thirst, the current need, makes him do something about it, namely getting something to drink. The drink satisfies the thirst, relegating the sensations of the mouth to ground. The person returns to his reading, again treating the book as figure. People also have personal emotional needs, and they must be satisfied. Some people, however, prevent emotional needs from assuming the appropriate figure and thereby contribute to their own suffering, just as a thirsty person is likely to enjoy his reading less if he does not get a drink of water. The healthy person, according to this formulation, is able to move flexibly from one figure to another, satisfying each particular need as it arises so that his behavior can be goal-directed and satisfying.

These processes are said to go on all the time; hence the Gestalt therapist can focus on what a client is doing right in the consulting room, here and now, without delving into the past. Consider a patient who seems ready to cry and yet does not. The Gestalt therapist will notice wetness in the eyes and perhaps grimacing around the mouth; he or she will conclude that the figure of crying is emerging but is being prevented from becoming the dominant figure in the person's perceptual-emotional field. The therapist can then point out to the person what is happening and, presumably, encourage him to cry, that is, to focus on the figure, excluding everything else by relegating it to the ground. As the person becomes more and more practiced in focusing on emergent needs, he will learn the general skill of fulfilling them as they arise.

### Gestalt therapy techniques

Gestalt therapy is noted for its emphasis on *techniques,* in contrast to their paucity in the insight therapies discussed so far. The techniques described here are but a small sample of current Gestalt practices. A general rule is to emphasize the present. Nothing exists but the now. The only things that can be coped with are faced in the present, although past and future experiences can also be brought into the present with the use of appropriate techniques.

The Gestalt therapist insists that the client talk in the present tense and direct his attention to current feelings and activities. Perls assumes further, as do other existentially oriented therapists, that people must bear continuing *responsibility* for what they are and what they are to become. One way to achieve this is by changing "it" language into "I" language.

*Therapist:* What do you hear in your voice?

*Patient:* My voice sounds like it is crying.

*Therapist:* Can you take responsibility for that by saying, I am crying? (Levitsky and Perls, 1970, p. 142).

This simple change in language supposedly makes it easier for the patient to assume responsibility for particular feelings and behavior and reduces his sense of being alienated from aspects of his very being. It helps the patient see himself as active rather than passive, as a responsible person rather than someone whose behavior is determined entirely by external events.

A convenient gambit for the Gestalt therapist is to have a client project and then talk to his projection of a feeling, or of a person, object, or situation. Thus, seeing that a patient is crying, the Gestalt therapist might ask him to regard the tears as being in a chair opposite him and to speak *to* the tears. This tactic often seems to help people confront their feelings. Indeed, to ask a person to talk *about* his tears is assumed to encourage him to establish still greater distance between himself and his feelings—something Gestalt therapists assert interferes with psychological well-being.

Another technique is to have the person behave opposite to the way he feels. Someone who is excessively timid might be asked during the therapy session to behave like an outgoing person. Perls assumes that the opposite side of the coin actually lies within the being of the person and that acting out feelings not usually expressed allows the person to make contact with a part of himself that has thus far been submerged.

During the therapy session Gestalt therapists often create unusual scenarios to externalize, to make more vivid and understandable, a problem they believe a client is having. In one session that we observed, a husband and wife sat together on a sofa, bickering about the woman's mother. The husband seemed very angry with his mother-in-law, and the therapist surmised that she was getting in the way of his relationship with his wife. The therapist wanted to demonstrate to the couple how frustrating this must be for both of them, and he also wished to goad both of them to do something about it. Without warning, he rose from his chair and wedged himself between the couple. Not a word was said. The husband looked puzzled, then hurt, and gradually became angry at the therapist. He asked him to move so that he could sit next to his wife again. The therapist shook his head. When the husband repeated his request, the therapist removed his jacket and placed it over the wife's head so that the husband could not even see her. A long silence followed, during which the husband grew more and more agitated. The wife meanwhile was sitting quietly, covered by the therapist's coat. Suddenly the husband stood up, walked past the therapist, and angrily removed the coat; then he pushed the therapist off the sofa. The therapist exploded in good-natured laughter. "I wondered how long it would take you to do something!" he roared.

The little game drove several points home in a way that mere words might not have. The husband—having been trained already by the therapist to get in better touch with his feelings and to express them without fear or embarrassment—reported tearfully that he had felt cut off from his wife by the therapist, in much the same way that he felt alienated from her by her mother. The mother was intruding, and he was not doing anything about it. He did not trust himself to assert his needs and to take action to satisfy them. The fact that he was able to remove the coat and the therapist as well made him wonder whether he might not behave similarly toward his mother-in-law. As he spoke, his wife began to sob; she confided to her husband that all along she had been wanting him to take charge of the problem with her mother. So far so good. But then the therapist turned to the woman and asked her why she had not removed the coat herself! The husband grinned as the therapist gently chided the wife for being unduly passive about her marital problems. By the end of the session, the clients, although emotionally drained, felt in better contact with each other and expressed resolve to work together actively to change their relationship with her mother.

The interpretation of dreams is another important part of Gestalt therapy. Gestalt analysis of them is quite different from the psychoanalytic. Rather than the dream being considered a rich source of symbolism relating to unconscious processes,

> *Every image in the dream, whether human, animal, vegetable, or mineral, is taken to represent an alienated portion of the self. By reexperiencing and retelling the dream*

*over and over again in the present tense, from the standpoint of each image, the patient can begin to reclaim these alienated fragments, and accept them, live with them, and express them more appropriately* (*Enright, 1970, p. 121*).

For example, a woman in Gestalt therapy dreamt of walking down a crooked path among tall, straight trees. The therapist asked her to *become* one of the trees, and this made her feel serene and more deeply rooted. She then expressed her desire for such security. When she was asked to become the crooked path, tears welled as she confronted the deviousness of the way in which she lived.

Once again, then, we see the attempt of the Gestalt therapist to externalize the feelings that a person has been customarily avoiding, so that he or she can become aware of them, more adequately confront them, and then decide to change them.

### The Gestalt therapy philosophy of life

As Naranjo (1970) has pointed out, an important aspect of Gestalt therapy is the philosophy of life that the therapist (perhaps unwittingly) conveys to the patient. Although Perls repeatedly emphasized that the therapist should not "lay his own trip" on the patient, nonetheless a patient in Gestalt therapy seems to be provided with what the therapist regards as a desirable mode of living. This mode for living has the following prescription.

1. Be concerned much more with the present rather than with your past or with the future.
2. Deal more with what is here than with what is absent.
3. Experience things rather than imagine them.
4. Feel rather than think.
5. Express feelings rather than justify or explain them, or judge those of others.
6. Open your awareness to pain as well as to pleasure.
7. Do not use the word should.
8. Take responsibility for your actions, feelings, and thoughts.
9. Surrender to being the kind of person you are.

This prescription, according to Naranjo, can be subsumed under the rubric of "living in the moment," or as Perls puts it, *living in the now.*

Those who knew or met Fritz Perls are aware that he seemed to personify the ideals of his therapy. He was a very present-oriented, earthy, spontaneous individual, who placed great emphasis on satisfying his own needs while at the same time respecting the needs of others. This philosophy is well summed up in the following poetic statement by Perls.

*I do my thing and you do your thing. I am not in this world to live up to your expectations. And you are not in this world to live up to mine. You are you and I am I. And if by chance we find each other, it's beautiful. If not, then not.*

### Evaluation

As with nearly every school of therapy, our initial criticism concerns the lack of evidence supporting the efficacy of the therapy. Again, it is worth emphasizing that this comment does not mean that people who go through such therapy are necessarily wasting their time. On the contrary, many people are undoubtedly helped by therapists who follow Perls's thinking and use his therapeutic techniques. Rather, we wish to caution that at least a part of the therapeutic improvement may be attributable to the placebo effect or to any number of other factors.

A second critical point is the gap between Perls's concepts and his techniques. This problem is common to all therapies, but there are special difficulties in relating the theoretical concepts of Gestalt therapy to the treatment actually given the patients. Our own reading of the Gestalt therapy literature suggests that these therapists spend much or most of their time urging clients to be more expressive, spontaneous, and much more responsive to their own needs and to the feelings of others. Perls describes this activity as making the person more attentive to emerging gestalts, and he thereby aligns his psychotherapy with the experimental findings of Gestalt psychology. It is open to question, however, whether Perls's description is the most accurate or parsimonious way of talking about the techniques, and, more importantly, whether such concepts help clients and assist in the effective training of good therapists.

Gestalt therapy does forcefully convey the existential message that a person is not a prisoner of his past, that he can at any time make the existential choice to be different, and that the therapist will not tolerate stagnation. No doubt this optimistic view helps many people change. If the person does not know how to behave differently, however, considerable damage can be done to an already miserable individual.

A third difficulty we see with Gestalt therapy is the same complaint voiced about Rogers's client-centered therapy; indeed, it may be common to all humanistic-existential therapies. According to humanists, people are, by their very nature, good and beautiful. If the belief is valid, it would be reasonable to trust this intrinsic good nature and to encourage direct expression of needs. But are people always good? Sometimes clients—especially those who are psychologically troubled—feel they must do something that, in the judgment of the professional, is not in their own best interests. Suppose that a client feels the need to murder someone or to engage in other behavior that, to outside observers, is surely undesirable. What is the therapist's responsibility? At what point does the therapist intervene and impose his or her judgment? We believe that Gestalt therapists do *not* abdicate all decisions to their clients and that they *do* exert considerable influence on them, if only by virtue of the models they themselves provide (recall our earlier comments on Perls as a person). It is likely that most people adopt the values of their therapists (Rosenthal, 1955), and it seems preferable to us to admit this social influence so that it can be dealt with, rather than to deny that such influence exists and perhaps allow for even greater "tyranny" of therapists over patients. This issue is discussed at length in Chapter 21.

## Summary

Insight therapies share the basic assumption that a person's behavior is disordered because he is not aware of what motivates his actions. Psychoanalysis and ego analysis tend to emphasize factors from the past, whereas most humanistic-existential approaches, such as those of Rogers and Perls, appear to emphasize the current determinants of behavior.

Consistent with Freud's second theory of neurosis, psychoanalysis tries to uncover childhood-based repressions so that infantile fears of libidinal expression can be examined by the adult ego in the light of present-day realities. Ego analysis puts more emphasis on the need of the patient to achieve greater control over the environment and over instinctual gratifications.

Rogers trusts the basic goodness of man's drive to actualize himself, and he proposes the creation of nonjudgmental conditions in therapy. Through their unconditional positive regard for their clients, therapists help clients to view themselves more accurately and to trust their own instincts for self-actualization. Existential therapists, influenced primarily by European existential philosophy, similarly regard man as having the innate ability to realize his potential, and they place heavy emphasis on his freedom to decide at any given moment to become different. Both Rogers and the existentialists assume that the only reality is the one perceived by the individual; thus the therapist must try at all times to view the world in the client's phenomenological frame of reference, rather than in his own.

The Gestalt therapy of Perls is usually regarded as humanistic-existential, yet it is different in important ways from the therapies of Rogers and other existentialists. Perls stresses living in the now, and the many techniques he and his followers have introduced try to help clients experience their current needs and feel comfortable about satisfying them as they emerge. The emphasis is on changing behavior, and yet considerable attention is directed toward increasing awareness of current motivation.

In addition to the specific criticisms we have made of each of these insight therapies, all have a common problem which impedes progress and refinement. Scientific data to support the claims of efficacy and the assertions that changes do occur for the reasons expounded by the various theorists are scarce. Some theorists—especially the existentialists—dismiss a priori and paradigmatically the need for and even the possibility of the kind of controlled research that most social scientists deem important. The ultimate question, especially in view of the large fees people pay to their therapists, is the very pragmatic one whether people are helped by the therapists. But even when patients do derive benefit, their improvement may be attributable at least in part to the ubiquitous placebo effect.

# chapter 19

## BEHAVIOR THERAPY



The insight-oriented therapies described in the preceding chapter all share the assumption that disordered behavior can be alleviated by enabling sufferers to know the reasons for their behavior. And yet behavior has sometimes been ignored during treatment, a neglect that opens them to criticism. The manner in which insight therapies developed and their lack of justifying principles also render them vulnerable. The theorists described in the preceding chapters have generally operated outside the mainstream of academic-experimental psychology. They were primarily practitioners, concerned with helping the individuals who turned to them for assistance, and were seldom well grounded in the methodology and principles of experimental psychology.

Throughout this book we have taken the view that the study of human behavior in general and abnormal behavior in particular should be scientific. Over the past two decades a method of treating abnormal behavior within a scientific framework has been developed. Called *behavior therapy* or behavior modification, it was initially restricted to procedures based on classical and operant conditioning. Today it has a broader base, all of experimental psychology (see Bandura, 1969; Kanfer and Phillips, 1970). Behavior therapy, as now conceived, is characterized more by its epistemological stance—its search for rigorous standards of proof—than by allegiance to any particular set of concepts (see Davison and Goldfried, 1973; Yates, 1970). In brief, behavior therapy is an attempt to study and change abnormal behavior by drawing on the discoveries made by experimental psychologists in their study of normal behavior.

Sometimes the term "behavior modification" has been used interchangeably with behavior therapy; people involved in operant conditioning have often preferred this term. But we have argued elsewhere (Davison and Stuart, 1975; Goldfried and Davison, 1976) that the term behavior therapy should be employed in order to differentiate this approach from others. After all, every therapy—whether it be psychoanalysis or psychosurgery—has as its ultimate goal the modification of behavior. In the recent past the work done by clinicians of other bents, who do not adhere to the standards of evidence and procedure that are the essence of behavior therapy, has been confused with the efforts of behavior therapists.

Just when behavior therapy first began to be developed is difficult to date. It is, in any event, not the case that some social scientist woke up one morning and proclaimed that from this day on people with psychological problems should be treated with techniques suggested by experimental findings. Rather, over many years people in the clinical field began to formulate a new set of assumptions about the best means of dealing with the problems that they encountered. We have found it helpful to examine four discernibly separate theoretical approaches and techniques that are applied in behavior therapy—counterconditioning, operant conditioning, modeling, and cognitive restructuring.

## Counterconditioning

In counterconditioning, illustrated in Figure 19.1, a response ($R_1$) to a given stimulus (S) is eliminated by eliciting different behavior ($R_2$) in the presence of that stimulus. For example, if a child is afraid ($R_1$) of a harmless animal (S), the therapist attempts to elicit a playful reaction ($R_2$) in the presence of the animal. Experimental evidence suggests that this counterconditioning, or substitution of a response, can eliminate $R_1$. An early and now famous clinical demonstration of counterconditioning was a case reported by Mary Cover Jones (1924). She successfully eliminated a little boy's fear of rabbits by feeding him in the presence of a rabbit. The animal was at first kept several feet away and then gradually moved closer on successive occasions. In this fashion the fear ($R_1$) produced by the rabbit (S) was "crowded out" by the stronger positive feelings associated with eating ($R_2$).

### Systematic Desensitization

Three decades later Joseph Wolpe (1958) employed similar techniques with fearful patients. He found that many of his clients, like the child treated by

FIGURE **19.1**
Schematic diagram of counterconditioning, whereby an original response ($R_1$) to a given stimulus (S) is eliminated by evoking a new response ($R_2$) to the same stimulus.

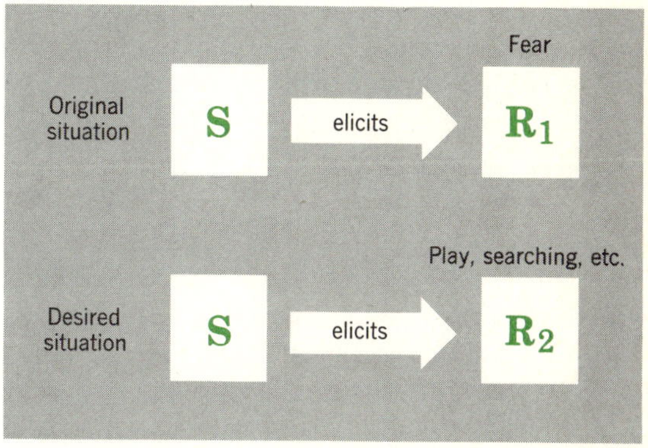

Joseph Wolpe, one of the pioneers in behavior therapy. He is known particularly for systematic desensitization, a widely applied behavioral technique.

Jones, could be encouraged to expose themselves gradually to the situation or object they feared if they were at the same time engaging in behavior that inhibited anxiety. Rather than have his patients eat, however, Wolpe taught them deep muscle relaxation. His training procedures were adapted from earlier pioneering work by Jacobson (1929), who had shown that strong emotional states like anxiety could be markedly inhibited if a person is in a state of deep relaxation. In his many experiments various autonomic indices as well as self-reports reflected reduction of anxiety in subjects who had been taught to let go of their muscles through a progressive program of contracting and relaxing muscle groups of the body.

Many of the fears felt by Wolpe's patients were so abstract—for example, fear of criticism or fear of failure—that it was impractical to confront them with *real-life* situations that would evoke these fears. Following earlier proposals by Salter (1949), Wolpe reasoned that he might have fearful patients *imagine* what they feared. Thus he formulated a new technique which he called *systematic desensitization,* a term originally applied to the medical procedure of administering increasing doses of allergens to hay fever and asthma sufferers. In systematic desensitization a deeply relaxed person is asked to imagine a graded series of anxiety-provoking situations; the relaxation tends to inhibit any anxiety that might otherwise be elicited by the imagined scenes. Over successive sessions a client is usually able to tolerate increasingly more difficult scenes as he or she climbs the hierarchy in imagination. As has been documented by Wolpe as well as by many other clinicians (for example, Goldfried and Davison, 1976), the ability to tolerate stressful imagery is generally followed by a reduction of anxiety in related real-life situations. The following case demonstrates how this clinical innovation has made it possible to treat a wider range of human neurotic fears and phobias than would have been feasible using only real-life stimuli.

The thirty-five-year-old substitute mail carrier who consulted us had dropped out of college sixteen years ago because of crippling fears of being criticized. Earlier, his disability had taken the form of extreme tension when faced with tests and speaking up in class. When we saw him, he was debilitated by fears of criticism in general and of evaluations of his mail-sorting performance in particular. As a consequence, his everyday activities were severely constricted and, though highly intelligent, he had apparently settled for an occupation that did not promise self-fulfillment.

After agreeing that a reduction in his unrealistic fears would be beneficial, the client was taught over several sessions to relax all the muscles of his body while in a reclining chair.

A list of anxiety-provoking scenes was also drawn up in consultation with the client.

You are saying "Good morning" to your boss.
You are standing in front of your sorting bin in the post office, and your supervisor asks why you are so slow.
You are only halfway through your route, and it is already 2:00 P.M.
As you are delivering Mrs. MacKenzie's mail, she opens her screen door and complains about how late you are.
Your wife criticizes you for bringing home the wrong kind of bread.
The officer at the bridge toll gate appears impatient as you fumble in your pocket for the correct change.

These and other scenes were arranged in an *anxiety hierarchy,* from least to most fear-evoking, analogous to the gradual manner in which Jones brought the feared rabbit closer and closer to the little boy. Desensitization proper began with the client being instructed first to relax deeply as he had been taught. Then he was to imagine the easiest item, remaining as relaxed as possible. After ten sessions the man was able to imagine the most distressing scene in the hierarchy without feeling anxious, and gradually his tensions in real life became markedly less.

In clinical practice systematic desensitization has proved effective with a great variety of anxiety-related problems. Indeed, many of the complaints described in Part II of this book appear to be amenable to the technique—phobias; obsessions and compulsions; psychophysiological disorders such as ulcer, hypertension, and asthma; reactive depression; and fears of sexual intimacy (Wolpe and Lazarus, 1966). Between therapy sessions clients are instructed to place themselves in progressively frightening real-life situations. These homework assignments help to move their adjustment from imagination to actuality (for example, Davison, 1968b; Sherman, 1972). Clients are also taught to use relaxation skills as a way of *coping with* anxieties as they arise in day-to-day living (for example, Goldfried and Trier, 1974).

Essential hypertension has been treated with Benson's (1975) Westernized version of transcendental medititation, a variant form of relaxation training. Hypertension sufferers acquire a daily habit of sitting quietly, concentrating on their breathing, and uttering silently to themselves a word like "One." The fact that blood pressure, and heart rate, can be lowered *during* such sessions came as no surprise. The muscle relaxation techniques of Edmund Jacobson (1929) had lowered them too. What is remarkable is the pervasiveness of the effect; overall blood pressure is apparently lowered during ordinary daily activities, as well as during the meditation sessions.

"LEAVE US ALONE! I AM A BEHAVIOR THERAPIST! I AM HELPING MY PATIENT OVERCOME A FEAR OF HEIGHTS."

In his best-selling book *The Relaxation*

## BOX 19.1 Therapy for Sexual Dysfunctions by Masters and Johnson

Masters and Johnson (1970) have not identified themselves as behavior therapists, but it seems appropriate for several reasons to include their work here. Many of their techniques have been used for some time by behavior therapists (for example, Wolpe, 1958). More importantly, their therapy procedures are based largely on their earlier laboratory work (Masters and Johnson, 1966), their focus is on current maintaining variables rather than on historical causes, and they are strongly committed to evaluating their clinical outcomes in as controlled a fashion as possible.

In Chapter 11 we saw that Masters and Johnson view fears about performance and assuming a spectator role as the most important variables in maintaining sexual dysfunction. Whatever the numerous historical factors entering into the development of a variety of sexual dysfunctions, they are all funneled into expression as these two common problems (see Figure 11.3, page 300.

The basic assumption is that sex will be enjoyed if fear does not interfere. The therapy attempts to reduce or eliminate fears of performance and to take the participants out of their maladaptive roles as spectators.

Couples participate in a two-week program of intensive therapy. Each day the couple meets with a dual-sex therapy team, the assumption being that men best understand men and women best understand women. For the first several days the experiences of all couples are the same, regardless of their specific problem. An important stipulation is that for the time being any sexual activity between the two partners is expressly forbidden. A complete social and sexual history is obtained during the first two days, and physical examinations are conducted so that any organic factors can either be excluded or be found and dealt with.

In the assessment interviews considerable attention is paid to the so-called "sexual value system," the ideas of each partner about what is acceptable and needed in a sexual relationship. Sometimes this sexual value system must be changed for one or both partners before sexual functioning can improve. For example, if one partner regards sexuality as ugly and unacceptable, it is doubtful whether even the most powerful therapy can help that person and the partner enjoy sex.

On the third day the therapists begin to offer interpretations about why problems have arisen and why they are continuing. In all cases the emphasis is on problems in the relationship, not on particular difficulties of either partner. A basic premise of the Masters and Johnson therapy is that " . . . there is no such thing as an uninvolved partner in any marriage in which there is some form of sexual inadequacy" (1970, p. 2). At this time the clients are introduced to the idea of the spectator role. They are told, for example, that an impotent male usually worries about how well or poorly he is doing rather than participating freely. It is pointed out to the couple that this pattern of observing himself, while totally understandable in context, is blocking his natural responses and greatly interfering with sexual enjoyment.

At the end of the third day an all-important assignment is given to the couple, namely to engage in "sensate focus." The couple is instructed to choose a time when they feel "a natural sense of warmth, unit compatibility . . . or even a shared sense of gamesmanship" (Masters and Johnson, 1970, p. 71). They are to undress and give each other pleasure by touching each other's bodies. The co-therapists appoint one marital partner to do the first "pleasuring" or "giving"; the partner who is "getting" is simply to enjoy being touched. The one being touched, however, is *not* required to feel a sexual response and, moreover, takes responsibility for immediately telling the partner if something becomes distracting or uncomfortable. Then the roles are switched. Attempts at intercourse are still forbidden. To Masters and Johnson this approach is a way of breaking up the frantic groping common among these couples. The sensate focus assignment may promote contact where none has existed for years; if so, it is a first step toward gradually reestablishing sexual intimacy.

Sensate focusing may uncover deep animosities that have hitherto remained hidden. Most of the time, however, partners begin to realize that encounters in bed can be intimate without necessarily being a prelude to sexual intercourse. On the second evening the partner being pleasured is instructed to give specific encouragement and direction by placing his or her hand on the hand of the giving partner in order to regulate pressure and rate of stroking. The touching of genitals and breasts is also now allowed. Still, however, there is no mention of an orgasm, and the prohibition on intercourse remains in effect. Diagrams are presented if the partners are ignorant of basic female and male anatomy, as they often are. After this second day of sensate focusing, treatment branches out according to the specific problem or problems of the couple. As an illustration, we will outline the therapy for orgasmic dysfunction in the female.

After the sensate focus exercises have made the couple more comfortable with each other in bed, the wife's attention is directed to maximizing her own sexual stimulation without trying to have an orgasm. As a result her own sexual excitement generally builds. The therapists give very explicit instructions about generally effective means of manually manipulating the female genital area, although ultimate decisions are made by the female partner, who is encouraged to make her wishes perfectly clear to the man, moment by moment. In the treatment of other dysfunctions, as in the treatment for this one, it is emphasized that at this stage having orgasms is not the focus of interaction between partners.

After the woman has begun to enjoy being pleasured in this way, the next step is to move the source of sensate pleasure from the man's hand on her body to his penis inside her vagina. She is told to place herself on top of the man and gently to insert the penis; she is encouraged simply to tune in to her feelings. When she feels inclined, she can begin slowly to move her pelvis. She is encouraged to regard the penis as something for her to play with, something that will provide her with pleasure. The male can also begin slowly to thrust. At all times, however, the wife must be able to decide when and what should happen next.

When the couple is able to maintain this containment for minutes at a time, without the man's thrusting forcefully toward orgasm, a major change has usually taken place in their sexual interactions: for perhaps the first time the woman has been allowed to feel and think sexually, and indeed selfishly, about her own pleasure. In their subsequent encounters most couples begin to have mutually satisfying intercourse.

Overall, the results have been extremely heartening: about 80 percent of the women who have undergone this therapy have been enabled to enjoy orgasms, sometimes for the first time in their lives.

Clinicians must be extremely sensitive in presenting these various treatment procedures to a couple whose problems may stretch back many years. Sometimes the couple discuss sex for the very first time at the Masters and Johnson clinic. The calm and open manner of the therapists puts the couple at ease, encouraging in them both a commitment to follow certain instructions, and a more open attitude toward sex and the activities that people may engage in together when making love. Although behavioral prescriptions are specific, the therapists can never lose sight of the atmosphere that must be maintained in the consulting room and, it is hoped, transferred over to the privacy of the bedroom, where much of the *actual* therapy takes place. As in other forms of behavior therapy, there is a strong emphasis on technique, but interpersonal factors set the stage for behavior to change.

In recent years sex clinics have sprung up everywhere, based in general on the Masters and Johnson model, and many researchers are investigating various aspects of the treatment package. One question being asked is whether a dual-sex therapy team is really necessary for all couples (Fordney-Settlage, 1975). Some clinicians now rely on electrically powered vibrators when treating female orgasmic dysfunction; with proper instruction many nonorgasmic women first learn to enjoy orgasms through self-stimulation with these little machines (Barbach, 1975; Dodson, 1974). The pursuit and enhancement of sexual pleasure for its own sake is being legitimized. Although some are concerned about this trend and dub it "sexual athletics," on the whole the relaxation of strictures regarding sexuality promises greater satisfaction for most people (Gagnon and Davison, 1974).

People practicing transcendental meditation in order to calm and relax themselves.

*Response,* Benson is appropriately cautious in drawing conclusions and in giving advice to hypertensive patients. But he does not conceal his enthusiasm for this nonmedical procedure, or his hope that in combination with antihypertensive drugs it may provide life-saving assistance to many millions of people suffering from essential hypertension.[1]

As with all the techniques described in this chapter, very rarely is only one procedure used exclusively. A person fearful of social interactions might well be given training in conversational and other social skills in addition to desensitization. Furthermore, the applicability of desensitization largely depends on the therapist's ingenuity in discovering the anxiety underlying a client's problems. For example, a client who is depressed and complains of feeling desperate and hopeless may fear sexual contact; the fear, then, would be the proper focus of desensitization. The behavior therapist's view of "underlying causes" is discussed at the end of this chapter (page 519).

## Assertion Training

Many people are unable to express positive or negative feelings to others and are thus crippled in their social encounters. For example, people can suffer great inconvenience because they find it difficult to ask for something that is their due. Salter (1949) assumes that the expression of resentment or appreciation can countercondition the anxiety associated with specific interpersonal situations. He therefore encourages socially inhibited people to express their feelings to others[2] in a graded fashion, thereby making each new situation less and less aversive; the result is akin to what is supposed to happen during desensitization. Recent experimental work confirms the earlier clinical findings (McFall and Marston, 1970; Linehan, Goldfried, and Goldfried, 1977).

Research has begun to focus on the components of nonassertive behavior. What can be discerned about nonassertive individuals that suggests treatment procedures? A study by Schwartz and Gottman (1976), for example, indicates that many nonassertive individuals know as well as do assertive people *what* to say in situations calling for self-expression. But they are inhibited by worry that others will not like them

[1] As encouraging as Benson's initial clinical findings are, optimism concerning the efficacy of this treatment has been tempered by the failure of better-controlled experiments (Surwit and Shapiro, 1976) to obtain similar results.

[2] Encouraging clients to assert themselves raises ethical and cultural issues. Some people may sincerely believe that self-denial is a greater good than self-enhancement. Others, those in the military, for example, may live in environments in which assertiveness is likely to meet with harsh punishment.

if they assert themselves or that they will hurt or offend others. An appropriate strategy would be to disabuse inhibited individuals of the belief that they will necessarily be rejected if they are "so bold" as to express their needs and desires, and to convince them that rejection in itself is not a catastrophe. To enjoy the fruits of self-expression, a person must stand the risk of meeting with disfavor from others (Rich and Schroeder, 1976).

*"Do you have any idea when the meek shall inherit the earth?"*

Drawing by Dana Fradon; © 1972 The New York Magazine, Inc.

## Aversive "Conditioning"

A related approach is *aversive conditioning,* which attempts to attach negative feelings to stimuli that are considered inappropriately attractive. The literature on classical aversive conditioning (that is, pairing a neutral or positive stim-

Andrew Salter, the originator of assertion training, which very often employs role playing to help the patient overcome passivity.

## BOX **19.2** Fighting Fear with Fear: Implosion Therapy

Systematic desensitization has fearful clients expose themselves to fear in a gradual fashion by imagining a series of episodes that become more frightening. Another means of reducing anxiety, called *implosion therapy* and sometimes *flooding,* is quite different. In this procedure the person immediately imagines himself in the most frightening of circumstances with no means of escape. This "sink or swim" approach is based on a classical conditioning view of phobias. People are assumed to have been conditioned to cues that are basically psychodynamic in nature. Stampfl and Levis (1967), as well as many analysts, assume that human fears originate in infantile aggression and sexuality. As the person matures, these fears become observable as common phobias. The differences from Wolpe's views are important: (1) whereas Wolpe (and most behavior therapists) do not concern themselves with the historical factors underlying fears, Stampfl believes it essential that patients confront them in therapy; (2) whereas Wolpe believes that patients should not be overwhelmed, Stampfl encourages people to become agitated with often bizarre images so that, presumably, the psychodynamic themes of sexuality and aggression can be confronted and the anxiety thereby extinguished. An implosion therapist might, for example, reduce a patient to tears and extreme fright by urging him to imagine his body being consumed by hideous mythical beasts of inconceivable proportions.

Not surprisingly, Stampfl's technique has been attacked by many behavior therapists as inhumane, vulgar, and needlessly cruel. *But* it has also become clear over the years that many fearful people can overcome their anxieties via implosion as well as through desensitization (for example, Barrett, 1969). Furthermore, the efficacy of exposure to fear alone, without the accompanying relaxation that is arranged for in desensitization, is supported by research with animals. Their fear of a stimulus that has previously been paired with shock can sometimes be rapidly extinguished if they are prevented from escaping it (Baum, 1970; Wilson and Davison, 1971; Stampfl and Lewis, 1967). Data on actual clinical populations (for example, Gelder et al., 1973) suggest that implosion and desensitization are equally effective in reducing a variety of phobias, although, understandably, implosive procedures are much more difficult for patients to undergo. Many behavior therapists are uncomfortable coupling psychoanalytic theory with otherwise "pure" behavioral techniques, but recent theorizing and research (see page 521) suggest that the two schools of thought may not be as inconsistent with each other as originally thought. We can expect behavioral researchers to continue to consider psychoanalytic thought seriously and to investigate whether it has relevance for behavior therapy.

ulus with an unpleasant unconditioned stimulus such as shock) of animals led therapists to believe that negative reactions can be conditioned in human beings, and they formulated treatment programs along these lines. For example, a boot fetishist (see page 282) might desire to be less attracted to the sight or feel of boots. To reduce the attraction, a therapist could give the client repeated electric shocks when pictures of boots are presented. The method is similar to desensiti-

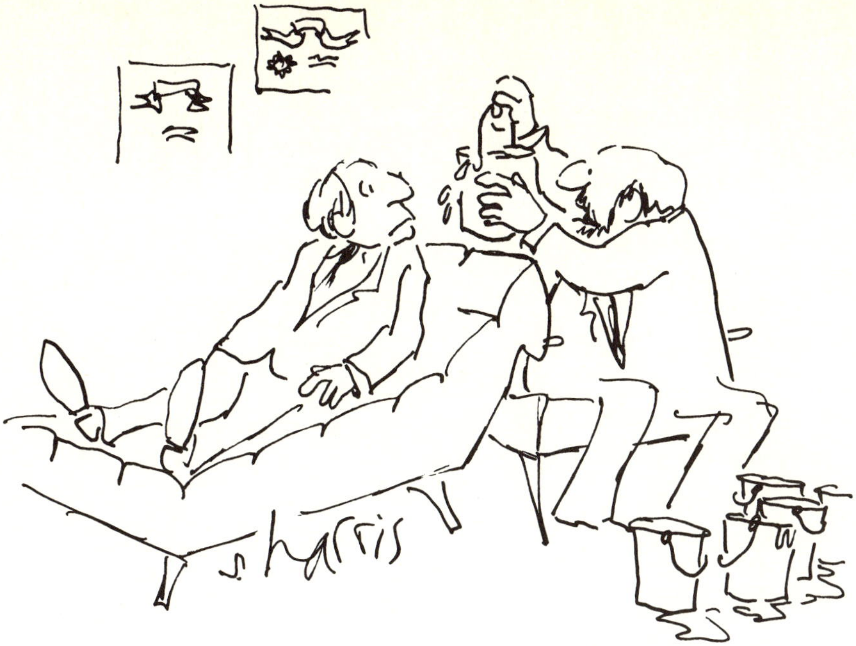


"TODAY WE'LL TRY AVERSION-THERAPY. EVERY TIME YOU SAY SOMETHING STUPID, I'LL SPILL A BUCKET OF WATER ON YOUR HEAD."

zation, but the goal is different, since the new response is an anxiety or aversive reaction and is substituted for a positive response. Among the problems dealt with in this way are overeating, smoking, excessive drinking, exhibitionism, and transvestism. Although some people have derived benefit from these procedures, the evidence does not indicate conclusively that these techniques are truly effective (Yates, 1975).

Perhaps the most widespread use of aversive procedures—and certainly the most controversial—is with homosexuals who desire to change their sexual orientation. Many behavior therapists view homosexuality as a problem of inappropriate positive attraction to same-sexed stimuli; therefore their therapeutic approach is to attempt to reduce this attraction.

Systematic research in this area has been done by Feldman and MacCulloch (1971). They have devised aversive techniques to discourage looking at homosexual stimuli. A homosexual man who desires to become less attracted to other men is asked to rate a series of pictures of males and females on a scale of increasing attractiveness. He is then presented with the slide of the least attractive male for a period of eight seconds, during which he can press a button to remove the male slide and thereby avoid a painful electric shock. Upon removal of the male slide, a "relief stimulus," a slide of the female he had previously rated as the most attractive, is presented. This procedure is followed in slide-by-slide fashion over several sessions, until the patient reliably avoids staring at the most appealing male slides.

Of their first forty-three male homosexual patients, more than half were judged to have become significantly more oriented toward heterosexual activities after an average of twenty aversive conditioning sessions. For example, thirteen were engaging in heterosexual intercourse whereas none had been before therapy. Many others had shifted to heterosexual fantasy if not actual heterosexual behavior.

These shifts are noteworthy in view of the admittedly limited nature of the therapy. Feldman and MacCulloch had intentionally excluded specific instruction in heterosexual behavior, which would seem to be necessary if a homosexual is to change his conduct beyond merely experiencing less sexual arousal when looking at another man. It must be noted, however, that neither the Feldman-MacCulloch therapy nor any other has completely eliminated homosexual feelings or behavior.

Relying on the power of the mind as did Wolpe in adapting Jones's treatment of the fearful child, behavior therapists have developed an aversive therapy to be practiced by clients through the exercise of the imagination. Lazarus (1958) formulated the first procedures for what was later given the name *covert sensitization*. The following is part of a treatment program that Cautela devised for alcoholics.

> You are walking into a bar. You decide to have a glass of beer. You are now walking toward the bar. As you are approaching the bar you have a funny feeling in the pit of your stomach. Your stomach feels all queasy and nauseous. Some liquid comes up your throat and it is very sour. You try to swallow it back down, but as you do this, food particles start coming up your throat to your mouth. You are now reaching the bar and you order a beer. As the bartender is pouring the beer, puke comes up into your mouth. You try to keep your mouth closed and swallow it down. You reach for the glass of beer to wash it down. As soon as your hand touches the glass, you can't hold it down any longer. You have to open your mouth and you puke. It goes all over your hand, all over the glass and the beer. You can see it floating around in the beer. Snots and mucus come out of your nose. Your shirt and pants are full of vomit. The bartender has some on his shirt. You notice people looking at you. You get sick again and you vomit some more and more. You turn away from the beer and immediately you start to feel better. As you run out of the bar room, you start to feel better and better. When you get out into clean fresh air you feel wonderful. You go home and clean yourself up (1966, p. 37).

The client agrees to imagine highly aversive situations over a number of sessions and at home as well, in the hope that his attraction to whatever causes him distress will be reduced by admittedly unpalatable fantasizing. Clinical evidence suggests that covert sensitization may help clients control habits such as overeating, drinking alcohol to excess, and smoking cigarettes.

Aversive conditioning is controversial for both ethical and scientific reasons. A great outcry has been raised about inflicting pain and discomfort on people, even when they ask for it. Perhaps the greatest ethical concern and anger have been voiced by the several gay liberation organizations; they hold that homosexuals who request painful treatment are actually seeking to punish themselves for behavior that a prejudiced society has convinced them is dirty. They accuse behavior therapists of impeding the acceptance of homosexuality as a legitimate life style when they accede to such requests (Silverstein, 1972). The issue is a difficult one to resolve and has led several behavior therapists to question whether therapists should ever agree to help homosexuals change their sexual orientation (see Box 21.4, page 595).

The scientific issue is whether the aversive

reactions acquired by human beings through shock and nausea are stable. As pointed out in Chapter 5, there is little evidence that a person will continue to react anxiously to an intrinsically harmless stimulus once he sees that he can no longer be shocked. Many behaviorists therefore assert that any beneficial outcomes of this treatment cannot be attributed to conditioning. Today fewer behavior therapists resort to these procedures.

A final caveat is in order. We have discussed these techniques as counterconditioning only because most workers favor explaining them as response substitution. A given technique, however, may achieve its effects for reasons quite different from those that are proposed by a particular theorist. Assertion training, for example, is considered an operant conditioning procedure by many workers. The client tries greater degrees of expressiveness and wins reward from the social environment. Aversive procedures are subject to different conceptualizations; some view these techniques as counterconditioning (Birk et al., 1971), but others (like Feldman and MacCulloch, 1971) see them as operant conditioning, for a shock or a noxious image punishes a particular response and discourages it. Behavior therapists have been attentive to this important question of how to conceptualize their treatments, as we shall demonstrate throughout this chapter.

## Operant Conditioning

In the 1950s a number of investigators, most of whom lived in the United States, suggested that therapists should try to shape overt behavior through rewards and punishments (Skinner, 1953). In the belief that they could through operant conditioning exercise some control over the complex, puzzling, often frenetic behavior of hospitalized patients, many experimentally minded psychologists determined to try to bring conceptual and practical order into the chaos of institutions for the severely disturbed. The following studies will give some of the flavor of this work.

### The Token Economy

Perhaps the most extensive and best-known work within the operant tradition was reported by Ayllon and his colleages (Ayllon and Azrin, 1968). The program was called the token economy. On the basis of earlier work that Staats and Staats (1963) had done with children, they set aside an entire ward of a mental hospital for a series of experiments in which rewards were provided for activities such as making beds and combing hair. Patients were systematically reinforced for their work by giving them plastic tokens that could later be exchanged for special privileges such as a private room or extra visits to the canteen. The entire life of each patient was as far as possible controlled by this regime.

These studies demonstrated how even markedly regressed adult hospital patients could be significantly affected by systematically manipulating reinforcement contingencies, that is, rewarding some behavior to increase its frequency, or ignoring or punishing other behavior to reduce its frequency. In order to show that a stimulus following behavior actually reinforces it, an experiment has to demonstrate not only that behavior increases when followed by a positive event, but also that behavior declines when nothing positive happens as a consequence. (Recall from Chapter 4 that the ABAB design can be employed to study the effect of contingencies.) Aylion and his associates demonstrated how contingencies affected the behavior of their ward patients. Figure 19.2 indicates that conduct such as brushing teeth and making beds markedly decreased when rewards were withdrawn, returning to a higher frequency when rewards were reinstated.

Since the publication of Ayllon's original hospital work, numerous similar programs have been instituted throughout the country. It is clear that at least short-term changes in overt behavior can be effected by manipulating the reinforcement contingencies of patients within the protected hospital setting. Whether the many deficits of adult mental patients, as detailed in Chapter 13, can be altered or compensated for through such procedures, however, is very much

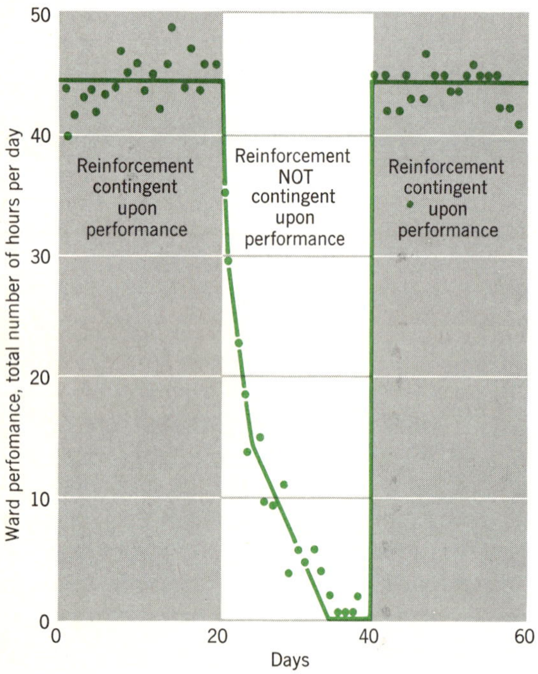


FIGURE **19.2**
When receiving tokens was the contingency, patients on a ward spent more time grooming themselves and doing chores than when they were given no reward. Adapted from Ayllon and Azrin, 1964.

an open question. This approach has also been criticized on historical and other grounds (see Box 19.3).

## Operant Work with Children

Some of the best operant conditioning behavior therapy has been done with children, perhaps because the kinds of problems most often encountered with youngsters "fit" especially well with an approach that institutes control through environmental contingencies. Children, after all, tend more than adults to be under continual supervision and (potential) control by others. At school their behavior is scrutinized by teachers, and when they come home parents frequently supervise their play and other social activities. In most instances the behavior therapist works with the parents and teachers in an effort to change the ways in which they reward and punish the children for whom they have responsibility. It is assumed that altering the reinforcement practices of the adults in a child's life will ultimately change the child's behavior.

The range of childhood problems dealt with through operant conditioning is very broad indeed, including aggression, bed-wetting, thumb-sucking, tantrums, asthmatic attacks, and poor school performance. In general, rates of improvement are superior to those reported for traditional forms of therapy (O'Leary, Turkewitz, and Taffel, 1973; Levitt, 1963). Operant behavior therapists must of course determine that the behavior being shaped or extinguished is in fact controllable through reward. A child who is crying because of physical pain should be attended to.

Encouraging results have been achieved by applying operant techniques to the training of retarded children. As we pointed out in Chapter 17, the labeling of children as "trainable" on the basis of an IQ score, meaning that they can only be taught self-care, may discourage attempts to teach them skills such as reading and writing. Many operant conditioners have challenged assumptions about the limited trainability of the re-

## BOX **19.3** Token Economies, Asylums, and the Metrics of Human Existence

In recent years questions have been raised about token economies in institutional settings. Some of these concern certain legal problems, and these are reviewed in detail in Chapter 21. Others have to do with the basic assumptions of these behavior control regimens (Gagnon and Davison, 1976).

David Rothman (1971), an historian, has traced the development of mental hospitals in this country during the nineteenth century. He shows that asylums of the time were instituted as they were because much of the madness of the day was assumed caused by the hurly-burly of a vigorous democratic and industrial society, which offered endless opportunities—and therefore possibilities for failure. Asylums were to be havens for those who could not keep up with the rapid economic and social expansion that had followed the industrial revolution.

Consider how different is this view of the mental hospital from the way token economies are organized. The disease, if you will, now becomes the doctor. The token economy is the nineteenth-century asylum on its head, for this innovation introduces into the hospital the very conditions that were assumed in the previous century to have caused mental disorders. Instead of protecting patients from the strains of an achievement-oriented, money-dominated society, the token economy introduces commercial relationships into the asylum.

But even if we are in sympathy with opposing the token economies on historical grounds, can we claim that they are necessarily bad? Can we really say that commercialism is likely to aggravate mental illness? After all, have we not made some progress in understanding mental disorder since the early nineteenth century? The reader may judge for himself by reflecting on the material presented in the preceding chapters of this book. It would seem that for the more serious disorders—schizophrenia, in particular—genetic factors and the biochemistry of the brain have provided and will provide the major clues to etiology, *not* the realm of environmental influences.

Other issues can be raised that are not tied to history. Token economies are effective in ward *management* (Goldfried and Davison, 1976; Hersen, 1976). They do seem to introduce order where there has been only chaos; helping a regressed schizophrenic dress herself and arrive on time to a hospital dining hall is a significant accomplishment. But what, in fact, do patients really learn on a token economy? According to Gagnon and Davison (1976),

*One thing that is learned is that producing certain kinds of behavior produces a stable response from the token-emitting behavioral engineer. . . . The value of any act is metrically stable, and its value can be compared to [that of] other acts*

> *[in] number of tokens. . . . [Is this a good thing for mental patients to learn if they are to be prepared for life outside the confines of the institution? Perhaps not.] The exchanges that characterize most conventional social life [suggest] that things do not come out even. . . . Life is* largely the capacity to tolerate interactions which have low predictability of outcome. . . . [*And*] staying out of asylums is a capacity to survive the fact that life is unjust: *sometimes you get what you pay for, sometimes you get more than you pay for, sometimes you get less than you pay for* (pp. 532–534, emphasis added).

Finally, a token regimen may encourage people to view themselves and others in ways that are undesirable. Human relationships and human feelings run the risk of being cheapened when reduced to a monetary metric. If a patient, for example, has to have twenty tokens to see a clergyman, will this adversely affect how he feels about religion? If thirty tokens are required for a weekend pass, how will a patient feel about the people she sees while she is on leave?

We are unaware of attempts by behavior therapists to answer such questions. In our view, the failure to do so does *not* represent callousness to the human condition; such an allegation would be unfair and incorrect. Rather, apparently because of their professional training, psychologists and psychiatrists are not inclined to view their work in historical and sociological contexts. Perhaps the kind of critical analysis summarized here will goad token economy workers into such considerations. Whatever the outcome, the beneficiaries will be those whom we are all trying to help.

tarded, much to the benefit of some retarded children and their families. Among other problems dealt with, they have been able to improve poor toilet habits (Minge and Ball, 1967) and hyperactive behavior (Doubros, 1966).

Perhaps the most significant and heartening advances have been in intellectual development. One example among many is a study by Ayllon and Kelly (1972). First they showed that measured IQ could be significantly raised in "trainable" retarded children (IQ below 55) simply by giving tokens as rewards for acceptable performances in the various subtests; the average gain was approximately 10 percent of the total possible score. Even more impressive were results from a six-week program at a school for retarded children. Two groups were carefully matched on IQ. One group was assigned to an experimental program while the control subjects continued in the ongoing academic program of the school. In the innovative program, which used specially designed materials to teach arithmetic, spelling, copying, and reading, children were reinforced with tokens depending on their achievements. The children were able to exchange their tokens for a variety of desirable things (soft drinks, candy, and extra privileges such as playing records and watching television).

Testing at the end of the six-week program showed that the IQ of the experimental subjects increased by an average of almost four points, whereas that of the control children actually decreased by nearly three points. Since the two groups had been carefully matched before the operant training program began, we can conclude that the program, whether the teaching materials, the token economy, or both, was responsible for the improvement.

Although programs such as these may offer hope to those responsible for the well-being of retarded children, their effectiveness must not be overestimated. The improvements in IQ shown in the Ayllon and Kelly study were statistically significant, but the children still remained retarded, that is, their posttreatment scores were still very far below average. Moreover, those designing remedial programs for retarded children and adults would do well to consider more systematically what specialists have discovered about the cognitive deficits of the retarded (see page 447). Even so, such programs—and scores of others tested throughout the country—do carry an important message, namely that one should not despair of making a beneficial impact on problems simply because procedures currently available have been unsuccessful.

## Biofeedback

A visit to the commercial exhibit area of any psychological or psychiatric convention will reveal a plentiful display of complex *biofeedback* apparatus, touted as efficient, even miraculous, means for helping people control one or another bodily-mental state. Basically, biofeedback gives a person prompt and exact information, otherwise unavailable, on muscle activity, brain waves, skin temperature, heart rate, blood pressure, and other bodily functions. It is assumed that a person can achieve greater voluntary control over these phenomena—most of which were once considered to be under involuntary control and completely unresponsive to will—if he or she knows immediately, through an auditory or

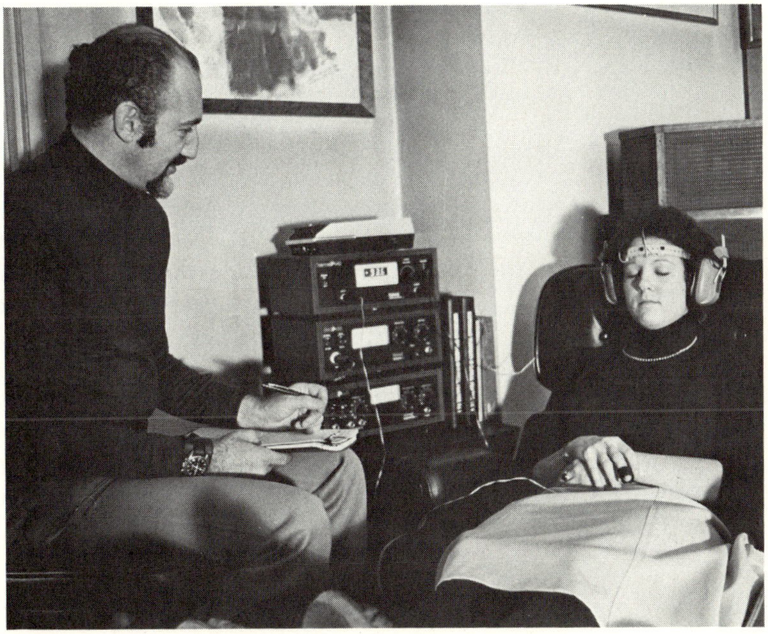

Biofeedback procedures are being applied in the treatment of a number of psychophysiological disorders. Shown here is a demonstration of techniques sometimes used to relieve headaches.

visual signal, whether a bodily activity is increasing or decreasing. Because anxiety has generally been viewed as a state involving the autonomic ("involuntary") nervous system, and because psychophysiological disorders (Chapter 7) afflict organs innervated by this system, it is obvious why researchers and clinicians have become intrigued with biofeedback.

Interest was spurred by a series of innovative experiments performed by Neal Miller and his colleagues (Miller, 1969). Initial findings indicated that most rats could indeed control via biofeedback such autonomically mediated responses as heart rate and dilation of blood vessels in the ear. But subsequent studies both in Miller's labs (Miller and Dworkin, 1974) and in those of other workers (Brener, 1974) cast these results into considerable doubt.

In a series of studies at Harvard Medical School, Shapiro, Schwartz, and Tursky demonstrated that human volunteers could achieve significant short-term changes in blood pressure and in heart rate (Schwartz, 1973; Shapiro, Tursky, and Schwartz, 1970). They found that some subjects could even be trained to increase their heart rate while decreasing blood pressure. Achievement of this fine-grained control lent still more impetus to biofeedback work with human beings and awakened hope that certain clinical disorders might be alleviated.

Once we move from the analogue studies just mentioned to the more challenging world of the clinic, at least three vital questions must be asked. First, even when biofeedback control over bodily events by normal subjects can be demonstrated, does this necessarily mean that similar control can be achieved by persons whose systems are *mal*functioning? Second, if actual patients can achieve some degree of control, will it be enough to make a difference? And third, can the control achieved by patients hooked up to and receiving immediate feedback from a remarkable apparatus be carried over to real-life situations in which they will have no special devices to inform them of their heartbeat and blood pressure?

The promise for biofeedback amelioration of essential hypertension, which has probably raised the most hopes, is as yet unfulfilled (Blanchard and Young, 1973, 1974; Yates, 1975). The highly touted training of the brain to produce alpha waves may similarly accomplish less than anticipated. The alpha state has been considered desirable for the feelings of calmness and well-being supposedly associated with it (Kamiya, 1968; Nowlis and Kamiya, 1970). Carefully controlled research, however, has usually failed to confirm earlier findings that the state can be induced or has demonstrated the central role played by subjects' expectations about the effects of alpha training (Glaros, 1975). There is no evidence that this treatment has helped patients.

The control of various forms of epilepsy has been attempted. Several patients have reduced the frequency of seizures during periods when they were receiving intensive biofeedback training to increase brain activity in the sensorimotor cortex, but this improvement did not always persist when training sessions were discontinued (Sterman, 1973). The question how to extend to real life beneficial effects achieved in the clinic plagues those studying biofeedback as it does other clinical researchers.

One form of treatment shows promise, however. A combination of at-home relaxation training and the reduction of tension in the frontalis muscles above the eyes through biofeedback can be effective in controlling tension headaches. An exemplary study by Budzynski and his associates (1973) demonstrated marked reductions both in frontalis contractions and in tension headaches in a group of adult patients who had suffered severely for several years. This improvement was not found in a control group of patients whose auditory feedback did not inform them of the true activity of the frontalis muscles. Instead, their bogus feedback was programmed to show consistently reduced contractions during training sessions, a manipulation to control for expectancy and placebo effects; the impressive clinical procedure—biofeedback machinery, white coats, and all—is quite persuasive. The clinical improvement of patients who had received true feedback persisted over an eighteen-month follow-up, suggesting that such training, when combined with home practice in relaxation, can have beneficial, long-term effects, even though people are no longer informed of their muscular contractions. Yet the fact that the treatment package also included relaxation training makes it impossible to attribute the gains to biofeedback alone (Blanchard and Young, 1974). Indeed, other studies applying biofeedback to tension headaches have clearly failed to produce any significant clinical relief (Elmore and Tursky, in press).

Even if biofeedback techniques are shown to produce meaningful improvements in patients, clinicians will have to remain mindful of the complexities of human problems. A person who has tension headaches, for example, probably also has a host of difficulties that contribute to them, such as marital problems. These will require attention. Similarly, a man with high blood pressure might have to alter a tense, driven life style before he can significantly reduce blood pressure through biofeedback. It is unwise, and a sign of naive clinical practice, to assume that one technique focused on a specific malfunction or problem will invariably cure the patient.

Finally, two observations on a theoretical level. Biofeedback has been discussed here because most investigators have assumed it to be a special case of operant conditioning. A measurable physiological change, like a reduction in heart rate, is followed by a signal denoting the change. This signal is assumed to function as a secondary reinforcer to increase the strength of the response. But it may be premature to conclude that biofeedback, when it works, does so for these reasons. More recent investigations (for example, Lang, 1974; Shapiro and Surwit, 1976) question how to conceptualize what is going on. Biofeedback may be effective because it allows better processing of information rather than because it rewards. Such questions are of more than theoretical interest, although their importance can readily be justified on this account alone. A better understanding of how something happens may suggest still more effective techniques.

A continuing problem with operant theory is its seeming capacity to include practically *anything* within its purview. If someone acquires a new skill, we look first for environmental reinforcers of a concrete sort, like money, food, or sex. If these are not found, a search is begun for more abstract events, such as receiving praise. If this hunt is similarly fruitless, people "find" reinforcers such as a feeling of well-being. Now awareness of internal events as they are monitored by highly sensitive bioelectric instruments—knowledge that the heart is slowing, blood pressure dropping, or contraction of the frontalis muscle diminishing—is similarly labeled a "reinforcer." We invite the reader to consider the following questions. Does regarding biofeedback as operant conditioning increase our understanding of biofeedback? Does it tell us what *kind* of feedback is best, auditory or visual, for example? Might some physiological systems be more responsive to certain kinds of feedback signals than to others (Elmore and Tursky, in press)? More generally, are there behavioral phenomena that are *not* amenable to an operant "explanation"? If there are not—and we sometimes believe this to be the case—can this view of human behavior be accused, as behaviorists have accused psychoanalytic theory, of explaining everything and therefore explaining nothing?

## Generalization of Treatment Effects

A problem common to all therapies, as we have indicated, is generalizing to real life whatever gains have been achieved in therapy. Insight therapists assume that the transfer of therapeutic effects is achieved through a restructuring of the personality. Being an environmentalist, a behavior therapist wonders how changes brought about by his or her manipulations can be made to persist once a client returns to his everyday situation—which often is assumed to have produced the problem in the first place!

Behavior therapists have tried to meet this challenge in several ways. Because laboratory findings indicate that intermittent reinforcement—rewarding behavior only a small portion of the time it appears—makes new behavior more enduring, many operant programs take care to move away from continuous schedules of reinforcement once desired behavior is occurring with satisfactory regularity. For example, if a teacher has succeeded in helping a disruptive boy spend more time in his seat by praising him generously for each arithmetic problem that he finishes there, he or she will gradually reward him for every other problem, and ultimately only infrequently. The hope is that the satisfactions of being a good pupil will make the child less dependent on the teacher's approval. Another strategy is to move from artificial reinforcers to those that occur naturally in the social environment. A token program might be maintained only long enough to encourage certain desired behavior, after which the person is weaned to natural reinforcers such as praise from peers.

Generalization can be effected by assigning the client a more active role. As an example, consider work done by Drabman, Spitalnik, and O'Leary (1973). In a three-month after-school program for disruptive young boys, the teacher rewarded nondisruptive classroom behavior and appropriate reading behavior. Then later the boys were allowed to self-rate their behavior according to the teacher's criteria and reward their own good conduct. That is, the pupils were taught that they could earn special privileges not only by behaving well when the teacher dispensed rewards but through honest evaluation of their own good behavior. The findings for the first part of the study were similar to those of many other studies. During token reinforcement imposed by the teacher, disruptive behavior decreased and academic behavior improved. *In addition,* and propitiously, this improvement generalized to periods of each class during which the child *himself judged* how well he was doing and *reinforced himself* accordingly; in other words, improved performance was extended to periods of time when the pupils were not under direct external control (see Box 19.4).

The implications are clear: at least with disruptive children, providing reinforcements for self-evaluated good behavior may be one effective way of improving behavior in situations in which the original controlling agent is absent.

An altogether different approach to the thorny problem of maintaining treatment gains once an individual leaves therapy comes from research on attribution, a subject usually studied by social psychologists. How a person explains to himself why he is behaving or has behaved in a particular way presumably helps to determine his subsequent behavior. Might not a person who has been in therapy and attributes improvement in his behavior to an external cause, such as a reinforcer from the environment, lose ground once what he considers the external justification for change is gone? In an analogue study on attribution and the ingestion of a "drug" (Davison and Valins, 1969), two groups of college undergraduates were given shock to determine how much they could bear. Then they took a prescribed "fast-acting vitamin compound" and were told that they would now be able to endure greater amounts of shock. And indeed they were, at least in their own minds. The experimenters surreptitiously altered the voltage levels to ensure this belief. Members of one group were then told that the capsule ingested was only a placebo, those of the other group that its effects would soon wear off. Those who believed that they had taken a placebo attributed to themselves the greater ability to withstand discomfort and endured higher levels of shock on a third test. Those who believed that the external agent was no longer effective were in the third round able to endure only lesser amounts of shock.

In an experiment with a similar design, conducted with people who were having trouble falling asleep, Davison, Tsujimoto, and Glaros (1973) obtained similar results, indicating that "real" problems may be treated by helping pa-

## BOX **19.4** Self-Control

One of the most exciting areas in behavior therapy is self-control (Goldfried and Merbaum, 1973; Mahoney, 1972). Much of the research and theory reviewed in this chapter seems to assume that the human being is a relatively passive recipient of stimulation from the environment. Given this apparent dependence on the external world, how can we account for behavior that appears to be autonomous, willed, and often contrary to what might be expected in a particular situation? How, for example, do we account for the fact that a person on a diet refrains from eating a luscious piece of chocolate cake even when hungry?

Psychoanalytic writers, including the ego analysts, handle the issue by positing within the organism some kind of internal agent. Thus many ego analysts assert that the ego can operate on its own power, making deliberate decisions for the entire psychic system—including decisions that go against the wishes of the id. Behaviorists, especially Skinner (1953), have objected to this "explanation," regarding it as simply a relabeling of the phenomena.

Perhaps the most widely accepted behavioral view of self-control is Skinner's: an organism engages in self-control when it arranges the environment so that only certain controlling stimuli are present. A person wishing to lose weight rids his or her home of fattening foods and avoids passing restaurants when hungry. Behavior remains a function of the environment, but the environment itself is seen as controlled by the organism.

A related behavioral conception of self-control is Bandura's (1969) explanation of aversive conditioning: rather than being passively conditioned to feel distaste for stimuli that have been paired with shock, a person learns a skill of aversive self-stimulation which he or she deliberately applies in real life. According to this view, a person resists a temptation by *deliberately* recalling the earlier aversive experience of being shocked or nauseated during therapy.

In our opinion, self-control places a strain on the behavioristic paradigm. In each of the last two paragraphs, a person is described as deciding something, arranging things, stimulating himself, and so forth. Each of these statements presupposes a conception of the person as an *initiator* of action, as the place where self-control *begins*.

Consider a cigarette box devised by Azrin and Powell (1968). This device allowed a smoker to obtain a cigarette only after a given period of time had passed, perhaps one hour. Many smokers were able to cut down on their cigarette use as the waiting period was gradually extended. But the smoker could at any time have broken the contract and sought cigarettes from other sources. This box, supposedly a device for increasing self-control, helps a person only if he or she is committed to using it, and smoking fewer cigarettes can be regarded as exercising self-control only if the person is *not* restrained by others to stay with the regime. For if smoking only cigarettes taken from the special box is under environmental control—the therapist's insistence that the smoker not seek another source—the control is external, not self-exercised.

What is only beginning to attract the attention of behaviorists is the *commitment* to change that a client must have (Davison, 1973; Kanfer and Karoly, 1972). Even the most powerful change procedure will have limited effect on a person who is not resolved to use it.

tients to attribute improvement to themselves. A clinical report by Levendusky and Pankratz (1975) confirms the benefits to patients of feeling they have improved through their own efforts.

What are the implications of attribution research? Since in behavior therapy most improvement seems to be controlled by environmental forces, especially therapy relying on operant manipulation, it might be wise for behavior therapists to help their clients feel more responsible. By encouraging an "I did it" attitude, therapists may help their clients to be less dependent on therapy and therapist and to maintain better their treatment gains. Insight therapies have always emphasized the desirability of patients' assuming primary responsibility for their improvement. Behavior therapists have only recently come to grips with the issue. And on a more general level, the question of attributing improvement underscores the importance of cognitive processes in behavior therapy, to be discussed later in this chapter.

## Modeling

Modeling is the third theoretical approach employed by behavior therapists. As we noted in Chapter 2, social learning generally encompasses not only classical and operant conditioning but also modeling. The importance of modeling and imitation in behavior is self-evident, for children as well as adults are able to acquire complex responses merely by watching others.

The effectiveness of modeling in clinical work was shown in a study by Bandura, Blanchard, and Ritter (1969). They were attempting to help people overcome their snake phobias. The researchers had fearful adults view both live and filmed confrontations of people and snakes. In these confrontations the models gradually moved closer to the animals. The fears of the patients were decidedly reduced. Other research has shown that children's fear of dogs (Hill, Liebert, and Mott, 1968) and of dentists (Adelson et al., 1972) can be reduced through modeling treatments. Some workers believe that such procedures are among the most powerful means for reducing neurotic fears (Franks and Wilson, 1974).

Some of the clinical work of Arnold Lazarus, one of the leading behavior therapists, may also be regarded as modeling treatment. In a procedure called *behavior rehearsal,* Lazarus (1971) demonstrates for a client how to handle a difficult interpersonal problem in a better way. The client observes the therapist's exemplary performance and then attempts to imitate it during the therapy session. By continual practice and observation, the client can frequently acquire entire repertoires of more effective and more satisfying behavior. Often videotape equipment can be creatively used to facilitate such modeling and imitation.

In recent years behavior therapy programs for psychotic patients have become increasingly sophisticated. They concentrate on helping patients develop social skills rather than on trying to eliminate their obvious erraticisms (see Goldsmith and McFall, 1975). One example is work done by

Bellack, Hersen, and Turner (1976). Three chronic schizophrenic patients were carefully observed for the frequency of appropriate assertive behavior in a variety of contrived social interactions. For instance, a given patient would be told to pretend that he had just returned home from a weekend trip to find that his lawn had been mowed. As he gets out of the car, his next-door neighbor approaches him and says that he has cut the patient's grass because he was already cutting his own. The patient must then respond to the situation. As expected, patients were initially not very good at making a socially appropriate response, which in this instance would have been some sort of thank-you. Training followed; the therapist encouraged the patient to respond, commenting helpfully on his efforts. If necessary, the therapist also modeled appropriate behavior so that the patient could observe and then try to imitate it. This combination of role playing, modeling, and positive reinforcement effected significant improvement in all three patients. There was even generalization to social situations that had not been worked on during the training. This study, and others like it, indicate that many severely disturbed patients can be taught directly new social behavior which may help them function better both inside *and outside* the hospital.

## Cognitive Restructuring

In the therapies discussed thus far, the emphasis has been on the direct manipulation of overt behavior and occasionally of covert behavior. Relatively little attention has been paid to direct alteration of the thinking and reasoning processes of the client. Perhaps as a reaction to insight therapy, behavior therapists initially discounted the importance of cognition, regarding any appeal to thinking and believing as a return to the "mentalism" that Watson vigorously objected to in the early part of the twentieth century (see page 41).

If behavior therapy is to be taken seriously as applying all experimental psychology, however, it should incorporate theory and research on cognitive processes. Indeed, in recent years behavior therapists have studied and manipulated these processes in their attempt to understand and modify overt and covert disturbed behavior (Mahoney, 1974). The following case illustrates the beneficial effects of cognitive restructuring.

A man had been diagnosed as paranoid schizophrenic, primarily because of his complaints of "pressure points" on his forehead and other parts of his body (Davison, 1966). He believed that these pressure points were signals from outside forces helping him to make decisions. These paranoid delusions had been resistant to drug treatment and other psychotherapeutic approaches. The behavior therapist, in examining the man's case history, hypothesized that the patient became very anxious and tense when he had to make a decision, that his anxiety took the form of muscular tension in certain bodily parts, and that the patient misconstrued the tension as "pressure points," signals from helpful spirits. Both patient and therapist agreed to explore the possibility that the pressure points were in fact part of a tension reaction to specific situations. For this purpose the therapist decided to teach the man deep muscle relaxation, with the hope that relaxation would enable him to control his tensions, including the pressure points.

But it was also important to have the man question his delusional system. So in the first session the therapist asked the patient to extend his right arm, clench his fist, and bend his wrist downward so as to bring the fist toward the inside of the forearm. The intent was to produce a feeling of tension in his forearm; this is precisely what happened, and the man noted that the feeling was quite similar to his pressure points.

Extensive relaxation training enabled the client to begin to control his anxiety in various situations within the hospital and at the same time to reduce the intensity of the pressure points. As he gained control over these feelings, he referred more and more to his pressure points as "sensations," and his conversation in general began to lose its earlier paranoid flavor.

Davison suggested that the relaxation training had been a means of enabling the patient to test a nonparanoid hypothesis, to see it confirmed, and thereby to shake off a belief about these sensations that had contributed to a diagnosis of paranoia.

## Rational-Emotive Therapy

For many years the clinical work of a New York psychotherapist, Albert Ellis, existed outside the mainstream of behavior therapy, but now it has begun to engage the interest of behavior therapists because it stresses cognition. The principal thesis of what Ellis calls rational-emotive therapy is that sustained emotional reactions are attributable to internal sentences that people repeat to themselves. For example, anxious persons may create their own problems by adopting unrealistic expectations, such as "I must win the love of everyone" (see page 151). Or a depressed woman may say to herself, several times a day, "What a worthless person I am." Ellis proposes that people interpret what is happening around them, that sometimes these interpretations can cause emotional turmoil, and that a therapist's attention should be focused on these internal sentences, rather than on historical causes or, indeed, overt behavior (Ellis, 1962).

Ellis lists a number of assumptions people can make that may lead to distress. One such notion is that people must be thoroughly competent in everything they do. Ellis suggests that many people actually believe this untenable assumption, and that they evaluate every event within this context. Thus, if a person makes an error, it becomes a catastrophe since it violates his deeply held conviction that he must be perfect. It sometimes comes as a shock to clients to realize that they actually believe such strictures and are as a result running their lives so that it becomes virtually impossible to live comfortably.

Albert Ellis's rational-emotive therapy is designed to help patients recognize the impossible "musts" they impose on themselves and become more realistic in their expectations.

Behavior therapists are just beginning to implement Ellis's rational-emotive therapy, which through talk helps the patient recognize and abandon irrational thought patterns. After becoming familiar with the client's problems, the therapist must present the basic rationale of treatment so that the client can understand and accept it. The following transcript is from a session with a young man who had inordinate fears about speaking in front of groups. The therapist guides the client to view his "inferiority complex" in terms of the unreasonable things he may be telling himself. The therapist's thoughts during the interview are indicated in italics.

*Client:* My primary difficulty is that I become very uptight when I have to speak in front of a group of people. I guess it's just my own inferiority complex.

*Therapist:* [*I don't want to get sidetracked at this point by talking about that conceptualization of his problem. I'll just try to finesse it and make a smooth transition to something else.*] I don't know if I would call it an inferiority complex but I do believe that people can, in a sense, bring on their own upset and anxiety in certain kinds of situations. When you're in a particular situation, your anxiety is often not the result of the situation itself, but rather the way in which you *interpret* the situation—what you tell yourself about the situation. For example, look at this pen. Does this pen make you nervous?

*Client:* No.

*Therapist:* Why not?

*Client:* It's just an object. It's just a pen.

*Therapist:* It can't hurt you?

*Client:* No. . . .

*Therapist:* It's really not the object that creates emotional upset in people, but rather what you *think* about the object. [*Hopefully, this Socratic-like dialogue will eventually bring him to the conclusion that self-statements can mediate emotional arousal.*] Now this holds true for . . . situations where emotional upset is caused by what a person tells himself about the situation. Take, for example, two people who are about to attend the same social gathering. Both of them may know exactly the same number of people at the party, but one person can be optimistic and relaxed about the situation, whereas the other one can be worried about how he will appear, and consequently be very anxious. [*I'll try to get him to verbalize the basic assumption that attitude or perception is most important here.*] So, when these two people walk into the place where the party is given, are their emotional reactions at all associated with the physical arrangements at the party?

*Client:* No, obviously not.

*Therapist:* What determines their reactions, then?

*Client:* They obviously have different attitudes toward the party.

*Therapist:* Exactly, and their attitudes—the ways in which they approach the situation—greatly influence their emotional reactions (Goldfried and Davison, 1976, pp. 163–165).

It can be argued that Ellis is preaching an ethical system, for he suggests that a great deal of emotional suffering is engendered by goals that *he* asserts are wrong. He proposes that these goals are subject to modification, and that by altering them a person can reduce subjective discomfort. Indeed, the reduction of stress can often improve performance so that, ironically, it more closely approximates the goal previously viewed as a "must" or a "should." Rational-emotive work appears at present to be one of the most promising and interesting areas in behavior therapy (for instance, Goldfried, Decenteceo, and Weinberg, 1974; Meichenbaum, 1972; Russell and Brandsma, 1974).

## Research in Systematic Desensitization

By now you should have some grasp of the scope of behavior therapy and its historical development. One of the most important characteristics of this field is its devotion to experimental investigation. The long-term goal is to build a scientifically based technology for changing behavior.[3]

Research in behavior therapy has become voluminous in recent years. Several journals are devoted entirely to this field, and many others frequently publish articles on behavior therapy. There are also several professional associations in the United States and abroad devoted to furthering interest in this approach to clinical work. In this section research in one subarea of behavior therapy, desensitization, will serve to illustrate the interplay between clinical and experimental work.

### Outcome Research in Desensitization

Laboratory workers became interested in studying desensitization because clinical reports indicated that the technique is effective in reducing, if not eliminating, neurotic fears. Psychologists and other mental health workers rightfully accord Wolpe enduring regard for his formulation and early development of this now widely applied therapy.

Initial steps in the experimental investigation of the procedure were taken by Lazovik and Lang (1960; Lang and Lazovik, 1963). They were concerned primarily with assessing the procedure under relatively controlled laboratory conditions. In the earlier clinical reports, improvement had been judged by the clinicians involved in the treatment, and other therapeutic procedures were usually employed along with desensitization. Lang and Lazovik decided that for greater control in evaluating desensitization of the simple phobia chosen, fear of snakes, testers who were not involved in the actual desensitization should measure the subjects' pretreatment and posttreatment ability to approach snakes. They also restricted treatment to desensitization. Their experiments showed that, indeed, desensitization can measurably and significantly reduce avoidance of a phobic object.

One of the most widely known and highly regarded experiments in systematic desensitization, and in psychotherapy research as a whole, was conducted by Gordon Paul (1966). His purpose was to compare systematic desensitization, a placebo, and insight therapy for their effectiveness in reducing unrealistic fear. He recruited students fearful of speaking in front of groups. Prior to treatment all students had to deliver a speech before an audience, and numerous measures of their anxiety were taken (self-reports, behavioral observations, and physiological measures; see page 81).

Students were then assigned to one of three different treatments. The first was systematic desensitization. The second was a placebo treatment. Subjects in this group met with a sympathetic therapist who led them to believe that a pill would reduce their overall sensitivity to stress. To convince them, Paul had them listen to a tape which the therapist told them had been used in training astronauts to function under stress. They listened to this "stress tape" for several sessions after ingesting the "tranquilizer." In reality, the pill was a placebo, and the tape contained various nonverbal sounds that had been shown in other research to be quite boring. In this way Paul raised subjects' expectations that their social anxieties could be lessened by taking a pill. The third treatment was insight therapy.

[3] That the most effective clinical procedures will be developed through science is an *assumption*. There is nothing inherent in the scientific method that guarantees victories for those studying human behavior. Because we have reached the moon and beyond by playing the science game does not mean that the same set of rules should he applied to human behavior. The existentialists, whose paradigm emphasizes free will, assume that the nature of man cannot be meaningfully probed by following the rules favored by the authors of this textbook. Although we are placing our bets on the scientific work described in this chapter, it nonetheless remains an article of faith that behavior therapy will prove the best means of treating disordered behavior.

Subjects met with skilled insight-oriented therapists to talk over their anxieties; the therapists were free to structure the sessions in any way they saw fit. All treatments were limited to five sessions, a number settled on by the insight therapists when they were asked how many sessions they would need to make a measurable impact on this kind of problem. An important feature of Paul's experimental design was training insight therapists to do systematic desensitization. In fact, insight therapists gave all three treatments. In this way Paul anticipated the criticism that any superiority of systematic desensitization could be attributed to greater enthusiasm shown by desensitization therapists.

The results of this important study revealed that subjects who had received systematic desensitization improved more than did the placebo and insight therapy subjects, who reacted about the same to their forms of therapy. Students receiving these two treatments did, however, show significant improvement. The results, then, indicated that systematic desensitization is superior to both insight therapy and to a placebo in lessening anxiety about making speeches. These results persisted in a two-year follow-up study (Paul, 1967).

## Process Research in Desensitization

These initial experiments did not consider what makes the procedure work. Subsequent experimenters, confident that the procedure was effective both in the clinic and under controlled laboratory conditions, have been conducting studies to try to discover the mechanisms that might account for the efficacy of the procedure. We shall describe one of them in some detail.

According to Wolpe's original formulation of the desensitization procedure, it works because relaxation inhibits the anxiety usually aroused by the frightening situations it is paired with through the subject's imaginings. In an experiment designed to evaluate this hypothesis, Davison (1968b) dismantled the desensitization procedure in the following way; if muscle relaxation is indeed important in reducing fear through desensitization, having subjects imagine graded anxiety-eliciting stimuli *without* accompanying relaxation should not be as effective. One group of snake phobics, the exposure group, did just this. They imagined a series of anxiety-evoking stimuli in the graded fashion typical in desensitization but without first learning deep muscle relaxation.

Another control situation was necessary to test the counterconditioning notions of Wolpe. The desensitization technique is applied within a clinical context in which clients expect to improve. To control for the placebo effect, a pseudodesensitization group was formed. These subjects received as much relaxation training as desensitization subjects, but the relaxation was not associated with anxiety-provoking stimuli. The imaginings of these pseudodesensitization subjects had nothing to do with their anxieties. Again, if the association of relaxation with situations *relevant* to the target behavior is important, this pseudodesensitization procedure should not be as beneficial as actual desensitization.

The third treatment in Davison's experiment was desensitization. Subjects in this group imagined a graded series of anxiety-evoking stimuli while their muscles were deeply relaxed. This group was expected to show more improvement than all the others if Wolpe's insistence on this contiguous pairing is indeed important. Finally, there was a fourth no-treatment group to control for the effects of having fear assessed. It is possible that a subject's fear of snakes will be reduced to a measurable degree merely by having that fear measured twice.

Another feature of the experimental design is important. In order to control for sheer amount of exposure to imagined stimuli, subjects in the exposure and the pseudodesensitization control groups were *yoked* to subjects in the desensitization group. That is, each desensitization subject, unbeknownst to her, had a "partner" in each of these two control groups whose number of scenes imagined was determined in advance by her own progress up the anxiety hierarchy. In this fashion, any differences among the groups

## BOX **19.5** Multimodal Therapy and the BASIC ID

Arnold A. Lazarus, one of the principal figures in behavior therapy.

For many years Arnold Lazarus has been among the most inventive of behavioral clinicians. He has been particularly concerned that behavior therapists remain *flexible,* not committing themselves to particular points of view regarding techniques or even to particular theories. He has now formulated this position in greater detail and given it the name *multimodal therapy*. It is an approach that aims to tailor therapy interventions to the full range of difficulties presented by clients. Lazarus (1973) proposes the acronym BASIC ID to help the clinician remember the seven modalities in which a given client may be having problems: behavior, affect, sensation, imagery, cognition, interpersonal relations, and drugs. Except for prescribed drugs, which are really an intervention rather than an aspect of the person's functioning, each represents a potential trouble spot for the clinician to attend to. Most clients, Lazarus suggests, have problems in several areas; in focusing on one or just a few of them, a therapist may overlook significant difficulties in others. A client who is depressed, for example, may also be disturbed by some of his or her interpersonal relationships.

But Lazarus develops multimodal therapy even further. He argues that the therapist must apply to the gamut of a patient's problems *any* techniques that promise to work; treatment should not be limited to behavior therapy procedures. Lazarus himself is not reluctant to employ techniques from nonbehavioral orientations. Psychoanalytic procedures, he argues, may be expecially well suited to alleviate problems of affect or cognition, whereas various behavior therapy techniques may be better suited to problems in overt behavior or in interpersonal relations. Table 19.1 is a "modality profile" adapted from one that was drawn up by Lazarus for a client.

As might be expected, Lazarus's proposals have not met with universal acceptance among behavior therapists. Some are worried that a "Do what you think will work" attitude will pollute the theoretical purity of behavior therapy and divert the attention of behavioral clinicians from their commitment to scientific formulations and evaluation. Further, the apparent antitheoretical flavor of his proposals disturbs those who believe that advances in therapy are made not only through clinical innovations of the sort people like Lazarus are so skillful in producing but by working methodically within a particular theoretical framework. In any event, Lazarus's suggestions serve to caution behavior therapists against being needlessly rigid in their clinical work. Given the very incomplete state of our knowledge of how best to help people, this warning is timely and valuable.

TABLE **19.1**

## Modality Profile for a Patient in Multimodal Therapy

(adapted from Lazarus, 1973).

| Modality | Problem | Proposed Treatment |
|---|---|---|
| Behavior | Frequent crying<br>Negative self-statements | Nonreinforcement<br>Positive self-talk assignments |
| Affect | Unable to express overt anger<br>Absence of enthusiasm and spontaneous joy<br>Emptiness and aloneness | Role playing<br>Positive imagery procedures<br>General relationship building |
| Sensation | Out of touch with most sensual pleasures<br>Frequent lower back pains | Sensate focus method<br>Orthopedic exercise |
| Imagery | Distressing scenes of sister's funeral | Desensitization |
| Cognition | Irrational self-talk:<br>"I am evil."<br>"I must suffer."<br>"I am inferior." | Deliberative rational disputation and corrective self-talk |
| Interpersonal relationships | Childlike dependence<br>Easily exploited and submissive | Specific self-sufficiency assignments<br>Assertion training |

TABLE **19.2**

Summary of Experimental Design To Determine Role of Counterconditioning in Systematic Desensitization
(from Davison, 1968b)

| Group | Pretreatment assessment ($E_1$) | Treatment procedure ($E_2$) | Posttreatment assessment ($E_1$) |
|---|---|---|---|
| Desensitization | Avoidance test with anxiety self-reports | Relaxation paired with graded imagined aversive stimuli | Avoidance test with anxiety self-reports |
| Pseudodesensitization | Same | Relaxation paired with imagined snake-irrelevant stimuli | Same |
| Exposure | Same | Graded imagined aversive stimuli without relaxation | Same |
| No treatment | Same | No treatment | Same |

could not be attributed to the number of stimuli imagined. The design of this experiment is summarized in Table 19.2.

The results revealed that desensitization subjects improved significantly more than did members of all other groups; and only when aversive stimuli were paired with relaxation was there any reduction in fear. These findings lend support to the idea that desensitization is effective because it involves counterconditioning, that is, because subjects imagine anxiety-evoking stimuli while they are responding in quite another way.

No single experiment, however, ever settles an issue. Several experiments have yielded findings that are inconsistent with a counterconditioning conceptualization of desensitization (for example, Waters, McDonald, and Koresko, 1972; Ross and Proctor, 1973); and more efficient variations of the original technique have been proposed (Goldfried and Davison, 1976). Behavior therapists maintain a high level of skepticism about their own clinical work, continuing to call into question issues that were thought to have been decided in earlier years. This is a healthy trend in clinical psychology, where all too often the pronouncements of innovative theoreticians are accorded such blind regard that careful analysis and experimentation are discouraged.

## Some Basic Issues in Behavior Therapy

We have reviewed both the development of theory and research in behavior therapy and the efforts expended to validate procedures and isolate the significant variables. The field is expanding each year; with such a proliferation of activity, everyone concerned with behavior therapy should remain aware of the problems and issues that transcend particular experimental findings. The following considerations, many of which have been alluded to earlier, need to be kept clearly in mind.

### The behavioral focus on current maintaining variables

An important defining characteristic of behavior therapy is its focus on current maintaining variables rather than on etiology. Masters and Johnson, for example, feel that performance fears and the spectator role are responsible for the maintenance of most human sexual dysfunctions, regardless of etiology (see again Figure 11.3). Religious orthodoxy and psychosexual trauma may well be important historical factors, but they are significant in the present only because they make people fearful about their sexual performance and prone to watch their sexual activities from a distance instead of losing themselves in the excitement of the moment. Behavior therapists tend to concentrate their attention on just such maintaining variables, regardless of what factors brought them into being.

### Internal behavior and cognition

In Chapter 4 we demonstrated that the inference of intervening processes and other explanatory fictions is useful in interpreting data and generating fruitful hypotheses. Behavior therapists are often thought to hold the radical behavioristic positions of Watson and Skinner, that it is not useful or legitimate to make inferences about internal processes of the organism. Our intent is to present a broader point of view as persuasively as we can, although not all contemporary behavior therapists (for example, Ullmann and Krasner, 1975; Bijou and Baer, 1961) agree on this issue.

The position we share with others (see Bandura, 1969; Kanfer and Phillips, 1970; Mahoney, 1974; Meyer and Chesser, 1970; Mischel, 1968; O'Leary and Wilson, 1975) is that behavior therapy, as applied experimental psychology, is legitimately concerned with internal as well as external events, provided the internal mediators are securely anchored to observable stimuli or responses. Behaviorists do not have to ignore the internal life of human beings; but they do differ from psychologists with other views in the rigor of their inferences and in the care they take to ensure that inferences are parsimonious as well as productive of good explanations and testable hypotheses.

### Underlying causes

A related misconception is that behavior therapy deals with symptoms whereas other therapies, particularly psychoanalytically oriented ones, are concerned with "root" or "underlying" causes. To many people a determinant of behavior that is assumed to lie in the unconscious or in the past is somehow more "underlying" or "basic" than a determinant that is anchored in the current environment. This conception fails to consider the fact that science searches for the most significant causes of behavior. If "underlying" is defined as "not immediately obvious," behavior therapists indeed search for underlying causes. If such causes are taken to be the most significant ones, that is, the controlling variables, the task of behavior therapists is the same as for all other therapists—to find the most significant causes (Bandura, 1969).

A clinical example will illustrate this point. A twenty-five-year-old man who had been discharged from a mental hospital was treated for problems that included occasional paranoid delusions. A careful behavioral assessment suggested to both client and therapist that these thoughts of persecution were triggered by considerable anxiety. Rather than working directly on the delusional episodes, then, the therapist desensitized the client to a variety of social situations in which others were likely to form adverse opinions of him. Such occasions seemed often to precede his paranoid "trips." As the client came gradually to be less upset about rejection and criticism, his paranoid thoughts dropped to near zero. Although there is of course no way of knowing whether desensitization to disturbing social situations was truly responsible for this outcome, the behavior therapist did search for an underlying cause as the strongest controlling variable.

### Broad-spectrum treatment

Our review of behavior therapy has necessarily been fragmented because we have dealt with separate techniques one at a time. In clinical practice, however, behavior therapists employ several procedures at once or sequentially in an attempt to deal with all the important controlling variables; this approach is generally referred to as *broad-spectrum behavior therapy* (Lazarus, 1971). For example, a woman fearful of leaving her home might well undergo desensitization by imagining herself walking out of her door and engaging in successive activities. Over the years, however, she may also have built up a dependent relationship with her husband. As she becomes bolder in venturing forth, this change in her behavior may disrupt the equilibrium of the relationship that she and her husband have worked out over the years. To attend only to her fear of leaving home would be incomplete behavior therapy (Lazarus, 1965) and might even lead to replacement of the agoraphobia with another difficulty that would serve to keep the woman at home—a problem frequently called "symptom substitution."

In a related vein, it is often said that behavior therapists invariably focus only on the patient's complaint as it was stated during the first interview. The facts are otherwise. A clinical graduate student was desensitizing an undergraduate for test anxiety. The client made good progress up the hierarchy of imagined situations but was not improving at all in the real world of test taking. The supervisor of the graduate student suggested that the therapist find out whether the client was studying for his tests. It turned out that he was not; worry about the health of his mother was markedly interfering with his attempts to study. Thus the goal of making the client nonchalant about taking tests was inappropriate, for he was approaching the tests themselves without adequate preparation. On the basis of additional assessment, the therapy shifted away from desensitization to a discussion of how the client could deal with his realistic fears about his mother's possible death.

### Relationship factors

Because of the scientific language typically employed in the literature on behavior therapy, behavior therapists are considered little if at all concerned with the therapist-client relationship: whether, for example, the client trusts the therapist, believes that he or she can be of assistance, and the like. Although behaviorists have, indeed, tried to emphasize the learning mechanisms that are brought into play by the various techniques, they have never discounted the importance of the client's feelings about the therapist (Goldfried and Davison, 1976). Research in behavior therapy has, in fact, already documented the importance of sometimes vaguely defined relationship factors. In the Paul (1966) study, for example, considerable and long-lasting improvement was observed in subjects who were given the placebo treatment in the context of a therapeutic relationship. Thus, although desensitization subjects improved more than did the others, the significant improvement in the placebo group demonstrates the substantial contribution of the warm, trusting relationship with a therapist.

A good therapeutic relationship is important for many reasons. It seems doubtful that clients will reveal deeply personal information if they do not trust or respect their therapists. Further, since behavior therapy cannot be imposed on an unwilling client, a therapist must obtain the cooperation of the client if there is to be any possibility at all that techniques will have their desired effect. In desensitization, for example, a client could readily sabotage the best efforts of the therapist by not imagining a particular scene, by not signaling anxiety appropriately, and by not practicing relaxation. And in virtually all other behavior therapy procedures clients are able to (and sometimes will) work against the therapist if relationship factors are neglected (Davison, 1973).

### Flesh on the theoretical skeleton

The issue of determining the most important controlling variables is related to another overlooked aspect of behavior therapy—indeed, of any therapy—namely moving from a general principle to a concrete clinical intervention.

To illustrate, let us consider a study in which undergraduates were trained to analyze the behavior of severely disturbed children in operant conditioning terms (Davison, 1964b). The students were encouraged to *assume* that the important determinants of these children's behavior were the consequences of that behavior. Armed with M & M candies as reinforcers, these student-therapists attempted to bring the behavior of the severely disturbed children under their control. Eventually, one child appeared to be losing interest in earning the candies. Working within a framework that required an effective reinforcer, the therapist looked around for another incentive. Luckily, he noticed that each time the child passed a window, she would pause for a moment to look at her reflection. The therapist obtained a mirror and was subsequently able to make "peeking into the mirror" the reinforcer for desired behavior; the peeks into the mirror were used in the same *functional* way as the M & M candies. Thus, *although guided by a general principle, the therapist had to rely on improvisation and inventiveness as demanded by the clinical situation.*

An outsider can get the impression that devising therapy along behavioral lines is easy and straightforward, that the application of a general principle to a particular case is a simple matter. Those who have worked as behavioral clinicians, however, know otherwise. Although a given theoretical framework helps to guide the clinician's thinking, it is by no means sufficient.

> *. . . The clinician in fact approaches his work with a given set, a framework for ordering the complex data that are his domain. But frameworks are insufficient. The clinician, like any other applied scientist, must fill out the theoretical skeleton. Individual cases present problems that always call for knowledge beyond basic psychological principles* (Lazarus and Davison, 1971, p. 203).

The preceding quotation from two behavior therapists is very similar to the following one from an article written by two experimental social psychologists.

> *In any experiment, the investigator chooses a procedure which he intuitively feels is an empirical realization of his conceptual variable. All experimental procedures are "contrived" in the sense that they are invented. Indeed, it can be said that the art of experimentation rests primarily on the skill of the investigator to judge the procedure which is the most accurate realization of his conceptual variable and has the greatest impact and the most credibility for the subject* (Aronson and Carlsmith, 1968, p. 25).

Thus behavior therapists are faced with the same kinds of decision-making challenges that their experimental colleagues face. There are no easy solutions in dealing with human problems.

### Psychoanalysis and behavior therapy—a rapprochement?

Is contemporary psychoanalysis compatible with behavior therapy? This question has been discussed for many years, and few professionals are optimistic about a meaningful rapprochement, arguing that these two points of view are incompatible paradigms. But recently Paul Wachtel (1977), an ego analyst, has offered a scheme that, in our view, holds considerable promise at least for establishing a dialogue between psychoanalytically oriented therapists and behavior therapists.

As indicated in Chapter 18, ego analysts place much more emphasis on current ego functioning than did Freud. Sullivan, for example, alerted his psychoanalytic colleagues to his belief that patients will feel better about themselves and function more effectively if they focus on problems in their current interpersonal behavior. But even Sullivan appears to have been ambivalent about the wisdom of working directly on how people act and feel in the present if this might mean they would not recover memories of repressed infantile conflicts. Wachtel, however, suggests that the therapist *should* help the client change his current behavior, not only so that he can feel better in the here and now but indeed so that he can *change* his childlike fears from the past. For example, if a client takes heart from being able to control present behavior, he may then uncover and alter his "woolly mammoth." By pointing out that a direct alteration of behavior may be able to help clients attain a more realistic understanding of their past repressed conflicts, traditionally the goal of psychoanalysis, Wachtel hopes to interest his analytic colleagues in the techniques employed by behavior therapists.

Similarly, Wachtel holds that behavior therapists can learn much from their analytic colleagues, especially concerning the *kinds* of problems people tend to develop. For example, psychoanalytic theory tells us that children have strong and usually ambivalent feelings about their parents, and that, presumably, some of these are so unpleasant that they are repressed, or at least are difficult to focus on and talk about openly. Suppose then that a behavior therapist is working with a male client who describes himself as fearful of heterosexual relationships. In most instances the therapist will work to help the client reduce his unrealistic anxieties and perhaps also offer training in social skills. But if the focus is exclusively on heterosexual anxiety, the therapist will not explore the possibility that the client is also *angry* at women. How might the therapist come to believe this? Wachtel suggests that the behavior therapist sensitive to the childhood conflicts that analysts focus on will question the client about his relationship with his mother. The client's reply or manner may give a hint of resentment. Assuming this happens, the therapist will then *see* the client differently. He will hypothesize that the client is not just fearful of women but angry at them as well, because he associates them with a mother who has been the object of both hate and love from early childhood. This additional information will presumably suggest a different behavioral intervention, for the anger must be dealt with.

Arnold Lazarus has been urging for years that behavior therapists adopt particular *techniques* from insight therapies. Gestalt therapists, for example, are very adept at helping people confront their feelings through a variety of highly innovative procedures (see page 485). Even though such techniques can hardly be said to have been derived from basic laboratory research, nonetheless they *appear to be effective* and should not be dismissed by behavior therapists simply because they come from a different therapeutic tradition. Moreover, it should be possible to conduct research on these procedures, something Gestalt therapists are not likely to do, and thereby evaluate when they are useful and why.

## Summary

In this chapter we have reviewed theory and research in behavior therapy, a branch of clinical psychology which attempts to apply the methodologies and principles of experimental psychology to the therapeutic modification of human behavior. Several subareas of this burgeoning field were surveyed: counterconditioning—eliciting a substitute response in the presence of a stimulus that evokes an undesired response; operant conditioning—teaching desired responses and discouraging undesired ones by applying the contingencies of reward and punishment; modeling—helping the client to acquire new responses and unlearn old ones by observing models; and cognitive restructuring—encouraging change in behavior by altering mediating thoughts. Masters and Johnson's method of treating human sexual inadequacies was summarized to show how the sensitivity of clinicians to human needs meshes well with specific behavioral techniques. Experimental work in systematic desensitization, a widely used technique for reducing unrealistic fears, was reviewed as a case study in behavior therapy research. Finally, several important issues in behavior therapy—such as the role of underlying causes, relationship factors, and the possibilities of integrating some parts of psychoanalytic theorizing into behavior therapy—were discussed in the hope of providing the reader with a better and more sophisticated grasp of a field that is both promising and controversial.

# chapter 20

## GROUP THERAPY, COMMUNITY PSYCHOLOGY, AND SOMATIC TREATMENT



A serious and continuing problem in the alleviation of human psychological suffering is the persistent shortage of mental health professionals (for example, Albee, 1969; Arnhoff, Rubinstein, and Speisman, 1969). Even overlooking the difficulties in defining mental disorder and in determining how many people need assistance, most writers agree that in the foreseeable future America's mental health needs are unlikely to be met. According to their present estimates of the incidence of disorder, the numbers trained and being trained will not be able to provide necessary services.

In this chapter we review three means of therapeutic intervention. Although different from one another in many important ways, they are similar in making far more efficient use of professional time than the one-to-one therapies reviewed in the preceding two chapters. In group therapy a professional treats a number of patients simultaneously; community psychology is oriented toward prevention and treats the problems of patients without removing them from their customary surroundings; and somatic treatments—drugs, electroconvulsive therapy, and surgery—do not require much time to administer. All three, then, are more economical than individual therapy. As we shall soon see, however, economy is not the primary reason that any of the three is chosen. Rather, each treatment has developed from a particular rationale for providing effective help.

## Group Therapy

A single therapist can obviously treat more people by seeing them in groups, and charge lower fees, than would be possible were he or she seeing them individually. But it would be a mistake to estimate the value of group therapy only in economic terms. Most group therapists regard their form of treatment as *uniquely* appropriate for accomplishing certain goals. For example, group members can learn vicariously (see page 44) when attention is focused on another participant. Social pressures, too, can be surprisingly strong in groups. If a therapist tells an individual client that his or her behavior seems hostile even when hostility is not intended, the message may be rejected; however, if three or four other people agree with the interpretation, the person may find it much more difficult to reject the observation. In addition, many people derive comfort and support solely from the knowledge that others have problems similar to their own.

As we saw in the two preceding chapters, the literature on one-to-one psychotherapy is confusing and extensive: so too is the information available on group therapy. Virtually every technique or theory employed in individual therapy has been, or can be, used for treating people in groups. Thus there are psychoanalytic groups (Slavson, 1950; Wolf, 1949), Gestalt groups (Perls, 1969), client-centered groups (Rogers, 1970), behavior therapy groups (Lazarus, 1968a; Paul and Shannon, 1966), and countless other kinds. We shall examine closely a few group psychotherapies in hopes of imparting some idea of the range of theories and procedures prevalent.

### Insight-Oriented Group Therapy

#### Moreno's psychodrama

J. L. Moreno, a Viennese psychiatrist, is said to have coined the term "group psychotherapy" in 1931. He was unquestionably one of the most influential and colorful figures in the field. The essence of the form of group therapy he introduced—psychodrama—is to have participants act out their feelings as if in a play. A male patient might be asked to converse with another group member playing the role of his father. By this means the patient is apparently helped to express his feelings and perceptions about his father more effectively than were he to try to verbalize them. "We must stimulate the patients to be concrete, and bring forth their feelings and thoughts in a structured form" (Moreno and Kipper, 1968, p. 56). Like other forms of group therapy, psychodrama makes unique use of the group as a vehicle for changing people. Group members provide a company of potential actors with whom to stage the dramatic presentations that presumably reveal people's true feelings and conflicts.

To facilitate therapeutic role taking, Moreno advised using an actual stage so that the members of the group are encouraged to view the proceedings as a kind of drama; the presence of an audience also contributes to the theatrical atmosphere. Moreno suggested many kinds of role taking to promote the expression and confrontation of true feelings. For example, the *mirroring technique* is designed for patients who have difficulty expressing themselves in action or in words: another person, an "auxiliary ego," portrays the patient as best he can, thereby furnishing him concrete information on how others view him. At all times the emphasis is on expressing in dramatic form true feelings about certain situations. The therapist is an important participant in these activities, sometimes actively directing the "play" so that therapeutic gain will be the maximum.

Should psychodrama be classified as insight or action-oriented therapy? Clearly, the therapist assumes responsibility for what happens during the session; furthermore, he or she goads the patients into specific behavior during treatment. On the other hand, the ultimate goal of the treatment was seen by Moreno as insight into motivation. Thus psychodrama appears to be an insight therapy that goes beyond the reliance on verbal interpretive methods of psychoanalysis but that still emphasizes the importance of helping patients achieve an understanding of their true motivations and needs.

Unfortunately, there is no body of research on psychodrama, so it is difficult to assess the efficacy of Moreno's ideas.

### Sensitivity training and encounter groups

Without question, one of the most exciting developments in clinical psychology and psychiatry is the sensitivity training group, or T-group, movement. Aronson (1972) differentiates the T-group from the more radical "encounter group," which grew in popularity primarily on the West coast at such places as the Esalen Institute. T-groups, he contends, tend to rely more on verbal procedures and to avoid the physical contact employed by many encounter groups. Aronson's distinction is not accepted by all workers, however. Rogers (1970) traces the development of encounter groups to his training of counselors at the University of Chicago in 1946, in which he emphasized personal growth and improved interpersonal communication. We would agree with his judgment that T-groups and encounter groups are usually impossible to distinguish one from the other nowadays.

The T-group was originally conceived in 1947 at the National Training Laboratories in Bethel, Maine. The impetus came from colleagues of Kurt Lewin, who was a famous social psychologist at MIT. The original groups were made up of people in industry, and the goal was to increase efficiency in business practices at the highest levels of management by making executives more aware of their impact on other people and of their own feelings about others. Over the past thirty years many people have participated in such groups, including no doubt some readers of this book.

The T-group is best viewed as educational. Generally speaking, members are encouraged to focus on their relationships to one another. Individuals are often drawn to T-groups because, even when apparently functioning quite well and without marked unhappiness, they feel that they are missing something in life or are perhaps concerned about interpersonal problems. Aronson lists some general goals of T-groups.

1. To develop a willingness to examine one's behavior and to experiment with new ways of behaving.
2. To learn more about people in general.
3. To become more authentic and honest in interpersonal relations.
4. To work cooperatively with people rather than assuming an authoritarian or submissive manner.
5. To develop the ability to resolve conflicts through logical and rational thinking rather than through coercion and manipulation of others.

In the most general terms T-groups and encounter groups provide a setting wherein people are encouraged to behave in an unguarded fashion. They are then helped to see how they come across to and affect others and to examine how they feel about their behavior. Aronson (1972) provides the following description of a group session getting started.

> *. . . He* [the leader] *. . . falls into silence. Minutes pass. They seem like hours. The group members may look at each other or out the window. Typically, participants may look at the trainer for guidance or direction. None is forthcoming. After several minutes, someone might express his discomfort. This may or may not be responded to. Eventually, in a typical group, someone will express annoyance at the leader: "I'm getting sick of this. This is a waste of time. How come you're not doing your job? What the hell are we paying you for? Why don't you tell us what we're supposed to do?" There may be a ripple of applause in the background. But someone else might jump in and ask the*

*first person why he is so bothered by a lack of direction—does he need someone to tell him what to do? And the T-group is off and running (p. 241).*

Levels of Communication Figure 20.1 is Aronson's schematic representation of a dyadic or two-person interaction. In our everyday lives we usually operate at level $P_3$, namely behaving in some verbal or nonverbal way toward another person. Usually the recipient of our $P_3$ behavior eventually responds at level $R_4$, evaluating us. There are obviously many points at which misjudgments can occur. For example, at level $R_3$ the recipient may misinterpret P's intention. Even though the person, a man, may feel warmly ($P_1$) toward his friend the recipient, he may have difficulty expressing warmth and therefore display sarcasm at $P_3$. The recipient may then interpret P's intention as a wish to hurt him ($R_3$), rather than as a desire to express warm feelings toward him. Without the open discussion of feelings that is encouraged in a T-group, the recipient can reject ($R_4$) the person as a nasty individual and never come to understand that the person really feels warmly ($P_1$) but has not learned to express his feelings ($P_3$) appropriately. Or the following might occur. A person may be expressing warm feelings in a totally open way, at $P_3$, but the recipient, for reasons of his own, may be so suspicious of any expression of warmth that he misinterprets ($R_3$) the person's intentions and rejects him instead of acknowledging and enjoying the expression of warmth. A properly run T-group encourages the participants to break down their interpersonal communications and reactions into all the various components so that they can examine their true feelings toward other persons and their perceptions of what they are receiving from them.

Within the T-group people talk frankly and listen to one another. Usually, the group works on the ongoing interaction, rather than examining past histories, as would be the case in a

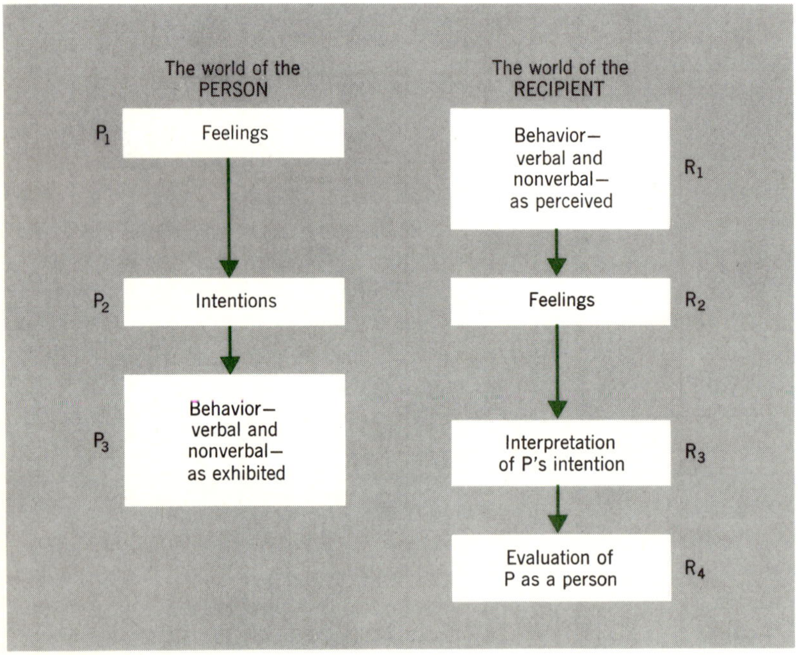


FIGURE **20.1**
Schematic representation of a two-person interaction. The diagram illustrates the different levels of communication possible. After Aronson, 1972.

psychoanalytically oriented group. The emphasis on openness is not necessarily a violation of a person's right to privacy, although there is little question that in some groups people feel pressured to reveal more about themselves than they might wish. Experienced and competent group leaders watch for undue coercion and direct the stream of conversation away from an individual when they sense excessive probing into the person's private feelings.

One of the principal tools for achieving the kind of learning desired in a T-group is immediate and open feedback from fellow group members, including the leader. Thus A may be continually interrupting B and yet be unaware of her dislike for B. Other group members, or the leader, might interject a comment to A that she is apparently having difficulty expressing certain feelings to B and perhaps would like to do so more directly than by interrupting him. Furthermore, A might be made aware of the negative impact that her constant interruptions have on B, perhaps even more negative than an honest expression of dislike would have.

**Role of T-group Leader** Let us now summarize what Aronson sees as the role and the function of the group leader in a T-group.

1. The leader or trainer is a full member of the group. His or her own feelings, reactions, and effects on others are as legitimate a subject of discourse as are those of any other group member. Unlike some group therapists, T-group leaders do not hold themselves aloof from their clients.
2. Being professionals, however, leaders are busy performing other functions as well. They may occasionally comment on what is going on in the group, or they may step in to help people with difficult encounters and to make certain that participants discuss their feelings about others rather than judging them.
3. On the assumption that discoveries made by one's self are more meaningful and longer-lasting than insights and observations doled out by experts, the group leader tries whenever possible not to intervene. At times, for example, he or she finds it best to remain silent.
4. Competent trainers will make every effort not to impose their will and ideas on the other participants, but they are of course aware of the very powerful position that they occupy in the group. It seems likely that some of the unfortunate abuses of encounter groups and T-groups can be attributed to the all-too-human tendency of some trainers to wield this power unwisely.

**Variations** Sensitivity or encounter groups vary in a number of ways. Rogers's (1970) groups tend to operate according to his individual client-centered therapy as outlined in Chapter 18; the leader tries to clarify the feelings of group members, on the assumption that growth can occur as people confront their emotions with honesty. The group leader—or "facilitator"—tends to be less active than in the T-groups Aronson describes. Some groups may meet for hours at a time, perhaps over a weekend, with little if any sleep allowed. Such *marathons* (Bach, 1966; Mintz, 1967; Stoller, 1968) rely on fatigue and extended exposure to a particular set of social conditions to weaken "defenses" and help the participants become more open. Many encounter group enthusiasts use exercises to break the ice (Schutz, 1967). For example, a man may be instructed to close his eyes and allow himself to be carried around by other group members, which is supposed to help him trust them. In another exercise two people stare into each other's eyes without speaking. Such maneuvers are meant to loosen people up, making clear to them that in this social setting feelings are to be expressed openly without censorship or fear of punishment. Bindrim (1968) introduced nudity as an aid to lowering defenses. Drug addict "Synanon" groups tend even to be brutal in the directness of their confrontations (Yablonsky, 1962).

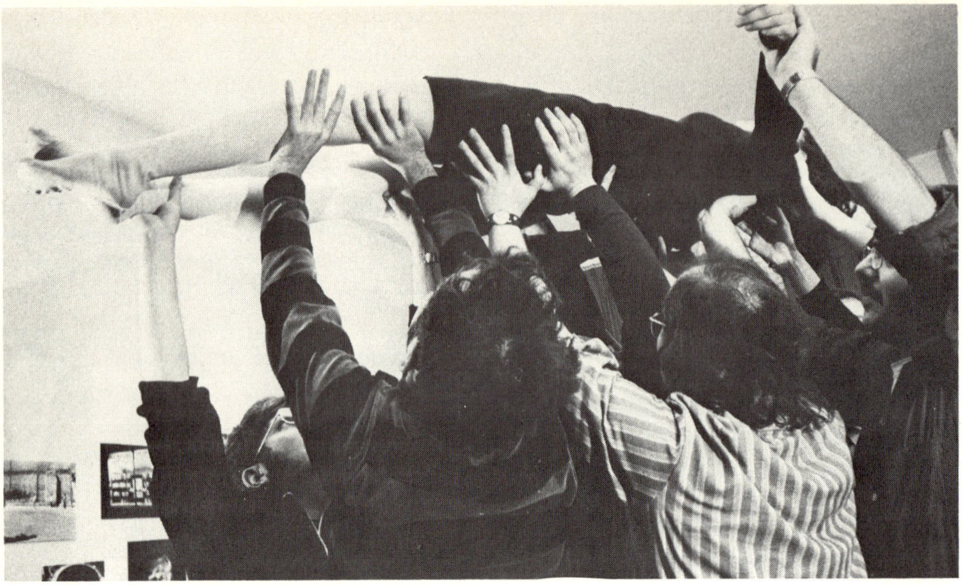

An encounter group exercise designed to foster trust.

Evaluation We turn now to research done on T-groups. Do they really work? Like other therapies, the T-group and encounter movement has its share of glowing testimonials.

> *I have known individuals for whom the encounter experience has meant almost miraculous change in the depth of their communication with spouse and children. Sometimes for the first time real feelings are shared. . . . I have seen teachers who have transformed their classroom . . . into a personal, caring, trusting, learning group, where students participate fully and openly in forming the curriculum and all the other aspects of their education. Tough business executives who described a particular business relationship as hopeless have gone home and changed it into a constructive one (Rogers, 1970, p. 71).*

Such observations, especially by a highly skilled and innovative clinician, contribute to the growing faith many people have in encounter groups. Comments of this nature do not, however, satisfy most scientists of human behavior.

Some critics have suggested that those who participate in T-groups learn only how to participate in T-groups. They are not able to transfer to real-life situations the insights and skills that have been acquired in a group (Houts and Serber, 1972). Transfer of learning is a difficult problem for, whether we like it or not, the real world is not set up to encourage openness and frankness. Those who are not operating by the rules of a T-group may be offended by the open and honest expression of feelings. Indeed, as Aronson reminds us, if someone insists that others be totally open when they do not want to be, he or she is being insensitive to their feelings and so really has *not* learned some of the essentials from what might have seemed a good T-group experience. Is this to say that T-group experiences can never transfer to the real world? Not necessarily, for a knowledge of how a person feels about others and comes across to them may be extremely useful in everyday activities, even though the overt behavior encouraged in a T-group is not continued.

Because the independent variables are so complex and difficult to control, it is extraordinarily difficult to do good research with T-groups. As with all psychotherapy research, there is little agreement on what are the best means of measuring success. There is wide disparity in how often groups meet and for how long, and the people assembled are quite diverse. Few studies have employed credible controls for the placebo effect. Most importantly, little attention is paid to what actually *happens* in the group. Mindful of these methodological shortcomings, Smith (1975) has offered the following tentative conclusions about groups that met for at least twenty hours and were compared to no-treatment controls.

1. T-group participants tend to view themselves more favorably after a group experience, and this effect often persists for months afterward.
2. Some studies suggest that group members come to view themselves as more in control of their behavior, more responsible for themselves.
3. There is little if any good evidence that T-groups help participants become more open-minded and less prejudiced.
4. Some documentation suggests that participants are more willing to disclose personal information about themselves.
5. Since the purpose of a sensitivity training group is to foster understanding of others and their needs, it is surprising how little evidence shows participants becoming more empathic.
6. Some evidence suggests that participants improve more than controls in communication skills.
7. Some data indicate that associates of former group participants see them as functioning better in their everyday activities. For example, they seem more relaxed, more communicative. But in most instances the observers knew that their friends and colleagues had been in a group program, thus weakening the import of this observation.

A sobering finding is the number of "casualties" from T-groups (for example, Yalom and Lieberman, 1971). Many people have reacted adversely to a leader's encouragement of confrontation or to his or her highly coercive and authoritarian manner. Moreover, as Serber (1972) has pointed out, a man with a serious deficiency in his interpersonal functioning, such as a painful degree of shyness, may have this fault pointed out to him by the group. If, as often seems to happen, the leader allows discussion to shift away from the man on the assumption that confrontation with the difficulty is sufficient in itself, the individual may very well leave the group feeling *worse* about himself. It appears that, like other interventions, group therapy can hurt as well as help (Bergin, 1966, 1971). Experiences in T-groups and encounter groups may affect people powerfully, but not always to the benefit of all participants.

## Behavior Therapy Groups

### Individualized behavior therapy in groups

Arnold Lazarus (1968a), a pioneer in group behavior therapy, has pointed out that a behavior therapist may, primarily for reasons of efficiency, choose to treat several people suffering from the same kind of problem by seeing them in a group rather than individually. The emphasis, as in one-to-one therapy, remains on interactions between the therapist and each individual patient or client.

Group desensitization (Lazarus, 1961; Paul and Shannon, 1966) is a good example of this individualized approach. A single therapist can teach deep muscle relaxation and present a hierarchy to each member of the group simultaneously, thus saving therapist time.

Another example of individualized behavior therapy in groups is Lazarus's (1968a) treatment of several impotent men in one group and of several frigid women in another group. Treatment for each group consisted of didactic discussion of sexual functioning, including noncoital methods of providing sexual pleasure to a partner, as well as group desensitization of related sexual fears. Therapeutic messages and instructions emanated from a single therapist to each of a number of people at the same time (Figure 20.2a).

### Assertion training groups

As we have seen, members of groups are also likely to interact with one another and provide a uniquely appropriate setting in which to bring about desirable behavioral changes (see Box 20.1). The lines of communication in such a group are among all participants, not just between therapist and participants (Figure 20.2b). Lazarus's assertion training groups are examples of this second type of behavior therapy group.

The assumption behind assertion training is that people can alleviate tension by learning to state their desires simply and without apology; and by expressing more openly their feelings of resentment as well as their warmth and cordiality. Group behavior therapy for nonassertive individuals attempts to reduce their anxiety about expressing their feelings toward others and to instill new habits of assertion within the educative atmosphere of the group.

Lazarus suggests that an assertion training group be composed of about ten people of the same sex. At the first meeting the behavior therapist describes the general goals of the therapy group, commenting particularly on the problems that nonassertiveness can create for individuals in our society. He also suggests that the therapy group can provide a good setting for cooperative problem solving. Like Rogers, he calls for honesty and acceptance within the group, hoping to eliminate the showmanship and falseness that often characterize ordinary social interaction. The therapist also prescribes constructive criticism and the diligent practice of new skills. Then members introduce themselves briefly, and the others are encouraged to comment on the manner in which they presented themselves, especially if it was apologetic.

Of particular importance are *assignments* carried out by the members *between group sessions:* attention is paid to behavior not just in the group but in real life as well. People are en-

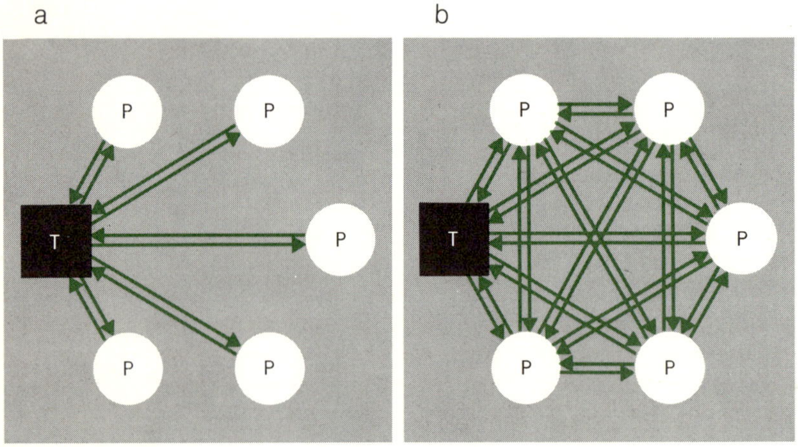


FIGURE **20.2**
Distinction between individualized group therapy (a) and group therapy in which interactions among all the members are regarded as important (b). Arrows indicate lines of communication and influence; T stands for therapist, P for patient.

## BOX **20.1** Encounter Group Exercises and Behavior Therapy

Behavior therapists have begun to consider the use of encounter group procedures for producing specified behavioral changes. Liberman (1972) has proposed a schema linking various exercises with behavioral goals, as illustrated in Table 20.1

### TABLE **20.1**
### The Use of Structured Exercises To Promote Behavioral Change in Groups
(adapted from Liberman, 1972)

| Exercise | Behavioral goal |
|---|---|
| One member breaks into circle of members with arms interlocked | To enable a new group member or an alienated member to feel part of the group (initiation) |
| Making noises, playing tag, simulating the playground activity of children | To reduce anxiety and diffidence in a beginning group; to warm up the group; to foster regression which may help members to suspend defensive behavior at least temporarily |
| Simulated karate, arm wrestling, other "combat" games | To dissipate hostile tensions between members, and to teach aggressive responses |
| Members acting in pairs confront each other with their exact feelings about one another | To teach emotional assertiveness; to desensitize anxiety attached to assertiveness |
| Tug of war | To teach teamwork and organized effort; to teach reciprocity in responding to the other team |
| Fantasy games and Gestalt exercises | To arouse affect and to give members the opportunity to work through a problem relationship emotionally—a corrective emotional experience |
| Members are instructed to express positive feelings to one another nonverbally | To teach individuals how to give and accept affection |
| Mirror game—mimicking the movements of a leader | To teach individuals to follow another's lead and to move in a way that others can easily follow |
| Members acting in pairs sum up and paraphrase partner's statements before going on to make their own statements | To teach each member to listen carefully and empathize with his or her partner |

couraged to describe both successful and unsuccessful attempts at assertive behavior in their everyday activities, and sometimes role playing is employed within the group to enable a person to improve upon past or anticipated performances. The emphasis is at all times on the benefits to be derived from appropriate and effective expression of both positive and negative feelings. If the therapist is sensitive and skillful, he or she is able to create an atmosphere in which group members begin to trust themselves to express criticism without fearing that they are hurting other people's feelings. Assertion groups may even be effective in reducing the compliant, withdrawn behavior of chronic schizophrenics (Bloomfield, 1973).

There are some similarities between Lazarus's assertion training groups and the sensitivity training groups described earlier, but an important difference is the attention Lazarus pays to between-session activities; people are trained within the group to make specific changes later, outside the group therapy setting. Although T-groups are similarly concerned with helping people change their everyday lives, as yet much less systematic attention has been paid to what clients do between group sessions.

## Family and Marital Therapy

The term *family therapy* does not denote a set procedure. Although the focus of therapy is on at least two members of a family, how the therapist views the problems, what techniques are chosen to alleviate them, how often family members are seen, and whether children and even grandparents are included are all variables of treatment. An example of marital therapy employing Gestalt techniques has already been provided (see page 486). Those who identify themselves as family therapists generally agree that faulty communication can be the cause of problems ranging from a poor marital relationship to misbehavior of a child at home or at school.

As an overall approach, family therapy seems to have begun with the work of John Bell, a psychologist working in the 1940s at the Mental Research Institute in Palo Alto, California. In the past thirty years an increasing number of mental health professionals have devoted their professional lives to this kind of work. During the 1960s the efforts of Virginia Satir, a psychiatric social worker, and Don Jackson, a psychiatrist, also at MRI, provided the field with fresh impetus. It is difficult to categorize the theoretical approach of the MRI people, but it is fair to say

Family therapists concentrate on the communication problems of distressed couples.

that their work has been much more behavioral in nature than insight-oriented. Faulty communication patterns are identified, and members of the family come to realize how their behavior affects their relations with others. They then devote their energies to making specific changes. Few family therapists are concerned with past history, and none believes that working with only one member of the family can be fruitful. Whatever the clinical problem, the family therapist views it as that of a *system,* the family, and therefore treated to the best advantage within this context.

Richard Stuart (1969) has provided an operant theory and what he calls operant-interpersonal therapy for work with troubled married couples. He conceives of marital problems in terms of negotiable exchanges of reinforcers between wife and husband. He therefore proposes that therapists encourage couples to make explicit reinforcement contracts with each other. For example, the husband can agree to show appreciation for his wife's efforts within or outside the home in exchange for her reinforcing him for his efforts at fathering. Similar operant analyses of marital problems—careful delineation of the specific behavior to be changed, and arrangement of positive reinforcement contingencies to shape new responses—are done by a clinical research team at the University of Oregon (Patterson, Hops, and Weiss, 1976).

Perhaps because the processes and outcomes of family therapy are so complex and often vague, controlled research on whether it works, with what kinds of problems, and how has only begun (Gottman et al., 1976; Weiss, Hops, and Patterson, 1973). A great virtue of most family therapists is their willingness to make their work public. It is commonplace to have therapy sessions videotaped, and several professional journals, such as *Family Process* and *Family Therapy,* publish detailed accounts of clinical work. Some professionals view family therapy as a revolution in the treatment of human psychological suffering. Whether it will indeed prove this dramatically effective remains to be seen.

## Community Psychology

The approach of community psychology is *seeking* rather than waiting (Rappaport and Chinsky, 1974). Waiting is the mode of nearly all therapies reviewed thus far. Professional persons with advanced degrees make themselves available in offices and hospitals to provide assistance to individuals who, usually out of extreme suffering, initiate the contact themselves or are referred by the courts. In the seeking mode, in contrast, mental health services are often provided outside of professional settings, in a person's own community; those who are troubled or are likely to be are actually sought out by these workers, some of whom are paraprofessionals supervised by psychologists or psychiarists. The emphasis is on early prevention of difficulties rather than the "repair work" commonly performed in the waiting mode.

But what does action-oriented community psychology offer people in their communities? Are the techniques employed by community psychologists different from those used in private practice so that a seeking mode makes especially good sense? The answer is complex.

Rappaport and Chinsky (1974) have proposed a scheme to clarify a too often confused area. They suggest that every type of mental health care has two components, the delivery and the conceptual. The delivery component relates to the difference between seeking and waiting, to an *attitude* about making services available. Community psychology has a seeking orientation. The conceptual component, on the other hand, consists of the theoretical and data-based underpinnings of the services. Two examples are psychoanalytic and learning approaches. Table 20.2 illustrates how these two conceptual modes combine with either style of delivery. For example, a twenty-four-hour-a-day "hotline" in a suicide prevention center would be in the community psychology seeking mode. But what specifically the people answering the phones say and do when a call comes in depends on the conceptual mode. One worker might be psycho-

TABLE **20.2**
## Some Possible Models for Mental Health Service
(adapted from Rappaport and Chinsky, 1974)

| Conceptual component* | Delivery component | |
|---|---|---|
| | Waiting mode | Seeking mode |
| Psychoanalytic conception | Psychodynamic explanations of abnormal behavior. Therapist waits for patient to contact him and then uses insight therapy. | Psychodynamic explanations of abnormal behavior. Professional attempts to prevent illness through public education and extends traditional treatments into community settings. |
| Behavioral conception | Learning theory interpretation of emotional dysfunction. Therapist waits for client to contact him and then uses techniques such as systematic desensitization. | Learning theory interpretation of emotional dysfunction. Professional extends services into the community through public education; trains various nonprofessionals in behavior therapy techniques and social-learning principles. |

* Listed here as examples are only two of a large number of possible conceptual components.

analytic in approach; another might construe suicide threats in learning terms. Clearly, these two workers would answer the calls differently—but both would be delivering community psychology. The conceptual components section of Table 20.2 could, of course, be expanded almost indefinitely. Whether a particular conceptual orientation is more suited to one of the two delivery modes than to the other is a separate, and crucial, question, one which creates ongoing controversy among community psychologists and psychiatrists.

### Values and the Question of Where To Intervene

In a recent effort to explain the essence of community psychology, Rappaport (1977) proposes that we view society as composed of four levels: the individual, the small group, the organization, and the institution. Therapists will intervene at a given level, depending on their values and goals for people. For example, if the therapist assumes that society itself is benign, human problems will be seen as failures to *adjust to* this benign system. Treatment will therefore attempt to change the *individual* so that he or she will fit into society. The goal is pursued in a number of ways—from behavior therapy to psychoanalysis to chemotherapy—but in all these modes of intervention society is considered good and people in need of adjustment to it. In contrast, human problems may be assumed to derive from interpersonal difficulties such as conflicts within families, work settings, and other *small groups*. Within the group framework the therapist will apply family and encounter therapy to help members communicate better. The therapist will *not* try to change only the individual because the problem is assumed to lie in group processes.

If the third level, that of *organizations,* is considered at fault, therapists have another view of human disorders. They "blame" the way units such as schools and prisons operate. To help a child who is failing in her academic work, for example, therapists examine the school curriculum and how it is implemented by principals and teachers; they do *not* provide remedial tutoring for the pupil. Community psychology operates at this level and at the *institutional* level, which is closely related to it but is more abstract and all-inclusive. Institutions refer not to physical entities such as school buildings and prisons but to the basic values and ideologies that characterize a society, its religion, and its politics. For example, the community psychologist may assert that people are unhappy because of a lopsided distribution of wealth and power. Professional efforts would then rightly be directed at political parties, the courts, legislatures, and the like, *not* to encourage them to function more efficiently but rather to change entirely their goals and basic assumptions so that they pursue a more equitable social distribution of wealth and power.

Rappaport's analysis makes it clear why some community workers tend to be impatient with individual and group therapy. They do not believe the problems lie with the individual or the group, and they even assert that by concentrating on these levels the therapist will overlook the real problems of organizations and institutions. For these reasons community psychologists work in the seeking mode and make no pretense, as some individual and group therapists unfortunately do, at being politically and ethically neutral.

## Community Mental Health Centers

### Goals and services

Why this shift to community activism in the treatment of mental disorders? For many years objections were raised about how few people could avail themselves of psychotherapeutic services, which were typically very expensive, in short supply, and apparently geared to so-called YAVIS clients—individuals who are young, attractive, verbal, intelligent, and successful. In addition, people came to believe that emotional difficulties could be better dealt with in their earliest stages of development, rather than after crises or complete deterioration. Indeed, "primary prevention" seeks to forestall problems altogether by changing the conditions that are assumed to cause them.

In the early years of this century, people considered insane were generally institutionalized in asylums or mental hospitals, human warehouses located miles from populated areas (see Box 20.2). But by the 1920s a number of "psychopathic hospitals" had been established in the midst of several American cities, under the supposition that individuals having difficulties coping with everyday problems should be treated early and in settings not so far removed from their homes. Additional impetus for treating mental disorders within the community was provided when the extent of the problem was revealed during World War II. Hundreds of thousands of draftees were judged to be unsuited for military service, and thousands more were later discharged with psychiatric disorders. Perhaps the greatest single impetus to this movement was a practical one; in 1963 President John F. Kennedy proposed a "bold new approach" to dealing with problems of mental illness, and Congress passed the Community Mental Health Centers Act funding hundreds of community-based centers across the country.

The principal objective of a community mental health center is to provide mental health care in a person's own community and at a cost that is not beyond the means of most people. The increased availability of clinical services presumably means that fewer individuals need be committed to institutions. In addition, the center is supposed to provide consultation and educational services to the local community.

How, specifically, are these goals approached? There are usually facilities for short-term inpa-

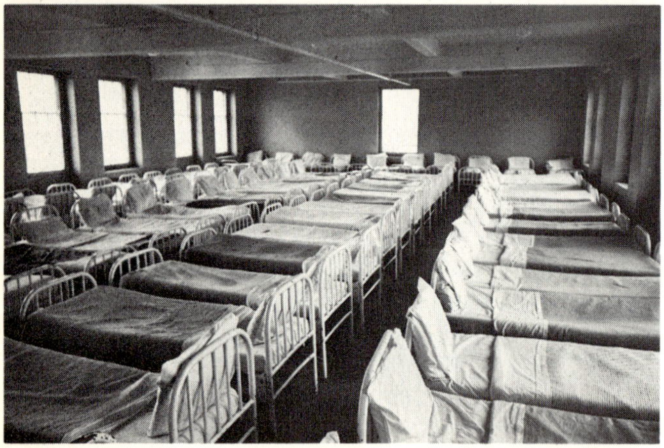

The top and center pictures are typical of state hospitals, outside and inside. Few patients can afford the obviously more favorable surroundings provided by private hospitals

## BOX 20.2 The Mental Hospital

Each year about two and a half million Americans are hospitalized for mental disorders. It has been estimated that one in ten people in this country will enter a mental hospital at least once (Atthowe, 1976). In Chapter 1 we reviewed some of the history of mental hospitals, and in Chapter 19 they were mentioned again in a critique of token economies. These institutions have been with us for many, many years, and, despite their problems, will probably continue to exist for some time to come.

Mental hospitals in this country are usually funded either by the federal government or by the various states. In fact, the term "state hospital" is taken to mean a *mental* hospital run by the state. They are often old, grim, and somewhat removed from major metropolitan centers. Their costs to society in economic terms are utterly staggering. Some Veterans Administration Hospitals and general medical hospitals also contain psychiatric wards.

In addition, there are private mental hospitals. Sheppard and Enoch Pratt near Baltimore, Maryland, and McLean Hospital, in Belmont, Massachusetts, are two of the most famous. The physical facilities of private hospitals tend to be superior to those of state hospitals for one simple reason: the private hospitals have more money. The daily costs to patients in these private institutions ran, in 1976, upward of $175 per day, a figure which did *not* include individual therapy sessions with a member of the professional staff! Although some patients may have medical insurance, usually with a ninety-day limit, such hospitals are clearly beyond the means of most citizens.

A somewhat specialized mental hospital is reserved for people who have been arrested and have been judged insane and unable to stand trial. They have not been sent to prison, but armed guards and tight security regiment their lives. Treatment of some kind is supposed to take place during their internment.

Many fine books and articles have been written about mental hospitals (Stanton and Schwartz, 1954; Goffman, 1961; Rosenhan, 1973; Moos, 1974). They agree with our own clinical experiences that, even in the best of hospitals, patients usually have precious little contact with psychiatrists or clinical psychologists. Most of a patient's days and evenings are spent either alone or in the company of other patients and of aides, individuals who often have little more than an elementary school education. The Rosenhan study of pseudopatients, described in Box 3.1 (page 57), provides some valuable insights on the attention patients receive, and Kesey's remarkable work of fiction, *One Flew over the Cuckoo's Nest,* although exaggerated, portrays vividly what life can be like inside one of these institutions. As with imprisonment, the overwhelming feeling is of helplessness and depersonalization. Patients sit endless hours in hallways waiting for dining halls to open, for medication to be given out, and for consultations with psychologists, social workers, and vocational counselors to begin.

Except for the most severely disturbed, patients have access to the various facilities of a hospital, ranging from woodworking shops to swimming pools, from gymnasia to the proverbial basketweaving shops. Most hospitals require patients to attend group therapy—here a general term indicating only that at least two patients are supposed to relate to each other or to a group leader in a separate room for a specified period of time. And for some patients there are the few sessions alone with a professional therapist.

By and large, in our opinion, the hospital serves primarily to isolate from the general community disturbed persons who are unable to adapt to social norms and whose life styles are not tolerated by society at large. The reasons for their maladaptations are the varied ones already discussed. Some writers (for example, Ullmann and Krasner, 1975) hold the view that people are placed in hospitals only because they are *labeled* sick or insane. But there is more to mental disorder than a diagnostic statement from a policeman, a judge, a teacher, or a psychiatrist. The vast majority of patients would be very much at a loss outside the haven and confines of a mental hospital.

One nagging problem is that institutionalization appears to become permanent once people have resided in mental hospitals for more than a year. Those discharged after two years of continuous hospitalization number only about 5 percent (Paul, 1969). The mental hospital has certainly not proved its worth by returning patients to the community. We recall asking a patient who had improved markedly over the previous several months why he was reluctant to be discharged. "Doc," he said earnestly, "it's a jungle out there." Although we cannot entirely disagree with his view, there nonetheless appear to be at least a few advantages to living on the outside. But this man—a veteran and chronic patient with a clinical folder more than two feet thick—had become so accustomed to the restrictions and care of various Veterans Administration hospitals that the prospect of leaving was as frightening to him as the prospect of entering a mental hospital is to those who have never lived in one.

One treatment now widely applied is "milieu therapy," in which the entire hospital becomes a "therapeutic community" (for example, Jones, 1953). All its ongoing activities and all its personnel become part of the treatment program. Milieu therapy appears to be a return to the moral practices of the eighteenth century. Social interaction and group activities are encouraged so that through group pressure the patients are directed toward normal functioning. Patients are treated as responsible human beings rather than custodial cases (Paul, 1969). They are expected to participate in their own readjustment, as well as that of their fellow patients. Open wards allow them considerable freedom. Evidence of the efficacy of milieu therapy, however, is scant.

In a milestone project at an Illinois state hospital, Paul and Lentz (1977) have recently demonstrated encouraging improvement in chronic "hard-core" patients through "social learning" therapy. A token economy, combined with other behavior therapy interventions, was tailored to the particular needs of each patient. A host of measures were taken on the behavior of both staff and patients over four and a half years of treatment, with an eighteen-month follow-up on patients who had been discharged. Since mental hospitals will be needed for the foreseeable future, especially by people who demonstrate time and again that they have difficulty functioning on the outside, Paul's work is of special importance. It suggests specific ways the chronic patient can be helped to cope better not only within the hospital but during periods of discharge as well.

One final observation. The first time that we toured a mental hospital during college, we were struck above all by the fact that most of the patients were not acting crazy. (What was going on in their heads is another matter.) Some were happy to see the bright, young, and occasionally frightened faces of their college visitors. Others were involved in watching television, playing cards, and flirting with the nurses or were lost in their own private reveries. Many of them seemed simply bored. After getting to know some of them through repeated visits, we learned that their reasons for being in the hospital were highly diverse. Some people had been committed. Others just had to "get away" from a bad marriage or a poor economic situation.* Some of the inmates appeared to be schizophrenic, others just depressed. A surprising number seemed little different from people who go to a private therapist or mental health clinic for treatment while continuing to hold down a job or run a household. But they had one important thing in common that must give pause before the mental hospital is considered a "solution." They were all labeled mental hospital patients, a title difficult to shake once it is bestowed.

* An extremely good predictor of mental hospitalization rates for the last hundred years has been the state of the economy (Brenner, 1973).

tient care, thereby providing an alternative to hospitalization. Generally, a twenty-four-hour walk-in crisis service offers "rap sessions" for younger members of the community. The centers are staffed by psychiatrists, psychologists, social workers, and nurses, and by paraprofessionals who live in the community and can help bridge the gap between the middle- and upper-middle-class professionals and community members to whom psychotherapy is sometimes an alien concept.

The first program involving paraprofessionals was probably that at Harvard University (Umbarger et al., 1962), in which students spent several hours per week as companions to patients in mental hospitals (see Guerney, 1969, for numerous examples of other programs). Community acceptance of these workers would seem to be a vital factor in community-based programs. An upper-middle-class psychiatrist whose residence is in the suburbs might well have difficulty establishing rapport with a lower-class ghetto resident. Yet a nonprofessional may not have all the qualities and talents necessary to make effective therapeutic interventions. Surely much depends on *what* the paraprofessional is supposed to do.

A wide range of services is included under the rubrics of "consultation" and "education." Consider an effort made by the Westside Community Mental Health Center in 1971 during enforced school busing in San Francisco.

> *We designed a program in which we placed a professional staff person on a school bus to ride to and from school with grade school children; in addition this staff person had streetcorner meetings with the parents about their busing concerns, and acted also as their advocate to the schools. Knowing the children would be experiencing separation anxiety in this [situation], we had our Hospital Art Department design coloring books with maps of the territory they would cover on the bus route; we attempted to introduce play materials and games that would be helpful*

*to the children, would encourage the children to carry "transitional objects" from home . . . such as dolls, teddy bears, special favorite toys. Our staff member met with the children before they boarded the bus, talked to them on the bus, again in their new schoolyard and on the way back home again (Heiman, 1973, p. 60).*

A mental health center might conceivably call a rent strike, should staff members decide that better housing would alleviate emotional suffering. Or suggestions might be made by a center's staff to change physical arrangements in a local factory in order to reduce the boredom or tension of performing particular kinds of work (see Box 20.3). Moreover, organized interventions such as these need not emanate solely from community mental health centers; mental health workers can operate readily from university departments, social welfare agencies, and even private offices.

## BOX **20.3** Environmental Psychology

Do you recall the last time you entered an air-conditioned building after suffering the heat and humidity of a mercilessly steamy summer day? What was your mood after being inside the cool haven for half an hour, compared to how you felt while walking outside? Have you ever visited some of the Gothic cathedrals in France and Germany? As you gazed upward to the soaring heights of the vaults, did you feel uplifted, exhilarated?

American psychology, since its beginning, has had a love affair with environmentalism. Over the past fifteen years the study of how elements of the physical environment affect thoughts, feelings, and behavior has involved psychologists in the domain of designers, architects, and urban planners. Their attempts to control behavior through control of environmental stimuli is now called environmental design or environmental management (see Sommer, 1969; Proshansky, Ittelson, and Rivlin, 1972). Given the community psychologists' appreciation of the importance of large social issues in behavior disorder, it is not surprising that they too want psychology applied in the planning of cities and mass transit systems, in the design of apartment and office buildings.

A fascinating example of research work in this field is a study done by Baum and Valins (1973). It investigated a proposal by Calhoun (1970) that within a given physical space there is a limit to the amount of social interaction that animals can tolerate before stress is created. Baum and Valins term as "unwanted social interaction" any degree of social contact among people that exceeds some optimal level; any environment that provides unwanted social interaction is regarded as crowded.

In an initial field study they found that students living in older dormitories on a university campus complained of more overcrowding than those living in newer ones. Furthermore, when confronted with miniature bedroom and lounge areas and asked to place miniature figures in them until "you would feel crowded if you were there," the residents of the older dormitories placed far fewer figures than did those from the newer dormitories, indicating that they would feel crowded with fewer people than would those in the newer dormitories. The subjects in this research study were freshmen who had been *assigned* to their dormitories, thus controlling for self-selection factors that might render the analysis of the data more ambiguous.

The effects of the physical environment on behavior is now being studied systematically by increasing numbers of psychologists.

In a subsequent study a subject coming either from the older dorms or from the newer residences was told to wait in a room in the laboratory with another subject. In reality the other student was the experimenter's "stooge." The hypothesis was that the students from the older accommodations, being more sensitive to crowding, would sit farther away from the stooge than those coming from newer dorms. This prediction was confirmed. Moreover, hidden observers counted the number of seconds within a five-minute period that each subject glanced in the direction of the stooge. Again significant differences emerged: "older-dorm" students looked at the stooge significantly less often than did "newer-dorm" students and, moreover, reported being more uncomfortable after the enforced waiting period.

Valins and Baum examined why students would feel more crowded in the older dormitories. The first obvious question was whether, in fact, older dormitories were more crowded in absolute terms than the newer dormitories. This seemed not to be the case with respect to numbers of people per square foot of living area. What differentiated the two sets of dormitories, however, was the *configuration* of the space. The older dormitories were constructed along traditional lines; a typical floor contained a number of bedrooms, with two students to a bedroom, each of which opened out directly onto the hall. All three dozen students on a given floor shared one large bathroom and lounge. By contrast, the newer dormitories, with a comparable number of students per floor, were arranged in individual suites with separate living areas and bathrooms to accommodate small groups of four to six students, again two to a bedroom. The residents of the older dormitories apparently had to interact daily with more people than did the residents of newer ones. Privacy was simply more difficult to obtain, and Baum and Valins assumed that such forced interaction with larger numbers of students brought unwanted social contacts. It did not seem surprising that the students in the older dorms felt more crowded.

Thus although provided with comparable amounts of physical space, students living in older dormitories were subjected to a far greater incidence of unwanted social interaction and were far more sensitive to crowding. The implications of such research are important. Among other things, it suggests that when architects design living quarters, they should take care to minimize unwanted social interaction by providing a certain degree of privacy. Investigations of this nature may cast light on the alarmingly high incidence of violence, emotional turmoil, and other problems that have come to characterize urban living.

Glass and Singer (1972), for example, document some of the deleterious effects of noise pollution. Their study (Cohen, Glass, and Singer, 1973) showed that the reading difficulties of elementary school children were associated with living in noisy apartments in New York City. Controlling for social class, they found that children who lived on the upper stories of a thirty-two story apartment house had higher reading scores than those living on the lower and noisier floors. Since research has shown that verbal skills are related to the ability to make auditory discriminations, they reasoned that noise was causing the reading problems. Indeed, children who had lived in the building fewer than four years were better readers than those who had lived there longer. Such research plus subjective impressions that excessive noise is distracting and unpleasant might encourage urban planners to insulate homes and apartments, which would also save energy and make them cheaper to heat and to air-condition.

### A behaviorally oriented CMHC

In Oxnard, California, Liberman and his colleagues (1974) have established the Behavior Analysis and Modification (BAM) Project. Staff employ a variety of behavior therapy techniques, including systematic desensitization, covert sensitization, assertion training, and token economies. Data are carefully collected on all patients before, during, and after treatment. For example, each week a staff person must complete a Behavioral Progress Record on each patient, indicating whether behavioral goals have been accomplished. The operant treatment of one of the patients in the day section of the Oxnard center is a good example of the carefully planned procedures.

> William was a . . . twenty-seven-year-old, single and unemployed man, diagnosed as schizophrenic. [Extremely withdrawn, he] had always lived with his parents, except for one brief hospitalization. William was not only socially withdrawn, but he actively removed himself from the presence of others. At his parents' home, most of his time was spent isolated in his room with the doors closed. He reported no friends, no social contacts, and he only left the house in the company of his parents.
>
> When he first came to the clinic, William spent a large amount of his time outside of the area of the clinic in which most of the activities took place. Not only did he stand in the hall, but William kept his eyes closed, and his fingers stuck in his ears.
>
> The first targeted [change in] behavior for William was [to be present] in the day room of the treatment center. A time sampling recording procedure was used whereby William's therapist observed him ten times during the day and recorded whether William was in the targeted area or not. A reversal design was planned to demonstrate experimental control

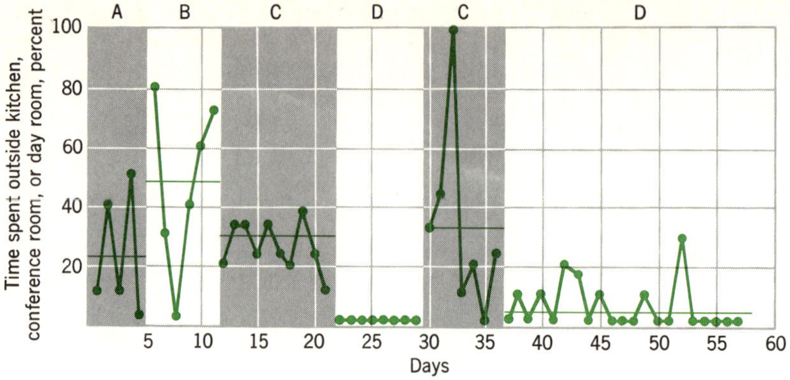


FIGURE **20.3**

Reducing the social isolation of a young male psychotic through contingency management. Condition A is the base line situation. In condition B coupons are earned by being near others; in C, time away from the clinic can be bought with the coupons; in D, time away from the clinic can still be bought with coupons, but social withdrawal costs the young man some of his earned coupons. After Liberman et al., 1974.

over this behavior. Figure 20.3 depicts the contingencies used and the results. . . .

. . . The procedures were as follows: For condition A, the therapist was simply to observe William on the predetermined schedule. This condition was the designated baseline phase. In condition B, William was paid coupons for being in the targeted area. The coupons were part of a regular, ongoing token economy at the center. The back-up reinforcers for the coupons were lunch, coffee, snacks, and excursions. In condition C, William was paid coupons but allowed to buy time off from the clinic . . . at the rate of one coupon for five minutes away. He could earn two coupons per observation or a maximum possible of twenty per day.

[The rules for condition D imposed a price on social withdrawal.] For each of the times William was observed outside of the targeted area, he was to relinquish two coupons. The reinforcement contingency was continued with William receiving two coupons with which he could buy time off from the clinic if he was in the day room. With the introduction of condition D, . . . observations of William outside the targeted area decreased to zero and remained there for eight days. At this point, the . . . cost procedure was removed; that is, condition C was reinstated. The effect was to increase the [number of times William was observed] away from people. With the reinstatement of . . . condition D, there was a gradual decrease and elimination of social isolation.

The results of the experiment are informative on several points. First, . . . experimental control was demonstrated over a targeted problem behavior of a patient in a day treatment center. Secondly, the results demonstrate the [importance of evaluating] a treatment program. The first two interventions that were used, conditions B and C, produced no change in William's behavior. It was only with the introduction of the third contingency that a desirable change was produced. In treatment settings many contingencies have to be tried before [an effective] one is found. Thirdly, the results demonstrated improvement in one target behavior, but did not show any changes in other behaviors, such as the amount of time William had his eyes open and the amount of time [he] spent in social conversation. [The various aspects of his antisocial behavior might have to be treated separately] (Liberman et al., 1974, pp. 112–114).

The series of reports from Liberman's BAM project are very promising. Treatment at the Oxnard Center, when compared with that at nearby centers not run along behavioral lines, was found more effective in increasing the social participation and in decreasing the isolation of chronic mental patients, who are typically withdrawn and apathetic. The underlying philosophy of the BAM project, a commitment to behavioral analyses of patients' problems and a systematic evaluation of therapeutic interventions, appears well suited to the general concept of a community mental health center. With continued experience it should be possible to refine treatments so that they are of maximum assistance to the greatest numbers of people—and this surely is the mandate of the original congressional act that set community mental health in motion in this country.

## Prevention in Community Psychology

Community psychology prevention programs assume that psychopathology may well have its genesis, at least in part, in social institutions, since they are powerful determinants of behavior. The attention of psychopathologists and other mental health workers should therefore be focused on how schools and other community environments provoke maladaptations and how these processes can be prevented.

### Teaching the facts about drugs

For some years educators, legislators, judges, and members of the clergy have been concerned about drug use among young people. They have made massive efforts to discourage young adults and children from trying marihuana, hashish, tranquilizers, alcohol, and LSD. They also attempt to help those already obtaining drugs from peers and from pushers to overcome their habit. In spite of these efforts, we saw in Chapter 10 that the use of marihuana, for example, has been increasing among teen-agers and adults in their early twenties. Is it possible that educational campaigns have no effect at all? Or, even more disquieting to those who deplore the prevalence of illicit drugs, that these campaigns actually *encourage* young people to use drugs?

Richard Stuart (1974) undertook a survey aimed at answering this difficult and politically loaded question. His reading of the literature indicated that although at least half the states require drug education in the public schools as a preventive measure, no one had determined the effects of these programs. Subjects in Stuart's study were 935 boys and girls in the seventh and ninth grades of an upper-middle-class suburban junior high school. With parental permission, these young people attended lectures and discussions on drugs one day a week for a period of ten weeks. The program was conducted by two female teachers in their mid-twenties, described by Stuart as ". . . casual in appearance and relaxed in style" (p. 191). The presentations and the occasional discussions conducted by the students themselves concerned the pharmacology of drugs and their physiological effects, as well as the social, psychological, and legal implications of their use. Some groups of students received information on "lesser drugs"—alcohol, tranquilizers such as Valium, marihuana, hashish, nicotine, and caffeine; some on "the major drugs"—LSD and other hard hallucinogens, amphetamines, barbiturates, and narcotics; and some on both. A carefully constructed questionnaire, which was filled out anonymously and which concerned present and past use and sale of the various drugs, worry about taking them, and acceptance of drug use as a nondeviant practice, was given prior to the program, immediately afterward, and four months later as a follow-up.

Very few students reported any experience with stimulants or narcotics; the evidence collected concerns alcohol, marihuana, and LSD. It is of potentially monumental importance. As compared to control subjects who did not participate in the drug education program, students who did increased their knowledge about drugs, indicating that the program did impart specific information, and *reported greater use of marihuana, LSD, and alcohol, as well as less worry*

## BOX 20.4 People's Liberation—An Aspect of Community Psychology

Life is change—this is one of the few things we can be certain of. Different demands, different joys, different sorrows, different challenges await us as we go through the life cycle. Much depends on where we grow up, how much money our families have, how sharp a mind we are born with, how well we apply ourselves in school and on our jobs—and luck. This book presents human problems that are fortunately remote from most of our personal lives, though there are surely readers who will find special significance in some of the material in these chapters. But we all experience unhappiness, groundless as well as reasonable fears, depression, perhaps even a touch of irrationality.

Let us spend some time, then, on ourselves, specifically on a set of life problems that confront all of us, those of sex roles and present shifts in them. Are sex roles a source of stress to little boys and little girls and to men and women? Could such stress underlie some of the unhappiness and occasional psychopathology that we encounter? Generalizations are especially risky when discussing social roles, for society is large and complex. But as a starting point, consider the following broad and contrasting codes for men and women that have applied and still do in much of contemporary Western culture.

**Men**

1. A man's worth is very much a function of how much money he earns, how much influence he has on his job and in society. A man who earns $30,000 is a better man than one who is on welfare.
2. Real men do not show emotion, nor are they especially aware of their own emotions and those of others. "Staying cool" is the ideal.
3. Real men are oriented to achievement.
4. It is not enough to attain a moderate success; a man must continually accomplish more.
5. The acquisition of power is the ultimate good, even though it means stepping on others.
6. Women are to be dominated, sexually and otherwise. To allow a woman to be in a superior position—at work or even in bed—is not as satisfying as being in control of her.
7. Being like a woman is to be avoided at all costs. The clearest violation of this standard is to have warm, possibly sexual feelings about another man, but it is also suspect to do "women's work," such as caring for children, keeping house, baking cookies.
8. Real men are decisive. Experiencing difficulty when making decisions is unmasculine.
9. Making mistakes is a serious violation of the male code.
10. Real men do not ask for help.

**Women**

1. A woman's worth is very much a function of how much money her husband (or boyfriend) earns, how much influence he has on his job or in society. A woman whose husband (or boyfriend) earns $30,000 is more valuable than one whose husband (or boyfriend) is on welfare.
2. Real women are in touch with their feelings and display emotion easily. They are emotionally supportive of others.
3. Real women are not achievement-oriented, except perhaps in maintaining well-run households.
4. True success is obtained vicariously. Women are content to bask in the glory of their husbands' and children's accomplishments and to effect change in society indirectly, for example, by collecting donations for charities.
5. Cooperation rather than the acquisition of power is the ultimate good for women.
6. Being dominant, sexually or otherwise, is eschewed. If a woman is in a superior position—at work or even in bed—she runs the risk of appearing to be emasculating.
7. A woman's feminity is lost through aggression, competitiveness, and other masculine traits. A woman should never appear more intelligent than her male peers.
8. Real women willingly allow their men to make the significant decisions that will shape family and social life.
9. Making mistakes enhances a woman's femininity, for it makes her appear more vulnerable.
10. Real women require assistance from others.

Readers of this book are no doubt familiar with the considerable women's liberation literature. The topics of this literature, which are also explored more personally in women's consciousness-raising groups, are the stereotypes of the female sex role code just summarized. Women support one another as sisters in their resolve to break through the needless constraints they feel are placed on them because they are females.

Closely tied to the women's movement is men's liberation. From what, you might ask, do men have to be liberated? Do they not enjoy most of society's rewards? The women's movement has forced men to question the male role, to ask themselves what are the parameters of masculinity? How "soft," for example, dare a man become before feeling threatened by the loss of his maleness? What are the emotional costs of constantly achieving and competing? What do men, and women, stand to gain if male sex role stereotypes are also challenged?

In the past few years men have been talking to one another in groups modeled after women's consciousness-raising sessions. In such groups a man is able, often for the first time, to relate to another man in a noncompetitive way. Support is given for expressing weakness and fear. Sexist attitudes are exposed—it does not take long for the word "girl" to be stricken from the vocabulary—and the male participants are encouraged to relate to other people in a more emotionally open fashion. The following is excerpted from a statement of purpose issued by the Men's Awareness Center of Long Island.

*Both Men and Women suffer the bondage of a tradition of belief that is both discriminating and oppressive. We must walk hand in hand, in common cause [of liberation. Our] essential purpose . . . is to provide insight into what it means to be a male in our society. . . . We have built a society in which we compete with one another, disconnect from each other and ourselves as feeling, responsive men and suffer the consequences of this alienation. We have cut ourselves off from the rich potentials of brotherhood and remain strangers to each other. . . .*

*Too long have we been estranged from ourselves; too long have we denied ourselves the inherent sensitivities of our sex; too long have we denied others this sensitivity. . . . The threat inherent in exposing our feelings, the fear of expressing emotion, can be overcome if and when we . . . support each other. . . .*

*Men interacting with men . . . paves the way for a firmer understanding of the way we relate to women. It is conceded that men have built a society, and continue to control it, out of an attitude of dominance. This sexist tradition is firmly ingrained in all males and it dictates the way men bond together. Sexism has been . . . the conditioning of all males since history was first recorded. For us today to question this prerogative . . . demands an undaunted effort at re-educating each and every one of us in the way we develop and implement our attitudes and value systems . . . and introduce them into our social structure. It could not and will not be possible unless men support men in their collective efforts to understand just what it really means to be a male in our society.*

—*F. Richard Vanacek*

Those active in both the women's and men's liberation movements believe that considerable pain and stress of everyday life can be traced to unnecessary rigid conceptions of sex roles. Learning that women will be considered aggressive if they seek to dominate, that men must not cry or ask for help, can limit the personal growth of men and women and cause needless questioning of an individual's masculinity or femininity. And it may underlie much of our anxiety and depression.

An additional source of strain is generally overlooked by those most deeply involved in people's liberation. Behavior does not change easily. An adult cannot turn himself or herself around as quickly and as completely as liberation rhetoric suggests. Habits of thought and action are "over-learned" by the time a person reaches maturity. A twenty-one-year-old woman may realize that she has every right to tell her lover what she desires from him, but her childhood learning that sexuality is suspect may inhibit her. A twenty-one-year old male may intellectually acknowledge that his feelings of vulnerability are part of the human condition, but awareness alone will not enable him to reveal to his close friends that he lacks confidence in himself. The process of shedding our socially acquired sex roles may itself generate stress and helplessness if changes are expected too quickly and completely.

*about their use,* after attending the special weekly classes. These differences persisted at follow-up. Furthermore, subjects in the program reported increased involvement in the sale of marihuana and LSD immediately afterward; their marihuana trafficking had not diminished at follow-up.

Stuart cautions that some students may have faked some of their answers, either because of or in spite of the fact that their responses could not be traced to them. But to collect a different kind of data would have posed serious problems concerning the civil rights of the participants, and the data might also have been subject to subpoena by the courts. As in all research, especially on a sensitive and complex issue such as this one, compromises must be made. The questionnaire did contain several checks on possible lying, and other results not summarized here strongly argue against the likelihood that the self-report answers were false. Moreover, the findings relate to *change* in use, not to absolute level; these students as a group were considerably below the national average in use of alcohol, LSD, and marihuana. Therefore it would be wrong to conclude that this drug education program unleashed a veritable orgy of drug taking in the community.

Even with these qualifications, however, Stuart seems justified in warning those who would decrease drug use among young people that education alone not only may fail to have the desired effect but may, as found here, actually increase the pattern of behavior deemed undesirable or dangerous. He suggests that instead attention be paid to ". . . sterile academic environments, unreinforcing home experiences, . . . a paucity of constructive . . . alternatives in the community" (p. 201).

### Suicide prevention centers and telephone crisis services

Another community agency is the suicide prevention center, modeled after the Los Angeles Suicide Prevention Center, founded in 1958 by Farberow and Shneidman. Staffed largely by nonprofessionals under the supervision of psychologists or psychiatrists, these centers attempt to provide twenty-four-hour consultation to people in suicidal crises. Usually the initial contact is made by telephone. The worker tries to assess the likelihood that the caller will actually make a serious suicide attempt and, most importantly, tries to establish personal contact that may dissuade the caller from suicide. The accompanying summary sheets used by telephone workers at the Suicide Prevention Center in Buffalo, New York, speed the recording of crucial bits of information.

Specialists hold that phone attendants in these centers should work toward the following goals (Speer, 1972).

1. "Tuning in," communicating empathy to the caller.
2. Conveying understanding of the problem.
3. Providing information regarding sources of help, for example, mental health clinics, psychologists, psychiatrists.
4. Obtaining an agreement form the caller to take some specific steps away from suicide, for example, making an appointment to come to the center itself.
5. Providing some degree of hope to the caller that the crisis will end and that life will not always appear so hopeless.

The potential value of such community facilities is made evident by data indicating that most suicides give warnings—"cries for help"—before taking their lives (see Chapter 8). Usually their pleas are directed first to relatives and friends, but many potential suicides are isolated from these sources of emotional support; a hotline service may save the lives of such individuals.

It is exceedingly difficult to do controlled reseach on suicide. Evaluating the effectiveness of suicide prevention centers is similarly problematic, for a large proportion of those who call are not heard from again. For example, Speer (1971)

SPCS, INC., BUFFALO, NEW YORK

INITIAL CONTACT SHEET (Telephone)

I. Identifying Information: (1-6) [ | | | | | ] Case No.________

(7) Line: 1 S 2 T 3 P (8-9) [ | ] Counselor________

(10-14) Date: [Mo. | Date | Yr.] (15) [ ] Day:____ (16-19) Call Began [hr. | min.] A/P [ ]

(20-22) Call Duration [min. | | ]

(24) [ ] 1 Caller: ( for self other ) 2 Other: Subject of Call________

Name:________ Name:________

Address:________ Address:________

Phone:________ Phone:________

(25) [ ] Catchment Area: Relationship to Caller________

(72-73) [ | | | ] Census Tract

Caller (or Subject of Call)

(26-27) Age: [ | ] (28) [ ] Sex: 1 M 2 F (29) [ ] Marital Status: 1 U 2 M 3 S 4 D 5 W

(30) [ ] Occupation:________ (32) [ ] Living Situation: ____Alone ____With:________

(31) [ ] Education:________

Affect and Behavior During Call: (33) [ ] Crying____ (34) [ ] Agitated____

(35) [ ] Hostile____ (36) [ ] Difficulty talking/unresponsive____

(37) [ ] Normal____ (38) [ ] Depressed____ (39) [ ] Intoxicated____

(40) [ ] Tripping____ (41) [ ] Other____

II. Identification of Problem (Check all Appropriate; double check primary problem):
(42-43) [ | ]

1 Alcoholism ____
2 Anxiety ____
3 Confusion ____
4 Depression ____
5 Drugs:
  Type ____
  Amount ____
6 Employment ____
7 Financial ____
8 Homeless/Stranded ____
9 Homicidal ____
Illegal Activities:
10 Theft ____
11 Assault ____
12 Other ____

13 Legal ____
14 Lonely ____
15 Medical Problems ____
16 Pregnancy ____
17 Reality Distortion ____
Relationship:
18 Marital ____
19 Parental ____
20 Dating ____
21 Family ____
22 Other ____
23 School ____

Sexual:
24 Heterosexual ____
25 Homosexual ____
26 Other ____
27 Social Withdrawal ____
28 Suicidal ____
29 Other ____

III. Assessment of Lethality:

A. Suicidal Behavior:

(44) [ ] Current Ideation: 0 1 2 3 4 5 None ____
(45) [ ] Current Suicidal Attempt (describe):________ None ____
(46) [ ] Other Suicidal Behavior (describe):________ None ____
(47) [ ] History of Attempts: Date ____ Method ____
Outcome________

B. Suicidal Plan:
(48) ☐ Specificity: 1.Vague_____ 2.Explicit_____
(49) ☐ Method: 1.Hi-Lethal_____ 2.Lo-Lethal_____ What:_____________________
(50) ☐ Availability of Means: 1.Yes____ 2.No_____ 3.Obtainable_____________

C. Resources:
(51) ☐ Internal (e.g. coping ability)_____________________________________
(52) ☐ External (e.g. significant other)__________________________________

D. (53) ☐ Communication: 1.Significant Other ____ 2.SPCS ____
3.Therapist elsewhere ____4.Other____

E. (54) ☐ Age: 1.Below 40______ 2.Above 40______
F. (55) ☐ Sex: 1.M___ 2.F___
G. (56) ☐ Marital Status: 1.U 2.M 3.S 4.D 5.W
H. (57) ☐ Physical Illness: 1.Yes___ 2.No___ What?____________________
I. (58) ☐ Drinking: 1.Yes___ 2.No___
J. (59) ☐ Recent Loss or Threat of Loss: 1.Yes___ 2.No___ What?____________
K. (60) ☐ Unexplained Change in Behavior: 1.Yes___ 2.No___
L. (61) ☐ Isolation: 1.Yes___ 2.No___
M. (62) ☐ Depression:
1.Trouble Sleeping___4.Hopelessness: Severe_____ Moderate_____
2.Loss of Appetite___ 5.Crying: Frequent_____
3.Loss of Weight___ 6.Crying: Uncontrollable_____
(63) ☐ Estimated Suicidal Risk: 1.Low___ 2.Mod.___ 3.High___ 4.Undet.___

IV. Disposition:
Resources Mobilized (check where appropriate)
(64) ☐ Traced____ (65) ☐ Rescue Squad____ (66) ☐ Police____ (67) ☐ Home Visit____
(68) ☐ Significant Other____ Who?__________________
(69) ☐ Appointment Made____ When?__________________
(70) ☐ Other:______________________________________

NARRATIVE SUMMARY (including Outcome and Recommendations):

(71) ☐ Follow-Up Requested: 1.Yes___ 2.No___

Outcome of Follow-Up:

(3/1/72)

found that more than 95 percent of callers did not use the service repeatedly. Does this mean that the phone contact helped so much that no further consultation was needed? Perhaps so, but it is also possible that many callers killed themselves after the phone call. One study (Weiner, 1969) found no differences in the suicide rates of cities with hotline services and of those without. Although numerous factors might have masked real differences, we cannot conclude from these data that the centers *have* demonstrated their effectiveness.

Speer (1972) attempted to evaluate one crisis phone service. His study sheds light on the kind of research people in the field are doing and on the difficulties such research poses. The subjects were thirty-four callers to a suicide prevention center who subsequently appeared for individual counseling. Some were asked to rate their feelings after the phone call that had led them to the center; others were asked how they had felt after the preceding plea for help, the last one made to a personal acquaintance, friend, or relative before they called the center. In this way Speer hoped to learn whether potential suicides derive more comfort and benefit from a service or from a friend or relative (who is presumably not trained in taking crisis calls).

The results are sobering: of the seven measures used, only one showed that calls to the center were significantly more helpful than calls to a friend. Speer concluded that, in this instance, there was no evidence of the superiority of a hotline service in achieving the goals specified for it.

Can anything else be said about this study? One possible confound in the design was not considered by Speer. When a person calls a crisis service, he or she may be decidedly more desperate than when phoning a friend or relative. Those who rated phone calls to the service may therefore have been reporting reactions felt in a far more unhappy and more suicidal mood than the individuals asked to remember their feelings after calls to friends. If so, there might very well be a significant difference in the efficacy of the two kinds of calls, a difference that would provide much-needed justification for the continuation or even the expansion of such centers.

Once again, we are left with little if any convincing evidence. Human lives are precious, however, and since many people who contact prevention centers weather a suicidal crisis successfully, there is at present no reason to discontinue these efforts.

## Residential Noninstitutional Programs

### Youth residences

Residential centers for disadvantaged youth have concentrated on teaching vocational and educational skills, even to those who have been diagnosed as having an antisocial personality or perhaps even schizophrenia. Some residental units have been located within a community itself (for example, Goldenberg, 1969) in the belief that training is most effective in a familiar urban setting. Other apparently effective work has been done in state schools located quite a distance from the homes of the attending youths. In view of the deleteriousness of reform schools and prisons—often being little more than training grounds where inmates learn how, when freed, to commit bigger and better crimes—it is heartening that noninstitutional programs are becoming more and more prevalent.

Most projects tend to be nonspecific in the actual techniques used. In contrast, one notable program, Cohen's National Training School project (Cohen and Filipczak, 1971), was organized exclusively along operant lines: residents earned privileges for criterion behavior, such as studying a certain number of hours.

Another excellent residental program carefully conceived along operant lines is one established by Montrose Wolf of the University of Kansas (Phillips et al., 1972). "Achievement Place," located in a middle-class community, is run by a young couple who act as surrogate

Residents of Achievement Place, an operantly run treatment center for delinquents, in a group discussion.

parents for about a dozen boys referred from the courts for delinquent behavior. At Achievement Place specific prosocial behavior earns a set amount of reinforcement. The program has allowed boys to return to their communities without the stigma and deterioration that all too often follow institutionalization in jails or state hospitals. The actual cost to county or state authorities for financing these small facilities is far less than that for traditional hospitals and prisons. Achievement Place has now been "exported" to numerous cities across the country.

### Halfway houses

Another kind of noninstitutional residence for people unable to function on their own is the halfway house. These are protected living units, typically located in large, formerly private residences. Here patients discharged from a mental hospital live, take their meals, and gradually return to ordinary community life by taking a part-time job or going to school. Living arrangements may be relatively unstructured; some houses set up money-making enterprises that help to train and support the residents. Depending on how well funded the halfway house is, the staff may include psychiatrists or clinical psychologists. The most important staff members are paraprofessionals, often graduate students in clinical psychology or social work who live in the house and act both as administrators and as friends to the residents. Group meetings, at which residents talk out their frustrations and learn to relate to others in honest and constructive ways, are often part of the routine.

Many people in mental hospitals neither profit from nor need the unnatural restraints that are intrinsic to closed institutions, yet they are not yet able to return to their families, to their university dormitories, and to their own apartments. The nation's requirements for effective halfway houses for ex-mental patients cannot be underestimated. Properly run ones are scarce. In several states there has been pressure from governors and from legislators to discharge as many hospital patients as possible. In the past twenty years these institutions have released almost half their nearly 600,000 residents. But discharge has all too often been bad for the patients. Some local communities object to the presence of shabbily dressed, often inappropriately behaving ex-patients in their neighborhoods. They have sometimes been exploited by entrepreneurs who, with state money, house them in unsanitary, poorly administered hotels and motels. Many ex-patients reenter the hospital in what has been termed the "revolving door" syndrome. Clearly, it is not enough merely to discharge mental patients. They must have out-patient services and a protective place to live (see Box 21.3, page 587).

## Overall Evaluation of Community Psychology Work

Community programs are difficult to evaluate because the questions being asked about large populations are extremely complicated and because the research examining the programs is usually inadequate. As with other efforts to evaluate therapeutic procedures, there is little agreement on indices of improvement. Community psychologists regard as crucial their attention to the sociocultural milieu as a determinant of behavior, both breakdown and improvement. But no evidence as yet indicates by what processes community programs may improve the milieu.

Community psychologists necessarily become social activists to some degree, which raises the danger that these well-meaning professionals may *impose* values and goals on their clients. John Kennedy's launching of the community mental health movement proclaimed that the federal government is rightfully concerned about improving the mental health of Americans. But what is mental health? Who is to decide? To what extent do the people being served by community psychologists have a say in how they are to be helped?

Problems of community mental health centers have been highlighted in a rather controversial critique by Ralph Nader's group (Holden, 1972). This report holds that the centers are based on a good and commendable set of ideas but that the implementation has been rather poor. Often the problem is one of old wine in new bottles. Nader's group pointed out that centers are usually controlled by psychiatrists whose training and outlook are tied to one-to-one therapy, typically along psychoanalytic lines; the "fit" between treatment and the problems of lower-income people who are the centers' primary constituencies is often loose. Liberman's BAM project, which was examined earlier, is a noteworthy exception.

Enthusiasm for community psychology must unfortunately be tempered with awareness of social reality—the conditions of deprivation that community psychologists assume produce and maintain disordered behavior. To train a black youngster for a specific vocational slot can have a beneficial long-term outcome for the individual only to the extent that society at large provides the appropriate opportunity to use these skills. Those who work in the community mental health movement are of course aware that racial and social prejudices play a central role in limiting the access of many minority groups to the rewards of the culture at large. Although efforts to improve the sociocultural milieu must of course continue if our society has any commitment to fostering social and mental well-being, programs may raise expectations that will only be dashed by the realities of the larger culture. This is the quandary of any mental health professional who ventures forth from the consulting room into the community.

# Somatic Treatment

All the therapeutic procedures considered thus far are psychological in nature; improvements in behavior are sought through techniques that provide new learning experiences, raise expectations for help, and facilitate insight. Behavior can also be affected by direct manipulation of the body. We saw a good illustration of the intimate relationship between mind and body in the discussion of psychophysiological disorders in Chapter 7. If psyche and soma are only two ways of talking about the same thing, it is reasonable to expect behavior to change when we intervene in certain bodily processes. Moreover, the many theories that blame psychopathology on physiological dysfunctions imply the efficacy of physiological treatments.

There are three major types of somatic treatment for abnormal behavior—drugs, surgical procedures, and convulsion therapies. Evidence indicates that *some* methods are effective in treating *some* behavioral problems. But, as we have cautioned many times before, this evidence does not in turn provide support for a physiological explanation of any of these disorders. In fact, somatic therapies have *not* usually been discovered through investigation of the physiology behind a particular disorder. Rather, the majority of the current treatments were discovered by accident, some, as we shall see, under almost bizarre circumstances.

## Drug Therapies

Four major categories of drugs have been used for some time in the amelioration of psychological disorders: minor tranquilizers, major tranquilizers, stimulants, and antidepressants. Table 20.3 gives examples of several widely used drugs in these categories, indicating the chemical groups that they belong to as well as both their generic and brand names. More recently a number of other drugs have been used for particular behavior disorders: lithium carbonate for manic-depressive psychosis, Antabuse for alcoholism, and methadone for heroin addiction.

Although we have reserved our discussion of therapeutic drugs for this chapter, the sad truth is that many of them could well have been mentioned in Chapter 10 on drug addiction and drug dependence. Methadone is a good example, for this drug is emerging as a possible alternative to heroin in the illicit drug trade. Even the minor tranquilizers can be abused, and some of them, like Miltown, are physically addictive over long periods of regular use. Both because of our psychological needs and because of the physiological realities of our bodies, human beings are all too prone to use psychoactive chemicals in self-defeating ways.

### Minor tranquilizers

As the name suggests, minor tranquilizers are used to reduce anxiety that is not of major proportions. They are usually prescribed for outpatients who suffer neurotic anxiety and psychosomatic disorders involving tension, and sometimes for the depressed individual who is also anxious. Barbiturates, which have been used to relieve anxiety since the turn of the century, were the first drugs in this category to gain widespread acceptance. But because of hazards such as addiction and undesirable side effects (see page 260), they were supplanted in the 1950s by a number of newly developed minor tranquilizers. The first of these was patented in 1952 by Berger and called meprobamate. It belongs to a group of drugs called the propanediols. The other principal group of minor tranquilizers consists of the benzodiazepines. Librium and Valium are the most prominent. The tranquilizer business has boomed throughout the intervening years, with numerous entries finding their way to the marketplace. Tranquilizers have become an accepted part of American culture, anxious businessmen and overtaxed parents being depicted as popping "happy" pills to get them through their trying days.

Because minor tranquilizers are usually prescribed for outpatients by general practitioners, arranging controlled research is very difficult,

TABLE **20.3**

Several Psychoactive Drugs Categorized by Their Effects on Behavior

| Effect group | Chemical group | Generic name | Trade name |
|---|---|---|---|
| Minor tranquilizers | propanediols | meprobamate | Miltown, Equanil |
| | benzodiazepines | chlordiazepoxide<br>diazepam | Librium<br>Valium |
| Major tranquilizers (antipsychotics) | phenothiazines | chlorpromazine<br>trifluoperazine<br>thioridazine | Thorazine<br>Stelazine<br>Mellaril |
| | butyrophenones | haloperidol | Haldol |
| | thioxanthenes | chlorprothixene | Taractan |
| Stimulants | amphetamines | dextroamphetamine | Dexedrine |
| | piperidyls | methylphenidate | Ritalin |
| Antidepressants | tricyclics | imipramine<br>amitriptyline<br>doxepin | Tofranil<br>Elavil<br>Sinequan |
| | monoamine oxidase inhibitors | phenelzine<br>tranylcypromine | Nardil<br>Parnate |

and little has been done (Greenblatt and Shader, 1972). But even so they are accepted as valuable therapeutic agents if they are not abused.

### Major tranquilizers

Phenothiazine, the nucleus of the phenothiazine drugs, was first produced by a German chemist in 1880 and was used to treat parasitic worm infections of the digestive system of animals. The drug went largely unnoticed until the 1940s, when the antihistamines were discovered by Bovet. The drugs with antihistaminic properties also have a phenothiazine nucleus. Antihistamines were prescribed to treat a variety of conditions ranging from the common cold and asthma to low blood pressure and shock. The French surgeon Laborit pioneered the use of antihistamines to reduce surgical shock. He noticed that they made his patients somewhat sleepy and less fearful about the impending operation. Laborit's work encouraged drug companies to reexamine antihistamines that had previously been rejected because they had stronger tranquilizing effects than antihistaminic. Shortly thereafter a French chemist, Charpentier, prepared a new phenothiazine derivative and called it chlorpromazine. It proved very effective in calming schizophrenics. As indicated earlier (see page 377), phenothiazines are now believed able to block impulse transmission in the dopaminergic pathways of the brain.

Chlorpromazine was first used therapeutically in the United States in 1954 and rapidly became the preferred treatment for schizophrenics. By 1970 over 85 percent of all patients in state mental hospitals were receiving chlorpromazine or one of the other phenothiazines. In recent years two other classes of drugs have also been given schizophrenics, butyrophenones and the thioxanthenes. Both seem generally as effective as the phenothiazines.

There is little doubt that the phenothiazines are useful in managing schizophrenic patients, and for this reason they are often referred to as antipsychotic drugs. In one study, conducted by the National Institute of Mental Health, patients newly admitted to nine different hospitals were randomly assigned to take one of four drugs on a double-blind basis (Cole, 1964a). Three of the drugs were different types of phenothiazine and the fourth was a placebo. The physicians in charge were allowed to adjust drug dosage to meet each patient's needs. During and after six weeks of treatment, three different measures were made of each patient: daily observations by ward personnel, a comprehensive rating by physician and nurse of severity of mental illness and improvement, and a one-hour diagnostic interview.

The ratings of improvement were as follows. None of the patients on any of the phenothiazines was rated as worse, 5 percent were rated as having shown no change, and 95 percent were rated as improved, with 75 percent of them considered much or very much improved. Of the patients on the placebo, 15 percent were rated as worse, 25 percent as having shown no change, and 60 percent as having improved, but only 10 percent of those who improved were in the "very much" category. On the basis of the psychiatric interview and daily observations, measurements on twenty-one variables such as social participation, confusion, and self-care were derived. As can be seen in Table 20.4, on thirteen of the twenty-one measures the drug patients were better than those on the placebo.

Such evidence is impressive. But is phenothiazine medication the preferred treatment when it is compared with other potential treatments a hospitalized schizophrenic patient might receive? In an attempt to answer this question, May (1968) assigned first-admission schizophrenic patients in a psychiatric hospital to one of five treatment groups.

1. Individual psychotherapy conducted by psychiatric residents.
2. Phenothiazine drugs.
3. Individual psychotherapy plus phenothiazine medication.
4. Electroconvulsive therapy (to be discussed later in this chapter).
5. Milieu therapy, in which the hospital administration tries to make the total living experience of the patient therapeutic.

Two classes of dependent variables were analyzed: clinical ratings of the patient's progress made by nurses and therapists, and data on release rate and length of time spent in the hospital. Drugs alone and the psychotherapy-plus-drugs combination were the two best treatments according to all the clinical measures. These two treatments were also superior both in shortening stay and in increasing the number of releases. Indeed, phenothiazines alone were found to be as effective as phenothiazines plus an extensive course of psychotherapy. At least when done by psychiatric residents, psychotherapy may well be superfluous for hospitalized schizophrenics.

Although the phenothiazine regimen reduces symptomatology so that the patient can be released from the hospital, it should not be viewed as a cure-all. What, for example, happens to a patient when he or she is discharged? Typically, patients are kept on so-called *maintenance doses* of the drug; they continue to take their medication and return to the hospital on occasion for adjustment of the dose level. But it turns out that released patients being maintained on phenothiazine medication may make only marginal adjustments to the community. The phenothiazines do not turn a socially incompetent schizophrenic with a poor premorbid history into a "pillar of the community." Furthermore, readmissions are frequent. The advent of the "phenothiazine era"

TABLE **20.4**
## Differences in Behavior of Phenothiazine and Placebo Patients in the NIMH Study
(from Cole, 1964a)

| Symptom or behavior | Placebo | Drug | Difference |
|---|---|---|---|
| Social participation | 0.49* | 1.51 | 1.02 |
| Confusion | 0.33 | 1.11 | 0.78 |
| Self-care | 0.13 | 0.88 | 0.75 |
| Hebephrenic symptoms | −0.13 | 0.58 | 0.71 |
| Agitation and tension | 0.27 | 0.95 | 0.68 |
| Slowed speed | −0.07 | 0.57 | 0.64 |
| Incoherent speech | −0.17 | 0.43 | 0.60 |
| Irritability | −0.20 | 0.40 | 0.60 |
| Indifference to environment | −0.05 | 0.45 | 0.50 |
| Hostility | 0.09 | 0.54 | 0.45 |
| Auditory hallucinations | 0.18 | 0.62 | 0.44 |
| Ideas of persecution | 0.36 | 0.78 | 0.42 |
| Disorientation | 0.16 | 0.37 | 0.21 |

* The higher the score, the greater the improvement. A minus score indicates deterioration.

probably reduced long-term institutionalization significantly. But in its place evolved the "revolving door" pattern of admission, discharge, and readmission so prevalent at this time.

Finally, the potentially serious side effects of phenothiazines must be noted. Patients generally report that taking the drug is disagreeable, causing dryness of the mouth, blurred vision, grogginess, and constipation. Perhaps this unpleasantness is one of the reasons maintenance programs have proved so difficult, for many patients simply discontinue taking the drugs. The voluntary fine musculatures feel rigid and twitchy, another distressing side effect. Additional drugs can suppress these symptoms, which resemble Parkinson's disease. In a muscular disturbance of older patients, called tardive dyskinesia, the mouth muscles involuntarily make sucking, lip-smacking, and chin-wagging motions. This syndrome affects from 10 to 15 percent of patients treated with phenothiazines for a long period of time. It does not respond to antiparkinsonian drugs and is irreversible. Among the other common side effects are low blood pressure and jaundice. In spite of the many difficulties, phenothiazines will undoubtedly continue to be the primary treatment for schizophrenics until something better is discovered. They are surely preferable to the straitjackets formerly used to restrain patients.

### Stimulants

One form of amphetamine, dextroamphetamine, and a piperidyl derivative, methylphenidate, are currently prescribed for hyperactive children. Their use for this purpose became controversial when a 1970 *Washington Post* article reported that between 5 to 10 percent of school children in Omaha, Nebraska, were receiving the stimulants (Maynard, 1970). The public became aroused and investigations followed. It became apparent that the use of stimulants for calming children was widespread, and that prescriptions were being written somewhat indiscriminately.

Shortly thereafter the Food and Drug Administration tightened its regulations.

The available evidence indeed indicates that stimulants are an effective treatment for hyperacvity (for example, Conners et al., 1972; Gittelman-Klein et al., 1976). In the Conners study 35 to 40 percent of the children showed dramatic improvement, and another 30 to 40 percent were moderately improved. The most frequent side effects of stimulants are decreased appetite and insomnia, but both are short-lived.

The therapeutic effectiveness of stimulants with hyperactive children has sometimes been termed paradoxical, for a stimulant is expected to energize, not calm. The research literature shows that stimulants have other effects, however, particularly on attention (Conners, 1972). The drugs improve the attention of hyperactive children, which makes them less distractible and calms them.

### Antidepressants

The *tricyclics* and the *monoamine oxidase* (MAO) *inhibitors* are two subcategories of antidepressants. Both classes of drugs were discovered serendipitously. Imipramine, a tricyclic, has a three-ring molecular structure similar to that of the phenothiazines; hence it was hoped that it might also be an effective treatment for schizophrenics. Early clinical work with the drug showed that it was of little value with schizophrenics, but it did produce an unexpected elevation in mood; for this reason it was subsequently used as an antidepressant. Tricyclics are now assumed to interfere with the reuptake of norepinephrine by the nerve cell after it has fired, thus keeping more of the neurotransmitter available at the synapse. The MAO inhibitor iproniazid was originally a treatment for tuberculosis. Because it improved the outlook of tubercular patients, it too was adopted as an antidepressant. The enzyme monoamine oxidase degrades monoamines of the central nervous system. Since a MAO inhibitor prevents this intracellular degradation, excess amounts of free norepinephrine and serotonin collect at the receptor sites (see Box 8.5, page 211). Thus both classes of drugs are considered to produce their therapeutic effects by raising levels of brain amines, facilitating neural transmission.

The available evidence suggests that the tricyclics are effective drugs to combat depression (Davis, Klerman, and Schildkraut, 1967). But it is also clear that tricyclics do not benefit *all* depressives. Thus research directed at determining which depressed patients are most likely to benefit from the drug is important. Some of this research has been carried out on so-called endogenous and exogenous depressives (Box 8.1, page 194). The tricyclic drugs were found more effective in relieving endogenous than exogenous depression (Lapolla and Jones, 1970; Raskin et al., 1970). Like the phenothiazines, the tricyclics also produce some undesirable side effects. These include dry mouth, constipation, dizziness, palpitations, and blurred vision.

In contrast to the tricyclics, the therapeutic effectiveness of the MAO inhibitors has not been well substantiated (Goodman and Gilman, 1970). For example, studies comparing a MAO inhibitor to a placebo that had been performed from 1958 to mid-1967 were reviewed. Fifteen studies demonstrated a statistically significant superiority of an MAO inhibitor over the placebo, but thirteen failed to demonstrate such superiority (Davis, Klerman, and Schildkraut, 1967).

Interest in MAO inhibitors appears to have declined in recent years, both because of the failure to demonstrate their effectiveness and because of their severe side effects. MAO inhibitors have greater toxicity than any other drug used for the treatment of psychological disorders; they are harmful to the liver, brain, and cardiovascular system. Moreover, these drugs have even been found to interact with other drugs and foods to cause death. Patients taking MAO inhibitors should avoid foods and beverages high in tyramine. Aromatic cheeses, avocado, beer, broad beans, Chianti wine, chicken livers, cream, game, lox, pickled herring, snails, and yeast extracts (Honigfeld and Howard, 1973) cannot be ingested, even in moderate amounts.

## Lithium carbonate

In this decade there has been great interest in the possibility of using lithium carbonate in the treatment of mania. The drug was discovered by Cade in 1949, who noted its sedative effect on guinea pigs. It was not used widely in the United States until more recently, however, for it had been judged dangerous after causing a few deaths. In these instances it had been ingested unrestrictedly as a salt substitute.

Although there is some evidence for the effectiveness of lithium carbonate as a treatment for mania, whether it is the best somatic treatment available is unclear. For example, in a double-blind experiment in which lithium was compared with chlorpromazine, 78 percent of the manics were helped by lithium but only 36 percent were helped by chlorpromazine (Johnson, Gershon, and Hekimian, 1968). But another study, also employing a double-blind methodology and also comparing lithium with chlorpromazine, did not find it to be more effective (Spring et al., 1970).

In addition to the claim that lithium subdues mania, it has also been proposed that the drug can lift depression and, when taken regularly, reduces the likelihood of subsequent manic and depressive episodes. Some evidence indeed supports these claims. Mendels, Secunda, and Dyson (1972), for example, found that lithium worked as well as a tricyclic in treating depression. In an evaluation of lithium as a maintenance treatment, Dunner, Stallone, and Fieve (1976) determined that it did reduce the frequency of manic episodes but had little effect on the recurrence of depression. Other studies, though, indicate that lithium does lessen the likelihood of depressive episodes (for example, Prien, Klett, and Caffey, 1973). The mode of action of lithium has not been established. Because of its toxicity, blood levels must be carefully monitored to avoid overdose.

## Antabuse (disulfiram)

Antabuse is frequently prescribed to treat alcoholism. Patients are instructed to take a daily dose of the substance, which alters the way alcohol is metabolized by the liver. If they then drink even a small amount of alcohol, a toxic metabolite with extremely aversive physiological effects collects in the bloodstream. The first reactions are likely to be intense flushing, heart palpitations, and great difficulty in breathing. These are followed by nausea, vomiting, and pallor as blood pressure falls; these conditions can last for several hours. In fact, should a goodly amount of alcohol be consumed, reactions can be severe enough to culminate in death. Antabuse, then, does not "cure" alcoholism; rather it creates a situation in which continued drinking is almost suicidal.

Data demonstrate the effectiveness of the treatment (for example, Bourne, Alford, and Bowcock, 1966). In one study that compared Antabuse with other treatments such as aversive conditioning, hypnotherapy, and milieu therapy (Wallerstein, 1957), Antabuse was found to be the most effective. A critical problem, however, lies in *motivating patients to stay on the drug.* Patients do not frequently volunteer for such treatment, and those who do often fail to take the Antabuse regularly. Thus, even though effective, Antabuse has been of limited usefulness in dealing with alcoholism (see Box 20.5).

## Methadone

Recent years have seen great interest in methadone, a synthetic narcotic, as a treatment for heroin addiction. The primary action of methadone is one of substitution, eliminating the craving for heroin and setting up a blockade to its effects so that "highs" are not experienced should heroin be taken. It will not eliminate addiction, for methadone itself is addicting.

The first major methadone program was established by Dole and Nyswander in 1964. Within five years they claimed to have successfully treated over a thousand heroin addicts (Dole, Nyswander, and Warner, 1968). People are admitted into their programs only if they are over eighteen years of age, have at least three years of addiction history, are not addicted to barbiturates

## BOX 20.5 Drugs Are Not Always Easy To Take

The use of Antabuse to treat excessive drinking by making ingestion of alcohol extremely unpleasant, if not dangerous, highlights a general problem in chemotherapy. Often the availability of apparently effective chemical agents blinds researchers and practitioners to the fact that patients may not want to take the medication. We have already mentioned the parkinsonianlike symptoms and other side effects of Thorazine. Indeed, it is fair to say that all drugs currently available exact a cost that can discourage prescribed use. An individual on Thorazine, for example, may have to be warned about driving a car, since the depressant, that is, tranquilizing, effects of this powerful drug increase reaction time and perhaps impair judgment as well. By the same token, a mood elevator such as Elavil may handicap the user in normal day-to-day activities. Antabuse seems to present a peculiar set of problems in that a heavy drinker must continue taking the drug regularly with full knowledge that imbibing his or her favorite beverage afterward will surely bring acute discomfort. The question then becomes how the clinician is to motivate the drinker to begin using the drug and remain with it. As we pointed out in our discussion of alcoholism (Chapter 10), people drink excessively for many reasons. A nonaddicted individual who seeks the numbing effects of alcohol may be unable to face life's problems. Perhaps his marital relationship is difficult, or perhaps his anxieties about dealing with authority figures are so great that, without his daily ration of martinis, he suffers distress of enormous proportions. If he is denied his crutch, what is he left with? For these and other reasons, to use Antabuse without taking care to help the person deal with the stresses that trigger drinking may be unwise and even antitherapteutic.

or alcohol, and have no psychiatric or epileptic complications. The treatment is divided into several phases, during which the addict moves from inpatient to outpatient status and finally back into the community.

Methadone appears to be relatively safe, its primary side effects being constipation and weight gain, and it is relatively inexpensive. Clearly, putting a heroin addict on a methadone maintenance regimen should reduce the likelihood of his or her involvement in criminal activity. As we have noted previously (see page 258), the high cost of maintaining a heroin habit leads many addicts into a life of crime. The methadone supplied by a treatment program is a substitute narcotic, legally administered. Additionally, methadone may not produce the same kind of euphoria that heroin does,[1] allowing addicts to make a better occupational adjustment.

In one of their studies of the drug, Dole and Nyswander selected twelve heroin addicts in the Rikers Island Prison in New York and put them on a methadone program. They were then released from prison. A follow-up seven months later determined that seven of the twelve were employed, five had some drug or law problem,

[1] Initially it was claimed that methadone does *not* produce a high. The black market that exists for it in New York City, however, suggests that it may, especially if used with other drugs.

and three were back in jail but not re-addicted. *All had discontinued using heroin.* In this case methadone was not a complete success, but given the usually much higher rate of re-addiction and involvement with the law, it appears to have been beneficial.

Methadone, however, is not a universally applicable treatment. Luria (1970), for example, estimates that it is successful in only between 10 to 20 percent of the addict population. Large numbers of addicts who go on a methadone program drop out. Another negative view has been offered by Dobbs (1971) in a report on a methadone program in Washington, D.C. Urine samples were routinely collected from these patients and analyzed for the presence of heroin. The majority of the 100 patients in his sample had at least one or more positive urine specimens, indicating continued use of heroin even while on methadone. These findings suggest that methadone may not exert as strong a blockage or cross-tolerance effect as had previously been supposed. Or addicts may alternate between methadone and heroin, even selling their unused doses of methadone on the black market. In view of these problems, an alternate drug, methadyl acetate, which has the same effects as methadone, was developed. Because it needs to be taken only three times per week (Ling et al., 1976), the addict can less conveniently alternate it with heroin. Finally, methadone replacement therapy has been attacked for merely changing a heroin addict into a methadone addict. The option of a substitute narcotic may discourage the development of programs that try to prevent or eliminate addiction to *any* kind of narcotic. This last criticism is a substantial one, but it should not obscure the usefulness of methadone maintenance treatment for some hard-core, criminal addicts.

## Psychosurgery

Scattered reports of surgery being performed to alter or remove parts of the brain supposedly responsible for abnormal behavior date back many years. The "modern era" of psychosurgery begins with the work of a Portugese neuropsychiatrist, Antonio de Egas Moniz. He had attended a scientific meeting in London in 1935 and was impressed by a report of Jacobsen and Fulton about brain surgery performed on two chimpanzees. The prefrontal areas of their cerebral cortexes had been removed. Before the operation the animals had been highly emotional and subject to violent temper tantrums when frustrated through experimentation. Afterward they were indifferent.

On the basis of this single case of two chimpanzees whose behavior was calmed through brain surgery, Moniz later persuaded a colleague, Almeida Lima, to operate on the frontal lobes of human patients. Within a few years a hundred lobotomies had been performed, and in 1949 Moniz shared a Nobel prize for this work. Moniz himself retired in 1944, partly because he had been rendered a hemiplegic by a bullet lodged in his spine. One of his lobotomized patients had shot him (Valenstein, 1973).

Lobotomy was introduced in the United States by Freeman and Watts; by 1950 they had operated on over a thousand patients. The rate picked up in the early 1950s, and Freeman later claimed that he had performed or supervised over 3500 lobotomies.

The original lobotomy was a very crude surgical procedure. In one of the two methods usually applied, a hole was drilled in each side of the head, and a blunt instrument was then inserted and rotated in an arc, destroying considerable white matter. In the other procedure, the transorbital technique, a surgical needle inserted into the brain through the thin structure separating the eye and the brain was similarly rotated (Figure 20.5). It is estimated that each of these techniques destroys about 120 square centimeters of brain tissue (Shevitz, 1976). The rationale behind both procedures was that the frontal cortex exaggerates the emotional responses produced in lower regions of the brain, in particular the thalamus and hypothalamus. Cutting the connections between these areas and the frontal cor-

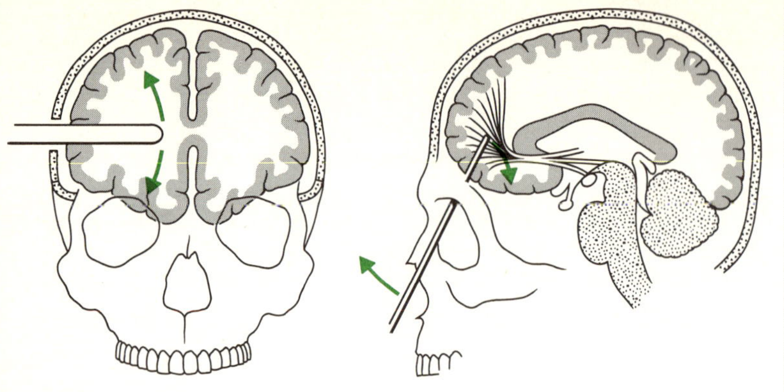


FIGURE **20.5**
Psychosurgeons attempt to eliminate especially troublesome behavior, such as violent psychotic episodes, by cutting the connections between the cortex of the frontal lobes and lower centers of the brain.

tex was assumed to have a calming effect.

As with most of the treatments we have discussed, there was an initial flurry of interest in psychosurgical procedures coupled with enthusiastic claims for their effectiveness. While the techniques were in relatively widespread use, they were applied to schizophrenics, to depressives, and less frequently to persons with personality disorders and to neurotics. Persons plagued by obsessions were more frequently operated on than other neurotics. The results of studies attempting to assess the efficacy of the treatment were unimpressive. For example, Robbin (1958, 1959) compared changes in lobotomy patients and controls. Lobotomy was found to produce a slightly greater discharge rate, but more of these patients were subsequently readmitted. Similarly, Barahal (1958) did a five-to-ten-year follow-up on 1000 lobotomy cases. His findings compelled him to publicize the high rate of undesirable side effects, such as seizures, extreme listlessness, stupor, and even death. In sum, these surgical procedures have little to recommend them; they lack demonstrated effectiveness and can have serious, *irreversible* consequences. With the advent of the phenothiazines in the mid-1950s, the popularity of lobotomy dropped off dramatically.

But newer surgical procedures have continued to be used in treating abnormal behavior. More precise techniques allow the frontal cortex to be separated from lower brain areas with a destruction of only 8 square centimeters of brain tissue (Shevitz, 1976). The procedure apparently has beneficial effects for some patients—notably those with severe depression, anxiety, and obsessive-compulsive disorders—and fewer undesirable side effects. Current thinking would limit these operations to patients with very severe, long-lasting problems that have not responded to any other treatment.

An even more controversial surgical procedure attempts to control violence and aggression. In the United States, Mark and Ervin (1970) have been its leading proponents. In their view a significant amount of human violence is initiated through brain malfunction, particularly of the amygdala. They implant electrodes into the amygdala in an attempt to locate the focus of the disorder. Then an electric current is passed through the electrodes, and portions of the amygdala are destroyed. Mark and Ervin have reported on the clinical effectiveness of their operation, as performed on ten violent people who also had temporal lobe epilepsy (Mark, Sweet, and Ervin, 1972). Valenstein (1973) has evaluated their report and found it wanting.

> In regard to the three patients who received unilateral lesions, it was reported that for some months after the operation, episodic violence was absent, but in two of the patients it was clear that assaultiveness was returning, one of them having remarked that his "old feelings were coming back" after he fractured the jaw of a fellow worker. The third patient's seizures were returning, but under a condition where he formerly would have been provoked into violence he attempted suicide.
>
> Better results are claimed for the seven patients receiving bilateral amygdala lesions, but the fact that it is necessary to destroy tissue at several brain sites raises some serious questions [about] the assertion by these investigators that they are destroying a specific trigger of the violence. Indeed, in another report Dr. Mark and his colleagues indicate that [they destroy tissue in a number of sites, depending on the patient]. Apparently there is considerable trial and error in the procedure; indeed, lesions are progressively enlarged until it appears that desirable results are obtained. [Few details] back up the impression [they try to convey that stimulating and recording with electrodes] provides a reliable basis for selecting the brain sites [to be destroyed]. Moreover, a close scrutiny of the data does not reveal results that are nearly as impressive as the summary statements would imply.
>
> Of the seven bilateral patients, one received no benefit at all, while another, in whom assaultiveness was absent for three years after the operation, became impotent and remained psychotic, continuing to have hallucinations. (This is not an uncommon result, as can be noted from Mark's comment at a symposium that "we found amygdaloidectomy in assaultive schizophrenic patients changes the assaultive character but not the schizophrenia.") A third patient developed a voracious appetite (hyperphagia) and gained thirty-five pounds in a little over three months. The patient still had seizures and rage attacks, but the latter were less frequent. A female patient who was suffering from uncontrollable fear (no evidence of violence is provided) was less incapacitated and able to hold a job, although the fears were not completely eliminated. In a fifth patient the assaultiveness disappeared for a year, but then "her intolerable assaultiveness recurred." A sixth patient had only been observed for a short period. The seventh patient is viewed as the most successful, but this is a very extreme case of a woman who received a head injury from a fall on ice. Afterward she had frequent seizures and physically assaulted almost everyone who came near her using her nails and teeth on delivery boys, a sick mother-in-law, her husband, and others. There was unquestionable evidence of brain damage. The bilateral amygdalectomy eliminated her rage attacks for seven years and reduced the seizure incidence from three to five a day to twenty a year (pp. 246–248).

The evidence, as reviewed by Valenstein, indicates that the enthusiasm of Mark and Ervin for their procedure is unwarranted. Yet in the same report they go on to speculate about developing tests to identify people who have brain dysfunctions that would make them likely candidates for their surgical techniques. In an earlier article they had even focused their attention on riots in metropolitan slums, suggesting that the rioters might have brain dysfunctions (Mark, Sweet, and Ervin, 1967). The title of an article eventually commenting on their proposal was predictable: "Threat to Blacks: Brain Surgery to Control Behavior" (*Ebony,* February 1973).

## Convulsive Therapy

Several people became interested in the therapeutic induction of convulsions, all during the same decade. Sakel, in the 1930s, had been experimenting with insulin injections as a means of reducing withdrawal symptoms in morphine addicts. In one patient the low blood sugar level produced by the insulin accidentally elicited a coma, and Sakel observed that afterward the patient's mental state was less confused. He continued to experiment with insulin-produced coma and reported that it could even reduce psychotic symptoms. The technique was soon in rather widespread use, both in Europe and North America.

At about the same time that Sakel began his work, Meduna came to the opinion that an "antagonism" existed between epilepsy and schizophrenia. He leapt from this conclusion, which we now know is incorrect, to propose that inducing a convulsion might cure schizophrenia. He chose the drug Metrazol for this purpose.

The originator of electroconvulsive shock therapy (ECT) was the Italian psychiatrist Cerletti. He had been interested in epilepsy and was seeking a means by which its seizures could be experimentally induced. The "solution" became apparent during a visit to a slaughterhouse, where Cerletti saw animals rendered unconscious by electric shocks administered to the head. Shortly thereafter he found that by applying electric shocks he could produce full tonic-clonic seizures in his laboratory. Not long after that he used the technique on a schizophrenic patient.

The electrical means of inducing a convulsion became the preferred method. The technique has remained essentially the same since its introduction by Cerletti, at least until recently. Electrodes are placed on each side of the patient's forehead, and a current of approximately 150 volts is allowed to pass between them for a period of about two seconds, inducing a grand mal seizure (see page 430). A period of electrical silence in the patient's brain follows; then there is a gradual resumption of the preconvulsive pattern.

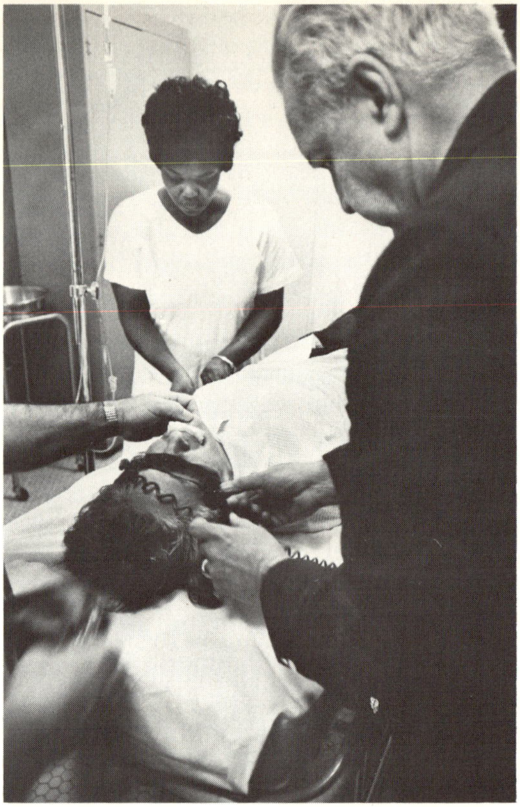

Patient being prepared for electroconvulsive therapy.

Patients nowadays are typically given a muscle relaxant beforehand to reduce the incidence of bone fractures and bruises occasionally suffered during ECT. The usual ECT regimen entails about ten treatments given at a rate of about three per week.

Following ECT the patient is often very confused and shows loss of memory both for happenings before the treatment and for whatever transpired within one hour afterward. The confusion and loss of memory generally disappear within several weeks.

A new development in ECT is unilateral shock, the application of shock to only one of the cerebral hemispheres, usually the nondominant one. Unilateral ECT causes less confusion and less impairment of memory. In most studies it has been found to be as therapeutically effective as the standard procedure (Inglis, 1969; Abrams, 1975).

Electroconvulsive therapy, although originally applied to both schizophrenics and depressed patients, is now used primarily for profoundly depressed people. As we saw previously when we reviewed the May (1968) study, phenothiazine medication is more effective for schizophrenics than is ECT. For severe depressives, though, ECT seems to be the most effective somatic treatment currently available. In one study depressed patients were randomly assigned to ECT, to one of the three drug therapies, or to a placebo drug. At the end of the treatment period, 76 percent of the patients in the ECT group were rated as improved, as were 44 percent of those in the drug groups and 42 percent of those in the placebo group (Greenblatt, Grosser, and Wechsler, 1964). The findings of many other studies generally confirm the effectiveness of ECT with profoundly depressed patients. Indeed, it is commonly regarded as the optimal treatment for severe depression (for example, Klerman, 1972), even though the mechanism by which it works is unknown.

In spite of the promise carefully administered ECT holds for deeply depressed patients, many professionals object to its use. A major problem is the fear that many patients have of ECT. In spite of amnesia for the episode, and even though muscle relaxants are given to prevent bone fractures, patients are often reluctant to undergo, or their families to sanction, such treatments, at least without considerable urging from the medical staff. The procedure is in truth violent in nature, although the amount of writhing and groaning has diminished greatly with the use of relaxants. ECT does entail the deliberate induction of a seizure and subsequent unconsciousness. Many people therefore consider the "cure" worse than the "disease." But it is difficult to dismiss ECT, since the evidence does indicate that it is effective in treating depression.

## Summary

Group therapy and community psychology share the important assumption that disordered behavior as well as normal is largely shaped by, or can at least be changed by, social variables such as group pressure. There is a great variety of both theory and method in group therapy and community psychology. Some group therapists aim at increased insight and heightened awareness, employing the techniques of psychodrama and encounter groups. Others focus on the group as a useful vehicle within which to apply behavior therapy. Community psychology encompasses many endeavors. What all seem to share is a seeking orientation—a venturing forth from the professional office to deal with human problems in a real-life setting. A number of innovative programs were described, but conclusive data regarding their effectiveness are not yet available.

For some of the somatic therapies, such as tranquilizers and ECT, there is evidence that they are effective, but for others, in particular psychosurgery, there are few data to commend them. Even when judged helpful, however, the somatic treatments should not be considered as effecting "complete cures." And side effects are frequent and unpleasant.

# chapter 21

## LEGAL AND ETHICAL ISSUES



Amendment 1 Congress shall make no law respecting an establishment of religion, or prohibiting the free exercise thereof; or abridging the freedom of speech, or of the press; or the right of the people peaceably to assemble, and to petition the Government for a redress of grievances.

Amendment 4 The right of the people to be secure in their persons, houses, papers, and effects, against unreasonable searches and seizures, shall not be violated. . . .

Amendment 5 No person . . . shall be compelled in any criminal case to be a witness against himself, nor be deprived of life, liberty, or property, without due process of law. . . .

Amendment 6 In all criminal prosecutions, the accused shall enjoy the right to a speedy and public trial . . . ; to be confronted with the witnesses against him; to have compulsory process for obtaining witnesses in his favor, and to have the Assistance of Counsel for his defense.

Amendment 8 Excessive bail shall not be required, nor excessive fines imposed, nor cruel and unusual punishments inflicted.

Amendment 13 . . . Neither slavery nor involuntary servitude, except as a punishment for crime whereof the party shall have been duly convicted, shall exist within the United States, or any place subject to their jurisdiction. . . .

Amendment 14 . . . No State shall . . . deprive any person of life, liberty, or property, without due process of law; nor deny to any person within its jurisdiction the equal protection of the laws.

Amendment 15 . . . The right of citizens of the United States to vote shall not be denied or abridged by the United States or by any State on account of race, color, or previous condition of servitude.

These elegant statements describe and protect some of the rights of American citizens and others residing in this country. Against what are these rights being protected? Be mindful of the circumstances under which most of these statements were issued. After the Constitutional Convention delegates had delineated the powers of government in 1787, the first Congress saw fit in 1789 to amend what they had framed and to set specific limits on the federal government. Amendments beyond the original ten have been added since that time. The philosophical ideal of American government has always been to allow citizens the maximum degree of liberty consistent with preserving order in the community at large.

We open our final chapter in this way because the legal and mental health systems collaborate continually, although often subtly, to deny a substantial proportion of our population their basic civil rights. With the best of intentions, judges, governing boards of hospitals, bar associations, and professional mental health groups have worked over the years to protect society at large from the actions of people designated as mentally ill and dangerous to themselves and others. But in so doing they have abrogated the rights of thousands of people in both criminal and civil commitment proceedings. Those who have broken the law, or who are alleged to have done so, can be committed to a prison hospital through *criminal commitment* proceedings. *Civil commitment* is a set of procedures by which a person who has not broken a law can be deprived of his or her liberty and incarcerated in a mental hospital, sometimes for long periods of time. In effect, both commitments remove individuals from the normal processes of the law.

## Criminal Commitment

We shall examine first the role of psychiatry and psychology in the criminal justice system. Almost as early as the concept of a *mens rea* or guilty mind and the rule "No crime without an evil intent" had begun to be accepted in English common law, insanity had to be taken into consideration, for a disordered mind may be regarded as unable to formulate and carry out a criminal purpose. At first insanity was not a trial defense, but the English crown sometimes granted pardons to people who had been convicted of homicide if they were judged completely and totally mad (Morris, 1968). By the reign of Edward I (1272–1307), the concept of insanity had begun to be argued in court and could lessen punishment. Then during the course of the fourteenth century it became the rule of law that a person proved to be wholly and continually mad could be defended against a criminal charge. But the unfortunates convicted as witches two and three centuries later could not offer this defense, for according to religious dogma they had made a voluntary and purposeful pact in delivering themselves to the devil.

After the religious dogma about witchcraft had lost its hold and mental illness became the province of medicine, the treatment of those regarded as mentally deranged improved. Even though the asylums (see page 16) were often brutalizing, incarceration in them was preferable to torture and death. Moreover, the insanity plea became better established in the courts, supposedly securing the legal status of the deranged. But even so their rights have not always been protected.

For more than a hundred years judges and lawyers have called on psychiatrists, and recently clinical psychologists as well, for assistance in dealing with criminal acts thought to have been committed when the accused was suffering extreme emotional upset or anguish. Are such emotionally disturbed perpetrators less criminally responsible than those who are not distraught but commit the same crimes? Should such individuals even be brought to trial for transgressions against society's laws? Although efforts to elicit professional opinions on these issues are undoubtedly well intentioned, injustices are sometimes done those whose emotional states and mental capacities have created doubts about their legal responsibility for their acts and about their competency to stand trial.

## Landmark Decisions on the Insanity Defense

A staggering amount of material has been written on the insanity defense, even though it is rarely successful. Only eleven cases, for example, were successfully defended on this basis in the state of New York in the 1960s.[1] Given the infrequency of acquittal by reason of insanity, why has so much been written on the issue? Alan A. Stone[2] (1975) has proposed an intriguing answer. Criminal law rests on the assumption that people have free will and that, if they do wrong, they have *chosen* to do so and should therefore be punished. "Our jurisprudence . . . while not oblivious to deterministic components, ultimately rests on a premise of freedom of will" (*United States* v. *Brawner*[3]). Stone suggests that the insanity defense strengthens the concept of free will by pointing to the few people who constitute an exception because they do not have it, namely those judged to be insane. These individuals are assumed to have diminished responsibility for their actions because of a mental defect, an inability to distinguish between right and wrong, or both. They lack the degree of free will that would justify holding them legally accountable for criminal acts. By exclusion, everyone else *has* free will! "The insanity defense is in every sense the exception that proves the rule. It allows the courts to treat every other defendant as someone who chose 'between good and evil'" (Stone, 1975, p. 222).

Historically, in modern Anglo-American criminal law, there have been three important court rulings that bear on the problems of legal responsibility and mental illness. The so-called "irresistible impulse" concept was formulated during an Ohio case in 1834, wherein it was decided that an insanity defense was legitimate if a pathological impulse or drive that the person could not control had compelled him to commit the criminal act. The irresistible impulse test was confirmed in two subsequent court cases, *Parsons* v. *State* and *Davis* v. *United States*.[4]

The second well-known concept, the McNaghten rule, was announced in the aftermath of a murder trail in England in 1843. Daniel McNaghten had mistaken the secretary of Sir Robert Peel for his employer, the British prime minister, whom McNaghten had been instructed to kill by the "voice of God." The judges ruled that ". . . . to establish a defence of insanity, it must be clearly proved that, at the time of the committing of the act, the party accused was labouring under such a defect of reason, from disease of the mind, as not to know the nature and quality of the act he was doing; or if he did know it, that he did not know he was doing what was wrong." This "right-wrong" concept has been applied in the United States for many years. It is the sole test in just fewer than half the states; in most other jurisdictions it is one of the standards and is often applied in conjunction with irresistible impulse.

The third decision, made in the 1954 case of *Durham* v. *United States*,[5] says that the "accused is not criminally responsible if his unlawful act was the product of mental disease or mental defect." David Bazelon, the presiding justice, be-

[1] The insanity defense may be pleaded more often in the future if capital punishments become prevalent again. Insanity has usually been claimed as a defense when the alternative was the death penalty.

[2] A principle source for our treatment of criminal and civil commitment is his excellent monograph *Mental Health and Law: A System in Transition*, published by the National Institute of Mental Health in 1975. It is strongly recommended to those who have special interest in the topic.

[3] United States v. Brawner, No. 22,714 (D.C. Cir. June 23, 1972).

[4] Parsons v. State, 2 So. 854, 866–67 (Ala. 1887); Davis v. United States, 165 U.S. 373, 378 (1897).

[5] Durham v. United States, 214 F. 2d 862, 876 (D.C. Cir. 1954).

lieved that by referring simply to mental illness he would leave the profession of psychiatry free to apply its full knowledge, no longer limited to considering impulses or knowledge of right and wrong. He did not incorporate in what would be called the Durham test any particular symptoms of mental disorder that might later become obsolete. The psychiatrist was accorded great liberty to convey to the court his or her own evaluation of the accused's mental condition.

In 1962 the American Law Institute (ALI) proposed its own guidelines, which were intended to be more specific and informative to lay jurors than the "mental disease or mental defect" of the Durham test.

> *1. A person is not responsible for criminal conduct if at the time of such conduct as a result of mental disease or defect he lacks substantial capacity either to appreciate the criminality (wrongfulness) of his conduct or to conform his conduct to the requirements of law.*
>
> *2. As used in the Article, the terms "mental disease or defect" do not include an abnormality manifested only by repeated criminal or otherwise antisocial conduct (The American Law Institute, 1962, p. 66).*

The first of the ALI guidelines combined the McNaghten rule and the irresistible-impulse concept. The second concerned those who are repeatedly in trouble with the law; they are not to be deemed mentally ill only because they keep committing crimes. The ALI test is being adopted in more and more states and is already the standard in all federal circuit courts of appeal.

Many issues are raised by the insanity defense, for in its application an abstract principle must be fit to specific life situations. As in all aspects of the law, terms can be defined in a number of ways—by the defendants, defense lawyers, prosecutors, judges, and, of course, jurors—and testimony can be presented in diverse fashion, depending on the skill of the interrogators and the intelligence of the witnesses.

Goldstein (1967), a law professor, has pointed out that in actual practice the McNaghten rule has not always restricted expert testimony of psychiatrists to the issue of whether the defendant knew right from wrong at the time he committed the crime. Goldstein has cited numerous cases in which psychiatrists and attorneys *interpreted* the McNaghten ruling in a way that allowed more general statements about mental illness—a practice that most textbooks tell us was permitted only after the Durham decision. For instance, a trial judge in Wisconsin, where the McNaghten right-wrong principle was operative, ruled that expert testimony offered to show that the defendant could not control his behavior was inadmissible as evidence. The judge stated that such evidence was relevant only to proving "irresistible impulse." The supreme court of Wisconsin overturned this ruling, however, arguing that evidence bearing on the defendant's inability to control himself should have been admitted: "Even under the right-wrong test, no evidence should be excluded which reasonably tends to show the mental condition of the defendant at the time of the offense" (Goldstein, 1967, p. 55).

A final point should be stressed. Only the defendant's mental condition *at the time the crime was committed* is in question. Consequently, retrospective, often speculative, judgment on the part of psychiatrists, attorneys, judges, and jurors is required.

## Case Example

To illustrate the problems that may be raised by an insanity plea, let us consider the case of Charles Rouse, as reported in a *New Republic* article by James Ridgeway (1967). Rouse, a twenty-year-old resident of Washington, D.C., was arrested one night while carrying a suitcase containing a .45 Colt automatic pistol, ammunition, two electric drills, and some razor blades. The maximum penalty for carrying such lethal weapons in the District of Columbia is one year, yet Rouse was confined much, much longer. How did this happen?

The Durham decision of 1954 applied in the District of Columbia. During his trial Rouse was examined by court psychiatrists and judged to be suffering from "antisocial reaction," sufficient grounds to be acquitted by reason of insanity according to the Durham test. Rouse received such an acquittal. But this "acquittal" did not lead to freedom. Rather, he was incarcerated in a federal mental hospital, St. Elizabeth's, in Washington, for psychotherapeutic treatment of his personality disorder. He was kept there for four years, *longer* than he would have been confined had no issues been raised about his sanity.

Those who favor close liaison between mental health workers and the courts argue that it would have been unjust to Rouse to hold him legally responsible for his misdemeanor, and that the most charitable and effective course of action—both for him and for society at large—was to treat the mental disorder that presumably had brought about the arrest in the first place. But how therapeutic was Rouse's forced hospitalization? After two years of confinement in St. Elizabeth's, Rouse had his attorney file a writ of habeas corpus, a procedure which an incarcerated person can institute in order to obtain a court hearing on whether continued detainment is justified. At this hearing Dr. E., Rouse's psychiatrist in the hospital, was asked to report on Rouse's behavior. The doctor cited examples of what he regarded as "poor judgment": Rouse had refused an invitation to leave maximum security and to move to less constricted areas of the prison hospital, preferring instead to seek relief through litigation and a court hearing. He had also left group therapy in a "cavalier manner," evidence, Dr. E. said, of lack of insight and poor judgment and of the continuing mental illness that had been the basis of his acquittal two years earlier.

The doctor also mentioned additional examples of what he considered to be diseased behavior, such as Rouse's reluctance to become involved with the other patients. "And because he does not get together with people I conclude that he is antisocial, antisocial since he cannot tolerate the anxiety that comes with having relationships with people" (p. 25). Dr. E. recommended to the judge that Rouse not be released yet, for "In my opinion if Mr. Rouse were placed at liberty at the present time it would be a precipitous thing to do and he would be dangerous to himself and to other people by virtue of his mental illness. I think he needs supervision over the long haul" (p. 25). Indeed, Dr. E. stated that, if released, Mr. Rouse would be likely to obtain guns and ammunition and to shoot someone.

In his defense, Rouse's attorney produced testimony by another psychiatrist who felt that further hospitalization would be *detrimental* and that Rouse should therefore be discharged. The judge, however, agreed with Dr. E., saying that Rouse had not taken advantage of the help available at St. Elizabeth's and that he was therefore not ready for release. Rouse was ultimately discharged on grounds that people under criminal commitment have a right to treatment and that his confinement at St. Elizabeth's amounted only to punishment.[6]

A number of general problems are highlighted by this case.

1. The judgment of psychiatrists and psychologists plays a crucial role in how long a person remains in a mental hospital for treatment of a problem that is said to have caused a criminal act. But professionals frequently *disagree* about the presence of a problem.

2. The hospital psychiatrist may interpret as evidence of continued mental illness any efforts made by the patient to escape from the hospital environment, even if by legal means. In Rouse's case it seemed as though almost everything he did was construed as symptomatic of his assumed illness.

3. Unorthodox behavior, particularly if it breaks a law, can be regarded as evidence of a dan-

[6] Rouse v. Cameron, 373 F. 2d 451 (D.C. Cir. 1966).

gerous mental disorder and can thereby remove the individual from the direct jurisdiction of the courts. It can cause the individual to be incarcerated for longer periods of time than he would have served had he been convicted and sentenced for the unlawful act.

Rouse's case is, of course, only one among many that could be discussed. Few others show forensic psychiatry[7] in as unfavorable a light. The record is bad enough, however, that many persons advocate reducing the role played by mental health professionals in the legal process. We shall discuss some of these issues later in the chapter.

"BUT YOU JUST CAN'T PLEAD INSANITY DUE TO AN EXTRA Y-CHROMOSOME IN A CASE OF EMBEZZLING."

## Competency To Stand Trial

The insanity defense concerns the accused's mental state *at the time of the crime.* A second issue, whether the person is competent to stand trial, concerns the defendant's mental condition *at the time of his or her trial.* Far greater numbers of people are committed to prison hospitals after being judged incompetent to stand trial than are tried and acquitted by reason of insanity. A Supreme Court case, *Pate* v. *Robinson,*[8] is the precedent for defense attorney, prosecutor, or judge to raise the question of mental illness whenever there is reason to believe that the accused's mental condition might interfere with the upcoming trial. Over the years most jurisdictions in this country have shown concern that the accused may be "presently insane and otherwise so mentally incompetent as to be unable to understand the proceedings against him or properly to assist in his own defense" (Pfeiffer, Eisenstein, and Dabbs, 1967, p. 322). Another way of stating this problem of competency is to say that the courts do not want a person to be brought to trial *in absentia,* which is a basic principle of English common law. A disturbed person can of course be physically present; what is referred to here is his or her mental state. If after examination the person is deemed too mentally ill to participate meaningfully in a trial, the trial is routinely delayed. The accused is incarcerated in a prison hospital with the hope that means of restoring adequate mental functioning can be found.

Being judged incompetent to stand trial can have severe consequences for the individual. Bail is automatically denied, even though it might be routinely granted if the question of incompetency had not been raised. The accused is incarcerated in a facility for the criminally insane for the pretrial examination; these institutions are typically the worst of hospitals. The accused may well lose employment and undergo the trauma of being separated from family and friends and from familiar surroundings for months or even longer. In fact, he *may* languish in the prison hospital for the rest of his life if he at no time in the future appears competent to stand trial (Stone, 1975)!

[7] This term refers to the activities of psychiatrists concerned with legal responsibility and criminal commitment. Psychologists have also become involved in legal proceedings.

[8] Pate v. Robinson, 383 U.S. 375 (1966).

Many psychiatrists, when asked to render a competency judgment, assume that if they judge the person to be mentally disturbed in any way, it follows that he or she cannot stand trial; thus have many people been deprived of their day in court. Robey (1965) has pointed out, however, that even a psychotic person may sufficiently understand his position in the legal proceedings to participate in them and to talk with his attorney rationally.[9] Robey proposes that a person be allowed to come to trial even though he may behave in a bizarre manner before and during the proceedings. The accused may be at a severe disadvantage if, during the trial, he is confused, deluded, hallucinating, and so on, but a somewhat inequitable trial may be preferable to being incarcerated until behavior is judged normal once again. It should be kept in mind that some of the people we are talking about are proved, once they have been brought to trial, *not* to have committed the crimes of which they were accused.

Fortunately, there is hope for reform. A 1972 Supreme Court case, *Jackson* v. *Indiana,*[10] concerned a mentally retarded deaf-mute man who was deemed not only incompetent to stand trial but unlikely ever to become competent. The Court ruled that the length of pretrial confinement should be limited; and, more importantly, since the defendant appeared unlikely ever to become competent, that the state should after this period either institute customary civil commitment proceedings or release the defendant. Legislation has been drafted in most states to define more precisely the minimal requirements for competency to stand trial, ending the latitude that has deprived thousands of people of their rights to due process (Amendment 14) and a speedy trial (Amendment 6).

[9] One novel option is now available in Massachusetts, although it has not been implemented. A defendant may have a provisional trial, even though he appears incompetent to stand trial. If acquitted, he would then not be committed for competency examination; if convicted, however, the trial would be considered void, and he would be referred as usual for pretrial observation. The provisional trial, in other words, takes place as though the defendant is competent, even in the face of grave doubts that he is (McGarry, 1972). An acquitted defendant would thereby avoid getting caught in the pretrial commitment morass, although his problems with society would not end were his demeanor indeed deranged. This right has until now proved illusory, probably because it poses the risk of two trials, which would be a great expense to both defendant and commonwealth.

[10] Jackson v. Indiana, 406 U.S. 715 (1972).

## Thomas S. Szasz and the Case Against Forensic Psychiatry and Psychology

### His polemic

"By codifying acts of violence as expressions of mental illness, we neatly rid ourselves of the task of dealing with criminal offenses as more or less rational, goal-directed acts, no different in principle from other forms of conduct" (Szasz, 1963, p. 141).

This quotation from one of Szasz's most widely read books enunciates the basic theme of his polemic against the weighty role that his own profession of psychiatry plays in the legal system. To understand the view of this outspoken and eloquent critic of forensic psychiatry, we must first of all examine the distinction made between *descriptive* and *ascriptive* responsibility. As Szasz points out, a person may be judged descriptively responsible in the sense that all agree a particular act was, in fact, performed by him. Assigning ascriptive responsibility, however, is a social judgment that society should inflict consequences upon someone deemed descriptively responsible. The court verdict of "not guilty by reason of insanity" says, first, that John Doe was descriptively responsible for commiting a crime, but second, that society will not ascribe legal responsibility to him and punish him for what he did. Killing in wartime is another example of this divergence between descriptive and ascriptive responsibilities. To murder the enemy as a member of a nation's armed forces is to be responsible for another person's death. Yet the soldier is not punished for his action and indeed may win honors for it.

To hold a person criminally responsible is to ascribe or attribute legal responsibility to him. A

Thomas S. Szasz, for years an outspoken critic of involuntary mental hospitalization. He has argued that psychiatrists should stop playing a central role in court proceedings.

Edward Oxford's attempt to assassinate Queen Victoria on June 10, 1840. The artist who drew this did not know that Oxford was not a "gentleman" but a waiter in a tavern.

given social group makes the judgment that the person who is descriptively responsible for a criminal act will receive criminal punishment. As Szasz points out, being criminally responsible is not a trait that is inherent in a person and that society uncovers. Rather, society at a given time and for a given criminal act decides that it will hold the perpetrator legally responsible and punish him.

Szasz goes on to suggest that psychiatry was assigned a role in the criminal courts when people acted in a way that was considered particularly irrational and threatening to society. According to Szasz, these exceptional cases all involved violence against people of high social rank. In shooting at a Lord Onslow in 1724, a man named Arnold was believed to have as little understanding of his murderous act as "a wild beast." Another man, James Hadfield, was deemed deranged for attempting to assassinate King George III in 1800 as he sat in a box at the Theatre Royal. And a third, Oxford by name, was regarded as insane for trying to kill Queen Victoria in 1840. The best-known case has already been mentioned, that of Daniel McNaghten (1843), who killed Sir Robert Peel's private secretary after mistaking him for Peel. In all these cases from English law, which forms the basis for all American law, people of low social rank openly attacked their superiors. Szasz believes that ". . . the issue of insanity may have been raised in these trials in order to obscure the social problems which the crimes intended to dramatize" (1963, p. 128).

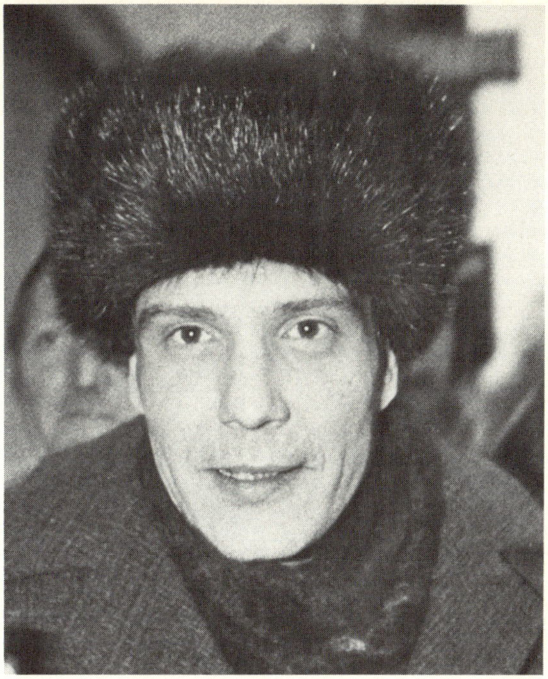

Zhores Medvedev (left) and Vladimir Bukovsky (right), Soviet dissidents who were detained by Russian authorities in mental hospitals for criticizing the government. (Left, The New York Times.)

Other cases here and abroad, such as the assassinations of John and Robert Kennedy, the South African prime minister Hendrik Verwoerd, and Martin Luther King, may to a degree reflect the social ills of today. Moreover, court proceedings in the Soviet Union are ominous. In *A Question of Madness,* the well-known Russian biochemist Zhores Medvedev (1972) told how Soviet psychiatrists collaborated with the state in attempting to muzzle his criticism of his government. They diagnosed him as suffering from paranoid delusions, split personality, and other mental ailments that would make it dangerous for him to be at large in society. In the years since, the confinement of political protesters for madness has, if anything, increased in the Soviet Union (see Box 21.1).

But pleas of insanity are made in far more ordinary cases. And of course Szasz does not claim that all these pleas involve some sort of silent conspiracy of the establishment to cover up social ills. Szasz sets forth a polemic much broader in scope. His basic concern is with individual freedom, which includes the right to *deviate* from prevailing mores. Far from advocating that people be held *less* accountable for antisocial acts, he argues that legal responsibility be extended to *all,* even to those whose actions are so far beyond the limits of convention that some people explain their behavior in terms of mental illness.

Szasz's villain is what he calls "psychoauthoritarianism." He traces all contemporary thought on the matter to Alexander and Staub (1929),

## BOX **21.1** General Svetlichny: "We Will Let Him Rot in the Insane Asylum!"

. . . I was arrested in 1963 for preparing two photocopies of [*Milovan*] Djilas's book "The New Class" and was placed in solitary confinement at the Lubyanks Prison. I was . . . summoned by General Svetlichny, who was then in charge of the Moscow K.G.B., and was offered [a chance] to repent and tell who gave me the book and who helped me make the photocopies. Then I would be released.

The obvious purpose of [this conversation] was to turn me into an informer and to make me cooperate with the authorities. But when nothing came of this, I was given a psychiatric examination, was declared mentally ill and was sent to Leningrad. I attribute my release to the fact that the Leningrad school [of psychiatry was disputing] with the Moscow school and [refuting] their diagnoses [of schizophrenia]. In February 1965 I was freed.

At the end of 1965, I was again arrested for organizing the first human rights demonstration, which took place on December 5 in defense of [Andrei] Sinyavsky and [Yuli] Daniel. . . . Up to that time, there had been no demonstrations since 1927 and the legislature forgot to foresee the proper measure of punishment for those who should take part in demonstrations. Consequently, there were no legal punitive means of punishment.

I was simply dispatched to one of the Moscow psychiatric hospitals with the intention that my old diagnosis be confirmed and then, without a new court hearing or investigation, I would again be sent to Leningrad as a person who had not as yet been fully "cured" from the previous time.

The K.G.B.'s calculations were undermined by honest young doctors at city hospital No. 13, who prepared an extensive report stating that I was not mentally ill. In spite of the doctors' conclusions, I was transferred to another city hospital, in accordance with the K.G.B.'s instructions.

In this hospital, the doctors also did not find me to be ill and insisted that I be released. And once again—upon the instructions of the K.G.B.—I was transferred, but this time to the Serbsky Institute. In the face of the well-supported conclusion provided by two hospitals, even the Serbsky Institute did not [dare] to declare me insane. . . . [But at] that very time, when my mother went to see General Svetlichny, he stomped his feet and screamed: "He will never be released! *We* will let him rot in the insane asylum!"

In the meantime, my case had attracted public attention and became well known in the West, thanks to the pronouncements made by Valery Tarsis and the activities of Amnesty International. Finally, the authorities were forced to appoint a neutral commission. But four professors who were specially summoned could not come to a unified conclusion. Two of them, representing Snezhnevsky's [Moscow] school, declared me to be mentally ill. The other two, opponents of his school, refuted their diagnosis.

I remained confined amid this situation for eight months, six of which were spent at the Serbsky Institute. You need not think that the dispute was strictly scientific: It was a matter of conformity or nonconformity of doctors, and the authorities could not find a sufficient number of conformists for a case which had attracted such publicity.

I was released after a representative of Amnesty International came to Moscow and went straight to Georgy Morozov, the director of the Serbsky Institute, and told him that if I were not immediately released, my case would be raised before the Bertrand Russell tribunal.

By the end of the 1960's, a well-established methodology of psychiatric repression had evolved . . . the K.G.B. provided the ideological direction, giving the instruction that opponents of the regime be declared insane, and the psychiatrists worked out an entire system with a diagnostic basis. By this time the Snezhnevsky school was in firm command of Soviet psychiatry.

The following categories of individuals were most liable to be declared "insane":

1. Prominent figures, whose trials would prove to be uncomfortable in the propagandistic sense.
2. So-called revisionists—that is, those who criticize the system from Marxist positions.
3. Persons who stood up for their convictions during the period of investigation, used legal means of defense and insisted on their right not to give any evidence whatsoever.
4. Believers, including those who faced purely political charges, without any "religious articles."

. . . In the 1970's political prisoners have been sent more and more often to psychiatric prison hospitals before the expiration of their camp sentences. This practice allows the authorities to lengthen their terms for an endless period of time.

Now another new method has emerged: the practice of giving psychiatric diagnoses to political prisoners prior to their release from camp. After being freed with such a diagnosis, a former prisoner always lives under the Damocles sword of compulsory hospitalization.

How do Soviet psychiatrists attempt to justify their complicity in such a widely developed system of psychiatric repression?

The main features of today's psychiatric prisons, of which psychiatrists can no longer claim to be unaware, include intensive treatment (with no regard to harmful effects), indefinite periods of confinement, the necessity of showing repentance in order to be freed, the discreditation of the person and his ideas, constant blackmail after the person's release, and his complete lack of any rights (such tested means of resistance as hunger strikes and the lodging of complaints, which are widely used in camps and prisons, serve only to burden a psychiatric diagnosis).

Under these conditions, every person who is arrested is afraid of being declared insane, and the threat of being sent to a psychiatric prison is used as blackmail during the period of investigation and during the course of the psychiatric examination (Bukovsky, 1977).

who argued that although the usual legal proceedings may be appropriate for "normal criminals," psychoanalysis should form the basis for handling "neurotic" criminals. They presented their position in a forthright manner.

> *We propose a more consistent application of the principle that not the deed but the doer should be punished. . . . The implementation of this principle requires expert diagnostic judgment which can be expected only from specially trained psychiatric experts. Before any sentence is imposed, a medical-legal diagnosis should be required. This would amount to an official recognition of unconscious motivations in all human behavior. The neurotic criminal obviously has a limited sense of responsibility. Primarily he is a sick person, and his delinquency is the outcome of his emotional disturbances. This fact, however, should not exempt him from the consequences of his action. If he is curable, he should be incarcerated for the duration of psychiatric treatment as long as he still represents a menace to society. If he is incurable, he belongs in a hospital for incurables for life (p. xiii).*

These are strong statements. Some have criticized Szasz for erecting a straw man, the assumption being that nowadays no one really believes the Alexander and Staub position to be well founded. In all likelihood, however, this view—with "psychotic" or "psychopathic" substituted for "neurotic"—still prevails, both in this country and elsewhere, to an extent that we cannot be complacent about its effects.

Of the many problems presented by the Alexander and Staub argument, Szasz suggests that the following are especially important.

1. Disputes in legal proceedings in which insanity is an issue are common; the prosecution and the defense routinely produce "expert" witnesses whose positions are diametrically opposed.
2. In view of the criticisms that have been made of Freud, a proposal for the "official recognition of unconscious motivations in all human behavior" seems an anachronism. To base important social judgments on a poorly tested theory appears almost foolhardy. It should be mentioned in passing that Freud himself recommended that psychological opinions *not* play a role in court.
3. It is *at least* open to question whether enforced psychotherapy can ever be meaningful and effective. Rouse's case is a good example of the undue power that a prison psychiatrist can have over a criminal entrusted to him for "treatment," and of the trouble that the patient can get into if he refuses psychotherapy.

Judge Bazelon, author of the Durham decision, is another target for Szasz's criticisms. Szasz accuses the judge of being naive about the quality of treatment available in mental hospitals, especially those reserved for criminals. He further castigates Bazelon for the fact that far too much power is placed in the hands of hospital psychiatrists. When the Durham test is applied, hospital psychiatrists are largely responsible for deciding when the individual is ready to be discharged. Finally, Szasz laments the impetus given by the Durham decision to a general denigration of the defendant. "Instead of recognizing the deviant as an individual different from those who would judge him, but nonetheless worthy of their respect, he is first discredited as a self-responsible human being and then subjected to humiliating punishment defined and disguised as treatment" (1963, p. 108).

### Evaluation of Szasz's position

As might be expected, Szasz has been answered by many whom he has criticized and by others who sincerely believe that psychiatry and psychology should have an important role in deciding how to deal with people whose criminal acts seem attributable to mental illness. When society acts with great certainty on the basis of "expert scientific opinion," however, particularly when that opinion denies to an individual the rights and respect accorded others in society, it may be well to let Szasz remind us that Sir Thomas Browne, a distinguished British physician, in 1664 testified in a court of law that witches did indeed exist, "as everyone knew."

And yet the abuses documented by Szasz should not blind us to the fact that—for whatever combination of physiological and psychological reasons—some people are, at times, a danger to others and to themselves. Although Szasz and others object to the mental illness metaphor as an explanation, it is difficult to deny that there is, indeed, madness in the world. People *do* occasionally imagine persecutors, whom they sometimes act against with force. Some people *do* hallucinate and on this basis may behave in a dangerous fashion. Our concern for the liberties of one individual has always been tempered with our concern for the rights of others.

But does it help a criminal acquitted by reason of insanity to place him in a prison mental hospital with an indeterminate sentence, pending his rehabilitation? The answer can surely not be an unqualified yes. Should such a person, then, be treated like any other convicted felon and be sent to a penitentiary? Considering the psychic damage that we know may occur in ordinary prisons, a yes to this question cannot be enthusiastic either. But a prison sentence is more often a finite term of incarceration. If we cannot demonstrate that people are rehabilitated in hospitals, perhaps it is just as well to rely on our prisons and on the efforts of penologists to improve these institutions and to find ways of helping inmates alter their behavior so that it will not be antisocial after release.[11]

[11] The treatment model, however, is being challenged by simple, old-fashioned retributive justice (Monahan, 1977). An emerging trend is to consider punishment rather than rehabilitation the primary purpose of imprisonment. The crime rates of prisoners who were given treatment, whether job training or psychotherapy, are no different after release from those of inmates who simply sat out their terms in their cells and led a routine prison life. Prisoners themselves have been agitating for finite sentences, rather than the indeterminate sentence that promises early parole depending on "rehabilitation."

## Civil Commitment

Civil commitment affects far greater numbers of people than criminal commitment. It is beyond the scope of this book to examine in detail the variety of state civil commitment laws and regulations. Each state has its own, and they are in almost constant flux. Our aim instead is to provide an overview that will give the reader a basic understandings of the issues and of the current directions of change.

In virtually all states of the union, a person can be committed to a mental hospital against his or her will if a judgment is made that he or she (1) is mentally ill and (2) is dangerous or needs treatment. At present, dangerousness to self or others is more often the second criterion, rather than the need for treatment.

Historically, governments have had the duty of protecting their citizens from harm. We take for granted the right and duty of government to set limits on our freedom for the sake of protecting us. Few drivers, for example, question the limits imposed on them by traffic signals. We usually go along with the Food and Drug Administration when it bans from uncontrolled use drugs that cause cancer in laboratory animals, although some people, to be sure, feel they have the right to decide for themselves what risks to take with their own bodies. Government, then, has a long-established right to protect us both from ourselves—the *parens patriae* power of the state; and from others—the police power of the state. Civil commitment is one further exercise of these powers.

Specific commitment procedures are generally of two types, formal and informal. Formal commitment is by order of a court. It can be requested by any responsible citizen; usually a relative or friend seeks the commitment. If the judge believes that there is good reason to pursue the matter, he or she will order a mental health examination. The person has the right to object to these attempts to "certify" him, and a court hearing can be scheduled to allow him to present evidence against commitment.

Informal, emergency commitment can be accomplished without initially involving the courts. For example, a hospital administrative board may decide that a voluntary patient requesting discharge is too disturbed and dangerous to be released. They are able to detain the patient with a temporary, informal commitment order. Any person acting wildly may be taken immediately to the state hospital by the police. Perhaps the most common informal commitment procedure is the "2PC" or "two physicians' certificate." In most states two physicians, not necessarily psychiatrists, can sign a certificate that will allow a person to be incarcerated for some period of time.[12]

## Faulty Instruments Cited in Jet That Crashed in Fog in Boston

WASHINGTON, Aug. 29 (AP) — A Delta Air Lines Jetliner that crashed into a seawall at Boston last month had a three-month history of problems with its radio and flight instruments, the National Transportation Safety Board disclosed today.

Problems with the instruments were reported seven times in the six-day period preceding the July 31 crash, the board said.

Eighty-eight of the 89 persons aboard the DC-9 jetliner died when the plane crashed sh... of a runway ... burned

Delta Air Lines DC-9 avionics configuration last April.

"Many of these complaints were of a recurring or chronic nature, dealing with the functioning of the flight director, the distance measuring equipment and one of the navigational receivers," the board said.

The safety board said that 14 jetliners were affected by the instrument modifications, which were made after Delta merged with Northeast Airlines last year. The board asked the Federal Aviation Adminstration t...estigate the modifications ...view the quality control

## Dangerousness: Problems in Definition and Prediction

The likelihood of committing a dangerous act is central to civil commitment, but is "dangerousness" easily defined? Stone (1975) suggests that, like beauty, it is in the eye of the beholder. Society punishes physical violence in the streets, for example, far more harshly than it punishes a business executive who knowingly neglects to replace defective gasoline tanks in an airplane (Geis and Monahan, 1976). White-collar dangerousness receives much less attention and retribution, even though it hurts more people.

The dangerousness standard varies greatly from state to state and is sometimes overly vague. In some states the danger need be only to property, not to other people. What must be borne in mind is that commitment is necessarily a form of preventive detention: the prediction is made that a person judged mentally ill may in the future behave in a dangerous manner and should therefore be detained. Ordinary prisoners, however, are released from penitentiaries, even though crime statistics show that most will commit additional crimes.

Studies have examined how good mental health professionals are at predicting that a person will commit a dangerous act (for example, Kozol, Boucher, and Garofalo, 1972; Stone, 1975; Monahan, 1973, 1976); they were found to be poor at making this judgment. Some workers have even argued that civil commitment for the purposes of preventive detention should be abolished. Apparently nothing important is being prevented! Monahan (in press), however, has carefully scrutinized these studies, and he has concluded that the professional's ability to predict violence is still an open question. Most of the studies had conformed to the following methodological pattern.

1. People were institutionalized for mental illness and for being a danger to the community.
2. While these people were in the hospital, some of them were again predicted to be violent if released into the community.
3. After a period of time, these people were released, thus putting together the conditions for "a natural experiment."

[12] Special issues are involved in the institutionalization and treatment of the mentally retarded, juveniles, drug addicts, and the aged. The reader is referred to Stone (1975) for an in-depth discussion and for guidance to the burgeoning legal literature.

4. Checks on the behavior of the released patients over the next several years did not reveal much dangerous behavior.

What is wrong with such research? Monahan points out that little if any consideration was given to changes that institutionalization itself might have effected. In the studies reviewed, the period of incarceration ranged from several months to fifteen years. Prolonged periods of enforced hospitalization might very well make patients more docile, if for no other reason than that they become that much older. Furthermore, the conditions in the open community where the predicted violence would be done can vary widely. We should not expect this kind of prediction to have great validity (see page 77).

> *Predictive validity tends to decrease as the gap increases between the behavior sampled on the prediction measure and the behavior that is being predicted. . . . The assessor who tries to predict the future without detailed information about the exact environmental conditions influencing the individual's criterion behavior may be . . . engaged in the process of hoping [rather] than of predicting* (Mischel, 1968, p. 140).

These studies, which have occasioned such pessimism about predicting whether a patient is dangerous, are therefore flawed. Yet they have also been used in arguments against emergency commitment. The fact of the matter is that neither these studies nor any others have examined this specific issue! Monahan, however, has theorized that prediction of dangerousness is probably far easier and surer in true emergency situations than after extended periods of hospitalization. When an emergency commitment is sought, the person may appear out of control and be threatening violence in his or her own living room. An outburst seems imminent. Thus, unlike the danger to society predicted in the studies previously examined, the violence requiring an emergency commitment is expected almost immediately and in a known situation. Commonsense tells us that such predictions of violence are likely to be very accurate. To test the validity of these expectations, we would have to leave alone half the people predicted to be immediately violent and later compare their behavior to that of persons hospitalized in such emergency circumstances. Such an experiment would be ethically irresponsible. Mental health professionals can only apply logic and make the most prudent judgments possible.

## Recent Trends for Greater Protection

The United States Constitution is a remarkable document. It lays down the basic duties of our elected federal officials and guarantees a set of civil rights. But there is often some distance between the abstract delineation of a civil right and its day-to-day implementation. Moreover, judges must *interpret* the Constitution as it bears on specific contemporary problems. Since nowhere in this cornerstone of our democracy is there specific mention of committed mental patients, lawyers and judges interpret various sections of the document to justify what they consider necessary changes in society's treatment of people whose mental health is in question.

In 1972 voluntary admissions to mental hospitals began to outnumber involuntary admissions. But it is still the case that two out of every five people admitted to a state or county mental hospital are there against their wishes. Moreover, it is impossible to know how many of those who admit themselves voluntarily do so under threat of civil commitment. The issue of enforced mental hospitalization is still very much with us. Even though psychiatrists, psychologists, the courts, and hospital staff are apparently growing more reluctant to commit, tens of thousands of mental patients are in hospitals against their will.

In a democratic society the most grievous wrong that can be suffered by a citizen is loss of liberty. The situation of mental patients is improving, however. The rights accorded to ordinary citizens, and even to criminals, are gradually being extended to those threatened with civil commitment or already hospitalized. No longer is it assumed that deprivation of liberty for purposes of mental health care is reason to deny to the individual all other rights. For example, a major court decision in Wisconsin, *Lessard v. Schmidt,*[13] provides that a person threatened with civil commitment has a right to counsel and to Fifth Amendment protection against self-incrimination. Moreover, it must be established beyond a reasonable doubt that the person is a danger to society. Although protection of the rights of the mentally ill will add tremendously to the burden of both civil courts and state and county mental hospital staffs, it is a price a free society will have to pay.

> *Given the record of past* [*criminal proceedings and*] *the tragic parody of legal commitment used to warehouse American citizens, it is . . . important that the individual feel sure that the* [*present*] *mental health system* [*in particular*] *cannot be so used and abused . . . for while the average citizen may have some confidence that if called by the Grand Inquisitor in the middle of the night and charged with a given robbery, he may have an alibi or be able to prove his innocence, he may be far less certain of his capacity, under the press of fear, to instantly prove his sanity* (Stone, 1975, p. 57).

The American Civil Liberties Union urges the retention of rights by people already hospitalized, in addition to pursuing vigorously the goal of reducing involuntary hospitalization. In a handbook published through the ACLU, Ennis and Siegel (1973) argue that committed patients should retain the right to vote, for their voting patterns have not been demonstrated to differ significantly from those of the communities from which they came. Ennis and Siegel argue also that, consistent with the Sixth Amendment, mental patients should have ready access to a lawyer, and that communications with their attorneys should be confidential. And they press for the right of patients to wear their own clothing and to retain control over their personal effects. These and other freedoms, for whose retention Szasz has also argued vigorously over the years, are now more often accorded mental patients (See Box 21.2).

One question that must certainly be asked, however, is whether the patient committed to a mental hospital is always best served by allowing him the privileges and choices that ordinary civil rights entail. Is it not inherent in the decision to commit that this individual is not able to make many determinations for himself? Those who inveigh against any reference to mental illness (for example Szasz, 1960; Ullmann and Krasner, 1975) find no problem in allowing people in mental hospitals to be treated as anyone else. But people sometimes *do* have problems thinking straight, they *do* sometimes need to be protected from themselves, others may take advantage of them, and they may even be harmed by others. Unfortunately, our knowledge of psychopathology is not sufficient for us to inform the legal profession what restraints on the liberty of mental patients are really necessary or even desirable.

### Right to treatment

One aspect of civil commitment has become controversial, the so-called right to treatment. If a person is deprived of liberty because he or she is mentally ill and is a danger to self or others, is not the state required to provide treatment to alleviate these problems? Is it not unconstitutional (and even indecent) to incarcerate someone without afterward providing the services he or she is supposed to need? This important question has been the subject of several recent court cases.

[13] Lessard v. Schmidt, 349 F. Supp. 1078 (E.D. Wis. 1972).

## BOX **21.2** Obtaining Patient's Rights

One of the realities of life, already mentioned, is the chasm that can exist between what is available in principle and what is available in actuality. Once there are laws, people often have to work to make these laws be of benefit to themselves. This may not be the way things should be, but it is indeed the way they are.

Information on the rights of mental patients is constantly updated by the ACLU and is available from them. Moreover, the Ennis and Siegel (1973) handbook informs mental patients of their rights and makes very practical suggestions on how to obtain these rights. Some of the advice may seem ruthless and conniving, but our adversary legal system requires such an approach. The system may not always be pretty, but it does seem to work better than anything else in protecting innocent parties.

Ennis and Siegel recommend several techniques to attorneys representing committed patients who wish to be released. To begin with, a patient's lawyer may request a court hearing in the hope that the hospital will simply release the patient. Psychiatrists dislike court appearances; the mere threat of being hauled before a judge may persuade members of a hospital staff to release the patient. If the hearing is held, other strategies are in order, such as challenging the credibility and impartiality of the psychiatrist who has determined that the patient is dangerous. The following exchange is proposed.

Q: Do you think he might even be dangerous to you?

*A*: Well, possibly. (If he says no, you can ask why he would be dangerous to others but not to the psychiatrist who recommends deprivation of his liberty.)

Q: In other words, you would feel personally safer if he were hospitalized than if he were at liberty, isn't that correct?

*A*: Well, yes.

Q: Then you are not completely disinterested in the outcome of this proceeding, are you? (pp. 293–294).

In *Wyatt* v. *Stickney*[14] an Alabama federal court ruled in 1972 that the only justification for the civil commitment of patients to a state mental hospital is treatment. As stated by Judge Johnson, "To deprive any citizen of his or her liberty upon the altruistic theory that the confinement is for humane and therapeutic reasons and then fail to provide adequate treatment violates the very fundamentals of due process." This ruling, upheld on appeal, is a milestone in the protection of people under civil commitment, at least to this extent: the state cannot simply put them away without meeting minimal standards of care, such as providing individualized treatment programs and suitable educational opportunities.

The *Wyatt* ruling and others like it, however, do not specify that the patient must obtain the *best* treatment, clearly an unrealistic requirement in view of how little is known about treatment. But some meaningful intervention must be attempted. These rulings acknowledge the state's obligation at least to eliminate the snake pits that have too long been an affront both to incarcerated patients and to the general population responsible for their establishment and maintenance.

In an even more celebrated case,[15] which eventually found its way to the Supreme Court, a civilly committed mental patient sued two state hospital doctors for his release and for money damages, on the grounds that he had been incarcerated against his will for fourteen years without being treated and without being dangerous to himself or to others. In January 1957, at the age of forty-nine, Kenneth Donaldson was committed to the Florida state hospital at Chattachoochee on petition by his father, who felt that his son was delusional. Donaldson was found at a court hearing to be a paranoid schizophrenic and was committed for "care, maintenance, and treatment." The Florida statute then in effect allowed for such commitment on the usual grounds of mental illness and dangerousness. "Dangerousness" could then be defined as inability to manage property and to protect oneself from being taken advantage of by others.

In 1971 Donaldson sued Dr. O'Connor, the hospital superintendent, and Dr. Gumanis, a hospital psychiatrist, for release. Evidence presented at the trial in a United States district court in Florida indicated that the hospital staff could have released Donaldson at any time following a determination that he was not a dangerous person. Testimony made it clear that at no time during his hospitalization had Donaldson's conduct posed any real danger to others or to himself. In fact, just before his commitment in 1957, he had been earning a living and taking adequate care of himself (and immediately upon discharge he secured a job in hotel administration). Nonetheless, O'Connor had repeatedly refused the patient's requests for release, feeling it was his duty to determine whether a committed patient could adapt successfully outside the institution. His judgment was that Donaldson could not. In deciding this question of "adjustment outside the institution," O'Connor went beyond a consideration of dangerousness on which most current state laws for commitment rest.

Several responsible people had attempted to obtain Donaldson's release by guaranteeing that they would look after him. For example, in 1963 a halfway house formally requested that Donaldson be released to its care, and between 1964 and 1968 a former college classmate asked more than once that the patient be released to his care. O'Connor refused, saying that the patient could be released only to his parents, who by this time were quite old and infirm.

The evidence indicated also that Donaldson received only custodial care during his hospitalization. No treatment that could conceivably alleviate or cure his assumed mental illness was undertaken. The "milieu therapy" that O'Connor claimed Donaldson was undergoing consisted, in actuality, of being kept in a large room with sixty

[14] Wyatt v. Stickney, 344 F. Supp. 373, 344 F. Supp. 387 (M.D. Ala, 1972).

[15] O'Connor v. Donaldson, 95 S. Ct. 2486 (1975).

Kenneth Donaldson, displaying a copy of the Supreme Court opinion stating that nondangerous mental patients cannot be confined against their will under civil commitment.

other patients, many of whom were under criminal commitment. Donaldson had been denied privileges to stroll around the hospital grounds or even to discuss his case with Dr. O'Connor.

The original trial and its appeal concluded that Donaldson was not dangerous and had been denied his constitutional right to treatment; O'Connor was found liable for a fine of $38,500. Throughout this litigation Donaldson declared he was neither dangerous nor mentally ill. *But,* went his claim, *even if* he were mentally ill, he should be released because he was not receiving treatment.

On appeal to the Supreme Court, it was ruled, on June 26, 1975, that "a State cannot constitutionally confine . . . a nondangerous individual who is capable of surviving safely in freedom by himself or with the help of willing and responsible family members or friends." In 1977 Donaldson ultimately settled for $20,000 from the estate of O'Connor, who had died during the appeals process, and from Dr. Gumanis. The money settlement was negotiated without any admission that the doctors were at fault. Donaldson may also sue for attorneys' fees as well, which is an important option. The award of legal fees would put teeth into the precedent established by the Supreme Court by making the representation of "other Donaldsons" more attractive to private attorneys (*Mental Health Law Project Summary of Activities,* 1977).

The Supreme Court decision on *O'Connor* v. *Donaldson* created a stir when it was issued, and it is certain to give mental health professionals pause in detaining patients. At the same time, the decision says less than some have assumed. Donaldson earned his release by convincing the Court that he was not dangerous to himself or others, and that he could survive outside the hospital with support from family and friends. But most states already require that patients be, in fact, considered dangerous, in addition to being judged mentally ill, if they are to be detained under civil commitment. By recognizing that mental illness by itself is not sufficient justification for continuation of hospitalization under civil commitment, the Court only confirmed statutes already in effect in most jurisdictions. The Court did not consider whether a nondangerous person could be civilly committed on the basis of needing treatment. Indeed, the Court was silent about the grounds for commitment in the first place.

Furthermore, the Court did not address the question what constitutes dangerousness. Given the problems already reviewed on this issue, we can appreciate the challenges that still await civil rights attorneys. Patients can still be detained against their will if judges can be convinced by lawyers and mental health professionals that they are, by some definition or other, dangerous in addition to being mentally ill. Moreover, although this decision is often cited as yet another affirmation of "right to treatment," the Supreme Court did not, in fact, rule on this issue. It did not recognize a constitutional right to treatment, although by the same token it did not deny it.

The *Donaldson* decision did say that a committed patient's status must be periodically reviewed, for the grounds on which a patient was initially committed cannot be assumed to continue in effect forever. In other words, people can change while in a mental hospital and may no longer require confinement. This seems straightforward enough! The Court reminded mental hospital officials that they must not forget their patients. It is a sad commentary on the mental hospital system that the Supreme Court of the United States saw the need to caution it about the obvious and routine (see Box 21.3).

### Right to refuse treatment

If a committed mental patient has the right to expect appropriate treatment, since he has lost his freedom because he needs help, does he have a right to *refuse* treatment, or a particular kind of treatment? The answer appears to be yes, but there are qualifications. A state hospital may have adequate staff to provide up-to-date chemotherapy as well as group therapy but lack the professional resources to offer individual therapy. Suppose that patient X refuses the available modalities and insists on individual therapy. Would he later be able to sue the hospital for not offering the specific services requested? If the patient has the right to refuse certain forms of treatment, how far should the courts go in ensuring this right, remaining at the same time realistic about the state's ability to provide alternatives? When should the judgment of a professional staff override the wishes of a patient, especially one who is grossly psychotic? Are the patient's best interests always served if he or she can veto the plans of those responsible for care (Stone, 1975)?

Electroconvulsive therapy is a form of treatment that patients often resist. Works of fiction, plus personal reports from people who have undergone ECT, generate strong emotional objections to it. State laws generally allow for ECT to be imposed on committed patients against their will, although in many instances the consent of a third party is required. In 1971 California, long one of the more progressive states on a variety of health and social issues, guaranteed patients the right to refuse ECT (as well as lobotomy). Yet this right could be revoked should the mental health professional in charge of the hospital find "good cause" to do so. In other words, the state giveth and the state taketh away!

In 1973 Massachusetts developed very strict guidelines for the administration of ECT. Informed written consent is required from *voluntary* patients, and they can at any later time withdraw consent given earlier. So far so good, but Stone (1975) points out some difficulties. What can a hospital do if an acutely suicidal, but voluntary, patient refuses ECT, which his psychiatrist believes is the best treatment for him? What if this patient also refuses the drugs his psychiatrist prescribes in lieu of ECT and goes on to commit suicide in the hospital? Should the hospital have provided close, round-the-clock surveillance of the patient? But what of the rights of the *other* patients, whose care might well have suffered because of the

## BOX **21.3** Releasing Mental Patients, to Their Benefit?

The cumulative impact of court rulings such as *Wyatt* v. *Stickney* and *O'Connor* v. *Donaldson* is to put mental health professionals on notice that they must be more careful about keeping people in mental hospitals against their will, and that they must attend more to the specific treatment needs of committed patients. Pressure is being put both on them and on state governments in particular to upgrade the quality of care in mental institutions. In view of the abuses that have been documented in hospital care, these are surely encouraging trends.

But the picture is not all that rosy. For judges to declare that patient care must meet certain minimal standards does not automatically translate into that praiseworthy goal. Long-term chronic patients are not especially attractive to psychiatrists and psychologists, which is no credit to the profession but nonetheless largely true. Furthermore, there is not an unlimited supply of money. Sadly enough, care of the mentally ill has never been one of government's high priorities. Nor is support of research in the social and behavioral sciences. As indicated in the previous chapter (page 553), many states have instead embarked on programs to discharge as many patients as possible from mental hospitals. The maxim has been "Treat them in the community," for it is best not to isolate patients for long periods in grim and forbidding asylums.

What *is* this "community" that former mental patients are supposed to find more helpful to them upon discharge? Who is to educate ordinary citizens not to be fearful of, or repulsed by, people who are shabbily dressed and often poorly groomed and who may on occasion act strangely? What are the most effective therapeutic procedures for helping these forgotten ones? Facilities outside the hospitals are not prepared to cope with the influx of former mental patients. In New York City in 1973, for example, an estimated 25,000 ex-mental patients were living on welfare in run-down hotels, without medication or other needed care (Stone, 1975). At the Public Hearing on the Problems of Deinstitutionalized Mental Patients in New York City, held October 5, 1977, mental health officials of New York State acknowledged that of the 100,000 mental patients released from their state hospitals since 1950, 30,000 are in Manhattan. Only 4000 of these people are receiving day services; 200 to 300 have supervised living. Integrating former patients into society at large and helping them cope with everyday living is a serious challenge to mental health professionals and laypeople alike.

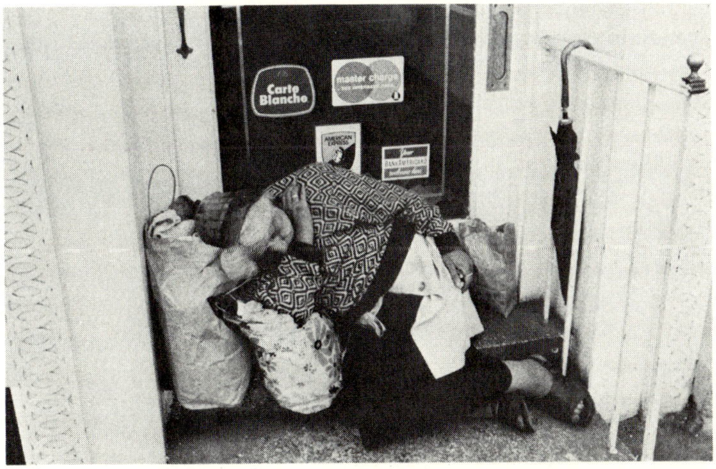

extra attention given the suicidal patient? A citizen may have the right to kill himself, but does he have the right to do it in a hospital? It is interesting that the civil commitment laws in Massachusetts allow a hospital to move for commitment when patients judged in dire need refuse shock treatment. Once committed, the patient is of course no longer voluntary and can be forced to undergo ECT if the responsible professional deems it advisable and necessary and if a relative or guardian consents.

Does civil commitment imply an incompetency that renders the patient incapable of forming reasonable opinions concerning therapies? The issue is similar to the problem in criminal commitment proceedings, when a judgment that the accused is mentally ill can deny him access to the courts. Stone believes that a civilly committed person may be competent to refuse a given treatment. He wisely proposes, though, that patients be given the right to refuse only certain treatments, those that are hazardous or very unpleasant, such as psychosurgery, ECT and any other convulsion therapy, aversion therapy, and chemotherapy with highly addictive drugs like methadone. Stone makes the point that these treatments are risky enough that patients should be allowed to refuse them—even patients under criminal commitment—and that refusal should be overridden only under the special scrutiny of the courts. At the same time, however, administration of less risky treatments would remain the option of the professional staff, with the patient having little to say about their use.[16]

[16] A resistant patient is able to ward off psychological therapies if he or she wishes, merely by refusing to participate. The high-risk techniques mentioned above are all somatic therapies, requiring little if any cooperation by the patient. What else in the armamentarium of clinical psychology and psychiatry could conceivably be *imposed* on an unwilling patient? The only answer seems to be the various psychoactive drugs, such as Thorazine. When patients are given their "meds" in mental hospitals, the drugs are often dissolved in liquid and must be drunk in the presence of a nurse or an aide, to ensure that they are being taken. Still, it is the common experience of those who have worked in mental hospitals that patients can manage to avoid taking their medication. Few treatments, then, can be forced on a patient. Unless staff members are able to enlist at least minimal cooperation, they can do little to help.

## Ethical Dilemmas in Therapy and Research

In this textbook we have examined a variety of theories and a multitude of data focusing on *what is* and *what is thought to be*. Ethics and values are a different order of discussion. They concern *what ought to be,* having sometimes little to do with what is. It is extremely important to recognize the difference. Within a given scientific paradigm we are able to examine what we believe is reality. As the study of philosophy and ethics reveals, however, the statements that people have made for thousands of years about what should be are a separate matter. The Ten Commandments are such statements. They are prescriptions and proscriptions about human conduct. For example, the eighth commandment, "Thou shalt not steal," in no way describes human conduct, for stealing is not uncommon. It is, instead, a pronouncement of an ideal that people *should* aspire to. The integrity of an ethical code that proscribes stealing does not depend on any evidence concerning the percentage of people who steal. Morals and data are two separate realms of discourse.

The legal trends reviewed thus far in this chapter place limits on the activities of mental health professionals. These legal constraints are important, for laws are one of society's strongest means of forcing all of us to behave in certain ways. Psychologists and psychiatrists also have professional and ethical constraints. All professional groups promulgate "shoulds" and "should nots," and by guidelines and mandates they limit to some degree what therapists and researchers do with their patients, clients, and subjects. Courts as well have ruled on some of these questions. We shall examine now the ethics of making psychological interventions into the lives of other human beings. More questions will be asked than can be answered.

### Ethical Restraints on Research

It is basic to science that what can be done is

likely to be attempted. The most reprehensible ethical insensitivity is documented in the brutal experiments conducted by certain German physicians on concentration camp prisoners during the Third Reich. One experiment, for example, investigated how long people lived when their heads were bashed repeatedly with a heavy stick. Even if important information might be obtained from this kind of atrocity, which seems extremely doubtful, such actions cannot be allowed. The Nuremberg trials, conducted by the Allies following the war, brought these and other barbarisms to light and meted our severe punishment to soldiers, physicians, and other Nazi officials who had engaged in or contributed to such actions, even when they claimed that they had merely been following orders.

It would be reassuring to be able to say that such gross violations of human decency take place only during incredible and cruel epochs such as the Third Reich, but unfortunately this is not the case. Spurred on by a blind enthusiasm for their work, researchers in this country have sometimes dealt with human subjects in reproachable ways.

Henry K. Beecher, a research professor at Harvard Medical School, surveyed medical research since 1945 and found that ". . . many of the patients [used as subjects in experiments] never had the risk satisfactorily explained to them, and . . . further hundreds have not known that they were the subjects of an experiment although grave consequences have been suffered as the direct result . . ." (1966, p. 1354). One experiment compared penicillin to a placebo as a treatment to prevent rheumatic fever. Even though penicillin had already been acknowledged as the drug of choice to give people with a streptococcal respiratory infection in order to protect them from later contracting rheumatic fever, placeboes were administered to 109 servicemen without their knowledge or permission. More men received penicillin than the placebo, but three members of the control group contracted serious illnesses—two cases of rheumatic fever and one of acute nephritis, a kidney disease—as compared to none of those who had received penicillin.

The training of scientists equips them splendidly to pose interesting questions, sometimes even important ones, and to design experiments that are as free as possible of confounds. They have no special qualifications, however, for deciding whether a particular line of inquiry that involves humankind *should* be followed. Society needs knowledge, and a scientist has a right in a democracy to seek that knowledge. The ordinary citizens employed as subjects in experiments must, however, be protected from unnecessary harm, risk, humiliation, and invasion of privacy. There are several international codes of ethics for the conduct of scientific research—the Nuremberg Code formulated in the aftermath of the Nazi war crime trials, the Declaration of Helsinki, and statements from the British Medical Research Council. Closer to home, in the early 1970s the Department of Health, Education and Welfare began to issue guidelines and regulations governing scientific research that employs human subjects. In addition, a blue-ribbon panel, the National Commission for the Protection of Human Subjects of Biomedical and Behavioral Research, conducted hearings and inquiries into restrictions that the federal government might impose on research performed with mental patients, prisoners, and children. And already for several years the proposals of behavioral researchers, many of whom conduct experiments related to psychopathology and therapy, have been reviewed for safety and general ethical propriety by "human subjects committees" in hospitals, universities, and research institutes. Such institutional review committees—and this is very significant—are composed not just of behavioral scientists but of citizens of the community, lawyers, students, and specialists in a variety of disciplines, such as professors of English, history, and comparative religion. They are able to block any research proposal or require modification of questionable aspects if in their collective judgment it will put participating subjects at too great risk.

## Informed Consent

Participation in research brings up the all-important concept of *informed consent.* Just as committed mental patients are gaining the right to refuse treatment, so may anyone refuse to be a subject in an experiment. The investigator must provide enough information to enable subjects to judge whether they want to take the risks inherent in being a participant. The prospective subjects must be legally capable of giving consent, and there must be no deceit or coercion in obtaining it. For example, an experimental psychologist might be interested in determining whether imagery will help college students associate one word with another. One group of subjects will be called upon to try to associate pairs of words in their minds by generating a fanciful image connecting the two, such as a CAT riding on a BICYCLE." The consent form will state that the experiment consists of sitting for half an hour in front of a screen, watching pairs of words being projected on it, and trying to learn the pairs by devising images that can connect them in memory. A prospective subject might decide, however, that such a session is likely to be boring and can, without penalty, decline to participate. In fact, review committees require that a subject be at liberty to withdraw from an experiment at any time, without penalty, although it is understandable that he or she would feel pressure not to do so.[17]

Paired-associates research is relatively innocuous, but what if the experiment poses real risks, such as ingesting a drug? Or the prospective subject may be a prisoner, a committed mental patient, or even a retarded child, unable to understand fully what is being asked. Such a subject may not feel free to refuse participation. And what of the rights of the researcher, which often are not as carefully considered as those of subjects, and of the cost to society of important research left undone? Will scientists become reluctant to undertake certain types of work because review committees make the process of obtaining informed consent unduly onerous and time-consuming?

Davison and Stuart (1975) have proposed a scheme (Table 21.1) that might protect subjects' rights when they participate in research, without hampering researchers in their quest for knowledge. In determining how careful the researchers must be when obtaining informed consent, Davison and Stuart would ask four questions. What is the level of risk? Little harm is likely in the kind of memory experiment mentioned earlier, but greater risk is inherent in a study that requires a subject to withstand electric shock applied to the fingers. Is the research of potential benefit to the subject or client? A subject might stand to gain a great deal from being in the study or to gain nothing directly, except the satisfaction of having helped a scientist find out something new. Is the technique an established one, whose risks and benefits are known or is it new and experimental, so that the researcher is unable to indicate how beneficial, harmful, or discomfiting participation might be? Is the subject realistically free to give consent or to refuse participation? A college student has great freedom to refuse, but a prisoner would probably feel considerable coercion to participate in an experiment if asked to do so.

These four question are not the only ones that might be asked, and the numbered consent procedures in Table 21.1 are merely suggestions. Clearly, the judgment of many other people would be needed to establish meaningful values and to work out a set of procedures. The scheme, however, may help human subjects committees to organize their thinking about the problem of obtaining informed consent in a variety of circumstances.

[17] It is not easy to demonstrate that a researcher has in fact obtained informed consent. Epstein and Lasagna (1969) found that only one-third of subjects volunteering for an experiment really understood what the experiment entailed. In a more elaborate study Stuart (in press) discovered that most college students could not accurately describe a simple experiment, even though it had just been explained to them and they had agreed to participate. A signature on a consent form is no assurance that informed consent has really been obtained, which poses a real challenge to investigators and members of review panels who are committed to upholding codes of ethics governing participation of human subjects in research.

TABLE **21.1**
## Guidelines for Protecting Subject's Right to Participate Only in Experiments of Own Choice

(after Davison and Stuart, 1975)

| Level of risk | Freedom to give consent | High potential benefit to subject: Established procedure | High potential benefit to subject: Experimental procedure | Low potential benefit to subject, high potential benefit to society: Established procedure | Low potential benefit to subject, high potential benefit to society: Experimental procedure |
|---|---|---|---|---|---|
| Low risk | Great freedom | 2–4* | 4 | 2–4 | 4–5 |
| | Feels some coercion | 5 | 5 | 5–6 | 7 |
| High risk | Great freedom | 4 | 5 | 5–6 | 7 |
| | Feels some coercion | 6 | 6 | 7 | 8 |

* The numbers indicate the degree of care that should be exercised in obtaining consent.

1. *No consent by the subject is necessary.* The investigator assures protection of the subject's rights. The nonobtrusive observation of traffic flow in public places or other public behavior might fall into this category. This procedure and the next are permissible only when a review panel has determined that the potential risk of harm to the anonymously observed subjects is nil.

2. *Subject is simply asked to sign a consent form for participation in research as a subject of observations, with no explanation of the nature of the study.* One example would be observing the supermarket shopping of individuals; an explanation of the objectives of the study might change relevant behavior.

3. *Subject is asked to sign a consent form for participation in research, with "debriefing" following participation.* Such a study might examine interpersonal behavior in public places; prior disclosure of the hypotheses could change behavior. A panel of experts would have to determine that subjects risked little in participating, including minimal humiliation following debriefing.

4. *Subject is asked to sign a consent form for participation in a project, after full disclosure of the objectives and methods of the research.* This procedure would be applied in efforts to evaluate treatment by randomly assigning subjects to experimental, to placebo control, and to no treatment control groups. A review panel must judge that risk of harm to control subjects is equal to or less than it would be were there no experiment.

5. *Subject is asked to sign a consent form for participation in a project, after full disclosure of the objectives and methods of the research and in the presence of at least one witness who is not involved in the research.* This procedure would be appropriate any time a review panel senses that subjects may feel obliged to participate. Research with adjudicated offenders could fall into this category.

6. *Subject is asked to sign a consent form for participation in a project, after full disclosure of the objectives and methods of the research and in the presence of witnesses. The consent is reviewed by an independent human subjects committee within the institution.* This procedure might be applied in the experimental evaluation of a program carrying out an institutional objective, for example, vocational training in prisons and mental hospitals.

7. *Subject is asked to sign a consent form for participation in a project, after full disclosure of the objectives and methods of the research and in the presence of witnesses. The consent is reviewed by an independent human subjects committee within the institution and by a similar committee outside the institution.* The procedure could be applied when the research concerns behavior changes that are not strictly related to institutional objectives, for example, a study of the role of repetition when mental patients are taught phrases in a foreign language.

8. *No consent is possible because the rights of subjects cannot be protected.*

## Treatment or Research?

What is the difference between treatment and research? This is a question that people attempting to replace old procedures with newer, possibly more effective methods must address, given the new Department of Health, Education and Welfare regulations on conducting research. Martin (1975) considered the following example. In school district A a teacher who has read about some of the token economy research in classrooms (for example, O'Leary and O'Leary, 1977) has adopted token reinforcement as a means of persuading a group of underachieving and often disruptive students to attend to their lessons. The results have been quite encouraging; the classroom is quieter, the students are in their seats more often, and their academic performance has improved. Moreover, the students themselves like the program. Is this an experiment? Should the teacher have obtained informed consent from the parents? A few miles away in school district B another teacher is also applying a token economy. The project is funded by a federal grant, calls itself experimental, and routinely obtained the informed consent that is commonplace for research. There is no doubt that *this* program is research, but does the similarity of district A's program to this one make it research as well?

Because of their relative newness, the application of behavioral procedures is likely to be construed as research, even though not so intended, and to be viewed with some apprehension. And yet we often take for granted—in fact, we applaud—an elementary school teacher who finds a novel way of exciting children about the learning process. "She's really a creative teacher. She doesn't content herself with the curriculum and the materials provided by the school board." To be sure, in many instances the difference between treatment and research is clear. For example, the drug Anectine, a paralytic agent often used to relax patients about to receive ECT, was imposed on a prisoner for a different purpose, to produce a frightening "unconditioned response" in an aversive conditioning endeavor. Although the drug is in routine use to protect ECT patients from physical harm, a judge ruled that employing it in this way raised serious constitutional questions and appeared to be cruel and unusual punishment.[18]

## Confidentiality and Privileged Communication—Who Is the Client?

When an individual consults a physician, a psychiatrist, or a clinical psychologist, he or she expects all that goes on in the session to remain confidential. Nothing will be revealed to a third party, excepting only to other professionals and those intimately involved in the treatment, such as a nurse or medical secretary. The ethical codes of the various helping professions dictate this confidentiality. The legal concept of privileged communication is even more protective of the patient or client; professionals can be punished by law if they divulge anything about a contact without the client's express permission. The client can therefore expect the law to protect the confidentiality of any communication that passes between himself and his therapist or doctor.

There are limits on both these protections. If a psychologist's client announces that he has just murdered someone, the psychologist is immediately released from the codes of confidentiality and privileged communication and indeed is expected to report the crime to the authorities. Under most circumstances, however, the client can confide in the psychologist and usually does.

But is it always clear to the clinician who the client is? In private therapy, when an adult pays a clinician a fee for help with a personal problem that has nothing to do with the legal system, the consulting individual is clearly the client, and the clinician is expected to maintain complete confidentiality about whatever transpires. But an individual may be referred to the clinician for an evaluation of his or her competency to stand trial. Or the clinician may be hired by an individual's family to assist in civil commitment proceedings. Perhaps the clinician is employed by a state mental hospital as a regular staff member and sees a particular patient about problems in controlling aggressive impulses. It should be clear, although it is alarming how seldom it *is* clear, that in these instances the clinician is serving more than one client. In addition to the patient, he or she is also serving the family or the state, and it is incumbent on the mental health professional to inform the patient that this is so. This dual allegiance does not necessarily indicate that the patient's own interests will be sacrificed, but it does mean that discussions will not inevitably remain secret and that the clinician may act in a way that displeases the individual. A patient being examined for commitment may, for example, confide in the clini-

[18] Mackey v. Procunier, 477 F. 2d 877 (9th Cir. 1973).

cian, revealing that she does, in fact, contemplate suicide and hears voices, as her family has suspected but never known for certain. This admission may later be used to justify a civil commitment to a mental hospital. In this case the patient will be protected from her own suicidal impulses, even though she asserts that she wants no such protection.

## Goals of Therapy

Ideally the client sets the goals for therapy, but in practice it is naive to assume that some are not imposed by the therapist and even go against the wishes of the client. School systems often want to institute programs that will teach children to "be still, be quiet, be docile" (Winett and Winkler, 1972, p. 499). Many behavior therapists have assumed that young children *should* be compliant, not only because the teacher can then run a more orderly class but because children are assumed to learn better when they are so. But do we really know that the most efficient and most enjoyable learning takes place when children are forced to remain quietly in their seats? Some advocates of "open classrooms" believe that curiosity and initiative, even in the youngest elementary school child, are at least as important as the acquisition of academic skills. Furthermore, perhaps the traditional skills of reading and writing are better imparted to youngsters when they have greater freedom to choose where and when they are to study. As is generally the case in psychology, evidence is less plentiful than are strongly held and vehemently defended opinions. But the issue is clear: any professionals consulted by a school system should be mindful of their own personal biases with respect to goals and be prepared to work toward different ones if the parents and school personnel so wish.[19]

A therapist working in a mental hospital has the quandary of deciding what will benefit patients. One of the *Wyatt* v. *Stickney* rulings states that patients must be paid at least the federal minimum wage for performing the janitorial, gardening, and other chores that have traditionally been assigned mental patients as a form of "occupational therapy." Further, any work must be done voluntarily. The *Wyatt* case revealed that in a particular hospital patients had become a cheap and captive "slave" labor force, responsible for the maintenance of the institution.

It might be argued that schizophrenic patients are better off mowing a lawn than languishing in bed, plagued by their imagined persecutors. And it might be argued further that cajoling or even forcing patients to learn how to sweep a hall, or fry an egg, or change the oil in a car will enhance their chances of ultimately becoming employable outside the institution. David Wexler (1973), a professor of law, has written a relevant paper, "Token and Taboo," which has received considerable attention from behavior therapists and from those working in the new law-and-behavior field. He points out that the *Wyatt* ruling, although intended to protect patients, might eventually work to their disadvantage. Directors of hospitals are always interested in running as efficient and economical an institution as possible, for this is what they are paid to do. Hitherto patient labor was attractive because it was, in fact, cheap. But seldom has it been as effective and efficient as labor that can be bought on the outside and brought into the hospital. If it is necessary to pay a federal minimum wage anyway, hospital administrators may choose to hire efficient employees. Patients may be deprived of valuable opportunities to learn new skills, and hospital life may become even more odious and boring.

And yet one long-term benefit is possible: mental health professionals will be forced to consider more carefully whether maintenance work is, in fact, helpful in preparing a patient for life outside the hospital. If such work can be shown to be truly rehabilitative, and not just a convenience to the institution, the *Wyatt* ruling

[19] Any therapist of course retains the option of *not* working for a client whose goals and proposed means of attaining them are abhorrent in his or her view.

might not preclude patients from performing it without pay.[20]

Much of the controversy about the goals of therapy concerns the institutionalized patient, whose freedom is obviously limited. But people who consult therapists voluntarily also operate within constraints on their freedom. The issue has been stated by Seymour Halleck (1971), a psychiatrist, who asserts that the neutrality of the therapist is a myth. In his opinion therapists influence their clients in ways that are subtle yet powerful.

> *At first glance, a model of psychiatric [or psychological] practice based on the contention that people should just be helped to learn to do the things they want to do seems uncomplicated and desirable. But it is an unobtainable model. Unlike a technician, a psychiatrist [or psychologist] cannot avoid communicating and at times imposing his own values upon his patients. The patient usually has considerable difficulty in finding the way in which he would wish to change his behavior, but as he talks to the psychiatrist his wants and needs become clearer. In the very process of defining his needs in the presence of a figure who is viewed as wise and authoritarian, the patient is profoundly influenced. He ends up wanting some of the things the psychiatrist thinks he should want (p. 19).*

Psychologists agree, and available data (for example, Rosenthal, 1955) support the contention, that patients are profoundly influenced by the values of their therapists. A person not only seeks out a therapist who suits his taste and meets what he believes are his needs but also adopts some of the ideals, sometimes even the mannerisms, of the therapist. Most therapists are keenly aware of this modeling after themselves, which surely increases the already heavy responsibilities of their professional role. Perry London (1964), a leading writer on the ethics of therapeutic intervention, has even suggested that therapists are contemporary society's secular priests, purveyors of values and ethics to help clients live "the good life" (see Box 21.4).

[20] On the other hand, once sweeping a floor is construed as treatment, patients who object to the work can invoke their legal right to refuse treatment. It does sometime appear that the law and the helping professions may be on a collision course.

## Choice of Techniques

The end does not justify the means. Most of us take in this maxim with our mother's milk. It is said to be intrinsic to a free society. In recent years questions concerning behavioral techniques have been debated among professionals and have even been the subject of court rulings. Perhaps because the various insight therapies are restricted to talking and listening, they have seldom been scrutinized as behavior therapy has. The very concreteness and specificity of behavioral techniques has called attention to them, as has their alignment with experimental psychology. Likening people to rats and pigeons and referring to each and every happening as a "stimulus" or "response" are offensive to some.

Certain behavioral techniques have been singled out by the courts. The token economy discussed in Chapter 19 is one. In their efforts to expedite the rehabilitation of mental patients (and prisoners as well), some behavior therapists offer them access to certain amenities as consequences for certain changes in behavior. A patient who wants to sleep in privacy can do so for 100 tokens, which may in turn be earned by attending group therapy every day for two weeks. Setting up such a contingency requires denial of a private room initially. But the *Wyatt* v. *Stickney* rulings suggest that privacy is an *absolute right* of a mental patient, and therefore it cannot be made *contingent* on anything the patient does or does not do. The patient should have it as a constitutional right. Also guaranteed by the *Wyatt* rulings and other decisions are three meals a day, without delay or deprivation. Earlier behavior therapists had made entry into a ward dining room contingent on certain behavior (Ayllon and Haughton, 1962).

# BOX **21.4** Not Can But Ought: The Treatment of Homosexuality

Several psychologists have argued that the social pressures on homosexuals to become heterosexual make it difficult to believe that the small minority of people who consult therapists for help in changing from same-sex to opposite-sex partners act with free choice (Silverstein, 1972; Davison, 1974, 1976; Begelman, 1975). Silverstein originally stated the problem in the following fashion.

*To suggest that a person comes voluntarily to change his sexual orientation is to ignore the powerful environmental stress, oppression if you will, that has been telling him for years that he should change. To grow up in a family where the word "homosexual" was whispered, to play in a playground and hear the words "faggot" and "queer," to go to church and hear of "sin" and then to college and hear of "illness," and finally to the counseling center that promises to "cure," is hardly* [to live in] *an environment of freedom and voluntary choice. The homosexual is expected to want to be changed and his application for treatment is implicitly praised as the first step toward "normal" behavior.*

*What brings* [homosexuals] *into the counseling center is guilt, shame, and the loneliness that comes from their secret. If you really wish to help them freely choose, I suggest you first desensitize them to their guilt. Allow them to dissolve the shame about their desires and actions and to feel comfortable with their sexuality. After that, let them choose, but not before. I don't know any more than you what would happen, but I think their choice would be more voluntary and free than it is at present* (p. 4).

It has further been suggested that the mere availability of change-of-orientation programs in a way condones the prejudice against homosexuality. Clinicians work to develop procedures and study their effects only if they are concerned about a problem to be dealt with by their techniques (Davison, 1976). The therapy literature contains scant material on helping homosexuals develop as individuals without changing their sexual orientation, in contrast to the many articles and books on how best to discourage homosexual behavior and substitute for it heterosexual patterns. Aversion therapy is apparently the most widely used behavioral technique (Davison and Wilson, 1973; Henkel and Lewis-Thomé, 1976). "What are we really saying to our clients when, on the one hand, we assure them that they are not abnormal and on the other hand, present them with an array of techniques, some of them painful, which are aimed at eliminating that set of feelings and behavior that we have just told them is okay?" (Davison, 1976, p. 161).

For these reasons it has been proposed that therapists refuse to help a homosexual become heterosexual even when such treatment is requested. This is obviously a radical proposal,

The struggle for gay rights is far from over. In June 1977 a referendum spearheaded by the entertainer Anita Bryant succeeded in repealing a homosexual rights law in Miami. Her "Save Our Children" crusade sounded the theme that gays should not be permitted in occupations like teaching. She is seen at the left with her husband, indicating that heterosexuality is number one. On the right is one of the many protest marches that followed the Miami election, this one in Manhattan.

and it has evoked some strong reactions. Gay-activist groups are understandably pleased, considering the suggestion concrete support for the belief that homosexuality per se is not a mental disorder. But many psychologists and psychiatrists are concerned about limiting the choices available to people seeking therapy. Why should a therapist decide for potential clients which options are to be available? Do not therapists have a responsibility to satisfy the needs expressed by their clients (Sturgis and Adams, in press)? A reply to this important criticism can be that therapists always decide what therapy they will offer by refusing to take clients whose goals they disagree with. Court rulings can also put constraints on the treatments available to patients. In *Kaimowitz* v. *Michigan Department of Mental Health,** for example, a state court held that a committed mental patient could not volunteer for psychosurgery, which he had hoped would eliminate fits of uncontrollable aggression and thereby gain him his release. The judge felt that, living in the coercive environment of a state hospital, the patient could not give informed consent to such a procedure. The request of a patient for a certain kind of treatment has never been sufficient justification for providing it (see Davison, in press).

It has been asserted that through continued research sex reorientation programs that are even more effective than those already available will probably be developed (Sturgis and Adams, in press). To discourage such work would deprive today's homosexuals of promising therapies and tomorrow's homosexuals of improved treatments. This objection, however, is not relevant. The fact that we *can* do something does not indicate that we *should*. The proposal to deny sexual reorientation therapy is philosophical-ethical in nature, not empirical. The decision whether we should change sexual orientation will have to be made on moral grounds.

Will numbers of people be hurt by eliminating the sex reorientation option? Some have raised the specter of an upsurge in suicides among homosexuals if therapists refuse to help them switch. These are very serious concerns, but they overlook the possibility, some would say the fact, that far greater numbers of people have been hurt over the years by the availability of sex reorientation programs. As already argued, the existence of these treatments is consistent with societal prejudices and discrimination against homosexuals.

The proponents who wish to terminate change-of-orientation programs believe that much good can come of their proposal. Homosexuals would be helped to think better of themselves, and greater efforts could be directed toward the problems homosexuals have, rather than to the problem of homosexuality.

*It would be nice if an alcoholic homosexual, for example, could be helped to reduce his or her drinking without having his or her sexual orientation questioned. It would be nice if a homosexual fearful of interpersonal relationships, or incompetent in them, could be helped without the therapist assuming that homosexuality lies at the root of the problem. It would be nice if a nonorgasmic or impotent homosexual could be helped as a heterosexual would be rather than* [*being guided*] *to change-of-orientation regimens . . . the hope* [*is*] *that therapists will concentrate their efforts on such* human *problems rather than focusing on the most obvious "maladjustment"—loving members of one's own sex (Davison, in press).*

* Kaimowitz v. Michigan Department of Mental Health, 42 U.S.L. Week 2063 (Mich. Cit. Ct., Wayne Cty. July 10, 1973).

These limitations on the choice of reinforcers met with a great outcry from some behavior therapists working in hospital settings. Many patients, they argued, are so regressed that the only way to motivate them is to use food as a primary reinforcer, which cannot be done if the Constitution is interpreted as forbidding hospital staff from ever delaying a meal or depriving a patient of food. Wexler (1973) suggests that these legal constraints only require behavior therapists to be more ingenious and inventive than they have been in the past. Staff may have to provide eggs for a patient's breakfast, but if the patient prefers them hard-boiled to soft-boiled, this choice can be made part of a contingency.

Of special concern is the use of aversive procedures. To some people the very term behavior therapy conjures up an image of the violent, Beethoven-loving protagonist in Kubrick's *Clockwork Orange,* eyes propped open with a torturous apparatus, being made nauseous by medicine while scenes of violence flashed on a screen and Beethoven's Ninth Symphony soared in his ears. Aversion conditioning programs do not reach this level of coercion and drama, but certainly any such procedure entails making the patient uncomfortable, sometimes extremely so. Making patients vomit or cringe with pain from electric shock applied to the extremities are two aversive techniques worthy of their name. Can there be any circumstances in which human beings allow themselves to inflict such pain on others?

Before too glibly exclaiming "No!" consider the following report.

> The patient was a nine-month-old baby who had already been hospitalized three times for treatment of vomiting and chronic rumination (regurgitating food and rechewing it in the mouth). A number of diagnostic tests, including an EEG, plus surgery to remove a cyst on the right kidney, had revealed no organic basis for the problems, and several treatments, including a special diet, had been attempted without success. When referred to Lang and Melamed (1969), two behavior therapists, the child was in critical condition and was being fed by tubes leading from the nose directly into the stomach. The attending physician had stated that the infant's life was in imminent danger if the vomiting could not be halted.
>
> Treatment consisted of delivering a series of one-second-long electric shocks to the infant's calf each time he showed signs of beginning to vomit. Sessions followed feeding and lasted under an hour. After just two sessions, shock was rarely required, for the infant learned quickly to stop vomiting in order to avoid the shock. By the sixth session he was able to fall asleep after eating. Nurses reported that the in-session inhibition of vomiting generalized as the infant progressively reduced his vomiting during the rest of the day and night. About two weeks later the mother began to assume some care of the hospitalized child, and shortly thereafter the patient was discharged with virtually complete elimination of the life-threatening pattern of behavior. Throughout the three weeks of treatment and observation, the child gained weight steadily. One month after discharge the child weighed twenty-one pounds and was rated as fully recovered by the attending physician. Five months later he weighed twenty-six pounds and was regarded as completely normal, both physically and psychologically.

Aversive conditioning procedures, like electroconvulsive therapy and psychosurgery, are subject to the greatest degree of regulation. A ruling of the *Wyatt* case, for example, forbids their use except with informed consent after consultation with a lawyer. Still being formulated are guidelines that professionals might adopt to ensure ethical practice. Mindful that short-term application of electric shock can sometimes keep retarded and autistic children from their self-destructive acts, Martin (1975) proposes that

> *The test should be that aversive therapy might be used where other therapy has not*

*worked, where it can be administered to save the individual from immediate and continuing self-injury, when it allows freedom from physical restraints which would otherwise be continued, when it can be administered for only a few short instances, and when its goal is to make other nonaversive therapy possible. Such an aversive program certainly requires consent from a guardian and immediate review of the results of* each separate administration (p. 77).[21]

Extra precautions such as these are necessary when treatment deliberately inflicts pain on a patient or client; they are especially necessary when the patient cannot realistically be expected to give informed consent. But should we be concerned only with physical pain? The anguish we suffer when a loved one dies is psychologically painful. It is perhaps more painful than an electric shock of 1500 microamperes. Who is to say? Since we allow that pain can be psychological, shall we permit a Gestalt therapist to make a patient cry by confronting him with feelings he has turned away from for years? Shall we forbid a psychoanalyst from guiding a patient to an insight that will likely cause great anguish, all the more so for the conflict's having been repressed for years?

## Concluding Comment

An underlying theme of this book concerns the nature of knowing. How do we decide that we understand a phenomenon? The branch of philosophy concerned with the methods and grounds for knowledge is called epistemology. The rules of the science game that govern our definition of and search for knowledge require theories that can be tested, experiments that can be replicated, and data that are public. But given the complexity of abnormal behavior and given the vast areas of ignorance, far more extensive than the domains that have already been mapped by science as it is currently practiced, we have great respect for theoreticians and clinicians, those inventive souls who make suppositions, offer hypotheses, follow hunches—all based on rather flimsy data but holding some promise that scientific knowledge will be forthcoming.

This final chapter demonstrates again something emphasized at the very beginning of this book, namely that the scientists who investigate behavior and the mental health professionals who give treatment are only human beings. They suffer from the same foibles that sometimes plague nonspecialists. They occasionally act with a certainty their evidence does not justify, and they sometimes fail to anticipate the moral and legal consequences of the ways in which they conduct research and apply the tentative findings of their young discipline.

The authors of this textbook hope that they have communicated in some measure their love for the subject matter and, more importantly, their commitment to the kind of questioning, doubting stance that wrests useful knowledge from nature and will yield more as new generations of scholars build upon the achievements of their predecessors.

[21] In addition to being humane, Martin's suggestions are consistent with an established legal principle which holds that therapy should begin with the technique that intrudes least on the patient's freedom and exposes him to the least possible risk (Morris, 1966).

## Summary

This final chapter dealt with legal and ethical issues in treatment and research. Some of the civil liberties of people are rather routinely set aside when judgments are made by mental health professionals and the courts that mental illness has played a role in determining their behavior. Criminal commitment sends a person to a hospital, either before a trial for an alleged crime, because he is deemed incompetent to stand trial; or after an acquittal by reason of insanity, because a mental defect, the inability to know right from wrong, or both are believed to have played a role in his committing a criminal act. A person who is considered ill and dangerous to himself and to others, though he has not broken a law, can be civilly committed to an institution. Recent court rulings have provided greater protection to all committed mental patients, particularly those under civil commitment: they have the right to counsel, Fifth Amendment protection against self-incrimination, the right to be treated, and even the right to refuse treatment, particularly any procedure that entails considerable risk. A number of moral issues in therapy and research were reviewed: ethical restraints on research, the duty of scientists to obtain informed consent from prospective human subjects, the question whether a program is treatment or research, the right of clients to confidentiality, the setting of therapy goals, and the choice of techniques.

# REFERENCES


Abel, G. G., Barlow, D. H., Blanchard, E. B., & Guild, D. The components of rapists' sexual arousal. *Archives of General Psychiatry,* in press.

Abraham, K. Notes on the psychoanalytical investigation and treatment of manic-depressive insanity and allied conditions, 1911. In E. Jones (Ed.), *Selected papers of Karl Abraham, M.D.* London: Hogarth Press, 1927.

Abrams, R. What's new in convulsive therapy? In S. Arieti & G. Chrzanowski (Eds.), *New dimensions in psychiatry.* New York: Wiley, 1975.

Abramson, L. Y., & Sackeim, H. A. A paradox in depression: Uncontrollability and self-blame. *Psychological Bulletin,* 1977, **84,** 839–851.

Abse, D. W. *Hysteria and related mental disorders.* Baltimore: Williams and Wilkins, 1966.

Adelson, R., Liebert, R. M., Poulos, R. W., & Herskovitz, A. A modelling film to reduce children's fear of dental treatment. *International Association of Dental Research Abstracts,* March 1972, 114.

Agras, S., Sylvester, D., & Oliveau, D. The epidemiology of common fears and phobias. Unpublished manuscript, 1969.

Akhter, S., Wig, N. N., Varma, V. K., Pershad, D., & Verma, S. K. A phenomenological analysis of symptoms in obsessive-compulsive neurosis. *British Journal of Psychiatry,* 1975, **127,** 342–348.

Akiskal, H. S., & McKinney, W. T. Overview of recent research in depression. *Archives of General Psychiatry,* 1975, **32,** 285–305.

Albee, G. W. We have been warned. In W. Ryan (Ed.), *Distress in the city.* Cleveland, Ohio: The Press of Case Western Reserve University, 1969.

Albee, G. W., Lane, E. A., & Reuter, J. M. Childhood intelligence of future schizophrenics and neighborhood peers. *Journal of Psychology,* 1964, **58,** 141–144.

Alexander, F. *Psychosomatic medicine.* New York: Norton, 1950.

Alexander, R., & Staub, H. *The criminal, the judge, and the public: A psychological analysis.* Glencoe, Ill.: The Free Press, 1929.

Alvarez, R. R. A comparison of the preferences of schizophrenics and normal subjects for rewarded and punished stimuli. Unpublished doctoral dissertation, Duke University, 1957.

American Law Institute. *Model penal code: Proposed official draft.* Philadelphia: The American Law Institute, 1962.

American Psychiatric Association. *Diagnostic and statistical manual of mental disorders.* (2nd ed.) Washington, D.C.: American Psychiatric Association, 1968.

Anastasi, A. *Psychological testing.* (3rd ed.) New York: Macmillan, 1968.

Angrist, B., Lee, H. K., & Gershon, S. The antagonism of amphetamine-induced symptomatology by a neuroleptic. *American Journal of Psychiatry,* 1974, **131,** 817–819.

*APA Monitor.* Marijuana—Here to stay? 1976, **7,** 5–10.

Arieti, S. *Interpretation of schizophrenia.* New York: Basic Books, 1955.

Arnhoff, F. N., Rubinstein, E. A., & Speisman, J. E. (Eds.) *Mental health manpower.* Chicago: Aldine, 1969.

Aronson, E. *The social animal.* San Francisco: Freeman, 1972.

Aronson, E., & Carlsmith, J. R. Experimentation in social psychology. In G. Lindzey & E. Aronson (Eds.), *The handbook of social psychology.* Vol. 2. *Research methods.* Menlo Park, Calif.: Addison-Wesley, 1968.

Asarnow, R. F., MacCrimmon, D. J., Cleghorn, J. M., & Steffy, R. A. The McMaster-Waterloo project: An attentional and clinical assessment of foster children at risk for schizophrenia. *Journal of Psychiatric Research,* 1977.

Ashcroft, G., Crawford, T., & Eccleston, E. 5–Hydroxyindole compounds in the cerebrospinal fluid of patients with psychiatric or neurological disease. *Lancet,* 1966, **2,** 1049–1052.

Atthowe, J. M. Treating the hospitalized person. In W. E. Craighead, A. E. Razdin, & M. J. Mahoney (Eds.), *Behavior modification: Principles, issues, and applications.* Boston: Houghton Mifflin, 1976.

Ausubel, D. P. Causes and types of narcotic addictions: A psychosocial view. *Psychiatric Quarterly,* 1961, **35,** 523–531. (a)

Ausubel, D. P. Personality disorder is disease. *American Psychologist,* 1961, **16,** 69–74. (b)

Ax, A. F. The physiological differentiation between fear and anger in humans. *Psychosomatic Medicine,* 1953, **15,** 433–442.

Ayllon, T., & Azrin, N. H. The measurement and reinforcement of behavior of psychotics. *Journal of the Experimental Analysis of Behavior,* 1965, **8,** 357–383.

Ayllon, T., & Azrin, N. H. *The token economy: A motivational system for therapy and rehabilitation.* New York: Appleton-Century-Crofts, 1968.

Ayllon, T., & Haughton, E. Control of the behavior of schizophrenic patients by food. *Journal of the Experimental Analysis of Behavior,* 1962, **5,** 343–352.

Ayllon, T., Haughton, E., & Hughes, H. B. Interpretation of symptoms: Fact or fiction? *Behaviour Research and Therapy,* 1965, **3,** 1–8.

Ayllon, T., & Kelly, K. Effects of reinforcement on standardized test performance. *Journal of Applied Behavior Analysis,* 1972, **4,** 477–484.

Azrin, N. H., & Powell, J. R. Behavioral engineering: The reduction of smoking behavior by conditioning apparatus and procedure. *Journal of Applied Behavior Analysis,* 1968, **1,** 193–200.

Bach, G. R. The marathon group: Intensive practice of intimate interactions. *Psychological Reports,* 1966, **181,** 995–1002.

Bagby, E. The etiology of phobias. *Journal of Abnormal Psychology,* 1922, **17,** 16–18.

Bancroft, J. H., Jones, G. H., & Pullan, B. R. A simple transducer for measuring penile erections, with comments on its use in the treatment of sexual disorders. *Behaviour Research and Therapy,* 1966, **4,** 239–241.

Bandura, A. *Principles of behavior modification.* New York: Holt, Rinehart and Winston, 1969.

Bandura, A. Psychotherapy based upon modelling principles. In A. E. Bergin & S. L. Garfield (Eds.), *Handbook of psychotherapy and behavior change.* New York: Wiley, 1971.

Bandura, A., Blanchard, E. B., & Ritter, B. Relative efficacy of desensitization and modelling approaches for inducing behavioral, affective, and attitudinal changes. *Journal of Personality and Social Psychology,* 1969, **13,** 173–199.

Bandura, A., & Menlove, F. L. Factors determining vicarious extinction of avoidance behavior through symbolic modeling. *Journal of Personality and Social Psychology,* 1968, **8,** 99–108.

Bandura, A., & Rosenthal, T. L. Vicarious classical conditioning as a function of arousal level. *Journal of Personality and Social Psychology,* 1966, **3,** 54–62.

Barahal, H. S. 1000 prefrontal lobotomies: Five-to-ten-year follow-up study. *Psychiatric Quarterly,* 1958, **32,** 653–678.

Barbach, L. G. *For yourself.* New York: Doubleday, 1975.

Barber, T. X. *Hypnosis: A scientific approach.* New York: Van Nostrand Reinhold, 1969.

Barber, T. X. *LSD, marihuana, yoga and hypnosis.* Chicago: Aldine, 1970.

Barber, T. X., & Calverley, D. S. Experimental studies in "hypnotic" behavior: Suggested deafness evaluated by delayed auditory feedback. *British Journal of Psychology,* 1964, **55,** 439–446.(a)

Barber, T. X., & Calverley, D. S. An experimental study of "hypnotic" (auditory and visual) hallucinations. *Journal of Abnormal and Social Psychology,* 1964, **63,** 13–20. (b)

Barber, T. X., & Silver, M. J. Fact, fiction, and the experimenter bias effect. *Psychological Bulletin, Monograph Supplement,* 1968, **70,** 1–29.

Barlow, D. H., Abel, G., Blanchard, E., & Mavissakalian, M. Plasma testosterone levels in male homosexuals: A failure to replicate. *Archives of Sexual Behavior,* 1974, **3,** 571–575.

Barlow, D. H., Becker, R., Leitenberg, H., & Agras, W. S. A mechanical strain gauge for recording penile circumference. *Journal of Applied Behavior Analysis,* 1970, **3,** 73–76.

Baron, R. A., & Byrne, D. *Social psychology: Understanding human interaction.* (2nd ed.) Boston: Allyn and Bacon, 1977.

Barrett, C. L. Systematic desensitization versus implosive therapy. *Journal of Abnormal Psychology,* 1969, **74,** 587–592.

Bartak, L., & Rutter, M. The use of personal pronouns by autistic children. *Journal of Autism and Childhood Schizophrenia,* 1974, **4,** 217–222.

Bartak, L., Rutter, M., & Cox, A. A comparative study of infantile autism and specific developmental language disorders: I. The children. *British Journal of Psychiatry,* 1975, **126,** 127–145.

Basedow, H. *The Australian aboriginal.* London: Adelaide, 1925.

Bateson, G., Jackson, D. D., Haley, J., & Weakland, J. Toward a theory of schizophrenia. *Behavioral Science,* 1956, **1,** 251–264.

Baum, A., & Valins, S. Residential environments, group size and crowding. *Proceedings of the 81st Annual Convention of the American Psychological Association.* Washington, D.C.: American Psychological Association, 1973.

Baum, M. Extinction of avoidance responding through response prevention (flooding). *Psychological Bulletin,* 1970, **74,** 276–284.

Beck, A. T. *Depression: Clinical, experimental and theoretical aspects.* New York: Harper and Row, 1967.

Beck, A. T. The core problem in depression: The cognitive triad. In J. Masserman (Ed.), *Depression: Theories and therapies.* New York: Grune and Stratton, 1970.

Beck, A. T. *Cognitive therapy and the emotional disorders.* New York: International Universities Press, 1976.

Beck, A. T., Laude, R., & Bohnert, M. Ideational components of anxiety neurosis. *Archives of General Psychiatry,* 1974, **31,** 319–325.

Beck, A. T., Ward, C. H., Mendelson, M., Mock, J. E., & Erbaugh, J. K. Reliability of psychiatric diagnosis: II. A study of consistency of clinical judgments and ratings. *American Journal of Psychiatry,* 1962, **119,** 351–357.

Becker, H. S. *Outsiders: Studies in the sociology of deviance.* New York: The Free Press, 1963.

Beecher, H. K. Ethics and clinical research. *New England Journal of Medicine,* 1966, **274,** 1354–1360.

Begelman, D. A. Ethical and legal issues of behavior modification. In M. Hersen, R. Eisler, & P. M. Miller (Eds.), *Progress in behavior modification.* New York: Academic Press, 1975.

Behar, M. Prevalence of malnutrition among preschool children of developing countries. In N. W. Scrimshaw & J. E. Gordon (Eds.), *Malnutrition, learning and behavior.* Cambridge, Mass.: M.I.T. Press, 1968.

Beisser, H. R., Glasser, N., & Grant, M. Psychosocial adjustment of children of schizophrenic mothers. *Journal of Nervous and Mental Disease,* 1967, **145,** 429–440.

Bellack, A. S., Hersen, M., & Turner, S. M. Generalization effects of social skills training in chronic schizophrenics: An experimental analysis. *Behaviour Research and Therapy,* 1976, **14,** 391–398.

Bellak, L., Hurvich, M., & Gediman, H. K. *Ego functions in schizophrenics, neurotics, and normals.* New York: Wiley, 1973.

Bellissimo, A., & Steffy, R. A. Redundancy-associated deficit in schizophrenic reaction time performance. *Journal of Abnormal Psychology,* 1972, **80,** 229–307.

Belliveau, F., & Richter, L. *Understanding "Human Sexual Inadequacy."* New York: Bantam, 1970.

Bem, D. J., & Allen, A. On predicting some of the people some of the time: The search for cross-situational consistencies in behavior. *Psychological Review,* 1974, **81,** 506–520.

Benda, C. E., Squires, N. D., Ogonik, M. J., & Wise, R. Personality factors in mild mental retardation: I. Family background and sociocultural patterns, *American Journal of Mental Deficiency,* 1963, **68,** 24–40.

Bender, L. Twenty years of research on schizophrenic children with special reference to those under twenty years of age. In G. Kaplan (Ed.), *Emotional problems of early childhood.* New York: Basic Books, 1955.

Bender, L. The life course of schizophrenic children. *Biological Psychiatry,* 1970, **2,** 165–172.

Bender, L. The life course of children with schizophrenia. *American Journal of Psychiatry,* 1973, **130,** 783–786.

Benjamin, H. Transvestism and trans-sexualism. *International Journal of Sexology,* 1953, **7,** 12–14.

Bennet, I. *Delinquent and neurotic children.* London: Tavistock Publications, 1960.

Benson, H. *The relaxation response.* New York: Morrow, 1975.

Bergin, A. E. Some implications of psychotherapy research for therapeutic practice. *Journal of Abnormal Psychology,* 1966, **71,** 235–246.

Bergin, A. E. The evaluation of therapeutic outcomes. In A. E. Bergin & S. L. Garfield (Eds.), *Handbook of psychotherapy and behavior change: An empirical analysis.* New York: Wiley, 1971.

Bergler, E. Personality traits of alcohol addicts. *Quarterly Journal of Studies on Alcohol,* 1946, **7,** 356–361.

Bergler, E. *Homosexuality: Disease or way of life.* New York: Hill and Wang, 1957.

Bernard, J. *The future of marriage.* New York: Bantam, 1973.

Bernstein, D. A. The modification of smoking behavior: A review. *Psychological Bulletin,* 1969, **71,** 418–440.

Berry, J. C. Antecedents of schizophrenia, impulsive character and alcoholism in males. Paper presented at the 75th Annual Convention of the American Psychological Association, Washington, D.C., 1967.

Bettelheim, B. *The informed heart.* New York: The Free Press, 1960.

Bettelheim, B. *The empty fortress.* New York: The Free Press, 1967.

Bibring, E. The mechanism of depression. In P. Greenacre (Ed.), *Affective disorders.* New York: International Universities Press, 1953.

Bieber, I., Dain, H. J., Dince, P. R., Drellich, M. G., Grand, H. C., Gundlach, R. H., Kremer, M. W., Rifkin, A. H., Wilbur, C. B., & Bieber, T. B. *Homosexuality: A psychoanalytical study.* New York: Random House, 1962.

Bijou, S. W., & Baer, D. M. *Child development.* Vol. 1. *A systematic and empirical theory.* New York: Appleton-Century-Crofts, 1961.

Bindrim, P. A report on a nude marathon: The effect of physical nudity upon the practice interaction in the marathon group. *Psychotherapy: Theory, Research and Practice,* 1968, **5,** 180–188.

Birk, L., Huddleston, W., Miller, E., & Cohler, B. Avoidance conditioning for homosexuality. *Archives of General Psychiatry,* 1971, **25,** 314–323.

Birk, L., Williams, G., Chasin, M., & Rose, L. Serum testosterone levels in homosexual men. *The New England Journal of Medicine,* 1973, **289,** 1236–1238.

Bitterman, M. E. Issues in the comparative psychology of learning. In R. B. Masterson, M. E. Bitterman, C. B. G. Campbell, & N. Hotten (Eds.), *The evolution of brain and behavior in veterbrates.* Hilldale, N.J.: Lawrence Erlbaum Associates, 1975.

Black, M., Freeman, B. J., & Montgomery, J. Systematic observation of play behavior in autistic children. *Journal of Autism and Childhood Schizophrenia,* 1975, **5,** 363–371.

Blanchard, E. B., & Young, L. D. Self-control of cardiac functioning: A promise as yet unfulfilled. *Psychological Bulletin,* 1973, **79,** 145–163.

Blanchard, E. B., & Young, L. D. Clinical applications of biofeedback training: A review of evidence. *Archives of General Psychiatry,* 1974, **30,** 573–589.

Bleke, R. R. Reward and punishment as determiners of reminiscence effects in schizophrenic and normal subjects. Unpublished doctoral dissertation, Duke University, 1953.

Bleuler, E. *Dementia praecox, or the group of schizophrenias,* 1911. English translation by J. Zinkin. New York: International Universities Press, 1950.

Bloomfield, H. H. Assertive training in an outpatient group of chronic schizophrenics: A preliminary report. *Behavior Therapy,* 1973, **4,** 277–281.

Bockhoven, J. *Moral treatment in American psychiatry.* New York: Springer, 1963.

Bogdan, R., & Taylor, S. The judged, not the judges: An insider's view of mental retardation. *American Psychologist,* 1976, **31,** 47–52.

Boll, T. J., Heaton, R., & Reitan, R. M. Neuropsychological and emotional correlates of Huntington's chorea. *Journal of Nervous and Mental Disease,* 1974, **158,** 61–69.

Bolles, R. C. Species-specific defense reactions and avoidance learning. *Psychological Review,* 1970, **77,** 32–48.

Bosch, G. *Infantile autism.* New York: Springer-Verlag, 1970.

Bourne, P. G., Alford, J. A., & Bowcock, J. Z. Treatment of skid row alcoholics with disulfiram. *Quarterly Journal of Studies on Alcohol,* 1966, **27,** 42–48.

Bower, G. H. Organizational factors in memory. *Cognitive psychology,* 1970, **1,** 18–46.

Bowers, K. S. Situationism in psychology: An analysis and a critique. *Psychological Review,* 1973, **80,** 307–336.

Bowers, M. B., Jr. Central dopamine turnover in schizophrenic syndromes. *Archives of General Psychiatry,* 1974, **31,** 50–54.

Brady, J. P., & Lind, D. L. Experimental analysis of hysterical blindness. *Archives of General Psychiatry,* 1961, **4,** 331–359.

Braginsky, B. M., Grosse, M., & Ring, K. Controlling outcomes through impression management: An experimental study of the manipulative tactics of mental patients. *Journal of Consulting Psychology,* 1966, **30,** 295–300.

Braginsky, D. D., & Braginsky, B. M. *Hansels and Gretels: Studies of children in institutions for the mentally retarded.* New York: Holt, Rinehart and Winston, 1971.

Bransford, J. D., & Johnson, M. K. Considerations of some problems of comprehension. In W. G. Chase (Ed.), *Visual information processing.* New York: Academic Press, 1973.

Brecher, E. M., & the Editors of *Consumer Reports. Licit and illicit drugs.* Mount Vernon, N.Y.: Consumers Union, 1972.

Brener, J. A general model of voluntary control applied to the phenomena of learned cardiovascular change. In P. A. Obrist, A. H. Black, J. Brener, & L. V. DiCara (Eds.), *Cardiovascular psychophysiology.* Chicago: Aldine, 1974.

Brenner, M. H. *Mental illness and the economy.* Cambridge, Mass.: Harvard University Press, 1973.

Briddell, D. W., & Wilson, G. T. Effects of alcohol and expectancy set on male sexual arousal. *Journal of Abnormal Psychology,* 1976, **85,** 225–234.

Bridger, W. H., & Mandel, I. J. Abolition of the PRE by instructions in GSR conditioning. *Journal of Experimental Psychology,* 1965, **69,** 476–482.

Brodie, H. K. H., & Leff, M. J. Bipolar depression: A comparative study of patient characteristics. *American Journal of Psychiatry,* 1971, **127,** 1086–1090.

Brodie, K. H., Gartrell, N., Doering, C., & Rhue, T. Plasma testosterone levels in heterosexual and homosexual men. *American Journal of Psychiatry,* 1974, **131,** 82–83.

Broen, W. E., & Storms, L. H. Lawful disorganization: The process underlying a schizophrenic syndrome. *Psychological Review,* 1966, **73,** 265–279.

Broverman, I. K., Broverman, D. M., & Clarkson, F. E. Sex-role stereotypes and clinical judgments of mental health. *Journal of Consulting and Clinical Psychology,* 1970, **34,** 1–7.

Brown, G. W. Length of hospital stay and schizophrenia: A review of statistical studies. *Acta Psychiatry et Neurology Scandanavia,* 1960, **35,** 414–430.

Brown, G. W., Birley, J. L. T., & Wing, J. K. Influence of family life on the course of schizophrenic disorders: A replication. *British Journal of Psychiatry,* 1972, **121,** 241–258.

Brown, G. W., Monck, E., Carstairs, G. M., & Wing, J. K. The influence of family life on the course of schizophrenic illness. *British Journal of Preventative and Social Medicine,* 1962, **16,** 55–68.

Brown, W. F. Heredity in the psychoneuroses. *Proceedings of the Royal Society of Medicine,* 1942, **35,** 785–790.

Brownmiller, S. *Against our will: Men, women and rape.* New York: Simon and Schuster, 1975.

Bruner, J. S., Olver, R. R., & Greenfield, P. M. (Eds.) *Studies in cognitive growth.* New York: Wiley, 1966.

Budzynski, T. H., Stoyva, J. M., Adler, C. S., & Mullaney, D. M. EMG biofeedback and tension headache: A controlled outcome study. *Psychosomatic Medicine,* 1973, **35,** 484–496.

Bukovsky, V. General Svetlichny: "We will let him rot in the insane asylum!" *New York Times,* May 3, 1977.

Bunney, W. E., Goodwin, F. K., & Murphy, D. L. The "Switch Process" in manic-depressive illness. *Archives of General Psychiatry,* 1972, **27,** 312–317.

Bunney, W. E., Murphy, D. L., Goodwin, F. K., & Borge, G. F. The switch process from depression to mania: Relationship to drugs which alter brain amines. *Lancet,* 1970, **1,** 1022.

Burton, R. *The anatomy of melancholy,* 1621. (13th ed.) London: Thomas Davison, White Friars, 1827.

Buss, A. H. *Psychopathology.* New York: Wiley, 1966.

Buss, A. H., & Lang, P. J. Psychological deficit in schizophrenia: I. Affect, reinforcement, and concept attainment. *Journal of Abnormal Psychology,* 1965, **70,** 2–24.

Cadoret, R. J., Winokur, G., & Clayton, P. J. Family history studies: VI. Depressive disease types. *Comprehensive Psychiatry,* 1971, **12,** 148–155.

Caldwell, D., Brane, A., & Beckett, P. Sleep patterns in normal and psychotic children. *Archives of General Psychiatry,* 1970, **22,** 500–503.

Calhoun, J. B. Space and the strategy of life. *Ekistics,* 1970, **29,** 425–437.

Cameron, N. *Personality development and psychopathology: A dynamic approach.* Boston: Houghton Mifflin, 1963.

Campbell, D., Sanderson, R. E., & Laverty, S. G. Characteristics of a conditioned response in human subjects during extinction trials following a single traumatic conditioning trial. *Journal of Abnormal and Social Psychology,* 1964, **68,** 627–639.

Campbell, M., Friedman, E., DeVito, E., Greenspan, L., & Collins, P. J. Blood serotonin in psychotic and brain damaged children. *Journal of Autism and Childhood Schizophrenia,* 1974, **4,** 33–41.

Cannon, W. E. "Voodoo" death. *American Anthropologist,* 1942, **44,** 169–182.

Cantwell, D. P. Genetic studies of hyperactive children. In R. Fieve, D. Rosenthal, & H. Brill (Eds.), *Genetic research in psychiatry.* Baltimore: Johns Hopkins University Press, 1975.

Cappell, H. An evaluation of tension models of alcohol consumption. In R. J. Gibbins, Y. Israel, H. Kalant, R. E. Popham, W. Schmidt, & R. G. Smart (Eds.), *Research advances in alcohol and drug problems,* Vol. 2. New York: Wiley, 1975.

Carpenter, W. T., Murphy, D. L., & Wyatt, R. J. Platelet monoamine oxidase activity in acute schizophrenia, *American Journal of Psychiatry,* 1975, **132,** 438–441.

Carr, A. T. Compulsive neurosis: Two psychophysiological studies. *Bulletin of the British Psychological Society,* 1971, **24,** 256–257.

Cashman, J. A. *The LSD story.* Greenwich, Conn.: Fawcett Publications, 1966.

Cautela, J. R. Treatment of compulsive behavior by covert sensitization. *Psychological Record,* 1966, **16,** 33–41.

Cavanaugh, D. K., Cohen, W., & Lang, P. J. The effect of "social censure" and "social approval" on the psychomotor performance of schizophrenics. *Journal of Abnormal and Social Psychology,* 1960, **60,** 213–218.

Cermak, L. S., & Butters, N. The role of interference and encoding in the short-term memory deficits of Korsakoff patients. *Neuropsychologia,* 1972, **10,** 89–96.

Chafetz, M. E. Addiction: II. Alcoholism. In A. M. Freedman & H. I. Kaplan (Eds.), *Comprehensive textbook of psychiatry.* Baltimore: Williams and Wilkins, 1967.

Chapman, L. J. Intrusion of associative responses into schizophrenic conceptual performance. *Journal of Abnormal and Social Psychology,* 1958, **56,** 374–379.

Chapman, L. J. The problem of selecting drug-free schizophrenics for research. *Journal of Consulting Psychology,* 1963, **27,** 540–542.

Chapman, L. J., & Chapman, J. P. Illusory correlation as an obstacle to the use of valid psychodiagnostic signs. *Journal of Abnormal Psychology,* 1969, **74,** 271–287.

Chapman, L. J., & Chapman, J. P. *Disordered thought in schizophrenia.* New York: Appleton-Century-Crofts, 1973.

Chapman, L. J., Chapman, J. P., & Miller, G. A. A theory of verbal behavior in schizophrenia. In B. A. Maher (Ed.), *Progress in experimental personality research,* Vol. 1. New York: Academic Press, 1964.

Chappell, D., Geis, G., Schafer, S., & Siegel, L. Forcible rape: A comparative study of offenses known to the police in Boston and Los Angeles. In J. M. Henslin (Ed.), *Studies in the sociology of sex.* New York: Appleton-Century-Crofts, 1971, 169–192.

Chein, I., Gerard, D. L., Lee, R. S., & Rosenfeld, E. *The road to H: Narcotics, delinquency, and social policy.* New York: Basic Books, 1964.

Chesler, P. *Women and madness.* Garden City, N.Y.: Doubleday, 1972.

Chesno, F. A., & Kilmann, P. R. Effects of stimulation intensity on sociopathic avoidance learning. *Journal of Abnormal Psychology,* 1975, **84,** 144–151.

Chodoff, P. The diagnosis of hysteria: An overview. *American Journal of Psychiatry,* 1974, **131,** 1073–1078.

Churchill, D. W. Psychotic children and behavior modification. *American Journal of Psychiatry,* 1969, **125,** 1585–1590.

Churchill, W. *Homosexual behavior among males: A cross-cultural and cross-species investigation.* Englewood Cliffs, N.J.: Prentice-Hall, 1967.

Clausen, J. A., & Kohn, M. L. Relation of schizophrenia to the social structure of a small city. In B. Pasamanick (Ed.), *Epidemiology of mental disorder.* Washington, D.C.: American Association for the Advancement of Science, 1959.

Cleckley, H. *The mask of sanity.* (4th ed.) St. Louis, Mo.: Mosby, 1964.

Cochrane, R. High blood pressure as a psychosomatic disorder: A selective review. *British Journal of Social and Clinical Psychology,* 1971, **10,** 61–72.

Cochrane, R. Hostility and neuroticism among unselected essential hypertensions. *Journal of Psychosomatic Research,* 1973, **17,** 215–218.

Coggins, W. J. The general health status of chronic cannabis smokers in Costa Rica. In S. Szara & M. Braude (Eds.), *Pharmacology of marihuana.* New York: Raven Press, in press.

Cohen, B. D., & Camhi, J. Schizophrenic performance in a word communication task. *Journal of Abnormal Psychology,* 1967, **72,** 240–246.

Cohen, B. D., Nachmani, G., & Rosenberg, S. Referent communication disturbances in acute schizophrenia. *Journal of Abnormal Psychology,* 1974, **83,** 1–14.

Cohen, H. L., & Filipczak, J. *A new learning environment.* San Francisco: Jossey-Bass, 1971.

Cohen, S., Glass, D., & Singer, J. E. Apartment noise, auditory discrimination, and reading ability in children. *Journal of Experimental Social Psychology,* 1973, **9,** 407–422.

Cole, J. O. Phenothiazine treatment in acute schizophrenia: Effectiveness. *Archives of General Psychiatry,* 1964, **10,** 246–261.

Coleman, J. C. *Abnormal psychology and modern life.* (5th ed.) Chicago: Scott, Foresman, 1976.

*Collaborative study of children treated for phenylketonuria, preliminary report 8.* Principal investigator: R. Koch. Presented at the Eleventh General Medicine Conference, Stateline, Nevada, February 1975.

Conger, J. J. The effects of alcohol on conflict behavior in the albino rat. *Quarterly Journal of Studies on Alcohol,* 1951, **12,** 1–29.

Conger, J. J., Sawrey, W. L., & Turrell, E. S. The role of social experience in the production of gastric ulcers in hooded rats in a conflict situation. *Journal of Abnormal and Social Psychology,* 1958, **57,** 214–220.

Conn, J. H., & Conn, R. N. Discussion of T. Barber's "Hypnosis as a causal variable in present-day psychology: A critical analysis." *Journal of Clinical and Experimental Hypnosis,* 1967, **15,** 106–110.

Conners, C. K. Pharmacotherapy of psychopathology in children. In H. C. Quay & J. S. Werry (Eds.), *Psychopathological disorders of childhood.* New York: Wiley, 1972.

Conners, C. K., Taylor, E., Meo, G., Kurtz, M., & Fournier, M. Magnesium pemoline and dextroamphetamine: A controlled study in children with minimal brain dysfunction. *Psychopharmacologia,* 1972, **26,** 321–336.

Cooper, J. E., Kendell, R. E., Gurland, B. J., Sharpe, L., Copeland, J. R. M., & Simon, R. *Psychiatric diagnosis in New York and London.* London: Oxford University Press, 1972.

Coppen, A. Prange, A. J., Whybrow, P. C., & Noguera, R. Abnormalities in indoleamines in affective disorders. *Archives of General Psychiatry,* 1972, **26,** 474–478.

Cory, D. W. *The homosexual in America: A subjective approach.* New York: Greenberg, 1951.

Costello, C. G. Dissimilarities between conditioned avoidance responses and phobias. *Psychological Review,* 1970, **77,** 250–254.

Cowan, P. A., Hoddinott, B. A., & Wright, B. A. Compliance and resistance in the conditioning of autistic children: An exploratory study. *Child Development,* 1965, **36,** 913–923.

Cox, A., Rutter, M., Newman, S., & Bartak, L. A comparative study of infantile autism and specific developmental language disorders: II. Parental characteristics. *British Journal of Psychiatry,* 1975, **126,** 146–159.

Creak, M., & Ini, S. Families of psychotic children. *Journal of Child Psychology and Psychiatry,* 1960, **1,** 157–175.

Crissey, M. S. Mental retardation: Past, present, and future. *American Psychologist,* 1975, **30,** 800–808.

Crompton, L. Homosexuals and the death penalty in colonial America. *Journal of Homosexuality,* 1976, **1,** 277–294.

Curtis, B. A., Jacobson, S., & Marcus, E. M. *An introduction to the neurosciences.* Philadelphia: Saunders, 1972.

Davis, J. M., Klerman, G., & Schildkraut, J. Drugs used in the treatment of depression. In L. Efron, J. O. Cole, D. Levine, & J. R. Wittenborn, *Psychopharmacology, A review of progress.* Washington, D.C.: U.S. Clearinghouse of Mental Health Information, 1967.

Davison, A. N., & Dobbing, J. Myelination as a vulnerable period in brain development. *British Medical Bulletin,* 1966, **22,** 40–44.

Davison, G. C. The negative effects of early exposure to suboptimal visual stimuli. *Journal of Personality,* 1964, **32,** 278–295. (a)

Davison, G. C. A social learning therapy programme with an autistic child. *Behaviour Research and Therapy,* 1964, **2,** 146–159. (b)

Davison, G. C. Differential relaxation and cognitive restructuring in therapy with a "paranoid schizophrenic" or "paranoid state." *Proceedings of the 74th Annual Convention of the American Psychological Association.* Washington, D.C.: American Psychological Association, 1966.

Davison, G. C. Elimination of a sadistic fantasy by a client-controlled counterconditioning technique. *Journal of Abnormal Psychology,* 1968, **73,** 84–90. (a)

Davison, G. C. Systematic desensitization as a counterconditioning process. *Journal of Abnormal Psychology,* 1968, **73,** 91–99. (b)

Davison, G. C. Appraisal of behavior modification techniques with adults in institutional settings. In C. M. Franks (Ed.), *Behavior therapy: Appraisal and status.* New York: McGraw-Hill, 1969.

Davison, G. C. Counter control in behavior modification. In L. A. Hamerlynck, L. C. Handy, & E. J. Mash (Eds.), *Behavior change: Methodology, concepts and practice.* Champaign, Ill.: Research Press, 1973.

Davison, G. C. Homosexuality: The ethical challenge. Presidential address to the Eighth Annual Convention of the Association for Advancement of Behavior Therapy, Chicago, 1974.

Davison, G. C. Homosexuality: The ethical challenge. *Journal of Consulting and Clinical Psychology,* 1976, **44,** 157–162.

Davison, G. C. Not can but ought: The treatment of homosexuality. *Journal of Consulting and Clinical Psychology,* in press.

Davison, G. C., & Goldfried, M. R. Postdoctoral training in clinical behavior therapy. Menninger Clinic Bulletin **17,** 1973.

Davison, G. C., & Stuart, R. B. Behavior therapy and civil liberties. *American Psychologist,* 1975, **30,** 755–763.

Davison, G. C., Tsujimoto, R. N., & Glaros, A. G. Attribution and the maintenance of behavior change in falling asleep. *Journal of Abnormal Psychology,* 1973, **82,** 124–133.

Davison, G. C., & Valins, S. Maintenance of self-attributed and drug-attributed behavior change. *Journal of Personality and Social Psychology,* 1969, **11,** 25–33.

Davison, G. C., & Wilson, G. T. Attitudes of behavior therapists toward homosexuality. *Behavior Therapy,* 1973, **4,** 686–696.

DeJong, R. N., & Sugar, O. *The yearbook of neurology and neurosurgery.* Chicago: Year Book Medical Publishers, 1971.

DeJong, R. N., & Sugar, O. *The yearbook of neurology and neurosurgery.* Chicago: Year Book Medical Publishers, 1972.

Dekker, E., & Groen, J. Reproducible psychogenic attacks of asthma. *Journal of Psychosomatic Research,* 1956, **1,** 58–67.

Dekker, E., Pelse, H. E., & Groen, J. Conditioning as a cause of asthmatic attacks. *Journal of Psychosomatic Research,* 1957, **2,** 97–108.

de Lint, J., & Schmidt, W. The epidemiology of alcoholism. In Y. Israel & J. Mardones (Eds.), *Biological basis of alcoholism.* New York: Wiley, 1971.

DeLuca, D., Cermak, L. S., & Butters, N. An analysis of Korsakoff patients' recall following various types of distractor activity. *Neuropsychologia,* 1975, **13,** 271–280.

DeMyer, M. The nature of the neuropsychological disability in autistic children. *Journal of Autism and Childhood Schizophrenia,* 1975, **5,** 109–127.

DeMyer, M., Barton, S., DeMyer, W. E., Norton, J. A., Allen, J., & Sterle, R. Prognosis in autism: A follow-up study. *Journal of Autism and Childhood Schizophrenia,* 1973, **3,** 199–246.

Denhoff, E. The natural history of children with minimal brain dysfunction. *Annals of the New York Academy of Sciences,* 1973, **205,** 188–205.

Deutsch, A. *The mentally ill in America.* New York: Columbia University Press, 1949.

Diamond, S., Baldwin, R., & Diamond, R. *Inhibition and choice.* New York: Harper and Row, 1963.

Dilling, C. A., & Rabin, A. I. Temporal experience in depressive states and schizophrenia. *Journal of Consulting Psychology,* 1967, **31,** 604–608.

Dobbs, W. H. Methadone treatment of heroin addicts. *Journal of the American Medical Association,* 1971, **218,** 1536–1541.

Dodson, B. *Liberating masturbation.* New York: Bodysex Designs, 1974.

Dokecki, P. R., Polidoro, L. G., & Cromwell, R. L. Commonality and stability of word association responses in good and poor premorbid schizophrenics. *Journal of Abnormal Psychology,* 1965, **70,** 312–316.

Dole, V. P., Nyswander, M. E., & Warner, A. Successful treatment of 750 criminal addicts. *Journal of the American Medical Association,* 1968, **206,** 2708–2711.

Doll, E. A. *Measurement of social competence: A manual for the Vineland Social Maturity Scale.* Circle Pines, Minn.: American Guidance Service, Inc., 1953.

Dollard, J., & Miller, N. E. *Personality and psychotherapy.* New York: McGraw-Hill, 1950.

Domino, E. F., Krause, R. R., & Bowers, J. Various enzymes involved with putative transmitters. *Archives of General Psychiatry,* 1973, **29,** 195–201.

Doubros, S. G. Behavior therapy with high level, institutionalized, retarded adolescents. *Exceptional Children,* 1966, **33,** 229–233.

Douglas, J. D. *The social meanings of suicide.* Princeton, N.J.: Princeton University Press, 1967.

Drabman, R. S., Spitalnik, R., & O'Leary, K. D. Teaching self-control to disruptive children. *Journal of Abnormal Psychology,* 1973, **82,** 10–16.

Dunham, H. W. *Community and schizophrenia: An epidemiological analysis.* Detroit: Wayne State University Press, 1965.

Dunner, D. L., Stallone, F., & Fieve, R. F. Lithium carbonate and affective disorders: A double-blind study of prophylaxis of depression in bipolar illness. *Archives of General Psychiatry,* 1976, **33,** 117–120.

Durkheim, E. *Suicide,* 1897. (2nd ed., 1930, in French.) English translation by J. A. Spaulding and G. Simpson. New York: The Free Press, 1951.

Eastman, C. Behavioral formulations of depression. *Psychological Review,* 1976, **83,** 277–291.

Edwards, A. L. *The social desirability variable in personality research.* New York: Dryden Press, 1957.

Eisenberg, L., & Kanner, L. Early infantile autism. *American Journal of Orthopsychiatry,* 1956, **26,** 556–566.

Ellenberger, H. F. The story of "Anna O": A critical review with new data. *Journal of the History of the Behavior Sciences,* 1972, **8,** 267–279.

Ellingson, R. J. Incidence of EEG abnormality among patients with mental disorders of apparently nonorganic origin: A criminal review. *American Journal of Psychiatry,* 1954, **111,** 263–275.

Ellis, A. *The folklore of sex.* New York: Grove Press, 1961.

Ellis, A. *Reason and emotion in psychotherapy.* New York: Lyle Stuart, 1962.

Elmore, A. M., & Tursky, B. The biofeedback hypothesis: An idea in search of a theory and method. In A. A. Sugerman & R. E. Tarter (Eds.), *Expanding dimensions of consciousness.* New York: Springer, in press.

Endler, N. S., Hunt, J. McV., & Rosenstein, A. J. An S-R inventory of anxiousness. *Psychological Monographs,* 1962, **76,** No. 536.

Engel, B. T., & Bickford, A. F. Response specificity: Stimulus response and individual response specificity in essential hypertension. *Archives of General Psychiatry,* 1961, **5,** 478–489.

English, H. B. Three cases of the "conditioned fear response." *Journal of Abnormal and Social Psychology,* 1929, **34,** 221–225.

Ennis, B., & Siegel, L. *The rights of mental patients.* American Civil Liberties Union Handbook Series. New York: Avon, 1973.

Enright, J. B. An introduction to Gestalt techniques. In J. Fagan & I. L. Shepherd (Eds.), *Gestalt therapy now: Theory, techniques, applications.* Palo Alto, Calif.: Science and Behavior Books, 1970.

Epstein, L. C., & Lasagna, L. Obtaining informed consent. *Archives of Internal Medicine,* 1969, **123,** 682–688.

Erikson, E. H. *Childhood and society.* New York: Norton, 1950.

Erlenmeyer-Kimling, L. A prospective study of children at risk for schizophrenia: Methodological considerations and some preliminary findings. In R. D. Wirt, G. Winokur, & M. Roff (Eds.), *Life history research in psychopathology,* Vol. 4. Minneapolis: University of Minnesota Press, 1975.

Ervin, F. R. Brain disorders. IV: Associated with convulsions. In A. M. Freedman & H. I. Kaplan (Eds.), *Comprehensive textbook of psychiatry.* Baltimore: Williams and Wilkins, 1967.

Evans, I. M. Classical conditioning. In M. P. Feldman & A. Broadhurst (Eds.), *Theoretical and experimental bases of the behaviour therapies.* New York: Wiley, 1976.

Evans, R. B. Childhood parental relationships of homosexual men. *Journal of Consulting and Clinical Psychology,* 1969, **33,** 129–135.

Eysenck, H. J. The effects of psychotherapy: An evaluation. *Journal of Consulting Psychology,* 1952, **16,** 319–324.

Eysenck, H. J. *Dynamics of anxiety and hysteria.* London: Routledge and Kegan Paul, 1957.

Eysenck, H. J. Classification and the problem of diagnosis. In H. J. Eysenck (Ed.), *Handbook of abnormal psychology.* London: Pitman, 1960.

Eysenck, H. J. *Fact and fiction in psychology.* Baltimore: Penguin, 1965.

Fagan, J., & Shepherd, I. L. (Eds.) *Gestalt therapy now: Theory, techniques, applications.* Palo Alto, Calif.: Science and Behavior Books, 1970.

Farina, A. *Abnormal psychology.* Englewood Cliffs, N.J.: Prentice-Hall, 1976.

Farkas, G., & Rosen, R. C. The effects of alcohol on elicited male sexual response. *Studies in Alcohol,* 1976, **37,** 265–272.

Feingold, B. F. *Introduction to clinical allergy.* Springfield, Ill.: Charles C Thomas, 1973.

Feldman, M. P., & MacCulloch, M. J. *Homosexual behavior: Therapy and assessment.* Oxford, England: Pergamon Press, 1971.

Fenichel, O. *The psychoanalytic theory of neurosis.* New York: Norton, 1945.

Ferster, C. B. Positive reinforcement and behavioral deficits of autistic children. *Child Development,* 1961, **32,** 437–456.

Ferster, C. B. Classification of behavioral pathology. In L. Krasner & L. P. Ullmann (Eds.), *Research in behavior modification.* New York: Holt, Rinehart and Winston, 1965.

Finney, J. C., Brandsma, J. M., Tondow, M., & LeMaistre, B. A study of transsexuals seeking gender reassignment. *American Journal of Psychiatry,* 1975, **132,** 962–964.

Florsheim, J., & Peterfreund, O. The intelligence of parents of psychotic children. *Journal of Autism and Childhood Schizophrenia,* 1974, **4,** 61–70.

Fontana, A. Familial etiology of schizophrenia: Is a scientific methodology possible? *Psychological Bulletin,* 1966, **66,** 214–228.

Ford, A. B. Casualties of our time. *Science,* 1970, **167,** 256–263.

Ford, C. S., & Beach, F. A. *Patterns of sexual behavior.* New York: Harper, 1951.

Ford, D. H., & Urban, H. B. *Systems of psychotherapy: A comparative study.* New York: Wiley, 1963.

Fordney-Settlage, D. S. Heterosexual dysfunction: Evaluation of treatment procedures. *Archives of Sexual Behavior,* 1975, **4,** 367–388.

Forsyth, R. P. Blood pressure responses to long-term avoidance schedules in the restrained rhesus monkey. *Psychosomatic Medicine,* 1969, **31,** 300–309.

Frank, G. A. The role of the family in the development of psychopathology. *Psychological Bulletin,* 1965, **64,** 191–208.

Frank, J. D. *Persuasion and healing.* (2nd ed.) Baltimore: Johns Hopkins University Press, 1973.

Franks, C. M., & Wilson, G. T. (Eds.) *Annual review of behavior therapy,* Vol. 2. New York: Brunner/Mazel, 1974.

Freed, E. X. Anxiety and conflict: Role of drug-dependent learning in the rat. *Quarterly Journal of Studies on Alcohol,* 1971, **32,** 13–29.

Freud, Anna. *The ego and mechanisms of defense.* New York: International Universities Press, 1946.

Freud, S. Three contributions to the theory of sex, 1905. In A. A. Brill (Ed.), *The basic writings of Sigmund Freud.* New York: Modern Library, 1938.

Freud, S. Analysis of a phobia in a five-year-old boy, 1909. In *Collected works of Sigmund Freud,* Vol. 10. London: Hogarth Press, 1955.

Freud, S. A case of paranoia running counter to the psychoanalytical theory of the disease, 1915. In *Collected papers,* Vol. 2. London: Hogarth Press, 1956.

Freud, S. Mourning and melancholia. 1917. In *Collected papers,* Vol. 4. London: Hogarth Press and the Institute of Psychoanalysis, 1950.

Freud, S. *The problem of anxiety,* 1926. New York: Norton, 1936.

Freud, S. Analysis terminable and interminable. *International Journal of Psychoanalysis,* 1937, **18,** 373–391.

Freud, S. *A general introduction to psychoanalysis.* New York: Garden City Publishing Company, 1949.

Freund, K. A laboratory method for diagnosing predominance of homo- and hetero-erotic interest in the male. *Behaviour Research and Therapy,* 1963, **1,** 85–93.

Friedhoff, A. J., & Van Winkle, E. Isolation and characterization of a compound from the urine of schizophrenics. *Nature,* 1962, **194,** 897–898.

Friedman, E., Shopsin, B., Sathananthan, G., & Gershon, S. Blood platelet monoamine oxidase activity in psychiatric patients. *American Journal of Psychiatry,* 1974, **131,** 1392–1394.

Frohman, C. E., Harmison, C. R., Arthur, R. E., & Gottlieb, J. S. Conformation of a unique plasma protein in schizophrenia. *Biological Psychiatry,* 1971, **3,** 113–121.

Gagnon, J. H. *Human sexualities.* Chicago: Scott, Foresman, 1977.

Gagnon, J. H., & Davison, G. C. Enhancement of sexual responsiveness in behavior therapy. Paper presented at the 82nd Annual Convention of the American Psychological Association, New Orleans, 1974.

Gagnon, J. H., & Davision, G. C. Asylums, the token economy, and the metrics of mental life. *Behavior Therapy,* 1976, **7,** 528–534.

Gagnon, J. H., & Simon, W. *Sexual conduct: The social origins of human sexuality.* Chicago: Aldine, 1973.

Gaines, J. The founder of Gestalt therapy: A sketch of Fritz Perls. *Psychology Today,* November 1974, **8,** 117–118.

Garcia, J., McGowan, B. K., & Green, K. F. Biological constraints on conditioning. In A. H. Black & W. F. Prokasy (Eds.), *Classical conditioning. II: Current research and theory.* New York: Appleton-Century-Crofts, 1972.

Garmezy, N. Approach and avoidance behavior of schizophrenic and normal subjects as a function of reward and punishment. *American Psychologist,* 1952, **7,** 334.

Garmezy, N. The prediction of performance in schizophrenia. In P. Hoch and J. Zubin (Eds.), *Psychopathology of schizophrenia.* New York: Grune and Stratton, 1966.

Garmezy, N. Vulnerability research and the issue of primary prevention. *American Journal of Orthopsychiatry,* 1971, **41,** 101–116.

Garrone, G. Étude statistique et genetique de la schizophrenie à Geneve de 1901 à 1950. *Journal de Genetique Humaine,* 1962, **11,** 89–219.

Gebhard, P. H. Situational factors affecting human sexual behavior. In F. A. Beach (Ed.), *Sex and behavior.* New York: Wiley, 1965.

Gebhard, P. H. Incidence of overt homosexuality in the United States and western Europe. In J. M. Livingood (Ed.), *National Institute of Mental Health Task Force on Homosexuality: Final report and background papers.* Rockville, Md.: National Institute of Mental Health, 1972.

Gebhard, P. H., Gagnon, J. H., Pomeroy, W. B., & Christenson, C. V. *Sex offenders.* New York: Harper and Row, 1965.

Geer, J. H., Davison, G. C., & Gatchel, R. I. Reduction of stress in humans through nonveridical perceived control of aversive stimulation. *Journal of Personality and Social Psychology,* 1970, **16,** 731–738.

Geer, J. H., Morokoff, P., & Greenwood, P. Sexual arousal in women: The development of a measuring device for vaginal blood volume. *Archives of Sexual Behavior,* 1974, **3,** 559–566.

Geis, G., & Monahan, J. The social ecology of violence. In T. Lickona (Ed.), *Moral development and behavior.* New York: Holt, Rinehart and Winston, 1976.

Geis, G., Wright, R., Garrett, T., & Wilson, P. R. Reported consequences of decriminalization of consensual adult homosexuality in seven American states. *Journal of Homosexuality,* 1976, **1,** 419–426.

Gelder, M. G., Bancroft, J. H. J., Gath, D. H., Johnston, D. W., Mathews, A. M., & Shaw, P. M. Specific and non-specific factors in behavior therapy. *British Journal of Psychiatry,* 1973, **123,** 445–462.

Gibbs, J. (Ed.) *Suicide.* New York: Harper and Row, 1968.

Ginsburg, H. P., & Opper, S. *Piaget's theory of intellectual development: An introduction.* Englewood Cliffs, N.J.: Prentice-Hall, 1969.

Gittelman-Klein, R., Klein, D. F., Katz, S., Saraf, K., & Pollack, E. Comparative effects of methylphenidate and thiordazine in hyperkinetic children. *Archives of General Psychiatry,* 1976, **33,** 1217–1231.

Gittleman, M., & Birch, H. G. Childhood schizophrenia: Intellect, neurologic status, perinatal risk, prognosis, and family pathology. *Archives of General Psychiatry,* 1967, **17,** 16–25.

Glaros, A. G. Expectation effects of subjects undergoing EEG alpha and beta wave feedback training. Unpublished doctoral dissertation, State University of New York at Stony Brook, 1975.

Glaser, G. H., Newman, R. J., & Schafer, R. Interictal psychosis in psychomotor–temporal lobe epilepsy: An EEG psychological study. In G. H. Glaser (Ed.), *EEG and behavior.* New York: Basic Books, 1963.

Glass, D., & Singer, J. E. *Urban stress: Experiments on noise and social stressors.* New York: Academic Press, 1972.

*A glossary of mental disorders.* Studies on Medical and Population Subjects 22. London: General Register Office, 1968.

Glover, E. *On the early development of mind.* New York: International Universities Press, 1956.

Goetzl, U., Green, R., Whybrow, P., & Jackson, R. X-linkage revisited. *Archives of General Psychiatry,* 1974, **31,** 665–671.

Goffman, E. *Asylums: Essays on the social situation of mental patients and other inmates.* Chicago: Aldine, 1962.

Goldberg, E. M., & Morrison, S. L. Schizophrenia and social class. *British Journal of Psychiatry,* 1963, **109,** 785–802.

Goldenberg, I. I. *Prospectus and guidelines for residential youth centers.* Washington, D.C.: U.S. Department of Labor, Office of Special Manpower Programs, 1969.

Goldfarb, W. *Childhood schizophrenia.* Cambridge, Mass.: Harvard University Press, 1961.

Goldfried, M. R., & Davison, G. C. *Clinical behavior therapy.* New York: Holt, Rinehart and Winston, 1976.

Goldfried, M. R., Decenteceo, E. T., & Weinberg, L. Systematic rational restructuring as a self-control technique. *Behavior Therapy,* 1974, **5,** 247–254.

Goldfried, M. R., & Merbaum, M. (Eds.) *Behavior change through self-control.* New York: Holt, Rinehart, and Winston, 1973.

Goldfried, M. R., & Sprafkin, J. N. *Behavior personality assessment.* Morristown, N.J.: General Learning Press, 1974.

Goldfried, M. R., Stricker, G., & Weiner, I. B. *Rorschach handbook of clinical and research applications.* Englewood Cliffs, N.J.: Prentice-Hall, 1971.

Goldfried, M. R., & Trier, C. S. Effectiveness of relaxation as an active coping skill. *Journal of Abnormal Psychology,* 1974, **83,** 348–355.

Goldsmith, J. B., & McFall, R. M. Development and evaluation of an interpersonal skill-training program for psychiatric patients. *Journal of Abnormal Psychology,* 1975, **83,** 51–58.

Goldstein, A. Opioid peptides (endorphins) in pituitary and brain. *Science,* 1976, **193,** 1081–1086.

Goldstein, A. S. *The insanity defense.* New Haven, Conn.: Yale University Press, 1967.

Goldstein, L., Sugarman, A. A., Stolberg, H., Murphree, H. B., & Pfeiffer, C. C. Electrocerebral activity in schizophrenics and non-psychotic subjects. *Electroencephalography and Clinical Neurophysiology,* 1965, **19,** 350–361.

Goodman, L., & Gilman, A. *The pharmacological basis of therapeutics.* (4th ed.) New York: Macmillan, 1970.

Goodwin, D. W., Crane, J. B., & Guze, S. B. Alcoholic "blackouts": A review and clinical study of 100 alcoholics. *American Journal of Psychiatry,* 1969, **126,** 191–198.

Goodwin, D. W., Powell, B., Bremer, D., Hoine, H., & Stern, J. Alcohol and recall: State dependent effects in man. *Science,* 1969, **163,** 1358–1360.

Goodwin, D. W., Schulsinger, F., Hermansen, L., Guze, S. B., & Winokur, G. A. Alcohol problems in adoptees raised apart from alcoholic biological parents. *Archives of General Psychiatry,* 1973, **128,** 239–243.

Gottesman, I. Differential inheritance of the psychoneuroses. *Eugenics Quarterly,* 1962, **9,** 223–227.

Gottesman, I., & Shields, J. *Schizophrenia and genetics: A twin study vantage point.* New York: Academic Press, 1972.

Gottman, J., Notarius, C., Gonso, J., & Markman, H. *A couple's guide to communication.* Champaign, Ill.: Research Press, 1976.

Gove, W., & Tudor, J. Adult sex roles and mental illness. *American Journal of Sociology,* 1973, **78,** 812–835.

Goyette, C. H., & Conners, C. K. Food additives and hyperkinesis. Paper presented at the 85th Annual Convention of the American Psychological Association, 1977.

Grace, W. J., & Graham, D. T. Relationship of specific attitudes and emotions to certain bodily diseases. *Psychosomatic Medicine,* 1952, **14,** 243–251.

Graham, D. T. Health, disease and the mind-body problem: Linguistic parallelism. *Psychosomatic Medicine,* 1967, **29,** 52–71.

Graham, D. T., Kabler, J. D., & Graham, F. K. Physiological responses to the suggestion of attitudes: Specificity of attitude hypothesis in psychosomatic disease. *Psychosomatic Medicine,* 1962, **24,** 159–169.

Graham, D. T., Stern, J. A., & Winokur, G. Experimental investigation of the specificity of attitude hypothesis in psychosomatic disease. *Psychosomatic Medicine,* 1958, **20,** 446–457.

Graham, P. J., Rutter, M. L., Yule, W., & Pless, I. B. Childhood asthma: A psychosomatic disorder? Some epidemiological considerations. *British Journal of Preventive Medicine,* 1967, **21,** 78–85.

Gray, J. *The psychology of fear and stress.* New York: McGraw-Hill, 1971.

Green, R. *Sexual identity conflict in children and adults.* New York: Basic Books, 1974.

Green, R., & Money, J. *Transsexualism and sex reassignment.* Baltimore: Johns Hopkins University Press, 1969.

Greenblatt, D. J., & Shader, R. I. The clinical choice of sedative-hypnotics. *Annals of Internal Medicine,* 1972, **77,** 91–100.

Greenblatt, M., Grosser, G. H., & Wechsler, H. Differential responses of hospitalized depressed patients to somatic therapy. *American Journal of Psychiatry,* 1964, **120,** 935–943.

Greenspan, K., Schildkraut, J. J., Gordon, E. K., Baer, L., Aronoff, M., & Durell, J. Catecholamine metabolism in affective disorders: III. MHPG and other catecholamine metabolites in patients treated with lithium carbonate. *Journal of Psychiatric Research,* 1970, **1,** 7.

Greer, S. Study of parental loss in neurotics and sociopaths. *Archives of General Psychiatry,* 1964, **11,** 177–180.

Greer, S. Learned helplessness in depressed, psychiatric, and normal subjects. Unpublished doctoral dissertation, State University of New York at Stony Book, 1976.

Grinker, R. R., & Spiegel, J. P. *Men under stress.* Philadelphia: Blakiston, 1945.

Gross, M. B., & Wilson, W. C. *Minimal brain dysfunction.* New York: Brunner/Mazel, 1974.

Grossman, H. (Ed.) *Manual on terminology and classification in mental retardation, 1973 revision.* Washington, D.C.: American Association on Mental Deficiency, 1973.

Gubbay, S., Lobascher, M., & Kingerlee, P. A neurological appraisal of autistic children: Results of a Western Australia survey. *Developmental Medicine and Child Neurology,* 1970, **12,** 422–429.

Guerney, B. G. (Ed.) *Psychotherapeutic agents: New roles for nonprofessionals, parents and teachers.* New York: Holt, Rinehart and Winston, 1969.

Gunderson, J. G., Arutry, J. H., Mosher, L. R., & Buchsbaum, S. Special report: Schizophrenia, 1973. *Schizophrenia Bulletin,* 1974, **2,** 15–54.

Gunn, J., & Fenton, G. *Lancet,* June 5, 1971, 1173–1176.

Haggard, E. Some conditions determining adjustment during and readjustment following experimentally induced stress. In S. Tomkins (Ed.), *Contemporary psychopathology.* Cambridge, Mass.: Harvard University Press, 1943.

Hall, C. S. *A primer of Freudian psychology.* New York: New American Library, 1964.

Halleck, S. L. *The politics of therapy.* New York: Science House, 1971.

Harburg, E., Erfurt, J. C., Hauenstein, L. S., Chape, C., Schull, W. J., & Schork, M. A. Socioecological stress, suppressed hostility, skin color, and black-white male blood pressure: Detroit. *Psychosomatic Medicine,* 1973, **35,** 276–296.

Hare, R. D. *Psychopathy: Theory and research.* New York: Wiley, 1970.

Harlow, H. F., & Harlow, M. K. Learning to love. *American Scientist,* 1966, **54,** 244–272.

Harrell, R. F., Woodyard, E., & Gates, A. D. *The effects of mothers' diets on the intelligence of offspring.* New York: Teachers College Press, Columbia University, 1955.

Harrington, A., & Sutton-Simon, K. Rape. In A. P. Goldstein, P. J. Monti, T. J. Sardino, & D. J. Green (Eds.), *Police crisis intervention.* Kalamazoo, Mich.: Behaviordelia, 1977.

Hartmann, H. *Ego psychology and the problem of adaptation.* New York: International Universities Press, 1958.

Hawley, C., & Buckley, R. Food dyes and hyperkinetic children. *Academic Therapy,* 1974, **10,** 27–32.

Hays, P. Etiological factors in manic-depressive psychoses. *Archives of General Psychiatry* 1976, **33,** 1187–1188.

Heath, R. G., & Krupp, I. M. Schizophrenia as an immunologic disorder. *Archives of General Psychiatry,* 1967, **16,** 1–33.

Heaton, R. K., & Victor, R. G. Personality characteristics associated with psychedelic flashbacks in natural and experimental settings. *Journal of Abnormal Psychology,* 1976, **85,** 83–90.

Heber, R. (Ed.) A manual on terminology and classification in mental retardation. (2nd ed.) *American Journal of Mental Deficiency, Monograph Supplement,* 1961.

Heber, R. *Epidemiology of mental retardation.* Springfield, Ill.: Charles C Thomas, 1970.

Hedblom, J. H. The female homosexual: Social and attitudinal dimensions. In J. A. McCaffrey (Ed.), *The homosexual dialectic.* Englewood Cliffs, N.J.: Prentice-Hall, 1972.

Heiman, N. M. Postdoctoral training in community mental health. Menninger Clinic Bulletin 17, 1973.

Held, J. M., & Cromwell, R. L. Premorbid adjustment in schizophrenia: An evaluation of a method and some general comments. *Journal of Nervous and Mental Disease,* 1968, **146,** 264–272.

Heller, J. *Something happened,* 1966. New York: Knopf, 1974.

Hempel, C. The theoretician's dilemma. In H. Feigl, M. Scriven, & G. Maxwell (Eds.), *Minnesota studies in the philosophy of science,* Vol. 2. Minneapolis: University of Minnesota Press, 1958.

Henkel, H., & Lewis-Thomé, J. *Verhaltenstherapie bei männlichen Homosexuellen.* Diplomarbeit der Studierenden der Psychologie, University of Marburg, 1976.

Henry, J. P., Stephens, P. M., Axelrod, J., & Miller, R. A. Effect of psychosocial stimulation on the enzymes involved in the biosynthesis and metabolism of noradrenaline and adrenaline. *Psychosomatic Medicine,* 1971, **23,** 227–237.

Herbert, J. Personality factors and bronchial asthma: A study of South African Indian children. *Journal of Psychosomatic Research,* 1965, **8,** 353–364.

Hermelin, B. *Recent psychological research.* In J. K. Wing (Ed.), *Early childhood autism: Clinical, educational, and social aspects.* Elmsford, N.Y.: Pergamon Press, 1966.

Hermelin, B., & O'Connor, N. Measures of occipital alpha rhythm in normal, subnormal, and autistic children. *British Journal of Psychiatry,* 1968, **114,** 603–610.

Hernández-Peón, R., Chávez-Ibarra, G., & Aguilar-Figueroa, E. Somatic evoked potentials in one case of hysterical anesthesia. *EEG and Clinical Neurophysiology,* 1963, **15,** 889–892.

Herrnstein, R. J. Method and theory in the study of avoidance. *Psychological Review,* 1969, **76,** 46–69.

Heston, L. L. Psychiatric disorders in foster home reared children of schizophrenic mothers. *British Journal of Psychiatry,* 1966, **112,** 819–825.

Hewett, F. M. Teaching speech to an autistic child through operant conditioning. *American Journal of Orthopsychiatry,* 1965, **33,** 927–936.

Higgins, G. Sexuality and the spinal cord injured patient. In J. LoPiccolo & L. LoPiccolo (Eds.), *Handbook of sex therapy.* New York: Plenum Press, in press.

Hilgard, E. R. *Hypnotic susceptibility.* New York: Harcourt Brace Jovanovich, 1965.

Hill, D. EEG in episodic psychotic and psychopathic behavior: A classification of data. *EEG and Clinical Neurophysiology,* 1952, **4,** 419–442.

Hill, J. H., Liebert, R. M., & Mott, D. E. W. Vicarious extinction of avoidance behavior through films: An initial test. *Psychological Reports,* 1968, **12,** 192.

Hinton, G. G. Childhood psychosis or mental retardation: A diagnostic dilemma: II. Pediatric and neurological aspects. *Canadian Medical Association Journal,* 1963, **89,** 1020–1024.

Hiroto, D. S., & Seligman, M. E. P. Generality of learned helplessness in man. *Journal of Personality and Social Psychology,* 1975, **31,** 311–327.

Hobbs, N. Helping disturbed children: Psychological and ecological strategies. *American Psychologist,* 1966, **21,** 1105–1115.

Hodapp, V., Weyer, G., & Becker, J. Situational stereotypy in essential hypertension patients. *Journal of Psychosomatic Research,* 1975, **19,** 113–121.

Hodgson, R. J., & Rachman, S. The effects of contamination and washing in obsessional patients. *Behaviour Research and Therapy,* 1972, **10,** 111–117.

Hoffman, M. *The gay world.* New York: Basic Books, 1968.

Hokanson, J. E., & Burgess, M. The effects of three types of aggression on vascular processes. *Journal of Abnormal and Social Psychology,* 1962, **65,** 446–449.

Hokanson, J. E., Burgess, M., & Cohen, M. F. Effects of displaced aggression on systolic blood pressure. *Journal of Abnormal and Social Psychology,* 1963, **67,** 214–218.

Hokanson, J. E., DeGood, D. E., Forrest, M. S., & Brittain, T. M. Availability of avoidance behaviors for modulating vascular-stress responses. *Journal of Personality and Social Psychology,* 1971, **19,** 60–68.

Hokanson, J. E., Willers, K. R., & Koropsak, E. Modification of autonomic responses during aggressive interchange. *Journal of Personality,* 1968, **36,** 386–404.

Holden, C. Nader on mental health centers: A movement that got bogged down. *Science,* 1972, **177,** 413–415.

Hollingshead, A. B., & Redlich, F. C. *Social class and mental illness: A community study.* New York: Wiley, 1958.

Holmes, T. H., & Rahe, R. H. The social readjustment rating scale. *Journal of Psychosomatic Research,* 1967, **11,** 213–218.

Holmes, T. S., & Holmes, T. H. Short-term intrusions into the life style routine. *Journal of Psychosomatic Research,* 1970, **14,** 121–132.

Honigfeld, G., & Howard, A. *Psychiatric drugs: A desk reference.* New York: Academic Press, 1973.

Horney, K. *Self-analysis.* New York: Norton, 1942.

Houts, P. S., & Serber, M. (Eds.) *After the turn-on, what? Learning perspectives on humanistic groups.* Champaign, Ill.: Research Press, 1972.

Huessy, H. R., Metoyer, M., & Townsend, M. 8–10 year follow-up of 84 children treated for behavioral disorder in rural Vermont. *Acta Paedopsychiatrica,* 1974, **40,** 230–235.

Humphreys, L. *Tearoom trade: Impersonal sex in public places.* Chicago: Aldine, 1970.

Hurley, R. L. *Poverty and mental retardation: A causal relationship.* New York: Random House, 1970.

Hutchings, B., & Mednick, S. A. Registered criminality in the adoptive and biological parents of registered male adoptees. In S. A. Mednick, F. Schulsinger, J. Higgins, & B. Bell (Eds.), *Genetics, environment and psychopathology.* New York: Elsevier, 1974.

Hutt, C., Hutt, S. J., Lee, D., & Ounsted, C. Arousal and childhood autism. *Nature,* 1964, **204,** 908–909.

Hutt, C., & Ounsted, C. The biological significance of gaze aversion with particular reference to the syndrome of infantile autism. *Behavioral Science,* 1966, **11,** 346–356.

Ikard, F. F., Green, D. E., & Horn, D. The development of a scale to differentiate between types of smoking as related to the management of affect. Paper presented at the annual meeting of the Eastern Psychological Association, Washington, D.C., 1968.

Inglis, J. Electrode placement and the effect of ECT on mood and memory in depression. *Canadian Psychiatric Association Journal,* 1969, **14,** 463–471.

Ingram, I. M. The obsessional personality and obsessional illness. *American Journal of Psychiatry,* 1961, **117,** 1016–1019.

Inhelder, B. *The diagnosis of reasoning in the mentally retarded.* (2nd ed.) New York: Chandler Publishing, 1968.

Innes, G., Millar, W. M., & Valentine, M. Emotion and blood pressure. *Journal of Mental Science,* 1959, **105,** 840–851.

Itil, T. M. Summary progress report of Grant MH20801. St. Louis, Mo., 1972.

Jacobson, E. *Progressive relaxation.* Chicago: University of Chicago Press, 1929.

Jarvik, M. E. The role of nicotine in the smoking habit. In W. A. Hunt (Ed.), *Learning mechanisms in smoking.* Chicago: Aldine, 1970.

Jeans, R. F. I. An independently validated case of multiple personality. *Journal of Abnormal Psychology,* 1976, **85,** 249–255.

Jellinek, E. M. Phases of alcohol addiction. *Quarterly Journal of Studies on Alcohol,* 1952, **13,** 673–684.

Jenkins, C. D. Psychologic and social precursors of coronary disease. *New England Journal of Medicine,* 1971, **284,** 244–255, 307–317.

Jersild, A. T., & Holmes, F. B. *Children's fears.* New York: Teachers College Press, Columbia University, 1935.

Jersild, A. T., Markey, F. V., & Jersild, C. L. Children's fears, dreams, wishes, daydreams, likes, dislikes, pleasant and unpleasant memories. In A. T. Jersild (Ed.), *Child psychology.* Englewood Cliffs, N.J.: Prentice-Hall, 1960.

Johnson, A. M., Falstein, E. I., Szurek, S. A., & Svendson, M. School phobia, *American Journal of Orthopsychiatry,* 1941, **11,** 701–702.

Johnson, G., Gershon, S., & Hekimian, L. Controlled evaluation in lithium and chlorpromazine in treatment of manic states. *Comprehensive Psychiatry,* 1968, **9,** 563–573.

Jones, B. M. Memory impairment on the ascending and descending limbs of the blood alcohol curve. *Journal of Abnormal Psychology,* 1973, **82,** 24–32.

Jones, B. M., & Parsons, O. A. Impaired abstracting ability in chronic alcoholics. *Archives of General Psychiatry,* 1971, **24,** 71–75.

Jones, B. M., & Parsons, O. A. Alcohol and consciousness: Getting high, coming down. *Psychology Today,* January 1975, **8,** 53–58.

Jones, E. *The life and work of Sigmund Freud,* Vol. 2. New York: Basic Books, 1955.

Jones, M. *The therapeutic community.* New York: Basic Books, 1953.

Jones, M. C. A laboratory study of fear: The case of Peter. *Pedagogical Seminary,* 1925, **31,** 308–315.

Jones, M. C. Personality correlates and antecedents of drinking patterns in males. *Journal of Consulting and Clinical Psychology,* 1968, **32,** 2–12.

Jones, M. C. Personality antecedents and correlates of drinking patterns in women. *Journal of Consulting and Clinical Psychology,* 1971, **36,** 61–70.

Kallmann, F. J. The genetics of psychosis. *American Journal of Human Genetics,* 1950, **2,** 385.

Kallmann, F. J. Twin and sibship study of overt male homosexuality. *American Journal of Human Genetics,* 1952, **4,** 136–146. (a)

Kallmann, F. J. Comparative twin study in the genetic aspects of male homosexuality. *Journal of Nervous and Mental Disease,* 1952, **115,** 283–298. (b)

Kallmann, F. J., & Roth, B. Genetic aspects of preadolescent schizophrenia. *American Journal of Psychiatry,* 1956, **112,** 599–606.

Kameny, F. E. Gay liberation and psychiatry. *Psychiatric Opinion,* 1971, **8,** 18–27.

Kamiya, J. Conscious control of brain waves. *Psychology Today,* April 1968, **1,** 56–61.

Kanfer, F. H., & Karoly, P. Self-control. A behavioristic excursion into the lion's den. *Behavior Therapy,* 1972, **3,** 398–416.

Kanfer, F. H., & Phillips, J. S. *Learning foundations of behavior therapy.* New York: Wiley, 1970.

Kanner, L. Autistic disturbances of affective contact. *Nervous Child,* 1943, **2,** 217–250.

Kanner, L. Problems of nosology and psychodynamics of early infantile autism. *American Journal of Orthopsychiatry,* 1949, **19,** 416–426.

Kanner, L. To what extent is early infantile autism determined by constitutional inadequacies? *Association for Research in Nervous and Mental Disease,* 1954, **33,** 378–385.

Kanner, L. Follow-up of eleven autistic children originally reported in 1943. In L. Kanner (Ed.), *Childhood psychosis: Initial studies and new insights.* Washington, D.C.: Winston-Wiley, 1973.

Kanner, L., & Eisenberg, L. Notes on the follow-up studies of autistic children. In P. Hoch & J. Zubin (Eds.), *Psychopathology of childhood.* New York: Grune and Stratton, 1955.

Kanner, L., & Lesser, L. Early infantile autism. *Pediatric Clinic of North America,* 1958, **5,** 711–730.

Kasl, S. V., & Cobb, S. Blood pressure changes in men undergoing job loss: A preliminary report. *Psychosomatic Medicine,* 1970, **6,** 95–106.

Katchadourian, H. A., & Lunde, D. T. *Fundamentals of human sexuality.* New York: Holt, Rinehart and Winston, 1972.

Kelly, E., & Zeller, B. Asthma and the psychiatrist. *Journal of Psychomatic Research,* 1969, **13,** 377–395.

Kennedy, W. A. School phobia: Rapid treatment of 50 cases. *Journal of Abnormal Psychology,* 1965, **70,** 285–289.

Kent, R. N., O'Leary, K. D., Diament, C., & Dietz, A. Expectation biases in observational evaluation of therapeutic change. *Journal of Consulting and Clinical Psychology,* 1974, **42,** 774–780.

Kessel, N., & Walton, A. *Alcoholism.* Baltimore: Penguin, 1965.

Kety, S. S. From rationalization to reason. *American Journal of Psychiatry,* 1974, **131,** 957–963.

Kety, S. S., Rosenthal, D., Wender, P. H., & Schulsinger, F. The types and prevalence of mental illness in the biological and adoptive families of adopted schizophrenics. In D. Rosenthal & S. S. Kety (Eds.), *The transmission of schizophrenia.* Elmsford, N.Y.: Pergamon Press, 1968.

Kimble, G. *Hilgard and Marquis' conditioning and learning.* New York: Appleton-Century-Crofts, 1961.

Kinsey, A. C., Pomeroy, W. B., & Martin, C. E. *Sexual behavior in the human male.* Philadelphia: Saunders, 1948.

Kinsey, A. C., Pomeroy, W. B., Martin, C. E., & Gebhard, P. H. *Sexual behavior in the human female.* Philadelphia: Saunders, 1953.

Kinsman, R. A., Spector, S. L., Shucard, D. W., & Luparello, T. J. Observations on patterns of subjective symptomatology of acute asthma. *Psychosomatic Medicine,* 1974, **36,** 129–143.

Klee, G. D., Bertino, J., Weintraub, W., & Calaway, E. The influence of varying dosage on the effects of lysergic acid diethylamide (LSD-25). *Journal of Nervous and Mental Disease,* 1961, **132,** 404–409.

Klee, G. D., & Weintraub, W. Paranoid reactions following lysergic acid diethylamide (LSD-25). In P. B. Bradley, P. Demicker, & C. Radonco-Thomas (Eds.), *Neuropsychopharmacology.* Amsterdam, Netherlands: Elsevier, 1959.

Kleeman, S. T. Psychiatric contributions in the treatment of asthma. *Annals of Allergy,* 1967, **25,** 611–619.

Klein, D. C., & Seligman, M. E. P. Reversal of performance deficits and perceptual deficits in learned helplessness and depression. *Journal of Abnormal Psychology,* 1976, **85,** 11–26.

Klein, M., Heimann, P., Isaacs, S., & Riviere, J. *Developments in psychoanalysis.* London: Hogarth Press, 1952.

Kleinmuntz, B. *Personality measurement: An introduction.* Homewood, Ill.: Dorsey Press, 1967.

Klerman, G. L. Drug therapy of clinical depressions. *Journal of Psychiatric Research,* 1972, **9,** 253–270.

Klerman, G. L., & Paykel, E. S. Depressive pattern, social background, and hospitalization. *Journal of Nervous and Mental Disease,* 1970, **150,** 466–478.

Kluger, J. M. Childhood asthma and the social milieu. *American Academy of Child Psychiatry,* 1969, **8,** 353–366.

Knapp, P. H. The asthmatic and his environment. *Journal of Nervous and Mental Disease,* 1969, **149,** 133–151.

Knight, R. P. The dynamics of chronic alcoholism. *Journal of Nervous and Mental Disease,* 1937, **86,** 538–548.

Koegel, R. L., & Wilhelm, H. Selective responding to the components of multiple visual cues by autistic children. *Journal of Experimental Child Psychology,* 1973, **15,** 442–453.

Kohn, M. L. Social class and schizophrenia: A critical review. In D. Rosenthal & S. S. Kety (Eds.), *The transmission of schizophrenia.* Elmsford, N.Y.: Pergamon Press, 1968.

Kolb, L. C. *Noyes' modern clinical psychiatry.* (7th ed.) Philadelphia: Saunders, 1968.

Kolodny, R. C., Masters, W. H., Hendryx, J., & Toro, G. Plasma testosterone and the semen analysis in male homosexuals. *New England Journal of Medicine,* 1971, **285,** 1170–1174.

Konig, P., & Godfrey, S. Prevalence of exercise-induced bronchial lability in families of children with asthma. *Archives of Diseases of Childhood,* 1973, **48,** 513.

Kopfstein, J. M., & Neale, J. M. A multivariate study of attention dysfunction in schizophrenia. *Journal of Abnormal Psychology,* 1972, **80,** 294–299.

Kozol, H., Boucher, R., & Garofalo, R. The diagnosis and treatment of dangerousness. *Crime and Delinquency,* 1972, **18,** 371–392.

Kranz, H. *Lebenschicksale krimineller Zwillinge.* Berlin: Springer-Verlag, 1936.

Kreitman, N., Sainsbury, P., Morrissey, J., Towers, J., & Scrivner, J. The reliability of psychiatric assessment: An analysis. *Journal of Mental Science,* 1961, **107,** 887–908.

Kuhn, T. S. *The Copernican revolution.* New York: Random House, 1959.

Kuhn, T. S. *The structure of scientific revolutions.* Chicago: University of Chicago Press, 1962.

Kuriansky, J. B., Deming, W. E., & Gurland, B. J. On trends in the diagnosis of schizophrenia. *American Journal of Psychiatry,* 1974, **131,** 402–407.

Kutchinsky, B. *Studies on pornography and sex crimes in Denmark.* Copenhagen: New Social Science Monographs, 1970.

Lacey, J. I. Somatic response patterning and stress: Some revisions of activation theory. In M. H. Appley & R. Trumball (Eds.), *Psychological stress.* New York: McGraw-Hill, 1967.

Lachman, S. J. *Psychosomatic disorders: A behavioristic interpretation.* New York: Wiley, 1972.

Laing, R. D. Is schizophrenia a disease? *International Journal of Social Psychiatry,* 1964, **10,** 184–193.

Lane, E. A., & Albee, G. W. Childhood intellectual differences between schizophrenic adults and their siblings. *American Journal of Orthopsychiatry,* 1965, **35,** 747–753.

Lang, A. R., Goeckner, D. J., Adessor, V. J., & Marlatt, G. A. Effects of alcohol on aggression in male social drinkers. *Journal of Abnormal Psychology,* 1975, **84,** 508–518.

Lang, P. J. The mechanics of desensitization and the laboratory study of fear. In C. M. Franks (Ed.), *Behavior therapy: Appraisal and status.* New York: McGraw-Hill, 1969.

Lang, P. J. Learned control of human heart rate in a computer directed environment. In P. A. Obrist, A. H. Black, J. Brener, & L. V. DiCara (Eds.), *Cardiovascular psychophysiology.* Chicago: Aldine, 1974.

Lang, P. J., & Lazovik, A. D. Experimental desensitization of a phobia. *Journal of Abnormal and Social Psychology,* 1963, **66,** 519–525.

Lang, P. J., & Melamed, B. G. Case report: Avoidance conditioning therapy of an infant with chronic ruminative vomiting. *Journal of Abnormal Psychology,* 1969, **74,** 1–8.

Lange, J. *Verbrechen als Schicksal.* Leipzig: Georg Thieme Verlag, 1929.

Langer, E. J., & Abelson, R. P. A patient by any other name . . . : Clinician group difference in labelling bias. *Journal of Consulting and Clinical Psychology,* 1974, **42,** 4–9.

Lapolla, A., & Jones, H. Placebo-control evaluation of desipramine in depression. *American Journal of Psychiatry,* 1970, **127,** 335–338.

Lasagna, L., Mosteller, F., Von Felsinger, J. M., & Beecher, H. K. A study of the placebo response. *American Journal of Medicine,* 1954, **16,** 770–779.

Lazarus, A. A. New methods of psychotherapy: A case study. *South African Medical Journal,* 1958, **33,** 660.

Lazarus, A. A. Group therapy of phobic disorders by systematic desensitization. *Journal of Abnormal and Social Psychology,* 1961, **63,** 504–510.

Lazarus, A. A. Behavior therapy, incomplete treatment, and symptom substitution. *Journal of Nervous and Mental Disease,* 1965, **140,** 80–86.

Lazarus, A. A. Behavior therapy in groups. In G. M. Gazda (Ed.), *Basic approaches to group psychotherapy and counseling.* Springfield, Ill.: Charles C Thomas, 1968. (a)

Lazarus, A. A. Learning theory and the treatment of depression. *Behavior Research and Therapy,* 1968, **6,** 83–89. (b)

Lazarus, A. A. *Behavior therapy and beyond.* New York: McGraw-Hill, 1971.

Lazarus, A. A. Multimodal behavior therapy: Treating the BASIC ID. *Journal of Nervous and Mental Disease,* 1973, **156,** 404–411.

Lazarus, A. A., & Davison, G. C. Clinical innovation in research and practice. In A. E. Bergin & S. L. Garfield (Eds.), *Handbook of psychotherapy and behavior change: An empirical analysis.* New York: Wiley, 1971.

Lazarus, A. A., Davison, G. C., & Polefka, D. Classical and operant factors in the treatment of a school phobia. *Journal of Abnormal Psychology,* 1965, **70,** 225–229.

Lazovik, A. D., & Lang, P. J. A laboratory demonstration of systematic desensitization psychotherapy. *Journal of Psychological Studies,* 1960, **11,** 238–247.

Leff, M., Roatch, J., & Bunney, W. E. Environmental factors preceding the onset of severe depressions. *Psychiatry,* 1970, **33,** 293–311.

Leitenberg, H., Agras, W. S., Barlow, D. H., & Oliveau, D. C. Contribution of selective positive reinforcement and therapeutic instructions to systematic desensitization therapy. *Journal of Abnormal Psychology,* 1969, **74,** 113–118.

Lemieux, G., Davignon, A., & Genest, J. Depressive states during rauwolfia therapy for arterial hypertension. *Canadian Medical Association Journal,* 1956, **74,** 522–526.

Leonard, C. V. Depression and suicidality. *Journal of Consulting and Clinical Psychology,* 1974, **42,** 98–104.

Lester, D. Attempts to predict suicidal risk using psychological tests. *Psychological Bulletin,* 1970, **74,** 1–17.

Lester, D., & Greenberg, L. Nutrition and the etiology of alcoholism. *Quarterly Journal of Studies on Alcohol,* 1952, **13,** 320–330.

Levendusky, P., & Pankratz, L. Self-control technique as an alternative pain medication. *Journal of Abnormal Psychology,* 1975, **84,** 165–168.

Levine, M. *A cognitive theory of learning: Research on hypothesis testing.* Hillsdale, N.J.: Lawrence Erlbaum Associates, 1975.

Levine, M., & Olson, R. P. Intelligence of parents of autistic children. *Journal of Abnormal Psychology,* 1968, **73,** 215–217.

Levitsky, A., & Perls, F. S. The rules and games of Gestalt therapy. In J. Fagan & I. L. Sherherd (Eds.), *Gestalt therapy now.* Palo Alto, Calif.: Science and Behavior Books, 1970.

Levitt, E. E. Psychotherapy with children: A further evaluation. *Behavior research and therapy,* 1963, **1,** 45–51.

Levy, L. H. *Psychological interpretation.* New York: Holt, Rinehart and Winston, 1963.

Lewinsohn, P. H. A behavioral approach to depression. In R. J. Friedman & M. M. Katz (Eds.), *The psychology of depression: Contemporary theory and research.* Washington, D.C.: Winston-Wiley, 1974.

Lewinsohn, P. H., & Libet, J. M. Pleasant events, activity schedules and depressions. *Journal of Abnormal Psychology,* 1972, **79,** 291–295.

Liberman, R. P. Learning interpersonal skills in groups: Harnessing the behavioristic horse to the humanistic wagon. In P. S. Houts & M. Serber (Eds.), *After the turn-on, what? Learning perspectives on humanistic groups.* Champaign, Ill.: Research Press, 1972.

Liberman, R. P., DeRisi, W. J., King, L. W., Eckman, T. A., & Wood, D. W. Behavioral measurement in a community mental health center. In P. O. Davidson, F. W. Clark, & L. A. Hamerlynck (Eds.), *Evaluation of behavioral programs in community, residential, and school settings.* Champaign, Ill.: Research Press, 1974.

Libet, J. M., & Lewinsohn, P. H. The concept of social skill with special reference to the behavior of depressed persons. *Journal of Consulting and Clinical Psychology,* 1973, **40,** 304–312.

Liebert, R. M., & Baron, R. A. Short-term effects of televised aggression on children's aggressive behavior. In J. P. Murray, E. A. Rubinstein, & G. A. Comstock (Eds.), *Television and social behavior,* Vol. 2. Washington, D.C.: U.S. Government Printing Office, 1972.

Liem, J. H. Effects of verbal communications of parents and children: A comparison of normal and schizophrenic families. *Journal of Consulting and Clinical Psychology,* 1974, **42,** 438–450.

Linehan, M. M., Goldfried, M. R., & Goldfried, A. P. Assertion therapy: Skill training or cognitive restructuring. Unpublished manuscript, 1977.

Ling, W., Charuvastra, V. C., Kaim, S. C., & Klett, C. J. Methadyl acetate and methandone as maintenance treatments for heroin addicts. *Archives of General Psychiatry,* 1976, **33,** 709–725.

Linton, H. B., & Langs, R. J. Empirical dimensions of LSD-25 reactions. *Archives of General Psychiatry,* 1964, **10,** 469–485.

Lockyer, L., & Rutter, M. A five-to-fifteen-year follow-up of infantile psychosis: III. Psychological characteristics. *British Journal of Psychiatry,* 1969, **115,** 865–882.

London, P. *The modes and morals of psychotherapy.* New York: Holt, Rinehart and Winston, 1964.

Loraine, J. A., Adamopoulos, D. A., Kirkham, E. E., Ismail, A. A. A., & Dove, G. A. Patterns of hormone excretion in male and female homosexuals. *Nature,* 1971, **234,** 552–555.

Lotter, V. Epidemiology of autistic conditions in young children: I. Prevalence. *Social Psychiatry,* 1966, **1,** 124–137.

Lotter, V. Factors related to outcome in autistic children. *Journal of Autism and Childhood Schizophrenia,* 1974, **4,** 263–277.

Lovaas, O. I., Freitag, G., Gold, V. J., & Kassorla, I. C. Experimental studies in childhood schizophrenia: Analysis of self-destructive behavior. *Journal of Experimental Child Psychology,* 1965, **2,** 67–84.

Lovass, O. I., Schreibman, L., Koegel, R., & Rehm, R. Selective responding by autistic children to multiple sensory input. *Journal of Abnormal Psychology,* 1971, **77,** 211–222.

Luborsky, L., & Spence, D. P. Quantitative research on psychoanalytic therapy. In A. E. Bergin & S. L. Garfield (Eds.), *Handbook of psychotherapy and behavior change: An empirical analysis.* New York: Wiley, 1971.

Lucchesi, B. R., Schuster, C. R., & Emley, G. S. The role of nicotine as a determinant of cigarette smoking frequency in man with observations of certain cardiovascular effects associated with the tobacco alkaloid. *Clinical Pharmacology and Therapeutics,* 1967, **8,** 789–796.

Luparello, T. J., McFadden, E. R., Lyons, H. A., & Bleecker, E. R. Psychologic factors and bronchial asthma. *New York State Journal of Medicine,* 1971, **71,** 2161–2165.

Luria, D. B. *Overcoming drugs: Program of action.* New York: McGraw-Hill, 1970.

Lyght, C. E. (Ed.) *The Merck manual of diagnosis and therapy.* (11th ed.) Rahway, N.J.: Merck Sharp and Dohme Research Laboratories, 1966.

Lykken, D. T. A study of anxiety in the sociopathic personality. *Journal of Abnormal and Social Psychology,* 1957, **55,** 6–10.

Lystad, M. M. Social mobility among selected groups of schizophrenics. *American Sociological Review,* 1957, **22,** 288–292.

MacDonald, M. L. The forgotten Americans: A sociopsychological analysis of aging and nursing homes. *American Journal of Community Psychology,* 1973, **3,** 272–292.

Maddi, S. R. The existential neurosis. *Journal of Abnormal Psychology,* 1967, **72,** 311–325.

Magee, B. *One in twenty: A study of homosexuality in men and women.* New York: Stein and Day, 1966.

Maher, B. A. *Principles of psychopathology: An experimental approach.* New York: McGraw-Hill, 1966.

Mahler, M. S. On child psychosis and schizophrenia: Autistic and symbiotic infantile psychoses. In *Psychoanalytic Study of the Child,* Vol. 7. New York: International Universities Press, 1952.

Mahoney, M. J. Research issues in self-management. *Behavior Therapy,* 1972, **3,** 45–63.

Mahoney, M. J. *Cognition and behavior modification.* Cambridge, Mass.: Ballinger, 1974.

Maier, N. R. F. *Frustration: The study of behavior without a goal.* New York: McGraw-Hill, 1949.

Main, T. F. Perception and ego-function. *British Journal of Medical Psychology,* 1958, **31,** 1–7.

Mandler, G. Anxiety. In D. L. Sills (Ed.), *International encyclopedia of the social sciences.* New York: Crowell Collier and Macmillan, 1966.

Mandler, G., & Sarason, S. B. A study of anxiety and learning. *Journal of Abnormal and Social Psychology,* 1952, **47,** 561–565.

*Marihuana and health: Fifth annual report to the U.S. Congress.* Rockville, Md.: National Institute on Drug Abuse, 1975.

Marin, P., & Cohen, A. Y. *Understanding drug use: An adult's guide to drugs and the young.* New York: Harper and Row, 1971.

Mark, V. H., & Ervin, F. R. *Violence and the brain.* New York: Harper and Row, 1970.

Mark, V. H., Sweet, W. H., & Ervin, F. R. Role of brain disease in riots and urban violence. *Journal of the American Medical Association,* 1967, **201,** 895.

Mark, V. H., Sweet, W. H., & Ervin, F. R. The effect of amygdalectomy on violent behavior in patients with temporal lobe epilepsy. In E. Hitchcock, L. Laitinen, & K. Vaernet (Eds.), *Psychosurgery.* Springfield, Ill.: Charles C Thomas, 1972.

Marks, I. M. *Fears and phobias.* New York: Academic Press, 1969.

Marks, I. M., & Gelder, M. G. Different onset ages in varieties of phobia. *American Journal of psychiatry,* 1966, **123,** 218, 221.

Marlatt, G. A., Demming, B., & Reid, J. B. Loss of control drinking in alcoholics: An experimental analogue. *Journal of Abnormal Psychology,* 1973, **81,** 233–241.

Marmor, J. Psychoanalytic therapy as an educational process: Common denominators in the therapeutic approaches of different psychoanalytic schools. In J. H. Masserman (Ed.), *Science and psychoanalysis*. Vol. 5. *Psychoanalytic education*. New York: Grune and Stratton, 1962.

Martin, B. The assessment of anxiety by physiological behavioral measures. *Psychological Bulletin,* 1961, **58,** 234–255.

Martin, D., & Lyon, P. *Lesbian/woman*. New York: Bantam, 1972.

Martin, R. *Legal challenges to behavior modification: Trends in schools, corrections, and mental health*. Champaign, Ill.: Research Press, 1975.

Masters, J. C., & Miller, D. E. Early infantile autism: A methodological critique. *Journal of Abnormal Psychology,* 1970, **75,** 342–343.

Masters, W. H., & Johnson, V. E. *Human sexual response*. Boston: Little, Brown, 1966.

Masters, W. H., & Johnson, V. E. *Human sexual inadequacy*. Boston: Little, Brown, 1970.

Mathe, A., & Knapp, P. Emotional and adrenal reactions of stress in bronchial asthma. *Psychosomatic Medicine,* 1971, **33,** 323–329.

Mausner, B. An ecological view of cigarette smoking. *Journal of Abnormal Psychology,* 1973, **81,** 115–126.

May, P. R. A. *Treatment of schizophrenia: A comparative study of five treatment methods*. New York: Science House, 1968.

Maynard, R. Omaha pupils given "behavior" drugs. *Washington Post,* June 29, 1970.

McCary, J. L. *Human sexuality*. New York: Van Nostrand Reinhold, 1967.

McClelland, D. C. Sources of hypertension in the drive for power. Paper presented as The Kittay Scientific Foundation Symposium "Psychopathology and Human Adaptation," New York, 1975.

McClelland, D. C., Davis, W. N., Kalin, R., & Wanner, E. *The drinking man*. New York: The Free Press, 1972.

McCord, W., & McCord, J. *The psychopath: An essay on the criminal mind*. New York: Van Nostrand Reinhold, 1964.

McCord, W., McCord, J., & Gudeman, J. Some current theories of alcoholism. *Quarterly Journal of Studies on Alcohol,* 1959, **20,** 727–749.

McCord, W., McCord, J., & Gudeman, J. *Origins of alcoholism*. Stanford, Calif.: Stanford University Press, 1960.

McFall, R. M., & Lillesand, D. B. Behavior rehearsal with modelling and coaching in assertion training. *Journal of Abnormal Psychology,* 1971, **77,** 313–323.

McFall, R. M., & Marston, A. R. An experimental investigation of behavior rehearsal in assertive training. *Journal of Abnormal Psychology,* 1970, **76,** 285–303.

McGarry, L. Competency to stand trial and mental illness. In *Crime and delinquency issues*. National Institute of Mental Health Monograph Series. Rockville Md.: DHEW Publication (HSM) 73–9105, 1972.

McGhie, A., & Chapman, J. S. Disorders of attention and perception in early schizophrenia. *British Journal of Medical Psychology,* 1961, **34,** 103–116.

McGuigan, F. J. Covert oral behavior and auditory hallucinations. *Psychophysiology,* 1966, **3,** 421–428.

McGuire, R. J., Carlisle, J. M., & Young, B. G. Sexual deviations as conditioned behaviour: A hypothesis. *Behaviour Research and Therapy,* 1965, **2,** 185–190.

McNeil, E. *The quiet furies*. Englewood Cliffs, N.J.: Prentice-Hall, 1967.

Mednick, B. R. Breakdown in high-risk subjects: Familial and early environmental factors. *Journal of Abnormal Psychology,* 1973, **82,** 469–475.

Mednick, S. A. A learning theory approach to research in schizophrenia. *Psychological Bulletin,* 1958, **55,** 316–327.

Mednick, S. A. A longitudinal study of children with high-risk for schizophrenia, *Mental Hygiene,* 1966, **50,** 522–535.

Mednick, S. A. Breakdown in individuals at high-risk for schizophrenia: Possible predispositional perinatal factors. *Mental Hygiene,* 1970, **54,** 50–63.

Mednick, S. A., & Schulsinger, F. Some premorbid characteristics related to breakdown in children with schizophrenic mothers. In D. Rosenthal & S. S. Kety (Eds.), *The transmission of schizophrenia*. Elmsford, N.Y.: Pergamon Press, 1968.

Medvedev, Z. *A question of madness*. New York: Knopf, 1972.

Meehl, P. E. Schizotaxia, schizotypy, schizophrenia. *American Psychologist,* 1962, **17,** 827–838.

Meichenbaum, D. Ways of modifying what clients say to themselves. *Rational Living,* 1972, **7,** 23–27.

Mello, N. K., & Mendelson, J. H. Experimentally induced intoxication in alcoholics: A comparison between programmed and spontaneous drinking. *Journal of Pharmacology and Experimental Therapy,* 1970, **173,** 101.

Mellor, C. S. First rank symptoms of schizophrenia. *British Journal of Psychiatry,* 1970, **117,** 15–23.

Meltzer, H. Y., Sachar, E. J., & Frantz, A. G. Serum prolactin levels in acutely psychotic patients: An indirect measurement of central dopaminergic activity. In E. Usdin (Ed.), *Neuropsychopharmacology of monoamines and their regulatory enzymes*. New York: Raven Press, 1974.

Mendels, J. *Concepts of depression*. New York: Wiley, 1970.

Mendels, J., & Cochrane, C. The nosology of depression: The endogenous-reactive concept. *American Journal of Psychiatry*, 1968, **124,** 1–11.

Mendels, J., Fieve, A., Fitzgerand, R. G., Ramsey, T. A., & Stokes, J. W. Biogenic amine metabolites in cerebrospinal fluid of depressed and manic patients. *Science*, 1972, **175,** 1380–1382.

Mendels, J., Secunda, S., & Dyson, W. A controlled study of the antidepressant effects of lithium carbonate. *Archives of General Psychiatry*, 1972, **26,** 154–157.

Mendels, J., Stinnett, J. L., Burns, D., & Frazer, A. Amine precursors and depression. *Archives of General Psychiatry*, 1975, **32,** 22–30.

Mendelson, J. H. Experimentally induced chronic intoxication and withdrawal in alcoholics. *Quarterly Journal of Studies on Alcohol*, Supplement 2, 1964.

Mendelson, W., Johnson, N., & Stewart, M. A. Hyperactive children as teenagers: A follow-up study. *Journal of Nervous and Mental Disease*, 1971, **153,** 273–279.

Mental Health Law Project, *Summary of Activities*, 1977, **2,** 1–2.

Metcalfe, M., & Goldman, E. Validation of an inventory for measuring depression. *British Journal of Psychiatry*, 1965, **111,** 240–242.

Metzner, R., Litwin, G., & Weil, G. M. The relation of expectation and mood to psilocybin reactions. *Psychedelic Review*, 1965, **5,** 3–39.

Meyer, V., & Chesser, E. S. *Behavior therapy in clinical psychiatry*. Baltimore: Penguin, 1970.

Mézey, A. G., & Cohen, S. I. The effect of depressive illness on time judgment and time experience. *Journal of Neurological and Neurosurgical Psychiatry*, 1961, **24,** 269–270.

Miklich, D. R., Rewey, H. H., Weiss, J. H., & Kolton, S. A preliminary investigation of psychophysiological responses to stress among different subgroups of asthmatic children. *Journal of Psychosomatic Research*, 1973, **17,** 1–8.

Milgram, N. A. Cognition and language in mental retardation: Directions and implications. In D. K. Routh (Ed.), *The experimental psychology of mental retardation*. Chicago: Aldine, 1973.

Miller, N. E. The influence of past experience upon the transfer of subsequent training. Unpublished doctoral dissertation, Yale University, 1935.

Miller, N. E. Studies of fear as an acquirable drive: I. Fear as motivation and fear-reduction as reinforcement in the learning of new responses. *Journal of Experimental Psychology*, 1948, **38,** 89–101.

Miller, N. E. Liberalization of basic S-R concepts: Extensions to conflict behavior, motivation, and social learning. In S. Koch (Ed.), *Psychology: A study of a science*, Vol. 2. New York: McGraw-Hill, 1959.

Miller, N. E. Learning of visceral and glandular responses. *Science*, 1969, **163,** 434–445.

Miller, N. E., & Dworkin, B. R. Visceral learning: Recent difficulties with curarized rats and significant problems for human research. In P. A. Obrist, A. H. Black, J. Brener, & L. V. DiCara (Eds.), *Cardiovascular psychophysiology*. Chicago: Aldine, 1974.

Miller, R. G., Palkes, H. S., & Stewart, M. A. Hyperactive children in suburban elementary schools. *Child Psychiatry and Human Development*, 1973, **4,** 121–127.

Miller, W. R. Learned helplessness in depressed and nondepressed students. Unpublished doctoral dissertation, University of Pennsylvania, 1974.

Miller, W. R. Psychological deficit in depression. *Psychological Bulletin*, 1975, **82,** 238–260.

Miller, W. R., & Seligman, M. E. P. Depression and the perception of reinforcement. *Journal of Abnormal Psychology*, 1973, **82,** 62–73.

Miller, W. R., Seligman, M. E. P., & Kurlander, H. M. Learned helplessness, depression, and anxiety. *Journal of Nervous and Mental Disease*, 1975, **161,** 347–357.

Milton, O., & Wahler, R. G. (Eds.) *Behavior disorders: Perspectives and trends*. (2nd ed.) Philadelphia: Lippincott, 1969.

Minge, M. R., & Ball, T. S. Teaching of self-help skills to profoundly retarded patients. *American Journal of Mental Deficiency*, 1957, **71,** 864–868.

Mintz, E. Time-extended marathon groups. *Psychotherapy*, 1967, **4,** 65–70.

Mintz, R. S. Psychotherapy of the suicidal patient. In H. L. P. Resnik (Ed.), *Suicidal behaviors*. Boston: Little, Brown, 1968.

Mintz, S., & Alpert, M. Imagery vividness, reality testing, and schizophrenic hallucinations. *Journal of Abnormal Psychology*, 1972, **79,** 310–316.

Mirsky, I. A. Physiologic, psychologic, and social determinants in the etiology of duodenal ulcer. *American Journal of Digestive Diseases,* 1958, **3,** 285–314.

Mischel, W. *Personality and assessment.* New York: Wiley, 1968.

Mischel, W. Toward a cognitive social learning reconceptualization of personality. *Psychological Review,* 1973, **80,** 252–283.

Mishler, E. G., & Waxler, N. E. *Interaction in families: An experimental study of family processes and schizophrenia.* New York: Wiley, 1968.

Mohr, J. W., Turner, R. E., & Jerry, M. B. *Pedophilia and exhibitionism.* Toronto: University of Toronto Press, 1964.

Monahan, J. The psychiatrization of criminal behavior. *Hospital and Community Psychiatry,* 1973, **24,** 105–107.

Monahan, J. The prevention of violence. In J. Monahan (Ed.), *Community mental health and the criminal justice system.* New York: Pergamon Press, 1976.

Monahan, J. Prisons: A wary verdict on rehabilitation. *Washington Post,* April 30, 1977, A13.

Monahan, J. Prediction research and the emergency commitment of dangerous mentally ill persons: A reconsideration. *American Journal of Psychiatry,* in press.

Moore, C., & Shiek, D. Toward a theory of early infantile autism. *Psychological Review,* 1971, **78,** 451–456.

Moos, R. H. *Evaluating treatment environments.* New York: Wiley, 1974.

Moreno, J. L., & Kipper, D. A. Group psychodrama and community-centered counseling. In G. M. Gazda (Ed.), *Basic approaches to group psychotherapy and group counseling.* Springfield, Ill.: Charles C Thomas, 1968.

Morris, A. A. Criminal insanity. *Washington Review,* 1968, **43,** 583–622.

Morris, J. *Conundrum.* New York: Harcourt Brace Jovanovitch, 1974.

Morris, N. Impediments to legal reform. *University of Chicago Law Review,* 1966, **33,** 627–656.

Morrison, J. R., & Stewart, M. A. A family study of the hyperactive child syndrome. *Biological Psychiatry,* 1971, **3,** 189–195.

Morrison, J. R., & Stewart, M. A. The psychiatric status of the legal families of adopted hyperactive children. *Archives of General Psychiatry,* 1973, **28,** 888–891.

Mowrer, O. H. A stimulus-response analysis of anxiety and its role as a reinforcing agent. *Psychological Review,* 1939, **46,** 553–565.

Mowrer, O. H. On the dual nature of learning—a reinterpretation of "conditioning" and "problem-solving." *Harvard Educational Review,* 1947, **17,** 102–148.

Mowrer, O. H., & Viek, P. An experimental analogue of fear from a sense of helplessness. *Journal of Abnormal and Social Psychology,* 1948, **43,** 193–200.

Murphy, D. L., & Wyatt, R. J. Reduced MAO activity in blood platelets from schizophrenic patients. *Nature,* 1972, **238,** 225–226.

Naranjo, C. Present-centeredness: Technique, prescription, and ideal. In J. Fagan & I. L. Shepherd (Eds.), *Gestalt therapy now: Theory, techniques, applications.* Palo Alto, Calif.: Science and Behavior Books, 1970.

Nathan, P. E., Titler, N. A., Lowenstein, L. W., Solomon, P., & Rossi, A. M. Behavioral analysis of chronic alcoholism. *Archives of General Psychiatry,* 1970, **22,** 419–430.

National Commission on Marihuana and Drug Abuse. *Marihuana: A signal of misunderstanding.* New York: The New American Library, 1972.

Neale, J. M. Perceptual span in schizophrenia. *Journal of Abnormal Psychology,* 1971, **77,** 196–204.

Neale, J. M., & Cromwell, R. L. Attention and schizophrenia. In B. A. Maher (Ed.), *Progress in experimental personality research,* Vol. 5. New York: Academic Press, 1970.

Neale, J. M., & Katahn, M. Anxiety, choice and stimulus uncertainty. *Journal of Personality,* 1968, **36,** 238–245.

Neale, J. M., & Liebert, R. M. Reinforcement therapy using aides and patients as behavioral technicians: A case report of a mute psychotic. *Perceptual and Motor Skills,* 1969, **28,** 835–839.

Neale, J. M., & Liebert, R. M. *Science and behavior: An introduction to methods of research.* Englewood Cliffs, N.J.: Prentice-Hall, 1973.

Nesbitt, P. D. Smoking, physiological arousal, and emotional response. *Journal of Personality and Social Psychology,* 1973, **25,** 137–144.

Neuhaus, E. C. A personality study of asthmatic and cardiac children. *Psychosomatic Medicine,* 1958, **20,** 181–186.

Newmark, C. S., Frerking, R. A., Cook, L., & Newmark, L. Endorsement of Ellis' irrational beliefs as a function of psychopathology. *Journal of Clinical Psychology,* 1973, **29,** 300–302.

Nowlis, D. P., & Kamiya, J. The control of electroencephalographic alpha rhythms through auditory feedback and the associated mental activity. *Psychophysiology,* 1970, **6,** 476–484.

Nunnally, J. C. *Psychometric theory.* New York: McGraw-Hill, 1967.

Nyhan, W. L. Disorders of nucleic acid metabolism. In G. E. Gaull (Ed.), *Biology of brain dysfunction.* New York: Plenum Press, 1973.

Öhman, A., Erixon, G., & Löfberg, I. Phobias and preparedness: Phobic versus neutral pictures as conditioned stimuli for human autonomic responses. *Journal of Abnormal Psychology,* 1975, **84,** 41–45.

O'Leary, K. D., & O'Leary, S. G. (Eds.) *Classroom management.* (2nd ed.) Elmsford, N.Y.: Pergamon Press, 1977.

O'Leary, K. D., Turkewitz, H., & Taffel, S. J. Parent and therapist evaluation of behavior therapy in a child psychological clinic. *Journal of Consulting and Clinical Psychology,* 1973, **41,** 289–293.

O'Leary, K. D., & Wilson, G. T. *Behavior therapy: Application and outcome.* Englewood Cliffs, N.J.: Prentice-Hall, 1975.

Oltmanns, T. F., O'Hayon, J., & Neale, J. M. The effects of anti-psychotic medication and diagnostic criteria on distractibility in schizophrenia. *Journal of Psychiatric Research,* in press.

Oltmanns, T. F., Weintraub, S., & Neale, J. M. Cognitive slippage in children vulnerable to schizophrenia. Paper presented at the 84th Annual Convention of the American Psychological Association, 1976.

Orne, M. T. The nature of hypnosis: Artifact and essence. *Journal of Abnormal and Social Psychology,* 1959, **58,** 277–299.

Orris, J. B. Visual monitoring performance in three subgroups of male delinquents. Unpublished M.A. thesis, University of Illinois, 1967.

Osgood, C. E., Luria, Z., & Smith, S. W. II. A blind analysis of another case of multiple personality using the semantic personality technique. *Journal of Abnormal Psychology,* 1976, **85,** 256–270.

Osgood, C. E., Suci, G. J., & Tannenbaum, P. H. *The measurement of meaning.* Urbana: University of Illinois Press, 1957.

Overton, D. A. State-dependent learning produced by depressant and atropine-like drugs. *Psychopharmacologia,* 1966, **10,** 6–31.

Pahnke, W. N. Drugs and mysticism. Unpublished doctoral dissertation, Harvard University, 1963.

Parker, N. Twins: A psychiatric study of a neurotic group. *Medical Journal of Australia,* 1964, **2,** 735–741.

Parsons, O. A. Brain damage in alcoholics: Altered states of consciousness. In M. M. Gross (Ed.), *Alcohol intoxication and withdrawal.* New York: Plenum Press, 1975.

Pasamanick, B., Rogers, M., & Lilienfeld, M. A. Pregnancy experience and the development of behavior disorder in children. *American Journal of Psychiatry,* 1956, **112,** 613–617.

Patterson, G. R., Ray, R. S., Shaw, D. A., & Cobb, J. *Manual for coding of family interactions.* New York: ASIS/NAPS, Microfiche Publications, 1969.

Patterson, G. R., Weiss, R. L., & Hops, H. Training of marital skills: Some problems and concepts. In H. Leitenberg (Ed.), *Handbook of behavior modification and behavior therapy.* Englewood Cliffs, N.J.: Prentice-Hall, 1976.

Paul, G. L. *Insight vs. desensitization in psychotherapy.* Stanford, Calif.: Stanford University Press, 1966.

Paul, G. L. Insight versus desensitization in psychotherapy two years after termination. *Journal of Consulting Psychology,* 1967, **31,** 333–348.

Paul, G. L. Chronic mental patient: Current status—future directions. *Psychological Bulletin,* 1969, **71,** 81–94.

Paul, G. L., & Lentz, R. J. *Psychosocial treatment of chronic mental patients: Milieu versus social learning programs.* Cambridge, Mass.: Harvard University Press, 1977.

Paul, G. L., & Shannon, D. T. Treatment of anxiety through systematic desensitization in therapy groups. *Journal of Abnormal Psychology,* 1966, **71,** 124–135.

Perls, F. S. *Gestalt therapy verbatim.* Moab, Utah: Real People Press, 1969.

Perls, F. S. Four lectures. In J. Fagan & I. L. Shepherd (Eds.), *Gestalt therapy now: Therapy, techniques, applications.* Palo Alto, Calif.: Science and Behavior Books, 1970.

Perls, F. S., Hefferline, R. F., & Goodman, P. *Gestalt therapy: Excitement and growth in the human personality.* New York: Julian Press, 1951.

Perris, L. The separation of bipolar (manic-depressive) from unipolar recurrent depressive psychoses. *Behavioral Neuropsychiatry,* 1969, **1,** 17–25.

Pervin, L. A. The need to predict and control under conditions of threat. *Journal of Personality,* 1963, **31,** 570–585.

Peters, J. E., & Stern, R. M. Specificity of attitude hypothesis in psychosomatic medicine: A reexamination. *Journal of Psychosomatic Research,* 1971, **15,** 129–135.

Pfeiffer, E., Eisenstein, R. B., & Dabbs, G. E. Mental competency evaluation for the federal courts: I. Methods and results. *Journal of Nervous and Mental Disease,* 1967, **144,** 320–328.

Phillips, E. L., Phillips, E. A., Fixsen, D. L., & Wolf, M. M. *The teaching-family handbook.* Lawrence, Kans.: Kansas Printing Service, 1972.

Phillips, L. Case history data and prognosis in schizophrenia. *Journal of Nervous and Mental Disease,* 1953, **117,** 515–525.

Piaget, J. *The origins of intelligence in children.* (2nd ed.) New York: International Universities Press, 1952.

Piaget, J. *The child's construction of reality.* London: Routledge and Kegan Paul, 1955.

Pinel, P. *A treatise on insanity,* 1801. English translation by D. D. Davis. New York: Hafner, 1962.

Pirsig, R. M. *Zen and the art of motorcycle maintenance: An inquiry into values.* New York: Morrow, 1974.

Pittman, D. J. The male house of prostitution. *Trans-Action,* 1971, **8,** 21–28.

Pokorny, A. D. Myths about suicide. In H. L. P. Resnik (Ed.), *Suicidal behaviors.* Boston: Little, Brown, 1968.

Pope, L. Motor activity in brain-injured children. *American Journal of Orthopsychiatry,* 1970, **40,** 761–770.

Post, R. M., Fink, E., Carpenter, W. T., & Goodwin, F. K. Cerebrospinal fluid amine metabolites in acute schizophrenia. *Archives of General Psychiatry,* 1975, **32,** 1063–1069.

Post, R. M., Kotin, J., Goodwin, F. K., & Gordon, E. K. Psychomotor activity and cerebrospinal fluid metabolites in affective illness. *American Journal of Psychiatry,* 1973, **129,** 67–72.

Prange, A. J., Wilson, I. C., Lynn, C. W., Alltop, L. B., Stikeleather, R. A., & Raleigh, N. C. L-Tryptophan in mania. *Archives of General Psychiatry,* 1974, **30,** 56–62.

Price, J. S. The genetics of depressive disorder. In A. Coppen & A. Walk (Eds.), *Recent developments in affective disorders.* British Journal of Psychiatry, Special Publication 2, 1968.

Price, R. H. *Abnormal behavior. Perspectives in conflict.* New York: Holt, Rinehart and Winston, 1972. (a)

Price, R. H. Psychological deficit versus impression management in schizophrenic word association performance. *Journal of Abnormal Psychology,* 1972, **79,** 123–137. (b)

Prien, R. F., Klett, C. J., & Caffey, E. M. Lithium carbonate and imipramine in prevention of effective episodes. *Archives of General Psychiatry,* 1973, **29,** 420–425.

Proctor, J. T. Hysteria in childhood. *American Journal of Orthopsychiatry,* 1958, **28,** 394–407.

Proshansky, H. M., Ittelson, W. M., & Rivlin, L. (Eds.) *Theory and research in environmental psychology.* New York: Holt, Rinehart and Winston, 1972.

*Public Hearing on the Problems of Deinstitutionalized Mental Patients in New York City, Transcript and Report.* New York: City Council, Olivieri and Stern, 1977.

Purcell, K., Brady, K., Chai, H., Muser, J., Molk, L., Gordon, N., & Means, J. The effect on asthma in children of experimental separation from the family. *Psychosomatic Medicine,* 1969, **31,** 144–164.

Purcell, K., & Weiss, J. H. Asthma. In C. G. Costello (Ed.), *Symptoms of psychopathology: A handbook.* New York: Wiley, 1970.

Quay, H. C. Psychopathic personality as pathological stimulus seeking. *American Journal of Psychiatry,* 1965, **122,** 180–183.

Rachman, S. Sexual fetishism: An experimental analogue. *Psychological Record,* 1966, **16,** 293–296.

Radloff, L. Sex differences in depression: The effects of occupation and marital status. *Sex Roles,* 1975, **1,** 249–265.

Rado, S. An adaptational view of sexual behavior. In P. Hoch & J. Zubin (Eds.), *Psychosexual development in health and disease.* New York: Grune and Stratton, 1949.

Rahe, R. H., & Holmes, T. H. Life crises and disease onset: A prospective study of life crises and health changes. Unpublished manuscript.

Rahe, R. H., & Lind, E. Psychosocial factors and sudden cardiac death: A pilot study. *Journal of Psychomatic Research,* 1971, **15,** 19–24.

Rapaport, D. *The organization and pathology of thought.* New York: Columbia University Press, 1951.

Rappaport, J. *Community psychology: Values, research, and action.* New York: Holt, Rinehart and Winston, 1977.

Rappaport, J., & Chinsky, J. M. Models for delivery of service from a historical and conceptual perspective. *Professional Psychology,* 1974, **5,** 42–50.

Rappaport, M. Competing voice messages: Effects of message load and drugs on the ability of acute schizophrenics to attend. *Archives of General Psychiatry,* 1967, **17,** 97–103.

Raskin, A., Schulterbrandt, J., Boothe, J., Reatig, N., & McKeon, J. Treatment, social and psychiatric variables related to symptom reduction in hospitalized depressives. In J. R. Wittenborn, S. Goldberg, & P. May (Eds.), *Psychopharmacology and the individual patient.* New York: Raven Press, 1970.

Rees, L. The significance of parental attitudes in childhood asthma. *Journal of Psychosomatic Research,* 1963, **7,** 181–190.

Rees, L. The significance of parental attitudes in childhood asthma. *Journal of Psychosomatic Research,* 1964, **7,** 253–262.

Regina v. Wilde (Central Criminal Court, Old Bailey, London, May 25, 1895). In H. Hyde (Ed.), *The Trials of Oscar Wilde.* New York: Dover, 1973.

Reid, E. C. Autopsychology of the manic-depressive. *Journal of Nervous and Mental Disease,* 1910, **37,** 606–620.

Reiss, A. J., Jr. The social integration of queers and peers. *Social Problems,* 1961, **9,** 102–120.

Reitan, R. M. Psychological deficits resulting from cerebral lesions in man. In J. M. Warren & K. Akert (Eds.), *The frontal granular cortex and behavior.* New York: McGraw-Hill, 1964.

Rescorla, R. A., & Solomon, R. L. Two-process learning theory: Relationships between Pavlovian conditioning and instrumental learning. *Psychological Review,* 1967, **74,** 151–182.

Resnik, H. L. P. (Ed.) *Suicidal behaviors.* Boston: Little, Brown, 1968.

Rich, A. R., & Schroeder, H. E. Research issues in assertiveness training. *Psychological Bulletin,* 1976, **83,** 1081–1096.

Richards, L. G., & Carroll, E. E. Illicit drug use and addiction in the United States: Review of available statistics. *Public Health Reports,* 1970, **85,** 1035–1041.

Richter, C. P. On the phenomenon of sudden death in animals and man. *Psychosomatic Medicine,* 1957, **19,** 191–198.

Ricks, D. M. The beginning of vocal communication in infants and autistic children. Unpublished dissertation, University of London, 1972.

Ridgeway, J. R. Who's fit to be free? *The New Republic,* 1967, **156,** 24–26.

Rimland, B. *Infantile autism.* New York: Appleton-Century-Crofts, 1964.

Rimland, B. Psychogenesis versus biogenesis: The issues and the evidence. In S. C. Plog & R. B. Edgerton (Eds.), *Changing perspectives in mental illness.* New York: Holt, Rinehart and Winston, 1969.

Rimland, B. The differentiation of childhood psychoses: An analysis of checklists for 2,218 psychotic children. *Journal of Autism and Childhood Schizophrenia,* 1971, **1,** 161–174.

Ringuette, E. L., & Kennedy, T. An experimental study of the double-bind hypothesis. *Journal of Abnormal Psychology,* 1966, **71,** 136–142.

Rizley, R. C. The perception of causality in depression: An attributional analysis of two cognitive theories of depression. Unpublished doctoral dissertation, Yale University, 1976.

Roback, H. B., McKee, E., & Webb, W. Psychopathology in female sex-change applicants and two help-seeking controls. *Journal of Abnormal Psychology,* in press.

Robbin, A. A. A controlled study of the effects of leucotomy. *Journal of Neurology, Neurosurgery, and Psychiatry,* 1958, **21,** 262–269.

Robbin, A. A. The value of leucotomy in relation to diagnosis. *Journal of Neurology, Neurosurgery, and Psychiatry,* 1959, **22,** 132–136.

Robey, A. Criteria for competency to stand trail: A checklist for psychiatrists. *American Journal of Psychiatry,* 1965, **122,** 616–622.

Robins, E., & Guze, S. Establishment of diagnostic validity in psychiatric illness: Its application to schizophrenia. *American Journal of Psychiatry,* 1970, **126,** 983–987.

Robins, L. N. *Deviant children grown up.* Baltimore, Md.: Williams and Wilkins, 1966.

Robinson, H. B., & Robinson, N. M. Mental retardation. In P. H. Mussen (Ed.), *Carmichael's manual of child psychology,* Vol. 2. (3rd ed.) New York: Wiley, 1970.

Robinson, N. M., & Robinson, H. B. *The mentally retarded child.* (2nd ed.) New York: McGraw-Hill, 1976.

Rodnick, E. H., & Garmezy, N. An experimental approach to the study of motivation in schizophrenia. In M. R. Jones (Ed.), *Nebraska symposium on motivation,* Vol. 5. Lincoln: University of Nebraska Press, 1957.

Rogers, C. R. *Counseling and psychotherapy: New concepts in practice.* Boston: Houghton Mifflin, 1942.

Rogers, C. R. *Client-centered therapy.* Boston: Houghton Mifflin, 1951.

Rogers, C. R. *On becoming a person: A therapist's view of psychotherapy.* Boston: Houghton Mifflin, 1961.

Rogers, C. R. *Carl Rogers on encounter groups.* New York: Harper and Row, 1970.

Rogers, C. R., Gendlin, G. T., Kiesler, D. V., & Truax, C. B. *The therapeutic relationship and its impact: A study of psychotherapy with schizophrenics.* Madison: University of Wisconsin Press, 1967.

Rokeach, M. *The three Christs of Ypsilanti.* New York: Knopf, 1964.

Rolf, J. E. The social and academic competence of children vulnerable to schizophrenia and other behavior disorders. *Journal of Abnormal Psychology,* 1972, **80,** 225–243.

Rosen, A., Hales, W. M., & Simon, W. Classification of suicidal patients. *Journal of Consulting Psychology,* 1954, **18,** 359–362.

Rosen, E., Fox, R., & Gregory, I. *Abnormal psychology.* (2nd ed.) Philadelphia: Saunders, 1972.

Rosenhan, D. L. On being sane in insane places. *Science,* 1973, **179,** 250–258.

Rosenthal, D. Changes in some moral values following psychotherapy. *Journal of Consulting Psychology,* 1955, **19,** 431–436.

Rosenthal, D. *Genetic theory and abnormal behavior.* New York: McGraw-Hill, 1970.

Rosenthal, R. *Experimenter bias in behavioral research.* New York: Appleton-Century-Crofts, 1966.

Rosenthal, R. Covert communication in the psychological experiment. *Psychological Bulletin,* 1967, **67,** 356–367.

Ross, A. O. *Psychological disorders of children: A behavioral approach to theory, research and therapy.* New York: McGraw-Hill, 1974.

Ross, D. M. Case study of a hyperactive four-year-old. Unpublished manuscript. Stanford University, 1961.

Ross, D. M., & Ross, S. A. *Hyperactivity: Research, theory, and action.* New York: Wiley, 1976.

Ross, S. M., & Proctor, S. Frequency and duration of hierarchy item exposure in a systematic desensitization analogue. *Behaviour Research and Therapy,* 1973, **11,** 309–312.

Roth, S., & Kubal, L. The effects of noncontingent reinforcement on tasks of differing importance: Facilitation and learned helplessness effects. *Journal of Personality and Social Psychology,* 1975, **32,** 680–691.

Rothman, D. *The discovery of the asylum.* New York: Harper and Row, 1971.

Rubin, V., & Comitas, L. *Ganja in Jamaica: A medical anthropological study of chronic marihuana use.* The Hague: Mouton, 1975.

Ruskin, A., Board, O. W., & Schaffer, R. L. Blast hypertension: Elevated arterial pressure in victims of the Texas City disaster. *American Journal of Medicine,* 1948, **4,** 228–236.

Russell, P. L., & Brandsma, J. M. A theoretical and empirical integration of the rational-emotive and classical conditioning theories. *Journal of Consulting and Clinical Psychology,* 1974, **42,** 389–397.

Rutter, M. The influence of organic and emotional factors on the origins, nature and outcome of childhood psychosis. *Developmental Medicine and Child Neurology,* 1965, **7,** 518–528.

Rutter, M. Prognosis: Psychotic children in adolescence and early adult life. In J. K. Wing (Ed.), *Childhood autism: Clinical, educational, and social aspects.* Elmsford, N.Y.: Pergamon Press, 1966.

Rutter, M. Psychotic disorders in early childhood. In A. J. Cooper (Ed.), *Recent developments in schizophrenia.* British Journal of Psychiatry, Special Publication 1, 1967.

Rutter, M. Concepts of autism: A review of research. *Journal of Child Psychology and Psychiatry,* 1968, **9,** 1–25.

Rutter, M. The development of infantile autism. *Psychological Medicine,* 1974, **4,** 147–163.

Rutter, M., & Lockyer, L. A five to fifteen year follow-up of infantile psychosis: I. Description of sample. *British Journal of Psychiatry,* 1967, **113,** 1169–1182.

Ryan, D. V., & Neale, J. M. Test taking sets and the performance of schizophrenics on laboratory tasks. *Journal of Abnormal Psychology,* 1973, **82,** 207–211.

Ryan, J. W., Steinberg, H. R., Green, R., Brown, J. D., & Durell, J. Controlled study of effects of plasma of schizophrenic and non-schizophrenic psychiatric patients on chicken erythrocytes. *Journal of Psychiatric Research,* 1968, **6,** 33–43.

Saghir, M. T., & Robins, E. Homosexuality: I. Sexual behavior of the female homosexual. *Archives of General Psychiatry,* 1969, **20,** 192–201.

Saghir, M. T., Robins, E., & Walbran, B. Homosexuality: II. Sexual behavior of the male homosexual. *Archives of General Psychiatry,* 1969, **21,** 219–229.

Salter, A. *Conditioned reflex therapy.* New York: Farrar, Straus, 1949.

Sandifer, M. G., Pettus, C., & Quade, D. A study of psychiatric diagnosis. *Journal of Nervous and Mental Disease,* 1964, **139,** 350–356.

Sarason, I. G. *Abnormal psychology: The problem of maladaptive behavior.* New York: Appleton-Century-Crofts, 1972.

Sarbin, T. R. Contributions to role-taking theory: I. Hypnotic behavior. *Psychological Review,* 1950, **57,** 255–270.

Sartorius, N., Shapiro, R., & Jablonsky, A. The international pilot study of schizophrenia. *Schizophrenia Bulletin,* 1974, **2,** 21–35.

Satterfield, J. H., Cantwell, D. P., Lesser, L. I., & Podosin, R. L. Physiological studies of the hyperactive child. *American Journal of Psychiatry,* 1972, **128,** 1418–1424.

Sawrey, W. L., & Weisz, J. D. An experimental method of producing gastric ulcers: Role of psychological factors in the production of gastric ulcers in the rat. *Journal of Comparative and Physiological Psychology,* 1956, **49,** 457–461.

Schachter, S. Nicotine regulation in heavy and light smokers. *Journal of Experimental Psychology General,* 1977, **106,** 5–12.

Schachter, S., Kozlowski, L. T., & Silverstein, B. Effects of urinary pH on cigarette smoking. *Journal of Experimental Psychology: General,* 1977, **106,** 13–19.

Schachter, S., & Latané, B. Crime, cognition, and the autonomic nervous system. In D. Levine (Ed.), *Nebraska symposium on motivation,* Vol. 12. Lincoln: University of Nebraska Press, 1964.

Schachter, S., Silverstein, B., Kozlowski, L. T., Herman, C. P., & Liebling, B. Effects of stress on cigarette smoking and urinary pH. *Journal of Experimental Psychology: General,* 1977, **106,** 24–30.

Schachter, S., Silverstein, B., & Perlik, D. Psychological and pharmacological explanations of smoking under stress. *Journal of Experimental Psychology: General,* 1977, **106,** 31–40.

Schain, R. J., & Reynard, C. L. Effects of a central stimulant drug (methylphenidate) in children with hyperactive behavior. *Pediatrics,* 1975, **55,** 709–716.

Scheerer, M., Rothman, E., & Goldstein, K. A case of "idiot savant": An experimental study of personality organization. *Psychological Monographs,* 1945, **58** (whole No. 269).

Schildkraut, J. J. The catecholamine hypothesis of affective disorders. *American Journal of Psychiatry,* 1965, **122,** 509–522.

Schmauk, F. J. Punishment, arousal, and avoidance learning in sociopaths. *Journal of Abnormal Psychology,* 1970, **76,** 443–453.

Schneider, K. *Clinical psychopathology.* New York: Grune and Stratton, 1959.

Schulsinger, F. Psychopathy: Heredity and environment. *International Journal of Mental Health,* 1972, **1,** 190–206.

Schur, E. M. Drug addiction in England and America. In D. Wakefield (Ed.), *The Addict.* Greenwich, Conn.: Fawcett Publications, 1965.

Schutz, W. C. *Joy.* New York: Grove Press, 1967.

Schwartz, G. E. Biofeedback as therapy: Some theoretical and practical issues. *American Psychologist,* 1973, **28,** 666–673.

Schwartz, M. A., Wyatt, R. J., Yang, H., & Neff, N. Multiple forms of monoamine oxidase in brain: A comparison of enzymatic activity in mentally normal and chronic schizophrenic individuals. *Archives of General Psychiatry,* 1974, **31,** 557–560.

Schwartz, M. S. The economic and spatial mobility of paranoid schizophrenics. Unpublished M.A. thesis, University of Chicago, 1946.

Schwartz, R. M., & Gottman, J. M. Toward a task analysis of assertive behavior. *Journal of Consulting and Clinical Psychology,* 1976, **44,** 910–920.

Sears, R. R., Maccoby, E. E., & Levin, H. *Patterns of child rearing.* Evanston, Ill.: Row, Peterson, 1957.

Segovia-Riquelma, N., Varela, A., & Mardones, J. Appetite for alcohol. In Y. Israel & J. Mardones (Eds.), *Biological basis of alcoholism.* New York: Wiley, 1971.

Seiden, R. H. Suicide: Preventable death. *Public Affairs Report,* 1974, **15,** 1–5.

Seligman, M. E. P. Phobias and preparedness. *Behavior Therapy,* 1971, **2,** 307–320.

Seligman, M. E. P. Fall into helplessness. *Psychology Today,* June 1973, **7,** 43–48.

Seligman, M. E. P. Depression and learned helplessness. In R. J. Friedman & M. M. Katz (Eds.), *The psychology of depression: Contemporary theory and research.* Washington, D.C.: Winston-Wiley, 1974.

Seligman, M. E. P. *Helplessness.* San Francisco: W. H. Freeman, 1975.

Seligman, M. E. P., & Hager, M. (Eds.) *Biological boundaries of learning.* New York: Appleton-Century-Crofts, 1972.

Selling, L. S. *Men against madness.* New York: Greenberg, Publisher, 1940.

Selye, H. *The stress of life.* New York: McGraw-Hill, 1956.

Serber, M. The experiential group as entertainment. In P. S. Houts & M. Serber (Eds.), *After the turn-on, what? Learning perspectives on humanistic groups.* Champaign, Ill.: Research Press, 1972.

Shaffer, H. R., & Emerson, P. E. Patterns of response to physical contact in early human development. *Journal of Child Psychology and Psychiatry,* 1964, **5,** 1–13.

Shakow, D. Segment set. *Archives of General Psychiatry,* 1962, **6,** 1–17.

Shakow, D. Psychological deficit in schizophrenia. *Behavioral Science,* 1963, **8,** 275–305.

Shapiro, A. K. A contribution to a history of the placebo effect. *Behavioral Science,* 1960, **5,** 109–135.

Shapiro, A. P. An experimental study of comparative responses of blood pressure to different noxious stimuli. *Journal of Chronic Diseases,* 1961, **13,** 293–311.

Shapiro, D., & Surwit, R. S. Learned control of physiological function and disease. In H. Leitenberger (Eds.), *Handbook of behavior modification and behavior therapy.* Englewood Cliffs, N.J.: Prentice-Hall, 1976.

Shapiro, D., Tursky, B., & Schwartz, G. E. Control of blood pressure in man by operant conditioning. *Circulation Research,* 1970, **26,** 127–132.

Sherman, A. R. Real-life exposure as a primary therapeutic factor in the desensitization treatment of fear. *Journal of Abnormal Psychology,* 1972, **79,** 19–28.

Shevitz, S. A. Psychosurgery: Some current observations. *American Journal of Psychiatry,* 1976, **133,** 266–270.

Shneidman, E. S. Suicide. In *Encyclopedia Britannica.* Chicago: Encyclopedia Britannica, 1973.

Shneidman, E. S., & Farberow, N. L. A psychological approach to the study of suicide notes. In E. S. Shneidman, N. L. Farberow, & R. E. Litman (Eds.), *The psychology of suicide.* New York: Jason Aronson, 1970.

Shneidman, E. S., Farberow, N. L., & Litman, R. E. (Eds.) *The psychology of suicide.* New York: Jason Aronson, 1970.

Shopsin, B., Friedman, E., & Gershon, S. Parachlorophenylalanine reversal of tranylcypromine effects in depressed patients. *Archives of General Psychiatry,* 1976, **33,** 811–819.

Silverstein, B., Kozlowski, L. T., & Schachter, S. Social life, cigarette smoking, and urinary pH. *Journal of Experimental Psychology: General,* 1977, **106,** 20–23.

Silverstein, C. Behavior modification and the gay community. Paper presented at the annual convention of the Association for Advancement of Behavior Therapy, New York City, 1972.

Simeons, A. T. W. *Man's presumptuous brain: An evolutionary interpretation of psychosomatic disease.* New York: Dutton, 1961.

Simon, W., & Gagnon, J. H. Psychosexual development. In J. H. Gagnon & W. Simon (Eds.), *The sexual scene.* Chicago: Aldine, 1970.

Simon, W., & Gilberstadt, H. Analysis of the personality structure of 26 actual suicides. *Journal of Nervous and Mental Disease,* 1958, **127,** 555–557.

Singer, M., & Wynne, L. C. Differentiating characteristics of the parents of childhood schizophrenics, childhood neurotics, and young adult schizophrenics. *American Journal of Psychiatry,* 1963, **120,** 234–243.

Sintchak, G. H., & Geer, J. H. A vaginal plethysmograph system. *Psychophysiology,* 1975, **12,** 113–115.

Sizemore, C. C., & Pittillo, E. S. *I'm Eve.* Garden City, N.Y.: Doubleday, 1977.

Skinner, B. F. *Science and human behavior.* New York: Macmillan, 1953.

Skinner, B. F. "Superstition" in the pigeon. *Journal of Experimental Psychology,* 1948, **38,** 168–172.

Skinner, H. A., Jackson, D. N., & Hoffman, H. Alcoholic personality types: Identification and correlates. *Journal of Abnormal Psychology,* 1974, **83,** 658–666.

Skrzypek, G. J. The effects of perceptual isolation and arousal on anxiety, complexity perference and novelty preference in psychopathic and neurotic delinquents. *Journal of Abnormal Psychology,* 1969, **74,** 321–329.

Slater, E. Erbpathologie des manisch-depressiven irreseins, Die Eltern und Kinder von Manisch-Depressiven. *Zeitschrift für die gesarnte Neurologie und Psychiatrie,* 1938, **163,** 1–47.

Slater, E. The thirty-fifth Maudsley lecture: Hysteria 311. *Journal of Mental Science,* 1961, **107,** 358–381.

Slater, E., & Glithero, E. A follow-up of patients diagnosed as suffering from hysteria. *Journal of Psychosomatic Research,* 1965, **9,** 9–13.

Slater, E., & Shields, J. Genetic aspects of anxiety. In M. H. Lader (Ed.), *Studies of anxiety.* Ashford, England: Headley Brothers, 1969.

Slavson, S. R. *Analytic group psychotherapy with children, adolescents and adults.* New York: Columbia University Press, 1950.

Sloane, R. B., Staples, F. R., Cristol, A. H., Yorkston, N. J., & Whipple, K. *Psychoanalysis versus behavior therapy.* Cambridge: Harvard University Press, 1975.

Smith, B. H. *Principles of clinical neurology.* Chicago: Year Book Medical Publishers, 1965.

Smith, P. B. Controlled studies of the outcome of sensitivity training. *Psychological Bulletin,* 1975, **82,** 597–622.

Snyder, S. H. *Madness and the brain.* New York: McGraw-Hill, 1974.

Snyder, S. H. The dopamine hypothesis of schizophrenia. *American Journal of Psychiatry,* 1976, **133,** 197–202.

Snyder, S. H., Banerjee, S. P., Yamamura, H. I., & Greenberg, D. Drugs, neurotransmitters, and schizophrenia. *Science,* 1974, **184,** 1243–1253.

Sommer, R. *Personal space: The behavioral basis of design.* Englewood Cliffs, N.J.: Prentice-Hall, 1969.

Spanos, N. P. Barber's reconceptualization of hypnosis: An evaluation of criticisms. *Journal of Experimental Research in Personality,* 1970, **4,** 241–258.

Speer, D. C. Rate of caller re-use of a telephone crisis service. *Crisis Intervention,* 1971, **3,** 83–86.

Speer, D. C. An evaluation of a telephone crisis service. Paper presented at the Midwestern Psychological Association meeting, Cleveland, Ohio, 1972.

Sperling, M. Conversion hysteria and conversion symptoms: A revision of classification and concepts. *Journal of the American Psychoanalytic Association,* 1973, **21,** 745–771.

Spitzer, R. L. On pseudoscience in science, logic in remission, and psychiatric diagnosis: A critique of Rosenhan's "On being sane in insane places." *Journal of Abnormal Psychology,* 1975, **84,** 442–452.

Spitzer, R. L. Personal communication, 1976.

Spitzer, R. L., & Endicott, J. Diagno. II: Further developments in a computer program for psychiatric diagnosis. *American Journal of Psychiatry,* 1969, **125,** 12–21.

Spitzer, R. L., Endicott, J., & Robins, E. *Research diagnostic criteria.* New York: Biometrics Research, 1975.

Spitzer, R. L., Endicott, J., Robins, E., Kuriansky, J., & Gurland, B. Preliminary report of the reliability of research diagnostic criteria applied to psychiatric records. In A. Sudilofsky, B. Beer, & S. Gershon (Eds.), *Prediction in psychopharmacology.* New York: Raven Press, 1976.

Spring, G., Schweid, D., Gray, G., Steinberg, J., & Horwitz, M. A double-blind comparison of lithium and chlorpromazine in the treatment of manic states. *American Journal of Psychiatry,* 1970, **126,** 1306–1309.

Srole, L., Langner, T. S., Michael, S. T., Opler, M. K., & Rennie, T. A. C. *Mental health in the metropolis: The midtown Manhattan study.* New York: McGraw-Hill, 1962.

Sroufe, L. A. Drug treatment of children with behavior problems. In F. Horowitz (Ed.), *Review of child development research.* Chicago: University of Chicago Press, 1975.

Staats, A. W., & Staats, C. K. *Complex human behavior.* New York: Holt, Rinehart and Winston, 1963.

Stampfl, T. C., & Levis, D. J. Essentials of implosive therapy: A learning-therapy-based psychodynamic behavior therapy. *Journal of Abnormal Psychology,* 1967, **72,** 496–503.

Stang, R. R. The etiology of Parkinson's disease. *Diseases of the Nervous System,* 1970, **31,** 381–390.

Stanton, A. H., & Schwartz, M. S. *The mental hospital.* New York: Basic Books, 1954.

Stanton, M. D., & Bardoni, A. Drug flashbacks: Reported frequency in a military population. *American Journal of Psychiatry,* 1972, **129,** 751–755.

Staub, E., Tursky, B., & Schwartz, G. E. Self-control and predictability: Their effects on reactions to aversive stimulation. *Journal of Personality and Social Psychology,* 1971, **18,** 157–162.

Stearns, J. *The sixth man.* New York: Macfadden-Bartell, 1961.

Steele, R. S. The physiological concomitants of psychogenic motive arousal in college males. Unpublished doctoral dissertation, Harvard University, 1973.

Stephens, J. H., & Kamp, M. On some aspects of hysteria: A clinical study. *Journal of Nervous and Mental Disease,* 1962, **134,** 305–315.

Sterman, H. B. Neurophysiologic and clinical studies of sensorimotor EEG biofeedback training: Some effects on epilepsy. *Seminars in Psychiatry,* 1973, **5,** 507–525.

Sternbach, R. A. *Principles of psychophysiology.* New York: Academic Press, 1966.

Stewart, M. A., Pitts, F. N., Craig, A. G., & Dieruf, W. The hyperactive child syndrome. *American Journal of Orthopsychiatry,* 1966, **36,** 861–867.

Stoller, F. H. Accelerated interaction: A time-limited approach based on the brief intensive group. *International Journal of Group Psychotherapy,* 1968, **18,** 220–235.

Stone, A. A. *Mental health and law: A system in transition.* Rockville, Md.: National Institute of Mental Health, 1975.

Stone, L. J., & Hokanson, J. E. Arousal reduction via self-punitive behavior. *Journal of Personality and Social Psychology,* 1969, **12,** 72–79.

Stuart, R. B. Operant-interpersonal treatment for marital discord. *Journal of Consulting and Clinical Psychology,* 1969, **33,** 675–682.

Stuart, R. B. Teaching facts about drugs: Pushing or preventing. *Journal of Educational Psychology,* 1974, **66,** 189–201.

Stuart, R. B. Protection of the right to informed consent to participate in research. *Behavior Therapy,* in press.

Sturgis, E. T., & Adams, H. E. The right to treatment: Issues in the treatment of homosexuality. *Journal of Consulting and Clinical Psychology,* in press.

Sullivan, H. S. *The interpersonal theory of psychiatry.* New York: Norton, 1953.

Surwit, R. S., & Shapiro, D. Cardiovascular biofeedback, muscle activity biofeedback and relaxation-meditation in the treatment of borderline hypertension. Paper presented at the annual meeting of the American Psychosomatic Society, March 26–28, 1976.

Szasz, T. S. The myth of mental illness. *American Psychologist,* 1960, **15,** 113–118.

Szasz, T. S. *Law, liberty, and psychiatry.* New York: Macmillan, 1963.

Szasz, T. S. (Ed.) *The age of madness: The history of involuntary hospitalization.* New York: Jason Aronson, 1974.

Tate, B. G., & Baroff, G. S. Aversive control of self-injurious behavior in a psychotic boy. *Behaviour Research and Therapy,* 1966, **4,** 281–287.

Taterks, S., & Kety, S. S. Study of correlation between electroencephalogram and psychological patterns in emotionally disturbed children. *Psychosomatic Medicine,* 1955, **17,** 62–72.

Taylor, J. A. A personality scale of manifest anxiety. *Journal of Abnormal and Social Psychology,* 1953, **48,** 285–290.

Taylor, J. K., & Hirt, M. Irrelevance of retention interval length and distractor-task similarity in schizophrenic cognitive interference. *Journal of Consulting and Clinical Psychology,* 1975, **43,** 281–285.

Terman, L. M. Kinsey's *Sexual Behavior in the Human Male:* Some comments and criticisms. *Psychological Bulletin,* 1948, **45,** 443–459.

Terry, B., & Wisniewski, H. Sans teeth, sans eyes, sans taste, sans everything. *Behavior Today,* March 25, 1974, **5,** 84.

Theodor, L. H., & Mandelcorn, M. S. Hysterical blindness: A case report and study using a modern psychophysical technique. *Journal of Abnormal Psychology,* 1973, **82,** 552–553.

Thigpen, C. H., & Cleckley, H. *The three faces of Eve.* Kingsport, Tenn.: Kingsport Press, 1954.

Thorndike, E. L. *The psychology of wants, interests and attitudes.* New York: Appleton, Century, 1935.

Tollefson, D. J. The relationship between the occurrence of fractures and life crisis events. Unpublished master of nursing thesis, University of Washington, Seattle, 1972.

Tramontana, J., & Stimbert, V. Some techniques of behavior modification with an autistic child. *Psychological Reports,* 1970, **27,** 498.

Treffert, D. A. The epidemiology of infantile autism. *Archives of General Psychiatry,* 1970, **22,** 431–438.

Treffert, D. A., McAndrew, J. B., & Dreifuerst, P. An inpatient treatment program and outcome for 57 autistic and schizophrenic children. *Journal of Autism and Childhood Schizophrenia,* 1973, **3,** 138–153.

Truax, C. B. Reinforcement and nonreinforcement in Rogerian psychotherapy. *Journal of Abnormal Psychology,* 1966, **71,** 1–9.

Truax, C. B., & Mitchell, K. M. Research on certain therapist interpersonal skills in relation to process and outcome. In A. E. Bergin & S. L. Garfield (Eds.), *Handbook of psychotherapy and behavior change.* New York: Wiley, 1971.

Tuckman, J., Kleiner, R. J., & Lavell, M. Emotional content of suicide notes. *American Journal of Psychiatry,* 1959, **116,** 59–63.

Turner, R. J., & Wagonfeld, M. O. Occupational mobility and schizophrenia. *American Sociological Review,* 1967, **32,** 104–113.

Ullman, L., & Krasner, L. *A psychological approach to abnormal behavior.* (2nd ed.) Englewood Cliffs, N.J.: Prentice-Hall, 1975.

Umbarger, C. C., Dalsimer, J. S., Morrison, A. P., & Breggin, P. R. *College students in a mental hospital.* New York: Grune and Stratton, 1962.

United States Department of Health, Education and Welfare. *Smoking and health.* Public Health Service Publication 1103. Washington, D.C.: U.S. Government Printing Office, 1964.

Valenstein, E. S. *Brain control.* New York: Wiley, 1973.

Van Praag, H., Korf, J., & Schut, D. Cerebral monamines and depression: An investigation with the probenecid technique. *Archives of General Psychiatry,* 1973, **28,** 827–831.

Von Felsinger, J. M., Lasagna, L., & Beecher, H. K. The response of normal men to lysergic acid derivatives. *Journal of Clinical and Experimental Psychopathology,* 1956, **17,** 414–428.

Von Wright, J. M., Pekanmaki, L., & Malin, S. Effects of conflict and stress on alcohol intake in rats. *Quarterly Journal of Studies on Alcohol,* 1971, **32,** 420–441.

Wachtel, P. *Psychoanalysis and behavior therapy: Toward an integration.* New York: Basic Books, 1977.

Waldfogel, S. Emotional crisis in a child. In A. Burton (Ed.), *Case studies in counseling and psychotherapy,* Englewood Cliffs, N.J.: Prentice-Hall, 1959.

Wallen, R. Gestalt therapy and Gestalt psychology. In J. Fagan & I. L. Shepherd (Eds.), *Gestalt therapy now: Theory, techniques, applications.* Palo Alto, Calif.: Science and Behavior Books, 1970.

Wallerstein, R. S. et al. *Hospital treatment of alcoholism: A comparative, experimental study.* New York: Basic Books, 1957.

Walters, C., Shurley, J. T., & Parsons, O. A. Difference in male and female responses to underwater sensory deprivation: An exploratory study. *Journal of Nervous and Mental Disease,* 1962, **135,** 302–310.

Ward, C. H., Beck, A. T., Mendelson, M., Mock, J. E., & Erbaugh, J. K. The psychiatric nomenclature: Reasons for diagnostic disagreement. *Archives of General Psychiatry,* 1962, **7,** 198–205.

Waters, W. F., McDonald, D. G., & Koresko, R. L. Psychophysiological responses during analogue systematic desensitization and nonrelation control procedures. *Behaviour Research and Therapy,* 1972, **10,** 381–399.

Watson, J. B. Psychology as the behaviorist views it. *Psychological Review,* 1913, **20,** 158–177.

Watson, J. B., & Rayner, R. Conditioned emotional reactions. *Journal of Experimental Psychology,* 1920, **3,** 1–14.

Watt, N. F., Stolorow, R. D., Lubensky, A. W., & McClelland, D. C. School adjustment and behavior of children hospitalized for schizophrenia as adults. *American Journal of Orthopsychiatry,* 1970, **40,** 637–657.

Webb, W. W. Conceptual ability of schizophrenics as a function of threat of failure. *Journal of Abnormal and Social Psychology,* 1955, **50,** 221–224.

Weinberg, G. *Society and the healthy homosexual.* New York: St. Martin's Press, 1972.

Weinberg, M. S. The male homosexual: Age-related variations in social and psychological characteristics. *Social Problems,* 1970, **17,** 527–537.

Weiner, B., Frieze, I., Kukla, A., Reed, L., Rest, S., & Rosenbaum, R. M. *Perceiving the causes of success and failure.* New York: General Learning Press, 1971.

Weiner, H., Thaler, M., Reiser, M. F., & Mirsky, I. A. Etiology of duodenal ulcer: I. Relation of specific psychological characteristics to rate of gastric secretion. *Psychosomatic Medicine,* 1957, **17,** 1–10.

Weiner, J. W. The effectiveness of a suicide prevention program. *Mental Hygiene,* 1969, **53,** 357–363.

Weintraub, S., Liebert, D., & Neale, J. M. Teacher ratings of children vulnerable to psychopathology. *American Journal of Orthopsychiatry,* 1975, **45,** 838–845.

Weiss, G., Minde, K., Werry, J. S., Douglas, V., & Nemeth, E. Studies on the hyperactive child: VIII. Five-year follow-up. *Archives of General Psychiatry,* 1971, **24,** 409–414.

Weiss, R. L., Hops, H., & Patterson, G. R. A framework for conceptualizing marital conflict: A technology for altering it, some data for evaluating it. In L. A. Hamerlynck, L. G. Handy, & E. J. Mash (Eds.), *Behavior change: The Fourth Banff Conference on Behavior Modification.* Champaign, Ill.: Research Press, 1973.

Weitzenhoffer, A. M., & Hilgard, E. R. *Stanford hypnotic susceptibility scale, Forms A and B.* Palo Alto, Calif.: Consulting Psychologists Press, 1959.

Wender, P. H., Rosenthal, R., Kety, S. S., Schulsinger, S., & Welner, J. Cross-fostering: A research strategy for clarifying the role of genetic and experiential factors in the etiology of schizophrenia. *Archives of General Psychiatry,* 1974, **30,** 121–128.

Werry, J. S., Weiss, G., & Douglas, V. Studies on the hyperactive child: I. Some preliminary findings. *Canadian Psychiatric Association Journal,* 1964, **9,** 120–130.

West, D. J. *Homosexuality.* Chicago: Aldine, 1967.

Wexler, D. B. Token and taboo: Behavior modification, token economies, and the law. *California Law Review,* 1973, **61,** 81–109.

White, W. A. *Outlines of psychiatry.* (13th ed.) New York: Nervous and Mental Disease Publishing Company, 1932.

Whitlock, F. A. The aetiology of hysteria. *Acta Psychiatrica Scandinavica,* 1967, **43,** 144–162.

Wickens, D. D., Allen, C. K., & Hill, F. A. Effects of instruction on extinction of the conditioned GSR. *Journal of Experimental Psychology,* 1963, **66,** 235–240.

Widom, C. S. A methodology for studying noninstitutionalized psychopaths. *Journal of Consulting and Clinical Psychology,* 1977, **45,** 674–683.

Wiener, G. Varying psychological sequelae of lead ingestion in children. *Public Health Reports,* 1970, **85,** 19–24.

Wiggins, J. Inconsistent socialization. *Psychological Reports,* 1968, **23,** 303–336.

Wilkins, R. H., & Brody, I. A. Alzheimer's disease. *Archives of Neurology,* 1969, **21,** 109–110.

Williams, H., & McNicol, K. N. Prevalence, natural history and relationship of wheezy bronchitis and asthma in children: An epidemiological study. *British Medical Journal,* 1969, **4,** 321–325.

Williams, R. J. Biochemical individuality and cellular nutrition. Prime factors in alcoholism. *Quarterly Journal of Studies on Alcohol,* 1959, **20,** 452–463.

Williams, W. S., & Jaco, E. G. An evaluation of functional

psychosis in old age. *American Journal of Psychiatry,* 1958, **110,** 910–916.

Wilson, G. T., & Davison, G. C. Aversion techniques in behavior therapy: Some theoretical and metatheoretical considerations. *Journal of Consulting and Clinical Psychology,* 1969, **33,** 327–329.

Wilson, G. T., & Davison, G. C. Processes of fear reduction in systematic desensitization: Animal studies. *Psychological Bulletin,* 1971, **76,** 1–14.

Wilson, G. T., & Lawson, D. M. The effects of alcohol on sexual arousal in women. *Journal of Abnormal Psychology,* 1976, **85,** 489–497.

Winett, R. A., & Winkler, R. C. Current behavior modification in the classroom: Be still, be quiet, be docile. *Journal of Applied Behavior Analysis,* 1972, **5,** 499–504.

Wing, J., Birley, J. L. T., Cooper, J. C., Graham, P., & Isaacs, A. D. Reliability of a procedure for measuring and classifying "present psychiatric state." *British Journal of Psychiatry,* 1967, **113,** 499–506.

Wing, L. The handicaps of autistic children: A comparative study. *Journal of Child Psychology and Psychiatry,* 1969, **10,** 1–40.

Wing, L. The syndrome of early childhood autism. *British Journal of Hospital Medicine,* September 1970, 381–392.

Winick, M., Rosso, P., & Waterlow, J. Cellular growth of cerebrum, cerebellum, and brain stem in normal and marasmic children. *Experimental Neurology,* 1970, **26,** 393–400.

Winokur, G., & Clayton, P. Family history studies: I. Two types of affective disorders separated according to genetic and clinical factors. In J. Wortis (Ed.), *Recent advances in biological psychiatry,* Vol. 9. New York: Plenum Press, 1967.

Winokur, G., Clayton, P. J., & Reich, T. *Manic-depressive illness.* St. Louis: Mosby, 1969.

Witkin, H. A., Mednick, S. A., Schulsinger, F., Bakkestrøm, E., Christiansen, K. O., Goodenough, D. R., Hirschhorn, K., Lundsteen, C., Owen, D. R., Philip, J., Rubin, D. B., & Stocking, M. Criminality in XYY and XXY men. *Science,* 1976, **193,** 547–555.

Wittman, C. Refugees from Amerika: A gay manifesto. *San Francisco Free Press,* January 7, 1970.

Wolberg, L. R. *The technique of psychotherapy.* New York: Grune and Stratton, 1954.

Wold, D. A. The adjustment of siblings to childhood leukemia. Unpublished medical thesis, University of Washington, Seattle, 1968.

Wolf, A. The psychoanalysis of group. *American Journal of Psychotherapy,* 1949, **3,** 16–50.

Wolf, M., Risley, T., & Mees, H. Application of operant conditioning procedures to the behavior problems of an autistic child. *Behaviour Research and Therapy,* 1964, **1,** 305–312.

Wolf, S., & Goodell, H., *Harold G. Wolff's stress and disease.* (2nd ed.) Springfield, Ill.: Charles C Thomas, 1968.

Wolpe, J. *Psychotherapy by reciprocal inhibition.* Stanford, Calif.: Stanford University Press, 1958.

Wolpe, J. *The practice of behavior therapy.* Elmsford, N.Y.: Pergamon Press, 1969.

Wolpe, J., & Lazarus, A. A. *Behavior therapy techniques: A guide to the treatment of neuroses.* Elmsford, N.Y.: Pergamon Press, 1966.

Wolpe, J., & Rachman, S. Psychoanalytic "evidence," a critique based on Freud's case of Little Hans. *Journal of Nervous and Mental Disease,* 1960, **131,** 135–147.

Woodruff, R. A., Clayton, P. J., & Guze, S. B. Hysteria: Studies of diagnosis, outcome and prevalence. *Journal of the American Medical Association,* 1971, **215,** 425–428.

Woodruff, R. A., Clayton, P. J., & Guze, S. B. Is everyone depressed? *American Journal of Psychiatry,* 1975, **132,** 627–628.

Woodruff, R. A., Goodwin, D. W., & Guze, S. B. *Psychiatric Diagnosis.* New York: Oxford University Press, 1974.

Wortis, J., Sersen, E. A., Floistad, I., & Astrup, C. Childhood and adult schizophrenia: Some clinical and experimental comparisons. *Pavlovian Journal of Biological Science,* 1974, **9,** 149–159.

Yablonsky, L. The anti-criminal society: Synanon. *Federal Probation,* 1962, **26,** 50–57.

Yablonsky, L. *Synanon: The tunnel back.* Baltimore: Penguin, 1967.

Yalom, I. D., & Lieberman, M. A. A study of encounter group casualities. *Archives of General Psychiatry,* 1971, **25,** 16–30.

Yates, A. J. *Behavior therapy.* New York: Wiley, 1970.

Yates, A. J. *Theory and practice in behavior therapy.* New York: Wiley, 1975.

Yurchenco, H. *A mighty hard road: The Woody Guthrie Story.* New York: McGraw-Hill, 1970.

Yuwiler, A., Ritvo, E., Geller, E., Glousman, R., Scheiderman, G., & Matsuno, D. Uptake and efflux of serotonin from platelets of autistic and nonautistic children. *Journal of Autism and Childhood Schizophrenia,* 1975, **5,** 83–98.

Zaslow, R. W., & Breger, L. A theory and treatment of autism. In L. Breger (Ed.), *Clinical cognitive psychology.* Englewood Cliffs, N.J.: Prentice-Hall, 1969..

Zerbin-Rudin, E. Endogene Psychosen. In P. Becker (Ed.), *Humangenetik: Ein kurzes handbuch in fünf banden,* Vol. 2. Stuttgart: Verlag, 1967.

Ziegler, F. J., Imboden, J. B., & Meyer, E. Contemporary conversion reactions: A clinical study. *American Journal of Psychiatry,* 1960, **116,** 901–910.

Zigler, E. Mental retardation. In P. London & D. Rosenhan (Eds.), *Foundations of abnormal psychology.* New York: Holt, Rinehart and Winston, 1968.

Zigler, E. Development versus difference theories of mental retardation and the problem of motivation. *American Journal of Mental Deficiency,* 1969, **73,** 536–556.

Zigler, E., Butterfield, E. C., & Capobianco, F. Institutionalization and the effectiveness of social reinforcement: A five- and eight-year follow-up study. *Developmental Psychology,* 1970, **3,** 255–263.

Zigler, E., & Phillips, L. Psychiatric diagnosis and symptomatology. *Journal of Abnormal and Social Psychology,* 1961, **63,** 69–75.

Zilboorg, G., & Henry, G. W. *A history of medical psychology.* New York: Norton, 1941.

Zung, W. W. K. A self-rating depression scale. *Archives of General Psychiatry,* 1965, **12,** 63–70.

# GLOSSARY

**Acetylcholine.** A *neurotransmitter*[1] of the central, somatomotor, and *parasympathetic* nervous systems and in the ganglia and the *neuron*–sweat gland junctions of the *sympathetic*.

**Acute schizophrenic.** Patient who has shown a rapid onset of schizophrenic behavior and has had little hospitalization.

**Addiction.** See *drug addiction*.

**Addison's disease.** An endocrine disorder produced by *cortisone*[1] insufficiency and marked by weight loss, fatigue, and a darkening of the skin.

**Adrenal glands.** Two small areas of tissue, located just above the kidneys; the inner core of each gland, the medulla, secretes *epinephrine* and *norepinephrine,* the outer cortex, *cortisone* and other steroid hormones.

**Adrenaline.** A hormone which is secreted by the *adrenal glands;* also called *epinephrine.*

**Adrenergic system.** All the nerve cells for which *norepinephrine* and *epinephrine* (and more broadly, other *monoamines, dopamine* and *serotonin*) are the transmitter substances, as opposed to the *cholinergic,* which consists of the nerve cells activated by *acetylcholine.*

**Affect.** A subjective feeling or emotional tone often accompanied by bodily expressions noticeable to others.

**Affective disorder.** A *psychosis* characterized by disabling mood disturbances.

**Affirming the consequent.** An error in logic by which, if A causes B on one occasion, it is assumed that A is the cause when B is observed on any other occasion.

**Agoraphobia.** A cluster of fears centering around being in open spaces and leaving the home.

**Alcoholism.** A behavioral disorder marked by continuous and excessive consumption of alcoholic beverages; a physiological dependence on alcohol. See *drug addiction.*

**Alkaloid.** Organic base found in seed plants, usually in mixture with a number of similar alkaloids; alkaloids are the active chemicals giving many drugs their medicinal properties and other powerful physiological effects.

**Alpha rhythm.** The dominant pattern (8 to 13 cps) of the *brain waves* of a resting but awake adult.

**Altruistic suicide.** As defined by Durkheim, self-annihilation that the person feels will serve a social purpose, such as the self-immolations practiced by Buddhist monks during the Vietnam war.

[1] Italicized words or variants of these terms are themselves defined elsewhere in the glossary.

**Alzheimer's disease.** A *presenile dementia* involving a progressive atrophy of cortical tissue and marked by speech impairment, involuntary movements of limbs, occasional *convulsions,* intellectual deterioration, and psychoticisms.

**Ambivalence.** The simultaneous holding of strong positive and negative emotional attitudes toward the same situation or person.

**American Law Institute Guidelines.** Rules proposing insanity to be a legitimate defense plea if during criminal conduct individual could not judge right from wrong or control his behavior as required by law. Repetitive criminal acts are disavowed as a sole criterion. Compare *McNaghten rule* and *irresistible impulse.*

**Amino acid.** One of a large class of organic compounds, important as the building blocks of proteins.

**Amnesia.** Total or partial loss of memory which can be associated with *hysteria,* an *organic brain syndrome,* or *hypnosis.* **Anterograde,** loss of memory for events that have just occurred. **Retrograde,** loss of memory for events immediately preceding a traumatic incident; and sometimes for events extending far back in time.

**Amphetamines.** A group of stimulating drugs which produce heightened levels of energy and, in large doses, nervousness, sleeplessness, and paranoid *delusions.*

**Anaclitic depression.** Profound sadness of an infant when separated from its mother for a prolonged period.

**Anal stage.** In psychoanalytic theory, the second *psychosexual stage,* occurring during the second year of life, during which the anus is considered to be the principal *erogenous zone.*

**Analgesia.** Insensitivity to pain without loss of consciousness; sometimes found in *hysterical conversion reaction.*

**Analogue experiment.** Experimental study of a phenomenon different from but related to the actual interests of the investigator.

**Analysand.** A person being psychoanalyzed.

**Analyst.** See *psychoanalyst.*

**Anesthesia.** Impairment or loss of sensation, usually of touch but sometimes of the other senses; often part of *hysterical conversion reaction.*

**Animal phobias.** Fear and avoidance of small animals.

**Anomic suicide.** As defined by Durkheim, self-annihilation triggered by the person's inability to cope with sudden and unfavorable change in his social situation.

**Anorexia.** A *psychophysiological disorder* characterized by the inability to eat or to retain any food or by a prolonged and severe diminution of appetite.

**Anoxia.** Deficiency in oxygen reaching the tissues severe enough to damage the brain permanently.

**Antabuse** (disulfiram). A drug which makes the drinking of alcohol produce nausea and other unpleasant effects.

**Anterograde amnesia.** Inability to form new memories after the brain has been damaged.

**Antidepressant.** A drug which alleviates *depression,* usually by energizing the patient and thus elevating mood.

**Antisocial personality.** A diagnosis applied to individuals who have repeated conflicts with society, are selfish, do not experience guilt, and are incapable of loyalty to others. The term is synonymous with sociopath and psychopath.

**Anxiety.** An unpleasant feeling of generalized fear and apprehension accompanied by increased physiological arousal. In learning theory considered a drive which mediates between a threatening situation and avoidance behavior. Anxiety can be assessed by self-report, by measuring physiological arousal, and by observing overt behavior.

**Anxiety neurosis.** Disorder in which *anxiety* is felt in so many situations that it appears to have no specific cause; in addition to diffuse anxiety, the patient may suffer acute attacks. Often referred to as *free-floating anxiety.*

**Anxiety problems.** A new diagnostic category in the current draft of DSM-III; encompasses several classes of disorders, such as *phobias* and *obsessions-compulsions,* in which *anxiety* is clearly a key debility.

**Aphasia.** Loss or impairment of the ability to use language because of lesions in the brain. **Executive,** difficulties in speaking or writing the words intended. **Receptive,** difficulties in understanding written or spoken language.

**Arousal.** A state of activation, either behavioral or physiological.

**Ascriptive responsibility.** The social judgment assigned to someone who has committed an illegal act and who, it is decided, should be punished for it; contrast with *descriptive responsibility.*

**Assertive training.** *Behavior therapy* procedures which attempt to help a person express more easily his legitimate feelings of resentment or approval.

**Asthma.** A *psychophysiological disorder* characterized by narrowing of the airways and increased secretion of mucus, which often cause breathing to be extremely labored and wheezy.

**Attention.** Maintenance of a readiness to respond; or focusing on relevant information.

**Attribution.** In psychology, the explanation a person has for his behavior.

**Aura.** Signal or warning of an impending epileptic *convulsion,* taking the form of dizziness or an unusual sensory experience.

**Autism.** Absorption in self or fantasy as a means of avoiding communication and escaping objective reality. See also *infantile autism.*

**Autonomic nervous system.** Division of the nervous system which regulates involuntary functions; innervates *endocrine glands, smooth muscle,* and heart muscle; initiates the physiological changes that are part of expression of emotion.

**Aversive conditioning.** A *behavior therapy* procedure which pairs a noxious stimulus, such as a shock, with situations that are undesirably attractive.

**Aversive stimulus.** A stimulus that elicits pain, fear, or avoidance.

**Avoidance learning.** An experimental procedure in which a neutral stimulus is paired with a noxious one so that the organism learns to avoid the previously neutral stimulus.

**Barbiturate.** A class of synthetic *sedative* drugs which are addictive and in large doses can cause death because the diaphragm relaxes almost completely.

**Basal ganglia.** Clusters of nerve cell bodies (*nuclei*) deep within the *cerebral hemispheres.* They are the lenticular nucleus, the caudate nucleus (collectively, the corpus striatum), the claustrum, and the amygdala.

**Behavior assessment.** Sampling of ongoing conditions, feelings, and overt behavior in their situational context, to be contrasted with the *projective test* and *personality inventory.*

**Behavior genetics.** The study of individual differences in behavior that are attributable in part to differences in genetic makeup.

**Behavior modification.** A term sometimes used interchangeably with *behavior therapy.*

**Behavior rehearsal.** A *behavior therapy* technique in which a client practices new behavior in the consulting room, often aided by demonstrations of the therapist.

**Behavior therapy.** A branch of psychotherapy narrowly conceived as the application of *classical* and *operant conditioning* to the alteration of clinical problems, but more broadly conceived as applied experimental psychology.

**Behaviorism.** School of psychology associated with John B. Watson, who proposed that observable behavior, not consciousness, is the proper subject matter of psychology. Currently, some who consider themselves behaviorists do use *mediational* concepts, provided they are firmly anchored to observables.

**Beriberi.** A deficiency disease attributed to lack of *thiamine* and marked by irritability, fatigue, insomnia, and weakened muscles.

**Beta rhythm.** The dominant pattern (14 to 25 cps) of *brain waves* found in an alert adult responding to a stimulus. See also *alpha rhythm*.

**Biofeedback.** A term referring to procedures that provide an individual immediate information of even minute changes in muscle activity, skin temperature, heart rate, blood pressure, and other somatic functions. It is assumed that voluntary control over these bodily processes can be achieved through this knowledge, thereby ameliorating to some extent certain psychophysiological disorders.

**Biophysical system.** As applied by Masters and Johnson, the part of the sexual response system that includes the genitalia and hormones.

**Bipolar depression.** A term applied to the disorder of people who have experienced episodes of both *mania* and *depression*. Also called bipolar-mood disorder and, in the current draft of DSM-III, bipolar affective disorder.

**Bisexual.** One who engages in both *heterosexual* and *homosexual* relations.

**Borderline mental retardation.** A limitation in mental development measured on IQ tests at between 68 and 83; people in this IQ range are usually not included in statistics on retardation and are able to achieve vocational and social competence.

**Brain wave.** Rhythmic fluctuations in voltage between parts of the brain produced by the spontaneous firings of its *neurons;* recorded by the *electroencephalograph*.

**Brainstem.** The part of the brain connecting the spinal cord with the *cerebrum;* contains the *pons* and *medulla oblongata* and functions as a neural relay station.

**Briquet's syndrome.** A disorder in which patients have multiple physical complaints and some true *conversion reactions;* histrionics, frequent hospitalizations, and unnecessary surgery are likely.

**Butch** (dyke). Slang terms for a *lesbian* whose dress and appearance are not feminine and who has assumed some aspects of the male role.

**Case study.** The collection of historical or biographical information on a single individual, often including his experiences in therapy.

**Castration.** Technically, surgical removal of the *testes* or ovaries, but in the vernacular may refer to removal of the *penis*.

**Castration anxiety.** Fear of having the genitals removed or injured.

**Catatonic immobility** (catatonia). Fixity of posture, sometimes grotesque, maintained for long periods with accompanying muscular rigidity, trancelike state of consciousness, and *waxy flexibility*.

**Catatonic schizophrenic.** Psychotic patient whose primary symptoms alternate between stuporous immobility and excited agitation.

**Catecholamines.** *Monoamine* compounds ($NH_2$), each having a catechol portion ($C_6H_6$); catecholamines known to be *neurotransmitters* of the central nervous system are *norepinephrine* and *dopamine;* another, *epinephrine,* is principally a hormone.

**Catechol-*O*-methyltransferase** (COMT). An enzyme which deactivates *catecholamines* in the *synapse*.

**Cathartic method.** Therapeutic procedure introduced by Breuer in late nineteenth century whereby a patient relives an earlier emotional catastrophe and reexperiences the tension and unhappiness.

**Central nervous system.** The part of the nervous system which in vertebrates consists of the brain and spinal cord and to which all sensory impulses are transmitted and from which motor impulses pass out; also supervises and coordinates the activities of the entire nervous system.

**Central sulcus.** A major fissure transversing the middle of the top and lateral surfaces of each *cerebral hemisphere,* dividing the *frontal lobe* from the *parietal*.

**Cerebellum.** An area of the hindbrain concerned with balance, posture, and motor coordination.

**Cerebral atherosclerosis.** A chronic disease impairing intellectual and emotional life and caused by a reduction in the brain's blood supply through a buildup of fatty deposits in the arteries.

**Cerebral cortex.** Thin outer covering of each of the *cerebral hemispheres,* highly convoluted, and made up of nerve cell bodies, which constitute the *gray matter* of the brain.

**Cerebral hemisphere.** Either of the two halves which make up the *cerebrum*.

**Cerebral hemorrhage.** Bleeding onto brain tissue from ruptured blood vessel.

**Cerebral thrombosis.** Formation of blood clot in cerebral artery, blocking circulation in that area of brain tissue and producing paralysis, loss of sensory functions, and even death.

**Cerebrum.** Two-lobed structure extending from the *brainstem* and constituting anterior part of brain. Largest and most recently developed portion of brain in man; coordinates sensory and motor activities as well as being seat of higher cognitive processes.

**Childhood schizophrenia.** A disorder usually distinguished from *infantile autism* and characterized by onset after age five, gross emotional impairment, perceptual distortions, and peculiar body movements.

**Chlorpromazine.** Generic term for one of the most widely used *major tranquilizers,* sold under the name *Thorazine.*

**Cholinergic system.** All the nerve cells for which *acetylcholine* is the transmitter substance, in contrast to the *adrenergic,* or more precisely the *monoaminergic.*

**Choreiform.** Pertaining to the involuntary, spasmodic, jerking movements of the limbs and head found in *Huntington's chorea* and other nervous disorders.

**Chromosomes.** Threadlike bodies within the nucleus of the cell, DNA being the principal constituent; regarded as carrying the *genes.*

**Chronic.** Of lengthy duration or recurring frequently, often with progressing seriousness.

**Chronic schizophrenic.** Psychotic patient who had deteriorated over a long period of time before diagnosis and who has usually been hospitalized for more than two years.

**Chronic undifferentiated schizophrenia.** A diagnosis frequently applied to patients who do not fit neatly into one of the other *schizophrenic* subcategories.

**Civil commitment.** Procedure whereby a person can be legally certified as mentally ill and hospitalized, even against his will.

**Clang association.** A stringing together of words because they are similar in sound, with no attention paid to their meaning, for example, "How are you Don, pawn, gone?"

**Classical conditioning.** A basic form of learning whereby a neutral stimulus is repeatedly paired with another stimulus (called the *unconditioned stimulus,* UCS) that naturally elicits a certain desired response (UCR). After repeated trials the neutral stimulus becomes a *conditioned stimulus* (CS) and evokes the same or similar response, called now the *conditioned response* (CR).

**Client-centered therapy.** A *humanistic-existential insight therapy,* developed by Carl Rogers, which emphasizes the importance of the therapist's understanding the client's subjective experiences and assisting him to increase his awareness of the current motivations for his behavior; the goal is not only to reduce anxieties but also to foster actualization of the client's potential.

**Climacteric.** The period of life in late middle age when the female's menstruation ceases and the sexual activity and competence of the male may be reduced.

**Clinical psychologist.** An individual who has usually earned a Ph.D. degree in psychology and whose training includes an internship in a mental hospital or clinic.

**Clitoris.** Small heavily innervated erectile structure located above the vaginal opening; primary site of female responsiveness to sexual stimulation.

**Clonic phase.** Stage of violent contortions and jerking of limbs in a *grand mal epileptic* attack.

**Cocaine.** A pain-reducing and stimulating *alkaloid* obtained from coca leaves; increases mental powers, produces euphoria, and heightens sexual desire.

**Cognition.** The process of knowing; the thinking, judging, reasoning, planning activities of the human mind. Behavior is now often explained as depending on the course these *symbolic processes* take.

**Cognitive restructuring.** A *behavior therapy* procedure which attempts to alter the manner in which the client thinks about his life so that he changes his overt behavior.

**Coitus.** Sexual intercourse.

**Colic.** A condition sometimes found in infants in which gas collects in the stomach and produces distress.

**Community mental health, community psychology.** An approach to therapy which emphasizes prevention and the seeking out of potential difficulties rather than waiting for troubled individuals to initiate consultation. The location for professional activities tends to be in the persons' natural surroundings rather than in the therapist's office.

**Competency to stand trial.** Legal decision whether a person can participate meaningfully in his own defense.

**Compulsion.** Irresistible impulse to repeat an irrational act over and over again.

**Concordance.** As applied in *behavior genetics,* the similarity in psychiatric diagnosis or in other traits in a pair of twins.

**Concrete operations stage.** Third period of intellectual development, ages seven to eleven, according to Piaget; the child has acquired well-organized cognitive systems, such as notions of time, space, and number.

**Concrete reasoning.** A pattern of thinking in which abstractions and generalizations cannot be made and terms and details of conversation are interpreted literally.

**Concussion.** A jarring injury to the brain produced by a blow to the head; usually involves a momentary loss of consciousness followed by transient disorientation and memory loss.

**Conditioned response** (CR). Response elicited by a given neutral stimulus (CS), after it has become conditioned by repeated contingent pairings with another stimulus (UCS) that naturally elicits this same or a similar response.

**Conditioned stimulus** (CS). A neutral stimulus which, after repeated contingent pairings with another stimulus (UCS) that naturally elicits a certain response (UCR), comes to elicit the same or a similar response, called the *conditioned response* (CR).

**Confabulation.** Filling in gaps in memory caused by brain dysfunction with made-up and often improbable stories which the subject accepts as true.

**Confounds.** Variables whose effects are so intermixed that they cannot be measured separately, making the design of the *experiment* internally invalid and its results impossible to interpret.

**Congenital.** Existing at or before birth but not acquired through heredity.

**Construct.** An entity inferred by a scientist to explain observed phenomena. See also *mediator*.

**Contingency.** A close relationship, especially of a causal nature, between two events, one of which regularly follows the other.

**Control group.** Subjects in an *experiment* for whom the *independent variable* is not manipulated, thus forming a base line against which the effects of the manipulation can be evaluated.

**Contusion, cerebral.** A bruising of neural tissue marked by swelling and hemorrhage and resulting in coma; may permanently impair intellectual functioning.

**Conversion reaction.** In DSM-II, a *hysterical neurosis,* and in the current draft of DSM-III, a *somatoform disorder;* paralysis, lack of sensation, sensory disturbances, and *analgesia* without organic *pathology*.

**Convulsion.** Violent and extensive twitching of the body caused by involuntary pathological muscle contractions.

**Convulsive therapy.** A biological therapy which induces *convulsions* by drugs or electric shock in hopes of effecting beneficial behavior change. See *electroconvulsive therapy*.

**Corpus callosum.** Large band of nerve fibers connecting the two *cerebral hemispheres*.

**Correlational method.** Research strategy used to establish whether two or more variables are related. Such relationships may be positive—as values for one variable increase, those for the other do also; or negative—as values for one variable increase, those for the other decrease.

**Cortisone.** A hormone secreted by the adrenal cortices.

**Co-twin.** In *behavior genetics* research using the *twin method,* the member of the pair who is tested later to determine whether he has the same diagnosis or trait discovered earlier in his birth partner, the *index case*.

**Counterconditioning.** Relearning achieved by eliciting a new response in the presence of a particular stimulus.

**Covert sensitization.** A form of aversive therapy in which the subject is told to imagine the undesirably attractive situations and activities at the same time that unpleasant feelings are induced by imagery.

**Cretinism.** Condition beginning in prenatal or early life characterized by *mental retardation* and physical deformities; caused by severe deficiency in the output of the *thyroid gland*.

**Critical period.** Stage of early development in which organism needs certain inputs and during which important irreversible patterns of behavior are acquired. See *imprinting*.

**Cultural-familial retardation.** Mild backwardness in mental development with no indication of brain pathology but evidence of similar limitation in at least one of the parents or siblings.

**Cunnilingus.** Oral stimulation of female genitalia.

**Cushing's syndrome.** An endocrine disorder usually affecting young women; produced by oversecretion of *cortisone* and marked by mood swings, irritability, agitation, and physical disfigurement.

**Defect theorist.** In the study of *mental retradation,* a person who believes that the cognitive processes of retardates are qualitatively different from those of normal individuals; contrast with *developmental theorist*.

**Defense mechanism.** In psychoanalytic theory, a reality-distorting strategy unconsciously adopted to protect the ego from anxiety.

**Delirium.** A state of great mental confusion marked by disorientation, clouding of consciousness, disordered speech, excitement, restlessness, and often *delusions* and *hallucinations*.

**Delirium tremens** (DTs). One of the *withdrawal symptoms* when a period of heavy alcohol consumption is terminated; marked by fever, sweating, trembling, cognitive impairment, and *hallucinations*.

**Delusion.** A belief contrary to reality, firmly held in spite of evidence to the contrary; common in paranoid disorders. **Of control,** belief that one is being manipulated by some external force such as radar, TV, or a creature from outer space. **Of grandeur,** belief that one is an especially important or powerful person. **Of persecution,** belief that one is being plotted against or oppressed by others.

**Dementia.** Progressive and marked deterioration of mental functioning.

**Dementia praecox.** An older term for *schizophrenia,* chosen to describe what was believed to be an incurable and progressive deterioration of mental functioning beginning in adolescence.

**Demographic variable.** Varying characteristic which is a vital or social statistic of an individual, sample group, or population, for example, age, sex, *socioeconomic status,* racial origin, education and the like.

**Demonology.** The doctrine that a person's abnormal behavior is caused by an autonomous evil spirit dwelling within him.

**Dependent variable.** In a psychological *experiment,* the behavior that is measured and is expected to change with manipulation of the *independent variable.*

**Depersonalization neurosis.** Disorder marked by feelings of unreality and estrangement from the self and the environment; patient may feel that he is someone else or is watching himself.

**Depression.** Emotional state marked by great sadness and apprehension, feelings of worthlessness and guilt, withdrawal from others, loss of sleep, appetite, and sexual desire, and either lethargy or agitation. Called depressive disorder in current draft of DSM-III.

**Depressive neurosis.** Reaction marked by excessive sadness that had its beginnings in a specific environmental event.

**Descriptive responsibility.** In legal proceedings, the social judgment assigned the accused, that he has performed an illegal act; contrast with *ascriptive responsibility.*

**Developmental theorist.** In the study of *mental retardation,* a person who believes that the cognitive development of retardates has simply been slower than that of normal individuals, not qualitatively different; contrast with *defect theorist.*

**Diathesis.** Constitutional *predisposition* toward a disease or abnormality.

**Diathesis-stress paradigm.** A theory which, as applied in psychopathology, assumes that individuals predisposed toward a particular mental disorder will be profoundly affected by stress and will then manifest abnormal behavior.

**Diencephalon.** Lower area of the forebrain containing the *thalamus* and *hypothalamus.*

**Directionality problem.** A difficulty in *correlational* research whereby it is known that two variables are related but it is unclear which is causing the other.

**Disease.** The medical concept that distinguishes an impairment of the normal state of the organism by its particular group of *symptoms* and its specific cause.

**Disorientation.** A state of mental confusion with respect to time, place, and identity of self, other persons, and objects.

**Displacement.** A *defense mechanism* whereby an emotional response is unconsciously redirected from a perhaps dangerous object or concept to a substitute less threatening to the *ego.*

**Dissociation.** A process whereby a group of mental processes is split off from the mainstream of consciousness, or behavior loses its relationship with the rest of the personality.

**Dissociative disorders.** A new diagnostic category in the current draft of DSM-III covering disorders that are clearly alterations in consciousness.

**Dissociative reaction.** In DSM-II, a *hysterical neurosis;* an alteration in consciousness manifested as *amnesia, fugue, multiple personality,* and *somnambulism.*

**Dizygotic (fraternal) twins.** Birth partners who have developed from separate fertilized eggs and who are only 50 percent alike genetically, no more so than siblings born from different pregnancies.

**Dominant gene.** One of a pair of *genes* which is stronger than the other and determines that the *trait* it fosters will prevail in the *phenotype.*

**Dopamine.** A *catecholamine* which is both a precursor of *norepinephrine* and itself a *neurotransmitter* of the central nervous system. Disturbances in certain of its tracts apparently figure in *schizophrenia* and *Parkinson's disease.*

**Double bind.** An interpersonal situation in which an individual is confronted, over long periods of time, by mutually inconsistent messages to which he must respond. Believed by some theorists to cause *schizophrenia.*

**Double-blind procedure.** A method for reducing the biasing effects of the expectations of subject and experimenter; neither is allowed to know whether the *independent variable* of the *experiment* is being applied to the particular subject.

**Down's syndrome** (mongolism). A form of *mental retardation* caused by an extra *chromosome.* The child's IQ is usually less than 50, his physical characteristics distinctive, the one most often noted being slanted eyes.

**Dream interpretation.** A key psychoanalytic technique in which the unconscious meanings of dream material are uncovered.

**Drive.** A *construct* explaining the motivation of behavior; or an internal physiological tension impelling an organism to activity.

**Drug addiction.** Physiological reliance on a drug developed through continual use; characterized by *tolerance* and *withdrawal symptoms*.

**Drug dependence.** Habitual use of a drug out of psychological but not physiological need; contrast with *drug addiction*.

**Drug use disorders.** A new diagnostic category in the current draft of DSM-III, covering the disorders of people who misuse drugs.

**DSM-II.** The current diagnostic and statistical manual of the American Psychiatric Association.

**Dualism.** Philosophical doctrine that man is both a mental and a physical being and that these two aspects are separate but interacting; advanced in its most definitive statement by Descartes. Contrast with *monism*.

**Durham decision.** A 1954 American court ruling that an accused person is not *ascriptively responsible* if his crime is judged attributable to mental disease or defect.

**Dysfunction.** Impairment or disturbance in the functioning of an organ or organ system.

**Dyshomophilia.** A new term in current draft of DSM-III; the disorder of people who are consciously distressed by their homosexual conduct and feelings through an internal conflict which is primary to any hurt felt in reaction to societal oppression.

**Dyspareunia.** Painful or difficult sexual intercourse, the pain or difficulty usually being caused by infection or a physical injury such as torn ligaments in the pelvic region.

**Echolalia.** The immediate and sometimes pathological repetition of the words of others; a speech problem often found in autistic children. In **delayed echolalia** this inappropriate echoing takes place hours or weeks later.

**Ego.** In psychoanalytic theory, the predominantly conscious part of the personality, responsible for decision making and for dealing with reality.

**Ego analysis.** An important set of modifications of classical *psychoanalysis,* based on a conception of the human being as having a stronger, more autonomous ego with gratifications independent of *id* satisfactions. Sometimes called ego psychology.

**Egoistic suicide.** As defined by Durkheim, self-annihilation committed because the individual feels extreme alienation from others and from society.

**Ejaculate.** To expel semen, typically during male orgasm.

**Ejaculatory incompetence.** Inability to *ejaculate*.

**Electra complex.** See *Oedipus complex*.

**Electrocardiograph.** Device for recording the electrical activity that occurs during the heartbeat.

**Electroconvulsive therapy** (ECT). Treatment which produces a *convulsion* by passing electric current through the brain; useful in alleviating profound *depression,* although typically an unpleasant and occasionally dangerous procedure.

**Electroencephalogram** (EEG). A graphic recording of electrical activity of the brain, usually that of the *cerebral cortex,* but sometimes the electrical activity of lower areas.

**Empathy.** Awareness and understanding of another's feelings and thoughts.

**Encephalitis.** Inflammation of brain tissue caused by a number of agents, the most important being several viruses carried by insects.

**Encephalitis lethargica.** Known as sleeping sickness. Form of encephalitis which occurred earlier in this century and was characterized by lethargy and prolonged periods of sleeping.

**Encounter group.** See *sensitivity group*.

**Endocrine gland.** Any of a number of ductless glands which release *hormones* directly into the blood or lymph. The secretions of some endocrine glands increase during emotional arousal.

**Endogenous.** Attributable to internal causes.

**Endogenous depression.** Profound sadness assumed to be caused by a biochemical malfunction in contrast to an environmental event; more recently regarded simply as having a more severe set of *symptoms* than *exogenous* or *neurotic depression*.

**Endorphins.** *Opiates* produced within the body; they may have an important role in the processes by which it builds up *tolerance* to drugs and is distressed by their withdrawal.

**Enticement.** Legal means of securing arrest whereby a police officer sets up a situation in which an illegal act can be committed but intent is in the mind of the person committing the crime.

**Entrapment.** Illegal means of arrest whereby the police officer sets up a situation that induces another person to perform an illegal act in which he might not otherwise engage.

**Environmental psychology.** A recent community-oriented psychology which assumes that people's feelings and behavior are importantly a function of their physical setting.

**Enzyme.** A complex protein produced by the cells to act as a catalyst in regulating metabolic activities.

**Epilepsy.** An altered state of consciousness accompanied by sudden changes in the usual rhythmical electrical activity of the brain. See also *grand mal, petit mal, Jacksonian,* and *psychomotor epilepsy.*

**Epinephrine.** Hormone (a *catecholamine*) secreted by the medulla of of the *adrenal gland;* its effects are similar, but not identical, to those of stimulating the *sympathetic* nerves; causes an increase in blood pressure, inhibits peristaltic movements, and liberates glucose from the liver. Also called *adrenaline.*

**Erogenous.** Capable of giving sexual pleasure when stimulated.

**Eros** (libido). Freud's term for the life-integrating instinct or force of the *id,* sometimes equated with sexual drive; compare *Thanatos.*

**Essential hypertension.** A *psychophysiological disorder* characterized by high blood pressure that cannot be traced to an organic cause; causes enlargement and degeneration of small arteries, enlargement of the heart, and kidney damage.

**Estrogen.** Female sex hormone produced especially in the ovaries; stimulates the development of and maintains the secondary sex characteristics, such as breast enlargement.

**Etiology.** All the factors that contribute to the development of an illness or disorder.

**Eugenics.** Science concerned with improving the hereditary qualities of the human race through social control of mating and reproduction.

**Ex post facto analysis.** In a psychological experiment, an attempt to reduce the *third-variable problem* by picking subjects who are matched on characteristics that may be *confounds.*

**Excitement phase.** As applied by Masters and Johnson, the first stage of sexual arousal which is initiated by any appropriate stimulus.

**Exhibitionism.** Marked preference for obtaining sexual gratification by exposing one's genitals to an unwilling observer.

**Existential analysis.** See *humanistic-existential therapy.*

**Existential neurosis.** Disorder in which patient feels alienation, considers life meaningless, and finds no activity worth selecting and pursuing. See also *premorbid personality.*

**Exogenous.** Attributable to external causes.

**Exogenous depression.** Profound sadness assumed to be caused by an environmental event.

**Exorcism.** Casting out of evil spirits by ritualistic chanting or torture.

**Experiment.** The most powerful research technique for determining causal relationships, requiring the manipulation of an *independent variable,* the measurement of a *dependent variable,* and the *random assignment* of subjects to the several different conditions being investigated.

**Extinction.** Elimination of a classically *conditioned response* by the omission of the *unconditioned stimulus.* In *operant conditioning,* the elimination of the conditioned response by the omission of *reinforcement.*

**Extradural hematoma.** Hemorrhage and swelling between the skull and dura mater when a *meningeal* artery is ruptured by a fractured bone of the skull.

**Family interaction method.** A procedure for studying family behavior by observing their interaction in a structured laboratory situation.

**Family method.** Research strategy in *behavior genetics* in which the frequency of a *trait* or of abnormal behavior is determined among relatives who have varying percentages of shared genetic background.

**Family therapy.** A form of *group therapy* in which the faulty communication patterns of members of a family are studied for correction.

**Fear-drive.** In the Mowrer-Miller theory, an unpleasant internal state which impels avoidance. The necessity to reduce a fear-drive can form the basis for new learning.

**Fear-response.** In the Mowrer-Miller theory, a response to a threatening or noxious situation which is covert and unobservable but which is assumed to function as a stimulus to produce measurable physiological changes in the body and observable overt behavior.

**Fellatio.** Oral stimulation of the *penis.*

**Fetishism.** Reliance on an inanimate object or a part of the body for sexual arousal.

**First-rank symptoms.** In *schizophrenia,* specific *delusions* and *hallucinations* proposed by Schneider as particularly important for its more exact diagnosis.

**Fixation.** In psychoanalytic theory, the arrest of *psychosexual* development at a particular stage through too much or too little gratification at that stage.

**Flat affect.** A deviation in emotional response wherein virtually no emotion is expressed whatever the stimuli, or emotional expressiveness is blunted; or a lack of expression and muscle tone in the face.

**Flight of ideas.** Rapid shift from one subject to another in conversation, with only superficial associative connections; a symptom of the manic phase of *manic-depressive psychosis.*

**Follow-up study.** A research procedure whereby individuals observed in an earlier investigation are contacted at a later time.

**Forced-choice selection.** Format of a *personality inventory* in which the response alternatives for each item are equated for social desirability.

**Forensic psychiatry.** The branch of psychiatry that deals with the legal questions raised by disordered behavior.

**Formal operations stage.** Final stage of intellectual development, eleven years and older, according to Piaget; the child becomes able to deal with the hypothetical; his thinking is not tied to concrete external objects.

**Free association.** A key psychoanalytic procedure, in which the *analysand* is encouraged to give free rein to his thoughts and feelings, verbalizing whatever comes into his mind without monitoring its content; the assumption is that, over time, hitherto repressed material will come forth for examination by the analysand and his *analyst.*

**Free-floating anxiety.** Continual anxiety not attributable to any specific situation or reasonable danger.

**Frontal lobe.** The forward or upper half of each *cerebral hemisphere,* in front of the *central sulcus;* active in reasoning and other higher mental processes.

**Fugue.** A *hysterical dissociative reaction* in which the individual flees to a new locality, sets up a totally new life, and is amnesic for his previous life, although he retains his faculties and appears normal to others.

**Functional psychosis.** A condition in which thought, behavior, and emotion are disturbed without known pathological changes in tissues or the conditions of the brain.

**Galvanic skin response** (GSR). Change in electric conductivity of the skin caused by increase in activity of sweat glands when the *sympathetic nervous system* is active, in particular when the organism is anxious.

**Gay.** A colloquial term for a *homosexual;* now often adopted by homosexuals who have openly announced their sexual orientation.

**Gay liberation.** The often militant movement seeking to achieve civil rights for homosexuals and recognition of the normality of *homosexuality.*

**Gender identity.** The individual's sense of being a man or a woman.

**Gene.** An ultramicroscopic area of the *chromosome;* the smallest physical unit of the DNA molecule that carries a piece of the information of heredity.

**General paresis.** See *neurosyphilis.*

**Genetic disease.** An abnormality determined at the moment of conception.

**Genetic identity or role disorders.** A new class in the current draft of DSM-III covering *transsexualism* and *transvestism.*

**Genital stage.** In psychoanalytic theory, the final *psychosexual stage* reached in adulthood, in which heterosexual interests predominate.

**Genotype.** An individual's unobservable, physiological genetic constitution; the totality of *genes* possessed by an individual. Compare *phenotype.*

**Gestalt therapy.** A *humanistic-existential insight therapy,* developed by Fritz Perls, which attempts to encourage clients to satisfy their emerging needs so that their innate goodness can be expressed.

**Gestation period.** The length of time, normally nine months in humans beings, during which a fertilized egg develops into an infant ready to be born.

**Glans.** The heavily innervated tip of the *penis.*

**Glove anesthesia.** An hysterical lack of sensation in the part of the hand that would usually be covered by a glove.

**Going in drag.** Dressing in female attire, usually with extensive makeup, by a male *homosexual.*

**Grand mal epilepsy.** The most severe form of *epilepsy,* involving loss of consciousness and violent *convulsions.*

**Graves' disease.** An endocrine disorder resulting from oversecretion of the hormone *thyroxin;* metabolic processes are speeded up, producing apprehension, restlessness, and irritability.

**Gray matter.** Neural tissue made up largely of nerve cell bodies; constitutes the cortex covering the *cerebral hemispheres,* the *nuclei* in lower brain areas, columns of the spinal cord, and the ganglia of the *autonomic nervous system.*

**Grimace.** Distorted facial expression, often a *symptom* of *schizophrenia.*

**Group therapy.** Method of treating psychological disorders whereby several persons are seen simultaneously by a single therapist.

**Gyrus.** A ridge or convolution of the *cerebral cortex*.

**Habituation.** In physiology, a process whereby an organism's response to the same stimulus temporarily lessens with repeated presentations.

**Hallucination.** A perception in any sensory modality without relevant and adequate external stimuli.

**Hallucinogen.** A drug or chemical whose effects include *hallucinations*. Hallucinogenic drugs such as *LSD, psilocybin,* and *mescaline* are often called *psychedelic*.

**Hashish.** The dried resin of the *Cannabis* plant, stronger in its effects than the dried leaves and stems which constitute *marihuana*.

**Hebephrenic schizophrenic.** Psychotic patient whose behavior is marked by silliness, incoherent speech, *hallucinations, delusions,* and considerable deterioration.

**Hermaphrodite.** A person with parts of both male and female genitalia.

**Heroin.** An extremely addictive *narcotic* drug derived from *morphine*.

**Heterophobia.** Fear of the opposite sex, considered by psychoanalysts and some learning theorists to be an explanation of *homosexuality*.

**Heterosexual.** One who engages in sexual relations with members of the opposite sex.

**High-risk method.** A research technique, used especially in the study of *schizophrenia,* involving the intensive examination of people who have a high probability of later becoming abnormal.

**Hives.** A transient skin condition characterized by slightly raised, itching patches; often considered a *psychophysiological disorder*.

**Homophobia.** Fear of *homosexuality*.

**Homosexuality.** Sexual desire or activity directed toward a member of one's own sex.

**Homovanillic acid.** A major metabolite of *dopamine*.

**Hormone.** A chemical substance produced by an *endocrine gland* and released into the blood or lymph for the purpose of controlling the function of a distant organ or organ system. Metabolism, growth, and development of secondary sexual characteristics are among the functions so controlled.

**Humanistic-existential therapy.** An *insight* psychotherapy which emphasizes the individual's subjective experiences, free will, and ever-present ability to decide on a new life course.

**Huntington's chorea.** A fatal *presenile dementia,* passed on by a single *dominant gene*. The *symptoms* include spasmodic jerking of the limbs, psychotic behavior, and mental deterioration.

**Hurler's syndrome** (gargoylism). An inherited physical and mental deterioration in which monopolysaccharides accumulate in the cells. Survival past the age of twenty is unusual.

**5-Hydroxyindoleacetic acid** (5-HIAA). The major metabolite of *serotonin* that is present in the cerebrospinal fluid.

**Hyperactivity.** A childhood disorder marked by an inability to inhibit movement in situations that call for it; problems in learning, attention, and relating to others are also common.

**Hypertension.** Abnormally high arterial blood pressure, with or without known organic causes. See *essential hypertension*.

**Hyperventilation.** Very rapid and deep breathing associated with high levels of anxiety; causes level of carbon dioxide in blood to be lowered, with possible loss of consciousness.

**Hypnosis.** A trancelike state or behavior resembling sleep, characterized primarily by increased suggestibility and induced by suggestion.

**Hypochondriacal neurosis.** A condition in which patient is preoccupied with bodily functions and imagined illnesses.

**Hypothalamus.** A collection of nuclei and fibers in the lower part of the *diencephalon;* concerned with the regulation of many visceral processes, such as metabolism, temperature, water balance, and so on.

**Hysteria** (hysterical state). Physical incapacity that makes no anatomical sense, for example, *glove anesthesia*. An older term for *hysterical conversion reaction*.

**Hysterical neurosis.** Disorder taking a variety of forms which can be grouped together as two types. **Conversion reaction,** paralysis, lack of sensation, sensory disturbances, and *analgesia* without organic *pathology*. **Dissociative reaction,** alteration in consciousness manifested as *amnesia, fugue, multiple personality,* and *somnambulism*.

**Hysterical personality.** The disorder of an immature, vain person, usually female, who is prone to histrionics, exaggeration, and willful seductiveness and seeks to be the center of attention.

**Id.** In psychoanalytic theory, that part of the personality present at birth, composed of all the energy of the *psyche* and expressed as biological urges which strive continually for gratification.

**Ideas of reference.** *Delusional* thinking which reads personal significance into seemingly trivial remarks and activities of others and completely unrelated events.

**Idiot savant.** An individual with a rare form of *mental retardation,* being extraordinarily talented in one or a few limited areas of intellectual achievement.

**Imipramine.** An *antidepressant* drug, one of the *tricyclic* group, effective primarily in alleviating *endogenous depression.*

**Implosion therapy.** A *behavior therapy* technique for reducing neurotic fears; the client is encouraged to imagine himself in the most frightening of situations and to visualize bizarre images, the assumption being that adult fears are traceable to *psychodynamic* themes of sex and aggression which must be confronted.

**Impotence—primary.** The physical or psychological condition of a male who has never had an erection sufficient for either heterosexual or homosexual intercourse. **Secondary,** inability of the male to have an erection sufficient for intercourse, although he has a history of at least one successful *intromission.*

**Imprinting.** The irreversible acquisition of behavior by a neonate of a social species during a *critical period* of development. The neonate is attracted to and mimics the first moving object seen, thereby acquiring specific patterns of behavior.

**In absentia.** Literally, "in one's absence." Courts are concerned that a person be able to participate personally and meaningfully in his own trial and not be tried *in absentia* because of a distracting mental disorder.

**In vivo.** As applied in psychology, taking place in a real-life situation.

**Inappropriate affect.** Emotional responses which are out of context, such as laughter when hearing sad news.

**Incest.** Sexual relations between close relatives for whom marriage is forbidden, most often between daughter and father or between brother and sister.

**Incidence.** In community studies of a particular disorder, the rate at which new cases occur in a given place at a given time; compare with *prevalence.*

**Incoherence.** In *schizophrenia,* a *thought disorder* wherein verbal expression is marked by disconnectedness, fragmented thoughts, jumbled phrases, and *neologisms.*

**Independent variable.** In a psychological *experiment,* the factor, experience, or treatment which is under the control of the experimenter and which is expected to have an effect on the subjects as assessed by changes in the *dependent variable.*

**Index case.** The person who in a genetic investigation bears the diagnosis or *trait* that the investigator is interested in. Same as *proband.*

**Indoleamines.** *Monoamine* compounds ($NH_2$), each containing an indole portion ($C_8H_7N$); indoleamines believed to act in neurotransmission are *serotonin* and tryptamine.

**Infantile autism.** A childhood disorder usually differentiated from *childhood schizophrenia* and marked by early and profound aloneness, a hedged inner world fended from all encroachments; *mutism* or *echolalic* speech; and intolerance of any change in routine or surroundings.

**Infectious disease.** Illness caused when a microorganism, such as a bacterium or a virus, invades the body, multiplies, and attacks a specific organ or organ system; pneumonia is an example.

**Insanity defense.** Legal argument that a defendant should not be held *ascriptively responsible* for an illegal act if the conduct is attributable to mental illness.

**Insight therapy.** A psychotherapy which attempts to impart to a patient greater awareness of what motivates his behavior, the assumption being that disordered behavior is caused by *repression* or other unconscious conflicts.

**Instrumental learning.** See *operant conditioning.*

**Intelligence quotient** (IQ). Technically now a deviation IQ, indicating how far an individual's raw score on an *intelligence test* falls away from the average raw score of his chronological age group.

**Intelligence test.** Standardized means of assessing a person's current mental abilities, for example, the Stanford-Binet test and the Wechsler Adult Intelligence Scale.

**Interpretation.** In *psychoanalysis,* a key procedure in which the *analyst* points out to the *analysand* where *resistances* exist and what certain dreams and verbalizations reveal about impulses repressed in the *unconscious.*

**Introjection.** In psychoanalytic theory, the unconscious incorporation of the values, attitudes, and qualities of another person into the individual's own ego structure.

**Intromission.** Insertion of *penis* into *vagina* or anus.

**Introspective method.** A procedure whereby trained subjects are asked to report on their conscious experiences; the principal method of study in early-twentieth-century psychology.

**Introversion-extroversion.** In Eysenck's theory of personality, a dimension referring for the most part to conditionability. Extroverts are said to acquire *conditioned responses* slowly and lose them rapidly: the reverse is true of introverts.

**Involutional melancholia.** An *affective disorder* characterized by profound sadness and occurring at a person's *climacteric* in late middle age.

**Irresistible impulse.** The term used in an 1834 Ohio court ruling on criminal responsibility in which it was decided that an *insanity defense* can be established by proving that the accused had an uncontrollable urge to perform the act.

**Jacksonian epilepsy.** A form of *epilepsy* in which muscle spasms are limited to a particular part of the body.

**Juvenile paresis.** A form of syphilis which is congenital and is similar to the adult disorder; the onset of deterioration is at twelve to fourteen years, after a symptom-free childhood.

**Klinefelter's syndrome.** A disorder of males in which an extra X *chromosome* usually keeps the testes small at puberty, may produce *mental retardation,* and may cause secondary female sex characteristics to develop.

**Korsakoff's psychosis.** A chronic brain disorder associated with *Wernicke's disease;* marked by loss of recent memories and associated *confabulation* and by additional lesions in the *thalamus.*

**La belle indifférence.** The blasé attitude *hysterics* often have toward their *symptoms.*

**Labile.** Easily moved or changed; quickly shifting from one emotion to another or easily aroused.

**Laceration.** A jagged wound; in the brain, a tearing of tissue by an object entering the skull, often causing paralysis, intellectual impairment, and even death.

**Latent stage.** In psychoanalytic theory, the fourth *psychosexual stage,* from ages six to twelve, during which id impulses play a minor role in motivation.

**Lateral sulcus.** A major horizontal fissure along the side of each *cerebral hemisphere,* separating the *frontal* and *parietal lobes* from the *temporal lobe.*

**Learned helplessness.** In learning experiments on *depression,* a concept referring to an animal's passive acceptance of discomfort after he has found that his responses do not provide a means of escape.

**Learning model.** As applied in abnormal psychology, a set of assumptions that abnormal behavior is learned in the same way as other human behavior.

**Lesbian.** Female *homosexual.*

**Lesch-Nyhan syndrome.** A serious kidney disease and *mental retardation* of male infants who receive a defective *gene* on the X *chromosome* from the mother. They become irritable after a few months, lose motor control, are self-mutilative by the second year, and die very young of renal and neurological damage.

**Lesion.** Any localized abnormal structural change in organ or tissue caused by disease or injury.

**Libido.** See *Eros.*

**Life Change Unit** (LCU) **score.** A score produced by totaling ratings of the stressfulness of recently experienced life events; high scores are found to be related to the contracting of a number of physical illnesses.

**Limbic system.** Lower parts of the *cerebrum* made up of primitive cortex; controls visceral and bodily changes associated with emotion and regulates drive-motivated behavior.

**Lithium carbonate.** A drug believed to be of some use in treating both *mania* and *depression.*

**Lobotomy.** A brain operation in which the nerve pathways between the *frontal lobes* of the brain and the *thalamus* and *hypothalamus* are cut in hopes of effecting beneficial behavioral change.

**Loose association.** In *schizophrenia,* an aspect of *thought disorder* wherein the patient has difficulty sticking to one topic and drifts off on a train of associations evoked by an idea from the past.

**LSD** (*d*-lysergic acid diethylamide). A drug synthesized in 1938 and discovered to be a *hallucinogen* in 1943; derived from lysergic acid, the principal constituent of the *alkaloids* of ergot, a grain fungus which in earlier centuries brought on epidemics of spasmodic ergotism, a nervous disorder sometimes marked by psychotic symptoms.

**Major tranquilizer.** A drug which strongly suppresses arousal and is used primarily to calm psychotic patients; also referred to as antipsychotic.

**Malingering.** Faking an incapacity in order to avoid work, often difficult to distinguish from a *hysterical conversion reaction.*

**Malleus Maleficarum** ("the witches' hammer"). A manual written by two Dominican monks in the fifteenth century to provide rules for identifying and trying witches.

**Mammillary body.** Either of two small rounded structures located in the *hypothalamus* and consisting of *nuclei.*

**Mania.** Emotional state of intense but unfounded elation evidenced in talkativeness, *flights of ideas,* and distractibility, in grandiose plans and spurts of purposeless activity. Called manic disorder in current draft of DSM-III.

**Manic-depressive illness, manic-depressive psychosis.** Originally described by Kraepelin; an *affective disorder* characterized by alternating moods of euphoria and profound sadness or by one of these moods.

**Maple Syrup Urine disease.** An inherited defect in *amino acid* metabolism causing *mental retardation* and death usually within first year.

**Marathon group.** A group session run continuously for a day or even longer, typically for *sensitivity training,* the assumption being that defenses can be worn down by the physical and psychological fatigue generated through intensive and continuous group interaction.

**Marihuana.** A nonaddictive *psychedelic* drug derived from the dried and ground leaves and stems of the female hemp plant, *Cannabis sativa.*

**Masochism.** Marked preference for obtaining or increasing sexual gratification through subjection to pain.

**Masturbation.** Self-stimulation of the genitals, typically to *orgasm.*

**McNaghten rule.** A British court decision of 1843 which stated that an *insanity defense* can be established by proving that the defendant did not know what he was doing or did not realize that it was wrong.

**Mediation theory.** In psychology, the view that certain stimuli do not directly initiate an overt response but activate an intervening process, which in turn initiates the response; an explanation of thinking, drives, emotions, and beliefs in terms of stimulus and response.

**Mediator.** In psychology, an inferred state intervening between the observable stimulus and response, being activated by the stimulus and in turn initiating the response; in more general terms, a thought, drive, emotion, or belief. Also called a *construct.*

**Medical model** (disease model). As applied in abnormal psychology, a set of assumptions that conceptualizes abnormal behavior as being similar to physical diseases.

**Medulla oblongata.** An area in the *brainstem* through which nerve fiber tracts ascend to or descend from higher brain centers.

**Megalomania.** Paranoid *delusion of grandeur* in which an individual believes himself to be an important person or to be carrying out great plans.

**Meninges.** The three layers of nonneural tissue that envelop the brain and spinal cord. They are the dura mater, the arachnoid, and the pia mater.

**Meningitis.** An inflammation of the *meninges* through infection, usually by a bacterium, or through irritation. **Meningococcal,** the epidemic form of the disease caused by *Neisseria meningitidis;* takes the life of 10 percent who contract it and causes cerebral palsy, hearing loss, speech defects, and other forms of permanent brain damage in one of four who recover.

**Mental age.** The numerical index of an individual's cognitive development determined by standardized *intelligence tests.*

**Mental retardation.** Subnormal intellectual functioning associated with impairment in social adjustment and beginning in childhood.

**Meprobamate.** Generic term for *Miltown,* a *minor tranquilizer,* the first introduced and one of the most widely used.

**Mescaline.** An *hallucinogen* and *alkaloid* which is the active ingredient of *peyote.*

**Metabolism.** The sum of the intracellular processes by which large molecules are broken down into smaller ones, releasing energy and wastes, and by which small molecules are built up into new living matter, consuming energy.

**Methadone.** A synthetic addictive *narcotic* for treating *heroin* addicts; acts as a substitute for heroin by eliminating its effects and the craving for it.

**Methedrine.** A very strong *amphetamine,* sometimes shot directly into the veins.

**3-Methoxy-4-hydroxyphenylethylene glycol** (MHPG). A major metabolite of *norepinephrine.*

**Midbrain.** The middle part of the brain which consists of a mass of nerve fiber tracts connecting the spinal cord and *pons, medulla,* and *cerebellum* to the *cerebral cortex.*

**Mild mental retardation.** A limitation in mental development measured on IQ tests at between 52 and 67; children with such a limitation are considered the educable mentally retarded and are placed in special classes.

**Milieu therapy.** Treatment procedure which attempts to make the total environment and all personnel and patients of the hospital a "therapeutic community," conducive to psychological improvement.

**Miltown.** Trade name for *meprobamate,* one of the principal *minor tranquilizers.*

**Minnesota Multiphasic Personality Inventory** (MMPI). A lengthy *personality inventory* by which an individual is diagnosed through his true-false replies to groups of statements indicating *anxiety, depression,* masculinity-femininity, and paranoia.

**Minor tranquilizer.** A drug which reduces moderate to low levels of *anxiety;* most often used with neurotic disorders.

**Mirroring.** A *psychodrama* technique in which an individual sees himself portrayed by another person, thereby acquiring a better idea of how he is viewed by others.

**Misdemeanor.** Illegal conduct which is not a gross violation of law; distinguished from a felony, which is punishable by a term in a state or federal prison. Vagrancy and "lewd and lascivious behavior" are examples.

**Mixed design.** A research strategy in which both *correlational* and *experimental* variables are used; assigning subjects from discrete populations to two experimental conditions is an example.

**Model.** A set of concepts from one domain applied to another by analogy. For example, in trying to understand the brain we may assume that in functions like a computer.

**Modeling.** Learning by observing and imitating the behavior of others.

**Moderate mental retardation.** A limitation in mental development measured on IQ tests at between 36 and 51; children with this degree of retardation are often institutionalized and their training is focused on self-care rather than development of intellectual skills.

**Mongolism.** See *Down's syndrome.*

**Monism.** Philosophical doctrine that ultimate reality is a unitary organic whole and that therefore mental and physical are one and the same. Contrast with *dualism.*

**Monoamine.** An organic compound containing nitrogen in one amino group ($NH_2$). Some of the known *neurotransmitters* of the central nervous system, called collectively brain amines, are *catecholamines* and *indoleamines,* which are monoamines.

**Monoamine oxidase** (MAO). An enzyme which deactivates *catecholamines* and *indoleamines* within the presynaptic *neuron,* indoleamines in the *synapse.*

**Monoamine oxidase inhibitors.** A group of *antidepressant* drugs which keep the enzyme *monoamine oxidase* from deactivating *neurotransmitters* of the central nervous system. With more *norepinephrine* and *serotonin* available in the *synapse,* mood is elevated.

**Monozygotic twins.** Genetically identical siblings who have developed from a single fertilized egg.

**Moral anxiety.** In psychoanalytic theory, the *ego's* fear of punishment for failure to adhere to the *superego's* standards of proper conduct.

**Moral treatment.** A therapeutic regimen, introduced by Philippe Pinel during the French Revolution, whereby mental patients were released from their restraints and were treated with compassion and dignity rather than with contempt and denigration.

**Morbidity risk.** The probability that an individual will develop a particular disorder.

**Morphine.** An addictive narcotic *alkaloid* extracted from *opium;* used primarily as an analgesic and as a *sedative.*

**Mourning work.** In Freud's theory of *depression,* the recall by a depressed person of memories associated with a lost one, serving to separate the individual from the deceased.

**Multimodal therapy.** Therapy introduced by Arnold Lazarus to encompass the seven modalities in which a client may experience difficulties—behavior, *affect,* sensation, imagery, *cognition,* interpersonal relations, and drugs—and to treat them through a variety of techniques, not all of them behavioral.

**Multiple-base-line design.** An experimental design in which two behaviors of a single subject are selected for study and a treatment is applied to one of them; the behavior that is not treated serves as a base line against which the effects of the treatment can be determined. Common design in operant research.

**Multiple personality.** A *hysterical dissociative reaction* in which an individual has distinctly different personalities at various times.

**Mutism.** The inability or refusal to speak.

**Myxedema.** An endocrine disorder of adults produced by thyroid deficiency; metabolic processes are slowed, and the patient becomes lethargic, slow-thinking, and depressed.

**Narcotic.** One of the addictive *sedative* drugs, for example, *morphine* and *heroin;* in moderate doses relieves pain and induces sleep.

**Negativism.** A tendency to behave in a manner opposite to the desires of others or to what is expected or requested.

**Neo-Freudian.** A person who has contributed to the modification and extension of Freudian theory.

**Neologism.** A word made up by the speaker that is usually meaningless to a listener.

**Neoplasm.** See *tumor.*

**Neurasthenic neurosis.** Disorder in which patient complains of chronic fatigue and weakness not attributable to illness or excessive physical activity; the simplest activities require great effort.

**Neurodermatitis.** Chronic disorder in which patches of the skin become inflamed; a *psychophysiological disorder.*

**Neurology.** The scientific study of the nervous system and especially its structure, functions, and abnormalities.

**Neuron.** A single nerve cell.

**Neurosis.** One of a large group of nonpsychotic disorders characterized by unrealistic *anxiety* and other associated problems, for example, phobic avoidances, *obsessions,* and *compulsions.*

**Neurosyphillis** (general paresis). Infection of the central nervous system by the spirochete *Treponema pallidum,* which destroys brain tissue; marked by eye disturbances, tremors, and disordered speech as well as severe intellectual deterioration and psychotic symptoms.

**Neurotic anxiety.** In psychoanalytic theory, fear of the consequences of expressing previously punished id impulses; more generally, unrealistic fear.

**Neurotic depression.** Excessive sadness which had its beginnings in a specific environmental event.

**Neuroticism.** In Eysenck's theory of personality, a dimension referring to the ease with which people can become autonomically aroused.

**Neurotransmitter.** Chemical substance important in transferring a nerve impulse from one *neuron* to another.

**Niacin.** One of the complex of B vitamins.

**Nicotine.** The principal *alkaloid* of tobacco.

**Niemann-Pick disease.** An inherited disorder of lipid (fat) metabolism, producing *mental retardation* and paralysis and bringing early death.

**Norepinephrine.** A *catecholamine* which is a *neurotransmitter* of the central nervous system. Disturbances in its tracts apparently figure in *depression* and *mania.* It is also a neurotransmitter secreted at the nerve endings of the *sympathetic nervous system;* and a hormone, liberated with *epinephrine* in the adrenal medulla and similar to it in action; and a strong vasoconstrictor.

**Normal curve.** As applied in psychology, the bell-shaped distribution of a measurable *trait* depicting most people in the middle and few at the extremes.

**Nosology.** A systematic classification of diseases.

**Nucleus.** In anatomy, a mass of nerve cell bodies (*gray matter*) within the brain or spinal cord by which descending nerve fibers connect with ascending nerve fibers.

**Object choice.** In the psychology of sex, the type of person or thing selected as a focus for sexual activity.

**Objective anxiety.** In psychoanalytic theory, the *ego's* reaction to danger in the external world; same as realistic fear.

**Obsession.** Intrusive and recurring thought which seems irrational and uncontrollable to the person experiencing it.

**Obsessive-compulsive neurosis.** Disorder in which mind is flooded with persistent and uncontrollable thoughts or the individual is compelled to repeat certain acts again and again.

**Occipital lobe.** The posterior area of each *cerebral hemisphere,* situated behind the *parietal* and above the *temporal lobes;* responsible for reception and analysis of visual information and for some visual memory.

**Oedipus complex.** In Freudian theory, the desire and conflict of the four-year-old male child who wants to possess his mother sexually and to eliminate the father rival. The threat of punishment from the father makes the boy *repress* these id impulses. Girls have a similar sexual desire for the father, which is repressed in analogous fashion and is called the Electra complex.

**Operant behavior.** A response which is supposedly voluntary and operates on the environment, modifying it so that a reward or goal is attained.

**Operant conditioning.** The acquisition or elimination of a response as a function of the environmental contingencies of *reward* and *punishment.*

**Operational definition.** A definition of a theoretical concept which equates it with a set of observable operations that can be measured.

**Opium.** The dried milky juice obtained from the immature fruit of the opium poppy. This addictive *narcotic* produces euphoria and drowsiness and reduces pain.

**Oral stage.** In psychoanalytic theory, the first *psychosexual stage* which extends into the second year, during which the mouth is the principal *erogenous* zone.

**Organic brain syndrome.** A mental disorder in which intellectual or emotional functioning or both are impaired through a *pathology* or dysfunction of the brain.

**Orgasm** (climax). The involuntary, intensely pleasurable, climactic phase in sexual arousal, lasting a number of seconds and usually involving muscular contractions and *ejaculation* in the male and similar contractions in the genitalia of the female.

**Outcome research.** Research on the effectiveness of psychotherapy. Contrast with *process research.*

**Paired-associates learning.** Retaining words in pairs by thinking up phrases that indelibly link the two words of each pair.

**Panic reaction.** In psychoanalytic theory, a sudden and inexplicable outburst of fear which is acute and overwhelming and may have disordering effects on the personality.

**Paradigm.** A set of basic assumptions that outline the universe of scientific inquiry, specifying both the concepts regarded as legitimate and the methods to be used in collecting and interpreting data.

**Paradigm clash.** The conflict created when a basically different set of assumptions threatens to replace a prevailing *paradigm,* for example, Copernicus' proposal that the sun—not the earth—is the center of the solar system.

**Paranoid schizophrenic.** Psychotic patient who has numerous systematized *delusions* as well as *hallucinations* and *ideas of reference.*

**Paranoid state.** A transitory *psychosis* characterized principally by *delusions of persecution* or *grandeur;* contact with reality is impaired but the patient's behavior is essentially normal except for the delusions.

**Paraphilias.** A new class in the current draft of DSM-III covering sexual attractions to unusual objects and sexual activities unusual in nature.

**Paraprofessional.** In clinical psychology, an individual lacking a doctoral degree but trained to perform certain functions usually reserved for clinicians, for example, a college student trained and supervised by a behavioral therapist to shape the behavior of autistic children through contingent reinforcers.

**Parasympathetic nervous system.** The division of the *autonomic nervous system* which is involved with maintenance; it controls many of the internal organs and is active primarily when the organism is not aroused.

**Parataxic distortion.** According to the ego analyst Harry Stack Sullivan, an unconscious misperception of reality stemming from a childhood disorganization in interpersonal relationships and extended to all later relationships.

**Parietal lobe.** The middle division of each *cerebral hemisphere,* situated behind the *central sulcus* and above the *lateral sulcus;* receiving center for sensations of the skin and of bodily positions.

**Parkinson's disease.** A *presenile dementia* characterized by uncontrollable and severe muscle tremors, a stiff gait, a masklike, expressionless face, and withdrawal.

**Pathology.** The anatomical, physiological, and psychological deviations of a disease or disorder; and the study of these abnormalities.

**Pearson product moment correlation coefficient (*r*).** A statistic, ranging in value from −1.00 to +1.00; the most common means of denoting a correlational relationship. The sign indicates whether the relationship is positive or negative; the magnitude indicates the strength of the relationship.

**Pedophilia.** Preference for obtaining sexual gratification through contact with youngsters defined legally as underage.

**Pellagra.** A deficiency disease produced by lack of *niacin;* marked by reddening of the skin on neck and hands and by *depression,* memory loss, and difficulty in concentration.

**Penile plethysmograph.** Device for recording changes in penile size and thus for detecting blood flow and erection.

**Penis.** The male organ of copulation.

**Peptic ulcer.** A lesion in the lining of the stomach or duodenum caused by excessive secretion of hydrochloric acid or susceptibility of the mucous membrane to its digestive action; generally regarded as a *psychophysiological disorder.*

**Personality disorders.** A heterogeneous diagnostic category for maladaptive patterns that are considered neither neurotic nor psychotic; some are self-defeating *traits* and others, in DSM-II, are social problems such as *alcoholism* and unconventional sexual practices.

**Personality inventory.** Self-report questionnaire by which examinee indicates whether statements assessing habitual behavioral tendencies apply to him.

**Petit mal epilepsy.** A form of *epilepsy* involving a momentary alteration in consciousness, more frequent in children than adults.

**Peyote.** A *hallucinogen* obtained from the root of the peyote cactus, the active ingredient being the *alkaloid mescaline.*

**Phallic stage.** In psychoanalytic theory, the third *psychosexual stage,* extending from ages three to six, during which maximal gratification is obtained from genital stimulation.

**Phenomenology.** As applied in psychology, the view that the phenomena of subjective experience should be studied because behavior is considered to be determined by how the subject perceives himself and the world rather than by objectively described reality.

**Phenothiazine.** Class name for a group of nonaddictive drugs which relieve psychotic symptoms and which are considered *major tranquilizers;* their molecular structure, like that of the *tricyclic drugs,* consists of three fused rings.

**Phenotype.** The totality of observable characteristics of a person; compare with *genotype.*

**Phenylketonuria** (PKU). A genetic disorder which, through a deficiency in a liver enzyme, phenylalanine hydroxylase, causes severe *mental retardation* unless phenylalanine can be largely restricted from diet until the age of six.

**Phillips Scale.** Series of questions which is filled out by the researcher from the case history of a schizophrenic and is used to assess his *premorbid adjustment.*

**Phobia.** Intense irrational fear and avoidance of specific objects and situations.

**Physiological paradigm.** A broad theoretical point of view holding that mental disorders are caused by aberrant *somatic* processes.

**Physiology.** Study of the functions and activities of living cells, tissues, and organs and of the physical and chemical phenomena involved.

**Pick's disease.** A *presenile dementia* involving diffuse atrophy of *frontal* and *temporal lobes,* impairing memory, concentration, and ability to think abstractly; eventually results in psychosis and death.

**Placebo.** Any therapy or inactive chemical agent, or any attribute or component of such a therapy or chemical, which affects a person's behavior for reasons having to do with his expectation of change.

**Placebo effect.** The action of a drug or psychological treatment that is not attributable to any specific operations of the agent. For example, a tranquilizer can reduce anxiety both because of its special biochemical action and because the recipient expects relief.

**Plateau phase.** In sexual arousal, the second stage during which excitement and tension have reached a stable high level before *orgasm.*

**Pleasure principle.** In psychoanalytic theory, the demanding manner by which the *id* operates, seeking immediate gratification of its needs.

**Pons.** An area in the *brainstem* containing nerve fiber tracts connecting the *cerebellum* with the spinal cord and with motor areas of the *cerebrum.*

**Positive spikes.** An EEG pattern recorded from the *temporal lobe* of the brain, with frequencies of 6 to 8 cps and 14 to 16 cps; often found in impulsive and aggressive people.

**Predisposition.** An inclination or tendency to respond in a certain way, either inborn or acquired; in abnormal psychology, a factor which lowers the ability to withstand stress and inclines some part of the individual's constitution toward *pathology.*

**Premature ejaculation.** Inability of the male to inhibit his *orgasm* long enough for mutually satisfying sexual relations.

**Premorbid adjustment.** In research on *schizophrenia,* the social and sexual adjustment of the individual before the onset or diagnosis of his *symptoms;* patients with good premorbid adjustment are those found to have been relatively normal earlier, but those with poor premorbid adjustment had inadequate interpersonal and sexual relations.

**Premorbid personality.** Maddi's term for a person who plays social roles well and satisfies his biological needs and yet has a feeling of emptiness and lack of fulfillment; he is regarded as a candidate for *existential neurosis.*

**Preoperational stage.** Second period of intellectual development, ages two to seven, according to Piaget; the child develops an internal representation of the external world but still is unable to manipulate ideas in an abstract fashion.

**Preparatory interval.** In a *reaction time test,* length of time between a warning signal and the actual stimulus for the response.

**Preparedness.** In *classical conditioning* theory, a biological *predisposition* to be especially sensitive to particular stimuli and to associate them readily with the *unconditioned stimulus.*

**Presenile dementia.** A degeneration of brain tissue occurring when the individual is in his forties or fifties and causing progressive mental deterioration.

**Prevalence.** In community studies of a disorder, the percent of a population that has it at a given time; compare with *incidence.*

**Primary impotence.** See *impotence.*

**Primary narcissism.** In psychoanalytic theory, the part of the *oral stage* of *psychosexual* development during which the ego has not yet differentiated from the *id.*

**Primary orgasmic dysfunction.** The incapacity of a woman who has never had an *orgasm,* either from masturbation or from intercourse.

**Primary process.** In psychoanalytic theory, one of the *id's* means of reducing tension, by imagining what it desires.

**Proband.** The person who in a genetic investigation bears the diagnosis or *trait* that the investigator is interested in. Same as *index case.*

**Process research.** Research on the psychological mechanisms by which a therapy may bring improvement. Compare *outcome research.*

**Profound mental retardation.** A limitation in mental development measured on IQ tests at less than 20; children with this degree of retardation require total supervision of all their activities.

**Prognosis.** A prediction of the likely course and outcome of an illness.

**Projection.** A *defense mechanism* whereby characteristics or desires unacceptable to the *ego* are attributed to someone else.

**Projective test.** A psychological assessment device employing a set of standard but vague stimuli, on the assumption that unstructured material will allow unconscious motivations and fears to be uncovered. The Rorschach series of inkblots is an example.

**Pronoun reversal.** A speech problem in which the child refers to himself as "he" or "you" and uses "I" or "me" in referring to others; often found in the speech of autistic children.

**Psilocybin.** A *psychedelic* drug extracted from the mushroom *Psilocybe mexicana.*

**Psyche.** The soul, spirit, or mind as distinguished from the body; in psychoanalytic theory, the totality of the *id, ego,* and *superego* including both conscious and unconscious components.

**Psychedelic.** A drug which expands consciousness; see also *hallucinogen.*

**Psychiatrist.** A physician (M.D. degree) who has taken specialized postdoctoral training, called a residency, in the diagnosis, treatment, and prevention of mental and emotional disorders.

**Psychoactive drug.** A chemical compound having a psychological effect, altering mood or thought processes; a *tranquilizer* is an example.

**Psychoanalysis.** A term applied primarily to the therapy procedures pioneered by Freud, entailing *free association, dream interpretation,* and working through of the *transference neurosis.* More recently the term has come to encompass the numerous variations on basic Freudian therapy.

**Psychoanalyst** (analyst). A therapist who has taken specialized postdoctoral training in psychoanalysis, after earning either an M.D. or a Ph.D.

**Psychodrama.** A kind of group psychotherapy, introduced by Moreno, in which patients play out, in theatrical settings, their feelings toward important figures and situations in their lives.

**Psychodynamic.** In psychoanalytic theory, relating to the mental and emotional forces and processes that develop in early childhood and their effects on behavior and mental states.

**Psychogenesis.** Development from psychological origins as distinguished from somatic origins; contrast with *somatogenesis.*

**Psychological autopsy.** Analysis of an individual's suicide through the examination of his letters and through interviews with friends and relatives in the hope of discovering why he took his life.

**Psychological deficit.** Term used to indicate that performance of a pertinent psychological process is below that expected of the normal person.

**Psychological test.** Standardized procedure designed to measure subject's performance of a particular task or to assess his personality.

**Psychomotor epilepsy.** Form of epileptic seizure in which the individual loses contact with the environment but appears conscious and performs some routine, repetitive act or engages in more complex activity.

**Psychopath.** See *antisocial personality.*

**Psychophysiological disorder.** A disorder with physical *symptoms* that may involve actual tissue damage, usually in one organ system, and that are produced in part by continued mobilization of the *autonomic nervous system* under stress. *Hives* and *ulcers* are examples.

**Psychosexual disorders.** A new diagnostic category in the current draft of DSM-III, consisting of three subcategories, *gender identity or role disorders, paraphilias,* and *psychosexual dysfunctions.*

**Psychosexual dysfunctions.** A new class in the current draft of DSM-III covering sexual inadequacies such as *impotence* and *dyspareunia.*

**Psychosexual stages.** In psychoanalytic theory, critical developmental phases which the individual passes through, each stage characterized by the body area providing maximal erotic gratification. The adult personality is formed by the pattern and intensity of instinctual gratification at each stage.

**Psychosexual trauma.** As applied by Masters and Johnson, earlier frightening or degrading sexual experience which is related to present sexual inadequacy.

**Psychosis.** A severe mental disorder in which thinking and emotion are so impaired that the individual is seriously out of contact with reality.

**Psychosocial system.** As applied by Masters and Johnson, the social, psychological, and cultural attitudes toward sexual responding.

**Psychosomatic disorder.** See *psychophysiological disorder.*

**Psychosurgery.** Any surgical technique in which neural pathways in the brain are cut in order to change behavior. See *lobotomy.*

**Psychotic depression.** Profound sadness marked by *delusions* and unjustified feelings of unworthiness.

**Psychoticism.** In Eysenck's theory of personality, a dimension referring to degree of contact with reality.

**Punishment.** In psychological experiments, any noxious stimulus imposed on the animal to reduce the probability that it will behave in the way deemed by the experimenter to be incorrect.

**Q-sort.** A personality test in which the respondent sorts a number of descriptive statements into categories ranging from "very characteristic" to "very uncharacteristic," depending on how they apply to him. Often used in research on *client-centered therapy*.

**Random assignment.** A method of assigning subjects to groups in an *experiment* that gives each subject an equal chance of being in each group. The procedure helps to ensure that groups are comparable before the experimental manipulation begins.

**Rape.** To force sexual intercourse on another person.

**Rational-emotive therapy.** *Cognitive restructuring, a behavior therapy* introduced by Albert Ellis and based on the assumption that much disordered behavior is a function of what people tell themselves. The therapy aims directly to alter the goals individuals set for themselves, particularly those that are unrealistic, such as "I must be universally loved."

**Raynaud's disease.** A *psychophysiological disorder* in which capillaries, especially of the fingers and toes, are subject to spasm; characterized by cold, moist hands, commonly accompanied by pain; may progress to local gangrene.

**Reaction formation.** A *defense mechanism* whereby an unconscious and unacceptable impulse or feeling which would cause anxiety is converted into its opposite so that it can become conscious and be expressed.

**Reaction time test.** A procedure for determining the interval between the application of a stimulus and the beginning of the subject's response.

**Recessive gene.** A *gene* which must be paired with one identical to it in order to determine a *trait* in the *phenotype*.

**Refractory phase.** Brief period after stimulation of a nerve, muscle, or other irritable element during which it is unresponsive to a second stimulus; or period after intercourse during which the male cannot have another *orgasm*.

**Regression.** A *defense mechanism* in which anxiety is avoided by retreating to the behavior patterns of an earlier *psychosexual stage*.

**Reinforcement.** In *operant conditioning,* increasing the probability that a response will recur either by presenting a contingent positive event or by removing a negative one; or any satisfying event or stimulus, which, by being contingent with a response, rewards and strengthens this response which precedes it and increases the probability that the subject will so respond again.

**Reliability.** The extent to which a test, measurement, or classification system produces the same scientific observation each time it is applied.

**Repression.** A *defense mechanism* whereby impulses and thoughts unacceptable to the ego are pushed into the *unconscious*.

**Resistance.** During *psychoanalysis,* the defensive tendency of the unconscious part of the ego to ward off from consciousness particularly threatening repressed material.

**Resistance to extinction.** The tendency of a *conditioned response* to persist in the absence of any *reinforcement*.

**Resolution phase.** In the sexual arousal cycle, the last stage during which sexual tensions abate.

**Response acquiescence.** A "yea"-saying *response set,* or agreeing with a question regardless of its content.

**Response deviation.** A tendency to answer questionnaire items in an uncommon way, regardless of their content.

**Response hierarchy.** The ordering of a series of responses according to the likelihood of their being elicited by a particular stimulus.

**Response set.** The tendency of an individual to respond in a particular way to questions or statements on a test—for example, with a "False"—regardless of the content of each query or statement.

**Reticular formation.** Network of *nuclei* and fibers in the central core of the *brainstem;* important in arousing the cortex and maintaining alertness, in the processing of incoming sensory stimulation, and in adjusting spinal reflexes.

**Retrograde amnesia.** Loss of memory for events immediately preceding a traumatic incident; and sometimes, after brain damage, for events extending far back in time.

**Retrospective report.** A recollection by an individual of a past event.

**Revealed-differences technique.** A procedure for studying family behavior by observing its members in a laboratory as they try to agree on an answer to a particular question.

**Reversal design** (ABAB design). An experimental design in which behavior is measured during a base line period (A), during a period when a treatment is introduced (B), during the reinstatement of the conditions that prevailed in the base line period (A), and finally during a reintroduction of the treatment (B). Common in operant research.

**Reward.** In psychological experiments, any satisfying event or stimulus which, by being contingent with a response, reinforces this response which it follows and increases the probability that the subject will so respond again.

**Rh factors.** Substances present in the red blood cells of most people. If Rh factors are present in the blood of a fetus but not in that of the mother, her system produces antibodies which may enter the bloodstream of the fetus and indirectly damage the brain.

**Rorschach test.** A *projective test* in which the examinee is instructed to interpret a series of ten inkblots reproduced on cards.

**Rubella** (German measles). An infectious disease which if contracted by the mother during the first three months of pregnancy has a high risk of causing *mental retardation* and physical deformity in the child.

**Sadism.** Marked preference for obtaining or increasing sexual gratification by inflicting pain on another person.

**Schizophrenia.** A group of psychotic disorders characterized by major disturbances in thought, emotion, and behavior—disordered thinking in which ideas are not logically related, perception and attention are faulty; bizarre disturbances in motor activity; impairment in the connection between perception and emotion, making emotionality flat, inappropriate, ambivalent, or labile; reduced tolerance for stress of interpersonal relations, causing patient to withdraw from people and reality, often into a fantasy life of *delusions* and *hallucinations.*

**Schizophrenogenic.** Causing or contributing to the development of *schizophrenia;* often applied to the cold, conflict-inducing mother who is alleged to make her children schizophrenic.

**School phobia.** An acute, irrational dread of attending school, usually accompanied by somatic complaints; the most common *phobia* of childhood.

**Secondary impotence.** See *impotence.*

**Secondary process.** The reality-based decision-making and problem-solving activities of the *ego;* compare with *primary process.*

**Sedative.** A drug which slows bodily activities, especially those of the central nervous system; used to reduce pain and tension and to induce relaxation and sleep.

**Senile dementia.** A form of *psychosis* brought on by progressive deterioration of the brain caused in part by aging; marked by carelessness in personal hygiene, memory impairment, and gross disorientation.

**Senile plaques.** Small areas of tissue degeneration in the brain, made up of granular material and filaments.

**Sensate focus.** Term applied to exercises prescribed at the beginning of the Masters and Johnson sex therapy program; partners are instructed to fondle each other to give pleasure but to refrain from intercourse, thus reducing anxiety about sexual performance.

**Sensitivity (encounter) group.** A small group of people who spend a period of time together both for therapy and for educational purposes; participants are encouraged or forced to examine their interpersonal functioning and their often-overlooked feelings about themselves and others.

**Sensorimotor stage.** First period of intellectual development, from birth to two years, according to Piaget; the child essentially knows by doing and has no internal representation of the world in symbols.

**Separation anxiety.** A fear experienced when a person is away from someone on whom he is very dependent; said to be important in *school phobia.*

**Serotonin.** An *indoleamine* which is a *neurotransmitter* of the central nervous system. Disturbances in its tracts apparently figure in *depression* and *mania.*

**Severe mental retardation.** A limitation in mental development measured in IQ tests at between 20 and 35; individuals so afflicted often cannot care for themselves, communicate only briefly, and are listless and inactive.

**Sex-change surgery.** Operation removing existing genitalia of a *transsexual* and constructing a substitute for the genitals of the opposite sex.

**Sexual value system.** As applied by Masters and Johnson, the activities that an individual holds to be acceptable and necessary in a sexual relationship.

**Shaping.** In *operant conditioning,* reinforcing responses that are successively closer approximations of the desired behavior.

**Shell shock.** A confused, disorientated state appearing in soldiers exposed to the strains of modern warfare.

**Sibling.** One of two or more persons having the same parents.

**Simple schizophrenic.** A person whose problems begin at an early age with withdrawal and apathy, and who becomes progressively more inaccessible and demented; *delusions* and *hallucinations* are infrequent.

**Single-subject experimental designs.** Designs for experiments conducted with a single subject; procedures include the *reversal* and *multiple-base-line* designs in operant research.

**Situational orgasmic dysfunction.** Inability of a woman to have an *orgasm* in particular situations.

**Skeletal (voluntary) muscle.** One of the muscles which

clothe the skeleton of the vertebrate, being attached to bone, and which are under voluntary control.

**Skinner box.** A laboratory apparatus in which an animal is placed for an *operant conditioning* experiment; contains a lever or other device which the animal must manipulate to obtain a reward or avoid punishment.

**Sleeping sickness.** See *encephalitis lethargica*.

**Slow brain waves.** The theta rhythm (4 to 7 cps) usually recorded by EEG from subcortical parts of the brain and the delta rhythm (less than 4 cps) normally recorded during deep sleep; sometimes recorded in awake sociopaths.

**Smooth (involuntary) muscle.** Thin sheets of muscle cells associated with *viscera* and walls of blood vessels; performs functions not under direct voluntary control.

**Social phobia.** Collection of fears linked to the presence of other people.

**Socioeconomic status.** Relative position in the community as determined by occupation, income, and amount of education.

**Sociopath.** See *antisocial personality*.

**Sodomy.** Originally, penetration of the male organ into the anus of another male; broadened in English law to include heterosexual anal intercourse and by some state statutes to cover all oral-genital contacts.

**Soma.** The totality of an organism's physical makeup.

**Somatic weakness.** Vulnerability of a particular organ or organ system to psychological stress and thereby to a particular *psychophysiological disorder*.

**Somatoform disorders.** A new diagnostic category in the current draft of DSM-III, encompassing *conversion reactions* and *Briquet's syndrome,* which are physical problems without an organic base.

**Somatogenesis.** Development from bodily origins as distinguished from psychological origins; compare with *psychogenesis*.

**Somnambulism.** Sleep walking with the necessary bodily movements controlled by an unknowing part of the person while the knowing mind sleeps or, in diurnal somnambulism, ceases most processes; identified in DSM-II as a *hysterical dissociative reaction*.

**Specitic-attitudes theory.** Hypothesis that certain attitudes are associated with certain *psychophysiological disorders,* for example, that a person who feels mistreated may develop *hives*.

**Specific-reaction theory.** Hypothesis that an individual develops a given *psychophysiological disorder* because of the innate tendency of his autonomic system to respond in a particular way to stress, for example, by increasing heart rate or developing tension in the forehead.

**Spectator role.** As applied by Masters and Johnson, a pattern of behavior in which the individual's focus on and concern for sexual performance impedes his natural sexual responses.

**Stability-lability.** A dimension of classifying the responsiveness of the *autonomic nervous system*. Labile individuals are those in whom a wide range of stimuli can elicit autonomic *arousal*. Stable individuals are not so easily aroused.

**Statistical model.** As applied in abnormal psychology, a set of assumptions by which a substantial deviation from the average is considered to be abnormal.

**Statistical significance.** A magnitude of difference that has a low probability of occurring by chance alone and is by convention regarded as important.

**Statutory rape.** Sexual intercourse, whether forced or not, with a female who is below an age fixed by local statute as that of consent.

**Stimulant.** A drug which increases alertness and motor activity and at the same time reduces fatigue, allowing an individual to remain awake for an extended period of time.

**Stress.** A stimulus which strains the physiological or psychological capacities of an organism.

**Stroke.** Sudden loss of consciousness and control followed by paralysis; caused by sudden anemia of a portion of the brain when a blood clot obstructs an artery or by hemorrhage into the brain when an artery ruptures.

**Subdural hematoma.** Hemorrhage and swelling of the arachnoid torn by a fractured bone of the skull.

**Sulcus** (fissure). A shallow furrow in the *cerebral cortex* separating adjacent convolutions or *gyri*.

**Superego.** In psychoanalytic theory, the part of the personality that acts as the conscience and reflects society's moral standards as they have been learned from parents and teachers.

**Symbiotic psychosis.** Disorder of childhood marked by extreme reluctance of the child to be separated from his mother.

**Symbolic process.** In behavioral analysis, an activity utilizing symbols.

**Sympathetic nervous system.** The division of the *autonomic nervous system* which acts on bodily systems—for example, speeding up the contractions of the blood vessels, slowing those of the intestines, and increasing the heartbeat—to prepare the organism for exertion, emotional stress, and extreme cold.

**Symptom.** An observable physiological or psychological manifestation of a *disease*.

**Synanon.** A residential mutual-help community, primarily for drug addicts, in which participants are held responsible for their behavior and encouraged, through harsh and direct feedback, to change their behavior.

**Synapse.** A small gap between two *neurons* where the nerve impulse passes from the axon of the first to the dendrites of the second.

**Syndrome.** A group or pattern of *symptoms* which tend to occur together in a particular *disease*.

**Systematic desensitization.** A major *behavior therapy* procedure which requires a fearful person, while deeply relaxed, to imagine a series of progressively more fearsome situations. The two responses of relaxation and fear are incompatible and fear is dispelled. Useful for treating psychological problems in which *neurotic anxiety* is the principal difficulty.

**Systematized delusion.** A highly organized set of mistaken beliefs which has become the dominant focus of the paranoid patient's life.

**Tachycardia.** Racing of the heart, often associated with high levels of anxiety.

**Tarantism.** Wild dancing mania, prevalent in the thirteenth century in western Europe; supposedly incited by the bite of a tarantula.

**Taraxein.** A protein (a gamma globulin) in the blood serum of schizophrenics, asserted by Heath to be responsible for their psychosis.

**Tay-Sachs disease.** A disorder of lipid (fat) metabolism causing severe *mental retardation,* muscular weakness, eventual blindness, and death in about the third year.

**Taylor Manifest Anxiety Scale.** Fifty items drawn from the MMPI as a self-report questionnaire to assess anxiety.

**Tearoom.** Homosexual term for a public toilet used for impersonal sexual encounters.

**Temporal lobe.** A large area of each *cerebral hemisphere* situated below the *lateral sulcus* and in front of the *occipital lobe;* contains primary auditory projection and association areas and general association areas.

**Testability.** The extent to which a scientific assertion is amenable to systematic testing.

**Testes.** Male reproductive glands or gonads; the site where sperm develop and are stored.

**Testosterone.** Male sex hormone secreted by the *testes;* responsible for the development of sex characteristics such as enlargement of the testes and growth of facial hair.

**Tetrahydrocannabinol** (THC). The major active chemical in *marihuana* and *hashish*.

**Thalamus.** A major brain relay station consisting of two egg-shaped lobes located in the *diencephalon;* receives impulses from all sensory areas except for the olfactory and transmits them to the *cerebrum*.

**Thanatos.** In psychoanalytic theory, the death instinct, which is the second of the two basic instincts within the *id,* the other being *Eros*.

**Thematic Apperception Test** (TAT). A *projective test* consisting of a set of black and white pictures reproduced on cards, each depicting a potentially emotion-laden situation. The examinee, presented with the cards one at a time, is instructed to make up a story about each situation.

**Thiamine.** One of the complex of B vitamins.

**Third-variable problem.** The difficulty in *correlational research* on two variables whereby their relationship may be attributable to a third variable.

**Thorazine.** Trade name for *chlorpromazine,* one of the *major tranquilizers* and a member of the *phenothiazine* group of drugs.

**Thought disorder.** The critical aspect to be looked for in diagnosing *schizophrenia;* evidenced by problems such as *incoherence, loose associations,* and *concrete reasoning* and speech marked by *neologisms* and *clang associations*.

**Thyroid gland.** Endocrine structure whose two lobes are located on either side of the windpipe; secretes *thyroxin*.

**Thyroxin.** Iodine-containing hormone secreted by the *thyroid gland;* participates in regulation of carbohydrate *metabolism,* thus determining the level of activity and in infants growth, development, and intelligence.

**Token economy.** A *behavior modification* procedure, based on *operant conditioning* principles, in which institutionalized patients are given artificial rewards such as poker chips for socially constructive behavior. The tokens themselves can be exchanged for desirable items and activities such as cigarettes and extra time away from the ward.

**Tolerance.** A physiological condition in which greater and greater amounts of an addictive drug are required to produce the same effect. See *drug addiction*.

**Tonic phase.** State of rigid muscular tension and suspended breathing in a *grand mal epileptic* attack.

**Trait.** A somatic characteristic or an enduring *predisposition* to respond in a particular way, distinguishing one individual from another.

**Tranquilizer.** A drug which reduces anxiety and agitation.

**Transference.** The venting of the *analysand's* emotions, either positive or negative, by his treating the *analyst* as the symbolic representative of someone important in his past. An example is the analysand's becoming angry with the analyst to release emotions actually felt toward his father.

**Transference neurosis.** A crucial and neurotic phase of *psychoanalysis* during which *analysand* reacts emotionally toward the *analyst,* treating him as a parent and reliving childhood experiences in his presence; enables both analyst and analysand to examine hitherto repressed conflicts in the light of present-day reality.

**Transsexual.** A person who believes that he is opposite in sex to his biological endowment.

**Transvestism.** The practice of dressing in the clothing of the opposite sex, usually for the purpose of sexual arousal.

**Trauma.** A severe physical injury or wound to the body caused by an external force; or a psychological shock having a lasting effect on mental life.

**Traumatic disease.** Illness produced by external assault such as poison, a blow, or stress, for example, a broken leg.

**Tremor.** An involuntary quivering of voluntary muscle, usually limited to small musculature of particular areas.

**Trephining.** A crude surgical practice of the Stone Age, whereby a hole was chipped in the skull of a person who was behaving peculiarly, presumably to allow the escape of evil spirits.

**Tricyclic drug.** One of a group of *antidepressants* so-called because the molecular structure of each is characterized by three fused rings; effective primarily in alleviating *endogenous depression.* Tricyclics are assumed to interfere with the reuptake of *norepinephrine* by the *neuron* after it has fired.

**Trisomy.** A condition wherein there are three rather than the usual pair of *chromosomes* within the cell nucleus.

**Tumor** (neoplasm). Abnormal growth which when located in the brain can be either malignant and directly destroy brain tissue, or benign and disrupt functioning by increasing intracranial pressure.

**Twin method.** Research strategy in *behavior genetics* in which *concordance* rates of *monozygotic* and *dizygotic* twins are compared.

**Two-factor theory.** Mowrer's theory of avoidance learning according to which (1) fear is attached to a neutral stimulus by pairing it with a noxious *unconditioned stimulus,* and (2) a person learns to escape the fear elicited by the *conditioned stimulus,* thereby avoiding the UCS. See *fear-drive.*

**Ulcer.** A break in skin or mucous membrane accompanied by tissue disintegration; in the stomach or duodenum, a lesion in the lining caused by excessive secretion of hydrochloric acid; generally regarded as a *psychophysiological disorder.*

**Unconditional positive regard.** According to Rogers, a crucial attitude for the client-centered therapist to adopt toward the client, who needs to feel accepted totally as a person in order to evaluate the extent to which his current behavior contributes to his self-actualization.

**Unconditioned stimulus** (UCS). A stimulus which elicits an instinctual, *unconditional response;* meat powder producing salivation is an example.

**Unconscious.** A state of unawareness without sensation or thought; in psychoanalytic theory, the part of the personality, in particular the *id* impulses, or id energy, of which the *ego* is unaware.

**Unipolar depression.** A term applied to the disorder of individuals who have experienced episodes of *depression* but not of *mania.*

**Vagina.** The sheathlike female genital organ which leads from the uterus to the external opening.

**Vaginal barrel.** The passageway of the vaginal canal leading from the external opening to the uterus.

**Vaginal orgasm.** Sexual climax experienced through stimulation of the *vagina.*

**Vaginal plethysmograph.** Device for recording the amount of blood in the walls of the *vagina* and thus for measuring arousal.

**Vaginismus.** Painful, spasmodic contractions of the outer third of the *vaginal barrel,* making insertion of the *penis* impossible or extremely difficult.

**Validity—internal.** The extent to which experimental results can be confidently attributed to the manipulation of the *independent variable.* **External,** the extent to which research results may be generalized to other populations and settings. As applied to psychiatric diagnoses, **concurrent,** the extent to which previously undiscovered features are found among patients with the same diagnosis; **predictive,** the extent to which predictions can be made about the future behavior of patients with the same diagnosis; **etiological,** the extent to which a disorder in a number of patients is found to have the same cause or causes.

**Variable.** A characteristic or aspect on which people, objects, events, or conditions vary.

**Vicarious conditioning.** Learning by observing the reactions of others to stimuli or through listening to what they say.

**Vineland Social Maturity Scale.** An instrument for assessing how many age-appropriate, socially adaptive behaviors a child engages in.

**Viscera.** The internal organs of the body located in the great cavity of the trunk proper.

**Vitamin.** Any of various organic substances which are as far as is known essential to the nutrition of many animals, acting usually in minute quantities to regulate various metabolic processes.

**Voodoo death.** The demise of a member of a primitive culture after breaking a tribal law or being cursed by the witch doctor.

**Voyeurism** (peeping). Marked preference for obtaining sexual gratification by watching others in a state of undress or having sexual relations.

**Waxy flexibility.** An aspect of *catatonia* in which the patient's limbs can be moved into a variety of positions, thereafter maintained for unusually long periods of time.

**Wernicke's disease.** A chronic brain disorder produced by a deficiency of B-complex vitamins; marked by confusion, drowsiness, partial paralysis of eye muscles, and unsteady gait and by lesions in the *pons, cerebellum,* and *mammillary bodies.* Chronic alcoholics are especially susceptible.

**Whirling response.** The tendency of the *child schizophrenic* to turn his entire body if his head is rotated by an examiner.

**White matter.** Neural tissue, particularly of the brain and spinal cord, consisting of tracts or bundles of myelinated (sheathed) nerve fibers.

**Withdrawal symptoms.** Negative physiological and psychological reactions evidenced when a person suddenly stops taking an addictive drug; cramps, restlessness, and even death are examples. See *drug addiction.*

**Word association test.** Experimental procedure in which a list of words is read to the subject who has been instructed to respond to each with the first word that comes to mind.

**Working through.** In *psychoanalysis,* the arduous, time-consuming process through which the *analysand* faces up to the validity of the *analyst's interpretations* and confronts hitherto repressed material until his problems are satisfactorily solved.

**XYY.** The sex *chromosome* designation of men with an extra male chromosome; a *genotype* thought at one time to predispose for violence but now considered less determinative in this regard.

**Zygote.** The fertilized egg cell formed when the male sperm and female ovum unite.

# PHOTO CREDITS

**Page ix:** Bob di Scal fani.

**Part One Opener**
Arthur Tress/Photo Researchers

**Chapter 1**
Page 7: David Mangurian. Page 8: Erwin Kramer/Photo Researchers. Page 9: (left) The Bettmann Archive, (right) New York Public Library Picture Collection. Page 10: Radio Times Hulton Picture Library. Page 12: (left) Radio Times Hulton Picture Library, (top right) Bildarchiv Preussicher Kulturbesitz, Germany, (bottom right) H. Roger-Viollet. Page 13: (left) Radio Times Hulton Picture Library, (right) H. Roger-Viollet. Page 14: Courtesy Commonwealth of Massachusetts. Page 15: (both) The Bettmann Archive. Page 16: Radio Times Hulton Picture Library. Page 17: Courtesy Sir John Soane's Museum, London. Page 18: (top and center) Brown Brothers, (bottom) H. Roger-Viollet. Page 19: (both) H. Roger-Viollet. Page 20: Radio Times Hulton Picture Library.

**Chapter 2**
Page 38: Sidney Harris. Page 41: (both) Culver Pictures. Page 44: Courtesy B. F. Skinner, photo by Kathy Bendo. Page 45: Courtesy Albert Bandura. Page 48 and 49: Sidney Harris.

**Chapter 3**
Page 71: Reprinted by permission of the publishers from Henry A. Murray, *Thematic Apperception Test,* Cambridge, Massachusetts: Harvard University Press. Copyright © 1943, by the President and Fellows of Harvard College, 1971 by Henry A. Murray. Page 73: Courtesy Dr. Henri F. Ellenberger.

**Chapter 4**
Page 103: Sidney Harris. Page 106: Sybil Shelton/Monkmeyer.

**Part Two Opener**
Marvin Lazarus/Photo Researchers

**Chapter 5**
Page 114: Victoria Beller-Smith/Photo Trends. Page 120: Sidney Harris. Page 122: (above) Courtesy Neal Miller, photo by Stella Kupferberg, (below) Courtesy O. H. Mowrer. Page 126: John Moss/Photo Trends.

**Chapter 6**
Page 135: New York Public Library Picture Collection. Page 143: (Box) Peter Menzel/Stock, Boston. Page 145: (top left and right) Kathy Bendo, (bottom) Rita Freed/Nancy Palmer. Page 149: Leo deWys, Inc. Page 153: Teri Leigh and John Ioan Gotman.

**Chapter 7**
Page 167: Courtesy Centraal Museum der Gemeente, Utrecht. Page 169: (top left) Peter Arnold, (top right) Arthur Tress/Woodfin Camp, (bottom left) Jean-Claude Lejeune/Stock, Boston, (bottom right) Arthur Tress/Photo Trends. Page 174: Courtesy of David C. McClelland. Page 176: Julius Weber. Page 177: Sidney Harris.

**Chapter 8**
Page 197: Courtesy Aaron T. Beck. Page 203: Marion Bernstein.

**Part Three Opener**
Arthur Tress/Photo Researchers

**Chapter 9**
Page 235: (both) Joel Gordon. Page 237: Courtesy S. Schachter, photo by Robert M. Krauss.

**Chapter 10**
Page 246: New York Public Library Picture Collection. Page 247: (both) New York Public Library Picture Collection. Page 248: (top left) Anne Dorfman, (top right) Charles Gatewood, (bottom) Mathias T. Oppersdorff/Photo Researchers. Page 249: Culver Pictures. Page 256: The Bettmann Archive. Page 257: Cary Wolinsky/Stock, Boston. Page 259: Henry Monroe/Black Star. Page 260: Sidney Harris. Page 261: Anne Dorfman. Page 264: Sidney Harris. Page 269: Culver Pictures. Page 273: Jeffrey Foxx/Woodfin Camp. Page 275: Sidney Harris.

**Chapter 11**
Page 283: Giancarlo Botti/Sygma. Page 284: (left) Courtesy Jude Patton, (center) Los Angeles Times, (right) Wide World Photos. Page 285: Tony Korody/Sygma. Page 288: (top) Charles Gatewood, (bottom) Mary Stuart Long. Page 293: Joel Gordon. Page 295: Bob Levin/Black Star.

**Chapter 12**
Page 305: Wide World Photos. Page 326: (top left) Vicki Lawrence/Stock, Boston.

**Part Four Opener**
Arthur Tress/Photo Researchers

**Chapter 13**
Page 333: (left) Radio Times Hulton Picture Library, (right) The Bettmann Archive. Page 339: Courtesy Mrs. Heidi Schneider. Page 342: Bill Bridges/Globe Photos. Page 345: Benyas/Black Star. Page 350: Courtesy Norman Garmezy, News Service, University of Minnesota.

**Chapter 14**
Page 363: James Gelvin/Black Star. Page 370: Courtesy David Rosenthal. Page 376: Christopher S. Johnson. Page 380: fotograf P. Schön Jensen.

**Chapter 15**
Page 387: Stephen J. Potter/Stock, Boston. Page 391: Marlis Müller. Page 405: (top) Marlis Müller, (bottom) Andy Mercado/Jeroboam.

**Part Five Opener**
Brett Weston/Rapho-Photo Researchers

**Chapter 16**
Page 421: (top) Dr. William C. Roberts, Dr. L. Maximilian Buja, Dr. Bernadine Healy Bulkley, from National Institutes of

Health, National Heart and Lung Institute, (center, bottom) Courtesy American Heart Association. Page 427: (top) Sepp Seitz/Magnum, (bottom) B. D. Vidibor/Photo Researchers.

**Chapter 17**
Page 442: Bill Stanton/Magnum. Page 447: Yves de Braine/Black Star. Page 453: Hank Lebo/Jeroboam. Page 454: Dr. Frank Lyman. Page 457: Armed Forces Institute of Pathology.

**Part Six Opener**
Arthur Tress/Photo Researchers

**Chapter 18**
Page 469: (both left) Edmund Engelman/Basic Books (right) Culver Pictures. Page 470: Stella Kupferberg. Page 473: Courtesy Lotte Jacobi. Page 474: William Alanson White Psychiatric Foundation. Copy of photo obtained from W. W. Norton. Page 478: The Bettmann Archive. Page 483: Courtesy Gestalt Institute of Cleveland.

**Chapter 19**
Page 493: Sidney Harris. Page 496: Ray Ellis/Photo Researchers. Page 497: Courtesy Andrew Salter, photo by Stella Kupferberg. Page 499: Sidney Harris. Page 505: Ray Ellis/Photo Researchers. Page 512: Courtesy Albert Ellis. Page 516: Van Bucher/Photo Researchers.

**Chapter 20**
Page 530: Hap Stewart/Jeroboam. Page 534: Optic Nerve/Jeroboam. Page 538: (top) Paul Fusco/Magnum, (center) Bill Stanton/Magnum, (bottom) Burk Uzzle/Magnum. Page 542: Norman Hurst/Stock, Boston. Page 552: Achievement Place, photo by Tom Plambeck. Page 564: Paul Fusco/Magnum.

**Chapter 21**
Page 572: Sidney Harris. Page 574: (left) Courtesy Thomas Szasz, photo by Gabor Szilasi, (right) New York Public Library Picture Collection. Page 575: (right) Melloul/Sygma. Page 580: New York Times. Page 585: Wide World Photos. page 587: F. D. Grunzweig/Photo Researchers. Page 596: (both) Bettye Lane.

**Color Plates**
Plate 1, spirochete: Reproduced with permission of Venereal Disease Control Division, Bureau of State Services, Center for Disease Control, Public Health Service, Department of Health, Education and Welfare.
Plate 1, brain section, Plates 2, 3, and 4: Courtesy Neuropathology, New York State Psychiatric Institute, State of New York Department of Mental Hygiene.

# QUOTATION CREDITS

Page 24, first column, line 9: Copyright © 1974, by Robert M. Pirsig. Reprinted by permission of William Morrow and Company.
Page 112, first column: Copyright © 1966, 1974, by Scapegoat Productions.
Pages 224–225, case of Dan: Copyright © 1967, by Prentice-Hall. Reprinted by permission.
Page 232, Table 9.1: Copyright © 1976, by the American Association of the Advancement of Science.
Page 294, second column top; pages 295, second column bottom, 296, first column: Copyright © 1970, by Fred Belliveau and Lin Richter. Reprinted by permission of Little, Brown and Company.
Pages 404, second column bottom, 405, second column top: Copyright © 1969, by Prentice-Hall. Reprinted by permission.
Page 419: Copyright © 1972, by W. B. Saunders Company.
Pages 424–425, case history: Copyright © 1970 by Henrietta Yurchenco and The Guthrie Children's Trust Fund. Reprinted by permission of McGraw-Hill Book Company. Pages 437–439, case history: Copyright © 1976, by the American Psychological Association. Reprinted by permission.
Page 513, dialogue: Copyright © 1976, by Holt, Rinehart and Winston. Reprinted by permission.

# NAME INDEX

# SUBJECT INDEX

*F*



*G*

*H*

*O*



*P*

*T*

*X*



*Z*